The American Legal Environment

INDIVIDUALS, BUSINESS LAW AND GOVERNMENT

Second Edition

The American Legal Environment

INDIVIDUALS, BUSINESS LAW AND GOVERNMENT

William T. Schantz, B.S., J.D., L.L.M. (Taxation)
Professor of Law, Portland State University/
Attorney at Law/Member of Oregon Bar

Janice E. Jackson, B.A., J.D.
Associate Professor of Law, Portland State University/
Attorney at Law/Member of Oregon Bar

West Publishing Company
St. Paul New York Los Angeles San Francisco

50 West Kellogg Boulevard
P.O. Box 43526
St. Paul, Minnesota 55164

Printed in the United States of America

96 95 94 93 92 91 90 89 8 7 6 5 4

Library of Congress Cataloging in Publication Data

Schantz, William T.
The American Legal Environment.

Includes index.
1. Law—United States—Cases. I. Jackson, Janice E.
II. Title.
KF385.A4S27 1984 349.73 83–25890
ISBN 0–314–72229–7 347.3

For Walter F. Henningsen—
outstanding businessman, sportsman, and friend

Contents in Brief

Contents

9

Contracts 547

11

Bailments, Sales, and Consumer Protection 713

12

Bankruptcy, Secured Creditors, and Accountants' Responsibilities 791

Table of Cases

Principal cases are in italic type. Nonprincipal cases are in roman type. References are to pages.

Foreword

It has been six years since I wrote an introduction to the first edition of Dr. Schantz's book. During the intervening years, society has changed and the laws have changed with it. Watergate has faded into the background. Domestic issues, the economy, and basic individual rights are the main concerns. Simultaneously, commercial law has become more complex, with the onset of litigation relating to the recession and the changes in corporate tax laws passed by the 97th Congress. The government, of course, has become ever more sophisticated in its application of administrative law by federal, state and local governments.

The population of the United States has passed through a period of alienation. As more and more people are touched by the law and begin to sense the effect of government on their personal lives, they are once again becoming involved. Sometimes, as large groups of citizens begin to involve themselves in political issues, they are susceptible to manipulation by established interests. This is understandable due to the complexity of the Executive, Legislative and Judicial branches of government. The myriad passageways of the American legal and governmental system can be very discouraging to a citizen.

If the trend toward de-centralization continues, American citizens will be required to expend more and more effort on the local level. This can be a mixed blessing, as it increases the number of authorities to whom an interested citizen must go for relief, but simultaneously, increases the influence of a single citizen or a small group of citizens.

The increased interest in government by the average citizen, the changing legal and social face of American society, and the age-old problem of coping with a legal and governmental system all require that today's average citizen be better informed than ever before. That is the purpose of *The*

American Legal Environment: Individuals, Business Law, and Government, Second Edition. This is a handbook for the college student and the involved citizen. It is designed to simplify the complex legal system into manageable concepts.

As a Senator, in the legislative branch, and a former Governor, in the executive, I know from first-hand experience of the many problems caused by complex laws. These were not and are not dry "legal questions"—they are people questions raising human issues. Many times in the past, such problems have been aggravated by a lack of understanding of the law. Had material been available to explain the basic legal issues, the affected individuals sometimes could have solved the matter themselves, or would have known that an attorney was needed. At least the basic knowledge would have been available.

Understanding our legal system, recognizing our legal rights, and mastering the basic legal language are all essential if people are to become conversant with our legal system—and they must if our government is to serve the people.

The authors of this text aim at the practical side of the law. Students and other lay people have felt helpless in the past when confronting these issues. Having an understanding of these matters—all so important in our daily lives—makes coping effectively with problems much easier.

As laws continue to expand in number, more people need to understand their effect. Just as additional lawyers will be needed for the actual legal work, a broader lay understanding must also be developed. Our laws must not scare people away. They must not be considered as tools to inhibit a person's rights. They must be just the opposite.

This was the task of the authors, and their book provides the framework for a thorough understanding of our legal system. The more the system is understood, the better the chance for orderly and smooth solutions to the many problems facing American society.

MARK O. HATFIELD
United States Senator from Oregon

"Nothing was illegal,
since there were no longer any laws."
George Orwell
1984

Preface

More than forty years ago George Orwell imagined a world in 1984 where there would be total government control with no freedom and no privacy ("Big Brother Is Watching You"). While the year 1984 has come and the world has changed tremendously in the last forty years with great technological advances, many more people, much more government, and constant international tension, the American legal system has survived still functioning as a democracy emphasizing and protecting individual rights, opportunities, and freedoms. The functioning of this system is perhaps the single most important factor in each of our lives.

Still few people seem to understand just how the law works. Young and old alike, they are cynical, skeptical, critical, and mostly very confused about the American legal system. They say and do outlandish things when they should do nothing; and they do nothing when their legal rights and remedies tell them to do everything. People are afraid of the law—and of lawyers. They know that legal advice is expensive, but they don't always know when to seek it. Frequently, they don't even realize that their rights have been violated. As a result, they go without advice they should have, or pay for advice they don't need at all. People are confused about where the law comes from, how lawyers find it, and what they do with it once they've got it. They don't understand how the courts and administrative agencies work, or what legal terms like tort and contract, indictment and impeachment, or res judicata and res ipsa loquitur really have to do with their lives.

And there is good reason for confusion. Our legal system is complicated—as complicated as any field of science. Education is the obvious answer. Even the system's loudest critics would be more effective and constructive in their criticism if they understood the law and how it works.

Yet not everyone can go to law school; and, certainly, not everyone who can wants to. The study of this text will not make lawyers out of you. But it should help eliminate your cynicism, your skepticism, and your confusion. It should destroy your fear of the law and the courts. And it should provide you with a good, basic understanding of our legal system—and, uniquely, a specific understanding of the many legal concepts that will help you recognize when you need a lawyer, when you do not, and if you do, what that lawyer will be doing for you. You can understand the law. You can protect your rights if you know what they are, and what legal machineries are available to help you enforce them.

And law is a fascinating subject to read about. It will always hold your interest because it involves your rights, your problems, and your remedies. Just think about some of the specifics: criminal cases involving murder and rape; torts like assault, battery, negligence, trespass and libel; business law with contracts, sales, corporations, insurance, checks and notes, antitrust, and the regulation of securities; the operation of government (including elections, recalls, impeachments, and administrative agencies); labor law strikes and boycotts; the environment; consumer protection; taxation; property bankruptcy; probate; birth and abortion; dying and death.

The law is here presented in easily readable fashion. From chapter to chapter, each basic legal principle is introduced by a question. After you read the section you should be able to answer the question. To help you understand what you read, the authors have carefully chosen and edited seven or more cases for each of the thirteen chapters that illustrate the workings and principles of our legal system. You will read some of the most famous—Abscam, Brown, Skokie, Johnny Carson, Miranda, Karen Quinlan, Nixon—as well as some of the most bizarre. And at the end of each chapter are eight review questions and eight to ten problems to which you can apply your new knowledge.

In this second edition, included within our description of the American legal environment, is a complete coverage of business law including the concepts of contracts, insurance, negotiable instruments, sales, agency, partnerships, corporations, securities regulation, antitrust, labor law, bankruptcy, secured transactions, trusts and estates. In these subject areas, where applicable, examples of questions from the law part of recent CPA exams are included.

The second edition also provides a greatly expanded coverage of administrative law, administrative agencies, and their relationship to and regulation of business.

A complete legal glossary is included as Appendix A and the United States Constitution is presented as Appendix B. Footnotes, which have been kept to a minimum, are numbered consecutively, beginning anew with each chapter, while footnotes in the case materials are from actual court opinions.

The text is believed the most unique of all undergraduate law books being the only one that truly covers all aspects of the legal environment, all procedures, the workings of American government, constitutional matters, administrative processes, business law subjects, torts, crimes, property, paralegal and law enforcement subjects. The comprehensive coverage presents a wealth of legal knowledge for use in any college course emphasizing American law.

ACKNOWLEDGMENTS

We wish to thank all the people who helped us with the Second Edition of *The American Legal Environment: Individuals, Business Law, and Government.*

United States Senator Mark O. Hatfield for once again writing the foreword. The Senator's lifetime of service to the American public sets a fine example for young people everywhere.

Portland State University students Wilson Lee, Nancy Price, and J. David Porter. Wilson and Nancy spent countless hours on the excellent glossary, and Dave worked long and hard to prepare the outstanding index.

Lewis and Clark law student Susan E. Snell for all her fine work in the administrative law and torts and crimes areas.

Finally, the West Publishing Company College Department for its support, encouragement, and superior production effort. Special thanks go to Ken Zeigler, the College Department manager, Jane Fischer, our editor, Mark Jacobsen, our production person, and Susan Brown, our copy editor.

Portland, Oregon — WTS
February, 1984 — JEJ

Note to Students

Law for college and university students recently has emphasized two broad subject areas: the so-called "legal environment" dealing with courts, government, procedures, and remedies; and traditional "business law" covering contracts, property, insurance, negotiable instruments, sales, agency, partnerships, corporations, securities, antitrust, bankruptcy, secured transactions, professional responsibility, trusts, wills, and estates.

Each of the the two broad subject areas has great practical importance and application for the student. It is necessary that an individual understand the legal environment—the operation of the American legal system—if he or she is to be able to enjoy the rights and privileges of that system. It is equally as important to know the rules, principles, and standards of the business law subject matter if one is to enter into transactions intelligently and prudently within our complex modern commercial world.

This text, we believe, is the first that completely covers both areas—the legal environment and business law.

This text will lend itself to a blending of subject matters if time does not allow for a complete coverage of all materials, so that your professor may select certain chapters or materials from certain chapters for inclusion within a one term, one semester, or one year law course.

The first five chapters, along with antitrust law within Chapter 7, consumer protection law within Chapter 11, and environmental law within Chapter 13, treat what is generally included within a legal environment course. The remaining materials in Chapters 6 through 13 cover traditional business law subject matters.

Several techniques are used in this text to make a more interesting study, provide easy readability, and give long lasting results—results that will enable you to make use of your understanding of law in the years to come.

SQ3R READING METHOD [1]

This method suggests that a student should use five steps in studying a text:

1. *Survey*—first read each heading in the chapter to see the main points which will be developed.
2. *Question*—turn each heading into a question before reading the text section that follows. In this book, each heading is already in the form of a question to facilitate the use of the SQ3R method.
3. *Read*—read the section following the question-heading having in mind finding the answer to the question.
4. *Recite*—having read the first section, look away from the book and try to answer the question. Use your own words in answering the question, but also realize that law is in large part a study of new words, and you must learn the language of law as you proceed in your study. If you can answer the question of the section and also know the key legal words, you will have attained your objective. If you can't do it, read the section over again until you can. It may be helpful to jot down key phrases or make a brief outline and save these notes. Repeat steps three and four for each section in the chapter.
5. *Review*—when all sections have been covered, look over your notes, if any, and go back to each question and again briefly recite each answer.

CASES

At the end of the text materials in each chapter you will find a number of actual opinions from appellate courts which serve as legal precedents in America. These cases were carefully chosen for their interest and relevancy. In Chapter 1, for example, you will find, among others, the Miranda, Village of Skokie, Karen Quinlan, and Abscam cases.

Law students often find that "briefing" cases helps them to understand and remember better. A brief is a summary of the case and is usually accomplished in about one page.

How to Brief a Case

While there is no definite form, many students use a four part approach as follows:

---

1. This SQ3R reading method was developed by Francis P. Robinson, Professor of Psychology at Ohio State University.

Facts In a paragraph or two summarize the facts before the court. It is as though you were briefly telling someone who has not read the case what the case is about.

Issue This is the main question that the court must decide and can be written in question form. It is as though you were the judge, and you are telling someone what the question is that you must decide to dispose of the case.

Answer This is what the court decided in response to the issue. It is for you to write what the judge decided in answering the question you presented as the issue. Frequently, it is simply a matter of writing the word "yes" or "no" followed by a few words of explanation.

Rule of law This is what the case stands for if it is to be used as a precedent in future cases. It is what you would tell someone in one sentence or so, and using the appropriate legal terms, what the case stands for in the sense of a rule to apply in the future.

Example of Brief

Facts Jones, hearing that Smith was interested in buying a shotgun for hunting purposes, called Smith and said he might be interested in selling an old gun his grandfather had owned. Responding to Smith's question, Jones said he might sell it for two or three hundred dollars. The next day Jones received a check for $300 from Smith in the mail. By that time, however, Jones had learned the gun was a valuable antique worth over $2500. Jones returned the check to Smith, and Smith sued Jones for breach of contract.

Issue Was a contract formed?

Answer No. Mutual assent required for the formation of a contract did not result.

Rule of law The offer required for mutual assent to form a contract must be a definite promise or undertaking and not merely a statement of possibility.

REVIEW QUESTIONS

At the end of the cases in each chapter, you will find eight review questions. These questions, which contain several related parts, provide a complete review of the chapter text. Answering these questions provides good preparation for class as well as good review for tests.

PROBLEMS

After the review questions, certain problems are presented. These are hypothetical situations involving controversies requiring your decision to resolve them through the application of the principles and rules of law contained in the chapter text. People situations bring reality into the law and make it more relevant to our day to day living.

CPA Problems

In Chapters 6 through 13, some of the problems are taken from the law part of the Uniform Certified Public Accountant test administered nationally twice a year. Both multiple choice and essay test questions are used. Many college and university students study business and accounting with intent to become CPAs. However, the questions from the law part of the CPA exam are very good law questions for all law students and valuable to all in a law study.

GLOSSARY

A glossary of significant legal terms is found as one of the appendices of this text.

UNITED STATES CONSTITUTION

The United States Constitution is another of the appendices. Our Constitution is the supreme law of the land; all other American law must be in harmony with the Constitution. You will need to become familiar with it as you study the American Legal Environment as the Constitution provides the basis for our rights, privileges, freedoms, and responsibilities.

The American Legal Environment

INDIVIDUALS, BUSINESS LAW AND GOVERNMENT

The law
Wherein, as in a magic mirror,
We see reflected,
Not only our own lives,
But the lives of all
Men that have been.
Oliver Wendell Holmes

1

The Meaning, Function, and Making of Law

HOW IMPORTANT IS LAW TO YOU AS AN INDIVIDUAL?

This three letter word law—is perhaps the most significant of all words to every individual in this world. Law exists in one form or another everywhere. No matter where you are born, be it Africa, Asia, America, or Australia, you are immediately subject to some law. Law formed a part of the ancient societies of primitive man, and it enters into every facet of living in modern civilizations. There is law relating to birth, marriage, and death. Law controls the ownership of property. It provides for the operation of schools, libraries, fire departments, police forces, armies, and navies. Law requires payment of taxes and the licensing of business. It controls traffic and pollution and provides punishment for what the law determines to be crime.

The existence of law is an established fact of life. Whether you live in China, Germany, Brazil, Russia, or the United States, what you do or do not do today, tomorrow, and each day during the rest of your life will be governed almost entirely by law. For law affects every aspect of your life. A good example is the seemingly simple act of going to work or to school on any particular day. If you travel in your car or on your bike, it is because the law permits you to contract for and own that item of what the law designates as personal property. Whatever your method of transportation, you are subject to traffic regulations. These laws determine your speed, cause you to stop at red lights, and give the right of way to pedestrians. Failure to observe these laws may result in arrest and fine or imprisonment.

Should you drive carelessly and cause an accident, the injured parties could successfully sue you because of law defining such driving as negligence.

Are you old enough to drive, to work, to vote, to drink, to contract, to get married, to own land, or to hold office? You can find your answer in the law. Do you qualify as an electrician, plumber, lawyer, doctor, or engineer? Again, the requirements are legally specified.

How important is law to you as an individual? Well, since the law affects every aspect of your life, it is of vital importance that you understand what it is and how it works. What are your rights? How are they protected? What is the due process that is required before your life, liberty, or property can be taken from you? Knowing the answers to these questions and to the many others included in the study of law is essential to successful living.

WHAT DOES THE WORD "LAW" MEAN?

Law is not an easy word to define. It is used in many different ways, has many different meanings, and has been defined, not without controversy, by many different people throughout the centuries.

The word law is used in connection with some aspect of almost every subject matter. In physics, we have Newton's law relating to bodies in motion. In mathematics, laws govern the order in which any operation proceeds, such as the law of the generation of the curve. There are laws of astronomy, such as Kepler's, that denote the method of planetary motions. In chemistry, Mendelejeff's law states that the properties of chemical elements are periodic functions of the atomic weights. Theology, too, is based on law—the law of God and the canon law of the Church. Political economy reveals Gresham's law that says "bad money drives out good." We have laws of nature, both physical and moral, the moral laws dealing with what is right and wrong. The word law is used to describe the legal profession itself, as "to enter the law"; and it describes individuals who are hired to enforce the law—i.e., the thief who sees the policeman coming on his motorcycle and says, "Let's get out of here. Here comes the law!" The word law describes almost any principle that should be obeyed, whether it be the law of hospitality or the law of grammar.

Although these examples are proper uses of the term law, they do not apply to law as we are concerned with it here. Still, the use of law in connection with physics, chemistry, astronomy, mathematics, theology, or morality does give us a clue as to what the law is within the framework of our study. For in these fields, it is always used to express rules or principles that govern conduct, action, or arrangement. In our study, too, law expresses such rules or principles. Law is some type of plan, method, scheme, or system of controlling the conduct of people. Within this plan or system of control there exist many rules and procedures. The plan need not be good—nor must it result in justice in order to be law. There was law in Nazi Germany during World War II, and there is law today in Libya, Iran, Poland, and within the most primitive tribes of the world. Law may be odious, repulsive, offensive, or extremely distasteful, but it is still law as long as it is an effective way of controlling the conduct of people. Law must guide, direct, manage, and restrain, in both personal behavior and deportment, those persons subject to it.

Law may therefore be defined as a system of control over the conduct of people.

DOES LAW REQUIRE POWER TO CONTROL?

To achieve a system of law, there must be built into that system some means of authority, control, or power to insure that people will act, for the most part, in the manner desired. Our definition of law assumes, therefore, the availability of machinery and procedures for enforcing conduct. This is one thing that separates law from ethics and religion. Ethics asks how people should treat others, and every religion tells its followers how to behave. Thus it is that Islam requires prayer five times daily, that Catholics insist on Mass every Sunday, that Mormons like to marry in the temple, and that Hindus may not eat beef. There is no question but what religion, whether it is Christianity, Judaism, Islam, Hinduism, Buddhism, or Confucianism, provides plans for controlling the conduct of its members. And there is no doubt that religion has been and continues to be a very strong force in the world. But religion, as a modern force that prescribes conduct, generally exists independently of law as we use that term, because there is no power or authority that requires one to observe the rules of any particular religion. There is nothing within the framework of any religion that insures that people will act according to its rules. In law, authority and power must be provided to guarantee that people will act in a certain way.

Imagine for a moment a world without law. Many people would undoubtedly act in much the same way as they do in a legal environment merely by following the rules of conscience, religion, and ethics. But even these people would occasionally have disputes needing settlement by orderly process of law—that is, by law with power to enforce the settlement. In addition, some persons would refuse to follow such generally accepted rules of conduct unless some power or authority required them to do so.

Now, the power or authority required to control human conduct effectively is not simply physical force. Certainly, physical force is sometimes used, as when one refuses to pay a fine or to go to jail, but the threat of force is usually sufficient. People feel mentally coerced to obey the law. They voluntarily obey it because, otherwise, they might have to pay that fine, go to jail, or suffer inconvenience or hardship. Or they may simply feel it is in their best interests or in the interests of society. But it is important to recognize that it is the ever-present authority with the power of its machinery and procedures that produces this result.

Power is necessary for effective control. As we shall see in the next section, this power may be lodged in the hands of one individual (e.g., a dictatorship), in the hands of a few (e.g., an oligarchy), or in the hands of all the people (e.g., a democracy).

WHAT SYSTEMS OF POWER AND CONTROL HAVE BEEN DEVISED?

In considering different systems of power and control it is necessary to look at three specific questions:

1. Who has the power?
2. Where does the power originate?
3. How is the power used?

Who has the power? The power can be held by one person, by a few persons, or by many persons. It is important to realize that having all the power in one person does not necessarily produce a bad result, bad law, or a bad way of controlling the conduct of people. Nor does having all the power in many people always produce a good result, good law, or a good way of controlling conduct. All three questions must be considered in describing legal systems and in deciding which produce good results.

Where does the power originate? Power may exist simply because it has been taken by force or by some other method not involving the consent of the people. A system is legitimate, in the sense of being authorized and sanctioned, only if the people have freely consented to the power structure within the system. When the people have not only consented to the power structure but have also given the power to elected representatives, the system is called a republic. It is this election of representatives who exercise the power that makes a system a republic.

Finally, how is the power used? If the people in authority benefit by reason of having the power at the expense of the people subject to that authority, the system is corrupt. This corruption exists whether the power is held by one, by a few, or by many and regardless of whether the power was originally taken by force or with the consent of the people.

Totalitarianism, or "total control," is not dependent on the number of persons in control. It is a system wherein the power structure controls every aspect of the lives of the people subject to it. Only one political party is usually allowed, and the system, by reasons of its complete control, permits little freedom. All means of communication, including newspaper, radio, and TV are controlled by those in power. Since the concept of private property is incompatible with totalitarianism, little private ownership exists. Totalitarianism existed in Germany under Adolf Hitler, and its exists today, to a lesser extent, in the Soviet Union and in the People's Republic of China.

Many terms apply to the various power structures that have been used or are now being used throughout the world to create and enforce law. If one person takes complete power and control without the consent of the people subject to that control, the form of government is called *autocracy*, and the ruler is a dictator since his or her power is unlimited. If this person occupies an inherited throne, he or she is also a monarch, and the government is a *monarchy*. There are, however, many limited monarchies, such as those in England and Sweden, where the power is actually in elected representatives who meet in national assembly in the manner of a republic. In the past, corrupt monarchies have been referred to as *tyrannies*, and there have been modern corrupt dictatorships (modern tyrants) in Germany under Adolf Hitler and in Russia under Joseph Stalin.

Historically, control was often lodged in the hands of a few individuals as opposed to just one. Those few, supposedly rulers of superior intelligence, ability, and character, were more often simply those who had the most wealth. This system was called an *aristocracy* and was used at times in the ancient Greek city-states. Corrupt aristocracies were called *oligarchies.* Today, small groups ruling in a totalitarian way in some communist dictatorships are properly considered oligarchies. There is, then, no real difference between a corrupt dictatorship and an oligarchy—both are corrupt and rule without limitation of power. However, an oligarchy requires a small group, while a corrupt dictatorship (referring to absolute authority or rule) usually describes one person in a position of power who uses that power in a corrupt and totalitarian manner.

A system in which the supreme power is in the hands of the people is a *democracy.* In a pure democracy, the people make the laws themselves. But pure democracy can work only in small groups simply because large groups on a national or even large city level can never get together and meet with any degree of efficiency. Thus, most democracies use the *republican* form of government where the people exert their power indirectly through elected representatives who make the law. The result of democracy in the world's republics—Switzerland, the United States, Canada, France, West Germany—has been the preservation of more individual freedom through the limitation of power. Many rights, including freedoms of speech, press, religion, assembly, privacy, and ownership of private property, are guaranteed. Life, liberty, and property may not be taken from the individual without due process of law.

However, the mere fact that power is lodged in large groups of people does not guarantee good results or freedom. There have been times in history when people have overthrown their governments, have eliminated freedom in rule through *mobocracy,* where unreasoning mobs of people exercise power and control at the expense of freedom.

Many systems of control, then, have been historically devised to control the conduct of people. Each form is law, ranging from the one-person dictatorship to the democracy within a republic. Nothing can be more important to the individual than the law—the system of control—under which he or she lives.

WHAT ARE THE LEGITIMATE AND PROPER FUNCTIONS OF LAW?

We have seen that throughout the world's history many different systems of control have been devised to control the conduct of people. Several different systems also exist today. Some have essentially eliminated freedom and have made slaves of the people. Others have provided too many rules—rules that infringe upon privacy and rules that eliminate incentive. Because of these results, some people believe it would be best if there were no government at all. This is called *anarchism*—the belief that there should be no government. In the past, anarchists have used violence to overthrow governments and to murder heads of state. This attempt to obliterate law has resulted in terror, loss of life, destruction of property, rule through mobocracy, and further loss of freedom, but it has never resulted in the elimination of law or government. The inescapable conclusion is that if people are to live together amicably, law must be an essential part of their lives. Today, the great increase in the world's population, together with tremendous advances in the fields of communication and transportation, make it almost impossible for the individual to isolate himself or herself. Every action one person takes affects others either directly or indirectly and may cause them involvement or even injury. Controversies and conflicts can and will result that must be settled in a peaceable manner. If they cannot be settled peaceably using rules of law, people will resort to other means and expose themselves to harm, enslavement, or death. We must have rules if we are to live together.

Yet, certainly, rules take away from our freedom. In fact, every time a rule is made, our freedom to act in a certain way is somewhat restricted. If there are too many rules, totalitarianism results, and there is very little freedom.

A very delicate job, then, belongs to those people in authority who must determine how far the rules can go before the cost becomes too great. And when we talk about cost, we are talking in terms of both cost in freedom and economic cost. If the cost in freedom is too great, then the rule is not warranted even if it achieves an otherwise desirable result. Consider, for example, the subject of "law and order," a phrase used oftentimes to describe the lessening or control of crime. It is a fact that many crimes take place after dark: specifically, many robberies, muggings, and rapes are committed after nine o'clock at night.

If we had a rule of law prohibiting people from being on the streets after nine o'clock at night, many of these crimes could not occur. Such a curfew would certainly reduce the number of robberies, muggings, and rapes, and this is a desirable result. But the cost in our freedom is too great. None of us would be willing to accept being locked in our houses every night at nine—this would simply take away too much of our freedom.

Every rule of law must be considered in this light. How much freedom will we lose if we have gun control laws? Or laws requiring us to wear seat belts, or to drive no faster than fifty miles an hour to conserve gasoline, or to quit driving in downtown core areas in order to lessen pollution? The cost of freedom, while perhaps acceptable in some of these areas, may be too great in others. Striking the delicate balance between law and freedom is a difficult task indeed. There is no question but what we must have law; but just as certainly, we must preserve as much of our freedom as possible while living in a modern world.

When we consider cost, freedom is, of course, the most important factor, but cost in terms of economics or money is also important. An otherwise desirable result may simply be too expensive in terms of dollars. If the nine o'clock curfew law was passed, how much would it cost to administer? How large a force would have to be hired and paid to make certain that people did stay in after curfew? Who would pay these costs? In recent times the budgets and deficits of government not only have been a constant concern but have been blamed for both recession and inflation.

Having concluded that we must have law and that law should not cost too much in terms of either freedom or money, we must now determine what legitimate things the law should achieve. What do we want the law to do for us? If we can determine its proper functions, then we can work to limit its authority—to keep control to the minimum and freedom to the maximum. What are the legitimate functions of law? There are four:

1. The settlement of disputes;
2. The establishment and maintenance of order;
3. The protection of the individual and his or her property;
4. The promotion of the general welfare.

The settlement of disputes is critical to a system of control. Even the most law-abiding citizen will occasionally get into a dispute with someone. Good neighbors for many years may suddenly discover that one has been occupying part of the other's land. Such a boundary dispute must be settled. Suppose your neighbor starts playing his or her stereo too loudly, begins burning rubbish in his or her back yard, or gets a barking dog with a bite to match. Such neighbors may believe they are well within their rights; you may not agree. You can fight it out with words or fists or guns—but a peaceful way under law is better. Disputes may arise from any kind of activity—from driving, from doing business, from recreation. A legal method to resolve conflicts peacefully must be available.

Just as essential to a system of control is the establishment and maintenance of order. Once a dispute makes its way to the courtroom, it must be settled, even there, under orderly rules of procedure. Thus it is that a defendant may not scream, yell, or otherwise disrupt the proceedings at hand. Order must be present or no result can be achieved. When a person drives an automobile, there must be rules to tell him or her which side of the street to drive on, when to stop at stop signs or red lights, and how fast to go. Without such rules tremendous traffic jams would result. There would be terrible accidents because drivers could not know what to expect from other drivers. There must be established rules of conduct for all drivers if order is to be achieved and chaos avoided. For example, without orderly plans for the development of land and cities, it would be possible for slaughter houses, steel mills, or paper manufacturers to crop up in the middle of residential areas. We have planning commissions and zoning laws to prevent this. The achievement of order, the establishment of a universal standard of conduct, permits all of us to operate daily with less confusion and anxiety and with a foreseeable expectation regarding the conduct of others.

The protection of person and property is perhaps even more important than the first two functions of law. Freedom to live without fear—fear that someone will steal your property, beat you, or perhaps kill you—is essential. Because people must respect each other, many laws deal with protection and security. People are not only punished for committing crime, whether it is stealing, beating, or killing, but they may also be sued by their victims for money damages. The law has created police departments and other so called "law enforcement" personnel, including the district attorney's office and the justice department, to protect people from crime and to help secure them in their person and property. This is not to say that there is no crime or that people are never hurt or that their things are never stolen. The function of law—to protect people and their possessions—is not carried out with perfection. But without law there would be much more crime, and many more people would be hurt, either physically or by loss of property. People would have to worry constantly about defending themselves and would have to carry weapons for protection. There would be no police to call. If you need a police officer, it is important that one be available. Even limited security and protection are much better than no security or protection at all. The law must provide for this.

The promotion of the general welfare involves activities that protect and help people as a group rather than as individuals. Criminal law, in addition to providing individual protection, certainly affects the entire public interest in the prevention and punishment of crime. Education laws, providing for public education at elementary, secondary, and college levels, introduce people to a better way of living. Many pollution laws have been passed in recent years regarding air, water, noise, and sanitation, all to promote the general welfare. Highways, bridges, parks, and other recreational facilities are constructed for public use. Conservation laws, health laws (such as Medicare, Social Security pensions, and disability benefits), unemployment compensation laws, Workers' Compensation laws, and numerous others fit within this function of law—the promotion of the general welfare.

WHAT ARE THE CHARACTERISTICS OF AN IDEAL SYSTEM OF LAW?

There have been and continue to be many different systems of law. Some, we might conclude, are bad—others better or even good. In making comparisons, however, certain characteristics stand out as "ideal" for all systems.

An ideal system of law must include at the least the following ten characteristics:

1. The law must be based on the free consent of the people subject to that system of control. The system cannot be forced upon them; rather, they must have free choice as to the plan or scheme under which they prefer to live.

2. The law must strive to achieve a system of limited control in order to preserve a maximum amount of freedom. The last thing a man or woman wants is total control over his or her life. People must be free to choose where they will live, what work they will do, and how they will think and act regarding religion, politics, economics, and government. Too much control stifles initiative and makes life uninteresting for the individual. Control must be such that most people will voluntarily comply with the rules without feeling their compliance unduly interferes with their freedom.

3. The law must stay within and effectively carry out the four legitimate functions we have previously defined—the settlement of disputes, the establishment of order, the protection of person and property, and the promotion of the general welfare.

4. The law must provide clearly defined sources of power based upon the consent of the people wherein the general power and authority are spelled out. No authority will be recognized unless it can be traced to such a source, and exercise of power will depend upon the popular consent found in these sources. Thus no one can exercise authority unless it is found within these general powers, and no one man or woman can legitimately move to control the conduct of others unless he or she is doing so with the consent of the people and within clearly defined sources spelling out the general authority.

5. The law must apply to all persons equally and without exception. No man or woman by reason of being in a particular governmental position, be it police chief, president, or supreme court judge, will be above the law. The law must apply to all, and every person must be equal before the eyes of the law. If anyone is given a superior or unique position because he or she has a government job or because he or she possesses greater wealth, then the law is corrupt.

6. The law must be knowable, understandable, and reasonable. People will accept the law only if they know and understand it to some considerable extent. Certainly not every individual will have the detailed knowledge and expertise of the lawyer. Yet basic knowledge and understanding of the law is important, and every individual should be given the opportunity to study and know the law in detail if he or she chooses to do so. In addition, the law must be reasonable to insure the voluntary compliance of those subject to it. If enough people feel a law is unreasonable, it will probably be neither effective nor enforceable.

7. The law must be flexible, adaptable, and changeable through orderly procedure. We live in a society of constant change—of new needs, new values, and new attitudes. The law must not be so rigid that it cannot adapt. But beyond mere adaptation, it must be possible to achieve substantial change in law through orderly procedure. If such change cannot be effected in a peaceful and orderly manner, the system contains a major defect. The ability to effect change by those subject to the law is essential. When changes cannot be so effected, revolution may result.

8. The law must provide for and encourage active and meaningful participation by the governed. All persons must be eligible to hold positions of authority. They must be able to vote to determine who will hold these positions of power. Participation in orderly, peaceful demonstrations or gatherings to influence law must be welcomed. It is vitally important that people be able to express themselves, to participate in the making and changing of law, and to vest the law with their continued consent.

9. The law must provide for rule by the majority of the people while, at the same time, safeguarding individual rights. This means that the majority will decide what constitutes the law only as long as their decisions do not threaten, impair, or destroy the fundamental rights of any one individual. Rule by majority is a necessary requirement, since it is unrealistic to expect that everyone will agree; as long as the majority agrees, a standard of conduct can be justifiably made for all. But this is true only if the majority does not oppress the minority. Those fundamental rights of all persons to life, assembly, due process, freedom of religion, equal opportunity, and liberty must be guaranteed even against a majority of people thinking otherwise. And protection against government itself must exist so that individual rights are protected first—so that a person cannot be sent to jail for what he is thinking or sent to jail without trial.

10. The law must provide for efficient and effective control without wasting the resources of its people. Without efficiency in operation, there is no effective control. If substantial voluntary compliance with the law is lacking, the system is not efficient. If effective control over violation of the rules is missing, the system again is not efficient. And if the system is full of red tape and bureaucracy with its excessive insistence on rigid routine and waste of money and time, then the system is not effective. The ideal system has limited control with minimum cost and maximum efficiency.

WHAT IS THE SYSTEM OF LAW IN THE UNITED STATES?

Colonial America resented the oppressive English law forced upon it by a mother country an ocean away. This law controlled the colonists' overseas trade and navigation, imposed taxation without representation, managed Indian affairs, and limited both their manufacturing and expansion—hardly a negligible interference. The colonists were angered by laws made for them in London with neither their consent nor involvement.

When, in 1763, England decided to keep a standing army in the colonies and to tax the colonists to pay for this army, a revolutionary spirit was born. This revolutionary zeal spread as England passed a series of acts that served only to infuriate the indignant colonists. In 1764, Parliament passed the Sugar Act requiring a three-penny tax on each gallon of molasses purchased by the colonies from other than English merchants. Then in 1765, the Quartering Act was passed which forced the colonists to provide living quarters for the English soldiers and to furnish them transportation and other items such as fuel and beer. At the same time, the Stamp Act required colonial America to buy tax stamps for legal documents and newspapers. This again was a taxing of the colonists without their consent or involvement. The Townshend Acts worsened an already deteriorating situation by taxing the tea, paper, and paint imported into the colonies. The colonists complained bitterly that "taxation without representation is tyranny."

In 1773, a group of colonists, disguised as Indians, raided the British vessels in the Boston harbor and threw the British tea into the water—an event known as the "Boston Tea Party." As a result, London passed the Intolerable Acts, which closed Boston Harbor to commerce, and the Restraining Act, which authorized the use of military force against the colonists and taking their leaders under arrest. British troops were ordered to march in April of 1775, and Paul Revere rode to give his legendary warning. The battle had begun! On July 4, 1776, the Declaration of Independence was adopted by the colonists who declared their independence from England. Major battles took place at Brandywine, Bunker Hill, Lexington, Saratoga, Yorktown, and elsewhere until 1782, when the war was over and America was free from English rule.

Along with freedom there came the responsibility to create a new system of law. The result? The legal system under which we live today in the United States. This system was born out of revolution against oppression—a struggle to achieve and insure freedom. Individual freedom was foremost in the minds of those who created the system of law in the United States. It is not surprising, then, that great emphasis was placed on guaranteeing personal liberty and on protecting the individual against the government itself by limiting its powers.

Two documents of American history illustrate the importance of individual freedom to those men who founded the American system of law. The following language is found in the Declaration of Independence:

> * * * [T]he history of the present King of Great Britain is a history of repeated injuries * * *, all having in direct object the establishment of an absolute Tyranny.
>
> * * * He has refused to pass laws for the accommodation of people * * * unless those people would relinquish the right of representation in the Legislature. * * *
>
> * * * He has obstructed the administration of justice. * * *
>
> * * * He has made Judges dependent on his will alone. * * *
>
> * * * He has kept among us, in times of peace, Standing Armies without the consent of our legislature.
>
> * * * He has combined with others to subject us to a jurisdiction * * * imposing taxes on us without our consent, * * * and depriving us of trial by jury.
>
> * * * He has plundered our seas, ravaged our Coasts, burnt our towns, and destroyed the lives of our people. * * *
>
> We hold these truths to be self-evident that all men are created equal, that they are endowed by their Creator with certain unalienable Rights, that among these are Life, Liberty, and the pursuit of Happiness. That to secure these rights, Governments are instituted among Men, deriving their just powers from the *consent of the governed.* [Emphasis supplied.]

And in the Constitution of the United States, the following is found:

> We the people of the United States, in order to form a more perfect Union, establish Justice, insure domestic tranquility, provide for the common defense, promote the general welfare, and secure the Blessings of Liberty to ourselves and our posterity do ordain and establish this Constitution for the United States of America.

In this Preamble to the Constitution the people originally consented to the law as established in the United States Constitution. Article VI, Section 2 of the Constitution states that the Constitution is the "supreme law" of the United States and all other United States law must be in harmony or such law is void. A legitimate system based on the continuing consent and continuing involvement of the governed is established, and the ultimate power continues to be vested in the people as a whole.

Only limited power is granted to the government through popular consent, the paramount purpose being to secure personal liberty and to maintain individual freedom. Article X of the Bill of Rights of the United States Constitution specifically states that:

> * * * [T]he powers not delegated to the United States by the Constitution, nor prohibited by it to the States, are reserved to the States respectively or to the people.

Governmental power is thus limited—power that has not been given to the government remains with the people. The real power, therefore, is with all of the people of the United States, each person being equal under the law.

Article XIV, Section 1, of the Constitution says that:

> * * * [A]ll persons born or naturalized in the United States, * * * are citizens of the United States * * * No state shall deprive any person of life, liberty or property without due process of law; nor deny to any person within its jurisdiction the equal protection of the laws.

The law, then, is with the consent of the governed. It is a government of limited power which guarantees individual liberty. The Constitution states that law is created to "* * * establish justice, insure domestic tranquility, provide for the common defense and promote the general welfare." These are the legitimate functions and purposes of law as we have previously defined them—the settlement of disputes, the establishment of order, the protection of person and property, and the promotion of the general welfare. All United States law is controlled by this language, and if a rule does not establish justice, secure the blessings of liberty, promote the general welfare, or provide for the common defense and domestic tranquility, it is unconstitutional and therefore invalid.

As we have seen, the constitutional system of law in the United States provides for a federal government which governs the people in all of the states and has only those limited powers granted to it by the states. The rest of the power is retained by the states and the people in them. As a result, each state has its own law controlled by a state constitution independent of federal law. State constitutions also provide for local control in county or city government.

Both federal and state constitutions provide for three branches of government with clearly defined general powers. The legislative branch "legislates" or creates specific laws—general rules of conduct consciously written for the general population. The executive branch carries the law into effect and superintends its enforcement. The judicial branch judges or applies the law to particular cases. Each branch is designed to make law, and each branch checks and balances the others so that none can abuse its power. Thus it is that senators, congressmen, judges, governors, presidents, and all other persons in positions of governmental authority can be removed from power. For example, the United States Constitution provides the following as to senators and congressmen:

> * * * Each House may determine the Rules of its Proceedings, punish its members for disorderly behavior, and with the concurrence of two thirds, expel a member.

State constitutions provide for the recall of public officers through special elections. Usually, 25 percent of those persons who voted in the preceding election in that district can sign a petition demanding a recall of the particular public official. Then a special election is held to determine whether or not he or she should be removed. Regarding the president, the federal Constitution provides:

> * * * The Senate shall have the sole power to try all impeachments * * *. When the President of the United States is tried, the Chief Justice shall preside; and no persons shall be convicted without the concurrence of two thirds of the members present.
>
> * * * Judgments in cases of impeachment shall not extend further than to removal from office, * * * but the party convicted shall nevertheless be liable and subject to indictment, trial, judgment and punishment according to law.

The system provides, therefore, that all persons are subject to the law and that we have a government of law—not of individuals.

The law in the United States is reasonably well known and understood by the public. This is so because the Constitution guarantees freedom of press, public trial, public assembly, and public record. The law is not hidden in any mysterious archives; law libraries, open to the public as well as to lawyers, contain complete texts of all constitutions, treaties, and statutes. The law is available to everyone to know and to understand. This is not to say that it is never complicated. It is extremely complicated at times, for it covers every aspect of living. It must do so to be effective.

In our system, the law is constantly changing. Legislatures meet to change old law and to write new law. Courts, greatly flexible, interpret the written law and adapt it to meet new problems and situations. Even the Constitution itself may be amended (and it has been several times) if three-fourths of the states agree on the need for such change. Significantly, this is orderly, peaceful change effected by the people through the system. This was not the case in colonial America under English rule. Nor was it true in Nazi Germany under Hitler, where rebellion and revolution would have been the only way to bring about change. In the United States, continuous change through the system eliminates any need for civil disobedience that may result in the breaking of law, violence, and bloodshed. This is not to suggest that the people should not meet in peaceable assembly or march in legal protest in order to influence the laws of the United States. The First Amendment of the Constitution provides for the "right of the people peaceably to assemble, and to petition the Government for a redress of grievances." In our recent history much has been achieved in protecting minority rights, ending the Vietnam war, and expressing concerns regarding the environment, nuclear power, and nuclear war through the voice of the American people and its impact upon elected representatives at the local, state, and national level.

All individuals may hold office in the United States. There are age requirements for some offices such as the presidency (thirty-five years), the Senate (thirty years), and the House of Representatives (twenty-five years). All persons are also eligible to vote for all offices generally at the age of eighteen years. They may also voice their opinions on many issues through use of initiative and referendum. These methods allow voters some direct control over lawmaking in the sense of pure democracy. Under the initiative, anyone may write a proposed law, and if he or she gets the required number of signatures supporting it in a petition, the proposal must be brought either before the legislature or before the people for a vote. So even though a legislature may refuse to consider a proposed law, the initiative can effect its consideration by the people themselves. It also allows minority groups to promote special interests since any group of voters may introduce the law.

In a referendum a proposed law is submitted to the people for approval. Many local governments require the submission of certain measures, especially those involving the expenditure of money. Local school board budget requests are a good example. Additionally, legislatures have the option to submit many bills for voter approval, and constitutional amendments must at times be so submitted. The people can, by petition, cause bills passed by the legislature to be referred to the vote of the people.

While initiative and referendum are not part of law in all states or at all local levels of government, the methods are used effectively in about half of the states. In Oregon, for example, initiative has been used over the years to abolish capital punishment, establish compulsory education, give women the right to vote, and create the first presidential preferential primary. It is not used on the national level, though there is some support for an amendment to the United States Constitution to permit national initiative. Such an amendment would permit any citizen or organization to draw up a bill and submit it to the U.S. attorney general. The would-be lawmaker would then have eighteen months to collect valid signatures from 3 percent (many states require higher percentages for local and state initiative measures) of those who voted in the previous presidential election (over two million signatures). When, and if, this was done, the measure would be submitted to the people on the next national ballot.

A majority vote is generally required to elect a government official or to approve a particular law brought before the voters on initiative or referendum. This is the basic United States system of majority rule. Numerous constitutional safeguards, however, protect the individual from oppression by the majority. The majority cannot through agreement take away any of the basic rights of the individual. For example, the federal Constitution provides:

> Congress shall make no law respecting an establishment of religion, or prohibiting the free exercise thereof; or abridging the freedom of speech, or of the press * * *
>
> The right of the people to be secure in their persons, houses, papers, and effects, against unreasonable searches and seizures, shall not be violated. * * *
>
> * * * Nor shall any person be subject for the same offense to be twice put in jeopardy of life or limb, nor shall be compelled in any criminal case to be a witness against himself, nor be deprived of life, liberty, or property without due process of law; nor shall private property be taken for public use without just compensation.
>
> In all criminal prosecutions, the accused shall enjoy the right to a speedy and public trial, by an impartial jury, * * * to have compulsory process for obtaining witnesses in his favor * * * and to have the assistance of counsel for his defense.

> Neither slavery nor involuntary servitude * * * shall exist within the United States.
>
> The right of citizens of United States to vote shall not be denied or abridged on account of race, color, or * * * sex.

In other words, the majority does take precedence in making laws and in choosing representatives. But this majority rule is so carefully restricted by constitutional guarantees of rights relating to life, liberty, property, and equal opportunity that fundamental individual rights and rights of minorities are not eliminated. We have, then, a democracy wherein the majority of people determine the system of control. This system, with built-in safeguards, protects the fundamental rights of the individual.

The system of law in the United States is properly called a constitutional system with a republican form of government. On paper, the system is close to ideal based as it is on the consent of the governed with direct and active involvement by the people and constitutional safeguards of individual rights. Its operation and administration, however, are less than ideal, for it depends on people for its accomplishment. We all must accept the limitations and imperfections of people. Since persons are not perfect and since the system must be operated by persons, the system will be operated imperfectly. Some corrupt individuals may achieve positions of power. There will at times be waste and inefficiency. Complete elimination of such abuse of power, waste, and inefficiency may be impossible. Still the built-in systems of checks and balance, the fact that all individuals are subject to the law, taken together with the constant vigilance of the free press make for far less corruption and waste than in most other systems. It is also important that the people subject to the law are not apathetic but remain constantly on the alert for signs of oppression or wrongdoing.

WHAT ARE THE SOURCES OF LAW IN THE UNITED STATES?

A person can act with authority under United States law only if he or she derives his or her power from well-defined sources of law. The sources of law in the United States are three:

1. Written law;
2. Common law; and
3. Administrative law.

The written law, as that term is used here, is narrowly defined to include federal and state constitutions, treaties made by the president with foreign nations, and statutes written and passed by the federal Congress, the state legislatures, or by local governmental units such as city or county commissions. To be "written," therefore, law must be found in one of three formal documents—a constitution, a treaty, or a statute.

A *constitution,* or supreme law of the area governed, sets out in formal written terms the fundamental system of power, i.e., the rules and principles for that area. We have the United States Constitution applying to all fifty states and separate constitutions controlling the local law of each individual state. A *treaty* is a formal written agreement between the United States and one or more foreign nations or sovereigns. It may relate to any number of subject matters including trade, defense, peace, fishing rights, or taxation. In the United States, treaties are made by the president with the advice and consent of the Senate. A *statute* is a formal written enactment of a legislative body, whether it be federal, state, city, or county. The power to write statutes, like the treaty making power, must be based on the constitution. If a statute or treaty is not made according to constitutional power, it is invalid.

Written law is a source of great power in the United States. It defines the specific powers of the president, congress, governors, and the legislatures; and it creates the courts and authorizes them to operate. The written law deals with many aspects of control including criminal, traffic, pollution, and zoning laws. But there are many situations that are not regulated by a constitution, treaty, or statute. And this is where common law comes into the picture. If you drive through a red light and a police officer stops you and gives you a ticket, he or she can do this because a statute (part of the written law) defines the running of the red light as a minor crime and gives the police officer authority to enforce the law. This is not common law because written law controls the situation. The judge knows what to do by looking to the written law. But if you are injured in an automobile accident because someone has very carelessly driven his or her car into yours, you may not be able to find any written law that assures your successful recovery of damages from the careless driver. Your recovery is dependent on the common law. Or say someone hits you in the nose or forces you to enter into an agreement that costs you injury or economic loss. There may be nothing in the written law that tells the judge that you have a remedy. Again, this is where common law applies.

Common law, then, comes into play when a judge has to make a decision—settle a dispute—without written law to guide him or her. The dispute must still be settled, or the law is not properly carrying out its functions. The judge will decide the case by looking to the rules of the common law—rules that were applied to similar cases in the past. This is how the common law developed and continues to develop. Judges decide matters initially according to what they believe most people would think is right and according to the customs and common beliefs of the community. If other judges follow this decision, the decision is considered a *precedent,* and if a large number of judges follow the precedent and decide the same question in the same way, it becomes part of the common law. These common law rules evolve without benefit of written law. They are just as much a part of our law and just as effective and binding as are the rules found in the written law's constitutions, treaties, and statutes. The common law rules are subject to change as the common beliefs in the community change. They can also be superseded and modified by statute. A statute that changes a common law rule effectively eliminates that rule from our legal system.

The third source of law in the United States is that which results from the work of an administrative agency. As previously stated, constitutions empower the legislative branches of government to make written rules called statutes, and they authorize the courts to apply these rules in deciding particular cases. It is simply impossible, however, for legislatures to make all the necessary rules or for courts to handle all of the cases. This is true for two reasons. First, the regulation of certain fields requires a nonlegal expertise. It is impossible for presidents, governors, senators, congressmen, or judges to know enough about technical fields or industries to make good rules for their proper regulation. Radio, TV, transportation, atomic energy, air and water pollution, aeronautics, and space exploration are all areas where nonlegal experts must do the rule making if we are to have rules that make sense. Thus, Congress creates an administrative agency such as the Federal Communications Commission to deal with the regulation of radio and TV, the Interstate Commerce Commission to deal with the transportation industry, or the Environmental Quality Commission—each with a specific job to do under the statute creating the agency. The agency makes rules and decides cases in the same manner as do legislatures and courts, and its rules and decisions are just as binding. The statute passed by the legislature gives the agency its general power to make detailed rules and regulations. When an agency decides a case, that is, resolves a dispute between parties or determines the rights of an individual, it is as much a part of our law as when a court does it. And this is the second reason for the creation of the administrative agency—to settle the thousands of mechanical questions that would otherwise overwhelm the courts by their volume. Often, a question can be determined simply by applying mechanical rules. Whether a person is entitled to social security benefits or benefits in a veterans hospital depends on his or her record under the social security law or as a veteran. The Social Security Administration or Veterans Administration can make these determinations without assistance from the courts. And this makes good sense because it allows the courts to devote their attention to more controversial matters.

All power to act within the United States system of law must be derived from written, common, or administrative law.

HOW DOES THE LAW RELATE TO BUSINESS?

The law relates to every aspect of a person's life. This, of course, applies both to the conducting of business and to the customer's dealings with business. The administration of business involves decision making. To make informed decisions, a business manager must understand the legal ramifications involved, or he or she may find himself or herself in trouble with customers, employees, or with the government. The consumer, too, must know when he or she is binding himself or herself to a contract to buy a product and what he or she can do if the product proves defective.

It is important to understand law in the full context of its legal environment—how does it apply to the individual's rights and duties, work, family, property, protection, procedures, and remedies. We have entitled this book *The American Legal Environment: Individuals, Business Law, and Government* because we hope to provide you with a rather complete basic understanding of the legal environment in the United States and, with such an understanding, the ability to achieve a better way of life.

WHAT DOES IT MEAN TO MAKE LAW?

Law is a system of control over the conduct of people. Developing the specifics of that system is called lawmaking and involves four distinct categories of activity:

1. Rule making (making general rules);
2. Interpreting (determining what the general rules mean);
3. Adjudicating (deciding cases or settling disputes); and
4. Executing (carrying out and enforcing the rules).

Rule making is the creation of principles governing conduct—principles that tell people what they can or cannot do. Rules are made either through legislation or through the common law. Legislation consists of general rules of conduct that are formally and solemnly written by an authorized branch of government. These rules may be made on the national level by Congress, on the state level by a state legislature, or on a local level by a county commission or city council. They may be called legislative acts, statutes, enactments, or ordinances, but they will always involve general rules of conduct that are consciously and formally declared (i.e., rendered authentic by following certain prescribed procedures) to be law. Legislation applies prospectively. It defines what the law shall be in future cases arising under it. So if the federal Congress decides that all cars must have certain antipollution devices on their exhaust pipes, this means that in the future cars must be so equipped. While legislation applies to the future, and universally to all people, the legal result in a court case applies to some past event as it relates to an individual or to a few specific people.

Rule making, however, is not confined to legislative branches of government but is also accomplished by the courts in creation of the common law. And these judicially created rules are just as binding as are the general rules of legislation. The administrative agency, too, makes rules in carrying out the job outlined in its enabling statute. The executive branches of government (governors, presidents, and the like) participate by instituting programs that urge creation of new legislation, by exercising veto powers over the legislative branches, and by making rules within the area of their own particular responsibilities. The people themselves share in rule making independently of the legislature through use of the initiative and referendum.

Ultimately, the general rules must be applied to specific fact situations. Well-formed rules, then, must be written in general, broad terms so as to apply to many different kinds of fact situations. If the rules are too specific, it is easy to find loopholes around them. But while it is important to use general terms, the result may be a certain difficulty in deciding whether the rule does in fact apply to a particular situation. Both written and common law rules must be interpreted. This job of interpretation belongs chiefly to the courts; but to some extent, those persons responsible for carrying out and enforcing the law aid in its interpretation by determining where it should be applied on a daily basis.

Adjudication, the act of settling disputes and controversies, means the ability to decide the case completely and to dispose of it. Judicial power, then, is power to decide and pronounce a final judgment with knowledge that the judgment will be enforced. In resolving a dispute, the court applies a general rule to a particular fact situation in order to reach a specific and final conclusion as to the rights and duties of the parties involved. "Settling" is the key word in understanding the meaning of adjudication. To settle means to reconcile, to make peace, or to change from a disturbed or troubled condition to one of quietness or tranquility. In other words, a great part of lawmaking is the settling of controversies between people in an orderly, peaceful, and final manner. Adjudication is primarily a job for the courts. But administrative agencies also adjudicate. If you are embroiled in a controversy with the Federal Trade Commission, the Social Security Board, or any one of more than a hundred other agencies, you must go all the way through the agency's procedures for deciding the dispute before you can take it to the courts for review of the agency's decision. Most such questions or disputes are settled without judicial participation—the agency itself adjudicates the matter.

The last activity involved in making law is execution of the law. To execute the law means to carry it into effect and to enforce the general rules. Rules can be made, interpreted, and applied and still fail to accomplish a result. Suppose a court determines that a person has wrongly injured you and must pay your hospital bill in the amount of $1,000. But what if he or she refuses to pay? Or say a court decides that a man is guilty of murder and sentences him to jail. But what if he does not go? A legislature can certainly make a general rule that all of us must drive no faster than fifty-five miles an hour or must not litter the highways. But what if we go faster than fifty-five miles or throw even more litter? You can see how important it is to effectuate the law—to carry it into effect, enforce it, and execute it. This is, for the most part, the job of the executive branches of government—the president and the governors with their many branches of investigative and prosecuting assistants (e.g., the police, the justice department, the attorney general, the district attorney, the FBI, and the sheriffs of various counties).

All aspects of lawmaking are important—making the general rules, interpreting them, applying them to particular fact situations through adjudication, and carrying them out and enforcing their results.

WHERE DOES THE POWER TO MAKE LAW ORIGINATE?

No person may engage in lawmaking in the United States unless he or she possesses the power or authority to do so. All power resides in the people of the United States who have consented to government under a constitutional system of law. The preamble of the Constitution, which we quoted earlier, states that the Constitution was established by the people and makes it clear that it is the people who hold the power—that they conduct the government through their representatives. The Constitution of the United States is the fundamental and supreme law of the land. Any law not in harmony with it is invalid. So to determine where the power to make law originates, the first place to look is the United States Constitution.

An overview of the Constitution reveals these parts:

- A *preamble* that expresses the consent of the people and the legitimate functions of law.

- *Article I,* with ten sections, that establishes the legislative branch of government with limited powers granted to Congress to make general rules for all the people.
- *Article II,* with four sections, that establishes the executive branch of government with limited power granted to the president to carry out and enforce the general rules as well as to participate in making those rules.
- *Article III,* with three sections that establish the judicial branch of government with limited power granted to the Supreme Court and other courts created by Congress to decide cases and controversies.
- *Article IV,* with four sections allowing new states to be admitted to the United States by Act of Congress, dealing with relations between the various states, making each state equal to every other state, forbidding any state to discriminate against citizens of other states in favor of its own (although reasonable differences in treatment are valid), and guaranteeing that each state shall have a republican form of government where representatives are elected by the people of each state.
- *Article V,* which provides for amendment of the Constitution.
- *Article VI,* which declares that the Constitution, the Acts of Congress made pursuant to the Constitution, and treaties made by the president are the supreme law of the land.
- Twenty-six *amendments* have been added to the Constitution. These amendments guarantee many individual rights and deal with miscellaneous items such as elections, income taxes, and prohibition. Particularly important with regard to the lawmaking power are amendments nine and ten which provide that powers not delegated to the federal government are retained by the states and by the people themselves.

The Constitution, then, provides Congress with power to make general rules within certain subject areas; the president with power to execute these rules; and the federal courts with power to interpret them and to decide cases and controversies on defined subject matters. All powers not specifically given to the federal Congress, the president, or the federal courts are reserved to the states and to the people. The states are also guaranteed a republican form of government. Each state has adopted its own constitution generally modeled after the federal one. A similar governmental structure provides for state legislative, executive, and judicial branches specifically defining the powers of each branch of government within the state. In addition, state constitutions provide for the creation of county and city governments, and it is in the constitution that the power to make law within such counties, cities, or towns originates.

The entire authority to make law must be traced to the federal and state constitutions. If someone purports to make law—that is, make rules, interpret them with authority, settle disputes, or enforce rules or decisions—his or her authority must come from one of these documents. For example, if the Chief of Police for the City of Portland, in the County of Multnomah, in the State of Oregon arrests someone for an alleged murder, and the District Attorney of that County prosecutes him, the Judge of the Circuit Court for that County finds him guilty, and the state policeman escorts him to prison—all of their lawmaking actions must be supported by powers traced to the Constitution. The federal Constitution, which became effective in 1788, reserves the power to prosecute and fix punishment for murder to each state. It also provides for the admission of new states into the Union by Act of Congress. The State of Oregon Constitution was framed by a convention of sixty delegates chosen by the people of the then Oregon Territory in September of 1857. On November 9 of the same year, the Constitution was approved by vote of the people. The Act of Congress admitting Oregon into the Union was approved in 1859, at which time the Oregon Constitution went into effect. This Constitution provides that the State of Oregon Legislature must institute a method whereby voters of any county may set up a county government and the voters of any city or town may provide for a city government. Based on these powers, the people of Multnomah County and of Portland, Oregon, have created both a county and city government (with formal county and city charters that are similar to constitutions) giving power to the Police Chief to make arrests for violations of the State Criminal Code. This Code, written by the State Legislature, empowers the District Attorney to prosecute for murder. The State Constitution and statutes enacted under it give the Judge power to conduct the trial and sentence the murderer to prison and authorize the state policeman to take the convicted murderer to prison.

The power to make law comes, therefore, from the people themselves who have agreed that the federal and state constitutions shall be their fundamental law. The constitutions set up three branches of government—legislative, executive, and judicial—each separate from the others—each with lawmaking functions and each checking and balancing the others.

In the next chapter we will deal with the interaction of the three branches with special emphasis on the jurisdiction of the courts and protection of individual rights.

Cases

Defending the Constitution in Chickasaw, Alabama.

MARSH v. STATE OF ALABAMA

Supreme Court of the United States, 1946.
326 U.S. 501, 66 S.Ct. 276, 90 L.Ed. 265.

Mr. Justice BLACK delivered the opinion of the Court.

In this case we are asked to decide whether a State, consistently with the First and Fourteenth Amendments, can impose criminal punishment on a person who undertakes to distribute religious literature on the premises of a company-owned town contrary to the wishes of the town's management. The town, a suburb of Mobile, Alabama, known as Chickasaw, is owned by the Gulf Shipbuilding Corporation. Except for that it has all the characteristics of any other American town. The property consists of residential buildings, streets, a system of sewers, a sewage disposal plant and a "business block" on which business places are situated. * * * Merchants and service establishments have rented the stores and business places on the business block and the United States uses one of the places as a post office from which six carriers deliver mail to the people of Chickasaw and the adjacent area. The town and the surrounding neighborhood * * * are thickly settled, and according to all indications the residents use the business block as their regular shopping center. * * * The town and its shopping district are accessible to and freely used by the public in general and there is nothing to distinguish them from any other town and shopping center except the fact that the title to the property belongs to a private corporation.

Appellant, a Jehovah's Witness, came onto the sidewalk we have just described, stood near the post-office and undertook to distribute religious literature. In the stores the corporation had posted a notice which read as follows: "This Is Private Property, and Without Written Permission, No Street, or House Vendor, Agent or Solicitation of Any Kind Will Be Permitted." Appellant was warned that she could not distribute the literature without a permit and told that no permit would be issued to her. She protested that the company rule could not be constitutionally applied so as to prohibit her from distributing religious writings. When she was asked to leave the sidewalk and Chickasaw she declined. The deputy sheriff arrested her and she was charged in the state court with violating * * * the 1940 Alabama Code which makes it a crime to enter or remain on the premises of another after having been warned not to do so. Appellant contended that to construe the state statute as applicable to her activities would abridge her right to freedom of press and religion contrary to the First and Fourteenth Amendments to the Constitution. This contention was rejected and she was convicted. [Her conviction was affirmed on appeal in the Alabama courts] * * *

Had the title to Chickasaw belonged not to a private but to a municipal corporation and had appellant been arrested for violating a municipal ordinance rather than a ruling by those appointed by the corporation to manage a company-town it would have been clear that appellant's conviction must be reversed. Under our decision in Lovell v. Griffin * * * and others which have followed that case neither a state nor a municipality can completely bar the distribution of literature containing religious or political ideas on its streets, sidewalks and public places or make the right to distribute dependent on a flat license tax or permit to be issued by an official who could deny it at will. We have also held that an ordinance completely prohibiting the dissemination of ideas on the city streets can not be justified on the ground that the municipality holds legal title to them. * * * And we have recognized that the preservation of a free society is so far dependent upon the right of each individual citizen to receive such literature as he himself might desire that a municipality could not without jeopardizing that vital individual freedom, prohibit door to door distribution of literature. * * * From these decisions it is clear that had the people of Chickasaw owned all the homes, and all the stores, and all the streets, and all the sidewalks, all those owners together could not have set up a municipal government with sufficient power to pass an ordinance completely barring the distribution of religious literature. Our question then narrows down to this: Can those people who live in or come to Chickasaw be denied freedom of press and religion simply because a single company has legal title to all the town? For it is the state's contention that the mere fact that all the property interests in the town are held by a single company is enough to give that company power, enforceable by a state statute, to abridge these freedoms.

We do not agree that the corporation's property interests settle the question. * * * Whether a corporation or a municipality owns or possesses the town the public in either case has an identical interest in the functioning of the community in such manner that the channels of communication remain free.

* * *

Many people in the United States live in company-owned towns. These people, just as residents of municipalities, are free citizens of their State and country. Just as all other citizens they must make decisions which affect the welfare of community and nation. To act as good citizens they must be informed. In order to enable them to be properly informed their information must be uncensored. There is no more reason for depriving these people of the liberties guaranteed by the First and Fourteenth Amendments than there is for curtailing these freedoms with respect to any other citizen.

When we balance the Constitutional rights of owners of property against those of the people to enjoy freedom of press and religion, as we must here, we remain mindful of the fact that the latter occupy a preferred position. As we have stated before, the right to exercise the liberties safeguarded by the First Amendment "lies at the foundation of free government by free men" * * *

Reversed and Remanded.

Anti-Soviet agitation and propaganda.

THE PEOPLE v. ALEXANDER GINZBURG [1]

On August 1, 1975 the thirty-five-nation Conference on Security and Cooperation in Europe (CSCE) signed a final agreement. Known as the Helsinki agreement, it was signed by the United States, Canada, the Soviet Union, and every Eastern and Western European nation except Albania. This agreement legitimized all national boundaries established in the aftermath of World War II including the Baltic States and East Germany. The Soviet Union signed the thirty-five-nation pact because it confirmed the "inviolability" of national frontiers of the Eastern European nations, a longstanding goal of the Soviet Union. The signing culminated two years of negotiation and also dealt with European security, economic cooperation, and human rights. Regarding the latter, the signed declaration specifically stated:

> The participating states will respect human rights and fundamental freedoms, including the freedom of thought, conscience, religion or belief, for all without distinction as to race, sex, language or religion.
>
> Within this framework the participating states will recognize and respect the freedom of the individual to profess and practice, alone or in community with others, religion or belief acting in accordance with the dictates of his own conscience.
>
> The participating states on whose territory national minorities exist will respect the right of persons belonging to such minorities to equality before the law, will afford them the full opportunity for the actual enjoyment of human rights and fundamental freedoms and will, in this manner, protect their legitimate interests in this sphere.

Shortly after the Helsinki signing, nine Soviet dissidents formed a committee to monitor Soviet compliance with the human rights provisions. Among the members of this "Public Group to Promote the Fulfillment of the Helsinki Accords in the U.S.S.R." were poet Alexander Ginzburg and Yelena Bonner Sakharov, wife of Andrei Sakharov, foremost builder of the Soviet Hydrogen bomb, winner of the 1975 Nobel Peace Prize, and a leader of the human rights movement in the U.S.S.R.

Alexander Ginzburg's father was an architect and ethnic Russian who died when Ginzburg was a child. His mother was Jewish, and as a gesture of defiance during Stalin's anti-Semitic regime, he took her name although his religion remained Russian Orthodox. He published underground poetry journals in the 1950s and twice was sent to prison and forced labor camps. The basis for a five-year sentence was the writing

1. References: *Facts on File, World News Digest with Index,* Facts on File, Inc., 119 W 57th St., New York, N.Y. August 9, 1975 and July 21, 1978; *The New York Times,* July 1, 11, 12, 13, 14, 1978; *Time, The Weekly News Magazine,* February 27, 1977, July 31, 1978, February 14, 1983.

of an unauthorized account of a dissenter's trial.

In February 1977, Alexander Ginzburg was arrested by the KGB (Komitet Sosudarstvennvi Bezopasnosti meaning Committee for State Security) and charged with the crime of "anti Soviet agitation and propaganda." On July 10, 1978 Ginzburg's trial began (in the Soviet Union a person may legally be held incommunicado for nine months before trial and the Supreme Soviet can further extend this time in individual cases) in Kaluga, 100 miles south of Moscow with the prosecutor asking for a ten-year prison term plus five years' internal exile (removal out of the Western part of the Soviet Union). The prosecutor claimed Ginzburg had circulated "slanderous inventions discrediting the Soviet State and socialist system" including the distribution of books (such as *The Gulag Archipelago*) by exiled Soviet author and Nobel laureate Alexander Solzhenitsyn.

The court heard twenty-five prosecution witnesses but refused to let Ginzburg call any witnesses in his own defense. While Ginzburg was allowed to have a lawyer, his attorney could only be someone first approved by the KGB. The trial was over in three days, and Ginzburg was sentenced to eight years in a forced labor camp.

Alexander Solzhenitsyn's wife Natilya has written the following:

> People in the West occasionally hear of the cruel conditions in Soviet labor camps: about prisoners being tortured by hunger and cold, about the denial of medical care to sick prisoners and about forced psychiatric treatment of perfectly sane people in mental hospitals. But very little is known about the frightening fate of political prisoners' families—of their wives and children and aged parents.
>
> In the U.S.S.R., a sentence for a political offense is always a sentence against the offender's family. Persecution against them starts immediately. Not only has the family lost its main provider but often the wife also loses her job. She has to feed her children, but she cannot find another job because there is but one employer—the state. * * *
>
> Such relentless pressure on political prisoners' families is not just the regime's revenge against those who oppose it. It is farsighted strategy. Those people who do not fear for themselves must fear for their families; they must know that their wives and children will go hungry, cold and homeless, will be subjected to humiliation, so it is better to give up any thought of dissent.

Does the display of the swastika amount to "fighting words"?

THE VILLAGE OF SKOKIE v. THE NATIONAL SOCIALIST PARTY

Supreme Court of Illinois, 1978.
69 Ill.2d 605, 14 Ill.Dec. 890, 373 N.E.2d 21.

Plaintiff, the village of Skokie, filed a complaint * * * seeking to enjoin defendants, the National Socialist Party of America (the American Nazi Party) and 10 individuals as "officers and members" of the party, from engaging in certain activities while conducting a demonstration within the village.

* * *

It is alleged in plaintiff's complaint that the "uniform of the National Socialist Party of America consists of the storm trooper uniform of the German Nazi Party embellished with the Nazi swastika"; that the plaintiff village has a population of about 70,000 persons of which approximately 40,500 persons are of "Jewish religion or Jewish ancestry" and of this latter number 5,000 to 7,000 are survivors of German concentration camps; that the defendant organization is "dedicated to the incitation of racial and religious hatred directed principally against individuals of Jewish faith or ancestry and non-Caucasians"; and that its members "have patterned their conduct, their uniform, their slogan and their tactics along the pattern of the German Nazi Party. * * *"

* * *

At the hearing on plaintiff's motion for an "emergency injunction" a resident of Skokie testified that he was a survivor of the Nazi holocaust. He further testified that the Jewish community in and around Skokie feels the purpose of the march in the "heart of the Jewish population" is to remind the two million survivors "that we are not through with you" and to show "that the Nazi threat is not over, it can happen again." Another resident of Skokie testified that as the result of defendants' announced intention to march in Skokie, 15 to 18 Jewish organizations, within the village and surrounding area, were called and a counterdemonstration of an estimated 12,000 to 15,000 people was scheduled for the same day. There was opinion evidence that defendants' planned demonstration in Skokie would result in violence.

* * *

In defining the constitutional rights of the parties who come before this court, we are, of course, bound by the pronouncements of the United States Supreme Court in its interpretation of the United States Constitution. * * * The decisions of that court, particularly *Cohen v. California* (1971), 403 U.S. 15, 91 S.Ct. 1780, 29 L.Ed.2d 284, in our opinion compel us to permit the demonstration as proposed, including display of the swastika.

"It is firmly settled that under our Constitution the public expression of ideas may not be prohibited merely because the ideas are themselves offensive to some of their hearers" * * * and it is entirely clear that the wearing of distinctive clothing can be symbolic expression of a thought or philosophy. The symbolic expression of thought falls within the free speech clause of the first amendment. * * *

The village of Skokie seeks * * * application of the "fighting words" doctrine. * * * That doctrine was designed to permit punishment of extremely hostile personal communication likely to cause immediate physical response, "no words being 'forbidden except such as have a direct tendency to cause acts of violence by the persons to whom, individually, the remark is addressed.'" * * * In *Cohen* the Supreme Court restated the description of fighting words as "those personally abusive epithets which, when addressed to the ordinary citizen, are, as a matter of common knowledge, inherently likely to provoke violent reaction." * * * Plaintiff urges, and the appellate court has held, that the exhibition of the Nazi symbol, the swastika, addresses to ordinary citizens a message which is tantamount to fighting words. Plaintiff further asks this court to * * * hold that the fighting-words doctrine permits a prior restraint on defendants' symbolic speech. In our judgment we are precluded from doing so.

In *Cohen*, defendant's conviction stemmed from wearing a jacket bearing the words "Fuck the Draft" in a Los Angeles County courthouse corridor. The Supreme Court for reasons we believe applicable here refused to find that the jacket inscription constituted fighting words. That court stated:

> The constitutional right of free expression is powerful medicine in a society as diverse and populous as ours. It is designed and intended to remove governmental restraints from the arena of public discussion. * * *
>
> * * * [W]e cannot indulge the facile assumption that one can forbid particular words without also running a substantial risk of suppressing ideas in the process. Indeed, governments might soon seize upon the censorship of particular words [emblems] as a convenient guise for banning the expression of unpopular views.

* * *

The display of the swastika, as offensive to the principles of a free nation as the memories it recalls may be, is symbolic political speech intended to convey to the public the beliefs of those who display it. It does not, in our opinion, fall within the definition of "fighting words," and that doctrine cannot be used here to overcome the heavy presumption against the constitutional validity of a prior restraint.

Nor can we find that the swastika, while not representing fighting words, is nevertheless so offensive and peace threatening to the public that its display can be enjoined. * * *

The *Cohen* court spoke to this subject:

> * * * While this Court has recognized that government may properly act in many situations to prohibit intrusion into the privacy of the home of unwelcome views and ideas which cannot be totally banned from the public dialogue, *e.g., Rowan v. Post Office Dept.,* 397 U.S. 728, 90 S.Ct. 1484, 25 L.Ed.2d 736 (1970), we have at the same time consistently stressed that 'we are often "captives" outside the sanctuary of the home and subject to objectionable speech.' * * * The ability of government, consonant with the Constitution, to shut off discourse solely to protect others from hearing it is, in other words, dependent upon a showing that substantial privacy interests are being invaded in an essentially intolerable manner.
>
> "* * * [T]he unpopularity of views, their shocking quality, their obnoxiousness, and even their alarming impact is not enough. Otherwise, the preacher of any strange doctrine could be stopped; the anti-racist himself could be suppressed, if he undertakes to speak in 'restricted' areas; and one who asks that public schools be open indiscriminately to all ethnic groups could be lawfully suppressed, if only he choose to speak where persuasion is needed most." [Rockwell v. Morris (1961)] 12 A.D.2d 272, 281–82, 211 N.Y.S.2d 25, 35–36.

* * * We accordingly, albeit reluctantly, conclude that the display of the swastika cannot be enjoined under the fighting-words exception to free speech, nor can anticipation of a hostile audience justify the prior restraint.

You have the right to remain silent.

MIRANDA v. ARIZONA

Supreme Court of the United States, 1966.
384 U.S. 436, 86 S.Ct. 1602, 16 L.Ed.2d 694.

[Four similar cases were brought together before the Supreme Court of the United States.] Mr. Chief Justice WARREN delivered the opinion of the Court.

I

The constitutional issue we decide in each of these cases is the admissibility of statements obtained from a defendant questioned while in custody or otherwise deprived of his freedom of action in any significant way. In each, the defendant was questioned by police officers, detectives, or a prosecuting attorney in a room in which he was cut off from the outside world. In none of these cases was the defendant given a full and effective warning of his rights at the outset of the interrogation process. In all the cases, the questioning elicited oral admissions, and in three of them, signed statements as well which were admitted at their trials. They all thus share salient features—incommunicado interrogation of individuals in a police-dominated atmosphere, resulting in self-incriminating statements without full warnings of constitutional rights.

* * * A valuable source of information about present police practices may be found in various police manuals and texts which document procedures employed with success in the past, and which recommend various other effective tactics. * * *

* * * The setting prescribed by the manuals and observed in practice becomes clear. In essence, it is this: To be alone with the subject is essential to prevent distraction and to deprive him of any outside support. The aura of confidence in his guilt undermines his will to resist. He merely confirms the preconceived story the police seek to have him describe. Patience and persistence, at times relentless questioning, are employed. To obtain a confession, the interrogator must "patiently maneuver himself or his quarry into a position from which the desired objective may be attained." When normal procedures fail to produce the needed result, the police may resort to deceptive strategems such as giving false legal advice. It is important to keep the subject off balance, for example, by trading on his

insecurity about himself or his surroundings. The police then persuade, trick, or cajole him out of exercising his constitutional rights.

* * * In each of the cases, the defendant was thrust into an unfamiliar atmosphere and run through menacing police interrogation procedures. * * * To be sure, the records do not evince overt physical coercion or patent psychological ploys. The fact remains that in none of these cases did the officers undertake to afford appropriate safeguards at the outset of the interrogation to insure that the statements were truly the product of free choice.

* * *

II

* * * The constitutional foundation underlying the privilege is the respect a government—state or federal—must accord to the dignity and integrity of its citizens. * * * Our accusatory system of criminal justice demands that the government seeking to punish an individual produce the evidence against him by its own independent labors, rather than by the cruel, simple expedient of compelling it from his own mouth. * * * In sum, the privilege is fulfilled only when the person is guaranteed the right "to remain silent unless he chooses to speak in the unfettered exercise of his own will."

* * *

III

Today, then, there can be no doubt that the Fifth Amendment privilege is available outside of criminal court proceedings and serves to protect persons in all settings in which their freedom of action is curtailed in any significant way from being compelled to incriminate themselves. We have concluded that without proper safeguards the process of in-custody interrogation of persons suspected or accused of crime contains inherently compelling pressures which work to undermine the individual's will to resist and to compel him to speak where he would not otherwise do so freely. * * *

We hold that when an individual is taken into custody or otherwise deprived of his freedom by the authorities in any significant way and is subjected to questioning, the privilege against self-incrimination is jeopardized. Procedural safeguards must be employed to protect the privilege and unless other fully effective means are adopted to notify the person of his right of silence and to assure that the exercise of the right will be scrupulously honored, the following measures are required. He must be warned prior to any questioning that he has the right to remain silent, that anything he says can be used against him in a court of law, that he has the right to the presence of an attorney, and that if he cannot afford an attorney one will be appointed for him prior to any questioning if he so desires. Opportunity to exercise these rights must be afforded to him throughout the interrogation. After such warnings have been given, and such opportunity afforded him, the individual may knowingly and intelligently waive these rights and agree to answer questions or make a statement. But unless and until such warnings and waiver are demonstrated by the prosecution at trial, no evidence obtained as a result of interrogation can be used against him. * * *

A probing search without a warrant.

UNITED STATES v. ROSS

Supreme Court of the United States, 1982.
456 U.S. 798, 102 S.Ct. 2157, 72 L.Ed.2d 572.

Justice STEVENS delivered the opinion of the Court.

In *Carroll v. United States*, 267 U.S. 132, 45 S.Ct. 280, 69 L.Ed. 543, the Court held that a warrantless search of an automobile stopped by police officers who had probable cause to believe the vehicle contained contraband was not unreasonable within the meaning of the Fourth Amendment. The Court in *Carroll* did not explicitly address the scope of the search that is permissible. In this case, we consider the extent to which police officers—who have legitimately stopped an automobile and who have probable cause to believe that contraband is concealed somewhere within it—may conduct a probing search of compartments and containers within the vehicle whose contents are not in plain view. We hold that they may conduct a search of the vehicle that is as thorough as a magistrate could authorize in a warrant "particularly describing the place to be searched."

In the evening of November 27, 1978, an informant who had previously proved to be reliable telephoned Detective Marcum of the District of Columbia Police Department and told him that an individual known as "Bandit" was selling narcotics kept in the trunk of a car parked at 439 Ridge Street. The informant stated that he had just observed "Bandit" complete a sale and that "Bandit" had told him that additional narcotics were in the trunk. The informant gave Marcum a detailed description of "Bandit" and stated that the car was a "purplish maroon" Chevrolet Malibu with District of Columbia license plates.

Accompanied by Detective Cassidy and Sergeant Gonzales, Marcum immediately drove to the area and found a maroon Malibu parked in front of 439 Ridge Street. A license check disclosed that the car was registered to Albert Ross; a computer check on Ross revealed that he fit the informant's description and used the alias "Bandit." In two passes through the neighborhood the officers did not observe anyone matching the informant's description. To avoid alerting persons on the street, they left the area.

The officers returned five minutes later and observed the maroon Malibu turning off Ridge Street onto Fourth Street. They pulled alongside the Malibu, noticed that the driver matched the informant's description, and stopped the car. Marcum and Cassidy told the driver—later identified as Albert Ross, the respondent in this action—to get out of the vehicle. While they searched Ross, Sergeant Gonzales discovered a bullet on the car's front seat. He searched the interior of the car and found a pistol in the glove compartment. Ross then was arrested and handcuffed. Detective Cassidy took Ross' keys and opened the trunk, where he found a closed brown paper bag. He opened the bag and discovered a number of glassine bags containing a white powder. Cassidy replaced the bag, closed the trunk, and drove the car to Headquarters.

At the police station Cassidy thoroughly searched the car. In addition to the "lunch-type" brown paper bag, Cassidy found in the trunk a zippered red leather pouch. He unzipped the pouch and discovered $3,200 in cash. The police laboratory later determined that the powder in the paper bag was heroin. No warrant was obtained.

Ross was charged with possession of heroin with intent to distribute, in violation of 21 U.S.C. § 841(a). Prior to trial, he moved to suppress the heroin found in the paper bag and the currency found in the leather pouch. After an evidentiary hearing, the District Court denied the motion to suppress. The heroin and currency were introduced in evidence at trial and Ross was convicted.

* * * [T]he Court of Appeals reversed the conviction. It held that the police had probable cause to stop and search Ross' car and that * * * the officers lawfully could search the automobile—including its trunk—without a warrant.

* * * [I]t held that the police should not have opened either container without first obtaining a warrant.

There is * * * no dispute among judges about the importance of striving for clarification in this area of the law. For countless vehicles are stopped on highways and public streets every day and our cases demonstrate that it is not uncommon for police officers to have probable cause to believe that contraband may be found in a stopped vehicle. In every such case a conflict is presented between the individual's constitutionally protected interest in privacy and the public interest in effective law enforcement.

* * * Given the nature of an automobile in transit, the Court [has] recognized that an immediate intrusion is necessary if

police officers are to secure the illicit substance. In this class of cases, the Court held that a warrantless search of an automobile is not unreasonable.

In defining the nature of this "exception" to the general rule that "[i]n cases where the securing of a warrant is reasonably practicable, it must be used," * * * the Court in *Carroll* emphasized the importance of the requirement that officers have probable cause to believe that the vehicle contains contraband. * * *

> "[T]hose lawfully within the country, entitled to use the public highways, have a right to free passage without interruption or search unless there is known to a competent official authorized to search, probable cause for believing that their vehicles are carrying contraband or illegal merchandise." *Id.*, at 153–154, 45 S.Ct., at 285.

Moreover, the probable cause determination must be based on objective facts that could justify the issuance of a warrant by a magistrate and not merely on the subjective good faith of the police officers. " '[A]s we have seen, good faith is not enough to constitute probable cause. That faith must be grounded on facts within knowledge of the [officer], which in the judgment of the court would make his faith reasonable.' "

In short, the exception to the warrant requirement established in *Carroll*—the scope of which we consider in this case—applies only to searches of vehicles that are supported by probable cause. In this class of cases, a search is not unreasonable if based on facts that would justify the issuance of a warrant, even though a warrant has not actually been obtained.

A lawful search of fixed premises generally extends to the entire area in which the object of the search may be found and is not limited by the possibility that separate acts of entry or opening may be required to complete the search. Thus, a warrant that authorizes an officer to search a home for illegal weapons also provides authority to open closets, chests, drawers, and containers in which the weapon might be found. A warrant to open a footlocker to search for marijuana would also authorize the opening of packages found inside. A warrant to search a vehicle would support a search of every part of the vehicle that might contain the object of the search. When a legitimate search is under way, and when its purpose and its limits have been precisely defined, nice distinctions between closets, drawers, and containers, in the case of a home, or between glove compartments, upholstered seats, trunks, and wrapped packages, in the case of a vehicle, must give way to the interest in the prompt and efficient completion of the task at hand.

* * * The scope of a warrantless search based on probable cause is no narrower—and no broader—than the scope of a search authorized by a warrant supported by probable cause. Only the prior approval of the magistrate is waived; the search otherwise is as the magistrate could authorize.[32]

The scope of a warrantless search of an automobile thus is not defined by the nature of the container in which the contraband is secreted. Rather, it is defined by the object of the search and the places in which there is probable cause to believe that it may be found. Just as probable cause to believe that a stolen lawnmower may be found in a garage will not support a warrant to search an upstairs bedroom, probable cause to believe that undocumented aliens are being transported in a van will not justify a warrantless search of a suitcase. Probable cause to believe that a container placed in the trunk of a taxi contains contraband or evidence does not justify a search of the entire cab.

We reaffirm the basic rule of Fourth Amendment jurisprudence stated by Justice

32. In choosing to search without a warrant on their own assessment of probable cause, police officers of course lose the protection that a warrant would provide to them in an action for damages brought by an individual claiming that the search was unconstitutional. Cf. *Monroe v. Pape*, 365 U.S. 167, 81 S.Ct. 473, 5 L.Ed.2d 492. Although an officer may establish that he acted in good faith in conducting the search by other evidence, a warrant issued by a magistrate normally suffices to establish it.

Stewart for a unanimous Court in *Mincey v. Arizona,* 437 U.S. 385, 390, 98 S.Ct. 2408, 2412, 57 L.Ed.2d 290:

> The Fourth Amendment proscribes all unreasonable searches and seizures, and it is a cardinal principle that 'searches conducted outside the judicial process, without prior approval by judge or magistrate, are *per se* unreasonable under the Fourth Amendment—subject only to a few specifically established and well-delineated exceptions.' * * *

The exception recognized in *Carroll* is unquestionably one that is "specifically established and well-delineated." We hold that the scope of the warrantless search authorized by that exception is no broader and no narrower than a magistrate could legitimately authorize by warrant. If probable cause justifies the search of a lawfully stopped vehicle, it justifies the search of every part of the vehicle and its contents that may conceal the object of the search.

The judgment of the Court of Appeals is reversed.

Bound, gagged, or thrown out of court.

ILLINOIS v. ALLEN

Supreme Court of the United States, 1970.
397 U.S. 337, 90 S.Ct. 1057, 25 L.Ed.2d 353.

Mr. Justice BLACK delivered the opinion of the Court. * * *

* * * One of the most basic of the rights guaranteed by the Confrontation Clause [of the Sixth Amendment] is the accused's right to be present in the courtroom at every stage of his trial. * * * The question presented in this case is whether an accused can claim the benefit of this constitutional right to remain in the courtroom while at the same time he engages in speech and conduct which is so noisy, disorderly, and disruptive that it is exceedingly difficult or wholly impossible to carry on the trial.

The issue arose in the following way. The respondent, Allen, was convicted by an Illinois jury of armed robbery and was sentenced to serve 10 to 30 years in the Illinois State Penitentiary. The evidence against him showed that on August 12, 1956, he entered a tavern in Illinois and, after ordering a drink, took $200 from the bartender at gunpoint. The Supreme Court of Illinois affirmed his conviction. * * * Later Allen filed a petition for a writ of habeas corpus in federal court alleging that he had been wrongfully deprived by the Illinois trial judge of his constitutional right to remain present throughout his trial. Finding no constitutional violation, the District Court declined to issue the writ. The Court of Appeals reversed. * * *

The facts surrounding Allen's expulsion from the courtroom are set out in the Court of Appeals' opinion sustaining Allen's contention:

> "After his indictment and during the pretrial stage, the petitioner [Allen] refused court-appointed counsel and indicated to the trial court on several occasions that he wished to conduct his own defense. * * *
>
> "The trial began on September 9, 1957. * * * [T]he petitioner began examining the first juror and continued at great length. Finally, the trial judge interrupted the petitioner, requesting him to confine his questions solely to matters relating to the prospective juror's qualifications. At that point, the petitioner started to argue with the judge in a most abusive and disrespectful manner. At last, and seemingly in desperation, the judge asked appointed counsel to proceed with the examination of the jurors. The petitioner continued to talk, proclaiming that the appointed attorney was not going to act as his lawyer. He terminated his remarks by saying, 'When I go out for lunchtime, you're [the judge] going to be a corpse here.' At that point he tore the file which his attorney had and threw the papers on the floor. The trial judge thereupon stated to the petitioner, 'One more outbreak of that sort and I'll remove you from the courtroom.' This warning had no effect on the petitioner. He continued to talk back to the judge, saying, 'There's not going to be no trial, either. I'm going to sit here and you're going to talk and you can bring your shackles out and straight

jacket and put them on me and tape my mouth, but it will do no good because there's not going to be no trial.' After more abusive remarks by the petitioner, the trial judge ordered the trial to proceed in the petitioner's absence. The petitioner was removed from the courtroom. * * *

"After a noon recess * * * the judge said that the petitioner would be permitted to remain in the courtroom if he 'behaved [himself] and [did] not interfere with the introduction of the case.' The jury was brought in and seated. Counsel for the petitioner then moved to exclude the witnesses from the courtroom. The [petitioner] protested this effort on the part of his attorney, saying: 'There is going to be no proceeding. I'm going to start talking and I'm going to keep on talking all through the trial. There's not going to be no trial like this.' * * * The trial judge thereupon ordered the petitioner removed from the courtroom." 413 F.2d, at 233–234.

After this second removal, Allen remained out of the courtroom during the presentation of the State's case-in-chief, except that he was brought in on several occasions for purposes of identification. * * * After the prosecution's case had been presented, the trial judge reiterated his promise to Allen that he could return to the courtroom whenever he agreed to conduct himself properly. Allen gave some assurances of proper conduct and was permitted to be present through the remainder of the trial, * * * which was conducted by his appointed counsel.

The Court of Appeals went on to hold that the Supreme Court of Illinois was wrong in ruling that Allen had by his conduct relinquished his constitutional right to be present * * *.

The Court of Appeals felt that the defendant's Sixth Amendment right to be present at his own trial was so "absolute" that, no matter how unruly or disruptive the defendant's conduct might be, he could never be held to have lost that right so long as he continued to insist upon it, as Allen clearly did. Therefore the Court of Appeals concluded that a trial judge could never expel a defendant from his own trial and that the judge's ultimate remedy when faced with an obstreperous defendant like Allen * * * is to bind and gag him. We cannot agree that the Sixth Amendment, the cases upon which the Court of Appeals relied, or any other cases of this Court so handicap a trial judge in conducting a criminal trial. We accept instead the statement of Mr. Justice Cardozo who * * * said: "No doubt the privilege [of personally confronting witnesses] may be lost by consent or at times even by misconduct." Although mindful that courts must indulge every reasonable presumption against the loss of constitutional rights, * * * we explicitly hold today that a defendant can lose his right to be present at trial if, after he has been warned by the judge that he will be removed if he continues his disruptive behavior, he nevertheless insists on conducting himself in a manner so disorderly, disruptive, and disrespectful of the court that his trial cannot be carried on with him in the courtroom. Once lost, the right to be present can, of course, be reclaimed as soon as the defendant is willing to conduct himself consistently with the decorum and respect inherent in the concept of courts and judicial proceedings.

* * *

We think there are at least three constitutionally permissible ways for a trial judge to handle an obstreperous defendant like Allen: (1) bind and gag him, thereby keeping him present; (2) cite him for contempt; (3) take him out of the courtroom until he promises to conduct himself properly.

* * *

* * * Trying a defendant for a crime while he sits bound and gagged before the judge and jury would to an extent comply with that part of the Sixth Amendment's purposes * * * but the use of this technique is itself something of an affront to the very dignity and decorum of judicial proceedings that the judge is seeking to uphold. * * * And criminal contempt has obvious

limitations as a sanction when the defendant is charged with a crime so serious that a very severe sentence such as death or life imprisonment is likely to be imposed. In such a case the defendant might not be affected by a mere contempt sentence when he ultimately faces a far more serious sanction. * * * Allen's behavior was clearly of such an extreme and aggravated nature as to justify either his removal from the courtroom or his total physical restraint. Prior to his removal he was repeatedly warned by the trial judge that he would be removed from the courtroom if he persisted in his unruly conduct and * * * Allen would not have been at all dissuaded by the trial judge's use of his criminal contempt powers. Allen was constantly informed that he could return to the trial when he would agree to conduct himself in an orderly manner. Under these circumstances we hold that Allen lost his right guaranteed by the Sixth and Fourteenth Amendments to be present throughout his trial.

It is not pleasant to hold that the respondent Allen was properly banished from the court for a part of his own trial. * * * [But] it would degrade our country and our judicial system to permit our courts to be bullied, insulted, and humiliated and their orderly progress thwarted and obstructed by defendants brought before them charged with crimes. * * * If our courts are to remain what the Founders intended, the citadels of justice, their proceedings cannot and must not be infected with the sort of scurrilous, abusive language and conduct paraded before the Illinois trial judge in this case. * * *

Reversed.

One person, one vote.

REYNOLDS v. SIMS

Supreme Court of the United States, 1964.
377 U.S. 533, 84 S.Ct. 1362, 12 L.Ed.2d 506.

Mr. Chief Justice WARREN delivered the opinion of the Court.

* * *

On July 21, 1962, the District Court held that the inequality of the existing representation in the Alabama Legislature violated the Equal Protection Clause of the Fourteenth Amendment * * * since population growth and shifts had converted the 1901 scheme, as perpetuated some 60 years later, into an invidiously discriminatory plan completely lacking in rationality. Under the existing provisions, applying 1960 census figures, only 25.1% of the State's total population resided in districts represented by a majority of the members of the Senate, and only 25.7% lived in counties which could elect a majority of the members of the House of Representatives. Population-variance ratios of up to about 41-to-1 existed in the Senate, and up to about 16-to-1 in the House. * * *

Undeniably the Constitution of the United States protects the right of all qualified citizens to vote, in state as well as in federal elections. * * * It has been repeatedly recognized that all qualified voters have a constitutionally protected right to vote, and to have their votes counted * * *.

The right to vote can neither be denied outright, * * * nor destroyed by alteration of ballots, * * * nor diluted by ballot-box stuffing * * *. The right to vote freely for the candidate of one's choice is of the essence of a democratic society, and any restrictions on that right strike at the heart of representative government. And the right of suffrage can be denied by a debasement or dilution of the weight of a citizen's vote just as effectively as by wholly prohibiting the free exercise of the franchise.

* * * Our problem, [in this case] is to ascertain whether there are any constitutionally [recognizable] principles which would justify departures from the basic standard of equality among voters in the apportionment of seats in state legislatures.

Legislators represent people, not trees or acres. Legislators are elected by voters, not farms or cities or economic interests. As long as ours is a representative form of government, and our legislatures are those instruments of government elected directly by and directly representative of the people, the right to elect legislators in a free and unimpaired fashion is a bedrock of our political system. * * * It would appear extraordinary to suggest that a State could be constitutionally permitted to enact a law providing that certain of the State's voters could vote two, five, or 10 times for their legislative representatives, while voters living elsewhere could vote only once. * * * Of course, the effect of state legislative districting schemes which give the same number of representatives to unequal numbers of constituents is identical. * * * The resulting discrimination against those individual voters living in disfavored areas is easily demonstrable mathematically. Their right to vote is simply not the same right to vote as that of those living in a favored part of the State. Two, five, or 10 of them must vote before the effect of their voting is equivalent to that of their favored neighbor. * * * Since the achieving of fair and effective representation for all citizens is concededly the basic aim of legislative apportionment, we conclude that the Equal Protection Clause guarantees the opportunity for equal participation by all voters in the election of state legislators. Diluting the weight of votes because of place of residence impairs basic constitutional rights under the Fourteenth Amendment just as much as invidious discriminations based upon factors such as race * * * or economic status * * *. Our constitutional system amply provides for the protection of minorities by means other than giving them majority control of state legislatures. And the democratic ideals of equality and majority rule, which have served this Nation so well in the past, are hardly of any less significance for the present and the future.

* * * Representation schemes once fair and equitable become archaic and outdated. But the basic principle of representative government remains, and must remain, unchanged—the weight of a citizen's vote cannot be made to depend on where he lives. * * *

* * * This is an essential part of the concept of a government of laws and not men. This is at the heart of Lincoln's vision of "government of the people, by the people, [and] for the people." The Equal Protection Clause demands no less than substantially equal state legislative representation for all citizens, of all places as well as of all races.

We hold that, as a basic constitutional standard, the Equal Protection Clause requires that the seats in both houses of a bicameral state legislature must be apportioned on a population basis. * * *

* * *

Affirmed and remanded.

The Supreme Court and the abortion controversy.

ROE v. WADE

Supreme Court of the United States, 1973.
410 U.S. 113, 93 S.Ct. 705, 35 L.Ed.2d 147.

Mr. Justice BLACKMUN delivered the opinion of the Court.

* * *

We forthwith acknowledge our awareness of the sensitive and emotional nature of the abortion controversy, of the vigorous opposing views, even among physicians, and of the deep and seemingly absolute convictions that the subject inspires. One's philosophy, one's experiences, one's exposure to the raw edges of human existence, one's religious training, one's attitudes toward life and family and their values, and the moral standards one establishes and seeks to observe, are all likely to influence and to color one's thinking and conclusions about abortion.

In addition, population growth, pollution, poverty, and racial overtones tend to complicate and not to simplify the problem.

Our task, of course, is to resolve the issue by constitutional measurement, free of emotion and of predilection. * * *

* * *

The principal thrust of appellant's attack on the Texas statutes is that they improperly invade a right, said to be possessed by the pregnant woman, to choose to terminate her pregnancy. * * *

* * *

The Constitution does not explicitly mention any right of privacy. [But] * * * the Court has recognized that a right of personal privacy, or a guarantee of certain areas or zones of privacy, does exist under the Constitution. In varying contexts, the Court or individual Justices have, indeed, found at least the roots of that right in the First Amendment, * * * in the Fourth and Fifth Amendments, * * * in the penumbras of the Bill of Rights, * * * in the Ninth Amendment, * * * or in the concept of liberty guaranteed by the first section of the Fourteenth Amendment, * * *. These decisions make it clear that only personal rights that can be deemed "fundamental" or "implicit in the concept of ordered liberty," * * * are included in this guarantee of personal privacy. They also make it clear that the right has some extension to activities relating to marriage, * * * procreation, * * * contraception, * * * family relationships, * * * and child rearing and education * * *.

This right of privacy, whether it be founded in the Fourteenth Amendment's concept of personal liberty and restrictions upon state action, as we feel it is, or, as the District Court determined in the Ninth Amendment's reservation of rights to the people, is broad enough to encompass a woman's decision whether or not to terminate her pregnancy. The detriment that the State would impose upon the pregnant woman by denying this choice altogether is apparent. Specific and direct harm medically diagnosable even in early pregnancy may be involved. Maternity, or additional offspring, may force upon the woman a distressful life and future. Psychological harm may be imminent. Mental and physical health may be taxed by child care. There is also the distress, for all concerned, associated with the unwanted child, and there is the problem of bringing a child into a family already unable, psychologically and otherwise, to care for it. In other cases, as in this one, the additional difficulties and continuing stigma of unwed motherhood may be involved. All these are factors the woman and her responsible physician necessarily will consider in consultation.

On the basis of elements such as these, appellants * * * argue that the woman's right is absolute and that she is entitled to terminate her pregnancy at whatever time, in whatever way, and for whatever reason she alone chooses. With this we do not agree. * * * The Court's decisions recognizing a right of privacy also acknowledge that some state regulation in areas protected by that right is appropriate. * * * [A] State may properly assert important interests in safeguarding health, in maintaining medical standards, and in protecting potential life. At some point in pregnancy, these respective interests become sufficiently compelling to sustain regulation of the factors that govern the abortion decision. * * *

We, therefore, conclude that the right of personal privacy includes the abortion decision, but that this right is not unqualified and must be considered against important state interests in regulation.

* * *

Where certain "fundamental rights" are involved, the Court has held that regulation limiting these rights may be justified only by a "compelling state interest," * * * and that legislative enactments must be narrowly drawn to express only the legitimate state interests at stake. * * *

* * *

A. The appellee * * * argue[s] that the fetus is a "person" within the language and meaning of the Fourteenth Amendment. * * * If this suggestion of personhood is established, the appellant's case, of course, collapses, for the fetus' right to life would then be guaranteed specifically by the Amendment. * * *

The Constitution does not define "person" in so many words. * * * [Where it is referred to there is no] assurance, that it has any possible prenatal application.

All this, together with our observation, * * * that throughout the major portion of the 19th century prevailing legal abortion practices were far freer than they are today, persuades us that the word "person," as used in the Fourteenth Amendment, does not include the unborn. * * *

* * *

B. The pregnant woman cannot be isolated in her privacy. She carries an embryo and, later, a fetus, * * *. The situation therefore is inherently different from marital intimacy, or bedroom possession of obscene material, or marriage, or procreation, or education, * * *. [I]t is reasonable and appropriate for a State to decide that at some point in time another interest, that of health of the mother or that of potential human life, becomes significantly involved. The woman's privacy is no longer sole and any right of privacy she possesses must be measured accordingly.

Texas urges that, apart from the Fourteenth Amendment, life begins at conception and is present throughout pregnancy, and that, therefore, the State has a compelling interest in protecting that life from and after conception. We need not resolve the difficult question of when life begins. When those trained in the respective disciplines of medicine, philosophy, and theology are unable to arrive at any consensus, the judiciary, at this point in the development of man's knowledge, is not in a position to speculate as to the answer.

In areas other than criminal abortion, the law has been reluctant to endorse any theory that life, as we recognize it, begins before live birth or to accord legal rights to the unborn except in narrowly defined situations and except when the rights are contingent upon live birth. * * * In short, the unborn have never been recognized in the law as persons in the whole sense.

In view of all this, we do not agree that, by adopting one theory of life, Texas may override the rights of the pregnant woman that are at stake. * * *

With respect to the State's important and legitimate interest in the health of the mother, the "compelling" point, in the light of present medical knowledge, is at approximately the end of the first trimester. This is so because of the now-established medical fact, * * * that until the end of the first trimester mortality in abortion may be less than mortality in normal childbirth. It follows that, from and after this point, a State may regulate the abortion procedure to the extent that the regulation reasonably relates to the preservation and protection of maternal health. Examples of permissible state regulation in this area are requirements as to the qualifications of the person who is to perform the abortion; as to the licensure of that person; as to the facility in which the procedure is to be performed, that is, whether it must be a hospital or may be a clinic or some other place of less-than-hospital status; as to the licensing of the facility; and the like.

This means, on the other hand, that, for the period of pregnancy prior to this "compelling" point, the attending physician, in consultation with his patient, is free to determine, without regulation by the State, that, in his medical judgment, the patient's pregnancy should be terminated. If that decision is reached, the judgment may be effectuated by an abortion free of interference by the State.

With respect to the State's important and legitimate interest in potential life, the "compelling" point is at viability. This is so because the fetus then presumably has the capability of meaningful life outside the mother's womb. State regulation protective of fetal life after viability thus has both logical and biological justifications. If the State is interested in protecting fetal life after viability, it may go so far as to proscribe abortion during that period, except when it is necessary to preserve the life or health of the mother.

Measured against these standards, * * * [the Texas statute] sweeps too broadly. The statute makes no distinction between abortions performed early in pregnancy and those performed later, and it limits to a single reason, "saving" the mother's life, the legal justification for the procedure.

* * *

To summarize and to repeat:

1. The state criminal abortion statute of the current Texas type, that excepts from criminality only a *life-saving* procedure on behalf of the mother, without regard to pregnancy stage and without recognition of the other interests involved, is violative of the Due Process Clause of the Fourteenth Amendment.

(a) For the stage prior to approximately the end of the first trimester, the abortion decision and its effectuation must be left to the medical judgment of the pregnant woman's attending physician.

(b) For the stage subsequent to approximately the end of the first trimester, the State, in promoting its interest in the health of the mother, may, if it chooses, regulate the abortion procedure in ways that are reasonably related to maternal health.

(c) For the stage subsequent to viability, the State in promoting its interest in the potentiality of human life may, if it chooses, regulate, and even proscribe, abortion except where it is necessary, in appropriate medical judgment, for the preservation of the life or health of the mother.

2. The State may define the term "physician" * * * to mean only a physician currently licensed by the State, and may proscribe any abortion by a person who is not a physician as so defined.

* * *

This holding, we feel, is consistent with the relative weights of the respective interests involved, with the lessons and examples of medical and legal history, with the lenity of the common law, and with the demands of the profound problems of the present day. The decision leaves the State free to place increasing restrictions on abortion as the period of pregnancy lengthens, so long as those restrictions are tailored to the recognized state interests. The decision vindicates the right of the physician to administer medical treatment according to his professional judgment up to the points where important state interests provide compelling justifications for intervention. Up to those points, the abortion decision in all its aspects is inherently, and primarily a medical decision, and basic responsibility for it must rest with the physician. If an individual practitioner abuses the privilege of exercising proper medical judgment, the usual remedies, judicial and intra-professional, are available.

* * *

It is so ordered.

The life-support system may be withdrawn.

In the Matter of KAREN QUINLAN, An Alleged Incompetent

Supreme Court of New Jersey, 1975.
70 N.J. 10, 355 A.2d 647.

The opinion of the Court was delivered by HUGHES, C. J.

The Litigation

The central figure in this tragic case is Karen Ann Quinlan, a New Jersey resident. At the age of 22, she lies in a debilitated and allegedly moribund state at Saint Clare's Hospital in Denville, New Jersey. The litigation has to do in final analysis, with her life,—its continuance or cessation,—and the responsibilities, rights and duties, with regard to any fateful decision concerning it, of her family, her guardian, her doctors, the hospital, the State through its law enforcement authorities, and finally the courts of justice.

* * * [T]he appellant (hereafter "plaintiff") Joseph Quinlan, Karen's father, had appealed the adverse judgment of the Chancery Division.

Due to extensive physical damage fully described in the able opinion of the trial judge, Judge Muir, supporting that judgment, Karen allegedly was incompetent. Joseph Quinlan sought the adjudication of that incompetency. He wished to be appointed guardian of the person and property of his daughter. It was proposed by him that such letters of guardianship, if granted, should contain an express power to him as guardian to authorize the discontinuance of all extraordinary medical procedures now allegedly sustaining Karen's vital processes and hence her life, since these measures, he asserted, present no hope of her eventual recovery.

* * *

On the night of April 15, 1975, for reasons still unclear, Karen Quinlan ceased breathing for at least two 15 minute periods. She received some ineffectual mouth-to-mouth resuscitation from friends. She was taken by ambulance to Newton Memorial Hospital. There she had a temperature of 100 degrees, her pupils were unreactive and she was unresponsive even to deep pain.

* * *

The matter is of transcendent importance, involving questions related to the definition and existence of death, the prolongation of life through artificial means developed by medical technology undreamed of in past generations of the practice of the healing arts; the impact of such durationally indeterminate and artificial life * * * prolongation on the rights of the incompetent, her family and society in general; the bearing of constitutional right and the scope of judicial responsibility, as to the appropriate response of an equity court of justice to the extraordinary prayer for relief of the plaintiff.

* * *

The further medical consensus was that Karen in addition to being comatose is in a chronic and persistent "vegetative" state, having no awareness of anything or anyone around her and existing at a primitive reflex level. Although she does have some brain stem function (ineffective for respiration) and has other reactions one normally associates with being alive, such as moving, reacting to light, sound and noxious stimuli, blinking her eyes, and the like, the quality of her feeling impulses is unknown. She grimaces, makes stereotyped cries and sounds and has chewing motions. Her blood pressure is normal.

* * *

From all of this evidence, and including the whole testimonial record, several basic findings in the physical area are mandated. Severe brain and associated damage, albeit of uncertain etiology, has left Karen in a chronic and persistent vegetative state. No form of treatment which can cure or improve that condition is known or available. As nearly as may be determined, considering the guarded area of remote uncertainties characteristic of most medical science predictions, she can *never* be restored to cognitive or sapient life. * * * * * * Her life * * * is sustained by the respirator and tubal feeding, and removal from the respirator would cause her death soon, although the time cannot be stated with more precision.

* * *

The Right of Privacy

It is the issue of the constitutional right of privacy that has given us most concern, in the exceptional circumstances of this case. Here a loving parent, *qua* parent and raising the rights of his incompetent and profoundly damaged daughter, probably irreversibly doomed to no more than a biologically vegetative remnant of life, is before the court. He seeks authorization to abandon specialized technological procedures which can only maintain for a time a body having no potential for resumption or continuance of other than a "vegetative" existence.

We have no doubt, in these unhappy circumstances, that if Karen were herself miraculously lucid for an interval (not altering the existing prognosis of the condition to which she would soon return) and perceptive of her irreversible condition, she could effectively decide upon discontinuance of the life-support apparatus, even if it meant the prospect of natural death. * * *

Although the Constitution does not explicitly mention a right of privacy, Supreme Court decisions have recognized that a right of personal privacy exists and that certain areas of privacy are guaranteed under the Constitution. * * *

* * * [T]his right is broad enough to encompass a patient's decision to decline medical treatment under certain circumstances, in much the same way as it is broad enough to encompass a woman's decision to terminate pregnancy under certain conditions. Roe v. Wade, 410 U.S. 113, 153, 93 S.Ct. 705, 727, 35 L.Ed.2d 147, 177 (1973).

Our affirmation of Karen's independent right of choice, however would ordinarily be based upon her competency to assert it. The sad truth, however, is that she is grossly incompetent and we cannot discern her * * * choice * * *. Nevertheless we have concluded that Karen's right of privacy may be asserted on her behalf by her guardian under the peculiar circumstances here present.

* * * Karen Quinlan is a 22 year old adult. Her right of privacy in respect of the matter before the Court is to be vindicated by Mr. Quinlan as guardian, as hereinabove determined.

* * *

Upon the concurrence of the guardian and family of Karen, should the responsible attending physicians conclude that there is no reasonable possibility of Karen's ever emerging from her present comatose condition to a cognitive, sapient state and that the life-support apparatus now being administered to Karen should be discontinued, they shall consult with the hospital "Ethics Committee" or like body of the institution in which Karen is then hospitalized. If that consultative body agrees that there is no reasonable possibility of Karen's ever emerging from her present comatose condition to a cognitive, sapient state, the present life-support system may be withdrawn and said action shall be without any civil or criminal liability therefor on the part of any participant, whether guardian, physician, hospital or others. We herewith specifically so hold.

"Ab"dul combined with the word "scam."

UNITED STATES v. MYERS

U.S. Court of Appeals, Second Circuit, 1982.
692 F.2d 823.

* * *

Now before us are appeals from judgments of conviction entered in the Eastern District of New York * * * in which four Congressmen and three co-defendants were found guilty of various offenses related to corruption of public office arising out of the Abscam investigation. * * * [( ]appellants Michael O. Myers, formerly Congressman from the First District of Pennsylvania; Angelo J. Errichetti, formerly Mayor of Camden, New Jersey; Louis Johanson, formerly a member of the City Council in Philadelphia, Pennsylvania; and Howard L. Criden, a law partner of Johanson's[;] * * * appellant Raymond F. Lederer, formerly Congressman from the Third District of Pennsylvania[;] * * * Frank Thompson, Jr., formerly Congressman from the Fourth District of New Jersey, and John M. Murphy, formerly Congressman from the Seventeenth District of New York[ )] * * * Though some of the three trials present distinct issues, all seven appellants raise questions of such similarity that we have found it appropriate to consider all of the claims in one opinion. For the reasons that follow, we have concluded that all of the judgments should be affirmed.

* * *

The charges stemmed from an elaborate undercover "sting" operation conducted by the Federal Bureau of Investigation. Three FBI agents and a private citizen, all acting in an undercover capacity, purported to be representatives of two Middle Eastern sheiks operating a fictitious entity known as Abdul Enterprises, Ltd. The undercover operatives let it be known that their principals were interested in investing money in the United States and immigrating to this country. The core allegation against Myers and his co-defendants was that on August 22, 1979, Myers received $50,000 in return for his promise to introduce private immigration bills permitting the sheiks to remain in the United States and to take other necessary action including intervention with the State Department. A jury trial was begun on August 11, 1980, and concluded on August 29, 1980. The jury convicted all four defendants on all three counts. Errichetti and Criden were each sentenced to concurrent terms of six years' imprisonment and fines totalling $40,000. Myers and Johanson were each sentenced to concurrent terms of three years' imprisonment and fines totalling $20,000.

* * *

The core allegation in [Lederer's] indictment was that on September 11, 1979, Lederer received $50,000 in return for his promise to help the sheiks with their immigration problems.

* * *

He was sentenced to concurrent terms of three years' imprisonment and fines totalling $20,000.

In a third indictment, Thompson and Murphy were charged, * * * with * * * conspiracy, bribery, and interstate travel counts. * * *

* * * Thompson was tentatively sentenced to the maximum allowable terms, pursuant to 18 U.S.C. § 4205(c), pending further consideration of his medical condition. Murphy was sentenced to concurrent terms of three years' imprisonment and fines totalling $20,000.

In the interim between the conclusion of the three trials and the sentencing of all appellants, Judge Pratt conducted a consolidated hearing to consider various claims by all seven appellants that the Government's conduct in the Abscam investigation and in the prosecution of the charges at trial violated rights protected by the Due Process Clause of the Fifth Amendment. In considering these allegations, Judge Pratt took testimony during a 16-day "due process" hearing conducted in January and February, 1981. Judge Pratt also permitted the seven appellants to rely upon evidence pertinent to their due process claims that had been presented in other proceedings stemming from the Abscam investigation. These included the record of the trial and the "due process" hearing concerning charges against former United States Senator Harrison A. Williams, Jr., of New Jersey, in the Eastern District of New York, and the trial and "due process hearing records of charges against former Philadelphia Councilmen Harry P. Jannotti and George X. Schwartz in the Eastern District of Pennsylvania (John P. Fullam, Judge), against former Congressman John W. Jenrette and a co-defendant in the District of Columbia (John G. Penn, Judge), and against former Congressman Richard Kelly and two co-defendants in the District of Columbia (William B. Bryant, Judge). Based upon this comprehensive record, Judge Pratt, in a detailed and thoughtful opinion, denied the due process contentions of the seven appellants as well as their multitude of other claims attacking the validity of their convictions. *United States v. Myers*, 527 F.Supp. 1206 (E.D.N.Y.1981).

* * *

The background of the Abscam operation is described by Judge Pratt as follows:

> "Abscam" is the code word given by the Federal Bureau of Investigation to an undercover "sting" operation conducted out of the FBI office at Hauppauge, Long Island, New York, under the supervision of agent John Good. Abscam began after Melvin Weinberg in 1977 was convicted in the Western District of Pennsylvania on his plea of guilty to fraud. In return for a sentence of probation Weinberg agreed to cooperate with the FBI in setting up an undercover operation. * * *
>
> * * * Initially, Weinberg worked directly under special agent John McCarthy who later was replaced by special agent Anthony

Amoroso. Both McCarthy and Amoroso worked undercover with Weinberg.

Weinberg was to present himself as a business agent for "Abdul Enterprises," an organization backed by two extremely wealthy Arab sheiks looking for American outlets for their cash. He would pass the word of big money available for deals to other con men and people who move between the legitimate and illegitimate. If criminal proposals appeared, appropriate action would be taken by the FBI.

Weinberg and the agents set up business in an office in Holbrook, Long Island. The FBI's code name "Abscam" came from the first two letters of "Abdul," combined with the word "scam."

At first Abscam's focus was upon stolen and forged securities and stolen art work. Other "investment" opportunities soon presented themselves, and quickly the investigation turned itself toward Atlantic City and the gambling casinos which were then being proposed and constructed. As word spread about Weinberg's contact with virtually inexhaustible Arab funds, Angelo Errichetti, who was both mayor of Camden, New Jersey, and a New Jersey state senator, came on the scene. Errichetti claimed to have extraordinary influence in obtaining gambling casino licenses, power over the commissioners who issued the licenses, connections with organized crime, ability to deal in narcotics, guns and counterfeit securities, as well as intimate knowledge of which members of the New Jersey legislature could be bought.

Errichetti brought to the undercover agents Howard Criden, a Philadelphia lawyer seeking to promote a gambling casino in Atlantic City. In July of 1979, Errichetti and Criden met with Weinberg and Amoroso on the sheiks' yacht in Florida to discuss financing for the proposed casino that a client of Criden's wanted to build. In the course of the day Amoroso and Errichetti discussed the problem that might be faced by the sheiks should a revolution occur in their country and should they want to come to the United States as permanent residents. Amoroso told Errichetti that he thought cooperation of public officials would be needed and that money would be no problem.

Immediately after this conversation Errichetti and Criden formed an alliance in which they undertook to produce for Amoroso and Weinberg public officials who, in return for money, were willing to use their influence with the government on the sheiks' behalf. Meetings were arranged at various locations in New York, Philadelphia and Washington where the FBI monitored the proceedings with concealed videotape cameras and microphones. Where videotape was not feasible audio recordings were used.

* * *

Criden told his law partners, Johanson and Ellis Cook, that Errichetti had told him they could make substantial sums of money if they knew any Congressmen who would be willing to meet the sheik or his representatives.

* * * The first meeting with Myers took place on August 22, 1979, at the Travelodge International Hotel near Kennedy Airport on Long Island.

* * * The meeting was recorded on videotape. Early in the conversation, Myers boasted of his influence in Congress. When Amoroso mentioned his conversation on the yacht with Errichetti concerning the sheiks' possible immigration problems, Myers replied, "Absolutely. Where I could be of help in this type of a matter, first of all, is private bills that can be introduced." Myers explained that delay was important in immigration matters and said, "[I]f I wanta keep somebody in the country, all I do is introduce a private bill." Later in the conversation, Amoroso told Myers that his employer was planning major investments in the United States, possibly including something in Philadelphia. Myers agreed with Amoroso that such an investment in his district would give him "a little protection," and added that it would provide a reason to go "full force and, ah, not that I won't otherwise," and the "perfect opportunity to raise hell before Congress." At the end of the meeting Amoroso handed Myers an envelope containing $50,000 in $100 bills. Amoroso said, "Spend it well"; Myers replied, "Pleasure."

* * *

Cook was then told that Myers had agreed to take only $15,000; of the remaining $20,000, Criden received $9,000 or $9,500, Johanson received $6,000 or $6,500, and Cook received $4,500.

* * *

At a subsequent meeting on January 24, * * * Myers vehemently complained about ending up with only $15,000, after expecting to retain $50,000 for himself out of an anticipated payment of $100,000. As Myers pointed out, "Who am I goin' to complain to . . . my congressman[?]"

* * * Myers acknowledged at his trial that he had retained $15,000 of the $50,000 handed to him by Amoroso. His defense, also adopted by his three co-defendants, was that all of his statements to Amoroso and Weinberg at the hotel on Long Island [were playacting].

* * *

Myers claimed he did not intend to fulfill any of the promises he made at the meeting. Over the Government's objection, Judge Pratt instructed the jury that they should convict the defendants at the *Myers* trial of bribery only if they found that Myers was not "playacting." The jury's verdicts constitute a rejection of Myers' defense.

* * *

Members of Congress enjoy no special constitutional rule that requires prior suspicion of criminal activity before they may be confronted with a governmentally created opportunity to commit a crime.

What is available in such circumstances is the traditional defense of entrapment, which prevents conviction of a person induced to commit a crime unless the prosecution can establish the person's predisposition to commit the crime.

* * *

The entrapment defense exonerates a defendant who engages in criminal behavior when the activity of government agents "implant[s] in the mind of an innocent person the disposition to commit the alleged offense and induce[s] its commission."

* * * But the defense of entrapment is not established simply because government agents "afford opportunities or facilities for the commission of the offense."

* * * The legal defense of entrapment is not established whenever a defendant is caught by a ruse.

Although the defense of entrapment was available to all seven appellants, none except Lederer elected to assert the defense at trial, or request a jury instruction on the issue. The defendants in the *Myers* and *Thompson-Murphy* trials made no attempt to avail themselves of the limited opportunity a defendant has to defend on the dual grounds of non-involvement and entrapment, *see United States v. Valencia,* 645 F.2d 1158, 1170–72 (2d Cir. 1980) (amended 1981). They claimed only that bribery had not occurred, the *Myers* defendants on the ground that Myers was only "playacting,"—pretending to promise official action—and Thompson and Murphy on the ground that proof was lacking that they had accepted money for promises of official action.

* * *

Although Lederer, having asserted the defense of entrapment at trial, can challenge the sufficiency of the evidence of his predisposition, his claim is without merit. In seeking only $5,000 for himself out of the $50,000 he received, Lederer displayed neither the greed of Myers nor the guile of Thompson and Murphy; nevertheless, the evidence at his trial fully entitled the jury to find his predisposition beyond a reasonable doubt. Predisposition may be established by "the accused's ready response to the inducement," *United States v. Viviano,* 437 F.2d 295, 299 (2d Cir.), *cert. denied,* 402 U.S. 983, 91 S.Ct. 1659, 29 L.Ed.2d 149 (1971); *United States v. Becker,* 62 F.2d 1007, 1008 (2d Cir. 1933). The videotape of the September 11 meeting reveals Lederer responding with alacrity. As he assured the sheik's representatives, "I'm not a Boy Scout."

* * *

Appellants contend that even if the traditional entrapment defense fails, whether factually in Lederer's case or procedurally as to the other appellants, the conduct of Abscam violated standards of due process because the Government's role in the investigation was excessive and fundamentally unfair.

* * * The appellants' claim of excessive governmental involvement in the instigation of criminal conduct is not supported by the facts. Though the "sting" was surely elaborate, its essential characteristic was the creation of an opportunity for the commission of crime by those willing to do so. The Government produced people with fictitious identities ready to pay bribes to Congressmen. Word of the availability of bribe money was made known. From that point on, the essential conduct of the agents and their paid informant was to see who showed up to take the bribes and videotape them in the act of doing so. Whatever may be the due process limit of governmental participation in crime, it was not reached here.

* * * Appellants contend that the size of the inducements offered to the Congressmen were excessive. They refer not to the $50,000 amounts of the bribes, but to the offers of financing multi-million dollar projects in the Congressmen's districts. We have considerable difficulty with the premise of this argument, which is that a Congressman is privileged to take a $50,000 bribe so long as he simultaneously believes he is bringing the benefits of investments to his district. The argument is an affront to all the law-abiding Members of Congress and state officials who consider it a normal part of their public responsibilities to promote business activity for the benefit of their constituents.

* * * Quite to the contrary, the evidence shows four Congressmen jumping at the chance to take a bribe and discussing investments in their districts as a convenient cover to justify their rendering of purchased legislative services. As Thompson said, anticipating possible criticism for helping the sheik, "I'm in a position to say well of course I'm helping this guy. Why shouldn't I help this guy . . . his money is helping my guys work everyday." Myers put it more bluntly: an investment in the district "gives me a little protection."

* * *

[T]he appellants contend that "playacting" is a defense to bribery. It is not. Since Myers appears to be the first public official in a reported federal decision to defend a bribery charge on the ground that he intended to keep the bribe but not to keep the promise he made to the bribe-payer, it is not surprising that the appellate reports have not dealt explicitly with the claim.

[T]he judgments appealed from are affirmed.

Review Questions

1. Is it essential that law exist? What are the costs of law? What should law accomplish? Explain your answers.

2. Should the majority always rule? Does an individual need protection against government itself? Explain your answers.

3. The word "law" is used in a variety of ways. What is the common characteristic in all of these uses? What is the definition of law as it relates to our study of law? How does "law" differ from religion?

4. What numbers are usually required to expel a member from a house of Congress, to recall an elected state official, to convict a president upon impeachment, and to amend the United States Constitution? Explain.

5. Relate the ten characteristics of an "ideal" system of law to the United States system of law.

6. Why are administrative agencies necessary? How do court cases differ from legislation? Explain your answers.

7. Distinguish and explain the four categories of activity involved in making law.

8. Define the following terms: adjudication, administrative law, common law, democracy, initiative, legislation, "legitimate" legal system, oligarchy, referendum, republic, totalitarianism, written law.

Problems

1. A special legislative session has been called to deal with a mounting statewide problem in Iron Will, U.S.A. During the past year, the number of deaths and injuries resulting from careless bicycling in, between, and through busy traffic intersections has doubled. Representative Jamus, a staunch conservative, has brought a bill before the House that will, if passed, ban the use of bicycles in all city areas for a ten-year period while new bicycle paths are under construction. Based upon your knowledge of the law, will Jamus's bill pass? What factors belong in a consideration of this proposed legislation?

2. Incumbent conservative state representative Sam Hatch is upset at local trial judge Nancy Miller for three different reasons. First of all, Representative Hatch was the author of a "gun control" statute requiring permits for carrying hand guns. After fisherperson John Fry was arrested while carrying a handgun without a permit while fishing on the Snake River ("for protection against snakes"), Judge Miller dismissed the charge as not being within the intent of the statute. Later, Judge Miller ruled that Sam Hatch's political opponent could sue Hatch for slander (Hatch, in making a campaign speech, untruthfully claimed his opponent had a prison record) even though there was no statute dealing with slander, basing her opinion on higher court decisions. Finally, when Hatch refused to control his outbursts in her court at the time of the proceeding resulting in the ruling, Judge Miller held him in contempt and fined him $250. Hatch says "the legislature makes the law not the judges, and Miller's actions are all illegal." Is he correct? Explain.

3. United States voters are outraged! President T. C. Cox, elected to office just eight months ago, has been caught expropriating public funds for his private collection of modern and impressionistic art. And while former sup-

porters had backed his campaign pledge to "advance the nation's culture" as a worthwhile one, they now feel tricked by such a flagrant misuse of the public trust. You are called in to advise a group of concerned citizens. What steps can they take to insure that justice is served upon the President?

4. Controversy abounds in Small Town, North Dakota, where local residents gather to debate the issue of obscenity—an issue the local legislature refuses to consider. Speakers are Phineas Phog, ardent crusader in the effort to keep smut and corruption out of news, movies, books, and assorted periodicals; and his opponent, Seymour Buchanan, who decries censorship in any form as the first step toward totalitarianism. Yet the majority of townspeople remain indifferent. While they desire a statute to define and limit obscenity, they want it based on a historical knowledge of the problem, and they want assurance that their efforts will not be useless in the face of a reluctant legislature. How would they go about researching this proposed legislation? Once a proposal is drafted, can voters demand it be put to a vote? Explain.

5. Members of the SMA (Students for Militant Action) comprise 9 percent of the student body at the University of Whitfield. Many of their views (for example, "student freedom at any cost") are frowned upon by the local police who are "sick and tired of those loudmouthed troublemakers over at the college." When it is discovered that SMA President, Jerry Barlow, is holding a series of "rap" sessions, the purpose of which is to arrive at a unified plan of action, the police, without benefit of search warrant, raid his apartment and seize all written proposals. Can the police use this evidence to prosecute SMA members on charges of conspiracy? Explain.

6. Assume the Supreme Court has ruled that state laws prohibiting the use and possession of marijuana are unconstitutional and void. Alarmed citizens have started a massive campaign to rally public opinion against this Supreme Court decision and have convinced 75 percent of the American public that the use of marijuana should be prohibited entirely. How can this majority sentiment prevail in light of the Supreme Court ruling? Is there any alternative to violence? Explain.

7. The "Egg 'n Honey Health Food" store, closed down by order of the Food and Drug Administration, poured time and money into upgrading the quality of its products. The storeowners now desire to reopen; they are satisfied that their store meets all FDA requirements. Must the owners of the "Egg 'n Honey" seek determination of this issue in the courts? Explain.

8. Sophomore student Lois Hardy has joined a local campus student organization called "Students Opposed to Nuclear Power." While she believes that nuclear power may constitute a definite threat to the environment, she is not certain of all the tactics proposed by her group. Many of the activities will be directed at a local noncampus political group known as "Citizens for Nuclear Power" which has an office in the city center and which believes that shutting down the local nuclear energy reactor plant will not only cause great problems for the poor and elderly because of higher costs for power, but will result in a loss of many jobs. Lois Hardy's student group plans the following activities in the next few months:

a. Organizing and holding large public meetings in the parks to discuss the question of nuclear reactors and their effects;
b. Picketing the headquarters of "Citizens for Nuclear Power" with students carrying signs and walking up and down in front of the office handing out leaflets to the public;
c. Sitting en masse on the main street of the city during rush hour traffic to bring attention to the nuclear power threat;
d. Breaking into the offices of "Citizens for Nuclear Power" at night in order to get a list of their membership and, then (over a period of many weeks), going to the houses of each of the members to stage protest meetings in the front yards of their individual homes;
e. Using their bodies to block all entrances to the local nuclear energy reactor plant so as to prevent its operation;
f. Collecting signatures from the voting public in order to place the issue of nuclear power on the next ballot;
g. Painting slogans demanding the end of nuclear power on all local public buildings;
h. Collecting signatures to recall the local mayor who supports nuclear power;
i. Calling in bomb threats to get public buildings evacuated so as to bring their cause to the greater attention of the media;
j. Sitting in and disrupting meetings of local legislative, judicial, and administrative hearings to make public officials more aware of the risks of nuclear power.

Should Lois Hardy participate in any or all of these activities as proper methods of political involvement? Explain your answers.

2

It is emphatically the province and duty of the judicial department to say what the law is.

Chief Justice John Marshall
Marbury v. Madison

Government, Courts, and Individual Rights

WHAT SPECIFIC CONSTITUTIONAL POWER RESTS WITH THE LEGISLATIVE BRANCH OF GOVERNMENT?

Article I, Section 1 of the United States Constitution states that "* * * all legislative powers herein granted shall be vested in a Congress of the United States, which shall consist of a Senate and a House of Representatives." Two important doctrines result from this section of the federal Constitution. First, Congress has only those specific powers that are enumerated in the Constitution; second, these powers belong only to the Congress and may not be transferred to the president or to the judicial branch. This last doctrine, the separation of powers, says that the Constitution divides the government into three branches—that it is a breach of this constitutional division if Congress either gives up its rule making power to one of the other branches or attempts by law to take on either the executive or judicial power. Congress may, however, delegate rule making power to an administrative agency as long as it is giving the agency only the power to "fill up the details" of the statute passed by Congress. Congress, then, does not have to furnish all the details. As long as it specifies in the statute the general purposes it wants to accomplish, the detail can be left to an administrative agency. Based on this principle, there are over a hundred administrative agencies that have made thousands of rules. Still, Congress must stay within the specific powers enumerated in the federal Constitution. What is not specifically granted is retained by the individual states and is subject to state rule making by state legislatures.

The powers of Congress are enumerated in Sections 8 and 9 of Article I of the Constitution. They may be classified as follows:

The Congress shall have the power to:

1. collect taxes;
2. pay the debts of the United States;
3. provide for the defense of the United States;
4. provide for the general welfare of the United States;
5. borrow money on the credit of the United States;
6. regulate commerce with foreign nations and among the states;
7. establish rules with regard to immigration and naturalization including the exclusion of aliens from the United States;
8. establish uniform rules on the subject of bankruptcy throughout the United States;
9. coin money and regulate its value and provide for punishment for counterfeiting;
10. fix the standard of weights and measures;
11. establish post offices and insure safe and prompt delivery of mail;
12. promote science and art by granting patents and copyrights;
13. establish additional federal courts inferior to the Supreme Court;
14. punish for piracy or felony on the high seas and for offenses against the law of the nation;
15. declare war and maintain armed forces;
16. govern the District of Columbia and other federal lands and properties;
17. and make all laws necessary and proper to carry out the powers enumerated in items one through sixteen.

These are the complete powers of Congress in making general rules for the population of the United States. All other powers are reserved to the states. The powers granted to Congress, however, have been very broadly construed. As a result, federal rule making power is very large. This is particularly true in connection with the commerce power (sixth on the list), which is the most important congressional power exercised in time of peace. This power, taken together with the necessary and proper clause power (number seventeen above), has enabled Congress to regulate any operation capable of affecting interstate commerce—e.g., highways, railways, navigation, labor, and minimum wage.

Additionally, Congress has broad powers of investigation, so it can determine what legislation should be enacted. This power is not expressly provided for in the Constitution and has been the subject of considerable controversy between the Congress and both the executive and judicial branches of government. In 1837, a committee appointed by the House of Representatives was given express power to send for persons and papers and to inquire into the way certain executive departments had been conducted. The Committee called upon President Andrew Jackson and various department heads for lists of persons appointed without the consent of the Senate and for an accounting of the sums of money paid to them. In refusing to comply, President Jackson stated that it was an invasion of the rights of the executive branch and that the doctrine of separation of powers must be preserved. The Supreme Court has stated in In re Chapman, 166 U.S. 661, 17 S.Ct. 677,

41 L.Ed. 1154 (1897), that Congress cannot pry into the private affairs of a citizen without showing that new legislation is contemplated. In 1973–1974, Congress investigated the so-called Watergate affair, demanding that President Nixon turn over certain presidential tapes. Nixon refused, again because of the doctrine of separation of powers (although he was later compelled to turn them over to the special Watergate Prosecutor—see the *Nixon* case at the end of the chapter). Still, congressional power to investigate is very broad, and when taken together with Congress's expressed constitutional powers, it becomes a most potent authority for the making of general rules.

The complete application of the doctrine of separation of powers provides that each branch of government (legislative, executive, and judicial) is separate from the others and equal to the others. For this reason, for example, the president does not have the power to make the general rules for the population of the United States. This power, as stated above, is given to the Congress in Article I of the Constitution. Nor does the president have the power to decide cases arising under the Constitution because this power is given to the Supreme Court under Article III. At the same time, the Congress and the Court must not invade the executive powers vested in the president under Article II.

State legislatures also have great power to make rules on all kinds of subject matter. Crime, divorce, adoption, transfer of property, mortgaging property, operation of business, banking, insurance, taxation, conservation, pollution, and many others—all are subject matters of state, county, and city rule making power.

WHAT ELSE DO CONSTITUTIONS DO BESIDES CREATE THE POWER TO MAKE LAW?

Both federal and state constitutions create legislative, executive, and judicial branches of government and vest them with power to make law. But it is important to recall that constitutions also limit the power of government, protect the individual from misuse of governmental authority, and guarantee fundamental individual rights. The following are some of the most important limitations, protections, and guarantees found in constitutions:

1. No person may be denied the writ of habeas corpus except in times of public danger or when martial law is in force. This prevents unjust imprisonment or detention by legal authorities. When a person is arrested, a writ of habeas corpus may be obtained from the court. This writ orders the police to produce the arrested person in court, and if no legal charge can be placed against him or her (that is, if there is no legal basis for continuing to hold the person), he or she must be freed.

2. No bill of attainder may be passed. This prevents a legislature from making any law that would inflict punishment on a person or group without judicial trial. In other words, a bill of attainder is a statute that "attaints" some person or group and thus takes away property or civil rights without a trial.

3. No ex post facto law may be passed. Every law that makes criminal an act that was innocent when done, or that inflicts a greater punishment than the law annexed to the crime at the time of its commission, is an ex post facto law. So, if your action is not criminal at the time you act, you cannot be punished when the same act is later made a crime. Nor can you be punished more severely for a crime than what is legally prescribed at the time you committed it.

4. No state may pass a law impairing the obligation of contract. This means that government cannot pass a law that changes or takes away the rights and duties of those persons who have made a valid contract or agreement—and we all do from time to time, whether it is merely the purchase of socks or a new record album. But while legislatures may not change our obligations and expectations under a contract, the states may still use their police power to make laws reasonably necessary to secure the health, safety, morals, comfort, or general welfare of the community. And this is so even where contracts may be affected. States may additionally exercise their power of eminent domain to take property for public use. (This includes property subject to a contract, which may be taken upon payment of due compensation.) Still, it is important to our freedom that the state may not pass a law that interferes with our ability to contract—to make agreements with one another—whether the agreement is to buy, sell, build, or provide a service.

5. No law may be passed respecting an establishment of religion or prohibiting the free exercise of religion. Neither the state nor the federal government can set up a church or pass laws that aid one religion or prefer one religion over another. No person can be forced to go to church or to remain away from church or to believe or disbelieve in any religion. Nor can he or she be punished for professing religious beliefs or disbeliefs or for church attendance or nonattendance.

6. No law may be passed abridging the freedom of speech or of the press. Freedom of speech, of course, is the ability to say what you believe, and while this freedom is guaranteed in the United States, it is not an absolute right. A person may not use speech in such a manner as to endanger the lives of others—as to yell "fire" in a crowded theater. And speech may be restricted if the restriction imposed is necessary to protect the state (the system of law that protects freedom of speech) from destruction or serious injury—political, economic, or moral. But the danger must be clear and imminent. Thus, a Chicago ordinance that permitted punishment for speech that "stirs the public to anger, invites disputes or brings about a condition of unrest" was held to be an unconstitutional restriction on the right of free speech. Justice Douglas wrote:

> A function of free speech under our system of government is to invite dispute. It may indeed best serve its high purpose when it induces a condition of unrest, creates dissatisfaction with conditions as they are, or even stirs people to anger. Speech is often provocative and challenging. It may strike at prejudices and preconceptions and have profound unsettling effects as it presses for acceptance of an idea. That is why freedom of speech, though not absolute * * * is nevertheless protected against censorship or punishment, unless shown likely to

> produce a clear and present danger of a serious substantive evil that rises far above public inconvenience, annoyance, or unrest. Terminiello v. Chicago, 337 U.S. 1, 69 S.Ct. 894, 93 L.Ed. 1131 (1949).

As to freedom of the press, the United States press has perhaps more freedom than any other in the world. There is no government censorship as was found in Spain under Fascist dictator Francisco Franco, for instance, where censors examined each publication with an eye to suppressing or banning it. There is no monopoly of printing and publishing in this country unlike in the U.S.S.R., where printing and publishing are subject to complete governmental control. In the Soviet Union the newspaper *Pravda,* for example, with its daily circulation of eleven million, is published by the Central Committee of the Soviet Communist Party and "toes the party line, hence the government line, on matters great and small." [1] The only censorship in the United States is that of public opinion (resulting in laws that curb the sale of obscene materials according to local community standards) and that which results from the law of libel (see Chapter 4).

7. No law may be passed preventing peaceable assembly. People may gather and hold meetings for a peaceful and lawful purpose. The Supreme Court has said that "the very idea of a government, republic in form, implies a right on the part of its citizens to meet peaceably for consultation in respect to public affairs and to petition for a redress of grievances." U. S. v. Cruikshank, 92 U.S. 542, 23 L.Ed. 588 (1876).

8. The government may not act to restrict the right of the people to be secure in their persons and homes from unreasonable search and seizure. This protects people from having their homes searched without a search warrant, and no warrants may be issued unless there is good reason to suspect a crime has been committed.

9. No person may be deprived of life, liberty, or property without due process of law. This means that no person will lose property or liberty unfairly. A person will be informed of the charges against him or her and have an opportunity to present his or her position. In all criminal cases a person is entitled to a speedy and public trial by jury, to have an attorney's representation and to cross examine witnesses. There are many other procedures and guarantees required for "due process." This term is considered more fully in Chapter 3.

10. No slavery or involuntary servitude is allowed except as punishment for crime, and all persons are entitled to equal protection of the laws. Thus, a person may not be compelled to labor for another in payment of a debt. Nor may legislation be passed that discriminates against some persons in favor of others. The Fourteenth Amendment requires:

> * * * [T]hat equal protection and security should be given to all under like circumstances in the enjoyment of their personal and civil rights; that all persons should be equally entitled to pursue their happiness and acquire and enjoy property, the prevention and redress of wrongs, and the enforcement of con-

---

1. *Time,* June 23, 1980, p. 56.

tracts; that no impediment should be interposed to the pursuits of anyone except as applied to the same pursuits by others under like circumstances; that no greater burdens should be laid upon one man than are laid upon others in the same calling and condition, and that in the administration of criminal justice no different or higher punishment should be imposed upon one than such as prescribed to all for like offenses. Barber v. Connolly, 113 U.S. 27, 31, 5 S.Ct. 357, 28 L.Ed. 923 (1885).

We have seen that the power to make law in the United States is shared by the legislative, judicial, and executive branches of government. Primary responsibility for writing the general rules rests with the legislature; complete responsibility for determining general rules of the common law is with the courts, as is primary responsibility for interpreting written and common law and deciding specific cases and controversies. The chief responsibility for carrying the law into effect and enforcing it belongs to the executive branches. All of these powers, however, are very much limited by constitutions which guarantee fundamental rights including the writ of habeas corpus, no bills of attainder or ex post facto laws, freedom of religion, press, and speech, due process, and equal protection under the law.

HOW DOES THE CONSTITUTION APPLY TO BUSINESS?

The United States Constitution has had and continues to have great effect upon the operation of American business. All provisions of the Constitution apply to the operation of business. We have seen in the *Marsh* case (Chapter 1) how the citizens of a town, owned by a business, could not be denied their First Amendment rights by that business. We have seen the impact of the constitutional right of privacy upon the operation of the medical profession and the business of medical technology (*Karen Quinlan* case, Chapter 1). It has been held in the case of Marshall v. Barlow's Inc., 436 U.S. 307, 98 S.Ct. 1816, 56 L.Ed.2d 305 (1978), that the Fourth Amendment protects commercial buildings as well as private homes and prevents building inspectors from inspecting for building code violations without search warrants if owners object to the inspections.

While all the Constitution has application to business as well as to individuals, certain provisions have had more substantial impact than others.

The Taxing Power

The Constitution provides that the Congress has the power to lay and collect taxes (Article I, Section 8). Congress may exercise its taxing power to promote any objective within a specific power granted to Congress in the Constitution. Revenue is raised through income, estate, gift, and other taxes, with business and employers paying approximately one-third to one-half of all federal taxes. Taxes are also used to regulate, as well as to raise revenue, with special taxes being imposed on dealers in firearms, for example. Every business person has to be continually aware of his or her responsibility to pay income taxes and to withhold income and social security taxes for his or her employees.

The Bankruptcy Power

Article I also grants Congress the power to establish uniform laws on the subject of bankruptcy. The 1979 bankruptcy act provides that individuals and business may go through voluntary or involuntary bankruptcy resulting in most of a debtor's assets being sold to pay off most debts to the extent possible, discharging further debt responsibility. The statute also allows business or individuals to reorganize and pay off debts over a time as an alternative to the usual bankruptcy procedure. State laws may not conflict with the bankruptcy laws of Congress because of the supremacy clause.

The Interstate Privileges and Immunities Clause

Article IV, Section 2, of the Constitution provides that "the citizens of each state shall be entitled to all privileges and immunities of citizens in the several states." This clause prohibits state discrimination against nonresidents of a state as to essential activities or basic rights including those associated with pursuing a livelihood. This has stopped states from preferring resident creditors (Blake v. McClung, 172 U.S. 239, 19 S.Ct. 165, 43 L.Ed. 432, 1898), from requiring higher fees from nonresidents to do business in a state than from residents (Toomer v. Witsell, 334 U.S. 179, 1948), and from giving hiring preference to residents over nonresidents (Hicklin v. Orbeck, 437 U.S. 518, 98 S.Ct. 2482, 57 L.Ed.2d 397, 1978).

The Interstate Commerce Clause

The commerce clause of Article I gives Congress the power "to regulate commerce with foreign nations, and among the several states and with the Indian tribes."

The United States Supreme Court, in what is called the "affectation doctrine," has determined that Congress has the power, under the commerce clause, to regulate any activity which has any *appreciable effect* upon interstate commerce. This is true even though the activity is carried on in only one state and even though the effect is only indirect. It is for this reason that Congress may regulate purely intrastate marketing of products because "the marketing of a local product in competition with that of a like commodity moving interstate may interfere with interstate commerce." (United States v. Wrightwood Dairy Company, 315 U.S. 110, 62 S.Ct. 523, 86 L.Ed. 726, 1942).

The Due Process Clause and Police Power

The Constitution protects against the deprivation of "life, liberty, or property without due process of law." At the same time, each state has the police power to enact legislation protecting or promoting the public health, welfare, safety, or morality. It does not violate due process for states to pass statutes specifying building construction requirements. Nor does it do so when statutes are passed to regulate the use of property through zoning, to regulate working conditions, or to regulate the sale of food, drug products, or the like.

The police powers provide substantial limitations upon the operation of business.

HOW DO THE BILL OF RIGHTS AND THE FOURTEENTH AMENDMENT RELATE?

The first ten amendments are referred to as the Bill of Rights. These amendments protect only against actions of the *federal* government. The First Amendment, for example, states that *Congress* shall make no law respecting an establishment of religion or abridging the freedom of speech or of the press or the right of the people peaceably to assemble. The amendments (Bill of Rights) do not prevent state or local government from making such laws.

However, the Fourteenth Amendment was adopted in 1868 and states in part:

> No state shall . . . deprive any person of life, liberty, or property without due process of law; nor deny to any person within its jurisdiction the equal protection of the laws.

The United States Supreme Court has held that the Bill of Rights is incorporated by the Fourteenth Amendment to the extent the rights are fundamental to the concepts of due process, liberty, and justice. Most provisions of the Bill of Rights have been incorporated and held applicable to state and local governments. Included are the First Amendment protections for religion, speech, assembly, and petition for grievances. So also are the Fourth Amendment provisions regarding arrest, search and seizure; the Fifth Amendment protections against double jeopardy, self-incrimination, and bar against taking property without just compensation; the Sixth Amendment rights to counsel in criminal prosecutions, confrontation and cross-examination of witnesses, speedy trial, public trial, jury trial, and compulsory process for obtaining witnesses; and the Eighth Amendment prohibition against cruel and unusual punishment.

WHAT IS THE SPECIFIC PROCEDURE USED IN WRITING THE GENERAL RULES OF LEGISLATION?

Before an idea can become a general rule of law, a great number of steps must be taken by the legislative body. Congress uses the following procedure to enact its statutes, and similar procedures are followed by state legislatures.

Step One Somebody has an idea for a law. It may be the senator or congressman himself or herself, or perhaps the president or some private citizen or group has made a recommendation. The idea must first be reduced to a writing called a bill.

Step Two The bill must be introduced in Congress. The Congress is composed of the Senate and the House of Representatives which meet in separate chambers in the Capitol in Washington, D.C. The Senate is composed of 100 members, two members being elected from each state; the House of Representatives has 435 members with state representation based on population. Thus, the number of each state's representatives may change after each national census, taken every ten years. Since membership is based on population, California or New York may have more than forty members, while Alaska or Nevada may have but one.

The bill may be introduced in either the Senate or in the House (an exception is made for revenue bills which must be introduced in the House as provided for in the Constitution). The bill is introduced by having it placed first in a basket called a "hopper." It is then read by the clerks to the membership of the House or Senate by title only, given a number, ordered to be printed, and referred to committee.

Step Three The bill is considered by an appropriate committee of the House or Senate. Both the House and the Senate have numerous committees to consider legislation because the entire Congress does not have time to consider the details of every bill introduced. The committee may either report the bill favorably, or may table it. If the bill is tabled, it is forgotten unless the majority of the Senate or House insist that it be brought before the full membership. Assuming the bill is reported favorably, it is put on the calendar for consideration by the full membership.

Step Four When the calendar date arrives, the bill is read in full (the second reading), and the Representatives or Senators, depending on which chamber it is in, first debate on whether or not to pass it—then they vote. If a majority vote for the bill, it is read a third time (by title only) and voted on again. If passed, it is sent on to the other chamber.

Step Five The other chamber, either the Senate or House, goes through the same process—first reading, committee consideration, second reading, third reading, and final approval. If the second house disagrees with the first, a conference committee composed of members of both houses will reconcile the differences, and the revised bill will be sent back to the House and Senate for final approval.

Step Six Once both the Senate and House have approved the bill, it is sent to the president for his signature. His signature approves the bill, and it becomes thereby the law of the land. The bill automatically becomes law if the president holds it for ten days without signing or vetoing it. In the case of a presidential veto, the bill is returned to Congress where, if both House and Senate vote to override the president's veto by a two-thirds majority, it still becomes law. If the bill reaches the president less than ten days before Congress adjourns, it cannot become law unless he signs it, and if he does not do so within the period remaining, the bill is automatically vetoed. This is known as a "pocket veto." On August 16, 1974, the U.S. Court of Appeals in

Washington, D.C. ruled that the pocket veto cannot be used when Congress has merely recessed. The following article explains what happened.

NIXON VETO OF MEDICAL EDUCATION BILL KILLED

By Linda Matthews [2]

WASHINGTON—In a victory for an attorney named Edward M. Kennedy, the U. S. Court of Appeals has invalidated former President Richard M. Nixon's pocket veto of a $225 million medical education bill.

The attorney, whose courtroom appearances have been rare, is better known as the senior senator from Massachusetts. The case was Kennedy's all the way: Not only did he argue it, but he was the plaintiff and had cosponsored the bill that Nixon vetoed.

No president can pocket veto a bill if Congress has merely recessed and has left behind at the Capitol employes authorized to receive a formal veto message from the chief executive, the court held.

By inference, the ruling limits a president's exercise of the pocket veto to end-of-the-session adjournments when Congress closes up shop and goes home for the remainder of the year.

The case turned on Article I, Section 7, Clause 2 of the Constitution, which states that a bill can be vetoed if a president returns it to Congress within 10 days, with a formal message, or if "the Congress by their adjournment prevent its return."

The latter procedure—nicknamed the pocket veto because presidents supposedly stuffed the bills in their pockets—has grown increasingly popular with chief executives in the past 40 years, as Congress has come to favor frequent, brief recesses.

President Franklin D. Roosevelt may go down as the champion pocket vetoer. He killed nine different bills with so-called "intrasession pocket vetoes," the kind outlawed Wednesday by the appeals court. President Dwight D. Eisenhower used the device seven times, President Lyndon B. Johnson twice, and Nixon on five occasions.

The reason for the pocket veto's popularity is clear: a president can get rid of legislation without explaining his reasons and without giving Congress an opportunity to override him. A normal veto can be reversed by two-thirds votes of both houses.

The appeals court delved deep into constitutional history and the Federalist Papers Wednesday before deciding that the "pocket veto power is an exception to the general rule that Congress may override" the president and thus must be narrowly construed.

The only purpose of the pocket veto, Circuit Court Judge Edward A. Tamm wrote for the court, was to insure that congressmen did not attempt to elude a formal veto by adjourning and making it impossible for the president to return the bill to them.

But such fears have no basis, and the pocket veto should have no place when Congress merely recesses and leaves employes behind to receive the president's message, Tamm said.

---

2. Copyright, 1974, Los Angeles Times. Reprinted by permission.

HOW IS IT DETERMINED WHAT THE GENERAL RULES OF LEGISLATION MEAN AND HOW THEY SHOULD BE APPLIED?

Statutes must be written in broad, general terms that will apply to a great number of fact situations. This, of course, results in the problem of interpretation—of trying to determine the exact meaning of these general statutes as they apply to the specific facts of each case. Interpretation is one of the activities of lawmaking, and it is a job for the courts. What does legislation mean? Several techniques are used in reaching such a determination.

First, judges will usually look to the legislative history of the statute. Congressional committees make and publish committee reports on prospective bills as they consider them. Courts will look at these reports and at reports of debate proceedings to determine exactly what situations the legislatures intended to cover by the statute, or exactly how they would have wanted the statute to apply to a particular fact situation. Still, questions left unresolved must be answered, and it is the courts who must ultimately decide whether or not the statute applies to the question at hand.

When there are doubts about the meaning of a statute or words used within a statute, the courts frequently use what are called "rules of construction" to determine the meaning. These rules of construction are for the most part rules of common law. In other words, they have been developed by the courts over hundreds of years and are now sufficiently accepted by the courts to be considered rules of law (rules of the common law since they are not generally written into statutory form). Occasionally, however, you will find that a legislature has written and passed a statute that governs the construction of statutes. This type of statute may be declaratory of the common law or may furnish additional rules for the courts to use in construing statutes.

Generally, the rules of construction result in either a strict or a liberal construction of the statute. If a court strictly construes a statute, it will find that most fact situations do not come within the scope of the statute and that cases will be excluded from its operation unless the statutory language makes it clear that the situation is included. A liberal construction of a statute gives the opposite result and permits extension of the statute to include a great number of cases.

The following are but a few of the great many rules of construction developed by the courts:

1. It is presumed that words in the statute are used in their ordinary and common sense, or in their special or technical sense if they have a well settled special or technical meaning. In other words, no special signficiance is attached to the fact that a word is used in a statute—it has the same meaning there as when used elsewhere.

2. The government, whether state or federal, is not included within the scope or application of a statute unless expressly named.

3. Statutes in general terms are construed to apply only to future situations, that is, prospectively to things coming into existence after the enactment of the statute.

4. Where the language of the statute is plain and unambiguous, the statute must be given effect according to its plain and obvious meaning.

5. Something may be within the letter of the statute yet not within the spirit of the statute nor within the intention of the legislature. Thus, an effort is made to give effect to the real intention of the legislative body even though contrary to the letter of the law.

6. The meaning of a doubtful word may be decided by looking at words with which it is associated.

7. That which is implied in a statute is as much a part of it as that which is expressed.

8. Criminal laws are strictly construed, that is, narrowly applied, since deciding that someone comes within the statute and is guilty of a crime results in the loss of his life, liberty, or property.

9. Remedial statutes are liberally construed—or broadly applied. Finding that someone comes within the statute is to remedy further, make better, or resolve the bad situation the legislature was trying to remedy.

10. When the language of a statute is ambiguous, the courts take into account all the facts and circumstances existing at the time of and leading up to the making of the law, including the history of that time, the customs of the community, the evils to be remedied, and the remedy provided.

11. Statutes which change the common law are to be strictly construed.

12. Statutes which are consistent with one another and which relate to the same subject matter are in pari materia and should be construed together and effect be given to them all, although they may contain no reference to one another and were passed at different times.

13. Where a general word in a statute follows particular and specific words of the same nature as itself, it takes its meaning from them and is presumed to be restricted to the same genus as those words. This rule is called ejusdem generis.

These thirteen rules, and others like them, are used to determine what statutory language means—to justify the court's result in applying a general rule to a particular fact situation.

Besides using rules of construction to decide the meaning of words found in statutes, most judges also apply two rules about words. The first rule states that words seldom have a single meaning. Most words have a variety of possible meanings depending on how the words are used. The question the judge should ask about a word used within a statute is not what is the "usual" meaning of the word, but, rather, "what can the word mean?" Unless an interpretation is clearly beyond the limits of a word's permissible meaning, the word may be given a meaning beyond its usual one as reported in the dictionary.

The second rule about words says that the context in which the word appears must be taken into account in deciding what the word means. When words appear in statutes, there are two contexts that must be considered. The first is textual context. This means that the judge should look not only at the sentence in which the word appears, but also at the larger units into which the statute is further divided including the paragraph, the section, the chapter, and the entire statute. A word appearing in a tax statute, for instance, may have an entirely different meaning than the same word appearing in a statute dealing with crime.

A word appearing in a statute must also be understood in light of its circumstantial context—that is, in view of all the relevant factors and conditions that were in existence at the time the statute was passed including social, political, economic, and technological circumstances. The idea is that the judge should interpret the word in such manner as to give effect to its underlying purpose as reflected in its textual and circumstantial contexts. In this way, the legislative intent will be carried out.

HOW IS IT DECIDED IF GENERAL RULES OF LEGISLATION ARE VALID AND CONSTITUTIONAL?

It is necessary on occasion to decide not only what a statute means but to determine its constitutionality as well. Article III of the Constitution, which establishes the judicial branch of the government and the powers of the Supreme Court, states the following: "Section 2.(1) The judicial power shall extend to all cases, in law and equity, arising under this constitution." This power to decide cases "arising under this constitution" is the basis for the Supreme Court's power to declare acts of Congress unconstitutional and invalid (the power is nowhere expressly provided for). This power is called "judicial review." It was first clearly defined in the famous case of Marbury v. Madison, 5 U.S. (1 Cranch) 137, 2 L.Ed. 60, by Chief Justice John Marshall in 1803. There, the Supreme Court ruled, for the first time, that an act of Congress was unconstitutional—that Congress had passed a bill and made rules dealing with a subject matter not within congressional powers.

Judicial review, one of the most important powers belonging to the courts, means that the judicial branch of government may determine that acts of the legislature or acts of executive branches of government are unconstitutional and therefore illegal. It means that courts may make law by striking down other law; the determination of unconstitutionality is itself law, and the ability to make that determination is significant in both federal and state courts. Judicial review has met with constant controversy, although its modern critics are more likely to criticize the court for how it exercises its power, rather than for exercising it at all. When the "nine old men" of the Court struck down President Franklin Roosevelt's New Deal legislation in the 1930s, they were attacked for being backward and conservative; yet conservative proponents of "law and order" in the 1960s branded the Warren Court (e.g., *Miranda* case) as a "bunch of soft liberals." But the decision in *Marbury v. Madison* has never been disturbed, and there is one fact both critic and ally can agree on: judicial review is an integral part of our legal system—and it is here to stay.

Judicial review serves as the basis for state court exercise of judicial review over local legislation to see if such legislation is in line with the state constitution. It is limited in both federal and state courts, however, by the "case and controversy" requirement. Courts will not look directly at statutes to review their constitutionality. A real case or controversy must first exist. There must be adverse parties with real interests at issue—parties who are fighting to achieve a particular result. Only where there is an honest and actual antagonistic fight for one's rights, and the constitutionality of a statute becomes important to determination of those rights, will the courts exercise judicial review and rule on the constitutionality of the statute. It is for this reason that the Court will not render an advisory opinion to the president or to Congress on the constitutionality of some contemplated legislation or action.

Closely related to the "case or controversy" requirement is the "doctrine of standing," requiring a person asserting the violation of a constitutional or statutory right to show a direct and immediate personal injury to himself or herself as a result of the challenged action. In other words, the individual bringing the case to the court must have a personal stake in the outcome and must show that his or her individual needs require a remedy, not merely that society has a problem. The broad problems of society are best solved through the political and legislative process as previously described and not by the courts. For example, in Warth v. Seldin, 422 U.S. 490, 95 S.Ct. 2197, 45 L.Ed.2d 343 (1975), low-income persons seeking to invalidate a town's restrictive zoning ordinance were held to lack standing because they failed to allege that they were personally unable to buy housing because of the statute. The Court concluded that voiding the ordinance might not have had any effect upon their ability to find affordable housing, and they would not benefit in any tangible way from the judicial intervention.

HOW DO THE GENERAL RULES OF THE COMMON LAW COME INTO BEING?

In the previous chapter we described common law as one of the three basic sources of law in the United States and stated that it provides us with many general rules. It has been called "unwritten law," and, of course, the key to understanding common law is to realize that this is law resulting from court decisions when there is no written law applicable to the particular fact situation. Yet, it is more than this—a rule of law becomes part of the common law only when it serves as a precedent for other legal decisions—that is, when other judges follow its reasoning in deciding their own cases. Courts also follow precedent in interpreting statutes (applying rules of construction that have been used in the past is one example) and in interpreting constitutions. Precedent, then, is not only crucial in the development of common law but is also significant in interpreting the written law. The use of precedent to decide present cases is known as the doctrine of stare decisis. This comes from the Latin phrase, "stare decisis et non quieta movere," which means "to adhere to precedents and not unsettle things that are settled." The doctrine of stare decisis refers not only to the use of precedents but to the principle itself that precedents *should be followed* in subsequent cases involving the same legal question. This emphasis on following precedent is an important one, for it brings more stability, certainty, and predictability into the law. But courts are not absolutely required to follow precedent—although they usually do. From time to time, they find that conditions have changed and that new precedent should be established. Just as legislatures must alter or abolish statutes to meet the needs of society, so too must courts be ready for change. Remember, one important characteristic of an ideal system of law is the ability to change. So, while uniformity and continuity are very important to law, the ability to make necessary change is just as vital.

Edward H. Levi, in his book, *An Introduction to Legal Reasoning,* states that the use of precedent involves a special kind of judicial reasoning by example. This process involves three steps:

1. The case decided in the past—that which is to serve as a precedent—is recognized as being similar to the current case.
2. The rule of the precedent case is stated.
3. The rule of the precedent case is applied to the current case.

The first step is the most difficult for the judge. Once he or she sees that there is a past case similar to the one before him, he or she can rather easily apply the rule of that case to the present one to come up with a result. Before lawyers go to court, they very thoroughly research past cases for favorable precedents. Lawyers for each side then try to convince the judge that the cases they have found are the same or similar to the case before the court and should therefore be used as precedents. At some point, the judge becomes convinced one way or the other, and the case is decided. The decision then becomes a precedent for future cases. That is the reasoning behind the principle of stare decisis, a principle extremely important to the making of common law and to the interpretation of written law.

WHO HAS POWER TO SETTLE DISPUTES BETWEEN PRIVATE PERSONS IN THE UNITED STATES?

While the courts have primary power to settle disputes in this country, some administrative agencies also make decisions involving the rights of private persons. The kinds of disputes that a particular court may settle (i.e., the subject matter jurisdiction of the court) are considered in a later section of this chapter, along with the procedural requirements of due process.

Every individual is faced with a variety of issues that may need settlement by law—crime, tort, contract, property, taxation, business, and domestic relations are to name but a few. Determination of these issues is called adjudication—a part of lawmaking. And its effect on the individual is more direct than is the making of the general rules or their interpretation. For example, if you are told conclusively by a court of law that you can back out of your record club membership because you are under eighteen years of age, or that the man who ran into your car has to pay for the damage he caused, or that you must go to jail for possession of marijuana, or that your wife has divorced you—you feel the direct application of the general rules of the law. Whenever a court decides a case, the result is called a judgment or a decree.

HOW ARE GENERAL RULES, JUDGMENTS, AND DECREES ENFORCED?

The general rules made by Congress and the specific decisions reached by courts would mean very little if they were unenforceable. Enforcement of these rules and decisions is left chiefly to the executive branches of government (several independent government agencies share in this responsibility).

The Constitution states that the "executive power shall be vested in a President" and that "he shall take care that the laws be faithfully executed." Under these express powers, the president is responsible for enforcing federal law, including acts of Congress, judgments of federal courts, and treaties with other countries. The president helps interpret the law as well by applying it to specific situations. Obviously, he cannot do the job alone. Within the White House and the Executive Office Building there are more than 1,000 persons working for the president. Volumes could be written on the construction and operation of the executive branch of government; we merely suggest the magnitude of the operation and the responsibilities involved by describing its two major components—the Executive Office and the Executive Departments.

The Executive Office includes nine specific bureaus or councils including the Office of Management and Budget, which prepares and supervises the administration of the billions of dollars spent to carry out the law; the National Security Council, which handles programs affecting the security of the United States (which in turn controls the CIA, Central Intelligence Agency, which evaluates and distributes intelligence relating to national security including counter-intelligence activities); the Council on Environmental Quality which develops and recommends to the president national policies which further environmental quality; the Office of Science and Technology, which evaluates the scientific and technological programs of the federal government; and the Office of the United States Trade Representative, which works to increase United States trade with other countries.

The following thirteen departments assist the president in administering the law: (1) State, (2) Treasury, (3) Defense, (4) Justice, (5) Interior, (6) Agriculture, (7) Commerce, (8) Labor, (9) Health and Human Services, (10) Housing and Urban Development, (11) Transportation, (12) Education, and (13) Energy. Each department is immense and so are its responsibilities. The Justice Department, for example, headed by the Attorney General, is responsibile for investigating violations of all federal laws. It has a tax division, a civil division, a land and natural resource division, an antitrust division, a criminal division, and a civil rights division. Its other departments include the FBI, the U.S. Parole Commission, The Immigration and Naturalization Service, the Board of Immigration Appeals, the Bureau of Prisons, the Community Relations Service, the Drug Enforcement Administration, the Pardon Attorney, and the Foreign Claims Settlement Commission (see figure 2–1). And this is but one department—there are twelve others plus all the parts of the Executive Office.

Numbers of independent agencies exist apart from the president. They are independent in the sense that they are not controlled by the president. These agencies have been created by Congress to carry out the written law and to operate in the fields of aeronautics and space, atomic energy, banking, civil service, communications, farm credit, home loans, interstate commerce, labor arbitration, securities and exchange, small business, veterans affairs, etc. Lawmaking agencies (rule making, decision making, and administration) include the Civil Aeronautics Board, Environmental Protection

FIGURE 2-1 THE DEPARTMENT OF JUSTICE

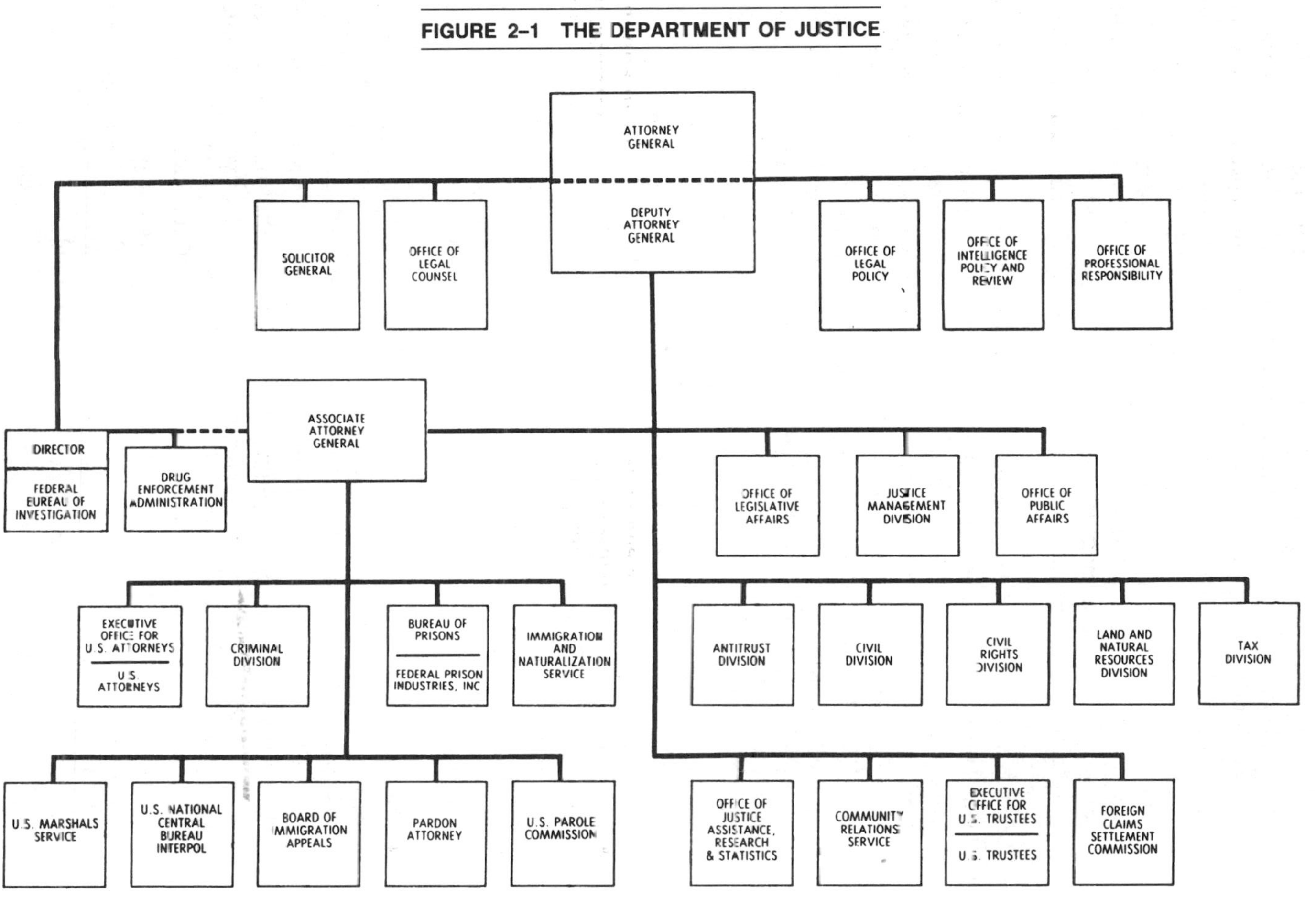

Source: United States Government Manual, 1982–83

Agency, Federal Communications Commission, Interstate Commerce Commission, National Labor Relations Board, Nuclear Regulatory Commission, Securities and Exchange Commission, Tennessee Valley Authority, Veterans Administration, and many, many more.

And this is only the federal law. There are countless other state and local governmental operations that enforce the law and carry it into effect. Governors and mayors have broad authority as do state and local agencies. The law must be carried out and enforced—and thousands of our citizens are involved in this aspect of lawmaking.

HOW IS IT DETERMINED IF THE RULES AND DECISIONS ARE PROPERLY AND EFFECTIVELY ENFORCED?

The federal and state system of law administration and enforcement is a fantastic one. This system undertakes to carry out and enforce the law as it is defined by the legislative and judicial branches of our government. As in any vast system, the possibility for abuse is considerable. The system must provide its own safeguards. Efforts are made to keep waste, corruption, and inefficiency to a minimum. The statutes themselves provide built-in checks; almost every governmental authority involved in administration of the law is required to operate with an internal control system including investigative and security personnel. The Justice Department actively investigates all governmental administration. In 1973, the Justice Department with FBI participation actively and vigorously investigated the famous Watergate burglary. This investigation resulted in the indictment and jailing of the Attorney General—the head of the Justice Department, and culminated in the resignation of President Richard M. Nixon himself. In 1981–82 a United States senator and several United States congressmen were convicted and sentenced to jail in the famous Abscam bribery and conspiracy cases (see the "*Abscam*" case in Chapter 1). At many times in our history, individuals in top governmental positions have been indicted and sent to prison, including legislators, judges, and members of the executive branch of government. This is not to say that everyone who breaks the law gets caught, but it does illustrate the fact that law applies to all people and that our system of carrying out and enforcing the law is substantially successful.

Judicial review also applies to enforcement of the law. The president must remain within his constitutional powers or the powers given him by Congress. More than once the Supreme Court has declared a president's acts void and illegal when undertaken outside of his designated authority. Administrative agencies, too, must not exceed the scope of power conferred by their statutes. If an agency attempts to go beyond these powers, the Supreme Court will declare its acts illegal and void.

The Constitution additionally guarantees individual rights in the areas of religion, speech, assembly, illegal search, and due process. If employees of the government violate these rights while trying to enforce the law, the employee and perhaps the government itself will be liable for the wrongdoing and have to pay in money damages to the injured individual.

HOW IS LAW MADE BETWEEN THE UNITED STATES AND OTHER COUNTRIES?

The Constitution of the United States gives power to make agreements with other countries to the president. Article II, Section 2, states that the president "shall have the power, by and with the advice and consent of the Senate, to make treaties, provided two-thirds of the Senators present concur." This power is of increasing importance as the United States assumes the role of world leader.

The Constitution also provides: "This Constitution and the Laws of the United States which shall be made in pursuance thereof; and all treaties made, or which shall be made, under the authority of the United States, shall be the supreme law of the land." While statutes passed by Congress must be made in pursuance of the Constitution and therefore subject to all of its limitations, treaties are not so restricted. They need only be made "under the authority of the United States" which means by the president with the advice and consent of the Senate. Thus, the president can enter into agreements with foreign countries without worrying about constitutional restrictions—the president can do things with a treaty that Congress cannot do with a statute. And this makes much sense. Not all countries have systems like ours with safeguards and restrictions. The president must be free to deal with these countries and make agreements in the best interests of the United States.

Treaties may include peace treaties that end wars; political treaties that deal with political alliances or settle political problems between countries; commercial treaties that deal with international business, fishing rights, navigation, trade tariffs, and other taxes; extradition treaties that deal with escaped criminals; confederation treaties that set up international organizations; and civil justice treaties that protect trademarks, patents, and copyrights.

Of course treaties cannot be enforced—most countries keep them as a matter of good faith and good business. Broken treaties have often been the cause of war. While there are some international courts such as the International Court of Justice which meets at The Hague to settle international disputes, no nation can be compelled to go before this court or to abide by its decisions. The United Nations, with its approximately 125-member nations including the United States, has had limited success in keeping peace and enforcing international agreements.

The president as commander-in-chief and chief foreign diplomat has authority to make executive agreements with foreign countries without the consent of Congress. Congress has further empowered the president to enter into reciprocal trade and arbitration agreements with foreign powers.

WHAT IS THE GENERAL LAW OF BUSINESS?

To understand how the general law of business has developed, it is necessary to go back hundreds of years to Europe to a time when business law was designated as "mercantile law" or "the law merchant." Before the common law courts existed in England, a system of so-called "mercantile courts" evolved to settle the disputes of the merchants and traders of the time. When disputes arose, these merchant courts promptly settled the issues so that the traveling merchants would not be detained. Their decisions were based on a system of rules, customs, and usages generally accepted by the merchants and traders themselves. The mercantile judges were frequently appointed at fairs where merchants came to sell their wares. The decisions were enforced by ostracizing any merchant who refused to accept them. The law merchant was forced to operate this way because early common law courts would not help the merchants resolve their disputes or help them enforce their own decisions. It was not until the eighteenth century that the law merchant was taken completely into the common law system. The common law decisions, by accepting the "law merchant," gave the force of law to the custom and usage of merchants. Business or commercial law, which has its roots completely in the customs and usages of the medieval merchants, has now been carried another step by the codification of the common law into statutory form.

Specifically, the various state legislatures in the United States have adopted what is called the Uniform Commercial Code. Under this Code, commercial law is governed to a great extent by written statute uniform in all the states. The Code is extremely detailed: its more than 400 sections cover many areas of commercial law with greatest emphasis on the law of sales and the use of checks and promissory notes. The purposes of the Code are stated as follows:

Section I–102

(1) This Act shall be liberally construed and applied to promote its underlying purposes and policies.
(2) Underlying purposes and policies of this Act are:
   (a) To simplify, clarify and modernize the law governing commercial transactions;
   (b) To permit the continued expansion of commercial practices through custom, usage and agreement of the parties;
   (c) To make uniform the law among the various jurisdictions.

Many areas of commercial law, however, remain unchanged by the Uniform Commercial Code and are still controlled by common law rules. Most contract law, for example, is based on common law and applies irrespective of the Uniform Commercial Code. Thus, both the Uniform Commercial Code and the common law are important in the study of business or commercial law.

HOW DOES THE SYSTEM OF CHECKS AND BALANCES WORK?

The legal system in the United States is one of checks and balances designed to diffuse control and responsibility among the several branches of government. Under this system of separation of powers, 435 congressmen are elected to the House of Representatives every two years and 100 senators to the Senate for six-year terms (a third of the Senate is thus elected every two years). Both chambers must agree before a general rule can become law.

The president and the executive branch exist separately and independently of the legislative branch. The president is elected to a four-year term of office and is prohibited from serving more than two terms. He must sign the bills passed by Congress, or they do not become law. But if he vetoes a bill, Congress can check him by overriding the veto if two-thirds of both houses agree. The president can also make treaties, but only if the Senate agrees—another check.

Judges, appointed for life, are independent of both other branches of government. The courts can declare laws passed by Congress or acts of the president unconstitutional—more checks. Yet the president appoints the judges with the Senate's consent, and Congress controls the courts' budgets—double check. Neither the courts nor the legislature possess a police force to enforce laws. And while the president has enforcement people under his jurisdiction, they operate independently of his judgment.

Congress can additionally impeach the president. It can investigate his activities or those of the courts, but both the president and the courts can refuse to cooperate if the separation of powers is threatened. The court must resolve these disputes—check—check—check. Congress can also create administrative agencies with power to make rules and decisions. The president appoints the people who serve on such an agency, and the court can determine if that agency has exceeded its power. Congress can withhold funds from the agency or terminate it completely. The president can remove its officers for failure to perform their duties properly.

And we have more checks. Locally, people not only vote for representatives but can also vote to recall them. They can use their powers of initiative and referendum. The Constitution specifically protects the rights of individuals against the government and prevents the majority from oppressing the minority. And the American Free Press maintains its constant vigilance on all aspects of government. There are many checks and balances but, unlike a game of chess, never a checkmate—supreme power remains with the people, and the law continues to apply to all persons whatever their positions of power.

WHAT IS THE PRIMARY CONCEPT WITHIN THE UNITED STATES LEGAL SYSTEM?

Each of you will have legal problems from time to time as you go through life. How will you resolve your disputes? If you are driving your car cautiously down the street when a drunk driver runs a red light and crashes into you, badly damaging your car and gravely injuring your person, what will you do if the driver refuses to pay for your expenses? Or say you buy a new, combination TV-stereo set for $1,500 cash, and the set does not work properly. What will you do if the seller refuses to repair it? Suppose someone beats you up because your hair is either too short or too long, and you end up in the hospital. Or someone agrees to build you a house for a certain price, does his job poorly, then ups the price. Or say your husband or wife

FIGURE 2–2 THE GOVERNMENT OF THE UNITED STATES

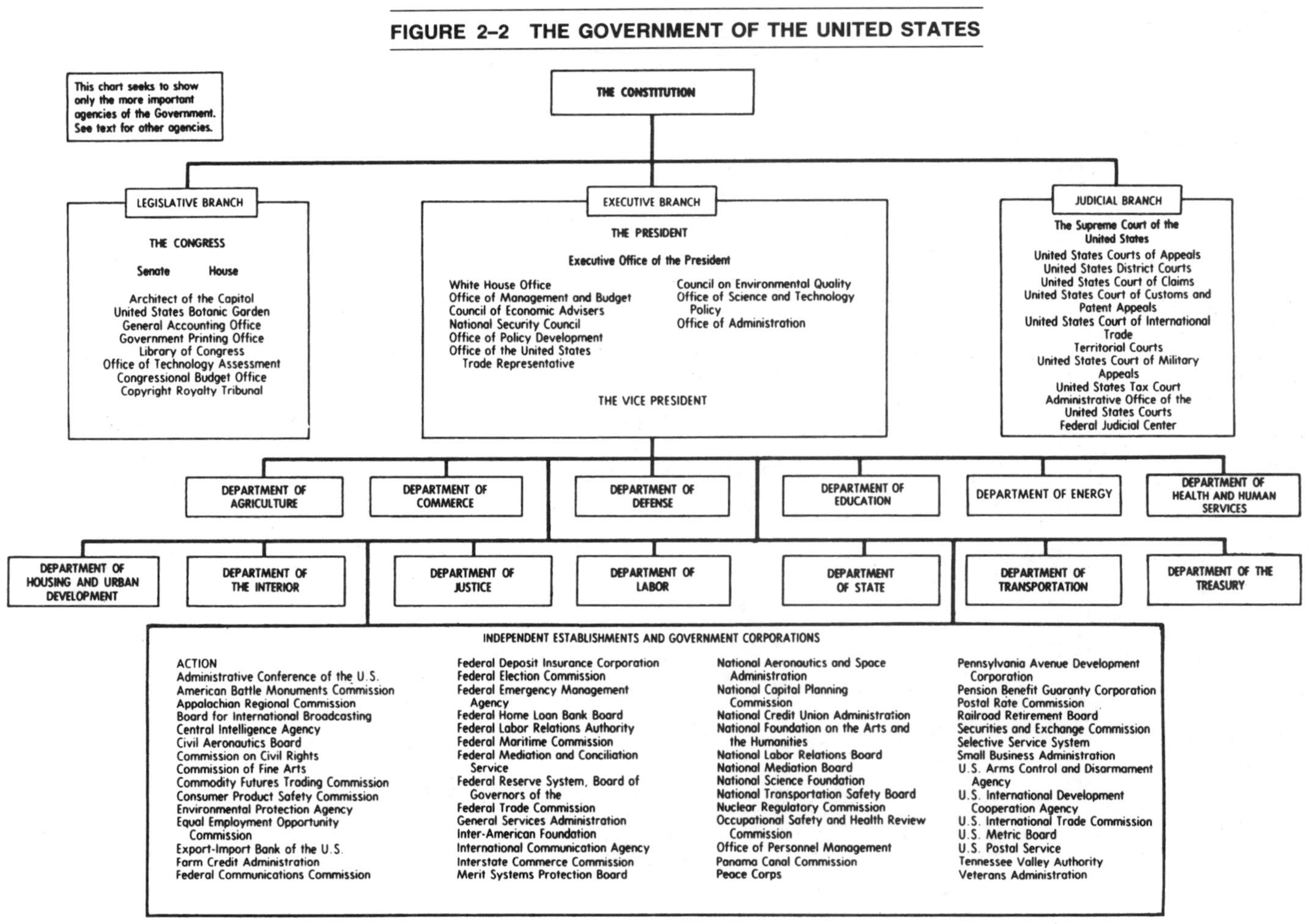
This chart seeks to show only the more important agencies of the Government. See text for other agencies.
THE CONSTITUTION
LEGISLATIVE BRANCH
THE CONGRESS
Senate House
Architect of the Capitol
United States Botanic Garden
General Accounting Office
Government Printing Office
Library of Congress
Office of Technology Assessment
Congressional Budget Office
Copyright Royalty Tribunal
EXECUTIVE BRANCH
THE PRESIDENT
Executive Office of the President
White House Office
Office of Management and Budget
Council of Economic Advisers
National Security Council
Office of Policy Development
Office of the United States Trade Representative
Council on Environmental Quality
Office of Science and Technology Policy
Office of Administration
THE VICE PRESIDENT
JUDICIAL BRANCH
The Supreme Court of the United States
United States Courts of Appeals
United States District Courts
United States Court of Claims
United States Court of Customs and Patent Appeals
United States Court of International Trade
Territorial Courts
United States Court of Military Appeals
United States Tax Court
Administrative Office of the United States Courts
Federal Judicial Center
DEPARTMENT OF AGRICULTURE
DEPARTMENT OF COMMERCE
DEPARTMENT OF DEFENSE
DEPARTMENT OF EDUCATION
DEPARTMENT OF ENERGY
DEPARTMENT OF HEALTH AND HUMAN SERVICES
DEPARTMENT OF HOUSING AND URBAN DEVELOPMENT
DEPARTMENT OF THE INTERIOR
DEPARTMENT OF JUSTICE
DEPARTMENT OF LABOR
DEPARTMENT OF STATE
DEPARTMENT OF TRANSPORTATION
DEPARTMENT OF THE TREASURY
INDEPENDENT ESTABLISHMENTS AND GOVERNMENT CORPORATIONS
ACTION
Administrative Conference of the U.S.
American Battle Monuments Commission
Appalachian Regional Commission
Board for International Broadcasting
Central Intelligence Agency
Civil Aeronautics Board
Commission on Civil Rights
Commission of Fine Arts
Commodity Futures Trading Commission
Consumer Product Safety Commission
Environmental Protection Agency
Equal Employment Opportunity Commission
Export-Import Bank of the U.S.
Farm Credit Administration
Federal Communications Commission
Federal Deposit Insurance Corporation
Federal Election Commission
Federal Emergency Management Agency
Federal Home Loan Bank Board
Federal Labor Relations Authority
Federal Maritime Commission
Federal Mediation and Conciliation Service
Federal Reserve System, Board of Governors of the
Federal Trade Commission
General Services Administration
Inter-American Foundation
International Communication Agency
Interstate Commerce Commission
Merit Systems Protection Board
National Aeronautics and Space Administration
National Capital Planning Commission
National Credit Union Administration
National Foundation on the Arts and the Humanities
National Labor Relations Board
National Mediation Board
National Science Foundation
National Transportation Safety Board
Nuclear Regulatory Commission
Occupational Safety and Health Review Commission
Office of Personnel Management
Panama Canal Commission
Peace Corps
Pennsylvania Avenue Development Corporation
Pension Benefit Guaranty Corporation
Postal Rate Commission
Railroad Retirement Board
Securities and Exchange Commission
Selective Service System
Small Business Administration
U.S. Arms Control and Disarmament Agency
U.S. International Development Cooperation Agency
U.S. International Trade Commission
U.S. Metric Board
U.S. Postal Service
Tennessee Valley Authority
Veterans Administration

Source: United States Government Manual, 1982–83

hits you, calls you names, and generally makes your life miserable. What will you do in these circumstances? What steps can you take if you are a victim of fraud, rape, slander, or theft?

An effective legal system must deal adequately with all of these problems and with the many others likely to arise during your lifetime. What do you do? Well, the natural and immediate answer is to see your lawyer. But what makes the lawyer so special? How does he or she know which specific rules and procedures apply to your fact situation? How does he or she understand the fantastic labyrinth of rules, decisions, standards, and principles that make up the law in the United States?

Certainly, the lawyer has spent at least three years studying the legal system in law school. But could he or she learn all the law in that period of time? The answer is no. For there are literally hundreds of thousands of written appellate court opinions that announce the law, hundreds of thousands of pages of statutes passed into law by state legislatures and the federal Congress, hundreds of thousands of administrative rulings and decisions. No lawyer can ever know all the law. *But the lawyer does understand the primary concept in our legal system, and he or she is able to recognize which specific legal concept applies to a particular fact situation.*

The word "concept" was used twice in that sentence—once to refer to the primary concept in our legal system and again to refer to the lawyer's ability to recognize specific legal concepts. It is very important to understand the meaning of concept as used here. The word "concept" comes from the Latin "conceptus," meaning "thing conceived." A concept is simply a general thought or idea. It is a mental formulation on a broad scale and in some detail.

We have referred to the primary concept of our law—that is, the fundamental or basic element of our entire legal system. This primary concept is the notion of *rights and duties.* Whatever situation we discuss—contract, sale, crime, tort, property, taxation, environment, consumer protection, trusts, estates, or probate—it all comes down to a discussion of rights and duties.

A right is a legal capacity to act or to demand action or forbearance on the part of another. If a right is a legal capacity to act—what is an act? Used in this sense, an act is a voluntary physical movement of a human being. But a right can also be the ability to demand action or forbearance on the part of another. A forbearance is a consciously willed absence of physical movement. And a forbearance can be a very valuable thing. If you have the ability—the right—to prevent someone from doing a certain thing, say, for instance, from selling a piece of land to anyone else but you, it can be worth a great deal of money to you.

A duty is a legal obligation to act or to refrain from acting. Rights and duties always go together. Whenever there is a right in one person or group, there is always a correlative duty in some other person or group.

The whole of our law, then, is a system of control that recognizes, creates, and enforces rights and duties. It may be classified into two parts: (1) the substantive law that defines rights and duties, and (2) the adjective law, or procedure by which rights and duties may be enforced. All legal concepts (specific subject matters of the law) are concerned with rights and duties and must be thought of in these terms.

WHAT IS A SPECIFIC LEGAL CONCEPT?

The lawyer uses a systematic approach to understand the great mass of opinions, rules, and decisions that make up our law. He or she recognizes and understands specific legal concepts. Again, a concept is but a general thought or idea conceived with some detail. But a legal concept is something more than this. It is a category—a specifically defined part of the whole law. And it is a division of law that has been authoritatively defined by the legislative, executive, or judicial branches of government. This division of law into parts or categories enables the lawyer to place his or her particular fact situation into a specific category or subject matter area. Certain rules, unique to that category or area of law, will then apply.

This, then, is the lawyer's special talent—the ability to categorize problems and resolve disputes. If you tell him or her you were hit by a drunk driver who ran a red light, he or she will recognize that negligence, a legal concept of tort law, is involved and will apply its rules and principles to your problem. His or her legal study has familiarized him or her with these rules and principles, and he or she knows where to look for any changes in the law.

If you tell your lawyer that your new TV-stereo does not work, he or she will place your fact situation within the concept of sales. He or she will not refer you to concepts of negligence, crime, or taxation—their rules and principles simply do not apply.

Suppose someone severely beats you. If you are to recover damages for your stay in the hospital, your lawyer must apply the rules and principles of another legal concept—the intentional tort of battery. Sales and negligence do not apply. In order to arrest your assailant, law enforcement officials must utilize the concept of crime, not tort, sales, or negligence.

If someone agrees to build you a house and then refuses to do so, the rules of contract law will control. And if you need a divorce, domestic relations law, with its rules on divorce, alimony, and child support, will provide the answers.

And so it is with every fact situation. Each must be placed within a specific legal concept defined in one or more of three legal sources—written, common, or administrative law. If there is no legal concept that provides a remedy in your particular situation, then you cannot win your case or obtain the result you desire. For instance, you may not like the looks of your neighbor because he is too fat. Can you sue to make him lose weight? The obvious answer is no. And it would be ridiculous if you could. There is no legal concept that recognizes your remedy in this situation and allows you to win—and this is true no matter how much your neighbor's obesity irritates you. But what if that same neighbor piles junk all over his yard and burns foul smelling rubbish? Can this fact situation be placed within a legal concept that provides you with a remedy? The answer here is yes. This is the tort of nuisance; your neighbor can be enjoined from such activity.

There are a great many legal concepts in our system of law. The lawyer, of course, studies these concepts in law school. Many of them are presented to you throughout this text, including torts, crimes, administrative law, partnerships, corporations, securities regulation, antitrust, property, contracts, insurance, sales, consumer protection, bankruptcy, taxes, and environmental law.

A legal concept, then, is a category defined by law into which fact situations can be placed with the result that certain rules and principles will apply. These categories are traditionally divided into areas of public and private law. Public law involves the rights of society as a whole and encompasses the legal concepts of criminal, administrative, and constitutional law. Where the public interest is directly involved, legal representation is by government agency. Private law, on the other hand, deals with the legal relationships existing between individuals. The two main legal concepts involved in private law are tort, which deal with wrongs committed by one person against another, and contracts, dealing with rights and duties of individuals created through their own agreement. Most civil actions between private parties deal either with tort or contract.

WHAT KINDS OF RIGHTS CAN A PERSON IN THE UNITED STATES HAVE?

The primary concept of our law is that of rights and duties. We have defined a right as a legal capacity to act—to do something voluntarily—or to demand that someone else act or not act. The protection and guarantee of individual rights is the most important single objective of our legal system.

There are two types of individual rights—personal rights and property rights. The difference between the two is in their transferability. If a right can be disposed of or transferred by gift, sale, or assignment, it is a property right. If it cannot be disposed of but can be exercised only by the person who possesses it (he or she cannot give or sell it to another), then it is a personal right.

Just as there are two types of rights—personal and property rights—so also are there two kinds of personal rights: first, those rights one has solely by virtue of being a person and citizen of this country, and second, those rights acquired through contract with another, but which rights cannot be sold or given away. Most contract rights are property rights and can be sold or transferred to another. Thus if you enter into a contract with a local used car company to buy a used Chevrolet, you can transfer your right to buy the car to your brother, and he can enforce his right. This is a contract right that is also a property right. But if you enter into a contract to work, say for a nightclub owner as a member of a performing musical group, the nightclub owner cannot transfer his or her right to have you work for him or her to another club owner. The right to have someone work for you is simply too personal to be transferred. Since this right cannot be transferred to another, it is a personal right, not a property right. So we see that both personal and property rights can be created by entering into agreements or contracts with others.

A good illustration of the personal rights you possess both as a person and as a citizen is found in the Bill of Rights—the first ten amendments to the U.S. Constitution. These amendments protect the fundamental freedoms of religion, speech, press, and assembly. They guarantee freedom from unreasonable search and seizure and assure the accused of a speedy trial by jury. The Fourteenth Amendment guarantees that no person shall be deprived of life, liberty, or property without due process of law. These rights, as well as the "civil rights" defined and guaranteed by statute, belong to you alone. They cannot be sold, given away, or transferred. They are personal rights, not property rights. The right to vote, to get married, to make a will—all are examples of personal rights. They belong only to you and may not be transferred.

Property rights are of two types as well. These are real property rights and personal property rights. Be careful not to confuse this last term, "personal property right," with the personal right we have just discussed.

The term "real" refers to the earth; real property rights refer to real estate, i.e., rights with respect to land and things permanently attached to land such as buildings and their fixtures. Personal property rights consist of all other property rights—transferable rights that are unconnected to land or things permanently attached to land.

Finally, personal property rights can also be broken down into two categories: tangibles ("choses in possession") or intangibles ("choses in action"). The tangible is a personal property right in something that has material substance—something that can be touched. The intangible, on the other hand, has no material substance. Rights in your books, clothes, and cars are examples of tangible personal property rights. Rights in things such as patents, copyrights, stocks, bonds, and contracts are examples of intangible personal property rights. Say you own a hundred shares of stock in a corporation like General Motors. You are given a stock certificate that evidences your ownership interest. But that piece of paper is not really what you own. You have an intangible personal property right—ownership of a very tiny part of one of the largest corporations in the world.

These, then, are all the rights you can have: *personal* and therefore nontransferable (because you are a person or because you have a nontransferable right under a contract); *property* and therefore transferable by gift, sale, or assignment—either *real property* (land and buildings) or *personal property* (either tangible or intangible).

HOW ARE RIGHTS ENFORCED?

We have seen that law is a system of control over the conduct of people and that the primary concept of our law is that of rights and duties. But rights are worthless unless they are protected and enforced. How is this accomplished?

Well, in the United States any person who has a right possesses, in addition, the capacity or ability to influence some other person with a corresponding duty. Again, rights and duties are correlative terms: for every right there is a duty, and for every duty there is a right. Once you have a legally recognized right, you are entitled to voluntary performance of the corresponding duty. But if that performance is not forthcoming, the law provides you with the courts and all available legal procedure to make certain that person performs. So if you are driving cautiously to work and a drunk driver smashes both you and your car, you have a right to be compensated in money for any damages you sustain. The drunk driver has a duty to pay for these damages. If he or she refuses to do so, you can influence his or her conduct by going to court and obtaining a judgment against him or her.

Similarly, if you enter into a contract to buy a combination TV-stereo and the set does not work, the law recognizes your right to get your money back or to have the seller put the set in good working condition. If the seller does not voluntarily respond and perform his or her duty, the law recognizes your capacity to influence the seller's conduct; you may force him or her to perform by using the courts and all available legal procedures.

WHAT IS THE DIFFERENCE BETWEEN A TRIAL COURT AND AN APPELLATE COURT?

The term "courts" has been used many times in the preceding pages. Courts not only resolve disputes, interpret written law, and establish principles of common law, but they are used as well to make people perform their duties. There are two basic types of courts—trial courts and appellate courts. Each has a different function, and it is important to understand the differences between them.

It is in the trial court that the matter in dispute is first considered and resolved. Witnesses are presented, exhibits and other evidence are introduced, first by the plaintiff to prove what he or she believes to be the facts—then by the defendant to disprove them. Television reruns of *Perry Mason* and *The Defenders* present a fairly accurate picture of how trials are conducted, with one exception. The surprise endings that frequently occur on TV seldom come up in the courtroom. Trial courts make an initial determination of the facts and attempt to settle the dispute once and for all. If both parties are satisfied with the decision made by the judge and/or jury, the case ends.

Appellate courts, on the other hand, are reviewing courts. They do not come into the picture until the trial court decision has already been made. The appellate court hears requests for reexamination of lower trial court decisions. The appellant (the loser in the trial court) tries to persuade the court of appeals that the trial court decided the case incorrectly, that the case should be reviewed, or that there should be a new trial. Instead of listening to witnesses, appellate courts study a typewritten record of the trial called a transcript which is prepared from notes taken down verbatim by a court reporter during the trial itself. Just as there are no witnesses, there are no juries. Lawyers alone participate by submitting written arguments called briefs and by arguing orally before the court.

All appellate court opinions are preserved in law libraries and are available to lawyers who seek precedents for future cases. You will recall that appellate courts follow case decisions from the past, i.e., apply rules of law from past cases to decide current ones. This is the doctrine of stare decisis, or the principle that prior decisions provide precedents that should be followed in subsequent cases involving the same question of law. The use of precedent is important both in the development of common law and in the interpretation of written law. Precedents are always established by appellate courts through their written opinions.

WHAT ARE THE TWO REQUIREMENTS OF "JURISDICTION"?

In the United States system, rights and duties exist only when based on legitimate sources of law. This is true for the courts as well. Your class, for example, could not today decide to be a court and try one of your professors for some criminal or tortious misconduct. Your class has no authority or power to do this, and a teacher has rights to "due process" that prevent this from taking place.

Before a court can settle a dispute, it must have power to do so. This power is termed "jurisdiction," and without proper jurisdiction, whatever the court does is meaningless. Jurisdiction refers, therefore, to the extent of a court's authority, power, or control.

Two requirements must be satisfied before a court has jurisdiction or power to settle the dispute. First, the case must fall within the designated powers of that court—designated in constitutions and statutes. Thus some courts can handle only minor crimes such as misdemeanors and money damage claims up to $2,500. Other courts can handle major crimes such as felonies and money claims of any amount. There are courts that deal only with domestic relations, such as divorce, or exclusively with tax, juvenile, or probate matters. If you go to the wrong court, proper jurisdiction will not exist, and you cannot obtain a hearing or a valid result.

And even if you go to the right court, it cannot hear the case until it also obtains jurisdiction over the defendant (the person you are suing). This is the second requirement of jurisdiction. The person bringing the suit is always called the plaintiff; the person being sued is the defendant. Whoever loses the case, if he or she appeals, is the appellant. And the winner in the trial court is called the appellee or respondent during the appeal.

Jurisdiction over the person of the defendant is obtained through service of process on the party being sued. Service or delivery of a summons notifies the defendant that he or she is being sued and commands him or her to appear in court or lose by default.

Both aspects of jurisdiction are considered in greater detail in the next few sections of this chapter.

WHAT COURTS HAVE POWER TO SETTLE WHAT KINDS OF DISPUTES?

A court must have power to consider a particular question before it can legitimately dispose of it. This, we have seen, is true for both the trial court and the appellate court. What are the powers of the various courts in the United States?

There are two systems of courts in the United States—the state system in each state and the federal system which is maintained by the federal government. The state system is of colonial origin: after the War for Independence, the existing courts continued to function and develop as state courts. Each state outlines its own court system in its constitution and statutes (laws made by the state legislatures). The federal court system is provided for in the United States Constitution which states that "the judicial power of the United States shall be vested in one Supreme Court, and in such inferior courts as the Congress shall from time to time ordain and establish." (Article III, Section 1.)

So we see, the dual sovereignty of our legal system characterizes our court system as well. Dual sovereignty refers to government at both the state and federal level. Thus we have a federal congress and state legislatures. We have a federal president and state governors. And we have a federal court system and a state court system—often referred to as "the dual court system." In each of these systems, there are both trial and appellate courts, and, under certain circumstances explained later in this section, it is possible to move from a state court to a federal court.

Let's look first at the state court system. There we find that while each state has both trial and appellate courts, not all state courts with similar functions have the same names in every state. In the state of Washington, for example, the main trial court is called the Superior Court, in Pennsylvania the Court of Common Pleas, in New York the Supreme Court, and in Oregon the Circuit Court. The New York Court of Appeals has the same function as the Oregon Supreme Court. But the basic framework in every state is the same. You should determine the names of the courts in your state, see what powers they have, and figure out where they fit within this framework. First is the lowest level trial court that is generally limited to cases involving minor crime or lesser amounts of dollar damages. These courts may be called justice courts, magistrate courts, police courts, traffic courts, district courts, etc. They have jurisdiction over minor crimes such as misdemeanors, where punishment is limited to short jail sentences (generally a year or less) in other than the state penitentiary and/or minor fines (perhaps up to $1,000). They also have jurisdiction over minor problems between individuals (civil actions) based on torts such as auto accidents resulting from negligence, or batteries (when someone beats on another), or beach of contract up to a certain amount—maybe $1,000 or $3,000, but not beyond a rather small figure.

These lower trial courts frequently have small claims divisions where the smallest kind of money claim can be disposed of in one final decision (there is usually no right to appeal from a small claims court). The elimination of an appeal in this instance is based simply on economics. The amount of the claim (usually from under $20 to as high as $700, $1,000, or more) is not large enough to justify further court proceedings. Thus the decision of a small claims court is final. But unless the amount involved is very small—say $200 or less—the plaintiff may, in some states, elect to bring his or her case in the regular division, rather than in the small claims division of the lower trial court. So it is up to him or her to make the choice. If the plaintiff does elect small claims, he or she usually represents himself or herself without a lawyer. While a person incurs little expense this way, the person is stuck with a final result. There are many advantages, however, to using the small claims court. It is generally effective in disposing of minor claims at almost no expense, it provides a method of achieving justice on minor matters that are too costly to handle otherwise; and it furnishes the average citizen with valuable experience and contact with the court system.

At the next level of the state court system is the main trial court with general jurisdiction over most other kinds of disputes or problems. These courts handle all serious crimes (felonies), all serious tort (wrongs) or contract cases, as well as tax, divorce, and probate (the transfer of a deceased person's property to those who have proper claim to it) problems, etc. In some states, an individual who loses a case in the lower trial court may choose to have a new trial in the higher court as a matter of right. But the loser will frequently elect not to because of the additional expense and because, having already lost once in the lower trial court, he or she may very well lose again when the same rules of law are applied to the situation once more.

Both the lower trial court of limited jurisdiction and the higher trial court of general jurisdiction (power to decide any kind of case) are found in each county of every state.

Trial court decisions are reviewed for error in state appellate courts. While a person always has a right to appeal from the higher trial court, he or she must file for appeal within a certain number of days (such as sixty days after the trial decision), or the trial decision becomes final. In an appellate court, remember, there is no trial. Judges consider oral and written arguments regarding mistakes of law made at the lower trial level to determine whether the trial decision should be affirmed, reversed, or a new trial ordered. Many states have more than one appellate court (a heavily populated state, for example, may have one or more intermediate reviewing courts).

Again, the final reviewing court in a state may be called the Supreme Court, the Supreme Court of Appeals, or the Court of Appeals, etc.

It is important to note that, with the exception of the small claims court, a person generally has a right to at least one trial and one appeal on any fact situation he or she can fit within a specific legal concept, whether it be crime, tort, contract, or property. This right to at least one trial and one appeal is basic to the concept of "due process"—that under the Fourteenth Amendment of the Constitution one may not have his or her life, liberty, or property taken away without "due process" of law.

The state court system, as described, decides most cases based on state constitutions, state statutes, and state common laws. The federal system, on the other hand, deals with one of two possible areas of jurisdiction or power. The first is based on what is called a *federal question*—federal, because it concerns the federal Constitution, a federal treaty entered into by the president, or a federal statute passed by Congress. The second, based on *diversity of citizenship,* is designed to prevent state court prejudice against a citizen of another state. In other words, where a citizen of New York is suing or is being sued by a citizen of California or any other state, the courts of the state where the case is to be decided may be prejudiced against the person from out of state. To prevent this, Congress passed a law that allows a dispute between citizens of different states to be brought in the federal trial courts. This is jurisdiction based on diversity of citizenship. The amount in controversy must equal or exceed $10,000. This jurisdictional amount is set simply because the federal courts could not handle all the cases that would otherwise result. But even if the amount involved is under $10,000, the parties will still receive at least one trial and one appeal (if desired) within the state court system. The jurisdictional amount of $10,000 applies to diversity of citizenship cases but no longer to federal question cases. In December of 1980, the $10,000 amount-in-controversy requirement in federal question cases was eliminated. In diversity cases there is no restriction on the subject matter at issue once the diversity of citizenship is established and the jurisdictional amount of $10,000 is present, with the exception that the federal court will, in no event, take jurisdiction of domestic relations (matrimonial status or child custody) or probate (estates of decedents or incompetent persons).

The district court is the basic federal trial court. It decides all federal questions and can hear all diversity of citizenship cases involving more than $10,000. Federal questions include federal crime (bank robbery, stealing cars and driving them over a state line, using the mails to defraud, federal narcotics violations, etc.), questions regarding interstate commerce, federal taxation, federal pollution standards, as well as a myriad of others. There are federal district courts in every state, in Puerto Rico, and in the District of Columbia, the Virgin Islands, the former Canal Zone, and Guam (where they also have local jurisdiction).

One other group must be considered along with the federal district courts—the administrative agencies. Administrative agencies are governmental authorities that are not courts or legislatures but that can decide cases like the courts or make rules like Congress. Having been created by Congress to carry out the detail of certain legislation, they are usually subject to review by the federal district courts (which are trial courts). Several of these agencies, however, are not so subject. Rather, they go directly on review to the federal appellate courts—the United States Courts of Appeal. Among the administrative agencies whose decisions are not subject to federal district court review are the Federal Trade Commission, the National Labor Relations Board, and the Securities and Exchange Commission.

Appeal from the federal district courts and these certain administrative agencies is to the U.S. Courts of Appeal. There are thirteen Courts of Appeal in the federal system, with each court responsible for hearing cases within a particular circuit (subject matter area or region of the country). Twelve of the courts (the eleven numbered circuits and the Court of Appeals for the District of Columbia as shown in Figure 3) have jurisdiction based on geography, with the eleven numbered circuits each covering several states in area. A decision of one of these twelve courts is binding within its geographical circuit. An appellant who is unhappy with a federal district court or administrative agency decision has a right to appeal to the circuit court for review. There are three judges on each circuit court (appellate courts always have an odd number of judges to prevent tie votes—three, five, seven, or, as on the U.S. Supreme Court, nine).

The U.S. Court of Appeals for the Federal Circuit—the so-called "Thirteenth Circuit"—is a relatively new court, having been created by the Federal Courts Improvement Act of 1982.[3] Unlike the other twelve circuit courts,

---

3. Formation of the court was accomplished by merging the former Court of Customs and Patent Appeals and the former Court of Claims (these courts were already housed in the same courts building, and the merger provided for more efficient administration). The U.S. Court of Appeals for the Federal Circuit inherited, in appellate form, substantially all the jurisdiction of the two courts abolished in the merger. Also, any cases originating in the U.S. district courts involving patent appeals or federal contract claims against the United States go to the Thirteenth Circuit for review. The legislative history of the Federal Courts Improvement Act reveals that the Thirteenth Circuit was created to provide a forum for appeals from throughout the country in areas of law where Congress determined there was a special need for national uniformity. Thus, in these areas, there is no chance of a "conflict" between circuits.

the jurisdiction of the Court of Appeals for the Federal Circuit is based on subject matter. The court has exclusive nationwide jurisdiction over certain kinds of cases—patent appeals, federal contract appeals, appeals from the U.S. Claims Court and Court of International Trade (see figure 2–3). A decision of the court is binding throughout the United States.

There are a few special courts in the federal system that deal only with certain subject matters. The United States Court of International Trade has jurisdiction over matters involving import transactions. For example, many federal statutes deal with duties or taxes imposed on goods that are transported in international trade. Disputes often arise between collectors for the United States Customs Service (an administrative agency) and importers and exporters. The United States Court of International Trade must settle these disputes. Appeals from this court are taken to the U.S. Court of Appeals for the Federal Circuit.

The United States Claims Court is a special court that deals only with claims against the United States government.[4] The claims may be based on breach of contract by the federal government, on tax refunds, on claims for just compensation for the taking of property, or upon any other claim founded upon the Constitution, an act of Congress, or any regulation by the executive branch of government. The Claims Court does not handle claims based on torts (wrongs) committed by employees of the federal government.

The United States Tax Court tries and adjudicates controversies involving the existence of deficiencies or overpayments in income, estate, or gift taxes in cases where deficiencies have been determined by the Commissioner of Internal Revenue. It is interesting that a taxpayer may have three different courts from which to choose regarding a federal tax controversy. He or she may go to the federal district court on the basis that the issue involves a federal question, to the Claims Court because it involves a claim against the United States government, or to the Tax Court. With the first two options the taxpayer must first pay the tax and then sue for a refund within a period of two years. With the Tax Court, the taxpayer may, without first paying the deficiency said to be owing by the Internal Revenue Service, ask the court to redetermine the deficiency to determine whether the Internal Revenue Service was correct. An appeal of a Tax Court decision may be taken to the U.S. Courts of Appeal.

Finally, within the federal system, is the United States Supreme Court, the highest court of the land. Appeals may be brought to this Court from

---

4. As previously noted, the Federal Court Improvements Act of 1982 technically abolished the old Court of Claims. The old Court of Claims functioned in many ways as both a "trial" court and an "appellate" court all in one, with traveling commissioners making initial findings of fact and conclusions of law and Court of Claims judges sitting in review of these decisions in Washington D.C. With the abolition of the court, the "appellate" function was transferred to the new U.S. Court of Appeals for the Federal Circuit, and a new court—called the U.S. Claims Court—was created to assume the "trial court" responsibilities of the old Court of Claims. The former commissioners of the old Court of Claims became the first judges of the new Claims Court. The former judges of the old court joined the former judges of the old Court of Customs and Patent Appeals to become the first judges of the new U.S. Court of Appeals for the Federal Circuit. The Federal Court Improvements Act of 1982 also gave the new Claims Court the power to grant certain equitable relief as well as money damages (the old Court of Claims could grant only money).

FIGURE 2-3 THE THIRTEEN FEDERAL JUDICIAL CIRCUITS

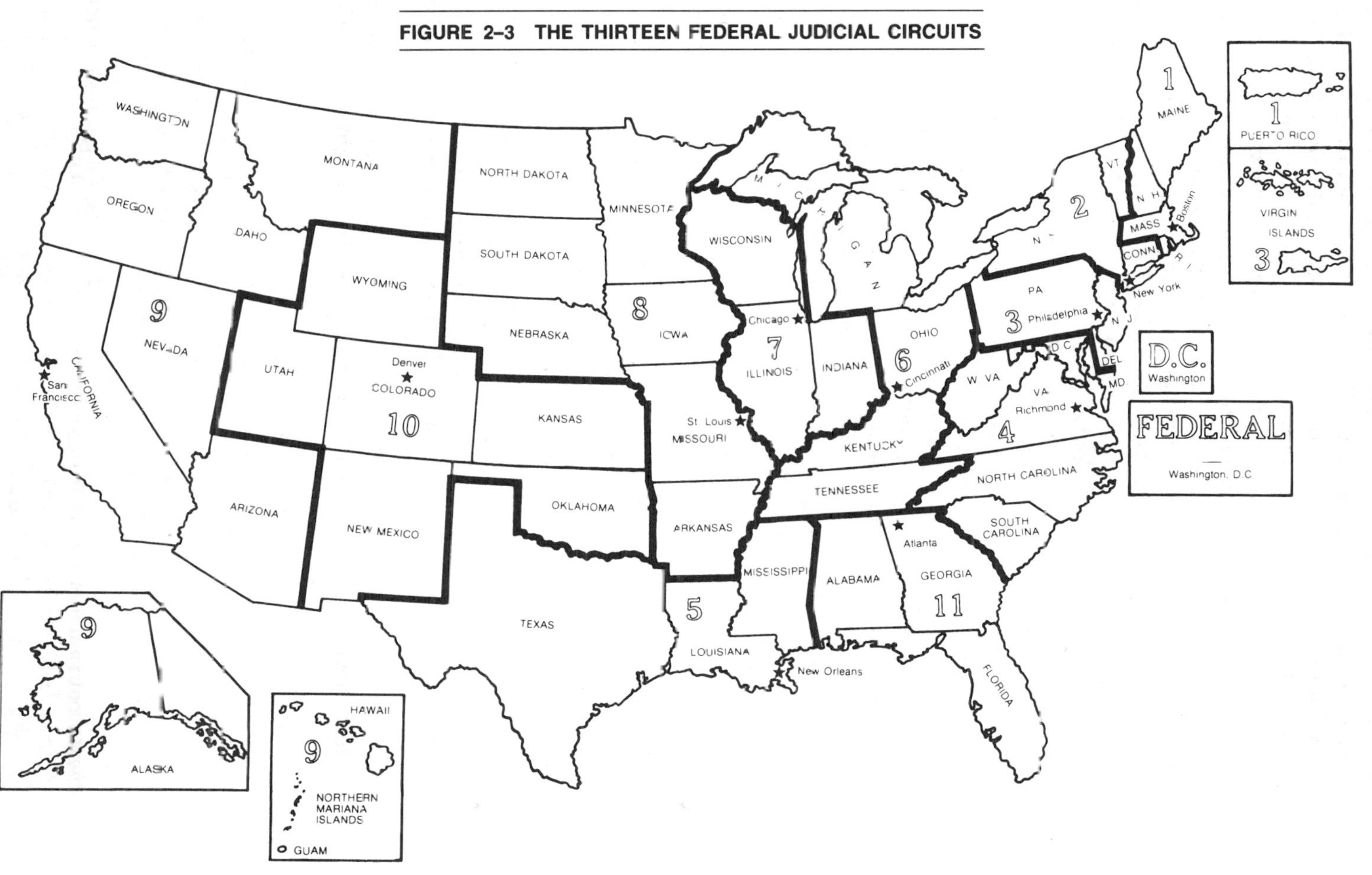

the thirteen U.S. Courts of Appeal and the highest courts of the various states. For the most part, however, the U.S. Supreme Court does not have to hear the appeals unless it chooses to do so. Judicial discretion is warranted because there has already been at least one trial and one appeal; further appeal to the Supreme Court is granted only in a case of substantial federal importance or where there is obvious conflict between decisions of two or more of the twelve U.S. circuit courts with geographically based jurisdiction. In other words, if the Court of Appeals for the Fifth Circuit holds differently than the Court of Appeals for the Ninth Circuit on the same question of law, the U.S. Supreme Court will probably straighten them out. To get to the Supreme Court from any of these appeals courts, it is necessary to file a "writ of certiorari" to the Court. This is a petition asking the Court to hear the case because there is a federal question involved. The decision of whether or not to hear the case is then left to the Court's discretion.

While the writ of certiorari is discretionary with the Supreme Court (and there is much more likelihood that the Court will deny the petition and not hear the case rather than grant the writ), the Supreme Court must hear an appeal from the highest court of a state if the state court has held a federal statute or treaty invalid or has upheld a state statute against the claim that it is unconstitutional or contrary to federal statute or treaty. Also an appeal to the United States Supreme Court may be taken as a matter of right if *any federal court* has held a federal statute invalid in a civil action to which the United States is a party, or if a *federal court of appeals* has held a state statute unconstitutional or repugnant to a federal statute or treaty.

In general, however, there is no right of appeal to the U.S. Supreme Court, and the possibility of getting there exists only through the writ of certiorari and then, only if the Court thinks the case is sufficiently important to hear. This discretionary power is necessary because of the great volume of cases urged on the Court each year for review. It would be impossible to hear them all. Each year the Court decides to hear about 200 of the approximate 5,000 cases that are filed. At least four of the nine justices must vote to grant certiorari, i.e., to hear the case. The vote is cast in secret conference with only the nine justices in attendance. If at least four of the justices do not believe the case is of substantial federal importance, it will not be heard.

In going from the state to the federal court system, we have so far considered going only from the highest court of the state to the U.S. Supreme Court for an additional appeal when a federal question of serious import is involved. It is also possible to transfer from a state trial court of general jurisdiction to the federal district court for trial if request is made prior to the start of trial and if the case could have been brought originally in the federal district court—that is, if the federal district court would have had power to hear the case to begin with because of a federal question or diversity of citizenship plus $10,000. This process is called "removal" to the federal court; but again, it can only be done prior to the beginning of trial in the state court and only by the defendant, since the plaintiff had an option to bring the case in the federal court in the first place.

Figure 2–4 illustrates the interrelationship between the state and federal court systems.

FIGURE 2–4 THE FEDERAL JUDICIAL SYSTEM

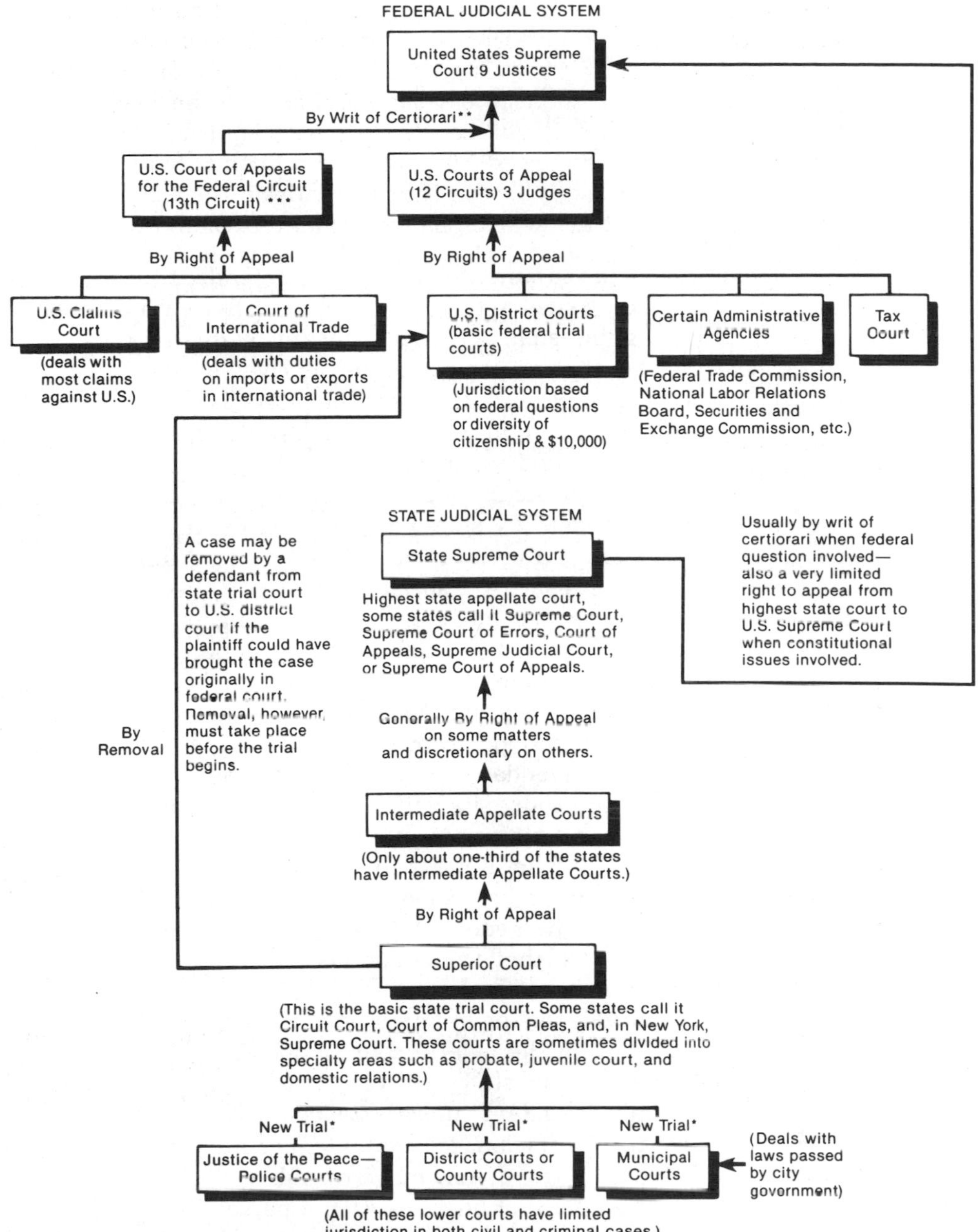

*A number of states do not provide for a new trial with these lower courts, but instead allow appeal by right directly to the appellate courts.

**An appeal to the United States Supreme Court may be taken as a matter of right if any federal court has held a federal statute invalid in a civil action to which the United States is a party or if a federal court of appeals has held a state statute unconstitutional or repugnant to a federal statute or treaty.

***Exclusive nationwide jurisdiction of patent appeals, federal contract appeals, and court of International Trade and Claims Court Appeals.

HOW DOES A COURT GET JURISDICTION OVER THE PERSON OF THE DEFENDANT?

Before a court can decide a case, it must have jurisdiction or power to do so. This not only requires the case to fall within an area of law over which the court has power but requires, in addition, that the court have jurisdiction over the person of the defendant. If the defendant can be found, he or she is served with a summons to "appear and defend." But occasionally, his or her whereabouts will be unknown; service, in this situation, can be accomplished by publication of notice and mailing a summons to the defendant's last known address.

The purpose of the summons is to give the defendant notice or knowledge that he or she is being sued and to provide him or her with an opportunity to be heard. This, again, is part of what is meant by due process. The Constitution clearly states that no person can be deprived of life, liberty, or property without due process of law. Unless a defendant is given notice of suit and a chance to be heard before his or her rights are determined in a courtroom, there is no jurisdiction and no due process of law.

How is this accomplished? Suppose that someone smashes into your car or refuses to service your TV-stereo as provided for in the contract of sale. You may have to bring a civil action against him. Your lawyer can commence the action by preparing a special document called a "complaint" (discussed in detail in the next chapter) and by filing it in the proper court. This complaint specifies what the defendant has done wrong; it "complains" to the court about his actions. Once the complaint has been properly filed, the clerk of the court issues a summons to the defendant commanding him to appear and defend the action. Copies of the summons and complaint must then be served on the defendant. Usually, either the sheriff or deputy of the county where the state court sits will serve the summons by delivering it to the defendant. In some states the summons may be served by any person who is over eighteen and not a party to the case. In the federal courts, only a U.S. Marshall or some other person specially appointed by the court can serve the defendant. The Federal Rules of Civil Procedure, which apply to the federal courts, state that the summons and copy of the complaint can either be handed to the defendant personally or left at his dwelling with some person of suitable age or in any other manner permitted by state statute of the state wherein the federal court is located.

State law varies. Some states are very strict and require actual physical delivery unless the defendant appears to be in hiding. Other states are much more liberal. California, for example, permits service to be made by (1) physical delivery to the defendant personally; (2) leaving the papers at his dwelling or usual place of business with a person at least eighteen years of age who is informed of the nature of the papers, and then mailing another copy to the defendant at the same place; (3) sending the papers by registered or certified air mail to any defendant who is out of the state; and (4) by publishing notice in the newspaper whenever any other measure is ineffective.

There are always special rules for minors, incompetents, and corporations.

Once the proper court has been chosen and the defendant has been notified through proper service of the summons, the defendant must respond within a certain period of time prescribed by statute, or he or she loses the case by default, and a default judgment will be rendered against him or her.

For many years a summons could not be served beyond the borders of the state in which it was issued. This is no longer true. If a citizen from a state 1,000 miles away from your state drives into your neighborhood and, because he is drunk, collides with your car, you may still be confined to the hospital when he returns home, a thousand miles away. Not only would it be highly difficult and very inconvenient for you to go to his state to sue him—it would be impractical as well—for your witnesses are here, in your own state. But if you could only sue him in your own state by serving him with a summons while he is present within its borders, you might be out of luck entirely, for, once gone, he might never return.

To solve this problem, states have adopted what are called "long arm" statutes which allow service of process on the defendant anywhere. These statutes reach the defendant and make him come back to the state where the basis for the suit took place. If he does not, default judgment is taken against him. Once a plaintiff has a valid judgment against a defendant, even a default judgment, it is final, and it may be enforced in any state where the defendant is residing or where he has property. This result is required by the Full Faith and Credit Clause of the United States Constitution. Article IV, Section 1 states in part: "Full faith and credit shall be given in each state to the public acts, records, and judicial proceedings of every other state." Remember, however, that the judgment must be a valid one to be enforceable in another state. This means that the court rendering the judgment had to have jurisdiction both as to subject matter and over the person of the defendant.

Long arm statutes, however, are not designed to cover every possible basis for a law suit. The typical statute limits service outside the state and makes a person come back and respond to its courts only when the suit arises from transmission of business in the state, commission of a tort (such as smashing your car negligently or hitting your nose intentionally), the ownership or use of real property in the state, contracting to sell insurance there, or the like. Additionally, the defendant must have certain minimum contacts or reasonable connection with the state so that maintenance of the case against him or her does not offend traditional notions of fair play and substantial justice. For example, the *New York Times* did not have to come to Alabama to defend a libel (tort) case after it published criticisms of a local Alabama official, even though it had a small number of subscribers in Alabama (New York Times Co. v. Connor, 365 F.2d 567 (5th Cir. 1966)). The *New York Times* was not considered to have sufficient contacts in Alabama to be doing business or to have committed a tort in Alabama for purposes of the long arm statute and jurisdiction over it as a defendant. Of course, this would not have prevented the plaintiff from going to New York and suing in that state.

Cases

Turning over the Watergate tapes for use as evidence in the trial of the Watergate burglars.

IN RE SUBPOENA TO NIXON

U.S. District Court, District of Columbia, 1973.
360 F.Supp. 1.

ORDER
SIRICA, Chief Judge

* * *

Ordered that respondent, President Richard M. Nixon, or any subordinate officer, official or employee with custody or control of the documents or objects listed in the grand jury subpoena *duces tecum* of July 23, 1973, served on respondent in this district, is hereby commanded to produce forthwith for the Court's examination *in camera,* the subpoenaed documents or objects which have not heretofore been produced to the grand jury. * * *

[A "subpoena duces tecum" is an order to produce evidence pertinent to the issues of a pending controversy. "In camera" is "in private" by the judge alone or in private hearing before the judge with all spectators excluded.] * * * In a letter to the Court dated July 25, 1973, the President advised that the tape recordings sought would not be provided, and by way of explanation wrote:

> * * * I follow the example of a long line of my predecessors as President of the United States who have consistently adhered to the position that the President is not subject to compulsory process from the courts.

UNITED STATES v. NIXON

Supreme Court of the United States, 1974.
418 U.S. 683, 94 S.Ct. 3090, 41 L.Ed.2d 1039.

Mr. Chief Justice BURGER delivered the opinion of the Court.

* * *

* * * [W]e turn to the claim that the subpoena should be quashed because it demands "confidential conversations between a President and his close advisors that would be inconsistent with the public interest to produce." * * * [A] broad claim that the separation of powers doctrine precludes judicial review.

In the performance of assigned constitutional duties each branch of the Government must initially interpret the Constitution, and the interpretation of its powers by any branch is due great respect from the others. The President's counsel, as we have noted, reads the Constitution as providing an absolute privilege of confidentiality for all presidential communications. Many decisions of this Court, however, have unequivocally reaffirmed the holding of Marbury v. Madison * * * that "it is emphatically the province and duty of the judicial department to say what the law is." * * *

* * *

Our system of government "requires that federal courts on occasion interpret the Constitution in a manner at variance with the construction given the document by another branch." * * * And in Baker v. Carr, * * * the Court stated:

> "[D]eciding whether a matter has in any measure been committed by the Constitution to another branch of government, or whether the action of that branch exceeds whatever authority has been committed, is itself a delicate exercise in constitutional interpretation, and is a responsibility of this Court as ultimate interpreter of the Constitution."

Notwithstanding the deference each branch must accord the others, the "judicial power of the United States" vested in the federal courts by Art. III, § 1 of the Constitution can no more be shared with the Executive Branch than the Chief Executive, for example, can share with the Judiciary the veto power, or the Congress share with the Judiciary the power to override a presidential veto. Any other conclusion would be contrary to the basic concept of separation of powers and the checks and balances that flow from the scheme of a tripartite government. * * * We therefore reaffirm that it is "emphatically the province and the duty" of this Court "to say what the law is" with respect to the claim of privilege presented in this case. * * *

In support of his claim of absolute privilege, the President's counsel urges two grounds one of which is common to all governments and one of which is peculiar to our system of separation of powers. The first ground is the valid need for protection of communications between high government officials and those who advise and assist them in the performance of their manifold duties; the importance of this confidentiality is too plain to require further discussion. Human experience teaches that those who expect public dissemination of their remarks may well temper candor with a concern for appearances and for their own interests to the detriment of the decisionmaking process. * * * [T]he privilege of confidentiality of presidential communications in the exercise of Art. II powers can be said to derive from the supremacy of each branch within its own assigned area of constitutional duties. Certain powers and privileges flow from the nature of enumerated powers; the protection of the confidentiality of presidential communications has similar constitutional underpinnings.

The second ground asserted * * * in support of the claim of absolute privilege rests on the doctrine of separation of powers. Here it is argued that the independence of the Executive Branch within its own sphere * * * insulates a president from a judicial subpoena in an ongoing criminal prosecution, and thereby protects confidential presidential communications.

However, neither the doctrine of separation of powers, nor the need for confidentiality of high level communications, without more, can sustain an absolute, unqualified presidential privilege of immunity from judicial process under all circumstances. * * *

* * * [W]hen the privilege depends solely on the broad, undifferentiated claim of public interest in the confidentiality of such conversations, a confrontation with other values arises. Absent a claim of need to protect military, diplomatic or sensitive national security secrets, we find it difficult to accept the argument that even the very important interest in confidentiality of presidential communications is significantly diminished by production of such material for *in camera* inspection with all the protection that a district court will be obliged to provide.

* * *

A President and those who assist him must be free to explore alternatives in the process of shaping policies and making decisions and to do so in a way many would be unwilling to express except privately. * * * The privilege [of confidentiality] is fundamental to the operation of government and inextricably rooted in the separation of powers under the Constitution. In Nixon v. Sirica, * * * the Court of Appeals held that such presidential communications are "presumptively privileged," * * * and this position is accepted by both parties in the present litigation. * * *

But this presumptive privilege must be considered in light of our historic commitment to the rule of law. This is nowhere more profoundly manifest than in our view that "the twofold aim [of criminal justice] is that guilt shall not escape or innocence suffer." * * * We have elected to employ an adversary system of criminal justice in which the parties contest all issues before a court of law. * * * The very integrity of the judicial system and public confidence in the system depend on full disclosure of all the facts, within the framework of the rules of evidence. To ensure that justice is done, it is imperative to the function of courts that compulsory process be available for the production of evidence needed either by the prosecution or by the defense.

Only recently the Court restated the ancient proposition of law * * *: "that the public * * * has a right to every man's evidence. * * *"

* * * The Sixth Amendment explicitly confers upon every defendant in a criminal trial the right "to be confronted with the witnesses against him" and to have compulsory process for obtaining witnesses in his favor. Moreover, the Fifth Amendment also guarantees that no person shall be deprived of liberty without due process of law. It is the manifest duty of the courts to vindicate those guarantees and to accomplish that it is essential that all relevant and admissible evidence be produced.

In this case we must weigh the importance of the general privilege of confidentiality of presidential communications in performance of his responsibilities against the inroads of such a privilege on the fair administration of criminal justice. The interest in preserving confidentiality is weighty indeed and entitled to great respect. However we cannot conclude that advisers will be moved to temper the candor of their remarks by the infrequent occasions of disclosure because of the possibility that such conversations will be called for in the context of a criminal prosecution.

On the other hand, the allowance of the privilege to withhold evidence that is demonstrably relevant in a criminal trial would cut deeply into the guarantee of due process of law and gravely impair the basic function of the courts. * * * Without access to specific facts a criminal prosecution may be totally frustrated. * * *

We conclude that when the ground for asserting privilege as to subpoenaed materials sought for use in a criminal trial is based only on the generalized interest in confidentiality, it cannot prevail over the fundamental demands of due process of law in the fair administration of criminal justice.

* * *

Affirmed.

[The Supreme Court ordered President Nixon to release the tape recordings for use as evidence at the trial of the Watergate burglars.]

The fine line of neutrality.

ENGEL v. VITALE

Supreme Court of the United States, 1962.
370 U.S. 421, 82 S.Ct. 1261, 8 L.Ed.2d 601.

Mr. Justice BLACK delivered the opinion of the Court.

The respondent Board of Education of Union Free School District No. 9, New Hyde Park, New York, acting in its official capacity under state law, directed the School District's principal to cause the following prayer to be said aloud by each class in the presence of a teacher at the beginning of each school day:

> Almighty God, we acknowledge our dependence upon Thee, and we beg Thy blessings upon us, our parents, our teachers and our Country.

This daily procedure was adopted on the recommendation of the State Board of Regents, a governmental agency * * * [with] broad supervisory, executive, and legislative powers over the State's public school system. These state officials composed the prayer which they recommended and published as a part of their "Statement on Moral and Spiritual Training in the Schools." * * *

Shortly after the practice of reciting the Regents' prayer was adopted by the School District, the parents of ten pupils brought this action in a New York State Court insisting that use of this official prayer in the public schools was contrary to the beliefs, religions, or religious practices of both themselves and their children. Among other things, these parents challenged the constitutionality of both the state law authorizing the School District to direct the use of prayer in public schools and the School District's regulation ordering the recitation of this particular prayer on the ground that these actions of official governmental agencies violate that part of the First Amendment of the Federal Constitution which commands that "Congress shall make no law respecting an establishment of religion"—a command which was "made applicable to the State of New York by the Fourteenth Amendment of the Constitution." * * *

We think that by using its public school system to encourage recitation of the Regents' prayer, the State of New York has adopted a practice wholly inconsistent with the Establishment Clause.

There can, of course, be no doubt that New York's program of daily classroom invocation of God's blessings as prescribed in the Regents' prayer is a religious activity. It is a solemn avowal of divine faith and supplication for the blessings of the Almighty. * * *

It is a matter of history that this very practice of establishing governmentally composed prayers for religious services was one of the reasons which caused many of our early colonists to leave England and seek religious freedom in America. * * *

It is an unfortunate fact of history that when some of the very groups which had most strenuously opposed the established Church of England found themselves sufficiently in control of colonial governments in this country to write their own prayers into law, they passed laws making their own religion the official religion of their respective colonies. * * *

By the time of the adoption of the Constitution, our history shows that there was a widespread awareness among many Americans of the dangers of a union of Church and State. These people knew, some of them from bitter personal experience, that one of the greatest dangers to the freedom of the individual to worship in his own way lay in the Government's placing its official stamp of approval upon one particular kind of prayer or one particular form of religious services. * * *

The First Amendment was added to the Constitution to stand as a guarantee that neither the power nor the prestige of the Federal Government would be used to control, support or influence the kinds of prayer the American people can say—that the people's religions must not be subjected to the pressures of government for change each time a new political administration is elected to office. Under that Amendment's prohibition against governmental establishment of religion, as reinforced by the provisions of the Fourteenth Amendment, government in this country, be it state or federal, is without power to prescribe by law any particular form of prayer which is to be used as an official prayer in carrying on any program of governmentally sponsored religious activity.

There can be no doubt that New York's state prayer program officially establishes the religious beliefs embodied in the Regents' prayer. * * * Neither the fact that the prayer may be denominationally neutral nor the fact that its observance on the part of the students is voluntary can serve to free it from the limitations of the Establishment Clause. * * *

When the power, prestige and financial support of government is placed behind a particular religious belief, the indirect coercive pressure upon religious minorities to conform to the prevailing officially approved religion is plain. But the purposes underlying the Establishment Clause go much further than that. Its first and most immediate purpose rested on the belief that a union of government and religion tends to destroy government and to degrade religion. * * *

It thus stands as an expression of principle on the part of the Founders of our Constitution that religion is too personal, too sacred, too holy, to permit its "unhallowed perversion" by a civil magistrate. Another purpose of the Establishment Clause rested upon an awareness of the historical fact that governmentally established religions and religious persecutions go hand in hand. * * * It was in large part to get completely away from this sort of systematic religious persecution that the Founders brought into being our Nation, our Constitution, and our Bill of Rights with its prohibition against any governmental establishment of religion. The New York laws officially prescribing the Regents' prayer are inconsistent both with the purposes of the Establishment Clause and with the Establishment Clause itself.

It has been argued that to apply the Constitution in such a way as to prohibit state laws respecting an establishment of religious services in public schools is to indicate a hostility toward religion or toward prayer. Nothing, of course, could be more wrong. * * *

* * * [The First Amendment] was written to quiet well-justified fears * * * arising out of an awareness that governments of the past had schackled men's tongues to make them speak only the religious thoughts that government wanted them to speak and to pray only to the God that government wanted them to pray to. It is neither sacrilegious nor antireligious to say that each separate government in this country should stay out of the business of writing or sanctioning official prayers and leave that purely religious function to the people themselves and to those the people choose to look to for religious guidance.

* * * To those who may subscribe to the view that because the Regents' official prayer is so brief and general there can be no danger to religious freedom in its governmental establishment, however, it may be appropriate to say in the words of James Madison, the author of the First Amendment:

> [I]t is proper to take alarm at the first experiment on our liberties. * * * Who does not see that the same authority which can establish Christianity, in exclusion of all other Religions, may establish with the same ease any particular sect of Christians, in exclusion of all other Sects?

* * *

Reversed and remanded.

The "legislative veto" case.

✔ IMMIGRATION AND NATURALIZATION SERVICE v. CHADHA

Supreme Court of the United States, 1983.
___ U.S. ___, 103 S.Ct. 2764, 77 L.Ed.2d 317.

Chief Justice BURGER delivered the opinion of the Court.

Chadha is an East Indian who was born in Kenya and holds a British passport. He was lawfully admitted to the United States in 1966 on a nonimmigrant student visa. His visa expired on June 30, 1972. On October 11, 1973, the District Director of the Immigration and Naturalization Service [INS] ordered Chadha to show cause why he should not be deported for having "remained in the United States for a longer time than permitted." [A] deportation hearing was held before an immigration judge on January 11, 1974. Chadha conceded that he was deportable for overstaying his visa and the hearing was adjourned to enable him to file an application for suspension of deportation * * *. [The law provides]:

> (a) As hereinafter prescribed in this section, the Attorney General may, in his discretion, suspend deportation and adjust the status to that of an alien lawfully admitted for permanent residence, in the case of an alien who applies to the Attorney General for suspension of deportation and—
>
> (1) is deportable under any law of the United States except the provisions specified in paragraph (2) of this subsection; has been physically present in the United States for a continuous period of not less than seven years immediately preceding the date of such application, and proves that during all of such period he was and is a person of good moral character; and is a person whose deportation would, in the opinion of the Attorney General, result in extreme hardship to the alien or to his spouse, parent, or child, who is a citizen of the United States or an alien lawfully admitted for permanent residence.

After Chadha submitted his application for suspension of deportation, the deportation hearing was resumed on February 7, 1974. On the basis of evidence adduced at the hearing, affidavits submitted with the application, and the results of a character investigation conducted by the INS, the immigration judge, on June 25, 1974, ordered that Chadha's deportation be suspended. The immigration judge found that Chadha met the requirements of § 244(a)(1): he had resided continuously in the United States for over seven years, was of good moral character, and would suffer "extreme hardship" if deported.

* * *

Once the Attorney General's recommendation for suspension of Chadha's deportation was conveyed to Congress, Congress had the power under § 244(c)(2) of the Act, 8 U.S.C. § 1254(c)(2), to veto the Attorney General's determination that Chadha should not be deported. Section 244(c)(2) provides:

> (2) In the case of an alien specified in paragraph (1) of subsection (a) of this subsection— if during the session of the Congress at which a case is reported, or prior to the close of the session of the Congress next following the session at which a case is reported, either the Senate or the House of Representatives passes a resolution stating in substance that it does not favor the suspension of such deportation, the Attorney General shall thereupon deport such alien or authorize the alien's voluntary departure at his own expense under the order of deportation in the manner provided by law. If, within the time above specified, neither the Senate nor the House of Representatives shall pass such a resolution, the Attorney General shall cancel deportation proceedings.

* * *

On December 12, 1975, Representative Eilberg, Chairman of the Judiciary Subcommittee on Immigration, Citizenship, and International Law, introduced a resolution opposing "the granting of permanent residence in the United States to [six] aliens", including Chadha. The resolution was referred to the House Committee on the Judiciary. On December 16, 1975, the resolution was discharged from further consideration by the House Committee on the Judiciary and submitted to the House of Representatives for a vote. The resolution had not been printed and was not made available to other Members of the House prior to or at the time it was voted on. So far as the record before us shows, the House consideration of the resolution was based on Representative Eilberg's statement from the floor that

> [i]t was the feeling of the committee, after reviewing 340 cases, that the aliens contained in the resolution [Chadha and five others] did not meet these statutory requirements, particularly as it relates to hardship; and it is the opinion of the committee that their deportation should not be suspended.

The resolution was passed without debate or recorded vote.

Since the House action was pursuant to § 244(c)(2), the resolution was not treated as an Article I legislative act; it was not submitted to the Senate or presented to the President for his action.

After the House veto of the Attorney General's decision to allow Chadha to remain in the United States, the immigration judge reopened the deportation proceedings to implement the House order deporting Chadha. Chadha moved to terminate the proceedings on the ground that § 244(c)(2) is unconstitutional. The immigration judge held that he had no authority to rule on the constitutional validity of § 244(c)(2). On November 8, 1976, Chadha was ordered deported pursuant to the House action.

Chadha appealed the deportation order to the Board of Immigration Appeals again contending that § 244(c)(2) is unconstitutional. The Board held that it had "no power to declare unconstitutional an act of Congress" and Chadha's appeal was dismissed.

Pursuant to § 106(a) of the Act, 8 U.S.C. § 1105a(a), Chadha filed a petition for review of the deportation order in the United

States Court of Appeals for the Ninth Circuit. The Immigration and Naturalization Service agreed with Chadha's position before the Court of Appeals and joined him in arguing that § 244(c)(2) is unconstitutional. In light of the importance of the question, the Court of Appeals invited both the Senate and the House of Representatives to file briefs *amici curiae.*

After full briefing and oral argument, the Court of Appeals held that the House was without constitutional authority to order Chadha's deportation; accordingly it directed the Attorney General "to cease and desist from taking any steps to deport this alien based upon the resolution enacted by the House of Representatives." The essence of its holding was that § 244(c)(2) violates the constitutional doctrine of separation of powers.

We granted certiorari * * * and we now affirm.

Before we address the important question of the constitutionality of the one-House veto provision of § 244(c)(2), we first consider several challenges to the authority of this Court to resolve the issue raised.

Appellate Jurisdiction

Both Houses of Congress contend that we are without jurisdiction under 28 U.S.C. § 1252 to entertain the INS appeal. Section 1252 provides:

> Any party may appeal to the Supreme Court from an interlocutory or final judgment, decree or order of any court of the United States, the United States District Court for the District of the Canal Zone, the District Court of Guam and the District Court of the Virgin Islands and any court of record of Puerto Rico, holding an Act of Congress unconstitutional in any civil action, suit, or proceeding to which the United States or any of its agencies, or any officer or employee thereof, as such officer or employee, is a party.

Parker v. *Levy,* 417 U.S. 733, 742 n. 10, 94 S.Ct. 2547, 2555 n. 10, 41 L.Ed.2d 439 (1974), makes clear that a court of appeals is a "court of the United States" for purposes of § 1252. It is likewise clear that the proceeding below was a "civil action, suit or proceeding," that the INS is an agency of the United States and was a party to the proceeding below, and that that proceeding held an Act of Congress—namely, the one-House veto provision in § 244(c)(2)—unconstitutional. The express requisites for an appeal under § 1252, therefore, have been met.

* * *

Standing

We must also reject the contention that Chadha lacks standing because a consequence of his prevailing will advance the interests of the Executive Branch in a separation of powers dispute with Congress, rather than simply Chadha's private interests. Chadha has demonstrated "injury in fact and a substantial likelihood that the judicial relief requested will prevent or redress the claimed injury . . . ." *Duke Power Co.* v. *Carolina Environmental Study Group,* 438 U.S. 59, 79, 98 S.Ct. 2620, 2633–2634, 57 L.Ed.2d 595 (1978). If the veto provision violates the Constitution, and is severable, the deportation order against Chadha will be cancelled. Chadha therefore has standing to challenge the order of the Executive mandated by the House veto.

* * *

Case or Controversy

It is also contended that this is not a genuine controversy but "a friendly, non-adversary, proceeding," *Ashwander* v. *Tennessee Valley Authority, supra,* 297 U.S., at 346, 56 S.Ct., at 482–483 (Brandeis, J., concurring), upon which the Court should not pass. This argument rests on the fact that Chadha and the INS take the same position on the constitutionality of the one-House veto. But it would be a curious result if, in the administration of justice, a person could be denied access to the courts because the Attorney General of the United States agreed with the legal arguments asserted by the individual.

A case or controversy is presented by this case. First, from the time of Congress' formal intervention, see note 5, *supra,* the concrete adverseness is beyond doubt. Congress is both a proper party to defend the constitutionality of § 244(c)(2) and a proper petitioner under § 1254(1). Second, prior to Congress' intervention, there was adequate Art. III adverseness even though the only parties were the INS and Chadha. We have already held that the INS's agreement with the Court of Appeals' decision that § 244(c)(2) is unconstitutional does not affect that agency's "aggrieved" status for purposes of appealing that decision under 28 U.S.C. § 1252, see *ante,* at 8–10. For similar reasons, the INS's agreement with Chadha's position does not alter the fact that the INS would have deported Chadha absent the Court of Appeals' judgment. We agree with the Court of Appeals that "Chadha has asserted a concrete controversy, and our decision will have real meaning: if we rule for Chadha, he will not be deported; if we uphold § 244(c)(2), the INS will execute its order and deport him."

* * *

The contentions on standing and justiciability have been fully examined and we are satisfied the parties are properly before us. The important issues have been fully briefed and twice argued. The Court's duty in this case, as Chief Justice Marshall declared in *Cohens* v. *Virginia,* 6 Wheat. 264, 404 (1821), is clear:

> Questions may occur which we would gladly avoid; but we cannot avoid them. All we can do is, to exercise our best judgment, and conscientiously to perform our duty.

We turn now to question whether action of one House of Congress under § 244(c)(2) violates strictures of the Constitution. We begin, of course, with the presumption that the challenged statute is valid. Its wisdom is not the concern of the courts; if a challenged action does not violate the Constitution, it must be sustained:

> "Once the meaning of an enactment is discerned and its constitutionality determined, the judicial process comes to an end. We do not sit as a committee of review, nor are we vested with the power of veto." *Tennessee Valley Authority* v. *Hill,* 437 U.S. 153, 194–195, 98 S.Ct. 2279, 2301–2302, 57 L.Ed.2d 117 (1978).

By the same token, the fact that a given law or procedure is efficient, convenient, and useful in facilitating functions of government, standing alone, will not save it if it is contrary to the Constitution. Convenience and efficiency are not the primary objectives—or the hallmarks—of democratic government and our inquiry is sharpened rather than blunted by the fact that Congressional veto provisions are appearing with increasing frequency in statutes which delegate authority to executive and independent agencies:

> Since 1932, when the first veto provision was enacted into law, 295 congressional veto-type procedures have been inserted in 196 different statutes as follows: from 1932 to 1939, five statutes were affected; from 1940–49, nineteen statutes; between 1950–59, thirty-four statutes; and from 1960–69, forty-nine. From the year 1970 through 1975, at least one hundred sixty-three such provisions were included in eighty-nine laws.

* * *

Explicit and unambiguous provisions of the Constitution prescribe and define the respective functions of the Congress and of the Executive in the legislative process. Since the precise terms of those familiar provisions are critical to the resolution of this case, we set them out verbatim. Art. I provides:

> "All legislative Powers herein granted shall be vested in a Congress of the United States, which shall consist of a Senate *and* a House of Representatives." Art. I, § 1. (Emphasis added).
>
> "Every Bill which shall have passed the House of Representatives *and* the Senate, *shall,* before it become a Law, be presented to

the President of the United States; . . ." Art. I, § 7, cl. 2. (Emphasis added).

"*Every* Order, Resolution, or Vote to which the Concurrence of the Senate and House of Representatives may be necessary (except on a question of Adjournment) *shall be* presented to the President of the United States; and before the Same shall take Effect, *shall be* approved by him, or being disapproved by him, *shall be* repassed by two thirds of the Senate and House of Representatives, according to the Rules and Limitations prescribed in the Case of a Bill." Art. I, § 7, cl. 3 (Emphasis added).

These provisions of Art. I are integral parts of the constitutional design for the separation of powers. We have recently noted that "[t]he principle of separation of powers was not simply an abstract generalization in the minds of the Framers: it was woven into the documents that they drafted in Philadelphia in the summer of 1787."

* * *

The President's role in the lawmaking process also reflects the Framers' careful efforts to check whatever propensity a particular Congress might have to enact oppressive, improvident, or ill-considered measures.

* * *

The Court also has observed that the Presentment Clauses serve the important purpose of assuring that a "national" perspective is grafted on the legislative process:

The President is a representative of the people just as the members of the Senate and of the House are, and it may be, at some times, on some subjects, that the President elected by all the people is rather more representative of them all than are the members of either body of the Legislature whose constituencies are local and not countrywide. . . . *Myers* v. *United States,* 272 U.S., at 123, 47 S.Ct., at 27.

The bicameral requirement of Art. I, §§ 1, 7 was of scarcely less concern to the Framers than was the Presidential veto and indeed the two concepts are interdependent. By providing that no law could take effect without the concurrence of the prescribed majority of the Members of both Houses, the Framers reemphasized their belief, already remarked upon in connection with the Presentment Clauses, that legislation should not be enacted unless it has been carefully and fully considered by the Nation's elected officials. In the Constitutional Convention debates on the need for a bicameral legislature, James Wilson, later to become a Justice of this Court, commented:

Despotism comes on mankind in different shapes. Sometimes in an Executive, sometimes in a military, one. Is there danger of a Legislative despotism? Theory & practice both proclaim it. If the Legislative authority be not restrained, there can be neither liberty nor stability; and it can only be restrained by dividing it within itself, into distinct and independent branches. In a single house there is no check, but the inadequate one, of the virtue & good sense of those who compose it.

* * *

These observations are consistent with what many of the Framers expressed, none more cogently than Hamilton in pointing up the need to divide and disperse power in order to protect liberty:

"In republican government, the legislative authority necessarily predominates. The remedy for this inconveniency is to divide the legislature into different branches; and to render them, by different modes of election and different principles of action, as little connected with each other as the nature of their common functions and their common dependence on the society will admit." The Federalist No. 51, at 324.

* * *

We see therefore that the Framers were acutely conscious that the bicameral requirement and the Presentment Clauses would serve essential constitutional functions. The President's participation in the legislative process was to protect the Executive Branch from Congress and to protect the whole people from improvident laws. The division of the Congress into two distinctive bodies assures that the legislative power would be exercised only after opportunity for full study and debate in separate settings. The President's unilateral veto power, in turn, was limited by the power of two thirds of both Houses of Congress to overrule a veto thereby precluding final arbitrary action of one person. It emerges clearly that the prescription for legislative action in Art. I, §§ 1, 7 represents the Framers' decision that the legislative power of the Federal government be exercised in accord with a single, finely wrought and exhaustively considered, procedure.

* * *

Congress made a deliberate choice to delegate to the Executive Branch, and specifically to the Attorney General, the authority to allow deportable aliens to remain in this country in certain specified circumstances. It is not disputed that this choice to delegate authority is precisely the kind of decision that can be implemented only in accordance with the procedures set out in Art. I. Disagreement with the Attorney General's decision on Chadha's deportation—that is, Congress' decision to deport Chadha—no less than Congress' original choice to delegate to the Attorney General the authority to make that decision, involves determinations of policy that Congress can implement in only one way; bicameral passage followed by presentment to the President. Congress must abide by its delegation of authority until that delegation is legislatively altered or revoked.

Finally, we see that when the Framers intended to authorize either House of Congress to act alone and outside of its prescribed bicameral legislative role, they narrowly and precisely defined the procedure for such action. There are but four provisions in the Constitution, explicit and unambiguous, by which one House may act alone with the unreviewable force of law, not subject to the President's veto:

(a) The House of Representatives alone was given the power to initiate impeachments. Art. I, § 2, cl. 6;

(b) The Senate alone was given the power to conduct trials following impeachment on charges initiated by the House and to convict following trial. Art. I, § 3, cl. 5;

(c) The Senate alone was given final unreviewable power to approve or to disapprove presidential appointments. Art. II, § 2, cl. 2;

(d) The Senate alone was given unreviewable power to ratify treaties negotiated by the President. Art. II, § 2, cl. 2.

Clearly, when the Draftsmen sought to confer special powers on one House, independent of the other House, or of the President, they did so in explicit, unambiguous terms. These carefully defined exceptions from presentment and bicameralism underscore the difference between the legislative functions of Congress and other unilateral but important and binding one-House acts provided for in the Constitution. These exceptions are narrow, explicit, and separately justified; none of them authorize the action challenged here. On the contrary, they provide further support for the conclusion that Congressional authority is not to be implied and for the conclusion that the veto provided for in § 244(c)(2) is not authorized by the constitutional design of the powers of the Legislative Branch.

Since it is clear that the action by the House under § 244(c)(2) was not within any of the express constitutional exceptions authorizing one House to act alone, and equally clear that it was an exercise of legislative power, that action was subject to the standards prescribed in Article I. The bicameral requirement, the Presentment Clauses, the President's veto, and Congress' power to override a veto were intended to erect enduring checks on each Branch and to protect the people from the improvident exercise of power by mandating certain prescribed steps. To preserve those checks, and maintain the separation of powers, the carefully defined limits on the power of each Branch must not be eroded. To accomplish what has been attempted by one House of Congress in this case requires action in conformity with the express procedures of the Constitution's prescription for legislative action:

passage by a majority of both Houses and presentment to the President.

The veto authorized by § 244(c)(2) doubtless has been in many respects a convenient shortcut; the "sharing" with the Executive by Congress of its authority over aliens in this manner is, on its face, an appealing compromise. In purely practical terms, it is obviously easier for action to be taken by one House without submission to the President; but it is crystal clear from the records of the Convention, contemporaneous writings and debates, that the Framers ranked other values higher than efficiency. The records of the Convention and debates in the States preceding ratification underscore the common desire to define and limit the exercise of the newly created federal powers affecting the states and the people. There is unmistakable expression of a determination that legislation by the national Congress be a step-by-step, deliberate and deliberative process.

The choices we discern as having been made in the Constitutional Convention impose burdens on governmental processes that often seem clumsy, inefficient, even unworkable, but those hard choices were consciously made by men who had lived under a form of government that permitted arbitrary governmental acts to go unchecked. There is no support in the Constitution or decisions of this Court for the proposition that the cumbersomeness and delays often encountered in complying with explicit Constitutional standards may be avoided, either by the Congress or by the President. With all the obvious flaws of delay, untidiness, and potential for abuse, we have not yet found a better way to preserve freedom than by making the exercise of power subject to the carefully crafted restraints spelled out in the Constitution.

V

We hold that the Congressional veto provision in § 244(c)(2) is severable from the Act and that it is unconstitutional. Accordingly, the judgment of the Court of Appeals is

Affirmed.

"For an immoral purpose."

CAMINETTI v. UNITED STATES

Supreme Court of the United States, 1917.
242 U.S. 470, 37 S.Ct. 192, 61 L.Ed. 442.

* * *

Mr. Justice DAY delivered the opinion of the court. * * *

[T]here was a conviction and sentence for violation of the so-called White Slave Traffic Act. * * *

In the Caminetti case, the * * * indictment * * * charged him with transporting and causing to be transported and aiding and assisting in obtaining transportation for a certain woman from Sacramento, California, to Reno, Nevada, in interstate commerce for the purpose of debauchery, and for an immoral purpose, to wit, that the aforesaid woman should be and become his mistress and concubine. * * * [D]efendant was found guilty and sentenced to imprisonment for eighteen months and to pay a fine of $1,500.00. Upon writ of error to the United States Circuit Court of Appeals for the Ninth Circuit, that judgment was affirmed. * * *

* * *

It is contended that the act of Congress is intended to reach only "commercialized vice," or the traffic in women for gain, and that the conduct * * * however reprehensible in morals, is not within the purview of the statute when properly construed in the light of its history and the purposes intended to be accomplished by its enactment. In * * * [Caminetti it was not] proved that the transportation was for gain or for the purpose of furnishing women for prostitution for hire, and it is insisted that, such being the case, the acts charged and proved, upon which conviction was had, do not come within the statute. * * *

It is specifically made an offense to knowingly transport or cause to be transported, etc., in interstate commerce, any woman or girl for the purpose of prostitution or debauchery, or for "any other immoral purpose," or with the intent and purpose to induce any such woman or girl to become a prostitute or to give herself up to debauchery, or to engage in any other immoral practice.

Statutory words are uniformly presumed, unless the contrary appears, to be used in their ordinary and usual sense, and with the meaning commonly attributed to them. To cause a woman or girl to be transported for the purposes of debauchery, and for an immoral purpose, to-wit, becoming a concubine or mistress, for which Caminetti [was] * * * convicted; * * * would seem by the very statement of the facts to embrace transportation for purposes denounced by the act, and therefore fairly within its meaning.

While such immoral purpose would be more culpable in morals and attributed to baser motives if accompanied with the expectation of pecuniary gain, such considerations do not prevent the lesser offense against morals of furnishing transportation in order that a woman may be debauched, or become a mistress or a concubine from being the execution of purposes within the meaning of this law. To say the contrary would shock the common understanding of what constitutes an immoral purpose when those terms are applied, as here, to sexual relations.

In United States v. Bitty * * * it was held that the act of Congress against the importation of alien women and girls for the purpose of prostitution "and any other immoral purpose" included the importation of an alien woman to live in concubinage with the person importing her. In that case this court said:

"All will admit that full effect must be given to the intention of Congress as gathered from the words of the statute. There can be no doubt as to what class was aimed at by the clause forbidding the importation of alien women for purposes of 'prostitution.' It refers to women who for hire or without hire offer their bodies to indiscriminate intercourse with men. The lives and example of such persons are in hostility to 'the idea of the family, as consisting in and springing from the union for life of one man and one woman in the holy estate of matrimony; the sure foundation of all that is stable and noble in our civilization; the best guaranty of that reverent morality which is the source of all beneficent progress in social and political improvement.' * * * Now the addition in the last statute of the words, 'or for any other immoral purpose,' after the word 'prostitution,' must have been made for some practical object. Those added words show beyond question that Congress had in view the protection of society against another class of alien women other than those who might be brought here merely for purposes of 'prostitution.' In forbidding, the importation of alien women 'for any other immoral purpose,' Congress evidently thought that there were purposes in connection with the importations of alien women which, as in the case of importations for prostitution, were to be deemed immoral. It may be admitted that in accordance with the familiar rule of *ejusdem generis,* the immoral purpose referred to by the words 'any other immoral purpose,' must be one of the same general class or kind as the particular purpose of 'prostitution' specified in the same clause of the statute. * * * But that rule cannot avail the accused in this case; for, the immoral purpose charged in the indictment is of the same general class or kind as the one that controls in the importation of an alien woman for the purpose strictly of prostitution. The prostitute may, in the popular sense, be more degraded in character than the concubine, but the latter none the less must be held to lead an immoral life, if any regard whatever be had to the views that are almost universally held in this country as to the relations which may rightfully, from the standpoint of morality, exist between man and woman in the matter of sexual intercourse."

* * *

It is further insisted that a different construction of the act than is to be gathered from reading it is necessary in order to save it from constitutional objections, fatal to its validity. The act has its constitutional sanction in the power of Congress over interstate commerce. The broad character of that authority was declared once for all in the judgment pronounced by this court, speaking by Chief Justice Marshall, in Gibbons v. Ogden, * * * and has since been steadily adhered to and applied to a variety of new conditions as they have arisen.

* * *

The transportation of passengers in interstate commerce, it has long been settled, is within the regulatory power of Congress, under the commerce clause of the Constitution, and the authority of Congress to keep the channels of interstate commerce free from immoral and injurious uses has been frequently sustained, and is no longer open to question.

* * *

The judgment * * * is

Affirmed.

Mr. Justice McKENNA, dissenting:

The transportation which is made unlawful is of a woman or girl "to become a prostitute or to give herself up to debauchery, or to engage in any other immoral practice." Our present concern is with the words "any other immoral practice," which, it is asserted, have a special office. The words are clear enough as general descriptions; they fail in particular designation; they are class words, not specifications. Are they controlled by those which precede them? If not, they are broader in generalization and include those that precede them, making them unnecessary and confusing. To what conclusion would this lead us? "Immoral" is a very comprehensive word. It means a dereliction of morals. In such sense it covers every form of vice, every form of conduct that is contrary to good order. It will hardly be contended that in this sweeping sense it is used in the statute. But, if not used in such sense, to what is it limited and by what limited? If it be admitted that it is limited at all, that ends the imperative effect assigned to it in the opinion of the court. But not insisting quite on that, we ask again, By what is it limited? By its context, necessarily, and the purpose of the statute.

For the context I must refer to the statute; of the purpose of the statute Congress itself has given us illumination. It devotes a section to the declaration that the "act shall be known and referred to as the 'White Slave Traffic Act.'" And its prominence gives it prevalence in the construction of the statute. It cannot be pushed aside or subordinated by indefinite words in other sentences, limited even there by the context. It is a peremptory rule of construction that all parts of a statute must be taken into account in ascertaining its meaning. * * * It is commercialized vice, immoralities having a mercenary purpose, and this is confirmed by other circumstances.

The author of the bill was Mr. Mann, and in reporting it from the House committee on interstate and foreign commerce he declared for the committee that it was not the purpose of the bill to interfere with or usurp in any way the police power of the states, and further, that it was not the intention of the bill to regulate prostitution or the places where prostitution or immorality was practised, which were said to be matters wholly within the power of the states, and over which the Federal government had no jurisdiction. And further explaining the bill, it was said that the sections of the act had been "so drawn that they are limited to the cases in which there is an act of transportation in interstate commerce of women for the purposes of prostitution." And again:

"The White Slave Trade.—A material portion of the legislation suggested and proposed is necessary to meet conditions which have arisen within the past few years. The legislation is needed to put a stop to a villainous interstate and international traffic in women and girls. The legislation is not needed or intended as an aid to the states in the exercise of their police powers in the suppression or regulation of immorality in general. It does not attempt to regulate the practice of voluntary prostitution, but aims solely to prevent panderers and procurers from compelling thousands of women and girls against their will and desire to enter and continue in a life of prostitution." Cong.Rec. vol. 50, pp. 3368, 3370.

In other words, it is vice as a business at which the law is directed, using interstate commerce as a facility to procure or distribute its victims.

In 1912 the sense of the Department of Justice was taken of the act in a case where a woman of twenty-four years went from Illinois, where she lived, to Minnesota, at the solicitation and expense of a man. She was there met by him and engaged with him in immoral practices like those for which petitioners were convicted. The assistant district attorney forwarded her statement to the Attorney General, with the comment that the element of traffic was absent from the transaction and that therefore, in his opinion, it was not "within the spirit and intent of the Mann Act."

* * * "[I]t is a familiar rule that a thing may be within the letter of the statute and yet not within the statute, because not within its spirit, nor within the intention of its makers." * * * Its principle is the simple one that the words of a statute will be extended or restricted to execute its purpose.

* * *

For these reasons I dissent from the opinion and judgment of the court. * * *

I am authorized to say that the Chief Justice and Mr. Justice CLARKE concur in this dissent.

Common law and the manufacturer.

MacPHERSON v. BUICK MOTOR CO.

Court of Appeals of New York, 1916.
217 N.Y. 382, 111 N.E. 1050.

[Appeal from a judgment entered in favor of the plaintiff.]

CARDOZO, J.

The defendant is a manufacturer of automobiles. It sold an automobile to a retail dealer. The retail dealer resold to the plaintiff. While the plaintiff was in the car it suddenly collapsed. He was thrown out and injured. One of the wheels was made of defective wood, and its spokes crumbled into fragments. The wheel was not made by the defendant; it was bought from another manufacturer. There is evidence, however, that its defects could have been discovered by reasonable inspection, and that inspection was omitted. * * * The charge is one, not of fraud, but of negligence. The question to be determined is whether the defendant owed a duty of care and vigilance to any one but the immediate purchaser.

The foundations of this branch of the law, at least in this state, were laid in Thomas v. Winchester, (6 N.Y. 397). * * * A poison was falsely labeled. The sale was made to a druggist, who in turn sold to a customer. The customer recovered damages from the seller who affixed the label. "The defendant's negligence," it was said, "put human life in imminent danger." A poison, falsely labeled, is likely to injure any one who gets it. Because the danger is to be foreseen, there is a duty to avoid the injury. * * * Thomas v. Winchester became quickly a landmark of the law. * * * [The Court next cites cases which expanded the principle of the *Thomas* case, holding defendants liable for an improperly constructed scaffold and for a coffee urn that exploded when the plaintiff heated it.]

* * * But whatever the rule in Thomas v. Winchester may once have been,

it has no longer that restricted meaning. A scaffold is not inherently a destructive instrument. It becomes destructive only if imperfectly constructed. A large coffee urn may have within itself, if negligently made, the potency of danger, yet no one thinks of it as an implement whose normal function is destruction. * * *

We hold, then, that the principle of Thomas v. Winchester is not limited to poisons, explosives, and things of like nature, to things which in their normal operation are implements of destruction. If the nature of a thing is such that it is reasonably certain to place life and limb in peril when negligently made, it is then a thing of danger. Its nature gives warning of the consequences to be expected. If to the element of danger there is added knowledge that the thing will be used by persons other than the purchaser, and used without new tests, then, irrespective of contract, the manufacturer of this thing of danger is under a duty to make it carefully.

* * * We have put aside the notion that the duty to safeguard life and limb, when the consequences of negligence may be foreseen, grows out of contract and nothing else. We have put the source of the obligation where it ought to be. We have put its source in the law.

From this survey of the decisions, there thus emerges a definition of the duty of a manufacturer which enables us to measure this defendant's liability. Beyond all question, the nature of an automobile gives warning of probable danger if its construction is defective. This automobile was designed to go 50 miles an hour. Unless its wheels were sound and strong, injury was almost certain. It was as much a thing of danger as a defective engine for a railroad. The defendant knew the danger. It knew also that the car would be used by persons other than the buyer. This was apparent * * * from the fact that the buyer was a dealer in cars, who bought to resell. The maker of this car supplied it for the use of purchasers from the dealer just as plainly as the contractor in Devlin v. Smith supplied the scaffold for use by the servants of the owner. The dealer was indeed the one person of whom it might be said with some approach to certainty that by him the car would not be used. Yet the defendant would have us say that he was the one person whom it was under a legal duty to protect. The law does not lead us to so inconsequent a conclusion. Precedents drawn from the days of travel by stagecoach do not fit the conditions of travel to-day. The principle that the danger must be imminent does not change, but the things subject to the principle do change. They are whatever the needs of life in a developing civilization require them to be.

* * *

The judgment should be affirmed, with costs.

"Let the manufacturer beware!"

GREENMAN v. YUBA POWER PRODUCTS, INC.

Supreme Court of California, 1963.
59 Cal.2d 57, 27 Cal.Rptr. 697, 377 P.2d 897.

TRAYNOR, Justice

Plaintiff brought this action for damages against the retailer and the manufacturer of a Shopsmith, a combination power tool that could be used as a saw, drill, and wood lathe. He saw a Shopsmith demonstrated by the retailer and studied a brochure prepared by the manufacturer. He decided he wanted a Shopsmith for his home workshop, and his wife bought and gave him one for Christmas in 1955. In 1957 he bought the necessary attachments to use the Shopsmith as a lathe for turning a large piece of wood he wished to make into a chalice. After he had worked on the piece of wood several times without difficulty, it suddenly flew out of the machine and struck him on the forehead, inflicting serious injuries. About ten and a half months later, he gave the retailer and the manufacturer written notice of claimed breaches of warranties and filed a complaint against them alleging such breaches and negligence.

* * * The jury returned a verdict for the retailer against plaintiff and for plaintiff against the manufacturer in the amount of $65,000. * * * The manufacturer and plaintiff appeal. Plaintiff seeks a reversal of the part of the judgment in favor of the retailer, however, only in the event that the part of the judgment against the manufacturer is reversed.

Plaintiff introduced substantial evidence that his injuries were caused by defective design and construction of the Shopsmith. His expert witnesses testified that inadequate set screws were used to hold parts of the machine together so that normal vibration caused the tailstock of the lathe to move away from the piece of wood being turned permitting it to fly out of the lathe. They also testified that there were other more positive ways of fastening the parts of the machine together, the use of which would have prevented the accident. The jury could therefore reasonably have concluded that the manufacturer negligently constructed the Shopsmith. The jury could also reasonably have concluded that statements in the manufacturer's brochure were untrue, that they constituted express warranties,[1] and that plaintiff's injuries were caused by their breach.

The manufacturer contends, however, that plaintiff did not give it notice of breach of warranty within a reasonable time and that therefore his cause of action for breach of warranty is barred by section 1769 of the Civil Code. * * *

The notice requirement * * * is not an appropriate one for the court to adopt in actions by injured consumers against manufacturers with whom they have not dealt. * * * "As between the immediate parties to the sale [the notice requirement] is a sound commercial rule, designed to protect the seller against unduly delayed claims for damages. As applied to personal injuries, and notice to a remote seller, it becomes a booby-trap for the unwary. The injured consumer is seldom 'steeped in the business practice which justifies the rule,' * * * and at least until he has had legal advice it will not occur to him to give notice to one with whom he has had no dealings." * * * We conclude, therefore, that even if plaintiff did not give timely notice of breach of warranty to the manufacturer, his cause of action based on the representations contained in the brochure was not barred.

Moreover, to impose strict liability on the manufacturer under the circumstances of this case, it was not necessary for plaintiff to establish an express warranty. * * * A manufacturer is strictly liable in tort when an article he places on the market, knowing that it is to be used without inspection for defects, proves to have a defect that causes injury to a human being. Recognized first in the case of unwholesome food products, such liability has now been extended to a variety of other products that create as great or greater hazards if defective. * * *

[Including a grinding wheel, a bottle, vaccine, insect spray, a surgical pin, an automobile, a skirt, a tire, a home permanent, hair dye, and an airplane.]

Although in these cases strict liability has usually been based on the theory of an express or implied warranty running from the manufacturer to the plaintiff, the abandonment of the requirement of a contract between them, the recognition that the liability is not assumed by agreement but imposed by law * * * and the refusal to permit

1. In this respect the trial court limited the jury to a consideration of two statements in the manufacturer's brochure. (1) "WHEN SHOPSMITH IS IN HORIZONTAL POSITION—Rugged construction of frame provides rigid support from end to end. Heavy centerless-ground steel tubing insures perfect alignment of components." (2) "SHOPSMITH maintains its accuracy because every component has positive locks that hold adjustments through rough or precision work."

the manufacturer to define the scope of its own responsibility for defective products * * * make clear that the liability is not one governed by the law of contract warranties but by the law of strict liability in tort. Accordingly, rules defining and governing warranties that were developed to meet the needs of commercial transactions cannot properly be invoked to govern the manufacturer's liability to those injured by their defective products unless those rules also serve the purposes for which such liability is imposed.

* * * The purpose of such liability is to insure that the costs of injuries resulting from defective products are borne by the manufacturers that put such products on the market rather than by the injured persons who are powerless to protect themselves. Sales warranties serve this purpose fitfully at best. * * * In the present case, for example, plaintiff was able to plead and prove an express warranty only because he read and relied on the representations of the Shopsmith's ruggedness contained in the manufacturer's brochure. Implicit in the machine's presence on the market, however, was a representation that it would safely do the jobs for which it was built. Under these circumstances, it should not be controlling whether plaintiff selected the machine because of the statements in the brochure, or because of the machine's own appearance of excellence that belied the defect lurking beneath the surface, or because he merely assumed that it would safely do the jobs it was built to do. It should not be controlling whether the details of the sales from manufacturer to retailer and from retailer to plaintiff's wife were such that one or more of the implied warranties of the sales act arose. * * * "The remedies of injured consumers ought not to be made to depend upon the intricacies of the law of sales." * * * To establish the manufacturer's liability it was sufficient that plaintiff proved that he was injured while using the Shopsmith in a way it was intended to be used as a result of a defect in design and manufacture of which plaintiff was not aware that made the Shopsmith unsafe for its intended use.

* * *

The judgment is affirmed.

For more than one year U.S. citizens are held as hostages by Iran.

UNITED STATES OF AMERICA v. IRAN

International Court of Justice
24 May 1980

CASE CONCERNING UNITED STATES DIPLOMATIC AND CONSULAR STAFF IN TEHRAN

Present: President Sir Humphrey WALDOCK; *Vice-President* ELIAS; *Judges* FORSTER, GROS, LACHS, MOROZOV, NAGENDRA SINGH, RUDA, MOSLER, TARAZI, ODA, AGO, EL-ERIAN, SETTE-CAMARA, BAXTER; *Registrar* AQUARONE.

[Fifteen judges from various parts of the world sit on the International Court of Justice.]

1. On 29 November 1979, the Legal Adviser of the Department of State of the United States of America handed to the Registrar an Application instituting proceedings against the Islamic Republic of Iran in respect of a dispute concerning the seizure and holding as hostages of members of the United States diplomatic and consular staff and certain other United States nationals.

* * *

"The United States requests the Court to adjudge and declare as follows:

(a) That the Government of Iran, * * * violated its international legal obligations to the United States as provided by

- Articles 22, 24, 25, 27, 29, 31, 37 and 47 of the Vienna Convention on Diplomatic Relations,
- Articles 28, 31, 33, 34, 36 and 40 of the Vienna Convention on Consular Relations,

■ Articles 4 and 7 of the Convention on the Prevention and Punishment of Crimes against Internationally Protected Persons, including Diplomatic Agents, and
■ Articles II(4), XIII, XVIII and XIX of the Treaty of Amity, Economic Relations, and Consular Rights between the United States and Iran, and
■ Articles 2(3), 2(4) and 33 of the Charter of the United Nations." * * *

* * *

12. The essential facts of the present case are, for the most part, matters of public knowledge which have received extensive coverage in the world press and in radio and television broadcasts from Iran and other countries.

* * *

15. In October 1979, the Government of the United States was contemplating permitting the former Shah of Iran, who was then in Mexico, to enter the United States for medical treatment. Officials of the United States Government feared that, in the political climate prevailing in Iran, the admission of the former Shah might increase the tension already existing between the two States, and *inter alia* result in * * * violence against the United States Embassy in Tehran, and it was decided for this reason to request assurances from the Government of Iran that adequate protection would be provided. * * *

When the United States Chargé d'affaires requested assurances that the Embassy and its personnel would be adequately protected, assurances were given by the Foreign Minister that the Government of Iran would fulfil its international obligation to protect the Embassy.

* * *

17. At approximately 10.30 a.m. on 4 November 1979, during the course of a demonstration of approximately 3,000 persons, the United States Embassy compound in Tehran was overrun by a strong armed group of several hundred people. The Iranian security personnel are reported to have simply disappeared from the scene; at all events it is established that they made no apparent effort to deter or prevent the demonstrators from seizing the Embassy's premises. The invading group (who subsequently described themselves as "Muslim Student Followers of the Imam's Policy", and who will hereafter be referred to as "the militants") gained access by force to the compound and to the ground floor of the Chancery building. Over two hours after the beginning of the attack, and after the militants had attempted to set fire to the Chancery building and to cut through the upstairs steel doors with a torch, they gained entry to the upper floor; one hour later they gained control of the main vault. The militants also seized the other buildings, including the various residences, on the Embassy compound. In the course of the attack, all the diplomatic and consular personnel and other persons present in the premises were seized as hostages, and detained in the Embassy compound; subsequently other United States personnel and one United States private citizen seized elsewhere in Tehran were brought to the compound and added to the number of hostages.

No attempt was made by the Iranian Government to clear the Embassy premises, to rescue the persons held hostage, or to persuade the militants to terminate their action against the Embassy. * * *

On 6 November 1979 a brief occupation of the Consulate of Iraq at Kermanshah occurred but was brought to an end on instructions of the Ayatollah Khomeini; no damage was done to the Consulate or its contents. On 1 January 1980 an attack was made on the Embassy in Tehran of the USSR by a large mob, but as a result of the protection given by the Iranian authorities to the Embassy, no serious damage was done.

23. Allegations have been made by the Government of the United States of inhumane treatment of hostages; * * * at the outset of the occupation of the Embassy some were paraded bound and blindfolded before hostile and chanting crowds; at least during the initial period of their captivity,

hostages were kept bound, and frequently blindfolded, denied mail or any communication with their government or with each other, subjected to interrogation, threatened with weapons. * * *

The Security Council then adopted resolution 457 (1979), calling on Iran to release the personnel of the Embassy immediately, to provide them with protection and to allow them to leave the country.

28. On 9 November 1979, the Permanent Representative of the United States to the United Nations addressed a letter to the President of the Security Council, requesting urgent consideration of what might be done to secure the release of the hostages and to restore the "sanctity of diplomatic personnel and establishments." The same day, the President of the Security Council made a public statement urging the release of the hostages, and the President of the General Assembly announced that he was sending a personal message to the Ayatollah Khomeini appealing for their release. * * *

30. Prior to the institution of the present proceedings, in addition to the approach made by the Government of the United States to the United Nations Security Council, that Government also took certain unilateral action in response to the actions for which it holds the Government of Iran responsible. On 10 November 1979, steps were taken to identify all Iranian students in the United States who were not in compliance with the terms of their entry visas, and to commence deportation proceedings against those who were in violation of applicable immigration laws and regulations. On 12 November 1979, the President of the United States ordered the discontinuation of all oil purchases from Iran for delivery to the United States. Believing that the Government of Iran was about to withdraw all Iranian funds from United States banks and to refuse to accept payment in dollars for oil, and to repudiate obligations owed to the United States and to United States nationals, the President on 14 November 1979 acted to block the very large official Iranian assets in the United States or in United States control, including deposits both in banks in the United States and in foreign branches and subsidiaries of United States banks. On 12 December 1979, after the institution of the present proceedings, the United States informed the Iranian Chargé d'affaires in Washington that the number of personnel assigned to the Iranian Embassy and consular posts in the United States was to be restricted.

* * *

32. During the night of 24–25 April 1980 the President of the United States set in motion, and subsequently terminated for technical reasons, an operation within Iranian territory designed to effect the rescue of the hostages by United States military units. In an announcement made on 25 April, President Carter explained that the operation had been planned over a long period as a humanitarian mission to rescue the hostages, and had finally been set in motion by him in the belief that the situation in Iran posed mounting dangers to the safety of the hostages and that their early release was highly unlikely. He stated that the operation had been under way in Iran when equipment failure compelled its termination; and that in the course of the withdrawal of the rescue forces two United States aircraft had collided in a remote desert location in Iran. He further stated that preparations for the rescue operations had been ordered for humanitarian reasons, to protect the national interests of the United States, and to alleviate international tensions. At the same time, he emphasized that the operation had not been motivated by hostility towards Iran or the Iranian people. * * *

The United States' claims here in question concern alleged violations by Iran of its obligations under several articles of the Vienna Conventions of 1961 and 1963 with respect to the privileges and immunities of the personnel, the inviolability of the premises and archives, and the provision of facilities for the performance of the functions of the

United States Embassy and Consulates in Iran.

* * *

54. No suggestion has been made by Iran that the 1955 Treaty was not in force on 4 November 1979 when the United States Embassy was overrun and its nationals taken hostage, or on 29 November when the United States submitted the dispute to the Court. The very purpose of a treaty of amity, and indeed of a treaty of establishment, is to promote friendly relations between the two countries concerned, and between their two peoples, more especially by mutual undertakings to ensure the protection and security of their nationals in each other's territory. It is precisely when difficulties arise that the treaty assumes its greatest importance, and the whole object of Article XXI, paragraph 2, of the 1955 Treaty was to establish the means for arriving at a friendly settlement of such difficulties by the Court or by other peaceful means. * * *

59. Previously, * * *, the religious leader of the country, the Ayatollah Khomeini, had made several public declarations inveighing against the United States as responsible for all his country's problems. In so doing, it would appear, the Ayatollah Khomeini was giving utterance to the general resentment felt by supporters of the revolution at the admission of the former Shah to the United States. The information before the Court also indicates that a spokesman for the militants, in explaining their action afterwards, did expressly refer to a message issued by the Ayatollah Khomeini, on 1 November 1979. In that message the Ayatollah Khomeini had declared that it was "up to the dear pupils, students and theological students to expand with all their might their attacks against the United States and Israel. * * *

By a number of provisions of the Vienna Conventions of 1961 and 1963, Iran was placed under the most categorical obligations, as a receiving State, to take appropriate steps to ensure the protection of the United States Embassy and Consulates, their staffs, their archives, their means of communication and the freedom of movement of the members of their staffs.

62. Thus, after solemnly proclaiming the inviolability of the premises of a diplomatic mission, Article 22 of the 1961 Convention continues in paragraph 2:

> *The receiving State is under a special duty to take all appropriate steps to protect the premises of the mission against any* intrusion or damage and to prevent any disturbance of the peace of the mission or impairment of its dignity. (Emphasis added.)

So, too, after proclaiming that the person of a diplomatic agent shall be inviolable, and that he shall not be liable to any form of arrest or detention, Article 29 provides:

> The receiving State shall treat him with due respect and *shall take all appropriate steps to prevent any attack on his person, freedom or dignity.* (Emphasis added.)

63. The facts * * * establish to the satisfaction of the Court that on 4 November 1979 the Iranian Government failed altogether to take any "appropriate steps" to protect the premises, staff and archives of the United States' mission against attack by the militants, and to take any steps either to prevent this attack or to stop it before it reached its completion.

* * *

In addition they show, in the opinion of the Court, that the failure of the Iranian Government to take such steps was due to more than mere negligence or lack of appropriate means.

* * *

66. As to the actual conduct of the Iranian authorities when faced with the events of 4 November 1979, the information before the Court establishes that, despite assurances previously given by them to the United States Government and despite repeated and urgent calls for help, they took no apparent steps either to prevent the militants from in-

vading the Embassy or to persuade or to compel them to withdraw. Furthermore, after the militants had forced an entry into the premises of the Embassy, the Iranian authorities made no effort to compel or even to persuade them to withdraw from the Embassy and to free the diplomatic and consular staff whom they had made prisoner. * * *

68. The Court is therefore led inevitably to conclude, in regard to the first phase of the events which has so far been considered, that on 4 November 1979 the Iranian authorities:

(a) were fully aware of their obligations under the conventions in force to take appropriate steps to protect the premises of the United States Embassy and its diplomatic and consular staff from any attack and from any infringement of their inviolability, and to ensure the security of such other persons as might be present on the said premises;
(b) were fully aware, as a result of the appeals for help made by the United States Embassy, of the urgent need for action on their part;
(c) had the means at their disposal to perform their obligations;
(d) completely failed to comply with these obligations.

* * * The Ayatollah * * * expressly forbade members of the Revolutionary Council and all responsible officials to meet the special representatives sent by President Carter to try and obtain the release of the hostages and evacuation of the Embassy.

* * *

74. The policy thus announced by the Ayatollah Khomeini, of maintaining the occupation of the Embassy and the detention of its inmates as hostages for the purpose of exerting pressure on the United States Government was complied with by other Iranian authorities and endorsed by them repeatedly in statements made in various contexts. * * * The militants, authors of the invasion and jailers of the hostages, had now become agents of the Iranian State for whose acts the State itself was internationally responsible. * * *

For these reasons,

THE COURT, * * *

Decides that the Government of the Islamic Republic of Iran must immediately take all steps to redress the situation resulting from the events of 4 November 1979 and what followed from these events, and to that end:

(a) must immediately terminate the unlawful detention of the United States Chargé d'affaires and other diplomatic and consular staff and other United States nationals now held hostage in Iran, and must immediately release each and every one and entrust them to the protecting Power (Article 45 of the 1961 Vienna Convention on Diplomatic Relations);
(b) must ensure that all the said persons have the necessary means of leaving Iranian territory, including means of transport;
(c) must immediately place in the hands of the protecting Power the premises, property, archives and documents of the United States Embassy in Tehran and of its Consulates in Iran; * * *

Decides that the Islamic Republic of Iran, by the conduct which the Court has set out in this Judgment, has violated in several respects, and is still violating, obligations owed by it to the United States of America under international conventions in force between the two countries, as well as under long-established rules of general international law; * * *

Decides that no member of the United States diplomatic or consular staff may be kept in Iran to be subjected to any form of judicial proceedings or to participate in them as a witness; * * *

Decides that the Government of the Islamic Republic of Iran is under an obligation to make reparation to the Government of the United States of America for the injury caused to the latter by the events of 4 November 1979 and what followed from these events; * * *

Decides that the form and amount of such reparation, failing agreement between the Parties, shall be settled by the Court, and reserves for this purpose the subsequent procedure in the case.

Done in English and in French, the English text being authoritative, at the Peace Palace, The Hague, this twenty-fourth day of May, one thousand nine hundred and eighty, in three copies, one of which will be placed in the archives of the Court, and the others transmitted to the Government of the United States of America and the Government of the Islamic Republic of Iran, respectively.

(Signed) Humphrey WALDOCK,
President.

(Signed) S. AQUARONE,
Registrar.

[Iran ignored this judgment, and the hostages were not released until many months later (fifteen months after being taken captive) and on the eve of President Reagan's inauguration after President Carter had left Washington, D.C.]

Keeping order in the courts.

CLEVELAND BOARD OF EDUCATION v. LaFLEUR

Supreme Court of the United States, 1974.
414 U.S. 632, 94 S.Ct. 791, 39 L.Ed.2d 52.

Mr. Justice STEWART delivered the opinion of the Court.

The respondents in No. 72–777 and the petitioner in No. 72–1129 are female public school teachers. During the 1970–1971 school year, each informed her local school board that she was pregnant; each was compelled by a mandatory maternity leave rule to quit her job without pay several months before the expected birth of her child. These cases call upon us to decide the constitutionality of the school boards' rules.

Jo Carol LaFleur and Ann Elizabeth Nelson, the respondents in No. 72–777, are junior high school teachers employed by the Board of Education of Cleveland, Ohio. Pursuant to a rule first adopted in 1952, the school board requires every pregnant school teacher to take a maternity leave without pay, beginning five months before the expected birth of her child. Application for such leave must be made no later than two weeks prior to the date of departure. A teacher on maternity leave is not allowed to return to work until the beginning of the next regular school semester which follows the date when her child attains the age of three months. A doctor's certificate attesting to the health of the teacher is a prerequisite to return; an additional physical examination may be required. The teacher on maternity leave is not promised re-employment after the birth of the child; she is merely given priority in reassignment to a position for which she is qualified. Failure to comply with the mandatory maternity leave provisions is grounds for dismissal.

Neither Mrs. LaFleur nor Mrs. Nelson wished to take an unpaid maternity leave; each wanted to continue teaching until the end of the school year. Because of the mandatory maternity leave rule, however, each was required to leave her job in March of 1971. * * * [T]he United States Court of Appeals for the Sixth Circuit [found] the Cleveland rules in violation of the Equal Protection Clause of the Fourteenth Amendment. * * *

The petitioner * * *, Susan Cohen, was employed by the School Board of Chesterfield County, Virginia. That school board's maternity leave regulation requires that a pregnant teacher leave work at least four months prior to the expected birth of her child. Notice in writing must be given to the school board at least six months prior to the expected birth date. A teacher on maternity leave is declared re-eligible for employment when she submits written notice from a physician that she is physically fit for re-employment, and when she can give assurances that care of the child will cause minimal interferences with her job responsibilities. The teacher is guaranteed re-employment no later than the first day of the school year following the date upon which she is declared re-eligible.

Mrs. Cohen informed the Chesterfield County Board in November 1970, that she was pregnant and expected the birth of her child about April 28, 1971. [The School Board denied her requests for a teaching extension] * * * [and] she was required to leave her teaching job on December 18, 1970. * * * [T]he Court of Appeals [for the Fourth Circuit] upheld the constitutionality of the challenged regulation in a 4–3 decision. * * *

We granted certiorari in both cases, * * * in order to resolve the conflict between the Courts of Appeals regarding the constitutionality of such mandatory maternity leave rules for public school teachers.

This Court has long recognized that freedom of personal choice in matters of marriage and family life is one of the liberties protected by the Due Process Clause of the Fourteenth Amendment. * * * As we noted in Eisenstadt v. Baird, * * * there is a right "to be free from unwarranted governmental intrusion into matters so fundamentally affecting a person as the decision whether to bear or beget a child."

By acting to penalize the pregnant teacher for deciding to bear a child, overly restrictive maternity leave regulations can constitute a heavy burden on the exercise of these protected freedoms. * * * [T]he Due Process Clause of the Fourteenth Amendment requires that such rules must not needlessly, arbitrarily, or capriciously impinge upon this vital area of a teacher's constitutional liberty.

* * *

[N]either the necessity for continuity of instruction nor the state interest in keeping physically unfit teachers out of the classroom can justify the sweeping mandatory leave regulations that the Cleveland and Chesterfield County School Boards have adopted.

* * *

For the reasons stated, we hold that the mandatory termination provisions of the Cleveland and Chesterfield County maternity regulations violate the Due Process Clause of the Fourteenth Amendment, because of their use of unwarranted conclusive presumptions that seriously burden the exercise of protected constitutional liberty. For similar reasons, we hold the three months' provision of the Cleveland return rule unconstitutional.

* * *

It is so ordered.

The "long arm" of the law must not offend traditional notions of fair play.

WORLD-WIDE VOLKSWAGEN CORP. v. WOODSON

Supreme Court of the United States, 1980.
444 U.S. 286, 100 S.Ct. 559, 62 L.Ed.2d 490.

MR. JUSTICE WHITE delivered the opinion of the Court.

The issue before us is whether, consistently with the Due Process Clause of the Fourteenth Amendment, an Oklahoma court may exercise * * * jurisdiction over a nonresident automobile retailer and its wholesale distributor in a products-liability action, when the defendants' only connection with Oklahoma is the fact that an automobile sold in New York to New York residents became involved in an accident in Oklahoma.

Respondents Harry and Kay Robinson purchased a new Audi automobile from petitioner Seaway Volkswagen, Inc. (Seaway), in Massena, N.Y., in 1976. The following year the Robinson family, who resided in New York, left that State for a new home in Arizona. As they passed through the State of Oklahoma, another car struck their Audi in the rear, causing a fire which severely burned Kay Robinson and her two children.

The Robinsons subsequently brought a products-liability action in the District Court for Creek County, Okla., claiming that their injuries resulted from defective design and placement of the Audi's gas tank and fuel system. They joined as defendants the automobile's manufacturer, Audi NSU Auto Union Aktiengesellschaft (Audi); its importer, Volkswagen of America, Inc. (Volkswagen); its regional distributor, petitioner World-Wide Volkswagen Corp. (World-Wide); and its retail dealer, petitioner Seaway. Seaway and World-Wide * * * [claimed] [3] that Oklahoma's exercise of jurisdiction over them would offend the limitations on the State's jurisdiction imposed by the Due Process Clause of the Fourteenth Amendment.

The facts presented to the District Court showed that World-Wide is incorporated and has its business office in New York. It distributes vehicles, parts, and accessories, under contract with Volkswagen, to retail dealers in New York, New Jersey, and Connecticut. Seaway, one of these retail dealers, is incorporated and has its place of business in New York. Insofar as the record reveals, Seaway and World-Wide are fully independent corporations whose relations with each other and with Volkswagen and Audi are contractual only. Respondents adduced no evidence that either World-Wide or Seaway does any business in Oklahoma, ships or sells any products to or in that State, has an agent to receive process there, or purchases advertisements in any media calculated to reach Oklahoma. In fact, as respondents' counsel conceded at oral argument, * * * there was no showing that any automobile sold by World-Wide or Seaway has ever entered Oklahoma with the single exception of the vehicle involved in the present case.

The Supreme Court of Oklahoma * * * [held] that personal jurisdiction over [World-Wide and Seaway] was authorized by Oklahoma's "long-arm" statute * * *.

The Due Process Clause of the Fourteenth Amendment limits the power of a state court to render a valid personal judgment against a nonresident defendant. *Kulko* v. *California Superior Court,* 436 U.S. 84, 91, 98 S.Ct. 1690, 1696, 56 L.Ed.2d 132 (1978). A judgment rendered in violation of due process is void in the rendering State and is not entitled to full faith and credit elsewhere. *Pennoyer* v. *Neff,* 95 U.S. 714, 732–733, 24 L.Ed. 565 (1878). Due process requires that the defendant be given adequate notice of the suit, *Mullane* v. *Central Hanover Trust Co.,* 339 U.S. 306, 313–314, 70 S.Ct. 652, 657, 94 L.Ed. 865 (1950), and be subject to the personal jurisdiction of the court, *International Shoe Co.* v. *Washington,* 326 U.S. 310, 66 S.Ct. 154, 90 L.Ed. 95 (1945). In the present case, it is not contended that notice was inadequate; the only question is whether these particular petitioners were subject to the jurisdiction of the Oklahoma courts.

As has long been settled, and as we reaffirm today, a state court may exercise personal jurisdiction over a nonresident defendant only so long as there exist "minimum contacts" between the defendant and the forum State.

* * * The concept of minimum contacts, in turn, can be seen to perform two related, but distinguishable, functions. It protects the defendant against the burdens of litigating in a distant or inconvenient forum. And it acts to ensure that the States, through their courts, do not reach out beyond the limits imposed on them by their status as coequal sovereigns in a federal system.

The protection against inconvenient litigation is typically described in terms of "reasonableness" or "fairness." We have said that the defendant's contacts with the forum State must be such that maintenance of the suit "does not offend 'traditional notions of fair play and substantial justice.'" *International Shoe Co.* v. *Washington, supra,* at 316, 66 S.Ct., at 158, quoting *Milliken* v. *Meyer,*

3. Volkswagen * * * unlike World-Wide and Seaway did not seek review in the Supreme Court of Oklahoma and is not a petitioner here. Both Volkswagen and Audi remain as defendants in the litigation pending before the District Court in Oklahoma.

311 U.S. 457, 463, 61 S.Ct. 339, 342, 85 L.Ed. 278 (1940). The relationship between the defendant and the forum must be such that it is "reasonable . . . to require the corporation to defend the particular suit which is brought there." * * *

Thus, the Due Process Clause "does not contemplate that a state may make binding a judgment * * * against an individual or corporate defendant with which the state has no contacts, ties, or relations."

* * * Petitioners carry on no activity whatsoever in Oklahoma. They close no sales and perform no services there. They avail themselves of none of the privileges and benefits of Oklahoma law. They solicit no business there either through salespersons or through advertising reasonably calculated to reach the State. Nor does the record show that they regularly sell cars at wholesale or retail to Oklahoma customers or residents or that they indirectly, through others, serve or seek to serve the Oklahoma market. In short, respondents seek to base jurisdiction on one, isolated occurrence and whatever inferences can be drawn therefrom: the fortuitous circumstance that a single Audi automobile, sold in New York to New York residents, happened to suffer an accident while passing through Oklahoma.

It is argued, however, that because an autombile is mobile by its very design and purpose it was "foreseeable" that the Robinsons' Audi would cause injury in Oklahoma. Yet "foreseeability" alone has never been a sufficient benchmark for personal jurisdiction under the Due Process Clause.

* * *

If foreseeability were the criterion, a local California tire retailer could be forced to defend in Pennsylvania when a blowout occurs there.

* * *

Because we find that petitioners have no "contacts, ties, or relations" with the State of Oklahoma, *International Shoe Co.* v. *Washington, supra,* at 319, 66 S.Ct., at 159, the judgment of the Supreme Court of Oklahoma is

Reversed.

Review Questions

1. How do the terms "primary" and "specific" legal concept relate to understanding American law? Explain. Describe and classify the various kinds of rights a United States citizen may have.

2. Are "custom and usage" important in commercial law? Explain. Name and explain how five provisions of the United States Constitution have particular impact on the doing of business. Explain how the Fourteenth Amendment relates to the Bill of Rights.

3. Where does the United States Supreme Court get the power to declare legislative or executive acts unconstitutional? What is this power called? Are there any limits on its use? Explain your answers.

4. When must the United States Supreme Court hear an appeal? When may a case be transferred from a state trial court to a federal trial court? When must a defendant citizen of another state return or lose by default? Explain your answers.

5. How does the seventeenth enumerated power of Congress relate to the others? What is the most important congressional power exercised by Congress in time of peace? Where in the Constitution is provided the congressional power to investigate? What is the extent of this investigative power? To what extent may a legislative body make a statute that affects contract rights? Explain your answers.

6. What is the difference between a trial court and an appellate court? What does any court need to settle a dispute? What is the specific power of the federal district court? The U.S. Claims Court? Explain your answers.

7. Name and explain five different techniques or items used or considered by judges in the interpretation of statutes.

8. Define the following terms: affectation doctrine, bill of attainder, doctrine of standing, ejusdem generis, ex post facto law, judicial review, pocket veto, reasoning by example, separation of powers doctrine, stare decisis, writ of certiorari, writ of habeas corpus.

Problems

1. Two merchants decide to enter into a contract or agreement for the sale of goods. As both are relatively new to the field of commercial law, they are somewhat hesitant to draw up the final agreement until they are satisfied that all provisions are on the legal "up and up." What source of law can you suggest that will clarify the law of sales for these merchants? Explain.

2. When Nick Pickering took over as editor-in-chief of the *Tri-Weekly Herald,* he was determined to expose the hidden scandals and bungling bureaucracy of state legislative officials. After one particularly critical editorial, the state legislature passed a statute creating a committee to censor all state news publications. An infuriated Pickering urged the state trial court to declare the statute unconstitutional as a denial of freedom of the press—a right guaranteed by the U.S. Constitution. The trial court refused to do so, and on appeal, the state supreme court affirmed that trial court decision. Must Pickering now surrender the *Herald* to legislative scrutiny? Explain.

3. Dr. Eileen Davidson, the frustrated head of the Solar Power Commission, decided to take matters into her own hands. The enabling statute which established the Commission in 1983 provided only that its members "research thoroughly" the problems of solar power with an eye to recommending legislation in that area. Dr. Davidson, spurred by the urgency of the power crisis, has issued several administrative orders, the provisions of which would forcefully encourage power producing industries to expand solar research. What "checks," if any, exist within the U.S. system of government that will prevent the Commission's continued exercise of unauthorized power? Explain.

4. Lisa Spall, an enthusiastic amateur candlemaker, agreed to sell twelve of her best wax creations to her neighbor, Henry Lord, for only ninety dollars. Henry promised to pay Lisa the money within three weeks' time; but a month passed, without word from Henry, and Lisa finally called to inquire about her missing payment. Henry, who had already burned seven of the twelve candles, replied indignantly that he had no intention of paying Lisa the ninety dollars—that, as her neighbor, he felt entitled to a gift once in a while. Lisa cannot afford to hire a lawyer to retrieve her ninety dollars. What possible alternative recourse does she have against Henry? Explain.

5. Three members of the women's liberation movement have been arrested and thrown in jail for criminal assault on the person of Governor T.J. Farnesworth, noted male chauvinist and proud of it. The indignant women are being prosecuted under a state statute designating such assault (upon the person of a public official) punishable by two years imprisonment and without benefit of trial by jury. As lawyer for defendants, you realize that cries of "sexist discrimination" will get you nowhere. Rather, you feel the statute itself, which eliminates trial by jury, is unfair, unjust, and violative of your defendants' rights. What legal doctrine can you urge to help them? Explain.

6. Fred Craven was minding his own business at his fraternity's annual, end-of-the-year beer bust, when he was suddenly physically attacked by Pete Francis, an out-of-state student who was "just visiting." Fred desires to bring a tort action for assault and battery against Pete in the state trial court for damages in the amount of $15,000, but he is concerned that the court may not have jurisdiction since Pete left the state the morning after the party. You are Fred's lawyer. Can he bring the action as planned? Explain.

In the same fact situation, assume that the state trial court has obtained proper jurisdiction over Pete. Pete returns to the state but fears that local prejudice against out-of-state students will prevent him from receiving a fair trial. You are Pete's lawyer. Counsel him.

7. Andy Foster was crossing the street at the corner of 11th and Pine when suddenly, without warning, he was struck to the ground by a speeding motorcycle. His injuries included two broken ribs and a not-so-mild concussion. But when seeking to recover damages from the cycle rider, lovely Miss Angela Stone, Andy can find no written law that would permit him recovery. He does find, however, a recent case in which another pedestrian, struck by a speeding van, was allowed to recover damages for negligence. Can Andy use this earlier case to persuade a judge that he is entitled to relief? What is the principle to be applied here? Name and explain the reasoning process involved.

8. A local statute recently passed in Sweeney Point, Missouri, prohibits the use of any motorized vehicle within the city's downtown core area between the hours of 3 p.m. and 7 p.m. This measure is widely supported by Sweeney residents who seek to reduce the record high pollution levels of the past six months. When the question arises as to whether this statute applies to government owned and operated vehicles in the downtown area (for example, the Sweeney Point Police Department is centrally located), how will the courts construe the statute's application? Name a rule that applies in this area.

Week 2
113-159
179-209

It is not without significance that most of the provisions of the Bill of Rights are procedural. . . . Steadfast adherence to strict procedural safeguards is our main assurance that there will be equal justice under law.

Justice Douglas
Joint Anti-Facist Refugee Committee v. McGrath
341 U.S. 123, 179 (1951).

3

Civil, Equitable, Criminal, and Other Procedure

WHAT SITUATIONS REQUIRE DIFFERENT LEGAL PROCEDURE?

Once a court has jurisdiction, it has power to settle the dispute. In this chapter we will consider just how courts and other governmental authorities reach final conclusions in the resolution of controversies. That is, we will deal with the adjective law—procedural law by which rights and duties are enforced.

The procedure followed, however, is not the same in every situation. In this chapter, for example, we will first describe the *civil action for money damages*. This action is the usual dispute between individuals. It may be based on breach of contract or tort. Or it may arise from a property dispute or any other legal concept involving private law. It is the "civil action" you bring, for example, when you sue someone for negligently driving his car into your own or for selling you that defective TV-stereo set.

But perhaps you seek a remedy in *equity* or file for divorce or dissolution of marriage in a *domestic relations* court. The procedures involved in these situations, as well as in *probate, crime, juvenile court,* and *impeachment* cases, are somewhat different. Yet much of what applies to the civil action for money damages applies to these situations as well, so it is very important to understand the civil action before you go on to the other procedures.

WHAT IS VENUE?

Before we consider specific procedure, there are four collateral subjects you must first understand. To begin with, if jurisdiction can be established in several places, where should trial be held? Venue refers to the proper or best place for trial when this situation arises. Remember, jurisdictional requirements are satisfied once the court has power over the subject matter (found in constitutions or statutes) and power over the person of the defendant (by service of summons). It is thus possible for several courts to obtain jurisdiction over the same case—each may have power to hear the same fact situation and to resolve the dispute. For instance, suppose you are a resident of San Diego, California and are seriously injured when a resident of Miami, Florida runs over you with his car. Your total damages exceed $50,000. Which courts may obtain jurisdiction? We know that any superior court in California has subject matter jurisdiction, and the State of California can obtain jurisdiction over the defendant with its long arm statute. The state courts of Florida probably have jurisdiction as well. But, in addition, federal courts in both California and Florida have jurisdiction because diversity of citizenship exists and the amount in controversy well exceeds the $10,000 limitation.

As plaintiff, you can sue in any of these courts if jurisdiction is your only consideration. But another question confronts you: which of these several courts is the best or proper place to handle the case? This is the problem of venue. Jurisdiction deals with the court's authority to exercise judicial power. Venue deals with the *place* where that power *should be exercised.* While the court must have jurisdiction (or what it does is meaningless and void), venue is mostly a matter of convenience. The purpose of venue is to prevent a plaintiff from forcing a defendant to a trial where it is difficult or burdensome for him or her to defend. The ability to object to venue is personal to the defendant; objection to venue may be raised only by the defendant. In federal courts and in many states, a request for a change in venue must be made in the defendant's first appearance before the court (usually this appearance would be by and through the defendant's attorney), or the defendant waives any improper venue. So if a court has proper jurisdiction and the defendant does not object to venue, the court can render a valid judgment.

Jurisdiction, then, affects the very power of the court to act, while venue is but a procedural matter. Determination of venue may be prescribed by statute; it may be based on avoiding possible prejudice; or it may simply involve matters of convenience. The federal statute states that proper venue is the district in which either plaintiff or defendant resides or the district where the injury occurred. State statutes regulating venue vary but generally provide that where land is involved, proper venue is in the county where the land is located. For most other actions, venue is in the county where the defendant resides.

Of course, venue can always be objected to on grounds of prejudice of either judge or prospective jury. This occurs frequently in criminal cases where substantial pretrial publicity makes it difficult for a defendant to receive a fair trial in a particular area of the country. A good example is the trial of Jack Ruby. Ruby was tried in Dallas County, Texas for killing Lee Harvey Oswald, the accused assassin of President John F. Kennedy. Although Ruby was convicted, the verdict was later reversed by an appellate court on the ground that defendant Ruby could not receive a fair trial in Dallas County. The trial court had made an error of law in refusing change of venue as requested by Ruby's lawyer.

Another ground for change of venue is the doctrine of "forum non conveniens." This simply means that the place selected for trial is not convenient. In deciding whether or not the change should be granted, the judge may consider the relative cost and inconvenience to the parties (plaintiff and defendant) and to the witnesses.

WHAT SUBSTANTIVE LAW MUST FEDERAL TRIAL COURTS FOLLOW?

The second subject relates to jurisdiction and venue when a federal court decides a diversity of citizenship case. You will recall that the federal district court has jurisdiction under one of two circumstances: (1) when a federal question is involved, and (2) when there is diversity of citizenship (plaintiff and defendant are from different states) and the plaintiff is asking for $10,000 or more in damages.

If the action involves a federal question—any claim or defense arising under the U.S. Constitution, U.S. treaties, or statutes—then federal law controls, and only federal law applies to that issue. This is true whether the federal question arises in a federal or in a state court. As stated in the supremacy clause, Article VI of the U.S. Constitution: "This constitution and the laws of the United States which shall be made in pursuance thereof * * * shall be the supreme law of the land and *the judges in every state shall be bound thereby.*" (Emphasis added.)

So there is really no problem in determining what substantive law a court must apply when a federal question is involved. Substantive law, as you will recall, deals with the definition of law—rights and duties, principles and standards. In this situation, federal law applies, and the United States Supreme Court has final say on what that law is.

But what about issues that do not involve a federal question? If diversity of citizenship exists, a federal court may be called upon to resolve the controversy anyway. So in the auto accident situation presented in the last section of this chapter in which the plaintiff and defendant are residents of San Diego and Miami, respectively, the federal court has both jurisdiction and proper venue. But the court cannot use the federal Constitution, a treaty, or a statute to determine whether or not the defendant was negligent. These sources of law simply do not apply when there is no federal question involved.

But what law does the federal court apply? Can the judge (in disregard of state law) exercise his or her discretion and decide the case according to his or her own notions of fairness and right? The answer is no. Whenever there is no federal question involved, the federal court must apply the substantive law of the state in which the court is located. Thus, in the diversity of citizenship case, the federal court decides what substantive law applies by looking to all applicable state statutes and by considering the opinions of the highest courts of the state in which the federal court is located. Federal procedural rules, embodied in the Federal Rules of Civil Procedure, still govern the operation of courtroom mechanics.

As a result, the federal court should reach the same result on nonfederal questions as the state court would have reached had it decided the case itself. This also means that no general federal common law results because federal questions involve interpretation of written law in the form of the U.S. Constitution, a treaty, or a federal statute, while diversity of citizenship cases are decided using only the substantive law, including the state common law, of the state wherein the federal court is located.

WHEN WILL THERE BE CHOICE OF LAW PROBLEMS?

The third subject is concerned with choice of law problems. Transactions or events that occur entirely within one state and involve only parties from that state present no choice of law problems. The law of that state will be applied to make the decision. Sometimes, however, one or more of the events occur outside the state where the case is brought, or one or more of the parties is from a different state. Additionally, the law of the one state on a particular subject may well be different from the other state since each state has established its own precedents interpreting the written law and making the common law. When all of this occurs, the court where the case is brought must apply conflict of law rules and decide to what extent, if any, it will recognize and apply another state's conflicting law to resolve the case.

There are a number of rules, mostly judge-made, used to decide what the choice of law should be in such cases. For many years when a tort was committed in a state other than where the tort case was being decided, the law of the state where the injury (the tort) took place was applied, even though not the same as the deciding state's law. The modern conflict of law principle no longer recognizes this "place of wrong" rule. Instead, the court deciding the case will look to the contacts and interests of each state involved and apply the law of the state having the most significant relationship with the parties and issues and whose interests would be most furthered by the application of its law. For example, in Reich v. Purcell, 67 Cal.2d 551, 63 Cal. Rptr. 31, 432 P.2d 727 (1967), a car accident occurred in Missouri, the "place of the wrong." The defendant-driver was a resident of California and was sued in California by the estates of decedents killed in the accident. The decedents had been residents of Ohio where their estates were being handled. If the plaintiffs won the case against the defendant, the money recovered would become part of the estates being administered in Ohio and would be distributed to decedents' families according to Ohio law. Missouri had a law limiting the amount that could be recovered for wrongful death. Ohio law had no such limitation in amount. California, in disregarding the "place of wrong" rule, applied the Ohio law saying that Missouri had no interest in having its limitation of damages applied since neither the plaintiffs nor the defendant resided there. Ohio had the dominant interest and most significant relationship because it was handling the distribution of the decedents' estates.

Choice of law problems involving contracts are settled by courts attempting to give effect to the expectation of the contracting parties through the application of the law of the state having the most significant relationship to the transaction and the parties.

When real property is involved, the law of the situs of the land will control; the state where the land is located is most interested in the marketability, transferability, value, and use of land located within its borders. With the sale of personal property, the Uniform Commercial Code specifies that reference is to be made to the law of the state with "appropriate relations" to the sale, i.e., the state having the most significant relation to the transaction and parties.

Criminal cases must always be heard in the state where the crime occurs and with an application of that particular state's criminal law.

Choice of law problems become even more complex when federal judges in diversity cases are applying the law of the state in which the federal court is located, and that law, under choice of law principles, requires the application of another state's law.

WHAT IS A CLASS ACTION?

The fourth subject is the class action.

Once in a while all of the ordinary rules of jurisdiction simply will not cover the situation. Certainly a person who has been wronged should be able to sue the person who has wronged him or her. But what if that person has injured not one but several hundred plaintiffs? Suppose that you are among 1,700 consumers who agree to buy transistor radios from an unscrupulous seller who lies about their quality. When the radios fall apart or stop working, each of you could sue for his or her seventy-five dollars—but many of you will not because it takes too much time or costs too much money. Can one consumer bring the action for all of you?

A class action is one brought by or against one or more members of a class or group of persons sharing a common interest. The common questions must predominate, and a class action will not be allowed where the individual issues, i.e., the issues to *each* member of the class, are found to be numerous and substantial. For example, in the case of City of San Jose v. Superior Court, 12 Cal.3d 447, 115 Cal.Rptr. 797, 525 P.2d 701 (1974), the owners of land next to an airport tried to bring a class action for damages to their land resulting from airport activities such as noise and pollution. The airport activities were common to all of the owners, but the right of each owner to recover involved too many individual factors such as the value of the property, its use, and its proximity to flight patterns. The class action was not permitted.

The Federal Rules of Civil Procedure for federal courts state that a class action may be brought only if:

1. The class is so numerous that joinder of all members is impracticable,
2. There are questions of law or fact common to the class,
3. The claims or defenses of the representative parties are typical of the claims or defenses of the class, and

4. The representative parties will fairly and adequately protect the interests of the class.

The Federal Rules also set down the duties of the judge, including the type of notice he or she must give to members of the class. While the matter of notice is left largely to the judge's discretion in determining the "due process" requirements of each situation, notice is mandatory in some cases; and, where this is so, the judge must inform each member of the class that he or she will be excluded from the class if so requested; otherwise, he or she will be bound by the judgment. For example, in a damages class action based on a predominant question common to the class, members of the class that can be identified through reasonable effort must be given individual notice. The notice, in such circumstances, must be mailed and must advise the class member not only of the nature of the claim and identity of the person representing the class, but also that the class member may request exclusion ("opt out"), but otherwise will be bound by the class action decision. The plaintiff representing the class initially must pay the costs of the notice; if he or she wins, recovery of such costs may be had from the defendant. Still, if the class is large, the cost of notice may prevent the bringing of the class action. In diversity of citizenship cases in federal court, each member of the class must have claims that equal or exceed $10,000, and aggregation of claims to meet the $10,000 figure is not permitted.

Several states have adopted the federal class action rule as part of their own law though they may have more flexible rules regarding notice requirements providing for greater application of notice by publication instead of requiring individual notice. Use of the class action has become widespread in areas of social control—antitrust litigation, civil rights, and consumer protection.

Now, assuming your state has similar rules to the federal rules on class actions, take another look at your claim against the fraudulent radio seller. The 1,700 members of your class are clearly ascertainable; it is not difficult to figure out who bought the radios from the seller. Each of you possesses an individual reason to sue, but it is based on a common question of fact—the fraudulent misrepresentations of the seller—he lied to each of you in the same way. Clearly, if some of the consumers are made parties to the action (i.e., plaintiffs bringing the case against the seller), they can successfully and fairly represent all of the consumers involved. Notice, of course, must be sent to each of you individually, and if any one of you requests exclusion, he or she will be excused from the judgment's binding effect. A class action in this situation is clearly superior to any other method of handling the loss of all the consumers. It avoids a multiplicity of law suits, yet provides each of you, whether or not you are actually there, with your "day in court" against the fraudulent seller.

WHAT ARE THE FOUR PROCEDURAL PARTS OF A CIVIL ACTION?

If you possess a right or legal capacity to influence someone's conduct, you may have to use the machinery of the courts and legal procedures to enforce your right. This process is called "litigation." Litigation is the carrying on

FIGURE 3–1 THE FOUR STAGES OF LITIGATION

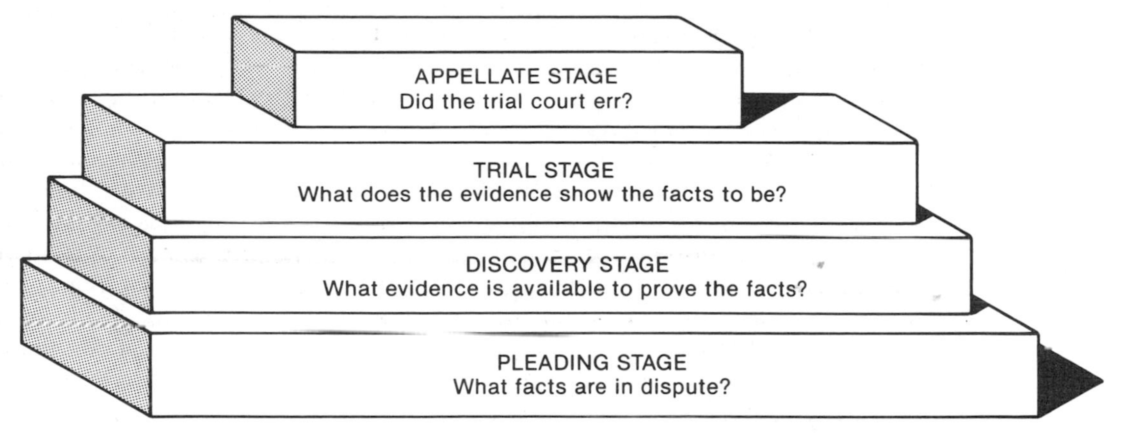

of a lawsuit. It is the courtroom contest for the purpose of enforcing a right. As shown in figure 3–1, litigation involves four stages or steps:

1. The *pleading* stage, which determines the facts at issue;
2. The *discovery* stage, which investigates the facts, prepares evidence for trial, and attempts to settle the controversy before trial;
3. The *trial* stage, which resolves the issues of fact; and, finally,
4. The *appellate* stage, which reviews the trial court proceedings for error.

Each stage of litigation is considered in detail in the following sections of this chapter.

WHAT IS THE "PLEADING" PART OF THE CIVIL ACTION?

The concept of fair play demands settlement of controversies or disputes according to orderly rules of procedure. But parties must first present their controversy to the court before it can be settled. How do they do this? In early England, the parties to a dispute would appear in court and orally shout out their positions as loudly as possible and usually at the same time as their opposition. As only confusion resulted, this was obviously not a good way to present a problem to the court.

Rules for orderly presentation soon developed. Parties were required to speak one at a time. As stated by Judge Curtis Bok: "In the whole history of law and order the longest step forward was taken by primitive man, when, as if by common consent, the tribe sat down in a circle and allowed one man to speak at a time. An accused who is shouted down has no rights whatever." Similarly, an accused who disrupts the orderly process of the court by shouting or otherwise misbehaving cannot receive "due process" of law. We saw this earlier in the case of *Illinois v. Allen* (see Chapter 1).

Equally important in maintaining order is the requirement that pleadings be reduced to writing. "Pleadings," or, simply, "pleading," is the name given to the process that brings the case initially before the court. This is a good name because it means exactly what it says. The parties are "pleading" their case. They are arguing for or against a position by presenting their version of the facts in writing.

The specifics of "pleading" vary to some extent from state to state. In the federal courts, pleadings are governed by the Federal Rules of Civil Procedure (a federal statute passed by Congress to govern civil action procedure in federal courts), which, you have learned, also governs the federal class action.

But the purpose of the pleadings is the same in every court, state and federal. Pleadings notify the parties and the court of the nature of the case before them. They define the controversy between the parties and narrow and formulate the issues in dispute. And, most important, pleadings set the boundary lines of the litigation: nothing should be introduced at trial that is not material to the disputed facts as contained in the pleadings. However, under modern practice, amendments of pleadings are usually allowed during trial or after trial as long as this does not cause substantial prejudice, inconvenience, expense, or unfairness to the other side. Also, a pretrial conference is often allowed or required by courts after the pleading and discovery stages are complete. This is done to further sharpen the issues in dispute, amend the pleadings if necessary to conform to the facts as developed in the discovery stage, encourage settlement of the case without trial, identify the witnesses to be called at the trial, and establish the trial agenda. The pretrial conference results in a pretrial order from the judge which supercedes the pleadings and controls the trial.

In the state court systems, there are often three basic pleadings: the "complaint," the "answer," and the "reply." The plaintiff files the first pleading, or complaint, to let the defendant know in detail why he or she is suing the defendant. This pleading is called a "complaint" because it "complains" about the defendant's actions. It sets forth reasons why the defendant should be compelled to respond to the plaintiff. The typical complaint sets forth the name of the court, the names of the parties to the dispute, a statement of the court's jurisdiction or power to hear the case, and a brief statement of the basic facts which form the basis for recovery. The complaint contains only allegations of fact—mere assertions that something is true without proof. The plaintiff alleges in the complaint that certain facts are true; that because they are true, he or she is entitled to money damages or other relief.

The original complaint is filed with the court that will hear the case. As you will recall from the last chapter, the defendant is furnished with a copy of the complaint at the time he or she receives the summons (see figures 3–2 and 3–3). The defendant then has a certain period of time to "answer"—ten, fifteen, thirty, or sixty days depending on where he or she is served and on what the rule of the particular state may be. If the defendant fails to answer in time, he or she loses the case by default. In the federal courts, the Federal Rules of Civil Procedure require the defendant to respond within twenty days after service of the summons and complaint.

The defendant's answer either admits or denies the specific facts alleged in the plaintiff's complaint. Whatever the defendant denies must be proved

FIGURE 3–2 THE SUMMONS

```
THE STATE OF WASHINGTON        SUPERIOR COURT       KING COUNTY
* * * * * * * * * * * * * * * * * * * * * * * * * * * * * * * * *

MARY PLAINTIFF, by her mother,  *
     her guardian,
                                *
                 Plaintiff,
                                *             SUMMONS
     vs.
                                *
THREE DOCTOR DEFENDANTS,
                                *
                 Defendants.

* * * * * * * * * * * * * * * * * * * * * * * * * * * * * * * * *
THE STATE OF WASHINGTON TO THE ABOVE NAMED DEFENDANTS:

         YOU ARE HEREBY SUMMONED to appear within twenty (20)
days after the service of this Summons upon you, if served
within the State of Washington, and within sixty (60) days
after said service if served without the State of Washington,
exclusive of the day of service, and defend the above
entitled action in the Superior Court of the State of
Washington, for the above County, and answer the complaint
of the plaintiff herein, and serve a copy of your answer
upon the undersigned, attorneys for plaintiff, at their
office below specified; and, in case of your failure so to
do, judgment will be rendered against you according to the
demand of the complaint, which will be filed with the Clerk
of the above entitled Court, and a copy of which is
herewith served upon you.


                              BY:_____________________________
                                 Attorneys for the Plaintiff
```

at trial by the plaintiff. Obviously, whatever he or she admits need not be proved in court, and if he or she admits that all the facts are true, there is no need for a trial at all because there are no facts at issue.

One method of response used by the defendant is the "general denial" of the entire complaint. The defendant, in effect, states that every single allegation in the complaint is false. As a result, the plaintiff must prove everything in court. Rule 11 of the Federal Rules of Civil Procedure, however, requires parties to exercise "good faith" in pleading. And since general denials are usually improper (as there is usually something in the complaint that is true), separate denials of specific allegations are generally called for.

In addition to admitting or denying portions of the complaint, the defendant can assert new facts in the answer by way of defense. For instance, if the complaint alleges that the defendant's negligence caused a bad car accident, the defendant can answer by first denying his or her own negligence and next by further alleging that the plaintiff's own negligence prompted the accident and damaged the defendant. If the defendant raises

FIGURE 3–3 THE COMPLAINT

THE STATE OF WASHINGTON SUPERIOR COURT KING COUNTY

* *

MARY PLAINTIFF, by her mother, her guardian, *

Plaintiff, *

vs. * COMPLAINT

THREE DOCTOR DEFENDANTS, *

Defendants. *

* *

Comes now the Plaintiff and for claim alleges:

I.

That MARY PLAINTIFF is an infant, born June 20, 1959; that her mother has been appointed the general guardian of Mary Plaintiff.

II.

That heretofore and on or about the 16th day of September, 1959, the infant plaintiff was hospitalized at a hospital in the State of Washington, and thereafter on or about the 15th day of October, 1959, underwent surgical and anaesthetic procedures by the defendant doctors, including specifically a thyrotomy for the removal or excision of a tumor in the course of which a plastic stent was placed in the throat of the plaintiff, and following which there was inserted or reinserted a tracheotomy tube. That the defendant doctors acted jointly and severally in connection with the surgery and in connection with the instructions to the recovery room.

III.

Following said operation, plaintiff was placed in a recovery room and while so confined suffered apnea and cardiac arrest. As a result of said apnea and cardiac arrest, infant plaintiff suffered loss of function of both arms and legs, loss and/or impairment of function of many muscles of the body, including muscles of speech, and is unable to stand, crawl or walk, and infant plaintiff's condition is permanent.

IV.

In the performance of the undertaking so assumed, defendant doctors failed and neglected to carefully, skillfully and properly treat and care for infant plaintiff in one or more of the following particulars:

1. Failure to cause themselves to be adequately informed as to the previous recent history of said child, particularly while in the hospital from and after September 16, 1959.

Figure 3-3 continued on next page

2. Failure to take appropriate steps to assure the maintenance of a proper and adequate airway in the recovery room.

3. Failure to use a proper sized plastic stent.

4. Failure to provide and require provision for appropriate recovery room supervision and attendance.

5. Failure to provide the recovery room in proper manner with adequate and correct recovery room instructions.

6. Failure to assign a physician to watch infant plaintiff, to be in constant attendance.

V.

As a direct and proximate result of the negligence of the defendant doctors, as aforesaid, infant plaintiff has been required to incur medical and hospital expenses for the rest of her life in an amount unknown at this time, as infant plaintiff will require continuous supervision, therapy, guidance and daily care for the remainder of her lifetime, will be unable to seek employment, and will always remain completely dependent upon others for her care and well being.

VI.

As a direct and proximate result of the negligence of defendant doctors, as aforesaid, infant plaintiff will suffer expenses, pain, suffering, disability, and other inconvenience for the remainder of her life, all to her general damage in the sum of One Million Seven Hundred Fifty Thousand and no/100 [$1,750,000.00] Dollars, together with special damages incurred to date. That the parents have relinquished to the infant child such causes of action as accrued to them as a result of this event.

WHEREFORE, Plaintiff prays judgment against the defendants and each of them for those special damages incurred to date of trial and proven at that time, but not to exceed the sum of One Hundred Thousand and no/100 [$100,000.00] Dollars, and for the further sum of future expenses, pain, suffering and disability to be proven at the time of trial, but not greater than One Million Seven Hundred Fifty Thousand and no/100 [$1,750,000.00] Dollars, and for costs and disbursements herein to be taxed.

BY: ______________________________
Attorneys for the Plaintiff

---

new matter in the answer, the plaintiff in many states must "reply" and either admit or deny the new facts alleged.

Once these pleadings are filed (i.e., the complaint, the answer, and the reply, where necessary), the case is said to be "at issue." Each party's contentions are known, and the boundary lines for trial have been set.

One final item about the pleading stage. In some situations, the plaintiff cannot win even if all the facts alleged in his or her complaint are true. We stated in the last chapter that a plaintiff can win his or her case only if the plaintiff can bring the fact situation within a specific legal concept that recognizes a right that he or she is entitled to enforce. We gave as an example the man who decides to sue his neighbor because he is too fat. Of course, he cannot win his case because there is no concept of law that acknowledges his claim or right against an obese neighbor. But suppose he writes a complaint and has a copy of the complaint together with a summons delivered to the fat neighbor. It would make no sense for the neighbor to "answer" and deny that he is too fat. What he should do is file a motion to dismiss the action based on the plaintiff's failure to state a claim upon which relief can be granted. This is called a demurrer in many state courts. Under the Federal Rules of Civil Procedure and in some states, it is called a motion to dismiss.

When the defendant files a demurrer or motion to dismiss, the judge must ask the following question: even if all the facts stated in the complaint are true, can the plaintiff win the case? If the answer is no, then the judge must sustain the demurrer or motion and dismiss the case. In our example, the neighbor may very well be excessively fat. His fatness may annoy the plaintiff. But even so, the plaintiff cannot win his case. The judge would sustain the demurrer with his response to the complaint: "So what? Even if this is true, no rule of law allows the plaintiff to recover against his fat neighbor."

WHAT IS THE "DISCOVERY" PART OF THE CIVIL ACTION?

The shouting matches in the early history of courts made it difficult to determine just what the cases were about. It was equally difficult for the adversaries to find out anything about their opponent's case. But while surprise was once a legitimate trial tactic, this is no longer so. Our present legal system provides "discovery" procedures that take the sporting aspect out of litigation and make certain that legal results are based on the true facts of the case—not on the skill of the attorneys.

It was not until the 1938 adoption of the Federal Rules of Civil Procedure that the philosophy of pretrial discovery was written into the law. These rules, adopted in whole or in part by a majority of the states, insure full disclosure of the facts prior to trial. They encourage pretrial settlement as well, for with both parties fully aware of the facts, one will often conclude that he or she cannot win the case.

In United States v. Procter and Gamble Co., 356 U.S. 677, 78 S.Ct. 983, 2 L.Ed.2d 1077 (1958), the U.S. Supreme Court stated that discovery rules "make a trial less a game of blind man's bluff and more a fair contest with the basic issues and facts disclosed to the fullest practicable extent." And in Burton v. Weyerhaeuser Timber Co., 1 F.R.D. 451 (D.Or.1941), the court emphasized that "surprise, both as a weapon of attack and defense, is not to be tolerated under the new Federal procedure."

Tools for discovery include the following:

1. Depositions;
2. Interrogatories;
3. Production of documents; and
4. Physical and mental examinations.

A deposition is testimony of a witness taken under oath but out of court, although the same question and answer method used in the courtroom is followed. A court reporter records the testimony so that a transcript can be provided. All parties to the case must be notified that the deposition is to be taken, so they can be present to cross-examine the witness. If necessary, a subpoena will be issued to compel a witness to appear (a subpoena is merely a court order requiring appearance to give testimony). In federal practice and in some states, depositions may be taken by telephone or recorded by videotape if the parties consent or the court so orders.

Interrogatories are written questions that must be answered under oath. One party may require them from another party but not from nonparty witnesses. Interrogatories are especially useful in obtaining descriptions of evidence in the possession of the adversary.

If a party desires, he or she may also request and receive for inspection and copying any document, writing, drawing, graph, chart, map, photo record, etc., in the hands of the opposing party.

When the mental or physical condition of a party is at issue, the court may order the party to submit to a complete physical or mental examination by a physician.

So in the typical auto accident case where you are sued for negligence, your lawyer can use discovery procedures to take the deposition of the plaintiff and other witnesses and require them to tell everything they know about the accident. He or she may demand production of doctor and hospital bills, garage repair bills, police reports, X-rays, etc., and he or she may copy all of them. Your attorney may even force the plaintiff to submit to a physical exam by a court appointed doctor.

If a party refuses to comply with discovery requests, the court may compel compliance, deem the facts established, dismiss the cause of action, or enter judgment by default.

For the federal district courts, the Judicial Panel on Multidistrict Litigation was created by Congress in 1968 so that civil actions involving one or more common questions of fact and pending in different districts could be transferred by the Panel for consolidated pretrial proceedings. The Panel is made up of seven federal circuit and district judges appointed by the Chief Justice of the United States Supreme Court.

It may happen, for example, that an airplane crash involves passengers from many parts of the United States with actions filed in several district courts. Or a defective product may have been sold and caused injuries to people in several states with a number of cases filed. In such circumstances the Panel may transfer all the cases to one district court so that discovery may be accomplished in a coordinated fashion and without unnecessary duplication and expense. The cases, once transferred, generally reach settlement or proceed to trial in the district to which they have been transferred. Since 1968 over 5,000 cases have been transferred and processed through this technique.

This has been important to business because, in addition to the common disaster and products liability cases, many cases have involved antitrust actions, stockholders' actions under securities laws, and patent, copyright, and trademark actions.

WHAT IS THE TRIAL PART OF THE CIVIL ACTION?

As previously stated, pretrial "discovery procedure" often results in out-of-court settlement, especially when the facts of the case show that one of the parties is very likely to lose. In this situation, the party can usually settle for less than it will cost if he or she loses in court. If settlement is impossible, the trial stage of litigation begins (it is important to remember, however, that a case may be settled at any time before, during, or even after trial—for example, when an appeal is being taken).

To understand the trial stage of a civil action, you must be able to answer these three questions:

1. What is meant by the adversary system, i.e., what are the proper functions of the judge, the jury, and the attorneys?
2. What is the actual procedure, i.e., how is the case presented and conducted?
3. What are the rules of evidence, i.e., what are the rules that establish which facts may or may not be presented to the jury?

What is the Adversary System?

The term "adversary" means opponent—one who opposes another in a battle, contest, or controversy. In an adversary system of law, each side is responsible for presenting his or her own side of the case, and each party must have an opportunity to be heard.

Legal procedure in the United States is based on the adversary system. The parties themselves, through their attorneys, are responsible for finding and presenting their own evidence and arguments. They alone must plan and execute their courtroom strategy; and the court's conclusions are based on what the parties have brought forth through witnesses, exhibits, and other evidence. If a party dislikes a particular witness, he or she does not have to use that witness. If he or she prefers to "skirt" or avoid certain questions, that choice is for the party to make. And this system is a very good one. Parties should be able to present their cases as they choose and in a manner that best represents their positions. Since each party's self-interest is at stake, it makes sense to leave each responsible for most of what happens to his or her case at trial. Experience shows that it is the best method for finding the truth and doing justice.

The parties then, through their attorneys, present the facts in their own way. They are restricted only by the rules of law regarding evidence and due process as discussed later in this section. But if the parties present their own cases, where does the judge come in? The judge is a referee. It is not the judge's job to get involved with strategy, planning, or presentation of evidence. His or her function is to keep the parties within the rules when asked to do so by a party who objects to what the other side is doing. If a party does not object, the judge should not do so for the party. Sometimes an attorney's strategy will include allowing objectionable evidence to come into court even though it could be kept out. And even if a judge thinks an attorney is inept, he or she should not interfere with the attorney's presentation of the case. Sometimes the attorney who appears most inept in the courtroom wins the greater number of his or her cases. The author remembers one case in particular where the attorney for the other side apologized to the jury in his closing arguments, stating that he knew he "was not very good" and he hoped that "the jury would not take out his inefficiency and inability to present the case" on his client. The jury not only ruled in his favor, but that attorney is now a superior court judge in the State of Washington.

Again, the trial judge is but a referee in a civil action before a jury. Just as a referee in a basketball game does not, out of sympathy, start shooting free throws for the losing team, so also must the trial judge remain neutral and allow the attorneys to play their own game. If the impartiality of a judge is questionable, he or she may be disqualified from a case upon motion of a party showing the judge's personal bias or involvement in the case.

The jury in a civil action is there simply to listen and observe and to make a decision based on what it hears. Jurors are not permitted to ask questions or even to discuss the case among themselves or with others until all the evidence has been presented. At that time, they are asked to make a decision based on what they have seen and heard. The judge may permit jurors to take notes during the trial and to use their notes during deliberations.

What is the Actual Trial Procedure?

Actual trial procedure involves these parts:

- Selection of a jury
- Opening statements
- Presentation of the plaintiff's case
- Motions for directed verdict
- Presentation of the defendant's case
- Plaintiff's rebuttal
- Defendant's answer to plaintiff's rebuttal
- Closing arguments
- Instructions to the jury
- Jury verdict
- Post-trial motions

Selection of jury The right to trial by jury is guaranteed in federal courts for both civil and criminal cases by the Sixth and Seventh Amendments to the U.S. Constitution. Trial by jury in state criminal prosecutions is secured by the Fourteenth Amendment and state constitutions generally provide for jury trial in civil cases.

While the traditional jury was made up of twelve persons, a decision of the United States Supreme Court states that this is not an absolute requirement: "The fact that the jury at common law was composed of precisely twelve is an historical accident, unnecessary to effect the purposes of the jury system and wholly without significance except to mystics." Williams v. Florida, 399 U.S. 78, 102, 90 S.Ct. 1893, 26 L.Ed.2d 446 (1970). Subsequently, juries can be less than twelve in number. Still, by federal statute, the number of jurors in a *federal criminal case* is twelve, and the United States Supreme Court has said that due process requires at least six jurors in a state criminal case. Ballew v. Georgia, 435 U.S. 223, 98 S.Ct. 1029, 55 L.Ed.2d 234 (1978). Many of the federal district courts have converted to juries of fewer than twelve in civil cases, and a majority of states now authorizes such juries in some or all civil trials. Nor in all state courts is it necessary for juries to reach unanimous verdicts. Some state statutes authorize verdicts by five-sixths of the jury (e.g., ten out of twelve); others require three-fourths or a simple majority. In federal courts the jury must render a unanimous decision in a civil case unless the parties otherwise agree. Federal criminal cases require a unanimous verdict. State criminal convictions have been upheld where not unanimous as long as based on a substantial majority of the jury (Johnson v. Louisiana, 406 U.S. 356, 92 S.Ct. 1620, 32 L.Ed.2d 152 (1972), which upheld a 9–3 verdict). Where a state jury is as small as six persons, the guilty verdict must be unanimous.

Jurors are first selected from lists of eligible citizens—generally from voter rolls. Whatever the method of selection, it must be at random and from a fair cross-section of the community. If any religious, racial, political, or ethnic group is systematically excluded from jury panels, there is a denial of equal protection of the law; voter lists must be supplemented if such groups are underrepresented or if there is underrepresentation by reason of sex or economic status.

Every person who is called for jury service has a duty to serve. While many people are at first reluctant because of the inconvenience involved, those who do serve nearly always find it to be a challenging, worthwhile experience. Still, excuse from service is allowed upon proof of hardship (such as loss of a job or substantial income or need to be at home with small children). And certain persons such as attorneys (who would tend to monopolize juries) and doctors (who are needed more in their profession) are often exempt from jury duty by statute. Jurors are usually paid, but the pay is small. A typical fee is fifteen dollars or twenty dollars a day plus mileage to the courthouse.

A large panel of jurors is always called to the courthouse. When a case is assigned to a courtroom for trial, a smaller group of prospective jurors is sent to that room. Their names are written on slips of paper, dropped in a box, and shuffled. The clerk of the court then draws out a sufficient number of names to make up a panel, and, as the names are called, the individuals take their places in the jury box. The prospective jury members must next swear to give true answers to all questions asked of them in the qualifying examination. This is designed to discover possible prejudice.

This question and answer session is called the "voir dire" examination. In some places the judge asks all the questions, in others only the attorneys, and in some, both. If, after questioning a prospective juror, an attorney feels that the party is not qualified to serve on the jury, he or she can "challenge" the juror for "cause." This challenge may be made on the basis that the prospective juror is related to a party or has a financial interest in the case or for any other reason that likely would make the juror unable to make an impartial decision. The judge must agree that the juror is not impartial before he or she will dismiss him or her and call another juror.

In addition to challenges for cause, which are unlimited in number, each side may excuse a certain number of jurors without stating any reason whatsoever. These are called "peremptory" challenges, and the number, fixed by statute or court rule, usually ranges from two to six. In the federal courts, the number of peremptory challenges is three. If you are an attorney, it is a good practice not to use all of your peremptory challenges—once you use the last one, the next person called may be much worse than the juror just excused. The "voir dire" examination continues until a full jury is empaneled. The court may also require the appointment of alternate jurors to serve in the event a regular juror dies or becomes sick or disabled. Practice varies as to whether alternate jurors are excused before, or take part in, jury deliberations.

Opening statements After the jury has been selected, the attorneys make their opening statements. These are statements that give the jury an overall picture of the case. Each attorney states what he or she expects to prove and how. The plaintiff's attorney makes his or her opening statement first. The attorney for the defendant can usually elect to make his or her opening statement immediately after the plaintiff finishes, or he or she can wait until the plaintiff completes presentation of the plaintiff's entire case. If the attorney elects to wait, he or she will make the opening statement prior to presenting the case for the defense. Although opening statements are not properly regarded as evidence, they do provide the jury with the essential facts of each side's case: they "outline" the case and make it easy for the jury to follow the evidence as presented. Opening statements are of increased importance because they create the first impression in the minds of the jurors.

Presentation of the plaintiff's case In trial of a lawsuit, the party with the burden of proof has the right to both open and close. This means that he or she is both first to speak to the jury in presenting and proving his or her case, and last to speak to the jury in making closing arguments. The plaintiff almost always has the burden of proof since the plaintiff is the one asking for damages or other relief. But on rare occasions, the defendant's answer in the pleading stage of litigation admits every allegation in the plaintiff's complaint. It further alleges by way of defense some new matter that is subsequently denied by the plaintiff's reply. The defendant, in this case, has the burden of proof as to the new matter, and he or she will be first to speak since the plaintiff has nothing left to prove.

In the usual case, however, the plaintiff is first to prove the facts alleged in the complaint. The evidence is presented by examining witnesses and by producing documents or other exhibits. When a witness is called, he or she is first placed under oath (i.e., he or she promises to tell the truth) and then questioned about facts with which he or she is familiar. These answers help establish the plaintiff's version of the facts. This questioning process is called the "direct examination." After the plaintiff completes the direct examination, the other side is given an opportunity to ask questions, or "cross examine" the witness. If you are an attorney, it is good practice never to ask questions in cross-examination to which you do not know the answers. The purpose of cross-examination is to test what has just been said in direct; because of this, cross-examination is sometimes called the "truth finder." But poor cross-examinations can hurt your case badly when an adverse witness further describes or repeats earlier responses that were not in your favor. After the cross-examination, the party calling the witness has another opportunity to ask questions. This is called the "redirect examination." The opposing party may "re-cross"-examine; and the other party may "re-redirect" and so on until someone stops. The examination is limited in each case to what was previously discussed. Thus, cross-examination is limited to those matters raised in the direct examination; redirect is limited to matters raised on cross; re-cross is limited to matters raised on redirect; etc. (see figure 3–4).

FIGURE 3–4 TESTIMONY CONTINUALLY NARROWS

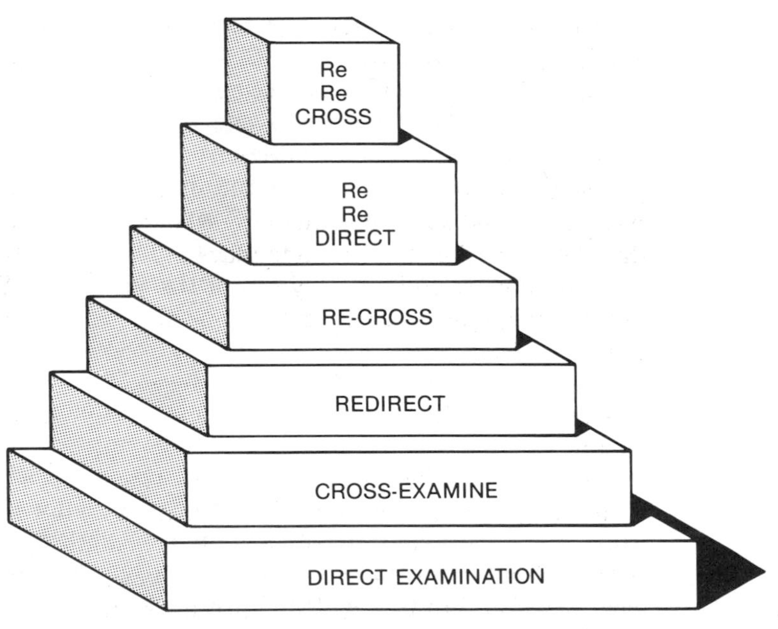

Witnesses may generally testify only as to matters they have actually observed. They may not give their opinions. But there is a very important exception to this rule—the use of the "expert" witness who is called specifically to give his or her opinion. The expert's testimony is often crucial to the lawyer's success and it is commonplace to use experts in all kinds of cases. To qualify as an expert witness, a person must possess substantial knowledge about a particular field or endeavor. This knowledge must be established in court. In one case, a paroled moonshiner was an expert witness—in another, a nuclear physicist. One famous expert, an entomologist (authority on bugs) was used in the so-called "coca-cola" cases where soft-drink bottlers were sued by consumers who found bugs in their beverages. In that kind of case, it was not difficult to prove that the company was liable: The question was—for how much? How much money should you recover if you drink a bug from a bottle of cola or uncola? The bug expert was asked if, in his opinion, a person would be badly hurt by eating a bug. The expert would explain that eating insects could be harmless. He would then take a live roach, pop it in his mouth, and chew it up. This, of course, graphically illustrated for the jury that the amount of money damages awarded should not be too high.

Medical doctors are frequently used in personal injury cases to give their opinions on the cause and extent of injury. Of course, both sides frequently present experts whose opinions contradict each other. When this happens, the differing opinions usually reflect genuine differences in professional points of view. Ultimately, the jury must decide which opinion is the correct one.

After presenting all his or her evidence, the plaintiff states that he or she has finished—that he or she "rests" the case.

Motion for directed verdict After the plaintiff rests his or her case, the defendant will frequently make a motion for a directed verdict. What the defendant is saying here is that the plaintiff has not proved his or her case and that, therefore, the plaintiff should lose. The judge must ask himself or herself whether or not the plaintiff could win at this point if further court proceedings were to cease. If the plaintiff could not win because he or she has not proved sufficient facts to do so, the judge will sustain the motion and direct the verdict for the defendant. The plaintiff will lose the case.

Say, for example, that you are the plaintiff. You are suing the defendant for negligently driving her car into yours. But when you finish your case, you have failed to prove that the defendant was driving the car at the time of the accident. Without such proof, you have no chance of winning the case, and the defendant's motion for directed verdict will be properly sustained by the judge.

The motion for directed verdict, then, resembles the demurrer in the pleading stage of litigation. Each says "so what?" to the plaintiff. The demurrer says "so what" to the complaint, claiming that the facts alleged, even if true, will not allow the plaintiff to win. The motion for directed verdict says "so what" to the evidence presented in court, asserting its insufficiency to win the case.

Presentation of the defendant's case If the motion for directed verdict is overruled, the defendant presents his or her evidence. He or she does this in the same manner as did the plaintiff with examination of witnesses, including experts, and presentation of documents and other exhibits. The plaintiff, of course, has the right to cross-examination and the defendant to redirect, etc. Also, the plaintiff may move for directed verdict against the defendant on the basis that the defendant's evidence was insufficient as a defense and the plaintiff should now win, without more, on the basis of the plaintiff's case. Assuming this motion is not granted, the case continues.

Plaintiff's rebuttal After the defendant has presented all of his or her evidence, the plaintiff may bring in rebuttal evidence.

Answer to plaintiff's rebuttal The defendant may bring in evidence to counter the rebuttal evidence to his or her case. Each side may contribute more evidence in this rebuttal/answer pattern until one side's evidence has been completely exhausted.

Closing arguments When all the evidence has been presented, the attorneys make closing arguments, or summations, to the jury. The plaintiff's attorney speaks first and last—he or she both opens the argument and closes it (the defendant's attorney argues in between). In the closing argument, the attorney for each side attacks his or her opponent's evidence for its unreliability. Each attorney may attempt to discredit his or her opponent's witnesses or may argue the case in words charged with emotion and eloquence. But each attorney must stay "within the record." That is, his or her arguments must be based upon facts supported by evidence introduced at the trial. Once the closing arguments are finished, it is time for jury instructions.

Instructions to the jury The jury bases its verdict on (1) the evidence presented at trial, and (2) the law as revealed in the judge's instructions to the jury on the rules, principles, and standards of the particular legal concept involved. In federal and most state courts, the jury instructions come after the closing arguments. In some state courts, the procedure is reversed, and the judge first instructs the jury before the closing arguments.

The verdict The jury reaches its verdict in the seclusion of the jury room. Once it is sent there to determine the verdict, it is "locked up." Jury members can no longer go home at night or even eat their meals alone. They must reach their verdict without outside contact; if they cannot agree by nighttime, they are provided with sleeping accommodations until they do agree. The verdict represents the jurors' agreement after detailed discussion and analysis. If the jury cannot agree upon a verdict after a reasonable period of time (usually several days), a mistrial will be declared, and a new trial ordered.

Once the verdict is reached, the jury is conducted back into court. The verdict is then delivered to the judge who reads it to the parties. At this time, it is common for the judge to "poll the jury" or ask each juror if the verdict is correct.

Post trial motions Obviously, error may occur in any trial. And if it does occur, the injured party has a right to appeal. The appellate stage of litigation is considered in the following section.

But before a party files for appeal, he or she may ask the judge who tried the case to grant a new trial. The party does this by filing a motion for a new trial within time limits prescribed by state or federal statute or by rules of the court. Under the Federal Rules of Civil Procedure, a motion for new trial must be filed within ten days of the entry of judgment.

The usual basis for requesting a new trial is that the verdict goes against the weight of the evidence. The judge will grant the new trial only if the evidence, as he or she views it, simply could not have resulted in the verdict reached by the jury. Or the judge may approve the jury's verdict but grant a "remittitur" which gives the plaintiff the option of either taking less in damages or of going through a new trial. Sometimes the judge will order a partial new trial which is restricted to redetermining the damages.

Of course, any legal error that will serve as grounds for an appeal will also serve as grounds for a motion for new trial. This includes erroneous jury instructions or erroneous judicial rulings in face of one party's objections to the admission of certain evidence. In this situation, however, the judge who made the ruling would have to agree that he or she was in error and that his or her error constitutes a basis for a new trial. This seldom occurs, and such questions are generally left to the appellate court for resolution.

What Are the Rules of Evidence?

The rules of evidence are designed to insure fair play in the courtroom by establishing which facts may or may not be presented to the jury. They make certain that disputes are settled according to the merits of the case. Having evolved over a long period of time, these rules may at first seem technical and difficult to understand. Their purpose, however, is a simple one—to allow the jury to hear only that evidence which is competent and relevant to the dispute. Rules of evidence seek to get at the truth by calm and careful reasoning; they strive to avoid decisions based on bias, prejudice, or irrelevant material.

The plaintiff must prove his or her case to the jury following these rules. This is called his or her burden of proof. The plaintiff does not have to prove the case beyond all doubt, however—only by a preponderance of the evidence (remember, we are dealing here with the civil action or controversy between private individuals, as opposed to the criminal case where the state must prove guilt beyond any reasonable doubt). The preponderance of the evidence in the civil case is the evidence that has greater weight and is most convincing in the minds of the jurors. To put it in percentage terms, this means proof by at least 51 percent. Or drawing a parallel to a game of basketball, a mere one-point win will satisfy your burden of proof. A famous lawyer once described the burden of proof in a civil action as that little amount of weight necessary to tip the scales of justice. He then held out his hands like a scale and said that all the plaintiff needs to do is tip the scale the tiniest little bit.

Many rules of evidence are rather rigid and restrictive. These are applied to protect the jury from hearing improper evidence.

You already know that the ordinary witness cannot give his or her opinion in court. Only the "expert" may do so. Jury verdicts should not be based on nonexpert opinions. Nor may the attorney prompt a witness by asking him or her a "leading question." A leading question is one that either contains the answer in the question, suggests the answer the attorney wants to hear, or is a question that can be answered yes or no. A leading question is unfair because it gives the witness a hint of the answer desired—it removes spontaneity from his or her courtroom response. And such a programmed response is not good proof in court. But while an attorney may not lead his or her own witnesses, leading questions are always allowed in cross-examination.

Hearsay evidence is not admissible because it is not based on the personal knowledge of the witness. Rather, the witness is testifying about a statement made by another person. Since that person is not present to be cross-examined, the hearsay statement may not come into court. Cross-examination is a basic right—the right to confrontation. You have a right to confront the witnesses against you and to cross-examine them about their testimony.

Only relevant evidence may be introduced in court. If you are suing someone for breach of contract because he or she sold you a bad TV-stereo, the fact that he or she once went through bankruptcy or was jailed three times for drunk driving is not relevant. It is not admissible as evidence. Such evidence might prompt the jurors to decide against the defendant, not because he or she breached the contract but because they are prejudiced against him or her.

Another rule of evidence is based on "privileged communication." These are confidential communications (made between persons in certain relationships) that do not have to be disclosed in court. Thus private communications between husband and wife, doctor and patient, clergy and penitent, and attorney and client are "privileged" by law in order that parties may speak freely without fear that their statements will be subsequently used against them.

The "best evidence" rule requires an attorney who refers to a written document, contract, or other writing to produce that writing as a courtroom exhibit. He or she may not simply tell about the writing in court.

Additional rules prevent the admission of certain evidence to the jury. For instance, if a defendant has liability insurance that covers negligent conduct, evidence of this fact is not admissible in court. If it were admissible, the jurors might find against the defendant because they know that the insurance company and not the defendant will pay the final judgment.

There are too many rules of evidence to cover all of them in this chapter. Just remember that all rules of evidence are designed to keep the jury from hearing evidence that is:

1. Irrelevant and immaterial to the facts at issue;
2. Repetitious of evidence already admitted;
3. Unreliable or not easily testable by cross-examination;

4. In violation of certain confidential relationships;
5. Or otherwise likely to influence or prejudice the jurors and cause them to decide the case on reasons other than its merits.

Remember, too, that the trial is an adversary proceeding. If the other side's attorney fails to object to the introduction of incompetent or prejudicial evidence, the jury will hear that evidence. It is up to the parties, through proper objections, to insure that the rules of evidence are faithfully followed.

WHAT IS THE APPELLATE PART OF THE CIVIL ACTION?

If one party believes that an error of law was made during the trial but is unable to convince the judge on post-trial motion that a new trial should be granted, he or she has a right to appeal to a higher court of law. The most common grounds for appeal include judicial errors in admitting evidence that should have been excluded (such as hearsay or privileged communication), or in refusing to admit evidence that should have been heard, or in failing to give proper jury instructions.

While appellate procedure may vary from state to state, the basic steps are as follows:

1. The lawyer lays the groundwork for appeal by objecting in trial at the time the error occurs. His objection makes the record if he or she later decides to appeal.
2. The appeal must be filed within prescribed time limits. Under the Federal Rules of Civil Procedure, notice of appeal must be filed within thirty days of the entry of judgment.
3. The appellant (the party who lost the case in the trial court and is now appealing) must serve notice of appeal on the respondent. He or she must also file a bond guaranteeing payment of the respondent's costs on appeal in case the judgment of the trial court is affirmed.
4. The entire record of the trial court must next be reduced to writing. The court reporter, who took down every word during the trial, transcribes his or her notes and prepares a complete trial transcript. This procedure may be very costly. Also included in the written record are the pleadings, verdict, and judgment. The appellate court, which neither hears from witnesses nor uses trial court procedure, will study the written record in great detail.
5. Written briefs are prepared by the attorneys for both sides. The appellant files the first brief, which is answered by the respondent's brief, which, in turn, may be replied to by the appellant. These briefs contain the parties' arguments as to why the case should be reversed or affirmed. The parties support their arguments with authority—cases and statutes urged by the attorneys as precedent for deciding the case in their respective favors.
6. In additon to reading the briefs, the appellate court listens to oral arguments from the attorneys. Each attorney is allotted a certain amount of time, ranging from thirty to sixty minutes, to get his or her points across. During that time, the appellate court judges question the attorneys about their positions.

7. After the oral arguments are completed, the judges retire to their chambers to take a vote of first impression. Based on this vote, the case is assigned by the chief judge to himself or herself or to one of the other judges for preparation of an opinion.

8. The finished opinion, which may take several weeks to prepare, is circulated among all the appellate court judges. If approved, it becomes the official opinion of the court. Judges who disagree may write dissenting opinions. Judges who agree for different reasons may write concurring opinions.

9. The opinion is announced. The losing party may then ask for a rehearing to try to convince the court that its conclusion is erroneous. If the rehearing is denied, the decision becomes final.

10. The appellate court decision is then sent to the trial court for enforcement. The lower court must either enforce its earlier verdict or hold a new trial. If it holds a new trial, the resulting verdict may also be appealed. And, as you saw from the previous chapter, there are several occasions where it is possible to appeal the decision of an appellate court to a higher court of appeal.

Appellate court decisions are important not only to the parties involved but to the entire United States legal system, for these decisions provide precedents for future cases. And it is here in the appellate court procedure that reasoning by example occurs. This reasoning applies, strengthens, changes, and establishes new precedent and principles of law. Many factors, such as history and custom, enter into this reasoning process. At times, the result desired is an important factor, and judges will decide that certain precedents must be overruled because changing times and increased social pressure demand a new result. Over the years, the needs and feelings of the people may change. The law must reflect these changes. We see this in many areas of law including civil rights, consumer protection, and environmental law.

WHAT IS MEANT BY RES JUDICATA?

Once a case is decided, appealed, and no further appeal is available, it would not make sense to allow the parties to start all over again. For this reason, a judgment is said to be final once all possibility of further appeal is gone. The matter cannot be considered again. This is the meaning of res judicata—literally, that the thing has been decided. As a principle of law, it means that a final decision in a civil action is conclusive. Further suits involving the same question of law between the same parties may not take place.

HOW IS THE FINAL JUDGMENT IN A CIVIL ACTION ENFORCED?

Suppose you receive a final judgment awarding you money damages against a defendant, but the defendant refuses to pay. How can you enforce the judgment?

Your first step is to obtain a writ of execution from the court. This writ is a routine court order that directs the appropriate officer (usually the sheriff) to take and sell as much of the defendant's property as is necessary to pay the judgment. The sheriff will sell the property at a public sale and deliver the proceeds to you. If the sale brings more than enough to cover the judgment, the balance goes to the defendant. All states have statutes excepting certain property from execution so that defendants will not lose everything. Defendants are typically allowed to keep clothes, tools, living quarters, and part of their current earnings. If a defendant does not have enough property to cover the judgment, he or she may file for bankruptcy and forever eliminate the judgment. On the other hand, if you cannot collect all of your judgment at the present time you may wait and collect it later when the defendant acquires property by work, inheritance, or otherwise. A judgment generally lasts for a long period of time—such as ten years by statute. And it can be renewed for additional periods of time.

WHAT IS THE DIFFERENCE BETWEEN MONEY ACTIONS AND EQUITY SUITS?

One final item must be added to a consideration of court power or jurisdiction, and that is the distinction between law and equity. Our system is based to a great extent on the legal system existing in England prior to the War for Independence. We inherited many rules of English law as well as a system of courts from which to begin and develop. The English law courts were established on a national scale by King Henry II at a time when life was more simple and justice quite crude. All power rested with the king who decided that the only way a person could use the courts was to buy a writ from him and present it to the court, which then had a duty to hear the case. Over a period of some 200 years extending into the sixteenth century, the English courts became very restrictive as to what cases they would consider. Personal, political, and civil rights as we understand them were not recognized. The final result was a peculiar one: no person could bring a case to prevent an injury to his or her property but only to obtain money damages for an injury already suffered. Monetary damages was the only relief available (the awarding of money damages has become known as "the remedy at law"). The law courts refused to require performance of any duty. They refused to issue an injunction (an order requiring a person to stop doing something or commanding him or her to perform a certain act). You can see that if someone was constantly burning stinking rubbish in his or her yard or trespassing on your property or calling you on the phone all night every night to keep you awake, you would want something more than money damages. You would want it stopped!

And that was the situation in England. When people needed other kinds of relief, they asked the all-powerful king for help. They based their requests on what was known as the "king's prerogative of grace"—an arbitrary power of the king to do good and dispense justice. They could not talk directly to the king so they did so through his Chancellor (the king's secretary) whose position originally corresponded more or less to that of the present English prime minister.

The Chancellor gave so many forms of relief that he finally became a judge and his department a court. Over the years, the High Court of Chancery developed into a very large system of courts existing separately from the courts of law. The rule of the Chancery Court was to provide relief when the remedy at law (money damages) was inadequate and to do always what was then considered right, just, and good. That is what equity means—giving justice and doing right. And that is why these separate courts became known as courts of equity.

Generally, in the United States, separate courts of law and equity were not established. *Each court, however, has the powers of both the law and equity courts of England.* Thus, each court is said to be hearing either an action at law or a suit in equity depending on what type of relief or damage the plaintiff asks for. If only money is requested, then the court is acting as a law court and will give only monetary relief. The last several sections of this chapter have dealt with the procedure used by the law court to determine whether money damages should be awarded. If someone wants other than money relief—injunction, specific performance, protection against patent infringement, stopping a nuisance or continued annoyance, etc.—then the court takes jurisdiction in equity and will grant a decree (not a judgment) ordering acts to be done or not to be done. The next section will describe the procedure of the equity court. Both actions at law and suits in equity involve private law—that is, cases brought between individuals as opposed to criminal cases where the state attempts to prove someone guilty of a crime and where the procedure involved is quite different.

WHAT PROCEDURE DOES A COURT OF EQUITY FOLLOW?

When the plaintiff asks for something other than money, the court must apply the principles of equity. When this occurs, there are several procedural changes in the four stages of litigation.

1. Pleading procedure is the same in equity as in the civil case for money. The complaint, answer, reply, demurrer, and motion to dismiss determine the facts at issue and set the boundary lines for dispute. Since the court does not apply rules of equity unless the remedy at law is inadequate, the plaintiff generally alleges this insufficiency in his or her complaint and spells out the other specific relief to which he or she feels entitled.

The defendant, in turn, objects to equity jurisdiction by answering that the remedy at law is adequate. Or he or she can file a demurrer or motion to dismiss the case.

So whenever you want to stop someone from doing something, such as, for example, trespassing on your land, you must allege in your complaint that money damage is insufficient—that you need an injunction commanding the defendant to stop what he or she is doing.

2. Discovery at law and in equity are exactly the same.
3. Trial follows the same orderly procedure but with several significant distinctions.

First, there is no jury. The judge decides the facts and applies the law accordingly. Determination of the proper remedy is left to his or her discretion.

Second, since there is no jury, the rules of evidence are substantially relaxed. The judge's legal training allows him or her to admit hearsay or otherwise irrelevant evidence and still differentiate between the competent and the incompetent. As a result, lawyers make fewer objections, and considerably more evidence is allowed into court.

Third, the judge applies equitable "maxims" or rules in an effort to do what is right, just, and best under the circumstances of the case. These maxims are often called rules of conscience. A well-known one is "Equity aids the vigilant." This means that a person who seeks equitable relief must do so quickly. For example, a statute of limitations may give you up to two years to bring a case based on tort. If the tort is nuisance (for instance, your neighbor annoys you by continually burning rubbish in his backyard), you will have two years' time in which to bring a civil action for money. But if you want an equitable injunction to stop the nuisance, you must be vigilant and ask for it soon after the nuisance begins. If you fail to do so, the court may refuse to grant the injunction. "He who comes into equity must do so with clean hands." Thus if a person is equally at fault, he cannot seek assistance based on the rules of conscience. For example, if you are burning rubbish in your own backyard, you cannot expect a court of equity to prohibit your neighbor from doing the same thing. "Equity assists ignorance but not carelessness." Nor will courts help the simply careless. If you are educated in the law but permit someone to take advantage of you because you are careless, you will get no help. But say you ignorantly sell an antique worth $10,000 for $100. The equity court might order the buyer to return your antique. It would be unconscionable not to do so.

Fourth, the judge in an equity suit issues a decree (as opposed to a judgment in a civil action for money). Since the decree calls for something other than the payment of money, it obviously cannot be enforced by selling the defendant's property. If the defendant refuses to comply with the order, the judge will hold him or her in "contempt of court" and fine or imprison him or her. So if your neighbor continues to burn rubbish after an injunction commands him to stop, he may well be fined or put in jail for a day, a week, or a month to force his compliance.

Fifth, a court will often issue an interlocutory or temporary injunction as soon as suit is filed. Immediate relief is granted even before a hearing on the merits of the case, because the court decides that the complained of conduct should not continue while the case is being heard. These preliminary injunctions are always under the control and discretion of the court and may be modified or dissolved at any time. Such injunctions are frequently made final if the court's decision on the merits is in favor of the plaintiff. But even a final or permanent injunction may be modified or dissolved as changed circumstances or conditions require. The principle of res judicata does not apply to the equitable decree or injunction, because such decrees or injunctions are not necessarily the final word in the case and, on further review, they may be modified.

WHAT IS DIVORCE PROCEDURE?

We pointed out earlier that much of our law is based on early English law. We inherited the English doctrines of law and equity, and although we did not create courts of law and equity as they existed in England, procedural differences do exist between our civil action for money damages and our civil action for equitable relief.

Our divorce law, too, is derived from the English and a little historical background brings to light several procedural differences here as well. After the Norman Conquest in 1066, the power to regulate marriage was placed in the hands of the Christian Church. Canon or church law controlled the marriage relationship, and ecclesiastical courts ruled on the validity of marriage and granted annulments and divorces sparingly. While ecclesiastical courts were never established in America and although English divorce law and procedure were not as fully embraced by our courts as were the doctrines of law and equity, the ecclesiastical law still has had its impact. The traditional grounds for divorce, such as adultery and cruelty, come from church law as well as do such traditional defenses to divorce as condonation (forgiveness—since the pardon of sins was considered intrinsically good) and recrimination (i.e., where both spouses had grounds for divorce, neither could get one—justified as a means of preserving marriage and families).

Many decisions, however, place divorce in the equity courts and rely upon equitable precedents to determine procedure. Still other courts state that divorce is primarily statutory. As a result, divorce law and procedure is a blend of equity, ecclasiastical law, and statutory law. Much of what we have described as civil and equitable procedure applies, therefore, to divorce. But there are some significant distinctions:

1. Minors may bring and defend divorce actions. In some jurisdictions, a guardian must be appointed to protect the minor's interests. In others, he or she is considered to have full legal capacity by reason of the marriage.

2. The defendant in a divorce action can be served by publication if the plaintiff seeks only dissolution of the marriage. But if he or she asks for alimony, child support, or division of the property, then personal service is required.

3. Federal courts have no jurisdiction to grant divorces or award alimony. But they may enforce alimony and property decrees rendered by state courts where there is diversity of citizenship and more than $10,000 involved.

4. Statutes generally require a "cooling off" period to encourage marital reconciliation. The parties must wait from twenty days to six months after filing the complaint before the court will hear the divorce and grant a decree dissolving the marriage.

5. But immediately from the time of filing for divorce, the court may grant preliminary or temporary injunctions to protect parties from harm or harassment, to provide temporary support, or even to prevent someone's departure from the state. So where either spouse has acted violently or has threatened to do so, the court may issue a preventive injunction.

6. There is no such thing as a default divorce in the normal sense of that term. Evidence showing that the plaintiff is entitled to a decree must always be presented even though the defendant does not appear to defend.

7. The privilege for confidential communications between husband and wife usually does not apply in divorce actions between spouses.

8. Divorce decrees are frequently interlocutory or temporary. They do not become final for a period of time varying from thirty days to one year. In a number of states the parties may not remarry during this time.

9. Most states have residency requirements for divorce stating that no person may file suit unless he or she has lived within the state for a period of at least ninety days to one year.

10. To prevent great hardship to either party, the court may modify alimony and child support decrees because of changed conditions. Res judicata applies only insofar as it relates to dissolution of the marriage. If the ex-spouse's income declines after the divorce and he or she is materially less able to pay the support, the payments may be reduced. On the other hand, if income substantially increases an ex-spouse may be entitled to a larger sum (if increased support is necessary to maintain him or her at the standard of living to which he or she became accustomed during the marriage).

The growing trend in more recent divorce legislation is toward the so-called "no fault" divorce laws. More than three-fourths of the states have passed such laws. These laws eliminate the traditional grounds for divorce. Parties need show only that "irreconcilable differences" exist between them and that these differences have "caused the irremediable breakdown of marriage." The quoted provisions are from the Oregon No Fault Divorce Law passed in 1971 which additionally states that "the court shall not receive evidence of specific acts of misconduct excepting where child custody is an issue and such evidence is relevant to that issue, or excepting at a hearing when the court finds such evidence necessary to prove irreconcilable differences." Nor may fault of the parties be considered in determining alimony, child support, or settlement of property. Oregon law does not even require the defendant to appear in court; he or she need only file a written answer to the plaintiff's petition. In other words, no fault laws put an end to the adversary nature of divorce proceedings where one spouse was required to show the other guilty of bad conduct. Fault is at issue only when a dispute arises over custody of the children or over the existence of irreconcilable differences. This greatly simplifies divorce procedure and effectively eliminates the outrageous influence of ecclasiastical dogmatism and the resulting bitterness when one spouse must accuse the other in court.

WHAT PROCEDURE APPLIES TO PROBATE CASES?

The legal concept of "probate" involves two unique problems: the administration of a dead person's estate, and guardianships and conservatorships. We consider each separately.

Estates

Our legal system recognizes a person's right to dispose of his or her property as he or she wishes. If an individual leaves a valid will at death, the courts will enforce it. But if he or she leaves no will, the property will pass according to the laws of intestacy to the nearest surviving relatives—first, to his or her spouse and children; if none, to parents; and if neither—to brothers and sisters. If a person dies without a will and without living relatives, then the property "escheats" or passes to the state in which he or she resides. This is because there is no living relative to inherit the property (state statutes gen-

FIGURE 3-5 TYPICAL LIMITS OF INTESTATE SUCCESSION

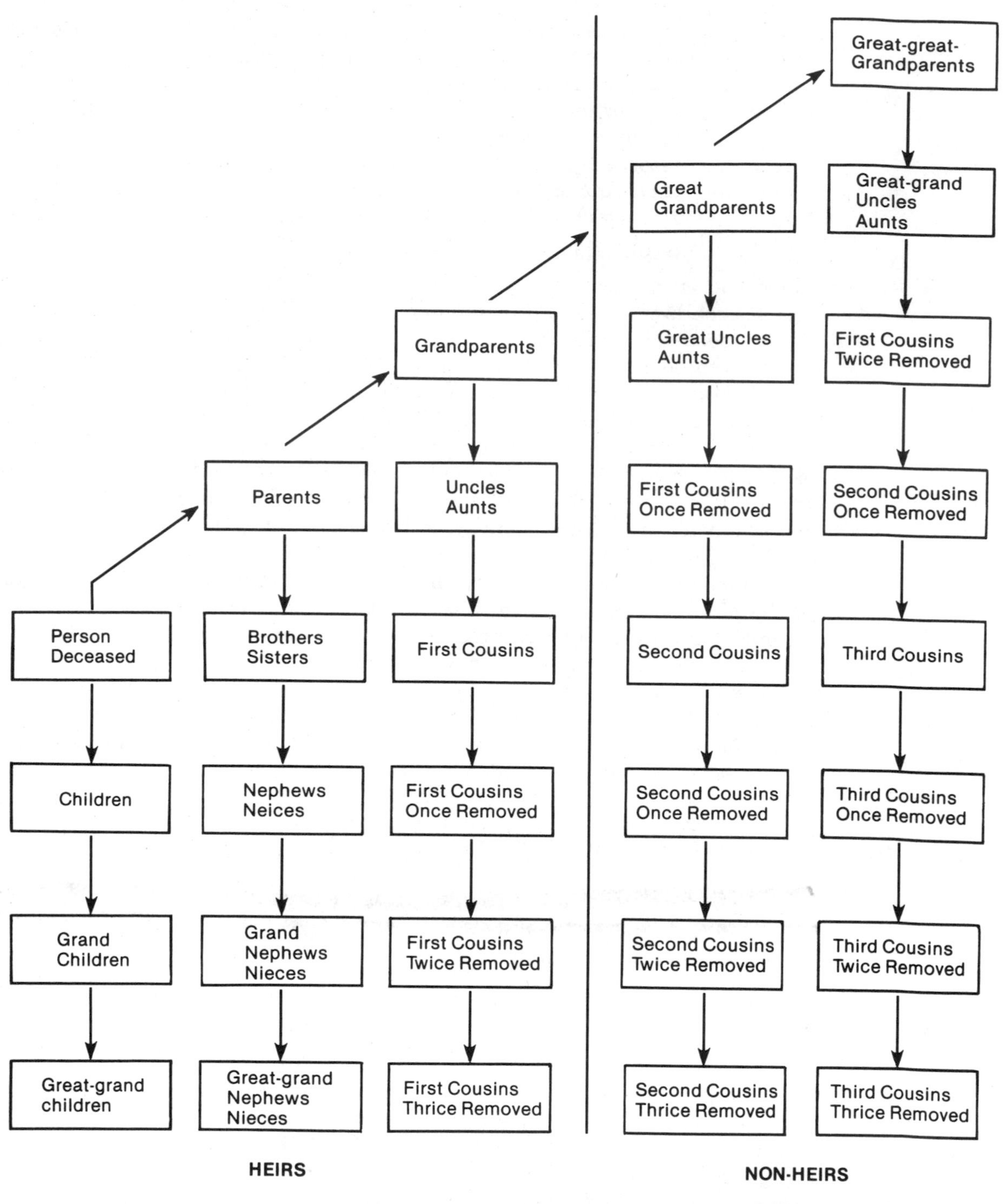

erally cut off the more remote relatives from inheriting, such as second cousins or great uncles and aunts).

In figure 3–5 note that the deceased's property will go first to children, then to grandchildren, then to great-grandchildren. It is only when there are none of these that the property will go to those listed in the second column, brothers and sisters, etc. And it is only when there are no living relatives in any of the first three columns that the property will escheat to the state. Individuals in the fourth and fifth columns are not closely enough related to be classified as heirs.

Note further that a wife or husband is not an "heir" because a spouse is not a blood relative. However, a wife or husband does receive the decedent's property—generally all of it if there are no children and half of it if there are children—if the decedent dies intestate.

Property seldom escheats to the state. Most people do have surviving relatives who receive their properties even in the absence of a will. And, of course, if there is a will, its provisions will be followed by the probate court, with one exception: a married person cannot prevent his or her surviving spouse from receiving a share of the property by leaving it all to someone else in a will. Statutes generally allow the spouse to contest the will and receive up to one-half of the deceased spouse's property.

Consider the following situation. A father dies and is survived by his wife, an unmarried daughter, and two grandchildren (the children of a daughter who predeceased him). The deceased may have a will leaving all his property to his wife or one-half to his wife and one-half to his daughter or grandchildren—that is, to any person or in any manner the deceased desired. If he has no will, state statute determines who gets the property. These statutes differ, but a typical one might provide the distribution of property illustrated in figure 3–6 when the decedent dies intestate.

FIGURE 3–6 A TYPICAL DISTRIBUTION OF PROPERTY

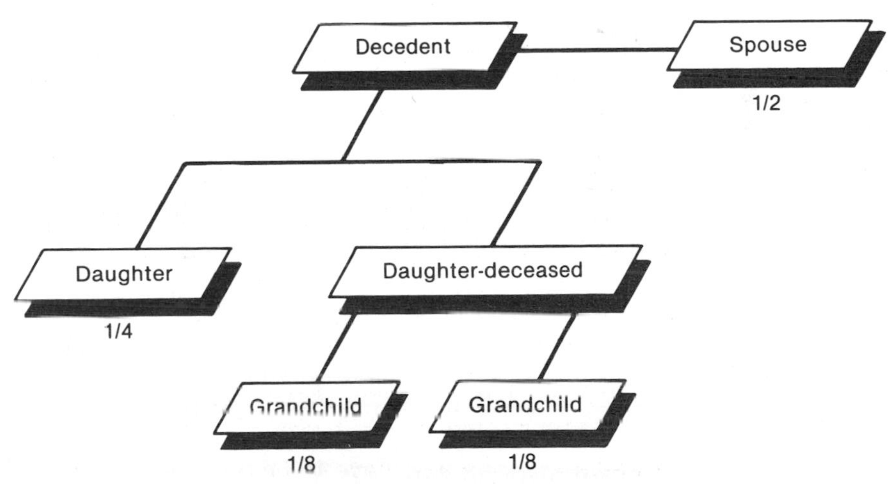

The main purpose of probate procedure is to get the decedent's property to its rightful owners. Say your father dies without a will. As his only living relative, you are entitled to his $10,000 savings account. But how do you get it? If you go down to the bank and proclaim your rights, the bank cannot give you the money because it has no way of knowing if your claim is a legal one. To obtain the money, you must follow regular probate procedure. This procedure safeguards the decedent's property—it protects those persons named by will or, if there is no will, those who take under the laws of intestate succession. Additionally protected are the decedent's creditors and government bodies claiming death or income taxes payable from the property.

The following is a brief summary of specific probate procedure:

1. A petition is first filed in the court with appropriate probate jurisdiction. Generally, the trial court of general jurisdiction handles probate matters. The petition contains:

a. The decedent's name, age, address, date and place of death, social security number, etc.;

b. Whether he or she died testate (with a will) or intestate (without a will);

c. Name and address of the person who will administer the estate (called the executor if there is a will and the administrator if there is no will or in some states "the personal representative" for either);

d. Names, relationships, and addresses of the heirs; and

e. Extent and nature of the assets.

2. If there is a will, proof of its validity must be furnished.

3. Upon appointment of the personal representative (executor or administrator), the estate is issued a number and formally opened as a legal entity.

4. The personal representative must notify the heirs that the estate has been opened.

5. Publication must be made in the decedent's county newspaper (e.g., once in each of four consecutive weeks). This gives creditors an opportunity to file claims, and they usually have from four to six months to do so.

6. The personal representative next files an inventory of the decedent's assets. Appraisal of the assets is frequently required.

7. Temporary support for spouse or children may be provided.

8. Claims, expenses, debts, and taxes are paid. If necessary, some properties will be sold to effect payment.

9. The remaining properties are distributed to the proper persons.

10. Accountings that show the following information are generally required:

a. The time covered;

b. Value of the inventoried property;

c. All money or property received during the period covered;

d. All disbursements made during this period;

e. A statement that taxes have been paid. (Estates are taxable entities that pay income taxes on income earned during administrations, and death taxes may also have to be paid—see Chapter 12.)

11. The estate is closed.

Guardianships and Conservatorships

The purpose of probate is to distribute the decedent's assets to his or her heirs free from the claims of creditors and as quickly as possible. The guardianship or conservatorship is created not for a dead person's estate but to protect and manage the property of a living person who cannot do it for himself or herself. A person may be too young, too old, or too ill to handle his or her own property. A person with such an incapacity is called a "ward." The guardian or conservator of the ward's property or estate must protect, preserve, and manage the estate and apply its proceeds toward the proper care of the ward and those persons to whom the ward owes a legal duty of support. Unlike probate procedure, which is concluded as rapidly as possible, the duties of the guardian or conservator continue as long as the ward remains incapacitated.

Guardians and conservators are very similar to court-appointed guardians for minors, incompetents, spendthrifts, or missing persons with property. A spendthrift is generally defined as a person whose excessive drinking, idleness, gambling, or debauchery spends, wastes, or so lessens his or her estate that the person or the person's family are exposed to want or suffering. An incompetent is any person who is unable to take care of himself or herself or his or her property for any reason, including mental illness, advanced age, and disease.

The term conservator applies to a person who is appointed upon petition of the ward himself or herself. In this case, the ward is mentally competent but feels unable to properly care for his or her property or business. The reasons may be physical, mental, or emotional.

Both guardians and conservators are closely supervised by the probate judge to make certain the ward's property is adequately protected. Both are concerned with the care, preservation, management, and disposition of the ward's estate.

Occasionally, a guardian is appointed to represent a ward in a single legal proceeding. He or she is called a guardian ad litem. For example, the interests of a minor or incompetent must be represented and protected by a guardian ad litem. So if a minor is injured in a car accident because of the defendant's negligence, the probate court must appoint a guardian ad litem to represent the minor before the case can even be filed on the minor's behalf.

WHAT IS CRIMINAL PROCEDURE?

A criminal conviction results in extremely grave consequences for the convicted individual who may be locked in jail for months, years, or for life. The criminal may even be sentenced to death if the statute providing for the death penalty meets the test of constitutionality. The law of criminal procedure is designed to protect the innocent from these harsh measures—from conviction, imprisonment, or death—even if some of the guilty go free as a result. True, the innocent are at times convicted, and certainly, this bias in their favor does permit many guilty persons to escape judgment altogether. But this is not a bad result! In a free society, it is more important to guarantee that those of us who do not commit crime are not arrested, convicted, and sent to jail than it is to put away those who do. The primary purpose of the rules of criminal procedure, then, is to insure the integrity and reliability of criminal trial.

Criminal procedure is perhaps best understood when divided into these three parts:

1. The burden of proof;
2. Obtaining the evidence; and
3. The actual procedural treatment of the defendant from time of arrest through appeal.

The Burden of Proof

"You are innocent until proved guilty." This well-known phrase accurately states a basic precept of our criminal law—a person charged with crime is presumed innocent under the law. It is up to the government to prove his or her guilt beyond a reasonable doubt. Section 1096 of the California Penal Code defines "reasonable doubt" as follows:

> It is not a mere possible doubt, because everything relating to human affairs, and depending on moral evidence, is open to some possible or imaginary doubt. It is that state of the case, which, after the entire comparison and consideration of all the evidence, leaves the minds of jurors in condition that they cannot say they feel an abiding conviction, to a moral certainty, of the truth of the charge.

Thus the prosecution must present strong evidence that creates within the mind of the jury an "abiding conviction to a moral certainty" that the person charged with crime has actually committed it. This degree of proof is much greater than the "mere preponderance" of the evidence required in the civil action for money damages (where just a bare tipping of the scales or a "one-point win" is sufficient).

Obtaining the Evidence

Law enforcement officials may not use just any method to obtain their evidence. There are several rules, constitutional in origin, that limit their sphere of action, and make certain that police tactics do not infringe upon our basic rights to privacy and freedom from harassment. Some of the more important safeguards are concerned with: searches and seizures, obtaining confessions, entrapment, and methods of identification.

Searches and seizures The Fourth Amendment of the United States Constitution states:

> The right of the people to be secure in their persons, houses, papers, and effects, against unreasonable searches and seizures, shall be not violated, and no warrants shall issue, but upon probable cause, supported by oath or affirmation, and particularly describing the place to be searched, and the person or things to be seized.

While evidence obtained during an unlawful search cannot be used in criminal prosecution (the Exclusionary Rule), a search and seizure authorized by a search warrant is a "reasonable search," and any evidence of the crime obtained from the search is admissible in court. Rule 41 of the Federal Rules of Criminal Procedure (the federal statute governing criminal prosecutions in federal courts) sets down the following procedure for obtaining a search warrant from a federal court:

1. Any judge within the district where the property to be searched is located may issue the warrant if he or she believes there is probable cause for doing so.
2. However, a warrant may be issued to search for and seize only:
   a. Property stolen in violation of federal law; or
   b. Property intended to be used or which has been used to commit a criminal offense.
3. The warrant must be executed and the search conducted within ten days of its issue date.

State procedure for obtaining a warrant is similar, though the grounds for issuing may be broader. But in addition to search by warrant, a state police officer who makes an arrest because he or she believes a crime has been or is being committed may conduct a search to protect himself or herself from hidden weapons and to prevent destruction of evidence. This includes "frisking" the suspect and searching an area into which the suspect might reach to grab a gun or destroy evidence. Also items in "plain view" and known to be evidence of a crime may be seized. Finally, a person who freely consents to a search cannot object when evidence found in the search is later used against him or her in court.

Confessions The Fifth Amendment of the Constitution states that "no person shall be compelled in any criminal case to be a witness against himself." The Fourteenth Amendment provides that a person's life, liberty, or property cannot be taken away without "due process of law." Construed together by the U. S. Supreme Court, these two amendments prevent the use of involuntary or coerced confessions in criminal trials. If a confession is not the result of a free and rational choice, it is coerced and, therefore, not admissible. And in the case of *Miranda v. Arizona* (see Chapter 1), the court held that "prior to any questioning the person must be warned that he has a right to remain silent, that any statement he does make may be used as evidence against him, and that he has a right to the presence of an attorney."

Entrapment—the use of informers Law enforcement officers often operate under cover or use paid informers to gather evidence and detect crime. This is especially true in crimes of vice involving two willing participants—e.g., narcotics, prostitution, and gambling. These crimes are difficult to control because there is usually no complaining victim. But use of informers and undercover agents can easily result in police abuse where the agent or informer induces the criminal conduct just to obtain a conviction. The police are guilty of entrapment when they cause someone to commit a crime by implanting the criminal idea in his or her mind. While there is nothing wrong with setting traps for persons bent on crime, the law does not allow police officers to instigate the crime itself. The courts ask whether the crime was the result of creative activity by the police which trapped an innocent person who was not otherwise predisposed to commit the crime. When a defendant asserts entrapment as a defense, the police may dispute him or her by introducing evidence of prior convictions for similar offenses in order to show a predisposition to commit the crime. Providing an opportunity to commit a crime to someone predisposed to commit it is not entrapment. That is why the undercover policewoman does not entrap a defendant who approaches her believing her to be a prostitute. The defendant is clearly predisposed to commit the crime.

Identification procedures Various procedures are used to identify a suspect as the person who committed the crime. While it does not violate the rights of an accused to make him or her stand in a "line-up," or say certain words, or put on special clothes that fit police descriptions of the criminal, the identification process must not be so unfair as to violate "due process." For example, it is unfair to draw attention to a very tall suspect by placing him or her in a line-up with very short men or women. This violates due process of law.

Once a person has been formally charged with a crime, the Supreme Court recognizes his or her right to have an attorney present during the identification line-up. This right, however, does not extend to the taking of fingerprints, handwriting exemplars, blood samples, or to the identification of the defendant from mug shots. And taking these samples does not violate the Fifth Amendment mandate that "no person shall be compelled in any criminal case to be a witness against himself."

The Actual Procedural Treatment of the Defendant from Time of Arrest through Appeal

From the time of arrest through appeal, the procedural treatment of a defendant involves the following:

- Pretrial procedure (similar in time to the pleading and discovery stage of the civil action), including arrest, arraignment, and certain special procedures;
- The trial—especially important because of the defendant's many constitutional rights that must be safeguarded;
- Judgment, sentencing, and treatment of the convicted person;
- Postconviction procedures; and
- Special rules and procedures dealing with criminal cases.

Pretrial procedure

Arrest A person is arrested when he or she is taken into custody to answer for the commission of a crime. This is the starting point of criminal procedure. A police officer commonly makes an arrest pursuant to an arrest warrant. But he or she can arrest a person without a warrant if the officer *reasonably believes* that the person has committed a felony (a private citizen can make the arrest if the person has *actually committed* a felony and either a police officer or a private citizen may arrest without a warrant any person who has *actually committed* a misdemeanor or has attempted to commit one in the presence of the citizen or officer, e.g., the shoplifter caught in the act).

A warrant for arrest may be obtained in one of two ways. First is by grand jury indictment. A grand jury is not like the fact-finding jury of a trial court. Rather, it is a "board of inquiry" that decides only if sufficient evidence exists to arrest someone for commission of a crime. In other words, the grand jury investigates or listens to evidence presented by the prosecutor (the district attorney, attorney general, or United States attorney, depending on the jurisdiction involved) and decides whether or not someone should be indicted. An indictment (also called a "true bill") is a formal written accusation that a person has committed a crime. It is signed by the foreman of the grand jury and is based on the jury's vote to indict. If the accused has not been taken into custody at the time of indictment, the judge issues a warrant for his or her arrest. This warrant is presented to the police officer who makes the actual arrest. Although the warrant's authority is confined to the territorial limit of the state in which it is issued, most states have adopted "Fresh Pursuit" statutes that allow police officers from one state to enter another when in fresh pursuit of a suspected felon (i.e., the officers must intend to arrest the person for a felony committed in the first state). A felony is generally defined as any crime punishable by death, by term of imprisonment exceeding one year, or by imprisonment in the state prison as opposed to a county or city jail. Any other crime is a misdemeanor (see Chapter 4). And where a person is accused of a mere misdemeanor, the police may not cross state lines to apprehend him or her. Even the person arrested for a felony must be "extradited" or brought back to the state where the crime took place. To accomplish this, the governor of that state must make formal demand upon the governor of the other state for the accused felon's return. Any crime is an extraditable offense.

When the police make an arrest without indictment by a grand jury (in which case a warrant was either obtained by some other method, or there was no warrant at all), the prosecutor in most states has an option to use the grand jury indictment anyway—and frequently does so. The grand jury meets to determine whether the accused has "probably" committed the crime even though he or she has already been taken into custody. Grand jury hearings are required in all federal felony cases by the Fifth Amendment of the Constitution which states: "No person shall be held to answer for a capital or otherwise infamous crime, unless on presentment or indictment of a Grand Jury."

A second method for obtaining a warrant is to file a complaint before a judge showing probable cause for arrest. A complaint is a sworn written statement by the police officer charging the offense and is based on his or her own observations and evidence. Once the complaint and arrest are made, the prosecutor may proceed with a hearing before the grand jury for an indictment or may make a formal written accusation of the crime called an "information." Like an indictment, the information must reasonably apprise the accused of the charges, so he or she has an opportunity to prepare and present his or her defense.

Bail A person arrested for a criminal misdemeanor may obtain release by posting bail in the amount designated in the court's bail schedule. When charged with a felony, however, release is not so simple. If the felony offense is bailable, the amount is usually fixed at the time of arraignment or at a preliminary hearing and is based on the nature of the crime, the previous record of the accused, and the likelihood of his or her fleeing the state if released. If the crime is of a very serious nature, it may not be bailable at all. The threat of danger to society should the accused flee or "jump bail" once released is far too high.

Generally, an individual may be released on his or her own recognizance (that is, without monetary bail) if the judge believes there is no danger of the person's not appearing for arraignment. Individuals may also be released to the custody of some person or organization designated by the court.

Arraignment Once the accused has been charged and arrested (the complaint, indictment, or information having been filed), he or she must be called into court and informed in public hearing of the charge against him or her. He or she must be given an opportunity to plead to the charge. This hearing is called the "arraignment." The defendant must be present; if he or she is out on bail and does not appear, a bench warrant is issued. At this time, the accused is informed of his or her constitutional rights, including the right to counsel. Once the indictment or information has been read, the defendant (the accused in the criminal case) may demurrer to the formal accusation (similar to the pleading stage of the civil case) if he or she believes that the facts stated do not constitute a crime. Or the defendant may file a motion to dismiss or set aside the charge or for change of venue. If the motions are dismissed, the defendant is asked to plead either "guilty" or "not guilty." A "not guilty" plea forces the state to prove at trial every specific charge in the indictment or information. A guilty plea is a complete admission of the charge and in some states a defendant is not allowed to enter such a plea to any offense punishable by death or life imprisonment. Where guilty pleas are made and accepted by the courts, no trial is necessary, and only sentencing of the defendant remains. Under Rule 11 of the Federal Rules of Criminal Procedure, the judge in a federal court cannot accept a plea of guilty without first talking to the defendant personally about his or her constitutional rights and determining that the plea is made voluntarily and with understanding of the nature of the charge and the consequences of the guilty plea. Of course, a guilty plea made involuntarily and without full understanding of its consequences violates due process of law under the Fourteenth Amendment of the Constitution.

Discovery If the defendant's attorney requests from the prosecution evidence that is favorable to the defendant, the prosecution must comply with the request. Failure to do so is a denial of due process of law. Due process also requires the prosecutor to disclose any evidence that would create reasonable doubt about the guilt of the defendant, even though the defendant's attorney has not requested it. United States v. Agurs, 427 U.S. 97, 96 S.Ct. 2392, 49 L.Ed.2d 342 (1976).

The Federal Rules of Criminal Procedure provide broad discovery techniques in criminal cases for the defense. State practice, on the other hand, varies as to what evidence (in possession of the prosecutor) the defense may see. Discovery by the prosecution is more limited because of the defendant's privilege against self-incrimination—the accused does not have to testify against himself or herself or help the state prove the charges.

The trial The following rights of the accused must be protected during the course of trial.

Right to an attorney The right to counsel in criminal cases is based on the Sixth and Fourteenth Amendments of the Constitution. If the accused cannot pay for his or her own attorney, the court must appoint one—to provide him or her with the same services available to the financially able defendant. This includes not only the right to counsel but also other services necessary to an effective defense, such as expert testimony.

Right to a speedy trial The Sixth and Fourteenth Amendments also require that "in all criminal prosecutions the accused shall enjoy the right to a speedy trial." What constitutes an unreasonable delay is determined from all the circumstances. Some states set specific time limits by statute. Under Section 1382 of the California Penal Code, for example, trial must be held within sixty days after indictment or filing of information.

Right to a fair and impartial trial Widespread publicity of an inflammatory nature by either newspaper or television may prevent a fair trial within a particular community. The defendant in this situation should ask for a change of venue before trial.

Inflammatory evidence may also prevent a fair trial, e.g., evidence of prior convictions. The same may result if the accused is required to wear prison clothes (Estelle v. Williams, 425 U.S. 501, 96 S.Ct. 1691, 48 L.Ed.2d 126, 1976) or is unnecessarily restrained in handcuffs or leg irons (State v. Borman, 529 S.W.2d 192, Mo.App.1975) in front of the jury.

Right to a trial by jury There is no right to trial by jury where the maximum penalty for conviction is a monetary fine or prison sentence of six months or less. But where the offense can result in a sentence of greater than six months, a jury trial must be offered to the accused, who can waive the right in all federal and in most state courts.

Right to a public trial Our legal system has always distrusted the concept of "secret trial." But if the reason is good enough, some or all of the courtroom spectators may be excluded from trial. For example, in a sex offense case (and in situations involving small children) where certain spectators might intimidate a witness and prevent him or her from testifying easily and honestly, the judge may legally order the spectators' exclusion. Friends and relatives of the accused, however, may never be kept from the courtroom. The Supreme Court held in the 1980 case of Richmond Newspapers v. Virginia, 100 S.Ct. 2814, that the public (including the press) has a right under the First and Fourteenth Amendments to be present at criminal trials unless there is an overriding interest determined by the trial judge that requires exclusion in order to protect the due process interests of the defendant.

Right against self-incrimination The accused in a criminal prosecution cannot be compelled to testify against himself or herself in either state or federal courts. Under the Fifth and Fourteenth Amendments of the Constitution, he or she may refuse to testify altogether. As one court put it: "He may stand mute, clothed in the presumption of innocence." 11 Cal.App.2d 650, 54 P.2d 43 (1963). But while the defendant cannot be forced to give oral testimony or to produce any documents, records, or other objects that might incriminate him or her, he or she can be compelled to submit to examinations for fingerprints, footprints, and samples of blood and urine. And any evidence thus obtained can be used against him or her in court. In addition, the defendant can be required to participate in line-ups, to put on certain articles of clothing, or to give handwriting exemplars. And finally, the accused waives the right to refuse to testify if he or she takes the stand in his or her own defense. The defendant must then answer all relevant inquiries (on cross-examination) about the crime with which he or she is charged.

Right to confrontation of witnesses The Sixth Amendment also provides that "the accused shall enjoy the right * * * to be confronted with witnesses against him." This means that he or she may cross-examine (through his or her attorney) any witnesses who appear and that the defendant has a right to be physically present in the courtroom when the witness is testifying. But if the accused acts in a disorderly or disrespectful manner, he or she forfeits this right and may be excluded from his or her own trial. (See *Illinois v. Allen,* Chapter 1.) The Sixth Amendment and due process clause of the Fourteenth Amendment also provide the defendant with the right to present his or her own witnesses and to otherwise make a defense to the charge. Thus, the accused has the right to subpoena witnesses the same as the prosecutor.

Another important rule is that the accused can neither be tried, sentenced, nor punished unless sane at the time of trial.

Judgment, sentencing, and treatment of convicted criminals Sentence in a criminal case is always imposed by the court (although in some states the jury recommends the punishment), and this must be done within a short period of time. A California statute, for example, provides for imposition of sentence within twenty-one days after the jury's finding of guilt. During the period of time from jury verdict to sentencing, probation officers usually conduct a presentence investigation and report to the court details of the defendant's background, prior criminal record, and family and financial circumstances. The officers recommend either that the defendant be placed on probation or sent to jail for a set period of time.

"Cruel and inhuman punishment" is prohibited by the Eighth and Fourteenth Amendments of the Constitution. As a result, sentences have been set aside where the punishment imposed was either too severe or where it did not "fit" the crime. The Supreme Court of the United States decided that a discretionary death penalty, applied infrequently and without deterrent effect, is "cruel and unusual punishment." Furman v. Georgia, 408 U.S. 238, 92 S.Ct. 2726, 33 L.Ed.2d 346 (1972). Also, the Court has held that mandatory capital punishment for certain types of homicides such as killing a police officer, with no provision for consideration of mitigating factors, is cruel and unusual. Woodson v. North Carolina, 428 U.S. 280, 96 S.Ct. 2978, 49 L.Ed.2d 944 (1976). And the death penalty for rape alone was held cruel and unusual because "grossly disproportionate" to the crime. Coker v. Georgia, 433 U.S. 584, 97 S.Ct. 2861, 53 L.Ed.2d 982 (1977). Still the death penalty is not always cruel and unusual punishment. If the statute provides adequate guidance as to aggravating and mitigating factors and further provides a review procedure insuring against discriminatory application, it will not be cruel and unusual. Gregg v. Georgia, 428 U.S. 153, 96 S.Ct. 2909, 49 L.Ed.2d 859 (1976). A number of states have abolished the death penalty by statute.

The "equal protection" clause of the Fourteenth Amendment forbids imposing greater punishment on a poor person than on a rich one. This means that a man or woman cannot be put into jail just because he or she is unable to pay a fine. In Illinois, a convicted person ordered to pay a fine as well as to serve a term of imprisonment was required by statute to remain in prison longer and "work off" the fine if he had no money to pay it. The U. S. Supreme Court declared this statute unconstitutional as a denial of equal protection of the laws. Williams v. Illinois, 399 U.S. 235, 90 S.Ct. 2018, 26 L.Ed.2d 586 (1970). A sentence of "sixty dollars or sixty days" is just as unconstitutional. Only when a person willfully refuses to pay a fine that he or she is financially able to pay can that person be sentenced to jail for nonpayment.

Postconviction procedures Upon conviction, the defendant may ask for a new trial. This motion is usually based on newly discovered evidence. And, of course, the defendant may always appeal his or her conviction. Under the Federal Rules, appeal from a criminal conviction must be taken within ten days following entry of judgment. The defendant may be released on bail if the court feels there is no substantial risk that he or she will flee and endanger the community.

The judgment of the appellate court is not necessarily the last word in a criminal case: the principles of "res judicata" do not apply to criminal cases the same way they apply to civil ones. Of course, it makes sense in a civil action—a tort or contract dispute between private individuals—that the case should be settled once and for all. But in the criminal case, where a mistake is uncovered only after the defendant has been sentenced and taken to jail, he or she should certainly not have to remain there because of the binding judgment rule. A convicted criminal can always seek further review of his or her case by petitioning for habeas corpus. The writ of habeas corpus, which serves as a remedy for any unlawful detention or imprisonment, specifies in writing why the petitioner should not remain in jail. The court must determine whether the writ should issue and, if it does issue, whether the prisoner should be released. The basis for release may be lack of jurisdiction of the trial court, unconstitutionality of the statute under which the prisoner was convicted, a sentence beyond that allowed for the offense, or violation of the prisoner's constitutional rights. The court's decision on the matter of habeas corpus can also be appealed to a higher court.

The right to appeal from a criminal conviction is guaranteed for the indigent as well as for the wealthy. If a person is too poor to pay for an attorney or for a transcript of the criminal trial proceedings, both must be provided—or there is a denial of due process of law. Due process also demands that in proceedings to revoke the defendant's probation or parole, the defendant be given notice of the preliminary hearing and a chance to speak out there on his or her own behalf. The defendant is additionally guaranteed a full hearing in front of the parole board with written notice of the parole violations charged against him or her, complete disclosure of unfavorable evidence, and the right to cross-examine adverse witnesses in front of a neutral hearing body.

Special rules and procedures dealing with criminal cases

Jurisdiction The court in a criminal case must have territorial jurisdiction (i.e., the crime must have occurred within the government's territorial boundaries). Thus for a state to prosecute a criminal defendant, the crime must have taken place within that state. This sounds easy, but there can be problems. Say that Joe is standing in the State of North Dakota and shoots Tom, who is standing in Minnesota where Tom dies. While the murder takes place in Minnesota and not North Dakota, North Dakota can punish Joe for the crime of shooting the gun. There are many rules of law to govern problems like this. Many state statutes, for example, provide that any person who commits a crime "in whole or in part" within the state may be there convicted of that crime.

The court has jurisdiction over the person of the defendant if the defendant is arrested within the state and brought before the court. If the defendant has left the state, the governor must demand his or her extradition before he or she can be arrested.

Venue Generally, the accused is properly tried in the county where the crime was committed. But again, problems can arise. Take for instance a murder case where the wound is inflicted in one county, the death occurs in another, and the body is found in a third. Each county is a proper place for trial; each has proper venue. And, of course, venue can always be changed to assure fair trial.

Double jeopardy Under the Fifth and Fourteenth Amendments of the Constitution, no person can be tried twice for the same offense. In other words, a person who has committed a crime can be subjected to only one trial and only one punishment for that crime. If found not guilty, he or she cannot be tried again. So if the state charges someone with murder and that person is acquitted, the state cannot later change the charge to manslaughter and have a second trial for the same act. But it is possible for a person to commit more than one crime with the same act (e.g., where there is more than one victim, there is more than one crime). The defendant in such a situation can be tried separately for each crime. Also, if two or more offenses are committed, the defendant may be tried separately for each as long as the second offense tried requires proof of some additional fact which the first did not. Breaking and entering a house to steal personal property and, while there, also raping the home owner is the commission of two separate crimes since proving the rape involves facts not needed to prove the burglary.

Statute of limitations Criminal prosecution must be initiated within certain set periods of time that vary from state to state. A misdemeanor action must typically begin within one year from commission of the crime and, for a felony, within three years with some exceptions (such as murder, where there is no time limit). The statutory period generally runs from the time the crime is committed, though in some states the statute of limitations on theft crimes does not begin to run until the theft is discovered.

HOW DOES THE PROCEDURE DIFFER WHEN A JUVENILE IS INVOLVED WITH CRIME?

On Wednesday, May 6, 1982 the body of an eleven-year-old girl was found in a wooded area less than 200 yards from her home in Cedar Mill, Oregon. The same day, a fifteen-year-old neighbor boy was taken into custody and taken to the Donald E. Long Juvenile Home. A petition accusing the boy of the juvenile equivalent of murder was filed in juvenile court. The public defender represented the boy at his arraignment. A search warrant had previously been obtained to search a locker room at the Cedar Park Intermediate School where pieces of a hockey stick, covered with blood and hair, were found. The boy attended the Cedar Park School.[1]

Juvenile court rules provide special protection for the young criminal offender. These courts are independently established in some states by state constitution or statute. In most states, however, they are simply branches of other courts.

Juvenile courts deal with delinquency (criminal conduct), truancy (absence from school without leave), incorrigibility, and neglect. They generally have statutory jurisdiction over children up to a certain age limit. Upper age limits are usually set at sixteen, seventeen, or eighteen. In some states, the accused must be less than this maximum age at the time of the offense—in others, at the time of the hearing. As a general rule, juvenile courts do not hear traffic matters.

While juvenile courts are primarily concerned with children charged with criminal conduct, they handle semidelinquents as well. The court may determine that "unruly children" of this type are "persons in need of supervision."

But only children who have violated the criminal law can be sent to reform school. The noncriminal juvenile who needs supervision, treatment, or rehabilitation is usually placed on probation under the supervision of a professionally trained probation officer. Community treatment, involving vocational guidance training, educational tutoring, and special recreation groups

---

1. *The Oregonian,* Vol. 132, No. 38,021, Oregonian Publishing Company, Portland, Oregon, Thursday, May 6, 1982.

is available in some locations. But if the semidelinquent child continues to be disruptive or incorrigible after he or she is placed on probation, the child may be returned to the juvenile court (as authorized by statute) and committed to an institution for juvenile delinquents.

The purpose of the juvenile court with both the juvenile delinquent and the semidelinquent is not to punish but to help the child—to rescue him or her from the danger of maturing into an adult criminal. In trying to accomplish this objective, juvenile courts have delved deeply into the social and psychological needs of the children before them. But they have frequently operated with such procedural informality that the Supreme Court of the United States was led to conclude that children adjudged as juvenile or semidelinquents have often been denied due process of law. Certainly, the Court states, it is all well and good to worry about the "welfare" of the juvenile or semidelinquent, but only after first making certain that the child is indeed guilty of the asserted behavior. Too often the juvenile court has accepted the child's guilt of either criminal or unruly conduct without requiring proof of that conduct and without using the same procedural safeguards used in adult criminal trials. Clearly, due process of law exists for everyone regardless of age. To safeguard the rights of juveniles, the Court set down the following rules for dealing with accused juvenile delinquents:

1. A police officer taking an alleged delinquent into custody may take him or her to the home of his or her parents, to a foster home, to a place maintained by an approved child welfare agency, or to a detention center for delinquents. If there is no detention center available, the child may be taken to jail, provided, first, that he or she can be kept separate from jailed adults and, second, that the juvenile court has specifically ordered the child jailed. Detention is permitted only where it is necessary to protect human life or property, to prevent the child from running away, or to supervise and return him or her to court (where there is no responsible parent or guardian).
2. The police are required to notify the parents of their child's arrest. If the parents obtain custody of the child, they must promise in writing to bring him or her to court or before a probation officer on the designated day.
3. The *Miranda* rights must be observed. Officials must inform the juvenile of his or her right to remain silent—that anything he or she does say can be used against him or her; that the child has a right to have an attorney present during discussions with the police; that if he or she cannot afford an attorney, one will be provided; and that he or she may stop answering questions at any time.
4. Where the juvenile is charged with a crime, the prosecution must prove guilt "beyond a reasonable doubt" and not by a mere preponderance of the evidence. In re Gault, 387 U.S. 1, 87 S.Ct. 1428, 18 L.Ed.2d 527 (1967).

The juvenile, however, does not have a right to trial by jury. As stated by the Supreme Court, trial by the judge alone may be just as fair and perhaps better for the juvenile.

Nor are juveniles entitled to public trials under the federal Constitution, the idea, again, being to protect the juvenile from adverse publicity.[2] In

2. At least one state, however, has interpreted its own state law as requiring all court proceedings—juvenile matters included—to be open to the public (Oregon).

most states if the child is over sixteen, he or she may be remanded to adult court (i.e., ordered tried in a normal criminal proceeding) and, if found guilty, then sentenced as an adult.

Probation is always a favored alternative to a reform institution. The period of probation generally does not exceed two years. If the child violates conditions of his or her probation, the probation may be revoked, and the child sent to the reform institution. Under recent legislation in many states, a juvenile sent to such an institution may be held in custody only for a period of time ranging from one to three years. In some states, the original commitment may continue until the child is twenty-one, at which time the child is released. An institutionalized child is often released before serving "his or her time" and is placed on parole under a probation program.

WHAT IS DUE PROCESS?

The Fourteenth Amendment of the Constitution states that your liberty and property cannot be taken away without due process of law. Procedural safeguard is the heart of due process. Six factors enter into its meaning.

Power Must Be Limited or Based on One or More of the Three Sources of Law.

The power to take away life, liberty, or property must be found in either written, common, or administrative law. If your neighbor burns smelly rubbish in his yard for several weeks, you cannot seize him and lock him up in your garage. Locking him up would deprive him of his liberty without due process of law. There is nothing in any source of law that gives you power to do so. But you can obtain an injunction from a court of equity. And if your neighbor then refuses to stop burning the rubbish, the judge has common law power to lock him up for contempt of court.

Reasonable Notice and Some Form of Hearing Must Be Provided.

Whoever has the power (whatever government officer or agency) must always give reasonable notice to the party whose life, liberty, or property is potentially affected. This party must also be provided with an opportunity to present his or her position in some kind of hearing.

Courts Must Be Available to Resolve Disputes.

Whenever a private dispute arises or a dispute between an individual and an official of the government, the parties must have ultimate access to the courts for resolution of their problem. The "dual court" state and federal court system is available for their use, and there is at least one trial and one appeal on almost any kind of problem. Again, your rubbish burning neighbor is entitled to his day in court if he wants it; to deny either of you access to the courts is to eliminate due process.

Courts Must Have Proper Jurisdiction.

A court must have jurisdiction before it can render a valid judgment or decree. Jurisdiction, you will recall, requires two things: the court must have power to hear the particular kind of case, and it must notify the defendant of the suit against him or her by serving him or her with a summons and a copy of the complaint. If your neighbor is not served with a summons by a court empowered to hear the case, any order the court issues is invalid, for it is issued without due process.

Established Rules of Evidence and Procedure Must Be Followed Within the Courtroom.

Courts must be careful that irrelevant, incompetent, or prejudicial evidence is not admitted in the courtroom—particularly in criminal cases and in jury cases involving money damages. Otherwise, decisions will not reflect the merits of the case. The fact that your neighbor drinks heavily or has been married six times is not relevant to a determination that the rubbish burning is a tort and must be stopped. Additionally, juries must be properly instructed in the law, and judges must referee these adversary proceedings, or due process does not exist.

Constitutional Rights Must Be Carefully Safeguarded.

Finally, those individual rights guaranteed by the Constitution must be protected—especially in the criminal case. The rights to counsel, to protection against improper search and seizure, to public trial by jury, to confront and cross-examine witnesses, the privilege against self-incrimination—all are essential to due process of law.

WHAT IS MEANT BY ARBITRATION AND MEDIATION?

We have learned about the procedures of the courts and the protections of due process. They are designed to achieve fair and correct results based only on competent evidence. They are available to anyone who becomes involved in a civil, equitable, divorce, probate, or criminal case. However, they are usually very time consuming and expensive.

Parties with disputes may be able to settle them without using these procedures. Apart from criminal matters, which must be handled by government prosecutors, individuals with disagreements may be able to resolve them by agreement. Civil cases arising from tort or contract are frequently settled by agreement even before a case is filed. And parties to a divorce often agree to property settlements without involving the courts.

As part of an agreement, individuals may bind themselves irrevocably to arbitration. This is a method using a neutral person or persons to resolve the problem. The parties select the arbitrator (or arbitrators) and present the case informally. A common practice is to use a panel of three arbitrators, each party selecting one and then the two arbitrators selecting the other. Arbitrators are not bound by established procedures or evidence. However, their decisions, called "awards," are binding on both sides as to the facts and the law. There is no judicial review or appeal except on allegations that the arbitrators were fraudulent, had conflicts of interest, or exceeded their authority.

Not only are arbitration procedures less formal, expensive, and time consuming, they also allow the use of experts in the areas of dispute. One can use a CPA, engineer, lawyer, or other type of expert where appropriate. In business, the consumer complaint is frequently handled through arbitration with the Better Business Bureau serving as the arbitrator. Arbitration is also often used in disputes involving international trade and in labor-management relations. In the public employee sector (e.g., police or fire fighters), arbitration is often required by statute since public employees are not allowed to strike. In the writing of business and labor-management contracts, the parties often agree in advance to submit all issues that may arise in the future to arbitration. Written arbitration agreements are referred to as "submission agreements." Many states have passed the Uniform Arbitration Act or other legislation covering arbitration procedures including submission, award, and enforcement of the award in the same manner as a court judgment.

Mediation differs from arbitration because the parties are not bound by the mediator's position. Instead, the mediator is brought in as a person skilled in settling disputes who offers help and an unbiased viewpoint which hopefully lead to a reasonable solution.

Several states are beginning to experiment with arbitration or mediation programs for civil lawsuits and other private disputes. The Oregon legislature, for example, in the summer of 1983, passed a statute for out-of-court handling of civil cases of $15,000 or less and to settle property disputes in divorce cases. The law still permits either party to use the regular court procedures if unhappy with the outcome, but with some penalty if he or she fails to improve his or her position. The law was passed after studies across the country showed that 90 to 95 percent of all participants in similar programs accepted the initial decision as final. Savings for participants in time and expense are very substantial.

Cases

Overdoing it in Los Angeles County.

DIAMOND v. GENERAL MOTORS CORP.

Court of Appeal of California, Second District, 1971.
20 Cal.App.3d 374, 97 Cal.Rptr. 639.

[The plaintiff brought a class action on behalf of himself and the residents of Los Angeles County for damages for and injunctive relief against pollution. The lower court in Los Angeles dismissed the suit. This dismissal was affirmed by the California Court of Appeals in the following opinion.]

FILES, Presiding Justice

This is an action brought by plaintiff "on behalf of himself and all other possessors of real property in, and residents of, the County of Los Angeles," as a class numbering 7,119,184 persons. The named defendants are 293 industrial corporations and municipalities who are alleged to have polluted the atmosphere of the county. * * * The complaint seeks billions of dollars in compensatory and punitive damages, and "an injunction permanently restraining defendants from emitting and discharging pollutants into the atmosphere of the County of Los Angeles." * * *

* * *

In substance, the automobile manufacturers are charged with negligently producing and distributing machines which are defective in that they emit harmful substances into the atmosphere; petroleum refiners are charged with manufacturing and distributing motor fuel which, in its intended use, pollutes the atmosphere; owners of industrial plants, steam generating plants, gasoline filling stations and airports are charged with unnecessarily discharging harmful substances and odors into the air. The conduct of the defendants is characterized as wilful, malicious and oppressive.

The complaint is plainly an attempt to deal with the problem of air pollution in Los Angeles County as a whole, as between all of the individuals in the county constituting a class of plaintiffs, and the industries which plaintiff believes to be responsible for the problem, as defendants. * * *

* * * [W]e believe the trial court properly concluded that the class action which plaintiff is attempting may not be maintained. This is a case where (1) there are significantly disparate interests within the alleged class; (2) the right of each member to recover (as well as the amount of his recovery) will depend upon substantial issues which must be litigated as between individual plaintiffs and defendants; and (3) the number of parties, the diversity of their interests, and the multiplicity of issues all in a single action would make the proceeding unmanageable.

* * *

The substance of the factual allegations * * * is that the defendants are maintaining a continuing public nuisance. * * * Civil Code section 3493 provides: "A private person may maintain an action for a public nuisance, if it is specially injurious to himself, but not otherwise." Plaintiff here attempts to bring his complaint within that statute by alleging that each member of the class has suffered special injury in that each "is prevented from enjoying his own unique property." * * * Plaintiff argues that he is simply combining here all of the special damage claims of the persons he proposes to represent. This means that plaintiff is trying to allege, in a single cause of action, 7,119,184 claims for * * * damages arising out of 7,119,184 special injuries.

Requiring plaintiff to state separately the seven million causes of action, and to plead factually the damage as to each, would in and of itself constitute a practical bar to this action. * * * Whether an individual has been specially injured in his person will depend largely upon proof relating to him alone—going to such matters as his general health, his occupation, place of residence, and activities. Whether a parcel of real property has been damaged will depend upon its unique characteristics, such as its location, physical features and use.

* * *

This complaint lacks the characteristics which were found to justify a class action in Vasquez v. Superior Court, * * * and Daar v. Yellow Cab Co. In *Daar* and *Vasquez* the class was composed of consumers or customers who had dealt with the defendants in an identifiable series of similar transactions. Here we have an aggregation of individual tort claims of persons classified only by their residence within a political subdivision of the state.

In *Daar* there was a single defendant and in *Vasquez* a single group of four defendants engaged in a common business scheme. Here we have hundreds of defendants each of whom is entitled to have its liability determined independently of each of the other defendants. In *Daar* and *Vasquez* the main issues upon which liability might rest were common to all members of the class, and the individually triable issues were relatively simple. Here the nature of the claim is such that substantial and difficult issues can only be resolved on an individual basis. * * *

* * * Everyone is interested in clean air.

* * * But in deciding whether the complaint states a cause of action on behalf of a class, the claimed efficacy of the group relief must be considered, since an important function of the class action is to provide an economical and effective group remedy. * * *

* * * The immediate effect of an injunction would be to halt the supply of goods and services essential to the life and comfort of the persons whom plaintiff seeks to represent. * * *

* * *

* * * Plaintiff is simply asking the court to do what the elected representatives of the people have not done: adopt stricter standards over the discharge of air contaminants in this county, and enforce them with the contempt power of the court.

* * *

We assume * * * that * * * anyone claiming to have sustained personal injury or property damage caused by an unreasonable discharge of contaminants into the atmosphere by one or more of the defendants could state a cause of action for his damages and for injunctive relief. But the class action attempted by plaintiff, as the purported representative of every resident of the county, is a wholly different kind of suit. The objective, which plaintiff envisions to justify his class action, is judicial regulation of the processes, products and volume of business of the major industries of the county.

* * *

A matter of morals.

HURLEY v. EDDINGFIELD

Supreme Court of Indiana, 1901.
156 Ind.App. 416, 59 N.E. 1058.

BAKER, J.

The appellant sued appellee for $10,000 damages for wrongfully causing the death of his intestate. The court sustained appellee's demurrer to the complaint, and this ruling is assigned as error.

The material facts alleged may be summarized thus: At and for years before decedent's death appellee was a practicing physician at Mace, in Montgomery county, duly licensed under the laws of the state. He held himself out to the public as a general practitioner of medicine. He had been decedent's family physician. Decedent became dangerously ill, and sent for appellee. The messenger informed appellee of decedent's violent sickness, tendered him his fee for his services, and stated to him that no other physician was procurable in time, and that decedent relied on him for attention. No other physician was procurable in time to be of any use, and decedent did rely on appellee for medical assistance. Without any reason whatever, appellee refused to render aid to decedent. No other patients were requiring appellee's immediate service, and he could have gone to the relief of decedent if he had been willing to do so. Death ensued, without decedent's fault, and wholly from appellee's wrongful act. The alleged wrongful act was appellee's refusal to enter into a contract of employment. Counsel do not contend that, before the enactment of the law regulating the practice of medicine, physicians were bound to render professional service to every one who applied. * * * The act regulating the practice of medicine provides for a board of examiners, standards of qualification, examinations, licenses to those found qualified, and penalties for practicing without license. * * * The act is a preventive, not a compulsive, measure. In obtaining the state's license (permission) to practice medicine, the state does not require, and the licensee does not engage, that he will practice at all or on other terms than he may choose to accept. * * * Judgment affirmed.

Parties to a dispute are responsible for presenting their own cases in court.

DREYER v. ERSHOWSKY

Supreme Court of New York, Appellate Division, 1913.
156 App.Div. 27, 140 N.Y.S. 819.

RICH, J.

This appeal is from a judgment in favor of the defendants, entered upon the verdict of a jury in an action to recover for negligence. It may be that upon the record here presented, and considering the method pursued in the trial of this action, a verdict for the defendants was not without justification. We are convinced, however, that the cause was so hastily disposed of that an injustice may have been done. The plaintiff was represented by skillful counsel, but was not permitted to have the facts elicited from his witnesses by the counsel employed to represent him and conduct his case. The ordinary and usual procedure in the trial of causes was disregarded. The learned justice who presided at the trial took it upon himself to conduct the examination of witnesses, and we feel that in taking from counsel, who was undoubtedly familiar with the case and knew what he expected to prove by his witnesses, the opportunity of trying his case the plaintiff has been deprived of his day in court.

The plaintiff was the first witness called upon the trial, and, after he had stated his place of residence and the nature of his business, the learned court interrupted the examination, and proceeded to question the witness as to the nature and cause of the accident and the extent of his injuries. The next witness was a physician and surgeon, and his examination in chief was also conducted by the court. The third witness for plaintiff was in defendants' employ at the time of the accident, and, after the witness had said in response to questions by the court that he saw plaintiff that day, counsel said:

"Would your honor permit me to conduct the examination?

"The Court: One moment, please. Get some facts first."

And the court proceeded to interrogate the witness as to the crucial questions involved. The record shows that counsel again asked to be permitted to examine the witness.

"Mr. Gottlieb: Won't your honor allow me to examine this witness?

"The Court: No."

Other witnesses were called for plaintiff and questioned by the court, when finally a witness was called in rebuttal. The record follows:

"Harry Weintraub, 102 Orchard Street, Manhattan, called as a witness in behalf of the plaintiff, being duly sworn, testified:

"By the Court: Q. Now, Weintraub, where were you on September 6, 1907?

"Mr. Gottlieb: Will your honor permit me to examine the witness?

"The Court: No; I am going to examine for a while.

"Mr. Gottlieb: I except [object].

"A. On the corner of Delancy and Forsyth street. Q. What were you doing there? A. I have been sitting on Mr. Rosenberg's wagon, moving van. Q. Who else was sitting on that moving van?

"Mr. Gottlieb: I object to your honor cross-examining the witness, if your honor please.

"Q. Who was sitting there?

"Mr. Gottlieb: I except [object].

"The Court: Counselor, you will sit down and not rise again until the court tells you.

"Mr. Gottlieb: I except [object]."

We think that the conduct of the court in refusing to permit counsel to conduct the examination of his witness was highly improper. * * * [I]t must be understood that we have not adopted in this country the practice of making the presiding judge the chief inquisitor. It is better to observe our time-honored custom of orderly judicial procedure, even at the expense of occasional delays; * * * it must not be forgotten that the trial of a lawsuit is an important event to the parties, and they must not only receive justice, but must be made to know that justice is being administered. The judge * * * should conduct the trial with such deliberation that the scales may be seen to balance at every stage in the progress of the trial.

We are of the opinion that the plaintiff has not had a fair opportunity of presenting his case, and the judgment and order must therefore be reversed and a new trial granted. * * *

Facing rejection.

BROWN v. BOARD OF EDUCATON OF TOPEKA

Supreme Court of the United States, 1954.
347 U.S. 483, 74 S.Ct. 686, 98 L.Ed. 873.

Mr. Chief Justice WARREN delivered the opinion of the Court.

These cases come to us from the States of Kansas, South Carolina, Virginia, and Delaware. They are premised on different facts and different local conditions, but a common legal question justifies their consideration together in this consolidated opinion.

In each of the cases, minors of the Negro race, through their legal representatives, seek the aid of the courts in obtaining admission to the public schools of their community on a nonsegregated basis. In each instance, they have been denied admission to schools attended by white children under laws requiring or permitting segregation according to race. This segregation was alleged to deprive the plaintiffs of the equal protection of the laws under the Fourteenth Amendment. In each of the cases other than the Delaware case, a three-judge federal district court denied relief to the plaintiffs on the so-called "separate but equal" doctrine announced by this Court in Plessy v. Ferguson. * * * Under that doctrine, equality of treatment is accorded when the races are provided substantially equal facilities, even though these facilities be separate. * * *

The plaintiffs contend that segregated public schools are not "equal" and cannot be made "equal," and that hence they are deprived of the equal protection of the laws. Because of the obvious importance of the question presented, the Court took jurisdiction. * * *

* * *

In approaching this problem, we cannot turn the clock back to 1868 when the Amendment was adopted, or even to 1896 when Plessy v. Ferguson was written. We must consider public education in the light of its full development and its present place in American life throughout the Nation. Only in this way can it be determined if segregation in public schools deprives these plaintiffs of the equal protection of the laws.

Today, education is perhaps the most important function of state and local governments. Compulsory school attendance laws and the great expenditures for education both demonstrate our recognition of the importance of education to our democratic society. It is required in the performance of our most basic public responsibilities, even service in the armed forces. It is the very foundation of good citizenship. Today it is a principal instrument in awakening the child to cultural values, in preparing him for later professional training, and in helping him to adjust normally to his environment. In these days, it is doubtful that any child may reasonably be expected to succeed in life if he is denied the opportunity of an education. Such an opportunity, where the state has undertaken to provide it, is a right which must be made available to all on equal terms.

We come then to the question presented: Does segregation of children in public schools solely on the basis of race, even though the physical facilities and other "tangible" factors may be equal, deprive the children of the minority group of equal educational opportunities? We believe that it does.

In Sweatt v. Painter * * * in finding that a segregated law school for Negroes could not provide them equal educational opportunities, this Court relied in large part on "those qualities which are incapable of objective measurement but which make for greatness in a law school." * * * Such considerations apply with added force to children in grade and high schools. To separate them from others of similar age and qualifications solely because of their race generates a feeling of inferiority as to their status in the community that may affect their hearts and minds in a way unlikely ever to be undone. * * * Whatever may have been the extent of psychological knowledge at the time of Plessy v. Ferguson, this finding is amply supported by modern authority. Any language in Plessy v. Ferguson contrary to this finding is rejected.

We conclude that in the field of public education the doctrine of "separate but equal" has no place. Separate educational facilities are inherently unequal. Therefore, we hold that the plaintiffs and others similarly situated for whom the actions have been brought are, by reason of the segregation complained of, deprived of the equal protection of the laws guaranteed by the Fourteenth Amendment. * * *

"Here's Johnny, The World's Foremost Commodian."

JOHN W. CARSON v. HERE'S JOHNNY PORTABLE TOILETS, INC.

United States Court of Appeals, Sixth Circuit, 1983.
698 F.2d 831.

* * *

Appellant, John W. Carson (Carson), is the host and star of "The Tonight Show," a well-known television program broadcast five nights a week by the National Broadcasting Company. Carson also appears as an entertainer in night clubs and theaters around the country. From the time he began hosting "The Tonight Show" in 1962, he has been introduced on the show each night with the phrase "Here's Johnny." This method of introduction was first used for Carson in 1957 when he hosted a daily television program for the American Broadcasting Company. The phrase "Here's Johnny" is generally associated with Carson by a substantial segment of the television viewing public. In 1967, Carson first authorized use of this phrase by an outside business venture, permitting it to be used by a chain of restaurants called "Here's Johnny Restaurants."

Appellant Johnny Carson Apparel, Inc. (Apparel), formed in 1970, manufactures and markets men's clothing to retail stores. Carson, the president of Apparel and owner of 20% of its stock, has licensed Apparel to use his name and picture, which appear on virtually all of Apparel's products and promotional material. Apparel has also used, with Carson's consent, the phrase "Here's Johnny" on labels for clothing and in advertising campaigns. In 1977, Apparel granted a license to Marcy Laboratories to use "Here's Johnny" as the name of a line of men's toiletries. The phrase "Here's Johnny" has never been registered by appellants as a trademark or service mark.

Appellee, Here's Johnny Portable Toilets, Inc., is a Michigan corporation engaged in the business of renting and selling "Here's Johnny" portable toilets. Appellee's founder was aware at the time he formed the corporation that "Here's Johnny" was the introductory slogan for Carson on "The Tonight Show." He indicated that he coupled the phrase with a second one, "The World's Foremost Commodian," to make "a good play on a phrase."

Shortly after appellee went into business in 1976, appellants brought this action alleging * * * invasion of privacy and publicity rights. They sought damages and an injunction prohibiting appellee's further use of the phrase "Here's Johnny" as a corporate name or in connection with the sale or rental of its portable toilets.

After a bench trial, the district court issued a memorandum opinion and order, Carson v. Here's Johnny Portable Toilets, Inc., 498 F.Supp. 71 (E.D.Mich.1980), which served as its findings of fact and conclusions of law. The court ordered the dismissal of the appellants' complaint.

* * * On the right of privacy and right of publicity theories, the court held that these rights extend only to a "name or likeness," and "Here's Johnny" did not qualify.

* * *

The right of publicity has developed to protect the commercial interest of celebrities in their identities. The theory of the right is that a celebrity's identity can be valuable in the promotion of products, and the celebrity has an interest that may be protected from the unauthorized commercial exploitation of that identity. In Memphis Development Foundation v. Factors Etc., Inc., 616 F.2d 956 (6th Cir.), cert. denied, 449 U.S. 953, 101 S.Ct. 358, 66 L.Ed.2d 217 (1980), we stated: "The famous have an exclusive legal right during life to control and profit from the commercial use of their name and personality." Id. at 957.

The district court dismissed appellants' claim based on the right of publicity because appellee does not use Carson's name or likeness. 498 F.Supp. at 77. It held that it "would not be prudent to allow recovery for a right of publicity claim which does not more specifically identify Johnny Carson." 498 F.Supp. at 78. We believe that, on the contrary, the district court's conception of the right of publicity is too narrow. The right of publicity, as we have stated, is that a celebrity has a protected pecuniary interest in the commercial exploitation of his identity. If the celebrity's identity is commercially exploited, there has been an invasion of his right whether or not his "name or likeness" is used. Carson's identity may be exploited even if his name, John W. Carson, or his picture is not used.

* * *

In Ali v. Playgirl, Inc., 447 F.Supp. 723 (S.D.N.Y.1978), Muhammad Ali, former heavyweight champion, sued Playgirl magazine under the New York "right of privacy" statute and also alleged a violation of his common law right of publicity. The magazine published a drawing of a nude, black male sitting on a stool in a corner of a boxing ring with hands taped and arms outstretched on the ropes. The district court concluded that Ali's right of publicity was invaded because the drawing sufficiently identified him in spite of the fact that the drawing was captioned "Mystery Man." The district court found that the identification of Ali was made certain because of an accompanying verse that identified the figure as "The Greatest." The district court took judicial notice of the fact that "Ali has regularly claimed that appellation for himself."

* * *

In this case, Earl Braxton, president and owner of Here's Johnny Portable Toilets, Inc., admitted that he knew that the phrase "Here's Johnny" had been used for years to introduce Carson. Moreover, in the opening statement in the district court, appellee's counsel stated:

Now, we've stipulated in this case that the public tends to associate the words "Johnny Carson," the words "Here's Johnny" with plaintiff, John Carson and Mr. Braxton, in his deposition, admitted that he knew that and probably absent that identification, he would not have chosen it.

That the "Here's Johnny" name was selected by Braxton because of its identification with Carson was the clear inference from Braxton's testimony irrespective of such admission in the opening statement.

We therefore conclude that, applying the correct legal standards, appellants are entitled to judgment. The proof showed without question that appellee had appropriated Carson's identity in connection with its corporate name and its product.

* * *

The judgment of the district court is vacated and the case remanded for further proceedings consistent with this opinion.

"I'm too drunk, I won't pass the test."

SOUTH DAKOTA v. MASON HENRY NEVILLE

Supreme Court of the United States, 1983.
— U.S. —, 103 S.Ct. 916, 74 L.Ed.2d 748.

JUSTICE O'CONNOR delivered the opinion of the Court.

Schmerber v. California, 384 U.S. 757, 86 S.Ct. 1826, 16 L.Ed.2d 908 (1966), held that a State could force a defendant to submit to a blood-alcohol test without violating the defendant's Fifth Amendment right against self-incrimination. We now address a question left open in *Schmerber,* and hold that the admission into evidence of a defendant's refusal to submit to such a test likewise does not offend the right against self-incrimination.

Two Madison, South Dakota police officers stopped respondent's car after they saw him fail to stop at a stop sign. The officers asked respondent for his driver's license and asked him to get out of the car. As he left the car, respondent staggered and fell against the car to support himself. The officers smelled alcohol on his breath. Respondent did not have a driver's license, and informed the officers that it was revoked after a previous driving-while-intoxicated conviction. The officers asked respondent to touch his finger to his nose and to walk a straight line. When respondent failed these field sobriety tests, he was placed under arrest and read his *Miranda* rights. Respondent acknowledged that he understood his rights and agreed to talk without a lawyer present. * * * Reading from the printed card, the officers then asked respondent to submit to a blood-alcohol test and warned him that he could lose his license if he refused. Respondent refused to take the test, stating "I'm too drunk, I won't pass the test." The officers again read the request to submit to a test, and then took respondent to the police station, where they read the request to submit a third time. Respondent continued to refuse to take the test, again saying he was too drunk to pass it.

South Dakota law specifically declares that refusal to submit to a blood-alcohol test "may be admissible into evidence at the trial." S.D.Comp.Laws Ann. § 32–23–10.1. Nevertheless, respondent sought to suppress all evidence of his refusal to take the blood-alcohol test. The circuit court granted the suppression motion for three reasons: the South Dakota statute allowing evidence of refusal violated respondent's federal constitutional rights; the officers failed to advise respondent that the refusal could be used against him at trial; and the refusal was irrelevant to the issues before the court. The State appealed from the entire order. The South Dakota Supreme Court affirmed the suppression of the act of refusal on the grounds that § 32–23–10.1, which allows the introduction of this evidence, violated the federal * * * privilege against self-incrimination.

* * *

Since other jurisdictions have found no Fifth Amendment violation from the admission of evidence of refusal to submit to blood-alcohol tests, we granted certiorari to resolve the conflict.

* * *

As part of its program to deter drinkers from driving, South Dakota has enacted an "implied consent" law. S.D.Comp.Laws Ann. § 32–23–10. This statute declares that any person operating a vehicle in South Dakota is deemed to have consented to a chemical test of the alcoholic content of his blood if arrested for driving while intoxicated. In *Schmerber v. California,* 384 U.S. 757, 86 S.Ct. 1826, 16 L.Ed.2d 908 (1966), this Court upheld a state-compelled blood test against a claim that it infringed the Fifth Amendment right against self-incrimination, made applicable to the States through the Fourteenth

Amendment. * * * We * * * held that the privilege bars the State only from compelling "communications" or "testimony." Since a blood test was "physical or real" evidence rather than testimonial evidence, we found it unprotected by the Fifth Amendment privilege.

Schmerber, then, clearly allows a State to force a person suspected of driving while intoxicated to submit to a blood alcohol test. South Dakota, however, has declined to authorize its police officers to administer a blood-alcohol test against the suspect's will. Rather, to avoid violent confrontations, the South Dakota statute permits a suspect to refuse the test, and indeed requires police officers to inform the suspect of his right to refuse. S.D.Comp.Laws Ann. § 32–23–10. This permission is not without a price, however. South Dakota law authorizes the department of public safety, after providing the person who has refused the test an opportunity for a hearing, to revoke for one year * * * the person's license to drive. * * * Such a penalty for refusing to take a blood-alcohol test is unquestionably legitimate. * * *

South Dakota further discourages the choice of refusal by allowing the refusal to be used against the defendant at trial. * * * *Schmerber* expressly reserved the question of whether evidence of refusal violated the privilege against self-incrimination. * * *

"[T]he Court has held repeatedly that the Fifth Amendment is limited to prohibiting the use of 'physical or moral compulsion' exerted on the person asserting the privilege." This coercion requirement comes directly from the constitutional language directing that no person "shall be *compelled* in any criminal case to be a witness against himself."

* * *

Here, the state did not directly compel respondent to refuse the test, for it gave him the choice of submitting to the test or refusing.

* * *

[T]he values behind the Fifth Amendment are not hindered when the state offers a suspect the choice of submitting to the blood-alcohol test or having his refusal used against him. The simple blood-alcohol test is so safe, painless, and commonplace, see *Schmerber,* 384 U.S., at 771, 86 S.Ct., at 1836, that respondent concedes, as he must, that the state could legitimately compel the suspect, against his will, to accede to the test. Given, then, that the offer of taking a blood-alcohol test is clearly legitimate, the action becomes no *less* legitimate when the State offers a second option of refusing the test, with the attendant penalties for making that choice. Nor is this a case where the State has subtly coerced respondent into choosing the option it had no right to compel, rather than offering a true choice. To the contrary, the State wants respondent to choose to take the test, for the inference of intoxication arising from a positive blood-alcohol test is far stronger than that arising from a refusal to take the test.

* * *

We hold, therefore, that a refusal to take a blood-alcohol test, after a police officer has lawfully requested it, is not an act coerced by the officer, and thus is not protected by the privilege against self-incrimination. * * *

[Also] we do not think it fundamentally unfair for South Dakota to use the refusal to take the test as evidence of guilt, even though respondent was not specifically warned that his refusal could be used against him at trial.

* * *

While the State did not actually warn respondent that the test results could be used against him, we hold that such a failure to warn was not the sort of implicit promise to forego use of evidence that would unfairly "trick" respondent if the evidence were later offered against him at trial. We therefore conclude that the use of evidence of refusal after these warnings comported with the fundamental fairness required by Due Process.

IV

The judgment of the South Dakota Supreme Court is reversed, and the case is remanded for further proceedings not inconsistent with this opinion.

Discovery is designed to ascertain the truth.

JONES v. SUPERIOR COURT OF NEVADA COUNTY

Supreme Court of California, 1962.
58 Cal.2d 56, 22 Cal.Rptr. 879, 372 P.2d 919.

TRAYNOR, Justice

On October 30, 1961, the day set for his trial on the charge of rape, petitioner filed a motion for continuance and an affidavit in which he alleged that he was and for a long time had been impotent and that he needed time to gather medical evidence including medical reports in connection with injuries he suffered in 1953 and 1954. The motion was granted. On November 3 the district attorney filed a motion for discovery, requesting petitioner and his attorney to make available to the prosecution: (1) the names and addresses of any and all physicians and surgeons subpoenaed to testify on behalf of petitioner with respect to certain injuries suffered by him in 1953 and 1954 and bearing on the question of whether or not petitioner is impotent; (2) the names and addresses of all physicians who have treated petitioner prior to the trial; (3) all reports of doctors or other reports pertaining to the physical condition of petitioner relating to said injuries and bearing on the question whether petitioner is impotent; and (4) all x-rays of petitioner taken immediately following the 1953 and 1954 injuries. The court granted the motion over petitioner's objection. Petitioner seeks a writ of prohibition to restrain enforcement of the trial court's order.

Discovery is designed to ascertain the truth * * * in criminal as well as in civil cases.

* * *

In People v. Riser, * * * we noted that "Originally at common law the accused in a criminal action could not compel production of documents or other evidence in the possession of the prosecution. Production was denied before trial on the ground that to compel the prosecution to reveal its evidence beforehand would enable the defendant to secure perjured testimony and fabricated evidence to meet the state's case. It was felt, furthermore, that to allow the defendant to compel production when the prosecution could not in its turn compel production from the defendant because of the privilege against self incrimination would unduly shift to the defendant's side a balance of advantages already heavily weighted in his favor. * * * Absent some governmental requirement that information be kept confidential for the purposes of effective law enforcement, the state has no interest in denying the accused access to all evidence that can throw light on issues in the case, and in particular it has no interest in convicting on the testimony of witnesses who have not been as rigorously cross-examined and as thoroughly impeached as the evidence permits. To deny flatly any right of production on the ground that an imbalance would be created between the advantages of prosecution and defense would be to lose sight of the true purpose of a criminal trial, the ascertainment of the facts." Similarly, absent the privilege against self-incrimination or other privileges provided by law, the defendant in a criminal case has no valid interest in denying the prosecution access to evidence that can throw light on issues in the case.

* * *

Petitioner contends, however, that the discovery order in this case violates the privilege against self-incrimination * * * and the attorney-client privilege. * * * It is settled that a defendant in a criminal case may not be compelled to testify * * * and it has generally been held that he may not be required to produce private documents in his possession.

Unlike an ordinary witness, a defendant need make no showing that the answer or document sought may be incriminating * * *, for the very fact that the prosecution seeks it, establishes that in the prosecution's view it may be incriminating.

* * *

Moreover, insofar as the prosecution seeks reports made or to be made by physicians to whom petitioner "was sent by his attorney for examination, as distinguished from advice and treatment," it would violate the attorney-client privilege, for such reports are communications from petitioner to his attorneys through such physicians.

* * *

The prosecution, however, is entitled to discover the names of the witnesses petitioner intends to call and any reports and x-rays he intends to introduce in evidence in support of his particular affirmative defense of impotence. A number of states have statutes permitting or requiring discovery in criminal cases of the identity of witnesses who are to be called to testify for a defendant in connection with a particular defense, such as an alibi.

* * *

Although such discovery may require a defendant to disclose information that would lead to effective rebuttal of his defense, these statutes have uniformly been upheld against the claim that they violate the privilege against self-incrimination.

* * *

The identity of the defense witnesses and the existence of any reports or x-rays the defense offers in evidence will necessarily be revealed at the trial. The witnesses will be subject to cross-examination, and the reports and x-rays subject to study and challenge. Learning the identity of the defense witnesses and of such reports and x-rays in advance merely enables the prosecution to perform its function at the trial more effectively. Thus, "the alibi statutes do not infringe on the privilege against self-incrimination. Rather, they set up a wholly reasonable rule of pleading which in no manner compels a defendant to give any evidence other than that which he will voluntarily and without compulsion give at trial. Such statutes do not violate the right of a defendant to be forever silent. Rather they say to the accused: If you don't intend to remain silent, if you expect to offer an alibi defense, then advance notice and whereabouts must be forthcoming; but if you personally and your potential witnesses elect to remain silent throughout the trial, we have no desire to break that silence by any requirement of this statute." (Dean, Advance Specification of Defense in Criminal Cases, 20 A.B.A.J. 435, 440.)

Insofar as the trial court's order herein requires petitioner to reveal the names and addresses of witnesses he intends to call and to produce reports and x-rays he intends to introduce in evidence to support his defense of impotence, it does not violate the privilege against self-incrimination. Nor to this extent does it violate the attorney-client privilege. It simply requires petitioner to disclose information that he will shortly reveal anyway. Such information is discoverable. The order, however, is not limited to the discovery of such information, and therefore cannot be enforced in its present form.

Let a peremptory writ of prohibition issue restraining the trial court from proceeding in a manner inconsistent with the views expressed herein.

Children should be seen, heard, and listened to.

IN RE GAULT

Supreme Court of the United States, 1967.
387 U.S. 1, 87 S.Ct. 1428, 18 L.Ed.2d 527.

Mr. Justice FORTAS delivered the opinion of the Court.

This is an appeal * * * from a judgment of the Supreme Court of Arizona affirming the dismissal of a petition for a writ of habeas corpus. * * * The petition sought the release of Gerald Francis Gault, appellants' 15-year-old son, who had been committed as a juvenile delinquent to the State Industrial School by the Juvenile Court of Gila County, Arizona. The Supreme Court of Arizona affirmed dismissal of the writ against various arguments which included an attack upon the constitutionality of the Arizona Juvenile Code because of its alleged denial of procedural due process rights to juveniles charged with being "delinquents." * * * It concluded that the proceedings ending in commitment of Gerald Gault did not offend those requirements. We do not agree, and we reverse. We begin with a statement of the facts.

On Monday, June 8, 1964, at about 10 a.m., Gerald Francis Gault and a friend, Ronald Lewis, were taken into custody by the Sheriff of Gila County. * * * The police action on June 8 was taken as the result of a verbal complaint by a neighbor of the boys, Mrs. Cook, about a telephone call made to her in which the caller or callers made lewd or indecent remarks. It will suffice for purposes of this opinion to say that the remarks or questions put to her were of the irritatingly offensive, adolescent, sex variety.

At the time Gerald was picked up, his mother and father were both at work. No notice that Gerald was being taken into custody was left at the home. No other steps were taken to advise them that their son had, in effect, been arrested. Gerald was taken to the Children's Detention Home. When his mother arrived home at about 6 o'clock, Gerald was not there. Gerald's older brother was sent to look for him at the trailer home of the Lewis family. He apparently learned then that Gerald was in custody. He so informed his mother. The two of them went to the Detention Home. The deputy probation officer, Flagg, who was also superintendent of the Detention Home, told Mrs. Gault "why Jerry was there" and said that a hearing would be held in Juvenile Court at 3 o'clock the following day, June 9.

* * *

On June 9, Gerald, his mother, his older brother, and Probation Officers Flagg and Henderson appeared before the Juvenile Judge in chambers. * * * No one was sworn at this hearing. No transcript or recording was made. No memorandum or record of the substance of the proceedings was prepared. Our information about the proceedings and the subsequent hearing on June 15, derives entirely from the testimony of the Juvenile Court Judge, Mr. and Mrs. Gault and Officer Flagg at the habeas corpus proceeding conducted two months later. From this, it appears that at the June 9 hearing Gerald was questioned by the judge about the telephone call. There was conflict as to what he said. * * * Judge McGhee testified that Gerald "admitted making one of these [lewd] statements." At the conclusion of the hearing, the judge said he would "think about it." Gerald was taken back to the Detention Home. He was not sent to his own home with his parents. On June 11 or 12, after having been detained since June 8, Gerald was released and driven home. * * * At 5 p.m. on the day of Gerald's release, Mrs. Gault received a note signed by Officer Flagg [informing her that further hearings were scheduled for Monday, June 15].

At the appointed time on Monday, June 15, Gerald, his father and mother, Ronald Lewis and his father, and Officers Flagg and Henderson were present before Judge McGhee. Witnesses at the habeas corpus proceeding differed in their recollections of Gerald's testimony at the June 15 hearing. * * * Again, the complainant, Mrs. Cook, was not present. * * * The Juvenile Judge said "she didn't have to be present at that hearing." The judge did not speak to Mrs. Cook or communicate with her at any time. Probation Officer Flagg had talked to her once—over the telephone on June 9.

* * * At the conclusion of the hearing, the judge committed Gerald as a juvenile delinquent to the State Industrial School "for the period of his minority [that is, until 21], unless sooner discharged by due process of law." An order to that effect was entered. It recites that "after a full hearing and due deliberation the Court finds that

said minor is a delinquent child, and that said minor is of the age of 15 years."

No appeal is permitted by Arizona law in juvenile cases. On August 3, 1964, a petition for a writ of habeas corpus was filed with the Supreme Court of Arizona and referred by it to the Superior Court for hearing.

At the habeas corpus hearing on August 17, Judge McGhee was vigorously cross-examined as to the basis for his actions. * * *

* * * In substance, he concluded that Gerald came within [an Arizona law that] * * * specifies that a "delinquent child" includes one "who has violated a law of the state or an ordinance or regulation of a political subdivision thereof." The law which Gerald was found to have violated * * * provides that a person who "in the presence or hearing of any woman or child * * * uses vulgar, abusive or obscene language, is guilty of a misdemeanor. * * *" The penalty specified in the Criminal Code, which would apply to an adult, is $5 to $50, or imprisonment for not more than two months. The judge also testified [that the law] * * * includes in the definition of a "delinquent child" one who, as the judge phrased it, is "habitually involved in immoral matters."

Asked about the basis for his conclusion that Gerald was "habitually involved in immoral matters," the judge testified, somewhat vaguely, that two years earlier * * * a "referral" was made concerning Gerald "where the boy had stolen a baseball glove from another boy and lied to the Police Department about it." * * * The judge also testified that Gerald had admitted making other nuisance phone calls in the past which, as the judge recalled the boy's testimony, were "silly calls, or funny calls, or something like that."

The Superior Court dismissed the writ, and appellants sought review in the Arizona Supreme Court. * * *

The Supreme Court handed down an elaborate and wide-ranging opinion affirming dismissal of the writ. * * * [Appellants] urge that we hold the Juvenile Code of Arizona invalid on its face or as applied in this case because, contrary to the Due Process Clause of the Fourteenth Amendment, the juvenile is taken from the custody of his parents and committed to a state institution pursuant to proceedings in which the Juvenile Court has virtually unlimited discretion, and in which the following basic rights are denied:

1. Notice of the charges;
2. Right to counsel;
3. Right to confrontation and cross-examination;
4. Privilege against self-incrimination;
5. Right to a transcript of the proceedings; and
6. Right to appellate review.

* * *

* * * The essential difference between Gerald's case and a normal criminal case is that safeguards available to adults were discarded in Gerald's case. * * *

If Gerald had been over 18, he would not have been subject to Juvenile Court proceedings. For the particular offense immediately involved, the maximum punishment would have been a fine of $5 to $50, or imprisonment in jail for not more than two months. Instead, he was committed to custody for a maximum of six years. If he had been over 18 and had committed an offense to which such a sentence might apply, he would have been entitled to substantial rights under the Constitution of the United States as well as under Arizona's laws and constitution. The United States Constitution would guarantee him rights and protections with respect to arrest, search, and seizure, and pretrial interrogation. It would assure him of specific notice of the charges and adequate time to decide his course of action and to prepare his defense. He would be entitled to clear advice that he could be represented by counsel, and, at least if a felony were involved, the State would be required to provide counsel if his parents were unable to afford it. If the court acted on the basis of his confession, careful procedures would be required to assure its voluntariness. If the case went to trial, confrontation and opportunity for cross-examination would be guaranteed. * * *

* * *

We now turn to the specific issues which are presented to us in the present case.

Notice of Charges

Appellants allege that the Arizona Juvenile Code is unconstitutional or alternatively that the proceedings before the Juvenile Court were constitutionally defective because of failure to provide adequate notice of the hearings. * * *

* * *

The Supreme Court of Arizona rejected appellants' claim that due process was denied. * * * It held that the appropriate rule is that "the infant and his parents or guardian will receive a petition only reciting a conclusion of delinquency. But no later than the initial hearing by the judge, they must be advised of the facts involved in the case. If the charges are denied, they must be given a reasonable period of time to prepare."

We cannot agree with the court's conclusion that adequate notice was given in this case. Notice, to comply with due process requirements, must be given sufficiently in advance of scheduled court proceedings so that reasonable opportunity to prepare will be afforded, and it must "set forth the alleged misconduct with particularity." * * * The "initial hearing" in the present case was a hearing on the merits. Notice at that time is not timely. * * *

* * * [Due process] does not allow a hearing to be held in which a youth's freedom and his parents' right to his custody are at stake without giving them timely notice, in advance of the hearing, of the specific issues that they must meet. Nor, in the circumstances of this case, can it reasonably be said that the requirement of notice was waived.

Right to Counsel

Appellants charge that the Juvenile Court proceedings were fatally defective because the court did not advise Gerald or his parents of their right to counsel, and proceeded with the hearing, the adjudication of delinquency and the order of commitment in the absence of counsel for the child and his parents or an express waiver of the right thereto. * * *

* * * There is no material difference in this respect between adult and juvenile proceedings of the sort here involved. * * *

* * * A proceeding where the issue is whether the child will be found to be "delinquent" and subjected to the loss of his liberty for years is comparable in seriousness to a felony prosecution. The juvenile needs the assistance of counsel to cope with problems of law, to make skilled inquiry into the facts, to insist upon regularity of the proceedings, and to ascertain whether he has a defense and to prepare and submit it. The child "requires the guiding hand of counsel at every step in the proceedings against him." * * *

We conclude that the Due Process Clause of the Fourteenth Amendment requires that in respect to proceedings to determine delinquency which may result in commitment to an institution in which the juvenile's freedom is curtailed, the child and his parents must be notified of the child's right to be represented by counsel retained by them, or if they are unable to afford counsel, that counsel will be appointed to represent the child.

* * *

Confrontation, Self-incrimination, Cross-examination

Appellants urge that the writ of habeas corpus should have been granted because of the denial of the rights of confrontation and cross-examination in the Juvenile Court hearings, and because the privilege against self-incrimination, was not observed. * * * If the confession is disregarded, appellants argue that the delinquency conclusion, since it was fundamentally based on a finding that Gerald had made lewd remarks during the phone call to Mrs. Cook, is fatally defective for failure to accord the rights of confrontation and cross-examination which the Due Process Clause of the Fourteenth Amendment of the Federal Constitution guarantees in state proceedings generally.

Our first question, then, is whether Gerald's admission was improperly obtained and relied on as the basis of decision, in conflict with the Federal Constitution. * * *

We shall assume that Gerald made admissions of the sort described by the Juvenile Court Judge, as quoted above. Neither Gerald nor his parents were advised that he did not have to testify or make a statement, or that an incriminating statement might result in his commitment as a "delinquent."

The Arizona Supreme Court rejected appellants' contention that Gerald had a right to be advised that he need not incriminate himself. It said: "We think the necessary flexibility for individualized treatment will be enhanced by a rule which does not require the judge to advise the infant of a privilege against self-incrimination."

In reviewing this conclusion of Arizona's Supreme Court, we emphasize again that we are here concerned only with a proceeding to determine whether a minor is a "delinquent" and which may result in commitment to a state institution. Specifically, the question is whether, in such a proceeding, an admission by the juvenile may be used against him in the absence of clear and unequivocal evidence that the admission was made with knowledge that he was not obliged to speak and would not be penalized for remaining silent. In light of Miranda v. State of Arizona, * * * we must also consider whether, if the privilege against self-incrimination is available, it can effectively be waived unless counsel is present or the right to counsel has been waived.

It has long been recognized that the eliciting and use of confessions or admissions require careful scrutiny. * * *

The privilege against self-incrimination is, of course, related to the question of the safeguards necessary to assure that admissions or confessions are reasonably trustworthy, that they are not the mere fruits of fear or coercion, but are reliable expressions of the truth. * * * One of its purposes is to prevent the state, whether by force or by psychological domination, from overcoming the mind and will of the person under investigation and depriving him of the freedom to decide whether to assist the state in securing his conviction.

It would indeed be surprising if the privilege against self-incrimination were available to hardened criminals but not to children. The language of the Fifth Amendment, applicable to the States by operation of the Fourteenth Amendment, is unequivocal and without exception. And the scope of the privilege is comprehensive. * * *

* * *

Against the application to juveniles of the right to silence, it is argued that juvenile proceedings are "civil" and not "criminal," and therefore the privilege should not apply. * * *

It would be entirely unrealistic to carve out of the Fifth Amendment all statements by juveniles on the ground that these cannot lead to "criminal" involvement. In the first place, juvenile proceedings to determine "delinquency," which may lead to commitment to a state institution, must be regarded as "criminal" for purposes of the privilege against self-incrimination. To hold otherwise would be to disregard substance because of the feeble enticement of the "civil" label-of-convenience which has been attached to juvenile proceedings. Indeed, in over half of the States, there is not even assurance that the juvenile will be kept in separate institutions, apart from adult "criminals." In those States juveniles may be placed in or transferred to adult penal institutions after having been found "delinquent" by a juvenile court. For this purpose, at least, commitment is a deprivation of liberty. It is incarceration against one's will, whether it is called "criminal" or "civil." And our Constitution guarantees that no person shall be "compelled" to be a witness against himself when he is threatened with deprivation of his liberty—a command which this Court has broadly applied and generously implemented in accordance with the teaching of the history of the privilege and its great office in mankind's battle for freedom.

* * *

We conclude that the constitutional privilege against self-incrimination is applicable in the case of juveniles as it is with respect to adults. We appreciate that special problems may arise with respect to waiver of the privilege by or on behalf of children, and that there may well be some differences in technique—but not in principle—depending upon the age of the child and the presence and competence of parents. The participation of counsel will, of course, assist the police, Juvenile Courts and appellate tribunals in administering the privilege. If counsel was not present for some permissible reason when an admission was obtained, the greatest care must be taken to assure that the admission was voluntary, in the sense not only that it was not coerced or suggested, but also that it was not the product of ignorance of rights or of adolescent fantasy, fright or despair.

The "confession" of Gerald Gault was first obtained by Officer Flagg, out of the presence of Gerald's parents, without counsel and without advising him of his right to silence, as far as appears. The judgment of the Juvenile Court was stated by the judge to be based on Gerald's admissions in court. Neither "admission" was reduced to writing, and, to say the least, the process by which the "admissions," were obtained and received must be characterized as lacking the certainty and order which are required of proceedings of such formidable consequences. Apart from the "admission," there was nothing upon which a judgment or finding might be based. There was no sworn testimony. * * *

* * * We now hold that, absent a valid confession, a determination of delinquency and an order of commitment to a state institution cannot be sustained in the absence of sworn testimony subjected to the opportunity for cross-examination in accordance with our law and constitutional requirements.

* * *

For the reasons stated, the judgment of the Supreme Court of Arizona is reversed and the cause remanded for further proceedings not inconsistent with this opinion. It is so ordered.

Judgment reversed and cause remanded with directions.

Review Questions

1. What are the roles of attorneys, juries, and judges in the adversary system of law? What party usually has the burden of proof? What method is used to limit the testimony of a particular witness? What may an expert do that a nonexpert may not? When are leading questions allowed? When is communication privileged? What is the purpose of rules of evidence? Explain your answers.

2. Are there any problems with "notice" in class actions? When will a class action not be allowed? What is the function of the Judicial Panel on Multidistrict Litigation? Explain your answers.

3. What is the purpose of venue? How does it differ from jurisdiction? Why is there no general federal common law? How are "choice of law" problems resolved? Explain your answers.

4. What numbers are required for a jury (1) in a federal criminal case, (2) for due process in a state criminal case, (3) for decision in a federal civil case, and (4) for decision in a federal criminal case? What is the number of peremptory challenges in the federal court? Within what time period must a motion for new trial be filed under the federal rules of civil procedure? An appeal under those rules? Under the federal rules of criminal procedure within what period of time must an appeal be filed?

5. How, when, and by whom may arrests be made? What special protection applies regarding obtaining evidence for use in criminal trials? What special rules of discovery apply to criminal cases? What special protections are afforded an accused during a criminal trial? Is the death penalty a "cruel and unusual" punishment? Are there special protections for juveniles charged with crime? Explain your answers.

6. How does a trial in equity differ from a trial at law? To what extent does "res judicata" apply to equity and divorce decrees? In "no fault" divorce when are specific acts of misconduct relevant? What is the main purpose of probating the estate of a decedent? What is the difference between a guardian and a conservator? Explain your answers.

7. What are the basic steps of an appeal? Explain.

8. Define the following terms: arbitration, best evidence rule, due process, escheat, interlocutory injunction, intestate, pretrial conference, recrimination, remittitur, spendthrift, supremacy clause, "the truth-finder."

Problems

1. Sixteen-year-old Minerva Ferdner was holding the third meeting of her just founded "Young Hellraisers" Club when newcomer Harry Wright (an undercover police rookie on orders to "break up those youth gangs before they break up the town") suggested "hotwiring" a car down on 4th and Benfield. Having "just checked out the neighborhood," Harry could persuasively assure the group that the unlocked car was theirs for the taking. When Minerva is later hauled into juvenile court for auto theft, she insists on public trial by jury where the whole world can proclaim her innocence. But does Minerva have any defense to the criminal conduct? And is she entitled to public trial by jury? Explain.

Assume that Minerva is found guilty of criminal auto theft. What alternatives are open to the juvenile court in reforming this young victim of her times?

2. Neill Barnes is served with a summons and a copy of a complaint charging him with negligence. What response should Neill make to this complaint in the following situations, and how does each response affect the plaintiff?

a. Every allegation in the complaint is untrue and unfounded;
b. Some allegations are true; others are false;
c. Every allegation is true, but there is some reason why Neill should not be held liable (i.e., he has a good defense);
d. Even if every allegation is true, the plaintiff cannot win his case.

What are the consequences of not responding at all?

In situation (c) above, the plaintiff has denied Neill's defense. Who has the burden of proof when this case goes to trial, and what is this burden?

3. Upon grand jury indictment for first-degree murder (a felony punishable by life imprisonment), a warrant was issued for the arrest of Luther Bradley. State police sighted Bradley near the state border and chased him ninety-six miles into the neighboring state before apprehending him. Were the officers justified in crossing state lines to make their arrest? Explain. What procedure must be followed to bring Bradley back to the state of the crime? After Bradley's return, is the court likely to release him on bail? Explain.

Trial is close at hand. But Bradley's lawyer fears that local press coverage has hopelessly prejudiced the community against the accused. What should he do to protect his client's interests?

Assume that Bradley is found guilty of first-degree murder, and his sentence is affirmed on appeal. New evidence is later discovered, however, that clears him of any part in the crime. But is Bradley entitled to another "day in court"? And how can he draw judicial attention to his changed situation? Explain.

4. Lou and Freda Armstrong, owners and operators of a houseboat rental service, intentionally overcharged each of sixty-five customers $250 for a two-week rental period. Upon discovering the overcharge, several customers expressed concern as to the best method of prosecuting their claim. What legal options are available to them?

5. Wealthy rug merchant James Ridgely III fatally crashed his small private aircraft on a business trip to Reno. His will divided his sizeable estate equally among his wife, Beatrice, his twenty-three-year-old son, James IV, and little Constance, his eight-year-old daughter. Constance, of course, is too young to understand her inheritance; James IV, a family man with two children, is usually too drunk to spend his wisely; and frail Beatrice, overcome by the emotional upset of her husband's death, feels too distraught to worry about financial affairs at all. How can Connie, James IV, and Beatrice handle their estates?

If James III had died without a will, how would his property be distributed? If he additionally left no surviving relatives?

6. Jason Grew was injured ($20,000 worth) in an auto collision with a tourist from out of state. Jason decided to bring a legal action in the federal district court of the defendant's home state, some 1,200 miles away, to make it difficult for the defendant to present a defense (favorable witnesses are all located at the scene of the accident) and to circumvent his own state's rule on contributory negligence, by which the plaintiff's slightest negligence is a complete bar to his recovery. The defendant's state also follows this rule, but Jason hopes to convince the federal court to permit recovery as the "more equitable thing to do." Assuming that Jason is guilty of contributory negligence, will the federal court permit him to recover damages? Explain. Is the defendant's home state the best place to handle this case? Explain.

Assume that a jury verdict for the defendant is affirmed on appeal. Can Jason bring his action again in another court of law? Explain your answer.

7. When their next door neighbors' teenaged son, Billy, formed a rock group with three of his friends, Joe and Donna Wilson had been first to encourage him. But seven months of extremely loud and continuous practice not only failed to improve the group's musical ability but had deprived the Wilsons of their nightly sleep as well. After waiting another six months to complain to Billy about the situation, they discovered that the group had just purchased a much larger amplifier to increase the volume, if not the quality, of their sound. Repeated complaints brought no relief from the young musicians who insisted that, after thirteen months of practice, they just had "too much time and effort invested" to give it all up. Can Joe and Donna obtain relief in a court of equity? Explain.

Assume the court has issued an injunction commanding the group to refrain from practicing after 11 P.M. Are the Wilsons helpless if the late night sessions continue in disregard of the decree? Explain.

8. When Susan Young found herself the defendant in a negligence action, she quickly called plaintiff Sid Harvey to see if he really had a case against her. Sid's complaint alleged only that Susan's careless driving had resulted in a collision with his car—that he was seriously injured in the amount of $15,000. But Sid refused to comment on his proof, stating that Susan could "just wait till we get to court to find out." He did mention some "damaging" photographs taken at the scene of the accident and two surprise witnesses who would soon tell all—but only in court. Susan seeks your advice. Must she wait till trial to examine Sid's case against her? Explain fully.

Assume that Susan examines the evidence and agrees that it is strong proof of her negligence. What would you advise her to do?

Assume, finally, that the case goes to trial, and Sid Harvey is awarded a judgment of $15,000. After four months go by, during which time Susan refuses to pay anything, Sid comes to Susan's home and demands payment. Susan replies saying: "I've got this house, the clothes on my back, a poorly paying job, and a tiny lot of land three miles down the road. Where am I going to get $15,000?" What options are available to Sid in enforcing the judgment against Susan? Explain.

It does not lie within the power of any judicial system to remedy all human wrongs. . . . ingratitude, avarice, broken faith, brutal words, and heartless disregard of the feelings of others—are beyond any effective legal remedy. . . .

William L. Prosser
Law of Torts

4

Business and Other Torts, Crimes, and Family Law

Torts

WHAT IS THE DIFFERENCE BETWEEN TORT AND CRIME?

A legal concept, as you will recall, is an authoritatively defined category into which cases or fact situations can be placed so that certain rules, principles, and standards apply. Tort and crime are two of these legal concepts. Both are broad categories covering a wide range of human activity; but, while they are distinct legal concepts, they are interrelated as well since the same act is frequently both a tort and a crime.

The word "tort" comes from the Latin word "tortus" meaning "twisted." In the French language, tort means "wrong." And that is what a tort is—some kind of wrong or twisted conduct—conduct that is *socially unreasonable.* Any time a person unreasonably interferes with another's interests, he or she is guilty of a tort. And there are many such torts or wrongs in our increasingly complex and crowded world. The purpose of tort law is to determine and adjust these losses, to afford compensation to an individual for injuries sustained as the result of tortious conduct.

A person who commits a crime frequently commits a tort as well, for most crimes involve socially unreasonable conduct, i.e., conduct that unreasonably interferes with someone else's interests. The crimes of murder, manslaughter, rape, robbery, burglary, and arson are all good examples of conduct that is both criminal and tortious.

Crime, unlike tort, is an offense against the public—all the people—and results in government prosecution of the accused. If convicted, the criminal is fined, imprisoned, or sentenced to death. This criminal prosecution is not designed to compensate the injured victim of the crime. To be sure, more and more judges today are ordering convicted criminals to make *restitution* to their victims (i.e., reimburse them for their actual loss). And some states have even established crime victims' compensation programs to provide relief to crime victims in specified cases. But restitution and victims' programs as they exist today fall far short of adequately compensating the victim of criminal activity. Suppose you are held up, mugged, and robbed. Besides losing your wallet (and the fifty dollars inside of it), you are hospitalized for a week with your injuries. The government will follow the criminal procedure described in Chapter 3 to convict your mugger and sentence him or her to jail. But in order to recover compensatory damages that will pay for your stay in the hospital and punitive damages that will punish the wrongdoer for his or her outrageous conduct, you must bring a civil action for the tort yourself, using a civil action procedure. Both the procedures and their objectives differ. Your burden of proof in the tort action (by a "mere preponderance" of the evidence) is much less than the state's burden in the criminal action (beyond a "reasonable doubt"). Because of this, it is possible for you to win your tort case while the state fails in its criminal prosecution for the same act, or vice versa. Frequently and unfortunately, the person guilty of the crime has no money or property. If that is the situation, it does no good to sue the wrongdoer for the tort because he or she is unable to pay a judgment.

At one time in England, both the tort and crime were considered by the same court at the same time. This has not been true in the United States, but because we did inherit our legal system from the English, we do find that some of our torts and crimes share the same name, such as "assault," "battery," and "trespass."

It is essential to differentiate between tort and crime—to remember that a tort is any socially unreasonable conduct for which a court of law will grant money damages to compensate an individual for his or her losses. Such conduct may be intentional or negligent. It certainly includes many types of criminal conduct such as murder, rape, and robbery. Crime, however, is an offense against the public; it results in a criminal proceeding designed to punish and reform the criminal. And it generally has little to do with compensating the victim of the crime.

WHAT ARE THE THREE THEORIES OF TORT LIABILITY?

A person may be held liable for tortious conduct on any of the following three grounds.

Intentional Interference with the Plaintiff's Interests

The intent required is not a hostile one but merely an intent to bring about a certain result. Even a defendant with good intentions is liable if the results of his or her actions are socially unreasonable: he or she intends to bring about certain results and is liable for any harm caused in doing so. But how do you tell what the defendant "intends" to do? Well, the defendant in a tort action is said to intend those results that a reasonable person in his or her position would believe substantially certain to follow from the actions. So while a person who shoots a gun into a crowd may hope that no one will be hurt, he or she is still liable to anyone who is injured because a reasonable person in his or her position would realize that harm is substantially certain to follow.

Negligence

A person is also liable for harm that results from his or her carelessness. It is an intentional tort if you run down a person with your car, desiring to hit him or her, or with knowledge that you are certain to do so. But if you merely run a person down carelessly when you fail to stop for a red light, you are guilty of negligence.

But remember, negligence is carelessness—and there is no liability for an unavoidable accident. This is an accident that occurs in the absence of negligence (i.e., one that would have occurred no matter how careful you were at the time). If a man suffers a heart attack at the wheel of his car and causes an accident, he is not liable for the damage unless he knew that he was likely to become sick and went ahead and drove the car anyway. Similarly, there is no negligence and no liability when a child dashes out in front of a car and a driver cannot avoid hitting her.

Negligence serves as the basis for liability in a great variety of situations, including the operation of motor vehicles, malpractice suits against professionals such as doctors or lawyers who have been careless in their work, and cases against landowners for injury to persons caused by their negligent acts. It is always based on a departure from a reasonable standard of conduct—the conduct of a reasonable, prudent person under the same or similar circumstances.

Strict Liability

This is liability without fault. Under certain circumstances, a defendant may be held responsible where his or her actions are neither intentional nor negligent. The person is held strictly liable simply because he or she caused the harmful result. Strict liability applies in situations where the defendant's conduct involves a very substantial risk of harm to others regardless of the precautions he or she takes. So where a person engages in blasting operations, the person is strictly liable for any harm that results.

WHAT INTENTIONAL BUSINESS OR COMMERCIAL TORTS ARE RECOGNIZED?

A commercial tort or business tort is socially unreasonable conduct that adversely affects a consumer, competitor, or other party. As with any other tort, the injured party may sue the tortfeasor (the businessperson who commits the tort) for money damages. The law recognizes six specific commercial or business wrongs.

The Commercial Tort of Infringing on Another's Trademark or Trade Name

According to the federal Lanham Act of 1946, a "trademark" is "any work, name, symbol, or device or any combination thereof adopted and used by a manufacturer or merchant to identify his goods and distinguish them from those manufactured or sold by others." Trade names, on the other hand, do not identify the goods themselves but rather relate to the business or business goodwill.

An exclusive twenty year right to use a trademark may be obtained by registering the mark with the U.S. Patent Office in Washington, D.C. If the right is infringed, the owner may obtain a court ordered injunction in addition to money damages. The twenty year right is renewable for additional twenty year periods indefinitely so long as the trademark is used in commerce.

Trade names, in contrast, are generally protected as common law property rights acquired by use of the name in connection with the business; or they may be protected under state registration laws. The use of the same or a deceptively similar trade name may be enjoined.

One reason the law protects trademarks and trade names is to protect consumers. Symbols and names relating to products provide valuable product identification for consumers and prevent unscrupulous businesses from "palming off" their goods as products of another. The idea is to protect consumers from buying goods they do not intend to buy. Knowing the trademark or trade name of a product makes it easy for a retailer to provide continuity of product quality. And by reference to trademarks and trade names, consumers can avoid buying products they have found to be unsatisfactory in the past.

The law also protects trademarks and trade names to protect manufacturers. A manufacturer who produces a superior product can use a trademark or trade name to identify the product; the mark or name will obviously have great value to the manufacturer. When another business copies the mark or name, it not only confuses the public, but it causes loss to the business that owns the mark or name. Such copying constitutes socially unreasonable conduct and is a tort—a commercial tort—for which the owner of the mark or name may obtain money damages. Section 35 of the Lanham Act specifically provides for tort damages relating to infringement of another's trademark as follows:

> Section 35. When a violation of any right of the registrant of a mark registered in the patent office shall have been established in any civil action arising under this Act, the plaintiff shall be entitled * * * to recover (1) defendant's profits, (2) any damages sustained by the plaintiff, and (3) the costs of the action. * * * In assessing damages the court may enter judgment, according to the circumstances of the case, for any sum above the amount found as actual damages, not exceeding three times such amount.

There are numerous examples in the law of the tort of infringing another's trademark or trade name. In Maier Brewing Co. v. Fleischmann Distilling Corp., 390 F.2d 117 (9th Cir.1968), the plaintiff Fleischmann successfully sued the defendant Brewing Company for selling beer under the same name and label as the plaintiff sold scotch whiskey ("Black and White"). In Armco Steel Corp. v. International Armament Corp., 249 F.Supp. 954 (D.C. D.C.1966), Armco Steel brought suit when the defendant used the name "Interarmco" to describe its products. And in Safeway Stores, Inc. v. Safeway Quality Foods, Inc., 433 F.2d 99 (7th Cir.1970), the plaintiff sued the defendant for using the same trade name "Safeway."

In cases brought under Section 35 of the Lanham Act, the plaintiff seeks an order enjoining the defendant from further use of the trademark; an order requiring the defendant to destroy or deliver up any products or containers bearing such mark; a judgment for the defendant's profits obtained from such use; and judgment for treble damages (i.e., three times the damages sustained by the plaintiff) together with the costs of the action including attorney's fees.

The Commercial Tort of Imitating Product Design or Product Packaging

Congress has created a patent system under which an inventor can obtain a patent to his or her invention (i.e., a monopoly or exclusive right to the invention) for a limited period of time (seventeen years). Anyone who infringes upon the patentee's right during this period is subject to court-ordered injunction and damages under the U.S. patent laws.

But many times it is not possible to patent an idea either because the idea is not something "new and never before used" or because it will not result in a "new and useful art, machine, manufacture, or composition of matter, or any new and useful improvement thereof." And sometimes an idea may simply be too costly to patent. Yet unpatented ideas are often very valuable and result in highly salable products. However, because the products have not been patented, they may be copied.

It is well established in the law that copying unpatented products and selling the copies does not in and of itself constitute a tort. The social policy favoring business competition and the availability of competing products for consumers is held sufficient justification for allowing the copying and sale. However, while business may copy unpatented products, it may not intentionally "palm off" the copies as being the "original" manufactured items. A false representation that the goods are the originals rather than copies, which representation is likely to confuse or deceive the public, constitutes the tort of unfair competition for which injunctive relief and damages may be sought. However, it must be emphasized that the mere inability of the public to tell two identical items apart will not support an award of damages—there must be some false representation or intentional "palming off" of the items as the originals.

The Commercial Tort of Misappropriating Another's Trade Secret

To obtain patent protection, a patent applicant must make full disclosure of his or her invention to the U.S. Patent Office. Assuming the patent is granted, it will be available publicly for anyone to inspect. In contrast, a "trade secret" is protected and kept exclusive by means of keeping it secret from the public. The *Restatement of Torts,* Section 757, Comment (b), (1939) defines a "trade secret" as follows:

> A trade secret may consist of any formula, pattern, device or compilation of information which is used in one's business, and which gives him an opportunity to obtain an advantage over competitors who do not know or use it. It may be a formula for a chemical compound, a process of manufacturing, treating or preserving materials, a pattern for a machine or other device, or a list of customers.

Thus, almost any knowledge or information can be a trade secret. Frequently, an inventor must make a choice between patenting a process or protecting it as a trade secret. If he or she chooses the latter course, protection will exist only as long as the process remains a secret.

The law provides limited protection for trade secrets. A business has responsibility not to appropriate *wrongfully* another's trade secrets, as by stealing them or inducing an employee or former employee of the other wrongfully to divulge the secrets. A wrongful appropriation will render the taker liable in tort damages. However, there is no liability where a business *rightfully* discovers another's trade secrets, as by independently developing the same ideas or studying the other party's marketed products. Once a product is placed on the market, anyone is free to look at it, reverse engineer it, take it apart, figure it out, and copy it. Remember, a trade secret is protected only so long as it remains secret.

However, substantial—not absolute—secrecy is all that is required. A business possessing a trade secret may entrust it to any number of individuals as long as the disclosure is made pursuant to an obligation of trust and confidence. For example, an employee has fiduciary duties to his or her employer by reason of the employment contract and may not divulge the employer's trade secrets. And, frequently, the employment contract expressly prohibits the employee from disclosing trade secrets upon leaving the employment. Such an agreement will be enforced by the courts unless it constitutes an unreasonable restraint on trade. In each case, the courts must balance the employer's interest in maintaining the secrecy of customer lists and other information with the employee's interest in using his or her job-learned skills in making a living.

Beyond prohibiting "palming off" of copies as originals and imposing liability for wrongfully appropriating another's trade secrets, the law favors full disclosure of ideas and inventions in order that competition may be fostered. True, the patent law grants a seventeen-year monopoly, but only in return for free availability and use of the invention at the end of the seventeen-year period.

The Commercial Tort of Misrepresentation and False Advertising

Fraud requires four things:

1. A material misrepresentation;
2. Intent on the part of the party making the misrepresentation that the other party rely on it;

3. Justifiable reliance by the other party (it would not be justifiable, for example, to rely upon a statement one knows to be false);
4. Inducement of the agreement by the misrepresentation (i.e., the misrepresentation must prompt the party to enter into the transaction).

In the area of commercial torts, false advertising that results in the purchase of goods will serve as the basis for a tort action based on misrepresentation. Of course, the misrepresentation must be of a material fact—something more than mere "puffing" of wares or a statement of opinion. And the buyer must rely on the false advertising in making the purchase. If the buyer was unaware of the advertising or did not rely on it (e.g., because he or she didn't believe it), there can be no recovery. The misrepresentation may be found in national advertising or on labels on the goods themselves.

Besides purchasers, competitors may also have a tort action against a business that falsely advertises; to recover, a competitor must show that the false advertising diverted customers away from his or her business.

The Commercial Tort of Product Defamation, Producer Defamation, or Invasion of Privacy

A businessperson may lawfully promote his or her product by critically comparing it to another's. However, the comparison must be honest and accurate. False assertions about another's product, made with intent to injure the other's business, constitute the tort of *disparagement.* Disparagement is similar to false advertising in that it involves giving false information to potential customers. It differs from false advertising in that the false statements are made about another's product and not one's own. A businessperson who disparages the quality, purity, or value of another's product is liable in tort for any pecuniary damage directly caused by the disparagement. If the false statements also defame the other party in the operation of his or her trade or business (by imputing dishonesty, fraud, deception, or other misconduct to the party so as to reflect poorly on his or her business character or reputation), the businessperson may additionally be liable for libel or slander (see following section).

With regard to the right of privacy, using another's name, portrait, or picture without his or her consent for purposes of trade or advertising constitutes a tortious invasion of the party's right of privacy and is compensable in damages as a commercial tort. A person's right to the exclusive use of his or her own name, portrait, or picture for these purposes is often referred to as a "right of publicity." The case of Haelan Laboratories, Inc. v. Topps Chewing Gum, Inc., 202 F.2d 866, 868 (2d Cir.1953) stated it this way:

> This right might be called a "right of publicity." For it is common knowledge that many prominent persons (especially actors and ballplayers), far from having their feelings bruised through public exposure of their likenesses, would feel sorely deprived if they no longer received money for authorizing advertisements, popularizing their countenances, displayed in newspapers, magazines, buses, trains, and subways. This right of publicity would usually yield them no money unless it could be made the subject of an exclusive grant which barred any other advertiser from using their pictures.

The Commercial "Prima Facie" Tort

Competition is inherently desirable within our economic system because it makes for better products at reduced costs. A person may be such a successful competitor that others simply cannot compete, and, generally, there is nothing tortious in this. But where the sole purpose of the competition is to use economic advantage to destroy the livelihood of another, it is a social wrong within the meaning of tort law—it is "unfair competition." And business has a responsibility to compete fairly. For example, in the famous case of Tuttle v. Buck, 107 Minn. 145, 119 N.W. 946 (1909), a banker set up a barber shop with the sole purpose of putting the local barber out of business. The court held that the banker had committed an actionable tort. The court said:

> The defendant is possessed of large means, and is engaged in the business of a banker in said village of Howard Lake . . . and is nowise interested in the occupation of a barber; yet in the pursuance of the wicked, malicious, and unlawful purpose * * *, and for the sole and only purpose of injuring the trade of the plaintiff, and of accomplishing his purpose and threats of ruining the plaintiff's said business and driving him out of said village, the defendant fitted up and furnished a barber shop in said village for conducting the trade of barbering * * * Said defendant * * * hired two barbers in succession for a stated salary, paid by him, to occupy said shop * * * with the sole design of injuring the plaintiff, and of destroying his said business, and not for the purpose of serving any legitimate interest of his own * * * and * * * to the plaintiff's damage in the sum of $10,000.
>
> * * * When a man starts an opposition place of business, not for the sake of profit to himself, but regardless of loss to himself, and for the sole purpose of driving his competitor out of business, and with the intention of himself retiring upon the accomplishment of his malevolent purpose, he is guilty of wanton wrong and an actionable tort.

Though the defendant's conduct in the *Tuttle* case did not fall within any established classification of tort, the court held that his conduct was "prima facie" (on its face) tortious. Remember, a tort is any socially unreasonable conduct, and any intentional act that is solely designed to damage another's property or trade is socially unreasonable and tortious whether or not it fits within any established tort classification. In the case of Ledwith v. International Paper Co., 64 N.Y.S.2d 810 (1946), the defendant acted from malicious motives to prevent the plaintiff from receiving an increase in pay, then to have the plaintiff demoted and later discharged. The court imposed liability on the defendant, stating that his conduct was a "prima facie" tort.

Two specific kinds of unfair or "prima facie" tortious competition are *interference with contractual relations* and *interference with prospective advantage.* A person interferes with a party's contractual relations when he or she intentionally causes a third party to breach an existing contract with a party. Thus, a person who induces a skilled worker to breach his or her employment contract has interfered with the employer's contractual relations and is liable in damages. The same is true of a retailer who persuades a supplier to breach a contract with another retailer so as to provide him or her with a commodity in short supply; the first retailer has interfered with the other's contractual relations and is liable to the party in damages.

A person interferes with another's prospective advantage when he or she intentionally deprives that other of an economic advantage that the person would otherwise have. This would include inducing another not to enter into a contract with the party. But the examples go far beyond this. In one case, the defendant destroyed the only bridge over to an island; this had the effect of severely injuring the plaintiff's business (i.e., depriving him of an economic advantage). In another case, the defendant fraudulently precipitated the plaintiff's election defeat. In still another case, a defendant telegraph company filed to deliver a message inviting the plaintiff to enter into an advantageous contract. Any method of unfair competition that results in a loss of profits may constitute interference with prospective advantage; a breach of trust, a boycott, an illegal conspiracy, threats or intimidation—all may be tortious within the meaning of "prima facie" tort.

WHAT ARE THE OTHER INTENTIONAL TORTS?

We describe here certain additional types of conduct that have been recognized as torts. But not all torts have names: any socially unreasonable conduct is a tort, and new torts are recognized from time to time.

Intentional Interference with the Person

Battery A battery is an unpermitted, offensive, or unprivileged touching of another's person. Examples include hitting, kicking, shooting, throwing an object that hits someone, or pulling a chair out from under a person just about to sit down. The gist of a battery action is not hostile intent but the absence of consent. So if a man kisses a woman while she is sleeping, he is liable for battery if their relationship is such that his kisses violate her dignity. And a doctor whose patient refuses to have his kidney removed commits a battery when he later removes the kidney after performing an altogether different, minor operation to which the patient has consented.

The touching need not be direct. Coming into contact with the plaintiff's clothing, with an object he or she is holding, or with a horse upon which the plaintiff is sitting is sufficient (e.g., a woman who was bucked off her horse and injured when the defendant struck the animal with a cane successfully sued for a battery). And the defendant who intends to batter one person and instead harms another is liable for battery to the injured party—the intent is said to "transfer" to that party.

Assault An assault is any act that places a person in actual apprehension or fear of an imminent battery. The defendant must have the ability to carry out the threat at the time it is made (or the plaintiff must reasonably think he or she does). It is an assault to aim a weapon at someone, to shoot at a person and miss (hitting the person is a battery), to chase him or her in a hostile manner, or to shake a fist at someone. Mere words, however violent, are generally insufficient. Nor do threats of future violence constitute assault. And if a person is totally unaware of the threat, there is no tortious assault at all because, without knowledge, the plaintiff cannot be in apprehension or fear of a battery. But even without knowledge of the threat, the same act may amount to criminal assault. Where someone waits in hiding to shoot another, points a gun, but is arrested before the intended victim learns of the act, he or she is guilty of criminal though not tortious assault since the intended victim was in no fear or apprehension of a battery.

False imprisonment False imprisonment takes place when one person confines another within a certain area and refuses to let him or her leave. No minimum or maximum time periods for confinement have been established, and complete restraint of freedom for even a very short period of time may constitute this tort. Arrest without legal authority is false imprisonment if there is present restraint of liberty. The restraint may be in a room, a building, a traveling automobile, or even in an entire city. False imprisonment also occurs when prison authorities fail to release someone at the end of his or her prison term. Many cases have been based on mistaken accusations of shoplifting: a person who is held and falsely accused has been improperly confined and may bring an action for the tort of false imprisonment. Merchants are thus advised to exercise great caution in restraining people and accusing them of this crime. Many merchants wait until the suspect has actually left the store with the merchandise before stopping him or her for questioning. Of course, it is a serious mistake and very socially unreasonable to accuse someone incorrectly and hold him or her for theft. The injured party may recover in a court of law for any damage to reputation or any humiliation or mental suffering he or she endures. Thus, if you are improperly accused of shoplifting and held at a store for investigation or arrest, the law of tort provides you with a remedy for your justified anger and strictly mental suffering.

Finally, the crime of kidnapping is also the tort of false imprisonment.

Infliction of mental or emotional distress Tort law also recognizes mental distress alone as a properly compensable injury. Thus a party may seek legal redress for outrageous acts that induce feelings of grief, anxiety, or shame even when unaccompanied by physical injury. "Common carriers," for example, are companies that provide public transportation by train, bus, or air. Because of the carriers' dealings with the public, courts impose upon them a higher standard of conduct, and common carriers have been held liable for mental disturbance caused their passengers by the profane, indecent, or grossly insulting language of their employees. But for individuals who do not deal with the general public, something more than mere insult, indignity, or hurt feelings is required to establish liability—some especially flagrant act of outrageous misconduct, something that exceeds the bounds of decent behavior. Intentional infliction of mental distress has been found where the defendant spread false rumors that the plaintiff's son had hanged himself; where the defendant made threatening telephone calls around the clock to the plaintiff; where, pretending to be the war department, he called the plaintiff with news that her husband had been killed in action; where he brought a mob to the plaintiff's home at night and theatened to lynch him unless he left town; and where the defendant wrapped up a gory dead rat to look like a loaf of bread and sent the package to the plaintiff to open. Many cases involve mishandling of dead bodies. Some have involved the outrageous conduct of bill collectors or the bullying tactics of landlords. Others are concerned with people who are especially susceptible to mental distress such as the elderly, the sick, small children, or pregnant women.

Defamation: libel and slander A person defames another by invading his or her interest in reputation and good name. Defamation may take either of two forms—libel (written defamation) or slander (oral defamation). Both libel and slander work a negative influence on the community's opinion of the plaintiff. In each, a defamatory statement must be communicated to someone other than the plaintiff. A defamatory communication is one that holds the plaintiff up to hatred, contempt, or ridicule, or that causes others to shun or avoid him or her. Defamatory statements injure the plaintiff's reputation, diminish his or her esteem, or induce derogatory feelings about him or her. Courts have held the following statements to be defamatory: that a person has been "raped," or has "attempted suicide," that he or she is "insane," "queer," a "bastard," a "coward," or a "liar."

While words, acts, or insults directed only at the plaintiff may provide a basis for a tort action of intentional infliction of mental distress, they are never sufficient to constitute slander or libel. "Publication" or communication to someone other than the person defamed is essential. This is not to say, however, that written or printed words are required. Publication demands only some written or oral communication (or even communication through gestures or visual exhibits) to some third party who hears and understands. Publication may be made to any third person, including the plaintiff's family or employees.

Slander or oral defamation must generally be supported by proof of "special" damage. In order to recover, the plaintiff must prove not only that he or she was slandered but that he or she suffered loss of customers, contracts, employment, or other pecuniary benefit or suffered serious illness or incurred substantial expense because of the slander. There are four exceptions to this rule, however; and the plaintiff may recover without proof of special damage if the slander imputes to the plaintiff a crime or a present, loathsome disease, or discredits the plaintiff in his or her business, trade, or profession, or imputes unchastity to a female plaintiff. If the defamation falls within one of these exceptions, the jury may award the plaintiff substantial damages without requiring proof that he or she suffered any actual loss. Libel or written defamation on the other hand, usually does not require proof of special damages. General damages are presumed from the publication of the libel.

Defenses to libel and slander, along with other defenses to intentional torts, are considered in the next section of this chapter. As will be seen, special rules are required for the media because of the interests of free press guaranteed by the First Amendment.

Invasion of the right to privacy A new development in tort law is the liability imposed for violating another's right to privacy. We have seen that it is a tort to use a person's name, portrait, or picture without his or her consent for purposes of trade or advertising.

Or a person may invade another's privacy by intruding on his or her solitude or seclusion. This includes searching a home without a warrant or wiretapping lines to eavesdrop on private conversations. A landlord who continually intrudes into a tenant's apartment is also guilty of this tort.

So too is public disclosure of private facts about a person an invasion of his or her privacy. The matter disclosed must be offensive to a reasonable person of ordinary sensibilities, and liability is imposed only when the fact made public is regarded by the community as highly objectionable. In one case, the defendant publicly removed the tires from the plaintiff's car because the plaintiff had failed to pay for them. The court stated that this was a "demonstrative publication" of the debt. Several cases have involved public exhibition of medical pictures of a plaintiff without permission.

In still other cases, the defendant has publicly and falsely attributed an opinion, poem, or work of art to the plaintiff. The defendant has invaded the plaintiff's right to privacy.

Intentional Interference with Property

Trespass to land Any physical entry upon the surface of another's land is a trespass. And this includes much more than just walking on the land. Since a building is considered part of the land, breaking into the building is a trespass. So too is flooding the land with water or shooting across it. Flying over land may be a trespass if it constitutes an unreasonable interference with the owner's actual use of the land. However, it is not a tort when the flight is authorized by federal law. Airport operations authorized by federal statute reflect a public interest that overrides the property rights of landowners near the airport. In such circumstances it may be possible to bring an action against the government based on what is called "inverse condemnation." Where the government acts to seriously damage or materially diminish the value of property, the owner of the property may sue the government defendant for its full value, even where there has been no physical occupancy or formal taking through the power of eminent domain. "Inverse condemnation" cases generally arise where highway construction has severely restricted the plaintiff's use of his or her property or where damage from low flying aircraft has materially diminished its value.

Trespass occurs as well where one person mines another's land or digs a tunnel under it. The tenant who remains on the land after the lease has expired is also a trespasser—he or she has no right to be there. And, finally, a person who successfully encourages others to trespass is also a trespasser.

Nuisance If the defendant uses property in a manner that unreasonably interferes with the plaintiff's use and enjoyment of his or her own land, the conduct is called a nuisance. Ownership or rightful occupation of land (e.g., renting an apartment) gives the owner or occupier the right to quiet enjoyment of the land. And any unreasonable interference with his or her comfort or convenience constitutes a private nuisance. Interference includes excessive noise, vibration, pollution, smoke, heat, odor, or fire hazard. A constantly howling dog, a stagnant swimming pool that smells or is full of mosquitoes, a bawdy house, a noisy heat pump—anything that disturbs the occupier's comfort or peace of mind is a nuisance. Of course, the test applied by the court is offensiveness or inconvenience to the normal person, not the landowner or occupier with peculiar sensitivities (e.g., a very elderly person who cannot tolerate a reasonable degree of noise).

While a trespass is a direct invasion of someone's land, a nuisance is a more indirect interference with the use of the land. Often, the defendant's conduct is both a trespass and a nuisance—a person who floods his or her neighbor's land directly invades the landowner's possession, and, in addition, completely deprives him or her of the use and enjoyment of the land.

In the operation of business, care must be taken to avoid creating nuisances. And a nuisance can involve a number of interferences. Operating a factory may create loud noise, smoke, air pollution, vibration, water pollution, and be a fire hazard all at the same time. In determining whether the defendant's conduct is unreasonable, and therefore a nuisance, several factors will be considered such as the values of the respective properties, the social benefits from allowing the condition to continue including any employment of others, and the cost to defendant to eliminate the condition.

Conversion Whereas trespass to land and nuisance are wrongful interferences with land, conversion and trespass to chattels are concerned with personal property—goods, things, or documents (e.g., books, clothing, cars, checks, notes, or stock certificates).

A person who seriously interferes with another's personal property may be forced by a court of law to purchase the property at its fair market value. Such an interference is called a conversion. If the interference is less than serious, it is called a trespass to the chattel rather than conversion, and a forced sale does not result.

The defendant, however, must intend to convert the property. If he or she intentionally steals it, destroys it, or seriously damages it, he or she is liable for the tort of conversion. But if the damage results from negligence, then the tort action must be based on negligence—not on conversion. Again, the intent required is not a conscious wrongdoing, but merely an intent to exercise control over the property inconsistent with the plaintiff's rights. Someone who unknowingly and with all good intentions buys stolen goods still commits a conversion; and if the true owner brings a tort action for the conversion, he or she must pay the owner the full value of the property even though he or she has already paid the thief.

Conversion always results in forced sale of the goods to the defendant. If someone intentionally destroys your typewriter, you can sue that person for conversion and force payment to you of the typewriter's full value—the defendant gets the destroyed typewriter in return. So if someone takes something from you that you want returned, you should not bring a conversion action for money damages. Rather, you should go to a court of equity and obtain a decree that requires the defendant to return your item to you. A request to the court for the return of specific goods is called a suit to "replevin" the goods.

Trespass to chattels If the interference is not serious enough to justify a forced sale of the property, the tort action is called a trespass to chattels.

Trespass to chattels is sometimes called "the little brother or sister of conversion." It provides recovery for intentional damage to a chattel that is insufficient to be classed as a conversion. Someone who takes a key and scratches paint off your automobile, for example, has not so damaged your car that he or she should be forced to purchase it. But the person has "trespassed to the chattel" and must pay for the damage.

WHAT ARE THE DEFENSES TO INTENTIONAL TORTS?

A defendant who engages in normally tortious conduct is not liable if he or she is privileged to commit the act. A defendant has a good defense to liability in the following situations.

Consent

When a person consents to the act that does the damage, there is generally no liability for the damage done. Consent is sometimes implied from the plaintiff's conduct. For example, a participant in a game or sporting event is generally held to consent to the physical contact normal to the game or event. And in emergency situations, an unconscious person impliedly consents to treatment in a hospital.

Thus it is possible to consent to a battery, a trespass, or to any other generally tortious conduct. But the defense is good only so long as the defendant remains within the boundaries of the consent given. A plaintiff may allow a defendant to dump fill dirt on his land, but it is still a trespass if he dumps pieces of concrete instead. And if a patient consents to a minor ear operation, her doctor commits a battery when he additionally removes the patient's tonsils without consent.

Self-Defense

A person is privileged to use whatever force is reasonably necessary to prevent harmful contact or confinement. This privilege to use force in self-defense extends not only to real danger but to apparent danger as well—as long as there is reasonable ground to believe that the danger is real.

Again, it is necessary to stay within the boundaries of the defense. Force cannot be used once the danger has passed. And revenge is always prohibited. Only that force necessary to prevent harm is allowed. A defendant cannot exert force likely to result in death or great bodily injury unless he or she is threatened by such force.

Defense of Others

This same privilege is available to the defendant who acts to protect others in real or apparent danger. There is always a risk of mistake, however, and a defendant who intervenes in a situation that does not require the use of force may be liable in damages.

Defense of Property

A person may also use reasonable force to protect property. The law, however, values life (even that of a thief) much more than it values property, and force that is likely to cause death or great bodily injury may never be used just to protect property. Nor can such force be exerted indirectly: spring guns and vicious watchdogs maintained for the protection of property interests alone do not fall within the scope of the defense privilege. While some jurisdictions prohibit the use of dangerous mechanical devices or dogs against mere trespassers or petty thiefs, they do permit their use to guard against commission of a felony (such as a burglary).

Recapture of Chattels

A person whose property has been wrongfully taken may use reasonable force to retake it if he or she does so immediately. As long as the owner is in "fresh pursuit" of the property, there is a privilege to use reasonable force; but if the pursuit stops at any time, the party must turn the chase over to law enforcement personnel.

Certainly, self-help provides a speedy remedy where the legal process may be slow and cumbersome. But caution is recommended. There is great risk involved in trying to recover goods that have been wrongfully taken—risk to the pursuer and risk of mistake. But where a person in fresh pursuit of his property breaks down a door, enters a building, and holds the thief captive until the thief can be taken into legal custody, the defense of "recapture of chattels" may be successfully asserted to the charges of trespass, battery, and false imprisonment.

Necessity

A person who acts to protect the entire community has a good defense to otherwise tortious conduct. If you shoot your neighbor's dog, for example, you are normally guilty of conversion. If brought to court, you must pay your neighbor the full value of the dog in exchange for the dead animal. But say the dog has rabies, and you shoot him to protect the public. In this case, you have a good defense—necessity. The same is true if you dynamite one house to stop a fire that threatens the town. Any trespass action against you will fail in the face of "necessity."

The interest protected, however, must be a public one. If you dynamite your neighbor's house strictly to save your own (assuming yours is the only house endangered by the fire), you are liable in damages for the trespass to your neighbor's house.

Legal Process

A police officer or other public officer who acts tortiously while attempting to arrest an individual under warrant or to seize his or her property under a writ of execution of judgment has a good defense to the conduct. But this is true only as long as the officer acts duly and properly: if he or she arrests the wrong person or employs unreasonable force, he or she is liable in damages. The officer or private citizen who makes an arrest without a warrant is protected by the rules discussed in the previous chapter dealing with criminal procedure. But a private citizen making a citizen's arrest must be very careful to have an adequate basis for doing so, or it may result in a tort of malicious prosecution. The following article reports such a case.

COURT AFFIRMS DINER AWARD [1]

Salem, Oregon—A Portland restaurant's failure to properly butter up a customer will cost the company $10,600, the Oregon Supreme Court ruled Thursday.

The court, affirming a Multnomah Circuit Court ruling, awarded Malcom D. Stroud of Portland $10,600 in damages in connection with an incident at Denny's Restaurant, 425 NE Hassalo St., on Nov. 8, 1972.

According to court records, Stroud, his wife and two friends visited the restaurant for a breakfast of sausage, hash brown potatoes, eggs and toast.

Stroud, however, objected when his toast was served with a frozen or refrigerated pat of butter instead of melted butter as stated in the menu, court records show.

When leaving the restaurant, Stroud tried to deduct 25 cents from the cost of his meal because of the menu discrepancy. The management of the restaurant called Portland police, according to court records.

The policeman who answered the call refused to arrest Stroud, however, and the cook at the restaurant made a citizen's arrest.

The charge later was dismissed, and Stroud later filed suit against the restaurant, charging malicious prosecution. His claim for damages was awarded by the circuit court, and the Court of Appeals, and the Supreme Court affirmed the damages.

Discipline

A parent or person who stands in the place of a parent may use reasonable force to discipline and control a child. Teachers are privileged to use force to maintain order in school. Again, force that exceeds what is reasonably necessary (child beating) is a battery.

Defenses to Defamation

There are two complete defenses to slander and libel called "absolute privilege" and "truth."

Absolute privilege Absolute privilege or immunity exists in a few limited situations where there is good reason to permit complete freedom of expression. A judge, for example, is absolutely privileged—he or she may not be held liable for slander or libel in his or her administration of the law. This privilege also extends to grand jurors, witnesses, lawyers, and parties in civil

1. Reprinted with permission of *The Oregonian,* Portland, Oregon.

and criminal cases. The purpose of the rule is to insure complete freedom of access to the courts, and it covers all matters relating to the litigation—pleadings, discovery, trial, and appeal. But statements concerning the case that are given to newspapers are not considered part of the proceeding, and they do not fall within the privilege.

Legislators are also absolutely immune from legal action for anything they say in the course of legislative proceedings. This extends, to some extent, to other officers as well—presidents, governors, and other superior officers in discharge of their responsibilities (see Chapter 5).

Truth Truth is a complete defense to a civil action for libel or slander in almost all jurisdictions. The defendant's motive generally makes no difference. Even the maliciously inspired find a complete defense in truth.

A few states, however (including Illinois, Pennsylvania, Maine, and New Hampshire), hold that truth is a defense only if the publication was made with good intentions.

But proving truth can be very difficult. Courts generally recognize the complete defense if the defendant can prove, if not every detail, at least the substantial truth of the statement.

Retraction Evidence of retraction of the defamatory statement generally reduces the plaintiff's damage award. Refusal to retract may result in a greater sum. But the retraction must be an honest effort to repair the wrong, or it serves no purpose whatsoever—a statement that a plaintiff "has not the manners of a hog" is not corrected by an assertion that he "has the manners of a hog."

Along these lines, a number of states have "retraction statutes" which apply to some media defendants. The California statute, for example, protects newspapers but not magazines. Such statutes typically provide that the particular defendant can be held liable for general damages (i.e., general harm to the plaintiff's reputation) only if it has failed to publish a retraction of the defamation. However, the defendant can still be held liable for special damages including damages for loss of employment or customers.

Constitutional Privilege Constitutional privilege presents an important defense in defamation and privacy cases involving public officials or matters of public concern. This defense is based on the First Amendment guarantees of freedom of speech and press. It extends to "fair comment" upon the conduct and qualifications of public officers and public employees. This comment is not limited to opinion but extends even to misstatements of fact if made for the public benefit and with an honest belief in their truth. A public official will be successful in a suit for libel or slander (relating to his or her official conduct or fitness for office) only where the defendant made the statement with knowledge of its falsity or in reckless disregard of its truth. The same rule applies to public figures and celebrities, including politicians, ball players, entertainers, famous inventors, authors, and war heroes. Even so, in 1981, popular comedienne Carol Burnett was able to meet this high burden and prove reckless disregard of the truth by the *National Enquirer* regarding a reported argument she supposedly had with Henry Kissinger in a Washington restaurant. She was awarded $1.6 million in damages by the jury (later reduced by remittitur). Still the press is given substantial protection in its coverage of the news and other matters of public interest. Someone who watches a murder take place (even of a member of his or her own family) is "news." He or she may be televised to the world—and he or she has no remedy for invasion of privacy.

WHAT IS NEGLIGENCE?

A person whose carelessness results in injury is liable for the tort of negligence. Negligence is unintentional conduct that falls below the standard established by law for the protection of others against unreasonably great risk of harm.

There is no liability, however, for an unforeseen, unavoidable accident. To constitute negligence, the risk must be foreseeable at the time the conduct occurs, and, in light of that risk, the defendant's actions must be unreasonable. Negligence, then, is failure to do what a reasonable person under the same or similar circumstances would do. The courts apply this "reasonable person" test to determine the defendant's liability for negligence. In an emergency situation, for example, a person's conduct may justly differ from the standard of conduct expected of a "reasonable" person under normal conditions. Thus it is not unreasonable to pull a person with broken bones out of a burning car—but if the car is not on fire, it may be more reasonable to wait for medical assistance.

The "reasonable person under similar circumstances" standard applies to all persons, with part of the circumstances being individual factors such as age or skills. Thus, if a child is involved, the standard is what can be expected of a reasonable person at that age and experience. If a physician is involved, the standard of care used is that customarily exercised by a physician in the same or a similar community.

The plaintiff must establish four elements to prove negligence:

1. He or she must show that the defendant has a duty to act according to a certain standard of conduct. This duty varies with the situation and circumstances. While a surgeon has a high duty of care to his or her patient, a landowner has very little duty to a trespassing adult. A driver's duty is to drive his or her car in a reasonable manner; but if he or she fails to and a pedestrian is injured, the driver is guilty of negligence. Under most "automobile guest statutes" (adopted in about one-half of the states), the same driver owes a lesser duty to a guest in his or her car than to a regular passenger. Say that you drive a friend to work or school and have an accident along the way. If your state has adopted a guest statute, you are liable for your friend's injuries only if your driving is grossly negligent. Of course, a person who shares expenses or pays for gasoline may not be a guest. In that case, your duty to him or her under the statute is greater, and you are liable for ordinary rather than gross negligence.

2. Once duty is established, the plaintiff must prove that the defendant breached the duty—that he or she failed to conform to the required standard of conduct.

3. Next, the plaintiff must prove that this breach of duty caused the injury. There must be a reasonably close causal connection between the breach and the injury, or there is no liability. The idea is to limit liability for the consequences of any act. If a hotel owner fails to install a fire escape, the owner has breached a duty to his or her guests. But if one of the guests dies in bed from smoke inhalation, the absence of a fire escape is not the proximate cause of the accident.

It is sometimes said that the defendant's conduct is not the cause of the injury if the event would have happened even in the absence of his or actions. The defendant's conduct *causes* the injury only where it is a material element or substantial factor in bringing the injury about.

When it is difficult or even impossible for a plaintiff to prove a breach of duty and/or causal connection between the breach and the damage done, the court sometimes helps the plaintiff out by applying the doctrine of "res ipsa loquitur"—a Latin phrase meaning "the thing speaks for itself." This doctrine allows the jury to infer the defendant's negligence without proof of his or her actions. Res ipsa loquitur applies only where the following conditions are met:

- The event must be one that normally does not occur in the absence of negligence;
- The injury must be caused by something within the exclusive control of the defendant;
- It must be impossible for the plaintiff to have negligently caused his or own injury; and
- Evidence of the event's true explanation must be more accessible to the defendant than to the plaintiff.

Thus when an elevator falls without warning, a commercial airliner disappears, a sponge is left inside a patient, or a patient's leg is surgically removed instead of his arm as agreed to—the doctrine of res ipsa loquitur may apply. Where it does apply, the plaintiff meets his or her burden of proof simply by showing the existence of the four conditions. And this is true even though the plaintiff cannot prove and perhaps does not know what really happened. After the plaintiff rests his or her case, the defendant must present evidence in defense or the jury will be allowed to "infer" or find negligence on this proof alone.

4. Finally, the plaintiff must prove that he or she suffered actual loss or damage.

WHAT ARE THE DEFENSES TO NEGLIGENCE?

The two most common defenses to negligence are contributory negligence and assumption of risk.

Contributory Negligence

Contributory negligence is conduct by the plaintiff that contributes to the harm he or she suffers—conduct that falls below the standard imposed by law for his or her own protection. In this case, both the plaintiff and defendant are at fault: each is guilty of negligence. In many courts, a plaintiff is completely barred from recovery if his or her own negligence has been a substantial factor in causing the injury. Under this rule, a plaintiff who continues to ride with a drunken driver at high speed after passing up a chance to leave the car cannot recover damages for his or her injuries. Many courts, however, hold that even where the plaintiff is negligent, he or she may still recover damages if the defendant had the "last clear chance" to avoid the harm.

Of course, the plaintiff must do whatever he or she can to avoid furthering the damage after the initial injury. This is called the *rule of avoidable consequences* and requires the plaintiff to obtain proper medical care after the accident. Where the plaintiff fails to act reasonably and thus worsens his or her situation, the court will deny recovery for the additional damage.

Oftentimes, the effect of the contributory negligence rule is to free the defendant from all liability even where his or her conduct has been a major factor in producing the injury. Because of this, a growing number of states refuse to enforce contributory negligence as a complete bar to recovery and have enacted statutes that apportion damage according to fault. There are some thirty to forty of these "comparative negligence" statutes presently in effect throughout the country (states adopting such statutes in recent years include Hawaii, Massachusetts, Oregon, Minnesota, New Hampshire, and Vermont). These statutes reduce the plaintiff's damages in proportion to his or her own negligence. Some specifically state the manner of apportionment: for example, if the defendant's fault is twice as great as the plaintiff's, then the plaintiff can recover two-thirds of his or her damages. Other statutes permit the jury to determine comparative fault.

Assumption of Risk

The plaintiff who assumes the risk of the defendant's negligence may be barred from recovery.

Where the plaintiff agrees with the defendant to accept the risk, he or she may be unable to recover damages if injury later results. So, if you join a club with a swimming pool and gym or rent a riding horse, you may have assumed the risk of any accidental injury likely to occur.

Many courts, however, hold such agreements void where one person is in a superior bargaining position. An employer, for example, cannot contract with his or her employees to make them assume the risk of the employer's negligence. Nor can public utilities, common carriers, and other public service companies contract away responsibility for their negligence. And it is contrary to public policy to allow hotel keepers, garagemen, and parking lot owners to do so by claiming that their customers have "assumed the risk."

Assumption of risk is generally not an express assumption, but one implied from the plaintiff's conduct. Spectators at sporting events "assume" the risk of flying baseballs or golf balls. They realize that no one will protect them from the obvious risks.

At times, the plaintiff knows that the defendant has been negligent; but, aware of the risk, he or she still voluntarily encounters it. A person who uses a stairway he or she knows to be unsafe, for example, assumes the risk of possible injury.

When a plaintiff knows about the risk and freely incurs it, the plaintiff is generally barred from recovery against the defendant. But where there is a *negligent* assumption of risk (as opposed to an agreed consent to the risk) in a state with a "comparative negligence" statute, the damages will probably be apportioned, and the defense will not provide a complete bar to recovery.

WHAT IS STRICT LIABILITY?

Tort liability is generally based on either intentional or negligent conduct. There is, however, a third theory of tort liability called strict liability that holds the defendant responsible for unintentional conduct he or she has taken every precaution to prevent. An informed social policy recognizes that some conduct is of great value to the community even where the risk of danger is extremely high. Yet, while the activity is tolerated, strict liability is imposed for any injury that results. You may take every precaution before conducting your blasting operations; even so, you may still be liable when someone is harmed. Strict liability is liability "without fault," and you are responsible for the harmful results of your conduct.

The three traditional areas of strict liability include animals, abnormally dangerous things, and food and drink. A fourth area—other product liability—has recently been added and is very important to business.

Animals

Trespassing animals A person who owns animals that are likely to roam and cause damage may be held strictly liable for the harm that results from their wanderings. While liability is imposed for animals like cattle, horses, and sheep, it does not extend to dogs and cats—in their case, negligence must first be established. In some western states, the rule is completely against strict liability; cattle graze at large on the range. And even within a particular state the rule may differ from county to county. Some states have either "fencing in" or "fencing out" statutes. "Fencing in" statutes (e.g., Arizona Code 50–606) compel animal owners to fence their animals in or face strict liability if they stray. "Fencing out" statutes (such as found in Colorado) protect the plaintiff who fences in his land by holding the defendant strictly liable when his animal breaks through the fence and causes damage. Otherwise, liability results only from intentional or negligent conduct.

Keeping dangerous animals A person who keeps a naturally wild animal (e.g., a tiger, bear, or monkey) or even a particular animal known to be vicious (such as a dog that bites or a horse that kicks) is strictly liable for any damage the animal causes. Statutes in some states, including Wisconsin, Connecticut, and Ohio impose absolute liability for certain types of damage inflicted by animals (e.g., dog bites) even where the animal has no known propensity for viciousness. These statutes reject the "one free bite" rule at least as to dogs. The statutes, however, generally do not protect trespassers on the defendant's property whose presence the owner had no reason to know of or anticipate.

Abnormally Dangerous Things

Certain activities are so dangerous that they involve serious risk of harm to others even when utmost care is exercised. Using explosives (or storing them in a city), crop-dusting, drilling oil wells in a populated area—all may fall within the rule. Two things are required: first, the act must be ultrahazardous, and second, the activity must be one unnatural to its surroundings. Certainly, the person who conducts blasting operations in the center of a city is strictly liable for any harm he or she causes. But one who blasts in an uninhabited area is probably liable only for his or her negligence.

Food and Drink

At the turn of the century, the sale of defective food was a considerable problem in this country. Negligence, however, was difficult to prove, particularly with respect to food purchased from wholesale or retail sellers. Common law thus developed to provide maximum protection for the consumer. It made the seller strictly liable for the food and drink he or she sold. This rule of strict liability (even in the absence of negligence) is now a well-established law in the United States.

Other Product Liability

Since 1960, strict liability for selling defective products has extended far beyond food and drink. It now applies to any kind of product that is recognizably dangerous to those who may come into contact with it.

The American Law Institute expressed this rule of strict liability for sale of dangerous products:

> 402 A Special liability of seller of products for physical harm to user or consumer.
>
> (1) One who sells any product in a defective condition unreasonably dangerous to the user or consumer or to his property is subject to liability for physical harm thereby caused to the ultimate user or consumer or to his property if
> (a) the seller is engaged in the business of selling such a product, and
> (b) if it is expected to and does reach the user or consumer without substantial change in the condition in which it is sold.
>
> (2) The rule stated in Subsection (1) applies although
> (a) the seller has exercised all possible care in the preparation and sale of the product, and
> (b) the user or consumer has not bought the product from or entered into any contractual relation with the seller.

More than two-thirds of the states now accept this rule as part of their common law. See *Greenman v. Yuba Power Products,* Chapter 2. The rule has been applied to power lathes, glass doors, automobiles, airplanes, and roller skates. Still, it does not apply universally to all products—there must be something wrong with the product that makes it unreasonably dangerous to those who come into contact with it. Product liability is further considered in Chapter 11, dealing with sales and consumer protection.

WHAT TYPES OF DAMAGES ARE RECOVERABLE IN A TORT ACTION?

A tort action may be based on intent, negligence, or strict liability. Its purpose in each case is to compensate the plaintiff for his or her loss. Determination of this loss is based on the law of damages—that is, the rules and standards used by courts to measure compensation for injury.

We are concerned here only with those rules and principles relating to tort damages, including personal injuries, punitive damages, injuries resulting in death, and miscellaneous rules for particular situations.

Personal Injuries

The measure of damages in a personal injury action includes the reasonable cost of care for doctors, nurses, hospital stay, and medicine, as well as for travel to and from the doctor's office or hospital. The expenses, however, must be traceable to the injury. Ordinary living expenses incurred during the period of disability are not included, as they would have existed even in the absence of injury.

When the injury forces the plaintiff to lose time from work, his or her lost earnings are a part of the damages. If the disability will continue into the future, the plaintiff may additionally recover for impairment of future earning capacity. The plaintiff, for example, may be awarded a very large damage award if he or she is unable to walk for the rest of his or her lifetime or if he or she will be physically restricted. The court determines the amount of the award by ascertaining the plaintiff's expected longevity prior to occurrence of the tort—how long, in view of the plaintiff's age and health, he or she could have expected to live. Life expectancy tables are used to assess this future loss.

The plaintiff who suffers bodily injury may also recover damages for past and future pain and for any serious mental suffering that accompanies it. This includes fright and shock at the time of injury, fear of the future, and humiliation caused by disfigurement. Of course, the pain may last for a lifetime, and, if this is so, damages may be recovered for all of the future suffering. But the law has no standard by which to measure pain and suffering in money. This determination is left to the jury's discretion, subject to appellate review for obvious error.

Punitive Damages

The concept of punishment generally does not enter into tort actions. The purpose of the action is to compensate completely the injured plaintiff by awarding him or her money or "compensatory" damages. Compensatory damages are not taxable income to the plaintiff as nothing has been done to earn the money. Rather, the damages make the plaintiff whole again—they replace what the defendant has taken away. And this is true even when the matter is settled out of court. An $8,000 settlement paid to you for your injury by a negligent driver's insurance company is not taxable income.

Contrasted with compensatory damages are "punitive damages." Also called exemplary damages or "smart money" (they make the defendant "hurt" or "smart"), punitive damages are designed to punish the defendant and to deter others from following his or her example. Punitive damages are awarded only when the defendant's act is absolutely outrageous. Aggravation, spite, or evil motive must exist. Because of this, punitive damages are not likely to be awarded for mere negligence. But they may be awarded for torts like battery, libel, or intentional interference with property, such as trespass, nuisance, or conversion when the conduct complained of is outrageous. Sometimes they are awarded for gross negligence. Whether to award them is always left to the jury's discretion. And the jury can award them for any kind of malicious, wanton, or oppressive misconduct that is actionable as a tort. Since they are a "windfall" to the plaintiff, they are taxable as income.

Injuries Resulting in Death

When an injured party died at common law, any right to bring a tort action died with him or her, and neither the estate nor the family could sue the person who caused the death. "Survival statutes" and "death injury acts" have changed this situation. These acts allow the personal representative of the decedent's estate (executor or administrator) and/or his or her surviving family members to bring an action for money damages for loss of the deceased. Some statutes limit loss to compensation for predeath injuries, i.e., pain and suffering of the injured person; loss of earnings, and expenses of care, treatment, and funeral. Other statutes provide additional damage for the deceased's loss of earnings during the period of his or her life expectancy. Damages may even include the family's loss of the deceased's personal services and attention, such as the moral and educational training of his or her children. About ten states grant punitive damages where the defendant's conduct in causing the death was malicious or wanton. And in about one-third of the states, there is a maximum limit set for recovery which varies from $5,000 to $25,000 or more.

As an example, on September 4, 1974 it was reported [2] that Eastern Airlines settled damage suits for $35 million. This tremendous amount was paid to survivors and next of kin after an Eastern Airlines jet crashed and killed 101 people. This crash occurred in the Everglades in Florida on December 29, 1972. Ninety-six passengers and five members of the crew were killed. Seventy-five people survived the crash.

Kenicho Golfur of New York City received the highest award in the amount of $850,000. Her back was broken in the crash, and her husband was killed. The average settlement was about $300,000.

The crash destroyed an $18 million jet. The National Transportation Safety Board ruled that the accident was caused by the crew which was in the cockpit of the airplane trying to replace a burned-out warning light and failed to notice the jet had lost altitude.

Eastern Airlines did have over $100 million in insurance, carried with four different insurance companies.

---

2. Associated Press News Article appearing in Portland, *Oregonian* newspaper, September 4, 1974; "Miami Fla. (AP)—Crash costs Eastern $35 Million Damages."

Miscellaneous Rules for Particular Situations

The plaintiff who has been falsely imprisoned is entitled to damages for loss of time, wounded feelings, humiliation, mental suffering, and injury to reputation.

In oral defamation cases (to recover for slander), material loss or "special damage" must be proved—injury to reputation, humiliation, and mental anguish are not enough. Exceptions, as pointed out before, include accusations of serious crime or present loathsome disease, accusations injurious to the plaintiff's business or profession, and charges of unchastity to a woman. Libel (written words) does not require proof of special damage, and the jury in these states can assess substantial damage upon the assumption that the plaintiff's reputation has been injured and his or her feelings wounded.

When personal property is wrongfully destroyed, the usual measure of damages is the value of the property at the time of destruction plus interest from the time of the injury.

And where the plaintiff has suffered no compensatory loss, he or she may still be awarded nominal damages (damages in a trivial amount) to recognize the defendant's wrong against him or her. Nominal damages result upon proof of most torts when actual loss cannot be proved. These include torts of violence against a person or his or her property, as well as trespass, libel, and nuisance—but not negligence.

The remedy at law for money damages, however, is not always adequate. If continuing trespass or nuisance exist, the plaintiff will want them stopped and must follow the equity procedure described in the previous chapter to obtain an equitable injunction.

Statutes of limitation in all our states set maximum time limits for bringing a tort action. The plaintiff who fails to bring an action within that time is barred from using the courts. Typically, the plaintiff must file a complaint within two years from the time of injury. Statutes of limitation vary from state to state and even within a state on different subject matters.

Crimes

WHAT IS A CRIME?

A crime is any act or omission prohibited by public law in order to protect the public. A crime is punishable by fine, imprisonment, or sentence of death.

HOW DOES CRIME RELATE TO BUSINESS?

The three main methods or ways of doing business are:

1. a sole proprietorship;
2. a partnership; or
3. a corporation.

A sole proprietorship is the least complicated with one person owning the business. A partnership is an association of two or more persons to carry on as co-owners a business for a profit. Sole proprietorships and partnerships do not exist as separate, independent entities apart from the people who own them. A corporation, on the other hand, is a separate legal entity existing independently and apart from the shareholders who own it. The laws controlling the doing of business using the partnership or corporate form are dealt with in Chapter 6 of this text. Here we are only concerned with crime as it relates to business. Several aspects are important.

First of all, individuals who operate businesses as sole proprietors or partners will be subject to licensing, zoning, and environmental laws. Violation may result in criminal penalty, usually in the nature of a fine. Thus, someone who, in operating a business, continually pollutes the air, may be subject to substantial fine and even to imprisonment if the violations are willful.

Secondly, some statutes provide that certain acts are criminal, whether done personally or through an employee. For example, the owner-operator of a restaurant-bar business may be held criminally responsible, with appropriate fine or temporary closure, for sale of liquor to minors even though the sale is by employees and even though the employees did not intentionally sell to minors.

Thirdly, a corporate entity can itself be held criminally responsible. Although a corporation obviously cannot be imprisoned, it can be fined for criminal activity. The threat of fine provides corporate managers with an incentive to take steps to avoid the commission of criminal offenses by corporate employees in the course of their employment. The fact that the corporation is held liable does not affect the criminal responsibility of the individual who actually committed the crime; both the corporation and the guilty employee may be convicted. Individuals cannot escape criminal liability on the basis that their criminal acts were undertaken on behalf of the corporation. The corporation may have a defense by establishing that the corporate employee who had supervisory responsibility over the subject matter of the offense used due diligence to prevent the crime from happening. Also, the most common type of crime for which a corporation is convicted involves strict liability, meaning no intent is required and even an accidental violation of the statute is a crime. These crimes usually have been "public welfare" offenses such as those involving polluting the air or water, selling adulterated food or drug products, contributing to the delinquency of children, bribing public officials, or trying to defraud consumers. They are usually less serious crimes in the sense of direct infringement on the rights of others and with regard to punishment. Still, occasionally corporations have been charged with very serious crime. In September of 1978 an Indiana prosecutor brought Ford Motor Company to trial on three reckless homicide charges. A van had smashed into the back of a 1973 Ford Pinto. The gas tank was ripped open, and gasoline splashed, ignited, and killed three young women. The homicide charge was based on the allegation that the three girls died as a result of a high-level corporate decision to risk human life for greater company profit. The issue was whether or not a corporation is capable of committing criminal homicide through the reckless design of products.

The prosecutor argued that conviction was necessary to "deter outrageous decisions to sacrifice human life for private profit." Although the jury ultimately ruled that Ford Motor Company was not guilty, the case remains a precedent for indicting corporations for serious non-strict liability crimes resulting from corporate decision making.

Fourthly, there are certain areas of criminal activity that relate to business or business persons more often than not. Many such crimes are described below.

Crimes Relating to Business

Securities fraud Before investment securities can be sold to the general public, they must be registered with the Securities and Exchange Commission (see Chapter 6). Willful violation of the securities laws, including misrepresentation regarding the offerings, subject the actor to possibly five years' imprisonment and/or a $10,000 fine.

Foreign bribery The Foreign Corrupt Practices Act was passed in 1977 as an aftermath to Watergate when the Special Prosecutor uncovered information indicating that certain corporations maintained secret "slush funds" to make payments to government officials and politicians both in the United States and in foreign countries. Thereafter, the Securities and Exchange Commission investigated further and discovered in 1975 that United Brands Corporation had arranged to pay bribes totaling $2.5 million to high officials of the government of Honduras in return for a 50 percent reduction in Honduras's export tax on bananas. After this, some 500 other American corporations admitted making similar payments to influence government decisions in foreign countries.

The Foreign Corrupt Practices Act makes it unlawful for American business firms, and those acting on their behalf, to make use of the mails or any means of interstate commerce in furtherance of any corrupt arrangement to pay a foreign official or politician to use his or her power or influence to assist such American firms in obtaining or retaining business for themselves or any other person. Any business firm which willfully violates the Foreign Corrupt Practices Act is subject to a fine of up to $1 million, and any individual violator is subject to a fine of up to $10,000 and imprisonment of up to five years.

Criminal antitrust The antitrust laws (Sherman Act, Clayton Act, Federal Trade Commission Act, and Robinson-Patman Act—see Chapter 7 for a detailed discussion) prohibit anticompetitive business practice that unreasonably restrains trade. Willful violations are crimes. The most common criminal violation of the antitrust law is price fixing; upwards of 80 percent of the criminal cases filed in antitrust charge conspiracies to fix prices.[3] Under the Sherman Act the maximum criminal penalty is a $100,000 fine and/or

3. The President's Commission on Law Enforcement and Administration of Justice—Task Force Report; Crime and Its Impact—An Assessment, 10, 9–10 (1967).

three years in jail for individual violators and up to $1 million in fines for corporations.

Bank fraud There are several areas of criminal activity involving banks. Anyone who gives or receives a bribe regarding bank loans or other bank transactions may be fined up to $5,000 and/or imprisoned not more than one year. Anyone who embezzles or otherwise willfully misapplies bank funds is subject to a fine of up to $5,000 or five years' imprisonment or both. This includes computerized embezzlement or manipulation of funds. And a person who willfully files a false statement to a bank or other federal credit institution faces fines, upon conviction, of up to $10,000 and/or imprisonment for two to five years.

Commercial bribery In more than half the states the bribing of an employee to influence conduct relating to his or her employer's business is the crime of commercial bribery. Both giving and receiving the bribe are illegal. Penalties vary from state to state with fines typically running from $500 to $5,000 and potential imprisonment of one year. Such bribes may also violate the antitrust laws if they have an anticompetitive effect. Payments of bribes or kickbacks (secret return of part of a sum received to individuals because of a buying or other transaction, e.g., "I buy from you, you pay me a secret commission back") may not be deducted as ordinary expenses by business and will be disallowed by the Internal Revenue Service.

Violation of the Hobbs Act The federal Hobbs Act provides that anyone who obstructs commerce by robbery or extortion shall be fined not more than $10,000 or imprisoned not more than twenty years or both. Extortion is payment under any kind of fear including economic duress, i.e., threats of economic harm. Thus, there have been indictments and convictions of public officials from mayors to police officers who have used their powers to shake down persons by refusing them the right to do business unless they pay tribute.

Violation of the Travel Act The Travel Act was enacted into law when Robert Kennedy was Attorney General in 1961 as part of his war on organized crime. The Travel Act makes it a crime to travel in interstate or foreign commerce or use any facility in interstate or foreign commerce, such as the mail, to carry on unlawful activity involving gambling, liquor, narcotics, prostitution, extortion, bribery, or arson. The penalty is up to a $10,000 fine and/or five years in prison. It is possible that the same act would be the basis for charges under state bribery or other statutes, the federal Hobbs Act, the federal Travel Act, or other federal acts such as the Foreign Corrupt Practices Act or statutes dealing with bank fraud, etc.

Violations of the Racketeer Influenced and Corrupt Organizations Act The Racketeer Influenced and Corrupt Organizations Act (RICO) is part of the Organized Crime Control Act of 1970. RICO makes it a crime to invest funds acquired through a pattern of racketeering in an enterprise engaged in interstate commerce. The law attempts to keep so-called "dirty" money out of legitimate business. The statute provides:

> It shall be unlawful for any person through a pattern of racketeering activity or through collection of an unlawful debt to acquire or maintain, directly or indirectly, any interest in or control of any enterprise which is engaged in, or the activities of which affect, interstate or foreign commerce.

"Pattern of racketeering activity" requires at least two acts of racketeering activity within ten years of each other. Crimes considered to be racketeering activity include, among others: murder, kidnapping, gambling, arson, robbery, bribery, sports bribery, extortion, narcotics dealing, counterfeiting, embezzlement from pension funds, Hobbs Act violations, Travel Act violations, interstate transportation of stolen property, white slave traffic (prostitution), and trafficking in contraband cigarettes.

The penalties for violation of RICO are interesting: first, each individual may be fined up to $25,000; second, he or she may be sentenced to jail for up to twenty years, thus removing the racketeer from further activity for a lengthy period; and, third, to prevent new people from taking the place of the convicted racketeer, forfeiture to the United States of property interests owned, controlled, or operated by the racketeer. The forfeiture provisions remove the economic base which made it possible to place "dirty money" into legitimate commerce and continue the activities while serving jail sentences.

Labor law violations It is a crime under the Labor Management Relations Act for management to make payments of money or other property to labor organizations (unions) or union officers. This applies to all payments including Christmas gifts and to indirect payments such as discounts on hotel rates or interest-free loans. The penalty is a fine up to $10,000 and/or imprisonment for not more than one year. See Chapter 7 for Labor Law.

Under the Labor Management Reporting and Disclosure Act (Landrum-Griffin Act), it is a crime for a union officer or employee to embezzle the money or property of a labor union. The penalty is $10,000 and/or five years.

Health care fraud The social security system provides substantial medical benefits to retired persons in the form of medicare programs. In the operation of this system, fraud has been uncovered including billing for services not rendered, misrepresentation of services rendered, double billing, and kickbacks from labs, pharmacies, or nursing homes. All are criminal acts with potential fines up to $25,000 and/or prison sentences up to five years.

Corporate tax fraud Any willful attempt to evade a federal tax may be punished upon conviction by a fine of not more than $10,000 plus imprisonment of not more than five years. In addition, the person responsible for the payment of corporate taxes may be subject to a penalty equal to the total amount of tax evaded.

Commercial espionage Earlier in this chapter we discussed the commercial tort of misappropriating another's trade secret. Under the National Stolen Property Act such misappropriation is also a federal crime if the trade secret is valued at $5,000 or more and has been transported in interstate commerce. A $10,000 and/or ten-year jail term penalty is provided. One who misappropriates a trade secret is also subject to state prosecution, the laws and penalties varying from state to state. Defendants have been convicted for stealing computer programs considered to be valuable trade secrets.

Violation of the Occupational Safety and Health Act The federal Occupational Safety and Health Act was passed in 1970. It gives the Secretary of Labor the power to promulgate and enforce safety standards for industries so as to reduce industrial accidents. The statute further provides that any employer who willfully violates any standard causing the death of an employee is subject to a $10,000 fine and/or six months in prison.

Food and drug violations The Federal Food, Drug, and Cosmetic Act prohibits misbranded and adulterated food and drugs from being sold or transported in interstate commerce. The act empowers FDA agents to make reasonable searches and to collect samples for testing. While individuals generally have a right to insist that search warrants be obtained prior to inspection, a complete refusal to permit inspection may result in criminal penalty of up to $1,000 in fines and/or one year in prison. Intentional misbranding or introduction of adulterated food or drugs may result in imprisonment of up to three years, a $10,000 fine, or both. Corporations, as entities, are subject to criminal liability as are corporate officers. However, no dealer can be prosecuted for shipping adulterated or misbranded goods in interstate commerce where he or she holds a guaranty from his or her seller that the goods are not adulterated or misbranded.

Environmental law violations There are a large number of statutes dealing with the environment including the Clean Air Act of 1977, the Clean Water Act of 1972, the Noise Control Act of 1972, the Solid Waste Disposal Act of 1965, the Federal Environmental Pesticide Control Act of 1972, and the Toxic Substance Act of 1976. These statutes are designed to prevent and control pollution and provide a number of criminal penalties including prison sentences for individuals and substantial fines for both corporations and individuals, e.g., $25,000 per violation per day. See Chapter 13 for detailed discussion of environmental law.

Mail and wire fraud Use of the mails, even intrastate, to further a scheme to defraud violates the federal mail fraud statute. Upon conviction, a person may be fined not more than $1,000 or imprisoned no more than five years or both. Each mailing in furtherance of a scheme to defraud is considered a separate criminal offense.

The wire fraud statute is similar to the mail fraud statute and makes criminal a transmission by wire, radio, or television in interstate commerce in furtherance of a scheme to defraud. Wire includes an interstate telephone call or telegram. Again the penalty is a fine up to $1,000 or imprisonment for up to five years or both.

HOW IS CRIME CLASSIFIED?

The federal Congress and all state legislatures have passed statutes defining and dealing with crime. While the specifics of the state and federal statutes vary, the general principles and applications remain the same. More than thirty of the states have passed all or part of the Model Penal Code.

This statute classifies crimes as felonies, misdemeanors, and petty misdemeanors. A crime is a felony if persons convicted thereof may be sentenced to imprisonment for a term in excess of one year. Otherwise a crime is a misdemeanor. Felonies and misdemeanors are further divided for purposes of maximum prison terms:

- *First-degree felonies:* twenty years or life imprisonment (and several states provide the death penalty for murder);
- *Second-degree felonies:* ten years;
- *Third-degree felonies:* five years;
- *Misdemeanors:* one year;
- *Petty misdemeanors:* thirty days.

Extended terms beyond these maximums are provided for persistent offenders ("three-time losers") and professional or dangerous criminals whose commitments are necessary for the protection of the public. While there is no statute of limitations for murder, a prosecution for a felony of the first degree must be commenced within six years after it is committed; other felonies, three years; misdemeanors, two years; and petty misdemeanors within six months.

In many states, a convicted felon is disqualified from holding public office. The felon loses his or her rights to vote, to serve on a jury, and to practice as an attorney. Political and civil rights are restored automatically upon final discharge from probation, parole, or imprisonment. In other states, conviction of a felony is grounds for divorce. None of these results follows conviction of a misdemeanor.

If only a fine can be imposed for an offense, it is not a crime but instead is termed a "violation." Conviction of a violation does not become a part of a criminal record.

WHAT ARE SOME SPECIFIC CRIMES AND THEIR PUNISHMENTS UNDER THE MODEL PENAL CODE?

Offenses Involving Danger to the Person

Criminal homicide A person is guilty of criminal homicide if he or she purposely, knowingly, or negligently causes the death of another human being. Criminal homicide is murder, manslaughter, or negligent homicide.

Murder—first-degree felony Murder results when criminal homicide is committed purposely or knowingly or recklessly under circumstances manifesting extreme indifference to the value of human life. Such recklessness and indifference are presumed if the actor is engaged or is an accomplice in the commission of robbery, rape, arson, burglary, kidnapping, or felonious escape. This is the felony murder rule. So the defendant who sets fire to an unoccupied house is guilty of murder when a fireman dies fighting the blaze. If a stranger rushes into the burning house to save someone trapped inside and is himself trapped, the defendant is again guilty of murder under the felony murder rule. When the armed robber's loaded gun accidentally goes off and kills a man, the robber, too, is guilty of felony murder.

For the felony murder rule to apply, the killing must be within the *res gestae* of the felony—that is, the homicide and the felony must be closely connected in point of time, place, and causal relation.

To establish murder the defendant's conduct must cause the death of a "living human being." Killing a fetus, then, is not murder unless the fetus has been "born alive." According to most courts, this means a fetus fully brought forth and with an independent circulation. Live birth and death by criminal agency must be proved beyond a reasonable doubt to sustain a conviction for murder.

Determination of when life ends is just as important. It may be murder to kill one who is already dying (mercy killing) or to accelerate another's death. The doctor who removes an organ for transplantation may be subject to criminal responsibility if he or she acts too soon. Some forty-five states have now passed the Uniform Anatomical Gift Act that authorizes the physician who tends the donor at his or her death or who certifies the death to determine when that death occurs. The determining physician may not participate in removal or transplantation procedures. And a person who acts in good faith under the act is not subject to criminal prosecution because of the transplant. Still, the exact time of death is not made clear in either science or law. It is often defined as the absence of heartbeat and respiration or as brain death. Yet a heart that has stopped beating will sometimes resume its natural rhythm and doctors disagree over how long an electroencephalograph must show flat brain waves before a person is dead (some say twenty-four hours is necessary for an irreversible coma). The apparent legal trend is toward adoption of brain death as the proper criterion for establishing time of death. But it is the doctor who must make the final decision in the individual case—not the courts. Some unresolved legal issues center around the use of life support systems to prolong the life of a person who prefers to die. See Chapter 1, In the Matter of Karen Quinlan.

At common law, death was murder only if it occurred within a year and a day from the time the injury was inflicted. Most states retain this limit on causation.

Manslaughter—second-degree felony Criminal homicide constitutes manslaughter when a homicide which would otherwise be murder is committed under the influence of extreme mental or emotional disturbance for which there is reasonable explanation or excuse. The reasonableness of such explanation or excuse is determined from the viewpoint of a person in the actor's situation under the circumstances as he or she believes them to be. Thus the law recognizes that a person may lose control of his or her senses and kill if sufficiently provoked, and, while it does not excuse the actions, it may reduce the crime from murder to manslaughter.

The provocation, however, must be reasonable. A person who is physically abused or unlawfully arrested or one who discovers his or her spouse committing adultery may be "reasonably provoked" into a state of passion. Being shot at is generally sufficient. For example, the intended victim who shoots his fleeing assailant in the back of the head and kills him is probably not guilty of murder: he has been provoked into a state of passion and is guilty only of manslaughter. Insulting words, on the other hand, even where accompanied by gestures, are generally insufficient to reduce murder to manslaughter. But informational words may be enough. Thus a wife's unexpected confession of adultery was sufficient to reduce her husband's crime to manslaughter when he killed her in a sudden heat of passion.

Of course, the homicide must take place before the passion subsides. Where the defendant has time to "cool off" before the fatal act, he or she is guilty of murder.

Negligent homicide—third-degree felony This usually involves very reckless or culpably negligent conduct. In one case, a nightclub owner was convicted of involuntary manslaughter when some 490 persons died in a fire on his premises because of inadequate exits and lack of other safety precautions. And where gross negligence in the operation of a motor vehicle results in death (e.g., driving when completely drunk and fatally injuring a pedestrian), the driver may be convicted of involuntary manslaughter or negligent homicide.

Kidnapping—first-degree felony A person is guilty of kidnapping if he or she unlawfully removes another from his or her place of residence or business, or unlawfully confines another for a substantial period in a place of isolation for ransom or as a shield or hostage, or to facilitate commission of any felony or flight thereafter, or to inflict bodily injury or terrorize the victim, or to interfere with the performance of any governmental or political function.

Aggravated assault—second-degree felony A person is guilty of aggravated assault if he or she attempts to cause serious bodily injury to another or causes such injury purposely, knowingly, or recklessly under circumstances manifesting extreme indifference to the value of human life.

Simple assault—misdemeanor A person is guilty of simple assault if he or she attempts to cause or purposely, knowingly, or recklessly causes bodily injury to another; or negligently causes bodily injury to another with a deadly weapon; or attempts by physical menace to put another in fear of imminent serious bodily injury.

Simple assault is a misdemeanor unless committed in a fight or scuffle entered into by mutual consent, in which case it is a petty misdemeanor.

Terroristic threats—third-degree felony Threatening to commit any crime of violence with purpose to terrorize another or to cause evacuation of a building, place of assembly, or facility of public transportation, or otherwise to cause serious public inconvenience is a third-degree felony under the Model Penal Code.

Sexual offenses

Rape—first-degree felony A male who has sexual intercourse with a female not his wife is guilty of rape if he compels her to submit by force or threat of imminent death, serious bodily injury, extreme pain, or kidnapping to be inflicted on anyone; or he has substantially impaired her power to control her conduct by administering drugs, intoxicants, or other means for the purpose of preventing resistance; or the female is unconscious; or the female is less than ten years old (some states use a different age such as twelve or fourteen). Sexual intercourse as used in the Model Penal Code includes oral and anal sex which is also referred to as deviate sexual intercourse. But a woman who consciously and validly consents to the act of intercourse, however tardily or reluctantly, has not been raped, even though she resists for a short period of time. The validity of her consent, however, is measured by her age and condition at the time of intercourse. There can be no consent where a woman is insane, idiotic, insensible, or asleep at the time of the act; and intercourse with her is rape even though she fails to resist.

In some states, statutes have been passed that allow for prosecution of a husband for rape of his own wife when she is compelled to submit by force. The difficulties of proof in such cases are very great, as they are in all rape and other sex related crimes where the alleged sexual activities have been carried out in private. Some statutes allow the defendant to offer evidence as a defense that the alleged victim had, prior to the time of the offense charged, engaged promiscuously in sexual relations with others. And sometimes the statutes state that no person shall be convicted of any felony based on sexual offenses upon the uncorroborated testimony of the alleged victim. Additional proof is required.

Corruption of minors and seduction—third-degree felony A male who has sexual intercourse with a female not his wife or any person who engages in deviate sexual intercourse or causes another to engage in deviate sexual intercourse is guilty of this offense if the other person is less than sixteen years old and the actor is at least four years older than the other person. Again, the ages for such crime vary from state to state.

In many states, the statutes make legal any sexual act between consenting adults (over eighteen years of age) with the exception of prostitution and incestuous activity.

Offenses against Property

Arson—second-degree felony A person is guilty of arson if he or she starts a fire or causes an explosion with the purpose of destroying a building or occupied structure of another; or destroying or damaging any property, whether his or her own or another's, to collect insurance for the loss.

Criminal mischief A person commits criminal mischief if he or she purposely or recklessly tampers with tangible property of another so as to endanger person or property. Criminal mischief is a felony of the third degree if the actor purposely causes pecuniary loss in excess of $5,000. It is a misdemeanor if less than $5,000 and over $100, or a petty misdemeanor if the loss is less than $100 and over $25. Otherwise it is a violation.

Burglary—second-degree felony A person is guilty of burglary if he or she enters a building or occupied structure with purpose to commit a crime therein, unless the premises are at the time open to the public or the actor is privileged to enter. Burglary is a second-degree felony only if it is perpetratod in the dwelling of another at night, or if in the course of committing the offense, the actor inflicts or attempts to inflict bodily harm on anyone or is armed with explosives or a deadly weapon. Otherwise it is a third-degree felony.

Criminal trespass A person commits an offense if, knowing that he or she is not privileged to do so, he or she enters or remains in any place as to which notice against trespass is given by actual communication, posting in a manner prescribed by law, or fencing or other enclosure manifestly designed to exclude intruders. This constitutes a petty misdemeanor if the offender defies an order to leave personally communicated to him or her by the owner of the premises or other authorized person. Otherwise it is a violation.

Robbery A person commits robbery if, in the course of committing a theft, he or she inflicts serious bodily injury upon another, or threatens another with or purposely puts him or her in fear of immediate serious bodily injury, or commits or threatens immediately to commit any felony of the first or second degree. The person is deemed "in the course of committing a theft" if it occurs in an attempt to commit theft or in flight after the attempt or commission. Robbery is a felony of the second degree, except that it is a felony of the first degree if, in the course of committing the theft, the actor attempts to kill anyone or purposely inflicts or attempts to inflict serious bodily injury.

Other theft offenses Theft constitutes a felony of the third degree if the amount involved exceeds $500 or if the property stolen is a firearm, automobile, airplane, motorcycle, motorboat, or other motor-propelled vehicle or, in the case of theft by receiving stolen property, if the receiver is in the business of buying or selling stolen property. Otherwise the theft is a misdemeanor. Again the figures will vary from state to state, but usually the amounts involved in thefts committed pursuant to one scheme or course of conduct may be aggregated in determining whether it will be a felony or a misdemeanor.

It is not a defense that theft was from the actor's spouse, except that misappropriation of household and personal effects is theft only if it occurs after the parties have ceased living together.

Theft by unlawful taking or disposition A person is guilty of theft if he or she unlawfully takes or exercises unlawful control over property of another with purpose to deprive him or her thereof.

Theft by deception A person is guilty of theft by deception if he or she purposely obtains property of another by deception. A person deceives if he or she purposely creates or reinforces a false impression, including false impressions as to law, value, intention, or other state of mind.

Theft by extortion A person is guilty of theft if he or she obtains property of another by threatening to inflict bodily injury on anyone, or accuse anyone of a criminal offense, or expose any secret tending to subject any person to hatred, contempt, or ridicule (blackmail).

Theft of property lost, mislaid, or delivered by mistake A person who comes into control of property of another that he or she knows to have been lost, mislaid, or delivered under a mistake is guilty of theft if, with purpose to deprive the owner thereof, he or she fails to take reasonable measures to restore the property to a person entitled to have it.

Receiving stolen property A person is guilty of theft if he or she purposely receives, retains, or disposes of property of another knowing that it has been stolen, unless the property is received with purpose to restore it to the owner.

Theft of services A person is guilty of theft if he or she purposely obtains services which he or she knows are available only for compensation, by deception or threat or other means to avoid payment for the service. Services include labor, professional service, transportation, telephone or other public service, accommodation in hotels, restaurants, or elsewhere, admission to exhibitions, use of vehicles or other movable property. Where compensation for service is ordinarily paid immediately upon the rendering of such service, as in the case of hotels and restaurants, refusal to pay or absconding without payment or offer to pay gives rise to a presumption that the service was obtained by deception as to intention to pay.

Forgery—third-degree felony A person is guilty of forgery if, with purpose to defraud or injure anyone or with knowledge that he or she is facilitating a fraud or injury, the actor alters any writing of another without his or her authority.

Tampering with records—misdemeanor A person commits a misdemeanor if, knowing that he has no privilege to do so, he falsifies, destroys, removes, or conceals any writing or record with purpose to deceive or injure anyone or to conceal any wrongdoing.

Credit cards A person commits an offense if he or she uses a credit card for the purpose of obtaining property or services with knowledge that the card is stolen or forged, or the card has been revoked or cancelled, or for any other reason his or her use of the card is unauthorized by the issuer. This offense is a felony of the third degree if the value of the property or services secured exceeds $500; otherwise it is a misdemeanor.

Deceptive business practices—misdemeanor A person commits a misdemeanor if, in the course of business, he or she:

1. Uses a false weight or measure;
2. Sells or delivers less than the represented quantity of any commodity or service;
3. Sells, offers, or exposes for sale adulterated or mislabeled commodities;
4. Makes a false or misleading statement in any advertisement addressed to the public;
5. Makes a false or misleading written statement for the purpose of obtaining property or credit;
6. Makes a false or misleading written statement for the purpose of promoting the sale of securities.

Other Offenses

Bigamy—misdemeanor A married person is guilty of bigamy if he or she contracts another marriage.

Perjury—third-degree felony A person is guilty of perjury if in any official proceeding he or she makes a false statement under oath, when the statement is material and he or she does not believe it to be true.

Tampering—third-degree felony A person commits an offense if, believing that an official proceeding or investigation is pending or about to be instituted, he or she attempts to induce a witness to testify falsely, or withhold any testimony, or elude legal process summoning him or her to testify, or absent himself or herself from any proceeding or investigation to which he or she has been legally summoned.

Hindering apprehension or prosecution—third-degree felony A person commits this offense if, with purpose to hinder the apprehension, prosecution, conviction, or punishment of another for crime, he or she:

1. Harbors or conceals the other;
2. Provides or aids in providing a weapon, transportation, disguise, or other means of avoiding apprehension or effecting escape;
3. Conceals or destroys evidence of the crime or tampers with a witness, informant, document or other source of information; [4]
4. Warns the other of impending discovery or apprehension;
5. Volunteers false information to a law enforcement officer.

---

4. The Watergate scandal is a case in point. Officials high in the Nixon Administration made substantial efforts to cover up their participation in the break-in of the Democratic National Headquarters. As a result, several of them were tried and convicted for crimes involving hindering prosecution.

Cruelty to animals—misdemeanor A person commits a misdemeanor if he or she purposely or recklessly subjects any animal to cruel mistreatment or subjects any animal in his or her custody to cruel neglect, or kills or injures any animal belonging to another without legal privilege or consent of the owner.

Prostitution—petty misdemeanor A person is guilty of prostitution, a petty misdemeanor, if he or she is an inmate of a house of prostitution or otherwise engages in sexual activity as a business.

Patronizing prostitutes—violation A person commits a violation if he hires a prostitute to engage in sexual activity with him or if he enters or remains in a house of prostitution for the purpose of engaging in sexual activity.

WHAT TWO ELEMENTS ARE NECESSARY TO COMMIT MOST CRIMES?

Commission of a crime generally requires two elements—a *mens rea* (criminal intent), and an *actus reus* (criminal act). Without these two ingredients, there is no crime. Bad thoughts alone are not enough; some type of act or omission to act is necessary. Thus a person who desires to rape, kill, or steal is not guilty of a crime as long as his or her thoughts are not reduced to action. But where he or she attempts to act or where he or she agrees to do so with another, there is criminal conduct: the attempt or conspiracy agreement constitutes the actus reus of the crime. Of course, a person can easily commit a crime simply by speaking (e.g., by committing perjury or orally hiring someone else to perform a criminal act).

While most crimes are affirmatively committed, some crimes are defined in terms of omission to act. A business person, for example, may fail to file a tax return, or a motorist may fail to stop at the scene of an accident in which he or she has been involved. A parent who neglects to feed a baby or to call a doctor when the child is sick may be guilty of criminal homicide if the child dies from lack of food or medical attention. But liability for nonaction may be imposed only where a legal duty to act can first be established. There is generally no legal duty to aid a person in peril even where the aid can be rendered easily and without danger. A person my therefore watch a child drown without risking criminal liability, and while a doctor may have a moral duty to help the sick or injured, the law does not impose a legal one.

But several areas of legal duty do exist. (1) There are duties based upon the family relationship. Parents have a legal duty to aid their small children, and spouses must aid each other. In Palmer v. State, 223 Md. 341, 164 A.2d 467 (1960), a mother was held criminally liable for standing by while her lover delivered a fatal beating to her baby—the mother had a legal duty to stop him. (2) Statutes, too, impose legal duties upon certain classes of people. For example, drivers involved in automobile accidents are commonly required to stop and render assistance (a person not involved in the accident has no duty to stop, but if he or she does stop and attempt to render aid, he or she may become liable in both tort and crime for doing an improper job).

Attempts, solicitations, and conspiracies (called inchoate crimes) are crimes in themselves. An *attempt* is a substantial step taken in a course of conduct planned to culminate in the commission of a crime. It requires (1) an intent to do an act or to bring about certain criminal consequences, and (2) an act in furtherance of that intent that goes beyond mere preparation. The following actions will result in conviction for attempt even where the crime is not completed: lying in wait; searching for or following the intended victim; enticing or seeking to entice him or her to go to the place for commission of the crime; reconnoitering the contemplated "scene" of the crime; unlawfully entering any structure, vehicle, or enclosure where the crime is to be committed; and possessing materials for use in commission of the crime that are specifically designed for the unlawful use or that serve no lawful purpose of the actor under the circumstance (e.g., an aspiring arsonist who arrives at the scene of his intended crime has no lawful use for inflammables). Where the evidence does not support conviction of a defendant charged with a completed crime, he or she may be convicted of unlawful attempt. One defense to "attempted crime" is complete abandonment of the criminal purpose. Thus, a person is not liable for attempt if, under circumstances manifesting a voluntary and complete renunciation of his or her criminal intent, he or she avoids commission of the crime by abandoning the criminal effort. Where mere abandonment is insufficient to accomplish an avoidance, he or she must do everything necessary to prevent commission of the attempted crime.

Criminal solicitation takes place when a person intentionally entices, advises, incites, orders, or otherwise encourages another person to commit a crime. A person is guilty of this crime if he or she intentionally commands or solicits another person to engage in or attempt to engage in conduct punishable as a felony or as a misdemeanor. Punishment for solicitation (like that for attempt) is generally one grade below the crime solicited. And again, renunciation is good defense if the solicitor persuades the person solicited not to commit the crime or otherwise prevents commission of the crime under circumstances manifesting a complete and voluntary renunciation of his or her criminal intent.

It is also criminal for two or more persons to conspire or combine to commit a crime. It is the unlawful combination or agreement that constitutes the offense—no further act is necessary. While renunciation by one conspirator provides that conspirator with a good defense to the crime, it does not affect the liability of other conspirators who fail to renounce their scheme. And if an individual does abandon the agreement, his or her participation in the conspiracy is terminated only when he or she advises the co-conspirators of a change of mind, or when he or she informs law enforcement authorities of the existence of the conspiracy and of his or her interest and participation therein.

To incur criminal liability for conduct, however, a person must generally act with the necessary "mens rea" or intent to commit the crime. A person who kills someone in mistaken self-defense does not intend to commit murder. Nor does one who accidentally takes another's property intend to commit theft. Many statutes specifically require a particular intent—without it, the defendant cannot be found guilty of the crime (e.g., a statute stating that a person is guilty of receiving stolen property only if he or she takes it "knowing that it was stolen"). Thus before an indictment charging assault with intent to murder, rape, or rob will be sustained, specific intent to commit these crimes must first be established. And in every prosecution for attempt to commit a crime, proof of the accused's intent to commit that particular crime must be introduced. Still, specific intent may be inferred from proof of the circumstances, and the principle that a person "intends" the natural and probable consequences of his or her act does apply. So in a prosecution for burglary, proof that the accused broke into the building and committed theft may be sufficient to establish specific intent to steal.

Motive is not an essential element of any crime. While it may establish the probability that someone committed a crime, the fact that a person has no motive or even that his or her motive is a good one is not important. Take euthanasia for example. Killing a person at his own request or to prevent him from suffering further is still criminal homicide. While the defendant's motive is good, he or she still "intends" to kill—the necessary "mens rea" that, taken together with the criminal act, constitutes the crime.

Many statutory crimes in the areas of negligence and strict liability do not require specific intent. A person may not intend to kill, but he or she is still guilty of negligent homicide if he or she acts in reckless disregard of a standard of conduct set down for the protection of others. So, too, will a motorist who exceeds the speed limit or drives without a taillight be convicted of these minor crimes and violations regardless of intent. The same applies to hunters or fisherpersons who violate statutes protecting game and fish and to individuals who unknowingly sell intoxicating liquors to minors. Defendants in some cases have been found guilty of even more serious crimes, including statutory rape, bigamy, or sale of narcotics, without proof of criminal intent. But for the most part, conviction of serious crimes, attempts, solicitations, or conspiracies require proof of both the mens rea and the actus reus.

WHEN IS SOMEONE GUILTY OF CRIME?

There are two areas of criminal law that help determine when an individual is guilty of crime. These are *responsibility* and *parties to crime.*

Responsibility

Responsibility is chiefly concerned with the subject of insanity (though intoxication and infancy are included as possible defenses). But the defense of insanity differs from other defenses; if insanity is successfully asserted, the defendant is usually committed to a mental institution. The term insanity is used very restrictively in its criminal sense. The medical practitioner or psychiatrist may well find that anyone who commits a serious crime suffers from some mental problem or disease. But if this medical standard were applied in criminal law, no one could be convicted of any crime. And while it is neither fair nor civilized to place insane individuals into jail for their acts, it just does not make sense to say that anyone who commits a crime is mentally ill and should not be prosecuted.

The leading case on insanity, known as *M'Naghten's* case, 8 Eng.Rep. 718 (1843), arose in England in 1843. In an attempt to murder English Prime Minister Sir Robert Peel, one M'Naghten had mistakenly killed Peel's private secretary instead. An appellate court acquitted M'Naghten of murder on the ground of insanity, defining the defense in the following words:

> To establish a defense on the ground of insanity, it must be clearly proved that, at the time of committing the act, the party accused was laboring under such a defect of reason, from disease of the mind, as not to know the nature or quality of the act he was doing, or if he did know it, that he did not know he was doing what was wrong.

Some states still apply the *M'Naghten* test. Under this test, a defendant cannot be convicted if, at the time he or she commited the act, the defendant was laboring under such a defect of reason from disease of the mind that he or she did not know the nature or quality of the act or did not know right from wrong. In Columbus, Ohio, on December 4, 1978, the famous Billy Milligan was found not guilty of double robberies and rapes by reason of insanity after evidence was accepted that Milligan was himself a victim of an uncontrolled mental illness involving his being twenty-four completely different personalities of all types, ages, and even sexes. The court concluded that Billy Milligan was unable to distinguish right from wrong or to understand what he was doing when taken over by multiple, different personalities as the crimes were committed.[5]

Some states have added the "irresistable impulse" test to their insanity defense laws: a defendant may assert the defense of insanity where mental disease has kept the defendant from controlling his or her conduct. A few jurisdictions have abandoned both the *M'Naghten* test and the *irresistable impulse* in favor of the so-called *Durham* rule which states that the accused is not criminally responsible for unlawful conduct produced by mental disease or mental defect. Still other states have adopted the more liberal Model Penal Code approach: "A person is not responsible for criminal conduct if at the time of such conduct as a result of mental disease or defect he or she lacks substantial capacity either to appreciate the criminality of his or her conduct or to conform his or her conduct to the requirements of law." The terms "mental disease or defect" do not include abnormality manifested only by repeated criminal or otherwise antisocial behavior. And if the court finds that the accused does suffer from mental disease or defect and that he or she poses a substantial threat, the accused may be committed to a mental hospital for custody, care, and treatment.

The legal trend had been toward adoption of the MPC's *substantial capacity* test, but recent controversy surrounding the use of the insanity defense has seen an effort in many areas of the country to "tighten up" or restrict the legal definition of insanity (à la M'Naghten where there is no defense at all if you knew that what you were doing was wrong). The controversy came to a head on June 21, 1982 when a U.S. district court jury in Washington, D.C. found John W. Hinckley, Jr., "not guilty by reason of in-

5. See *The Minds of Billy Milligan,* by Daniel Keys, Bantam Books, New York, 1981.

sanity" on all charges arising out of his assassination attempt on President Ronald Reagan on March 30, 1981. The jury's verdict, based on the "substantial capacity" test, was met with a storm of protest, and U.S. Attorney General William French Smith called for a change in the law permitting acquittal in such cases. One of the sought after changes concerned the placement of the burden of proof of insanity: in the Hinckley trial, prosecutors had to prove that Hinckley was *sane* to obtain a conviction. In most states following the MPC approach, the burden is on the defendant who asserts insanity to prove that he or she was *insane* at the time of commission of the act.

Automatism is a defense closely related to insanity. A person who engages in otherwise criminal conduct is not guilty when his or her act is committed in a state of unconsciousness or semi-consciousness. These states of less than full awareness include epileptic and post-epileptic states, conditions associated with organic brain disease, and concussional states following head injuries. The somnambulist who wanders nightly is a classic victim of automatism. Metabolic disorders such as anoxia and hypoglycemia, as well as drug-induced states of semi-consciousness, may also result in automatic activity.

In the English case of Regina v. Charlson [1955] 1 All.E.R. 859, a man struck his ten-year-old son with a mallet, then threw the boy out of a window. Evidence showed that the man suffered from a cerebral tumor which made him subject to fits of impulsive violence. He was acquitted on the defense of automatism (insanity was not asserted, though it, too, might have been a successful defense).

Voluntary or involuntary intoxication is also a good defense to crime when it eliminates the necessary mens rea or criminal intent. Of course, this defense is of little value where intoxication is an element of the crime, and the defendant charged with being drunk in a public place or with driving under the influence of alcohol must look elsewhere for assistance.

Finally, children up to a certain age are generally considered incapable of committing crime. They are tried, not as adults, but in juvenile courts where concern is for their welfare—not their punishment. While determination of juvenile delinquency is a civil rather than a criminal matter, juveniles are still entitled to full protection of their constitutional rights (see Chapter 3).

Parties to Crime

Another important rule of criminal law states that if several persons combine or conspire to commit a crime, or if they command or counsel a crime or aid and abet in any attempt to commit a crime each is responsible for all acts committed by all partners in execution of the common purpose so long as the acts are a natural or probable consequence of the unlawful combination or undertaking. So if several persons combine to commit a burglary and one of them murders the owner of the house in order to accomplish the common purpose which is to steal, each is guilty of murder. This result, of course, fits together with the felony murder rule. The criminal mastermind who stays at home while his four co-conspirators rob the bank is as guilty as his partners are of any act committed in carrying out the crime. Even if one of the partners disobeys an order not to carry a loaded gun and kills a bank teller as a result, all are guilty of murder under the felony murder rule and the rule concerning parties to a crime. But an individual who comes into the picture *only after* the crime has been committed and then aids or assists the person who has committed the felony is not guilty of the crime itself. He or she is called an accessory after the fact, and the crime is against the state and public justice.

WHAT ARE THE PURPOSES OF THE CRIMINAL LAW?

It is often said that the ultimate end of criminal law is the prevention of harm to individual and social interests. These particular goals stand out:

- Deterrence to discourage others from committing crime by making an example of offenders or by authorizing severe punishment for commission of crime;
- Incapacitation to remove offenders from society and thus deny them any further opportunity to commit crime;
- Rehabilitation to prepare offenders for return to society and to a useful life;
- Retribution to inflict justly deserved punishment. Some courts reject retribution as a proper goal of criminal law.

Criminal law in its broadest sense seeks to prevent injury to the public health, safety, morals, and welfare. It uses punishment and the threat of punishment to achieve its purposes.

Family Law

WHAT IS FAMILY LAW AND HOW DOES IT RELATE TO BUSINESS?

Family law is a concept that deals with marriage, children, and divorce. All have important implications regarding property, support, and tax matters which, in turn, affect the individual's business, i.e., his or her making a living.

As we shall learn in the next section, in community property states marriage will immediately have effect on future property rights. And in all states, having children will create obligations of support. When divorce requires property settlements, these may split business ownerships. There may be continuing obligations of support for an ex-spouse after marriage.

It is also a fact that in recent years thousands of people throughout the country have decided to live together without being married. This has resulted in a new term being coined: "posslq" standing for "person of the opposite sex sharing living quarters." Contrary to rumor, such relationships, in and of themselves, do not create legal right or obligation in either party. This can result in heartbreak and hardship when such a relationship ends, as neither party is entitled to share in the other's property or to continuing support from the other. The only way this can be changed is if the parties enter into a valid contract regarding property and support (see Chapter 9 and the *Lee Marvin* case). Unfortunately, most individuals do not think to enter into a contract and, without the protections of marriage, are left with no legal interest in each other's property, business, or income.

WHAT IS COMMUNITY PROPERTY?

In forty-two of the fifty states the fact of marriage will not cause a sharing in the ownership of properties acquired thereafter or in a splitting of the income of each spouse (however, rights and sharing will result if there is a divorce or a death of either spouse).

Community property is recognized only in eight states: Arizona, California, Idaho, Louisiana, Nevada, New Mexico, Texas, and Washington. The theory behind community property is that a husband and wife form a "community." All property, other than separate property, acquired by the spouses during the existence of the community is "community property" belonging to both spouses equally in undivided one-half shares.

Separate Property

Because community property, by definition, excludes *separate property,* it is important to understand "separate property" as that term is used in community property states. Separate property refers to property belonging entirely to one spouse who is free to sell the property or otherwise use or dispose of it without regard to the wishes of the other spouse. Separate property may be acquired in a variety of ways.

In the absence of "community" Property acquired by either spouse prior to the marriage is separate property and remains separate throughout the marriage. Also, any property either spouse acquires after dissolution of the marriage is separate.

In the presence of "community" The following types of property are separate property even when acquired by the husband or wife during marriage:

- Property a spouse receives as a gift or inheritance;
- Rents, dividends, or other income from separate property (e.g., rent income from an apartment house the wife acquired prior to marriage);
- Gains from sales or exchanges of separate property, as well as any property received in exchange for separate property;
- Earnings from a "sole trader" business (most community property states have what are called "sole trader" statutes that permit a spouse who formally alleges the other spouse to be incompetent or improvident to go into busi-

ness for himself or herself. The purpose of such statutes is to insulate the petitioner spouse's earnings from the incompetent spouse's debts.);

- Money damages recovered by a spouse for personal injuries inflicted by the other spouse (damages recovered from anyone else are community property).

Separate property created by agreement The spouses are free to designate what would normally be community property as separate property and vice versa by agreement prior to or during marriage.

What rights does each spouse have with regard to community property? Each has an undivided one-half interest in all community property arising out of the marriage relationship, and each has equal rights in management and control of the property. Both spouses must consent to any transfer of an interest in the property—neither is free to transfer his or her interest irrespective of the wishes of the other. Each spouse is free to will his or her share of the community property as he or she sees fit. Where a decedent spouse fails to dispose of his or her community property by will, the surviving spouse is entitled to all the community property.

In the event the parties obtain a divorce, the community property is usually divided equally between husband and wife regardless of the cause of dissolution. However, the court cannot award one spouse's separate property to the other, although the court may consider the value of the separate assets in determining how much alimony or child support should be paid.

DOES ANY RESPONSIBILITY RESULT TO PEOPLE DOING BUSINESS AS SOLE PROPRIETORS BY REASON OF FAMILY LAW?

At first blush, one might wonder whether a sole proprietor, being an individual business owner, has any legal responsibility to himself or herself. The answer is yes. A person who has been successful in accumulating some wealth has a legal responsibility to maintain sufficient property so that he or she or his or her family does not become a charge of the state. Thus, if a sole proprietor becomes incompetent or is a spendthrift (remember from the previous chapter that a spendthrift is a person whose excessive drinking, idleness, gambling, or debauchery so spends, wastes, or lessens the person's estate that he or she or his or her family is exposed to want or suffering), the court, as we have seen in Chapter 3, may appoint a guardian to handle his or her affairs (e.g., upon petition of an adult child to prevent the parent from squandering his or her assets). This is most obvious where the sole proprietor is married. A married person with children owes certain support obligations to his or her family. Statutes in most states provide that family expenses, including children's education expenses, are the responsibility of both spouses.

A variety of remedies are used to enforce support responsibilities. A child, through his or her attorney, may sue the parent directly in a civil suit if support is not provided. And in most states, criminal nonsupport statutes make it a misdemeanor for a parent to refuse to support his or her children if he or she is financially able to do so. And, again, if the parent is incompetent or a spendthrift, a child, through his or her attorney, may petition the court to appoint a guardian to manage the parent's properties and business affairs.

WHEN CAN A PERSON GET A DIVORCE?

For many years, the law looked upon divorce as an evil: marriage, it seemed to say, should be preserved and continued except under the most extreme circumstances. But after a time, divorce was recognized as a necessary, though regrettable, procedure that could be attributed to the fault of one or both of the parties. State divorce statutes reflected this attitude by listing the traditional grounds (invariably mixed up with fault) that could lead to dissolution of marriage. Some of these statutes are still intact. But in a growing number of states, the parties may end their marriage by consent (without alleging and proving any of the traditional grounds for divorce) by alleging that "irreconcilable differences" have led to the "irremediable" breakdown of their marriage. The traditional grounds for divorce include:

■ *Adultery:* Adultery is usually defined as "voluntary sexual intercourse of a married person with a person other than the offender's husband or wife." While it is a grounds for divorce in several states, it is seldom used—and for obvious reasons. (Until 1967, adultery was the *only* ground for absolute divorce in New York.)

■ *Desertion:* Called "abandonment" in some states, desertion is a continuous and uninterrupted separation that lasts for a period of time, varying from one to five years.

■ *Cruelty:* Cruelty—usually "extreme cruelty" or "cruel and inhuman" treatment—was the most widely used grounds for divorce until states began to add the "no-fault" and "irreconcilable differences" language to their statutes (the term "cruelty" had come to mean serious and irreconcilable differences even before the new language was added).

The most significant change in divorce law has been the widespread addition of the "irreconcilable differences" and "no-fault" provisions in statutes defining grounds for divorce. The typical statutory language is as follows: "The dissolution of a marriage may be decreed when irreconcilable differences between the parties have caused the irremediable breakdown of the marriage."

About two-thirds of the states now include "irreconcilable differences" as a grounds for divorce. The statutes also abolish the principle of "fault" of the parties in deciding whether the marriage should be ended and in dividing up the property. A typical statute might provide:

1. The doctrines of fault and of in pari delicto are abolished in suits for dissolution of a marriage.
2. The court shall not receive evidence of specific acts of misconduct, excepting where child custody is an issue and such evidence is relevant to that issue, or excepting at a hearing when the court finds such evidence necessary to prove irreconcilable differences.
3. In dividing, awarding, and distributing the real and personal property (or both) of the parties (or of either of them) between the parties and in fixing

the amount and duration of the contribution one party is to make to the support of the other (i.e., alimony), the court shall not consider the fault, if any, of either of the parties in causing grounds for the annulment or dissolution of the marriage.

WHAT SUPPORT OBLIGATIONS MAY ARISE OUT OF A DISSOLUTION OF MARRIAGE?

Both alimony and child support may be ordered as part of the dissolution of marriage process. Alimony, often called spousal support, refers to payments made by one spouse for the support of the other spouse following the dissolution of marriage. In awarding alimony, certain factors are commonly taken into account.

- *Age* The age of the spouses at the time of divorce may be an important factor (e.g., is the wife or husband too old to find work or become employable?)
- *Health* The health of the parties may also be an important consideration. If the wife is too ill to work, she will need support; the husband who is ill will not be able to provide it.
- *The length of the marriage* The court is more likely to award alimony where the parties have been married a long time. Following marriages of shorter duration, alimony may be awarded on a temporary basis to assist in education or retraining enabling the recipient spouse to become self-supporting.

In the past, where alimony was awarded, it was generally the husband who was required to pay. In fact, statutes in some states provided that *only* the husband could be ordered to pay alimony. However, such laws have been held to be discriminatory, and today, either spouse may be ordered to pay alimony depending on his or her financial ability and the needs of the other spouse.

Either spouse may also be ordered to make child support payments to the custodial spouse (i.e., the spouse who receives custody of the children, although a growing number of couples today retain joint custody of their children following a divorce). In determining the award, the court will look at the family's income level and standard of living prior to the divorce. The court's objective is to provide the child with adequate food, shelter, clothing, medical care, and education.

Both alimony and child support orders may be modified upon proof of changed circumstances (the authority to modify them is granted by statute in many states). Regarding alimony, assume that the husband has been ordered to make spousal support payments.[6] The alimony order or decree may be modified as follows:

1. *The wife's remarriage* The new husband then assumes the duty of support.

---

6. If the wife were ordered to make the payments, the same basic results would apply but in reverse.

2. *The husband's remarriage* An ex-husband who remarries may find it very difficult to support "two" families at the same standard of living. Some courts reduce the first wife's alimony because of this. Still others follow no hard and fast rule but say that the first wife's alimony should be reduced where the second wife is placed under such undue hardship that she must go to work to help meet the alimony payments.
3. *The wife's changed needs* The alimony award may be increased to meet the wife's changed needs (e.g., a sudden illness) or reduced to reflect a substantial inheritance or other increase in her income.
4. *The husband's changed income* If the husband's income materially declines and he is unable to pay the alimony in full, his payments may be reduced, but where his income substantially increases, there is usually no resulting increase in alimony. It is neither fair nor sensible to increase the alimony just because the husband prospers after the marriage has ended. The alimony should be based on the husband's position at the time of the divorce as long as the wife's needs are provided for. The wife is not entitled to share in the husband's increased productivity as he carries on his life without her.
5. *The husband's death* Generally, the payment of alimony ends with the husband's death.

Child support orders can also be modified when circumstances change. The remarriage of the custodial spouse generally does not affect the duty of the paying spouse to continue to support his or her children (unlike the effect of remarriage on the duty to pay alimony). But if the custodial spouse's new husband or wife adopts the children, the new spouse will assume responsibility for their support, and the ex-spouse's obligation will be terminated.

Also, the duty of child support will generally terminate when the child comes of legal age (e.g., eighteen years), although statutes in some states provide that the duty will continue until the child turns twenty-one, regardless of the technical age of majority, so long as he or she remains in school. Another exception arises where the child is so physically or mentally disabled that he or she cannot take care of himself or herself, in which case the duty of support will continue on through the child's adult years.

HOW ARE ALIMONY AND CHILD SUPPORT ORDERS ENFORCED?

Where a husband or wife refuses to meet his or her alimony or child support obligations, the court will enforce its order with a contempt proceeding. Usually, the spouse entitled to payment initiates the proceeding by setting forth the terms of the decree and showing that the defendant spouse has breached them. After the defendant is personally served, he or she must appear in a hearing before the court. And if the spouse is found to be in contempt, he or she faces fine or imprisonment. In one case, a young man-about-town was several days late with his alimony check (and for the fourth or fifth time) when he was commanded to appear in court and explain why. He did so in a very flippant manner: "Why Judge, I only wanted to punish my ex-wife a little." After spending a week in the county jail, the young man has not since been a minute late with his payments (while the Constitution prohibits imprisonment for nonpayment of debts, alimony is not considered a "debt" but an "obligation" arising out of marriage).

The Uniform Reciprocal Enforcement of Support Act, in force in almost every state, provides another means of enforcing child support orders. This is most important to the spouse who finds himself or herself with a valid decree of support in one state and an ex-spouse living in another. Under the statute, the recipient spouse may bring an action in the state where he or she lives and have it "forwarded" to the proper official in the ex-spouse's state. The courts of that state will then order the ex-spouse to make the child support payments or be held in contempt of court.

Finally, in cases where a dependent child is receiving welfare, the Internal Revenue Service is authorized by law to deduct unpaid child support from any tax refund owing to the spouse obliged to pay the support and use it to reimburse the welfare agency.

ARE THERE ANY TAX IMPLICATIONS TO A DISSOLUTION OF MARRIAGE?

Divorce decrees frequently contain property settlements in addition to orders of support. The form of the settlement varies with the situation. One spouse may be ordered to transfer either real or personal property to the other, or he or she may be required to pay cash in a lump sum or in installments.

Whatever the situation may be—alimony and child support decrees or settlement of property—neither spouse can afford to ignore the tax consequences involved.

Alimony

Section 71 of the Internal Revenue Code provides that certain payments (generally known as alimony) are taxable to the spouse receiving the alimony and deductible to the spouse paying the alimony. For example, suppose that a husband has been ordered to pay alimony to his wife. To qualify as taxable income to the wife (and to be, therefore, deductible to the husband), the alimony must be payable in what are called "periodic" payments. Periodic payments are payments of a fixed amount for an indefinite period of time. Thus a payment of $200 a month for the wife's lifetime is a periodic payment—it is taxable to the wife and deductible to her husband. But a specific sum of money received in installments over a definite period of time is not periodic. Thus an order to pay $10,000 to the wife in yearly installments of $2,000 for a period of five years is not periodic—is not taxable to the wife. But even installment payments for a specific sum are considered "periodic" where the payments extend for more than ten years' time. The wife, however, will never be taxed in one year on more than 10 percent of the total amount she is to receive—no matter how much she is paid per installment—and her husband can deduct no more. So if the wife is to receive a total property settlement of $60,000 to be paid $10,000 the first year and $5,000 a year over the next ten years, she will be taxed on no more than $6,000 the first year (10 percent of the $60,000 total), and that is the amount her husband can deduct from his income. During each of the next ten years, the wife will report her entire payment of $5,000, and her husband will deduct an equal amount since it is less than 10 percent of the total.

Another form of periodic payment is one that is certain as to time but uncertain as to amount. An example is an award of alimony measured by, say, 15 percent of the husband's income for the next six years. Here, the duration of payment is determined, but the amount is indefinite. This form of award qualifies as a "periodic" payment and is taxable to the wife and deductible to the husband.

Child Support Payments

Child support payments are not taxable to the receiving spouse or deductible to the paying spouse.

To qualify as a child support payment, the award must be specifically designated for the support of children. In other words, if the wife is to receive $500 a month for life or until she remarries and nothing in the decree indicates that the money is for the support of her children, all the payments are considered alimony, even where there are dependent children living with the wife. However, where there is a mixed award, say of $500 (i.e., $250 designated as alimony and $250 designated as child support), a partial payment of $350 a month instead of the full $500 is considered as full payment of the child support—and only $100 of alimony.

Personal Exemptions for Children after Divorce

Another important tax consideration in the divorce situation revolves around the taking of the personal exemption for dependent children. The personal exemption is a flat allowance that a taxpayer may deduct in computing his or her taxable income. The exemption is currently $1,000 per dependent in 1982–1983. In addition to exemptions for the taxpayer and his or her spouse (where a joint return is filed), the taxpayer is also entitled to an equal exemption for each qualified dependent. A qualified dependent is a person related to the taxpayer in a certain way or a member of his or her household dependent on the taxpayer for at least 50 percent of his or her support. Of course, children qualify in most families—the problem arises when there has been a divorce and the child lives with one spouse, while the other makes payments for the child's support. Which spouse can claim the child as a dependent?

Generally, the parent who has custody of the child for the greater portion of the year is entitled to the dependency exemption where: (1) the parents are divorced or legally separated or are separated under a written separation agreement; (2) the parents together furnish more than one-half of the child's support for the year; and (3) the child is in custody of either or both of the parents for more than one-half of the year.

There are two exceptions to the general rule. First, if the divorce or separation decree or written agreement between the parents specifically states that the parent without custody can still have the exemption, that parent will get the exemption if he or she contributes at least $600 to the child's support during the year (the noncustodial parent is here entitled to the exemption even though his or her contribution is less than one-half of the child's support). Second, the noncustodial parent is entitled to the exemption if he or she contributes $1,200 or more in child support (regardless of the number of children) during the year, and the custodial parent fails to establish by a clear preponderance of the evidence that he or she provided more.

Taxable Transfers

Another important tax consideration at the time of divorce is the possibility that income may result by reason of giving up property in a property settlement. For example, if a husband transfers property to his wife in settling his obligation to support her or for her release of any rights to his other property or estate, he will have a taxable gain to the extent of the difference between what he paid for the property transferred and its fair market value. So if a husband transferred a ranch for which he paid $100,000 (his tax basis) to his wife in a property settlement so that he has no further obligation of support, and the ranch is now worth $1,000,000, the husband has a taxable gain of $900,000. The tax basis to the wife would be $1,000,000, and she would have no gain on the transfer.

WHAT IS THE TAX DEDUCTION FOR TWO-EARNER MARRIED COUPLES?

For several years there has been a controversy about paying federal income taxes as two single taxpayers versus paying as a married couple. A number of couples in the country have even periodically gotten divorced and remarried to pay a lesser amount of total income taxes when both have been working. For years beginning in 1983, the law now provides a special deduction to offset the fact that a married couple, both working, would usually have paid a higher tax than two single taxpayers with the same income. This was called the "marriage penalty." To relieve this, the law now allows a deduction of 10 percent of the lesser of $30,000 or the earned income of the spouse with the lower income. The result is that if each spouse is earning at least $30,000, there will be a deduction of $3,000. If one spouse earns less than $30,000, the deduction will be 10 percent of what that spouse earns.

Cases

Can one copy what is not patented?

SEARS, ROEBUCK & CO. v. STIFFEL CO.

Supreme Court of the United States, 1964.
376 U.S. 225, 84 S.Ct. 784, 11 L.Ed.2d 661.

Mr. Justice BLACK delivered the opinion of the Court.

The question in this case is whether a State's unfair competition law can, consistently with the federal patent laws, impose liability for or prohibit the copying of an article which is protected by neither a federal patent nor a copyright. The respondent, Stiffel Company, secured design and mechanical patents on a "pole lamp"—a vertical tube having lamp fixtures along the outside, the tube being made so that it will stand upright between the floor and ceiling of a room. Pole lamps proved a decided commercial success, and soon after Stiffel brought them on the market Sears, Roebuck & Company put on the market a substantially identical lamp, which it sold more cheaply, Sears' retail price being about the same as Stiffel's wholesale price. Stiffel then brought this action against Sears in the United States District Court for the Northern District of Illinois, claiming in its first count that by copying its design Sears had infringed Stiffel's patents and in its second count that by selling copies of Stiffel's lamp Sears had caused confusion in the trade as to the source of the lamps and had thereby engaged in unfair competition under Illinois law. There was evidence that identifying tags were not attached to the Sears lamps although labels appeared on the cartons in which they were delivered to customers, that customers had asked Stiffel whether its lamps differed from Sears', and that in two cases customers who had bought Stiffel lamps had complained to Stiffel on learning that Sears was selling substantially identical lamps at a much lower price.

The District Court, after holding the patents invalid for want of invention, went on to find as a fact that Sears' lamp was "a substantially exact copy" of Stiffel's and that the two lamps were so much alike, both in appearance and in functional details, "that confusion between them is likely, and some confusion has already occurred." On these findings the court held Sears guilty of unfair competition, enjoined Sears "from unfairly competing with [Stiffel] by selling or attempting to sell pole lamps identical to or confusingly similar to" Stiffel's lamp, and ordered an accounting to fix profits and damages resulting from Sears' "unfair competition."

The Court of Appeals affirmed.[1] 313 F.2d 115. That court held that, to make out a case of unfair competition under Illinois law, there was no need to show that Sears had been "palming off" its lamps as Stiffel lamps; Stiffel had only to prove that there was a "likelihood of confusion as to the source of the products"—that the two articles were sufficiently identical that customers could not tell who had made a particular one. Impressed by the "remarkable sameness of appearance" of the lamps, the Court of Appeals upheld the trial court's findings of likelihood of confusion and some actual confusion, findings which the appellate court construed to mean confusion "as to the source of the lamps." The Court of Appeals thought this enough under Illinois law to sustain the trial court's holding of unfair competition, and thus held Sears liable under Illinois law for doing no more than copying and marketing an unpatented article. We granted certiorari to consider whether this use of a State's law of unfair competi-

1. No review is sought here of the ruling affirming the District Court's holding that the patent is invalid.

tion is compatible with the federal patent law.

Before the Constitution was adopted, some States had granted patents either by special act or by general statute, but when the Constitution was adopted provision for a federal patent law was made one of the enumerated powers of Congress because, as Madison put it in The Federalist No. 43, the States "cannot separately make effectual provision" for either patents or copyrights. That constitutional provision is Art. I, § 8, cl. 8, which empowers Congress "To promote the Progress of Science and useful Arts, by securing for limited Times to Authors and Inventors the exclusive Right to their respective Writings and Discoveries." Pursuant to this constitutional authority, Congress in 1790 enacted the first federal patent and copyright law, 1 Stat. 109, and ever since that time has fixed the conditions upon which patents and copyrights shall be granted. These laws, like other laws of the United States enacted pursuant to constitutional authority, are the supreme law of the land. When state law touches upon the area of these federal statutes, it is "familiar doctrine" that the federal policy "may not be set at naught, or its benefits denied" by the state law. This is true, of course, even if the state law is enacted in the exercise of otherwise undoubted state power.

The grant of a patent is the grant of a statutory monopoly; indeed, the grant of patents in England was an explicit exception to the statute of James I prohibiting monopolies. Patents are not given as favors, as was the case of monopolies given by the Tudor monarchs but are meant to encourage invention by rewarding the inventor with the right, limited to a term of years fixed by the patent, to exclude others from the use of his invention. During that period of time no one may make use, or sell the patented product without the patentee's authority. But in rewarding useful invention, the "rights and welfare of the community must be fairly dealt with and effectually guarded." To that end the prerequisites to obtaining a patent are strictly observed, and when the patent has issued the limitations on its exercise are equally strictly enforced. To begin with, a genuine "invention" or "discovery" must be demonstrated "lest in the constant demand for new appliances the heavy hand of tribute be laid on each slight technological advance in an art." Once the patent issues, it is strictly construed. [I]t cannot be used to secure any monopoly beyond that contained in the patent, the patentee's control over the product when it leaves his hands is sharply limited, and the patent monopoly may not be used in disregard of the antitrust laws. Finally, and especially relevant here, when the patent expires the monopoly created by it expires, too, and the right to make the article—including the right to make it in precisely the shape it carried when patented—passes to the public.

Thus the patent system is one in which uniform federal standards are carefully used to promote invention while at the same time preserving free competition. Obviously a State could not, consistently with the Supremacy Clause of the Constitution, extend the life of a patent beyond its expiration date or give a patent on an article which lacked the level of invention required for federal patents. To do either would run counter to the policy of Congress of granting patents only to true inventions, and then only for a limited time. Just as a State cannot encroach upon the federal patent laws directly, it cannot, under some other law, such as that forbidding unfair competition, give protection of a kind that clashes with the objectives of the federal patent laws.

In the present case the "pole lamp" sold by Stiffel has been held not to be entitled to the protection of either a mechanical or a design patent. An unpatentable article, like an article on which the patent has expired, is in the public domain and may be made and sold by whoever chooses to do so. What Sears did was to copy Stiffel's design and to sell lamps almost identical to those sold by Stiffel. This it had every right to do under the federal patent laws. That Stiffel originated the pole lamp and made it popular is immaterial. "Sharing in the goodwill of an article unprotected by patent or trademark is the exercise of a right possessed by all—and in the free exercise of which the consuming public is deeply interested." To allow a State by use of its law of unfair competition to prevent the copying of an article which represents too slight an advance to be patented would be to permit the State to block off from the public something which federal law has said belongs to the public. The result would be that while federal law grants only * * * 17 years' protection to genuine inventions, States could allow perpetual protection to articles too lacking in novelty to merit any patent at all under federal constitutional standards. This would be too great an encroachment on the federal patent system to be tolerated.

Sears has been held liable here for unfair competition because of a finding of likelihood of confusion based only on the fact that Sears' lamp was copied from Stiffel's unpatented lamp and that consequently the two looked exactly alike. Of course there could be "confusion" as to who had manufactured these nearly identical articles. But mere inability of the public to tell two identical articles apart is not enough to support an injunction against copying or an award of damages for copying that which the federal patent laws permit to be copied. Doubtless a State may, in appropriate circumstances, require that goods, whether patented or unpatented, be labeled or that other precautionary steps be taken to prevent customers from being misled as to the source, just as it may protect businesses in the use of their trademarks, labels, or distinctive dress in the packaging of goods so as to prevent others, by imitating such markings, from misleading purchasers as to the source of the goods. But because of the federal patent laws a State may not, when the article is unpatented and uncopyrighted, prohibit the copying of the article itself or award damages for such copying. The judgment below did both and in so doing gave Stiffel the equivalent of a patent monopoly on its unpatented lamp. That was error, and Sears is entitled to a judgment in its favor.

Reversed.

The "Golden Fleece of the Month Award."

HUTCHINSON v. PROXMIRE

Supreme Court of the United States, 1979.
443 U.S. 111, 99 S.Ct. 2675, 61 L.Ed.2d 411.

Respondent Proxmire is a United States Senator from Wisconsin. In March 1975, he initiated the "Golden Fleece of the Month Award" to publicize what he perceived to be the most egregious examples of wasteful governmental spending. The second such award, in April 1975, went to the National Science Foundation, the National Aeronautics and Space Administration, and the Office of Naval Research, for spending almost half a million dollars during the preceding seven years to fund Hutchinson's research.

* * *

The bulk of Hutchinson's research was devoted to the study of emotional behavior. In particular, he sought an objective measure of aggression, concentrating upon the behavior patterns of certain animals, such as the clenching of jaws when they were exposed to various aggravating stressful stimuli. The National Aeronautics and Space Agency and the Navy were interested in the potential of this research for resolving problems associated with confining humans in close quarters for extended periods of time in space and undersea exploration.

The Golden Fleece Award to the agencies that had sponsored Hutchinson's research was based upon research done for Proxmire by Schwartz.

* * *

After contacting a number of federal and state agencies, Schwartz helped to prepare a speech for Proxmire to present in the Senate on April 18, 1975; the text was then incorporated into an advance press release, with only the addition of introductory and concluding sentences. Copies were sent to a mailing list of 275 members of the news media throughout the United States and abroad.

Schwartz telephoned Hutchinson before releasing the speech to tell him of the award; Hutchinson protested that the release contained an inaccurate and incomplete summary of his research. Schwartz replied that he thought the summary was fair.

In the speech, Proxmire described the federal grants for Hutchinson's research, concluding with the following comment:

> "The funding of this nonsense makes me almost angry enough to scream and kick or even clench my jaw. It seems to me it is outrageous.
>
> "Dr. Hutchinson's studies should make the taxpayers as well as his monkeys grind their teeth. In fact, the good doctor has made a fortune from his monkeys and in the process made a monkey out of the American taxpayer.
>
> "It is time for the Federal Government to get out of this 'monkey business.' In view of the transparent worthlessness of Hutchinson's study of jaw-grinding and biting by angry or hard-drinking monkeys, it is time we put a stop to the bite Hutchinson and the bureaucrats who fund him have been taking of the taxpayer." 121 Cong.Rec. 10803 (1975).

In May 1975, Proxmire referred to his Golden Fleece Awards in a newsletter sent to about 100,000 people whose names were on a mailing list that included constituents in Wisconsin as well as persons in other states. The newsletter repeated the essence of the speech and the press release. Later in 1975, Proxmire appeared on a television interview program where he referred to Hutchinson's research, though he did not mention Hutchinson by name.

On April 16, 1976, Hutchinson filed this suit in United States District Court in Wisconsin. In Count I he alleges that as a result of the actions of Proxmire and Schwartz he has "suffered a loss of respect in his profession, has suffered injury to his feelings, has been humiliated, held up to public scorn, suffered extreme mental anguish and physical illness and pain to his person. Further, he has suffered a loss of income and ability to earn income in the future." Count II alleges that the respondents' conduct has interfered with Hutchinson's contractual relationships with supporters of his research. He later amended the complaint to add an allegation that his rights of privacy and peace and tranquility have been infringed.

Respondents moved for a change of venue and for summary judgment. In their motion for summary judgment they asserted that all of their acts and utterances were protected by the Speech or Debate Clause. In addition, they asserted that their criticism of the spending of public funds was privileged under the Free Speech Clause of the First Amendment. They argued that Hutchinson was both a public figure and a public official, and therefore would be obliged to prove the existence of "actual malice." Respondents contended that the facts of this case would not support a finding of actual malice.

Without ruling on venue, the District Court granted respondents' motion for summary judgment. 431 F.Supp. 1311 (W.D. Wis.1977). In so ruling, the District Court relied on both grounds urged by respondents.

* * *

The Court of Appeals affirmed, holding that the Speech or Debate Clause protected the statements made in the press release and in the newsletters.

* * *

[Article 1, Section 6 of the United States Constitution states: "The Senators and Representatives shall * * * be privileged * * * for any speech or debate in either house. * * *"]

The Speech or Debate Clause has been directly passed on by this Court relatively few times in 190 years.

* * *

Literal reading of the Clause would, of course, confine its protection narrowly to a

"Speech or Debate *in* either House." But the Court has given the Clause a practical rather than a strictly literal reading which would limit the protection to utterances made within the four walls of either Chamber. Thus, we have held that committee hearings are protected, even if held outside the Chambers; committee reports are also protected.

* * *

The gloss going beyond a strictly literal reading of the Clause has not, however, departed from the objective of protecting only legislative activities. In Thomas Jefferson's view:

> "[The privilege] is restrained to things done in the House in a Parliamentary course . . . . For [the Member] is not to have privilege contra morem parliamentarium, to exceed the bounds and limits of his place and duty." T. Jefferson, A Manual of Parliamentary Practice 20 (1854), reprinted in The Complete Jefferson 704 (S. Padover ed. 1943).

* * *

More recently we expressed a similar definition of the scope of the Clause:

> "Legislative acts are not all-encompassing. The heart of the Clause is speech or debate in either House. Insofar as the Clause is construed to reach other matters, *they must be an integral part of the deliberative and communicative processes* by which Members participate *in committee and House proceedings* with respect to the consideration and passage or rejection of proposed legislation or with respect to other matters which the Constitution places within the jurisdiction of either House. As the Court of Appeals put it, the courts have extended the privilege to matters beyond pure speech or debate in either House, but 'only when necessary to prevent indirect impairment of such deliberations.' "

* * *

Indeed, the precedents abundantly support the conclusion that a Member may be held liable for republishing defamatory statements originally made in either House. We perceive no basis for departing from that long-established rule.

* * *

We reach a similar conclusion here. A speech by Proxmire in the Senate would be wholly immune and would be available to other Members of Congress and the public in the Congressional Record. But neither the newsletters nor the press release was "essential to the deliberations of the Senate" and neither was part of the deliberative process.

* * *

Since *New York Times Co. v. Sullivan,* 376 U.S. 254, 84 S.Ct. 710, 11 L.Ed.2d 686 (1964), this Court has sought to define the accommodation required to assure the vigorous debate on public issues that the First Amendment was designed to protect while at the same time affording protection to the reputations of individuals.

* * *

In *Gertz v. Robert Welch, Inc.,* the Court offered a general definition of "public figures":

> "For the most part those who attain this status [of public figure] have assumed roles of especial prominence in the affairs of society. Some occupy positions of such persuasive power and influence that they are deemed public figures for all purposes. More commonly, those classed as public figures have thrust themselves to the forefront of particular public controversies in order to influence the resolution of the issues involved. In either event, they invite attention and comment." * * *

On this record, Hutchinson's activities and public profile are much like those of countless members of his profession. His published writings reach a relatively small category of professionals concerned with research in human behavior. To the extent the subject of his published writings became a matter of controversy, it was a consequence of the Golden Fleece Award. Clearly, those charged with defamation cannot, by their own conduct, create their own defense by making the claimant a public figure. * * *

Reversed and remanded.

The "kissing case."

HODGES v. NOFSINGER

District Court of Appeal of Florida, 1966.
183 So.2d 14.

Action against automobile driver to recover for injuries sustained by passenger-owner when driver kissed her and automobile veered across the road into a canal. The Circuit Court * * * entered final judgment on a verdict for plaintiff, and defendant appealed. * * *

SWANN, Judge

The defendant Gary C. Hodges, appeals from a final judgment entered for the plaintiff, Mary Nofsinger, after a jury trial, in the sum of $7,500.00 The sole question on appeal is whether the plaintiff was guilty of contributory negligence, as a matter of law, thereby precluding her from any recovery from the defendant in this cause.

The parties have referred to this as the "kissing case." The defendant's version of the facts on appeal are as follows. The parties had seen each other many times prior to the accident. The plaintiff was a single woman, about twenty-five years of age, and the defendant was a member of the United States Air Force, stationed at Homestead, Florida at the time the accident occurred. On that day, the defendant and a friend went to the plaintiff's house. The friend had to return to the base early, but the defendant wanted to stay and the plaintiff agreed to take him back to the base in her automobile later in the evening.

At about 8:00 P.M. they departed for Homestead with the defendant driving the plaintiff's car and the plaintiff sitting close to him on the front seat, "about the middle of the car." She testified that the defendant drove normally, and made the following answers to questions propounded at trial:

* * *

"Q. From the time you got onto Allapattah Drive up to the time of the accident, describe what happened.

"A. Well, we were just driving along Allapattah, and Gary kissed me, and we went off the road into the canal."

* * *

"Q. You didn't protest or object, or push Gary away at all during the kissing, did you?
"A. No, I didn't."

* * *

" 'A. The kissing occurred for a number of seconds, and we hit right then. I mean there was no pause in between.' "

* * *

"Q. * * * Would you please tell me, please, isn't it a fact that you did kiss fully on the mouth?

"A. The kiss was fully on the mouth."

* * *

"Q. And the kiss continued for a number of seconds, didn't it?

"A. I felt at the time that it did.

"Q. And it endured up to the time of the accident?

"A. Yes."

* * *

"Q. This wasn't the first time you kissed, was it?

"A. No."

* * *

The defendant contends that on these facts and circumstances the plaintiff cooperated in the kissing, with a reckless disregard for her safety, and was therefore guilty of contributory negligence as a matter of law.

The plaintiff sets forth the facts in a different light than those of the defendant. The plaintiff contends, and submitted to the jury, the same preliminary factual situation as the defendant. The essential difference in the evidence of the parties is summarized as follows. The defendant was driving in a normal manner, looking straight ahead, and suddenly, without any prior conversation or warning, the defendant kissed the plaintiff. This surprised her and she did not react or cooperate. She did not have an opportunity to protest or object to the defendant's kissing her before the car veered across the road through a guard rail and into a canal, which resulted in her injuries.

It is apparent from the testimony that there are conflicts in the evidence as to the issue of contributory negligence; that is, whether the plaintiff cooperated in the kiss, or whether she was so surprised that she did not have time in which to protest or object to the actions of the defendant. The conflicting evidence on this issue was properly submitted to the jury to be resolved by it. * * *

On appeal by the defendant from a final judgment based on a jury verdict, all testimony and proper inferences therefrom are required to be construed most favorably to the plaintiff. * * *

* * * Inasmuch as we are required to construe the testimony and proper inferences therefrom most favorably to the plaintiff, we cannot say on appeal that the plaintiff was guilty of contributory negligence, as a matter of law.

* * *

[The reason the testimony was construed in favor of the plaintiff was because the plaintiff won in the trial court. Had the defendant won in the trial court, the appellate court would have construed the testimony and proper inferences therefrom most favorably to the defendant. This is because the appellate court, unlike the jury, does not actually see and hear the witnesses but must rely on the transcript of the trial.]

For the reasons stated, the judgment appealed from is therefore

Affirmed.

Does a corporation charged with criminal violation have a privilege against self-incrimination?

UNITED STATES v. PINKSTON-HOLLAR, INC.

United States District Court, District of Kansas, 1976.
4 O.S.H.C. 1697.

This is a criminal proceeding brought pursuant to the Occupational Safety and Health Act of 1970. The matter now is before the Court for consideration of several motions filed by the defendants whereby they seek suppression of evidence and dismissal or amendment of the Information.

* * *

The Information charges that the defendants willfully failed to provide proper safety equipment for one of their employees as required by law and that such failure resulted in the accidental death of this employee. 29 U.S.C. Secs. 655, 666(e). The accident in question occurred on January 29, 1975, at a construction site near Goddard, Kansas, and was immediately reported to the Wichita office of the Occupational Safety and Health Administration (OSHA) by the defendant Robert Pinkston. This office then assigned an OSHA compliance officer to inspect the job site and investigate the reported accident. The officer's investigation commenced the day following the accident, January 30, 1975, and continued every working day for approximately one week. The investigation consisted primarily of personal conversations with fellow employees of the deceased and with Robert Pinkston, vice president of the defendant corporation. Eventually, on February 11, 1975, the matter was referred to OSHA's Regional Solicitor's Office for possible criminal prosecution.

It is clear that under Section 17 of the Occupational Safety and Health Act, 29 U.S.C. Sec. 666, both civil and criminal penalties may result from an investigation of an employer by OSHA. The facts indicate, however, that at no time did the compliance officer inform either defendant in this case that there was a possibility of criminal prosecution arising from his investigation. The facts further show that the defendants fully cooperated with the officer in his investigation, making themselves and their employees available to him, in order that they might mitigate possible civil penalties arising from the occurrence in question. The compliance officer nevertheless conducted his investigation without giving the defendants warnings as noted in *Miranda v. Arizo-*

na, 384 U.S. 436, 16 L.Ed.2d 694, 86 S.Ct. 1602 (1966).

The defendants contend in their first motion that the compliance officer's failure to warn them of the criminal nature of the investigation and of their rights under the Constitution requires suppression of any evidence elicited from the defendants or their employees.

Miranda v. Arizona, of course, set forth a procedure which must be followed by the Government in certain circumstances when interrogating a criminal suspect protected by the Fifth Amendment privilege against self-incrimination. This procedure, however, is required *ipso facto* only when the suspect has been taken into the Government's custody or is otherwise deprived of his freedom by the Government. * * * There is no evidence in this case that either defendant had been taken into custody during the investigation in question, even if it be assumed that a corporation can ever be "in custody." *Beckwith*, however, points out that in any case, to determine compliance with Fifth Amendment, incriminating statements of a criminal suspect must be analyzed to determine whether they were volunteered or coerced in light of the surrounding circumstances.

To begin, we note that the corporation, Pinkston-Hollar, Inc., has no Fifth Amendment privileges against self-incrimination. A corporation, as such, cannot be "coerced" or compelled as can an individual. The privilege, furthermore, is a personal one, applying only to natural individuals, and cannot be utilized by an organization such as a corporation. * * *

The defendant Robert Pinkston appears to be claiming that the compliance officer's failure to tell him of the criminal nature of the investigation was a deception which vitiated any voluntariness in the statements Pinkston made during the officer's interviews. Pinkston volunteered the information, he says, believing the investigation was in the interest of civil justice only. This may or may not have been true. We find, however, that at the time Pinkston made any possibly incriminating remarks to the officer no criminal investigation was in process.

* * *

From the notes and records prepared by the compliance officer of his investigation, it appears that Pinkston made only three disclosures which could possibly have implicated him in the offense charged: (1) that Hulsey had been the employee of Pinkston-Hollar, Inc., (2) that he, Pinkston, was an officer of the defendant corporation, and (3) that he, Pinkston, had an interest in safety and personally instructed new employees in safety precautions. These disclosures were made on the morning of January 30, 1975, the first date of the investigation, at a time when the compliance officer was merely trying to ascertain what had happened. There was no crime evident at the time as opposed to OSHA's interest in its civil jurisdiction. Not until the next day, January 31, 1975 did the officer begin to suspect that a willful and criminal violation of the Act may have occurred. By this time, Pinkston had made all the statements which might be deemed incriminating. The circumstances therefore do not support a theory of coercion by deception.

* * * Pinkston points out that he has been charged under 29 U.S.C. Sec. 666(e) and 18 U.S.C. Sec. 2 as an aider and abettor of the defendant corporation. He contends that he cannot be charged as an abettor because in all matters respecting the incident in question he acted as the agent of the defendant corporation and therefore the two were the same. He claims that in acting for the corporation he could not have abetted it in crime. A corporation, of course, acts only through its officers and agents. It would appear, therefore, that responsible corporate officials who have the power to prevent or correct violations of the Occupational Safety and Health Act may be prosecuted in the same sense as they may be under the Federal Food, Drug, and Cosmetic Act of 1938.

* * *

The final motion is for dismissal or amendment of the Information for failure to track the language of the criminal statute. The statute proscribes willful violation of OSHA regulations promulgated by the Secretary of Labor. The regulation allegedly violated requires the use of safety nets at workplaces which are more than 25 feet above the ground when the use of "ladders, scaffolds, catch platforms, temporary floors, safety lines, or safety belts is impractical." 29 C.F.R. Sec. 1926.105(a).

* * *

We find that the Information in this case adequately advises the defendants of the offense charged. * * *

IT IS THEREFORE ORDERED that the motions of the defendants for suppression of evidence and dismissal of the Information be, and the same are hereby,

Overruled.

Is bribery of a private employee a federal crime?

PERRIN v. UNITED STATES

Supreme Court of the United States, 1979.
444 U.S. 37, 100 S.Ct. 311, 62 L.Ed.2d 199.

Mr. Chief Justice BURGER delivered the opinion of the Court.

We granted certiorari to resolve a Circuit conflict on whether commercial bribery of private employees prohibited by a state criminal statute constitutes "bribery . . . in violation of the laws of the State in which committed" within the meaning of the Travel Act.

Petitioner Vincent Perrin and four codefendants were indicted in the Eastern District of Louisiana for violating the Travel Act, [which] provides in part:

> "(a) Whoever travels in interstate or foreign commerce or uses any facility in interstate or foreign commerce, including the mail, with intent to—
>
> "(1) distribute the proceeds of any unlawful activity; or
>
> "(2) commit any crime of violence to further any unlawful activity; or
>
> "(3) otherwise promote, manage, establish, carry on, or facilitate the promotion, management, establishment, or carrying on, of any unlawful activity,
>
> "and thereafter performs or attempts to perform any of the acts specified in subparagraphs (1), (2), and (3), shall be fined not more than $10,000 or imprisoned for not more than five years, or both.
>
> "(b) As used in this subsection 'unlawful activity' means (1) any business enterprise involving gambling, liquor on which the Federal excise tax has not been paid, narcotics * * * or prostitution offenses in violation of the laws of the State in which they are committed or of the United States, or (2) extortion, bribery, or arson in violation of the laws of the State in which committed or of the United States."

The indictment charged that Perrin and his codefendants used the facilities of interstate commerce for the purpose of promoting a commercial bribery scheme in violation of the laws of the State of Louisiana.

* * *

The Government's evidence at trial was that Perrin, David Levy, and Duffy LaFont engaged in a scheme to exploit geological data obtained from the Petty-Ray Geophysical Co. Petty-Ray, a Louisiana-based company, was in the business of conducting geological explorations and selling the data to oil companies. At trial, company executives testified that confidentiality was imperative to the conduct of their business. The economic value of exploration data would be undermined if its confidentiality were not protected. Moreover, public disclosure after sale would interfere with the contractual rights of the purchaser and would otherwise injure Petty-Ray's relationship with its customers.

In June 1975 LaFont importuned Roger Willis, an employee of Petty-Ray, to steal confidential geological exploration data from his employer. In exchange, LaFont promised Willis a percentage of the profits of a corporation which had been created to exploit the stolen information. Perrin, a consulting geologist, was brought into the scheme to interpret and analyze the data.

In late July 1975 Perrin met with Willis, LaFont, and Levy.

* * *

After the meeting, Willis contacted the Federal Bureau of Investigation and disclosed the details of the scheme. Willis agreed to permit conversations between himself and the other participants to be recorded. Forty-seven tapes were made, a large number of which were played to the jury.

The United States Court of Appeals for the Fifth Circuit affirmed Perrin's conviction, rejecting his contention that Congress intended "bribery" in the Act to include only bribery of public officials.

* * *

The Travel Act was one of several bills enacted into law by the 87th Congress as part of the Attorney General's 1961 legislative program directed against "organized crime." Then Attorney General Robert Kennedy testified at Senate and House hearings that federal legislation was needed to aid state and local governments which were no longer able to cope with the increasingly complex and interstate nature of large-scale, multiparty crime. The stated intent was to "dry up" traditional sources of funds for such illegal activities.

* * *

In this country, by the time the Travel Act was enacted in 1961, federal and state statutes had extended the term bribery well beyond its common-law meaning.

* * *

[B]y 1961 the common understanding and meaning of "bribery" had extended beyond its early common-law definitions. In 42 States and in federal legislation, "bribery" included the bribery of individuals acting in a private capacity. It was against this background that the Travel Act was passed.

* * *

Petitioner also contends that commercial bribery is a "management" or "white-collar" offense not generally associated with organized criminal activities. * * * From this, he argues that Congress could not have intended to encompass commercial bribery within § 1952 [The Travel Act].

* * *

The notion that bribery of private persons is unrelated or unknown to what is called "organized crime" has no foundation. The hearings on the Travel Act make clear that a major area of congressional concern was with the infiltration by organized crime into legitimate activities. * * * Legitimate businesses had come to be used as a means for highly organized criminal activities to hide income derived from illegal sources. Moreover, Committees investigating these activities found that those who infiltrated legitimate businesses often used the same criminal techniques to expand their operations and sales in the legitimate enterprises. Thus, in discussing the infiltration of organized groups into nongambling amusement games, the McClellan Committee reported that the organization achieved its holdings in legitimate business by "force, terror and the corruption of management, union and public officials." * * *

Indeed, the McClellan Committee in 1960, like the Kefauver Committee in 1950–1951, documented numerous specific instances of the use of commercial bribery by these organized groups to control legitimate businesses. The McClellan Committee, for example, reported that a particular "shylocking" operation began in New York when persons were able to obtain a substantial unsecured line of credit at a New York bank "by making gifts to two of the bank officials." The Kefauver Committee explored, among numerous others, the relationship between a high-ranking official of the Ford Motor Co. and persons believed to be members of organized illegal groups. Its evidence suggested that organized crime had exploited that relationship to obtain Ford dealerships and hauling contracts.

* * *

There can be little doubt that Congress recognized in 1961 that bribery of private persons was widely used in highly organized criminal efforts to infiltrate and gain control of legitimate businesses, an area of special concern of Congress in enacting the Travel Act.

* * *

We hold that Congress intended "bribery . . . in violation of the laws of the State in which committed" as used in the Travel Act to encompass conduct in violation of state commercial bribery statutes. Accordingly, the judgment of the Court of Appeals is

Affirmed.

Conducting an interstate pornography business through a pattern of racketeering activity.

UNITED STATES v. THEVIS

United States Court of Appeals, Fifth Circuit, 1982.
665 F.2d 616.

KRAVITCH, Circuit Judge

Appellants Michael Thevis and Global Industries, Inc. [Global] were convicted by a jury of violating the Racketeer Influenced and Corrupt Organizations Act [RICO]. Thevis and appellants Anna Jeanette Evans and Alton Bart Hood were convicted of conspiracy to violate the civil rights of Roger Dean Underhill under 18 U.S.C. § 241 by preventing him from testifying at trial.

[The government also sought forfeiture of all assets of the corporate defendant, various real estate properties, contract rights, property rights, and interests in various publishing ventures.]

* * *

The original indictment in this case, filed on June 10, 1978, named Michael G. Thevis, Global Industries, Inc., * * * as defendants. The central allegation was that Thevis and the corporations had conducted an interstate pornography business through a pattern of racketeering activity. Roger Dean Underhill, a principal witness before the grand jury, was named as an unindicted co-conspirator. On October 25, 1979, the grand jury returned a superseding indictment which added a charge that Thevis, Jeanette Evans and Bart Hood conspired to murder Underhill in order to prevent his testimony.

* * *

The trial lasted approximately eight weeks and produced a voluminous record.[3]

In the 1960's, Michael Thevis organized and controlled a group of corporations whose principal purpose was the profitable distribution of adult books and films. Underhill met Thevis in the fall of 1967 and became a Thevis employee. Together, Underhill and Thevis developed a profitable peep-show machine that was manufactured and distributed by two Thevis-controlled corporations, Automatic Enterprises and Cinematics. The government offered evidence as to five separate acts of racketeering in the conduct of this peep-show enterprise. These acts were the murders of two competitors in the adult entertainment business, two separate acts of arson against competitors, and the murders of Underhill and a bystander, Isaac Galanti.

The Hanna Murder

Kenneth "Jap" Hanna owned several adult book stores in Atlanta. On November 13, 1970, Thevis called Underhill at 8:30 a.m. and told him to come to work immediately. When Underhill arrived, Thevis stated that he had shot Ken Hanna and left the body in the trunk of Hanna's car in Thevis' warehouse. In his haste to dispose of the body, Thevis had left the car keys in Hanna's pocket, locked in the trunk. Thevis asked Underhill, a trained locksmith, to open the trunk and retrieve the keys. Thevis and

3. The record on appeal consisted of 118 volumes comprising nearly 16,000 pages.

Underhill then drove the car containing Hanna's body to the Atlanta airport parking lot and left it. Afterwards, Underhill took various steps to dispose of any incriminating evidence, including burning the moving pad on which Hanna's body had lain and replacing several bloody floor boards in the warehouse. In addition, he bought a welding torch outfit and melted the gun, the trunk lock, Hanna's car keys, some Mexican coins which had been in Hanna's possession, and a screwdriver. That night Underhill dumped the melted objects and the bloody boards in the Chattahoochee River.

* * *

The Mayes Murder

Jimmy Mayes was employed by Thevis and Underhill to build peep shows. Underhill paid Mayes by giving him a percentage of his stock in the peep-show corporations. When Thevis took away half of Underhill's and Mayes' shares, Mayes became enraged and threatened to kill Thevis. In December of 1972, Thevis ordered Underhill to kill Mayes and gave him a gun for that purpose. Underhill had a chance to shoot Mayes one night, but could not pull the trigger. At Thevis' instruction, Underhill then hired Bill Mahar to do the job. Mahar told Underhill that he was going to kill Mayes by putting a pipe bomb in his truck. The bomb went off just before midnight, and literally blew Mayes to pieces.

Thevis was at this time in the hospital due to injuries sustained in a motorcycle accident. On the day of the murder, Underhill advised Thevis that the explosion would take place that night. After the explosion, Underhill went to the scene and found a piece of bone and a gold pin. He showed this evidence to Thevis in the hospital; Thevis said that he planned to make the bone into a paperweight. The day after the murder, Thevis instructed his nephew, Mann Chandler, to give Underhill money from Thevis' safe to pay Mahar.

The Louisville Arson

Nat Bailer, a competitor of Cinematics in the peep-show industry, owned a warehouse in Louisville, Kentucky. Thevis ordered Underhill to go to Louisville and burn the warehouse. On the weekend of April 27, 1976, Underhill drove to Louisville and, with two Thevis employees, Clifford Wilson and Robert Mitchum, set fire to the warehouse. Returning from Louisville, Underhill called Thevis and reported their success. The former Mrs. Underhill corroborated Underhill's out of town trip on April 27, 197[6]. She also noticed that he was dirty and smokey when he returned and remembered that he wanted to get rid of the clothes he was wearing.

The Fayetteville Arson

In 1972, Thevis operated an adult bookstore in Fayetteville, North Carolina. Herman Womack owned a competing bookstore just one block away. Thevis told Underhill to burn down the competitor. On September 19, 1972, Underhill and Mahar drove to Fayetteville and accomplished the arson by drilling a hole in the roof of the building pouring gasoline down into the interior, and igniting it with a water pistol used as a flame thrower. Afterwards Thevis gave Underhill $1,500 with which he paid Mahar for the successful arson.

The Underhill-Galanti Murders

Under duress from Thevis, Underhill sold his interest in Cinematics to Thevis in 1971, but remained on Thevis' payroll (at about $50 per week) until Underhill went to prison in 1974. In 1975 Underhill filed a civil RICO suit against Thevis. While Underhill was in prison, the government sought unsuccessfully to get Underhill's cooperation in its investigation of Thevis. Underhill was paroled in January 1977 without having reached any specific agreement with the government. Following his parole, Underhill was granted immunity and began to cooperate. He gave lengthy recorded statements to the FBI in January 1977 and testified before a federal grand jury in May 1977. In

June 1977, Underhill visited Thevis in the federal prison in Springfield, Missouri. Underhill wore a shoe mike provided by the FBI and recorded his conversation with Thevis. During this conversation Underhill told Thevis of his interviews with the FBI and that he had taken and passed a polygraph examination.

On April 28, 1978, Thevis escaped from the New Albany, Indiana, jail where he was confined during the trial of a civil case arising from the Louisville arson. Soon after his escape, he contacted defendants Evans and Hood. Jeanette Evans, a real estate agent in Marietta, Georgia, was a close personal friend of Thevis. Bart Hood, her cousin, was a detective in the Summerville, South Carolina, police department. Evans and Hood assisted Thevis in establishing several aliases, in obtaining an apartment, a VISA credit card, and safe-deposit boxes [and guns].

On October 21, 1978, Irene Williams, Underhill's fiancee, joined him at an Atlanta motel. Underhill intended to enter the Federal Witness Protection Program shortly, but wanted to sell [some] property first. Ms. Williams and Underhill spent two days cleaning up the property. On Wednesday, October 25, Underhill left Williams at approximately 11:30 a.m. to keep an appointment to show the property to Isaac N. Galanti. At about noon, Williams and her two children drove to meet Underhill. When she arrived, she noticed the gate was down and then found the bodies of Underhill and Galanti. She ran across the street to the residence of Henry and Pearl Stumminger.

* * *

Thevis and Evans were arrested on November 9, 1978 in Bloomfield, Connecticut. A search of their persons and their car yielded firearms, $411,000 in cash, and over one million dollars worth of jewelry. A search of a rental locker in South Windsor, Connecticut disclosed a transcript of interviews the FBI had conducted with Underhill. Fingerprint analysis revealed over 100 of Thevis' fingerprints and palm prints throughout the transcript and one of Evans' fingerprints on an inside page of the transcript.

Immediately after his arrest, Thevis was confined in a federal prison in Danbury, Connecticut. His cellmate, Bernard McCarthy, testified that Thevis had confessed to the murder of Underhill. According to McCarthy, Thevis told him that he had lured Underhill to his property by breaking the fence down, where he "assassinated" Underhill and his "bodyguard" with a shotgun. Thevis explained that he killed Underhill because Underhill intended to testify against him, and that Underhill was to enter the marshal's protection service the following Monday.

* * *

Appellants make three separate arguments that the trial court erred in construing RICO. First, they claim that the trial court should have struck the Underhill-Galanti murders from Counts One and Two of the indictment (the RICO charges) because the evidence failed to show that Thevis was "associated with" the enterprise at the time of the murders, and because the murders were not acts through which Thevis conducted the affairs of the enterprise.

This contention is without merit. As this court noted in *United States v. Elliott*, * * * proof of association with a RICO enterprise may depend wholly on circumstantial evidence. The record in this case contains such evidence. Although Thevis had purportedly sold his interest in the pornography business to his secretary, Laverne Bowden, for $16 million dollars, the note securing the sale was always in default. Thevis, therefore, could foreclose at any time and regain his interest in the business. Rodney Glen Smith, a cellmate of Thevis in 1977, testified that despite the "sale," Thevis stated he still "controlled" his pornography empire; given the terms of the "sale" and the fact Thevis had contacted Ms. Bowden after his escape from jail in 1978, one could infer that Thevis' interest in the success of the pornography enterprise continued until the Underhill murder. The murder itself, moreover, neatly advanced Thevis' interests in the enterprise. The original indictment in the case sought forfeiture of all the assets of Global and Fidelity under RICO forfeiture provisions. The Underhill murder was designed to prevent the government's key witness from testifying at trial, thus imperiling the government's entire RICO case and preventing both RICO criminal convictions and forfeiture. The murder, therefore, protected the integrity of the enterprise. Keeping the enterprise together was inextricably tied to furthering its business; hence the Underhill murder was a proper predicate act.

* * *

Appellants' second argument is that the term "enterprise" as used in RICO does not include the specific association charged in this case. The RICO definitions section, states that an enterprise "includes any individual, partnership, corporation, association, or other legal entity, and any union or other group of individuals associated in fact although not a legal entity * * *" Appellants contend that because the indictment described the enterprise as "a group of individuals associated in fact with various corporations," the enterprise alleged did not fall within the literal bounds of the statutory classifications. We reject this claim.

Appellants' final argument is that RICO was not intended to apply to illegitimate enterprises such as the association alleged here. The Supreme Court has now decided this issue in *United States v. Turkette*, * * *, holding that RICO applies to both illegitimate and legitimate enterprises.

* * *

Having determined that the charges in the indictment were proper, we proceed to consider appellants' various evidentiary claims. One of their major contentions is that the trial court erroneously admitted certain transcripts of Underhill's grand jury testimony and FBI interviews as substantive evidence of guilt on the RICO charges.

* * *

The court held that although admitting the evidence under Rule 804(b)(5) would have violated Thevis' confrontation rights under the sixth amendment, the government had established by "clear and convincing" evidence that Thevis had caused Underhill's death; hence, Thevis had waived his confrontation rights. * * *

The sixth amendment to the Constitution provides in part that "in all criminal prosecutions, the accused shall enjoy the right * * * to be confronted with the witnesses against him * * *." All parties to this appeal agree that this right may be waived in a proper case.

* * * A waiver of a constitutional right is ordinarily valid only if there is "an intentional relinquishment of a known right or privilege."

* * * The accused, however, may also waive his confrontation rights indirectly, such as by absenting himself from trial, *Taylor v. United States*, 414 U.S. 17, 94 S.Ct. 194, 38 L.Ed.2d 174 (1973), or engaging in contumacious conduct which requires his removal from the courtroom. *Illinois v. Allen* [see Chapter 1].

We conclude that a defendant who causes a witness to be unavailable for trial for the purpose of preventing that witness from testifying also waives his right to confrontation.

* * * [W]hen confrontation becomes impossible due to the actions of the very person who would assert the right, logic dictates that the right has been waived. The law simply cannot countenance a defendant deriving benefits from murdering the chief witness against him. To permit such subversion of a criminal prosecution "would be contrary to public policy, common sense, and the underlying purpose of the confrontation clause," *United States v. Carlson*, 547 F.2d 1346, 1359 (8th Cir. 1976), *cert. denied*, 431 U.S. 914, 97 S.Ct. 2174, 53 L.Ed.2d 224 (1977), and make a mockery of the system of justice that the right was designed to protect.

* * *

In accordance with our decision we affirm the convictions of all defendants on all counts.

Affirmed.

Can a nontriggerman guilty of felony murder be sentenced to death?

ENMUND v. FLORIDA

Supreme Court of the United States, 1982.
458 U.S. 782, 102 S.Ct. 3368, 73 L.Ed.2d 1140.

Justice WHITE delivered the opinion of the Court.

The facts of this case, taken principally from the opinion of the Florida Supreme Court, are as follows. On April 1, 1975, at approximately 7:45 a.m., Thomas and Eunice Kersey, aged 86 and 74, were robbed and fatally shot at their farmhouse in central Florida. The evidence showed that Sampson and Jeanette Armstrong had gone to the back door of the Kersey house and asked for water for an overheated car. When Mr. Kersey came out of the house, Sampson Armstrong grabbed him, pointed a gun at him, and told Jeanette Armstrong to take his money. Mr. Kersey cried for help, and his wife came out of the house with a gun and shot Jeanette Armstrong, wounding her. Sampson Armstrong, and perhaps Jeanette Armstrong, then shot and killed both of the Kerseys, dragged them into the kitchen, and took their money and fled.

Two witnesses testified that they drove past the Kersey house between 7:30 and 7:40 a.m. and saw a large cream or yellow-colored car parked beside the road about 200 yards from the house and that a man was sitting in the car. Another witness testified that at approximately 6:45 a.m. he saw Ida Jean Shaw, petitioner's common-law wife and Jeanette Armstrong's mother, driving a yellow Buick with a vinyl top which belonged to her and petitioner Earl Enmund. Enmund was a passenger in the car along with an unidentified woman. At about 8 a.m. the same witness saw the car return at a high rate of speed. Enmund was driving, Ida Jean Shaw was in the front seat, and one of the other two people in the car was lying down across the back seat.

Enmund, Sampson Armstrong, and Jeanette Armstrong were indicted for the first-degree murder and robbery of the Kerseys. Enmund and Sampson Armstrong were tried together.[1] The prosecutor maintained in his closing argument that "Sampson Armstrong killed the old people." The judge instructed the jury that "[t]he killing of a human being while engaged in the perpetration of or in the attempt to perpetrate the offense of robbery is murder in the first degree even though there is no premeditated design or intent to kill." He went on to instruct them that

> "In order to obtain a conviction of first degree murder while engaging in the perpetration of or in the attempted perpetration of the crime of robbery, the evidence must establish beyond a reasonable doubt that the defendant was actually present and was actively aiding and abetting the robbery or attempted robbery, and that the unlawful killing occurred in the perpetration of or in the attempted perpetration of the robbery."

The jury found both Enmund and Sampson Armstrong guilty of two counts of first-degree murder and one count of robbery. A separate sentencing hearing was held and the jury recommended the death penalty for both defendants under the Florida procedure whereby the jury advises the trial judge whether to impose the death penalty. * * * The trial judge then sentenced Enmund to death on the two counts of first-degree murder. * * * The trial judge found four statutory aggravating circumstances: the capital felony was committed while Enmund was engaged in or was an ac-

1. Jeanette Armstrong's trial was severed and she was convicted of two counts of second-degree murder and one count of robbery and sentenced to three consecutive life sentences. *Enmund v. State,* 399 So.2d 1362, 1371 (Fla.1981).

complice in the commission of an armed robbery, * * * the capital felony was committed for pecuniary gain, it was especially heinous, atrocious, or cruel, * * *; and Enmund was previously convicted of a felony involving the use or threat of violence, * * *. Enmund was therefore sentenced to death on each of the murder counts.

The Florida Supreme Court affirmed Enmund's conviction and sentences. It found * * * that the interaction of the "felony murder rule and the law of principals combine to make a felon generally responsible for the lethal acts of his co-felon."

* * *

It was thus irrelevant to Enmund's challenge to the death sentence that he did not himself kill and was not present at the killings; also beside the point was whether he intended that the Kerseys be killed or anticipated that lethal force would or might be used if necessary to effectuate the robbery or a safe escape. We have concluded that imposition of the death penalty in these circumstances is inconsistent with the Eighth and Fourteenth Amendments.

The Cruel and Unusual Punishment Clause of the Eighth Amendment is directed, in part, "against all punishments which by their excessive length or severity are greatly disproportioned to the offenses charged."

* * *

This Court most recently held a punishment excessive in relation to the crime charged in *Coker v. Georgia*. There the plurality opinion concluded that the imposition of the death penalty for the rape of an adult woman "is grossly disproportionate and excessive punishment for the crime of rape and is therefore forbidden by the Eighth Amendment as cruel and unusual punishment."

* * *

Thirty-six state and federal jurisdictions presently authorize the death penalty. Of these, only nine jurisdictions authorize imposition of the death penalty solely for participation in a robbery in which another robber takes life.

* * * In each of these nine states, a non-triggerman guilty of felony murder cannot be sentenced to death for the felony murder absent aggravating circumstances above and beyond the felony murder itself.

* * *

In *Gregg v. Georgia* the prevailing opinion observed that "[t]he death penalty is said to serve two principal social purposes: retribution and deterrence of capital crimes by prospective offenders." * * * Unless the death penalty when applied to those in Enmund's position measurably contributes to one or both of these goals, it "is nothing more than the purposeless and needless imposition of pain and suffering," and hence an unconstitutional punishment. * * * We are quite unconvinced, however, that the threat that the death penalty will be imposed for murder will measurably deter one who does not kill and has no intention or purpose that life will be taken. Instead, it seems likely that "capital punishment can serve as a deterrent only when murder is the result of premeditation and deliberation." * * *

As for retribution as a justification for executing Enmund, we think this very much depends on the degree of Enmund's culpability—what Enmund's intentions, expectations, and actions were. American criminal law has long considered a defendant's intention—and therefore his moral guilt—to be critical to "the degree of [his] criminal culpability," and the Court has found criminal penalties to be unconstitutionally excessive in the absence of intentional wrongdoing.

For purposes of imposing the death penalty, Enmund's criminal culpability must be limited to his participation in the robbery, and his punishment must be tailored to his personal responsibility and moral guilt. Putting Enmund to death to avenge two killings that he did not commit and had no intention of committing or causing does not measurably contribute to the retributive end of ensuring that the criminal gets his just deserts.

Because the Florida Supreme Court affirmed the death penalty in this case in the absence of proof that Enmund killed or attempted to kill, and regardless of whether Enmund intended or contemplated that life would be taken, we reverse the judgment upholding the death penalty and remand for further proceedings not inconsistent with this opinion.

So Ordered.

Justice BRENNAN, concurring.

I join the Court's opinion. However, I adhere to my view that the death penalty is in all circumstances cruel and unusual punishment prohibited by the Eighth and Fourteenth Amendments. See *Gregg v. Georgia,* 428 U.S. 153, 227, 96 S.Ct. 2909, 2950, 49 L.Ed.2d 859 (1976) (dissenting opinion).

Justice O'CONNOR, with whom THE CHIEF JUSTICE, Justice POWELL, and Justice REHNQUIST join, dissenting.

Today the Court holds that the Eighth Amendment prohibits a State from executing a convicted felony murderer. I dissent from this holding. * * *

Ida Jean Shaw testified that on March 31 the petitioner and the two Armstrongs were staying at her house. When she awoke on April 1, the day of the murders, the petitioner, Jeanette, and Sampson, as well as Shaw's 1969 yellow Buick, were gone. A little after eight o'clock, either the petitioner or Sampson Armstrong entered the house and told her that Jeanette had been shot. After learning that Jeanette had been shot during a robbery, Shaw asked the petitioner "why he did it." Enmund answered that he had decided to rob Thomas Kersey after he had seen Kersey's money a few weeks earlier.[5] At the same time, Sampson Armstrong volunteered that he had made sure that the Kerseys were dead.

Ida Jean Shaw also testified that, pursuant to the petitioner's and Sampson Armstrong's instructions, she had disposed of a .22 caliber pistol that she normally kept in her car, as well as a .38 caliber pistol belonging to the Armstrongs. The murder weapons were never recovered.

* * *

[T]he murders were especially heinous, atrocious, or cruel because the Kerseys had been shot in a prone position in an effort to eliminate them as witnesses. * * * * * * [T]he evidence clearly showed that the petitioner was an accomplice to the capital felony and that his participation had not been "relatively minor," but had been major in that he "planned the capital felony and actively participated in an attempt to avoid detection by disposing of the murder weapons." * * *

Considering these factors, the trial court concluded that the "aggravating circumstances of these capital felonies outweigh the mitigating circumstances," and imposed the death penalty for each count of murder. * * * The court sentenced the petitioner to life imprisonment for the robbery.

* * *

[I]t cannot be disputed that he is responsible, along with Sampson and Jeanette Armstrong, for the murders of the Kerseys. There is no dispute that their lives were unjustifiably taken, and that the petitioner, as one who aided and abetted the armed robbery, is legally liable for their deaths.

* * *

Accordingly, I conclude that the death penalty is not disproportionate to the crime of felony murder, even though the defendant did not actually kill or intend to kill his victims.

5. Thomas Kersey normally kept large sums of money in his wallet and indiscriminately showed the cash to people he dealt with. A few weeks before his murder, Kersey revealed the contents of his wallet to the petitioner and bragged that at any time he could "dig up $15,000, $16,000." 399 So.2d, at 1365.

Should ex-wives pay alimony?

ORR v. ORR

Supreme Court of the United States, 1979.
440 U.S. 268, 99 S.Ct. 1102, 59 L.Ed.2d 306.

Mr. Justice BRENNAN delivered the opinion of the Court.

The question presented is the constitutionality of Alabama alimony statutes which provide that husbands, but not wives, may be required to pay alimony upon divorce.

On February 26, 1974, a final decree of divorce was entered, dissolving the marriage of William and Lillian Orr. That decree directed appellant, Mr. Orr, to pay appellee, Mrs. Orr, $1,240 per month in alimony. On July 28, 1976, Mrs. Orr initiated a contempt proceeding in the Circuit Court of Lee County, Ala., alleging that Mr. Orr was in arrears in his alimony payments. On August 19, 1976, at the hearing on Mrs. Orr's petition, Mr. Orr submitted in his defense a motion requesting that Alabama's alimony statutes be declared unconstitutional because they authorize courts to place an obligation of alimony upon husbands but never upon wives. The Circuit Court denied Mr. Orr's motion and entered judgment against him for $5,524, covering back alimony and attorney fees. Relying solely upon his federal constitutional claim, Mr. Orr appealed the judgment. On March 16, 1977, the Court of Civil Appeals of Alabama sustained the constitutionality of the Alabama statutes, 351 So.2d 904.

* * *

We now hold the challenged Alabama statutes unconstitutional and reverse. * * *

In authorizing the imposition of alimony obligations on husbands, but not on wives, the Alabama statutory scheme "provides that different treatment be accorded * * * on the basis of * * * sex; it thus establishes a classification subject to scrutiny under the Equal Protection Clause." * * * The fact that the classification expressly discriminates against men rather than women does not protect it from scrutiny. * * * "To withstand scrutiny" under the Equal Protection Clause, " 'classifications by gender must serve important governmental objectives and must be substantially related to achievement of those objectives.' "

* * *

Appellant views the Alabama alimony statutes as effectively announcing the State's preference for an allocation of family responsibilities under which the wife plays a dependent role, and as seeking for their objective the reinforcement of that model among the State's citizens. * * * We agree, as he urges, that prior cases settle that this purpose cannot sustain the statutes. * * * [T]he "old notio[n]" that "generally it is the man's primary responsibility to provide a home and its essentials," can no longer justify a statute that discriminates on the basis of gender. "No longer is the female destined solely for the home and the rearing of the family, and only the male for the marketplace and the world of ideas." * * *

There is no reason, therefore, to use sex as a proxy for need. Needy males could be helped along with needy females with little if any additional burden on the State.

* * *

Moreover, use of a gender classification actually produces perverse results in this case. As compared to a gender-neutral law placing alimony obligations on the spouse able to pay, the present Alabama statutes give an advantage only to the financially secure wife whose husband is in need. Although such a wife might have to pay alimony under a gender-neutral statute, the present statutes exempt her from that obligation. * * *

A gender-based classification which, as compared to a gender-neutral one, generates additional benefits only for those it has no reason to prefer cannot survive equal protection scrutiny.

Legislative classifications which distribute benefits and burdens on the basis of gender carry the inherent risk of reinforcing the stereotypes about the "proper place" of women and their need for special protection.

* * *

Where, as here, the State's compensatory and ameliorative purposes are as well served by a gender-neutral classification as one that gender classifies and therefore carries with it the baggage of sexual stereotypes, the State cannot be permitted to classify on the basis of sex.

* * *

Having found Alabama's alimony statutes unconstitutional, we reverse the judgment below and remand the cause for further proceedings not inconsistent with this opinion.

Review Questions

1. How does criminal responsibility differ for corporations versus partnerships or sole proprietorships? Does corporate criminal responsibility affect individual criminal responsibility? A corporation is usually convicted of what type of crime? What does the Foreign Corrupt Practices Act make unlawful? What is the most common criminal violation of the antitrust laws? Is there any tax effect if bribes or "kickbacks" are paid? What is the purpose of RICO? Is there any way a dealer can prevent prosecution for shipping adulterated goods in interstate commerce? Explain your answers.

2. Why does the law protect trademarks and trade names? What remedies are provided under the Lanham Act? Does copying an unpatentable product and selling it constitute a tort? How much secrecy is required to protect a trade secret? What are the four elements of fraud? What is the difference between disparagement and false advertising? Explain your answers.

3. How long is the protection for a registered trademark or trade name? A patent? What is the possible maximum penalty for violation of the securities laws? The Foreign Corrupt Practices Act? The Sherman Act? What is the maximum penalty for computerized embezzlement or other manipulation of bank funds? For violation of the Hobbs Act? What are the possible penalties for violation of RICO? Within what period of time must a prosecution for a felony commence under the Model Penal Code? A misdemeanor? To constitute murder under the common law, the death must result within what period of time after the injury? What is the punishment for solicitation or attempt to commit a crime?

4. Explain the "reasonable person" standard used to determine negligence. What are the four elements of negligence? How does "last clear chance," "the rule of avoidable consequences," and "comparative negligence" relate to contributory negligence? How does intentional assumption of risk differ from negligent assumption of risk? Explain your answers.

5. In most states does marriage itself require legal sharing of property or income? In community property states, is all property acquired by a husband or wife "community"? What are the rights of each spouse in community property? Is a child entitled to support from parents? For how long? What factors are taken into account in awarding alimony upon dissolution of marriage? What are the tax consequences of alimony payments? Are child support payments deductible? Are transfers of property in divorce settlements ever taxable? What factors enter into modification of alimony or child support decrees? Explain your answers.

6. How are crimes classified under the Model Penal Code? What is the difference between murder, manslaughter, and negligent homicide? What kind of crime under the Model Penal Code would it be, if any, to call in a bomb threat causing the evacuation of a school or hospital? When is a burglary a second-degree felony? Can the unauthorized use of someone else's credit card be a serious crime? What crimes were involved in the Watergate scandal? When may criminal liability for nonaction be imposed? Is motive an essential element of a crime? What are the tests for criminal insanity? How does an accessory after the fact differ from the parties to a crime? Explain your answers.

7. Explain the three different bases for tort liability. Does an intentional tort require hostility? Will an owner of animals be held liable for damage done by them? How about a person who sells a defective product? What is necessary to establish liability for the intentional infliction of mental or emotional distress? When are special damages not required to be proved in defamation cases? Are there any special defenses to defamation? How is it decided whether a defendant's activity constitutes a nuisance? How does trespass to chattels relate to conversion? May the same force be used to defend property as people? How about using force to discipline a child? Explain your answers.

8. Define the following terms: automatism, deceptive business practices, felony murder rule, inchoate crime, marriage penalty, prima facie tortious competition, posslq, publication, res ipsa loquitur, smart money, sole trader business, the National Stolen Property Act.

Problems

1. Oliver's Shoes, Inc. markets a pair of wooden sandals with a specially designed arch that serves to exercise the foot and keep it in good health. Though the sandals are not patented, they sell well across the country under the trademark of "Lo-Mar" Sandals. Percy Enterprises, in an effort to increase its profits, manufactures and sells a wooden sandal that is identical in appearance to the "Lo-Mar" shoes. The Percy Company sells the shoes under the name "Low-Marr" Sandals; it does a good business as many consumers who intend to buy the Oliver Company product pick up the Percy shoes by mistake. When Oliver Shoes discovers what Percy Enterprises is up to, it seeks your legal advice. What rights, if any, does the Company have against

Percy Enterprises? Explain fully. Would your answer differ if the Oliver Company's product was patented? Explain.

2. Percy Enterprises also manufactures and sells a canvas sports shoe which directly competes with a shoe sold by Paulson Bros. Shoes. To increase its sales at Paulson's expense, the Percy Company tells several retail shoe stores that the Paulson manufacturing process is "shoddy" and that the Paulson Company is on its last financial legs. The Percy Company, in fact, has no knowledge about the Paulson operation or finances; nevertheless, its sales increase and Paulsons' sales decrease. The Percy Company also advertises its shoes as being "the first choice of sports favorite Jim Doherty." Jim Doherty, in fact, knows nothing about the shoes, and has not consented to having his name used for advertising purposes. What rights, if any, does Paulson Bros. Shoes have against the Percy Company? Explain fully. What rights, if any, does Jim Doherty have against the Percy Company? Explain fully.

3. Marsha McKenzie marries Greg Brown. After their marriage, Marsha sells her streamfront property and the adjoining tract and places the proceeds in a savings account in her own name; Greg does not join her in the transfer. Over the years, Greg and Marsha acquire a home, expensive furnishings, and a beachhouse. Both Greg and Marsha help pay for these items (however, Marsha works only part-time and does not contribute as much as Greg). After Greg and Marsha have been married forty years, Greg receives a small inheritance from his father and uses the money to purchase a new car. Not long after, Marsha sells the beachhouse to Bill O'Connell without telling Greg about the sale. Greg dies a few weeks later leaving a will giving "whatever interest in real or personal property I may own to my sister Ruth." Assuming community property law applies, answer the following:

a. As between Ruth and Marsha, who owns the savings account proceeds? The house and furnishings? The new car? Explain all your answers.
b. As between Ruth, Marsha, and Bill O'Connell, who owns the beachhouse? Explain.

How would your answer differ if Greg and Marsha were not legally married but were only "living together"? Explain.

4. Luther Guest arrived home unexpectedly early from a New York business trip to find his wife, Patricia, in a more than compromising position with the local grocer. Enraged, Luther grabbed a pistol from the bureau drawer and shot them—dead. Moments later, a stunned Luther sobbed in remorse. Is Luther guilty of murder? Would your answer differ if upon discovering the adulterous liaison, Luther had left the house in anger, returning several hours later to kill the now contrite Patricia? Explain.

5. Dennis Hendersen, sitting in a parked car with Cynthia Jones, shook with anger. Not only had Cynthia turned him down twice for a date, but now that she had gone out with him, she refused his kisses. "Well, I'll show her," he muttered, as he grabbed the protesting girl and kissed her soundly. Cynthia slapped him in return and demanded to go home immediately. But Dennis only laughed. He proceeded to drive through town at breakneck speed ignoring the girl's pleas to be let out of the car, until an hour later, when he deposited her on a busy street corner. What tort actions can Cynthia bring against her unruly suitor? Is the jury likely to award her punitive damages? Can Dennis recover from Cynthia for the slap in the face? Explain.

Cynthia has confided her troubles with Dennis to her older brother, Dale. Infuriated, Dale tracks Dennis down at the local singles bar, shoves him up against the wall, and shakes a fist menacingly in his face, stating—"If you ever come near my sister again, Hendersen, I'll kill you." Dennis is all apologetic, but as soon as Dale turns to leave, he picks up an empty wine decanter and breaks it over Dale's head. What torts have been committed by Dale? Was Dennis justified in hitting him? Explain.

6. Tired of supporting her still struggling artist husband, Steve, after fifteen years of marriage, Debbie Goodrich falls easy prey to the southern drawl and "nouveau hip" attire of B. J. Dorsey, renowned "money man" and president of B. J. Dorsey Enterprises, Inc. (where Debbie works as a high salaried executive vice president). Dorsey's sweet-talking ways have convinced the determined Debbie to leave that "no account drain on her income" and to move in with B. J. himself in his neighboring ranch-style home. Left with two young children and the balance of a small savings account, Steve waits five years for Debbie to come to her senses and return home. When she fails to, he sues for divorce. But is Steve entitled to a divorce under the traditional divorce laws of his state? And is the court likely to award him alimony and child support? Suppose Steve gets an award—can Debbie escape payment by running off to another state with B. J.? Explain. Can Steve also convince the court that he is entitled to all or most of Debbie's property since she was at fault in leaving him? Explain. A few years later, Steve prospers financially in the art world and decides to remarry. Assuming that Debbie has been forced to contribute to his (and their children's) support up to this time, must Debbie continue to do so now? Explain.

7. a. Ambrose Copeland had watched the wealthy Reuben Marshall take his evening stroll every night for the last two weeks: certainly, robbing the old gentleman would be an easy task. On the night of his intended crime, Copeland followed Marshall deep into Laplander Park and was just about ready to accost his victim when the sudden appearance of an on-duty policeman frightened him away. Is Copeland guilty of criminal conduct? Explain.

b. Keith Fitzsimmons angrily pushes the elderly Clement Hennessey out of his way while leaving the corner diner. When Hennessey decides to file criminal charges against him, Fitzsimmons plans to "beat the rap" by asserting insanity as a defense: witness his repeated criminal convictions (Fitzsimmons has been in and out of jail for as long as he can remember). What crime has Fitzsimmons committed? And is insanity, applying the Model Penal Code approach, a good defense? Explain.

8. Leslie Hayes was overjoyed with her new Chinese red sportscar. But Leslie had dawdled too long on her first "test drive" and had only an hour to get to work. On impulse, she cut across the private road running through old Mrs. Hinkley's estate, hoping the forbidden route would save her those extra five minutes. Mrs. Hinkley, peering through an upstairs window, shook her fist at the unwelcome intruder. Back on the open road, Leslie negligently drove her car through a red light and ran into another car driven by Daniel Hayden. Hayden, severely injured, will be paralyzed for life. In an action against Leslie for negligence, what is Hayden's measure of damages?

Mrs. Hinkley, noted for her absentmindedness, forgets all about Leslie's short cut across her property. When she remembers it three years later, she decides to bring legal action against her. What action should she bring? What possible defense is open to Leslie? If the case goes to trial and Mrs. Hinkley can prove no actual damage to her property, can she still recover damages? Explain.

"The circumstance that the national legislature has through so many generations . . . seen wisdom in the administrative process suggests that bureaucracy may after all have its admissible virtues. . . ."

Walter Gellhorn and Clark Byse
Administrative Law

5

Administrative Law and Government Agencies

WHAT ARE ADMINISTRATIVE AGENCIES AND WHY ARE THEY ESSENTIAL?

As we have previously discussed in Chapters 2 and 3, constitutions empower the legislative branches of government to make written rules called statutes, and they authorize the courts to apply these rules in deciding particular cases. It is simply impossible, however, for legislatures to make all the necessary rules or for courts to handle all of the cases. This is true for two reasons. First, the regulation of certain fields requires a nonlegal expertise. It is impossible for presidents, governors, senators, congressmen, or judges to know enough about technical fields or industries to make good rules for their proper regulation. Radio, TV, transportation, atomic energy, air and water pollution, aeronautics, and space exploration are all areas where nonlegal experts must do the rule making if we are to have rules that make sense. Thus, Congress creates an administrative agency such as the Federal Communications Commission to deal with the regulation of radio and TV, the Interstate Commerce Commission to deal with the transportation industry, or the Environmental Protection Agency—each with a specific job to do under the statute creating the agency. The agency makes rules and decides cases in the same manner as do legislatures and courts, and its rules and decisions are just as binding. The statute passed by the legislature gives the agency its general power to make detailed rules and regulations. When an agency decides a case, that is, resolves a dispute between parties or determines the rights of an individual, it is as much a part of our law as when a court does it. And this is the second reason for the creation of the administrative agency—to settle the thousands of mechanical questions that would otherwise overwhelm the courts by their volume. Often, a question can be determined simply by applying mechanical rules. Whether a man is entitled to social security benefits or benefits in a veterans hospital depends on his record under the social security law or as a veteran. The Social Security Administration or Veterans Administration can make these determinations without assistance from the courts. And this makes good sense because it allows the courts to devote their attention to more controversial matters.

An administrative agency is any government authority that is not a court or legislature but that acts like one by making rules or deciding cases. An agency may be called a commission, board, bureau, authority, office, officer, administrator, department, division, or agency; and if the president or other public official is given power to make rules or decide cases, then he or she, too, is an administrative agency.

Administrative agencies affect all of us much more than do courts or legislatures. While many people live out their entire lives without ever suing or being sued in court, every individual is constantly affected by administrative law. Agencies protect us against false advertising; unfair trade practices; unwholesome food (particularly meat and poultry); adulterated food; mislabeled drugs; air and water pollution; loss of income while unemployed; fraud in the sale of securities or land; disregard of the public interest in radio and TV broadcasting; excessive utility rates for gas, electricity, and telephone; unreasonable rates and schedules by railroads, buses, and airlines; improper building and wiring in construction jobs; less than minimum wages; hunger and poverty; uncompensated injuries incurred on the job; unsafe public transportation; unsafe roads, bridges, and elevators; unsafe automobiles, toys, and other products; unsanitary restaurants and hospitals; sale of narcotics; and sale of certain firearms. And this list is far from complete.

Agencies dispose of many times the number of court-handled cases. In a recent year, civil trials in all federal courts numbered just over 8,000, while agencies formally disposed of over 90,000 cases. And in a typical year, informal decisions by state and federal agencies run to the hundreds of millions. The Social Security Administration itself deals with more than 5 million applications yearly. More than 99 percent of these cases (dealing with retirement pensions, medicare protection, disability income for disabled persons of any age, death benefits, etc.) are disposed of informally—that is, without hearing before an examiner. Yet each decision, formal or otherwise, legally binds some individual, and unless he or she appeals that decision, the result is just as conclusive as any courtroom determination.

No one is sure just how many hundreds of agencies exist at the federal, state, and local level. Included, however, are insurance commissions, zoning agencies, departments of agriculture and labor, and numbers of occupational licensing agencies. State boards of education, local school boards, and school principals make rules for schools around the country. These rules are part of the law. They tell students when the school year begins, what a passing grade is, and what subjects are required for graduation. School "administrators" decide what constitutes improper dress or behavior on school grounds, and what actions will serve as a basis for suspension or expulsion. Since these are legal decisions, they are both conclusive and binding on the students. But you may challenge their validity, initially, by appealing within the administrative agency itself and, finally, by taking your case to the courts for review. Recently in Oregon, for example, an administrative decision requiring a high school student to cut his hair was appealed to the local Circuit Court after the agency's decision was upheld by the local school board. The Circuit Court affirmed the decision, but its decision was later reversed on appeal to a higher court of law (see *Neuhaus v. Federico,* presented at the end of this chapter).

The whole of this chapter will deal with administrative law and governmental agencies. By way of introduction, four aspects of administrative law should be familiar.

Rule Making

An administrative agency is legislatively created by an enabling statute, a statute that brings the agency into being and enables it to operate. While the enabling statute must provide the agency with standards of operation, these standards may be very broad. The agency can fill in the detail by establishing its own specific rules. But while the agency is pretty much free to determine how it will carry out its assigned tasks, the agency must maintain appropriate safeguards for the individuals who come into contact with it. The agency generally publishes its proposed rules and invites interested persons to submit their written comments. Employees of the agency then check through the comments and revise the rules for republication. Once republished, the rules generally do not become final for thirty days to allow for additional comment or protest. The ultimate result is a set of rules that describe the purpose, organization, procedure, and practice of the agency.

The agency also makes specific rules that interpret existing law. For example, in Skidmore v. Swift and Co., 323 U.S. 134, 65 S.Ct. 161, 89 L.Ed. 124 (1944), the Wage and Hour Administrator of the Department of Labor ruled that time spent by firemen eating and sleeping while down at the station house is not employment time under the minimum wage law. The Court agreed that this was a proper rule of the agency. Such specific rules are validly made by the hundreds of agencies across the land. Of course, agency rules are always subject to judicial review by the courts.

Investigation

Administrative agencies must have access to any factual materials they need to carry out their programs. Agencies may therefore subpoena records, reports, and other materials so long as the records demanded are reasonably relevant to the matter in issue.

Hearing by Examiner

The most significant aspect of administrative procedure is use of the "hearing examiner." If a question cannot be settled informally, a hearing is scheduled. Prior to the hearing, the case is assigned to an examiner. Similar to a judge, the examiner usually sits alone as presiding officer. He or she administers oaths, issues subpoenas, and regulates the hearing itself. Upon completion of the hearing, the parties generally submit written arguments (briefs) to the examiner along with their own findings of fact and legal conclusions. The examiner studies this material, then prepares his or her "initial decision" both as to law and fact. A copy of the decision is given to all the parties to the hearing who may then submit to the agency additional arguments against the examiner's decision. The parties may also present oral arguments to the heads of the agency who make the final decision, usually in consultation with the examiner (who frequently participates in the preparation of the final report or agency decision). In federal agencies, under the Federal "Administrative Procedure Act" originally passed in 1947, the hearing examiners are called "administrative law judges."

Judicial Review

It is a general rule that administrative remedies must be exhausted before a court can review the action of an agency. In other words, if the agency has its own built-in method of review (appeal through the agency itself), a party must pursue that method before he or she can go to the courts for review. Once the decision is final and there is no further review within the agency, the courts may be asked to review the decision by trial in a trial court or by direct appellate review in a court of appeals, depending on what the particular agency's statute prescribes.

As a matter of historical significance, it should be realized that government agencies have often been created to handle a current problem or to solve serious social problems. In 1914, the Federal Trade Commission was created because of monopolies. More recently nuclear energy has created new agencies, as have racial discrimination and environmental conditions. Specialized staffing, expertise, and flexibility help in dealing with each situation. One must not forget, however, that each agency is working with its own unique problems using limited resources.

WHAT IS THE DELEGATION DOCTRINE?

Agencies are often given, at the same time, broad powers which are characteristic of each of the three branches of government. Not only do they have legislative power to make rules which may carry penalties for violation, but also executive power to investigate for violation of the rules, and judicial power to settle disputes arising from the rules. Many of these administrative agencies are unattached to any of the three branches of government and operate independently after being created by Congress and after their commissioners are appointed by the president.

As we have indicated earlier, the broad delegations of combined powers are necessary because Congress is unable to provide the detailed rules and day-to-day administration necessary in many fields of endeavor. Effective regulation often requires the exercise of all three kinds of power—legislative, executive, and judicial—by the same governing agency on a day-to-day basis. Providing all of these powers in one agency allows for greater uniformity and flexibility. Business can then plan its operations with some degree of certainty and expectancy.

Delegating combined powers to independent agencies conflicts somewhat with the separation of powers principle and checks and balances process explained in Chapter 2. The purpose of separation of powers and checks and balances is to provide control and accountability over government power. As long as this is provided over government agencies, government operates more effectively and efficiently with agencies than without them. The delegation of powers is constitutional as long as adequate standards are provided within the enabling statute that narrow and confine the agency's power so the courts can determine generally (the standards do not have to be precise) what that agency is to accomplish. Additionally, the statute must make certain there are procedural due process protections, so that an administrative agency may not deprive a person of liberty or property without providing reasonable opportunity to know and challenge the agency's decision before it becomes final. There must be safeguards to assure basic fairness.

The courts are more willing to sustain delegation of powers to an agency when the subject matter with which the agency is concerned involves a new, technical, and rapidly changing area and where the details can't be easily anticipated or understood by Congress. It is often difficult for Congress to foresee exactly what an agency will need to do, and it is unworkable to constantly revise the agency's enabling statute. Yet Congress must, in its delegation, always provide controls and accountability over the agency.

Congress, in the National Environmental Policy Act of 1969, made it a requirement that all federal agencies consider the environmental impact of all major decisions. And accountability will reach directly to Congress anytime an agency does not perform according to public expectancy. Congress controls the "purse strings" and can budget an agency out of existence. Or it can restructure it substantially. As an example, the Atomic Energy Commission was created initially to oversee a very technical emerging scientific industry, but after several years of operation was terminated by Congress because it was not considered to be handling effectively the safety and environmental aspects of nuclear power. It was replaced by the Nuclear Regulatory Commission which itself has been intensely criticized by reason of the Three Mile Island accident in 1979.

A few agencies, dealing with disability or welfare benefit programs, are not subject to as much control through annual budget appropriations because the level of their annual expenditures is fixed in their enabling statutes according to some formula or entitlements for beneficiaries.

One agency, the General Accounting Office, has as its main function the job of reviewing other agency activity. The GAO was originally created to conduct financial audits of other agencies, but now also reviews and evaluates agency programs. Along the same line, most agencies are also subject to "Sunset" laws (varying greatly from agency to agency) which provide that an established agency will go out of existence after a fixed period of time unless Congress reestablishes it. This forces Congress to reexamine the effectiveness of an agency from time to time.

WHAT EXECUTIVE BRANCH CONTROLS EXIST OVER ADMINISTRATIVE AGENCIES?

Under Article II of the U.S. Constitution, the president has the power to appoint and remove high-ranking federal officers. The extent of this power is limited by some of the enabling statutes which provide, in many of the independent agencies, for commissioners to be appointed for fixed periods of years, not the same as the president's term of office. Typically, the statutes also provide that only a certain number of the commissioners (e.g., three out of five) may be from the same political party, and that the commissioners may be removed only for "inefficiency, neglect of duty, or malfeasance in office." Still, a newly elected president generally has the opportunity to make a number of key agency appointments during his or her term of office.

Presidents may also change the chairpersons within the independent agencies and thereby change policy. President Carter, for example, did this with the Nuclear Regulatory Commission after the Three Mile Island accident.

The president may submit reorganization plans to Congress under the Reorganization Act. Such plans may transfer functions from one department to another, and if Congress does not vote to reject the plan within a fixed period of time, the transfer becomes effective. This is how the Environmental Protection Agency came into being when the President submitted a plan to consolidate in one new agency what had previously been handled by a number of different executive departments.

Within the White House itself is the Office of Management and Budget, which has the responsibility of sending up to Congress an annual executive budget. In determining the specifics of this budget, the Office of Management and Budget asks for and receives budget requests from the individual agencies and changes them according to administrative priorities. It also looks at any requests agencies have for changes in substantive law and helps with proposals to Congress that are in accord with the particular president's views.

WHAT ARE THE "FREEDOM OF INFORMATION ACT," THE "GOVERNMENT IN THE SUNSHINE ACT," AND THE "PRIVACY ACT"?

How easy is it for a person to find out about the inner activities of a government agency? Well, two statutes have been passed by Congress to make it relatively easy to get information regarding agency activities. The 1966 Freedom of Information Act provides that "any person" has the right to see and to copy government records. There are some exemptions including protections for national security, invasion of personal privacy, and protection of trade secrets. Even within the exemptions, the agency cannot withhold the information unless it shows some specific threat to a private or governmental interest.

The Freedom of Information Act states in part:

> Each agency, in accordance with published rules, shall make available for public inspection and copying—

> (A) final opinions, including concurring and dissenting opinions, as well as orders, made in adjudication of cases;
>
> (B) those statements of policy and interpretations which have been adopted by the agency and are not published in the Federal Register; and
>
> (C) administrative staff manuals and instructions to staff that affect a member of the public.
>
> * * * On complaint, the district court of the United States * * * has jurisdiction to enjoin the agency from withholding agency records and to order the production of any agency records improperly withheld from the complainant. In such a case the court * * * may examine the contents of such agency records * * * to determine whether such records or any part thereof shall be withheld under any of the exemptions. * * *
>
> In the event of noncompliance with the order of the court, the district court may punish for contempt the responsible employee.

Generally, an agency must react to a request to see and copy records within ten days of the making of the request.

The Government in the Sunshine Act was passed in 1976 and requires most meetings of agencies to be open to the public. Again similar exemptions are provided, but apart from the exemptions, the statute states that "every portion of every meeting of an agency shall be open to public observation."

The Privacy Act of 1974 allows individuals to inspect any files that administrative agencies have on them. It also permits individuals to correct any erroneous or incomplete records.

TO WHAT EXTENT MAY A GOVERNMENT AGENCY GATHER INFORMATION?

In the previous section we have explained the importance of private parties' being able, under the Freedom of Information and Sunshine Acts, to obtain information from government agencies. It is also important that agencies have information if they are to regulate properly and make good decisions. Yet, in the United States, the citizenry considers freedom from governmental intrusion essential to liberty. The people are afraid that private information about them may be misused by government. Thus, while the agencies are given the ability to investigate and require information to be disclosed, their powers are subject to constitutional and other limitations to prevent abuse.

Agencies use several techniques for gathering data including the issuing of subpoenas for documents or testimony. Parties may contest the legality of the requests directly to the agency and, if the agency does not agree, then to the courts. If the court upholds a subpoena, it will issue an order supporting it. A person who does not comply will be held in contempt of court. Subpoenas and/or search warrants will not be enforced or granted by the courts unless the information sought by the agency is relevant to a lawful subject of investigation within the agency powers specified in the enabling statute. Subpoenas must also adequately describe the items the agency wants to see, and the request must not be unreasonably burdensome in the sense of cost, disruption of business, or loss of trade secrets.

If there is a risk of a criminal penalty being imposed, a person has a right within the Fifth Amendment not to provide information that may incriminate him or her. However, this protection does not apply when the only penalties possible are civil and there is no crime involved. Also, the Fifth Amendment cannot be asserted by a corporation or on behalf of a corporation because it is a right that is available only to protect natural persons. And an agency can seek approval from the attorney general to immunize a witness from prosecution for crime, and then compel him or her to testify. The attorney general generally will not give approval unless he or she first determines that the testimony is necessary to protect the public interest.

The functions of many agencies involve making inspections for purposes of safety, sanitation, or protection of the environment. If a person does not consent to a search, the agency generally has to seek a search warrant from a court before making the inspection.

WHAT ARE THE INFORMAL FUNCTIONS OF GOVERNMENT AGENCIES?

Most administrative decisions are made without formality. And informal action is generally not subject to much by way of procedural safeguard. After an informal action is taken, of course, an individual may be able to utilize the Freedom of Information Act and the Privacy Act to discover what information was used in making the informal decision. But these statutes do not permit the party to contest the basis for the agency action. To do so, one must go on to a higher level of administration or to the courts.

A far greater number of cases are settled informally with administrative agencies than are contested. Many agencies have developed informal settlement and negotiation procedures, and some have codified these procedures into their rules of practice and even provide interested members of the public with an opportunity to make comment upon proposed settlements. When an administrator determines to settle a case on some basis, it is considered to be within his or her discretionary function and generally is not reviewable by the courts. The settlement will take the form of a "consent order," with the party's agreeing to comply with the order so as to affect a remedy but without admitting that he or she has committed any violation of law. Because this is not an admission of wrongdoing, if a third party later sues by reason of the same facts, the consent order does not prevent a denial of legal liability.

Of course, it is necessary for administrative agencies to process large numbers of claims and applications including many dealing with welfare, social security, veterans' benefits, tax refunds, etc. Formal hearings are requested in only a very small part of the many claims processed.

Similarly, administrative agencies also informally perform many tests and inspections to determine if cars, planes, and trains comply with safety rules; if foods and drugs are contaminated; if drivers are qualified to drive and pilots to fly; if industry is in compliance with environmental standards; and to help consumers make intelligent choices. And agencies have authority to remove products from the market or to take away licenses or to seize adulterated or misbranded foods when the public must be protected. This can be done without first having a formal hearing or trial as long as the agency holds a full hearing promptly thereafter.

In a number of industries, including securities, banking, communication, and transportation, there is a continuing supervision by government agencies on an informal basis.

Agencies provide advice and other information to the public when asked to do so. The legal and technical advice provided by government agencies is essential to the operation of small business which would otherwise have great difficulty in knowing and meeting many of the requirements of law.

The government also spends a large amount of money through grants and contracts to private industry. It also manages about a third of the land making up the United States which is actually owned by the government. Most of these activities involving grants, contracts, and land management are accomplished informally by administrative agencies.

WHEN DOES A PERSON HAVE A RIGHT TO AN ADMINISTRATIVE HEARING?

The Fifth and Fourteenth Amendments provide that no person shall "be deprived of life, liberty, or property, without due process of law." Due process requires fairness, including adequate notice and an opportunity to be heard. Some government entitlements including certain welfare benefits, licenses to practice a profession or to drive, public education, and some public employment have been held "property" subject to due process. A few agencies dealing with prisons or as parole boards have powers to restrict individual "liberty" directly and must worry about due process. Otherwise, due process protections are generally not involved in the "liberty" context because injured individuals usually do not worry about a hearing before an agency when "liberty" has been violated, but instead bring tort actions against the individuals who deprived them of their "liberty." Only where defamation or other tort action (see Chapter 4) is precluded is an individual likely to allege an issue involving denial of due process because of loss of liberty (with the exception of the prison and parole areas).

The fact of requiring a notice and hearing (due process) may also depend on the immediate harm that would otherwise result if none were provided. Thus, an agency, depriving a person of his or her welfare benefits or high school classes or discontinuing water or heating for even a short period of time, may cause such severe loss as to require a hearing first.

Hearings, when required, do not have to be of a full-fledged-trial type to meet due process standards, but there must be sufficient notice to inform interested parties of the nature of the potential loss of property or liberty and afford them opportunity to object. Sometimes hearings are not considered necessary at all because they would add nothing, as where there are no facts in issue or where a determination is based on highly technical facts (the drugging of a racehorse or actual medical disability of a claimant) or strictly clerical facts (losing a driver's license based on a point system on conviction of certain offenses). Also, the opportunity to be heard must be tailored to the capacities and circumstances of those who are to be heard. Some people can't present their positions in writing and must do so orally.

The question of whether or not a person has a right to counsel at administrative hearings is not settled. Under the federal Administrative Procedure Act a "person compelled to appear in person before an agency or representative thereof is entitled to be accompanied, represented, and advised by counsel." Note that this applies only to federal agencies and only to compulsory appearance. State and local agencies may not have such a rule, and appearances may be voluntary before any agency. It has even been held (Madera v. Board of Education, 386 F.2d 778 (2d Cir.1967)) that the presence of an attorney might prevent the agency from accomplishing its purpose, as when parents of a suspended student meet with school officials for purposes of working out disciplinary problems. Generally, the courts have concluded that due process does not require the appointment of counsel for indigent participants in agency hearings. This is largely because it would be prohibitively expensive for an agency operating under limited appropriations from the legislative branch.

Due process does require that the decision be made by an impartial person with no personal stake in the outcome. Still it does not prevent administrators from participating in both the investigative and decision-making process. And the same officials are often expected both to make policy and to decide particular disputes. For an agency to carry out its delegated functions it must, by necessity, often be involved in all of these activities: rule making, investigating, prosecuting, and decision making. Constitutionally, no strict separation of functions can be or has been required, as long as there is no denial of basic fairness.

Finally, due process does require the agency to give some explanation of its decision to persons who are affected by the decision. Such explanation need not always be with any formality or even in writing.

Sometimes a formal evidentiary hearing is required by reason of due process protections against the taking of property or liberty. More often, such formal evidentiary hearings are required by statute. For example, the Federal Trade Commission Act provides that under certain circumstances the Commission will issue a complaint and provide the party with a hearing who may then "show cause why an order should not be entered by the Commission." When a federal enabling statute requires such a hearing, then the federal Administrative Procedure Act's adjudication procedures must be followed. More than 200,000 formal hearings are handled by administrative law judges each year.

In such procedures, the following rules apply:

1. The Administrative Procedure Act provides that "persons entitled to notice of an agency hearing shall be timely informed." This means notice of the time, place, and issues. However, the statute does not require the same technical pleading and procedure as in the civil case described in Chapter 3. Administrative law judges operate with greater latitude than do other judges. Where an agency has two or more parties competing for the same interest, as sometimes happens in broadcasting, air carrier, routing, pipeline certifying, utility franchising, etc., the hearings of the parties may be consolidated into one comparative hearing to see who is best qualified.

2. The Administrative Procedure Act does not provide discovery techniques to the parties beyond the Freedom of Information Act. Within their own operating rules, agencies vary widely on the extent to which discovery is allowed. Some agencies have found that allowing liberal discovery caused stalling by the parties and considerable cost and delay. Also, the agency's own staff usually does much of the work of discovery, and the Freedom of Information Act allows the parties to see the materials gathered.

3. The actual formal evidentiary hearing of an agency is very close to that of a trial court (see Chapter 3): attorneys represent the parties, witnesses are cross-examined, exhibits are presented, objections and ruling are made. The parties also submit proposed findings and conclusions to the administrative law judge who renders a decision which may be appealed to the heads of the agency. However, the Administrative Procedure Act also provides that "an agency may, when a party will not be prejudiced thereby, adopt procedures for the submission of all or part of the evidence in written form." Because of the submission of much more by way of written evidence, rather than having the parties directly testify, more time can be devoted to questioning and cross-examination to clarify the evidence submitted. The Administrative Procedure Act provides that a party may "conduct such cross-examination as may be required for a full and true disclosure of the facts."

Evidentiary rules in administrative hearings are also otherwise more liberal than in courts. The Administrative Procedure Act provides that any "oral or documentary evidence may be received" (this would include hearsay evidence), "but the agency as a matter of policy shall provide for the exclusion of irrelevant, immaterial, or unduly repetitious evidence." The rules are more liberal because there is less risk of unfairness when the decision is to be made by experts in administrative law areas rather than by juries in civil cases.

4. The administrative law judge conducts the hearing and renders an "initial" or "recommended" decision. The administrative law judge does not have to conduct the hearing as an adversary contest, as in the civil case described in Chapter 3, and need not be a passive referee as within such adversary system. Instead the administrative law judge usually takes an active part in the proceeding and questions witnesses and otherwise does what is necessary to find the relevant facts.

The difference between an "initial" and "recommended" decision is that the initial decision does not have to be reviewed by the agency heads and becomes the final agency action unless it is so reviewed, while the recommended decision must always be reviewed by the agency heads. And while the decision by the administrative law judge will always be given importance by the agency heads, it will not be sustained as easily as an appellate court sustains a trial court decision. This is because the Administrative Procedure Act specifies that on "appeal from or review of the initial decision, the agency has all the powers which it would have in making the initial decision." This is important because an agency has the responsibility for both making broad policy as well as deciding individual disputes, and overriding considerations may be most important in such areas as price fixing, consumer protection, securities regulation, and the environment. This may cause the agency heads to have a bias necessary to protect the public interest.

At the same time, the Administrative Procedure Act does provide that any employee who is "engaged in the performance of investigative or prosecuting functions" cannot take any part or otherwise be involved in deciding an individual case. Other employees who were not involved in such activity (adversary) may be consulted even by the administrative law judge regarding the evidence on record. However, additional nonrecord evidence itself is not allowed to be brought in by such employees because the Administrative Procedure Act states that the "transcript of testimony and exhibits, together with all papers and requests filed in the proceeding, constitutes the exclusive record for decision."

5. The Administrative Procedure Act requires all decisions to include "findings and conclusions, and the reasons or basis therefor, on all the material issues of fact, law, or discretion presented on the record." This makes for more accountability and discipline in the agency and allows for a meaningful judicial review if the courts have to take a look at the administrative decision. The Administrative Procedure Act provides that reviewing courts should set aside such decisions when "unsupported by substantial evidence." This test requires such a court to look at the entire record including the initial or recommended decision of the administrative law judge whether or not it was reversed by the agency heads.

WHAT IS THE IMPORTANCE OF GOVERNMENT AGENCY "RULE MAKING" ACTIVITIES?

Many enabling statutes creating agencies require the agencies to promulgate general regulatory rules. This has been particularly true in recent years in the environmental and consumer protection areas of law. General rules are designed for uniform voluntary compliance by entire industries, all business firms, or the entire population. They provide guidance for business and others in advance and prevent many individual cases from ever arising. They are the same as the statutes of Congress in that they have general and prospective application, are standards of conduct for all to follow, and are backed by legal penalties.

The Administrative Procedure Act defines a rule as "the whole or a part of an agency statement of general or particular applicability and future effect designed to implement, interpret, or prescribe law or policy." Within this definition, we see that in addition to "legislative" rules, agencies also write "interpretative" rules which simply interpret already existing parts of the statute the agency has jurisdiction to administer. For example, the Commissioner of Internal Revenue issues a substantial volume of regulations containing what the Commissioner believes is the proper interpretation of the Internal Revenue Code. Interpretative rules do not prevent a party in a later case from presenting evidence to show that the agency's interpretation of the statutory law was incorrect. Interpretative rules are merely positions an agency has taken as to the meaning of particular parts of a statute, and the agency's position may or may not be sustained by the courts. On the other hand, reviewing courts let legislative rules stand as long as they are made within the agency's jurisdiction as set down in its enabling statute.

The Administrative Procedure Act requires certain procedures for rule making by government agencies. The basic rule making procedure is called "informal" or "notice-and-comment" rule making. With legislative rule making (where, as previously explained, the agency rules have the same effect as laws passed by Congress), the agency is required to use this notice-and-comment procedure. There are three procedural requirements: (1) the agency must give prior notice (usually in the Federal Register) with a description of the subjects and issues involved; (2) the agency must provide interested persons an opportunity to participate by submitting written comments; and (3) the final rules issued by the agency must be accompanied by a concise general statement of its reasons for the rules. While the agency is not required to hold any oral hearings, many agencies often do so.

There are several permissible (as opposed to being mandatory) exemptions to the notice-and-comment procedure, including rule-making proceedings relating to agency management or personnel or to public property, loans, grants, benefits, or contracts; military or foreign policy; interpretative rules; general statements of agency policy; and situations where it can be specifically shown that public participation would not accomplish anything or would be harmful (usually where the subject matter is trivial or time is of the essence).

More is required than informal notice-and-comment procedure when Congress states specifically in the enabling statute that the agency rules are "to be made on the record after opportunity for an agency hearing." Section 553(c) of the Administrative Procedure Act. A trial-type hearing is then required with testimony and cross-examination. This is called "rule making on a record" or "formal rule making." Congress has also provided in some enabling statutes for different specific forms of rule making procedure.

TO WHAT EXTENT ARE ADMINISTRATIVE AGENCIES SUBJECT TO JUDICIAL REVIEW?

You will recall from Chapter 2 that federal court jurisdiction includes federal questions, and that, since 1980, the $10,000 jurisdictional amount has been eliminated for federal questions (although it still applies to diversity of citizenship cases). Thus any action involving a federal question, including those brought against federal agencies or agency personnel, may be brought without regard to the dollar value of the plaintiff's claim. An exception is made under the Consumer Product Safety Act where the $10,000 amount-in-controversy requirement, based on violations of consumer product safety rules, has been retained.

Federal questions against agencies might include injunctions to require or set aside agency acts, as well as money damages for harm caused by agency acts. However, most federal administrative orders must be appealed within a short time period (usually within sixty days), or they become final. And judicial review is not available at all under the Administrative Procedure Act when "statutes preclude review" or the decision is "committed to agency discretion by law." Section 701 of the Administrative Procedure Act. For example, Congress has provided that "the decisions of the administrator on any question of law or fact under any law administered by the Veterans Administration providing benefits for veterans and their dependents or survivors shall be final and conclusive and no court shall have power or jurisdiction to review any such decision." But not many statutes are phrased by

Congress to preclude all judicial review, and the courts are reluctant to accept a complete cutting off of review or a very short time limitation within which to bring appeals for review of administrative decisions.

Courts will sometimes accept that agency action should not be reviewed because the action was solely within the agency's discretion and therefore not reviewable. This often is the situation with issues of national defense or foreign policy where secrecy is considered important or where the decision is considered within the political or legislative function as opposed to judicial. Managerial day-to-day decisions made for purposes of operating the agency itself are also frequently considered within the discretion of the agency and not reviewable.

Even if the administrative action is reviewable, the plaintiff must also have standing to seek judicial review (again see Chapter 2 for a discussion of "standing"). To have standing, the plaintiff must show injury in fact. This can be a showing of economic harm such as by the creation of additional competition for the plaintiff. For example, in Association of Data Processing Service Organizations v. Camp, 397 U.S. 150, 90 S.Ct. 827, 25 L.Ed.2d 184 (1970), the Comptroller of the Currency allowed national banks to perform data processing services despite a statute that appeared to prohibit the offering of such services. The resulting economic injury to persons in the data processing business was sufficient to satisfy the standing requirement of injury in fact. Injury in fact can also be noneconomic in nature. In Sierra Club v. Morton, 405 U.S. 727, 92 S.Ct. 1361, 31 L.Ed.2d 836 (1972), the Supreme Court held that threats to aesthetic, recreational, or environmental interests could be sufficient injury for standing. Unfortunately for the plaintiff in that case, the pleadings were defective because they failed to allege that any of the Sierra Club members actually used the wilderness area affected by the proposed agency activity of building a ski resort and public highway on federal lands.

Finally, even though the agency's decision is reviewable and even though the plaintiff has standing, the plaintiff may still not get judicial review if his or her timing is wrong. Two doctrines apply: exhaustion of administrative remedies and ripeness for review.

Where a party still has the right to further administrative hearing or administrative review, courts will not review on the ground that there has not been an exhaustion of administrative remedies. Judicial intervention is not necessary because the agency may correct any error at a later stage of the administrative process.

Similarly, the courts may conclude that the issue is not "ripe" for review, i.e., that the agency needs to have additional experience with the entire problem area before the courts get involved. Sometimes an agency will make a decision that causes companies or persons to act in a certain new manner. Courts may conclude that some experience is necessary under the new requirements before review can be properly accomplished, and they will not review immediately when the first persons affected go to court seeking a determination that they do not have to comply.

Rule making by agencies is also reviewable by courts, and courts may set aside rules that are considered arbitrary or irrational. Where the rules result from a "formal" rule making proceeding, the courts allow the rules to stand if supported by "substantial evidence." Rules adopted under informal "notice-and-comment" procedures will stand unless held "arbitrary and capricious."

MAY A PERSON SEEK MONEY DAMAGES AS A RESULT OF THE ACT OF AN ADMINISTRATIVE AGENCY?

Governmental Immunity

Under the English common law system the king was the law: since he "could do no wrong," his subjects could not sue him. We inherited this English common law, and, in 1821, the U.S. Supreme Court held that the federal government cannot be sued without its consent. The federal government has since given complete statutory consent (in the Federal Tort Claims Act of 1946) to liability for the negligent or wrongful acts or omissions of its employees acting within the scope of their employment. But as stipulated in the Act, federal immunity still exists in several areas. Originally, the Act provided that no suit for "any claim arising out of assault, battery, false imprisonment, false arrest, malicious prosecution, abuse of process, libel, slander, misrepresentation, deceit or interference with contract rights" could be maintained. However, the Federal Tort Claims Act was amended in 1974 to make the government liable for certain intentional torts committed by law enforcement officers. Today, a person may sue the United States for injuries arising out of an assault, battery, false imprisonment, false arrest, abuse of process, or malicious prosecution committed by such an officer.

The government is not liable, and has not consented to liability, for "discretionary" acts of policy makers. Only decisions made at the "operational" level of government may serve as a basis for liability. The distinction between "discretionary" and "operational" was made clear in United Air Lines v. Wiener, 335 F.2d 379, 393 (9th Cir.1964). As stated in the case, a "discretionary" decision is not basis for suit against the government while a "not discretionary" decision is.

> Discretionary to undertake fire fighting, lighthouse rescue, or wrecked ship marking services, but not discretionary to conduct such operations negligently; discretionary to admit a patient to an army hospital, but not discretionary to treat the patient in a negligent manner; discretionary to establish a post office in a particular location, but not to negligently fail to establish handrails; discretionary to establish control towers at airports and to undertake air traffic separation, but not to conduct the same negligently; discretionary to reactivate an airbase, but not to construct a drainage and disposal system thereon in a negligent fashion; and discretionary for the CAS to conduct a survey in low flying, twin engine airplane, but not for pilots thereof to fly negligently.

Nor is strict liability in any of its traditional areas (e.g., wild animals or ultrahazardous activities) imposed upon the federal government.

States, too, share in this governmental immunity. Since a state is composed of all the people within the state, it cannot be sued by any one of them without its consent. And while states have consented to some liability (which varies from state to state), few states match the federal government in breadth of consent.

Municipalities are also immune from suit for "governmental" functions. A city, therefore, is not responsible even for the intentional torts of its police officers such as battery, trespass, false imprisonment, or gross negligence in making arrests. The same is generally true for firefighters and public school custodians. Of course, the individual officer or employee who commits the tort is personally liable, though oftentimes he or she has no money with which to pay the damages. Cities, however, are liable for the negligent torts of their employees engaged in "proprietary" rather than "governmental" work—that is, work or services that could have been provided by a private business such as supplying water, electricity, or operating an airport or a hospital. But the operation of parks and playgrounds is considered "governmental," and the city is not liable for torts committed by its park employees.

Again, many states have abolished municipal immunity to some extent by case decision or statute. Several states, including Iowa, Oregon, New York, Utah, and Washington, have abolished some state immunity. Where this has been done, the city and state governments can be sued for most negligent torts of their employees as long as the case is not based on a negligent, "discretionary" policy decision. So, if state officers improperly design a highway, this is a discretionary action, and the state cannot be held liable for any damage that results. But if the same highway is improperly maintained, the state is liable for any accident caused by the improper maintenance.

While the trend in the law is toward abrogation of governmental immunity, the higher ranked administrative and public officials in government are generally fully immune from liability for torts committed in the performance of official functions. Judges are granted complete immunity for their judicial acts because they must be free to decide cases and make legal decisions without fear of later liability. The same immunity applies to members of the federal Congress, to state and municipal legislators, and to the highest executive and administrative officers in government. Lower administrative officials are immune to tort actions based on their discretionary decisions. But if their acts do not involve personal judgment, the officers are liable in a court of law. Such government officials may also be liable in damages under the Civil Rights Act if they "knew or reasonably should have known" that their actions would violate a plaintiff's basic constitutional rights. This statute provides liability when a citizen is deprived of his or her rights under the federal Constitution or federal statutes by one acting under color of state law. To avoid liability, these lesser government officials must demonstrate that their actions were reasonable in light of the information available to them at the time of their acts. And local government entities such as cities have been held to have no immunity from suit under the Civil Rights Act, Owen v. City of Independence, 445 U.S. 622, 100 S.Ct. 1398, 63 L.Ed.2d 673 (1980).

Finally, some of the most recent enabling statutes provide for private actions by individuals to enforce agency rules or standards. For example, the Clean Air Act permits any person to bring a civil suit against any government official or private party who is claimed to be violating air pollution standards established under the Act.

WHAT ARE THE SPECIFIC FUNCTIONS OF THE INDEPENDENT FEDERAL AGENCIES?

The independent administrative agencies of the federal government may be categorized into five functional areas:

1. Business regulation,
2. International trade regulation,
3. Safety and environmental protection,
4. Government operation, and
5. Miscellaneous.

The *main* agencies within these groups will be described in the remainder of this chapter. Remember that we are dealing here with the *independent* agencies and that there are many additional federal agencies within the thirteen executive departments.

Business Regulation

The Federal Trade Commission Of all the federal agencies, the Federal Trade Commission has the broadest authority over domestic business practices. It is an independent law enforcement agency charged by Congress with protecting consumers and business persons against anticompetitive behavior and unfair and deceptive business practices.

The Commission has authority to stop business practices that restrict competition or that deceive or otherwise injure consumers. Such practices may be terminated by cease and desist orders issued after an administrative hearing or by injunctions issued by the federal courts upon application by the Commission.

In addition, the FTC defines practices that violate the law so that business persons may know their legal obligations and consumers may recognize those business practices against which legal recourse is available. The Commission does this through Trade Regulation Rules and Industry Guides issued periodically as "dos and don'ts" to business and industry and through business advice—called Advisory Opinions—given to individuals and corporations requesting it.

Both business persons and the general public may participate in the shaping of Trade Regulation Rules and Industry Guides. Before a rule or guide is officially issued, any interested individual or group may comment on its provisions either in writing or at a public hearing. Ample notice of these hearings is given through news releases and by publication in the Federal Register.

In their final form, Advisory Opinions, Trade Regulation Rules, and Industry Guides are widely publicized, so that businesses, industries, and consumers affected, as well as trade associations and others who are interested, will be aware of the Commission's actions. The Commission is authorized to sue for civil penalties and to obtain redress, including damages, for violation of such rules.

When law violations are individual rather than industrywide, the FTC may enter orders to halt false advertising or fraudulent selling or to prevent a business person or corporation from using unfair tactics against competitors. The Commission itself has no authority to imprison or fine. However, if one of its final cease and desist orders or Trade Regulation Rules is violated, it can seek civil penalties in federal court of up to $10,000 a day for each violation. It can also seek redress for those who have been harmed by unfair or deceptive acts or practices. Redress may include cancellation or reformation of contracts, refunds of money, return of property, and payment of damage.

Each of the Federal Trade Commission's five commissioners is appointed for a term of seven years by the president of the United States, with the advice and consent of the United States Senate. The president designates one of the commissioners as chairman. Not more than three commissioners may be members of the same party. Their terms are staggered to assure continuity of experience and to keep the Commission nonpartisan.

Within the FTC, its Bureau of Competition is responsible for enforcing the antitrust laws. It investigates and, when necessary, litigates matters arising under the Clayton Act and restraint of trade matters under Section 5 of the Federal Trade Commission Act. The Bureau also seeks to discover and remedy anticompetitive practices and to eliminate unreasonable or unfair restraints of trade resulting from illegal business methods (see Chapter 7).

The FTC's Bureau of Consumer Protection, on the other hand, investigates and litigates cases involving acts or practices alleged to be deceptive or unfair to consumers. It guides and counsels businesspersons, consumers, and federal, state, and local officials to promote understanding and encourage compliance with trade laws. The Bureau also develops and administers a nationwide education program to alert the public to deceptive trade practices and to the role a citizen can play in correcting them.

The full organization chart of the Federal Trade Commission is presented in figure 5–1.

The Federal Trade Commission's principal functions are:

1. To promote free and fair competition in interstate commerce through prevention of general trade restraints such as price-fixing agreements, boycotts, illegal combinations of competitors, and other unfair methods of competition;

2. To safeguard the public by preventing the dissemination of false or deceptive advertisements of consumer products or use of other unfair or deceptive practices;

3. To achieve true credit cost disclosure by consumer creditors (retailers, finance companies, nonfederal credit unions, and other creditors not specifically regulated by another government agency) to assure a meaningful basis for informed credit decisions, and to regulate the issuance and liability of credit cards so as to prohibit their fraudulent use in or affecting commerce; and

4. To protect consumers against circulation of inaccurate or obsolete credit reports and to insure that consumer reporting agencies exercise their responsibilities in a manner that is fair and equitable.

FIGURE 5–1 THE FEDERAL TRADE COMMISSION

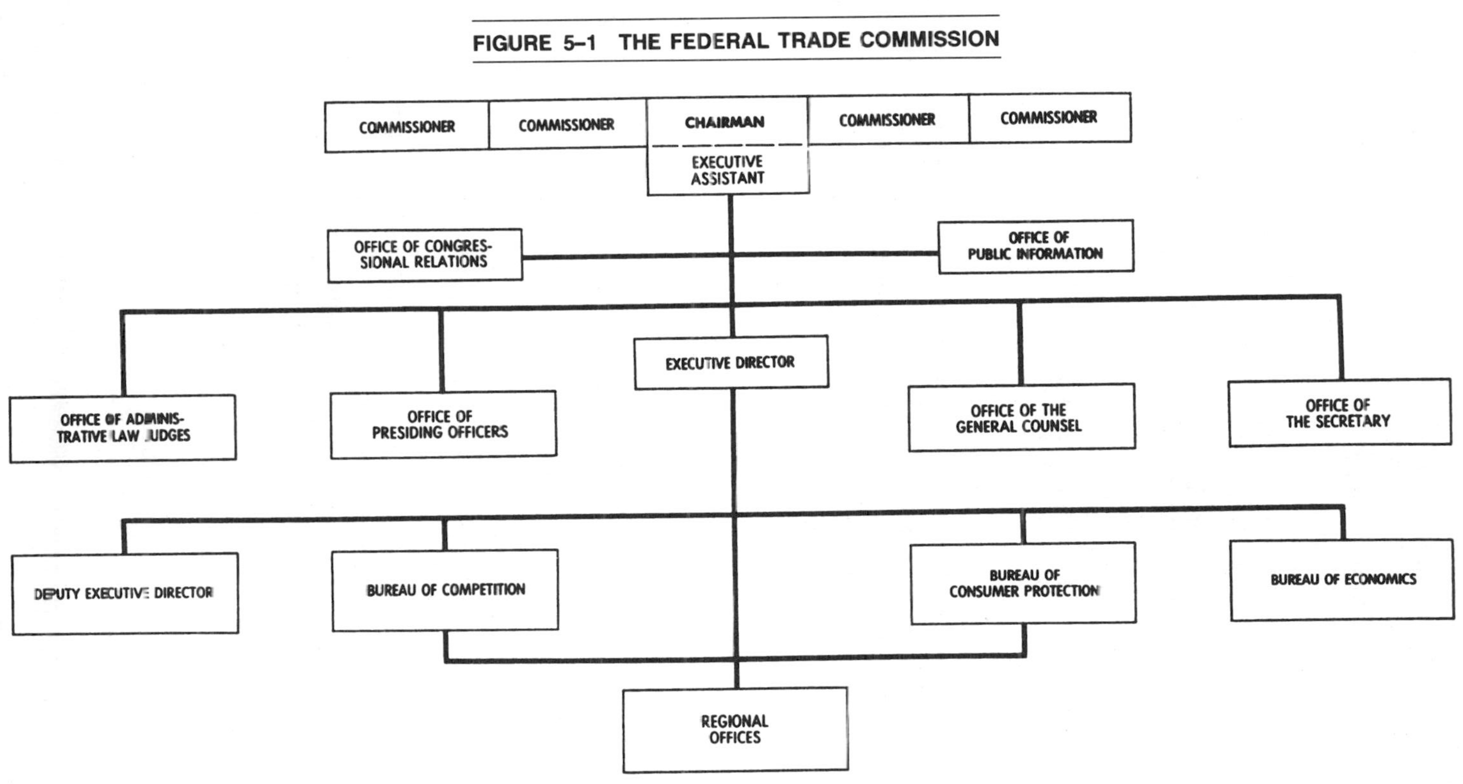

Source: United States Government Manual, 1982–83

Figures 5–2 and 5–3 provide a description of the typical procedures followed by the Federal Trade Commission in developing a Trade Regulation Rule (figure 5–2) and in handling a specific case (figure 5–3).

The National Labor Relations Board

Also: Related Agencies:

- *Federal Mediation and Conciliation Service,* and
- *National Mediation Board.*

The National Labor Relations Board, an independent federal agency established in 1935, administers the nation's principal labor relations law.

FIGURE 5–2 HOW AN FTC TRADE REGULATION IS DEVELOPED

An FTC Regulation Rule is a statement of general or particular applicability which defines unfair or deceptive acts or practices within the meaning of Section 5 of the Federal Trade Commission Act. FTC Trade Regulation Rule proceedings are commenced by the Commission either upon its own initiative or in response to a written petition by any interested person stating reasonable grounds.

An investigation takes place prior to the formal commencement of the proceedings to determine whether such action is warranted. Once a determination to propose a rule has been made, a presiding officer is appointed to conduct the public proceedings.

Formal commencement begins with publication in the *Federal Register* of an initial notice of proposed rule making. This notice includes the substance of the proposed rule or a description of the issues involved, the legal authority for the proposed rule, the particular reason for it, and an invitation to interested persons to propose specific issues and to comment on the proposed rule.

After sufficient time for receiving comments and proposed issues from interested persons, the presiding officer publishes a final notice in the *Federal Register.* This indicates the designated issues upon which limited cross-examination may be permitted, the time and place of informal hearings, and instructions for those wishing to appear at the hearings.

Informal hearings are then held to receive the views of interested persons. After the hearings have been completed, the presiding officer prepares a summary of the record and initial findings and conclusions with regard to those issues designated by the presiding officer and such other findings and conclusions as he or she sees fit. The FTC staff then prepares a report containing its recommendations based upon the rule making record, taking into account the presiding officer's findings. Both of these reports are placed on the public record for sixty days for public comment.

Next, the Commission reviews the rule making record, including the reports of the presiding officer and the staff. The Commission may issue, modify, or decline to issue the proposed rule. If it determines to issue a rule, it must adopt a Statement of Basis and Purpose to accompany the rule. The final rule is published in the *Federal Register.* Once a rule is promulgated, any interested person has sixty days to petition the appropriate U.S. Court of Appeals for judicial review of the rule.

Source: Federal Trade Commission

FIGURE 5–3 HOW A FEDERAL TRADE COMMISSION CASE IS HANDLED

Formal FTC complaints develop from Commission investigations. The investigations may be initiated by the Commission or they may arise from letters sent to the FTC by businesspersons or consumers citing alleged illegal practices. These letters are called "applications for complaints" to distinguish them from formal complaints brought by the Commission.

Applications for complaints also come from members of Congress, other federal, state, and local government agencies, and trade associations.

Each application is reviewed to determine whether the practice questioned involves violation of a law administered by the FTC.

If it does, an investigation is begun. This may start with correspondence from the Commission requiring the business concerned to file a special report, or with a request of a subpoena for information by the staff of a bureau or regional office.

From the information obtained during the investigation, the decision is made either to close the case or to issue a complaint, along with a proposed cease and desist order.

Cases can also be settled by consent order, a formal document signed by the business person or company involved certifying that the challenged practices will be corrected or discontinued. The public has the opportunity to comment on a proposed consent order and the Commission takes these comments into consideration before the order is finally issued. Violations of consent orders can result in assessment of civil penalties.

Cases which are not settled are litigated before an FTC Administrative Law Judge. Following hearings, either the respondent or the Commission's complaint counsel can appeal the judge's initial decision to the five Commissioners.

The Commission hears the argument and announces its decision: to issue a cease and desist order or to dismiss some or all of the charges.

If the Administrative Law Judge's initial decision is not appealed, it may be adopted—with or without modifications—by the Commission. FTC staff cannot appeal an adverse decision by the Commission.

If a cease and desist order is issued, the respondent has sixty days to appeal the Commission's decision to a U.S. Court of Appeals. Either side may ultimately file for certiorari to the United States Supreme Court.

Source: Federal Trade Commission

This statute, the National Labor Relations Act, generally applies to all interstate commerce except railroads and airlines. These two are covered by the Railway Labor Act.

The purpose of the National Labor Relations Act is to reduce interruptions in commerce caused by industrial strife. It seeks to do this by providing orderly processes for protecting and implementing the respective rights of employees, employers, and unions in their relations with one another. The achievement of this aim is the job of the NLRB.

The NLRB has two primary functions: (1) to determine and implement, through secret-ballot elections, the free choice by employees as to whether they wish to be represented by a union and, if so, by which one; and (2) to prevent and remedy unlawful acts, called unfair labor practices, by either employers or unions. These include employer unfair labor practices such as interference with employees' freedom to organize and bargain collectively, domination of unions, antiunion discrimination, and refusal to bargain; and union unfair labor practices such as intimidation of employees, restraint or coercion of employers, refusal to bargain collectively, and engaging in certain types of strikes and picketing (see Chapter 7).

The National Labor Relations Board does not act on its own motion in either function. It processes only those charges of unfair labor practices and petitions for employee elections which may be filed with it at one of its Regional Offices or other smaller field offices.

Each year the NLRB receives more than 50,000 cases of all kinds. Some two-thirds are unfair labor practice charges. Over the years, charges filed against employers have outnumbered those filed against unions by about two to one. Charges are filed by individual workers, employers, and unions.

Since its establishment, the NLRB has processed more than 350,000 cases alleging violation of the Act's prohibitions against unfair labor practices. And it has conducted more than 250,000 secret-ballot employee self-determination elections in appropriate worker groups.

The NLRB has five Board members and a general counsel, each appointed by the president with Senate consent. The Board members are appointed to five-year terms, the term of one member expiring each year. The statute specifies that the president shall designate one member to serve as chairman of the Board. The general counsel is appointed to a four-year term. Reappointments may be made, and members of the Board often serve for more than one term.

Headquartered in Washington, the NLRB has thirty-three Regional Offices and sixteen smaller field offices throughout the country. Total Washington and field staffs number approximately 3,000.

The NLRB's judicial functions are separate, by law, from its prosecuting functions. The five-member Board acts primarily as a quasi-judicial body in deciding cases upon formal records, generally upon review from decisions of regional directors or administrative law judges. The general counsel is responsible for the investigation and prosecution of charges of violations of the Act, and he or she has general supervision of the Regional Offices.

The NLRB has no statutory independent power of enforcement of its orders, but it may seek enforcement in the United States Courts of Appeals. Similarly, parties aggrieved by its orders may seek judicial review in the courts.

The Federal Mediation and Conciliation Service The Federal Mediation and Conciliation Service is another independent agency involved with labor-management problems. It is separate and independent from the National Labor Relations Board. This agency provides mediation assistance in preventing and settling collective bargaining controversies. For this purpose, the agency has federal mediators, known as commissioners, stationed strategically throughout the country.

Thus, the Federal Mediation and Conciliation Service helps prevent disruptions in the flow of interstate commerce caused by labor-management disputes by providing mediators to assist disputing parties in the resolution of

FIGURE 5–4 THE PROCEDURES OF THE NATIONAL LABOR RELATIONS BOARD

Upon the filing of an unfair labor practice charge with an NLRB Regional Office, members of the professional staff of that office investigate circumstances from which the charge arises in order to determine whether formal proceedings are warranted. Approximately one-third of the unfair labor practice allegations are found, after investigation, to require legal disposition. In such a case, the Regional Office works with the parties in an attempt to achieve a voluntary settlement adequate to remedy the alleged violation. A large number of cases are settled at this stage. If a case cannot be settled, then a formal complaint is issued, and the case is heard before an Administrative Law Judge.

NLRB Administrative Law Judges conduct formal hearings and issue decisions which may be appealed to the five-member Board; if they are not appealed, the Administrative Law Judges' recommended orders become orders of the Board.

The NLRB's emphasis on voluntary disposition of cases at all stages means that only about 5 percent of the unfair labor practice charges originally filed with the Regional Offices are litigated all the way through to a decision of the Board. The Board is still called on to decide more than 1,200 unfair labor practice cases and some 700 representation cases each year.

In representation election cases, the thirty-three Regional Directors have the authority to process all petitions, rule on contested issues, and direct elections or dismiss the requests, subject to review by the Board on limited grounds. The NLRB, through its Regional Offices, conducts some 9,000 representation elections a year in which more than half a million employees exercise their choice by secret ballot.

Source: National Labor Relations Board

their differences. The service can intervene on its own motion or by invitation of either side in a dispute. Mediators have no law enforcement authority and rely wholly on persuasive techniques.

The Labor-Management Relations Act requires that parties to a labor dispute must file a dispute notice if agreement is not reached thirty days in advance of a contract termination or reopening date. The notice must be filed with the Federal Mediation and Conciliation Service. The notice alerts the Service to possible bargaining trouble. If the case falls within the jurisdiction of the Service, the regional office then assigns a mediator to check with the employer and union involved to see whether assistance is required.

While methods and circumstances vary, the mediator generally will confer first with one of the parties involved and then with the other to get their versions of the pending difficulties. Then with these problems firmly in mind, the mediator usually will call joint conferences with the employer and union representatives. Often the mediator can get stalled negotiations going again, improve the bargaining atmosphere, encourage mutual discussions, explore alternative solutions, suggest specific contract clauses that have worked well elsewhere, and provide needed economic data and other information.

In addition to mediation services, the Federal Mediation and Conciliation Service helps employers and unions in selecting arbitrators to adjudicate labor-management disputes by maintaining a large roster of qualified arbitrators. When an employer and a union need an arbitrator, they only need to notify the Service, and the Service will provide at no charge a listing of qualified arbitrators in their area who are available to hear the dispute. When the parties have agreed on one name from the list, they notify the Service and it notifies the arbitrator. The Federal Mediation and Conciliation Service roster of arbitrators is made up of private citizens (not government employees) who meet certain standards of training and experience, most of whom have held responsible positions related to collective bargaining. The arbitration process ultimately results in a binding agreement for both parties.

In the summer of 1981, by way of example, the Federal Mediation and Conciliation Service mediated a settlement of the baseball strike, worked unsuccessfully to settle the walkout of the Professional Air Traffic Controllers' Organization, prevented a strike in the postal union and by the Hotel and Restaurant Employees Union (6,000 maids, bartenders, waiters, waitresses, and busboys) in the nation's capital.

The National Mediation Board The National Mediation Board is an independent agency created to handle all labor-management collective bargaining problems in the railroads and airlines. This Board does for the transportation industry what the National Labor Relations Board and the Federal Mediation and Conciliation Service do for other U.S. businesses in labor-management relations. Some 200 railroad and airline mediation cases are closed by the Board each year along with some 150 railroad and airline employee representation disputes.

After the recent passage of the Milwaukee Railroad Restructuring Act and the Rock Island Railroad Transition and Employee Assistance Act, the Board's mediatory services resulted in agreement on employee protective benefits. And the growing number of mergers and acquisitions, formation of new carriers, and intrastate airlines expanding into interstate operations, prompted by sweeping deregulatory changes, caused a number of representation disputes involving trunk, regional, commuter, charter, and foreign airlines.

The Securities and Exchange Commission The Securities and Exchange Commission was created on July 2, 1934 by an act of Congress entitled the Securities Exchange Act of 1934. It is an independent commission composed of five members, not more than three of whom may be members of the same political party. They are appointed by the president, with the advice and consent of the Senate, for five-year terms, the terms being staggered so that one expires each year. The chairperson is designated by the president.

The SEC's staff is composed of lawyers, accountants, security analysts and examiners, engineers, and other professionals, together with administrative and clerical employees.

The laws administered by the Commission relate in general to the field of securities and finance and seek to provide protection for investors and the public in their securities transactions. These securities laws are designed to facilitate informed investment analyses and prudent and discriminating investment decisions by the investing public. Before a public offering of securities can be made, a registration statement must be filed with the Commission by the issuer setting forth certain required information. The purpose of registration is to provide disclosure of financial and other information on the basis of which investors may appraise the merits of the securities. To that end, investors must be furnished a prospectus containing the most important data set forth in the registration statement to enable them to evaluate the securities. (See Chapter 6 for a complete description of the securities laws, i.e., the Securities Act of 1933 and the Securities Exchange Act of 1934).

The SEC also serves as advisor to federal courts in corporate reorganization proceedings under Chapter 11 of the Bankruptcy Reform Act of 1978.

The Interstate Commerce Commission The Interstate Commerce Commission is an independent agency responsible for regulating interstate surface transportation to assure that the American public has adequate and efficient transportation systems. The ICC holds jurisdiction over some 20,000 for-hire companies providing surface transportation in the United States. These companies include railroads, trucking companies, bus lines, water carriers, coal slurry pipelines, freight forwarders, and transportation brokers.

The ICC is directed by eleven commissioners appointed by the president and confirmed by the Senate for seven-year terms. The president designates one of the commissioners to serve as chairperson, and the commissioners elect the vice-chairperson on an annual basis.

The ICC maintains an Office of Consumer Protection to handle complaints and inquiries from the public. Each year it deals with over 50,000 complaints and 25,000 inquiries.

Field offices are maintained in fifty-six cities to audit carrier accounts, monitor the utilization of railroad freight cars in order to avoid severe shortages, investigate violations of the Interstate Commerce Act and related laws, and provide assistance to the public in its use of regulated carriers which provide transportation by railroad, highway, and waterway.

In the transportation economics area, the Commission settles controversies over rates and charges among competing and like modes of transportation, shippers, and receivers of freight, passengers, and others. It rules upon applications for mergers, consolidations, acquisitions of control, and the sale of carriers and issuance of their securities. It prescribes accounting rules, awards reparations, and administers laws relating to railroad bankruptcy. It acts to prevent unlawful discrimination, destructive competition, and rebating. It also has jurisdiction over the use, control, supply, movement, distribution, exchange, and return of railroad equipment.

In the transportation service area, the Commission grants the right to operate to railroads, trucking companies, bus lines, freight forwarders, water carriers, and transportation brokers. It also approves applications to construct and abandon railroad lines.

Although public hearings on matters before the Commission may be held at any point throughout the country, final decisions are made at the Washington, D.C. headquarters in all formal proceedings. These cases include rulings upon rate changes, applications to engage in for-hire transport, carrier mergers, adversary proceedings on complaint actions, and punitive measures taken in enforcement matters.

Consumer protection programs involve assuring that the public obtains full measure of all transportation services to which entitlement is guaranteed by the Interstate Commerce Act. This law ensures that rates will be fair and service will be reasonable. Discrimination, preferential treatment, or prejudicial actions by carriers are illegal, and instances of such violations may be brought to the attention of the Commission at any field office.

The Commission also maintains a Small Business Assistance Office to help the small businessowner or transportation firm in such matters as how to file protests on rates, how to file for new operating authority or extensions, or how to get adequate service where there is none.

The Federal Communications Commission The Federal Communications Commission was created to regulate interstate and foreign communications by wire and radio in the public interest. The scope of the regulation includes radio and television broadcasting; telephone, telegraph, and cable television operation; two-way radio and radio operators; and satellite communication.

The Broadcast Bureau of the FCC administers the regulatory program for the following broadcast services: standard (AM), frequency modulation (FM), television, instructional TV, experimental, international shortwave, and related auxiliary services; issues construction permits, operating licenses, and renewals or transfers of licenses; and oversees compliance by broadcasters with statutes and commission policies.

The Commission's regulation of cable television includes rules relating to broadcast signal carriage, quality of service delivered, access to and use of cable channels for the delivery of nonbroadcast programing, and limitations on state and local restrictions on the delivery of interstate programming.

Much of the investigative and enforcement work of the FCC is carried out by its field staff. The Field Operations Bureau has six regional offices, thirty field offices, and thirteen monitoring stations. It also operates a nationwide fleet of mobile monitoring vehicles for technical enforcement purposes. Monitoring stations maintain continuous surveillance of the radio spectrum, detecting unlicensed operation and activities or nonconforming transmission, and furnish radio bearings on ships and planes in distress.

While the FCC is prohibited by law from censoring program content, it does have many regulatory responsibilities in the program area. For example, it requires licensees to attempt to ascertain and serve the programming tastes, needs, and desires of their communities. Licensees are also obligated to comply with statutes, rules, and policies relating to program content, such as identification of all sponsored broadcast matter.

The Federal Communications Commission also requires licensees to make available equal opportunities for use of broadcast facilities by political candidates. It also enforces rules on personal attacks, editorials endorsing or opposing political candidates, station identification, identification of recorded programs, and publicly declared commission policies on fairness in the presentation of controversial issues. The FCC requires licensees to prevent use of their facilities for false or misleading advertising.

The FCC conducts inquiries and investigations, and licensees who have violated FCC statutes, rules, or policies are subject to sanctions including loss of license and fines up to $10,000.

The Commission limits the number of broadcasting outlets that any one individual or company may own to a total of seven AM, seven FM, and seven TV stations (only five of which can be VHF). The same owner cannot operate more than one station of the same kind in the same place.

The Commission is required to "study new uses for radio, provide for experimental uses of frequencies, and generally encourage the larger and more effective use of radio in the public interest." Cooperation is maintained with government and commercial research and development groups. In connection with its research activities, the FCC operates a laboratory at Laurel, Maryland.

The Commission also supervises the Emergency Broadcast System to notify and instruct the public in the event of enemy attack. This system is put to peacetime use for broadcasting information and instructions about local and statewide emergencies.

The Federal Reserve System The Federal Reserve System, the central bank of the United States, is charged with administering and making policy for the nation's credit and monetary affairs. The system consists of five parts: the Board of Governors in Washington; the twelve Federal Reserve Banks, their twenty-five branches and other facilities situated throughout the country; the Federal Open Market Committee; the Federal Advisory Council; and the member commercial banks, which include all national banks and state-chartered banks that have voluntarily joined the System.

Board supervisory powers are vested in the Board of Governors, which has its offices in Washington. The Board is composed of seven members appointed by the president by and with the advice and consent of the Senate. The Board is given the power to fix the requirements concerning reserves to be maintained by member banks against deposits and the power to determine the maximum rate of interest that may be paid by member banks on their time and savings deposits. Also, the Board of Governors reviews and determines the discount rates charged by the Federal Reserve Banks on their discounts and advances. For the purpose of preventing excessive use of credit for the purchase or carrying of securities, the Board is authorized to regulate the amount of credit that may be initially extended and subsequently maintained on any security (margin requirements). The Board is also authorized to make examinations of the Federal Reserve Banks and to require statements and reports from such banks. And the Board has jurisdiction over the admission of state banks and trust companies to membership in the Federal Reserve System, the termination of membership of such banks, and the establishment of branches by such banks.

The Board of Governors has authority to issue cease and desist orders in connection with violations of law or unsafe or unsound banking practices by member state banks and to remove directors or officers of such banks in certain circumstances. It may, at its discretion, suspend member banks from the use of the credit facilities of the Federal Reserve System for making undue use of bank credit for speculative purposes or for any other purpose inconsistent with the maintenance of sound credit conditions.

Each member of the Board of Governors is also a member of the Federal Open Market Committee, whose membership, in addition, includes five representatives of the Reserve Banks, each such representative being elected annually. Purchases and sales of securities in the open market are undertaken to supply the bank reserves to support the credit and money needed for long term economic growth, to offset cyclical economic swings, and to accommodate seasonal demands of businesses and consumers for money and credit.

The Federal Advisory Council acts in an advisory capacity, conferring with the Board of Governors on general business conditions and making recommendations concerning matters within the Board's jurisdiction. The Council is composed of twelve members, one from each Federal Reserve district being selected annually by the board of directors of the Reserve Bank of the district.

In figures 5–5 and 5–6, the organization of the Federal Reserve System and its relation to instruments of credit policy are presented.

FIGURE 5–5 ORGANIZATION OF THE FEDERAL RESERVE SYSTEM

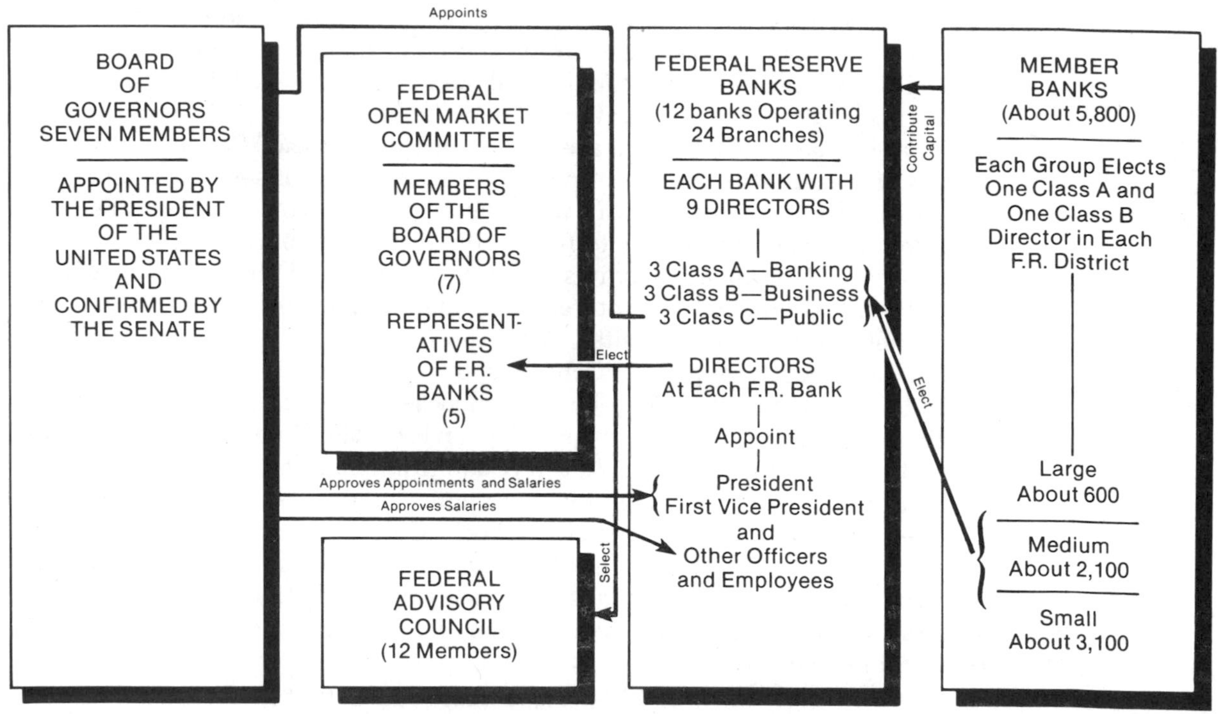

Source: The Federal Reserve System Board of Governors

FIGURE 5–6 FEDERAL RESERVE'S RELATION TO INSTRUMENTS OF CREDIT POLICY

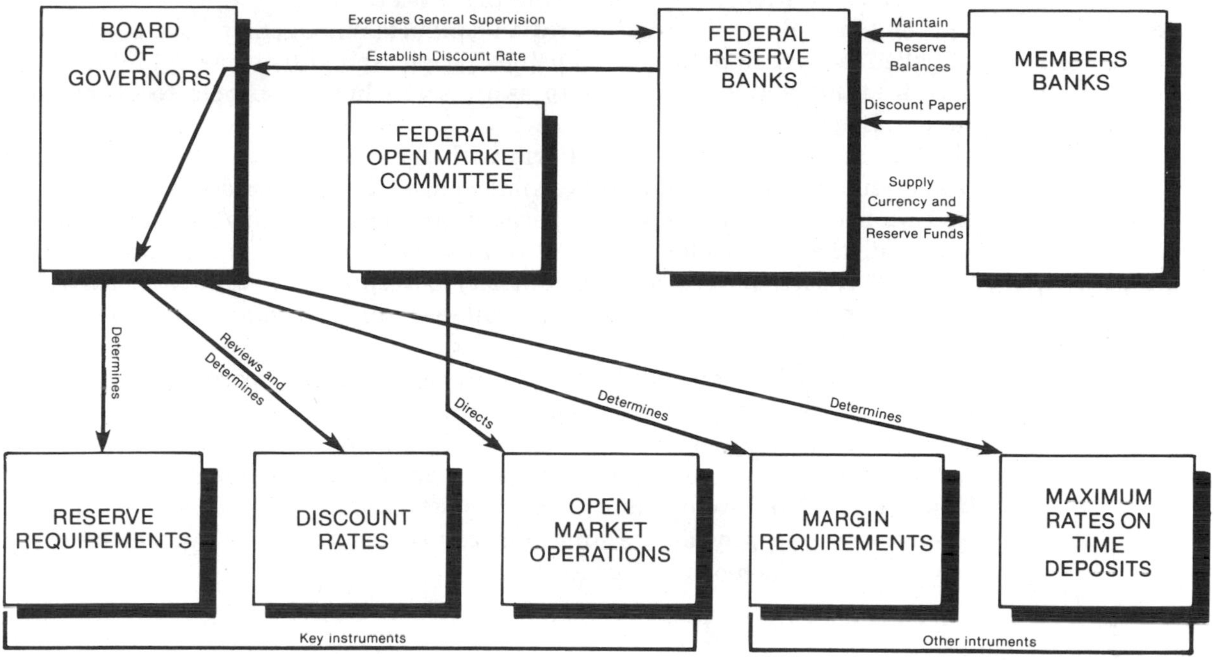

Source: The Federal Reserve System Board of Governors

Small Business Administration The Small Business Administration provides loans to small business concerns to help them finance plant construction or expansion and acquire equipment and working capital. Farming enterprises are included within the term "small business concerns."

The victims of floods, riots, civil disorders, and other catastrophes are provided with loans to aid them in repairing, rebuilding, or replacing their homes, businesses, or other property. Loans are provided to assist small businesses which have sustained substantial economic injury resulting from a major disaster or such natural disasters as excessive rainfall or drought, have been economically injured by an urban renewal or highway construction program or by any construction program conducted with federal, state, or local funds.

The agency is also authorized to make loans to assist small firms in meeting federal air or water pollution standards and to make special loans to handicapped individuals and nonprofit organizations employing the handicapped in the production of goods or services.

The SBA may finance small firms that manufacture or develop specific energy measures and may make loans to small firms suffering economic injury as the result of energy shortages.

The SBA provides a wide range of services to small firms to help them obtain and fulfill government contracts. It sets aside suitable government purchases for competitive award to small business concerns and provides an appeal procedure for a low-bidding small firm whose ability to perform a contract is questioned by the contracting officer.

The Small Business Administration conducts management courses for established as well as prospective businesspeople and enlists the volunteer aid of retired and active executives to assist small businesspeople to overcome their management problems.

SBA has also combined its efforts with those of private industry, banks, local communities, and other government agencies to increase substantially the number of minority owned, operated, and managed businesses and also to provide the chances for success of those businesses. In its field offices, the agency will describe to potential minority entrepreneurs how all of the services and programs of the SBA are available to help them become business managers.

The SBA's Women's Business Enterprise Division operates to develop and coordinate a national program to increase the numbers and enhance the profitability and job-creation potential of women-owned businesses while making maximum use of existing government and private sector resources. This WBED also develops and recommends national pilot programs in the private sector to provide training and counseling in the management and financing of women-owned businesses.

International Trade Regulation

United States International Trade Commission The United States International Trade Commission, created by Congress in 1916 with six commissioners, furnishes studies, reports, and recommendations involving international trade and tariffs to the president, the Congress, and other government agencies. In this capacity, the Commission conducts a variety of investigations pertaining to the international policies of the United States.

The International Trade Commission performs a number of functions pursuant to the Tariff Act of 1930, the Agricultural Adjustment Act, the Trade Expansion Act of 1962, the Trade Act of 1974, and the Trade Agreements Act of 1979. These functions include:

Import relief for domestic industries The Commission conducts investigations upon petition on behalf of an industry to determine whether an article is being imported into the United States in such increased quantities as to be a substantial cause of serious injury to the domestic competing industry. If the Commission's finding is affirmative, the president can take action to provide import relief, such as an increase in duties (import taxes) or establishment of quantitative restrictions.

Unfair practices in import trade The Commission conducts investigations to determine whether unfair methods of competition or unfair acts are being committed in the importation of articles into the United States. If the Commission determines that the effect is to injure or to restrain or monopolize trade and commerce, it may issue orders excluding the articles from entry or issue cease and desist orders. The president may disapprove these actions within sixty days after issuance.

Imports sold at less than fair value The Commission conducts investigations to determine whether there is a reasonable indication that an industry in the United States is materially injured by reason of imports sold or likely to be sold at less than fair value. If the Commission's determination is affirmative, an order may be issued under which a dumping duty is imposed on the articles sold at less than fair value.

Trade and tariff issues The Commission advises the president as to the probable economic effect on the domestic industry and consumers of modification of duties and other barriers to trade which may be considered for inclusion in any proposed trade agreements with foreign countries.

The Commission also has broad powers to study and investigate all factors relating to U.S. foreign trade, their effect on domestic production, employment, and consumption, and the competitiveness of U.S. products. It also furnishes reports and investigations on such matters for and at the request of the president, the House Ways and Means Committee, and the Senate Finance Committee.

Federal Maritime Commission The Federal Maritime Commission is an independent regulatory agency responsible for U.S. domestic offshore and foreign waterborne commerce (over 95 percent of U.S. foreign trade is waterborne). Its major functions include:

- The regulation of ocean carrier ratemaking in the U.S. foreign and domestic offshore trades, assuring that only the rates on file with the Commission are charged;
- Investigation of discriminatory rates and practices among shippers, carriers, terminal operators, and freight forwarders;
- Licensing of independent ocean freight forwarders;
- Passenger vessel certification;
- Certification of vessels to ensure financial responsibility for pollution by oil and hazardous substances; and
- Certification of financial responsibility of shipowners and operators to pay judgments for personal injury or death or to refund fares in the event of nonperformance of voyages.

The Commission's most visible activities occur through its enforcement of Section 15 of the Shipping Act. Section 15 exempts ocean carrier conferences from the Sherman and Clayton antitrust laws. In order to prevent abuses of concerted ratemaking authority, the Federal Maritime Commission evaluates all agreements between or among entities subject to the Shipping Act.

The Export-Import Bank The Export-Import Bank of the United States, known as Eximbank, facilitates and aids in financing exports of United States goods and services. Eximbank has implemented a variety of programs to meet the needs of the U.S. exporting community according to the size of the transaction. These programs take the form of direct lending or the issuance of guarantees and insurance, so that exporters and private banks can extend appropriate financing without taking undue risks. Eximbank's direct lending program is limited to larger sales of U.S. products and services around the world. The guarantees, insurance, and discount programs have been designed to assist exporters in smaller sales of products and services.

The Bank is authorized to have outstanding, at any one time, dollar loans, guarantees, and insurance in an aggregate amount not in excess of $40 billion.

Exim financial services support a broad cross-section of products and projects—from industrial raw materials and farm products, computers, and farm machinery to cement plants, power generating plants, and commercial jet aircraft. It provides direct loans at fixed interest rates for long terms, project-financing supports for the export of "turnkey" projects such as manufacturing, electric power and petrochemical plants, and large mining and construction operations, as well as short term financing (up to six months) or medium term (six months to five years).

The Export-Import Bank is self-sustaining and does not receive appropriations from the Congress. The Bank was capitalized in 1945 with $1 billion subscribed by the United States. Since that time it has paid dividends to the Treasury amounting to more than $1 billion and produced retained earnings of more than $2 billion.

The Bank normally requires that overseas buyers make cash payments of at least 15 percent of the U.S. contract price. In some cases, the Bank also requires exporters to retain a portion (usually 10 percent) of the financing. Guarantees of repayment may also be required from a government institution in the buyer's country.

While Exim is an independent agency, it has been prohibited by Congress from financing sales to South Africa's government but may do business with private importers in South Africa provided that they meet certain fair employment practices. Exim may not do business with any Communist country unless the president determines that doing so would be in the national interest. In other countries, Exim can deny credit applications for nonfinancial or noncommercial reasons only if the president determines that such action would be in the national interest. Among the factors that Congress has directed the president to consider in making such determinations are the United States' policy regarding international terrorism, environmental protection, nuclear nonproliferation, and human rights. Exim cannot provide financing for the sale of goods for military use to any economically less developed country.

Safety and Environmental Protection

The United States Environmental Protection Agency The United States Environmental Protection Agency (EPA) is responsible for executing federal laws aimed at protecting the environment. EPA was formed in 1970 to consolidate in one agency much of the federal authority and expertise in controlling pollution and dealing with other threats to life and the environment. The agency's mission is to control and abate pollution in the areas of air, water, solid waste, noise, radiation, and toxic substances.

Within the agency, the Office of Enforcement is responsible for insuring compliance with EPA's regulations. EPA's enforcement philosophy has been to encourage voluntary compliance by communities and private industry and, as mandated by federal environmental laws, to encourage state and local governments to perform direct enforcement activities needed to meet environmental standards. If state and local agencies fail to produce effective plans for pollution abatement or if they do not enforce the programs they do develop, EPA generally is authorized to do so under provisions of major environmental laws (see Chapter 13 for a discussion of the statutes dealing with the environment).

In addition, enforcement functions of a national character are carried out by EPA because delegation to the states is not practical. EPA, for example, inspects and tests automobiles before, during, and after production to insure compliance with air pollution control standards. The agency also can require the recall of automobile or truck models that fail to meet these standards. EPA also maintains a staff of inspectors who spot check compliance with unloaded gasoline regulations, monitor air and water quality, check radiation levels, and collect other data to use in enforcing environmental laws. The agency also has created a special task force to clean up existing hazardous waste sites.

EPA additionally assesses the compliance of other federal departments and agencies with the laws EPA administers. The major assessment tool is the Environmental Impact Statement, which must be prepared for any federal activity significantly affecting environmental quality. Agencies are thus required to internalize consideration of the environmental repercussions of their activities. Figure 5–7 presents the structure of the Environmental Protection Agency.

Consumer Product Safety Commission Some 36 million Americans are injured and 30,000 killed each year in accidents related to consumer products at a cost estimated at $9.5 billion annually. Many of these injuries and deaths occur when consumers are using products commonly found in most homes such as bicycles, power lawn mowers, toys, household chemicals, television sets, appliances, power tools, etc. To reduce the number and severity of these injuries, Congress enacted the Consumer Product Safety Act which President Nixon signed into law on October 27, 1972. The Consumer Product Safety Commission was activated as an independent federal regulatory agency on May 14, 1973.

The Commission is responsible for implementing not only the Consumer Product Safety Act but also the Federal Hazardous Substances Act, the

FIGURE 5–7 THE ENVIRONMENTAL PROTECTION AGENCY

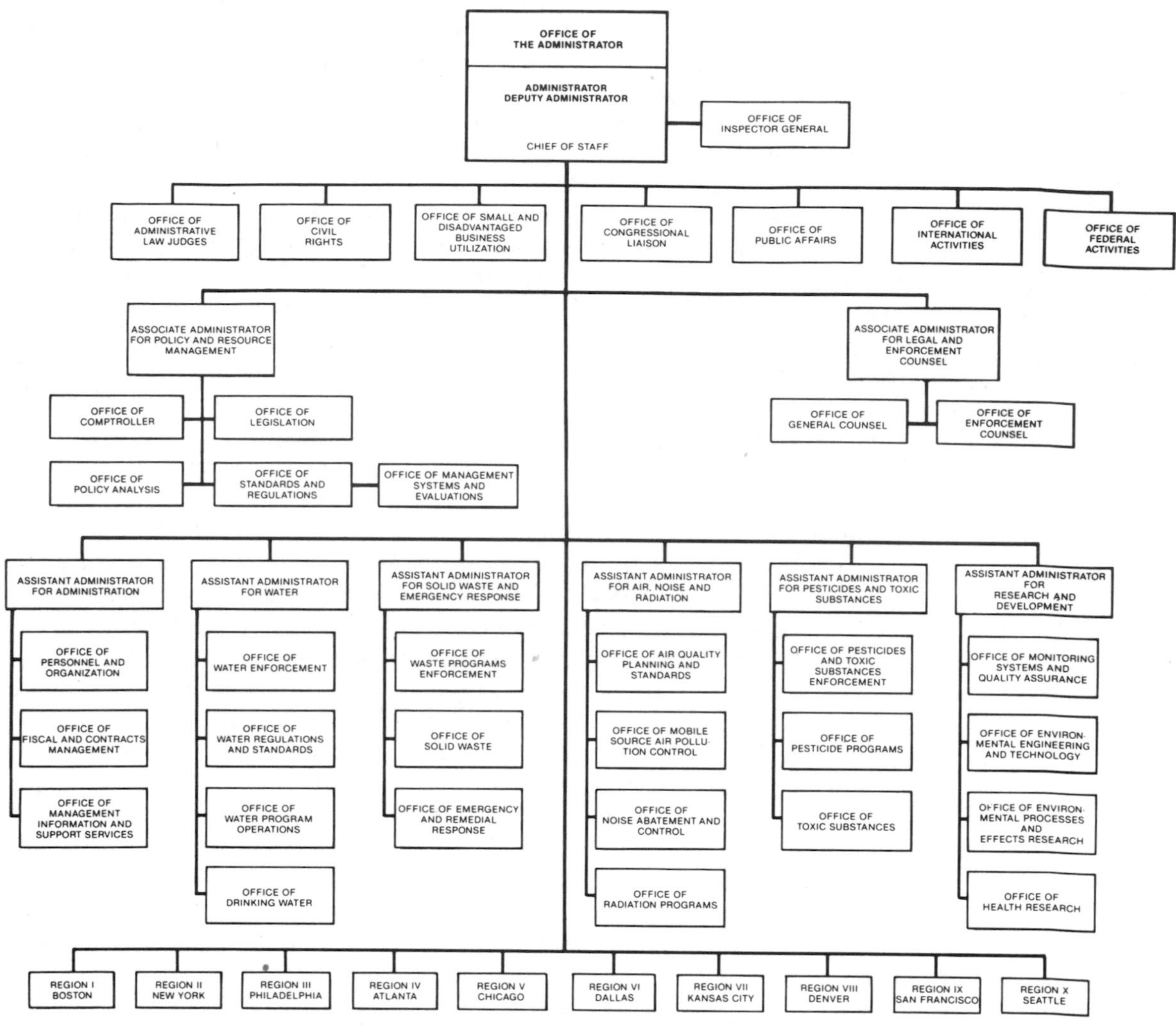

Source: United States Government Manual, 1982–83

Poison Prevention Packaging Act, the Flammable Fabrics Act, and the Refrigerator Safety Act.

The Commission:

- Issues and enforces mandatory product safety regulations;
- Bans unsafe products when safety standards are not feasible;
- Initiates recalls of hazardous products;
- Helps industry develop voluntary safety standards; and
- Conducts applied research and develops test methods for unsafe products.

Under Commission regulations:

■ Architectural glazing materials, such as glass patio doors, are required to be made of materials, which, if broken, are less likely to inflict injury than ordinary glass;

■ Matchbooks are required to conform to a Commission safety standard which requires placement of the friction strip on the outside back cover and prescribes other safety features;

■ Unsafe refuse bins which may be tipped over and injure children have been banned;

■ Unsafe bicycles have been banned, and safety requirements have been enacted to help reduce approximately one-half million related accidents every year;

■ Paint containing high levels of lead and toys and furniture bearing such paint have been banned to reduce the risk of lead poisoning in children;

■ Safety packaging is required for containers of potentially dangerous drugs and household chemicals. The number of childhood poisonings by aspirin, for example, dropped 55 percent since 1972.

■ Asbestos-containing patching compounds and asbestos-containing artificial fireplace ashes were banned because inhalable asbestos fibers may cause cancer; and

■ Lawn mowers must meet a safety standard covering walk-behind, rotary power mowers intended for consumer use.

The Commission's toll-free HOTLINE receives approximately 300,000 calls a year from consumers. To report a product-related injury, a hazardous product, or to request information, consumers may call toll free from anywhere in the continental U.S. 800–638–8326.

The Commission's enforcement authorities under the five acts it administers include: injunctions to prevent violations of safety-related laws and regulations; seizures of products that are in violation of regulations; cease and desist orders; mandatory and voluntary recalls of hazardous products; and civil and criminal penalties. Any person who knowingly commits a prohibited act is subject to a civil fine up to $2,000 for each violation (fines for multiple violations run up to $50,000), and criminal penalties for any person who "knowingly and willfully" violates the Act are a fine up to $50,000 and imprisonment up to one year or both.

Section 14 of the Act requires the manufacturer to conduct a "reasonable testing program" to make certain that his or her product conforms to established safety standards. After the product has been tested, the manufacturer must provide the distributor or retailer with a certificate stating that all applicable consumer protection safety standards have been met.

Section 15 of the Act requires the manufacturer to take corrective steps if he or she learns that his or her product is defective. If the manufacturer, distributor, or retailer knows that the product is defective or that it is not in compliance with safety rules, he or she must inform the Consumer Product Safety Commission immediately.

The Commission can then order the manufacturer: (1) to make the product safe, or to repair its defect; (2) to replace the product with an equivalent safe product; or (3) to refund the purchase price of the product less a reasonable allowance for use.

The Nuclear Regulatory Commission The Nuclear Regulatory Commission came into being on January 19, 1975 when the Atomic Energy Commission was abolished. President Ford, on signing the legislation, stated in part:

> The highly technical nature of our nuclear facilities and the special potential hazards which are involved in the use of nuclear fuels fully warrant the creation of an independent and technically competent regulatory agency to assure adequate protection of public health and safety. NRC will be fully empowered to see to it that reactors using nuclear materials will be properly and safely designed, constructed and operated to guarantee against hazards to the public from leakage or accident.

The Nuclear Regulatory Commission is headed by a five-member commission appointed by the president and confirmed by the Senate for five-year terms.

Within the agency, its Office of Nuclear Reactor Regulation evaluates applications for permits to build and licenses to operate nuclear reactors. Its review of applications encompasses the safety, safeguards, and environmental aspects of nuclear facilities. Many requirements are imposed to achieve safety objectives. These include a comprehensive quality assurance program for the design, construction, and operation of the plant; multiple safety systems and physical barriers to prevent the uncontrolled release of radioactivity; and extensive testing and inspection of plant and equipment and systems.

Where approval has been granted in licensing reviews, the office then issues construction permits and operating licenses.

The Office of Nuclear Safety and Safeguards licenses and regulates fuel-cycle facilities, the transport and handling of nuclear materials, and the safeguarding of nuclear facilities and materials.

This responsibility includes the development of programs for protecting nuclear materials from diversion and nuclear facilities from sabotage.

The Office of Nuclear Regulatory Research has two primary responsibilities: (1) to administer the research program which serves as a basis for the Nuclear Regulatory Commission to confirm the safety, safeguards, and environmental assessments made in performance of its regulatory functions; and (2) to develop regulations, criteria, guides, standards, and codes defining the siting, design, construction, operation, decommissioning, and safeguarding of nuclear reactors and other nuclear facilities, as well as the storage, processing, transporting, safeguarding, and use of nuclear materials.

The research effort includes programs in water reactor safety, probabilistic risk assessment, the behavior of nuclear fuel, computer codes to predict the nature and consequences of severe accident damage to reactor fuel and containment systems, advance safety technology relating to high temperature, gas-colleged reactors and liquid metal fast-breeder reactors, and fuel-cycle, environmental, and waste management areas.

The Nuclear Regulatory Commission's inspection function is carried out by its Office of Inspection and Enforcement to assure that nuclear facilities and other licensees comply with NRC requirements for health and safety, security of nuclear materials and facilities, and environmental protection. This is achieved by inspecting the quality assurance systems of licensees as well as conducting, on a sampling basis, an inspection of licensed activities.

The NRC is also implementing a program of resident inspectors for operating nuclear power plants and many of those under construction. Some fuel facilities are also staffed with resident inspectors. The resident inspectors are assisted in their inspections by technical specialists based in the regional offices. These specialist inspections include such areas as environmental monitoring, emergency planning, radiation protection, security and in-service inspection of nuclear components.

The Office of Inspection and Enforcement also investigates accidents and incidents at licensed facilities as well as complaints or allegations from licensee employees or members of the public concerning activities of NRC licensees.

When appropriate, this office carries out enforcement actions including notices of violations requiring corrective action, imposition of fines, or modifications, supension, or revocation of licenses.

Government Operation

General Services Administration At one time, dozens of agencies were involved in carrying out the government's internal business, such as buying supplies, constructing buildings, providing computers and communications, and keeping records. In 1949, Congress created one agency—the General Services Administration—to handle the government's internal business affairs. Today, GSA is an agency of over 37,000 people organized like a large corporation to manage the multibillion dollar annual business of the federal government. It is the government's builder and landlord, wholesaler and retailer, transportation expediter, communications and data-processing expert, property and utilities manager, and historian and records keeper. It is organized into six services: Public Buildings, Federal Supply, Transportation and Public Utilities, Automated Data and Telecommunications, Federal Property Resources, and National Archives and Records.

The Public Buildings Service manages federally owned and leased space in 10,000 buildings. It designs and constructs new buildings and restores historic ones. It is concerned with energy conservation, fire safety, environ mental protection, safe and healthy workspace, accessibility for the handicapped, and overall efficiency.

Buying, storing, and distributing all that's needed for day to day government work is the job of the Federal Supply Service in GSA. Some of the 4.2 million items on its shopping list are pencils and paper, typewriters, cars, furniture, tools, light bulbs, paints, and household appliances. It also obtains services from calculator repairs to carpet cleaning. Each year Federal Supply spends about $3 billion on behalf of other agencies. Through special procurement procedures, this Service channels millions of federal dollars into areas of high unemployment and attempts to create new opportunities for small, minority and women-owned businesses. It also purchases items from workshops for the handicapped and from Federal Prison Industries. Sixteen depots and sixty-nine retail stores handle storage and distribution aided by a computerized order and followup system.

The Transportation and Public Utilities Service oversees federal travel and transportation services and the rates federal agencies must pay for public utilities such as water and electricity. The Service also operates a fleet of more than 88,000 cars, vans, and trucks for federal business.

The Automated Data and Telecommunications Service oversees the procurement and management of data-processing and telecommunications equipment and services for the federal government. The Service operates, for federal use, the world's largest private telephone network, with more than a million telephones in over 2,000 locations throughout the fifty states. It transmits some 230 million long-distance calls a year. It is also the federal disaster communications coordinator and maintains special emergency communications teams throughout the country. And it provides "secure" communications to federal agencies such as the Drug Enforcement Administration and the U.S. Customs Service.

The Federal Property Resources Service manages the use of government property from typewriters to helicopters. Anything not used by one agency is transferred to another if possible. When federal use is exhausted, personal property is offered for donation to eligible state and local nonprofit organizations or for sale to the public. Surplus real estate may be donated for public recreation or airports or sold for development. This Service also stores, inspects, and maintains the national stockpile of strategic and critical materials held to protect U.S. industry from a sudden cutoff during a war or other national emergency.

The National Archives and Records Service is the keeper of the nation's history and preserves historic documents in Washington and in eleven regional archives. Fifteen federal records centers around the country store agency records—those with no historic value are put on microfilm.

The GSA also maintains Business Service Centers in major cities across the country which offer advice to business persons on how to do business with the government. The Consumer Information Center provides information to consumers and the Federal Information Center provides information on other federal programs.

General Accounting Office The General Accounting Office is headed by the Comptroller General of the United States. GAO is required by statute to assist Congress by reviewing the operations of essentially all government agencies. GAO makes audits and evaluations of programs, activities, and financial operations of federal departments and agencies and their contractors and grantees. Audits and program evaluations include independent factfinding and onsite verification and analysis.

The GAO staff is multidisciplinary and includes evaluators, auditors, attorneys, actuaries and other mathematical scientists, claims adjudicators and examiners, engineers, computer and information specialists, economists and other social scientists, personnel management specialists, as well as members of a variety of other disciplines. The staff is permanently located in twenty-two regional offices and suboffices throughout the United States and in four offices around the world. In Washington, D.C., auditors and evaluators are stationed at over seventy agency locations. GAO has contracted for access to a variety of computerized data bases and also has access to various econometric and manipulative models to help GAO staff forecast the impact of program alternatives. These resources allow GAO to perform audits and evaluations in just about any subject area. GAO audits not only include examining accounting records and financial transactions and statements, but also checking for compliance with applicable laws and regulations, examining the efficiency and economy of operations, and reviewing the results of operations to evaluate whether desired results, including legislatively prescribed objectives, have been effectively achieved.

During any year, the General Accounting Office will issue about 1,000 reports on audits or special studies. About three-fourths of these are submitted to the Congress, the rest to federal agencies. Most of these reports recommend congressional or agency actions necessary to correct problems and improve federal programs and activities. The reports are available from the U.S. General Accounting Office with the first five copies free of charge. GAO publishes a list of the reports under more than forty subject areas from "computers" to "defense procurement" to "employment and training" to "foreign aid" to "justice and law enforcement" to "nuclear energy" to "social programs and benefits" to "weapons acquisition process."

U.S. Office of Personnel Management

Also: Related Agencies:

- *Merit Systems Protection Board,* and
- *Federal Labor Relations Authority.*

The U.S. Office of Personnel Management is the central personnel agency of the federal government. It is charged with recruiting, training, job classification, employee productivity, and pay and benefits administration. OPM also administers federal employee retirement and insurance programs, and it exercises management leadership in labor relations, affirmative action, and employee utilization.

OPM is an independent agency with some 8,200 employees headed by a director and deputy director appointed by the president and confirmed by the Senate. The director is the president's chief advisor in civilian federal employment matters, and OPM is the primary agency for helping the president carry out the responsibilities of managing the federal work force.

Together with the Merit Systems Protection Board, OPM administers the Civil Service Reform Act which became effective in 1979.

The Merit Systems Protection Board The Merit Systems Protection Board is an independent agency created to safeguard both the merit system and individual employees against abuses and unfair personnel actions. The Civil Service Reform Act requires agencies to inform employees of the critical elements and performance standards of their jobs and requires agencies to provide written warnings to employees prior to the initiation of demotion or removal actions based on poor performance. Adverse actions, such as removals of federal employees, suspensions for over fourteen days, or reductions in grade or pay, may be appealed to the Merit Systems Protection Board.

The Federal Labor Relations Authority The Federal Labor Relations Authority oversees the creation of bargaining units, supervises elections, and deals with labor-management issues in federal agencies. The Civil Service Reform Act affirms the basic rights of federal employees to form, join, and assist labor organizations (or to refrain from doing so). It prohibits strikes and work slowdowns, as well as picketing that interferes with government operations. The Act also provides for court enforcement of Federal Labor Relations Authority decisions and orders, including judicial review in unfair labor practice cases.

Miscellaneous

ACTION This is the principal agency in the federal government for administering volunteer service programs. ACTION consists of a Washington, D.C. headquarters, and ten domestic regional offices, supporting forty-nine individual state offices. Peace Corps, administered by ACTION, consists of a Washington, D.C. headquarters and overseas operations in sixty-three countries.

ACTION includes, among others, the following programs:

Foster Grandparent Program The Foster Grandparent Program was created to offer older men and women opportunities for close relationships with children having special or exceptional needs. It is an opportunity for older Americans to continue serving their communities and themselves in an active and meaningful capacity. Foster grandparents work in schools and hospitals for retarded, disturbed, and handicapped children, in day care centers, corrections institutions, in homes for disadvantaged, dependent, or neglected children, and other settings within the community.

Foster grandparents are low-income persons, at least sixty years of age, and come from every kind of background. They receive both preservice orientation and in-service instruction. Volunteers serve twenty hours per week, receive a stipend of forty dollars per week, as well as provisions for reimbursement of travel costs, a meal each day, accident and liability insurance coverage, and a yearly physical examination.

Retired Senior Volunteer Program The purpose of Retired Senior Volunteer Program is to create a variety of meaningful opportunities for persons of retirement age to participate, through volunteer service, more fully in the life of their communities. Volunteers must be at least sixty years of age and be willing and able to serve on a regular basis. There are no income or educational requirements. They perform various services according to community need (and their preference) in a variety of settings, including schools, courts, and health care, rehabilitation, day care, youth, and other community centers.

Urban Crime Prevention Program The Urban Crime Prevention Program utilizes volunteers through private, nonprofit organizations in cities of 150,000 or more to develop crime prevention projects for low and moderate income neighborhoods. Initiated in 1980, UCPP focuses primarily on community dispute settlement, arson, property crime victimization, and victim/witness assistance as well as locally designed crime prevention projects. Volunteers in the UCPP may be community residents who volunteer a few hours a week, full-time volunteers who receive a living allowance, or members of established volunteer organizations whose interests coincide with those of local projects.

Peace Corps On creating the Peace Corps, the Congress declared that its mission was to promote world peace and friendship; to help the peoples of other countries in meeting their needs for trained manpower; to help promote a better understanding of the American people on the part of the peoples served; and to promote a better understanding of other peoples on the part of the American people. Peace Corps programming is directed toward meeting the basic needs of those living in the poorest areas of the countries in which the Peace Corps operates.

Men and women of all ages and walks of life are trained over a nine-to-fourteen-week period in the appropriate local language, the technical skills necessary for the particular job, and the cross-cultural skills needed. They are then placed overseas in countries whose needs are critical, and who request volunteers to aid in their economic and social development. Volunteers serve for a period of two years, living among the people with whom they work. Volunteers are expected to become a part of the community and to demonstrate, through their voluntary service, that people can be an important impetus for change.

More than 6,000 volunteers serve in sixty-three countries throughout Latin America, Africa, the Near East, Asia, and the Pacific. These volunteers work primarily in the areas of agriculture/rural development, health, and education.

International Communications Agency The U.S. International Communications Agency came into being on April 1, 1978. Its director reports to the president of the United States and receives policy guidance from the Secretary of State. The agency maintains 201 posts in 125 countries. The purposes of the agency are:

- To give foreign peoples the best possible understanding of our policies and our intentions and sufficient information about American society and culture to comprehend why we have chosen certain policies over others;
- To encourage the broadest possible exchange of people and ideas between our country and other nations;
- To help insure that our government adequately understands foreign public opinion and culture for policy-making purposes, and to assist individual Americans and institutions in learning about other nations and cultures; and
- To prepare for and conduct negotiations on cultural exchanges with other governments.

The International Communications Agency employs some 8,000 people, about half of them foreign nationals who work overseas. Communication is accomplished through:

Personal contact Agency officers serving abroad provide most direct personal links with opinion leaders in the countries to which they are assigned. They also promote contacts between these opinion leaders and visiting American experts.

Exchange activities The Fulbright Program involves the annual exchange of approximately 1,500 U.S. and foreign predoctoral students and approximately 1,200 professors, senior scholars, and researchers. In addition, there is an exchange of approximately 800 elementary and secondary school teachers conducted by the Department of Education, and the Hubert H. Humphrey Fellowship Program provides mid-career professionals from Third World Countries a year of specially designed graduate level training at selected U.S. universities.

International visitors Invitations are extended annually by U.S. chiefs of mission to about 1,500 foreign leaders in government, labor, mass media, science, education, and other fields to visit their counterparts in the United States for periods of up to thirty days. About 500 of these foreign leaders participate in multiregional projects on such topics as energy, food systems, environment, communications, and the role of women. Programming these visitors in the communities to which they travel involves more than 100,000 U.S. volunteers and ninety community organizations.

American participants The International Communications Agency sends selected Americans, called "American participants," overseas for short-term speaking programs. These Americans help inform experts abroad of developments in the United States in economics, foreign policy, political and social processes, the arts and humanities, and science and technology. Some 600 American experts take part in the program each year.

Performing and fine arts Under its "Arts America" program and in conjunction with the National Endowment for the Arts, the agency assists qualified artists and performing groups in arranging private tours overseas.

American studies and language The agency facilitates English language instruction at many binational and cultural centers. More than 350,000 foreign citizens attend English-language classes at agency-assisted facilities abroad annually.

Libraries and books The agency maintains some 128 libraries and reading rooms in more than seventy-nine countries. They contain about 825,000 books and 22,000 periodical subscriptions, which are used by some 9 million visitors annually. The focus is on materials that will help people in foreign countries learn about the United States, its people, history, and culture.

Radio The Voice of America is the agency's broadcasting element, sending out over 900 hours of programming a week in English and thirty-eight other languages via short and medium wave to an estimated 67 million listeners. The backbone of the programming is news and news analysis, but there are also programs to portray various aspects of American society and to take advantage of the popularity overseas of American music.

Films and television The agency acquires and produces videotape programs and films for foreign distribution. These are shown by USICA posts to audiences overseas and are sometimes also distributed through foreign media and commercial theaters abroad. In addition, the agency provides foreign TV stations with news clips of events in the United States.

Publications The agency publishes ten magazines and some commercial bulletins in twenty languages, most of them printed at Regional Service Centers in Manila and Mexico City. The contents consist largely of reprints from American periodicals. Pamphlets, leaflets, printed exhibits, and posters also are distributed in more than 100 countries.

Exhibitions The agency produces an average of thirteen major exhibits a year, including solo exhibitions and major displays in international trade fairs and special international promotions.

The Federal Emergency Management Agency The Federal Emergency Management Agency is the central point of contact within the federal government for a wide range of emergency management activities in both peace and war. The director of FEMA reports to the president and works closely in emergency matters with the National Security Council, the Cabinet, and the White House staff. FEMA has a staffing level of approximately 2,500. There are ten regional offices located around the United States.

Because highly trained emergency managers are essential to effective emergency management, the agency operates its National Emergency Training Center in Emmitsburg, Maryland. On this campus are the Emergency Management Institute, which offers training in the areas of national security, technological hazards, natural hazards, and emergency processes, and the National Fire Academy, which offers training to the nation's fire service and allied professionals in fire prevention and control activities.

The FEMA coordinates civil emergency preparedness for nuclear attack, nuclear power plant accidents, and nuclear weapons accidents and coordinates mobilization of resources during national security emergencies. It also operates the federal aid programs for presidentially declared disasters and emergencies. And the agency administers national flood insurance, crime insurance, and riot reinsurance programs.

The United States Commission on Civil Rights The United States Commission on Civil Rights is an independent, bipartisan, fact-finding agency established under the Civil Rights Act of 1957. The Commission investigates sworn allegations that certain citizens are being deprived of their right to vote by reason of color, race, religion, sex, age, handicap, or national origin or by reason of fraud. It also serves as a national clearinghouse for information in respect to discrimination or denials of equal protection because of color, race, religion, sex, age, handicap, or national origin. Since it lacks enforcement powers that would enable it to apply specific remedies in individual cases, it refers the many complaints it receives to the appropriate government agency for action. In 1982, the Commission was very active in the process resulting in a ten-year extension of the Voting Rights Act which prohibits states and political subdivisions from maintaining or establishing voting practices which have the effect of discriminating against individuals on the basis of their race, color, or language.

The Equal Employment Opportunity Commission The U.S. Equal Employment Opportunity Commission was created by Title VII of the Civil Rights Act of 1964. It is responsible for the enforcement of Title VII which prohibits employment discrimination on the basis of race, color, religion, sex, or national origin. It also administers the Age Discrimination in Employment Act and the Equal Pay Act.

EEOC has five commissioners and a general counsel appointed by the president and confirmed by the Senate. Commissioners are appointed for five-year staggered terms. The EEOC staff receives and investigates employment discrimination charges and, if cause is found, attempts to conciliate the charges. When conciliation is not achieved, the commission may file lawsuits in federal district court against private employers, labor organizations, and employment agencies.

Employment discrimination by private employers, state and local governments, educational institutions, and labor organizations having fifteen or more employees is prohibited. So also is employment discrimination by the federal government, private and public employment agencies, and joint labor-management committees for apprenticeship and training. It is unlawful for an employer to discriminate with regard to classified advertisements, recruitment, testing, hiring or firing, compensation, assignment, classification of employees, transfer, promotion, layoff, recall, use of company facilities, training and apprenticeship programs, fringe benefits such as life and health insurance, pay, retirement plans, disability leaves, or other terms and conditions of employment or to retaliate against individuals who oppose unlawful employment practices or attempt to exercise their rights under the statute.

It is unlawful for labor unions to discriminate with regard to applications for membership, segregation or classification of members, referrals for employment, training and apprenticeship programs, other discriminatory conduct, classified advertisements or to retaliate against individuals who oppose unlawful employment practices.

Remedies under Title VII may include requiring an employer, union, or employment agency to end discriminatory practices and systems, to institute equal employment practices and systems, and in some cases, to provide specific financial or other compensation for victims of discrimination. Remedies may involve reinstatement, hiring, reassignment, promotion, training, seniority rights, backpay, and other compensation and benefits. The maximum backpay award under Title VII is two years prior to the filing of the charge. Affirmative action plans, which may include goals and timetables for increasing the number of minorities and women in an employer's workforce, also may be required.

The Equal Pay Act protects women and men against pay discrimination based on sex. It prohibits sex discrimination in the payment of wages to women and men performing substantially equal work in the same establishment. However, the law does not apply to pay differences based on factors other than sex (e.g., seniority, merit, or systems that reward worker productivity). Penalties for employer violations of the Equal Pay Act include payment of back wages, interest, liquidated damages, attorney's fees, and court costs. Criminal penalties may also apply. Suit may be brought by EEOC or by the complainant. Back wages may be recovered for a period of two years prior to filing of suit, except in the case of willful violation, where three years of backpay may be recovered. Under the EPA, confidentiality of all complainants is protected, and employers are prohibited from retaliating against any employee who files a complaint or participates in an investigation. Equal Pay complaints can be taken in person, by mail, or over the telephone at any EEOC district or area office.

The Age Discrimination in Employment Act protects workers aged forty to seventy from arbitrary age discrimination in hiring, discharge, pay, promotions, fringe benefits, and other aspects of employment. It applies to private employers of twenty or more workers; federal, state, local governments and employment agencies; and labor organizations with twenty-five or more members. The law does not apply if an age requirement or limit is: (1) a bona fide job qualification, (2) part of a bona fide seniority system or employee benefit plan, or (3) based on reasonable factors other than age. Filing requirements, penalties, etc., are similar to those under the Equal Pay Act.

A person who believes that he or she has been discriminated against under any of these statutes when applying for a job, on the job, or in the terms and conditions of employment because of race, color, religion, sex, national origin, or age may file a charge of discrimination against the employer at any field office of the U.S. Equal Employment Opportunity Commission (the offices are located in forty-nine cities throughout the United States). Federal employees must file with their own agency. The individual complainant is counseled as to what to expect while the charge is being investigated. The charge itself is put into writing, and the employer is notified to come to a fact-finding conference to discuss the allegations in the charge. Information obtained at the fact-finding conference is used to help resolve the charge with a settlement. If settlement is impossible or inappropriate, the charge is investigated further by a Continued Investigation and Conciliation Unit. Most charges are conciliated or settled before the case actually goes to trial. If the commission decides to litigate, a lawsuit is filed in federal district court. If the commission decides not to litigate itself, a right to sue letter is issued which permits the individual to take the case to federal court.

Cases

The president will have all of the necessary weapons needed to control inflation.

AMALGAMATED MEAT CUTTERS v. CONNALLY

United States District Court, District of Columbia, 1971.
337 F.Supp. 737.

In this litigation Plaintiff Union, the Amalgamated Meat Cutters suing on its own behalf and on behalf of its affiliated local unions, attacks the constitutionality of the Economic Stabilization Act of 1970.[1]
* * *

Two different actions are consolidated in the complaint. Count II seeks to require the major meat packing companies to perform their obligations, under their 1970 collective bargaining agreements with the Union, to grant a general wage increase of twenty-five cents an hour effective September 6, 1971. The Union asserts this wage increase was agreed upon in April 1970 after long and difficult negotiations, that the parties carefully weighed alternative benefits and concessions before agreeing on the specific provisions, and that its inclusion was decisive in obtaining the Union's acceptance. The employers respond that the implementation of the wage increase obligation would violate Executive Order 11615, 36 F.R. 15727, promulgated by President Nixon August 15, 1971.

This Executive Order, Stabilization of Prices, Rents, Wages and Salaries, establishes a 90-day price-wage freeze, a requirement that "prices, rents, wages and salaries

1. This title may be cited as the "Economic Stabilization Act of 1970."

§ 202. *Presidential authority*

(a) The President is authorized to issue such orders and regulations as he may deem appropriate to stabilize prices, rents, wages, and salaries at levels not less than those prevailing on May 25, 1970. Such orders and regulations may provide for the making of such adjustments as may be necessary to prevent gross inequities.

§ 203. *Delegation*

The President may delegate the performance of any function under this title to such officers, departments, and agencies of the United States as he may deem appropriate.

§ 204. *Penalty*

Whoever willfully violates any order or regulation under this title shall be fined not more than $5,000.

shall be stabilized for a period of 90 days" at levels no greater than the highest rates pertaining to a substantial volume of actual transactions by the seller of commodities or services involved in a specified base period preceding August 15. The Union's position is that this defense is insufficient as a matter of law because the Act is unconstitutional and the Executive Order invalid.

The broader aspect of the controversy before us appears in Count I of the complaint, an action brought against John B. Connally, who as Secretary of the Treasury is Chairman of the Cost of Living Council, and the other officials constituting the Council. In Executive Order 11615 President Nixon established the Cost of Living Council "which shall act as an agency of the United States," specified that it shall be composed of certain designated officials as members and "delegated to the Council all of the powers conferred on the President by the Economic Stabilization Act of 1970."

The main claim of the Union is that the Act unconstitutionally delegates legislative power to the President, in violation of the general constitutional principle of the Separation of Powers, and in contravention of Article I, Section I of the Constitution, which provides: "All legislative Powers herein granted shall be vested in a Congress of the United States."

* * * [I]t is difficult to define the line which separates legislative power to make laws, from administrative authority to make regulations." There is no analytical difference, no difference in kind, between the legislative function—of prescribing rules for the future—that is exercised by the legislature or by the agency implementing the authority conferred by the legislature. The problem is one of limits

* * *

The issue is whether the legislative description of the task assigned "sufficiently marks the field within which the Administrator is to act so that it may be known whether he has kept within it in compliance with the legislative will."

* * * Concepts of control and accountability define the constitutional requirement. The principle permitting a delegation of legislative power, if there has been sufficient demarcation of the field to permit a judgment whether the agency has kept within the legislative will, establishes a principle of accountability under which compatibility with the legislative design may be ascertained not only by Congress but by the courts and the public. That principle was conjoined in *Yakus* with a recognition that the burden is on the party who assails the legislature's choice of means for effecting its purpose, a burden that is met "[o]nly if we could say that there is an absence of standards for the guidance of the Administrator's action, so that it would be impossible in a proper proceeding to ascertain whether the will of Congress has been obeyed[12]."

These doctrines have been applied to sustain legislation that delegated broad authority indeed in order to assure requisite flexibility to the officials or agencies designated to discharge the tasks assigned by the Congress. New York Central Securities Corp. v. United States, 287 U.S. 12, 24, 53 S.Ct. 45, 77 L.Ed. 138 (1932) (permitting consolidation of carriers when "in the public interest"); FPC v. Hope Natural Gas Co., 320 U.S. 591, 600, 64 S.Ct. 281, 88 L.Ed. 333 (1944) ("just and reasonable" rates for natural gas); Nat'l Broadcasting Co. v. United States, 319 U.S. 190, 225–226, 63 S.Ct. 997, 87 L.Ed. 1344 (1943) (licensing of radio communications "as public convenience, interest or necessity requires").

* * *

Under these governing concepts we can not say that in the Act before us there is such an absence of standards that it would be impossible to ascertain whether the will of Congress has been obeyed.

In some respects, indeed, Congress has been precise in its limitations. The Presi-

12. Yakus v. United States, 321 U.S. at 426, 64 S.Ct. at 668.

dent is given an authority to stabilize prices and wages by § 202(a) of the Act, but not at levels less than those prevailing on May 25, 1970.

* * *

Congress gave the President broad authority to stabilize prices, rents, wages and salaries, but in effect it contemplated that controls to achieve broad stabilization would begin with a regulation applicable to the entire economy. While the subject matter was broad, the technique was relatively confined. Confronted with the continuing and escalating inflation, Congress made its will relatively plain, by giving the President authority to halt the inflationary escalation with the issuance of a regulation providing across-the-board controls. The House Banking and Currency Committee Report specifically envisaged a 3-month "freeze" to get "a handle on inflation."

* * *

The House Report states (at p. 10) that the provisions were proposed so that "the President will have all of the necessary weapons needed to control inflation." And the Committee added:

> No one can doubt that inflation is still on a rampage in our economy. The cost-of-living figures released on July 22 indicated that prices have risen in the first half of this year at a 6 percent annual rate. Granted that this rate of increase is insignificantly less than that experienced in the first half of last year, this in no way provides any solace to the unemployed, the aged, and others living on fixed incomes, and the wage earner who finds his wages continually eroded by increases in the cost of living. This same inflation is responsible for the housing depression, the balance-of-payments crisis and the current liquidity squeeze.

* * * We see no merit in the contention that the Act is constitutionally defective because the timing of the imposition of controls was delegated to the President.

* * * Congress * * * sought in the national interest to have the right remedy available on a standby basis, if the President should wish to adopt that prescription, following his further reflection and taking into account future developments and experience.

* * *

Finally the House Report takes cognizance, in support of delegation of "timing" to the President, that Congress might not be in session when action was requisite.

* * *

The claim of undue delegation of legislative power broadly raises the challenge of undue power in the Executive and thus naturally involves consideration of the interrelated questions of the availability of appropriate restraints through provisions for administrative procedure and judicial review. * * *

The safeguarding of meaningful judicial review is one of the primary functions of the doctrine prohibiting undue delegation of legislative powers.

* * *

[C]hallenges may be made under the provisions for judicial review in the Administrative Procedure Act, 5 U.S.C. §§ 701–706.

* * *

We have no occasion to expatiate on these familiar provisions and principles for judicial review of agency actions, or to determine what kinds of agency action under the 1970 Act may be classified as "final" and reviewable, or when some court remedy other than direct review may be "adequate." We merely note that we see no indication whatever, * * * that the actions taken under the 1970 Act are removed from the judicial review provisions of 5 U.S.C. §§ 701–706. * * * They provide that a person suffering legal wrong because of agency action is entitled to review thereof, 5 U.S.C. § 702. Judicial review is provided for final agency action for which there is no other adequate remedy in court, 5 U.S.C. § 704.

When the impact of regulations is direct and immediate, so that the controversy is "ripe" for judicial resolution, these provisions of 5 U.S.C. §§ 701–706, permit pre-enforcement judicial review.

* * *

Our view of the applicable law makes it clear that plaintiff's motion for injunctive relief must be denied.

So ordered.

The "squeal rule" of the Department of Health and Human Services requiring notification to parents when contraceptives were prescribed to minors was beyond the powers of the agency.

PLANNED PARENTHOOD FEDERATION OF AMERICA, INC. v. HECKLER

United States Court of Appeal, District of Columbia Circuit, 1983.
712 F.2d 650.

WRIGHT, Circuit Judge

At issue in this case is the validity of regulations recently issued by the Secretary of the Department of Health and Human Services (HHS) requiring all providers of family planning services which receive funds under Title X of the Public Health Service Act (1) to notify parents or guardians within ten working days of prescribing contraceptives to unemancipated minors; (2) to comply with state laws requiring parental notice of, or consent to, the provision of any family planning services to minors; and (3) to consider minors who wish to receive services on the basis of their parents' financial resources, rather than their own. Numerous organizations and individuals joined in a consolidated action in the District Court to enjoin the Secretary from enforcing these regulations. The lower court entered a preliminary, and then a final, injunction prohibiting enforcement of the new regulations on the ground that they constitute invalid agency action in excess of statutory authority. Because we agree that the regulations are fundamentally inconsistent with Congress' intent and purpose in enacting Title X and are therefore beyond the limits of the Secretary's delegated authority, we affirm the decision below.

In 1970 Congress enacted Title X of the Public Health Service Act to establish a nationwide program with the express purpose of making "comprehensive family planning services readily available to all persons desiring such services." Congress authorized the Department of Health, Education and Welfare (HEW) to make grants and enter into contracts with public or nonprofit entities to assist in the establishment of family planning projects that offer a broad range of family planning methods, including the provision of prescription and nonprescription contraceptive drugs and devices. The Title X program was originally funded for three years, but has since been reauthorized and refunded continuously.

In light of the breadth of the statutory language and clear congressional intent that *all* persons receive such services, Title X grantees have served the teenage population from the inception of the program. Following enactment of Title X, however, Congress frequently expressed its increasing concern about the still unmet family planning needs of sexually active teenagers in this country. Ultimately, Congress in 1978 amended the statute itself to require that Title X projects offer "a broad range of acceptable and effective family planning methods and services (*including * * * services for adolescents*)." While this amendment simply codified accepted past practice, the added language clearly reflected Congress' intent to place "a special emphasis on preventing unwanted pregnancies among sexually active adolescents."

In 1981 Congress again amended Title X, this time to require by statute that grantees encourage family participation in their Title X programs. With this additional language, Section 300(a) of the Act now reads:

> The Secretary is authorized to make grants to and enter into contracts with public or nonprofit private entities to assist in the establishment and operation of voluntary family planning projects which shall offer a broad range of acceptable and effective family planning methods and services (including natural family planning methods, infertility services, and services for adolescents). *To the extent practical, entities which receive grants or contracts under this subsection shall encourage family participation in projects assisted under this subsection.*

42 U.S.C. § 300(a) (amendment emphasized).

On February 22, 1982 the Secretary published for public comment modifications of certain regulations governing Title X grants. Proposed as a means of implementing Congress' 1981 amendment to Title X, the new regulations seek to mandate the encouragement of family participation in three basic ways. First, and most significantly, they require Title X grantees to notify a parent or guardian within 10 working days of initially prescribing contraceptives to an unemancipated minor. Without verification that such notice was received, no further prescriptions may be provided to the minor.

Second, the regulations require Title X recipients to comply with any *state* law that mandates notification or consent of parent or guardian upon provision of family planning services to a minor. Finally, the new regulations redefine the statutory phrase "low-income family" so as to require Title X grantees to consider the economic eligibility of minors on the basis of their parents', rather than their own, financial resources.

As the Department itself acknowledged, public response to the proposed regulations was "overwhelming." Over 120,000 individuals and organizations contributed to the public comment. Among those opposing the proposed regulations were 19 major medical associations, including the American Medical Association and the American Psychiatric Association, 40 states, and the District of Columbia. On January 26, 1983 HHS nevertheless promulgated the final regulations, virtually unchanged. They were accompanied by a 15-page preamble that generally discussed the comments submitted and the reasons for the new rules. The regulations were to take effect on February 25, 1983.

On February 18, 1983 the District Court, * * * concluded that the regulations requiring parental notification "are outside the scope of the agency's authorizing legislation, and are therefore invalid." The court also held that the other two requirements—compliance with state parental notification and consent laws and redefinition of adolescent financial eligibility—are similarly invalid for violating the intent of Title X. Since the court found that the regulations were promulgated in excess of statutory authority, it did not rule on plaintiffs' allegations that the regulations are arbitrary and capricious and abridge the constitutional privacy rights of mature minors.

* * *

This appeal presents a straightforward issue of statutory construction. Urging reversal of the decision below, appellants, the Secretary and HHS, argue that the new regulations are perfectly consistent with the language and intent of the 1981 amendment to Title X and are therefore not in excess of statutory authority. Before addressing the merits of this assertion, we outline briefly this court's scope of review.

An essential function of the reviewing court is to guard against bureaucratic excesses by ensuring that administrative agencies remain within the bounds of their delegated authority. To that end, it falls within the province of this court to interpret the proper limits of Congress' delegation of authority in Title X and to determine whether the challenged regulations traverse those limits. As appellants duly point out, the rulemaking authority that Congress has delegated to the Secretary is broad indeed:

> Grants and contracts made under this subchapter shall be made in accordance with such regulations as the Secretary may promulgate. * * *

42 U.S.C. § 300a–4(a).

Yet, however sweeping this delegation of authority, it is not unlimited. We will declare regulations in excess of statutory authority if they "bear[ ] no relationship to any recognized concept of" the particular statutory terms at issue. Agency action must be found to be consistent with the congressional purposes underlying the authorizing statute. In short, these regulations can be sustained only if this "reviewing court [is] reasonably able to conclude that the grant of authority contemplates the regulations issued."

Appellants further contend that, in construing the reaches of Title X, we must give great deference to the Secretary's own interpretation of the statute. While courts frequently do give substantial deference to the administering agency's interpretation of its statute, the deference accorded does vary from case to case, and under certain circumstances can dissipate altogether:

> [D]eference must have limits where, as here, application of the [agency's statutory interpretation] would be inconsistent with an obvious congressional intent * * *. Courts need not defer to an administrative construction of a statute where there are "compelling indications that it is wrong."

In the present case there are indeed "compelling indications" that the Secretary has misconstrued Congress' intent in enacting the 1981 amendment to Title X. Our own careful review of the language of the statute and its legislative history makes it clear that these regulations not only violate Congress' specific intent as to the issue of parental notification, but also undermine the fundamental purposes of the Title X program. It is to this statutory analysis we now turn.

"[T]he starting point for interpreting a statute is the language of the statute itself." The 1981 amendment to Title X consists of just one simple sentence:

> To the extent practical, entities which receive grants or contracts under this subsection shall encourage family participation in projects assisted under this subsection.

According to the Secretary, the statute's use of the word "shall" imposes a nondiscretionary duty upon Title X grantees to communicate with the teenager's parents so as to involve them in their child's contraceptive decisions. We cannot agree. Certainly the use of the word "shall" presumptively implies some type of mandatory obligation on grantees. But the nature of that obligation is defined by the word "encourage." As the District Court noted, Congress' choice of this permissive and nonobligatory term is in itself revealing. Had Congress intended to mandate parental involvement, it could easily have done so with more appropriate and less ambiguous language such as "shall *require* family participation" or "shall *notify* the family."

Indeed, the very concept of encouragement is further weakened by the use of a qualifier "to the extent practical." While no specific content may be given that phrase from the face of the statute, its use indicates Congress' intent that the goal of encouraging family participation may well have to give way to other, more practical considerations. Contrary to appellant's assertions, then, the express language of the statute certainly does not lend support to the Secretary's interpretation of the amendment as "reasonably contemplat[ing]" a parental notification requirement.

Our inquiry into the congressional intent behind the 1981 amendment need not end with a simple parsing of the express terms of the statute. Although we find that the "plain meaning" of the statute is clear from its terms, we note that the legislative history is equally illuminating in this case. In particular, because appellants attach meaning to the fact that the statute does not expressly indicate precisely *how* Title X entities "shall encourage" family participation, reference to the legislative history is essential.

The Conference Committee report accompanying the 1981 amendment specifically addressed the new sentence:

> The conferees believe that, *while family involvement is not mandated*, it is important

> that families participate in the activities authorized by this title as much as possible. It is the intent of the conferees that *grantees will encourage participants* in Title X programs to *include their families* in counseling and involve them in decisions about services.

We find this Conference Report statement to be a crystal-clear and unequivocal expression of congressional intent—an intent that controls the Secretary in the exercise of her or his rulemaking authority. Several points emerge from the Conference Committee's explanation of the amendment. In enacting the amendment to encourage family participation, Congress most definitely did *not* intend to *mandate* family involvement. It is impossible to conceive of a more intelligible way to convey that meaning than the comment made by the committee. Thus, to the extent that the parental notification requirement of the new regulations operates to *require* family involvement, it is inconsistent with Congress' intent.

* * *

Congress * * * has long recognized not only the importance of family involvement, but the crucial importance as well of preserving patient confidentiality in the Title X program. In 1972 the Secretary first promulgated a regulation to ensure doctor-patient confidentiality in Title X programs. These regulations remain in effect unchanged.

Congress was fully aware of this consistent administrative practice and in particular recognized the critical role played by the assurance of confidentiality in attracting adolescents to the clinics. For example, the Senate report accompanying the 1977 reauthorization of Title X expressly acknowledged that teenagers more readily seek family planning services at Title X facilities precisely because of the policy of patient confidentiality:

> [T]he Committee believes HEW must not overlook the preference of many individuals, particularly the teenage target group, for family planning clinics as the initial entry point to family planning information and services. This preference is due partially to the greater degree of *teenage confidence in the confidentiality which can be assured by a family planning clinic* and in the proficiency of the family planning services provided in a clinic specializing in those and related services.

Thus Congress made clear that confidentiality was essential to attract adolescents to the Title X clinics; without such assurances, one of the primary purposes of Title X—to make family planning services readily available to teenagers—would be severely undermined.

* * *

Having determined that the new regulations' parental notification requirement is inconsistent with Congress' intent in Title X and finds no support in Title XX, we need not tarry long in disposing of appellants' arguments as to the other two requirements.

The Secretary's requirement that Title X grantees comply with prevailing state law as to parental notification or consent constitutes an invalid delegation of authority to the states. As the District Court found:

> Although Congress is free to permit the states to establish eligibility requirements for recipients of Title X funds, Congress has not delegated that power to the states. Title X does not provide, or suggest, that states are permitted to determine eligibility criteria for participants in Title X programs. * * *

In the absence of Congress' express authorization to HHS to in turn empower the states to set eligibility criteria, the Secretary has no power to do so. Therefore, in enacting such a regulation in this case the Secretary has exceeded the limits of Congress' delegated authority.

Furthermore, even if Congress had authorized the Secretary to delegate to the states the power to set eligibility standards, the state laws would still have to conform with the existing requirements of Title X and its regulations. It is elementary that under the Supremacy Clause of the Constitution states are not permitted to establish eligibility standards for federal assistance programs that conflict with the existing federal statutory or regulatory scheme. * * *

Since we have concluded that, the continuing policies of Title X prohibit the Secretary from requiring parental notification, the states would likewise be precluded from imposing similar conditions.

The elimination of the current regulation as to teenagers' financial eligibility is clearly entailed by the Secretary's imposition of the parental notification requirement. The new regulation deletes the following: "[U]nemancipated minors who wish to receive services on a confidential basis must be considered on the basis of their own resources." If the confidentiality of adolescents is no longer to be respected, then the above requirement is logically unnecessary.

However, since the parental notification requirement is invalid, then so too is this change in determining financial eligibility. We thus agree with the reasoning of the District Court: the regulation requiring that an adolescent's eligibility for services be based on her parents', rather than her own, income is invalid "because it has the same effect as the parental notification requirement." Clearly, if a minor must obtain financial information from her parents to determine her own eligibility for family planning services, the regulation denies her the requisite confidentiality and operates as a *de facto* parental notification requirement. Indeed, if the parents do not meet the eligibility standards and the minor has no funds of her own, the regulation may operate as a *de facto* parental *consent* rule; by withholding funds, the parents can prevent the teenager from receiving any contraceptive services at Title X clinics. Either way, the regulation operates as a deterrent to teenage access to contraceptive services, thereby undermining Title X's goal of reducing the teenage pregnancy rate.

Moreover, the regulation also conflicts with Title X's specific admonition that the Secretary define "low-income" families in such a way as to insure that "economic status shall not be a deterrent to participation in the programs assisted under [Title X]." Reflecting its general concern about the problems of adolescent pregnancy, Congress clearly intended to include *all* adolescents—not just those from low-income families—among the groups benefited by Title X. In short, the new financial eligibility requirement conflicts with the basic purpose and express provisions of Title X, finds no basis elsewhere in the Act, and is therefore invalid.

This court is, of course, fully aware that these Title X regulations are at the center of a great whirlwind of public controversy. No doubt the moral and political wisdom of the Secretary's actions will remain in dispute for some time to come. The legality of those actions, however, should not. Our review of Title X and its legislative history leads to the inescapable conclusion that the Secretary exceeded the bounds of statutory authority by promulgating regulations that contravene congressional intent.

We hold that the challenged regulations are unlawful. The judgment of the District Court enjoining enforcement of the regulations is therefore

Affirmed.

No warrantless search of the working areas of the business.

MARSHALL v. BARLOW'S INC.

Supreme Court of the United States, 1978.
436 U.S. 307, 98 S.Ct. 1816, 56 L.Ed.2d 305.

Mr. Justice WHITE delivered the opinion of the Court.

Section 8(a) of the Occupational Safety and Health Act of 1970 (OSHA or Act) empowers agents of the Secretary of Labor (Secretary) to search the work area of any employment facility within the Act's jurisdiction. The purpose of the search is to inspect for safety hazards and violations of OSHA regulations. No search warrant or other process is expressly required under the Act.

On the morning of September 11, 1975, an OSHA inspector entered the customer service area of Barlow's Inc., an electrical and plumbing installation business located in Pocatello, Idaho. The president and general manager, Ferrol G. "Bill" Barlow, was on hand; and the OSHA inspector, after showing his credentials, informed Mr. Barlow that he wished to conduct a search of the working areas of the business. Mr. Barlow inquired whether any complaint had been received about his company. The inspector answered no, but that Barlow's Inc., had simply turned up in the agency's selection process. The inspector again asked to enter the nonpublic area of the business; Mr. Barlow's response was to inquire whether the inspector had a search warrant. The inspector had none. Thereupon, Mr. Barlow refused the inspector admission to the employee area of his business. He said he was relying on his rights as guaranteed by the Fourth Amendment of the United States Constitution.

Three months later, the Secretary petitioned the United States District Court for the District of Idaho to issue an order compelling Mr. Barlow to admit the inspector. The requested order was issued on December 30, 1975, and was presented to Mr. Barlow on January 5, 1976. Mr. Barlow again refused admission, and he sought his own injunctive relief against the warrantless searches assertedly permitted by OSHA. A three-judge court was convened. On December 30, 1976, it ruled in Mr. Barlow's favor.

* * *

[T]he court held that the Fourth Amendment required a warrant for the type of search involved here and that the statutory authorization for warrantless inspections was unconstitutional. An injunction against searches or inspections pursuant to § (8)a was entered. The Secretary appealed.

* * *

The Warrant Clause of the Fourth Amendment protects commercial buildings as well as private homes. To hold otherwise would belie the origin of that Amendment, and the American colonial experience.

The general warrant was a recurring point of contention in the Colonies immediately preceding the Revolution. The particular offensiveness it engendered was accutely felt by the merchants and businessmen whose premises and products were inspected for compliance with the several parliamentary revenue measures that most irritated the colonists.

* * *

Against this background, it is untenable that the ban on warrantless searches was not intended to shield places of business as well as of residence.

* * *

The businessman like the occupant of a residence, has a constitutional right to go about his business free from unreasonable official entries upon his private commercial property. The businessman, too, has that right placed in jeopardy if the decision to enter and inspect for violation of regulatory laws can be made and enforced by the inspector in the field without official authority evidenced by a warrant." *See v. City of Seattle, supra,* 387 U.S., at 543, 87 S.Ct., at 1739. * * * [T]he Fourth Amendment prohibition against unreasonable searches protects against warrantless intrusions during civil as well as criminal investigations. *Ibid.* The reason is found in the "basic purpose of this Amendment . . . [which] is to safeguard the privacy and security of individuals against arbitrary invasions by governmental officials." *Camara, supra,* 387 U.S., at 528, 87 S.Ct. at 1730. If the government intrudes on a person's property, the privacy interest suffers whether the government's motivation is to investigate violations of criminal laws or breaches of other statutory or regulatory standards. * * *

The Secretary also attempts to derive support for a *Colonnade-Biswell*-type exception by drawing analogies from the field of labor law.

[However,] [t]he owner of a business has not, by the necessary utilization of employees in his operation, thrown open the areas where employees alone are permitted to the warrantless scrutiny of Government agents. That an employee is free to report, and the Government is free to use, any evidence of noncompliance with OSHA that the employee observes furnishes no justification for federal agents to enter a place of business from which the public is restricted and to conduct their own warrantless search.

* * * Whether the Secretary proceeds to secure a warrant, with or without prior notice, his entitlement to inspect will not depend on his demonstrating probable cause to believe that conditions in violation of OSHA exist on the premises. Probable cause in the criminal law sense is not required. For purposes of an administrative search such as this, probable cause justifying the issuance of a warrant may be based not only on specific evidence of an existing violation but also on a showing that "reasonable legislative or administrative standards for conducting an . . . inspection are satisfied with respect to a particular [establishment.]"

* * *

A warrant showing that a specific business has been chosen for an OSHA search on the basis of a general administrative plan for the enforcement of the Act derived from neutral sources such as, for example, dispersion of employees in various types of industries across a given area, and the desired frequency of searches in any of the lesser divisions of the area, would protect an employer's Fourth Amendment rights. We doubt that the consumption of enforcement energies in the obtaining of such warrants will exceed manageable proportions.

* * * Nor do we agree that the incremental protections afforded the employer's privacy by a warrant are so marginal that they fail to justify the administrative burdens that may be entailed. The authority to make warrantless searches devolves almost unbridled discretion upon executive and administrative officers, particularly those in the field, as to when to search and whom to search. A warrant, by contrast, would provide assurances from a neutral officer that the inspection is reasonable under the Constitution, is authorized by statute, and is pursuant to an administrative plan containing specific neutral criteria. Also, a warrant would then and there advise the owner of the scope and objects of the search, beyond which limits the inspector is not expected to proceed. These are important functions for a warrant to perform, functions which underlie the Court's prior decisions that the Warrant Clause applies to inspections for compliance with regulatory statutes.

* * *

We conclude that the concerns expressed by the Secretary do not suffice to justify warrantless inspections under OSHA or vitiate the general constitutional requirement that for a search to be reasonable a warrant must be obtained.

We hold that Barlow's was entitled to a declaratory judgment that the Act is unconstitutional insofar as it purports to authorize inspections without warrant or its equivalent and to an injunction enjoining the Act's enforcement to that extent. The judgment of the District Court is therefore affirmed.

So ordered.

An evidentiary hearing may not be the most effective method of decision making in all circumstances.

MATHEWS v. ELDRIDGE

Supreme Court of the United States, 1976.
424 U.S. 319, 96 S.Ct. 893, 47 L.Ed.2d 18.

Mr. Justice POWELL delivered the opinion of the Court.

The issue in this case is whether the Due Process Clause of the Fifth Amendment requires that prior to the termination of Social Security disability benefit payments the recipient be afforded an opportunity for an evidentiary hearing.

Cash benefits are provided to workers during periods in which they are completely disabled under the disability insurance benefits program. * * * Respondent Eldridge was first awarded benefits in June 1968. In March 1972, he received a questionnaire from the state agency charged with monitoring his medical condition. Eldridge completed the questionnaire, indicating that his condition had not improved and identifying the medical sources, including physicians, from whom he had received treatment recently. The state agency then obtained reports from his physician and a psychiatric consultant. After considering these reports and other information in his file the agency informed Eldrige by letter that it had made a tentative determination that his disability had ceased in May 1972. The letter included a statement of reasons for the proposed termination of benefits, and advised Eldridge that he might request reasonable time in which to obtain and submit additional information pertaining to his condition.

In his written response, Eldridge disputed one characterization of his medical condition and indicated that the agency already had enough evidence to establish his disability. The state agency then made its final determination that he had ceased to be disabled in May 1972. This determination was accepted by the Social Security Administration (SSA), which notified Eldridge in July that his benefits would terminate after that month. The notification also advised him of his right to seek reconsideration by the state agency of this initial determination within six months.

Instead of requesting reconsideration Eldridge commenced this action challenging the constitutional validity of the administrative procedures established by the Secretary of Health, Education, and Welfare for assessing whether there exists a continuing disability. He sought an immediate reinstatement of benefits pending a hearing on the issue of his disability. * * * The Secretary moved to dismiss on the grounds that Eldridge's benefits had been terminated in accordance with valid administrative regulations and procedures and that he had failed to exhaust available remedies. In support of his contention that due process requires a pretermination hearing, Eldridge relied exclusively upon this Court's decision in *Goldberg v. Kelly,* 397 U.S. 254, 90 S.Ct. 1011, 25 L.Ed.2d 287 (1970), which established a right to an "evidentiary hearing" prior to termination of welfare benefits. The Secretary contended that *Goldberg* was not controlling since eligibility for disability benefits, unlike eligibility for welfare benefits, is not based on financial need and since issues of credibility and veracity do not play a significant role in the disability entitlement decision, which turns primarily on medical evidence.

The District Court concluded that the administrative procedures pursuant to which the Secretary had terminated Eldridge's benefits abridged his right to procedural due process. * * * [T]he District Court held that prior to termination of benefits Eldridge had to be afforded an evidentiary hearing. * * *

At the outset we are confronted by a question as to whether the District Court had jurisdiction over this suit.

* * * The only avenue for judicial review is 42 U.S.C. § 405(g), which requires exhaustion of the administrative remedies provided under the Act as a jurisdictional prerequisite. * * *

On its face § 405(g) bars judicial review of any denial of a claim of disability benefits until after a "final decision."

* * *

We conclude that the denial of Eldridge's request for benefits constitutes a final decision for purposes of § 405(g) jurisdiction over his constitutional claim.

* * *

Procedural due process imposes constraints on governmental decisions which deprive individuals of "liberty" or "property" interests within the meaning of the Due Process Clause of the Fifth or Fourteenth Amendment. The Secretary does not contend that procedural due process is inapplicable to terminations of Social Security disability benefits. * * *

Rather, the Secretary contends that the existing administrative procedures, detailed below, provide all the process that is constitutionally due before a recipient can be deprived of that interest.

* * * The fundamental requirement of due process is the opportunity to be heard "at a meaningful time and in a meaningful manner."

* * *

Eldridge agrees that the review procedures available to a claimant before the initial determination of ineligibility becomes final would be adequate if disability benefits were not terminated until after the evidentiary hearing stage of the administrative process. The dispute centers upon what process is due prior to the initial termination of benefits, pending review.

In recent years this Court increasingly has had occasion to consider the extent to which due process requires an evidentiary hearing prior to the deprivation of some type of property interest even if such a hearing is provided thereafter. In only one case, *Goldberg v. Kelly,* 397 U.S., at 266–271, 90 S.Ct., at 1019–1022, 25 L.Ed.2d 287, has the Court held that a hearing closely approximating a judicial trial is necessary.

* * *

Since a recipient whose benefits are terminated is awarded full retroactive relief if he ultimately prevails, his sole interest is in the uninterrupted receipt of this source of income pending final administrative decision on his claim. His potential injury is thus similar in nature to that of the welfare recipient in *Goldberg.* * * *

Only in *Goldberg* has the Court held that due process requires an evidentiary hearing prior to a temporary deprivation. It was emphasized there that welfare assistance is given to persons on the very margin of subsistence:

> The crucial factor in this context—a factor not present in the case of . . . virtually anyone else whose governmental entitlements are ended—is that termination of aid pending resolution of a controversy over eligibility may deprive an *eligible* recipient of the very means by which to live while he waits.

* * *

Eligibility for disability benefits, in contrast, is not based upon financial need. Indeed, it is wholly unrelated to the worker's income or support from many other sources, such as earnings of other family members, workmen's compensation awards, tort claims awards, savings, private insurance, public or private pensions, veterans' benefits, food stamps, public assistance, or the "many other important programs, both public and private, which contain provisions for disability payments affecting a substantial portion of the work force . . . ."

* * *

In addition to the possibility of access to private resources, other forms of government assistance will become available where the termination of disability benefits places a worker or his family below the subsistence level.

* * *

In view of these potential sources of temporary income, there is less reason here than in *Goldberg* to depart from the ordinary principle, established by our decisions, that something less than an evidentiary hearing is sufficient prior to adverse administrative action.

* * *

An additional factor to be considered here is the fairness and reliability of the existing pretermination procedures, and the probable value, if any, of additional procedural safeguards. Central to the evaluation of any administrative process is the nature of the relevant inquiry.

In order to remain eligible for benefits the disabled worker must demonstrate by means of "medically acceptable clinical and laboratory diagnostic techniques," * * * that he is unable "to engage in any substantial gainful activity by reason of any *medically determinable* physical or mental impairment . . . ." * * * In short, a medical assessment of the worker's physical or mental condition is required. This is a more sharply focused and easily documented decision than the typical determination of welfare entitlement. In the latter case, a wide variety of information may be deemed relevant, and issues of witness credibility and veracity often are critical to the decisionmaking process. *Goldberg* noted that in such circumstances "written submissions are a wholly unsatisfactory basis for decision."

By contrast, the decision whether to discontinue disability benefits will turn, in most cases, upon "routine, standard, and unbiased medical reports by physician specialists," * * * concerning a subject whom they have personally examined.

* * *

The potential value of an evidentiary hearing, or even oral presentation to the decisionmaker, is substantially less in this context than in *Goldberg.*

The decision in *Goldberg* also was based on the Court's conclusion that written submissions were an inadequate substitute for oral presentation because they did not provide an effective means for the recipient to communicate his case to the decisionmaker. Written submissions were viewed as an unrealistic option, for most recipients lacked the "educational attainment necessary to write effectively" and could not afford professional assistance. In addition, such submissions would not provide the "flexibility of oral presentations" or "permit the recipient to mold his argument to the issues the decision maker appears to regard as important." * * * In the context of the disability-benefits-entitlement assessment the administrative procedures under review here fully answer these objections.

The detailed questionnaire which the state agency periodically sends the recipient identifies with particularity the information relevant to the entitlement decision, and the recipient is invited to obtain assistance from the local SSA office in completing the questionnaire. More important, the information critical to the entitlement decision usually is derived from medical sources, such as the treating physician. Such sources are likely to be able to communicate more effectively through written documents than are welfare recipients or the lay witnesses supporting their cause. The conclusions of physicians often are supported by X-rays and the results of clinical or laboratory tests, information typically more amenable to written than to oral presentation. * * *

A further safeguard against mistake is the policy of allowing the disability recipient's representative full access to all information relied upon by the state agency. In addition, prior to the cutoff of benefits the agency informs the recipient of its tentative assessment, the reasons therefor, and provides a summary of the evidence that it considers most relevant. Opportunity is then afforded the recipient to submit additional evidence or arguments, enabling him to challenge directly the accuracy of information in his file as well as the correctness of the agency's tentative conclusions. These procedures, again as contrasted with those before the Court in *Goldberg,* enable the recipient to "mold" his argument to respond to the precise issues which the decisionmaker regards as crucial.

* * *

We reiterate the wise admonishment of Mr. Justice Frankfurter that differences in the origin and function of administrative agencies "preclude wholesale transplantation of the rules of procedure, trial and review which have evolved from the history and experience of courts."

The judicial model of an evidentiary hearing is neither a required, nor even the most effective, method of decisionmaking in all circumstances. The essence of due process is the requirement that "a person in jeopardy of serious loss [be given] notice of the case against him and opportunity to meet it." * * * All that is necessary is that the procedures be tailored, in light of the decision to be made, to "the capacities and circumstances of those who are to be heard," * * * to insure that they are given a meaningful opportunity to present their case. In assessing what process is due in this case, substantial weight must be given to the good-faith judgments of the individuals charged by Congress with the administration of social welfare programs that the procedures they have provided assure fair consideration of the entitlement claims of individuals. * * * This is especially so where, as here, the prescribed procedures not only provide the claimant with an effective process for asserting his claim prior to any administrative action, but also assure a right to an evidentiary hearing, as well as to subsequent judicial review, before the denial of his claim becomes final. * * *

We conclude that an evidentiary hearing is not required prior to the termination of disability benefits and that the present administrative procedures fully comport with due process.

The judgment of the Court of Appeals is

Reversed.

The FCC regulatory authority over cable television is not carte blanche.

HOME BOX OFFICE, INC. v. FEDERAL COMMUNICATIONS COMMISSION

United States Court of Appeals, District of Columbia Circuit, 1977.
567 F.2d 9.

In these 15 cases, consolidated for purposes of argument and decision, petitioners challenge various facets of four orders of the Federal Communications Commission which, taken together, regulate and limit the program fare "cablecasters" and "subscription broadcast television stations" may offer to the public for a fee set on a per-program or per-channel basis. * * *

At the heart of these cases are the Commission's "pay cable" rules. * * * The effect of these rules is to restrict sharply the ability of cablecasters to present feature film and sports programs if a separate program or channel charge is made for this material. In addition, the rules prohibit cablecasters from devoting more than 90 percent of their cablecast hours to movie and sports programs and further bar cablecasters from showing commercial advertising on cable channels on which programs are presented for a direct charge to the viewer. Virtually identical restrictions apply to subscription broadcast television.

* * *

[D]espite the latitude which must be given the Commission to deal with evolving technology, its regulatory authority over cable television is not a *carte blanche.* Unless these regulations are "justified by reasons which are properly the concern of [the Commission]," * * * they must be set aside.

* * *

[T]he Commission may only exercise authority over cable television to the extent "reasonably ancillary" to the Commission's jurisdiction over broadcast television.

* * *

The purpose of the Commission's pay cable rules is to prevent "siphoning" of feature film and sports material from conventional broadcast television to pay cable. Although there is dispute over the effectiveness of the rules, it is clear that their thrust is to prevent *any* competition by pay cable entrepreneurs for film or sports material that either has been shown on conventional television or is likely to be shown there. How such an effect furthers any legitimate goal of the Communications Act is not clear.

* * *

[We must] require that the Commission state clearly the harm which its regulations seek to remedy and its reasons for supposing that this harm exists.

* * *

[E]ach of the orders challenged here is the product of * * * informal rule making governed by Section 4 of the Administrative Procedure Act. * * *

We have recently had occasion to review at length our obligation to set aside agency action which is "arbitrary, capricious, an abuse of discretion, or otherwise not in accordance with law * * *."

* * * It is axiomatic that we may not substitute our judgment for that of the agency. * * * Yet our review must be "searching and careful," and we must ensure both that the Commission has adequately considered all relevant factors, and that it has demonstrated a "rational connection between the facts found and the choice made."

Equally important, an agency must comply with the procedures set out in Section 4 of the APA. * * *

The APA sets out three procedural requirements: notice of the proposed rulemaking, an opportunity for interested persons to comment, and "a concise general statement of [the] basis and purpose" of the rules ultimately adopted. 5 U.S.C. § 553(b)–(c). As interpreted by recent decisions of this court, these procedural requirements are intended to assist judicial review as well as to provide fair treatment for persons affected by a rule.

To this end there must be an *exchange* of views, information, and criticism between interested persons and the agency.

* * * Consequently, the notice required by the APA, or information subsequently supplied to the public, must disclose in detail the thinking that has animated the form of a proposed rule and the data upon which that rule is based.

* * * Moreover, a dialogue is a two-way street: the opportunity to comment is meaningless unless the agency responds to significant points raised by the public. * * *

At the outset, we must consider whether the Commission has made out a case for undertaking rulemaking at all since a "regulation perfectly reasonable and appropriate in the face of a given problem may be highly capricious if that problem does not exist." * * * Here the Commission has framed the problem it is addressing as

> how cablecasting can best be regulated to provide a beneficial supplement to over-the-air broadcasting without at the same time undermining the continued operation of that "free" television service.

* * * To state the problem this way, however, is to gloss over the fact that the Commission has in no way justified its position that cable television must be a supplement to, rather than an equal of, broadcast television. Such an artificial narrowing of the scope of the regulatory problem is itself arbitrary and capricious and is ground for reversal.

* * * The Justice Department and other petitioners have repeatedly pointed out that the conventional television industry is highly concentrated and is, therefore, likely to enjoy substantial monopoly and monopsony power.

* * *

"[C]ompetition is less rigorous in television than elsewhere in the economy."

* * *

[T]he Commission did not consider whether conventional television broadcasters could pay more for feature film and sports material than at present without pushing their profits below a competitive return on investment and, consequently, it could not properly conclude that siphoning would occur because it could not know whether or how much broadcasters, faced with competition, would increase their expenditures by reducing alleged monopoly profits. * * *

Equally important, the pay cable rules taken as a whole scarcely demonstrate a consistent solicitude for the poor. Thus, although "free" home viewing relies upon advertiser-supported programming, the Commission has in this proceeding barred cable firms from offering advertising in connection with subscription operations. As a result, the Commission forecloses the possibility that some combination of user fees and advertising might make subscription cable television available to the poor, giving them access to the diverse programming cable may potentially bring.

* * * We are thus left with the conclusion that, if the Commission is serious about helping the poor, its regulations are arbitrary; but if it is serious about its rules, it cannot really be relying on harm to the poor. Whatever may be the ultimate validity of this argument, its principal defect on this review is that there is no record evidence to support it.

* * *

It is apparently uncontested that a number of participants before the Commission sought out individual commissioners or Commission employees for the purpose of discussing *ex parte* and in confidence the merits of the rules under review here. In fact, the Commission itself solicited such communications in its notices of proposed rulemaking and, without discussing the nature, substance, or importance of what was said, argues before us that we should simply ignore these communications.

* * * To give a flavor of the effect of these contacts, * * * we think it useful to quote at length from the brief. * * *

> [*Ex parte*] presentations have in fact been made at crucial stages of the proceeding. Thus, in early 1974, then-Chairman Burch sought to complete action in this proceeding. Because the Commission was "leaning" in its deliberations towards relaxing the existing rules "with 'wildcard' rights for 'blockbuster' movies," American Broadcasting Company's representatives contacted "key members of Congress," who in turn successfully pressured the Commission not to take such action. Further, in the final crucial decisional period, the tentative course to be taken by the Commission would leak after each non-public meeting, and industry representatives would rush to make *ex parte* presentations to the Commissioners and staff. On March 10, 1975, the trade journals state that "word of last week's changes . . . got out during the week, and both broadcast and cable lobbyists rushed to the Commission, unhappy with some facets."

* * *

Although it is impossible to draw any firm conclusions about the effect of *ex parte* presentations upon the ultimate shape of the pay cable rules, the evidence is certainly consistent with often-voiced claims of undue industry influence over Commission proceedings, and we are particularly concerned that the final shaping of the rules we are reviewing here may have been by compromise among the contending industry forces, rather than by exercise of the independent discretion in the public interest the Communications Act vests in individual commissioners. * * * Our concern is heightened by the submission of the Commission's Broadcast Bureau to this court which states that in December 1974 broadcast representatives "described the kind of pay cable regulation that, in their view, broadcasters 'could live with.'" If actual positions were not revealed in public comments, as this statement would suggest, and, further, if the Commission relied on these apparently more candid private discussions in framing the final pay cable rules, then the elaborate public discussion in these dockets has been reduced to a sham.

Even the possibility that there is here one administrative record for the public and this court and another for the Commission and those "in the know" is intolerable. Whatever the law may have been in the past, there can now be no doubt that implicit in the decision to treat the promulgation of rules as a "final" event in an ongoing process of administration is an assumption that an act of reasoned judgment has occurred, an assumption which further contemplates the existence of a body of material—documents, comments, transcripts, and statements in various forms declaring agency expertise or policy—with reference to which such judgment was exercised. Against this material, "the full administrative record that was before [an agency official] at the time he made his decision," * * * it is the obligation of this court to test the actions of the Commission for arbitrariness or inconsistency with delegated authority. * * * Yet here agency secrecy stands between us and fulfillment of our obligation. * * * [T]he public record must reflect what representations were made to an agency so that relevant information supporting or refuting those representations may be brought to the attention of the reviewing courts by persons participating in agency proceedings. This course is obviously foreclosed if communications are made to the agency in secret and the agency itself does not disclose the information presented. Moreover, where, as here, an agency justifies its actions by reference only to information in the public file while failing to disclose the substance of other relevant information that has been presented to it, a reviewing court cannot presume that the agency has acted properly, * * * but must treat the agency's justifications as a fictional account of the actual decisionmaking process and must perforce find its actions arbitrary.

* * *

Equally important is the inconsistency of secrecy with fundamental notions of fairness implicit in due process and with the ideal of reasoned decisionmaking on the merits which undergirds all of our administrative law. * * * In the Government in the Sunshine Act, for example, Congress has declared it to be "the policy of the United States that the public is entitled to the fullest practicable information regarding the decisionmaking processes of the Federal Government," * * * and has taken steps to guard against *ex parte* contacts in formal agency proceedings.

* * *

From what has been said above, it should be clear that information gathered *ex parte* from the public which becomes relevant to a rulemaking will have to be disclosed at some time. On the other hand, we recognize that informal contacts between agencies and the public are the "bread and butter" of the process of administration and are completely appropriate so long as they do not frustrate judicial review or raise serious questions of fairness. Reconciliation of these considerations in a manner which will reduce procedural uncertainty leads us to conclude that communications which are received prior to issuance of a formal notice of rulemaking do not, in general, have to be put in a public file. Of course, if the information contained in such a communication forms the basis for agency action, then, under well established principles, that information must be disclosed to the public in some form. Once a notice of proposed rulemaking has been issued, however, any agency official or employee who is or may reasonably be expected to be involved in the decisional process of the rulemaking proceeding, should "refus[e] to discuss matters relating to the disposition of a [rulemaking proceeding] with any interested private party, or an attorney or agent for any such party, prior to the [agency's] decision." * * * If *ex parte* contacts nonetheless occur, we think that any written document or a summary of any oral communication must be placed in the public file established for each rulemaking docket immediately after the communication is received so that interested parties may comment thereon.

* * *

The regulations * * * are set aside * * *.

The National Highway Traffic Safety Administration was "arbitrary and capricious" in removing the requirement of airbags for new cars.

UNITED STATES DEPARTMENT OF TRANSPORTATION v. STATE FARM MUTUAL AUTOMOBILE INSURANCE CO.

Supreme Court of the United States, 1983.
— U.S. —, 103 S.Ct. 2856, 77 L.Ed.2d 443.

JUSTICE WHITE delivered the opinion of the Court.

The development of the automobile gave Americans unprecedented freedom to travel, but exacted a high price for enhanced mobility. Since 1929, motor vehicles have been the leading cause of accidental deaths and injuries in the United States. In 1982, 46,300 Americans died in motor vehicle accidents and hundreds of thousands more were maimed and injured. While a consensus exists that the current loss of life on our highways is unacceptably high, improving safety does not admit to easy solution. In 1966, Congress decided that at least part of the answer lies in improving the design and safety features of the vehicle itself. But much of the technology for building safer cars was undeveloped or untested. Before changes in automobile design could be mandated, the effectiveness of these changes had to be studied, their costs examined, and public acceptance considered. This task called for considerable expertise and Congress responded by enacting the National Traffic and Motor Vehicle Safety Act of 1966. The Act, created for the purpose of "reduc[ing] traffic accidents and deaths and injuries to persons resulting from traffic accidents," directs the Secretary of Transportation or his delegate to issue motor vehicle safety standards that "shall be practicable, shall meet the need for motor vehicle safety, and shall be stated in objective terms." In issuing these standards, the Secretary is directed to consider "relevant available motor vehicle safety data," whether the proposed standard "is reasonable, practicable and appropriate" for the particular type of motor vehicle, and the "extent to which such standards will contribute to carrying out the purposes" of the Act.

The Act also authorizes judicial review under the provisions of the Administrative Procedure Act (APA), 5 U.S.C. § 706 (1976), of all "orders establishing, amending, or revoking a Federal motor vehicle safety standard." Under this authority, we review today whether NHTSA [National Highway Traffic Safety Administration] acted arbitrarily and capriciously in revoking the requirement in Motor Vehicle Safety Standard 208 that new motor vehicles produced after September 1982 be equipped with passive restraints to protect the safety of the occupants of the vehicle in the event of a collision. Briefly summarized, we hold that the agency failed to present an adequate basis and explanation for rescinding the passive restraint requirement and that the agency must either consider the matter further or adhere to or amend Standard 208 along lines which its analysis supports.

The regulation whose rescission is at issue bears a complex and convoluted history. Over the course of approximately 60 rulemaking notices, the requirement has been imposed, amended, rescinded, reimposed, and now rescinded again.

As originally issued by the Department of Transportation in 1967, Standard 208 simply required the installation of seatbelts in all automobiles. It soon became apparent that the level of seatbelt use was too low to reduce traffic injuries to an acceptable level. The Department therefore began consideration of "passive occupant restraint systems"—devices that do not depend for their effectiveness upon any action taken by the occupant except that necessary to operate the vehicle. Two types of automatic crash protection emerged: automatic seatbelts and airbags. The automatic seatbelt is a traditional safety belt, which when fastened to the interior of the door remains attached without impeding entry or exist from the vehicle, and deploys automatically without any action on the part of the passenger. The airbag is an inflatable device concealed in the dashboard and steering column. It automatically inflates when a sensor indicates that deceleration forces from an accident have exceeded a preset minimum, then rapidly deflates to dissipate those forces. The life-saving potential of these devices was immediately recognized, and in 1977, after substantial on-the-road experience with both devices, it was estimated by NHTSA that passive restraints could prevent approximately 12,000 deaths and over 100,000 serious injuries annually.

In 1969, the Department formally proposed a standard requiring the installation of passive restraints. In 1970, the agency revised Standard 208 to include passive protection requirements * * *. The Modified Standard mandated the phasing in of passive restraints beginning with large cars in model year 1982 and extending to all cars by model year 1984. The two principal systems that would satisfy the Standard were airbags and passive belts; the choice of which system to install was left to the manufacturers. In *Pacific Legal Foundation* v. *Dep't of Transportation,* 593 F.2d 1338 (CADC), the Court of Appeals upheld Modified Standard 208 as a rational nonarbitrary regulation consistent with the agency's mandate under the Act.

Over the next several years, the automobile industry geared up to comply with Modified Standard 208. As late as July, 1980, NHTSA reported:

> "On the road experience in thousands of vehicles equipped with airbags and automatic safety belts has confirmed agency estimates of the life-saving and injury-preventing benefits of such systems. When all cars are equipped with automatic crash protection systems, each year an estimated 9,000 more lives will be saved and tens of thousands of serious injuries will be prevented." NHTSA, Automobile Occupant Crash Protection, Progress Report No. 3, p. 4 (App. 1627).

In February 1981, however, Secretary of Transportation Andrew Lewis reopened the rulemaking due to changed economic circumstances and, in particular, the difficulties of the automobile industry. Two months later, the agency ordered a one-year delay in the application of the standard to large cars, extending the deadline to September 1982, and at the same time, proposed the possible rescission of the entire standard. After receiving written comments and holding public hearings, NHTSA issued a final rule (Notice 25) that rescinded the passive restraint requirement contained in Modified Standard 208.

In a statement explaining the rescission, NHTSA maintained that it was no longer able to find, as it had in 1977, that the automatic restraint requirement would produce significant safety benefits. Notice 25, 46 Fed.Reg. 53,419 (Oct. 29, 1981). This judgment reflected not a change of opinion on the effectiveness of the technology, but a change in plans by the automobile industry. In 1977, the agency had assumed that airbags would be installed in 60% of all new cars and automatic seatbelts in 40%. By 1981 it became apparent that automobile manufacturers planned to install the automatic seatbelts in approximately 99% of the new cars. For this reason, the life-saving potential of airbags would not be realized. Moreover, it now appeared that the overwhelming majority of passive belts planned to be installed by manufacturers could be detached easily and left that way permanently. Passive belts, once detached, then required "the same type of affirmative action that is the stumbling block to obtaining high usage levels of manual belts." For this reason, the agency concluded that there was no longer a basis for reliably predicting that the standard would lead to any significant increased usage of restraints at all.

* * *

State Farm Mutual Automobile Insurance Co. and the National Association of Independent Insurers filed petitions for review of NHTSA's rescission of the passive restraint standard. The United States Court of Appeals for the District of Columbia Circuit held that the agency's rescission of the passive restraint requirement was arbitrary and capricious.

* * *

The Department of Transportation accepts the applicability of the "arbitrary and capricious" standard. It argues that under this standard, a reviewing court may not set aside an agency rule that is rational, based on consideration of the relevant factors and within the scope of the authority delegated to the agency by the statute. We do not disagree with this formulation. The scope of review under the "arbitrary and capricious" standard is narrow and a court is not to substitute its judgment for that of the agency. Nevertheless, the agency must examine the relevant data and articulate a satisfactory explanation for its action including a "rational connection between the facts found and the choice made." In reviewing that explanation, we must "consider whether the decision was based on a consideration of the relevant factors and whether there has been a clear error of judgment." Normally, an agency rule would be arbitrary and capricious if the agency has relied on factors which Congress has not intended it to consider, entirely failed to consider an important aspect of the problem, offered an explanation for its decision that runs counter to the evidence before the agency, or is so implausible that it could not be ascribed to a difference in view or the product of agency expertise. The reviewing court should not attempt itself to make up for such deficiencies: "We may not supply a reasoned basis for the agency's action that the agency itself has not given." We will, however, uphold a decision of less than ideal clarity "if the agency's path may reasonably be discerned."

* * *

The ultimate question before us is whether NHTSA's rescission of the passive restraint requirement of Standard 208 was arbitrary and capricious. We conclude, as did the Court of Appeals, that it was. We also conclude, * * * that further consideration of the issue by the agency is therefore required.

* * *

The first and most obvious reason for finding the rescission arbitrary and capricious is that NHTSA apparently gave no consideration whatever to modifying the Standard to require that airbag technology be utilized. Standard 208 sought to achieve automatic crash protection by requiring automobile manufacturers to install either of two passive restraint devices: airbags or automatic seatbelts. There was no suggestion in the long rulemaking process that led to Standard 208 that if only one of these options were feasible, no passive restraint standard should be promulgated. Indeed, the agency's original proposed standard contemplated the installation of inflatable restraints in all cars. Automatic belts were added as a means of complying with the standard because they were believed to be as effective as airbags in achieving the goal of occupant crash protection. At that time, the passive belt approved by the agency could not be detached. Only later, at a manufacturer's behest, did the agency approve of the detachability feature—and only after assurances that the feature would not compromise the safety benefits of the restraint. Although it was then foreseen that 60% of the new cars would contain airbags and 40% would have automatic seatbelts, the ratio between the two was not significant as long as the passive belt would also assure greater passenger safety.

The agency has now determined that the detachable automatic belts will not attain anticipated safety benefits because so many individuals will detach the mechanism. Even if this conclusion were acceptable in its entirety, standing alone it would not justify any more than an amendment of Standard 208 to disallow compliance by means of the one technology which will not provide effective passenger protection. It does not cast doubt on the need for a passive restraint standard or upon the efficacy of airbag technology. In its most recent rule-making, the agency again acknowledged the life-saving potential of the airbag:

> "The agency has no basis at this time for changing its earlier conclusions in 1976 and 1977 that basic airbag technology is sound and has been sufficiently demonstrated to be effective in those vehicles in current use. . . ." NHTSA Final Regulatory Impact Analysis (RIA) at XI–4 (App. 264).

Given the effectiveness ascribed to airbag technology by the agency, the mandate of the Safety Act to achieve traffic safety would suggest that the logical response to the faults of detachable seatbelts would be to require the installation of airbags. At the very least this alternative way of achieving the objectives of the Act should have been addressed and adequate reasons given for its abandonment. But the agency not only did not require compliance through airbags, it did not even consider the possibility in its 1981 rulemaking. Not one sentence of its rulemaking statement discusses the airbags-only option. Because, as the Court of Appeals stated, "NHTSA's . . . analysis of airbags was nonexistent," what we said in *Burlington Truck Lines* v. *United States,* 371 U.S., at 167, 83 S.Ct., at 245, is apropos here:

> "There are no findings and no analysis here to justify the choice made, no indication of the basis on which the [agency] exercised its expert discretion. We are not prepared to and the Administrative Procedure Act will not permit us to accept such . . . practice. . . . Expert discretion is the lifeblood of the administrative process, but 'unless we make the requirements for administrative action strict and demanding, *expertise,* the strength of modern government, can become a monster which rules with no practical limits on its discretion."

We have frequently reiterated that an agency must cogently explain why it has exercised its discretion in a given manner.

The automobile industry has opted for the passive belt over the airbag, but surely it is not enough that the regulated industry has eschewed a given safety device. For nearly a decade, the automobile industry waged the regulatory equivalent of war against the airbag and lost—the inflatable restraint was proven sufficiently effective. Now the automobile industry has decided to employ a seatbelt system which will not meet the safety objectives of Standard 208. This hardly constitutes cause to revoke the standard itself. Indeed, the Motor Vehicle Safety Act was necessary because the industry was not sufficiently responsive to safety concerns. The Act intended that safety standards not depend on current technology and could be "technology-forcing" in the sense of inducing the development of superior safety design. If, under the statute, the agency should not defer to the industry's failure to develop safer cars, which it surely should not do, *a fortiori* it may not revoke a safety standard which can be satisfied by current technology simply because the industry has opted for an ineffective seatbelt design.

Although the agency did not address the mandatory airbags option and the Court of Appeals noted that "airbags seem to have none of the problems that NHTSA identified in passive seatbelts," petitioners recite a number of difficulties that they believe would be posed by a mandatory airbag standard. These range from questions concerning the installation of airbags in small cars to that of adverse public reaction. But these are not the agency's reasons for rejecting a mandatory airbag standard. Not having discussed the possibility, the agency submitted no reasons at all. The short—and sufficient—answer to petitioners' submission is that the courts may not accept appellate counsel's *post hoc* rationalizations for agency action. It is well-established that an agency's action must be upheld, if at all, on the basis articulated by the agency itself. * * * We do not require today any specific procedures which NHTSA must follow. Nor do we broadly require an agency to consider all policy alternatives in reaching decision. It is true that a rulemaking "cannot be found wanting simply because the agency failed to include every alternative device and thought conceivable by the mind of man . . . regardless of how uncommon or unknown that alternative may have been. . . ." 435 U.S., at 551, 98 S.Ct., at 1215–1216. But the airbag is more than a policy alternative to the passive restraint standard; it is a technological alternative within the ambit of the existing standard. We hold only that given the judgment made in 1977 that airbags are an effective and cost-beneficial life-saving technology, the mandatory passive-restraint rule may not be abandoned without any consideration whatsoever of an airbags-only requirement.

"An agency's view of what is in the public interest may change, either with or without a change in circumstances. But an agency changing its course must supply a reasoned analysis . . ." [W]e * * * conclude that the agency has failed to supply the requisite "reasoned analysis" in this case. [W]e * * * remand the case to the NHTSA for further consideration consistent with this opinion.

So ordered.

Government officials may not, with impunity, discharge their duties in such manner as to violate the United States Constitution.

BUTZ v. ECONOMOU

Supreme Court of the United States, 1978.
438 U.S. 478, 98 S.Ct. 2894, 57 L.Ed.2d 895.

Mr. Justice WHITE delivered the opinion of the Court.

This case concerns the personal immunity of federal officials in the Executive Branch from claims for damages arising from their violations of citizens' constitutional rights. Respondent filed suit against a number of officials in the Department of Agriculture claiming that they had instituted an investigation and an administrative proceeding against him in retaliation for his criticism of that agency. The District Court dismissed the action on the ground that the individual defendants, as federal officials, were entitled to absolute immunity for all discretionary acts within the scope of their authority. The Court of Appeals reversed, holding that the defendants were entitled only to the qualified immunity available to their counterparts in state government. * * * Because of the importance of immunity doctrine to both the vindication of constitutional guarantees and the effective functioning of government, we granted certiorari. * * *

Respondent controls Arthur N. Economou and Co., Inc., which was at one time registered with the Department of Agriculture as a commodity futures commission merchant. Most of respondent's factual allegations in this lawsuit focus on an earlier administrative proceeding in which the Department of Agriculture sought to revoke or suspend the company's registration. On February 19, 1970, following an audit, the Department of Agriculture issued an administrative complaint alleging that respondent, while a registered merchant, had willfully failed to maintain the minimum financial requirements prescribed by the Department.

* * *

While the administrative complaint was pending * * *, respondent filed this lawsuit in Federal District Court, * * * seeking damages. Named as defendants were the individuals who had served as Secretary and Assistant Secretary of Agriculture during the relevant events; the Judicial Officer and Chief Hearing Examiner; several officials in the Commodity Exchange Authority; the Agriculture Department attorney who had prosecuted the enforcement proceeding; and several of the auditors who had investigated respondent or were witnesses against respondent.

The complaint stated that prior to the issuance of the administrative complaints respondent had been "sharply critical of the staff and operations of Defendants and carried on a vociferous campaign for the reform of Defendant Commodity Exchange Authority to obtain more effective regulation of commodity trading." The complaint also stated that, some time prior to the issuance of the February 19 complaint, respondent and his company had ceased to engage in activities regulated by the defendants. The complaint charged that each of the administrative complaints had been issued without the notice or warning required by law; that the defendants had furnished the complaints "to interested persons and others without furnishing respondent's answers as well"; and that following the issuance of the amended complaint, the defendants had issued a "deceptive" press release that "falsely indicated to the public that [respondent's] financial resources had deteriorated, when Defendants knew that their statement was untrue and so acknowledge[d] previously that said assertion was untrue."

The complaint then presented 10 "causes of action," some of which purported to state claims for damages under the United States Constitution. For example, the first "cause of action" alleged that respondent had been denied due process of law because the defendants had instituted unauthorized proceedings against him without proper notice and with the knowledge that respondent was no longer subject to their regulatory jurisdiction. The third "cause of action" stated that by means of such actions "the Defendants discouraged and chilled the campaign of criticism [plaintiff] directed against them, and thereby deprived the [plaintiff] of [his] rights to free expression guaranteed by the First Amendment of the United States Constitution."

* * *

The single submission by the United States on behalf of petitioners is that all of the federal officials sued in this case are absolutely immune from any liability for damages even if in the course of enforcing the relevant statutes they infringed respondent's constitutional rights and even if the violation was knowing and deliberate. Although the position is earnestly and ably presented by the United States, we are quite sure that it is unsound and consequently reject it.

In *Bivens v. Six Unknown Fed. Narcotics Agents,* the victim of an arrest and search claimed to be violative of the Fourth Amendment brought suit for damages against the responsible federal agents. * * * We held that a violation of the Fourth Amendment by federal agents gives rise to a cause of action for damages consequent upon the unconstitutional conduct.

* * *

Our system of jurisprudence rests on the assumption that all individuals, whatever their position in government, are subject to federal law:

> No man in this country is so high that he is above the law. No officer of the law may set that law at defiance with impunity. All the officers of the government from the highest to the lowest, are creatures of the law, and are bound to obey it. * * *

In light of this principle, federal officials who seek absolute exemption from personal liability for unconstitutional conduct must bear the burden of showing that public policy requires an exemption of that scope.

This is not to say that considerations of public policy fail to support a limited immunity for federal executive officials. We consider here * * * the need to protect officials who are required to exercise their discretion and the related public interest in encouraging the vigorous exercise of official authority. Yet * * * it is not unfair to hold liable the official who knows or should know he is acting outside the law, and that insisting on an awareness of clearly established constitutional limits will not unduly interfere with the exercise of official judgment. We therefore hold that, in a suit for damages arising from unconstitutional action, federal executive officials exercising discretion are entitled only to qualified immunity * * *, subject to those exceptional situations where it is demonstrated that absolute immunity is essential for the conduct of the public business.

* * * Federal officials will not be liable for mere mistakes in judgment, whether the mistake is one of fact or one of law. But we see no substantial basis for holding, as the United States would have us do, that executive officers generally may with impunity discharge their duties in a way that is known to them to violate the United States Constitution or in a manner that they should know transgresses a clearly established constitutional rule. The principle should prove as workable in suits against federal officials as it has in the context of suits against state officials. Insubstantial lawsuits can be quickly terminated. * * *

[F]irm application of the Federal Rules of Civil Procedure will ensure that federal officials are not harassed by frivolous lawsuits.

Although a qualified immunity from damages liability should be the general rule for executive officials charged with constitutional violations, our decisions recognize that there are some officials whose special functions require a full exemption from liability.

In *Bradley v. Fisher,* the Court analyzed the need for absolute immunity to protect judges from lawsuits claiming that their decisions had been tainted by improper motives.

* * *

Judges were often called to decide "[c]ontroversies involving not merely great pecuniary interests, but the liberty and character of the parties, and consequently exciting the deepest feelings." * * * If a civil action could be maintained against a judge by virtue of an allegation of malice, judges would lose "that independence without which no judiciary can either be respectable or useful." Thus, judges were held to be immune from civil suit "for malice or corruption in their action whilst exercising their judicial functions within the general scope of their jurisdiction."

* * *

Judges have absolute immunity not because of their particular location within the Government but because of the special nature of their responsibilities. This point is underlined by the fact that prosecutors—themselves members of the Executive Branch—are also absolutely immune. "It is the functional comparability of their judgments to those of the judge that has resulted in both grand jurors and prosecutors being referred to as 'quasi-judicial' officers, and their immunities being termed 'quasi-judicial' as well."

The cluster of immunities protecting the various participants in judge-supervised trials stems from the characteristics of the judicial process rather than its location. As the *Bradley* Court suggested, 13 Wall., at 348–349, controversies sufficiently intense to erupt in litigation are not easily capped by a judicial decree. The loser in one forum will frequently seek another, charging the participants in the first with unconstitutional animus. * * * Absolute immunity is thus necessary to assure that judges, advocates, and witnesses can perform their respective functions without harassment or intimidation.

At the same time, the safeguards built into the judicial process tend to reduce the need for private damages actions as a means of controlling unconstitutional conduct. The insulation of the judge from political influence, the importance of precedent in resolving controversies, the adversary nature of the process, and the correctability of error on appeal are just a few of the many checks on malicious action by judges. Advocates are restrained not only by their professional obligations, but by the knowledge that their assertions will be contested by their adversaries in open court. Jurors are carefully screened to remove all possibility of bias. Witnesses are, of course, subject to the rigors of cross-examination and the penalty of perjury. Because these features of the judicial process tend to enhance the reliability of information and the impartiality of the decisionmaking process, there is a less pressing need for individual suits to correct constitutional error.

We think that adjudication within a federal administrative agency shares enough of the characteristics of the judicial process that those who participate in such adjudication should also be immune from suits for damages. The conflicts which federal hearing examiners seek to resolve are every bit as fractious as those which come to court. As the *Bradley* opinion points out: "When the controversy involves questions affecting large amounts of property or relates to a matter of general public concern, or touches the interests of numerous parties, the disappointment occasioned by an adverse decision, often finds vent in imputations of [malice]."

Moreover, federal administrative law requires that agency adjudication contain many of the same safeguards as are available in the judicial process. The proceedings are adversary in nature. * * * They are conducted before a trier of fact insulated from political influence. * * * A party is entitled to present his case by oral or documentary evidence, and the transcript of testimony and exhibits together with the pleadings constitute the exclusive record for decision. The parties are entitled to know the findings and conclusions on all of the issues of fact, law, or discretion presented on the record.

There can be little doubt that the role of the modern federal hearing examiner or administrative law judge within this framework is "functionally comparable" to that of a judge. His powers are often, if not generally, comparable to those of a trial judge: He may issue subpoenas, rule on proffers of evidence, regulate the course of the hearing, and make or recommend decisions. See § 556(c). More importantly, the process of agency adjudication is currently structured so as to assure that the hearing examiner exercises his independent judgment on the evidence before him, free from pressures by the parties or other officials within the agency. Prior to the Administrative Procedure Act, there was considerable concern that persons hearing administrative cases at the trial level could not exercise independent judgment because they were required to perform prosecutorial and investigative functions as well as their judicial work, * * * and because they were often subordinate to executive officials within the agency.

* * * Since the securing of fair and competent hearing personnel was viewed as "the heart of formal administrative adjudication," * * * the Administrative Procedure Act contains a number of provisions designed to guarantee the independence of hearing examiners. They may not perform duties inconsistent with their duties as hearing examiners. * * * When conducting a hearing under § 5 of the APA, * * * a hearing examiner is not responsible to, or subject to the supervision or direction of, employees or agents engaged in the performance of investigative or prosecution functions for the agency. * * * Nor may a hearing examiner consult any person or party, including other agency officials, concerning a fact at issue in the hearing, unless on notice and opportunity for all parties to participate. Hearing examiners must be assigned to cases in rotation so far as is practicable. They may be removed only for good cause established and determined by the Civil Service Commission after a hearing on the record. Their pay is also controlled by the Civil Service Commission.

In light of these safeguards, we think that the risk of an unconstitutional act by one presiding at an agency hearing is clearly outweighed by the importance of preserving the independent judgment of these men and women. We therefore hold that persons subject to these restraints and performing adjudicatory functions within a federal agency are entitled to absolute immunity from damages liability for their judicial acts. Those who complain of error in such proceedings must seek agency or judicial review.

We also believe that agency officials performing certain functions analogous to those of a prosecutor should be able to claim absolute immunity with respect to such acts. The decision to initiate administrative proceedings against an individual or corporation is very much like the prosecutor's decision to initiate or move forward with a criminal prosecution. An agency official, like a prosecutor, may have broad discretion in deciding whether a proceeding should be brought and what sanctions should be sought. The Commodity Futures Trading Commission, for example, may initiate proceedings whenever it has "reason to believe" that any person "is violating or has violated any of the provisions of this chapter or of the rules, regulations, or orders of the Commission." * * * A range of sanctions is open to it.

The discretion which executive officials exercise with respect to the initiation of administrative proceedings might be distorted if their immunity from damages arising from that decision was less than complete. * * * While there is not likely to be anyone willing and legally able to seek damages from the officials if they do *not* authorize the administrative proceeding, * * * there is a serious danger that the decision to authorize proceedings will provoke a retaliatory response. An individual targeted by an administrative proceeding will react angrily and may seek vengeance in the courts. A corporation will muster all of its financial and legal resources in an effort to prevent administrative sanctions. "When millions may turn on regulatory decisions, there is a strong incentive to counter-attack."

The defendant in an enforcement proceeding has ample opportunity to challenge the legality of the proceeding. An administrator's decision to proceed with a case is subject to scrutiny in the proceeding itself. The respondent may present his evidence to an impartial trier of fact and obtain an independent judgment as to whether the prosecution is justified. His claims that the proceeding is unconstitutional may also be heard by the courts. Indeed, respondent in this case was able to quash the administrative order entered against him by means of judicial review. See *Economou v. U.S. Department of Agriculture,* 494 F.2d 519 (C.A.2 1974).

We believe that agency officials must make the decision to move forward with an administrative proceeding free from intimidation or harassment. Because the legal remedies already available to the defendant in such a proceeding provide sufficient checks on agency zeal, we hold that those officials who are responsible for the decision to initiate or continue a proceeding subject to agency adjudication are entitled to absolute immunity from damages liability for their parts in that decision.

We turn finally to the role of an agency attorney in conducting a trial and presenting evidence on the record to the trier of fact. We can see no substantial difference between the function of the agency attorney in presenting evidence in an agency hearing and the function of the prosecutor who brings evidence before a court. In either case, the evidence will be subject to attack through cross-examination, rebuttal, or reinterpretation by opposing counsel. Evidence which is false or unpersuasive should be rejected upon analysis by an impartial trier of fact. If agency attorneys were held personally liable in damages as guarantors of the quality of their evidence, they might hesitate to bring forward some witnesses or documents. "This is particularly so because it is very difficult if not impossible for attorneys to be absolutely certain of the objective truth or falsity of the testimony which they present."

* * * Apart from the possible unfairness to agency personnel, the agency would often be denied relevant evidence. * * *. Administrative agencies can act in the public interest only if they can adjudicate on the basis of a complete record. We therefore hold that an agency attorney who arranges for the presentation of evidence on the record in the course of an adjudication is absolutely immune from suits based on the introduction of such evidence. * * *

There remains the task of applying the foregoing principles to the claims against the particular petitioner-defendants involved in this case. * * *

[We] remand the case to the District Court for further proceedings consistent with this opinion.

So ordered.[1]

1. In the case of Nixon v. Fitzgerald, — U.S. —, 102 S.Ct. 2690, 73 L.Ed.2d 349 (1982), the Court held:

> Applying the principles of our cases to claims of this kind, we hold that petitioner, as a former President of the United States, is entitled to absolute immunity from damages liability predicated on his official acts. We consider this immunity a functionally mandated incident of the President's unique office, rooted in the constitutional tradition of the separation of powers and supported by our history. * * *
>
> The President occupies a unique position in the constitutional scheme. Article II of the Constitution provides that "[t]he executive Power shall be vested in a President of the United States . . . ." This grant of authority establishes the President as the chief constitutional officer of the Executive Branch, entrusted with supervisory and policy responsibilities of utmost discretion and sensitivity. These include the enforcement of federal law—it is the President who is charged constitutionally to "take care that the laws be faithfully executed"; the conduct of foreign affairs—a realm in which the Court has recognized that "[i]t would be intolerable that courts, without the relevant information, should review and perhaps nullify actions of the Executive taken on information properly held secret"; and management of the Executive Branch—a task for which "imperative reasons requir[e] an unrestricted power [in the President] to remove the most important of his subordinates in their most important duties."
>
> The President's unique status under the Constitution distinguishes him from other executive officials.
>
> * * *
>
> Because of the singular importance of the President's duties, diversion of his energies by concern with private lawsuits would raise unique risks to the effective functioning of government. As is the case with prosecutors and judges—for whom absolute immunity now is established—a President must concern himself with matters likely to "arouse the most intense feelings." * * * Yet, as our decisions have recognized, it is in precisely such cases that there exists the greatest public interest in providing an official "the maximum ability to deal fearlessly and impartially with" the duties of his office. * * * This concern is compelling where the officeholder must make the most sensitive and far-reaching decisions entrusted to any official under our constitutional system. Nor can the sheer prominence of the President's office be ignored. In view of the visibility of his office and the effect of his actions on countless people, the President would be an easily identifiable target for suits for civil damages. Cognizance of this personal vulnerability frequently could distract a President from his public duties, to the detriment not only of the President and his office but also the Nation that the Presidency was designed to serve.
>
> In view of the special nature of the President's constitutional office and functions, we think it appropriate to recognize absolute Presidential immunity from damages liability for acts within the "outer perimeter" of his official responsibility.
>
> Under the Constitution and laws of the United States the President has discretionary responsibilities in a broad variety of areas, many of them highly sensitive. In many cases it would be difficult to determine which of the President's innumerable "functions" encompassed a particular action. In this case, for example, respondent argues that he was dismissed in retaliation for his testimony to Congress—a violation of 5 U.S.C. § 7211 and 18 U.S.C. § 1505. The Air Force, however, has claimed that the underlying reorganization was undertaken to promote efficiency. Assuming that the petitioner Nixon ordered the reorganization in which respondent lost his job, an inquiry into the President's motives could not be avoided under the kind of "functional" theory asserted both by respondent and the dissent. Inquiries of this kind could be highly intrusive.
>
> Here respondent argues that petitioner Nixon would have acted outside the outer perimeter of his duties by ordering the discharge of an employee who was lawfully entitled to retain his job in the absence of "such cause as will promote the efficiency of the service." * * * Because Congress has granted this legislative protection, respondent argues, no federal official could, within the outer perimeter of his duties of office, cause Fitzgerald to be dismissed without satisfying this standard in prescribed statutory proceedings.
>
> This construction would subject the President to trial on virtually every allegation that an action was unlawful, or was taken for a forbidden purpose. Adoption of this construction thus would deprive absolute immunity of its intended effect. It clearly is within the President's constitutional and statutory authority to prescribe the manner in which the Secretary will conduct the business of the Air Force. * * * Because this mandate of office must include the authority to prescribe reorganizations and reductions in force, we conclude that petitioner's alleged wrongful acts lay well within the outer perimeter of his authority.
>
> A rule of absolute immunity for the President will not leave the Nation without sufficient protection against misconduct on the part of the chief executive. There remains the constitutional remedy of impeachment. In addition, there are formal and informal checks on Presidential action that do not apply with equal force to other executive officials. The President is subjected to constant scrutiny by

The expense and annoyance of litigation is part of the social burden of living under government.

FEDERAL TRADE COMMISSION v. STANDARD OIL CO. OF CALIFORNIA

Supreme Court of the United States, 1980.
449 U.S. 232, 101 S.Ct. 488, 66 L.Ed 2d 416.

Justice Powell delivered the opinion of the Court.

This case presents the question whether the issuance of a complaint by the Federal Trade Commission is "final agency action" subject to judicial review before administrative adjudication concludes.

On July 18, 1973, the Federal Trade Commission issued and served upon eight major oil companies, including Standard Oil Company of California (Socal), a complaint averring that the Commission had "reason to believe" that the companies were violating § 5 of the Federal Trade Commission Act, * * * and stating the Commission's charges in that respect. The Commission issued the complaint under authority of § 5(b) of the Act, * * * which provides:

> "Whenever the Commission shall have reason to believe that any . . . person, partnership, or corporation has been or is using any unfair method of competition or unfair or deceptive act or practice in or affecting commerce, and if it shall appear to the Commission that a proceeding by it in respect thereof would be to the interest of the public, it shall issue and serve upon such person, partnership, or corporation a complaint stating its charges in that respect and containing a notice of a hearing . . ."

An adjudication of the complaint's charges began soon thereafter before an Administrative Law Judge, and is still pending.

On May 1, 1975, Socal filed a complaint against the Commission in the District Court for the Northern District of California, alleging that the Commission had issued its complaint without having "reason to believe" that Socal was violating the Act. Socal sought an order declaring that the issuance of the complaint was unlawful and requiring that the complaint be withdrawn. Socal had sought this relief from the Commission and been denied. In support of its allegation and request, Socal recited a series of events that preceded the issuance of the complaint and several events that followed. In Socal's estimation, the only inference to be drawn from these events was that the Commission lacked sufficient evidence when it issued the complaint to warrant a belief that Socal was violating the Act.

The gist of Socal's recitation of events preceding the issuance of the complaint is that political pressure for a public explanation of the gasoline shortages of 1973 forced the Commission to issue a complaint against the major oil companies despite insufficient investigation. The series of events began on May 31, 1973. As of that day, the Commission had not examined any employees, documents, or books of Socal's, although the Commission had announced in December 1971, that it intended to investigate possible violations of the Federal Trade Commission Act in the petroleum industry.

The District Court dismissed Socal's complaint on the ground that "a review of preliminary decisions made by administrative agencies, except under most unusual circumstances, would be productive of nothing more than chaos." The Court of Appeals for the Ninth Circuit reversed and * * * held that the issuance of the complaint was "final agency action" under § 10(c) of the APA. * * *

the press. Vigilant oversight by Congress also may serve to deter Presidential abuses of office, as well as to make credible the threat of impeachment. Other incentives to avoid misconduct may include a desire to earn re-election, the need to maintain prestige as an element of Presidential influence, and a President's traditional concern for his historical stature.

The existence of alternative remedies and deterrents establishes that absolute immunity will not place the President "above the law." For the President, as for judges and prosecutors, absolute immunity merely precludes a particular private remedy for alleged misconduct in order to advance compelling public ends.

We granted the Commission's petition for a writ of certiorari because of the importance of the questions raised by Socal's request for judicial review of the complaint before the conclusion of the adjudication.

The Commission averred in its complaint that it had reason to believe that Socal was violating the Act. That averment is subject to judicial review before the conclusion of administrative adjudication only if the issuance of the complaint was "final agency action" or otherwise was "directly reviewable" under § 10(c) of the APA. * * * We conclude that the issuance of the complaint was neither. * * *

The Commission's issuance of its complaint was not "final agency action." * * * "[T]he cases dealing with judicial review of administrative actions have interpreted the 'finality' element in a pragmatic way." In Abbott Laboratories, for example, the publication of certain regulations by the Commissioner of Food and Drugs was held to be final agency action subject to judicial review * * * prior to any Government action for enforcement. The regulations required manufacturers of prescription drugs to print certain information on drug labels and advertisements. The regulations were "definitive" statements of the Commission's position, * * * and had a "direct and immediate . . . effect on the day-to-day business" of the complaining parties. * * * They had "the status of law" and "immediate compliance with their terms was expected." In addition, the question presented by the challenge to the regulations was a "legal issue . . . fit for judicial resolution." * * * Finally, because the parties seeking the declaratory judgment represented almost all the parties affected by the regulations, "a pre-enforcement challenge . . . [was] calculated to speed enforcement" of the relevant Act. * * *

The issuance of the complaint in this case, however, is materially different.

By its terms, the Commission's averment of "reason to believe" that Socal was violating the Act is not a definitive statement of position. It represents a threshold determination that further inquiry is warranted and that a complaint should initiate proceedings. To be sure, the issuance of the complaint is definitive on the question whether the Commission avers reason to believe that the respondent to the complaint is violating the Act. But the extent to which the respondent may challenge the complaint and its charges proves that the averment of reason to believe is not "definitive" in a comparable manner to the regulations in Abbott Laboratories.

* * *

Section 5 of the Act, requires that the complaint contain a notice of hearing at which the respondent may present evidence and testimony before an administrative law judge to refute the Commission's charges. Either party to the adjudication may appeal an adverse decision of the administrative law judge to the full Commission, * * * which then may dismiss the complaint. * * * If instead the Commission enters an order requiring the respondent to cease and desist from engaging in the challenged practice, the respondent still is not bound by the Commission's decision until judicial review is complete or the opportunity to seek review has lapsed. * * * Thus, the averment of reason to believe is a prerequisite to a definitive agency position on the question whether Socal violated the Act, but itself is a determination only that adjudicatory proceedings will commence.

Serving only to initiate the proceedings, the issuance of the complaint averring reason to believe has no legal force comparable to that of the regulation at issue in Abbott Laboratories, nor any comparable effect upon Socal's daily business. The regulations in Abbott Laboratories forced manufacturers to "risk serious criminal and civil penalties" for noncompliance, * * * or "change all their labels, advertisements, and promotional materials; . . . destroy stocks of printed matter; and . . . invest heavily in new printing type and new supplies." * * * Socal does not contend that the issuance of the complaint had any such legal or practical effect, except to impose upon Socal the burden of responding to the charges made against it. Although this burden certainly is substantial, it is different in kind and legal effect from the burdens attending what heretofore has been considered to be final agency action.

In contrast to the complaint's lack of legal or practical effect upon Socal, the effect of the judicial review sought by Socal is likely to be interference with the proper functioning of the agency and a burden for the courts. Judicial intervention into the agency process denies the agency an opportunity to correct its own mistakes and to apply its expertise. * * * Intervention also leads to piecemeal review which at the least is inefficient and upon completion of the agency process might prove to have been unnecessary.

Furthermore, unlike the review in Abbott Laboratories, judicial review to determine whether the Commission decided that it had the requisite reason to believe would delay resolution of the ultimate question whether the Act was violated. Finally, every respondent to a Commission complaint could make the claim that Socal had made.

In sum, the Commission's issuance of a complaint averring reason to believe that Socal was violating the Act is not a definitive ruling or regulation. It had no legal force or practical effect upon Socal's daily business other than the disruptions that accompany any major litigation.

Because the Commission's issuance of a complaint averring reason to believe that Socal has violated the Act is not "final agency action" under § 10(c) of the APA, it is not judicially reviewable before administrative adjudication concludes. We therefore reverse the Court of Appeals and remand for the dismissal of the complaint.

It is so ordered.

Review Questions

1. To what extent may an agency conduct its functions secretly? Are agency investigative powers subject to any limitations? Is most administrative agency work accomplished using formal procedure? When is a formal procedure required? Is a person entitled to a lawyer at administrative hearings? Explain your answers.

2. What rules apply to a formal evidentiary hearing under the federal Administrative Procedure Act? How is a Federal Trade Commission case handled? What are the procedures of the National Labor Relations Board? Explain or outline your answers.

3. Why is it impossible for the legislatures and courts to make all rules and resolve all cases? How is an administrative agency created? To what extent may legislative, executive, and judicial powers be delegated to administrative agencies? Must there be strict separation of powers within an agency? What legislative and executive checks exist over administrative agencies? Explain your answers.

4. What problems may arise, if any, in seeking judicial review of administrative agency actions in the federal courts? Explain your answers.

5. To what extent may government be sued for acts of its employees? May the employees themselves be sued? Explain your answers.

6. What are the functions of general regulatory rules? What are the procedural requirements for rule making by agencies under the federal Administrative Procedure Act? Is a trial-type hearing ever required in this rulemaking activity? When, if ever, will rule making by agencies be set aside by courts? Explain your answers.

7. How does the FTC enforce its cease and desist orders? What are the eight subject areas handled by the FTC's Bureau of Consumer Protection? What are the two primary functions of the NLRB? Do the mediators of the Federal Mediation and Conciliation Service have law enforcement authority? Does the work of the SEC ever relate to bankruptcy? What is the function of the ICC in the transportation service and consumer protection areas? What agency has responsibility to provide information to the public regarding enemy attack or other emergency? What agency sets margin requirements in the purchase and carrying of securities? Where can a potential minority or woman entrepreneur receive government assistance regarding business management? What agency sometimes issues orders excluding the importation of articles into the United States? Are such orders subject to change? What agency prevents price fixing by ocean carriers? What agency is prohibited by Congress from dealing with South Africa and Communist countries? Why? And why is it that this agency receives no appropriations from Congress? What is the function of the Office of Environmental Review? What agency has barred paint containing high levels of lead so as to reduce lead poisoning in children? How does the NRC assure that licensees comply with health and safety requirements? What agency handles the government's internal business affairs? What office within what agency is the keeper of the nation's history? Which agency assists Congress by reviewing the operations of the other agencies? Which agency is primarily responsible for managing the federal work force? Under what agency does the Peace Corps operate and to accomplish what purpose? What is the Fulbright program? Which federal agency maintains libraries in other countries? What is the function of the United States Commission on Civil Rights? Which federal agency deals with Title VII of the Civil Rights Act? What is the Equal Pay Act?

8. Define the following terms: administrative agency, administrative law judge, delegation doctrine, discretionary act, Environmental Impact Statement, exhaustion of administrative remedies, initial decision, interpretative rules, notice-and-comment rule making, ripeness for review, "Sunset" law, Voice of America.

Problems

1. Assume a "liquor control commission" has been recently established for the District of Columbia and is subject to the federal Administrative Procedure Act. An investigation officer has issued an order to close up "Joe's Bar" because of allegations that minors are served there as a matter of course. Joe denies this. He wants to keep his District of Columbia liquor license to operate. He wonders why he wasn't even told about the problem, and he wants to talk to the commission, bring an attorney with him, and have someone other than the investigator make the decision. Is he entitled to any of these things? What rules should apply? Explain.

2. Local administrative agency supervisor Brenda Hall found Tom Jensen Cannery, Inc. to be violating labeling regulations in placing thousands of "sugar-free" labels on cases of fruit canned in sugar syrup. Tom Jensen, president, voluntarily agreed to pay a substantial fine and correct the situation. Later, Lois Nelson, a diabetic, became very sick on the fruit and is suing the corporation. Tom says he is not liable because of his settlement with the government agency. In the alternative, he now wants to appeal the settlement made with the agency to the courts. What results? Explain.

3. Assume that Jim Watts is the manager of the newly created Indian Fish Commission. He has ruled that Indians may use power boats (previously no motor boats were allowed) to catch fish that border or run through Indian Reservations or federally owned lands. Watts feels that this should be allowed for two fishing seasons on an experimental basis to see if it will or will not cause problems. The American Wilderness Association, without making an effort to talk to Watts, his supervisors, or the Fish Commission members themselves, has filed a complaint in District Court objecting to the decision. Might the Association have any problem? Explain.

4. United States Senator Thompson has been upset about the steel industry and its relationship with the steel workers. She has introduced a bill in the Senate creating a new agency to regulate the steel industry. The statute gives the National Steel Regulatory Commission the power "to manage the steel industry to protect the steel workers as needed." It is anticipated that the agency would, when it deemed it necessary, send management teams into steel company executive offices to replace corporate management and to direct the day-to-day activities of management with specific ability to discard union contracts and allocate business profits and assets in any manner necessary to provide high levels of income to the steel workers. Is this statute likely to be acceptable within administrative law principles? Explain.

5. Federal employees of the newly created "Controlled Substances Commission" believe that several million dollars worth of marijuana is being grown in the southern part of your state. The agency, without consultation with any other government officials, sends 400 armed investigators to check all 134 large farms in this area having the investigators arrive at 5:30 in the morning for surprise purposes. Though all of the farmers protest, the searches of the farms are made. In some cases force is used, and some farmers, their wives, and children are injured. Marijuana is found and destroyed on twenty-three farms. The Commission has four meetings in the next three weeks to review its operations, and though many of the farmers want to attend, the meetings are closed to the public and held in secret. Files are opened for all 134 farms, but the farmers are not allowed to see them when they request to do so. What are the legal issues involved? Explain.

6. President Stellges, starting his first term in office in January, has immediately fired three members of the Federal Trade Commission because they are not members of his political party. In firing them he has made a number of public statements about their "fascist" philosophy and "Hitler" tactics. They are suing him for slander. Will the firings stand up? Will the slander suit be successful? Explain.

7. Assume that Congress has created a new agency to deal with the problems of United States farmers producing an excess of wheat, corn, and similar crops. The newly appointed five-person commission has met over the last several months and, without benefit of any public input, issued 280 pages of rules which restrict the amount of acreage that can be used to grow certain crops. Farmers everywhere are complaining. Have they a legal basis for complaint? Explain.

8. Assume the federal agency dealing with the management of the United States National Parks decides to build a wild life enclosure of several hundred acres within a national park for tourists to drive through. The federal engineers decide to include a grizzly bear area in one end of the enclosed area to be well marked by "danger" signs. After the first year, and at the end of the first winter when the park is reopened, the "danger" signs had all fallen and needed to be replaced. Park personnel did not get around to doing this, although signs were ready and available at the park maintenance building, until seven weeks after the park was opened. In the interim, Barbara Evans, a tourist in a car with a convertible top, stopped in the grizzly bear area not knowing of the danger. A bear ripped the top of the car and mauled Barbara causing her serious injury before forest rangers saved her. She is suing the federal government contending that the grizzly bear area should never have been a part of the wild life enclosure, that injury by wild animals is an area of strict liability in tort (see Chapter 4), and that the failure to put up the signs also makes the federal government liable. Is she correct in her contentions? Explain.

"The term 'business' has no definite or legal meaning. [O]ccasional, single, or isolated activities do not constitute business. . . . Labor, business and work are not synonyms."

Henry Campbell Black
Black's Law Dictionary

6

Partnerships, Corporations, and the Regulation of Securities

WHAT ARE THE THREE MAIN WAYS OF DOING BUSINESS?

When we talk of "doing business," we mean only those who actually own the business and therefore participate in its profits and losses. It is the business owners who are concerned with the structure of the business or its internal operation; they are interested in the possible ways of doing business and in the legal ramifications of each method. For it is they—the owners—who must make the determination as to the form of business organization to be used.

The three main methods or ways of doing business are:

1. A sole proprietorship;
2. A partnership; or
3. A corporation.

A sole proprietorship is a "one person" operation: one person (the "sole proprietor") owns and operates the business. Generally speaking, any kind of business may be operated as a sole proprietorship—a grocery store, hardware store, law practice, plumbing company, auto-body shop, etc. A sole proprietorship is the least complicated form of business organization with no body of law directly governing it (i.e., there is no "sole proprietorship law" as there is contract law, tort law, negotiable instruments law, sales law, agency law, and the like). The result is that there are no formal requirements for going into business as a sole proprietor. However, a sole proprietorship, like any other form of business organization (including partnerships and corporations), is subject to regulation by city, county, state, and federal governments. For example, a sole proprietor generally has to obtain a city, county, and/or state business license in order to operate his or her business. Zoning laws may prevent the proprietor from locating his or her business in a particular area; the proprietor's operation will be subject to environmental laws, consumer protection laws, antitrust and labor laws. And if the sole proprietor hires employees or agents to work or contract for him or her, all the rules of employer-employee law and agency law will apply. (But, again, all forms of business organizations are subject to these rules.)

In contrast to the sole proprietorship, there is a great body of law governing the partnership method of doing business. A partnership is an association of two or more persons ("partners") to carry on as co-owners a business for profit. A partnership is based on a private contract (written, oral, or implied) between the partners, specifying how the business is to be operated, and how the profits and losses are to be divided. Permission from the state to operate as a partnership is not required.

In forty-eight out of the fifty states, partnerships are subject to the Uniform Partnership Act (UPA).[1] The Act deals with the nature of partnership, relations between partners and persons dealing with the partnership, property rights of partners, and dissolution and winding up of a partnership.

A sole proprietor and a partnership have one important element in common—unlimited risk. By this is meant that, for purposes of liability, the personal assets of a sole proprietor or partner [2] are lumped together with his or her business assets. It follows that if a sole proprietor or partner incurs a large contract debt or is held liable for the negligent act of his or her employee, every nonexempt asset (see Chapter 12) the sole proprietor or partner owns may be taken to pay the debt or to satisfy the liability judgment. Of course, to a large extent, the risks of liability can be covered by insurance. Still, the cost of insurance may be prohibitive and the insurance coverage inadequate. For example, say that a small town druggist (a sole proprietor) is sued for $1.5 million because his employee-pharmacist misfilled a prescription. The druggist's insurance coverage is far less than $1.5 million, and the drugstore's total assets amount to less than $100,000. All the druggist's personal assets will be at stake in the case.

Limited liability is one of the major attractions of the corporate method of doing business. A corporation is an "artificial person"—i.e., a legal entity that is separate and distinct from its owners. A corporation enables its owners, called shareholders, to limit their liability to the amount of their investment in the corporation.

As with partnerships, there is a large body of law (partly common and partly statutory) governing corporations. The requirements for becoming a corporation are much more formalized than for either a sole proprietorship or partnership. Generally, to incorporate a business, it is necessary to file

1. Only Georgia and Louisiana have not passed the UPA.

2. The single exception is for a partner who qualifies as a "limited partner" under the Uniform Limited Partnership Act. As will be seen later in the chapter, a "limited partner" is liable only to the extent of his or her investment in the partnership.

"articles of incorporation" (a statement of purpose, powers, and ownership rights) with the state corporation commissioner's office. If the articles are in proper form, the state will issue a corporate *charter,* which is a legal document creating the corporation and authorizing it to operate. The Model Business Corporation Act governing corporations has been passed in whole or in part by thirty-four states.

Regarding taxes, a sole proprietor must compute income and social security taxes on his or her net profits. This is done on or before April 15 of each year, using "Form 1040 U.S. Individual Income Tax Return" along with "Schedule C Profit or (Loss) from Business or Profession" and "Schedule SE Computation of Social Security Self-Employment Tax."

On the other hand, with regard to taxes, the partnership itself pays no taxes. Rather, it files a mere *information* return with the government ("Form 1065, U.S. Partnership Return of Income"), specifying how much income the partnership had for the year and what each partner's share of the income is. The reporting and payment of taxes on the income is left to the individual partners: each must report his or her share of the partnership income on his or her personal income tax return (Form 1040, Schedule E). Each partner will be taxed on his or her share whether or not it was actually distributed to him or her during the course of the year.

Each partner's share of the income must be reported on a Schedule K–1 (one for each partner) to be filed along with Form 1065. Ultimately, the information contained on the K–1 will be compared with the partner's personal income tax return (Form 1040, Schedule E).

Because a corporation is a legal entity, it must report and pay taxes on its net income. In recent years, the first $25,000 of corporate income has been taxed at a rate varying from 15 percent to 17 percent; income over $25,000 has been taxed at rates that reach 46 percent on income over $100,000.[3] And there may be state tax on the corporate income as well. It is only the balance—what is left after taxes—that may be paid to the owners (the shareholders) as dividends. This corporate income in the form of dividends is then taxed a second time as each shareholder must report his or her dividends as income on his or her personal income tax return. This "double taxation" may be one disadvantage of using the corporate form of business organization.

To some extent a small corporation owned by shareholders who are its officers may avoid corporate tax by paying salaries to the officers. These wages are deductible from gross profit as an expense of doing business, and if this results in no corporate net profit, there is no corporate tax. Of course, the salaries must be "reasonable" to be deductible under the law. A high salary looks to be unreasonable anytime there exists a relationship between

3. The rates in 1983 were as follows:

Taxable Income	1983
$ 1–$ 25,000	15%
25,001– 50,000	18%
50,001– 75,000	30%
75,001– 100,000	40%
over 100,000	46%

the parties in addition to that of employer and employee (e.g., in the sole proprietorship situation, where the employee is a son or daughter of the sole proprietor; in the corporate situation, where the employee is a shareholder of the corporation). There is no precise rule as to what is reasonable: the test is the amount of compensation that like enterprises would ordinarily pay for like services. Obviously, if a shareholder has nothing to do with corporate operations, a salary to the shareholder is unjustified. And where a corporation has a history of paying little or no dividends, a high salary paid even to a working shareholder may be declared unreasonable (in which case the excessive portion of the salary will be disallowed as a deduction).

Thus, it is sometimes impossible for a corporation to avoid paying corporate tax simply by paying salaries to employees. There may be too much net profit, and high salaries may not be justified. Even so, it may be possible for the corporation to escape payment of corporate tax by electing to be taxed, not as a corporation, but as a partnership under Subchapter S of the federal Internal Revenue Code (the IRC, the basic tax law of the United States, is divided into many chapters and subchapters). Subchapter S provides that certain "small business corporations" may elect to be taxed as a partnership. (As you will recall, a partnership pays no taxes but files a mere information return, and each partner reports his or her share of the partnership income on his or her personal tax return whether or not it is received during the year.)

For a corporation to qualify as a Subchapter S corporation, it must meet the following specific requirements:

1. The corporation must have no more than thirty-five shareholders.[4] The number thirty-five corresponds to the private placement exemption under federal securities law (see later section of this chapter).
2. Each shareholder of the corporation must be an individual (or the estate of a deceased individual) and not a corporation, partnership, or trust (with the exception of a "grantor trust" or a trust receiving the stock of a deceased shareholder under a will for a period not to exceed sixty days—see Chapter 13 on trusts).
3. The corporation must have no more than one class of stock[5] (e.g., it cannot have both common and preferred stock as defined later in this chapter).
4. The corporation must be a domestic corporation. A corporation existing under the laws of a jurisdiction outside the United States cannot qualify.

A corporation that meets the above requirements can elect to be taxed as a partnership under Subchapter S. However, all the shareholders must consent to the election.

Like a partnership, a Subchapter S corporation pays no taxes but files a mere information return (Form 1120(S), reporting each individual shareholder's share of the corporate income on special, attached K–1 schedules. And like partners, each shareholder must report his or her share of the corporate

---

4. For purposes of this test, husband and wife and their estates are treated as one shareholder.

5. The Subchapter S Revision Act of 1982 provides that differences in voting rights between the shares of common stock shall not create a second class of stock.

income on his or her personal income tax return. Also, like partners, each is taxed on his or her share whether or not it was distributed to him or her during the course of the year.

WHAT IS THE NATURE OF A PARTNERSHIP?

There are four elements to the definition of a partnership:

1. There must be at least two persons (or partners);
2. Each must have an ownership interest (not necessarily equal) in the business;
3. The parties must intend to carry on the business together; and
4. They must associate in order to make a profit (parties who associate for nonprofit purposes are not partners).

The fact that a person receives a share of the profits from an unincorporated business is considered prima facie evidence that the person is a partner in the business. The effect of showing that a person has received profits from an unincorporated business is to raise a rebuttable presumption of partnership. However, the UPA, Section 7, states that no such inference shall be drawn if such profits were received as payment of a debt, as wages of an employee, as rent to a landlord, as an annuity to a widow or representative of a deceased partner, or as the consideration for the sale of goodwill of a business. Goodwill is the intangible value in a business beyond its book value; a buyer is willing to purchase goodwill because it represents future potential earnings based on the previous record of the business.

For a partnership to exist, the co-owners must intend to carry on together a business for profit. As used here, "business" means an enterprise involving continuous and on-going activity for an indefinite period of time. It does not refer to a single business transaction or ownership of property requiring a limited management. The latter type of activity is properly termed a "joint venture" and is a much more informal arrangement than a partnership. For example, if three people (joint adventurers) with separate, full-time occupations get together for the purpose of building an apartment house (which they intend to co-own and comanage), the arrangement is a joint venture and not a partnership. However, it should be realized that for all intents and purposes, a joint venture is treated the same under the law as a partnership. Partners and joint venturers have much the same rights and liabilities, and where appropriate, the courts will apply the Uniform Partnership Act to issues arising from joint venture arrangements. The only practical difference between a partner and joint venturer is that the latter does not file a partnership tax return, but instead shows his or her profits on his or her personal return as investment earnings or other income.

Under the common law, a partnership is considered to be an aggregate of individuals rather than a separate entity. A corporation is deemed to be an entity—an artificial person—existing separate and distinct from the shareholders who own it. Generally speaking, the Uniform Partnership Act follows the aggregate theory of partnerships; however, the UPA also applies an entity theory to a limited extent for purposes of convenience. The UPA allows a partnership to be sued as an entity (i.e., in the partnership name). However, in some states, a judgment obtained against the partnership alone is enforceable only against partnership assets and not against the personal assets of the individual partners. For this reason, suit is usually brought against both the partnership and the individual partners.

Secondly, under Section 8(3) of the Uniform Partnership Act, a partnership can hold and convey real property as an entity (i.e., in its own name). Where real property is acquired in the partnership name, it must be conveyed in the partnership name and not in the names of the individual partners.

And for accounting purposes, partnership assets, liabilities, and ownership, as well as all business transactions, are accounted for separately and distinct from the personal assets and liabilities of the individual partners.

A partnership is also treated as an entity for purposes of going through bankruptcy. This may be done without involving the personal assets of the individual partners. But, remember, the individual partners are liable for the partnership debts, and every partner (with the exception of a limited partner) exposes all of his or her personal assets to liability for the debts. So if partnership debts exceed partnership assets, the creditors of the partnership may look to the individual assets of each partner.

Finally, it sometimes occurs that the partners' personal assets are brought into court along with the partnership assets, and creditors of the partnership and creditors of the individual partners both claim an interest in all the assets. Under Section 40(h) of the UPA, the partnership creditors are given a prior right to the partnership assets, while the creditors of the individual partners are given a prior right to the personal assets of their individual debtors. This is referred to as the *marshaling* of partnership assets (*marshaling* being the arranging or ranking of assets in a certain order toward payment of debts).

A partnership is formed by *contract* between or among the partners. The agreement is referred to as the *articles of partnership* or *articles of co-partnership*. The articles usually include the name of the partnership, the capital contributions of each partner, a plan for division of profits and losses among the partners, the rights, if any, of the partners to withdraw from the partnership (and the terms, conditions, and notice requirements for withdrawal), and a provision for determining the value of a partner's "interest in the partnership" upon the partner's death or withdrawal from the partnership.

The partnership name may not be the same as or deceptively similar to the name of an already existing partnership. Nor may a partnership name include a term or phrase that is likely to mislead the public into thinking the business is a corporation. Also, any business operating under an assumed name (whether a sole proprietorship or partnership) is generally required to file a certificate with the state setting forth the assumed name of the business along with the true names and addresses of the business owners. Failure to file the required certificate may result in fine, imprisonment, or both; and the business itself may be disallowed from using the courts to enforce its contract rights against third parties (some states allow the business to "cure" the defect by filing the certificate prior to initiating any legal action).

WHAT IS A PARTNERSHIP BY ESTOPPEL?

The principle of estoppel states that a party may be estopped (in effect—stopped) from asserting a position that is true because the party has led another to believe that something else was true. The principle applies with full force to partnership law. Suppose that a person who is not a partner purports to be one or knowingly allows another to misrepresent that he or she is a partner. If a third party extends credit or other consideration in reliance on the misrepresentation, the purported partner will be estopped from denying the existence of a partnership. However, this person is not a partner in fact (estoppel does not establish an actual partnership) and has no right to interfere in the business or assist in its management, being a partner for liability purposes for that transaction only.

WHAT LEGAL RELATIONSHIP EXISTS BETWEEN THE PARTNERS?

Each partner is a fiduciary of every other partner. A fiduciary is a person in a position of trust and confidence with another. Thus, a partner may not compete with the partnership (e.g., engage in a competitive business) or "self-deal" in partnership transactions without the consent of *all* the partners. If the partner does so, he or she will have to account to the partnership for any profits derived.

The partners are free to apportion management rights and responsibilities in any manner they desire in the partnership agreement. Where the partnership agreement is silent as to the specifics of management and control, UPA Section 18 governs, and the partners are deemed to have equal rights. This is so even though the partners are entitled to different percentages of the profits. In the event of a disagreement as to operations, a majority vote of the partners will be decisive with one exception: if the proposed act is contrary to a specific provision of the partnership agreement, *all* the partners must consent to the act or it cannot be done.

In almost all cases, the partnership agreement provides a plan for division of profits and losses among the partners. However, in the absence of such a plan, the partners are held to share profits and losses equally.

A partner is entitled to a formal accounting if he or she is wrongfully excluded from the partnership business, or other circumstances render an accounting just and reasonable.

As to property rights in the partnership, three aspects must be considered:

1. Each partner's ownership interest in specific partnership property;
2. Each partner's "interest in the partnership" (i.e., his or her right to partnership profits and surplus); and
3. Each partner's right as to distributions by the partnership.

Specific Partnership Property

As to ownership of partnership property, each partner has equal rights to the property in the form of concurrent ownership called tenancy in partnership. The incidents of ownership are as follows:

1. Each partner has an equal right to possession of the partnership property for partnership purposes (as opposed to private purposes or interests of the individual partners);
2. All partners must join in any transfer of an interest in partnership property;
3. Partnership property is not subject to any property interests of spouses or families;
4. Partnership property is subject only to the claims of creditors of the partnership—not to claims of creditors of the individual partners; and
5. Partnership property is not part of the deceased partner's estate; upon the death of a partner, the remaining partners automatically receive the decedent's interest in the partnership property.

Survivorship is the most important feature of a tenancy in partnership; when a partner dies, the remaining partners automatically acquire his or her interest in the partnership property. Of course, the surviving partners have a duty to account to the deceased's estate for the value of the deceased's *interest in the partnership.* In so doing, the survivors will, in effect, pay over the full value of the deceased's interest in the specific partnership property—however, the survivors will be able to keep the specific assets in case they want to continue the business as a new partnership.

A Partner's "Interest in the Partnership"

This brings us to the second property right of each partner—his or her *interest in the partnership* which is figured from the partner's capital account as reflected by the partnership balance sheet. It includes any capital contributions and advances made by the partner to the partnership (an "advance" is a capital contribution beyond the amount the partner agreed to contribute in the partnership agreement).

A partner's interest in the partnership is always classified as *personal property* even where all the partnership assets are real property. The classification of the interest as personal property can make a difference, particularly where a decedent partner leaves all his or her personal property to one beneficiary and all his or her real property to another.

A partner is free to assign (transfer) his or her interest in the partnership: the assignee (transferee) does not become a partner by virtue of the assignment but merely succeeds to the partner's rights as to profits and surplus.

A judgment creditor of an individual partner, though he or she may not reach specific partnership property, may obtain a charging order against the partner's interest in the partnership. Under the charging order, future distributions in respect of the partner's interest must be paid to the creditor until the judgment is satisfied. In some cases, the courts will even order sale of the partner's interest to satisfy the judgment.

Rights as to Distributions

In any particular year, a partner may or may not receive his or her share of profits by way of cash or property distributions. As you already know, a partner is taxed on his or her share of profits whether or not he or she actually receives them. When a partnership is dissolved, any partner who has not actually received his or her full share of profits is entitled to payment in full of the share as part of his or her interest in the partnership (however, as will be seen in the section on termination of partnerships, partnership debts and liabilities must be satisfied first).

Upon dissolution, a partner is also entitled to the return of his or her capital investment (part of his or her interest in the partnership) along with any advances made to the partnership.

WHAT LEGAL RELATIONSHIP EXISTS BETWEEN THE PARTNERS AND THIRD PARTIES?

We move now to the legal relationship existing between the partners and third parties (i.e., nonpartners). This is an important area of partnership law, as the purpose of a partnership is to do business with third parties. There are two aspects to the relationship that must be considered:

1. The authority of partners as agents to contract with third parties, and
2. The liability of partners to third parties.

Authority of Partners as Agents

Every partner is an agent of the partnership with respect to the ordinary partnership business. It follows that any routine business contract entered into by a partner with a third party is binding on the partnership. Any nonbusiness-related contract or contract outside the ordinary scope of the business is not binding on the partnership.

Because it is normal to the appearance of a partner to be able to bind the partnership in ordinary business matters, a partner will have apparent authority to do so notwithstanding any secret limitation on his or her authority.

Liability of Partners to Third Parties

The liability of partners to third parties varies depending on whether it is contract liability or tort liability.

Contract liability Partners are jointly liable on all partnership contracts. By this is meant that they are liable together as a group on contracts; they are not liable individually. It follows that all partners are "necessary parties" to any action involving a contract—if one partner is named in a suit to enforce a contract, all must be named. Of course, a creditor of the partnership may always proceed against the partnership itself by filing suit in the partnership name. But if the creditor names only the partnership and not the individual partners, any judgment obtained will bind only the partnership assets.

The fact that the partners are jointly liable does not mean that each must pay an equal amount and no more of any judgment obtained against them. If there are ten partners and only two have assets (the others being bankrupt), the two with assets will have to pay the entire judgment (beyond whatever the partnership assets will cover). This is so though all the partners are jointly liable and all are named in the contract action. Of course, any partner who pays more than his or her share of the losses as set by the partnership agreement will have a right to contribution from the other partners.

The rule of joint liability also applies to an incoming partner who is held liable even for debts that existed before he or she came into the partnership. However, the incoming partner is liable for such pre-existing debts only to the extent of his or her investment in the partnership (in other words, his or her liability must be satisfied out of partnership assets).

Because the contract liability of partners is joint, a release of one partner by a creditor serves to release all partners (a "release" is a contract not to hold the partner liable on the debt).

Tort liability In contrast to their joint liability on contract obligations, partners are jointly and severally liable for partnership torts. That is to say, the partners are liable not only together as a group but also individually. Thus, the tort victim may sue all the partners together or a single partner (without joining the other partners). However, if the particular tort requires proof of malice or bad intent (e.g., fraud or misrepresentation), each partner who is held liable must be shown to have had the specific intent or malice. Of course, negligence, which is the most common tort, has no specific intent requirement, and each partner is jointly and severally liable without regard to intent.

Finally, the release of one partner by the victim of the tort does not serve to release any other partner. The partners, in this case, are jointly and severally liable, and each may be held without regard to the liability of any other partner.

HOW IS A PARTNERSHIP TERMINATED?

The term "dissolution" has a special meaning in the law of partnership. It refers not to the actual termination of the partnership, but to the beginning of the "winding up" of the partnership business preliminary to termination. Prior to dissolution, a partnership is "carrying on business"; after dissolution, it is "winding up" business. The "winding up" process may be lengthy and cumbersome, as where all the partners disband, all the assets are sold, and all business operations cease. Or it may be short and rather easily accomplished, as where only one partner leaves and the others continue the business as a new partnership—the "winding up" here being simply to account to the withdrawing partner for the value of his or her interest in the partnership. Once the "winding up" is complete, the dissolved partnership is terminated.

Events Triggering Dissolution of a Partnership

In all cases the following events will trigger dissolution of a partnership, although the "winding up" process will vary depending on the circumstances.

The express will of a partner Any partner may, at any time dissolve the partnership. Of course, a partner who prematurely dissolves a partnership may be breaching the partnership agreement and be liable in damages to the other partners. And though the original partnership is dissolved, the other partners have a right, under UPA Section 38(2), to continue the business in the partnership name (but as a new partnership, upon payment to the breaching partner of the value of his or her partnership interest less any recoverable damages). Here, "winding up" is a relatively easy matter.

Expulsion of a partner A partnership dissolves if the partners expel one of their members; to continue in business, the remaining partners must effect a new partnership agreement. Whether the expulsion will constitute a breach of contract, entitling the expelled partner to damages, depends on the partnership agreement.

Death or bankruptcy of a partner The personal services and credit of each partner are considered essential to a partnership. It follows that the death or bankruptcy of a partner dissolves the partnership.

Illegality A partnership usually dissolves if its operations become illegal (e.g., where a court decision or a statute makes the partnership business unlawful). However, the partnership may waive dissolution and simply return to a legal business activity.

Judicial decree The courts will order dissolution whenever:

1. A partner has been declared insane in any judicial proceeding or is otherwise shown to be of unsound mind;
2. A partner is incapable of performing his or her partnership duties;
3. A partner is guilty of improper conduct which adversely affects the partnership business or the interests of the partners;
4. The partnership can continue operating only at a loss; or
5. Dissolution is the only way to protect the interests of an assignee or a judgment creditor with a charging order against a partner's interest in the partnership.

In the event of a complete liquidation of the partnership and when partnership debts and liabilities exceed assets, the partners will contribute according to their share in the profits. If any partner is insolvent, the remaining partners will have to make up his or her share, again sharing the loss proportionately according to the partnership agreement.

In settling accounts between the partners after dissolution, the liabilities of the partnership rank in order of payment as follows:

1. Those owing to creditors other than partners;
2. Those owing to partners other than for capital and profits;
3. Those owing to partners in respect of capital;
4. Those owing to partners in respect of profits.

WHAT IS A LIMITED PARTNERSHIP?

A limited partnership is a partnership consisting of one or more general (regular) partners and one or more limited partners. Unlike a general partner who has unlimited liability, a limited partner is liable only to the extent of his or her investment in the partnership—the limited partner's personal assets are not subject to liability. However, in exchange for limited liability, the limited partner forfeits the right to act as an agent of the partnership and to participate in the partnership management. If a limited partner takes part in management of the partnership, he or she will become liable as a general partner.

Under Section 13 of the Uniform Limited Partnership Act, which has been adopted by thirty-nine states,[6] a limited partner may loan money to the partnership or otherwise transact business with the partnership. A limited partner who does so will be treated the same as any other partnership creditor.

Whereas there are no prescribed formalities for entering into a regular partnership, the ULPA requires parties forming a limited partnership to prepare and execute a certificate setting forth, among other things, the name of the partnership, the character or kind of business involved, the location of the principal office, the names and addresses of all partners and their capital contributions, and the designation of each partner as either "general" or "limited." The purpose of the certificate is to put potential creditors of the partnership on notice that some of the partners have limited liability. The certificate must be filed with the appropriate state and/or county official in the location where the business is to operate.

It should be pointed out that unless the partnership agreement provides to the contrary, a limited partner may rightfully demand the return of his or her contribution upon dissolution of the partnership or anytime after he or she has given six months' notice in writing to all other partners. However, the limited partner shall not receive any part of his or her contribution until all liabilities, except liabilities to partners, have been paid or there remains sufficient partnership property with which to pay them.

In settling accounts after dissolution, the liabilities of the partnership shall be entitled to payment in the following order:

1. Those to creditors in the order of priority as provided by law (remember that a limited partner who makes bona fide loans to a partnership is treated the same as other creditors as to those loans);
2. Those to limited partners in respect to their share of the profits and other compensation by way of income on their contributions;
3. Those to limited partners in respect to the capital of their contributions;
4. Those to general partners other than for capital and profits;
5. Those to general partners in respect to profits;
6. Those to general partners in respect to capital.

---

6. Ten states (Arkansas, Colorado, Connecticut, Maryland, Minnesota, Montana, Nebraska, Washington, West Virginia, and Wyoming) have adopted the Revised Uniform Limited Partnership Act. This revised statute specifies several activities in which a limited partner may engage without being considered as taking part in management or control so as to lose limited liability. These include being a contractor, agent, or employee of the limited partnership, consulting with and advising a general partner with respect to the partnership business, and voting on such partnership matters as dissolution, transfer of assets outside the ordinary course of business, or changing the nature of the business. Also, under this revised act, limited partners who do participate in management will have unlimited liability only to persons who actually know of such participation. It is expected that more states will pass the revised act as time goes on.

(Note the substantial difference in order of payment for a regular partnership and a limited partnership.)

WHAT ARE THE CHARACTERISTICS OF A CORPORATION?

The corporate form of business organization offers certain advantages that the sole proprietorship and partnership methods do not. Being a legal entity, a corporation has rights and liabilities that are separate and distinct from those of its shareholders; the assets and liabilities of a corporation belong to the corporation—not to the shareholders. The legal entity offers five advantages.

Advantages of Incorporation

Limited liability A person who invests in a corporation (i.e., purchases corporate stock) becomes an owner of the corporation and is called a shareholder or stockholder. Unlike a sole proprietor or partner, a shareholder enjoys limited liability—i.e., a shareholder is liable only to the extent of his or her investment in the corporation; his or her personal assets are not subject to liability. The corporation as an entity is responsible for its own debts.

Separation of ownership from management Another important advantage of a corporation is that ownership is completely separable from management (important because many people want to invest in a business but have no desire or ability to participate in management). Although shareholders have no right by virtue of being shareholders to participate in management of the corporation, they do have a right to elect a board of directors which, in turn, chooses corporate officers. It is the directors and officers who are responsible for corporate management. Of course, if they choose, the shareholders may serve as directors and officers (assuming they can get elected or appointed). But the important thing is that not a single one of them *need* participate in business management.

Ease of transferring ownership interests The corporate form of business organization also makes for ease of transferring ownership interests. Think about the problems involved when a sole proprietor sells his or her business. He or she personally owns every item of business inventory and other property. The sole proprietor must attach a value to each item of personal property and transfer each item. Where the total business or a major part of it is to be sold, the rules on "bulk sales" apply requiring the seller-transferor to furnish the buyer-transferee with a list of the existing creditors of the business. The buyer must give notice of the sale to the listed creditors. Observing the legal formalities takes time, and weeks or even months may elapse before the new owner can take over the business. At least for a time, business operations will cease or slow down considerably.

Along the same lines, if a partner leaves the partnership, a dissolution and winding up is required, which in many cases will halt or slow down business operations, at least temporarily.

Now think about the situation where a sole proprietor or partner dies. The sole proprietorship or partnership comes to an end. And the interest of the deceased sole proprietor or partner must be probated. "Probate" is the process by which a decedent's property is listed, valued, taxed (death taxes), and distributed to the decedent's rightful heirs or beneficiaries. Thus, every item of the deceased sole proprietor's inventory must be listed and valued for probate purposes. Similarly, the deceased partner's interest in the partnership must be probated, and the partnership wound up.

In contrast to both a sole proprietor and a partner, a shareholder of a corporation can easily transfer his or her ownership interest inter vivos (during life) or at death without disrupting the corporate operations in any way. This is because a shareholder owns—not an interest in any specific corporate property (remember, the corporation as an entity owns its own property) or a right to participate in corporate management—but an intangible personal property interest in the entire corporation. The shareholder's interest is represented by a stock certificate which evidences the number of corporate shares owned. Thus, during his or her lifetime, a shareholder may transfer all or part of his or her stock (e.g., by sale or gift) without affecting the corporate operations. The shareholder merely endorses the stock certificate over to the transferee (there is a place on the back of the certificate for the transferor-owner to sign); the certificate is then delivered to the corporation which issues a new stock certificate to the new owner. Obviously, this is much easier than worrying about the individual business assets. And it does not halt or slow down business operations. Furthermore, if the transferor has held the stock long enough to qualify for long-term capital gain treatment (one year), sale of the stock may result in a tax advantage to the seller (generally only 40 percent of long-term gain is taxed for income tax purposes, resulting in a maximum effective tax rate of 20 percent). The sale of the individual assets held in a sole proprietorship or partnership may well result in higher taxes.

Suppose that a shareholder dies. Certainly, his or her stock must be valued and listed for probate purposes. But this is much simpler than valuing and listing individual business assets. Moreover, it does not disrupt the corporate business operations, which brings us to the fourth advantage of the corporate method of doing business—perpetual life.

Perpetual life Because a corporation is a legal entity and not an aggregate of its individual shareholders, it is capable of perpetual life. In other words, a corporation, being an artificial person, is immune from death. It may have generations of different shareholders.

Ease of raising capital Finally, a corporation does not have the limited financial resources of a sole proprietorship or partnership. If a corporation wants to raise capital (e.g., to start or expand the business), it can offer stock for sale. And it can have literally thousands of shareholders. (The fact that management is completely separable from ownership makes it possible for a corporation to raise capital without risking automatic interference in its management.)

IS THE CORPORATE FORM ALWAYS EFFECTIVE TO LIMIT THE LIABILITY OF THE SHAREHOLDERS?

The rights and liabilities of a corporation are separate and distinct from those of its shareholders. The corporate entity is said to be like a "veil" in that it shields the shareholders from corporate debts and other obligations. Thus, if a judgment is entered against the corporation, the shareholders will be liable only to the extent of their investment in the corporation; their personal assets will not be subject to liability.

However, the "corporate veil" operates only if the business is conducted in good faith. If the corporate entity is being used to defraud people or to achieve other injustice, the courts will "pierce" (set aside) the corporate veil and hold the shareholders personally liable for the corporate debts and other obligations. Generally, the courts will pierce the corporate veil only where the corporation is not operating as a true legal entity, but is really the "alter ego" of its shareholders who are using the corporate form as a "shell" or "vehicle" to control private interests and assets, or debts, and where failure to pierce the corporate veil would result in fraud or other injustice. Yet, so long as the corporation is adequately financed, complies with all formation and record keeping requirements, conducts itself on a corporate and not on a personal basis, and has a legal purpose and objective, its shareholders will certainly enjoy limited liability. This is so even though it is a one shareholder or family corporation.

HOW DOES A CORPORATION SELL ITS OWNERSHIP?

A corporation sells its ownership by issuing shares of stock. The articles of incorporation filed with the state corporation commissioner to create the corporation must state how many shares can be issued (i.e., how many are authorized by the corporation). Say that a corporation is authorized to issue 1,000 shares of stock. It issues all the shares; you buy 200. You own 20 percent of the corporation (but remember, you have no interest in the specific corporate property—the corporation as an entity owns this—you own a 20 percent intangible personal property interest in the entire corporation).

The articles must also state whether the stock is to be *par value* or *no-par value.* Par value stock is stock that is assigned a specific value (such as $100 a share or $10 a share) which is stated on the stock certificate. The initial board of directors determines what the par value should be. Par value shares cannot legally be issued unless the corporation receives consideration for the shares equal to the par value (i.e., the value stated on the certificate). If the corporation is unsuccessful, the value of a shareholder's interest (the difference between corporate assets and liabilities times the shareholder's percentage share) will decrease and become far smaller than the par value stated on the certificate.

No-par value stock is stock that is issued without any stated value on the certificate. The board of directors determines what amount of cash or other consideration is to be accepted for what number of shares. Say that a corporation issues 100 shares of no-par value stock. One investor contributes $25,000 capital for 25 percent (25 shares) of the stock, so do two other investors. An inventor who has patented a new machine gives the patent to the corporation for the remaining 25 percent of its shares. The intangible personal property right represented by the patent is treated as having a value equal to the cash contributions of the other investors even though its actual value cannot be ascertained.

The issuance of stock by a corporation for less than full and adequate consideration results in *watered stock.* This usually results when par value stock is issued in return for property (other than cash) or services having a fair value less than the par or stated value of the stock. Statutes generally provide that stock may be issued for money, property, or past services rendered; it may not be issued for services to be performed in the future (i.e., future services).

The most frequent issue before the courts in watered stock cases is whether creditors of an insolvent corporation can collect the amount of the "water" (i.e., the difference between the consideration given and the par or stated value of the stock) from the shareholder who transferred the property or services to the corporation in exchange for the stock. Most courts provide that only creditors who extended credit after issuance of the watered shares can collect the amount of the "water" from the shareholder; creditors who extended credit before issuance of the shares cannot.

In any event, before proceeding against the shareholder, a creditor must first reduce his or her claim against the corporation to judgment and then try to collect the judgment. An exception arises where the corporation has been declared bankrupt by a federal bankruptcy court; the creditor, in this case, may proceed directly against the shareholder without first going against the corporation.

Suppose that the shareholder has sold or otherwise transferred the watered stock. The transferee is not liable for the amount of the water unless he or she had knowledge of it at the time of the transfer.

Whether stock is par value or no-par value, its book value is determined by dividing the value of the corporate assets less liabilities by the number of shares of stock issued by the corporation. Obviously, the book value of stock changes constantly, reflecting the profits and losses of the business. And it often differs substantially from the market value of the stock. The market value is the price that a willing buyer would pay a willing seller for the stock, neither party being under any compulsion to buy or sell. For example, though the book value of the inventor's stock is $750 a share, a willing buyer might be eager to pay $1,200 or even $2,000 a share if the patent (and hence the corporation) has great potential.

The articles of incorporation must also specify the classes of stock to be issued and the number of shares of each class. A corporation may issue two basic classes of stock: *common stock* and *preferred stock.*

Common and Preferred Stock

Common stock is the ordinary stock of a corporation. If only one class of stock is authorized, it will, in effect, be common, and the common stockholders will have complete, unrestricted voting rights. They will also be entitled to share ratably in any dividends that are distributed and in such net assets as are distributed upon dissolution of the corporation.

If more than one class of stock is authorized, the articles must set forth the preferences, limitations, and relative rights of each class. Shares with preferences as to earnings (dividends) or net assets (liquidation) or both are termed *preferred stock.* Shares with no preference as to earnings and/or net assets are termed *common stock.* Except as otherwise provided by the articles of incorporation, all classes of stock enjoy equal rights as to voting, dividends, and net assets. The articles typically provide otherwise as follows:

Voting rights At least one class of shares must have complete, unrestricted voting rights. Usually, the articles provide that the common stock is the "voting stock" (i.e., that the common stockholders have the right to elect the board of directors; the preferred stock has no voting rights). However, there is nothing to prevent the articles from making the preferred stock voting, the common nonvoting, or authorizing two classes of common stock or preferred stock, one of which is voting and one of which is nonvoting.

Dividends Dividends are the means by which shareholders participate in corporate earnings (net profit). A dividend is a distribution of cash or other property (sometimes stock) made by a corporation to its shareholders. The board of directors determines whether or not a dividend should be declared in any particular year, and in a nonprofit year, the decision is likely to be against paying one.

Some corporations pay dividends every year, while others seldom pay dividends. However, the fact that a corporation pays few dividends does not necessarily make the company a bad investment. People invest in corporations, not only for dividends, but also to share in growth of the company. If a corporation, rather than pay dividends, reinvests its income profitably (e.g., by adding more factories or purchasing more inventory), the stockholders will be able to watch the value of their stock go up and up.

The articles of incorporation generally give preferred stockholders a preference (i.e., a preferred position) on dividends, the "preference" being that the preferred stockholders will be paid a stated annual rate of dividend (e.g., 6 percent) before any dividend is paid to the common stockholders.

Distribution of net assets on dissolution of the corporation A second preference common to preferred stock is one on the assets of a corporation in the event of dissolution. Typically, the preference states that after creditors have been paid, but before the common stockholders receive anything, the preferred stockholders must receive the par value of their stock from the corporate assets or the par value plus a premium. The common stockholders are entitled to any surplus remaining.

While the preferred stockholders are guaranteed a specific sum of money upon liquidation of the corporation, that is the maximum amount they will receive. It is the common stockholders who, by receiving the surplus, will participate in growth of the corporation. Some corporations have increased in value many hundreds of times since they first came into existence. To enable preferred stockholders to share in corporate growth, they are often given *conversion rights*—i.e., rights to convert their stock to common stock at certain times or under certain circumstances.

WHAT ARE THE FUNCTIONS OF CORPORATE PROMOTERS?

A great many corporations are formed from existing sole proprietorships or partnerships needing no extra capital to convert over into the corporate form. Still others are organized by individuals who plan to own all the corporate stock themselves: the incorporators neither want nor need any other shareholders. A lesser number of corporations are started from scratch by individuals who do need to raise capital—or at least obtain the promise of capital—in order to go into business as a corporation. In the latter case, the people who participate in forming the corporation, selling its stock, and organizing its initial business activities are referred to in law as corporate *promoters.*

Promoters are fiduciaries of the corporation they form. If a promoter sells his or her own property to the corporation for cash or stock, he or she must disclose to the corporation (1) what property is being sold; (2) the fact that he or she owns the property; and (3) the amount of profit that he or she stands to make from the sale. A failure to disclose these things constitutes a fraud on the corporation. The disclosure must be made either to an independent board of directors (meaning a majority of the board's directors who are disinterested) or to all existing stockholders plus any people then known to be planning to become stockholders.

As will be seen later in the chapter, disclosure problems have been obviated to a great extent by state and federal statutes regulating the issuance of securities. These statutes require complete disclosure of all factors affecting the value of property received by a corporation in exchange for its stock.

In organizing a corporation, promoters often enter into contracts on behalf of the business prior to issuance of the corporate charter. For example, the promoters might negotiate to purchase an office building for use as the main place of business. Or they might negotiate contracts to purchase inventory. To what extent is the corporation liable on these contracts?

The corporation is liable only if it ratifies or adopts the contracts after issuance of the corporate charter. The ratification may be express (e.g., where the board of directors passes a resolution ratifying the contract), or it may be implied (e.g., where the corporation moves into the office building or accepts delivery of the inventory). Following the ratification, the corporation may enforce the contract against the third party.

As for the promoters, they have no personal liability on preincorporation contracts so long as they make it clear at the time of contracting that they are contracting *on behalf of the corporation only and not for themselves personally.* The third party, in this case, relies solely on the credit of the proposed corporation and has no claim against the promoters personally (e.g., the third party cannot hold the promoters liable if the corporation is never formed or if it otherwise fails to ratify or carry out the contract). It follows that the promoters have no ability to enforce the contract against the third party if the corporation is not formed.

WHAT IS THE LAW REGARDING STOCK SUBSCRIPTIONS?

A *stock subscription* is an agreement by a party called a "subscriber" to purchase a certain amount of capital stock of a corporation. If the corporation is in existence at the time of the subscription, the agreement is an enforceable contract. However, promoters of a corporation frequently arrange for stock subscriptions before the corporation comes into existence. The majority rule is that a preincorporation stock subscription is a mere offer by the subscriber and not an enforceable contract: the corporation is not yet in existence and, hence, cannot accept the offer. The subscription becomes an enforceable contract only at such time as the corporation is formed and accepts the offer.

A minority of courts feel that revocability of preincorporation stock subscriptions is contrary to public policy. They point out that other shareholders rely on the subscriptions in subscribing for their own shares, and that revocation often results in undercapitalization of the corporation. Accordingly, the minority courts hold that a preincorporation stock subscription is more than a mere offer to purchase shares when the corporation is formed—it is also a contract between or among the subscribers and, as such, is binding. If a subscriber fails to go through with his or her stock subscription following formation of the corporation, the other subscribers may sue him or her and recovery money damages.

Statutes in other states simply make preincorporation stock subscriptions irrevocable for a certain period of time (e.g., ninety days or six months). The Model Business Corporation Act makes them irrevocable for six months.

WHAT IS AN "ULTRA VIRES" ACT BY A CORPORATION?

In filing the articles of incorporation, the corporate purpose or purposes must be stated. Once the corporate charter is issued, the corporation has express power to perform any legal act required to carry out its purposes. The corporation also has whatever power is conferred upon corporations generally by the state corporation statute—e.g., power to own property, to buy and sell, to sue and be sued, etc.

An "ultra vires" act is one that goes beyond the powers of the corporation (the term "ultra vires" obviously has little meaning where the corporation's stated purpose is "to engage in any lawful activity"). Often in the past, a corporation would try to assert a plea of ultra vires as a defense to a contract action brought against the corporation. Generally, the corporation would enter into a contract beyond the scope of its power (i.e., an ultra vires contract). Later, wanting to get out of the contract, the corporation would assert that the agreement was ultra vires and, hence, not binding on the corporation. Today, most corporation statutes expressly provide that ultra vires may not be raised as a defense to an existing contract. If what would be an ultra vires contract is still in the negotiating stage, the shareholders may go to court to enjoin (stop) the corporation from entering into it. But once the corporation has entered into the contract, neither the corporation itself nor the shareholders may set it aside on the grounds that it is ultra vires. However, the corporation (or the shareholders themselves in a "derivative" action, as will be explained in a later section) may bring an action against the directors and/or officers who authorized the ultra vires act to recover any loss that results to the corporation.

HOW IS A CORPORATION MANAGED AND CONTROLLED?

The Shareholders

The shareholders of a corporation have no right or power by virtue of being shareholders to participate directly in management of the corporation. However, they do exercise indirect control over corporate management through their voting rights. The shareholders elect the board of directors which is directly responsible for managing the corporation. The shareholders can also vote to amend the articles of incorporation or the corporate bylaws or to dissolve the corporation, etc. And though the board has sole power to manage the day-to-day business affairs of the corporation (and to contract on behalf of the corporation), the board cannot make major changes in corporate structure or business operations without shareholder approval.

The Board of Directors

The board of directors is responsible for managing the corporation. The directors are fiduciaries of the corporation and, as such, are held to high standards of good faith; they must exercise reasonable care and diligence in all matters relating to corporate management. Because directors often have many business interests in addition to their directorship, they are not held to an impossible standard—rather, the "business judgment rule" is applied. The rule states that a director is personally liable for an erroneous business judgment that results in loss to the corporation only if the director acted fraudulently or in bad faith. Thus, the standard of care required is one of honest judgment. So long as a director makes an honest judgment, he or she will not be personally liable even if the judgment proves to be in error. However, a director who makes no effort to acquire sufficient facts on which to base his or her judgment does not act honestly and in good faith and will be personally liable to the corporation for any loss that results from the judgment. Examples of "bad faith" judgments include the reckless hiring of dishonest employees and the failure to purchase adequate insurance to provide against foreseeable casualty. And it is generally considered a "bad faith" judgment for a director to authorize a corporate loan to a director, officer, or shareholder of the corporation. In most states, a director who does so without approval of at least two-thirds of the shareholders is held to guarantee repayment of the loan.

The Officers

The officers of a corporation are elected by the board of directors which also sets their terms of office and salaries. The officers generally include a president, vice-president, secretary, and treasurer; however, there are sometimes many more officers. The officers have power to bind the corporation to contracts within the ordinary scope of the corporate business. Like directors, officers are fiduciaries of the corporation and have fiduciary duties of good faith, loyalty, and honesty. Because of their day-to-day familiarity with the corporate affairs, officers are generally held to a higher standard of care than are directors.

WHAT ARE THE RULES REGARDING CONFLICTS OF INTEREST?

As fiduciaries, directors and officers have a duty of loyalty requiring them not to take advantage of the corporation for their own interests. In other words, directors and officers must not use their positions within the corporation to gain personally. When their personal interests conflict with those of the corporation, there is said to be a conflict of interest. There are five major areas where a conflict of interest may arise.

1. *A director or officer enters into a personal business transaction with the corporation.* A director or officer who contracts personally with the corporation is in much the same position as a promoter who does so. If the director or officer fails to make full disclosure regarding the contract to an independent board of directors, the corporation will have a right to rescind the contract or sue the director or officer for money damages (the corporation's measure of damages being the amount of unfair profit made on the transaction by the director or officer).
2. *A director serves on the boards of two corporations that deal with each other (called an "interlocking directorate").* Most courts hold that contracts between such corporations are valid unless one of the corporations took undue advantage of the other or acted fraudulently by reason of having its director on the board of the other corporation.
3. *A director or officer personally takes advantage of a business opportunity that would be advantageous to the corporation (the "corporate opportunity" doctrine).* The corporate opportunity doctrine states that a director or officer must offer the corporation a "right of first refusal" on any business opportunity that he or she learns of that would be of benefit to the corporation. For example, say that a director learns that a large warehouse is up for sale. Though the corporation would have many uses for such a warehouse, the director fails to disclose the opportunity and purchases the warehouse for himself or herself. The corporation, in this case, may legally force the director to convey the property to the corporation at the director's expense (the courts will impose a "constructive trust" on the property in favor of the corporation—see Chapter 13). Or if the director has already sold the property to another, the corporation may sue the director for money damages and collect all the profits the director made on the transaction.
4. *A director or officer becomes an owner of a competing business.* Anytime a director or officer becomes an owner of a competing business, there is a conflict of interest. The director or officer may not continue to serve as a director or officer.
5. *A director, officer, employee, or other "insider" uses inside information to make "insider profits."* Directors, by virtue of sitting on the board, often

acquire information affecting the value of the corporation and its stock. Officers, employees, and large shareholders of the corporation may also have access to such "insider information." The federal Securities Exchange Act of 1934 provides for recovery of insider profits in the following ways.

Rule 10b–5

Rule 10b–5 promulgated by the Securities and Exchange Commission states that it is unlawful to use a "manipulative or deceptive device" including a "misstatement or *omission* of any material fact in connection with the purchase or sale of any security in interstate commerce." Rule 10b–5 applies to every sale or resale of securities, including the first such sale. It applies to any failure to disclose material "inside" information. Examples of material inside information would include knowledge of imminent merger, changes in dividend rates, new product development, discovery of new resources, anticipated legal action, etc. Under the rule, anyone who possesses such inside information must disclose it. Thus, a broker who receives inside information from someone in the corporation must disclose the information when buying or selling the corporate stock.

The interstate commerce requirement means only that some instrumentality of interstate commerce must be used in connection with the purchase or sale—e.g., the mail or telegraph. Even a purely intrastate telephone call (a call made entirely within one state) will do.

Any buyer or seller—even a member of the investing public—who is injured by an insider's violation of Rule 10b–5 may sue to rescind the purchase or sale or to recover money damages. If several people have been injured, they may bring a single class action to recover damages for the entire group.

Rule of Section 16

Section 16 of the Securities Exchange Act of 1934 applies only to securities that must be registered under the Act. A corporation must register whenever it is engaged in interstate commerce and either lists its securities on a national securities exchange *or* has at least 500 shareholders and total assets of at least $3,000,000. Section 16 requires an insider of such a corporation—called a "covered" corporation—to disclose any short-term profits he or she makes on the corporate stock. The section defines "short-term" or "short swing" profits as any profits made by an insider as the result of the purchase and sale of the covered corporation's stock within six months of each other. For purposes of the section, an "insider" includes not only a director or officer of the corporation but also any shareholder who owns at least 10 percent or more of the corporate stock at the time of the purchase and sale.

Under Section 16, all short swing profits made by an insider belong to the corporation—there are no exceptions. The law raises a conclusive presumption that the profits resulted from inside information; no evidence to the contrary will be considered. Thus, it makes no difference that the profits resulted from normal market conditions only, that the insider had good motives, or even that the insider had no inside information at all.

Short swing profits belong to the corporation, not to the shareholders. However, if the corporation refuses to bring legal action to recover the profits, the shareholders may bring action on behalf of the corporation (this is a "derivative" suit, as will be explained in a later section).

In determining whether short swing profits have been made, any pair of transactions occurring within a six-month period may be looked to: losses from other transactions occurring within the same period may be disregarded. (In other words, though the insider's dealings show an overall loss, any profit made from a particular pair of transactions will still be short swing profits belonging to the corporation.)

WHAT ARE THE RIGHTS AND RESPONSIBILITIES OF SHAREHOLDERS?

The owners of a corporation (i.e., the "shareholders" or "stockholders") have no interest in specific corporate property, nor do they have any direct voice in corporate management. However, shareholders do have certain basic rights.

The Basic Rights of Shareholders

Dividends Shareholders have no legal right to dividends. The declaring of dividends is a matter within the discretion of the board of directors. However, if a large surplus has accumulated and the directors refuse to declare a dividend, their refusal may be held in violation of their fiduciary duties (in which case the courts may order payment of a dividend upon petition of the shareholders). Dividends may be declared and paid only out of *current profits* (the profits of the year) or *earned surplus* (undistributed profits from previous years). They may not be declared and paid out of *stated capital.* Stated capital refers to the total par value of all issued par value shares plus the total value received for all no-par value shares. Any amount paid for par value stock over and above its par value is called *capital surplus.* Generally, dividends may be paid out of capital surplus only if (1) there is no earned surplus available, and (2) the distribution will not render the corporation insolvent. For purposes of declaring and paying dividends, a corporation is insolvent when it is unable to meet its debts as they fall due. Sometimes, the board of directors will set aside a portion of "earned surplus" for special purposes (e.g., to retire a specific debt, acquire specific property, or maintain a fund required by a creditor as a condition to the granting of credit. Such surplus is referred to as *restricted surplus* and is not available for the payment of dividends.

No dividends of any kind may be paid if the corporation is insolvent or would become so by payment of a dividend.

Redemption of shares A corporation *redeems* shares when it purchases shares of its stock from shareholders and cancels the shares. A corporation has no power to redeem absent express authorization in the articles of incorporation. And redemption is never allowed where a corporation has only one class of stock such as common (to permit redemption in such a case would be to allow the directors to eliminate the very shareholders to whom they are responsible for managing the corporation).

The right to redeem is often built into preferred stock to enable the corporation to ultimately eliminate that class of stock (and its dividend and liquidation preferences) for the benefit of the common stockholders.

Corporate redemption should not be confused with corporate *repurchase* of shares. A corporation repurchases shares when it buys shares of stock from shareholders but does not cancel the shares. Though the stock remains authorized and issued, it is no longer outstanding (i.e., held by shareholders); rather, it is held by the corporation itself and is known as *treasury stock.* Treasury stock cannot be voted, it does not participate in dividends, and it has none of the other rights of stock held by the shareholders. However, it can be reissued by the corporation at a later time (redeemed shares, on the other hand, are cancelled and cannot be reissued). Moreover, treasury stock can be resold without worrying about receiving full consideration for the shares: the stock will not be considered "watered" so long as the original issue complied with the requirement that full value be received.

Unlike the power to redeem shares, the power to repurchase exists independently of the articles of incorporation: a corporation is deemed to have inherent power to repurchase its own shares.

Pre-emptive rights It is possible for a corporation to change the proportionate interests of its shareholders by issuing new shares of stock to new owners or by issuing new shares to old shareholders but in amounts disproportionate to their ownership interests. To enable shareholders to prevent a decrease in their proportionate ownership interest, all states recognize what are called "pre-emptive rights" of shareholders. A "pre-emptive right" is a shareholder's right to "pre-empt" his or her share of any new issue of corporate stock. In other words, the shareholders must be given the opportunity to purchase a percentage amount of the new issue equal to his or her present holdings; in this way, the shareholder can prevent a decrease in his or her proportionate ownership interest. A pre-emptive right is a right of first refusal only, and if the shareholder does not purchase his or her share of the stock, it may be sold to others. The resale of treasury stock is not subject to pre-emptive rights.

Inspection of corporate records In most states, the shareholders have a statutory right to make a reasonable inspection of the corporate records (financial reports, minutes of meetings, and any other records reflecting the corporate business and management). A shareholder has no right to inspect at an unreasonable time or for any purpose adverse to the corporate interest. For example, a shareholder may not inspect the corporate records to acquire information allowing him or her to go into a competing business. However, it is generally accepted that a shareholder may inspect shareholder lists for the purpose of contacting the shareholders to undertake a change in control of the corporation.

Voting rights The corporate bylaws generally provide for an annual meeting of the shareholders. Bylaws are adopted by the board of directors after the articles of incorporation have been filed with the state and the corporate charter has been issued. They are written rules (usually many pages) governing corporate activities and operations. At the annual meeting of shareholders, the shareholders will elect a new board of directors and vote on any other business matters within their power—e.g., to amend the articles or bylaws, dissolve the corporation, etc.

Straight voting Each common stockholder generally has the right to cast one vote for each share of stock that he or she owns. This is called straight voting. In all matters other than the election of directors, straight voting is the method used.

Cumulative voting Obviously, if straight voting is used to elect the board of directors, any group of shareholders with at least 51 percent of the shares will be able to elect all the directors. To ensure shareholders with less than 51 percent some representation on the board, all states now require or at least allow the use of cumulative voting. Under cumulative voting, each share of common stock has as many votes as there are directors to be elected. And a shareholder can distribute his or her votes among the candidates in any way that he or she chooses. That is to say, he or she may "cumulate" his or her votes: he or she may cast them all for one director, or half for one and half for another, or in any other desired combination.

Proxy voting In all states, shareholders have a right to vote by proxy. A proxy is a power of attorney given by a shareholder to another party authorizing the party to exercise the voting rights of the shares. The use of proxies enables minority shareholders to obtain enough votes to gain representation on the board of directors; majority shareholders frequently solicit proxies as well.

To prevent abuse of proxies, the federal Securities and Exchange Commission has adopted certain proxy rules pursuant to authority conferred by Section 14 of the Securities Exchange Act of 1934. Rule 14(a) states that anyone who is soliciting proxies covering registered securities must set forth complete information regarding the matters to be voted on and must identify all the participants involved in the proxy solicitation. If corporate management is soliciting proxies, it must also include an opposition statement of up to 200 words from any minority interest that wants to make one. And if the minority wants to make an independent solicitation, management must cooperate by supplying a list of the corporate shareholders or by mailing the solicitations for the minority.

Additional protection of minority shareholders To this point, we have seen that minority shareholders find protection in cumulative voting and pre-emptive rights. Now we find that they are further protected by reason of their fiduciary relationship with the majority. The majority shareholders are fiduciaries of the minority. As fiduciaries, they have a duty to use their power in the interests of all the shareholders—not to use it to produce a profit for themselves at the expense of the minority (by paying dividends, setting salaries, and otherwise controlling the corporation in their favor).

There may even be a breach of fiduciary duty where the majority sells its shares to outsiders who take over control of the corporation. Ordinarily, the majority (like any other seller) is entitled to sell its shares so as to make the best deal possible for itself. But the majority breaches its fiduciary duty to the minority if it makes the sale notwithstanding its knowledge of "special facts" indicating that the minority's interest will sharply decline in value as a result of the sale (e.g., where the majority knows that the buyer plans to limit expansion of the corporation by confining his or her sales to a single buyer under his or her control).

Some courts go so far as to state that whenever control of the corporation is material, the majority must exercise "inherent fairness" and give the minority shareholders an "equal opportunity" to sell their shares on the same terms as the majority.

Finally, the majority breaches its fiduciary duty to the minority where it takes advantage of inside information to purchase minority shares.

Court actions or suits by shareholders Shareholders sometimes find it necessary to bring legal action against directors, officers, or majority shareholders who have injured them personally (e.g., where the majority breaches its fiduciary duty to the minority). If several shareholders have been injured, they may use a single class action to recover for the entire group.

Occasionally, however, it is not the shareholders who have been injured by the actions of others, but the corporation itself. For example, a director who takes personal advantage of a corporate opportunity or makes swing profits or violates the proxy rules promulgated by the Securities and Exchange Commission breaches his or her fiduciary duties to the corporation. And, as you know, a corporation may sue in its own name to recover damages.

But suppose that the corporation refuses to sue. The directors, who are responsible for bringing suit for the corporation, may well refuse to take legal action if it means suing one of their own members or a corporate officer for mismanagement. The shareholders, in this case, cannot sue as individuals because they have not been damaged as individuals. However, one or more shareholders can bring an action on behalf of the corporation to recover damages for the corporation. Such a proceeding is called a *derivative suit* because it derives from the corporation's cause of action.

A shareholder may bring a derivative suit only after he or she has made written demand upon the directors to take legal action, and the directors either refuse or fail to take action within a reasonable time. That is to say, a shareholder must give the corporation an opportunity to bring legal action before taking it upon himself or herself to sue on behalf of the corporation.

ARE THERE ANY SPECIAL RULES ON CORPORATE MERGERS AND CONSOLIDATIONS?

A *merger* takes place when an existing corporation absorbs one or more existing corporations: the absorbing corporation survives the merger; the absorbed corporations cease to exist.

A *consolidation* occurs when a new corporation is formed from one or more existing corporations: the new or consolidated corporation absorbs the existing corporations which cease to exist as separate entities.

The surviving or consolidated corporation succeeds to all the rights and liabilities of the absorbed corporations. After the merger or consolidation, the shareholders of the absorbed corporations own stock in the surviving or new corporation. Most states require shareholder approval of a proposed merger or consolidation by at least two-thirds of the shareholders of each corporation involved in the transaction. And, in most states, minority shareholders who vote against a proposed merger or consolidation have a statutory remedy: the dissenters can require the corporation in which they own stock to purchase their shares at fair market value as a condition precedent to merger or consolidation. For a minority shareholder to take advantage of this remedy, he or she must (1) file an objection to the proposed merger or consolidation before the shareholders meeting at which the proposal is to be considered; (2) vote against the proposal; and (3) make written demand upon the corporation to purchase his or her shares at a price to be determined by appraisal.

In a merger or consolidation, the surviving or consolidated corporation acquires the *stock* of the absorbed corporations. As an alternative to merger or consolidation, an existing corporation may simply purchase the assets of another corporation. Only a majority of the shareholders of the selling corporation must consent to the purchase; shareholders of the purchasing corporation need not approve. And, in most states, dissenters have no rights to be bought out as they do in a merger or consolidation.

Or a corporation may gain voting control of another corporation by purchasing at least 51 percent of its stock. In this case, the controlled corporation will continue to operate as a subsidiary of the controlling corporation. No shareholder approval is required.

WHAT ARE THE RULES ON DISSOLUTION AND LIQUIDATION OF A CORPORATION?

Dissolution of a corporation may be voluntary or involuntary. A corporation voluntarily dissolves when its directors meet and pass a resolution to dissolve and liquidate; the resolution must be ratified by a majority of the shareholders who are entitled to vote. Following ratification, the directors must file a certificate of dissolution with the proper state official, usually the corporation commissioner.

The state itself may force the corporation into involuntary dissolution by bringing what is called a "quo warranto" action to require forfeiture of the corporate charter. Usually, the state will do this only where the corporation engages in ultra vires activity or fails to properly organize and operate following issuance of the charter.

Creditors of a corporation cannot force the corporation into involuntary dissolution. But once dissolution has begun, the creditors' interests must be protected. To begin with, the corporation must notify the creditors of the dissolution and liquidation activity. It must carry out any existing contracts with the creditors (dissolution does not excuse performance of existing contracts). And the corporation must pay the creditors in full before paying the shareholders anything. But, remember, the shareholders of the corporation have limited liability and are not responsible for corporate debts. If the corporation has insufficient assets to pay all its creditors, the creditors cannot look to the individual shareholders for payment. However, if the corporation pays the shareholders first before paying the creditors, the creditors can trace the assets into the hands of the shareholders and require their return for distribution to the creditors.

After all creditors have been paid in full, the shareholders are entitled to their proportionate shares of the net assets of the corporation.

WHAT ARE SECURITIES WITHIN THE MEANING OF THE FEDERAL SECURITIES LAWS?

The most common form of security is the share of stock that a person owns in a corporation. However, the term "security" not only covers "equity" (ownership) interests but also "debt" interests—money loans made in the form of promissory notes, bonds, debentures, etc. A *bond* is simply a borrower's written promise given in return for money (or its equivalent) to pay a fixed sum of money (the face value of the bond or bond "principal") at a specified future time (the "maturity" date), with stated interest payable at fixed intervals. Corporations and governmental bodies issue bonds to raise revenue. Corporate bonds are frequently "convertible"—i.e., they may be exchanged for a stated number of common shares at certain times and under certain circumstances. *Debentures* are bonds that are not secured by specific assets.

But the term "security" is not restricted to shares, notes, bonds, and debentures. It covers any offering that constitutes an "investment" regardless of its form and regardless of whether it is oral or written. The basic test of whether something is a security is whether "the person *invests* his or her money in a common enterprise and is led to expect profits from the efforts of the promoter or a third party." Securities and Exchange Commission v. W.J. Howey Co., 328 U.S. 293, 66 S.Ct. 1100, 90 L.Ed.2d 1244 (1970).

Recent court holdings have expanded the definition of "security" to include the regulation of "pyramid" sale schemes in which an investor-buyer is obligated to persuade others to buy before he or she can receive any return on his or her investment (e.g., the typical "chain letter" scheme).

WHY IS IT NECESSARY TO REGULATE SECURITIES?

Because securities are intangibles, they are peculiarly susceptible to abuse and may be used to defraud naive and unsophisticated investors. The value of a share of corporate common stock, for example, depends on the value of the corporation. The value of a note depends on the ability of the maker to pay the note. If inaccurate or incomplete information regarding the securities is provided to the investing public, investors can be easily misled or defrauded.

To prevent this, the securities laws require full disclosure of all material facts surrounding the initial issuance ("primary offering") of securities and their subsequent resale in "secondary offerings" (many shares of publicly held corporations are traded thousands of times in the stock market). The latter is accomplished by requiring a continuous flow of information about the issuer of the securities. Antifraud provisions in the laws provide a civil action remedy for investors who are defrauded in the purchase or sale of securities.

WHY WOULD A CLOSELY HELD CORPORATION DECIDE TO SELL ITS SHARES TO THE PUBLIC?

A closely held corporation might decide to sell its shares to the public for any or all of the following reasons:

1. The corporation needs additional money in order to expand or diversify.
2. The shareholders of the corporation want to convert a portion of their stock to money so as to be able to invest in other companies. (They don't want all of their investment income dependent on the earnings of a single enterprise—they don't want all their "eggs in one basket.") Establishing a public market for their shares allows the shareholders to sell and liquidate their holdings at most any time.
3. The shareholders anticipate estate tax problems when one or more of their number pass away. By selling some of their holdings to the public the shareholders will not only establish a share value for estate tax purposes but will generate some liquidity (cash) with which to pay the death taxes.
4. Having publicly owned shares establishes a share value for purposes of merger or consolidation and makes a corporation more attractive for such purposes. Many closely held corporations will merge with publicly owned corporations so as to be sure of receiving readily marketable shares.
5. Having publicly owned shares makes it easier for a corporation to attract and hold key management people. One way that a corporation tries to attract and keep key management is by giving key executives and employees stock options. A stock option is simply a right to purchase so many shares of stock at a certain price. An executive or employee can exercise a stock option after the stock has gone up in value and thus share in the results of his or her successful management efforts. Stock options are particularly attractive to business executives when the stock has a public market and the executives can see its value going up on a daily basis.
6. Finally, a corporation with publicly owned securities generally has an easier time borrowing funds at low interest rates. Financial institutions prefer to make loans to such corporations because the public market for the corporation's shares provides the corporation with an additional source of equity capital, reducing the risk that the corporation will be unable to meet its loan commitments.

So you see, there are many reasons why a closely held corporation might want to sell its shares to the public. However, to make a "public offering," a corporation must strictly comply with all applicable state and federal securities laws.

WHAT FEDERAL LAW CONTROLS "PUBLIC OFFERINGS" OF SECURITIES?

The federal Securities Act of 1933 controls "public offerings" of securities. Often called the "truth in securities" law, it is essentially a "disclosure" statute. Section 5 of the Act states that no security may be offered or sold to the public through the use of the mail or any other means of interstate commerce unless the security is first *registered* with the Securities and Exchange Commission (the SEC). However, as will be discussed in a later section, certain securities and securities transactions are exempt from the registration requirements of the Act, including offers or sales by persons other than issuers, underwriters, or dealers (all defined below). The result is that most resales of securities by ordinary investors are exempt from registration as routine trading transactions or "casual sales." Thus, from a practical standpoint, the 1933 Act requires registration chiefly in the case of *primary offerings* (i.e., initial sales of securities to the public for the first time), although some *secondary offerings* (i.e., resales) that do not qualify as casual sales or routine trading transactions have no exemption to claim and must also satisfy the registration requirement.

So in studying securities, start out with the idea that any offer or sale of a security to the public is covered and requires registration unless a specific exemption can be found. The purpose of the registration is to provide full and fair disclosure of all material facts regarding the securities to be offered for sale. While the Securities Act does not give the SEC any power to prohibit public offerings of securities, it does give the Commission power to require the issuer of securities to make full disclosure of all material facts regarding the securities.

The Requirements of the Registration Statement

An issuer of securities (i.e., one who issues or proposes to issue securities) "registers" them by filing a registration statement with the SEC. The statement consists of two parts: first, a *prospectus* or pamphlet summarizing the key information contained in the registration statement (a copy of the prospectus must be furnished to every purchaser of the securities); and, second, *Part II* of the statement which must set forth extensive information about the securities and the issuer of the securities (Part II remains on file with the SEC but is available for public inspection).

The Securities Act specifically requires thirty-two items of information in the registration statement, and it authorizes the SEC to require whatever additional information it deems necessary for full disclosure. To facilitate the filing of the registration statement, the SEC has promulgated Form S–1 as the basic form for use in registering a proposed securities offering. Form S–1 runs to more than fifty pages of instructions and usually results in many times that number of pages when the registration statement is complete.

Information required includes the principal purposes for which the net proceeds to the registrant from the securities to be offered are intended to be used. The business done and intended to be done by the registrant must be described including competitive conditions in the industry and principal products produced and services rendered by the registrant. If the registrant was organized within the past five years, the names of the promoters, and the nature and amount of anything of value received by each promoter directly or indirectly from the registrant must be furnished. Also, any material legal proceedings must be described. Recent balance sheets as well as profit and loss and source and application of funds statements are required and must be certified by an independent certified or public accountant to guarantee an independent evaluation of the validity of the statements. An accountant is not "independent" for purposes of certifying financial statements included in a registration statement if he or she is (or was during the period under review) a director or officer of the issuer-corporation or if he or she holds a significant ownership interest in the corporation (significant with respect to the total capital of the corporation or the accountant's own personal fortune).

As you can see, the preparation of a registration statement is a very substantial undertaking. Remember that the objective of the Securities Act is to provide prospective investors with all the information they need to make intelligent, informed decisions about investing in securities. This is a difficult goal to accomplish because the issuer may resist telling all (to do so may guarantee that no one will invest). Also, many investors are financially unsophisticated and do not understand complex financial terminology or financial statements.

The Registration Process with the SEC

Once prepared, the registration statement must be filed with the main office of the SEC. The SEC is charged with the responsibility of enforcing and administering the federal securities laws, including the 1933 Securities Act and the 1934 Securities Exchange Act (see Chapter 5 for a description of this agency).

Unless the SEC orders to the contrary, a registration statement becomes effective automatically twenty days after it is filed with the Commission. While Section 5(c) of the Securities Act prohibits any offers to sell or to buy securities before the registration statement is filed, the Act permits offers but not sales during the twenty-day "waiting period" between filing and effectiveness. There are no restrictions on oral offers made during this period, but written offers may be made only through a "preliminary prospectus."

The outside front cover page of the preliminary prospectus must bear in red ink the following legend:

> A REGISTRATION STATEMENT RELATING TO THESE SECURITIES HAS BEEN FILED WITH THE SECURITIES AND EXCHANGE COMMISSION BUT HAS NOT YET BECOME EFFECTIVE. INFORMATION CONTAINED HEREIN IS SUBJECT TO COMPLETION OR AMENDMENT. THESE SECURITIES MAY NOT BE SOLD NOR MAY OFFERS TO BUY BE ACCEPTED PRIOR TO THE TIME THE REGISTRATION STATEMENT BECOMES EFFECTIVE. THIS PROSPECTUS SHALL NOT CONSTITUTE AN OFFER TO SELL OR THE SOLICITATION OF AN OFFER TO BUY NOR SHALL THERE BE ANY SALES OF THESE SECURITIES IN ANY STATE IN WHICH SUCH OFFER, SOLICITATION OR SALE WOULD BE UNLAWFUL PRIOR TO REGISTRATION OR QUALIFICATION UNDER THE SECURITIES LAWS OF ANY SUCH STATE.

A preliminary prospectus is often called a "red herring" prospectus because of the requirement that the legend be printed in red ink.

The SEC uses the twenty-day waiting period to review the registration statement. If it is readily apparent that the statement fails to accomplish the basic purpose of the Securities Act—that is, assure the public of adequate reliable information about the securities offered for sale—the SEC will notify the issuer in writing that it will spend no further time reviewing the statement and that no detailed comments about the statement will be forthcoming. (Generally, this occurs only where the statement is very poorly prepared or has glaring gaps in disclosure of required material). Such written notice from the SEC is called a "bed bug" letter.

An issuer who receives a "bed bug" letter must either rewrite the registration statement or forego the public offering.

Where the registration statement complies in most, but not all respects with the statutory requirements, the SEC will issue detailed comments as to how the statement can be brought into full conformity with the requirements. The Commission may require supplemental information, including letters from the issuer's chief executive officer, accountants, and managing underwriter (where the issue is being handled by underwriters) acknowledging that the parties are aware of their statutory responsibilities under the Securities Act. (An "underwriter" is a financing specialist—frequently a stock brokerage house—who is paid to offer advice regarding the need for public financing, the best types of securities to offer, the best time to offer them, and the best operating price. Usually, the underwriter determines the manner of distributing the securities and participates in the distribution. The actual distribution is often accomplished through a *syndicate* which is an association of brokerage firms with each member firm offering the securities to its customers.)

In any event, the statutory burden of full disclosure always remains on the issuer, the issuer's directors, the underwriter, the accountants, and any other experts named in the registration statement. *The burden never shifts to the SEC.* Even after the registration statement has become effective, there must be printed on the outside front cover page of the prospectus, in boldface at least as large as 10-point modern type, the following statement:

> THESE SECURITIES HAVE NOT BEEN APPROVED OR DISAPPROVED BY THE SECURITIES AND EXCHANGE COMMISSION. NOR HAS THE COMMISSION PASSED UPON THE ACCURACY OR ADEQUACY OF THIS PROSPECTUS. ANY REPRESENTATION TO THE CONTRARY IS A CRIMINAL OFFENSE.

Once a registration statement becomes effective, the securities covered by the statement may be sold, but a copy of the final prospectus must be delivered to each purchaser.

Exemptions under the Securities Act of 1933

Certain securities and securities transactions are exempt from the registration requirements of the Securities Act of 1933. A number of these are discussed below.

Securities issued or guaranteed by the government For example, government bonds, the proceeds of which are to be used for such things as sewage, parking, airports, docks, or sports facilities, are exempt.

Securities issued by banks Banks are regulated by other agencies including the Federal Reserve Board described in Chapter 5.

Short-term commercial paper Negotiable promissory notes and drafts that arise out of current business transactions or the proceeds of which are to be used for current operations are exempt so long as they will mature within nine months of their issuance date. Not included within the exemption are notes and drafts the proceeds of which are to be used to construct a plant, purchase equipment, or fund real estate development (this would be long-term capital investment as opposed to current operations).

Securities issued by nonprofit organizations Securities that are issued by religious, educational, or other charitable, nonprofit organizations are exempt.

Securities issued by savings and loan associations Like banks, savings and loan associations are supervised by other state and federal agencies and are exempt from the registration provisions of the Securities Act. The same is true of farmers' cooperative associations.

Securities issued by common carriers Common carriers are regulated by the Interstate Commerce Commission (see Chapter 5) and are exempt from the registration requirements of the Securities Act of 1933.

Insurance policies Insurance policies issued by insurance companies are not considered securities within the meaning of the 1933 Securities Act and are, therefore, not subject to the federal registration requirements. Of course, stock or other securities issued by insurance companies are subject to the registration requirements.

Securities exchanged with existing security holders Securities that are exchanged by an issuer with the issuer's existing security holders exclusively are exempt from federal registration requirements so long as no commissions are made or given on the exchange. For example, stock dividends, stock splits, the exchange of one class of stock for another—all fall within the exemption.

Intrastate offerings of securities Section 3(a)(11) of the Securities Act of 1933 exempts intrastate offerings of securities from the Section 5 registration requirements. An intrastate offering is an issue that is offered and sold only to residents within one state by an issuer who resides and does business within the state or, in the case of a corporation, is incorporated in and doing business in the state. The exemption is intended to facilitate local financing of local business operations.

To this end, SEC has adopted Rule 147 which establishes guidelines for companies that want to be certain they meet the requirements for the intrastate offering exemption. Rule 147 is said to be a "safe harbor" rule: an issuer who follows the guidelines sails in safe water and will generally qualify for the exemption. The Rule, however, is not exclusive, and a company that fails to comply with all of its requirements may still qualify for the intrastate exemption (although it will certainly be more difficult to establish).

Rule 147 requires the following:

1. The issuer must be incorporated or organized in the state in which it is making the offering.
2. The issuer must carry out a significant portion of its business in the state. The issuer satisfies this requirement if it derives 80 percent of its gross revenues from the state, locates 80 percent of its assets there, uses 80 percent of its net proceeds in the state, and maintains its principal office there.
3. The issuer must make offers and sales only to residents of the state. One sale or even one offer to sell to a nonresident may render the entire issue ineligible for the exemption.
4. Sales as well as resales to nonresidents are prohibited during the time the securities are being offered and sold by the issuer and for an additional period of nine months following the issuer's last sale (resales to residents are not restricted).
5. Precautions must be taken against sales and resales to nonresidents, including the placing of a restrictive legend on the securities certificate stating that the securities have not been registered and that resales can only be made to residents. Additionally, the issuer should obtain a written statement from each purchaser as to his or her residence and should lodge a stop transfer instruction with the stock transfer agent for the securities in question.

Note that there is no fixed limit on the size of an intrastate offering or the number of purchasers. If an issue qualifies as intrastate, the fact that the issuer used the mails intrastate in making the offering will not destroy the exemption.

But realize that even though no registration is required for an intrastate offering under the federal Securities Act of 1933, state securities laws (called "Blue Sky" laws) may well require registration before the intrastate offering can be made. Blue Sky laws require similar procedures.

Transactions by any person other than an issuer or underwriter This is also referred to as the "casual sales" exemption. The Securities Act specifically exempts from its registration requirements transactions by any person other than an issuer or underwriter. The exemption is frequently referred to as the "casual sales" exemption because it permits investors to make casual sales of their securities without registration. The exemption is limited to what are termed "routine trading transactions." This allows people across the country to buy and sell stock on the market, for example through the New York or American Stock Exchanges, without worrying about going through the registration process.

To qualify for the exemption, a person must not be an issuer or an underwriter. An issuer is any person who issues or proposes to issue a security (e.g., this would include corporate promoters). "Issuer" also includes, for purposes of the casual sales exemption, any *control person* (i.e., any person who directly or indirectly controls the issuer, also called an *affiliate*).

In strict terms, an underwriter is any person who (1) has purchased or participated in the purchase of securities from an issuer with a view to distributing any security; (2) offers or sells securities for an issuer in connection with the distribution of any security; or (3) participates in underwriting the distribution of any security.[7] A person is an underwriter if he or she purchases securities from a control person with a view toward, or offers or sells for a control person in connection with, the distribution of any security. As little as 10 percent or less may establish control where the remainder of the corporate stock is widely held.

Thus, secondary distributions of securities held by control persons are subject to the registration and prospectus requirements of the 1933 Act. They are considered to have as much potential for fraud and abuse as initial public offerings by issuers. However, SEC Rule 144 does permit control persons to sell strictly limited quantities of their securities without registration (generally not to exceed during any three month period 1 percent of the total class of shares outstanding) if they sell them exclusively through brokers' transactions, do not solicit or arrange for solicitation of orders, and make no payments other than to a broker who executes the order to sell. Also, there must be available to purchasers adequate information about the securities and the issuer of the securities. And the control person must file notice of intent to make the sale with the SEC at the same time as he or she places the order to sell with the broker.

Small offerings under Regulation A (not over $1.5 million) Section 3(b) of the Securities Act authorizes the SEC to exempt from registration certain public offerings where the securities to be offered involve relatively small dollar amounts. Under this provision, the SEC has adopted Regulation A, which provides that if the total amount of offerings made by an issuer during any twelve month period does not exceed $1.5 million, the offering is exempt from the usual registration requirements. However, under Regulation A, the issuer must still file a simplified "registration statement" for the small offering consisting of a notification, offering circular, and exhibits with the SEC's regional office in the area where the company's principal business activities are conducted.

Thus, there is not a complete exemption for small offerings but merely a simplified form of registration. It is often called the "short form" of registration, since the offering circular, which is similar in content to a prospectus, must be supplied to each purchaser and the securities issued may be freely traded following the Regulation A issuance. The principal advantage of a Regulation A offering as opposed to a full registration is that the required financial statements are simpler and need not be audited.

---

7. Corporate directors or officers who participate in the distribution of securities may be deemed underwriters if they receive commissions or payments over and above their regular salaries.

All types of companies may use Regulation A, with the exception of investment companies registered or required to be registered under the Investment Company Act of 1940.

It should be noted that Regulation A, in addition to being available to issuer companies, is also available on a limited basis to shareholders who desire to make resales of their securities but cannot find an exemption from registration. With respect to affiliates (control persons), the general rule under Regulation A is that securities offered by an issuer and its affiliates must not together exceed the $1.5 million ceiling. Moreover, any one affiliate may issue no more than $100,000 of securities in a one year period. The affiliate must also have the issuer's permission to make the issuance, based on a finding by the issuer that the affiliate's offering will not interfere with any financing efforts contemplated by the issuer under Regulation A during the following one year period.

Regarding shareholders other than affiliates, they may also use Regulation A to offer $100,000 of securities each during a one year period (where the sales don't qualify as casual sales). However, the aggregate amount offered by all such shareholders in any one year period may not exceed $300,000. But note that their offerings, unlike those of affiliates, are not included in the issuer's $1.5 million ceiling.

Similar to filing under Regulation A is registration using a relatively new form—the S–18—which allows issuers to make a public offering up to $5 million without going through the full S–1 registration requirements. Form S–18 was adopted by the SEC in April, 1979 as an alternative to S–1. It is available for the registration of securities to be sold to the public for cash not exceeding an aggregate offering price of $5 million, provided that the issuer is not subject to the SEC's continuous reporting requirements under the Securities Exchange Act of 1934 (as you will recall, these are issuers with at least 500 shareholders of equity securities and total assets of at least $3 million). Form S–18 offers reduced disclosure requirements and a less expensive registration process for the smaller issuer who desires to gain access to the public capital markets.

While many of the requirements for an S–18 registration statement are the same as those for a full registration, Form S–18 does permit a qualifying issuer to provide audited financial statements for two fiscal years as opposed to three as required under Form S–1; to include less extensive narrative disclosure, particularly in the area of description of the business; and to file with the SEC's regional office nearest the place where the company's principal business operations are conducted. The advantage to regional filing is that the local office may be more familiar with the local business community and financial environment as well as the background and history of the company.

Like Regulation A, Form S–18 may also be used by selling shareholders such as affiliates who cannot find an exemption from registration; they may use S–18 to offer up to $1.5 million (e.g., an affiliate who desires to offer or sell more than Rule 144 would permit without registration).

Limited Offers under Regulation D In March, 1982, the SEC adopted Regulation D under Sections 4(2) and 3(b) of the Securities Act of 1933 to coordinate various "limited offering" exemptions and streamline the existing requirements applicable to private offers and sales of securities (i.e., offers and sales not amounting to "public" offerings requiring registration). Regulation D establishes three exemptions from registration in Rules 504, 505, and 506.[8]

It is important to realize at the outset that transactions exempt by virtue of Regulation D are not exempt from the antifraud or civil liability provisions of the federal securities laws (as discussed below). Also, the rules are available only to issuers of securities, not including affiliates (control persons) in this case or any other person for resale of the issuer's securities. The rules provide an exemption only for the transactions in which the securities are offered or sold by the issuer, not for the securities themselves. As a result, the securities are "restricted" securities, and resales must be accomplished through registration or some exemption from the registration requirements.

Offers and sales made more than six months before the start of a Regulation D offering or more than six months after completion will not be "integrated" (i.e., considered part of the Regulation D offering) so long as, during those six month periods, there are no offers or sales of securities by or for the issuer that are of the same or a similar class as those offered or sold under Regulation D. If they are, they will be integrated and counted as part of the offering. In questionable cases, the SEC will consider the following factors to determine whether offerings should be integrated:

1. whether the sales are part of a single plan of financing;
2. whether the sales involve issuance of the same class of securities;
3. whether the sales have been made at or about the same time;
4. whether the same type of consideration is received; and
5. whether the sales are made for the same general purposes.

Rule 504—Exemption for limited offers and sales of securities not exceeding $500,000 The exemption provided by Rule 504 is available to issuers other than covered corporations (those subject to registration and continuing disclosure under the 1934 Act) and investment companies. Under the Rule, qualified issuers may offer up to $500,000 of securities in a twelve month period to any number of issuers without going through registration. The rationale for the Rule is to provide an exemption for offers and sales made by small issuers in raising small amounts of capital. Due to the small size and limited character of the offering, it is felt that no public purpose is served by requiring registration. The specific requirements for the exemption include;

1. The aggregate offering price must not exceed $500,000 in twelve months.
2. The offering must not be made through any form of general solicitation or general advertising which includes, but is not limited to, any advertisement, article, notice, or other communication published in any newspaper, maga-

8. Rule 504 replaced the former Rule 240 ("very small offerings"), Rule 505 the former Rule 242, and Rule 506 the former Rule 146 dealing with private placements.

zine, or similar media or broadcast over television or radio; or any seminar or meeting where attendance has been solicited through general advertising.
3. The issuer must exercise reasonable care to assure that the purchasers of the securities are not underwriters but rather are buying for investment. Precautions that should be taken include, but are not limited to, reasonable inquiry to determine if the purchaser is acquiring the securities for himself or herself or for other persons; written disclosure to each purchaser prior to sale that the securities have not been registered under the Act, and therefore cannot be resold unless they are registered or unless an exemption is available; and placement of a legend on the securities certificate stating that the securities have not been registered under the Act and setting forth or referring to the restrictions on transferability and sale of the securities.
4. The issuer must notify the SEC within fifteen days after the first sale of the securities, using Form D.

Requirements two and three above are waived where the offers and sales are made exclusively in one or more states each of which provides for the registration of the securities and requires the delivery of a disclosure document before sale. The securities, in such case, will not be restricted.

Rule 504 does not require that any specified disclosure concerning the securities be provided to purchasers. However, the businessperson should take care that sufficient information is provided to meet the full disclosure obligations which exist under the antifraud provisions of the securities laws.

Rule 505—Exemption for limited offers and sales of securities not exceeding $5 million Rule 505 was adopted by the SEC to provide small businesses with more flexibility in raising capital than is available under Rule 504. Rule 505 provides a limited offering exemption available to all issuers other than investment companies for sales of securities up to $5 million in any twelve month period without registration. The specific requirements for the exemption include:

1. The aggregate offering price must not exceed $5 million in any twelve month period.
2. The issuer must reasonably believe there are no more than thirty-five purchasers. However, in calculating the number of purchasers, "accredited investors" are not included.[9] Under Regulation D, "accredited investor" is defined to include banks, insurance companies, registered investment companies, business development companies, or small business investment companies, and certain employee benefit plans for which investment decisions are made by a bank, insurance company, or registered investment adviser; any employee benefit plan within the meaning of Title I of the Employee Retirement Income Security Act with total assets in excess of $5 million; private business development companies; charitable organizations with assets in ex-

9. Also not included are (1) any relative, spouse, or relative of the spouse of a purchaser who has the same principal residence as the purchaser; (2) any trust or estate in which a purchaser and any of the persons related to him or her collectively have more than 50 percent of the beneficial interest; or (3) any corporation or other organization of which a purchaser and any of the persons related to him or her collectively are beneficial owners of more than 50 percent of the equity securities or equity interests.

cess of $5 million; directors, executive officers, and general partners of the issuer; persons purchasing at least $150,000 of securities, where the total purchase price does not exceed 20 percent of the purchaser's net worth; natural persons with a net worth of at least $1 million; and natural persons with an income of at least $200,000 per year for two years preceding the offering and for the year in which the offering is made.

3. The offering must not be made through any form of general solicitation or general advertising as defined above.

4. Where the offering involves one or more nonaccredited investors, the issuer must furnish *all* purchasers with information regarding the issuer, its business, and the securities offered. Where only accredited investors are involved, there are no specific information requirements. This is because accredited investors, by definition, are financially sophisticated and are in a position to demand whatever information they deem necessary from the issuer.

5. The issuer must exercise reasonable care to assure that the purchasers of the securities are not underwriters but rather are buying for investment, taking the same precautions as outlined above.

6. The issuer must notify the SEC within fifteen days after the first sale of the securities, using Form D.

Rule 506—Exemption for limited offers and sales without regard to dollar amount of the offering This is the so-called "private placement" exemption. Section 4(2) of the Securities Act of 1933 provides an exemption from registration for "transactions by an issuer not involving any public offering." Because of the uncertainty as to the precise limits of this private placement exemption, the SEC adopted Rule 506 under Regulation D as a "safe harbor" rule, providing objective standards upon which businesspersons can rely in order to qualify for the exemption. Unlike Rules 504 and 505, Rule 506 is available to any issuer. The specific requirements for the exemption include:

1. The issuer must reasonably believe that there are no more than thirty-five purchasers of securities (but, again, not including accredited investors in calculation of the thirty-five).

2. The issuer must reasonably believe immediately prior to making any sale that each purchaser who is not an accredited investor either alone or with his or her purchaser representative has such knowledge and experience in financial and business matters that he or she is capable of evaluating the merits and risk of the investment.

3. The offering must not be made through any form of general solicitation or general advertising.

4. Where the offering involves one or more accredited investors, the issuer must furnish *all* purchasers with information regarding the issuer, its business, and the securities offered (the same kind of information as would be provided in a registration statement). Where only accredited investors are involved, there are no specific information requirements.

5. The issuer shall exercise reasonable care to assure that purchasers of the securities are not underwriters but rather are buying for investment. Generally, the issuer requires the purchaser to sign "investment letters" stating that they are buying for investment only (for this reason, shares issued pursuant to the private placement exemption are commonly referred to as "lettered stock"). The securities themselves generally bear a legend calling attention to the fact that the purchasers represented that they were purchasing for investment pursuant to the private placement exemption. The legend has the effect of making the securities largely unmarketable.

6. The issuer must notify the SEC within fifteen days after the first sale of the securities, using Form D.

Notice that under Rule 506, there is no ceiling on the amount which may be raised by the offering. Also notice that the securities may be sold to an unlimited number of accredited investors.[10] Of course, Rule 506 does add a new requirement—that the issuer must believe that any nonaccredited investor has sufficient financial sophistication to appreciate the risks of the investment. That determination is sometimes difficult to make and need not be made under a 505 limited offer.

Resale of restricted securities Subject to the limited exception noted with regard to Rule 504, securities acquired under Regulation D limited offering exemptions are restricted securities and must be registered prior to resale or else an exemption from registration found. SEC Rule 144 provides one such exemption. It provides that restricted securities held by a control person or other purchaser may be resold without being deemed part of a public distribution (offering) if certain conditions are met. First, the securities must be owned and fully paid for for a period of at least two years prior to resale. (This insures that the investor purchased for investment rather than for public distribution.)[11] Second, the amount of securities sold during any three month period generally must not exceed 1 percent of the class outstanding.[12] Third, the sale may be made only through brokers' transactions. Fourth, there must be available to the public current information about the issuer of the securities. And finally, notice of the sale must be filed with the SEC on a prescribed form concurrently with the sale.

Ordinary investors (persons other than issuers, control persons, or brokers or dealers) may also sell restricted securities pursuant to SEC Rule 237 without registration if the issuer has been an active business concern for at least five years, the seller has fully owned the securities for at least the same

---

10. The Small Business Investment Incentive Act of 1980 created a new statutory exemption from registration under the Securities Act of 1933—Section 4(6)—for transactions involving offers and sales of securities by any issuer solely to one or more accredited investors where the total offering price of each issue does not exceed $5 million, the offering is not made by any form of advertising or public solicitation, and notice is given on Form D. Section 4(6) does not contain any specific disclosure requirements. However, the adoption of Rule 506 under Regulation D in 1982 appears to have removed any special benefit from using 4(6) as any offering that would qualify for exemption under Section 4(6) would also appear to qualify under Rule 506.

11. You will recall from our "casual sales" exemption discussion that control persons can also use Rule 144 to resell nonrestricted securities. The same basic requirements apply except that there is no two year holding period.

12. In some cases, the volume limitations will not apply to sales of restricted securites by noncontrol persons who have fully owned the securities for at least three or four years and the securities are either listed on a national securities exchange or are securities of a "covered" corporation.

period of time, sales of the issuer's securities during a one year period do not exceed the lesser of $50,000 or the proceeds from sale of 1 percent of the issuer's shares outstanding in that class of securities, and the sales transactions are negotiated other than through a broker or dealer.

Finally, don't forget that Regulation A and Form S–18 may also be used for resales by shareholders, including control persons, without going through the full S–1 requirements.

Dealer and broker transactions Generally, a dealer or broker is anyone who engages in the business of offering, buying, selling, or otherwise dealing or trading in securities issued by another. The 1933 Act expressly exempts all brokers' transactions that are executed upon an *unsolicited customer's order* to buy or sell securities. The customer gives the order; there is no solicitation from the broker. The broker-dealer exemption is designed to insure that individuals may dispose of their securities freely without registration and to assure an open market for securities at all times. However, the exemption applies only to the dealer's or broker's part of the transaction—the customer must find his or her own exemption from registration or he or she will be liable under the Act (usually, the customer can rely on the "casual sales" exemption).

Dealers and brokers are not exempt when they acquire issued securities during the distribution period and solicit purchasers for the securities. Under the SEC "40-day" rule, brokers or dealers who solicit sales of securities within forty days after the effective date of a registration statement covering the securities must comply with the same prospectus requirements as issuers and underwriters of the securities.

Any person who claims one of the exemptions above has the burden of establishing all the facts necessary to support the exemption. If there is the slightest variation from the exemption requirements, the basis for the exemption may be gone, and, if so, every offer or sale will violate Section 5 of the Securities Act. A person who violates Section 5 is liable to the purchaser and must refund the full purchase price. A consideration of civil liabilities follows.

The Civil Liability of People Who Fail to Make Full Disclosure

Section 5 of the Securities Act of 1933 makes it unlawful for any person to sell nonexempt securities in interstate commerce unless a registration statement covering the securities has been filed with the SEC and is in effect. Section 11 of the Act puts teeth into the law by providing civil liabilities "on account of any false registration statement."

Under Section 11, *any person* who acquires a security issued pursuant to a registration statement (including the prospectus) containing a misrepresentation or omission of a material fact may sue *any or all persons* connected with the preparation or publication of the statement. The term "material" has been interpreted by the courts to mean "a fact which if it had been correctly stated or disclosed would have deterred or tended to deter the average prudent investor from purchasing the securities in question." Escott v. BarChris Construction Corp., 283 F.Supp. 643 (S.D.N.Y.1968).

FIGURE 6–1 PUBLIC OFFERINGS OF SECURITIES

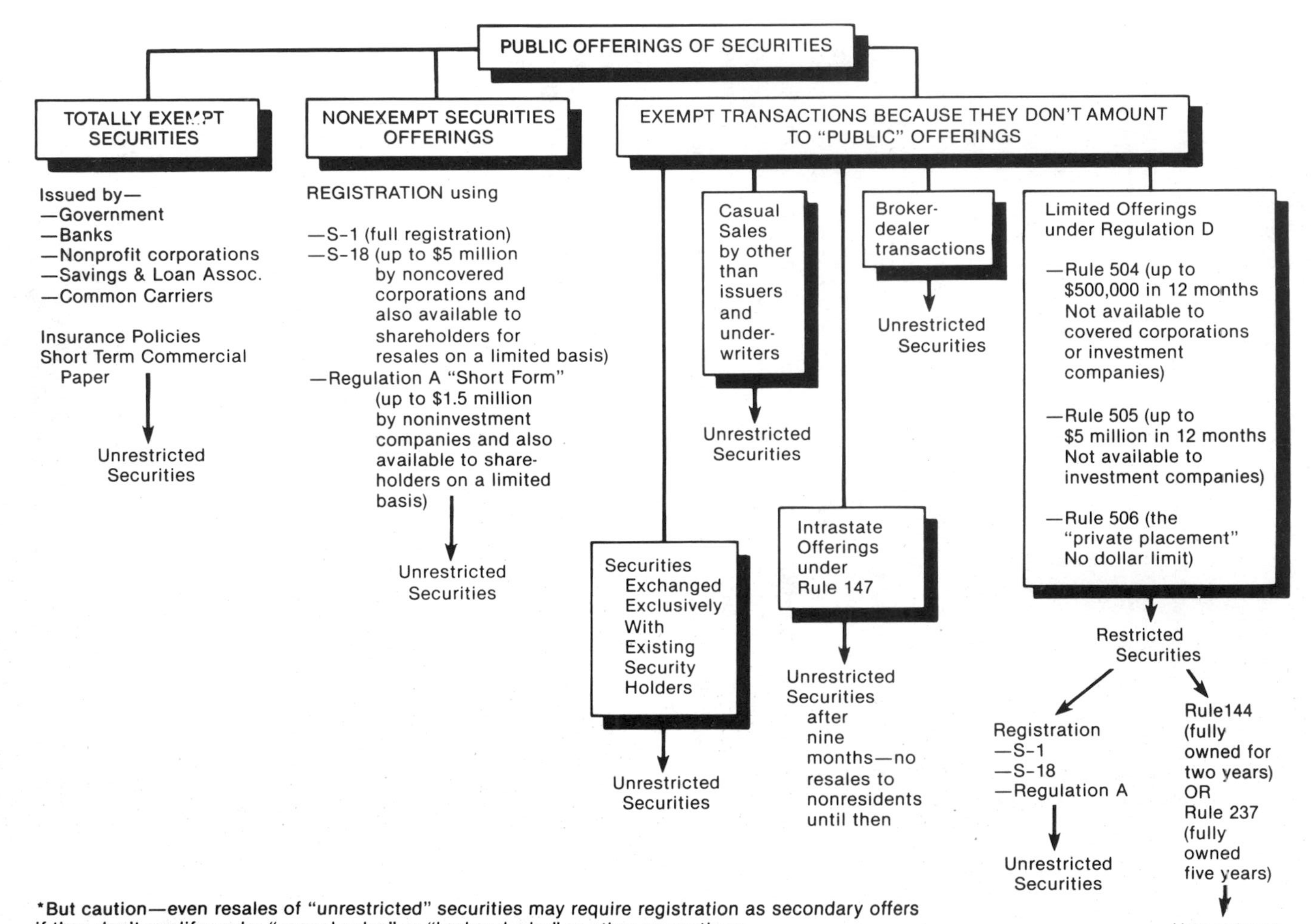

*But caution—even resales of "unrestricted" securities may require registration as secondary offers if they don't qualify under "casual sales" or "broker-dealer" or other exemptions.
The only exception is for totally exempt securities which never require registration.

The right to sue under Section 11 is thus not limited to the original issuee (purchaser) of the security—any person who subsequently acquires the security from the original issuee or his or her transferee may also sue under the Section. To recover, the security holder must prove only that some material fact was omitted or misrepresented in the registration statement, resulting in money loss to the security holder. The security holder does not have to prove that he or she relied on the omission or misrepresentation in making the purchase.

As to who is liable under Section 11, the *issuer* of the securities (including control persons under Section 11) is strictly liable for any loss resulting from the omission or misrepresentation (i.e., the issuer is liable regardless of how much care he or she exercised in preparing and publishing the statement). Also liable, but not strictly so, are (1) any *underwriter* of the securities, (2) any person who *signed* the registration statement, (3) *officers, directors, or partners* of the issuer at the time the registration statement was filed (including those who agreed to be named and were named on the registration statement as prospective directors or partners), and (4) any *professional* such as an accountant, engineer, appraiser, or the like who is named in the registration statement as having certified the portion of the statement containing the omission or misrepresentation.

The people listed in (1) through (4) above are not strictly liable under Section 11 but are liable only if they failed to exercise "due diligence" with respect to the information contained in the registration statement. As to the portions of the registration statement made on the authority of an expert, "due diligence" is established as long as the defendant had no reasonable ground to disbelieve the expert's statements. As to all other portions, the burden is on the defendant to show that he or she personally investigated the accuracy of the statement—he or she cannot escape liability on the basis that he or she accepted the management's representations at face value.

The type and extent of investigation required of a particular defendant depends on his or her degree of expertise as well as his or her relationship to the issuer. Obviously, a director who is actively engaged in management of the business will have more responsibility than a director who has little to do with management. As for an accountant, he or she is expected to use the generally accepted principles of the accounting profession in making his or her expert judgment.

Note that a defendant has a good defense to liability under Section 11 if he or she can show that the purchaser had knowledge of the misstatement or omission at the time of making the purchase. The defendant also has a good defense to the extent that he or she can show that the security declined in value for reasons apart from the misstatement or omission (e.g., where the entire industry is depressed, and all stocks have declined in value).

In bringing actions under Section 11, the buyer's measure of damages is the difference between the amount the buyer paid for the security (not exceeding the price at which the security was offered to the public) and the security's fair market value at the time the suit is brought or, if the security is resold prior to initiation of the suit, its resale price. In no case will the buyer's measure of damages exceed the public offering price of the securities.

ARE THERE ANY RULES GOVERNING DEALINGS IN SECURITIES AFTER THEIR INITIAL ISSUE?

As we have seen, the Securities Act of 1933 controls public offerings of securities: the Act requires full disclosure through use of a registration statement, including a prospectus. It covers both primary offerings of securities (i.e., initial issues) as well as those secondary offerings (i.e., resales) that cannot find an exemption from registration (e.g., secondary distributions by control persons that don't qualify as casual sales).

The Securities Exchange Act of 1934, on the other hand, governs dealings in securities subsequent to their initial issue. It requires all "covered corporations" (again, all companies that list their shares on a national securities exchange [13] *or* that have at least 500 shareholders of equity securities and total assets of at least $3 million) to register their securities with the SEC and file quarterly reports with the Commission providing a complete up-to-date statement of all business operations and matters affecting the value of the securities. The information required in the reports closely parallels that required in the 1933 Act registration statement, including detailed information as to the nature of the registrant's business, any significant changes in the business during the preceding fiscal year, a description of the physical properties of the registrant, current financial reports, identification of the registrant's executive directors and officers and their holdings in the corporation, and identification of other principal holders of the corporate securities.

Also, any person who owns more than 5 percent of any class of securities of a covered corporation must file an individual report with the SEC disclosing his or her holdings. In this way, the investing public has access to information that will help it spot attempts by an investor to take over corporate management by gaining control of at least 51 percent of the voting stock. Along these same lines, it is unlawful under the 1934 Act for any party to use any means of interstate commerce to attempt to gain control of a covered corporation by means of a *tender offer* without making prior disclosure to the SEC. A tender offer is a general offer to purchase the securities of a corporation, with the offer made directly to the corporation's shareholders. The SEC requires prior disclosure of the background and identity of the person making the offer, the sources and amounts of any consideration to be used, any present or future plans for the purchased securities, the number of shares owned, and the existence of any contracts, arrangements, or other understandings relating to the issuer or its securities. The tender offer rule does not apply if, after completing the offer, the offeror is not the owner of at least 5 percent or more of the class of security purchased.

---

13. An exchange is an organization which provides a marketplace or facilities for bringing together purchasers and sellers of securities. There are more than a dozen national exchanges which must meet standards set by the SEC. And the exchanges themselves set strict standards for listing corporations (e.g., the New York Stock Exchange requires a corporation to have at least 2,000 shareholders and $16 million of assets). The practical result is that corporations that list their shares on a national exchange will always meet the second test of having at least 500 shareholders and total assets of at least $3 million.

It is also unlawful under the 1934 Act for any person making a tender offer or defending against one to make any untrue statement concerning the offer or to engage in any fraudulent, deceptive, or manipulative acts or practices in connection with the offer.

And finally, don't forget that covered corporations are also subject to the 1934 Act provisions relating to proxies (Section 14) and short swing profits (Section 16) as discussed previously in the chapter.

WHAT CIVIL LIABILITY IS PROVIDED UNDER THE SECURITIES EXCHANGE ACT OF 1934?

The SEC has promulgated Rule 10b–5 as the basic antifraud provision of the Securities Exchange Act (the Rule was referred to earlier in connection with recovery of insider profits). The Rule provides:

> It shall be unlawful for any person, directly or indirectly, by the use of any means or instrumentality of interstate commerce, or of the mails, or of any facility of any national securities exchange,
>
> (1) to employ any device, scheme, or artifice to defraud,
>
> (2) to make any (oral or written) untrue statement of a material fact or to omit to state a material fact necessary in order to make the statements made, in the light of circumstances, under which they were made, not misleading, or
>
> (3) to engage in any act, practice, or course of business which operates or would operate as a fraud or deceit upon any person in connection with the purchase or sale of any security.

The language of Rule 10b–5 is all-encompassing. So long as the interstate commerce requirement is met ("the use of any means or instrumentality of interstate commerce, or of the mails, or of any facility of any national securities exchange"), the Rule applies to *any* purchase or sale by *any* person of *any* security. There are no exemptions. All securities—whether publicly traded, or closely held, registered or unregistered, listed or traded over the counter—fall within the scope of the Rule.

The Rule covers not only the original issuance of securities but also every subsequent resale—even a redemption or repurchase by the issuer corporation. It applies to every transfer or exchange of securities, including the "exchange of stock" that occurs in a merger or consolidation.

As to who may sue under the Rule, any *buyer* or *seller* of securities who suffers a money loss as the result of another's fraudulent activity in connection with the purchase or sale may sue (under Section 11 of the 1933 Act, only the *buyer* may sue).

As to who may be sued, any person who violates the Rule may be whether or not he or she actively participated in the purchase or sale. All that is required is that the party's activity be "connected with" the purchase or sale (meaning any activity that would cause a reasonable investor to rely thereon in making a purchase or sale). No privity between the plaintiff and the defendant (i.e., no contract or other direct dealing) is required. Depending on the circumstances, any of the following may be sued: buyer, seller, issuer, underwriter, broker, accountant, lawyer, even a complete outsider (e.g., a stock brokerage house that publishes false information concerning a security prompting a purchaser to buy the security from another party).

To recover under Rule 10b–5, the plaintiff purchaser or seller must prove that:

1. The defendant misrepresented or failed to disclose a material fact or otherwise acted so as to cheat or defraud the plaintiff in connection with the purchase or sale. An alleged omission or misrepresentation may be oral or written; the latter may be found in a registration statement, prospectus, annual report, proxy statement, press release, or any other document.
2. The omission or misrepresentation was material (such that a reasonable investor would have attached importance to it in deciding whether to purchase or sell).
3. The defendant's activity was intentional (which, in some cases, may include a situation where the defendant acted in reckless disregard of the truth).
4. The plaintiff relied on the defendant's manipulative or deceptive device or conduct in making the purchase or sale (contrast this with the antifraud provisions of the 1933 Act—Section 11, where reliance need not be shown).

Rule 10b–5 has been given a very expansive interpretation by the courts and is the leading antifraud provision of the federal securities acts. It has been applied to hold accountable underwriters, dealers, accountants, and lawyers who have published misleading information about securities. Issuer corporations have sued their promoters under Rule 10b–5 to recover for "watered stock" violations (i.e., where the promoters have transferred overvalued personal property to the corporation in exchange for shares). Shareholders have brought class actions to recover for 10b–5 violations. They have maintained derivative suits (on behalf of the corporation) under the Rule against corporate directors who have engaged in fraudulent activity in connection with the purchase or sale of securities to the shareholders.

Under Rule 10b–5 any buyer or seller who is injured by another's manipulative or deceptive activity may sue to rescind the transaction (if privity exists between the plaintiff and defendant) or to recovery money damages. For example, a seller who sues for damages under 10b–5 is entitled to the difference between the price he or she received for the securities and the price he or she would have received had there been no fraud.

Also any person who willfully violates the 1934 Act may, upon conviction, be fined from $5,000 to $10,000 or imprisoned not more than five years or both.

WHAT IS THE FOREIGN CORRUPT PRACTICES ACT?

The Foreign Corrupt Practices Act was passed by Congress in 1977 as an amendment to the Securities Exchange Act of 1934. The Act is designed to prevent the use of corporate funds for corrupt purposes. Among other things, the Act requires companies that are subject to the registration and continuing disclosure requirements of the Securities Exchange Act of 1934 (those with 500 shareholders and $3 million of assets) to maintain strict accounting standards and management control over their assets.

The statute imposes affirmative duties on such companies to maintain books, records, and accounts which, in reasonable detail, accurately and fairly reflect the transactions of the corporation; and it requires them to design an adequate system of internal accounting controls to assure, among other things, that the assets of the issuer are used for proper corporate purposes.

The Foreign Corrupt Practices Act also makes it a crime for any U.S. company (not just covered corporations) to bribe a foreign government official for specified corrupt purposes. Under the Act, it is unlawful for a corporation to make corrupt use of the mails or other means of interstate commerce in furtherance of an offer, payment, promise to pay, or authorization of payment of anything of value to any foreign official, foreign political party, candidate for foreign political office, or any other person which the issuer knows or has reason to know will make such an offer, promise, or payment. The purpose of the payment must be to influence an act or decision of a foreign official, party, candidate, etc., to use his or her influence to affect a government act or decision so as to assist the corporation in obtaining, retaining, or directing business to any person. The word "corruptly" connotes an evil motive or purpose—an intent wrongfully to influence the recipient. It is no defense that the payment was demanded as a price for gaining entry into a market or to obtain a contract since, at some point, the U.S. company would have to make a conscious decision whether or not to bribe. Companies violating the criminal prohibitions face a maximum fine of $1 million. Individuals acting on behalf of such companies face a maximum fine of $10,000 and five years in jail.

Cases

Partner Dooley made it clear that he was "voting no."

SUMMERS v. DOOLEY

Supreme Court of Idaho, 1971.
94 Idaho 87, 481 P.2d 318.

DONALDSON, Justice

This lawsuit tried in the district court, involves a claim by one partner against the other for $6,000. The complaining partner asserts that he has been required to pay out more than $11,000 in expenses without any reimbursement from either the partnership funds or his partner. The expenditure in question was incurred by the complaining partner (John Summers, plaintiff-appellant) for the purpose of hiring an additional employee. The trial court denied him any relief except for ordering that he be entitled to one half $966.72 which it found to be a legitimate partnership expense.

The pertinent facts leading to this lawsuit are as follows. Summers entered into a partnership agreement with Dooley (defendant-respondent) in 1958 for the purpose of operating a trash collection business. The business was operated by the two men and when either was unable to work, the nonworking partner provided a replacement at his own expense. In 1962, Dooley became unable to work and, at his own expense, hired an employee to take his place. In July, 1966, Summers approached his partner Dooley regarding the hiring of an additional employee but Dooley refused. Nevertheless, on his own initiative, Summers hired the man and paid him out of his own pocket. Dooley, upon discovering that Summers had hired an additional man, objected, stating that he did not feel additional labor was necessary and refused to pay for the new employee out of the partnership funds. Summers continued to operate the business using the third man and in October of 1967 instituted suit in the district court for $6,000 against his partner, the gravamen of the complaint being that Summers has been required to pay out more than $11,000 in expenses, incurred in the hiring of the additional man, without any reimbursement from either the partnership funds or his partner. After trial before the court, sitting without a jury, Summers was granted only partial relief and he has appealed. He urges in essence that the trial court erred by failing to conclude that he should be reimbursed for expenses and costs connected in the employment of extra help in the partnership business.

The principal thrust of appellant's contention is that in spite of the fact that one of the two partners refused to consent to the hiring of additional help, nonetheless, the non-consenting partner retained profits earned by the labors of the third man and therefore the non-consenting partner should be estopped from denying the need and value of the employee, and has by his behavior ratified the act of the other partner who hired the additional man.

The issue presented for decision by this appeal is whether an equal partner in a two man partnership has the authority to hire a new employee in disregard of the objection of the other partner and then attempt to charge the dissenting partner with the costs incurred as a result of his unilateral decision.

The State of Idaho has enacted specific statutes with respect to the legal concept known as "partnership." Therefore any solution of partnership problems should logically begin with an application of the relevant code provision.

In the instant case the record indicates that although Summers requested his partner Dooley to agree to the hiring of a third man, such requests were not honored. In fact Dooley made it clear that he was "voting no" with regard to the hiring of an additional employee.

An application of the relevant statutory provisions and pertinent case law to the factual situation presented by the instant case indicates that the trial court was correct in its disposal of the issue since a majority of the partners did not consent to the hiring of the third man. I.C. § 53–318(8) provides:

> "Any difference arising as to ordinary matters connected with the partnership business may be decided by a *majority of the partners*. * * *" (emphasis supplied.)

* * * A careful reading of the statutory provision indicates that subsection 5 bestows *equal rights in the management and conduct of the partnership business* upon all of the partners. The concept of equality between partners with respect to management of business affairs is a central theme and recurs throughout the Uniform Partnership Law, I.C. § 53–301 et seq., which has been enacted in this jurisdiction. Thus the only reasonable interpretation of I.C. § 53–318(8) is that business differences must be decided by a majority of the partners provided no other agreement between the partners speaks to the issues.

A noted scholar has dealt precisely with the issue to be decided.

> "* * * if the partners are equally divided, those who forbid a change must have their way." Walter B. Lindley, A Treatise on the Law of Partnership, Ch. II, § iii, ¶ 24–8, p. 403 (1924). See also, W. Shumaker, A Treatise on the Law of Partnership, § 97, p. 266.

In the case at bar one of the partners continually voiced objection to the hiring of the third man. He did not sit idly by and acquiesce in the actions of his partner. Under these circumstances it is manifestly unjust to permit recovery of an expense which was incurred individually and not for the benefit of the partnership but rather for the benefit of one partner.

Judgment affirmed.

Was the continuation of the newspaper after the death of the partners an act of winding up the partnership?

KING v. STODDARD

California Court of Appeal, First District, Division 3, 1972.
28 Cal.App.3d 708, 104 Cal.Rptr. 903.

Harold C. BROWN, Associate Justice

This is an appeal from a judgment in the sum of $12,370 rendered in favor of respondents, Harley King and Stanford White, for accounting services performed for the Walnut Kernel, a newspaper. The action was brought against the executors of two deceased partners who owned the newspaper.

The question presented on this appeal is whether the continuation of the newspaper after the death of the partners was an act of winding up the partnership under Corporations Code section 15035 so as to render the estate of the partners liable for an accountant's bill incurred subsequent to the death of the partners.

The facts: Prior to 1962, the newspaper, Walnut Kernel, was operated as a general partnership in which Lyman E. Stoddard, Sr., and Alda S. Stoddard owned a 51 percent interest as community property, and their son, Lyman E. Stoddard, Jr., owned 49 percent. On January 3, 1963, Alda S. Stoddard died and her daughter, Nancy Gans, was appointed executrix. After the death of Alda S. Stoddard, no formal winding up of the partnership took place. On February 13, 1964, Lyman E. Stoddard, Sr., died, and his son, John L. Stoddard, was appointed executor.

The operation of the business continued after the death of Lyman E. Stoddard, Sr.; Lyman E. Stoddard Jr., operated it as the sole surviving partner. John L. Stoddard, who was then acting on behalf of both estates, considered his duty was to obtain the winding up of partnership affairs as quickly as possible. He was not satisfied with the continuation of the business and when his brother, Lyman, Jr., did not wind up the business, John made some unsuccessful attempts to sell it himself. In 1965 he brought an action against his brother, Lyman, Jr., to force an accounting and liquidation of the assets of the partnership. The case was dismissed before trial upon agreement of the parties which became effective September 6, 1966. In the written agreement, the parties settled their accounts with each other. Lyman E. Stoddard, Jr., agreed to be responsible for all debts arising out of the business since February 13, 1964. The agreement was approved by the probate court. The business was in a weak financial condition after Lyman E. Stoddard, Sr.'s, death and was eventually discontinued.

For approximately 10 years prior to the death of Alda S. Stoddard, the respondents, King and White, and their predecessors had been accountants for the Walnut Kernel. They continued to do the accounting after the deaths of Alda and Lyman, Sr. The appellants were aware that respondents were continuing their work. One of the respondents, King, testified that he understood that respondents would be paid at such time as the estates were in a liquid condition allowing payment and that he would not have continued to render the services had he known that the estates would not be responsible.

John L. Stoddard and Nancy Gans, the executors, did not individually participate in the operation of the partnership business in any manner. The court concluded they were not individually liable.

The court found the estate of Alda S. Stoddard liable for the accounting services rendered by appellants during the period of time following her death—1963 to 1968. The court also found the estate of Lyman E. Stoddard, Sr., jointly liable with the estate of Alda S. Stoddard for the accounting services rendered by appellants following his death—1964 to 1968. * * * The estate's liability was predicated upon the court's finding that the services were rendered during the process of winding up the partnership operation of the Walnut Kernel newspaper. We have concluded that the trial court erred and that the continuation of the business was not a winding up of the affairs of the partnership.

The partnership was dissolved by operation of law upon the deaths of Alda and Lyman E. Stoddard, Sr. Corporations Code section 15029 provides that dissolution of a partnership is "* * * caused by any partner ceasing to be associated in the carrying on as distinguished from the winding up of the business." Death is one of the causes of dissolution. Dissolution, however, does not terminate the partnership which "* * * continues until the winding up of partnership affairs is completed." (Corp. Code, § 15030.)

"In general a dissolution operates only with respect to future transactions; as to everything past the partnership continues until all pre-existing matters are terminated." Although the general rule is that a partner has no authority to bind his copartners to new obligations after dissolution section 15035 of the Corporations Code provides that "[a]fter dissolution a partner can bind the partnership * * * (a) By any act appropriate for winding up partnership affairs * * *."

It is this latter provision upon which the court based its decision that the estates of the deceased partners were liable for the accounting services performed after dissolution. The court found that "LYMAN STODDARD, JR.'S continuation of the WALNUT KERNEL business was an appropriate act for winding up the partnership, since the assets of the business would have substantial value only if it was a going business. It was to the advantage of the partnership that the business be maintained as a going business."

Respondents, as accountants, had performed services both before and after the dissolution. The services, however, were a continuation of the accounting services pursuant to the ordinary course of the operation of the business. Respondent King testified that he was "* * * doing work for the activity of the newspaper, the financial activity of the newspaper" and that he was doing the same type of work as he had always performed for the Walnut Kernel. The exhibits which support his bill for services indicate that he did not, or was not able to, break down his services into categories which would separate ordinary accounting services from those related to a winding up of the partnership. The court, however, found that the continuation of the business itself was an "act appropriate for winding up partnership affairs."

We disagree with this finding. It is probably true that there might have been advantages to the partnership to sell the business as a going business, but the indefinite continuation of the partnership business is contrary to the requirement for winding up of the affairs upon dissolution. In Harvey v. Harvey, 90 Cal.App.2d 549, 554, 203 P.2d 112, 115–116, the court disapproved a finding that the business and assets of a partnership were of such character as to render its liquidation impracticable and inadvisable until a purchaser could be found. The court stated: "In effect it [the finding] authorizes the indefinite continuation of the partnership after the death of a partner, a procedure not in accordance with section 571 of the Probate Code. Respondents counter with the argument that the business is such that it cannot be wound up profitably, and the estate given its share. But this argument overlooks the distinction between winding up a business and winding up the partnership interest in that business."

There are few cases which illustrate acts approved as "appropriate for winding up partnership affairs" under either the California Corporations Code or the identical section 35 of the Uniform Partnership Act. (See Stump v. Tipps, 120 Cal.App.2d 418, 261 P.2d 315 [assignment of partnership property to repay partnership debt]; Cooley v. Miller & Lux, 168 Cal. 120, 142 P. 83 [disposition of partnership property]; Leh v. General Petroleum Corporation, 165 F.Supp. 933 (S.D. Cal.1958) [maintenance of action for damages on behalf of the partnership]; In re Heller's Estate, 319 Pa. 135, 178 A. 681 [execution of renewal notes after death of partner].)

Even if we assume that a situation might exist where continuation of the business for a period would be appropriate to winding up the partnership interest, such a situation did not exist here. The record reflects the fact that the surviving partner was not taking action to wind up the partnership as was his duty under Probate Code section 571, nor did the estates consent in any way to a delay. Rather, their insistence on winding up took the form of an effort to sell the business and a suit to require an accounting. There is nothing in the record upon which to base the argument made by respondents that appellants consented to their continued employment. The fact that they did not object is of no relevance. They had no right to direct and did not participate in the operation of the business. Therefore, the determination that the acts of the accountants were rendered during a winding up process is not based upon substantial evidence.

* * *

We conclude that the services of respondents were rendered after the dissolution resulting from the deaths of the partners, Lyman, Sr., and Alda Stoddard, and do not constitute services during the "winding up" processes of the partnership within the meaning of section 15031 of the Corporations Code. The claim for those services, therefore, are not chargeable to the partnership.

The judgment is reversed.

Russell and Andrews took part in the control of the business—limited or general partners?

HOLZMAN v. DE ESCAMILLA

California Court of Appeal, Fourth District, 1948.
86 Cal.App.2d 858, 195 P.2d 833.

MARKS, Justice

This is an appeal by James L. Russell and H.W. Andrews from a judgment decreeing they were general partners in Hacienda Farms, Limited, a limited partnership, from February 27 to December 1, 1943, and as such were liable as general partners to the creditors of the partnership.

Early in 1943, Hacienda Farms, Limited, was organized as a limited partnership (Secs. 2477 et seq., Civil Code) with Ricardo de Escamilla as the general partner and James L. Russell and H.W. Andrews as limited partners.

The partnership went into bankruptcy in December, 1943, and Lawrence Holzman was appointed and qualified as trustee of the estate of the bankrupt. On November 13, 1944, he brought this action for the purpose of determining that Russell and Andrews, by taking part in the control of the partnership business, had become liable as general partners to the creditors of the partnership. The trial court found in favor of the plaintiff on this issue and rendered judgment to the effect that the three defendants were liable as general partners.

The findings supporting the judgment are so fully supported by the testimony of certain witnesses, although contradicted by Russell and Andrews, that we need mention but a small part of it. * * *

De Escamilla was raising beans on farm lands near Escondido at the time the partnership was formed. The partnership continued raising vegetable and truck crops which were marketed principally through a produce concern controlled by Andrews.

The record shows the following testimony of de Escamilla:

"A. We put in some tomatoes.

"Q. Did you have a conversation or conversations with Mr. Andrews or Mr. Russell before planting the tomatoes? A. We always conferred and agreed as to what crops we would put in. * * *

"Q. Who determined that it was advisable to plant watermelons? A. Mr. Andrews. * * *

"Q. Who determined that string beans should be planted? A. All of us. There was never any planting done—except the first crop that was put into the partnership as an asset by myself, there was never any crop that was planted or contemplated in planting that wasn't thoroughly discussed and agreed upon by the three of us; particularly Andrews and myself."

De Escamilla further testified that Russell and Andrews came to the farms about twice a week and consulted about the crops to be planted. He did not want to plant peppers or egg plant because, as he said, "I don't like that country for peppers or egg plant; no, sir," but he was overruled and those crops were planted. The same is true of the watermelons.

Shortly before October 15, 1943, Andrews and Russell requested de Escamilla to resign as manager, which he did, and Harry Miller was appointed in his place.

Hacienda Farms, Limited, maintained two bank accounts, one in a San Diego bank and another in an Escondido bank. It was provided that checks could be drawn on the signatures of any two of the three partners. It is stated in plaintiff's brief, without any contradiction * * * that money was withdrawn on twenty checks signed by Russell and Andrews and that all other checks except three bore the signatures of de Escamilla, the general partner, and one of the other defendants. The general partner had no power to withdraw money without the signature of one of the limited partners.

Section 2483 of the Civil Code provides as follows:

"A limited partner shall not become liable as a general partner, unless, in addition to the exercise of his rights and powers as a limited partner, he takes part in the control of the business."

The foregoing illustrations sufficiently show that Russell and Andrews both took "part in the control of the business." The manner of withdrawing money from the bank accounts is particularly illuminating. The two men had absolute power to withdraw all the partnership funds in the banks without the knowledge or consent of the general partner. Either Russell or Andrews could take control of the business from de Escamilla by refusing to sign checks for bills contracted by him and thus limit his activities in the management of the business. They required him to resign as manager and selected his successor. They were active in dictating the crops to be planted, some of them against the wish of Escamilla. This clearly shows they took part in the control of the business of the partnership and thus became liable as general partners.

Judgment affirmed.

"Perfect candor, full disclosure, the utmost good faith, and the strictest honesty are required of promoters."

FRICK v. HOWARD

Supreme Court of Wisconsin, 1964.
23 Wisc.2d 86, 126 N.W.2d 619.

Action to foreclose a mortgage on real estate. Plaintiff-respondent is the assignee of the promoter of a corporation. The * * * mortgage being foreclosed was executed by the corporation in favor of the promoter and his wife when they sold certain real estate located in the city of Milwaukee to the corporation. Defendant-appellant is the receiver of the corporation.

On January 24, 1958, Michael D. Preston, an attorney, entered into a contract to purchase real estate located at 3816 West Wisconsin Avenue, Milwaukee. The purchase price was $240,000. Preston agreed to pay $5,000 down, $65,000 on the date of closing, and the vendor agreed to take back a purchase money mortgage for $170,000. On April 1, 1958, Preston organized Pan American Motel, Inc. He subscribed to one share of capital stock of the corporation. The stated value of this one share of stock was $1,000.

* * *

On September 1, 1958, Pan American Motel, Inc. offered to purchase the real estate in question from Preston and his wife for $350,000. The terms of the offer were $70,000 on closing; that the corporation would assume the outstanding mortgage of $170,000; and that the corporation would execute a note and mortgage in the sum of $110,000 to make up the balance of the purchase price. * * * The offer was accepted and carried out according to its terms. * * *

In order to construct a motel on the premises the corporation negotiated a $550,000 construction loan with First Federal Savings and Loan Association. A mortgage securing this loan was recorded on July 2, 1959. Preston recorded his mortgage on September 17, 1959.

* * * On December 8, 1961 * * * the mortgage of April 1, 1959 was assigned by Preston and his wife to the plaintiff. The plaintiff paid $72,500 for the mortgage. * * * On September 15, 1961 an appraisal of the assets of the corporation was made by the American Appraisal Company. * * * A letter from the American Appraisal Company * * * stated that the fair value for investment purposes of the property was $1,200,000. At this time a motel had been erected on the real estate and Pan American Motel, Inc. was a going concern. On January 16, 1962 the defendant was appointed receiver of the corporation * * * [the corporation being in financial difficulty]. On July 10, 1962 plaintiff recorded his mortgage assignment from Preston.

In his complaint plaintiff * * * asked for foreclosure of the 1959 mortgage and a deficiency judgment against the corporation. The defense was violation of a fiduciary duty to the corporation on the part of plaintiff's assignor and a contention that the mortgage was a fraudulent conveyance.

* * *

From a judgment of foreclosure in favor of the plaintiff for the amount of $77,159.57 defendant appeals.

BEILFUSS, Justice

* * *

Did Preston, as a promoter, breach a fiduciary duty to the corporation? It appears without dispute that Preston was the organizer and promotor of the Pan American Motel, Inc.

He entered into the contract to purchase land for $240,000 on January 24, 1958. The terms were—$5,000 down payment, $65,000 at the closing of the sale and purchase money mortgage back in the amount of $170,000. He borrowed the $5,000 down payment. * * * He organized the corporation April 1, 1958 and was its sole stockholder until September 3, 1958. * * * To pay for the land he withdrew at least $61,000 of the $65,000 closing payment from the corporation and gave the mortgage for $170,000. Three days later, September 1, 1958, the corporation offered him $350,000 for the land. The offer was accepted and the corporation paid Preston $70,000 by cancellation of his debt of $35,000 to the corporation, issuing 35 shares of its stock to him, assuming the $170,000 mortgage, and giving him a note and mortgage for $110,000. The offer was signed by Preston as seller and Frank J. Mack for the corporation. At the time the offer to purchase was made by the corporation Preston was, as far as the record reveals, the sole stockholder and completely dominated the affairs of the corporation. There was a board of directors consisting of Preston and two others but the record does not show they owned any stock or that they were in any way independent of Preston. On April 1, 1959 the note of $110,000 and mortgage were signed by Preston as president of the corporation and by Frank J. Mack as secretary payable to Preston and his wife.

The trial court found that Preston committed a fraud upon the corporation but that the transaction was not secret.

The fact that the transaction was not secret does not in all instances relieve a promoter of his fiduciary obligation to the corporation.

> "The promoters may deal with the corporation, but they must deal fairly, the burden of proof of fairness being on them. When they deal with the corporation, it must have independent directors; and the promoters cannot also be directors or dominate them as representatives of the other adversely interested parties.
>
> "Perfect candor, full disclosure, good faith, in fact, the utmost good faith, and the strictest honesty are required of promoters, and their dealings must be open and fair, or without undue advantage taken.
>
> "It is the duty of the promoters to retain in their hands the property which is to constitute corporate assets until the corporation is formed, to cause it to be formed within a reasonable time, and then to turn over to it the assets so held * * *." * * *
>
> "As a result of the fiduciary relation or relation of trust and confidence sustained by a promoter, an unfair advantage taken or secret profit gained thereby is a fraud. * * *"
>
> "*Conditions Requisite to Valid Sale.* A promoter cannot act as both seller and buyer. Hence, where he seeks to sell property to the corporation, he must, if he wishes to retain his profit, provide the corporation with an independent board of directors in no wise under his control and make a full disclosure to the corporation through them, or make a full disclosure of all material facts to each original subscriber for stock in the corporation, or procure a ratification of the sale, after disclosure of its circumstances, by the completely established corporation. * * *"
>
> "From the foregoing we deduce this: If one or more persons acquire property, intending to promote the organization of a corporation to purchase it from them at a profit to themselves and effect such purpose, limiting the membership to interested parties till the transaction is completed between them and the corporation, intending thereafter to cause the balance of the capital stock to be sold to outsiders, they being kept in ignorance of the true nature of such transaction, and effecting such intent, they are guilty of actionable fraud upon the corporation and responsible to it for the gains made. * * *

It is clear that at the time of the sale of the land to the corporation, and the execution of the note and mortgage, that the corporation had no independent board of directors. The actions of the corporation were completely dominated by Preston. The transaction to sell the land held for a very short period of time was controlled by Preston both as buyer and seller. This was not an agreement between an independent buyer and seller dealing at arm's length. Preston as an individual selling the property had a personal financial interest to obtain the highest price available; Preston as the alter ego of Pan American Motel, Inc. had a financial interest to purchase the property at the lowest price available. There could be no meeting of the minds.

The fact that the land may or may not have been worth more than $240,000 cannot override Preston's fiduciary obligation as a promoter of the corporation. In this instance where he completely dominated the corporation at the time of the transaction it was his fiduciary obligation to give the corporation the benefit of his bargain, if it was one. If Preston had provided the corporation with a board of directors who could have acted independently and at arm's length the situation might have been different. For Preston to obtain a profit of $110,000 for himself under the circumstances herein is unconscionable and a violation of his fiduciary obligation and as such a fraud upon the corporation.

* * *

Frick, the assignee of Preston, contends that the land sale transaction was subsequently ratified by the corporation and, therefore, the defense of constructive fraud by the promoter is no longer available. The burden of proof to show ratification and to show that it was the act of an independent board of directors was upon Preston's assignee. He has not met this burden. In any event the creditors cannot be bound by a ratification in which they had no voice.

Judgment reversed with directions to dismiss the complaint.

Could the minority shareholder compel payment of dividends?

DOHERTY v. MUTUAL WAREHOUSE

United States Court of Appeals, Fifth Circuit, 1958.
255 F.2d 489.

RIVES, Circuit Judge

This action is by a minority shareholder against a corporation to compel declaration and payment of dividends. * * *

* * *

In Alabama, the law is well settled that a court of equity will not interfere with the internal business management of corporate affairs by the board of directors so long as they keep within the scope of the charter powers, and are not guilty of fraud, maladministration, or abuse of discretion.

The district court made the following among other findings of fact:

> 3. The original capital of the corporation was $15,000.00, and as of the end of the year 1955 the surplus of the corporation was $188,738.38.
>
> 4. Prior to the year 1955, the management of the corporation had determined that for sound business reasons the corporation should accumulate a surplus of $200,000.00. At the end of the year 1956 the surplus of the corporation, for the first time exceeded $200,000.00; the surplus being $206,314.30. Early in 1957 the directors of the corporation declared a dividend of $6,000.00 to stockholders of record—being a $40.00 dividend for each share of outstanding stock.
>
> 5. The decision not to declare a dividend for the year 1955 and to use the profits of the corporation in the business was not an abuse of discretion, and such refusal to declare a dividend was not arbitrary, nor was there any bad faith, or fraud or maladministration destructive or injurious to the corporation. The decision not to declare a dividend for 1955 and to accumulate surplus was consistent with the character and needs of the business. At all times here material the directors, officers and management of the corporation have acted fairly and in the utmost good faith in the handling of the business, management and corporate affairs of the corporation in the interest of the corporation.

This Court should not set aside those findings of fact unless it determines that they are clearly erroneous. After carefully reading and studying the record in the light of the briefs and oral argument, we find ourselves in entire agreement with the district court. No good purpose would be served by a more detailed discussion of the evidence. The judgment was right, and it is

Affirmed.

Bowling for dollars.

ESCOTT v. BARCHRIS CONSTRUCTION CORP.

United States District Court, S.D. New York, 1968.
283 F.Supp. 643.

McLEAN, District Judge

This is an action by purchasers of $5^1/_2$ per cent convertible subordinated fifteen year debentures of BarChris Construction Corporation (BarChris). Plaintiffs purport to sue on their own behalf and "on behalf of all other and present and former holders" of the debentures. When the action was begun on October 25, 1962, there were nine plaintiffs. Others were subsequently permitted to intervene. At the time of the trial, there were over sixty.

The action is brought under Section 11 of the Securities Act of 1933. Plaintiffs allege that the registration statement with respect to these debentures filed with the Securities and Exchange Commission, which became effective on May 16, 1961, contained material false statements and material omissions.

Defendants fall into three categories: (1) the persons who signed the registration statement; (2) the underwriters, consisting of eight investment banking firms, led by Drexel & Co. (Drexel); and (3) BarChris's auditors, Peat, Marwick, Mitchell & Co. (Peat, Marwick).

The signers, in addition to BarChris itself, were the nine directors of BarChris, plus its controller, defendant Trilling, who was not a director.

* * *

At the time relevant here, BarChris was engaged primarily in the construction of bowling alleys, somewhat euphemistically referred to as "bowling centers." These were rather elaborate affairs. They contained not only a number of alleys or "lanes," but also, in most cases, bar and restaurant facilities.

* * *

The introduction of automatic pin setting machines in 1952 gave a marked stimulus to bowling. It rapidly became a popular sport, with the result that "bowling centers" began to appear throughout the country in rapidly increasing numbers. BarChris benefitted from this increased interest in bowling. Its construction operations expanded rapidly. It is estimated that in 1960 BarChris installed approximately three per cent of all lanes built in the United States.

BarChris's sales increased dramatically from 1956 to 1960. According to the prospectus, net sales, in round figures, in 1956 were some $800,000, in 1957 $1,300,000, in 1958 $1,700,000. In 1959 they increased to over $3,300,000, and by 1960 they had leaped to over $9,165,000.

For some years the business had exceeded the managerial capacity of its founders. Vitolo and Pugliese are each men of limited education. Vitolo did not get beyond high school. Pugliese ended his schooling in seventh grade. Pugliese devoted his time to supervising the actual construction work. Vitolo was concerned primarily with obtaining new business. Neither was equipped to handle financial matters.

* * *

Rather early in their career they enlisted the aid of Russo, who was trained as an accountant. He first joined them in the days of the partnership, left for a time, and returned as an officer and director of B & C Bowling Alley Builders, Inc. in 1958. He eventually became executive vice president of BarChris. In that capacity he handled many of the transactions which figure in this case.

In 1959 BarChris hired Kircher, a certified public accountant who had been employed by Peat, Marwick. He started as controller and became treasurer in 1960. In October of that year, another ex-Peat, Marwick employee, Trilling, succeeded Kircher as controller. At approximately the same time Birnbaum, a young attorney, was hired as house counsel. He became secretary on April 17, 1961.

In general, BarChris's method of operation was to enter into a contract with a customer, receive from him at that time a comparatively small down payment on the purchase price, and proceed to construct and equip the bowling alley. When the work was finished and the building delivered, the customer paid the balance of the contract price in notes, payable in installments over a period of years. BarChris discounted these notes with a factor and received part of their face amount in cash. The factor held back part as a reserve.

In 1960 BarChris began a practice which has been referred to throughout this case as the "alternative method of financing." In substance this was a sale and leaseback arrangement. It involved a distinction between the "interior" of a building and the building itself, i.e., the outer shell. In instances in which this method applied, BarChris would build and install what it referred to as the "interior package." Actually this amounted to constructing and installing the equipment in a building. When it was completed, it would sell the interior to a factor, James Talcott Inc. (Talcott), who would pay BarChris the full contract price therefor. The factor then proceeded to lease the interior either directly to BarChris's customer or back to a subsidiary of BarChris. In the latter case, the subsidiary in turn would lease it to the customer.

Under either financing method, BarChris was compelled to expend considerable sums in defraying the cost of construction before it received reimbursement. As a consequence, BarChris was in constant need of cash to finance its operations, a need which grew more pressing as operations expanded.

In December 1959, BarChris sold 560,000 shares of common stock to the public at $3.00 per share. This issue was underwritten by Peter Morgan & Company, one of the present defendants.

By early 1961, BarChris needed additional working capital. The proceeds of the sale of the debentures involved in this action were to be devoted, in part at least, to fill that need.

The registration statement of the debentures, in preliminary form, was filed with the Securities and Exchange Commission on March 30, 1961. A first amendment was filed on May 11 and a second on May 16. The registration statement became effective on May 16. The closing of the financing took place on May 24. On that day BarChris received the net proceeds of the financing.

By that time BarChris was experiencing difficulties in collecting amounts due from some of its customers. Some of them were in arrears in payments due to factors on their discounted notes. As time went on those difficulties increased. Although BarChris continued to build alleys in 1961 and 1962, it became increasingly apparent that the industry was overbuilt. Operators of alleys, often inadequately financed, began to fail. Precisely when the tide turned is a matter of dispute, but at any rate, it was painfully apparent in 1962.

In May of that year BarChris made an abortive attempt to raise more money by the sale of common stock. It filed with the Securities and Exchange Commission a registration statement for the stock issue which it later withdrew. In October 1962 BarChris came to the end of the road. On October 29, 1962, it filed in this court a petition for an arrangement under Chapter XI of the Bankruptcy Act. BarChris defaulted in the payment of the interest due on November 1, 1962 on the debentures.

* * *

Peat, Marwick, BarChris's auditors, who had previously audited BarChris's annual balance sheet and earnings figures for 1958 and 1959, did the same for 1960. These figures were set forth in the registration statement. * * *

The registration statement in its final form contained a prospectus as well as other information.

* * *

The prospectus contained, among other things, a description of BarChris's business, a description of its real property, some material pertaining to certain of it subsidiaries, and remarks about various other aspects of its affairs. It also contained financial information. It included a consolidated balance sheet as of December 31, 1960, with elaborate explanatory notes. These figures had been audited by Peat, Marwick.

* * *

Plaintiffs challenge the accuracy of a number of these figures. They also charge that the text of the prospectus, apart from the figures, was false in a number of respects, and that material information was omitted.

* * *

I find that the 1960 sales figure of $9,165,320, as stated in page 4 of the prospectus, was inaccurate. The total figure, instead of $9,165,320, should have been $8,511,420.

It necessarily follows that the figure for net operating income for 1960 appearing on page 4 of the prospectus was also incorrect. * * *

The net operating income, instead of $1,742,801, should have been $1,496,196.

Since the net operating income figure was incorrect, it necessarily follows that the ultimate result of the entire table, i.e., the earnings per share figure, was incorrect.

* * *

The prospectus contained a balance sheet as of December 31, 1960 of BarChris and consolidated subsidiaries. This was audited by Peat, Marwick. Plaintiffs attack its accuracy on a variety of grounds.

They charge that current assets were grossly overstated because several items were incorrectly classified as current.

Cash on hand as of December 31, 1960, as per the balance sheet, amounted to $285,482. This amount actually was on hand on that day. But plaintiffs contend, and I believe correctly, that certain rather peculiar circumstances relating to this cash balance should have been disclosed.

* * *

On December 22, 1960, at Russo's request, Talcott released * * * $147,466.80 to BarChris Financial Corporation temporarily, on the latter's agreement to redeposit it with Talcott not later than January 16, 1961, so that Talcott could continue to hold it as security. BarChris Financial Corporation then paid $145,000 of this sum to BarChris, which put it into one of BarChris's bank accounts. It was thus reflected in the cash balance as of December 31, 1960.

Plaintiffs claim that this transaction was arranged by Russo in order to increase BarChris's cash temporarily, so that its financial condition would look better on December 31, 1960. No other explanation was offered by defendants and I can see none.

* * *

Plaintiffs also complain about a receivable due from Federal Lanes representing a down payment under its contract for the purchase of an alley. The amount was $125,000. It had been overdue since July 31, 1960. As it turned out, BarChris never did collect this $125,000. Federal eventually went into bankruptcy. Plaintiffs say that the uncollectibility of this debt was so obvious on December 31, 1960 that a full reserve should have been set up against it, thereby reducing current assets accordingly.

* * * I believe that the prospects for Federal were so bad, even on December 31, 1960, that some reserve should have been set up against the probability that this $125,000 would never be collected. * * *

The prospectus stated on page 5 that BarChris "is engaged in the design, manufacture, construction, installation, modernizing and repair of bowling alleys and the manufacture and sale of related equipment * * *." Plaintiffs claim that this was misleading because it did not reveal that BarChris was also engaged in operating bowling alleys. * * *

Operating an alley is obviously quite a different business from constructing one, with different problems and different risks. There is not a word of this in the prospectus. It was something that purchasers of the debentures were entitled to know. I find, therefore, that the omission of any reference to this subject rendered the description of BarChris's business incomplete and therefore misleading.

* * *

It is a prerequisite to liability under Section 11 of the Act that the fact which is falsely stated in a registration statement, or the fact that is omitted when it should have been stated to avoid misleading, be "material." The regulations of the Securities and Exchange Commission pertaining to the registration of securities define the word as follows:

> The term "material", when used to qualify a requirement for the furnishing of informa-

> tion as to any subject, limits the information required to those matters as to which an average prudent investor ought reasonably to be informed before purchasing the security registered.

What are "matters as to which an average prudent investor ought reasonably to be informed"? It seems obvious that they are matters which such an investor needs to know before he can make an intelligent, informed decision whether or not to buy the security.

* * *

The average prudent investor is not concerned with minor inaccuracies or with errors as to matters which are of no interest to him. The facts which tend to deter him from purchasing a security are facts which have an important bearing upon the nature or condition of the issuing corporation or its business.

Judged by this test, there is no doubt that many of the misstatements and omissions in this prospectus were material. * * *

[The court found all of the defendants liable for violating Section 11 of the Securities Act of 1933. None was able to show "due diligence" as a defense.]

[As to damages, the court said] [s]ection 11(a) provides that when a registration statement contains an untrue statement of a material fact or omits to state a material fact, "any person acquiring such security * * * may * * * sue." Section 11(e) provides that:

> The suit authorized under subsection (a) may be to recover such damages as shall represent the difference between the amount paid for the security (not exceeding the price at which the security was offered to the public) and (1) the value thereof as of the time such suit was brought, or (2) the price at which such security shall have been disposed of in the market before suit, or (3) the price at which such security shall have been disposed of after suit but before judgment if such damages shall be less than the damages representing the difference between the amount paid for the security (not exceeding the price at which the security was offered to the public) and the value thereof as of the time such suit was brought * * *.

Section 11(e) then sets forth a proviso reading as follows:

> Provided, that if the defendant proves that any portion or all of such damages represents other than the depreciation in value of such security resulting from such part of the registration statement, with respect to which his liability is asserted, not being true or omitting to state a material fact required to be stated therein or necessary to make the statements therein not misleading, such portion of or all such damages shall not be recoverable.

Each defendant in one form or another has relied upon this proviso as a complete defense. Each maintains that the entire damage suffered by each and every plaintiff was caused by factors other than the material falsities and omissions of the registration statement. These factors, in brief, were the decline in the bowling industry which came about because of the fact that the industry was overbuilt and because popular enthusiasm for bowling diminished.

These adverse conditions had begun before these debentures were issued. * * * BarChris's financial position, as we have seen, was materially worse in May 1961 then it had been on December 31, 1960.

As time went on, conditions grew worse, both for BarChris and the industry. The receipts of alley operators diminished. New construction of alleys fell off. By 1962 it had almost ceased.

There is a wide disparity in the factual pattern of purchases and sales of BarChris debentures by the plaintiffs in this action. Some plaintiffs bought theirs when the debentures were first issued on May 16, 1961. Others bought theirs later in 1961. Still others purchased theirs at various dates in 1962, some even as late as September 1962, shortly before BarChris went into Chapter XI. In at least one instance, a plaintiff purchased debentures after BarChris was in Chapter XI.

There is a similar disparity as to sales. Some plaintiffs sold their debentures in 1961. Others sold theirs in 1962. Others never sold them.

The position taken by defendants in their affirmative defenses is an extreme one which cannot be sustained. I cannot say that the entire damage suffered by every plaintiff was caused by factors other than the errors and omissions of the registration statement for which these defendants are responsible. As to some plaintiffs, or as to part of the damage sustained by others, that may be true. The only practicable course is to defer decision of this issue until the claim of each individual plaintiff is separately considered. As stated at the outset, this opinion is devoted only to matters common to all plaintiffs.

* * *

Defendants' motions to dismiss this action, upon which decision was reserved at the trial, are denied. * * *

* * *

So ordered.

Is the independent auditor liable even though he or she does not benefit from the inflated price of the security?

DRAKE v. THOR POWER TOOL CO.

United States District Court, N.D. Illinois, E.D., 1967.
282 F.Supp. 94.

PARSONS, District Judge

Plaintiff Drake complains that he purchased Thor stock through the facilities of the New York Stock Exchange at a time when the assets and profits of Defendant Thor were being fictitiously reported in its financial statements and thereupon promulgated to the public as well as to Thor's stockholders, and that when the true financial condition became known the price of Thor shares as then traded on the New York and Midwest Stock Exchanges dropped precipitously. Thor is charged with falsification of its inventory and sales figures and issuing financial statements reflecting such false figures. Peat, Marwick, Mitchell & Co., Thor's independent accounting firm, is charged with applying inappropriate accounting procedures with respect to the Thor audits and uttering untrue certifications of Thor's false financial statements. The cause is a class action on behalf of certain persons similar to plaintiff who had bought and subsequently sold their shares. * * *

A Rule10b–5 claim is alleged * * * under * * * the Securities Exchange Act of 1934. * * *

The Defendant, Peat, Marwick, has filed a motion to dismiss the action. * * *

Section 10(b) of the 1934 Act, provides:

> It shall be unlawful for any person, directly or indirectly, by the use of any means or instrumentality of interstate commerce or of the mails, or of any facility of any national securities exchange—
>
> (b) To use or employ in connection with the purchase or sale of any security registered on a national securities exchange or any security not so registered, any manipulative or deceptive device or contrivance in contravention of such rules and regulations as the Commission may prescribe as necessary or appropriate in the public interest or for the protection of investors.

Rule 10b–5 as promulgated by the Securities and Exchange Commission, provides:

> It shall be unlawful for any person, directly or indirectly, by the use of any means or instrumentality of interstate commerce, or of the mails, or of any facility of any national securities exchange—
>
> (a) To employ any device, scheme or artifice to defraud.
>
> (b) To make any untrue statement of a material fact or to omit to state a material fact necessary in order to make the statement made, in the light of the circumstances under which they were made, not misleading, or
>
> (c) To engage in any act, practice, or course of business which operates or would

operate as a fraud or deceit upon any person, in connection with the purchase or sale of any security.

* * * The Federal securities legislation was designed to protect the investor, maintain integrity and honesty in the securities market, and curb "unnecessary, unwise, and destructive speculation." Where Congress expressly created civil liabilities to implement these policies, two aims predominated: to compensate the innocent investor who had lost money on falsely valued securities and to deter the proscribed practices by effective civil sanctions which complemented injunctive and criminal remedies. * * *

Neither congressional intent nor the statutory scheme will be distorted by granting the plaintiffs a remedy under Rule 10b–5. The Rule functions as a reservoir in an interstate economy with transactions occurring all over the country in situations where there simply would not be a remedy without it. Rule 10b–5 is particularly applicable to this case.

* * *

Section 10(b) and Rule 10b–5 are aimed at prohibiting fraudulent schemes in trading in securities and were designed in protecting both investors and the public interest. * * *

* * * The purpose of the financial statements is to inform the man on the street, and the underlying policy of the Securities and Exchange Acts and of Rule 10b–5 is to assure that he can have truthful information in buying securities. * * * [T]he defendants have set themselves up to be independent certified public auditors. As such, they have assumed a peculiar relationship with the investing public. * * *

Defendant Peat, Marwick, in independently auditing Thor's financial statement, remains liable regardless of whether it had benefited from the supposedly inflated market price. * * *

In Fischer et al. v. Kletz et al., 266 F.Supp. 180 (S.D.N.Y.1967), which also involved the Defendant Peat, Marwick in an allegation that it failed to disclose that financial statements which it certified contained false and misleading figures and that interim statements were false and misleading[,] Judge Tyler refused to dismiss a common law fraud allegation and also found the defendant liable under Rule 10b–5. The Court clearly placed no weight on the absence of any allegation of gain.

* * *

The Court denies Defendant's Motion to Dismiss.

Review Questions

1. What is the specific responsibility of a corporate promoter selling his or her own property to the corporation, and to what extent are the corporation and promoter bound on contracts made for the corporation by a corporate promoter? Is a stock subscription irrevocable? When can shareholders do something about "ultra vires" acts? As to management, what are the specific responsibilities of shareholders, directors, and officers? Summarize the five potential conflicts of interest that corporate officers or directors may face? Explain your answers.

2. To what extent may a partner bind the partnership, and how and to what extent are partners, including "incoming partners," liable for partnership debt? How does dissolution change a partnership? What events may cause dissolution? Are there any risks in being a limited partner? Is there more or less formality in setting up a limited versus a general partnership? Is there any difference in the order of payment of liabilities in a general versus a limited partnership? Explain your answers.

3. What is the test for definition of "security" within the Securities Act of 1933? Why would a closely held corporation go public? What is the purpose of the Securities Act of 1933? How is this purpose accomplished? What are the "intrastate," "casual sales," "small offerings under Regulation A," "Regulation D," and "dealer and broker transaction" exemptions under the Securities Act? What is the difference in potential civil liability under Section 11 of the Securities Act of 1933 and Rule 10b–5 under the Securities Exchange Act of 1934? What does the Foreign Corrupt Practices Act require and prohibit? Explain your answers.

4. What is the one important element that a sole proprietorship and partnership have in common? How does this differ from the corporation? How is a partnership taxed? A corporation? Is a corporation ever taxed as a partnership? To what extent are salaries deductible by corporations? What are the requirements of Subchapter S elections? Explain your answers.

5. What are five characteristics of a corporation that may make it an advantageous method of doing business? Must a shareholder participate in the management of a corporation? Will partnership ownership interests or corporate stock ever be classified as real property? When, if ever, will the courts pierce the corporate veil? What is the difference between par value and no-par value stock? Between common and preferred stock? Is "book value" of stock the same as "market value"? What stock generally participates in the growth of the corporation? Explain your answers.

6. To what extent is a partnership treated as an entity? Are there any rules regarding partnership names? When must all partners consent to a partnership act? Must partners share equally in partnership profits or losses? What are the incidents of ownership in a tenancy in partnership? Does a judgment creditor or assignee of an individual partner have rights to partnership assets? Explain your answers.

7. Explain the shareholder rights regarding dividends, redemption, preemption, inspection, and voting. What is the difference between merger and consolidation, and are there protections in this area for minority shareholders? Explain.

8. Define the following terms: corporate opportunity doctrine, cumulative voting, derivative suit, fiduciary, joint venture, marshaling of partnership assets, partnership by estoppel, quo warranto action, "red herring" prospectus, treasury stock, ultra vires act, watered stock.

Problems

1. Executive Office Supply Co., is a limited partnership consisting of three general partners (Mike Miller, Bob Bishop, and Jean Carpenter) and two limited partners (Dick Pierce and Vera Vaughn). On March 1, Vera agrees to work full-time managing the partnership; she immediately begins making important management decisions. On March 3, in order to obtain a $25,000 bank loan for the business, Mike and Bob falsely tell First State Bank that Peter Hunter, a well-known and prosperous businessman, is a general partner in the firm. Though Peter knows that Mike and Bob are wrongfully using his name, he does not inform the bank, and the bank makes the loan in reliance on the misrepresentation. On March 5, Sara Carter, an employee of Executive Office Supply, negligently runs the company delivery truck into an auto driven by Fred Jensen. Fred is seriously injured, and his claim against the company amounts to $85,000. On March 10, Jean Carpenter withdraws from the partnership in order to go into the office supply business on her own. Purportedly acting on behalf of Executive Office Supply, Jean purchases $25,000 worth of inventory on credit from Martex Manufacturing Company. Jean has dealt with the Martex Company on behalf of Executive Office Supply many times in the past; Martex has no knowledge that Jean has withdrawn from the partnership. Meanwhile, Bob Bishop feels that he is being unfairly excluded from management decisions and that he is not receiving his full share of partnership income. He demands a formal accounting.

a. Who is liable on the $25,000 bank loan from First State Bank? To what extent is each person liable? Explain.
b. Who is liable to Fred Jensen for Sara Carter's negligence? To what extent is each person liable? Explain.
c. What is the effect of Jean Carpenter's withdrawal from the partnership?
d. Who, if anyone, is bound by Jean's contract with Martex Manufacturing Company? To what extent are they bound? Explain.
e. Does Bob Bishop have a right to a formal accounting? Explain.
f. Assuming that the whole matter is taken to court and that creditors of both the partnership and the individual partners are claiming the partnership assets and the assets of the individual partners, how will the court determine priorities among creditors?

2. Midas Marx owns 75 percent of the shares in the closely held Marx, Inc.; his brother Martin owns the remaining 25 percent. Martin Marx, his sister Molly, and his other brother Milton serve as directors of the corporation. Martin is also president of the corporation, Molly is vice-president, and Milton is secretary-treasurer. The corporation decides to make a public offering of $10,000,000 of common stock in the corporation to residents in a three-state area. Martin, acting on behalf of the corporation, prepares a registration statement (including a prospectus) covering the proposed securities offering and files it with the SEC. Although Martin knows that another company's new invention will soon render one of Marx's major products obsolete, he makes no mention of this fact in the registration statement. The statement nevertheless passes SEC scrutiny, and it becomes effective twenty days after filing. Molly Marx, who is being paid a $1,000 bonus over and above her regular salary for helping sell the securities, telephones Norma Carswell and persuades her to purchase $10,000 worth of stock. Norma, who will invest in anything, does not read the prospectus covering the securities and does not take Marx's product line into consideration in making the purchase. When it becomes apparent that Marx omitted information concerning its product line from the registration statement and the securities decline in value, Norma's attorney advises her to sue under the federal securities laws. Marx, however, contends that the SEC approved the statement, relieving Marx of any responsibility for omissions of fact. What are Norma's rights, if any, against Marx, Inc., Midas, Martin, Molly, and Milton Marx under Section 12 of the federal Securities Act of 1933? Under Section 10(b) of the Securities Exchange Act of 1934? Explain fully, discussing the liability of each party separately.

3. Delwood is the Central American representative of Massive Manufacturing, Inc., a large diversified conglomerate listed on the New York Stock Exchange. Certain key foreign government and large foreign manufacturing company contracts were in the crucial stages of bidding and negotiation. During this crucial time, Feldspar, the CEO of Massive, summoned Delwood to the company's home office for an urgent consultation. At the meeting, Feldspar told Delwood that corporate sales and profits were lagging and something definitely had to be done. He told Delwood that his job was on the line and that unless major contracts were obtained, he would have to reluctantly accept his resignation. Feldspar indicated he was aware of both the competition and the legal problems that were involved. Nevertheless, he told Delwood "do what is necessary in order to obtain the business." Delwood flew back to Central America the next day and began to implement what he believed to be the instructions he had received from Feldspar. He first contacted influential members of the ruling parties of the various countries and indicated that large discretionary contributions to their re-election campaign funds would be forthcoming if Massive's bids for foreign government contracts were approved. Next, he contacted the large foreign manufacturers and indicated that loans were available to them on a nonrepayment basis if they placed their business with Massive. These payments were to be accounted for by charging certain nebulous accounts or by listing the payments as legitimate loans to purchasers. In any event, the true nature of the expenditures were not to be shown on the books. All this was accomplished, and Massive's sales improved markedly in Central America.

Two years later the Securities and Exchange Commission discovered the facts described above.

Required: Answer the following, setting forth reasons for any conclusions stated.

What are the legal implications of the above to Delwood, Feldspar, and Massive Manufacturing?

Source: CPA Exam, May 1981, # 4.a.

4. Davis and Clay are licensed real estate brokers. They entered into a contract with Wilkins, a licensed building contractor, to construct and market residential housing. Under the terms of the contract, Davis and Clay were to secure suitable building sites, furnish prospective purchasers with plans and specifications, pay for appliances and venetian blinds and drapes, obtain purchasers, and assist in arranging for financing. Wilkins was to furnish the labor, material, and supervision necessary to construct the houses. In accordance with the agreement, Davis and Clay were to be reimbursed for their expenditures. Net profits from the sale of each house were to be divided 80 percent to Wilkins, 10 percent to Davis, and 10 percent to Clay. The parties also agreed that each was to be free to carry on his own business simultaneously and that such action would not be considered a conflict of interest. In addition, the agreement provided that their relationship was as independent contractors, pooling their interests for the limited purposes described above.

Ace Lumber Company sold lumber to Wilkins on credit from mid-1980 until February 1981. Ace did not learn of the agreement between Davis, Clay, and Wilkins until April 1981, when an involuntary bankruptcy petition was filed against Wilkins and an order for relief entered. Ace Lumber has demanded payment from Davis and Clay. The lumber was used in the construction of a house pursuant to the agreement between the parties.

Required: Answer the following, setting forth reasons for any conclusions stated.

In the event Ace sues Davis and Clay as well as Wilkins, will Ace prevail? Discuss the legal basis upon which Ace will rely in asserting liability.

Source: CPA Exam, May 1981, # 5.a.

5. Lawler is a retired film producer. She had a reputation in the film industry for aggressiveness and shrewdness; she was also considered somewhat overbearing. Cyclone Artistic Film Productions, a growing independent producer, obtained the film rights to "Claws," a recent bestseller. Cyclone has decided to syndicate the production of "Claws." Therefore, it created a limited partnership, Claws Productions, with Harper, Von Hinden and Graham, the three ranking executives of Cyclone, serving as general partners. The three general partners each contributed $50,000 to the partnership capital. One hundred limited partnership interests were offered to the public at $50,000 each. Lawler was offered the opportunity to invest in the venture. Intrigued by the book and restless in her retirement, she decided to purchase ten limited partnership interests for $500,000. She was the largest purchaser of the limited partnership interests of Claws Productions. All went well initially for the venture, but midway through production, some major problems arose. Lawler, having nothing else to do and having invested a considerable amount of money in the venture, began to take an increasingly active interest in the film's production.

She frequently began to appear on the set and made numerous suggestions on handling the various problems that were encountered. When the production still seemed to be proceeding with difficulty, Lawler volunteered her services to the general partners who as a result of her reputation and financial commitment to "Claws" decided to invite her to join them in their executive deliberations. This she did, and her personality insured an active participation.

"Claws" turned out to be a box office disaster, and its production costs were considered to be somewhat extraordinary even by Hollywood standards. The limited partnership is bankrupt, and the creditors have sued Claws Productions, Harper, Von Hinden, Graham, and Lawler.

Required: Answer the following, setting forth reasons for any conclusions stated.

What are the legal implications and liabilities of *each* of the above parties as a result of the above facts?

Source: CPA Exam, May 1981, # 5.b.

6. William Harrelson is president of the Billings Corporation, a medium-size manufacturer of yogurt. While serving as president, Harrelson learns of an interesting new yogurt product loaded with vitamin additives and with a potentially huge market. He immediately forms another corporation, the Wexler Corporation, to produce and market the new product. In his zeal, however, Harrelson overextends his personal credit and utilizes Billings's credit, along with its plant and employees, as needed, to produce the new product. The new product becomes a big success. As a result, Harrelson's Wexler stock is presently worth millions of dollars.

Required: Answer the following, setting forth reasons for any conclusions stated.

Billings's shareholders contend that Harrelson's actions are improper and seek a remedy against him. Will they succeed and what remedies are available to them?

Source: CPA Exam, November 1981, # 3.a.

7. Three independent sole proprietors decided to pool their resources and form a partnership. The business assets and liabilities of each were transferred to the partnership. The partnership commenced business on September 1, 1981, but the parties did not execute a formal partnership agreement until October 15, 1981. Which of the following is correct?

a. The existing creditors must consent to the transfer of the individual business assets to the partnership.
b. The partnership began its existence on September 1, 1981.
c. If the partnership's duration is indefinite, the partnership agreement must be in writing and signed.
d. In the absence of a partnership agreement specifically covering division of losses among the partners, they will be deemed to share them in accordance with their capital contributions.

Source: CPA Exam, May 1982, # 1(1).

8. A court is most likely to disregard the corporate entity and hold shareholders personally liable when

a. The owner-officers of the corporation do *not* treat it as a separate entity.

b. A parent corporation creates a wholly owned subsidiary in order to isolate the high risk portion of its business in the subsidiary.
c. A sole proprietor incorporates his business to limit his liability.
d. The corporation has elected, under Subchapter S, *not* to pay any corporate tax on its income but, instead, to have the shareholders pay tax on it.

Source: CPA Exam, May 1982, # 1(8).

9. Under the Foreign Corrupt Practices Act, an action may be brought which seeks

a. Treble damages by a private party.
b. Injunctive relief by a private party.
c. Criminal sanctions against both the corporation and its officers by the Department of Justice.
d. Damages and injunctive relief by the Securities and Exchange Commission.

Source: CPA Exam, November 1982, # 1(30).

10. Which of the following statements concerning the scope of Section 10(b) of the Securities Exchange Act of 1934 is correct?

a. In order to come within its scope, a transaction must have taken place on a national stock exchange.
b. It applies exclusively to securities of corporations registered under the Securities Exchange Act of 1934.
c. There is an exemption from its application for securities registered under the Securities Act of 1933.
d. It applies to purchases as well as sales of securities in interstate commerce.

Source: CPA Exam, November 1980, # 1(42).

7

If you become an employer, give every employee the full equivalent of his share in the product. Don't live in a boastful luxury based on taking more from the world than you give.
Will Durant

Employee, Antitrust, and Labor Law

WHY WORK AND AT WHAT KIND OF JOB?

From time immemorial people have worked in order to survive. Up until 10,000 to 12,000 years ago, all the human populations throughout the world relied on foraging for subsistence. This means that people relied on natural reserves for the food and other materials essential to their lives. The foragers had little choice in their work—they were either hunters or gatherers. And even within this limited area of work, there was generally a division of labor on the basis of sex and age. The pattern in many foraging societies, for example, was for men to hunt and women to collect. The women were generally the major collectors, and their labor provided more than two-thirds of the calories consumed by band members. Old people in these societies did little work but were greatly respected because of their contributions to the band during their younger years. Among the active workers, those most skilled and successful at their jobs received the most respect. Thus the best hunters and collectors were more highly prized and respected than were the mediocre workers. And so it is today.

Yet we have come a long way from the time of the forager to the *Future Shock* described by Alvin Toffler in his bestselling description of the constantly changing, super-industrialized world in which we presently live. The creative ability of people has gone far beyond the fashioning of simple implements for the procurement of food and the building of shelter. The human being's great mental capacity and distinctive ability to communicate have resulted in an extremely advanced society of great accomplishments and complex lifestyles. We still must work in order to subsist—we need to eat and keep warm—but our choice of livelihood is considerable. There are thousands of ways to make a living.

The job market in the United States has changed more than a little since the following advertisement was run by the United States Post Office department in 1860 in search of "qualified Pony Express" riders.

> Wanted, Young skinny wiry fellows not over 18. Must be expert riders, willing to risk death daily. Orphans preferred. Wages $25.00 per week.

The *Occupational Outlook Handbook,* published by the U.S. Bureau of Labor Statistics (copies of the current edition may be obtained from the Superintendent of Documents, U.S. Government Printing Office, Washington, D.C. 20402), presents a study of nearly 1,000 occupations and thirty major industries within the United States. The handbook includes information on employment outlook and earnings (both past and prospective), as well as information on the nature of the work and what is required by way of training or other qualifications. Anyone who is undecided about how to make a living will find this handbook to be worthwhile reading material.

Why work? The answer is obvious. You must have an income if you are to have a home, a car, a balanced diet of wholesome food, adequate medical and dental care, travel, and entertainment.

At what kind of a job? Each individual must answer that question for himself or herself. The financial security that comes from a high income job may not make for happiness if you have to give up so much of your time to work that you have little or no time for anything else. Still most people spend as much as half of their waking hours on the job. So it is important to do something that you enjoy.

One factor is clearly relevant. The more education you have, the more income you will realize. The figures in table 7–1 are taken from a recent United States Department of Commerce, Bureau of the Census, *Current Population Report.*

Another important consideration is that no matter what work you choose, you will carry out your job as either an employee or an independent contractor. These are legal terms with legal definitions that have great significance for all who work. About 70 percent of the work force in this country is made up of employees—the rest, 30 percent, is composed of self-employed independent contractors. The difference between the two categories and the resulting legal distinctions will be explored in the text sections that follow.

A third factor coming into play and affecting your work is what is considered by some to be the single outstanding characteristic of modern American society. This is the growth of massive concentrations of people, resources, and power in the form of big business corporations, labor unions, and government agencies: the corporations are the employers; the unions represent the employees; and the agencies regulate both. In this chapter we will consider the law surrounding the employment relation as well as the law affecting labor unions (labor law) and that regulating big business (antitrust law).

TABLE 7-1 MEDIAN MONEY INCOME OF PERSONS WITH INCOME, BY SEX, RACE, AND EDUCATIONAL ATTAINMENT: 1975 AND 1980

	1975					
	Male			Female		
Item	Total	White	Black	Total	White	Black
Median Income, total	*9,426*	*9,891*	*5,967*	*3,642*	*3,703*	*3,250*
Elementary school:						
Less than 8 years	4,628	4,843	3,871	2,248	2,342	2,027
8 years	6,515	6,640	5,149	2,620	2,621	2,676
High school:						
1–3 years	7,447	7,864	5,356	2,995	2,997	2,997
4 years	10,167	10,463	7,468	4,153	4,143	4,234
College:						
1–3 years	10,412	10,656	8,300	4,306	4,238	5,165
4 years	14,350	14,656	10,573	7,001	6,700	8,461
5 or more years	17,476	17,622	14,539	10,143	10,047	10,900

	1980					
	Male			Female		
Item	Total	White	Black	Total	White	Black
Median Income, total	*14,296*	*15,117*	*8,983*	*5,749*	*5,819*	*5,114*
Elementary school:						
Less than 8 years	7,035	7,572	5,302	3,643	3,725	3,432
8 years	8,960	9,235	6,773	4,177	4,256	3,684
High school:						
1–3 years	9,924	10,531	6,783	4,242	4,308	3,994
4 years	14,583	15,176	10,479	6,080	6,048	6,115
College:						
1–3 years	15,674	16,252	11,761	6,985	6,872	7,735
4 years	22,173	22,724	15,648	10,119	9,936	11,664
5 or more years	26,927	27,235	21,085	15,108	15,042	16,354

[a] For persons 18 years old and over. Based on Current Population Survey

Source: U.S. Bureau of the Census, *Current Population Reports*, series P–60, Nos. 105 and 132.

WHAT IS THE DIFFERENCE BETWEEN AN EMPLOYEE AND AN INDEPENDENT CONTRACTOR?

What is modernly called the employer-employee relationship was referred to, in old common law terminology, as the relationship of "master-servant." The use of these terms—master and servant—is still legally correct, and judges, lawyers, and law students frequently and correctly describe what the layman thinks of as "employer-employee" in terms of "master-servant."

A servant is a person employed to render services of any type to a master who retains control or the right to control the servant in how he or she renders the services. And this is the essential feature of the master-servant relationship: the master, at all times, retains control or the right to control the physical activities of the servant in the performance of his or her required employment duties. The master is said to have the right to direct both the method and the mode of the service, and the servant is said to be entirely under the control of the master and without independent discretion. Still, this does not mean that the master must actually stand by and constantly observe and supervise the work. Rather, it means merely that the relationship presupposes a right on the part of the master to have the work performed in such manner as he or she directs and a correlative duty on the part of the servant to perform in the manner directed. The crucial element of the relationship is the "right to control."

The term "servant," as used above, includes all persons of whatever rank or position who are subject to the "right of control." The term "servant" is therefore synonymous with "employee." Almost everyone is an employee at one time or another, working subject to the control of an employer.

An employee (servant) is to be distinguished from an independent contractor in that, while the independent contractor works physically for the employer, the employer has no right to control the contractor in how he or she does the work. The independent contractor exercises an independent occupation or calling. He or she contracts with the employer only as to the results to be accomplished—not as to the method, mode, or means whereby the work is to be done. The independent contractor, it is often stated, is hired to do a job for a price. While the finished job must meet certain specifications, the manner and method of doing the work is left entirely up to the contractor. The independent contractor usually works for a lump sum, while the employee is paid by the hour. In addition, the independent contractor generally possesses a high degree of skill or expertise that the employer does not have—thus it would not make sense for the employer to have a right to control the contractor in how the work is done. And while the independent contractor usually owns his or her own business, uses his or her own tools, and furnishes his or her own place to work, the employee generally relies upon the employer to provide these things.

Still, the "right of control" test is the most important consideration in determining whether a particular worker is an employee or an independent contractor. And even the specially skilled man or woman who provides his or her own tools and works for a lump sum is still an employee and not an independent contractor where the employer retains the right of control.

A worker's classification as either an employee or an independent contractor has several important legal consequences in the areas of tort liability and taxation.

Tort Liability

The most important reason for distinguishing between the employee and the independent contractor is that the doctrine of "respondeat superior," which applies to the former, does not apply to the latter. The doctrine of respondeat superior means simply that the master or employer must respond in damages for all torts committed by his or her employees while acting within the scope of their employment. Thus whenever an employee tortiously injures a third person while acting within the scope of his or her employment, the injured party may bring an action at law against either the employee or the employer or both. The employee is directly liable for his or her wrongful act, and the employer is liable vicariously under the legal doctrine of respondeat superior.

Of common law origin, this doctrine developed at a time when the servant was viewed as the property of the master. Since the master had absolute control over the servant's acts, it was considered only fair to hold him or her responsible for any injury that resulted from those acts. Of course, the servant or employee is no longer considered the property of the master or employer, but the doctrine of respondeat superior still makes sense as a matter of good social policy. The doctrine is justified under two theories: (1) the "deep pocket" doctrine which states that public policy is furthered if an injured person is presented with the most effective relief available. As the employee's financial resources are extremely limited in comparison with those of the employer, the injured party should be able to proceed against the employer who, in terms of finances, has the "deeper pocket"; and (2) the "entrepreneur theory" which says that, since the employer has created the risk of harm by hiring the employee to work he or she should assume full financial responsibility if the employee's tortious scope of employment conduct causes injury to a third party. The employer can protect himself or herself against this risk by passing the cost of liability (along with the other costs of doing business) on to the consumers who use the products or services. This is good social policy because it "forces" employers to more closely regulate and supervise their employees' work. And with closer employee supervision, the risk of injuries to the public is substantially reduced.

The employer is liable for the torts of employees committed within the scope of employment notwithstanding the employer's exercise of due care in hiring the employee and in supervising his or her acts. The only requirements for liability are that the person committing the tort is, in fact, an employee (someone over whom the employer has the right of control in the doing of the work) and that the employee is acting within the scope of the employment at the time he or she commits the tort. An employee is acting within the scope of employment if, at the time of commission of the tort he or she is intending to serve the master and is doing the work in the usual and normal way. Suppose, for example, that an employee truck driver drives his or her truck negligently while delivering the employer's goods and injures a third party. The employee, at the time of the injury, is intending to serve the master by delivering the goods and he or she is delivering the goods in the usual and normal way—by transporting them in the employer's truck. The employee's negligent driving is a risk of doing business, and the employer is thus liable in damages to the injured third party. The result is to the contrary, however, where the employee "borrows" the truck to take his or her family on a weekend outing and negligently drives the vehicle into an unfortunate pedestrian. The employee, in this case, is not intending to serve the master, and he or she is not within the scope of employment. The employer is therefore not liable to the injured pedestrian.

The scope of employment requirement is a necessary limitation on employer liability: it insures that the employer will be held liable only for those torts committed by his or her employee while engaged in work of the type the employee was hired to perform during the hours he or she was hired to perform it in.

In determining whether a particular employee was acting within the scope of employment (intending to serve the employer and doing the work in the usual and normal way) at the time of commission of a tort, the following factors are taken into account: (1) Was the act authorized, or was it incidental to an act authorized by the employer? (2) The time, place, and purpose of the act. (3) Was the act one commonly done by employees on behalf of their employers? (4) To what extent were the employer's interests advanced by the act that resulted in the tort? (5) To what extent were the private interests of the employee involved? (6) Did the employer furnish the means or the instrumentality with which the injury was inflicted (the truck, machine, tool, etc.)? (7) Did the employer have reason to know that the employee would do the act in question? (8) Had the employee ever done this act before while employed by this employer? (9) Did the act involve crime as well as tort? (10) Was the act a way of doing what the employee was hired [1] to do, or was it totally unrelated to his or her duties and no way of doing the job at all?

Under these rules, an employer is seldom held responsible for an employee's intentional torts (as opposed to a negligent tort or trespass tort). This is because most employers do not hire employees to fight with customers or to commit intentional assaults and batteries upon them. Still, there are exceptions. An employee hired to keep order in a cocktail lounge, for example, may commit a battery upon a customer while trying to calm him or her down. Since the employee is intending to serve the master in keeping order and is doing the job in the usual and normal way (with physical force, where necessary), the employee is within the scope of employment, and the employer is liable for the customer's injuries.

Generally, an employer is not liable for the crimes of his or her employees unless the employer has in some way directed, participated in, or approved the criminal act. Exceptions to this rule arise, however, where the illegal sale of liquor is involved or where the purity and branding of foods or the accuracy and range of prices and weights is at issue.

In summary, two elements must be shown in order to establish vicarious liability on the part of an employer for the torts of any particular employee.

1. The "master-servant" (employer-employee) relationship must be shown to exist between the party whose act caused the injury and the person sought to be held liable therefor (the right to control).

2. And it must be shown that the employee's wrongful act was committed within the scope of employment (i.e., while intending to serve the employer and while doing the job in the usual and normal way).

The doctrine of "respondeat superior" does not apply where tortious acts are committed by an independent contractor. Thus an employer is not vi-

---

1. However, it should be understood that "hired" does not require any payment of money or other compensation. A person will be a servant so long as there is a *right to control* in the employer. Thus, a son or daughter at the wheel of the family car will make his or her parents liable under the doctrine of respondeat superior if the child is negligent while carrying out family business for the parents.

cariously liable for injuries to third persons caused by the independent contractor's negligent acts. Again, the following factors are generally taken into account in determining whether an individual is an employee or an independent contractor.

1. How much control the employer may exercise over the details of the work (according to the agreement with the person performing the work);
2. Whether or not the party doing the work has his or her own occupation or business distinct from that of the employer;
3. Whether the kind of work at issue is usually done under direction or by a specialist without any supervision;
4. Whether the person doing the work furnishes his or her own tools and own place to work;
5. How long the person has been employed—for one job or for a continuous period of time;
6. The method of payment—by the hour or by the job;
7. How much skill is required to accomplish the work.

While the employer is never vicariously liable for the independent contractor's tort, there are situations in which the employer may be held liable for his or her own negligence in permitting the contractor to come on to the employer's premises to do dangerous work that results in injury to the general public—injury that could have been avoided if the employer had taken the proper precautions.

For example, suppose an employer hires an independent contractor to wash the windows on his or her building. While performing the job, the contractor drops a bucket on a customer's head from some six stories up. If the employer failed to warn customers with signs or by roping off the area beneath the contractor, he or she will be liable for the customer's injury. But this is not vicarious liability—this is liability for the employer's own negligence.

Also, where the work contracted is of a highly dangerous nature, the employer will be held liable for any injuries that result. The employer cannot avoid or delegate the potential liability involved with such work by contracting to have it done by an independent contractor. In application, this generally involves some kind of "ultrahazardous activity" for which strict liability is imposed under the law of torts (see Chapter 4 for ultrahazardous activities including the transport of highly volatile chemicals, crop spraying, drilling oil wells, blasting, etc.). Thus if an employer hires an independent contractor in the blasting business to blast some stumps out of his or her land, and the blast (though set off carefully) hurls a large piece of rock on to the plaintiff's roof, damaging the house, the employer is strictly liable for the damage even though both the employer and the independent contractor acted carefully and without negligence.

A final situation in which the employer is liable for injuries caused by an independent contractor is where the employer is negligent in selecting the particular independent contractor or in permitting him or her to undertake the activity in question.

Taxation

The second significant legal difference between the employee and the independent contractor is in the area of taxation. The tax consequences resulting from a worker's classification as either an employee or an independent contractor vary in three areas: (1) withholding for social security purposes; (2) withholding for income tax purposes; and (3) income tax deductions.

WHAT ARE THE SOCIAL SECURITY REQUIREMENTS FOR EMPLOYEES VERSUS INDEPENDENT CONTRACTORS?

Social security law provides for three kinds of benefits for nearly all workers in the United States. These are "retirement," "survivors," and "disability" benefits, and all three are paid for through the social security tax. Thus if you retire at the age of sixty-two or sixty-five, you will receive monthly retirement benefits if you have a sufficient work record. In the event of your death at any age, certain members of your family will receive insurance payments if you are covered at the time of your death under the social security system. And if you become totally disabled and are unable to work, you may be eligible for monthly payments if you have been covered under the social security program for the required period of time.

Both employees and independent contractors must pay social security tax. But it makes a substantial difference to employers, employees, and independent contractors just what classification they find themselves in.

Under the Federal Insurance Contributions Act (FICA), all employers are required to pay social security tax on their employees' wages (including bonuses and commissions) up to a certain fixed payment. The employee must pay an equal amount of tax, but his or her payment is automatically deducted and withheld from each salary or wage payment made by his or her employer. The employer must then file a quarterly return (Form 941) by the last day of the month following the quarter covered by the return, and he or she must deposit the social security taxes (both the employer's share and the tax withheld from the employees' wages) into an authorized bank with Federal Tax Deposit Form 501. Large employers deposit the tax funds weekly, and small employers pay them every quarter when they file their quarterly return.

It must be emphasized that an employer is liable for payment of the tax that must be withheld from employee wages—even where the employer fails to withhold the tax and pays what should have been withheld to the employees. The employer, in this case, will still have to pay both the *employer* and the *employee* shares. Of course, the employer will have a right to reimbursement from the employees. And an employer may also be liable for penalties and interest for failure to collect a tax, failure to file a return, failure to deposit taxes, nonpayment of tax, fraud in connection with withholding statements, or failure to supply taxpayer identification numbers.

As you can see, it is essential for employers to keep accurate records of all wages paid to employees. While no particular form of accounting is prescribed, the system used must show that the employer's tax liability was correctly figured and that the proper amount of tax was paid.

Independent contractors pay a higher social security tax than do employees. But, in their case, there is no "matching" payment by employers—employers pay social security tax only on behalf of employees. Again, the tax is levied on the same fixed amount of the independent contractor's income as on the employee's income; the independent contractor's income is called self-employment income under the social security system. The independent contractor must file an annual return of his or her self-employment income on the same date as he or she files his or her regular income tax return. And even if the contractor has no income tax to pay on his or her self-employment income (because of high medical expense deductions, interest deductions, or the like), he or she will still have to pay social security tax.

Thus, the basic idea of social security is simple: during working years, employees, their employers, and self-employed people pay social security taxes. This money is placed into trust fund accounts and is used to pay benefits to the millions already on social security and to pay administrative costs of the program. Ultimately, when today's workers' earnings stop or are reduced because of retirement, death, or disability, benefits will be paid to them from taxes paid by people in covered work and self-employment at that time.

Part of the social security taxes goes for hospital insurance under the Medicare program (as discussed below, a government sponsored program of hospital and medical coverage) so workers and their dependents will have help in paying their hospital bills when they become eligible for the program. The medical insurance portion of Medicare is financed in part by premiums paid by the people who have enrolled for this protection and, in part, by amounts from the federal government. The government's share of the medical insurance and certain other social security costs comes from general revenues and not from social security taxes.

As long as a person has earnings that are covered by law (and investment income is generally not covered as not being compensation for personal services actually rendered in the sense of wages or self-employment income), he or she continues to pay social security taxes regardless of age and even though receiving social security benefits.

Since the early 1970s, the social security system had been paying out more in benefits than had been collected in taxes. To make up the shortfall, the system had been drawing from its trust fund reserves. In 1981, with projections showing that by late 1982 the system was in danger of failing to have enough money to pay benefits, President Reagan appointed a bipartisan National Commission on Social Security Reform to review the social security system's financing problems and to recommend a course of action. The Commission reported its findings and recommendations in January, 1983 and legislation embodying the Commission's basic proposals was enacted into law. The changes in the law are designed to restore financial stability to the social security system both in the short run and in the long-term future.

Table 7–2 shows the present and future social security tax rates as scheduled by the 1983 legislation. Notice that the self-employment tax rates are equal to the combined employee and employer rates.

TABLE 7–2 SOCIAL SECURITY TAX RATES

Years	Cash Benefits	Hospital Insurance	Total
Tax Rate for Employees and Employers (Each) (Percent of Covered Earnings)			
1983	5.40	1.30	6.70
1984	5.70	1.30	7.00
1985	5.70	1.35	7.05
1986–87	5.70	1.45	7.15
1988–89	6.06	1.45	7.51
1990 and after	6.20	1.45	7.65
Tax Rate for Self-Employed Persons			
1983	8.05	1.30	9.35
1984	11.40	2.60	14.00
1985	11.40	2.70	14.10
1986–87	11.40	2.90	14.30
1988–89	12.12	2.90	15.02
1990 and after	12.40	2.90	15.30

Each person's wages and self-employment income are entered on his or her social security record throughout the working years. This record of earnings is used to determine eligibility for benefits and the amount of cash benefits to be received.

The maximum amount of annual earnings that counts for social security (i.e., the wage base) was $37,800 in 1984. The base will rise automatically in future years as earning levels rise. Every year, the increase in the average covered wages will be figured, and if wage levels have increased since the base was last set, the base will be raised—but only if there is an automatic benefit increase the same year.

Currently, nine out of ten workers in the United States are earning protection under social security, and about one out of every six persons in the country receives a monthly social security check. Additionally, over 24 million people sixty-five and over have health insurance under Medicare. Another 3 million disabled persons under sixty-five are also covered by Medicare.

Under social security, a person is considered disabled if he or she has a severe physical or mental condition which prevents the person from working and is expected to last (or has lasted) for at least twelve months, or is expected to result in death. Benefits start for the sixth full month of disability and continue as long as the person is disabled and unable to perform gainful work. Cases are reviewed periodically to make certain the person receiving benefits remains disabled. If the worker dies, survivors' benefits can be paid to certain members of the worker's family. A lump-sum payment (generally $255) can also be made but only if there is an eligible surviving widow, widower, or entitled child.

Monthly social security benefits are also paid to certain dependents of a worker who has retired, become disabled, or died. If a worker is receiving retirement or disability benefits, monthly benefits can also run to his or her unmarried children under eighteen (under nineteen if full-time high school students), unmarried children eighteen or over who were severely disabled before twenty-two years of age and who continue to be disabled, a wife or husband aged sixty-two or over, and to a wife or husband under sixty-two who is caring for a child under sixteen who is receiving a benefit based on the retired or disabled worker's earnings. In the case of a deceased worker, monthly benefits can be paid to his or her unmarried children under eighteen (under nineteen if full-time high school students), unmarried children eighteen or over who were severely disabled before twenty-two and who continue to be disabled, a widow or widower sixty or over, a widow or widower fifty or older who becomes disabled not later than seven years after the worker's death, a widow or widower or surviving divorced mother or father if caring for the deceased worker's child either under sixteen or disabled who is receiving a benefit based on the earnings of the deceased worker, or dependent parents sixty-two or older.

Benefits can also go to a divorced spouse at sixty-two or over, a surviving divorced spouse at sixty, or to a disabled surviving divorced spouse fifty or older if the marriage lasted ten years or more. Under certain conditions, children may be eligible for social security benefits based on a grandparent's earnings.

Starting in January, 1985, a divorced spouse who has been divorced at least two years can receive benefits at sixty-two whether or not his or her former spouse receives them. However, the former spouse must be eligible for social security benefits regardless of whether he or she has retired.

Generally, a marriage must have lasted at least one year before dependents of a retired or disabled worker can get monthly benefits; survivors can get benefits in most cases if the marriage lasted at least nine months.

Regarding Medicare, two parts—hospital insurance and medical insurance—help protect people sixty-five and over from the high costs of health care. Disabled people under sixty-five who have been entitled to social security disability benefits for twenty-four or more months are also eligible for Medicare. Insured workers and their dependents who need dialysis treatment or a kidney transplant because of permanent kidney failure also have Medicare protection.

The hospital insurance portion of Medicare helps pay the cost of inpatient hospital care and certain kinds of followup care. The medical insurance portion helps pay the cost of physicians' services, outpatient hospital services, and for certain other medical items and services not covered by hospital insurance. People who have medical insurance pay a monthly premium. More than two-thirds of the costs of the medical insurance premium is paid from general revenues of the federal government. The basic premium was $12.20 a month through December of 1983 (this will change from time to time to reflect the cost of living).

Any person eligible for a social security benefit as a worker, dependent, or survivor, is eligible for hospital insurance protection upon reaching the age of sixty-five. And people sixty-five or over who have not worked long enough to be eligible for social security can still obtain Medicare protection by enrolling and paying a monthly premium.

TABLE 7–3 WORK CREDIT FOR RETIREMENT BENEFITS

If you reach 62 in year	Years you need
1981	$7^1/_2$
1982	$7^3/_4$
1983	8
1987	9
1991 or later	10

As stated previously, before a person can receive monthly cash benefits under social security, he or she must have credit for a certain amount of work under the program. The exact amount of work credit depends on age. Social security credit is measured in "quarters of coverage." Employees and self-employed persons receive quarters of coverage for a specific dollar amount of covered annual earnings (in 1984, employees and self-employed received one quarter of coverage for each $370 of covered annual earnings). No more than four quarters of coverage can be credited for a year. The amount of earnings needed to obtain a quarter of coverage will increase automatically in the future to keep pace with average wages. Table 7–3 shows how much credit is needed for benefits.

A person who becomes disabled before the age of twenty-four needs credit for only one and one-half years of work in the three year period prior to the disability. If disabled between twenty-four and thirty-one, the person generally needs credit for at least five years of work out of the ten years preceding the disability. Workers disabled at an older age generally need more credit.

As of January 1, 1984, social security coverage was extended to all employees of nonprofit organizations and to new federal employees. Termination of social security coverage for employees of state and local governments is also prohibited by the federal law.

Having enough work credit means only that some benefit will be received. The exact amount of the benefit depends on earnings over a period of years. In figuring benefits for workers who reach sixty-two, become disabled, or die, actual earnings for past years are adjusted to take account of changes in average wages, and a formula is applied to the average to obtain the benefit rate. This method is intended to insure that benefits will reflect changes in wage levels over a working lifetime. This is important because average wages in the economy can change greatly over a thirty to forty year period.

Following are examples of 1983 benefits: a person reaching sixty-five in 1983 would have a possible monthly retirement benefit of as much as $709; a person reaching sixty-two in 1983 would have a possible monthly retirement benefit of as much as $526. A person becoming disabled in 1983 could have a benefit as high as $795 a month, again depending on age and past earnings. Survivors of a worker who died in 1983 could expect to receive as much as $1,393 a month for a family of three or more. There is no fixed minimum benefit amount for workers who reach sixty-two, become disabled, or die after 1981 as rates are determined on each worker's earnings covered by social security. Benefits for people on the rolls will increase automatically each January as the cost of living rises. Each year, living costs will be compared with those of the year before. If living costs have increased three percent or more, benefits will be increased by the same amount.

Starting with the increase payable in January, 1985, if the balance in the social security trust funds is below fifteen percent (twenty percent beginning with the January 1990 increase) of the total amount required to pay benefits for the year, the annual increase will be based on the increase in average wages if lower than the increase in cost of living.

If a person qualifies for checks on the record of more than one worker (for example, on one's own work and one's spouse's), he or she will get an amount equal to the larger of the two amounts.

Starting with 1984, up to one-half of a person's benefits may be subject to the federal income tax for any year in which his or her adjusted gross income for federal tax purposes plus nontaxable interest income and one-half of social security benefits exceeds a base amount. The base amount is $25,000 for an individual, $32,000 for a couple filing jointly. The amount of benefits subject to tax will be the smaller of one-half the benefits, or one-half the amount of combined income (adjusted gross income plus one-half of total benefits) in excess of the base amount.

Under social security, a person may retire as early as sixty-two years of age, but the retirement check will be reduced permanently. Payment amounts are also reduced if a wife, husband, widow, or widower starts getting payments before sixty-five. The amount of reduction depends on the number of months a person gets benefits before reaching sixty-five. If one starts the benefits early, he or she will get about the same value in total benefits over the years, but in smaller amounts to take account of the longer period of receipt. Starting in 2000, the age at which full benefits are payable will be increased in gradual steps until it reaches sixty-seven. This will affect persons born in 1938 and later as shown in table 7–4. When this change is fully phased in, a worker can still receive benefits at sixty-two, but the benefit rate will be lower than the current rate at age sixty-two. Now a person retiring at sixty-two receives eighty percent of the amount payable at sixty-five. When the increase in the retirement age becomes fully effective,

TABLE 7–4 AGE FOR FULL RETIREMENT BENEFITS

If you were born in	Retirement Age (year/months)
1938	65/2
1939	65/4
1940	65/6
1941	65/8
1942	65/10
1943–1954	66/0
1955	66/2
1956	66/4
1957	66/6
1958	66/8
1959	66/10
1960 and after	67

a worker retiring at age sixty-two will receive a benefit equal to seventy percent of the age sixty-seven benefit.

If a person returns to work and is under seventy years of age, his or her earnings may affect social security benefits. However, a person may receive all benefits if his or her earnings do not exceed the annual exempt amount. The annual exempt amount for 1984 was $6,960 for people sixty-five or over and $5,160 for people under sixty-five. If earnings go over the annual exempt amount, the Social Security Administration withholds $1 in benefits for each $2 of earnings above the limit. Starting in 1990, $1 in benefits will be withheld for each $3 in earnings above the limit for people sixty-five and over. Beginning in the year 2000, the age at which this withholding rate applies will increase as the retirement age increases. Income from savings, most investments, or insurance does not affect benefits, as "earnings" for purposes of reduction of benefits refers generally to compensation for personal services actually rendered.

In future years, the annual exempt amounts will increase automatically as the level of average wages rises.

HOW DO YOU DISTINGUISH BETWEEN AN EMPLOYEE AND AN INDEPENDENT CONTRACTOR?

Generally, the common law "right of control" test is used to distinguish between employees and independent contractors for purposes of the social security law. Special provisions in the law, however, provide that the following workers are "employees" regardless of who has the right of control, so long as the workers perform services for pay in the prescribed circumstances.

1. A full-time traveling or city salesperson is an employee if he or she solicits orders for one employer from wholesalers, retailers, contractors, hotels, restaurants, and the like for merchandise and business supplies. The salesperson's entire or principal business activity must be devoted to solicitation for one employer (the multiple-line salesperson is thus not an "employee" under this social security law). Of course, if the employer has the right to control the salesperson's manner or method of doing his or her job, the salesperson is an employee under the common law "right of control" test. But even where he or she fails this test, the salesperson is still an "employee" for social security purposes if he or she works full-time for one employer.

2. An agent-driver or commission-driver is an "employee" if he or she distributes meats, vegetables, fruits, bakery goods, or beverages (except milk) or if he or she handles laundry or drycleaning for his or her employer. This includes the person who operates his or her own truck or the company's truck, who serves customers designated by the company as well as those solicited on his or her own, and whose pay is either a commission on sales or simply the difference between the price he or she charges customers and the price he or she pays to the company for the product or service.

3. A full-time life insurance salesperson is an "employee" for social security purposes regardless of who has the right to control so long as the salesperson's entire or principal business activity is devoted to soliciting life insurance for one insurance company.

4. A homeworker is an employee if he or she meets the common law test or if he or she satisfies each of the following requirements:

a. The homeworker does work according to specifications furnished by the person for whom the services are performed. The homeworker's materials are furnished by that person, and they must later be returned either to that person or to his or her designee; and

b. He or she is paid at least fifty dollars cash in any calendar quarter.

These four exceptions to the common law test do not apply where the worker in question has a substantial investment in the facilities used in connection with his or her job (other than facilities for transportation), or where the services are in the nature of a single transaction and not part of a continuing relationship with the employer.

Social security law also specifically includes "any officer" of a corporation as an employee. Partners, on the other hand, are not employees of the partnership, and their shares of partnership earnings are subject not to the employer-employee tax but to the self-employment tax on independent contractors.

WHAT ARE THE INCOME TAX WITHHOLDING REQUIREMENTS FOR EMPLOYEES VS. INDEPENDENT CONTRACTORS?

Every employer who pays wages to an employee must withhold from the wages paid an amount determined according to government tables like the one presented in figure 7–1. As with social security taxes, the employer is required to withhold income taxes only if the legal relationship of employer-employee exists: the employer need not withhold income taxes from wages paid to an independent contractor. Again, the same common law tests control. There is generally an employer-employee relationship when the person for whom services are performed has the right to control and direct the individual who performs the services not only as to the result to be accomplished, but also as to the details and means of performance. The employer does not have to actually direct or control the way the services are performed—it is enough that he or she has the right to do so. Individuals who are in fact partners, independent contractors, or sole proprietors of a business are not subject to withholding on their drawings or earnings.

HOW DO INCOME TAX DEDUCTIONS DIFFER BETWEEN AN EMPLOYEE AND AN INDEPENDENT CONTRACTOR?

Deductions are important to all of us. This is because every deduction an individual is permitted to take under the law reduces his or her amount of income; and since the tax rate is applied against the amount of income, the lower the income, the lower the tax.

An employee can take only limited deductions with respect to his or her employment. Only those expenses required for the job are allowed. Thus the cost and maintenance of uniforms and work clothes are deductible if the clothes are required as a condition of employment and are not suitable for

FIGURE 7–1 A GOVERNMENT WITHHOLDING TABLE

SINGLE Persons—MONTHLY Payroll Period

And the wages are—		And the number of withholding allowances claimed is—										
At least	But less than	0	1	2	3	4	5	6	7	8	9	10
		The amount of income tax to be withheld shall be—										
$0	$116	$0	$0	$0	$0	$0	$0	$0	$0	$0	$0	$0
116	120	.20	0	0	0	0	0	0	0	0	0	0
120	124	.60	0	0	0	0	0	0	0	0	0	0
124	128	1.10	0	0	0	0	0	0	0	0	0	0
128	132	1.60	0	0	0	0	0	0	0	0	0	0
132	136	2.10	0	0	0	0	0	0	0	0	0	0
136	140	2.60	0	0	0	0	0	0	0	0	0	0
140	144	3.00	0	0	0	0	0	0	0	0	0	0
144	148	3.50	0	0	0	0	0	0	0	0	0	0
148	152	4.00	0	0	0	0	0	0	0	0	0	0
152	156	4.50	0	0	0	0	0	0	0	0	0	0
156	160	5.00	0	0	0	0	0	0	0	0	0	0
160	164	5.40	0	0	0	0	0	0	0	0	0	0
164	168	5.90	0	0	0	0	0	0	0	0	0	0
168	172	6.40	0	0	0	0	0	0	0	0	0	0
172	176	6.90	0	0	0	0	0	0	0	0	0	0
176	180	7.40	0	0	0	0	0	0	0	0	0	0
180	184	7.80	0	0	0	0	0	0	0	0	0	0
184	188	8.30	0	0	0	0	0	0	0	0	0	0
188	192	8.80	0	0	0	0	0	0	0	0	0	0
*	*	*			*	*	*			*	*	*
2,520	2,560	551.40	523.00	494.70	467.40	442.40	417.40	392.40	367.40	342.40	319.60	298.80
2,560	2,600	565.00	536.60	508.30	480.00	454.40	429.40	404.40	379.40	354.40	329.60	308.80
2,600	2,640	578.60	550.20	521.90	493.60	466.40	441.40	416.40	391.40	366.40	341.40	318.80
2,640	2,680	592.20	563.80	535.50	507.20	478.80	453.40	428.40	403.40	378.40	353.40	328.80
2,680	2,720	605.80	577.40	549.10	520.80	492.40	465.40	440.40	415.40	390.40	365.40	340.40
2,720	2,760	619.40	591.00	562.70	534.40	506.00	477.70	452.40	427.40	402.40	377.40	352.40
2,760	2,800	633.60	604.60	576.30	548.00	519.60	491.30	464.40	439.40	414.40	389.40	364.40
2,800	2,840	648.40	618.20	589.90	561.60	533.20	504.90	476.60	451.40	426.40	401.40	376.40
2,840	2,880	663.20	632.40	603.50	575.20	546.80	518.50	490.20	463.40	438.40	413.40	388.40
2,880	2,920	678.00	647.20	617.10	588.80	560.40	532.10	503.80	475.40	450.40	425.40	400.40
2,920	2,960	692.80	662.00	631.10	602.40	574.00	545.70	517.40	489.00	462.40	437.40	412.40
2,960	3,000	707.60	676.80	645.90	616.00	587.60	559.30	531.00	502.60	474.40	449.40	424.40
3,000	3,040	722.40	691.60	660.70	629.90	601.20	572.90	544.60	516.20	487.90	461.40	436.40
3,040	3,080	737.20	706.40	675.50	644.70	614.80	586.50	558.20	529.80	501.50	473.40	448.40
3,080	3,120	752.00	721.20	690.30	659.50	628.70	600.10	571.80	543.40	515.10	486.80	460.40
3,120	3,160	766.80	736.00	705.10	674.30	643.50	613.70	585.40	557.00	528.70	500.40	472.40
3,160	3,200	781.60	750.80	719.90	689.10	658.30	627.40	599.00	570.60	542.30	514.00	485.60
3,200	3,240	796.40	765.60	734.70	703.90	673.10	642.20	612.60	584.20	555.90	527.60	499.20
3,240	3,280	811.20	780.40	749.50	718.70	687.90	657.00	626.20	597.80	569.50	541.20	512.80
3,280	3,320	826.00	795.20	764.30	733.50	702.70	671.80	641.00	611.40	583.10	554.80	526.40
3,320	3,360	840.80	810.00	779.10	748.30	717.50	686.60	655.80	625.00	596.70	568.40	540.00
3,360	3,400	855.60	824.80	793.90	763.10	732.30	701.40	670.60	639.80	610.30	582.00	553.60
3,400	3,440	870.40	839.60	808.70	777.90	747.10	716.20	685.40	654.60	623.90	595.60	567.20
3,440	3,480	885.20	854.40	823.50	792.70	761.90	731.00	700.20	669.40	638.50	609.20	580.80
3,480	3,520	900.00	869.20	838.30	807.50	776.70	745.80	715.00	684.20	653.30	622.80	594.40
3,520	3,560	914.80	884.00	853.10	822.30	791.50	760.60	729.80	699.00	668.10	637.30	608.00
3,560	3,600	929.60	898.80	867.90	837.10	806.30	775.40	744.60	713.80	682.90	652.10	621.60
3,600	3,640	944.40	913.60	882.70	851.90	821.10	790.20	759.40	728.60	697.70	666.90	636.10
		37 percent of the excess over $3,640 plus—										
$3,640 and over		951.80	921.00	890.10	859.30	828.50	797.60	766.80	736.00	705.10	674.30	643.50

Source: Internal Revenue Service

regular wearing apparel off duty or away from work. Labor union dues paid as a condition of employment are also deductible. But expenses of training for a career, securing a license, or commuting expenses to and from work are not.

An independent contractor, on the other hand, can deduct any expense incurred in carrying on his or her trade, business, or profession. Only two requirements must be met: (1) the expense must be directly connected with the taxpayer's trade, business, or profession; and (2) it must be reasonable in amount. Expenses incurred for repairs, rent, advertising, insurance, travel, and entertainment, for example, are all included within this category.

By now it should be apparent that the classification of a worker as either an employee or an independent contractor has important consequences in the areas of vicarious liability for the worker's torts, withholding for social security and income tax purposes, and income tax deductions.

Consider the following situation. Your author once had a friend and client who was a high school music and band teacher in a small town some forty or fifty miles away from a very large city. When an out-of-town minister asked the teacher to act as the organist and choir director at his church in the city, the teacher sought your author's advice. The job would require the teacher to make one trip into the city each week on a Tuesday night to practice with the choir and to remain there all Sunday morning to lead the choir and play the organ. The church minister offered to pay the teacher $150 a month for this service.

Now is the teacher an employee or an independent contractor if he accepts this job as choir director? And does his classification make a difference? All parties agreed that, if possible, the teacher should be classified as an independent contractor. The minister, in that case, would not have to withhold income taxes from the $150 a month fee. Nor would he have to withhold and "match" social security taxes. And the church would not face liability if its new choir director accidentally (but negligently) struck some choir member in the eye while directing the choir. Finally, as an independent contractor, the "choir director" could deduct the expenses he incurred in commuting to the city twice a week to practice and lead the choir.

A contract was drafted specifically stating that the choir director would be in complete charge of the practices—he alone would decide what music he would use and what and when he would play on Sundays. The director was further described in the contract as an independent contractor and not an employee. It was specifically agreed in writing that he was hired to do a job for a price and that the minister would have no right to control his manner and method of performance. Finally, a lump sum payment of $450 was agreed upon and inserted into the contract to cover a three-month period of time.

Today, the minister and the choir director continue to use this contract, entering into a new one every quarter. Since the minister has no right of control, the choir director is clearly an independent contractor. This saves the minister all the trouble of social security and income tax withholding, and it eliminates his potential liability under the doctrine of respondeat superior. And it makes for greater cash income for the choir director who can claim additional deductions against his income.

WHAT HAPPENS IF A WORKER IS INJURED ON THE JOB?

We have already seen that where an employee injures some member of the public while acting within the scope of his employment, the employer is liable under the doctrine of respondeat superior.

But who must bear the loss if the employee is injured while on the job?

Workers' Compensation

By 1900, industrial accidents were at an all-time high in this country. An enormous number of workers were injured on the job every year. Some were injured as a result of their employer's carelessness in providing unsafe working conditions. But many other accidents were simply unavoidable and not due to any negligence on the part of the employer. Where the injured employee could prove that the accident resulted from the employer's negligence, he or she could recover damages. But negligence was extremely difficult to prove since the employer had available an "unholy trio" of defenses—the fellow-servant rule, assumption of risk, and contributory negligence. The fellow-servant rule made it clear that respondeat superior did not apply where an employee injured, not a member of the general public, but a fellow employee. The injured employee, in this case, could not recover damages from the employer but was left to his or her remedies against the frequently penniless fellow servant. The employer could also assert, to bar recovery, that the employee "assumed the risk" of unsafe working conditions by accepting the employment. This defense was especially effective where the employee knew of the unsafe condition and nevertheless remained on the job. And, finally, where the employee's own carelessness contributed to or increased his or her injury, the employer could plead "contributory negligence" and successfully prevent recovery. But negligence was not only a difficult charge to prove, it was timely and expensive as well. And even where the injured employee had a good claim, the expense and delay of litigation often prompted the employee to accept a compromise settlement for a fraction of the full value of his or her claim. And where the accident was "unavoidable," the employee could not recover at all.

But was it fair to expect the injured worker to shoulder his or her own accident costs? Obviously not, as the average worker seldom has sufficient savings to tide him or her over in the event of serious injury. Someone else had to assume this burden. The only question was who—the worker's relatives? The state or federal government? Some organized charity? Or the employer (even though not negligent)? Ultimately, it was decided that the employer should bear the cost since he or she created the risk. Of course, the cost can be anticipated and passed on to the public by means of higher prices. Or the employer can spread the cost by purchasing liability insurance.

Workers' Compensation thus rests upon the economic principle that those persons who enjoy the product of a business should ultimately bear the cost of industrial accidents incident to the manufacture, preparation, and distribution of the product or service. It makes no difference who is at fault. The injured employee is guaranteed under his or her state Workers' Compensation statute at least a minimum sum to use for medical expense and support after each and every accident.

Workers' Compensation statutes provide for the injured worker to receive an amount worked out in advance by a state agency. The agency predetermines specific amounts for varying injuries and additionally grants limited amounts of compensation for periods of time depending on the extent and length of disability. The worker who receives an award is not entitled to further compensation. And he or she cannot bring suit against the employer for additional recovery. In other words, the employee will recover Workers' Compensation no matter who is at fault in the injury, but recovery will be limited to an amount deemed proper by the state administrative agency for that kind of injury and that period of disability. (However, it should be pointed out that if a third party is at fault in causing the injury, the worker can sue the third party and recover further.) This system of Workers' Compensation protects all the workers in America and handles over 2 million worker injuries each year (it is interesting to note that there is a growing movement to place auto accidents under a similar type of no-fault provision throughout the country).

The purpose of this limited, no-fault recovery is to mitigate the disastrous economic effects of a work-related injury by providing for payments of money to or for the benefit of an injured employee. These payments are called "benefits," and each state has its own schedule of benefit payments. All states furnish medical aid for injured employees. This includes, in addition to the cost of the service of physicians and nurses, hospitalization expenses, the cost of recuperation equipment such as crutches, the cost of prosthetic devices such as artificial arms, false teeth, and similar aids. More than a billion dollars of medical expenses are paid each year under Workers' Compensation statutes.

The amount of disability benefits granted depends on whether the disability is partial or total and whether it is temporary or permanent. Maximum weekly benefits for total disability range from around $100 a week in some states to over $500 a week in others. A number of states provide for payment of a percentage of lost wages (from 50 to 90 percent); others set maximum dollar amounts. And while some states cover the injured employee for as long as he or she is disabled, still others have maximum periods of payment. The present trend is to extend coverage for the entire period of disability.

Certain types of injuries involving permanent, partial disability are specifically covered in state statutes and are commonly referred to as "scheduled injuries." This means that the injury is one listed on a schedule in the law for which a predetermined amount of compensation is made payable. Typical scheduled injuries include loss of an arm, an eye, a leg, or other bodily members.

Death benefits are also payable to cover burial expenses and to take care of the deceased worker's family. Monthly benefits to a surviving spouse will generally be based on a percentage of the deceased worker's gross monthly wage (e.g., 60 percent of gross monthly wage up to a maximum amount such as $700). Dependent children's benefits may run at a particular dollar figure per child or a percentage of the gross wages (e.g., $150 a month for the first two dependent children and $50 a month for children in excess of two) with ceilings for a family of a maximum amount such as $1,000, $1,400, or the like. If a surviving spouse remarries, some states provide for a lump sum final payment of $5,000 to $7,500. Some states even provide for deferral of this lump sum to see if the second marriage lasts; if it does not, the spouse can go back to receiving the benefits by reason of the work-related death of the first spouse.

Methods of providing the money for the injured worker vary from state to state. Some states require the employer to obtain insurance protection from a private insurance company. In other states, the employer must contribute money for each employee into a state insurance fund which serves as the exclusive source for payment of compensation claims. Still other states permit the employer at his or her option to either participate in the state fund, to secure protection from a private insurer, or to establish himself or herself as a self-insurer.[2]

Again, it is important to distinguish between the employee who is covered under the Workers' Compensation statutes and the independent contractor who is not. Statutes also generally exclude from coverage workers who are not regular employees but are hired only as "casual" laborers—i.e., for an isolated job of a temporary nature. Statutes throughout the states, however, vary greatly on this subject.

It is also important to note that an injury is compensable only where it "arises out of and in the course of employment." An employee who is injured Sunday afternoon while at home fixing his or her TV set is not injured on the job, and Workers' Compensation is not available. Still, there is often a fine line between what is in the course and what is out. For example, an employee who takes his or her meals off work premises on his or her own time is generally regarded as outside the course of employment both while eating the meal and while proceeding to and from the eating place. But an employee who is injured in an organized recreational activity or sporting event that has been acquiesced in by the employer and that takes place on the premises during a period of rest or recreation is considered to be within the course of employment and thus covered by Workers' Compensation.

In summary, Workers' Compensation statutes (which have been enacted in all our states) provide limited, no-fault recovery for any covered employee who is injured or killed on the job. Whereas under the old common law, the employer could escape all liability by asserting in defense the fellow-servant rule, assumption of risk, or contributory negligence, these three defenses are not available to the employer under Workers' Compensation statutes. In most states, the injured employee will receive benefits even where the injury is a result of his or her own negligence, stupidity, drunkenness, or fight with a fellow worker (a few states, however, do deny or limit recovery where the injury results from the employee's willful misconduct).

WHAT IS UNEMPLOYMENT COMPENSATION?

Injury is not the only risk of employment. Perhaps as great a risk is the possibility of becoming unemployed. In terms of numbers, for example, it certainly affects more of our working population. Less than twenty workers per 100,000 suffer disabling injuries each year in this country. But in some recent years, the unemployment rate has been running 8 to 10 percent and

2. An employer who fails to obtain the required Workers' Compensation coverage may be sued by the employee, and the employer cannot assent the "unholy trio" of defenses. In some states, the state will pay the employee's claim and bring suit against the employer for reimbursement.

higher with over 8,000 per 100,000 workers out of work. Even in prosperous times, when our unemployment rate stabilizes at a low 4 percent, 4,000 out of every 100,000 workers are still out of a job. And a growing proportion of our unemployed are teenagers and young women in the twenty to twenty-four-year-old age bracket.

The unemployment compensation system is a complicated combination of federal and state law designed to protect the worker against complete loss of income when he or she is out of work and suitable replacement work is not available. Only the worker with a history of working experience will qualify for unemployment compensation, because only he or she can suffer a "wage loss" within the meaning of the unemployment legislation.

Basically, what is required under the unemployment compensation law is the payment of an unemployment tax on the payrolls of all employers who have in any year as few as one employee for as little as eighteen weeks in a calendar year or who have a payroll of as little as $225 in any calendar quarter. The federal tax rate has been 3.5 percent on the first $7,000 of the employee's annual wages, but is 6.2 percent on the first $7,000 of wages after December 31, 1984. Agricultural employers and those who hire domestic employees in their private homes are exceptions to the above criteria. Agricultural employers must pay the tax if they have ten or more employees on any one day in each of twenty different calendar weeks in any calendar year or have cash payroll for farm workers of $20,000 or more during a calendar quarter. Those who hire domestic employees in their private homes must pay the tax if they have a payroll of $1,000 or more cash wages in any calendar quarter. College students performing paid services for the college while attending classes are not covered by the unemployment tax law.

The tax is paid by the employer—not by the employee (that is, it is not withheld from the employee's salary as is the income tax and the social security tax). The unemployment tax is properly considered an expense of doing business.

To be eligible for unemployment compensation benefits, an unemployed worker must qualify under his or her own state statute. Generally, he or she must be unemployed, have filed a claim for benefits, be able and available for work, and have been previously employed for a specified period of time. While the law varies somewhat from state to state, generally a person must have had at least fifteen to twenty weeks of work coverage to qualify and base wages of $700 or more. The weekly benefits will depend on the total wages paid during the base year and may run from $50 to $150 a week and for 6 months to a year. But an individual whose unemployment is due to: (1) having been discharged for misconduct connected with his or her work, or (2) having left work voluntarily without good cause, or (3) having failed without good cause, either to apply for available suitable work when so directed by the employment officer or to accept suitable work when offered shall be disqualified from the receipt of benefits.

Most of the unemployment tax goes to a state employment division. The federal law provides forgiveness of as much as 5.4 percent of the 6.2 percent tax (as of 1985) if that amount is paid to a particular state (as long as the state's unemployment law conforms to federal law) so that each state can administer its own unemployment tax program. A state may also have a higher wage base than $7,000 (e.g., Oregon's base of $13,000 in 1984 and $14,000 in 1985). Although only a small part of the tax is actually paid over to the federal government (i.e., .8 percent), this builds up a federal loan fund that may be made available to a state if it does not have sufficient money to provide unemployment benefits. These loans must be paid back by the state or the federal rate will go up for that state to collect them.

Generally, claimants will receive a maximum of twenty-six times their weekly benefit amount (a weekly benefit amount may be computed, for example, on the basis of 1.25 percent of the total base year wages but with a fixed lower limit of and an upper limit of 60 percent of the state's average weekly wage). During periods of abnormally high unemployment, extended benefits may be provided, although they may be at less than the amount payable on a regular claim. In 1983 for example, some states because of very high unemployment extended the twenty-six week period by an additional thirteen weeks which was followed by a federal extension of an additional sixteen weeks (making it possible to receive unemployment benefits for as long as fifty-five weeks).

The rate of tax that employers pay is not necessarily the same. Generally, new employers will start at the maximum rate. Then, each employer's tax rate will be recomputed every year. The new rate is based on "experience" (meaning unemployment benefit charges against the employer's account) from past years. Fewer charges resulting from employment benefits paid a particular employers' workers result in lower experience and a lower tax. Rates may be as low as 2 percent for employers with low experience history.

Individuals who are unemployed are not required to accept any jobs that are available, but only suitable jobs based on previous qualifications and experience. However, individuals who are on extended benefits (beyond the usual twenty-six week period) are subject to stricter eligibility requirements and must generally accept any job they are capable of performing as long as the pay exceeds their weekly benefit amount (and meets minimum wage requirements).

WHAT ARE THE RULES REGARDING WAGES, HOURS, AND WORKING CONDITIONS?

The following exchange took place in 1911 between a Pennsylvania judge and a little girl named Helen Susscak who was an eight-year-old textile mill employee:

Judge. "Helen, what time do you go to work?"

Helen. "Half after 6 evenin's."

Judge. "When do you come home from the mill?"

Helen. "Half after 6 mornin's."

Judge. "How far do you live from the mill?"

Helen. "I don't know. I guess it mostly takes an hour to git there."

Judge. "And the inspector tells me it's across lonely fields exposed to storms that sweep down the valley. What's your pay, Helen?"

Helen. "I gits 3 cents an hour, sir."

Judge. "If my arithmetic is good that is almost 36 cents for a night's work. Well, now, we do indeed find the flesh and blood of little children coined into money."

The above incident was recounted by Senators Javits of New York and Williams of New Jersey at the time the 1966 Amendments to the Fair Labor Standards Act were being considered. The original Fair Labor Standards Act was the product of the "New Deal" of the 1930s. In May of 1937, President Franklin Roosevelt sent to Congress a wage-hour proposal stressing the necessity of conserving "our primary resources of manpower by controlling maximum hours, minimum wages, the evil of child labor and the exploitation of unorganized labor." Senator Hugo L. Black (who became justice of the Supreme Court in 1938 where he served some forty-five years before his death in 1972) of Alabama introduced an appropriate bill in the Senate, where the bill was ultimately passed as the Fair Labor Standards Act of 1938. The purpose of the Act was to guarantee certain minimum working conditions, particularly a minimum wage and a maximum length work week. The minimum wage was set at $3.35 an hour by Congress beginning January 1, 1981, having been increased many times over the years (from 35 cents an hour when the Act was originally passed) because of inflation.

The Fair Labor Standards Act (FLSA) is primarily a wage and hour law. The following are its most important substantive provisions:

Sec. 6(a) Every employer shall pay to each of his employees who in any work week in an enterprise engaged in commerce or in the production of goods for commerce, wages at the following rates:

(1) not less than $3.35 an hour.

Sec. 7(a)(1) * * * No employer shall employ any of his employees who in any work week is engaged in commerce or in the production of goods for commerce, or is employed in an enterprise engaged in commerce * * * for a work week longer than forty hours, unless such employee receives compensation for his employment in excess of the hours above specified at a rate not less than one and one-half time the regular rate at which he is employed.

Sec. 12(c) No employer shall employ any oppressive child labor in commerce or in the production of goods for commerce.

Sec. 16(a) Any person who willfully violates any of the provisions * * * shall upon conviction thereof be subject to a fine of not more than $10,000 or to imprisonment for not more than six months or both.

Sec. 3(1) "Oppressive child labor" means a condition of employment under which (1) any employee under the age of sixteen years is employed by an employer (other than a parent * * *) in any occupation, or (2) any employee between the ages of sixteen and eighteen years is employed by an employer in any occupation which the Secretary of Labor shall find and by order declare to be particularly hazardous for the employment of children between such ages or detrimental to their health or well-being.

Sec. 12(a) No producer, manufacturer, or dealer shall ship or deliver for shipment in commerce any goods produced in an establishment situated in the

United States in or about which within thirty days prior to the removal of such goods therefrom any oppressive child labor has been employed. * * *

Exemptions [only two exemptions are listed—there are many more]

Sec. 13(a) The provisions of sections 6 * * * and 7 (wages and hours) shall not apply with respect to—

(1) any employee employed in a bona fide executive, administrative, or professional capacity * * *; or

(2) any employee employed by any retail or service establishment * * * if more than 50 per centum of such establishment's annual dollar volume of sales of goods or services is made within the State in which the establishment is located. * * * [This exemption applies only to establishments doing $362,500 or less of business annually.]

The Fair Labor Standards Act strictly regulates "child labor." Minors may not be employed in "oppressive" labor—i.e., occupations particularly hazardous for them or detrimental to their health and well-being. Notice that the statute prohibits a wholesaler from delivering goods to a dealer in another state where the wholesaler knows that oppressive child labor was used in manufacturing the goods. For minors between the ages of sixteen and eighteen, prohibited jobs include logging, roofing, meat packing or slaughtering, and building demolition. For persons between fourteen and sixteen, some employment is permitted under regulations provided by the secretary of labor. Employment in occupations other than mining or manufacturing, for example, is allowed so long as it does not interfere with the schooling, health, or well-being of the fourteen to sixteen-year-old. Permissible categories include office and clerical work, retailing, price marking and shelving, deliveries by foot or using a bicycle, garden work, and gasoline station work as long as the minor does not work in the pits or racks.

ARE THERE LAWS PROHIBITING JOB DISCRIMINATION?

The answer is yes. Job discrimination on grounds of race, color, religion, sex, national origin, and age is unlawful under federal law. Various state laws expand this list and include other characteristics such as creed and ancestry. Title VII of the Civil Rights Act of 1964 is the most important federal law designed to eliminate discriminatory employment practices. You will recall our discussion of Title VII and other job discrimination laws from Chapter 5 in connection with the work of the EEOC (Equal Employment Opportunity Commission). Title VII applies to employers of fifteen or more employees. Section 703 of the statute states:

Sec. 703. (a) It shall be an unlawful employment practice for an employer—

(1) to fail or refuse to hire or to discharge any individual or otherwise to discriminate against any individual with respect to his compensation, terms, conditions, or privileges of employment, because of such individual's race, color, religion, sex or national origin; or

(2) to limit, segregate, or classify his employees or applicants for employment in any way which would deprive any individual of employment opportunities or otherwise adversely affect his status as an employee, because of such individual's race, color, religion, sex, or national origin.

On October 31, 1979, President Carter signed into law a pregnancy disability amendment to Title VII. The change in the law expands the definition of "sex" discrimination to include discrimination on the basis of "pregnancy, childbirth, or related medical conditions." Among other things, the amendment does the following:

1. Requires employers to treat pregnancy and childbirth the same as other causes of disability under fringe benefit plans;
2. Prohibits terminating or refusing to hire or promote a woman solely because she is pregnant;
3. Bars mandatory leaves for pregnant women arbitrarily set at a certain time in their pregnancy and not based on their inability to work; and
4. Protects the reinstatement rights of women on leave for pregnancy-related reasons, including credit for previous service and accrued retirement benefits, and accumulated seniority.

Sex discrimination under Title VII also includes sexual harassment on the job (i.e., the conditioning of employment or terms of employment on sexual favors, including the creation of a hostile working environment infused with sexual proposition or innuendo).

The types of practices that are outlawed by Title VII are outlawed with respect to age discrimination by the Age Discrimination in Employment Act of 1967. Originally, the provisions of the Act were limited to individuals who were at least forty years of age but less than sixty-five. However, the Age Discrimination in Employment Act Amendments of 1978 raised the upper age limit on coverage from sixty-five to seventy and prohibited the forced retirement based on age of employees below the age of seventy. The law applies only to employers of twenty or more workers. The amendments (a) forbid a seniority system or employee benefit plan to require or permit the involuntary retirement of an employee under the age of seventy; (b) permit the compulsory retirement at age sixty-five of employees employed in a bona fide executive or high policy-making position and entitled to a pension of at least $27,000 per year; and (c) eliminate the maximum age for retirement of seventy that presently applies to U.S. government employees.

The 1978 Amendments do not preclude an employer from terminating an employee for cause. Any employee, including an older person, who is incompetent or unable to perform his or her job is not protected under the Act from being discharged or retired. This fact may prompt the firing of some older workers who would have been kept on the job prior to the passage of the amendments. Many employers have tolerated less than acceptable work performance from older employees simply because they were near retirement age (on the other hand, prior to passage of the amendments, many capable persons were forced to retire simply because of their age). Of course, in terminating employees for cause, the same performance standards must be applied to all employees—not special standards for older employees—or this itself will violate the Act as being age discrimination.

The Age Discrimination in Employment Act does not prevent discrimination on the basis of age where age is a bona fide occupational qualification reasonably necessary to the normal operation of the business (as in piloting a plane or playing professional ball). But where it is not an occupational qualification (e.g., where a flight attendant is concerned), a person cannot be hired or fired because of his or her age.

Along the same line, Title VII, Section 706(g) of the Civil Rights Act of 1964 authorizes federal district courts to correct unlawful discriminatory practices by enjoining them and ordering such "affirmative action as may be appropriate." The statute especially provides for the "reinstatement or hiring of employees, with or without back pay," and adds the additional ability to give "any other equitable relief as the court deems appropriate."

The Civil Rights Act of 1968 also states that:

> (b) Whoever, whether or not acting under color of law, by force or threat of force willfully injures, intimidates or interferes with, or attempts to injure, intimidate or interfere with
>
> (2) any person because of his race, color, religion or national origin and because he is or has been—
>
> (c) applying for or enjoying employment, or any perquisite thereof, by any private employer or any agency of any State or subdivision thereof, or joining or using the services or advantages of any labor organization, hiring hall, or employment agency;
>
> * * * shall be fined not more than $1,000 or imprisoned not more than one year or both; and if bodily injury results shall be fined not more than $10,000, or imprisoned not more than ten years, or both; and if death results shall be subject to imprisonment for any term of years or for life.

Discrimination in pay and other employment practices is still permitted under these laws if it is done in conformance with a bona fide (a) seniority system; (b) merit system; (c) a system that measures earnings by quantity or quality of production; (d) a system that distinguishes among employees who work in different locations; or (e) a system based on the results of a professionally developed ability test related to the work in question.

WHAT IS MEANT BY "AFFIRMATIVE ACTION"?

"Affirmative Action" is a program initiated by the federal government to eliminate discrimination in employment against women and minorities. By threatening to terminate supply and research contracts, the federal government (particularly the Departments of Education and of Health and Human Services) has pressured employers to take specific steps to hire and promote minorities and women in percentages roughly equal to their representation in the local community. Though "affirmative action" results in reverse discrimination against white male employees and white male applicants, the justification for the program is found in the conclusion that such white males can find other jobs more easily than can women and minorities—if necessary, in firms where federal contracts have not been entered into and where the government does not have this corrective weapon available. Some opponents of the program maintain that there should be no discrimination against anyone and that the Civil Rights Act should be administered with neutrality. These opponents believe that employment and promotion should be based on merit. Proponents, on the other hand, believe that steps should be taken to catch women and minorities up even at the expense of reverse discrimination.

In 1977, Congress passed the Public Works employment plan which requires 10 percent of the work on federally funded local public works projects to be performed by minority contractors or subcontractors. The U.S. Supreme Court has upheld this law as being constitutional. The Court has also upheld a corporation's voluntary affirmative action program establishing an on-the-job training program for production workers and requiring 50 percent of the trainees to be black until such time as the percentage of black skilled craft workers in the plant approximates the percentage of blacks in the local labor force. The Court ruled that the program was legal and in accord with the mandates of the Civil Rights Act of 1964 (see United Steelworkers of America v. Weber, 443 U.S. 193, 99 S.Ct. 2721, 61 L.Ed.2d 480 (1979)).

Antitrust and Labor Law

INTRODUCTION

In the 1800s, the social theory of "laissez-faire" prevailed in the United States. The basic rule of "laissez-faire" was that people are best served by letting them go about their business with as little government interference as possible. In a free market, laissez-faire theorists insisted, individuals can pursue their own self-interests, and unfettered competition will maintain prices and wages at the proper levels. In the case of prices, firms will compete for the consumer's dollar, and, as to wages, workers will compete for jobs and bargain individually with employers to obtain the best working conditions possible. Laissez-faire, however, did not and could not work. Neither competition nor individual bargaining can produce the desired results where the parties are not even close to being evenly matched. If a very large firm competes with a very small one, for example, the small firm will end up going under, and competition will be effectively eliminated. And if the large firm bargains individually with its workers, it is in a position to dictate terms of employment, and it will frequently do so to the detriment of the employees. By the late 1800s, it had become increasingly clear that government regulation was necessary both for purposes of maintaining competition and for protecting the rights of unorganized employees. Beginning with the Sherman Act in 1890, many laws have been enacted to accomplish these objectives.

The remainder of this chapter will deal, first, with the antitrust laws that are designed to outlaw or control business practices tending to restrain trade and impair free competition. And second, it will deal with labor law—the laws designed to protect the rights of employees to self-organize and bargain collectively with their employers.

Antitrust and labor law are of interest to all people whether they are business persons, consumers, employers, or employees. Antitrust law is designed to insure competition in business. Competition means better consumer products at lower prices. Antitrust law achieves its goal by prohibiting anticompetitive business practices and unfair methods of competition.

Labor law, on the other hand, is designed to keep the peace between workers and management—i.e., between employers and their employees. Business persons and employees alike need to know about the rights of employees to organize and bargain collectively.

Antitrust and labor law are treated together here because, historically, they were closely tied together. Let us begin our study by looking back to post-Civil War America.

WHAT WAS BUSINESS LIKE IN POST-CIVIL WAR AMERICA?

After the Civil War ended in 1865 and until 1914, the American economy underwent a period of rapid industrialization. Hundreds of new corporations emerged during this time—corporations larger than ever before, and "industrial empires" flourished under the control of a few powerful individuals. As these industrial giants gained monopolistic control of the marketplace, they began to charge the public more while, at the same time, giving them less. Public dissatisfaction soon turned to outrage as the "giants" used unfair methods to force their smaller competitors out of business. Frequently, for example, they cut prices to such an extent that the small competitors simply could not afford to stay in business. But once the competition was gone, prices would skyrocket. Farmers, too, found much to complain about in the way the "giants" ran business. The role of agriculture had greatly diminished throughout the country. With lower prices for their crops and higher costs for the manufactured goods and railroad services they so desperately needed, the farmers began to organize and make demands upon the industrial "giants."

The individual worker, however, had little or no ability to bargain with the "giant": the personal relationship that had once existed between employer and employee had come to an end with industrialization. At the same time, the Western frontier disappeared and thousands of workers began to migrate to the cities where they became more and more dependent on wages for survival. Unskilled European immigrants also came into the country in droves and began to flood the labor market.

The net result was that "big" business—really big business—had everything going for it at the expense of the two groups making up the bulk of the population—the consumers and the workers. These groups suffered low wages and high prices all because of monopoly—the elimination of effective competition.

The common law (unwritten law) was completely ineffective in dealing with the competitive abuses crying out for reform. While the common law outlawed certain combinations between companies or corporations and thus rendered them unenforceable (the companies could not force each other to combine by going to court after entering into such an agreement—theirs would be an illegal bargain, and they would be left in pari delicto—i.e., "in equal fault" and without remedy), it did not provide an absolute prohibition against unfair competition that could be enforced by both government and private parties. Statutory laws—acts of Congress—were urgently needed.

WAS THE SHERMAN ANTITRUST ACT INITIALLY EFFECTIVE IN CURBING THE ABUSES OF BIG BUSINESS?

Under strong public pressure to curtail business abuses, Congress passed the Sherman Antitrust Act in 1890. This Act is still in effect today, and, along with a few other statutes, it forms our basic antitrust law. Although the Sherman Act was designed to outlaw certain types of big business conduct (notably monopolies and monopolizing), big business wielded great power; and, as unbelievable as it may seem, the Act was first used not against big business, but against organized labor. How did this come about?

Well, in 1880, both workers and farmers joined in the first effort to organize against the abuses of the new industrial society. Their organization was called the Knights of Labor, and it included workers from almost every kind of occupation—skilled and unskilled laborers, farmers, and even small businesspersons. Membership in the Knights had grown to 700,000 by 1886, only to break down and almost disappear by 1890: the alliance between groups as diverse as workers and farmers simply could not hold together. In 1886, skilled workers formed the American Federation of Labor and elected the renowned Samuel Gompers as the organization's first president. Gompers led the AFL for the next forty years and greatly influenced the development of labor unions in this country. The AFL was composed of national craft unions, and by 1914 had more than 2,000,000 members concentrated in skilled trades and a few industries.

During the 1880s, business went to court to get injunctions against labor union activity—and business usually won. In the case of Vegelahn v. Guntner, 167 Mass. 92, 44 N.E. 1077 (1896), for example, the court agreed with managment that employee picketing had to be stopped, for "no one can lawfully prevent employers or persons wishing to be employed from the exercise of their rights." And courts throughout the country repeatedly insisted that employers had the right to "be free of molestation."

After passage of the Sherman Act in 1890, it was not difficult to convince an already biased court system that unions posed a greater threat than did big business. In 1893, for example, the American Railway Union was organized under the leadership of Eugene Debs. The purpose of the union was to organize railroad industry employees. When the Pullman Palace Car Company refused to negotiate with the union, many employees walked off the job, and much violence and damage resulted. Finally, a Sherman Act injunction was obtained against the union, and Debs and others were jailed for failing to obey it. The court held that the Sherman Act language prohibiting "combinations or conspiracies in restraint of trade" applied to labor union as well as business activities. This was in 1894.

During the next twenty years up until 1914, the Sherman Act was used as a strike-breaking weapon against the labor union. And in the "Danbury Hatters" case (Loewe v. Lawlor, 208 U.S. 274, 28 S.Ct. 301, 52 L.Ed. 488,

1908), the United States Supreme Court seemed to say that trade unions themselves were illegal under the Sherman Act.

WHAT HAPPENED IN 1914?

When Congress passed the Sherman Act in 1890, it did not intend to use the Act against labor unions. What it did intend was to curb the abuses of big business. But the court interpreted the Sherman Act so that not only was it not used to curb big business abuses, but it was used to prevent effective labor union organization. By 1914, Congress was clearly unhappy with these results. And the public was furious! Two acts were passed to make it clear that big business unfair competition had to stop and that antitrust laws were not to be used against labor organizations. These acts were the Clayton Act and the Federal Trade Commission Act (presented in detail later in this chapter).

The Clayton Act is often called "labor's Magna Carta" because of two sections of the Act which apply specifically to labor organizations:

- Section 6 provides that antitrust laws are not to be interpreted so as to prohibit the existence of labor organizations from "lawfully carrying out the legitimate objects thereof." This section effectively exempts labor unions and agricultural organizations from the Sherman and Clayton Acts.
- Section 20 specifically prohibits the use of injunctions by the federal courts in any case between an employer and employees or between employers or employees involving a dispute over terms and conditions of employment.

Union membership rose sharply after passage of the Clayton Act. Today, union members number in the millions. As you can see, the antitrust laws and labor's first efforts to organize were closely tied together from post-Civil War times up until the passage of the Clayton Act in 1914. Since that time, however, antitrust laws have generally been used to curb anticompetitive behavior on the part of business. And labor law has gone its own way with other federal statutes. Because of this, we will now consider antitrust and labor law independently of each other in the text sections that follow.

Antitrust Law

WHAT IS THE PURPOSE OF ANTITRUST LAW?

Antitrust law is founded on three basic statutes: the Sherman Act, the Clayton Act, and the Federal Trade Commission Act.

The Sherman Act makes unlawful "every contract, combination or conspiracy *in restraint of trade* in interstate or foreign commerce." It also prohibits monopolizing and attempts to monopolize. Violators of the Act are subject to fine or imprisonment, or both. A person found guilty may be fined up to $100,000 and imprisoned up to three years. A corporation may be fined $1 million for each offense. And the federal district courts are empowered to issue injunctions restraining violations. Anyone injured by a violation is entitled to recover in a civil action treble damages (i.e., three times the amount of the actual loss sustained).

In addition, a final legal sanction under the Sherman Act provides that any property being transported from one state to another as a part of a violation may be seized by the government and forfeited to the United States.

More specific is the Clayton Act which prohibits certain practices *if* they "substantially lessen competition." Price discrimination, mergers and consolidations, "tie-in" sales, and exclusive dealing arrangements are all prohibited where they are found to be anticompetitive in nature (the specifics of this anticompetitive behavior will be considered later in this chapter). Under Section 2 of the Clayton Act (as amended by the Robinson-Patman Act), it is unlawful for any person engaged in commerce to discriminate in price between different purchasers of commodities of like grade and quality, where the effect may be substantially to lessen competition or tend to create a monopoly or to injure, destroy, or prevent competition with any person who either grants or knowingly receives the benefits of such discrimination, or with the customers of either of them. Both the seller who offers and the buyer who knowingly receives discriminatory prices are held guilty of violating this part of the Clayton Act.

Section 3 of the Clayton Act prohibits sales on condition that the buyer not deal with competitors of the seller where the effect may be substantially to lessen competition or tend to create a monopoly.

Section 7 of the Clayton Act prohibits acquisitions or mergers where the effect may be substantially to lessen competition or tend to create a monopoly.

And Section 8 of the Clayton Act states that "no person shall at the same time be a director in two or more corporations, any one of which has capital aggregating more than $1,000,000 * * * if such corporations are or shall have been theretofore, by virtue of their business and location of operation, competitors, so that the elimination of competition by agreement between them would constitute a violation of any of the provisions of any of the antitrust laws."

The Clayton Act, unlike the Sherman Act, does not provide for criminal penalty or for forfeiture of property. However it does provide for government injunction and treble damages. Additionally, it gives private persons the ability to seek injunctions for violations. Also it provides that a final decision for the United States that a person or firm has violated the antitrust laws is prima facie evidence of a violation for purposes of a private suit for treble damages.

The Federal Trade Commission Act (passed in 1914 at the same time as the Clayton Act) created the Federal Trade Commission. You will recall from Chapter 5 that this administrative agency is broadly authorized to enforce the antitrust laws, including both the Sherman and Clayton Acts. In addition, the FTC may, on its own, identify and restrain any anticompetitive business or corporate conduct. Section 5 of the Federal Trade Commission Act prohibits "unfair methods of competition in or affecting commerce and unfair or deceptive acts or practices in or affecting commerce." This language is so broad that it has been held to mean that the Federal Trade Commission may determine what methods of competition are undesirable and prohibit even conduct that does not in itself violate the antitrust laws. The Commission initiates enforcement proceedings by serving a complaint on the alleged violator. If the Federal Trade Commission finds a violation of the antitrust laws, it issues a "cease and desist order" which becomes final unless the defendant seeks judicial review. The FTC may bring a civil action seeking penalties of up to $10,000 per day for violation of a final cease and desist order.

WHAT IS THE DIFFERENCE BETWEEN "THE RULE OF REASON" AND "PER SE" VIOLATIONS?

The Sherman Act provides that "*every* contract, combination * * * or conspiracy in restraint of trade" is illegal. In Standard Oil Co. v. United States, 221 U.S. 1, 31 S.Ct. 502, 55 L.Ed. 619 (1911), the Supreme Court interpreted this to include only agreements that *unreasonably* restrain trade. This has become known as "the Rule of Reason." The Rule requires a case-by-case examination of the "reasonableness" of any particular agreement or combination among competitors. The courts consider several factors in deciding if a restraint is unreasonable including the structure of the industry, the particular firm's position in the industry, the duration of the restraint, and the reasons why it was used.

Having adopted the Rule of Reason in the Standard Oil case, the Supreme Court, in subsequent cases, decided that certain types of business agreements among competitors would be held unreasonable as a matter of law. In other words, these practices were held "illegal per se." The Court concluded that certain agreements will always result in a substantial restraint of trade and must always be prohibited. No case-by-case inquiry into reasonableness is necessary. Thus, price fixing is always bad and never reasonable. Conduct may be "per se" illegal under the Sherman, Clayton, or Federal Trade Commission Act. When an action is declared "per se" illegal, establishing its existence is all that is necessary to prove a violation of the antitrust laws. This simplifies the trial and limits the issues. A Rule of Reason analysis will be much more complicated because of the necessity of proving the action unreasonable if it is to be a violation. Also, the "per se" rulings have provided business with definite guidelines and standards because specific conduct is known to be illegal. There is far less predictability when the Rule of Reason must be applied to the conduct to see if it has caused an "unreasonable" restraint of trade.

WHAT SPECIFIC PRACTICES FALL WITHIN THE MEANING OF UNFAIR COMPETITION?

"Unfair competition" includes, but is not limited to, the following.

Monopolizing

Probably all of you have played the game of "Monopoly" wherein your chief goal was to gain control of the most property and drive your competitors out of business. The kinds of "ruthless tactics" that enabled you to win the game, however, would not be permitted in real life—the government would not let you get away with them. Monopoly power is defined as the power to control prices or exclude competitors in a particular market. But unless the monopolist deliberately and purposefully exercises his or her monopoly power to acquire or maintain the market, there is no "unfair competition" in the sense of an antitrust violation. Innocent or natural monopolies are not illegal (e.g., a small town newspaper where the town market can support only one paper; a professional basketball team in a city where there are insufficient sports fans to support more than one team; or a manufacturer who alone possesses the particular facilities required to supply a market). Still, even though monopoly power is acquired innocently, if it is then used in a "ruthless, predatory, or exclusionary" way, it is a violation of the Sherman Act. Ovitron Corp. v. General Motors, 295 F.Supp. 373 (D.C.N.Y.1969).

Courts consider the share of the market that an alleged monopolist has presently acquired to determine illegality. Market shares of 70 to 90 percent have been held to be monopoly power, but circumstances might be such that less percentages could suffice. Also, to determine whether a company has monopoly power the "relevant" market must be defined in terms of the "product" market and the "geographic" market. The geographic market is generally defined by the area in which the defendant and competing sellers sell the product, and the question is asked as to what geographic area prospective customers can look for the product or service. This may be a local, regional, or national market. Product market, on the other hand, is determined by consumer preferences, and the question is asked as to what products are reasonably interchangeable. In United States v. E.I. duPont, 351 U.S. 377, 76 S.Ct. 994, 100 L.Ed. 1264 (1956), the Supreme Court, considering whether duPont had a monopoly in cellophane, held that the relevant market was all flexible wrapping material, not merely cellophane wrapping material, stressing the functional interchangeability of the products.

Remember, however, that even if monopoly power is found, there is no violation unless it is shown that the monopolist deliberately and purposefully exercised his or her monopoly power to acquire or maintain the market. This will include exclusionary conduct restricting others from competing, such as by continually increasing production to supply all demand and keep competitors out, or by refusing to supply products or services in a reasonable and nondiscriminatory manner.

Monopoly buying power, called monopsony power, can be as illegal as monopoly selling power. A buyer can't use monopsony (buying) power in one area to require concessions or preferences in other areas that are injurious to his or her competitors in those areas.

Attempts to Monopolize

The U.S. Supreme Court has defined "attempt to monopolize" as "the employment of methods, means, and practices which would, if successful, accomplish monopolization." An attempt is illegal, however, only where it involves "unfair conduct" and not merely good business know-how. Sometimes, for example, a really good competitor can eliminate his or her competition without doing anything unfair, and there is certainly nothing wrong with this. But a businessperson who tries to induce others to boycott his or her competitors or who uses discriminatory pricing in an effort to drive the competitors out of business is guilty of unfair conduct—of an attempt to monopolize. He or she may be enjoined by a court of equity, criminally prosecuted, or sued in a civil action for treble damages.

Horizontal Restraints of Trade

Competitors in the same industry who get together and agree to eliminate or lessen the competition between or among themselves are said to create a horizontal restraint of trade. For example, if Ford, General Motors, and Chrysler collaborate (get together and agree) to fix auto prices or to divide up the U.S. market for cars, they are creating a horizontal restraint of trade, since all compete directly in the auto market. Horizontal restraints of trade may take any of the following shapes:

Price fixing among competitors The U.S. Supreme Court has stated that "any combination or agreement between competitors, formed for the purpose and with the effect of raising, depressing, fixing, pegging, or stabilizing the price of a commodity in interstate or foreign commerce is illegal per se." Thus it is no defense that the price fixed was a "reasonable" price: "price fixing" among competitors is simply illegal under antitrust law.

Examples of illegal price fixing include the minimum fee schedule adopted by the bar association of the State of Virginia, Goldfarb v. Virginia State Bar, 421 U.S. 773, 95 S.Ct. 2004, 44 L.Ed.2d 572 (1975); an agreement among auto dealers to use the same list prices from which to bargain with potential buyers, Plymouth Dealers Association v. United States, 279 F.2d 128 (9th Cir.1960); and an agreement by buyers on the prices they will offer to sellers, Mandeville Island Farms v. American Crystal Sugar, 334 U.S. 219, 68 S.Ct. 996, 92 L.Ed. 1328 (1948). Also, agreements between competitors limiting sales or production are illegal price fixing agreements as are their agreements to prohibit competitive bidding.

Division of markets Any agreement among businesses performing similar services or dealing in similar products to divide up and share the available market is also illegal per se. And, just as with price fixing, no justifications or defenses are allowed.

Illegal division of market agreements include agreements dividing markets on the basis of geographical areas or on the basis of customers or products. All are illegal per se.

Group boycotts People are generally free to refuse to deal with others—except where their action constitutes "unfair competition." Any agreement among a group of competitors not to deal with a person or firm outside the group is an unlawful group boycott. And a group boycott, like price fixing and division of markets, is illegal per se.

Exchange of information among competitors on prices, costs, production, inventories, etc. An agreement to fix prices, divide markets, or boycott certain goods may be inferred from an exchange of information among competitors. In the case of American Column and Lumber Co. v. United States, 257 U.S. 377, 42 S.Ct. 114, 66 L.Ed. 284 (1921), for example, the Court held unlawful an exchange of product, inventory, and current price list information among 365 hardwood manufacturers who controlled one-third of the market. The Court's decision was influenced by the fact that, after the exchange, prices among the group increased substantially.

It is simply not a good idea for business competitors to exchange any information on prices. Even though business persons are members of the same trade or professional associations, exchange of information within the association may well constitute an unreasonable restraint of trade—and this is particularly true if the information deals with prices. Information other than price may not result in anticompetitive restraints, but it too will be suspect. In litigation, the courts will ask whether the exchange lessened competition in the market causing the users of the products or services involved to have less choice or to pay more. If so and if unreasonable, the exchange will be a violation of antitrust law under the Rule of Reason.

Vertical Restraints of Trade

Unlike a horizontal restraint of trade which involves anticompetitive agreements within the same level of industry, a vertical restraint refers to anticompetitive dealings on different levels. For example, before a car is sold to a consumer:

1. The iron ore is mined;
2. The ore is refined into steel ingots;
3. The ingots are processed into sheets of steel;
4. The steel, along with fabrics, paints, etc., is manufactured into an automobile;
5. The auto is distributed to a dealer; and
6. The dealer holds the auto for sale.

None of these processes directly compete on a horizontal level. Rather, the relationships are "vertical"—on different levels of industry—and some vertical restraints of trade are illegal.

Resale price maintenance by sellers It is a per se violation of antitrust law for a seller (e.g., a manufacturer) to set by contract the price at which the buyer (e.g., the retailer) can resell his or her product. In some states, however, until 1975, "State Fair Trade Laws" exempted from illegality resale price maintenance agreements as to commodities which: (1) bore the trade mark, brand, or name of the producer or distributor, and (2) were in free and open competition with other commodities of the same general class. Thus in a Fair Trade Law state, General Electric Company could have validly obtained a local department store's agreement not to sell GE toasters for less than thirty-five dollars each. Some states went so far as to say that any seller who knew about such a valid agreement was bound by it—*whether he or she signed it or not!* On December 12, 1975 the "Consumer Goods Pricing Act of 1975" was passed by the federal Congress. This law repealed the federal antitrust exemptions which had permitted the "State Fair Trade Laws." Thus, this legalized price fixing has been eliminated from the law.

Resale price maintenance agreements are illegal whether the seller sets minimum or maximum prices. While manufacturers are free to announce "suggested retail prices," they must be suggestions only, and they can't be a part of an agreement. Any forcing of customers to adhere to the prices by threatening suspension or no further dealing is illegal.

Exclusive distributors Generally one may pick and choose his or her dealers or distributors. However, if the seller has no competitors in the market (no interbrand competition), a monopoly may result in the area unless he or she has other dealers in the area (intrabrand competition). In such situations, the Rule of Reason will be applied to see if there is an unreasonable restraint of trade.

Customer and territorial restrictions Prior to 1977, the Supreme Court had ruled that it was a per se antitrust violation for a manufacturer to impose territorial and customer restrictions upon its dealers. This meant, for example, that a manufacturer could not require his or her dealers to resell his or her products "only to customers residing" within a certain geographical area.

In 1977 in Continental T.V., Inc. v. GTE Sylvania, Inc., 433 U.S. 36, 97 S.Ct. 2549, 53 L.Ed.2d 568 (1977) the Supreme Court held that the Rule of Reason should be used to determine the legality of customer and territorial vertical restraints. The Court said that certain nonprice vertical restrictions may cause interbrand competition even though they eliminate intrabrand competition. When there are substitutes available for the product through interbrand competition, the intrabrand competition is not so important. This is the more so where a new product is entering the market, where a product has special features (e.g., requiring special refrigeration or care to preserve quality), or where a failing company needs such agreements to prevent going into bankruptcy. Under such circumstances using the Rule of Reason approach, the agreements restricting customers, territories, or locations may not result in unreasonable restraints of trade.

Tying agreements In a tying agreement, a seller refuses to sell one of his or her products (the "tying" product) to a customer unless the customer agrees to buy a second product (the "tied" product) as well. Tying agreements are illegal per se under the Clayton Act. Thus it is a violation of antitrust law for a computer manufacturer to "tie" the use of its computer cards to the purchase of its computers. The Sherman Act makes tie-ins involving services, intangibles, or real property also illegal per se.

Three requirements are necessary if a tying agreement is to be illegal: (1) There must be two separate products (or services, etc.)—the desired tying product and the tied product which the buyer otherwise might not buy; (2) The seller must have enough market power to cause competition to be restrained in the tied product; and (3) The agreement tying the products must affect commerce not insubstantially. Once these facts are established, there is per se illegality.

Requirement contracts Buyers and sellers sometimes agree that the buyer will sell only the seller's products. Such agreements provide a source of certain supply to a buyer and are not per se illegal. Instead the courts ask whether the dollar amount involved is so substantial as to cause an anticompetitive effect or whether the share of the market foreclosed by the agreement is so large as to cause anticompetitive effect.

The above list of anticompetitive behavior is not exclusive. Remember, the Federal Trade Commission may find that certain conduct is an "unfair method of competition," even though it violates neither the letter nor the spirit of existing antitrust laws. And once the Commission identifies the new anticompetitive behavior, it may issue a cease and desist order against it. Of course, Federal Trade Commission decisions are always subject to judicial review by the United States Circuit Courts of Appeal.

ARE THERE SPECIAL ANTITRUST RULES REGARDING MERGERS, CONSOLIDATIONS, OR OTHER ACQUISITIONS?

Any merger or consolidation (horizontal or vertical) that restrains competition is illegal. For example, a merger which results in a firm's controlling an undue percentage share of the market will substantially lessen competition and is thus subject to an injunction.

The Celler-Kefauver Act of 1950 was an amendment to Section 7 of the Clayton Act and made it illegal "to substantially lessen competition in any line of commerce in any section of the country" by acquiring "the stock or part of the assets of another corporation also engaging in commerce." The courts have given broad definition to the meaning of "line of commerce," again emphasizing the interchangeability of products as in the monopoly cases. However, the courts have found it easier to hold a substantial lessening of competition, and therefore an illegal merger, than to find an illegal monopoly under the Sherman Act.

"Section of the country" has been defined as the geographic area where competition is immediately and directly affected. The relevant market area may be local, regional, or national. If there is a reasonable likelihood of a substantial lessening of competition because of the merger, consolidation, or other acquisition, Section 7 will be applied to prevent the combination. The basic intent of the law is to prefer efficiency achieved through internal expansion rather than through combination. Internal expansion will preserve competition and perhaps make it better.

The Hart-Scott-Rodino Antitrust Improvements Act of 1976 is also an amendment to the Clayton Act and provides a thirty-day premerger notification. The purpose of the premerger notification is to allow the Federal Trade Commission and the Justice Department to enjoin mergers which may have anticompetitive effects. If the acquiring company has sales or assets of $100 million or more and the company to be acquired has sales or assets of $10 million or more, they must inform the Federal Trade Commission of the proposed merger thirty days before the merger is to take place. During the thirty-day period the Federal Trade Commission and Justice Department will look at the proposal and may request additional items of information before deciding whether or not to seek an injunction against the combination.

The Department of Justice also has issued a set of "merger guidelines." While they are not binding on the courts, they are frequently used by them when the legality of mergers is at issue. There are three separate areas: horizontal mergers, vertical mergers, and conglomerate mergers.

Horizontal Mergers

When competitors combine, there is a horizontal merger. These are companies performing similarly in producing or distributing comparable goods or services. And there may be a violation of Section 7 even when a very small competitor is acquired by a dominant competitor because the small competitor in fact provided aggressive competition. The law is designed to prevent concentration of business, and even though the result of a horizontal merger may be to acquire less than 10 percent of the relevant market, it may still substantially lessen competition and be held illegal.

The Department of Justice guidelines for horizontal mergers look to market shares of both firms.

1. In markets that are highly concentrated, as where the four largest companies account for at least 75 percent of the market, mergers will be challenged where the acquiring and acquired firm have market shares of 4 percent and 4 percent or more; 10 percent and 2 percent or more; or 15 percent and 1 percent or more.
2. In markets that are less concentrated the percentages used are 5 percent and 5 percent or more; 10 percent and 4 percent or more; 15 percent and 3 percent or more; 20 percent and 2 percent or more; 25 percent and 1 percent or more.
3. In markets that are getting more concentrated, i.e., where any grouping of the two to eight largest companies shows an increase of 7 percent or more of the market over the last five to ten years, a challenge will be made of any acquisition by any member of the group of a competitor with a market share of 2 percent or more.
4. Finally, an injunction will be sought in any unusual circumstance such as where a "disruptive" competitor or firm with unusual competitive potential is being acquired.

The fact that one of the companies faces bankruptcy unless there is a merger may prevent the merger from being challenged.

Vertical Mergers

Vertical mergers involve acquisition of firms not directly competing but involving different levels of activity regarding services, a product, or its parts. Vertical mergers may eliminate competitors who are not integrated in the same manner. When retail outlets are acquired by a manufacturer, there is usually a substantial lessening of competition in the retail market. And when a large buyer acquires a supplier, there is no competition from other suppliers.

The Department of Justice guidelines for vertical mergers look to the extent to which other potential customers are foreclosed and challenge any merger of a supplying firm with 10 percent or more of the sales in a market and a purchasing firm or firms with 6 percent or more of the purchases in the supplying firm's market, unless it is clear that there will be no substantial lessening of competition as a result.

Conglomerate Mergers

Conglomerate mergers are all types of mergers that are not classified as horizontal or vertical mergers. They put different kinds of business into a centralized control and make firms larger and more powerful. A conglomerate merger may eliminate potential competitors who are said to be "waiting in the wings." Thus, in FTC v. Proctor & Gamble, 386 U.S. 586, 87 S.Ct. 1224, 18 L.Ed.2d 303 (1967), the acquisition of a liquid bleach manufacturer by Proctor and Gamble, a large soap manufacturer, would eliminate the soap company as a potential entrant into the liquid bleach business. This, in turn, would cause the firms already in the bleach market from making price and output decisions in as competitive a manner to keep the "wings" from out of the market. The Court forced Proctor and Gamble to divest itself of Clorox saying, additionally, that Clorox, already holding 48 percent of the bleach market, could take unfair advantage over competitors because of the availability of Proctor and Gamble resources.

The Department of Justice guidelines for conglomerate mergers provide that a challenge will be made when a firm that potentially might enter a market is joined with a firm with 25 percent or more of that market or one of two firms which together have 50 percent or more of this market. The Department will also challenge conglomerate mergers designed to facilitate reciprocal buying arrangements and any others that may produce substantial anticompetitive effect.

Regarding conglomerate mergers, legislation has been introduced in Congress to prohibit mergers between companies (1) with assets or sales exceeding $2 billion each, (2) with assets or sales exceeding $350 million each, or (3) where one has assets or sales exceeding $350 million and the other company has 20 percent or more net sales in any significant market. Defenses to (2) or (3) would include proving the transaction would make competition better or showing that within one year of the transaction there was a divesting of assets equal to those being acquired. As this text is being written, whether or not such legislation will be passed is an open question.

WHAT IS THE ROBINSON-PATMAN ACT?

The Robinson-Patman Act was passed by Congress in 1936 as an amendment to the Clayton Act; it is properly thought of as part of the Clayton Act. Robinson-Patman specifically outlaws certain activities by buyers and sellers. With regard to sellers, the Act makes it unlawful for any seller engaged in commerce *directly* or *indirectly* to discriminate in prices charged to purchasers on the sale of commodities of like grade and quality where the effect *may be* to injure, destroy, or prevent competition. Prior to passage of Robinson-Patman, the Clayton Act had already outlawed price discrimination intended to drive *direct* competitors out of the market—i.e., price discrimination designed to do what is called "primary line" injury. Thus, it was unlawful under the original Clayton Act for large nationwide firms to engage in local price cutting in an effort to injure smaller local competitors or force them out of the market. But it was unclear whether the original Clayton Act covered what is called "secondary line" injury—i.e., competition at the buyer's level. Secondary line injury occurs where one buyer is given a more favorable price than his or her competitors. For example, for a manufacturer to give a better price to chain stores than to the chain stores' small store competitors is price discrimination at the secondary level. The Robinson-Patman Act outlaws this kind of discrimination.

Unlawful secondary line discrimination results because a customer who receives a better price is able to resell at a lower price than his or her competitors. For example, in FTC v. Morton Salt Co., 334 U.S. 37, 68 S.Ct. 822, 92 L.Ed. 1196 (1948), it was held that even though salt represents a very small portion of a retail grocer's business, the effect of selling salt at a reduced price to a favored buyer was to allow that grocer to divert business and cause competitive injury.

And even if a favored buyer does not sell at a lower price than his or her competitors, it may still be unlawful because the favored party may have lower manufacturing costs than his or her competitors and thus achieve a higher profit—again with the result that competition is injured.

The Robinson-Patman Act also provides that a seller who provides or pays for advertising (e.g., handbills, window and floor displays, demonstrations, and the like) must do so through a plan under which all buyers are notified and can receive a payment or service proportional to their purchases. In other words, a seller who offers advertising services for his or her products must offer them to all buyers on proportionally equal terms (i.e., on terms based on the buyers' relative volume of purchases and the relative amount of sales of the seller's products). To do otherwise is a per se violation of the Robinson-Patman Act—no showing of adverse competitive effect is required.

With regard to buyers, the Robinson-Patman Act makes it per se unlawful for a buyer to exact price concessions in the form of brokerage commissions either personally or through an agent. This is unlawful regardless of its effect on competition.

There are two important defenses to Robinson-Patman violations:

Justification based on cost There is no violation of Robinson-Patman if prices are different because costs are different. The Act states that "differentials which make only due allowance for differences in the cost of manufacture, sale, or delivery resulting from the differing methods or quantities" in which commodities are sold or delivered do not result in illegal price discrimination. Rather, the differences are *functional discounts*. Some purchasers may have special needs requiring special manufacture and justifying additional costs. And others may merit a higher charge because of higher freight and delivery costs (e.g., a buyer who receives large quantities in carload lots).

However, the defense based on difference in costs applies only to the price discrimination portion of Robinson-Patman. It is no defense to the granting of a brokerage payment or to discriminatory payments for advertising or to discriminatory promotional services.

Justification based on meeting competition It is a complete defense to a charge of price discrimination or of furnishing unequal advertising or promotional payments or services that the action was taken to meet a competitor's equally low price or to match a competitor's advertising or promotional services or facilities (however, it is no defense to a charge of providing brokerage payments).

The defense is available even though the price charged is somewhat lower than the competitor's so long as it is shown that the price was set based on a reasonable belief that it was required to meet the competitor's price. This is because competitors may not be able to determine all the information needed to come up with identical prices. And if they exchange information to do so, the exchange itself may be a violation of the Sherman Act.

One final note about Robinson-Patman. The statute specifically applies to both buyers and sellers. Section 2(f) of the Clayton Act, as amended by Robinson-Patman, makes it unlawful for a buyer "knowingly to induce or receive a discrimination in price which is prohibited. * * *" Section 2(c) provides that it is unlawful "to receive or accept" as well as "to pay or grant" brokerage commissions as price concessions. A violation of Robinson-Patman, like any other Clayton Act violation, may result in fine, imprisonment, or both for the offender and treble damages for the injured party or parties.

Labor Law

WHAT IS LABOR LAW?

Labor law is designed to control and govern the continuous process by which workers and management decide the terms and conditions of employment. It is based almost entirely on federal statutes passed by Congress during the last forty-five years. The idea behind labor law is to keep peace between workers and management through the process known as *collective bargaining*—i.e., the settlement of industrial disputes through peaceful negotiation between employers and employee representatives. Successful collective bargaining requires two things: (1) self-organization of employees, and (2) equal bargaining power between workers and management. Labor law encourages and promotes these goals by placing statutory limitations on employer interference with the right of employees to self-organize and bargain collectively. And, because unions, too, may abuse their power, labor law also acts to curb and control certain union activities.

WHAT FEDERAL STATUTES MAKE UP OUR "LABOR LAW"?

Labor law is presently based on four statutes:

1. The Norris-LaGuardia Act of 1932;
2. The National-Labor Relations Act (or Wagner Act) of 1935;
3. The Labor Management Relations (or Taft-Hartley Act) of 1947; and
4. The Labor-Management Reporting and Disclosure (or Landrum-Griffin) Act of 1959.

The Norris-LaGuardia Act declares that the worker "though he should be free to decline to associate with his fellows must have full freedom of association, self-organization, and designation of representatives of his own choosing, to negotiate the terms and conditions of his employment; and must be free from the interference, restraint, or coercion of employers of labor in these activities." The Norris-LaGuardia Act thus promotes union organization and collective bargaining; it permits unions to exert effective economic pressure against employers.

The National Labor Relations Act of 1935 guarantees employees the right (1) to form, join, or assist labor organizations; (2) to bargain collectively with the employer; and (3) to engage in concerted activity for the purpose of collective bargaining or mutual aid and protection. The National Labor Relations Act is the heart of labor law. Just twelve years after its passage in 1935, union membership had increased from 3 million to 15 million employees.

After World War II came to an end, unions began to strike on a nationwide basis in some of our most important industries, including coal mining, oil refining, lumber, rail, auto, etc. The strikes were designed to force employers into making great concessions at a time when almost every kind of product was in very short supply. This was a poor time for employees to take their employers to task. The War was over. Americans had been waiting patiently to start living again—to be able to buy the many things they had done so long without. When organized labor used strikes to force higher wages and other concessions at this peak of consumer demand, the general public turned with fury on the unions. They blamed the unions, and they blamed the strikes for delays in the production of consumer goods. Growing sentiment arose to prohibit or, at the least, restrict certain union activities. Congress responded with the third major part of our labor legislation—the Taft-Hartley Act of 1947.

The Taft-Hartley Act enables the government to combat union "unfair labor practices" and to intervene in strikes that threaten the national welfare. The Federal Mediation and Conciliation Service, created by the Act to assist in labor disputes, must be notified by labor and/or management anytime either party desires to make a change in the terms or conditions of employment as previously fixed by a collective bargaining agreement (see Chapter 5).

Taft-Hartley also authorizes the president to intervene in labor disputes by appointing a Board of Inquiry to investigate and report on the issues involved. If the president concludes from the report that the national health, welfare, or security of the country is threatened, he may ask a federal district court to issue an eighty-day injunction against the strike or work stoppage. Where granted, the injunction will dissolve within the eighty days, and the strike may thereafter continue.

Taft-Hartley additionally outlaws the *closed shop.* In a closed shop, union membership is a condition of employment—that is, membership is required before hiring. Membership in a *union shop* is also compulsory, but only *after* employment. And union shop arrangements are legal so long as there is a thirty-day "grace" period after hiring before membership is required. Thus a collective bargaining agreement between labor and management may require new employees, as a condition of their employment, to join the union "on or after" the thirtieth day of employment. But it cannot require them to join the union before they are hired.

During the 1950s, the Senate investigated a number of unions on charges of corruption, unethical behavior, and a lack of democratic procedures. The result of the investigation was the Landrum-Griffin Act passed in 1959 to protect the rights and interests of individual workers as well as of the public from infringement by powerful union leaders. Landrum-Griffin makes specific election procedures mandatory for unions, and it requires substantial disclosures by labor unions and their officers. The Act also provides penalties for fraud or corruption or misuse of union funds.

WHAT ARE THE GOALS OF LABOR LAW?

The goals of labor law are four:

1. Industrial peace—continued production uninterrupted by strikes and lockouts.
2. Collective bargaining—the settlement of industrial disputes through peaceful negotiations between employers and employee representatives. Where collective bargaining proves ineffective to settle a dispute, other methods of settlement, including conciliation and mediation through the Federal Mediation and Conciliation Service, and waiting or "cooling off" periods should be attempted.
3. Self-organization of employees—self-organization accomplished free from employer interference and union coercion.
4. Quick settlement of disputes that imperil the national health or safety.

With these four goals in mind, let us consider some of the specific problems that arise in labor-management relations.

HOW DO FEDERAL LABOR LAW STATUTES PROTECT EMPLOYEES?

Protection of the right of employees to band together to form unions and to bargain collectively is the underlying purpose of the National Labor Relations Act. The job of implementing this protection is given to the National Labor Relations Board along with its general counsel (made up of a great many lawyers) and its numerous field agents. The Board itself is composed of five members, each appointed by the president of the United States (with Senate approval) to serve for a term of five years. The two major functions of the Board are (1) to determine employee representation for industries, and (2) to decide whether certain challenged actions are unfair labor practices.

Representation cases refer to the actual decision as to which union is representing the workers. The law states that the employer must bargain collectively when asked to do so by his or her workers' designated representative. The workers must select this representative by secret ballot in an election administered by the National Labor Relations Board. Before an election can be held, the Board must first determine the appropriate bargaining unit—that is, which group of employees makes up the union. Similarity of skills is generally the most important factor here since it usually reflects a similarity of problems and interests among the employees. The law specifically prohibits the Board, however, from placing professional employees with nonprofessionals and from placing plant guards (who enforce security rules) with other employees. After the Board determines who belongs in the bargaining unit, it will direct an election in which the employees pick the union they want to represent them. Administration of the election is delegated by the Board to its field agents and regional directors. Once the regional director certifies the results, his or her decision is final unless a party seeks review by the full National Labor Relations Board.

In "unfair labor practice" cases, the Board's authority is more formally exercised. A trial or hearing examiner conducts a hearing on the issues involved and enters a report with recommended findings and suggested remedies. If neither party objects to the report, it becomes the decision of the Board. Where objections are filed, the Board assumes complete control over the case, reviews the record, and makes its own determination. A party who objects to the Board's decision may appeal his or her case to the United States Court of Appeals.

If the National Labor Relations Board believes that an injunction is necessary to put an end to the unfair labor practice, it will go to the federal district court and allege: (1) the filing of an unfair labor practice charge; (2) the issuance of a complaint on the charge; (3) the facts supporting the charge; and (4) the likelihood that the unfair practice will continue unless an injunction is issued to restrain it. If the court agrees with the Board, the injunction will issue. (See Chapter 5 for a description of the NLRB.)

WHAT ARE SOME UNFAIR LABOR PRACTICES?

Employer Questioning of Employees

It is not an unfair labor practice for an employer to merely question an employee about his or her union activities. But if he or she uses spies or informers to obtain such information, the employer does run afoul of the law. And while an employer can make and enforce rules that prevent an employee from distributing union literature or soliciting union membership during the employee's working hours or in areas where work is being performed, the employer cannot ban such activities altogether. The employee's right to pursue union activities during nonwork hours and in nonwork areas must be recognized.

Suppose an employer releases antiunion literature containing false statements. The release, in itself, is not an unfair labor practice, but the Board will set aside an election in which the release or other propaganda has made it impossible for the employees to reach a free and fair decision on the issues or the candidates.

Union Coercion of Employees

Unions, too, must respect the rights of employees. Section 8(b) of the National Labor Relations Act prohibits a union from restraining or otherwise coercing employees in the exercise of their right to self-organize. In one case, for example, a union representative trying to organize workers stated that "those who do not join the union will lose their jobs" and that "we have ways of dealing with people like you guys." The representative's statements were found to be unfair labor practices.

Section 8(b)(1)(A) of the NLRA also prohibits unions or their agents from threatening employees with physical harm or committing actual violence upon them for refusal to cooperate with union directives. The Section applies to any threat of bodily harm and even to destruction of company property by a union agent (on the theory that the destruction constitutes an implied threat of physical violence to the employees). And although peaceful picketing does not amount to coercion for purposes of the Act, mass picketing calculated to deter nonstrikers from working does violate the Section, as does the blocking of plant entrances and exits.

Employer or Union Discrimination

It is illegal for either employers or unions to use discrimination as a means of denying employees their rights to self-organize. Thus an employer may not legally hire or fire an employee on the basis of his or her membership or lack of membership in a labor union. Nor may an employer discharge, lay off, transfer, or otherwise change terms of employment in order to encourage or discourage union membership. It is also unlawful for a union to cause or attempt to cause an employer to discriminate against an employee.

In summary, the National Labor Relations Act provides that it is an unfair labor practice to do the following.

Employers

To—

1. Interfere with, restrain, or coerce employees in the exercise of their rights to form, join, or assist unions or to bargain collectively or to act in any concerted fashion for their mutual aid or protection or to interfere, restrain, or coerce employees who choose to refrain from any such union activities.
2. Dominate or interfere with the formation or administration of any labor organization or to contribute financial or other support to it.
3. Discriminate in hiring, in granting tenure, or regarding any other condition of employment in order to encourage or discourage union membership (but remember, the "union shop" is an exception to this rule).

4. Discriminate against any employee because he or she has filed charges or given testimony under the Act (such as by firing the employee or discriminating against him or her with respect to pay or promotion).
5. Refuse to bargain with a labor organization that represents a majority of the employees in the bargaining unit.

Unions

To—

1. Restrain or coerce employees in their right to join or to refuse to join a union.
2. Restrain or otherwise coerce an employer in his or her selection of a collective bargaining representative who will arbitrate or adjust grievances on behalf of the company.
3. Cause or attempt to cause an employer to discriminate against an employee in violation of the rule that an employer shall not discriminate in order to encourage or discourage union membership.
4. Refuse to bargain collectively in good faith with an employer.
5. Strike or terminate a contract without giving notice to the employer and to the Federal Mediation and Conciliation Service.

WHAT IS THE LAW ON COLLECTIVE BARGAINING?

A union that is duly elected by a majority of employees has exclusive authority to represent all employees on matters properly the subject of collective bargaining. The employer must bargain directly with the certified union—he or she may not negotiate individual contracts with his or her employees. The employees, too, are bound by the union election and must thereafter deal with their employer through their elected union representatives. Because unions are not infallible and may abuse their power, the law provides that the union has a duty to bargain fairly on behalf of all employees (including nonunion members). Failure to do so constitutes an unfair labor practice.

It is also an unfair labor practice for employers or unions to refuse to bargain at all or to refuse to bargain "in good faith." Each side must make a sincere effort to reach an agreement and must actively participate in negotiations to that end. An employer who has a "take it or leave it" attitude or offers terms that no responsible employee representative could accept is not bargaining in good faith.

WHAT ARE THE THREE SUBJECTS OF COLLECTIVE BARGAINING?

The National Labor Relations Act divides collective bargaining into three subject matter areas, compulsory subjects, permissive subjects, and illegal subjects.

Compulsory subjects These are areas where bargaining is required by statute. NLRA Section 8(d) requires employers and unions to bargain collectively on "wages, hours, and other terms and conditions of employment, or the negotiation of an agreement or any question arising thereunder." Retirement plan benefits fall within the meaning of "wages, rates of pay, hours of employment or other conditions of employment" and are thus the proper subject of compulsory collective bargaining.

Permissive subjects These are subjects that fall within the discretion of the employer and the union who may choose whether or not to bargain about them. Subjects such as corporate structure, general business practice, and plant location, for example, may be the subject of collective bargaining, but they don't have to be.

Illegal subjects These are areas forbidden to the employer and union who cannot bargain here because it would be illegal to do so (e.g., an attempt to bargain about a "closed shop" as outlawed by the Taft-Hartley Act).

HOW CAN A COLLECTIVE BARGAINING AGREEMENT BE CHANGED OR TERMINATED?

Suppose the employer or the union wants to change or terminate a collective bargaining agreement. The party desiring the change must do the following:

1. Notify the other party in writing of his or her desire to make the change at least sixty days prior to the expiration date of the contract;
2. Offer to meet and confer with the other party for the purpose of negotiating a new or altered contract;
3. Notify the appropriate federal and state mediation agencies within thirty days of the first notice, unless an agreement has been reached by that time;
4. Continue in full force and effect, without resorting to strike or lockout, all the terms and conditions of the existing contract for the period of sixty days after the first notice is given or until the expiration date of the contract, whichever occurs later.

HOW ARE COLLECTIVE BARGAINING AGREEMENTS ENFORCED?

Under the Taft-Hartley Act, a union may sue or be sued on behalf of the employees it represents. Thus either party (employer or union) may sue the other for breach of the collective bargaining agreement. The suit may be brought in any federal district court having jurisdiction over the parties, regardless of diversity of citizenship or federal jurisdictional amount.

WHAT IS THE LAW ON STRIKES AND PICKETING?

The National Labor Relations Act guarantees employees the right to strike and picket. The Act further provides that strikers retain their status as "employees" even while on strike. Of course, the employees can always agree with their employer not to strike as part of a collective bargaining agreement.

Still, a strike or boycott is illegal if its objective is to enforce what would amount to an unfair labor practice (e.g., a strike to force the employer to discriminate against employees on the basis of race).

And under the NLRA, the following strikes are also illegal:

1. *Violent strikes* Strikes that are violent in nature receive no protection under the law. Sitdown strikes, where workers occupy the employer's premises and refuse to work, are also illegal. And strikers found guilty of violence in connection with a strike may be discharged.

2. *Strikes occurring prior to expiration of the sixty-day cooling off period* The NLRA makes it unlawful for a union to strike to terminate or change a collective bargaining agreement without first giving the employer sixty days' notice thereof and offering to negotiate a new contract. The reason for the notice requirement is to create a "cooling off" period during which time tempers may "cool" and a drastic strike may be averted. Where the contract is for a fixed term, the union cannot strike prior to the contract termination date, and it may strike then only if the sixty days' notice requirement has been met.

3. *Partial strikes* Employees may either continue to work and negotiate, or they can strike, but they cannot remain on the job and occasionally disrupt or shut down the employer's operations.

4. *Strikes undertaken to force employers to make other nonunion employees join the union.*

5. *Strikes undertaken to force an employer to pay for unnecessary services* Called "featherbedding," this is the practice of forcing employers to hire or retain more workers than the employer needs to operate his or her business.

CAN AN EMPLOYER HIRE REPLACEMENTS DURING A STRIKE AND REFUSE TO TAKE THE STRIKERS BACK AFTER THE STRIKE IS OVER?

It is an unfair labor practice under the NLRA for an employer to interfere with his or her employees' right to strike. Obviously, workers would be reluctant to strike if they thought they might lose their jobs as a result. Yet, on the other side of the coin, the employer has a legitimate right and interest in keeping his or her business operating when workers walk off the job. Certainly, it is not unreasonable for the employer to hire other employees to work in place of the strikers. But what happens when the strike is over, and the strikers desire to return to their jobs? The answer here depends on why the workers strike in the first place. If the workers strike because of an *unfair labor practice,* they are entitled to come back to work even if it is necessary to fire their replacements. But if the workers strike only for increased benefits (such as higher wages), the employer does not have to reinstate them if replacements have taken over their jobs.

Employers may also discharge employees for "slowdowns," partial strikes, or "wildcat strikes." A slowdown occurs when workers remain on the job but refuse to perform their duties or to work at the regular pace. A partial strike takes place when employees come to work but, after working a short time, feign illness or other disability in order to cause a work stoppage. And a "wildcat strike" arises when a minority of union members strike without union authorization.

As far as picketing is concerned, any picketing carried out by violent means is unlawful. The National Labor Relations Act additionally prohibits mass picketing designed to deter employees from entering or leaving a plant as well as any picketing accompanied by threats or violence. Obstructing plant entrances to keep nonstrikers from entering or leaving is also unlawful.

WHAT REQUIREMENTS MUST A UNION ELECTION MEET?

The Landrum-Griffin Act of 1959 was passed in part to guarantee fair union elections. The Act sets forth the following minimal requirements for conducting the nomination and election of union officials in a free and democratic manner:

1. All union members in good standing must be allowed to vote ("one person, one vote").
2. Local officers must be elected at least every three years and national officers every five.
3. Union officers must be elected by secret ballot.
4. Reasonable opportunity to nominate candidates must be provided.
5. Every union member in good standing must be eligible to be a candidate, subject to reasonable qualifications uniformly imposed.
6. Members must be notified at least fifteen days prior to the election.
7. If the union distributes campaign literature, it must do so at the expense of the candidates and without discrimination between or among them.
8. Adequate safeguards must be provided for the election itself, including the right of any candidate to have observers at the polls and at the ballot counting.
9. Candidates must not use union funds to finance their campaigns.

Landrum-Griffin authorizes the secretary of labor in conjunction with the courts to protect the rights of union members in connection with union elections. Although the secretary may initiate his or her own investigation into election violations, the secretary usually acts upon complaints filed by disgruntled members of the union. If, upon investigation, the secretary finds "probable cause" to believe the law was violated, he or she will bring suit in federal court (within sixty days of the complaint's filing date) to set aside the election. The federal court will then decide whether the law was violated, and if it decides that it was, a new election will be ordered. The secretary of labor will supervise the new election and certify the names of the winners to the court.

WHAT ABOUT CORRUPTION IN UNIONS?

The Landrum-Griffin Act also requires union disclosure of certain basic information, including the names of officers and union finance materials. This information must be made available to union members. Willful violation of the Act's reporting provisions is punishable by a fine of up to $10,000 and/or imprisonment for up to one year. The secretary of labor has the right to inspect union records and to question such persons as he or she believes necessary to determine if violations have occurred.

Title V of the Landrum-Griffin Act, entitled "Safeguards for Labor Organizations," imposes fiduciary duties upon union officers, agents, shop stewards, and other union representatives. Union officials are also prohibited from using union funds for personal expenditures and from acquiring financial or other interests that conflict with the interests of the labor union. To help enforce these provisions, the law permits individual union members to sue union officials for damages, for an accounting, or for any other relief appropriate where the union itself fails to do so. Union officials found guilty of embezzling, stealing, or otherwise willfully misappropriating union funds may be fined up to $10,000 and imprisoned up to five years.

Cases

Does the doctrine of respondeat superior apply?

NAWROCKI v. COLE

Supreme Court of Washington,
Department 2, 1952.
41 Wn.2d 474, 249 P.2d 969.

OLSON, Justice

A jury returned a verdict in favor of plaintiff for damages incurred in an automobile collision. * * * [D]efendant has appealed. J.T. Cole is the sole defendant, his wife having died before the trial.

His appeal presents two principal questions: (1) Was a mechanic he employed to repair his car, and who was testing it on the highway when the collision occurred, an independent contractor [i.e., does the doctrine of respondeat superior apply] and (2) was defendant himself negligent in having his car driven on the highway when, as plaintiff alleges, "he knew that said automobile had serious motor trouble and might be stalled on said highway"?

During the evening in question, defendant and two guests were returning to Tacoma from Wilbur in defendant's automobile. As they approached Ellensburg, the motor ceased to function properly. It operated jerkily, and the car could be driven only at slow speeds, estimated by defendant to be from five or ten miles an hour to thirty or thirty-five miles an hour. It did not stop entirely, nor was it necessary to drive the car in low gear.

Defendant arrived at a garage in Ellensburg late in the evening. He told the mechanic how the car had operated and asked him to find the trouble and repair it. The mechanic proceeded to work on the motor, and it was running smoothly when he presented a bill for his services. Defendant did not pay the bill or accept the car, but asked the mechanic to take it out on the highway and test it to be sure that it was operating properly.

The mechanic, accompanied by one of the defendant's guests, then drove the car onto the main traveled highway leading out of Ellensburg. After he had gone about one mile, the motor again ceased to function properly, and it was impossible to accelerate the car. He then decided that the fuel pump was the source of the trouble, and, as he was returning to the garage, plaintiff, going in the same direction, drove his automobile into the rear of defendant's car. Plaintiff testified that, before the collision, defendant's car was stopped on the highway and that he saw no lights on it. Some rain had fallen during the evening, and the pavement was wet. Visibility was poor because of haze or fog in the vicinity of the collision.

An independent contractor is one who, in the pursuit of an independent business, undertakes to perform a specified piece of work or to render a particular service for another, without submitting to control in the manner of performance. The principal question is, who has the right to control the manner of doing the work? The independence of the relation is not affected by a reservation, by the one ordering the work, of a right to supervise it merely to determine whether or not it is done according to the contract.

* * *

The evidence * * * establishes that the mechanic was engaged in an independent business, that of repairing automobiles. He undertook a specified piece of work, the repair of defendant's car. Defendant did not know what had to be done, and the mechanic was free from his direction or control regarding the details or the manner of repair. Defendant was concerned only with the result of the work and did not supervise it, except to request that the car be tested to determine whether the work of repair was completed. Neither defendant nor his guest, who rode with the mechanic during the test, specified or controlled the exact place or kind of test to be made. The test became part of the work of repair, and the mechanic did what he determined, from the test, was necessary to finish his job. Not until then did he complete his work, deliver the car to defendant, and receive his pay.

Upon these facts the mechanic became an independent contractor, as a matter of law, when he accepted defendant's car for repair. Defendant's request that the car be tested did not change this relationship, as plaintiff contends, and it prevailed until the car was redelivered to defendant. * * *

Therefore, because the negligence, if any, of the mechanic, an independent contractor, cannot be imputed to defendant [not being a servant, respondeat superior does not apply, and there is no vicarious liability], if the judgment can be sustained, it must be upon the alleged negligence of defendant himself.

An automobile is not *per se* a dangerous instrumentality. It may become such if it is so mechanically defective as to render it liable to become uncontrollable on the highway.

The case at bar is not pleaded on a theory of strict or absolute liability. It is rested upon the alleged negligence of defendant. The standard of conduct required of defendant upon this theory of the case may be defined by stating the essential elements of plaintiff's proof, if he is to recover. They are that, at the time defendant's automobile went upon the highway, (1) it was defective, (2) defendant knew or, as a reasonable man, should have known of the defect and of the reasonable likelihood that it would cause injury, (3) the defect proximately caused the injury to plaintiff, and (4) the damages he sustained.

Upon this issue, the evidence is undisputed that defendant's car did not stop on the highway, nor did its lights cease to function, before he delivered it to the garage for repair. The motor was operating smoothly, and all of the lights, both front and rear, were burning when the mechanic drove the car out of the garage to test it. * * * [W]e find no fact or reasonable inference from the facts or circumstances in this case, to sustain a verdict adverse to defendant upon the second essential element of plaintiff's proof.

Neither of the issues we have discussed should have been submitted to the jury. The judgment is reversed, and the cause is remanded to the trial court for the entry of judgment in favor of defendant, notwithstanding the verdict of the jury.

"A rock, the size of a brick."

GIEM v. WILLIAMS

Supreme Court of Arkansas, 1949.
215 Ark. 705, 222 S.W.2d 800.

McFADDIN, Justice

This is an action instituted by appellee, as widow and administratrix, to recover damages for the death of Joe Williams.

Giem and Associates, hereinafter called appellants, obtained a contract to construct a dormitory on the campus of the University of Arkansas in Fayetteville. Appellants sublet the excavation work to Carl Tune. Joe Williams (hereinafter called deceased) went to the place of construction to apply to appellants' superintendent for work as a carpenter. While in appellants' shed on the premises, Williams was struck on the head by a large rock which had been hurled through the roof of the building as the result of blasting then being done by Tune in the excavation work. Williams died three days later as a result of his injuries; and this action ensued. * * *

The plaintiff (appellee) tried the case on the theory that the defendants (appellants) were liable for * * * failure to see that Tune, even as independent contractor, exercised proper care in the use of the explosives in excavation work. Appellants, for defense, claimed (a) that there was no negligence on their part; (b) that Tune was an independent contractor for whose acts appellants were not liable. * * * The trial resulted in a verdict against appellants for $8950. From an unavailing motion for new trial, there is this appeal, presenting questions as to the law, the evidence and the amount of the verdict.

* * *

Appellee's instruction number 2 presented to the jury for decision the question, whether appellants, by claiming that Tune was an independent contractor, could thereby escape liability for his negligence, if any, in the inherently dangerous blasting. * * * Appellee's instruction number 4 presented to the jury for decision, whether the blasting—under the facts and circumstances in this case—was of such nature that the duty of appellants, as to proper care, could not be delegated. * * * These instructions presented the law as to the liability, if any, of appellants.

* * * From all of the authorities, we conclude the law to be:

* * *

(c) that appellants, in having blasting done in the excavation for the dormitory, near a well-traveled street and in a populous center, could not escape liability, for failure to use proper care, through the claim that the blasting had been entrusted to an independent contractor;

(d) that if Tune (the independent contractor) failed to use proper care to prevent injury by missiles from the explosion, then such failure—under the facts herein—would be negligence imputed to appellants. * * *

* * *

II. *Sufficiency of the Evidence to Sustain Recovery Against Appellants.* In addition to the facts previously stated, there was evidence tending to show:

(1) that appellants had erected at the place of construction, about 160 feet from where Tune was excavating, the ordinary contractor's shed, which was a frame building about 12 feet wide and 30 feet long, and with a frame roof and roofing paper thereon;

(2) that the deceased and his fellow carpenter (Lindler), having learned that carpenters would soon be needed on the work, went to the place of construction in Lindler's car, which they parked on the street near appellants' shed;

(3) that deceased and Lindler, in proceeding towards the shed, met Nordstrom, appellants' superintendent, and were discussing with him the employment of carpenters, when Tune came up and advised Lindler: "You had better move your car;

you are liable to get some glass broke, because they are going to shoot."

(4) that Lindler then drove his car a distance of 30 or 40 feet from where it had been parked, sat in the car until the blasting had been accomplished, and then returned to Nordstrom to complete the interrupted conversation;

(5) that when Lindler went to move his car Nordstrom and the deceased stepped into appellants' shed and were standing there "shoulder to shoulder" when the blasting occurred;

(6) that a rock "the size of a brick" crashed through the roof of the shed and struck the deceased on the head, causing the injuries which resulted in his death three days later;

(7) that in the excavation work Tune at that time was using three sticks of dynamite in each of four holes, the detonators of the dynamite being exploded simultaneously by an electric current;

(8) that the fact that dynamite was being used for such excavation was known to appellants and Nordstrom, and the test holes for such use were shown on the plan furnished to Tune by appellants;

(9) that Tune used no mat or cushion (other than sand) over the holes for protection of the public against flying missiles, although he had on the location materials for constructing such mats; and

(10) that such mats should be used in blasting in populous places such as where this excavating was being done.

* * *

There was also a jury question as to whether the appellants' superintendent, Nordstrom, used proper care in selecting the shed as a place of safety and impliedly inviting deceased therein, when Nordstrom knew—or in the exercise of ordinary care, should have known—that Tune was not using mats or cushions over the holes in which the dynamite was to be exploded. Just because Nordstrom was personally willing to take the chance of injury by missiles from the blast does not furnish a criterion of due care by appellants towards an implied invitee.

* * *

Finding no error, the judgment is affirmed.

Youthful exuberance put out the claimant's eye.

CRILLY v. BALLOU

Supreme Court of Michigan, 1958.
353 Mich. 303, 91 N.W.2d 493.

SMITH, Justice

Once more we consider the great remedial statute, the workmen's compensation act. The case before us involves a boy of some 16 years. He and a teen-age friend had been employed by a contractor engaged in roofing and siding work. From time to time they would throw shingles and nails back and forth at each other. These acts, assaults in point of law, arose from youthful exuberance, rather than from vindictiveness, or animosity. Nevertheless, the last shingle thrown put out the claimant's eye. He claims compensation. In opposition it is said that the injury did not arise out of and in the course of the employment.

We are here in the general area of the assault cases. The particular type of assault now before us is in the sportive assault. Its labels are as varied as the acts themselves. It is sometimes called fooling, or practical-joking, horseplay, or larking. It knows no bounds of occupation or calling, or time, or location, as its very terminology reveals. Thus the larking of the English youths, when undertaken on the great ships of sail, with their towering masts so nearly scraping the sky itself, became "skylarking." Whatever the term employed, however, this particular kind of assault is, for the purpose of the social evils sought to be remedied by this act, governed by principles essentially similar to those applicable to the malicious assault. The workman blinded on the job by a fellow worker may console himself to some degree if the blinding were merely sportive, not malicious, but his family's loss of income recognizes no such distinction, nor does the economic burden necessarily assumed by charity, public or private, in the extreme cases. * * *

The arguments against recovery in this type of case are well known. In the first place it may be said that the employee was not hired to throw shingles, or nails, but to work. * * * Since, then, the employee was not hired to throw things (nails, rolls, apples, hot ashes, or stones, to cite a few instances from the reported cases) if he was injured in so doing, it is argued that he was injured "outside the scope of his employment." Or, it is sometimes said, the injury received under such circumstances, arose from the workman's own fault, or possibly, the fault of a fellow workman. * * *

What is all this talk of fault, of negligence, of scope of employment, of foreseeability, of implied authority? We once lived in a paradise of these concepts, a veritable legalistic Garden of Eden, so completely out of touch with the realities of industrial life that those who came before us for succor, the halt and the blind, the victims of industrial accidents, were almost invariably turned away empty handed. It was the reaction of our people to these unrecompensed injuries that found expression in the workmen's compensation acts. * * * Compensation * * * was not to be barred by fault, or neglect, or inattention, that is, for the mere human failings of the workman. In short, no longer need the workman be free from fault to receive recompense. The family of the careless worker, as well as him more careful, knew privation and sorrow when injury stopped income. True, the injured workman would not get full "damages" as that term is used in the law. The amount of his recovery was carefully circumscribed. * * * [T]he workman has given up his common-law action, and can no longer seek damages from a jury. However, there was a giving on both sides. In return for the workman's limited monetary recovery he got the certainty of adequate compensatory payments without recourse to litigation.

* * *

So it is that we get to the assault cases, a type of case involving, just as clearly as in event of negligence, a degree of culpability, of fault, on the part of the workman, either the claimant himself, or his fellow workers. The earliest of the sportive assault (the fooling, or horseplay, or skylarking) cases denied recovery. Their reasoning reveals their misconceptions. Armitage v. Lancashire & Yorkshire Ry. Co., [1902] 2 K.B. 178, involved three boys. Two were larking. A third was hit in the eye by a piece of iron thrown by one of the larking pair. Recovery was denied: "This was a wrongful act entirely outside the scope of the employment." Here, it will be noted, the court is falling back upon a concept (scope of employment) entirely foreign, both in origin and application, to the principles underlying the passage of compensation legislation. Scope of employment has its uses, it is true, in the application of the doctrine of *respondeat superior*. But compensation does not involve *respondeat superior* and recovery in compensation cases turns not on the common-law concept of scope of employment but upon the statutory requirement of course of employment. The two concepts have a different content. In fact, distinguished students of the subject have stated that, "perhaps the most important guide" for the interpretation of the expression "arising out of and in the course of his employment" is to "realize that it should be sharply differentiated from the technical phrase 'scope of employment' designed to circumscribe the area of vicarious liability to third persons."

* * *

* * * Labor is not a commodity. Labor is people, men, women, and, as this case so tragically shows, children. They have great virtues, for they are made in God's im-

age, but they have grievous faults, for they are far from perfect. They quarrel, they fight, they are sometimes abusive, even profane. They are hired to work, and work they do, as our industrial might attests. Yet they work not always carefully, for they are heedless, not always with a single-minded devotion to duty, for they are thoughtless. There was a time when employers could say to an injured employee, I hired you to be careful, not careless. I hired you to work, not to fight, or play. I hired the best in you, not the worst. I hired the good, not the evil. I hired the virtue, not the vice. Such sophistry was, for a time, accepted. It was true that the boy in Mr. Justice Cardozo's case (Leonbruno, supra,) was not hired to throw apples, any more than the boys before us were hired to throw shingles. But what was hired, a boy or a robot? The answer is simple and it points to our solution: the employer hired a human being, with all his reactions and his imperfections. Going to the job does not sanctify him. At home or at work, give a man a curse and he will anger, give a teenage boy an apple core and he will throw it. The workman "brings to his work," as we said, dissenting in Salmon v. Bagley Laundry Company, 344 Mich. 471, 487, 74 N.W.2d 1, 8, "* * * all of his human characteristics, his frailties as well as his virtues. We cannot, either actually or legally, make the precise excisions of the surgeon. We cannot remove from him, and put to work for his employer, only his strength. His strength goes hand in hand with his temper. It is impossible for us to employ only the grace and charm of the female worker. We hire as well her lively curiosity. We collect these people by the hundreds, even thousands, and we put them to work, sometimes amid noise and vibration, sometimes in smoke and steam. They get tired. They get hungry. They get thirsty. They have to go to the toilet. The day wears on and tempers grow short. Relief is sought in horseplay. Trips to the water cooler and coffee urn grow in number and duration. This is the course of employment. 'Course of employment' is not a sterile form of words. It is descriptive of life in the industrial age. These human deviations from the course of the automaton do not suspend the employer-employee relationship. They are not departures from employment, but the very substance of it. They are the inevitable concomitants of the working relationship and conditions which produce the product. Its cost must reflect the fatigue, the irritations, and sometimes the blood that went into it. It is here that we find the explanation for the horseplay cases, the curiosity cases, and the assault cases."

Herein lies our answer. For the purposes of the compensation act the concept of course of employment is more comprehensive than the assigned work at the lathe. It includes an employee's ministrations to his own human needs: he must eat; concessions to his own human frailties: he must rest, must now and then have a break, and he sometimes, even on the job, plays practical jokes on his fellows. Course of employment is not scope of employment. The former, as the cases so clearly reveal, is a way of life in a working environment. If the injury results from the work itself, or from the stresses, the tensions, the associations, of the working environments, human as well as material, it is compensable. Why? Because those are the ingredients of the product itself. It carries to the market with it, on its price tag stained and scarred, its human as well as its material costs. So says the statute. It does not become us to ignore its plain commands.

We need not undertake to define the outer limits of compensability. We rule on the case before us. The requirement that there be a causal connection between the work, or the incidents thereof, the working conditions, and the injury, serves to exclude the purely personal, nonwork-connected, disputes, such as that which arose after one Harry Elrod attempted to "date" the wife of a fellow workman whom he had met in a tavern the night preceding the altercation. Elrod v. Union Bleachery, 204 S.C. 481. Excluded, also, under the terms of the statute are acts of such gross and reprehensible nature as to constitute intentional and wilful misconduct. This presents a situation of an entirely different character than that presented by the playful shove or the roundhouse punch, no matter how tragic may be the latter's unexpected results. And this exclusion of acts of a degree of moral turpitude, it will be observed, is by the legislature itself, not a judicial retrogression to principles of tort. Further than this in definition we do not attempt to go. The precise future line of demarcation will be marked out, in the traditional manner, by the case-to-case decisions.

[W]e specifically hold that injuries received in assaults, either sportive or malicious, are not, by reason of such fact alone, beyond the realm of compensability. If arising out of the employment and received in the course thereof they are compensable.

* * *

The order of the workmen's compensation appeal board is reversed and the cause remanded for entry of an order in accordance herewith. * * *

"Any man in his right mind would want to rape you."

BUNDY v. JACKSON

United States Court of Appeals, District of Columbia Circuit.
Argued March 26, 1980. Decided Jan. 12, 1981.

J. SKELLY WRIGHT, Chief Judge

In *Barnes v. Costle*, 561 F.2d 983 (D.C.Cir. 1977), we held that an employer who abolished a female employee's job to retaliate against the employee's resistance of his sexual advances violated Title VII of the Civil Rights Act of 1964. The appellant in this case asserts some claims encompassed by the *Barnes* decision, arguing that her rejection of unsolicited and offensive sexual advances from several supervisors in her agency caused those supervisors unjustifiably to delay and block promotions to which she was entitled. Equally important, however, appellant asks us to extend *Barnes* by holding that an employer violates Title VII merely by subjecting female employees to sexual harassment, even if the employee's resistance to that harassment does not cause the employer to deprive her of any tangible job benefits.

The District Court in this case made an express finding of fact that in appellant's agency "the making of improper sexual advances to female employees [was] standard operating procedure, a fact of life, a normal condition of employment," and that the director of the agency, to whom she complained of the harassment, failed to investigate her complaints or take them seriously. Nevertheless, the District Court refused to grant appellant any declaratory or injunctive relief, concluding that sexual harassment does not in itself represent discrimination "with respect to * * * terms, conditions, or privileges of employment" within the meaning of Title VII. Further, the court denied appellant's request for back pay to compensate for the allegedly improper delay in her promotion to GS-9, and for elevation to GS-11 and back pay for the delay in that promotion, holding that the employer had independent, legitimate reasons for delaying and denying the promotions.

Because we believe the District Court wrongly construed Title VII on the claim for declaratory and injunctive relief and failed to apply the proper burden of proof analysis to the promotion claims, we reverse.

Appellant Sandra Bundy is now, and was at the time she filed her lawsuit, a Vocational Rehabilitation Specialist, level GS-9, with the District of Columbia Department of Corrections (the agency). Bundy began with the agency as a GS-4 Personnel Clerk in 1970, was promoted to GS-5 that same year, * * * and achieved her current GS-9 level in 1976, one year after she filed her formal complaint of sexual harassment with the agency. In recent years Bundy's chief task has been to find jobs for former criminal offenders.

The District Court's finding that sexual intimidation was a "normal condition of employment" in Bundy's agency finds ample support in the District Court's own chronology of Bundy's experiences there. Those experiences began in 1972 when Bundy, still a GS-5, received and rejected sexual propositions from Delbert Jackson, then a fellow employee at the agency but now its Director and the named defendant in this lawsuit in his official capacity. It was two years later, however, that the sexual intimidation Bundy suffered began to intertwine directly with her employment, when she received propositions from two of her supervisors, Arthur Burton and James Gainey.

Burton began sexually harassing Bundy in June 1974, continually calling her into his office to request that she spend the workday afternoon with him at his apartment and to question her about her sexual proclivities.[2] Shortly after becoming her first-line supervisor Gainey also began making sexual advances to Bundy, asking her to join him at a motel and on a trip to the Bahamas. Bundy complained about these advances to Lawrence Swain, who supervised both Burton and Gainey. Swain casually dismissed Bundy's complaints, telling her that "any man in his right mind would want to rape you," and then proceeding himself to request that she begin a sexual relationship with him in his apartment. Bundy rejected his request.

We add that, although the District Court made no explicit findings as to harassment of other female employees, its finding that harassment was "standard operating procedure" finds ample support in record evidence that Bundy was not the only woman subjected to sexual intimidation by male supervisors.

In denying Bundy any relief, the District Court found that Bundy's supervisors did not take the "game" of sexually propositioning female employees "seriously," and that Bundy's rejection of their advances did not evoke in them any motive to take any action against her. The record, however, contains nothing to support this view, and indeed some evidence directly belies it. For example, after Bundy complained to Swain, Burton began to derogate her for alleged malingering and poor work performance, though she had not previously received any such criticism. Burton also arranged a meeting with Bundy and Gainey to discuss Bundy's alleged abuse of leave, though he did not pursue his charges at this meeting.

Beyond these actions, Bundy's supervisors at least created the impression that they were impeding her promotion because she had offended them, and they certainly did nothing to help her pursue her harassment claims through established channels. Bundy became eligible for promotion to GS-9 in January 1975. When she contacted Gainey to inquire about a promotion he referred her to Burton, who then referred her back to Gainey, who then told her that because of a promotion freeze he could not recommend her for a promotion. One month later, however, Bundy learned that the personnel office had indeed recommended other employees for promotion despite the freeze. * * * Bundy then informally consulted an Equal Employment Opportunity (EEO) Officer who was working in her office, and then requested a meeting with Claude Burgin, Swain's supervisor. On February 18, 1975 Bundy met with Burton and Burgin and told the latter that Burton and Gainey had sexually harassed her and denied her a

2. Burton called Bundy into his office to ask about her weekend activities and, in particular, whether she liked horses. When she responded that she indeed rode horses, he said that he had heard that women rode horses to obtain sexual relief. He told her he had books and pictures at home to support this theory and suggested that she come to his apartment to see them. Burton specifically asked her to come to his apartment to look at the books and pictures during the workday afternoon instead of performing her job-related field activities. Moreover, he repeated his importunings by telephone after obtaining Bundy's unlisted home number.

promotion because she had resisted their advances. Burgin simply responded that she was denied the promotion because her work was unsatisfactory, and that she was free to pursue the matter further if she cared to. Bundy then informally complained about the sexual harassment to Aquila Gilmore, the Chief EEO Officer in the agency. Gilmore, however, simply advised that her charges might be difficult to prove, and cautioned her against bringing unwarranted complaints. He never brought the issue to the attention of Delbert Jackson, by then Director of the agency. * * * Bundy was finally promoted to GS-9 in July 1976. Having received "satisfactory" ratings for her work performance, she became eligible for promotion to GS-11 in July 1977, but has not yet received that promotion.

Bundy filed her complaint in the District Court on August 3, 1977.[6]

* * *

The key provision of Title VII states:

> It shall be an unlawful employment practice for an employer—
>
> (1) to fail or refuse to hire or to discharge any individual, or otherwise to discriminate against any individual with respect to [her] compensation, terms, conditions, or privileges of employment, because of such individual's * * * sex * *[.]

The specific provision of Title VII applying to employment with the District of Columbia, as well as to a federal agency as in *Barnes v. Costle, supra*, states:

> All personnel actions affecting employees * * * in those units of the Government of the District of Columbia having positions in the competitive service * * * shall be made free from any discrimination based on race, color, religion, sex, or national origin.

Despite the difference in language between these two sections, we have held that Title VII places the same restrictions on federal and District of Columbia agencies as it does on private employers, and so we may construe the latter provision in terms of the former. We infer that the District Court in this case did the same, and that it refused Bundy declaratory and injunctive relief because it believed that sexual harassment not leading to loss or denial of tangible employment benefits for the harassed employee fell outside the scope of discrimination with respect to "terms, conditions, or privileges of employment."

Because Paulette Barnes had had her job terminated after she refused her supervisor's sexual importunings, we were not required in *Barnes* to construe the phrase "terms, conditions, or privileges of employment." Instead, our task of statutory construction in *Barnes* was to determine whether the disparate treatment Barnes suffered was "based on * * * sex." We heard arguments there that whatever harm Barnes suffered was not *sex* discrimination, since Barnes' supervisor terminated her job because she had refused sexual advances, not because she was a woman. We rejected those arguments as disingenuous in the extreme. The supervisor in that case made demands of Barnes that he would not have made of male employees. "*But for* her womanhood * * * [Barnes'] participation in sexual activity would never have been solicited. To say, then, that she was victimized in her employment simply because she declined the invitation is to ignore the asserted fact that she was invited only because she was a woman subordinate to the inviter in the hierarchy of agency personnel." Id. at 990 (emphasis added; footnotes omitted).[7]

6. Since the agency took no final action on her complaint, and since she waited more than 180 days after she filed the complaint with the agency, Bundy fully exhausted her administrative remedies before proceeding in District Court. 42 U.S.C. § 2000e–16(c) (1976); Civil Service Commission Regulations § 713.281, Federal Personnel Manual Supp. 990–1 (1978).

7. We also rejected the argument that sexual harassment could not be gender discrimination simply because a woman could also harass a man, or because any homosexual supervisor could harass an employee of the same gender. We noted that in each instance the question is one of but-for causation: would the complaining employee have suffered the harassment had he or she been of a different gender? *Barnes v. Costle*, 561 F.2d 983, 990 n. 55 (D.C.Cir.1977). Only by a *reductio ad absurdum* could we imagine a case of harassment that is not sex discrimination—where a bisexual supervisor harasses men and women alike. Id.

We thus made clear in *Barnes* that sex discrimination within the meaning of Title VII is not limited to disparate treatment founded solely or categorically on gender. Rather, discrimination is *sex* discrimination whenever sex is for no legitimate reason a substantial factor in the discrimination.

* * *

We thus have no difficulty inferring that Bundy suffered discrimination on the basis of sex. Moreover, applying *Barnes*, we have no difficulty ascribing the harassment—the "standard operating procedure"—to Bundy's employer, the agency. Although Delbert Jackson himself appears not to have used his position as Director to harass Bundy, an employer is liable for discriminatory acts committed by supervisory personnel, and there is obviously no dispute that the men who harassed Bundy were her supervisors. *Barnes* did suggest that the employer might be relieved of liability if the supervisor committing the harassment did so in contravention of the employer's policy and without the employer's knowledge, and if the employer moved promptly and effectively to rectify the offense. Here, however, Delbert Jackson and other officials in the agency who had some control over employment and promotion decisions had full notice of harassment committed by agency supervisors and did virtually nothing to stop or even investigate the practice. And though there was ample evidence in this case that at least two other women in the agency suffered from this harassment, *Barnes* makes clear that the employer could be held liable even if Bundy were the only victim, since Congress intended Title VII to protect *individuals* against class-based prejudice.

We thus readily conclude that Bundy's employer discriminated against her on the basis of sex. What remains is the novel question whether the sexual harassment of the sort Bundy suffered amounted by itself to sex discrimination with respect to the "*terms, conditions, or privileges of employment.*" Though no court has as yet so held, we believe that an affirmative answer follows ineluctably from numerous cases finding Title VII violations where an employer created or condoned a substantially discriminatory work *environment*, regardless of whether the complaining employees lost any tangible job benefits as a result of the discrimination.

Bundy's claim on this score is essentially that "conditions of employment" include the psychological and emotional work environment—that the sexually stereotyped insults and demeaning propositions to which she was indisputably subjected and which caused her anxiety and debilitation, illegally poisoned that environment. This claim invokes the Title VII principle enunciated by Judge Goldberg in *Rogers v. Equal Employment Opportunity Com'n*, 454 F.2d 234 (5th Cir.1971). The plaintiff in *Rogers*, a Hispanic, did not claim that her employer, a firm of opticians, had deprived her of any tangible job benefit. Rather, she claimed that by giving discriminatory service to its Hispanic *clients* the firm created a discriminatory and offensive work environment for its Hispanic *employees*. Granting that the express language of Title VII did not mention this situation, Judge Goldberg stated:

> Congress chose neither to enumerate specific discriminatory practices, nor to elucidate in extenso the parameter of such nefarious activities. Rather, it pursued the path of wisdom by being unconstrictive, knowing that constant change is the order of our day and that the seemingly reasonable practices of the present can easily become the injustices of the morrow. Time was when employment discrimination tended to be viewed as a series of isolated and distinguishable events, manifesting itself, for example, in an employer's practices of hiring, firing, and promoting. But today employment discrimination is a far more complex and pervasive phenomenon, as the nuances and subtleties of discriminatory employment practices are no longer confined to bread and butter issues. As wages and hours of employment take subordinate roles in management-labor relationships, the modern employee makes ever-increasing demands in the nature of intangible fringe benefits. Recognizing the importance of these benefits,

> we should neither ignore their need for protection, nor blind ourselves to their potential misuse.

454 F.2d at 238. The Fifth Circuit then concluded that the employer had indeed violated Title VII, Judge Goldberg explaining that "terms, conditions, or privileges of employment"

> is an expansive concept which sweeps within its protective ambit the practice of creating a work environment heavily charged with ethnic or racial discrimination. * * * One can readily envision working environments so heavily polluted with discrimination as to destroy completely the emotional and psychological stability of minority group workers * * *.

Accord, Carroll v. Talman Federal Savings & Loan Ass'n, (7th Cir.1979), (forcing female bank employees to wear uniforms while allowing males to wear own suits violates Title VII by perpetuating demeaning sexual stereotypes; "terms and conditions of employment" mean more than tangible compensation and benefits); *Cariddi v. Kansas City Chiefs Football Club, Inc.,* (8th Cir.1977) (though employee could only prove isolated incidents, a pattern of offensive ethnic slurs would violate his Title VII rights); *Firefighters Institute for Racial Equality v. City of St. Louis,* (8th Cir.1977) (segregated employee eating clubs condoned—though not organized or regulated—by employer violate Title VII by creating discriminatory work environment); *Gray v. Greyhound Lines, East,* (D.C.Cir.1976) (pattern of racial slurs violates Title VII rights to nondiscriminatory environment); *United States v. City of Buffalo,* (W.D.N.Y.1978) (black employees entitled to work environment free of racial abuse and insult); *Compston v. Borden, Inc.,* (S.D.Ohio 1976) (demeaning religious slurs by supervisor violate Title VII); *Harrington v. Vandalia-Butler Board of Educ.* (6th Cir. 1978), (giving female physical education teachers inferior locker and shower facilities is illegal discrimination; Title VII reaches "actual working conditions," not just equal opportunity for employment); *Waters v. Heublein, Inc.,* (9th Cir.1977) (white plaintiff has standing to sue employer who discriminates against blacks, since she has statutory right to work environment free of racial prejudice); *Swint v. Pullman-Standard,* (5th Cir.1976) (discriminatory job assignments violate Title VII even where no discrimination in salary; Title VII claimant need not prove tangible economic harm).

The relevance of these "discriminatory environment" cases to sexual harassment is beyond serious dispute. Racial or ethnic discrimination against a company's minority clients may reflect no intent to discriminate directly against the company's minority employees, but in poisoning the atmosphere of employment it violates Title VII. Sexual stereotyping through discriminatory dress requirements may be benign in intent, and may offend women only in a general, atmospheric manner, yet it violates Title VII. Racial slurs, though intentional and directed at individuals, may still be just verbal insults, yet they too may create Title VII liability. How then can sexual harassment, which injects the most demeaning sexual stereotypes into the general work environment and which always represents an intentional assault on an individual's innermost privacy, not be illegal?

* * * [U]nless we extend the *Barnes* holding, an employer could sexually harass a female employee with impugnity by carefully stopping short of firing the employee or taking any other tangible actions against her in response to her resistance, thereby creating the impression—the one received by the District Court in this case—that the employer did not take the ritual of harassment and resistance "seriously."

Indeed, so long as women remain inferiors in the employment hierarchy, they may have little recourse against harassment beyond the legal recourse Bundy seeks in this case. The law may allow a woman to prove that her resistance to the harassment cost her her job or some economic benefit, but this will do her no good if the employer never takes such tangible actions against her.

> And this, in turn, means that so long as the sexual situation is constructed with enough coerciveness, subtlety, suddenness, or onesidedness to negate the effectiveness of the woman's refusal, or so long as her refusals are simply ignored while her job is formally undisturbed, she is not considered to have been sexually harassed.

* * *

It hardly helps that the remote prospect of legal relief under *Barnes* remains available if she objects so powerfully that she provokes the employer into firing her.

* * *

Bundy proved that she was the victim of a practice of sexual harassment and a discriminatory work environment permitted by her employer. Her rights under Title VII were therefore violated. We thus reverse the District Court's holding on this issue and remand it to that court so it can fashion appropriate injunctive relief. And on this novel issue, we think it advisable to offer the District Court guidance in framing its decree.

The Final Guidelines on Sexual Harassment in the Workplace (*Guidelines*) issued by the Equal Employment Opportunity Commission on November 10, 1980, offer a useful basis for injunctive relief in this case. Those Guidelines define sexual harassment broadly:

> Unwelcome sexual advances, requests for sexual favors, and other verbal or physical conduct of a sexual nature constitute sexual harassment when (1) submission to such conduct is made either explicitly or implicitly a term or condition of an individual's employment, (2) submission to or rejection of such conduct by an individual is used as the basis for employment decisions affecting such individual, or (3) such conduct has the purpose or effect of unreasonably interfering with an individual's work performance or creating an intimidating, hostile, or offensive work environment.

* * *

The Guidelines go on to reaffirm that an employer is responsible for discriminatory acts of its agents and supervisory employees with respect to sexual harassment just as with other forms of discrimination, regardless of whether the employer authorized or knew or even should have known of the acts, and also remains responsible for sexual harassment committed by nonsupervisory employees if the employer authorized, knew of, or should have known of such harassment. The general goal of these Guidelines is *preventive*. An employer may negate liability by taking "immediate and appropriate corrective action" when it learns of any illegal harassment, but the employer should fashion rules within its firm or agency to ensure that such corrective action never becomes necessary.

Applying these Guidelines to the present case, we believe that the Director of the agency should be ordered to raise affirmatively the subject of sexual harassment with all his employees and inform all employees that sexual harassment violates Title VII of the Civil Rights Act of 1964, [and] the Guidelines of the EEOC. The Director should also establish and publicize a scheme whereby harassed employees may complain to the Director immediately and confidentially. The Director should promptly take all necessary steps to investigate and correct any harassment, including warnings and appropriate discipline directed at the offending party, and should generally develop other means of preventing harassment within the agency.

Perhaps the most important part of the preventive remedy will be a prompt and effective procedure for hearing, adjudicating, and remedying complaints of sexual harassment within the agency. Fortunately, the District Court need not establish an entire new procedural mechanism for harassment complaints. Under regulations promulgated by the Equal Employment Opportunity Commission, the Department of Corrections, like all other federal and District of Columbia agencies, is required to establish procedures for adjudication of complaints of denial of equal employment opportunity, whether the ground of discrimination is race, color, religion, sex, or national origin. The required procedures guarantee the complainant a prompt and effective investigation, an opportunity for informal adjustment of the discrimination, and, if necessary, a formal evidentiary hearing. Moreover, if the complaint proves meritorious the agency may be required to take disciplinary action against any employee found to have committed discriminatory acts. Finally, the agency must inform any employee denied relief within the agency of his or her right to file a civil action in the District Court.

* * *

Beyond claiming that the sexual harassment she suffered was illegal in itself, Bundy claims that her supervisors illegally retaliated against her refusal of their sexual propositions by delaying her promotion to GS-9 level, and that they continue to retaliate by denying her a promotion to GS-11. Bundy thus requests back pay for the delay in promotion to both levels, and an order requiring her immediate promotion to GS-11. The District Court held against Bundy on these claims, essentially finding that the supervisors were not offended by Bundy's refusal of their advances, and hence had no motive to retaliate against her, and that Bundy's flawed qualifications and work performance gave them legitimate reasons for delaying and denying the promotions. Bundy now argues that the District Court's factual findings were clearly erroneous, * * *.

* * *

To establish a prima facie case of illegal denial of promotion in retaliation against the plaintiff's refusal of sexual advances by her supervisors, the plaintiff must show (1) that she was a victim of a pattern or practice of sexual harassment attributable to her employer (Bundy has, of course, already shown this); and (2) that she applied for and was denied a promotion for which she was technically eligible and of which she had a reasonable expectation. If the prima facie case is made out, the employer then must bear the burden of showing, by clear and convincing evidence, that he had legitimate nondiscriminatory reasons for denying the claimant the promotion.

* * *

Applying these principles, we remand the case to the District Court for further proceedings consistent with this opinion.

So ordered.

An affirmative action plan collectively bargained by an employer and a union.

UNITED STEELWORKERS v. WEBER

Supreme Court of the United States, 1979.
443 U.S. 193, 99 S.Ct. 2721, 61 L.Ed. 480.

Mr. Justice BRENNAN delivered the opinion of the Court.

Challenged here is the legality of an affirmative action plan—collectively bargained by an employer and a union— that reserves for black employees 50% of the openings in an in-plant craft training program until the percentage of black craft workers in the plant is commensurate with the percentage of blacks in the local labor force. The question for decision is whether Congress, in Title VII of the Civil Rights Act of 1964 as amended, 42 U.S.C.A. § 2000e, left employers and unions in the private sector free to take such race-conscious steps to eliminate manifest racial imbalances in traditionally segregated job categories. We hold that Title VII does not prohibit such race-conscious affirmative action plans.

In 1974 petitioner United Steelworkers of America (USWA) and petitioner Kaiser Aluminum & Chemical Corporation (Kaiser) entered into a master collective-bargaining agreement covering terms and conditions of employment at 15 Kaiser plants. The agreement contained, *inter alia*, an affirmative action plan designed to eliminate conspicuous racial imbalances in Kaiser's then almost exclusively white craft work forces. Black craft hiring goals were set for each Kaiser plant equal to the percentage of blacks in the respective local labor forces. To enable plants to meet these goals, on-the-job training programs were established to teach unskilled production workers—black and white—the skills necessary to become craft workers. The plan reserved for black employees 50% of the openings in these newly created in-plant training programs.

This case arose from the operation of the plan at Kaiser's plant in Gramercy, La. Until 1974 Kaiser hired as craft workers for that plant only persons who had had prior craft experience. Because blacks had long been excluded from craft unions, few were able to present such credentials. As a consequence, prior to 1974 only 1.83% (five out of 273) of the skilled craft workers at the Gramercy plant were black, even though the work force in the Gramercy area was approximately 39% black.

Pursuant to the national agreement Kaiser altered its craft hiring practice in the Gramercy plant. Rather than hiring already trained outsiders, Kaiser established a training program to train its production workers to fill craft openings. Selection of craft trainees was made on the basis of seniority, with the proviso that at least 50% of the new trainees were to be black until the percentage of black skilled craft workers in the Gramercy plant approximated the percentage of blacks in the local labor force.

During 1974, the first year of the operation of the Kaiser-USWA affirmative action plan, 13 craft trainees were selected from Gramercy's production work force. Of these, 7 were black and 6 white. The most junior black selected into the program had less seniority than several white production workers whose bids for admission were rejected. Thereafter one of those white production workers, respondent Brian Weber, instituted this class action in the United States District Court for the Eastern District of Louisiana.

The complaint alleged that the filling of craft trainee positions at the Gramercy plant pursuant to the affirmative action program had resulted in junior black employees receiving training in preference to more senior white employees, thus discriminating against respondent and other similarly situated white employees in violation of §§ 703(a)[2] and (d)[3] of Title VII. The District Court held that the plan violated Title VII, entered a judgment in favor of the plaintiff class, and granted a permanent injunction prohibiting Kaiser and the USWA "from denying plaintiffs, Brian F. Weber and all other members of the class, access to on-the-job training programs on the basis of race." A divided panel of the Court of Appeals for the Fifth Circuit affirmed, holding that all employment preferences based upon race, including those preferences incidental to bona fide affirmative action plans, violated Title VII's prohibition against racial discrimination in employment. We granted certiorari. We reverse.

2. Section 703(a), 42 U.S.C.A. § 2000e–2(a), provides:

"(a) It shall be an unlawful employment practice for an employer—

"(1) to fail or refuse to hire or to discharge any individual, or otherwise to discriminate against any individual with respect to his compensation, terms, conditions, or privileges of employment, because of such individual's race, color, religion, sex, or national origin; or

"(2) to limit, segregate, or classify his employees or applicants for employment in any way which would deprive or tend to deprive any individual of employment opportunities or otherwise adversely affect his status as an employee, because of such individual's race, color, religion, sex, or national origin."

3. Section 703(d), 42 U.S.C.A. § 2000e–2(d), provides:

"It shall be an unlawful employment practice for any employer, labor organization, or joint labor-management committee controlling apprenticeship or other training or retraining, including on-the-job training programs to discriminate against any individual because of his race, color, religion, sex, or national origin in admission to, or employment in, any program established to provide apprenticeship or other training."

We emphasize at the outset the narrowness of our inquiry. Since the Kaiser-USWA plan does not involve state action, this case does not present an alleged violation of the Equal Protection Clause of the Constitution. Further, since the Kaiser-USWA plan was adopted voluntarily, we are not concerned with what Title VII requires or with what a court might order to remedy a past proven violation of the Act. The only question before us is the narrow statutory issue of whether Title VII *forbids* private employers and unions from voluntarily agreeing upon bona fide affirmative action plans that accord racial preferences in the manner and for the purpose provided in the Kaiser-USWA plan. That question was expressly left open in McDonald v. Santa Fe Trail Trans. Co., 427 U.S. 273, 281 n. 8, 96 S.Ct. 2574, 2579, 49 L.Ed.2d 493 (1976) which held, in a case not involving affirmative action, that Title VII protects whites as well as blacks from certain forms of racial discrimination.

Respondent argues that Congress intended in Title VII to prohibit all race-conscious affirmative action plans. Respondent's argument rests upon a literal interpretation of § 703(a) and (d) of the Act. Those sections make it unlawful to "discriminate * * * because of * * * race" in hiring and in the selection of apprentices for training programs. Since, the argument runs, McDonald v. Santa Fe Trail Trans. Co., supra, settled that Title VII forbids discrimination against whites as well as blacks, and since the Kaiser-USWA affirmative action plan operates to discriminate against white employees solely because they are white, it follows that the Kaiser-USWA plan violates Title VII.

Respondent's argument is not without force. But it overlooks the significance of the fact that the Kaiser-USWA plan is an affirmative action plan voluntarily adopted by private parties to eliminate traditional patterns of racial segregation. In this context respondent's reliance upon a literal construction of § 703(a) and (d) and upon *McDonald* is misplaced. It is a "familiar rule that a thing may be within the letter of the statute and yet not within the statute, because not within its spirit nor within the intention of its makers." The prohibition against racial discrimination in § 703(a) and (d) of Title VII must therefore be read against the background of the legislative history of Title VII and the historical context from which the Act arose. Examination of those sources makes clear that an interpretation of the sections that forbade all race-conscious affirmative action would "bring about an end completely at variance with the purpose of the statute" and must be rejected.

Congress' primary concern in enacting the prohibition against racial discrimination in Title VII of the Civil Rights Act of 1964 was with "the plight of the Negro in our economy." 110 Cong.Rec. 6548 (remarks of Sen. Humphrey). Before 1964, blacks were largely relegated to "unskilled and semi-skilled jobs." Id., at 6548 (remarks of Sen. Humphrey); id., at 7204 (remarks of Sen. Clark); id., at 7279–7280 (remarks of Sen. Kennedy). Because of automation the number of such jobs was rapidly decreasing. See 110 Cong.Rec., at 6548 (remarks of Sen. Humphrey); id., at 7204 (remarks of Sen. Clark). As a consequence "the relative position of the Negro worker [was] steadily worsening. In 1947 the non-white unemployment rate was only 64 percent higher than the white rate; in 1962 it was 124 percent higher." Id., at 6547 (remarks of Sen. Humphrey). Congress considered this a serious social problem. As Senator Clark told the Senate:

> "The rate of Negro unemployment has gone up consistently as compared with white unemployment for the past 15 years. This is a social malaise and a social situation which we should not tolerate. That is one of the principal reasons why this bill should pass." Id., at 7220.

Congress feared that the goals of the Civil Rights Act—the integration of blacks into the mainstream of American society—could not be achieved unless this trend were reversed. And Congress recognized that that would not be possible unless blacks were able to secure jobs "which have a future." As Senator Humphrey explained to the Senate:

> "What good does it do a Negro to be able to eat in a fine restaurant if he cannot afford to pay the bill? What good does it do him to be accepted in a hotel that is too expensive for his modest income? How can a Negro child be motivated to take full advantage of integrated educational facilities if he has no hope of getting a job where he can use that education?" Id., at 6547.
>
> * * *
>
> "Without a job, one cannot afford public convenience and accommodations. Income from employment may be necessary to further a man's education, or that of his children. If his children have no hope of getting a good job, what will motivate them to take advantage of educational opportunities?" Id., at 6552.
>
> * * *

Accordingly, it was clear to Congress that "the crux of the problem [was] to open employment opportunities for Negroes in occupations which have been traditionally closed to them," id., at 6548 (remarks of Sen. Humphrey), and it was to this problem that Title VII's prohibition against racial discrimination in employment was primarily addressed.

* * *

Given this legislative history, we cannot agree with respondent that Congress intended to prohibit the private sector from taking effective steps to accomplish the goal that Congress designed Title VII to achieve. * * * It would be ironic indeed if a law triggered by a Nation's concern over centuries of racial injustice and intended to improve the lot of those who had "been excluded from the American dream for so long" 110 Cong.Rec., at 6552 (remarks of Sen. Humphrey), constituted the first legislative prohibition of all voluntary, private, race-conscious efforts to abolish traditional pattens of racial segregation and hierarchy.

Our conclusion is further reinforced by examination of the language and legislative history of § 703(j) of Title VII.[5] Opponents of Title VII raised two related arguments against the bill. First, they argued that the Act would be interpreted to *require* employers with racially imbalanced work forces to grant preferential treatment to racial minorities in order to integrate. Second, they argued that employers with racially imbalanced work forces would grant preferential treatment to racial minorities, even if not required to do so by the Act. See 110 Cong.Rec. 8618–8619 (remarks of Sen. Sparkman). Had Congress meant to prohibit all race-conscious affirmative action, as respondent urges, it easily could have answered both objections by providing that Title VII would not require or *permit* racially preferential integration efforts. But Congress did not choose such a course. Rather Congress added § 703(j) which addresses only the first objection. The section provides that nothing contained in Title VII "shall be interpreted to *require* any employer * * * to grant preferential treatment * * * to any group because of the race * * * of such * * * group on account of" a defacto racial imbalance in the employ-

5. Section 703(j) of Title VII, 42 U.S.C.A. § 2000e–2(j), provides:

> "Nothing contained in this subchapter shall be interpreted to require any employer, employment agency, labor organization, or joint labor-management committee subject to this subchapter to grant preferential treatment to any individual or to any group because of the race, color, religion, sex, national origin of such individual or group on account of an imbalance which may exist with respect to the total number or percentage of persons of any race, color, religion, sex, or national origin employed by any employer, referred or classified for employment by any employment agency or labor organization, admitted to membership or classified by any labor organization, or admitted to, or employed in, any apprenticeship or other training program, in comparison with the total number or percentage of persons of such race, color, religion, sex, or national origin in any community, State, section, or other area, or in the available work force in any community, State, section, or other area."

er's work force. The section does *not* state that "nothing in Title VII shall be interpreted to *permit*" voluntary affirmative efforts to correct racial imbalances. The natural inference is that Congress chose not to forbid all voluntary race-conscious affirmative action.

* * * In view of this legislative history and in view of Congress' desire to avoid undue federal regulation of private businesses, use of the word "require" rather than the phrase "require or permit" in § 703(j) fortifies the conclusion that Congress did not intend to limit traditional business freedom to such a degree as to prohibit all voluntary, race-conscious affirmative action.

We therefore hold that Title VII's prohibition in § 703(a) and (d) against racial discrimination does not condemn all private, voluntary, race-conscious affirmative action plans.

We need not today define in detail the line of demarcation between permissible and impermissible affirmative action plans. It suffices to hold that the challenged Kaiser-USWA affirmative action plan falls on the permissible side of the line. The purposes of the plan mirror those of the statute. Both were designed to break down old patterns of racial segregation and hierarchy. Both were structured to "open employment opportunities for Negroes in occupations which have been traditionally closed to them."

At the same time the plan does not unnecessarily trammel the interests of the white employees. The plan does not require the discharge of white workers and their replacement with new black hires. Nor does the plan create an absolute bar to the advancement of white employees; half of those trained in the program will be white. Moreover, the plan is a temporary measure; it is not intended to maintain racial balance, but simply to eliminate a manifest racial imbalance. Preferential selection of craft trainees at the Gramercy plant will end as soon as the percentage of black skilled craft workers in the Gramercy plant approximates the percentage of blacks in the local labor force.

We conclude, therefore, that the adoption of the Kaiser-USWA plan for the Gramercy plant falls within the area of discretion left by Title VII to the private sector voluntarily to adopt affirmative action plans designed to eliminate conspicuous racial imbalance in traditionally segregated job categories. Accordingly, the judgment of the Court of Appeals for the Fifth Circuit is

Reversed.

The beer is made by the aseptic brewing process which requires refrigerated marketing.

ADOLPH COORS CO. v. FEDERAL TRADE COMMISSION

United States Court of Appeals,
Tenth Circuit, 1974.
497 F.2d 1178.

BARRETT, Circuit Judge

Adolph Coors Company appeals an Order to Cease and Desist issued by the Federal Trade Commission. The FTC filed a complaint alleging that Coors was engaged in anticompetitive practices in violation of Section 5 of the Federal Trade Commission Act.[1] An Initial Decision was issued by the Administrative Law Judge after hearings were conducted in Denver extending over a period of thirty days. The Law Judge found that Coors had not violated the Act. He recommended that the complaint be dismissed. The FTC appealed the Initial Decision to the

1. Section 5 of the Federal Trade Commission Act, 15 U.S.C.A. § 45, provides in part:

(a)(1) Unfair methods of competition in commerce, and unfair or deceptive acts or practices in commerce, are declared unlawful.

* * *

(6) The Commission is empowered and directed to prevent persons, partnerships, or corporations, * * * from using unfair methods of competition in commerce and unfair or deceptive acts or practices in commerce.

five-member Federal Trade Commission. The Commission substituted its findings for those of the Law Judge and found, as a matter of Law, that Coors had violated Section 5 of the Act.

Adolph Coors Company, a Colorado corporation, is engaged in brewing, distribution and sale of beer, using the trade name of "Coors." Coors has one brewery in Golden, Colorado, and distributes its beer in an eleven-state area. The beer is sold to the distributors who in turn sell to retailers. While Coors is the fourth largest beer brewer in the United States, it alone among the nation's some 70 brewers is a "shipping" brewery, i.e., Coors ships all of the beer brewed at its single "regional" brewing plant at Golden, Colorado, F.O.B. to the various distributors in Arizona, California, Colorado, Idaho, Kansas, Nevada, New Mexico, Oklahoma, Texas (some counties only), Utah and Wyoming. In 1971 the average barrel of Coors beer traveled 961 miles to its market place.

The beer is made by the aseptic brewing process which requires refrigerated marketing. It is uncontroverted that Coors beer is substantially more expensive than any other beer consumed in the United States, and yet because of its popularity, Coors has climbed from the 49th largest brewery in 1948 to its number 4 position today. Coors maintains market leadership in total sales against all competitors except in its territory served in Texas. Because of the delicacy of the product, it is essential that the refrigeration controls and expeditious marketing techniques be strictly monitored. Once the beer is delivered to the distributors, this obligation is assumed by them under an agreement with Coors. It is the distributor who is required to protect the "integrity" of the Coors beer quality by guarding against a retailer's failure to rotate the beer, and failure to insure proper refrigerated storage. Coors beer retained over 90 days must be destroyed.

Coors has 35 area representatives to help market the product. Each representative is assigned certain distributors to work with and to see that Coors' Policy Manual is followed. The price Coors charges to its distributors is set by Coors. Coors suggests to its distributors and retailers the price at which to sell its beer.

Each distributor is assigned a territory in which to market Coors' products. Coors may reduce the territory or add distributors to a particular territory. There are 166 independent distributors and one wholly owned subsidiary company.

In 1964 Coors eliminated sales to central warehouse accounts. Central warehouse accounts are either retailers such as large chain supermarkets who buy for redelivery to their own outlets, or independents who purchase for redelivery to nonaffiliated retail outlets or retailer warehouses.

Coors favors draught accounts. It has a draught policy in which tavern owners are given 30 days to discontinue handling other brands of light draught beer. If the owner-retailer continues to sell another brand of light draught beer, Coors discontinues its supply of light draught beer to the tavern.

The contract between Coors and the distributors enables Coors to cancel its contract for any breach by the distributor, with a five-day notice. Either Coors or the distributor may cancel the contract without cause with a 30-day notice.

Coors contends that: (1) it did not engage in wholesale or retail price fixing; (2) its vertically imposed territories are reasonable and legal; (3) it has no policy of requiring exclusive draught accounts; (4) it has the right to protect its quality product and not distribute its beer through central warehousing; (5) its contract termination rights are reasonable and legal. * * *

Coors contends that it did not engage in price fixing agreements with its distributors. Its practices are set out in the Coors Policy Manual which states as follows.

> In order to maintain a successful wholesale or retail business, pricing integrity is essential. Pricing integrity will result in an adequate and equitable profit to both Distributor and retailer and is fair to the ultimate consumer.

> It is the policy of the Adolph Coors Company to suggest, if it so chooses, to either the wholesaler or retailer level, suggested minimum pricing. We reserve the right to further that policy by simply refusing to deal with anyone who doesn't adhere to said policy.
>
> The Adolph Coors Company and its agents must only state the policy. They cannot make agreements, threaten, coerce, or intimidate wholesalers or retailers in any manner. They can enforce the policy only by reserving the right to refuse to deal with those who don't adhere to the suggested prices.

Coors' sales manager, Harvey Gorman, testified that the product is controlled by agreeing individually with each distributor. This policy is enforced by a provision in the contract between Coors and the distributor enabling Coors to terminate a distributorship in 30 days without cause. Since there are about 7,000 applicants for distributorships, any distributor who does not conform to Coors' pricing policies could readily be replaced. Coors' area representatives constantly obtain wholesale price information and send the information to the home office in Golden. The area representatives also resolve any conflicts between the prices proposed by a distributor and those suggested by Coors.

John Hemphill, a former Coors distributor, testified that he would only go so far in making a request to use his own prices, knowing that Coors could terminate him in 30 days. He also testified that a Coors' area representative told him that the best thing for him to do is not to be a distributor if he could not agree to Coors' policies on pricing and territories. * * *

Jay Wagnon, a Coors' distributor, testified that Coors insisted on controlling distributor price increases and that when he refused to adopt wholesale prices suggested by the Coors' area representative he was summoned to Golden and requested to change his prices. He stated that Coors' personnel told him to bring his prices in line with Coors' recommendations or they could put another distributor in his area. He testified that he was afraid; that he had been threatened; and that he therefore conformed to the suggested prices. * * *

Jay Thurman, a former distributor, testified that he was given pricing sheets by the area representative which were to be followed. He was told that if the prices were changed, it would go through Mr. Straight, a Coors official, who, in turn, would determine if the changes were justified.

Peter Tinetti, a former distributor, testified that Coors sent him the prices at which to sell Coors beer.

The area representatives submitted reports to the Golden headquarters about agreements or understandings they had made with distributors on wholesale prices.

Price fixing is illegal *per se* under the Sherman Antitrust Act. Price fixing is also illegal *per se* under Section 5 of the Federal Trade Commission Act. Prices are fixed when they are agreed upon. The agreement to fix prices renders the conspiracy illegal. The agreement may be inferred or implied from the acts and conduct of the parties, as well as from surrounding circumstances.

> * * * [T]he test * * * is whether the agreement, or conduct, interferes with the freedom of sellers or traders in such a manner as to prohibit or restrain their ability to sell in accordance with their own judgment, and not what particular effect the agreement or conduct, has on the actual prices.

* * *

There is substantial evidence from the record as a whole to support the Commission's findings of price fixing agreements between Coors and its distributors.

Coors also challenges the Commission's finding that Coors has a resale price maintenance program and that it has in some cases secured adherence to its suggested retail prices by unlawful means. There is substantial evidence to support the Commission's finding.

Coors' policy is to establish pricing integrity which means that a certain profit is allowed on each level of resale. Pricing integrity is not possible with price discounting. Coors implements pricing integrity by refusing to deal with anyone not adhering to its price suggestions. A Coors' area representative threatened to refuse further sales to an offending retailer unless he would adhere to the prices suggested by Coors. Coors used its distributors to secure retailers' adherence to suggested minimum prices. One area representative reported that a retailer was cut off by a distributor because the retailer was advertising Coors beer at cut prices. Another area representative reported that a distributor planned to take appropriate action against a retailer who refused to sell at suggested prices. A distributor reported that Coors beer was not delivered to a retailer who cut prices. An area representative reported that action would be taken against a retailer who refused to raise his prices to a profit level.

Mr. Letcher, a retailer, testified that he was selling Coors at special weekend prices and that he was warned by the Coors distributor to discontinue the practice. Letcher refused to cooperate and the distributor terminated deliveries to his store. The distributor told Letcher that deliveries would be received if he would agree not to discount the beer, and that Letcher might lose the retail account if he continued to discount the beer. Letcher was also told by the distributor that Coors does not tolerate price cutting. Letcher sold his business. The distributor resumed deliveries to the new owners who agreed not to discount the beer. The distributor did not act independently in cutting off Letcher as Coors suggests, but cut him off in accordance with Coors' pricing policies.

United States Supreme Court decisions hold that if a manufacturer advances beyond a simple refusal to deal and takes affirmative action to secure compliance with its prices, a combination in violation of Section 1 of the Sherman Antitrust Act and Section 5 of the Federal Trade Commission Act occurs. Any trespass on the independence of a reseller or wholesaler to set his own prices is a violation of the Sherman Act. A seller may refuse to deal with one failing to adhere to its specified prices, but where a concerted effort is used to interfere with the distributors' pricing independence and to compel them to adhere to suggested prices, there is a violation of the Sherman Antitrust Act. A manufacturer may choose those to whom it will sell to as long as its conduct has no monopolistic purposes.

The Commission found that:

> * * * [Coors] has pursued a policy of fixing, controlling and maintaining prices at which Coors beer is sold at both the wholesale and retail level, that in furtherance of this policy it has engaged in various acts and practices such as: suggested resale prices to both distributors and retailers, checking prices at which distributors and retailers sell Coors beer, advising distributors and retailers that it is contrary to Coors pricing policy for them to deviate from prices approved by respondent, threatening to terminate distributorships and threatening to force distributors to sell their businesses for refusing to adhere to suggested retail prices, entering into agreements and understandings with distributors as to the wholesale prices which the distributors will charge for Coors beer, joining with distributors in attempting to coerce retailers to refrain from selling Coors beer at prices below those approved by respondent, encouraging distributors to prevent retail price cutting by refusing to deliver Coors beer to price cutters, or to reduce the amount of beer delivered, and entering into agreements and understandings with retailers as to the retail prices or range of prices at which such retailers will sell Coors beer.

There is substantial evidence in the record to support the Commission's findings.

II.

Coors alleges that its vertically imposed territories are reasonable and legal. The Commission held that Coors vigorously enforces its territorial restrictions and that it has engaged in unlawful price fixing which is:

> * * * [S]trong grounds for presuming that the most injurious effects of vertical territori-

al divisions may be operative, and, therefore, for holding the entire arrangement of territories with price fixing illegal per se.

The Coors' distributor contract provides, in part, as follows:

> While this agreement is in effect the Distributor will conduct the business of wholesale distribution of Coors Beer in the above territory only. * * *

In United States v. Arnold, Schwinn & Co., 388 U.S. 365, 87 S.Ct. 1856, 18 L.Ed.2d 1249 (1967), the United States brought an antitrust action against Arnold, Schwinn & Co., an association of Schwinn distributors and a Schwinn distributor, seeking a declaratory judgment to invalidate the distribution franchising system of its products. Schwinn bicycles are shipped directly to franchised retailers who agree to sell only to ultimate consumers. Schwinn also distributed its bicycles to franchised distributors who agreed not to resell to anyone outside their assigned territories. The Court held that:

> Under the Sherman Act, it is unreasonable without more for a manufacturer to seek to restrict and confine areas or persons with whom an article may be traded after the manufacturer has parted with dominion over it. Such restraints are so obviously destructive of competition that their mere existence is enough. If the manufacturer parts with dominion over his product or transfers risk of loss to another, he may not reserve control over its destiny or the conditions of its resale.

The rule of law in *Schwinn* is clear and unequivocal.

> Once the manufacturer has parted with title and risk, he has parted with dominion over the product, and his effort thereafter to restrict territory or persons to whom the product may be transferred—whether by explicit agreement or by silent combination or understanding with his vendee—is a *per se* violation of § 1 of the Sherman Act.

Coors, a manufacturer, enters into an agreement with its distributors to distribute Coors beer in the assigned territory only. Coors maintains that the territorial restrictions are necessary to retain the quality and proper refrigerated handling of its beer, and that the territorial restrictions are legal. However, since Coors parts with title and risk to the product when it sells and delivers the beer to distributors, and thus has parted with dominion over the product, its further effort to restrict the territories or persons to whom the product can be transferred is a *per se* violation of Section 1 of the Sherman Act and Section 5 of the Federal Trade Commission Act. Coors may still condition its sales to distributors and others upon maintenance of procedures necessary to control the quality of the product.

Although we are compelled to follow the *Schwinn per se* rule rendering Coors' territorial restrictions on resale illegal *per se*, we believe that the *per se* rule should yield to situations where a unique product requires territorial restrictions to remain in business. For example, speed of delivery, quality control of the product, refrigerated delivery, and condition of the Coors product at the time of delivery may justify restraints on trade that would be unreasonable when applied to marketing standardized products. Perhaps the Supreme Court may see the wisdom of grafting an exception to the *per se* rule when a product is unique and where the manufacturer can justify its territorial restraints under the rule of reason.

The dissenters in *Schwinn* contended that the new *per se* rule cannot be justified, automatically invalidating vertical restraints in a distribution system based on sales to wholesalers and retailers.

> * * * [T]he Court has, *sua sponte* created a bluntly indiscriminate and destructive weapon which can be used to dismantle a vast variety of distributional systems—competitive and anticompetitive, reasonable and unreasonable.

Thus we are foreclosed from considering the reasonableness of the restriction or its business justification. We are cognizant of the unpredictability which is created in relationship to the Coors operation. [The Supreme Court did change the Schwinn *per se* rule in the case of Continental T.V. Inc. v. GTE Sylvania, Inc., 433 U.S. 36, 97 S.Ct. 2549, 53 L.Ed.2d 568 (1977).]

Coors contends that it has no policy of requiring exclusive draught accounts. The Commission found that Coors combined with its distributors in the practice of encouraging and coercing retailers to sell Coors draught beer to the exclusion of light draught beer competitors in violation of Section 5 of the Federal Trade Commission Act.

Mr. Coors testified that exclusive draught accounts were desirable. Several distributors testified that the purpose of obtaining exclusive draught accounts is to encourage draught customers to buy beer to take home. To implement the policy, Coors threatened to terminate a retailer's supply of Coors draught beer unless he eliminated competitive draught beers within 30 days. Coors' distributors did, in fact, take out their Coors draught beer if the retailer did not comply with the policy.

The policy of pursuing an exclusive draught policy violates Section 5 of the Federal Trade Commission Act. There is substantial evidence in the record to support the Commission's finding.

Coors asserts that it has the right to protect its quality product and not distribute its beer through central warehousing. The Commission held that Coors' prohibition of central warehouse sales, or a requirement that wholesale prices to those accounts equal those to other retailers is a substantial restraint on the capacity of the distributor to resell to whomever he chooses and threatens the same anticompetitive results as other illegal restraints on alienation. Therefore, the Commission found that the practices are unfair methods of competition in violation of Section 5 of the Federal Trade Commission Act.

The central warehouse method of distribution involves purchase by the warehouser of beer from the brewer or the distributor. The beer is delivered by the retailer to its outlets. This method of distribution could cut the price of the beer to the retailer and consumer. Coors eliminated sales to central warehouse accounts in 1964. The distributors viewed central warehousing as a threat to the integrity of their territorial restrictions. Coors alleges that sales to central warehousers affects the quality of its beer because of poor procedures used by the warehousers.

The Order imposed by the FTC does not prevent Coors' distributors from conditioning its sales to central warehouse accounts on the maintenance of procedures necessary to the quality control of its products. The Order only enjoins Coors from requiring its distributors from refusing to sell to central warehouse accounts. The restriction by Coors, limiting those with whom the distributors may deal, amounts to a restriction on resale and violates the mandates of *Schwinn* and the Federal Trade Commission Act. There is substantial evidence in the record to support the FTC's finding.

Coors alleges that its contract termination rights are reasonable and legal and that its conduct in the rare instances of its use has been proper and legal in every respect. The Commission held that:

> Whether or not any actual terminations of Coors distributors, or sales forced by threat of termination can be ascribed entirely, solely and unambiguously to the failure of the terminated or coerced distributor to participate in an antitrust violation, it is abundantly clear from the record in this case that Coors representatives have used the explicit or implicit threat of speedy termination in often successful efforts to force the acquiescence of its distributors in anti-competitive behavior.

The Coors distributor contract provides in part as follows:

> This agreement and any supplements now or hereafter effective (whether fixing prices and terms to the Distributor, or otherwise) may be cancelled in entirety at any time by the Company for any breach by the Distributor on five (5) days' written notice to the Distributor. This agreement and such supplements may be cancelled in entirety by either party without cause upon the giving of notice to

that effect to the other party, in which event termination shall become effective thirty (30) days after delivery or the mailing of the written notice of cancellation, whichever first occurs. * * *

The Commission held that Coors used the threat of speedy termination to force its distributors into anticompetitive behavior. There is substantial evidence in the record to support the Commission's holding.

Coors has the right to terminate distributors according to the contract provisions which the distributors have agreed to. However, it may not use the contract termination provisions to force its distributors into anticompetitive behavior.

[Affirmed.]

Some proof of its accuracy.

NATIONAL LABOR RELATIONS BOARD v. TRUITT MANUFACTURING CO.

Supreme Court of the United States, 1956.
351 U.S. 149, 76 S.Ct. 753, 100 L.Ed. 1027.

Mr. Justice BLACK delivered the opinion of the Court.

The National Labor Relations Act makes it an unfair labor practice for an employer to refuse to bargain in good faith with the representative of his employees.

The question presented by this case is whether the National Labor Relations Board may find that an employer has not bargained in good faith where the employer claims it cannot afford to pay higher wages but refuses requests to produce information substantiating its claim.

The dispute here arose when a union representing certain of respondent's employees asked for a wage increase of 10 cents per hour. The company answered that it could not afford to pay such an increase, it was undercapitalized, had never paid dividends, and that an increase of more than $2^1/_2$ cents per hour would put it out of business. The union asked the company to produce some evidence substantiating these statements, requesting permission to have a certified public accountant examine the company's books, financial data, etc. This request being denied, the union asked that the company submit "full and complete information with respect to its financial standing and profits," insisting that such information was pertinent and essential for the employees to determine whether or not they should continue to press their demand for a wage increase. * * * The company refused all the requests. * * *

On the basis of these facts the National Labor Relations Board found that the company had "failed to bargain in good faith with respect to wages in violation of Section 8(a)(5) of the Act." * * * The Board ordered the company to supply the union with such information as would "substantiate the Respondent's position of its economic inability to pay the requested wage increase." * * *

* * *

We think that in determining whether the obligation of good-faith bargaining has been met the Board has a right to consider an employer's refusal to give information about its financial status. While Congress did not compel agreement between employers and bargaining representatives, it did require collective bargaining in the hope that agreements would result. Section 204(a)(1) of the Act admonishes both employers and employees to "exert every reasonable effort to make and maintain agreements concerning rates of pay, hours, and working conditions * * *." In their effort to reach an agreement here both the union and the company treated the company's ability to pay increased wages as highly relevant. The ability of an employer to increase wages without injury to his business is a commonly considered factor in wage negotiations. Claims for increased wages have sometimes been abandoned because of an employer's unsatisfactory business condition; employees have even voted to accept wage decreases because of such conditions.

Good-faith bargaining necessarily requires that claims made by either bargainer should be honest claims. This is true about an asserted inability to pay an increase in wages. If such an argument is important enough to present in the give and take of bargaining, it is important enough to require some sort of proof of its accuracy. And it would certainly not be farfetched for a trier of fact to reach the conclusion that bargaining lacks good faith when an employer mechanically repeats a claim of inability to pay without making the slightest effort to substantiate the claim. * * * We agree with the Board that a refusal to attempt to substantiate a claim of inability to pay increased wages may support a finding of a failure to bargain in good faith.

The Board concluded that under the facts and circumstances of this case the respondent was guilty of an unfair labor practice in failing to bargain in good faith. * * *

[We affirm the Board's decision.]

Is the promise of "permanent employment" only an argument that "this is war" and essentially meaningless?

BELKNAP, INC. v. HALE

Supreme Court of the United States, 1983.
— U.S. —, 103 S.Ct. 3172, 77 L.Ed.2d 798.

Justice WHITE delivered the opinion of the Court.

The federal labor relations laws recognize both economic strikes and strikes to protest unfair labor practices. Where employees have engaged in an economic strike, the employer may hire permanent replacements whom it need not discharge even if the strikers offer to return to work unconditionally. If the work stoppage is an unfair labor practice strike, the employer must discharge any replacements in order to accommodate returning strikers. In this case we must decide whether the National Labor Relations Act (the NLRA or the Act) preempts a misrepresentation and breach-of-contract action against the employer brought in state court by strike replacements who were displaced by reinstated strikers after having been offered and accepted jobs on a permanent basis and assured they would not be fired to accommodate returning strikers.

Petitioner Belknap, Inc., is a corporation engaged in the sale of hardware products and certain building materials. A bargaining unit consisting of all of Belknap's warehouse and maintenance employees selected International Brotherhood of Teamsters Local No. 89 (Union) as their collective bargaining representative. In 1975, the Union and Belknap entered into an agreement which was to expire on January 31, 1978. The two opened negotiations for a new contract shortly before the expiration of the 1975 agreement, but reached an impasse. On February 1, 1978, approximately 400 Belknap employees represented by Local 89 went out on strike. Belknap then granted a wage increase, effective February 1, for union employees who stayed on the job.

Shortly after the strike began, Belknap placed an advertisement in a local newspaper seeking applicants to "permanently replace striking warehouse and maintenance employees." [1] A large number of people responded to the offer and were hired. After each replacement was hired, Belknap presented to the replacement the following statement for his signature:

> "I, the undersigned, acknowledge and agree that I as of this date have been employed by

1. The advertisement said:

PERMANENT EMPLOYEES WANTED
BELKNAP, INC.

OPENINGS AVAILABLE FOR QUALIFIED PERSONS LOOKING FOR EMPLOYMENT TO PERMANENTLY REPLACE STRIKING WAREHOUSE AND MAINTENANCE EMPLOYEES.

> Belknap, Inc. at its Louisville, Kentucky, facility as a regular full time permanent replacement to permanently replace ______ in the job classification of ________."

On March 7, Local 89 filed unfair labor practice charges against petitioner Belknap. The charge was based on the unilateral wage increase granted by Belknap. Belknap countered with charges of its own. On April 4, the company distributed a letter which said, in relevant part:

> TO ALL PERMANENT REPLACEMENT EMPLOYEES
>
> * * *
>
> We recognize that many of you continue to be concerned about your status as an employee. The company's position on this matter has not changed nor do we expect it to change. You will continue to be permanent replacement employees so long as you conduct yourselves in accordance with the policies and practices that are in effect here at Belknap.
>
> * * *
>
> We continue to meet and negotiate in good faith with the Union. It is our hope and desire that a mutually acceptable agreement can be reached in the near future. However, we have made it clear to the Union that we have no intention of getting rid of the permanent replacement employees just in order to provide jobs for the replaced strikers if and when the Union calls off the strike.

On April 27, the Regional Director issued a complaint against Belknap, asserting that the unilateral increase violated §§ 8(a)(1), 8(a)(3), and 8(a)(5) of the Act.[2] Three days later, on April 7, the company again addressed the strike replacements:

> We want to make it perfectly clear, once again, that there will be no change in your employment status as a result of the charge by the National Labor Relations Board, which has been reported in this week's newspapers.
>
> We do not believe there is any substance to the charge and we feel confident we can prove in the court's satisfaction that our intent and actions are completely within the law.

A hearing on the unfair labor practice charges was scheduled for July 19. The Regional Director convened a settlement conference shortly before the hearing was to take place. He explained that if a strike settlement could be reached, he would agree to the withdrawal and dismissal of the unfair labor practice charges and complaints against both the Company and the Union. During these discussions the parties made various concessions, leaving one major issue unresolved, the recall of the striking workers. The parties finally agreed that the Company would, at a minimum, reinstate 35 strikers per week. The settlement agreement was then reduced to writing. Petitioner laid off the replacements, including the twelve respondents, in order to make room for the returning strikers.

Respondents sued Belknap in the Jefferson County, Kentucky, Circuit Court for misrepresentation and breach of contract. Belknap, they alleged, had proclaimed that it was hiring permanent employees, knowing both that the assertion was false and that respondents would detrimentally rely on it. The alternative claim was that Belknap was liable for breaching its contracts with respondents by firing them as a result of its agreement with Local 89. Each respondent asked for $250,000 in compensatory damages, and an equal amount in punitive damages.

Belknap, after unsuccessfully seeking to remove the suit to federal court, moved for

2. Section 8(a) of the National Labor Relations Act, 29 U.S.C. § 158(a) provides, in relevant part:

> (a) It shall be an unfair labor practice for an employer
> (1) to interfere with, restrain, or coerce employees in the exercise of the rights guaranteed in section 157 of this title; . . .
> (3) by discrimination in regard to hire or tenure of employment or any term or condition of employment to encourage or discourage membership in any labor organization; . . .
> (5) to refuse to bargain collectively with the representatives of his employees, subject to the provisions of section 159(a) of this title.

summary judgment, on the ground that respondents' causes of action were preempted by the NLRA. The trial court agreed and granted summary judgment. The Kentucky Court of Appeals reversed. The court first concluded that preemption was inappropriate because Belknap's alleged activities were not unfair labor practices. Belknap's action was not prohibited by 29 U.S.C. § 158(a)(3), which makes unlawful discrimination in personnel decisions for the purpose of encouraging or discouraging membership in a particular union, since plaintiffs did not seek membership in any labor organization. Relying on *Linn* v. *Plant Guard Workers*, 383 U.S. 53, 86 S.Ct. 657, 15 L.Ed.2d 582 (1966), the court also concluded that the suit was not preempted because the contract and misrepresentation claims were of only peripheral concern to the NLRA and were deeply rooted in local law.

We granted Belknap's petition for certiorari, 457 U.S. 1131, 102 S.Ct. 2956, 73 L.Ed. 2d 1347 (1982). We affirm.

* * *

It is asserted that Congress intended the respective conduct of the Union and Belknap during the strike beginning on February 1 " 'to be controlled by the free play of economic forces' ", *Machinists* v. *Wisconsin Employment Relations Commission*, *supra*, at 140, quoting *NLRB* v. *Nash-Finch*, 404 U.S. 138, 144, 92 S.Ct. 373, 377, 30 L.Ed.2d 328 (1971), and that entertaining the action against Belknap was an impermissible attempt by the Kentucky courts to regulate and burden one of the employer's primary weapons during an economic strike, that is, the right to hire permanent replacements. To permit the suit filed in this case to proceed would upset the delicate balance of forces established by the federal law. Subjecting the employer to costly suits for damages under state law for entering into settlements calling for the return of strikers would also conflict with the federal labor policy favoring the settlement of labor disputes. These arguments, it is urged, are valid whether or not a strike is an economic strike.

We are unpersuaded. It is true that the federal law permits, but does not require, the employer to hire replacements during a stike, replacements that it need not discharge in order to reinstate strikers if it hires the replacements on a "permanent" basis within the meaning of the federal labor law. But when an employer attempts to exercise this very privilege by promising the replacements that they will not be discharged to make room for returning strikers, it surely does not follow that the employer's otherwise valid promises of permanent employment are nullified by federal law and its otherwise actionable misrepresentations may not be pursued. We find unacceptable the notion that the federal law on the one hand insists on promises of permanent employment if the employer anticipates keeping the replacements in preference to returning strikers, but on the other hand forecloses damage suits for the employer's breach of these very promises. Even more mystifying is the suggestion that the federal law shields the employer from damages suits for misrepresentations that are made during the process of securing permanent replacements and are actionable under state law.

Arguments that entertaining suits by innocent third parties for breach of contract or for misrepresentation will "burden" the employer's right to hire permanent replacements are no more than arguments that "this is war", that "anything goes", and that promises of permanent employment that under federal law the employer is free to keep, if it so chooses, are essentially meaningless. It is one thing to hold that the federal law intended to leave the employer and the union free to use their economic weapons against one another, but is quite another to hold that either the employer or the union is also free to injure innocent third parties without regard to the normal rules of law governing those relationships. We cannot agree * * * that Congress intended such a lawless regime.

The argument that entertaining suits like this will interfere with the asserted policy of the federal law favoring settlement of labor disputes fares no better. This is just another way of asserting that the employer need not answer for its repeated assurances of permanent employment or for its otherwise actionable misrepresentations to secure permanent replacements. We do not think that the normal contractual rights and other usual legal interests of the replacements can be so easily disposed of by broad-brush assertions that no legal rights may accrue to them during a strike because the federal law has privileged the "permanent" hiring of replacements and encourages settlement.

In defense of this position, Belknap, * * * urges that permitting the state suit where employers may, after the beginning of a strike, either be ordered to reinstate strikers or find it advisable to sign agreements providing for reinstatement of strikers, will deter employers from making permanent offers of employment or at the very least force them to condition their offer by stating the circumstances under which replacements must be fired. This would considerably weaken the employer's position during the strike, it is said, because without assuring permanent employment, it would be difficult to secure sufficient replacements to keep the business operating. Indeed, as the Board interprets the law, the employer must reinstate strikers at the conclusion of even a purely economic strike unless it has hired "permanent" replacements, that is, hired in a manner that would "show that the men [and women] who replaced the strikers were regarded by themselves and the [employer] as having received their jobs on a permanent basis."

We remain unconvinced. If serious detriment will result to the employer from conditioning offers so as to avoid a breach of contract if the employer is forced by Board order to reinstate strikers or if the employer settles on terms requiring such reinstatement, much the same result would follow from Belknap's and the Board's construction of the Act. Their view is that, as a matter of federal law, an employer may terminate replacements, without liability to them, in the event of settlement or Board decision that the strike is an unfair labor practice strike. Any offer of permanent employment to replacements is thus necessarily conditional and nonpermanent. This view of the law would inevitably become widely known and would deter honest employers from making promises that they know they are not legally obligated to keep. Also, many putative replacements would know that the proffered job is, in important respects, nonpermanent and may not accept employment for that reason. It is doubtful, with respect to the employer's ability to hire, that there would be a substantial difference between the effect of the Board's preferred rule and a rule that would subject the employer to damages liability unless it suitably conditions its offers of employment made to replacements.

Belknap counters that conditioning offers in such manner will render replacements non-permanent employees subject to discharge to make way for strikers at the conclusion or settlement of a purely economic strike, which would not be the case if replacements had been hired on a "permanent" basis as the Board now understands that term. The balance of power would thus be distorted if the employer is forced to condition its offers for its own protection. Under Belknap's submission, however, which is to some extent supported by the Board, Belknap's promises, although in form assuring permanent employment, would as a matter of law be non-permanent to the same extent as they would be if expressly conditioned on the eventuality of settlement requiring reinstatement of strikers and on its obligation to reinstate unfair labor practice strikers. As we have said, we cannot believe that Congress determined that the employer must be free to deceive by promising permanent employment knowing tht it may choose to reinstate strikers or may be forced to do so by the Board.

* * * The Board suggests that such a conditional offer "might" render the replacements only temporary hires that the employ-

er would be required to discharge at the conclusion of a purely economic strike. But the permanent-hiring requirement is designed to protect the strikers, who retain their employee status and are entitled to reinstatement unless they have been permanently replaced. That protection is unnecessary if the employer is ordered to reinstate them because of the commission of unfair labor practices. It is also meaningless if the employer settles with the union and agrees to reinstate strikers. But the protection is of great moment if the employer is not found guilty of unfair practices, does not settle with the union, or settles without a promise to reinstate. In that eventuality, the employer, although he has prevailed in the strike, may refuse reinstatement only if he has hired replacements on a permanent basis. If he has promised to keep the replacements on in such a situation, discharging them to make way for selected strikers whom he deems more experienced or more efficient would breach his contract with the replacements. Those contracts, it seems to us, create a sufficiently permanent arrangement to permit the prevailing employer to abide by its promises.

We perceive no substantial impact on the availability of settlement of economic or unfair labor practice strikes if the employer is careful to protect itself against suits like this in the course of contracting with strike replacements. Its risk of liability if it discharges replacements pursuant to a settlement or to a Board order would then be minimal. We fail to understand why in such circumstances the employer would be any less willing to settle the strike than it would be under the regime proposed by Belknap and the Board, which as a matter of law, would permit it to settle without liability for misrepresentation or for breach of contract.

Belknap and its supporters, the Board and the AFL–CIO, offer no substantial case authority for the proposition that the *Machinists* rationale forecloses this suit. Surely *Machinists* did not deal with solemn promises of permanent employment, made to innocent replacements, that the employer was free to make and keep under federal law. *J.I. Case, Co.* v. *NLRB*, 321 U.S. 332 (1944), suggests that individual contracts of employment must give way to otherwise valid provisions of the collective bargaining contract, but it was careful to say that the Board "has no power to adjudicate the validity or effect of such contracts except as to their effect on matters within its jurisdiction". There, the cease-and-desist order, as modified, stated that the discontinuance of the individual contracts was "without prejudice to the assertion of any legal rights the employee may have acquired under such contract or to any defenses thereto by the employer."

* * *

The complaint issued by the Regional Director alleged that on or about February 1, Belknap unilaterally put into effect a 50¢-per-hour wage increase, that such action constituted unfair labor practices under §§ 8(a)(1), 8(a)(3) and 8(a)(5), and that the strike was prolonged by these violations. If these allegations could have been sustained, the strike would have been an unfair labor practice strike almost from the very start. From that time forward, Belknap's advertised offers of permanent employment to replacements would arguably have been unfair labor practices since they could be viewed as threats to refuse to reinstate unfair labor practice strikers. Furthermore, if the strike had been an unfair labor practice strike, Belknap would have been forced to reinstate the strikers rather than keep replacements on the job. Belknap submits that its offers of permanent employment to respondents were therefore arguably unfair labor practices, the adjudication of which were within the exclusive jurisdiction of the Board, and that discharging respondents to make way for strikers was protected activity since it was no more than the federal law required in the event the unfair labor practices were proved.

Respondents do not dispute that it was the Board's exclusive business to determine, one, whether Belknap's unilateral wage increase was an unfair labor practice, which would have converted the strike into an unfair labor practice strike that required the reinstatement of strikers, and, two, whether Belknap also committed unfair labor practices by offering permanent employment to respondents. They submit, however, that under our cases, properly read, their actions for fraud and breach of contract, are not preempted. We agree with respondents.

Under *Garmon*, a state may regulate conduct that is of only peripheral concern to the Act or which is so deeply rooted in local law that the courts should not assume that Congress intended to preempt the application of state law. In *Linn* v. *Plant Guard Workers*, 383 U.S. 53, 86 S.Ct. 657, 15 L.Ed. 2d 582 (1966), we held that false and malicious statements in the course of a labor dispute were actionable under state law if injurious to reputation, even though such statements were in themselves unfair labor practices adjudicable by the Board. Likewise, in *Farmer* v. *Carpenters*, 430 U.S. 290, 97 S.Ct. 1056, 51 L.Ed.2d 338 (1977), we held that the Act did not preempt a state action for intentionally inflicting emotional distress, even though a major part of the cause of action consisted of conduct that was arguably an unfair labor practice. Finally, in *Sears, Roebuck & Co.* v. *Carpenters*, 436 U.S. 180, 98 S.Ct. 1745, 56 L.Ed.2d 209 (1978), we held that a state trespass action was permissible and not preempted, since the action concerned only the location of the picketing while the arguable unfair labor practice would focus on the object of the picketing. In that case, we emphasized that a critical inquiry in applying the *Garmon* rules, where the conduct at issue in the state litigation is said to be arguably prohibited by the Act and hence within the exclusive jurisdiction of the NLRB, is whether the controvery presented to the state court is identical with that which could be presented to the Board. There the state court and Board controversies could not fairly be called identical. This is also the case here.

* * * The strikers cannot secure reinstatement, or indeed any relief, by suing for misrepresentation in state court. The state courts in no way offer them an alternative forum for obtaining relief that the Board can provide. The same was true in *Sears* and *Farmers*. Hence, it appears to us that maintaining the misrepresentation action would not interfere with the Board's determination of matters within its jurisdiction and that such an action is of no more than peripheral concern to the Board and the federal law. At the same time, Kentucky surely has a substantial interest in protecting its citizens from misrepresentations that have caused them grievous harm. It is no less true here than it was in *Linn* v. *Plant Guard Workers*, *supra*, at 63, 86 S.Ct., 663 that "[t]he injury" remedied by the state law "has no relevance to the Board's function" and that "[t]he Board can award no damages, impose no penalty, or give any other relief" to the plaintiffs in this case. The state interests involved in this case clearly outweigh any possible interference with the Board's function that may result from permitting the action for misrepresentation to proceed.

Neither can we accept the assertion that the breach of contract claim is preempted. The claimed breach is the discharge of respondents to make way for strikers, an action allegedly contrary to promises that were binding under state law. As we have said, respondents do not deny that had the strike been adjudicated an unfair labor practice strike Belknap would have been required to reinstate the strikers, an obligation that the state could not negate. But respondents do assert that such an adjudication has not been made, that Belknap prevented such an adjudication by settling with the Union and voluntarily agreeing to reinstate strikers, and that, in any event, the reinstatement of strikers, even if ordered by the Board, would only prevent the specific performance of Belknap's promises to respondents, not immunize Belknap from responding in damages from its breach of its otherwise enforceable contracts.

For the most part, we agree with respondents. We have already concluded that the federal law does not expressly or impliedly privilege an employer, as part of a settlement with a union, to discharge replacements in breach of its promises of permanent employment. Also, even had there been no settlement and the Board had ordered reinstatement of what it held to be unfair labor practice strikers, the suit for damages for breach of contract could still be maintained without in any way prejudicing the jurisdiction of the Board or the interest of the federal law in insuring the replacement of strikers. The interests of the Board and the NLRA, on the one hand, and the interest of the state in providing a remedy to its citizens for breach of contract, on the other, are "discrete" concerns. We see no basis for holding that permitting the contract cause of action will conflict with the rights of either the strikers or the employer or would frustrate any policy of the federal labor laws.

* * *

[T]he decision of the Kentucky Court of Appeals is

Affirmed.

"Ma Bell is a cheap mother."

SOUTHWESTERN BELL TELEPHONE CO.

200 NLRB No. 101, Case No. 14–CA–6595,
Samuel M. Singer,
Administrative Law Judge, 1972.

Before MILLER, KENNEDY and PENELLO.

Judge's Findings and Conclusions

A telephone company was charged with violating Section 8(a)(1) and (3) of the Act by directing employees to leave its premises unless they ceased displaying sweatshirts containing a slogan that the employer deemed objectionable.

It is stipulated that, during discussions toward a new bargaining agreement, employees appeared at work wearing sweatshirts with the slogan, "Ma Bell is a Cheap Mother." It is further stipulated that the slogan is capable of more than a single interpretation, with one of those meanings being considered obscene, derisive and insulting. Even some employees complained that the shirts were vulgar and in poor taste.

The employees wearing the shirts were directed to leave unless they removed the shirts or somehow covered up the slogans. All of the shirt-wearers chose to leave. The company did not pay them for the time they lost. The company told workers and the union that the men were not suspended, but could return to work whenever they satisfied the directive.

The union did not encourage, but neither did it discourage the wearing of the shirts. The union sponsored and distributed other insignia such as "big potato" buttons and automobile stickers. It did approve "Cheap Mother" bumper stickers. The company never prohibited the wearing of union insignia or slogans of any kind other than the "Cheap Mother" slogan. It did not object to the "big potato" buttons. No employee was ever previously disciplined for union activity. The employer has encouraged employees to wear sweatshirts with company slogans.

Section 7 of the Act guarantees to employees the right to engage in concerted activities for the purpose of collective bargaining or other mutual aid or protection. The fact that the employees wore the shirts on the first day of contract negotiations clearly shows that their objective was to support the union's bargaining position. It is not material that the union did not sponsor the activity or that the sweatshirts did not name the union, since employees can act concertedly for their mutual aid or protection independently of a union.

However, some concerted activities may be so "indefensible" as to warrant the disciplining of participants. Although the display of union insignia at work is a valid form of concerted or union activity, considerations of plant production or discipline may justify restrictions on such activity.

It is acknowledged that the slogan had a double interpretation and that the word "mother" can be used in a derisive and insulting manner. Management officials thought the slogan vulgar and profane, and designed to taunt supervisors. In view of the controversial nature of the language and its susceptibility to a derisive and profane construction, management could legitimately ban the use of the "provocative" slogan as a reasonable precaution against discord and bitterness between employees and management, and to assure plant discipline. The subjective intent of the employees is not controlling.

The offensive language was worn on shirts to be exposed to employees and management for the entire working day. The fact that supervisors may occasionally use an obscene epithet to give vent to strong feelings does not legitimize such a continuous display. The company's directive was a reasonable and protected management prerogative. It did not matter that the order came before the actual disruption of discipline.

There is no merit to the contention that the slogan was privileged free speech. The protection of the Act is not co-extensive with the protection accorded citizens under the Constitution or other laws. The Act deals only with the employer-employee relationship. "Freedom of Speech" does not preclude an employer from prohibiting the distribution of defamatory and insulting statements that tend to disrupt discipline.

It is noted that the company has never been known as an antiunion employer, and that the employees were not discharged or disciplined for wearing the sweatshirts, except to the extent they lost wages for the hours they chose to be absent from the plant.

It is concluded that the employer did not violate either Section 8(a)(1) or (3) of the Act. The employer's request that the slogans be removed or covered up was unrelated to opposition to protected concerted activity.

Board's Decision

The Board has decided to affirm the rulings, findings, and conclusions of the Administrative Law Judge and to adopt his recommended order.

Review Questions

1. Is natural monopoly power always illegal? Is it possible for buyers to engage in illegal price fixing? Is the exchange of information by business competitors illegal per se? What is the difference between a vertical and horizontal restraint of trade? Is the announcing of "suggested retail prices" by manufacturers illegal? How about manufacturers' setting minimum or maximum prices for retailers? Is it a per se violation for a manufacturer to impose territorial or customer restrictions upon its dealers? What is required for a tying agreement to be per se illegal? What is the basic preference of the Celler Kefauver Act regarding business expansion? When must premerger notification be made to the FTC? When will the Department of Justice challenge mergers? How does the Robinson-Patman Act make buyer activity illegal? What are two defenses to Robinson-Patman violations? Explain your answers.

2. What is the most important element in defining the master-servant relationship? Is "hiring" necessary? How is the independent contractor different? How can you tell if one is an independent contractor or a servant?

What two theories justify the doctrine of respondeat superior? Does the doctrine make for good social policy? What does it mean to be "acting within the scope of employment"? What factors are taken into account in determining whether an employee was within the scope of employment? When will an employer be liable for an employee's crimes? Is an employer ever liable for injuries caused by the tortious acts of an independent contractor? Explain your answers.

3. Upon what economic principle does the law of Workers' Compensation rest? Is an injured worker covered by Workers' Compensation allowed to sue his or her employer? May he or she sue a third party who caused the injury? What is the difference between "course" of employment and "scope" of employment? Does the employer or employee pay unemployment taxes? What are the general requirements for eligibility for unemployment compensation benefits? Does it matter how a person became unemployed? Explain your answers.

4. Why is it difficult for "laissez-faire" to work? Why didn't the common law prevent monopoly? Against whom was the Sherman Act first used? Why has the Clayton Act been called "labor's Magna Carta"? What legal sanctions may be imposed under the Sherman Act? When is anticompetitive behavior illegal under the Clayton Act? May the FTC prohibit anticompetitive behavior even though it is not specifically prohibited by the Clayton Act? Is a "per se" or a "rule of reason" violation easier to prove? Explain your answers.

5. Which statute is the heart of labor law? What does it guarantee? Under what statute may the president stop a strike? Under what circumstances? What are the goals of labor law? What is the difference between a representative case and an unfair labor practice case? How does the National Labor Relations Board get an injunction to end an unfair labor practice? Can an employer completely ban employee union activity? Is picketing an unfair labor practice? Can an employer contribute financial support to a union? Do unions bargain only for union members? Must employers bargain with unions on all business subject matter? How is an existing collective bargaining agreement changed, and when can a strike be called? When are strikes illegal? Must strikers be hired back? May union officials use union funds to pay for their campaigns in union elections? Under what law and circumstances will the secretary of labor set aside a union election? Explain your answers.

6. What is the purpose of the Fair Labor Standards Act? Are there any exemptions to the Fair Labor Standards Act requirements? Is any employment permitted for persons aged fourteen to sixteen? How does the law protect against job discrimination on account of race, color, religion, sex, and national origin? What is the age where a person may be forced to retire? Are there exceptions where age may be used as a basis for ending employment? Upon what basis may discrimination in pay and other employment practices be permitted? Explain your answers.

7. What benefits are provided by social security? What social security taxes must be paid? Are there special rules for determining who is an employee for social security tax purposes? Are these "employees" ever considered independent contractors? Are partners or corporate officers considered employees for purposes of the social security tax or for income tax withholding? Are there differences in income tax deductions for employees versus independent contractors? Explain your answers.

8. Define the following terms: affirmative action, casual laborers, closed shop, collective bargaining, "disruptive" competitor, "featherbedding," intrabrand competition, monopsony, oppressive child labor, Pregnancy Disability Amendment, "relevant" market, respondeat superior, "scheduled" injuries, "secondary line" injury, the "unholy trio" of defenses, "wildcat" strike.

Problems

1. For several years, Clyde Markum has had an arrangement with Ralph Hoy whereby Ralph is to sell Clyde's fresh eggs and vegetables to local produce markets. Ralph uses his own truck to pick up the produce and make the deliveries; he is paid on a commission basis, and he works hard to solicit new customers. He does his job as he sees fit without direction from Clyde Markum. One day while Ralph is on his way to the Markum farm to pick up a truckload of eggs and vegetables, he carelessly runs his truck into a car driven by Libby Connors. Libby's car is damaged beyond repair, and Libby herself is seriously injured. Libby sues both Ralph Hoy and Clyde Markum for money damages for her injuries. Result? Explain.

Ralph Hoy is also injured in the accident and will be permanently disabled. Can Ralph recover under Workers' Compensation? Explain. Can Ralph recover unemployment compensation for any portion of the six-month period he spends in the hospital? Explain. Can he recover social security disability benefits? Explain. For purposes of social security law, is Ralph an employee or an independent contractor? Explain. Does his classification for social security purposes make a difference? Explain.

2. Erica Becker performs secretarial work (typing and filing) for Lawson Furniture Store. Erica works Monday through Friday from 8 A.M. to 5 P.M.; she is paid $225/week for her services. Erica's supervisor, Carol Landis, rates Erica as one of the best secretaries around. To improve her shorthand skills, Erica signs up for a nightclass at the local business college. She also joins the employee union, paying $10 a month in union dues. One day at work, Carol tells Erica to hand deliver an important written contract to Mrs. Ferguson who lives across town. Erica takes the company car, and, on her way to Mrs. Ferguson's, she negligently runs the car into Maurice Lambert, a young bicycle rider. After seeing Maurice off to the hospital, Erica delivers the contract to Mrs. Ferguson. Though it is only 3:30 P.M., Erica takes the company car and goes to visit her sister, Ginny. At 4:30 P.M., Erica leaves Ginny's house and starts home (Erica plans to return the company car the following day). Erica, however, is still a little shaken up from her earlier accident, and she negligently runs the company car into a parked truck belonging to Jerry Ellis.

a. Maurice Lambert sues both Erica Becker and Lawson Furniture for his injuries. Result? Explain.
b. Jerry Ellis sues both Erica and Lawson Furniture for the damage to his truck. Result? Explain.
c. Assuming Erica is injured in the first accident, can she recover from Lawson Furniture for her injuries under modern law? Under common law? Explain.
d. Assuming Erica is injured in the second accident, can she recover from Lawson Furniture for her injuries under modern law? Under common law? Explain.
e. Can Erica deduct the cost of the nightclass and the union dues from her gross income for purposes of federal income tax? Explain.

3. Lawson Furniture Company hires Richard Robel to come out to the office and repair the photocopy machine. The Company agrees to pay Richard, who makes a living out of repair work, $75 for his efforts. Richard arrives at the office with his own tools and sets to work on the machine. Before long, Anna Lawson, the owner of the Company, asks Richard if he will help load some furniture on the company truck. Richard agrees and follows the foreman's direction in loading the coffee tables, lamps, and other furniture items. While helping with the loading, Richard carelessly drops a heavy coffee table right on the foot of Mary Overmyer, a visitor to the Company. Mike Oliphant, a company employee, calls Richard a "stupid fool," and Richard socks him in the nose. Richard then apologizes and returns to repairing the photocopy machine. The machine is located on the second floor near an open railing. While working on the machine, Richard carelessly drops a heavy wrench on the head of Myra Parker, a business customer downstairs on the second floor. Myra was not aware that repair work was going on upstairs; she is seriously injured. The Lawson Company immediately fires Mike Oliphant and Richard Robel for causing trouble. It also fires sixty-year-old Simon Rider because his work production has fallen below company standards. And it hires Candy Harris because she is a female and there are more males than females working at the plant; Sam Johnson, who is just as qualified as Candy, complains when she is hired instead of him.

a. Mary Overmyer sues both Richard Robel and Lawson Furniture for damages for her injuries. Result? Explain.
b. Myra Parker sues both Richard Robel and Lawson Furniture for damages for her injuries. Result? Explain.
c. Can Mike Oliphant recover for injury to his nose from Lawson Furniture under modern law? Under common law? Explain.
d. Can Mike recover unemployment compensation until he finds another job? Can Richard Robel do so? Explain.
e. Simon Rider claims that he was the victim of age discrimination. A valid contention? Explain.
f. Sam Johnson claims that he was the victim of sex discrimination. A valid contention? Explain.

4. a. The employees of "Buy Smart" Grocery Stores decide to strike for higher wages. Their current contract is set to expire on June 1, so on May 15, the employees' union notifies Buy Smart in writing of their intention to strike for higher wages. The union offers to meet and confer with representatives of Buy Smart for the purpose of negotiating a new contract. On June 1, the employees' union has not yet reached an agreement with Buy Smart, so the employees go on strike. What are Buy Smart's legal rights, if any, against the employees? Assuming Buy Smart hires replacement workers during the strike, does it have to fire the replacements and allow the strikers to return when the strike is over? Explain.

   b. Suppose instead that the Buy Smart employees strike because of several threats made by management to discourage new employees from joining the union. A total of 500 workers walk off the job. They take turns picketing the Buy Smart Stores in a peaceable and orderly fashion. Assuming Buy Smart hires replacement workers during the strike, does it have to fire the replacements and allow the strikers to return when the strike is over? Explain. Would your answer differ if fifty of the striking employees had blocked the store entrances and exits during the strike and verbally and physically abused both Buy Smart customers and management? Explain.

   c. After the strike, it comes to light that Union President Dolores Fisher threatened several employees with physical harm unless they would agree to help picket the stores. It is also discovered that Dolores used union funds to finance her re-election campaign and that she has been using union monies for personal travel expenditures. What are the union members' rights, if any, against Dolores Fisher? What action, if any, would you advise them to take?

5. a. After comparing prices, products, and inventories with fellow textile manufacturers, Gina Roberts and Waldo Cunningham, Harriet Topper decides to raise her prices substantially. Gina and Waldo quickly follow suit. Legal? Explain. Does it matter to your answer whether or not the increase in price is a reasonable one? Explain. Suppose that after comparing the business information, Gina, Waldo, and Harriet agree to divide the textile market equally among themselves and sell their products at approximately the same prices. Again, is this legal? What issues are involved here?

   b. Textile manufacturer Gina Roberts deals primarily in cottons and synthetics. Gina agrees to supply retailer, Jim Humphries, with twenty-five bolts of Roberts's top quality cotton cloth only if Jim will also purchase 2,400 spools of Roberts's Grade A cotton thread. When Jim agrees, Gina also insists, as a part of the contract of sale, that Jim resell the cloth for no less than three dollars a yard and the thread for no less than three dollars per one dozen spools. Is Gina's contract with Jim a legal one? Explain.

   c. Textile manufacturer Harriet Topper is less than pleased when the Griggs Textile Company opens up and provides her with some pretty stiff competition. As Harriet, who has been in business for a number of years, has substantial savings to fall back on, she simply cuts her prices until the fledgling Griggs Company cannot compete financially and still remain in business. What rights, if any, does the owner of Griggs Textiles have against Harriet? What action is the Federal Trade Commission likely to take with regard to Harriet's activities? In your answer, assume, first, that Griggs Textiles has already been forced to shut down operations; and, second, that the Company is still in operation, but fading fast.

6. In 1979 Banner was one of thirty-eight retail Marco gasoline stations in greater Fort Wayne, Massachusetts, and one of eight such stations in its particular sales territory. The nearest competing Marco station was eleven blocks away. Banner's supplier, Marvel Company, was a major integrated refiner and distributor of petroleum products. Like other Marco stations in Fort Wayne, Banner purchases gasoline from Marvel at 94.1 cents per gallon and resold it at 98.9 cents per gallon.

In September of 1979 Best by Test Oil Company, operator of a chain of sixty-five retail gasoline stations, opened its only Best by Test station in Fort Wayne diagonally across the street from Banner and began selling its gasoline at 96.9 cents per gallon. Best by Test was exclusively a retailer and did not compete with Marvel. This differential of 2 cents per gallon between Banner's and Best by Test's retail prices was the normal differential between "major" and "nonmajor" brands of gasoline. Subsequently however, beginning in December, Best by Test from time to time reduced its price, sometimes to 91.9 cents or 90.9 cents per gallon, and on each occasion Banner's sales suffered. Banner sought assistance from Marvel to meet Best by Test's competition. After four months of watchful waiting, Marvel gave Banner a discount of 1.7 cents per gallon in April 1980 to permit the latter to reduce its retail price to 95.9 cents per gallon to counter a Best by Test retail price of 94.9 cents per gallon, later lowered to 93.9 cents per gallon. At this point, other Marco dealers, located within a three-and-one-half-mile radius of Banner, suffered substantial declines in sales; they had not received any discount from Marvel and had not reduced their retail prices. They observed some of their former customers buying gasoline from Banner. Those Marco retail stations which suffered losses as a result of Marvel's pricing policies have claimed a violation of federal antitrust law by Marvel and have brought legal action against it to recover damages.

Required: Answer the following, setting forth reasons for any conclusions stated.

a. Will the Marco retail stations which suffered losses prevail?

b. What probable defense will Marvel assert in order to avoid liability?

Source: CPA Exam, November 1980, #2.b.

7. Higgins Corporation sells coffee to chain stores and independent grocers. It offers two types of discounts. For the chain stores, Higgins offers a substantial flat discount regardless of volume purchased. For the independent grocers, Higgins grants only volume discounts, on a sliding-scale basis. Higgins received a cease and desist order from the Federal Trade Commission (FTC) and has retained Daniel Chapman, CPA, to assist Higgins in its defense. Basically, the FTC contends that Higgins's discount practices are in violation of the Robinson-Patman Act and thus must be enjoined. Higgins's management has decided not to plead possible defenses of "changed conditions" or "meeting competition" but rather focus exclusively on the "cost justification" defense. Chapman is concerned about the nature and effect of cost data he should obtain.

Required: Answer the following, setting forth reasons for any conclusions stated.

a. Discuss the key issues and problems faced in a cost justification defense.
b. Suppose instead that Higgins had sold coffee under its own brand name to independent grocers and under a private label to chain stores at a lower price. What ramifications, if any, would this have under a Robinson-Patman action?

Source: CPA Exam, May 1983, #3.a.

8. The United States Department of Justice has alleged that Variable Resources, Inc., the largest manufacturer and seller of variable speed drive motors, is a monopolist. It is seeking an injunction ordering divestiture by Variable of a significant portion of its manufacturing facilities. Variable denies it has monopolized the variable speed drive motor market. Which of the following statements is correct insofar as the government's action against Variable is concerned?

a. The government must prove that Variable is the sole source of a significant portion of the market.
b. In order to establish monopolization, the government must prove that Variable has at least 75 percent of the market.
c. If Variable has the power to control prices or exclude competition, it has monopoly power.
d. As long as Variable has not been a party to a contract, combination, or conspiracy in restraint of trade, it can not be found to be guilty of monopolization.

Source: CPA Exam, May 1982, #1(27).

9. Which of the following regarding workers' compensation is correct?

a. A purpose of workers' compensation is for the employer to assume a definite liability in exchange for the employee's giving up his common law rights.
b. It applies to workers engaged in or affecting interstate commerce only.
c. It is optional in most jurisdictions.
d. Once workers' compensation has been adopted by the employer, the amount of damages recoverable is based upon comparative negligence.

Source: CPA Exam, November 1982, #1(26).

10. Which of the following is a part of the social security law?

a. A self-employed person must contribute an annual amount which is less than the combined contributions of an employee and his or her employer.

b. Upon the death of an employee prior to his retirement, his estate is entitled to receive the amount attributable to his contributions as a death benefit.
c. Social security benefits must be fully funded and payments, current and future, must constitutionally come only from social security taxes.
d. Social security benefits are taxable as income when they exceed the individual's total contributions.

Source: CPA Exam, May 1983, #1(35).

8

It is generally recognized that property includes the right of acquisition, the right of dominion, the right of possession, the right of use and enjoyment, the right of exclusion, and the right of disposition.

73 Corpus Juris Secundum, 142

The Ownership of Property

WHAT IS PROPERTY?

The common law has traditionally recognized two types of individual rights—personal rights and property rights. The difference between the two is found in their transferability. If a right can be disposed of or transferred by gift, sale, or assignment, it is a property right. If a right cannot be disposed of but can be exercised only by the person possessing it (i.e., the owner cannot give it away or sell it to another), it is a personal right. Personal, nontransferable rights include such Bill of Rights protections as freedoms of religion, speech, press, and assembly. Civil rights are nontransferable and so are rights to vote, to marry, and to make a will.

Property or transferable rights, on the other hand, include real property rights and personal property rights. The term "real" refers to the earth; accordingly, real property rights are rights with respect to real estate (land and things permanently attached to land such as buildings and their fixtures).

An additional and important factor in distinguishing between real and personal property is the *time* involved. Unless an individual's interest in land can last forever or at least for the duration of the individual's lifetime, the interest is classified as personal property. This rule that any interest in land of potentially infinite or lifetime duration is real property and any other interest is personal property stems from early English common law; the rule was later adopted into the United States legal system.

Thus, at early English common law, a landowner who was wrongfully deprived of possession of his or her land could bring a legal action to regain possession only if he or she owned what was termed a "freehold estate" (i.e., an interest in land of potentially infinite or lifetime duration). An interest of potentially infinite duration was and is referred to legally as a "fee" interest. An interest of lifetime duration was and is referred to legally as a "life estate." The owner of a fee interest or life estate could bring a case in court called a "real action" to recover possession of the property. The owner of less than a freehold estate (e.g., the owner of a "leasehold" interest, i.e., an interest in land for a limited period—months, years, etc.) could bring only what was termed a "personal action" to recover money damages, not the property itself.

And that is where the terms "real property" and "real estate" have come from—from law defining real property as land interests of potentially infinite (fee interest) or lifetime (life estate) duration. All other property is personal property. For this reason, an interest in land that is limited to a term for years (a typical lease or rental agreement) is not real property but is called a "chattel real." It is a chattel interest in real property. This is not to say that, modernly, a person who is wrongfully deprived of possession of land that he or she has leased for a period of years cannot regain possession of the land in the courts—but only that historically he or she could not do so through a real action. However, it is still correct to classify interests in land that are less than fee or life estate interests as personal property.

WHEN DO MINERALS, TREES, CROPS, AND THE LIKE CHANGE FROM REAL TO PERSONAL PROPERTY?

The Uniform Commercial Code provides the definition of goods at section 2–105:

> "Goods" means all things (including specially manufactured goods) which are movable at the time of identification to the contract for sale. "Goods" also includes the unborn young of animals and growing crops and other identified things attached to realty as described in the section on goods to be severed from realty (Section 2–107).

As a result of the UCC definition, "goods, which are always and without exception classified as personal property, include animals and their unborn young, growing crops, timber, and other things to be severed from land or realty.

The timing of when crops, timber, minerals, structures, and the like change from real estate to personal property is controlled by Section 2–107 of the UCC which says:

> A contract for the sale of minerals or the like (including oil or gas) or structure or its materials to be removed from realty is a contract for the sale of goods * * * *if they are to be severed by the seller.* * * *
>
> A contract for the sale apart from the land of growing crops or other things attached to realty and capable of severance without material harm thereto, but not described in subsection (1) or of timber to be cut is a contract for the sale of goods

* * * *whether the subject matter is to be severed by the buyer or by the seller* even though it forms part of the realty at the time of contracting.

WHAT IS THE LAW ON FIXTURES?

A fixture is an article, once personal property, that has become so closely connected to real property as to lose its status as a chattel and become a part of the land. The first and most important test in determining whether a particular item of personal property has become a fixture is the annexor's intent in having added the chattel to the realty. Did the annexor (person adding the property) intend to make a permanent improvement to the land? If he or she did, that intent will be controlling, and the chattel added to the property will be a legal fixture. It is not the annexor's secret or undisclosed intent that is considered, but rather the annexor's apparent intent as evidenced by his or her conduct and statements at the time of the annexation.

The only time the annexor's intent to make a permanent improvement will be disregarded is where the annexation is wrongful because the annexor does not own the chattel he or she adds to the real property. It is simply not fair to deprive the chattel owner of his or her personal property just because the annexor intended permanently and wrongfully to add the property to his or her (or another's) land. An exception to this rule arises where the chattel loses its identity by incorporation. For example, where a single stolen brick is built into a wall containing many hundreds of bricks, it would obviously be impossible to identify and recover the specfic stolen property. The stolen brick, in this case becomes the property of the landowner (under the laws of "accession" as explained later in this chapter).

Wrongful annexations aside, if the annexor's intent were discoverable in every situation, it would be an easy matter to determine whether a particular item of personal property had become a legal fixture when attached to the land. The annexor's intent, however, is not always readily apparent, and the courts must frequently look to other tests (tests that are said indirectly to prove intent) to make this determination.

The second test used by the courts to determine whether or not a chattel is a legal fixture is the manner in which the article is affixed to the real estate. If the article is so permanently attached to the land or a building on the land that it cannot be removed without causing substantial injury to the real property, it will be a fixture unless a contrary intent on the part of the annexor can be shown.

The third test of a legal fixture is the adaptability of the chattel to the real estate, particularly to the land's business use or other specifically intended purpose. Thus, an item installed in a building to carry out the purpose for which the building was constructed (e.g., a screen in a movie theater) will usually be considered a fixture.

Without regard to the three fixture tests it is the law that a tenant (a renter of land, buildings, or apartments) may remove any chattels he or she installs on leased premises regardless of whether the chattels are used in a trade or business. The tenant's only obligation is to repair or pay for any damage to the realty caused by the removal of the chattels. Where removal would result in irreparable damage to the real property, removal cannot be made.

WHAT DIFFERENCE DOES IT MAKE WHETHER SOMETHING IS CLASSIFIED AS REAL OR PERSONAL PROPERTY?

There are seven very practical reasons why it is important to determine whether an article is real property or personal property.

Sales and Other Transfers of Real Estate

Because fixtures are real, not personal property, they are included in any sale or other transfer of the realty. Thus, the classification of property as either chattel or fixture is crucial to determining whether or not the sale or transfer includes the built-in appliances, the air-conditioning system, the built-in stereo set, the TV antenna, the storm windows, the rugs, the hanging lamps, etc.

Eminent Domain Condemnation Proceedings

The Fifth Amendment of the United States Constitution states that property shall not be taken for public use without just compensation. Thus, in eminent domain or condemnation proceedings by the government, the government must reimburse the landlord for the reasonable value of his or her real property. Whether the government must pay the landlord the reasonable value of chattels affixed to the land or whether the landlord must remove the chattels as personal property depends upon the classification of the chattels as personal property or fixtures.

Creditors' Rights

A buyer purchasing chattels on credit may give a security interest to the seller of the chattel (called a "chattel mortgage" in the past, a security interest gives the security interest holder the right to repossess the chattel if the buyer gets behind in payments). If the chattel is later attached to realty so as to become a fixture, the rights of the security interest holder may be placed in jeopardy (assuming proper filings have not been made to protect the security interest—see Chapter 11). If the chattel is not a fixture, the seller's security interest is paramount.

The same kind of problem may result where a mortgage is placed on the real property, making the real estate subject to sale if the mortgage debt is not repaid. Whether chattels subsequently attached to the real estate are subject to sale in the event of a mortgage default will again depend on whether or not the chattels are classified as personal property or fixtures.

Taxation

Most states levy taxes on both real estate and personal property (although the personal property tax often applies only to business). The applicable tax rates will vary depending upon the classification of the property as either real property or personal property.

Distribution of Property at Death

Frequently, a decedent (dead person) will leave a will providing for distribution of his or her real property to one beneficiary and his or her personal property to another. The classification of the decedent's property interests as either real or personal property will thus substantially affect the survivors' interests.

Requirements for Transfer of Property

While certain formalities are required to transfer real estate, including the execution and delivery of a written document called a deed as described hereafter, personal property may be transferred without any formality whatsoever (e.g., it is possible to sell a TV set by merely delivering it to the buyer in exchange for cash).

In addition, the rule that an oral contract or agreement to buy or sell an interest in real property will not be enforceable in court unless it is evidenced by a written memorandum containing the essential terms of the agreement does not apply to contracts to buy or sell personal property unless the value of the personal property equals or exceeds $500 (see the later section in this chapter dealing with the Statute of Frauds).

Determination of Applicable Law

Real property is generally governed by the law of the location of the real estate without regard to where the real property owner resides. In contrast, personal property is controlled by the law of the owner's domicile (or residence) no matter where the personal property is located. Thus, if a person living in Oregon and owning property in Florida dies without a will, the laws of Florida will govern the distribution of any real estate located in Florida, while the laws of Oregon will govern the distribution of any personal property located there.

HOW IS A LANDLORD–TENANT RELATIONSHIP CREATED?

A landlord-tenant relationship arises only from what is termed a "lease." A "lease" is a binding agreement by a real property owner, called a landlord, to rent real property to a second party, called a tenant, coupled with a conveyance or transfer to the tenant of the right to exclusive possession of the property. A lease is thus both a contract (binding agreement) and a conveyance (transfer), and it is the ony method by which the landlord-tenant relationship may be created. Other legal concepts may involve the right to *use* real property, but they are not lease agreements because they do not result in the transfer of the right to exclusive possession. For example, a person who rents a hotel or motel room is not a tenant but is a licensee (the holder of a license). The brief period of use of the room, together with the high degree of control reserved by the hotel or motel management, indicates that a mere privilege to use the premises was intended rather than a transfer of the right to exclusive possession. Similarly, a lodger's contract for a room and board is not a lease but a mere license to use the room. And an employee who lives on his or her employer's premises as a condition of employment is a licensee and not a tenant.

In close cases where the intent of the parties is not clear, the courts will look at the following factors to determine whether a particular relationship is a lease or a license:

1. What the parties themselves call the agreement;
2. Whether the agreement calls for the payment of rent (indicates a lease);
3. Whether the agreement gives possession for a term (a definite period) or for an unlimited time (the former suggests a lease, the latter a license);
4. The specificity with which the real property is described (the more specific the description, the more likely a lease);
5. The limitations, if any, on the use of the real property (excessive limitation indicates a license).

The determination of whether the relationship is a lease or license is important because a tenant possesses legal rights far superior to those of a licensee. Not only is the tenant entitled to exclusive possession of the property (as opposed to mere use), but he or she has a right to notice prior to eviction unless the lease specifies a definite ending date. The licensee, on the other hand, has no right to notice. And, whereas the tenant can justifiably use reasonable force (called "self-help") to remove trespassers from the leased premises, the licensee must look to the licensor for their removal. Finally, a lease agreement is not affected by the landlord's conveyance (transfer) of the land to a third party, but a conveyance does serve to terminate a license.

While many lease agreements are put into writing as a matter of course, only lease agreements for periods greater than one year (in a few states, three years) have to be written in order to be enforceable.

The most common form of leasehold estate will be a "tenancy for years" or a "tenancy from period to period." A tenancy or estate for years is a tenancy that has a fixed or definite beginning and end at the time of creation of the tenancy. Thus, a tenancy created to last a specific number of days, weeks, months, or years is an estate for years. Because both parties know from the outset exactly when the tenancy will end, the tenancy terminates automatically without either party's giving notice.

A tenancy from period to period is an estate that continues from year to year, or from month to month, or for other successive fractions of a year until terminated by proper notice from either party. The beginning date of the tenancy as well as the period of the estate (i.e., yearly, monthly, weekly) are always certain—it is only the ending date that is unknown. Proper notice must always be given to terminate a periodic tenancy. In a month-to-month tenancy, written notice given thirty days in advance of the desired termination date is usually sufficient to terminate the tenancy and the thirty-day notice period can begin and end at any time. For a year to year tenancy, while some statutes require only a thirty-day notice given at any time, other statutes insist upon a sixty-day written notice prior to the end of the term.

CAN A LANDLORD LEGALLY REFUSE TO RENT TO SOMEONE?

The federal Fair Housing Act of 1968 prohibits a landlord from refusing to sell or rent to an individual on the basis of race, color, religion, or national origin. Most states also have statutes prohibiting discrimination on these grounds in the rental or sale of real property, and many states additionally outlaw discrimination on grounds of sex, age, handicap, or having children.

Along the same line, the Civil Rights Act of 1866 states: "All citizens of the United States shall have the same right, in every state and Territory, as is enjoyed by the white citizens thereof to inherit, purchase, lease, sell, hold, and convey real and personal property." In the 1968 case of Jones v. Mayer Co., 392 U.S. 409, 88 S.Ct. 2186, 20 L.Ed.2d 1189 (1968), the U.S. Supreme Court held that this Act of Congress bars all racial discrimination, private as well as public, in the sale or rental of property. An individual who has been discriminated against may complain to the Department of Housing and Urban Development which will investigate the complaint and try to eliminate the complained of conduct. The injured party may also go to federal court and obtain an injunction requiring the other party to stop discriminating. Or the injured party may simply petition the court for money damages from the wrongdoer in an amount to cover the actual loss suffered plus up to $1,000 in "punitive" damages (punitive damages are "penalty" damages that vary in amount according to the outrageousness of the wrongdoer's conduct). If the injured party cannot afford to hire an attorney, the court will appoint a lawyer to assist the party with his or her discrimination case.

WHAT ARE THE RIGHTS AND DUTIES OF LANDLORDS AND TENANTS?

The lease relationship creates certain rights and duties in both the landlord and tenant. A landlord, to begin with, has a duty to transfer possession to the tenant at the beginning of the tenancy. The landlord also has a duty to provide the tenant with quiet, uninterrupted possession and enjoyment of the real property during the period of the lease agreement. This is called the landlord's "covenant" or promise of quiet enjoyment. If during the term of the lease the landlord wrongfully evicts the tenant (or allows another to do so) from all or any portion of the real estate, the tenant is completely excused from paying rent until possession of the property is restored. If the landlord so seriously interferes with the tenant's use and enjoyment of the real estate that the tenant is forced to leave the property, the landlord is said to have made a *"constructive eviction,"* which, like a regular eviction, relieves the tenant of any further obligation to pay rent. Examples of constructive eviction by the landlord include turning off heat, electricity, or water; making excessive noise; permitting the building to become infested with rats; and failing to provide air conditioning in windowless buildings.

In addition to the landlord's covenant of quiet enjoyment is the landlord's "implied" covenant of habitability of the premises. Landlord-tenant law implies a promise on the part of the landlord that the premises are, at least initially, in a habitable (i.e., liveable) condition. The law recognizes that the tenant typically has little or no opportunity to inspect the premises and determine whether there are any defects in plumbing, heating, etc., before he or she takes possession of the property. "Habitability" is generally defined as meaning compliance with the local housing code. A housing code is a city, county, or state statute that establishes certain minimum standards to be met by dwellings intended for human occupancy, including specifics as to space requirements and essential facilities, e.g., bathroom, kitchen, utilities.

And while modern landlord-tenant law holds the tenant accountable for "affirmative" and "permissive" waste of the property ("affirmative" waste is a voluntary act on the part of the tenant that damages the premises, such as breaking down a door while "permissive" waste is a negligent failure to act on the part of the tenant which results in damage or decay to the property, such as carelessly leaving a window open durig a rainstorm, thereby ruining the wallpaper of the leased premises), the law imposes an affirmative duty of repair upon the landlord, generally extending the landlord's covenant of habitability throughout the period of the lease. Thus, it is up to the landlord to maintain the premsies in a "tenantable" condition that complies with the local housing code. Several states have additionally defined by statute "essential services" that the landlord must provide, including proper facilities for lighting, heating, water, etc.

Assuming the landlord fails to maintain the premises, can the tenant withhold payment of rent? Under the common law, the answer is no. At common law, the rights and duties of the landlord and tenant are said to be "independent" of each other; if the landlord or the tenant breaches a covenant (promise), the other party may not, in turn, breach a covenant but can only seek relief in court. The only exception, under the common law, was in the case of a breach of the covenant of quiet enjoyment, i.e., the wrongful eviction previously described.

However, to some extent, the rule of independent covenants has been changed by modern landlord-tenant statutes. For example, in many states, if the landlord fails to make needed repairs, the tenant has a legal right to withhold payment of the rent, placing it into a fund unavailable to the landlord until the repairs are made; use all or part of the rent to make the repairs, paying to the landlord only what is left; or petition the court to place the building in "receivership" and appoint a "receiver" to collect the rent and make the necessary repairs. To give force to these tenants' remedies, recent statutes and court holdings in many states prohibit a landlord from retaliating against a tenant who uses the remedies by giving the tenant notice of eviction. Prohibitions against retaliatory eviction are particularly important to the month-to-month tenant who, in the normal case, may be given thirty days' written notice at anytime for any reason.

Despite the landlord's responsibility for maintaining the leased premises in a habitable condition, the landlord is generally not liable for injury that occurs on the property to the tenant or the tenant's guests. One exception to this rule arises where the injury occurs as a result of a concealed dangerous condition (e.g., rotting floor) that the landlord knew about at the beginning of the tenancy and failed to disclose to the tenant. A landlord is also liable for injury to a tenant or tenant's guest resulting from the defective condition of "common areas" adjacent to the leased premises that remain under the landlord's control (e.g., elevators, stairways, or hallways in an apartment building).

Let us move now from landlord obligation and duties to the tenant's duty to pay rent. Every tenant shares this duty even where no express promise to pay rent can be found (in which case, the duty is to pay a "reasonable rental value"). Occasionally, premises rented for commercial or business use by the tenant will utilize what is termed a "percentage lease" in which the tenant pays not only a minimum monthly rent but also, at the end of the business year, a percentage of the tenant's gross receipts. Because the rent (which varies) is necessarily dependent on the success of the tenant's business, it is generally said that the tenant has a duty to use reasonable diligence to produce as many receipts as possible.

What are the landlord's rights if the tenant fails to pay his or her rent? At common law, the landlord had an unlimited right called the right of "distress" to enter the leased property and seize the tenant's chattels, holding them until the rent was paid (and, if necessary, selling them to collect the unpaid rent). Modernly, the right of "distress" has been strictly limited by statute in most states, and some states have altogether abolished it.

States that have abolished distress generally permit the landlord to remove the tenant's property from the leased premises only where the tenancy agreement has come to an end and it is necessary to clear out the dwelling unit in order to rent to a new tenant. The landlord, in this case, has a duty to store any chattels he or she removes from the premises and to give the tenant ample time and opportunity to claim them. If the tenant fails to claim the property in a reasonable time and the goods must ultimately be sold, the landlord is entitled to reasonable storage costs only—he or she cannot apply the proceeds of the sale against the tenant's unpaid rent. And any surplus proceeds after deduction for storage must be returned to the tenant. The landlord's sole remedy with regard to the unpaid rent is to sue the tenant in court for breach of the rental agreement.

The right of "distress" aside, can the landlord legally use force to retake possession of the leased premises from a tenant who is behind in his or her rent? In a majority of states, the answer is no, and a tenant ousted by force may generally sue to recover money damages and/or possession of the premises. Nearly every state, however, has enacted a summary (brief and informal) statutory procedure by which a landlord can legally evict a tenant in default on his or her rent. Called an "*unlawful detainer proceeding,*" this statutory procedure requires the landlord to give notice to the tenant that he or she must pay all rent due within a short period of time (typically three to ten days) or else the tenant must vacate the premises. If the tenant fails to pay the rent within the specified time and refuses to move, the landlord files suit in court asking for an order directing the tenant to give up possession of the property. The tenant then has up to five days' time in which to file an "answer" to the landlord, raising any applicable defenses to payment (such as use of the rent to make needed repairs). If the tenant fails to file an answer, any defenses raised must be proved in the courtroom hearing, or the tenant will lose there as well. Where the tenant loses either by default or decision, the landlord will receive a "writ of possession" from the court ordering the sheriff to direct the tenant to move and, if the tenant fails to move, physically to oust him or her from the property.

WHAT IF THE TENANT LEAVES THE LEASED PREMISES PRIOR TO THE END OF THE TERM?

Sometimes a tenant finds it necessary to leave the leased premises prior to the end of the term (e.g., where the tenant finds employment in another city or has to move for personal or family reasons). A *surrender* occurs where the tenant voluntarily gives up possession of the premises, and the landlord accepts possession with *intent* that the lease be terminated. The tenant in this case is excused from any further obligation under the lease agreement.

However, many times the landlord refuses to accept possession and terminate the agreement, and the tenant simply *abandons* the premises. Generally speaking, the landlord has two options in this situation. First, he or she may let the premises sit idle and sue the tenant for the rent as it falls due (the majority rule is that the landlord is not obligated to relet the premises). Or the landlord may retake possession of the premises, relet them, and hold the original tenant for the difference between the old rental and the new rental. Under the majority rule, the landlord's retaking of possession does not effect a surrender so long as the landlord notifies the tenant of his or her intention to relet the premises and to hold the tenant responsible for any deficit in rent. A minority of jurisdictions give the landlord a third option and allow him or her to sue at once for all rent due under the entire period of the lease (set off by the reasonable rental value of the premises for that period). These common law remedies have been codified by statute in a number of states.

WHAT ARE THE NEWEST TRENDS IN LANDLORD TENANT LAW?

The Uniform Residential Landlord Tenant Act (URLTA), a modern statutory breakthrough for tenants, has been adopted (although with some variation) in some thirteen states (including Alaska, Arizona, Delaware, Florida, Hawaii, Kansas, Kentucky, Nebraska, New Mexico, Ohio, Oregon, Virginia, and Washington), and several other state legislatures are likely to pass the Act in the near future. The URLTA includes the following important provisions:

1. An express warranty of habitability requiring the landlord to "comply with the requirements of applicable housing codes materially affecting health and safety." This means that the landlord must maintain the premises in a safe and habitable condition and provide essential services, including water, heat, electricity, etc.
2. A provision permitting the tenant to make minor repairs (after notice to the landlord who fails to make the repair) and deduct their cost from the next rental payment (generally up to $100 or one-half the monthly rent payment, whichever is greater). There is some variation from state to state with respect to the kinds of repairs that can be made, with some states limit-

ing repairs to utilities and essential services. Another common limitation is that repairs can be made only once every twelve-month period.

3. A provision abolishing the landlord's "distress" (seizing the tenant's personal property and "distraint" (locking the tenant behind in rent out of the real property). Where the landlord acts in disregard of the statute to seize the tenant's property or to lock the tenant out of the premises, the tenant may generally recover money damages in an amount three times his or her monthly rent, or treble damages (i.e., three times the actual loss suffered) plus attorney's fees. (But, remember, the landlord does have a legal right to "store" the goods of a tenant who has abandoned the leasehold premises.)

4. A provision prohibiting the landlord from taking retaliatory action against a tenant who attempts to organize other tenants, joins a tenants' union, or reports a housing code violation by the landlord. Retaliatory intent is presumed where landlord action (including raising rent, decreasing services, or evicting the tenant) follows the tenant activity within a certain period of time (usually six months). Up to that time, the burden is on the landlord to disprove retaliatory motives; after that time, the legal burden shifts and it is up to the tenant to prove retaliatory intent.

5. A provision limiting security deposits collected by the landlord to an amount no greater than one month's rent. Any deductions from the deposit must be fairly made and itemized in writing; all unclaimed amounts must be returned to the tenant within fourteen days of termination of the tenancy. If the landlord fails to comply with the URLTA provisions, the tenant may recover twice the amount of his or her rent money damages.

6. A provision prohibiting the landlord from turning off the utility services of a tenant in default on rent payments.

WHAT ARE THE WAYS TO ACQUIRE OWNERSHIP OF PERSONAL PROPERTY?

Ownership of personal property is most commonly acquired by purchase. The purchase and sale of goods is governed by the law of contracts and sales (see Chapter 11 for the specifics on the law of sales). The purchase and sale of corporate stock is strictly regulated by the federal Securities and Exchange Commission (as we have seen in Chapter 6). Drafts, notes, and checks are controlled by the law of negotiable instruments (Chapter 10).

There are several other ways (apart from purchase and sale) of acquiring ownership of personal property. For example, a person may acquire ownership of abandoned property or wild things (e.g., fish, birds, and other wild animals that belong to no one) simply by taking the property into legal possession. The finder of lost property may ultimately acquire title if the true owner cannot be located. And a person may obtain ownership of personal property by means of accession, confusion, gift, patent, or copyright law. In each of these situations an individual acquires ownership of personal property by means other than purchase.

Ownership of property (real or personal) is generally referred to as "title." And it is important to realize that title is not a written paper. It is a legal concept indicating ownership—that is, legally protected interest in property good as against the whole world. Ownership or title may be evidenced by a written "document of title" or "title certificate" (and usually is in the case of large items like cars, boats, and airplanes), but these papers are merely evidence of ownership and are not required. The owner of a book, a table, a lamp, or a TV set may possess nothing in writing to indicate ownership, but he or she will possess title (a legally protected interest in the property) nonetheless.

Title or ownership is important because it confers upon the owner of the property the exclusive right to use, possess, and dispose of the property. Disposition encompasses lifetime transfers as well as distribution to heirs and beneficiaries upon the owner's death.

Like title or ownership, "possession" is a legal term with a special meaning. To possess personal property legally, a person must: (1) intend to exercise control over the chattel and (2) phyiscally control the chattel to an appreciable extent (i.e., exercise a sufficient amount of physical control over the property). Both factors are essential to establishing legal possession. For example, a person who is unaware of the existence of a chattel within his or her physical control (e.g., a valuable ring in the pocket of an old coat) does not intend to possess the property and is not in legal possession of the chattel (the result would be contrary if the individual consciously intended to possess the contents of the coat's pocket, whatever they might be). And a person who picks up an article from the street or from a store counter (e.g., a necktie or a book), examines it, and ultimately discards it has *custody only* and not legal possession because there is neither intent to exercise control over the item nor sufficient physical control of the property. The same is true of an individual who tries on clothing to determine whether or not to buy.

Proof of possession—legal possession—is extremely important in cases involving the acquisition of title to wild things, abandoned property, and other property found on public and private premises.

Wild Things

In the vast majority of cases, possession alone will not establish ownership of property. But where wild animals (*ferae naturae*), as opposed to domestic animals (*domitae naturae*), are concerned, legal possession of the animals (including fish found in rivers, lakes, and oceans) will generally be sufficient to vest all title and ownership rights in the possessing party. Until wild things are taken into possession, they belong to no one. Once reduced to possession, it is essential that the law protect the possessor's exclusive use and enjoyment of the property by recognizing the possessor as the party with legal title. Of course, this is subject to statutory restrictions dealing with the licensing of hunters and fisherpeople and regulating seasons, bag limits, and fish and game conservation.

Also one must remember that legal possession demands sufficient physical control of the property coupled with an intent to control or possess it. This is not to say that actual physical control of a wild animal is always necessary to obtain title. While merely chasing a wild animal with intent to possess it will never constitute legal possession, no matter how close the pursuit may be, a hunter who is in fresh pursuit of a wild animal that he or she has mortally wounded is the legal owner of the animal despite the intervention of an outsider who completes the kill and captures the wild thing. The hunter's actual physical possession of the animal is close to inevitable, and there exists "sufficient" physical control to establish legal possession and ownership. Similarly, a party who confines a wild animal in an enclosed place under the party's private control and takes reasonable precautions to prevent the animal from escaping has exercised sufficient physical control (coupled with intent to control) to establish legal possession and ownership.

Suppose a wild animal that is reduced to possession escapes from its owner. Unless the animal has been tamed or domesticated to the point that it will eventually return to the place of its captivity, the animal reverts to its wild state and again belongs to no one. Thus, wild pigeons trained as homing pigeons remain the property of their owner though they fly freely far from the owner's land, while a red fox that escapes from its cage with no intention of returning reverts to nature and is wild once more. A single exception to the general rule arises where a formerly wild animal, not native to its place of captivity (e.g., an elephant housed in a private zoo in Anaheim, California), escapes from its owner-captor. Though the animal has no intention of returning to its place of captivity, the owner retains title and has superior rights to anyone who subsequently captures the animal.

Finally, it must be mentioned that a landowner has a common law right to any wild animals (including birds or fish) that are taken from his or her land by trespassers. Many landowners post "no hunting" and "no fishing" signs to help enforce this right.

Abandoned Property

A person who intentionally relinquishes ownership and possession of a chattel without placing title in someone else is said to "abandon" the personal property. (Real property, on the other hand, can never be abandoned.) The common law rule is that abandoned personal property belongs to no one, and the first person to take the property into legal possession (i.e., the first person to exercise sufficient physical control over the property with intent to acquire ownership) obtains legal title.

The common law rule has been changed by statute in some states, the statutes declaring that all abandoned property belongs to the state. Any person who finds abandoned property must report the discovery to the appropriate state agency. If it chooses, the agency may disclaim the state's interest in the abandoned property and award the property to the finder.

Acquiring title to personal property by taking possession of wild things or abandoned property is known in the law as acquiring title by *"occupation."*

Finders

Closely related to the subject of abandoned property is the law regarding finders of personal property.

Lost property Lost property differs from abandoned property in two ways. First, while abandoned property is intentionally and permanently given up by its owner, lost property is unintentionally and accidentally lost or left behind by its owner through carelessness, inadvertence, or neglect. The owner of lost property has no intention of relinquishing title or possession of the property—the owner simply has no idea where the property is. Second, whereas abandoned property belongs to the first person to take it into legal possession, lost property does not belong to the finder or person first to possess it; it continues to belong to the true owner.

Treasure trove Treasure trove, to be distinguished from both abandoned and lost property, is defined as coin or bullion (and, modernly, paper money) found buried in the ground. Treasure trove is not abandoned property because the owner who buried it had no intention of relinquishing his or her rights in the money or gold. And it is not lost property because there was nothing accidental about its burial in the soil—the owner intentionally hid the treasure in the ground, fully expecting to return for it at a later date but, for some unexplained reason, failing to return.

Modernly, unless a state by statute claims title to all or part of any treasure trove discovered within its boundaries (and several states do), the finder will obtain title and become the owner of the property.

Objects other than treasure trove found embedded in the soil are given, not to the finder of the property, but to the owner of the land, called the owner of the locus in quo. The property is given to the landowner rather than the finder because the property is considered to be a part of the soil itself. For example, in Allred v. Biegel, 240 Mo.App. 818, 219 S.W.2d 665 (1949), an ancient Indian canoe found embedded in the soil was awarded to the landowner, not the finder. It makes no difference whether the article was originally lost or abandoned (or mislaid as defined in the next section), if it is embedded in the soil and the true owner cannot be found, the owner of the locus in quo will acquire title. The article is classified as "part of the land."

Mislaid or Misplaced Property

Mislaid property is property that the owner has voluntarily and intentionally put down in a particular location, only to subsequently forget where he or she has placed the property. The property is not abandoned because the owner intends to reclaim it and it is not lost because the owner intentionally set it down. When mislaid property is found, the general rule is that the owner of the "locus in quo," i.e., the owner of the place where the chattel is found, possesses superior rights to the finder. The theory behind the rule is that once the true owner remembers where he or she mislaid the chattel, the true owner will return to that place in search of the mislaid property. If the owner of the "locus in quo" has possession of the property, the true owner will have little difficulty in locating his or her chattel. And if the true owner never returns to claim the property, the owner of the "locus in quo" (rather than the finder) is entitled to ownership for having cared for the property in anticipation of the true owner's return.

In cases where it is difficult to determine whether goods are lost or misplaced, the courts will carefully scrutinize the physical placement of the goods at the time of their discovery. For example, goods found on a table, in a drawer, under a mattress, or in a forgotten vault or other secret place indicate intentional placement by the owner and are more likely mislaid than lost. Goods found on the floor or on the ground, on the other hand, suggest an accidental separation from their owner and are probably lost rather than mislaid.

In all but a few states, lost property found on public or semipublic property goes to the finder rather than the owner of the locus in quo. The finder of the lost chattel has superior rights to all but the true owner (including the owner of the locus in quo) and will ultimately obtain title if the true owner cannot be located. For example an umbrella or other item of personal property lost and found in a restaurant or theater or on a bus or train will belong to the finder unless the true owner can be located to claim it. Oftentimes, and particularly where the item is left on a public conveyance, such as a bus or train, the property will be classified as mislaid rather than lost (if at all logically possible) in order to give the true owner every opportunity to return and collect his or her property from the owner of the locus in quo.

Where lost property is found not on public but on private property, the states are divided on whether the finder or the owner of the locus in quo has the superior rights.

Also, as a means of discouraging trespassing, it is generally held that a trespasser on real property has no rights, and this holds true for a trespassing finder. The owner of the locus in quo will always have the superior claim. Thus, a finder who is wrongfully present on the land at the time of making the discovery acquires no legal rights to possession or ownership of the property whether the chattel is abandoned, lost, mislaid, treasure trove, or property other than treasure trove embedded in the gound. The owner of the locus in quo and, in some cases, the state will always have a superior claim.

Where the finder is rightfully present on the land (as is the case with a social guest of the landlord, a business visitor, and any other person present on the property with the landowner's permission), the finder generally acquires rights to possession and title as outlined above. However, an exception arises where the finder also happens to be an employee of the landowner who finds the property during the course of employment and who either (1) has a duty to turn over to the employer any personal property found on the land; or (2) knows or should know as a reasonable person that the landowner intends to exercise control with respect to everything found on the real property. If these conditions are satisfied, the employer-landowner will always be entitled to possession of the chattel (and ultimately title if the true owner cannot be located) even in situations that would ordinarily place superior rights in the finder of the property (e.g., lost property on semipublic land). Of course, where the property is mislaid, rather than lost, the owner of the locus in quo will be entitled to possession over the finder in any case.

When does an employee have a duty to turn over to the employer-landowner any personal property found on the premises? An easy example is a hotel maid who discovers a watch while cleaning a rented hotel room. Another is a country club janitor who finds a club member's ring while cleaning out the swimming pool. In each case, the employee has a duty to turn the property over to the employer—the owner of the locus in quo—because the true owner is likely to look to the employer for return of the missing article.

When does an employer-landowner intend to exercise control over everything found on the premises? Generally, the existence of a contract duty on the part of the employer to care for property brought onto his or her business premises indicates such intent. For example, an employee of an owner-operator of a safe-deposit vault has good reason to know that his or her employer intends to exercise control over any property found on the premises. The employer has a contract duty to care for customers' property brought into the vault area, and customers who lose property will look to the employer for the property's return. Because of this, the employer (the owner of the locus in quo), and not the employee who discovers the property, has superior rights to possession and ultimately title. Another example is an owner-operator of a large deep freeze area containing many individual frozen food lockers. Again the employer has a contract duty to care for customers' property brought onto the business premises and if an employee finds a "lost" package of frozen meat on the floor of the deep freeze area, the employer is entitled to possession of the meat and ultimately title if the true owner cannot be found.

Statutes in many states require a finder of lost property (not including abandoned, mislaid, or treasure trove property) to report the discovery to the appropriate state official (usually the county clerk) within ten to fifteen days after making the discovery. The finder must also advertise the find by posting notices and/or placing ads in the county newspaper. If the true owner does not turn up to claim the property within six months to one year's time, the finder will acquire title to the lost property.

A finder who fails to follow the statutory procedure and simply keeps the lost property is generally liable, upon discovery, for twice the amount of the chattel's value (usually, the finder is required to reimburse the owner for the full value of the chattel and to pay a "penalty" of one-half the chattel's value to the owner and one-half to the county).

Before we move on to other methods of acquiring ownership of personal property, it is necessary to point out two other principles pertaining to finders of *lost* personal property.

1. A person who finds lost property has no legal obligation to take charge of the property. However, if the finder does take charge of the chattel, he or she has a duty to use reasonable care to preserve the chattel and to make reasonable efforts to locate the true owner. The finder holds the property as a *bailee* for the true owner. A bailment may be defined as the rightful possession of another's personal property. As will be explained in Chapter 11, a bailment which is not based on a contract (as in the finder situation) is called a "gratuitous" bailment. If the finder (the gratuitous bailee) fails to search for the true owner or fails to restore the chattel to the owner once the owner is located, the finder will be liable for conversion of the property.

2. A finder of lost property is not entitled to compensation for his or her services absent a statute providing for compensation or an offer of reward extended by the chattel owner. However, the finder is entitled to reimbursement from the owner for actual expenses incurred in protecting and preserving the property and in advertising to locate the owner. But the right of reimbursement does not confer a "possessory lien" upon the finder. If the owner refuses to reimburse the finder, the finder's sole remedy is to bring a legal action in court against the owner to recover money damages—the finder cannot retain possession of the property until the owner agrees to reimburse him or her nor can the finder sell the owner's property and collect reimbursement from the sales proceeds. A "lien," incidentally, is simply a claim or charge against real or personal property that secures the payment of a debt or other promised performance. A "possessory lien" is a claim or charge against property that is in the lienholder's possession, allowing the creditor to hold the property until the owner discharges the indebtedness owing.

Accession

Literally, *accession* means "something added." As a legal concept, accession refers to a means of acquiring ownership or title to personal property that is "added to" property already in existence. For example, (1) the owner of animals (including birds and fish) gains title to any offspring of the animals; (2) a person who plants and cultivates crops becomes the owner of the crops he or she harvests; (3) a person who contracts to have an article of personal property repaired becomes the owner of any materials added to the chattel during the course of the repair; and (4) a person who provides another with all the materials for manufacture of an article obtains title to the finished product.

Also, a person who innocently and mistakenly takes another's personal property and adds a very great deal of material and/or labor to it will generally acquire title to the property under the rules of accession. In determining whether the innocent wrongdoer has added sufficient parts and/or labor to justify a transfer of title, courts make use of the following two rules:

Loss of identity rule This is also called the doctrine of "specification." Ordinarily, title will pass to the innocent trespasser if the chattel has lost its original identity and has been converted into a new species (e.g., grapes changed into wine, wheat into flour, or clay into bricks).

Relative value rule Additionally, title will generally pass to the innocent trespasser when there is a great increase in the value of the chattel as a result of the accession. There is no generally accepted formula for measuring a "sufficient increase" in value (although several courts have held that an increase in the property's value by five or six times will be sufficient). The court simply determines whether it would work a tremendous hardship on the innocent trespasser or otherwise result in a gross injustice to permit the original owner to retain title to the property.

Where title automatically passes to the innocent trespasser, the owner's sole remedy is to sue the trespasser for conversion. The measure of damages (the amount the original owner can recover from the innocent trespasser or from a third person who has purchased the enhanced property from the innocent trespasser) will be the original value of the property *before* the addition of materials and/or labor.

With a willful wrongdoer, as opposed to the innocent trespasser, the general rule is that a willful trespasser who deliberately takes another's personal property and adds materials and/or labor to it cannot acquire title by accession even where there is a change in species of the property or a substantial increase in value of the chattel. The innocent party is entitled to return of his or her property along with any additions made by the willful trespasser. However, in most states, where the goods or materials of two different owners are added together or incorporated, title to the resulting product will go to the owner of the "principal thing" or chattel without regard to the parties' fault or wrongfulness. Generally, if the materials added by the trespasser increase the value of the innocent party's property by more than 50 percent, title will pass to the trespasser as owner of the principal thing (i.e., as owner of the most valuable property). For example, if a willful trespasser steals paint and uses it to paint his or her car, the trespasser will not lose the car but will acquire title to the paint added to the car. Of course, the owner of the paint will have the right to sue the trespasser for the value of the paint in a legal action for conversion, but the owner cannot demand return of the property (the paint) itself.

The most recent trend in the law is to recognize another exception to the general rule where the willful trespasser adds not primarily materials but labor to the innocent party's property to produce a chattel of much greater value. For example, a thief who paints a masterpiece upon a stolen canvas or carves a stolen block of wood into a valuable work of art may well obtain title to the finished product through the laws of accession.

There is no accession and no passage of title or ownership where materials attached to the primary chattel can be removed without causing significant harm to the chattel and without changing the original nature of the property.

If the personal property added to the primary chattel is subject to a security interest in a third party, accession will not operate to extinguish the third party's interest: the security interest will prevail even over the interest of the original owner under Section 9–314 of the Uniform Commercial Code.

Confusion

In a very few situations, title or ownership of personal property may be acquired by means of confusion. Confusion exists where goods owned by different parties are intermingled so that the property of each is no longer separable or distinguishable. Confusion is like accession in that it involves the contribution of distinct parts to a new integral; it is unlike accession in that there is an intermingling only. In accession, the goods of one party are either so changed by the labor of another as to form a new or more valuable chattel, or so physically united to the primary chattel as to become a constituent part of it. In confusion, the goods of each owner retain their original form and characteristics; it is only because of the circumstance of intermingling that each party's goods can no longer be identified, separated, and returned to their proper owners.

There is no confusion so long as each party's property can be identified and returned. Nor is there confusion resulting in a change of ownership where fungible goods are mixed together and the percentage of each party's contribution to the mass is known. "Fungible" goods are goods of the same quality and value, any one unit of which is the same as any other unit, which goods are customarily sold by weight and measure. Examples are grain, oil, or minerals of the same grade. So long as each party knows how much he or she has contributed to the mass, it makes no difference that different goods are in fact returned to each owner—all the goods are identical.

The only time legal confusion exists is where goods are indistinguishably intermixed by one of the owners, rendering the goods inseparable. Where the owner intermixes the goods inadvertently without any wrongful intent or willful purpose, no forfeiture will result if it is possible to determine the original values or quantities of the properties intermixed. Where this is impossible, the loss falls on the party who caused the intermixture, and that party loses title to his or her goods.

Where the owner willfully and wrongfully or fraudulently intermixes the goods so as to render them indistinguishable, the wrongdoer forfeits his or her goods entirely. The innocent party or parties acquire complete ownership or title to the goods and have no obligation to compensate the wrongdoer in any way.

For example, in one case, a logger who had borrowed a great deal of money from a sawmill operator had stored his unmarked and unbranded logs in a slough adjacent to the sawmiller's place of business. Fearing that the logger would not repay him, the sawmiller intentionally and wrongfully intermixed his own unbranded and unmarked logs with those of the logger and subsequently claimed title to them all. The court denied the sawmiller's claim and held that, since the number of logs each party owned could not be exactly (or even close to exactly) determined, the legal concept of confusion applied, and the logger acquired title to all the logs.

Gift

Defined legally, a gift is a voluntary transfer of ownership of property without consideration.

Inter vivos gift To make an effective inter vivos (i.e., lifetime) gift requires three things: (1) proper donative intent on the part of the donor or giftgiver; (2) legal delivery of the gift to the donee or recipient; and (3) proper acceptance of the gift by the donee.

To have the requisite donative intent the donor must have present mental capacity at the time of making the gift (i.e., he or she may not be incapacitated due to mental illness) and must intend to make an immediate, effective transfer of his or her property interest to the donee. The usual method of delivery is physical transfer of the chattel to the donee. But where appropriate, the donor can make a "constructive" delivery of the gift property by delivering to the donee the means by which the donee can gain control of the personal property (e.g., handing over the keys to a car or the passbook to a savings account). A written document, called a deed of gift, containing words of itent to make a present gift is sufficient without more to constitute a valid delivery of personal property.

Gift causa mortis A gift causa mortis is a conditional gift of personal property made by a person anticipating imminent death. The gift is conditional in that the donee who receives the gift will be entitled to keep the property only if the donor does in fact die as anticipated, the donee survives the donor, and the donor does not revoke the gift before he or she dies. Also, there must generally be an actual physical delivery of the property or a written deed of gift. Unlike an inter vivos gift, a gift causa mortis is always revocable by the donor who can revoke it at any time before he or she dies. And the gift is automatically revoked if the donor does not die from the illness or peril that prompted him or her to make the gift.

The concept of gift causa mortis applies to personal property only—not to real property. And this rule works both ways. For example, if a donor attempts to make a gift causa mortis out of the contents of a box containing, in addition to items of personal property, a deed to real property, the gift will not be valid as to the deed. And if the same donor executes and delivers the deed to the donee, intending the delivery to be a revocable gift causa mortis, the gift will not be revocable upon the owner's recovery but will constitute an effective inter vivos gift.

An effective gift causa mortis will prevail over a provision in the donor's will transferring the subject of the gift to a different person. Because of this, the law generally requires an actual physical delivery of the property or a written deed of gift (constructive delivery being insufficient). And while the gift causa mortis is automatically revoked if the donor does not die from the illness or peril that prompted him or her to make the gift, the fact that the donor recovers will not affect the rights of a third party who purchased the gift property from the donee in good faith without knowing that the gift was subject to revocation. The donee's sale of the goods to a bona fide purchaser cuts off the donor's ability to revoke the gift, and the donor probably has no further rights or recourse even against the donee.

Trademarks

You will also recall from Chapter 4 that the law provides protection against unauthorized appropriation of a trademark or trade name. The federal Lanham Act of 1946 defines a "trademark" as any "work, name, symbol, or device or any combination thereof adopted and used by a manufacturer or merchant to identify his goods and distinguish them from those manufactured or sold by others." Trade names, on the other hand, do not identify the goods themselves but, rather, relate to the business or business goodwill. A person may obtain an exclusive twenty year right to use a trademark by registering the mark with the U.S. Patent Office in Washington, D.C. The right is renewable indefinitely for additional twenty year periods so long as the mark is used in commerce. If the right is infringed, the owner may obtain a court-ordered injunction in addition to money damages (although damages will be permitted only where the owner's own use of the mark is accompanied by a statement that it is "registered in the U.S. Patent Office"). Trade names are generally protected as common law property rights or under state registration laws. Infringement may result in injunction and/or damages.

Patents

A patent may be granted for "any new and useful art, machine, manufacture, or composition of matter, or any new and useful improvement thereof." The Commissioner of Patents in Washington, D.C. issues the patent giving the patentee an exclusive right to make, use, and sell the invention for seventeen years. As you will recall from Chapter 4 dealing with business torts, anyone who infringes upon the patentee's right will be subject to court-ordered injunction and damages.

A patent cannot be granted for an idea only, and to obtain a patent, the following procedure must be strictly complied with:

1. The inventor must file a written application for a patent with the Commissioner of Patents in Washington, D.C.;
2. The application must contain:
   a. A written description of the invention or discovery;
   b. A precise specification of the part, improvement, or change that the inventor claims to be new;
   c. The applicant's affidavit (sworn statement) that he or she believes the invention or discovery to be new and never before known or used; and
   d. A copy of a drawing of the discovery (where a drawing is possible) or sample if the invention is a composition of matter.

Copyrights

The owner or author of literary, dramatic, musical, artistic, and other intellectual works may obtain federal statutory copyright protection for the work, i.e., the exclusive right to use, print, reprint, sell, copy, revise, transform, record, and perform the work publicly for the period of the author's life, plus an additional fifty years. However, the copyright statute also provides that even though the copyright owner has exclusive rights to use, sell, copy, etc., the copyrighted material, others are entitled to make "fair use" of the copyrighted work. Section 107 of the statute states: "a copyrighted work, including such use by reproduction in copies of phonorecords or by any other means specified by that section, for purposes such as criticism, comment, news reporting, teaching (including multiple copies for classroom use), scholarship, or research, is not an infringement of copyright." The statute also permits any library to make one copy of a copyrighted work without the copy's constituting an infringement of the copyright.

What may be copyrighted? Books, directories, periodicals, newspapers, lectures, sermons, dramatic or musical compositions, maps, works of art, motion pictures, etc. The only requirement is that the item be original. It does not have to be useful or novel or have literary merit or artistic value.

Anyone who infringes the author's statutory copyright is subject to a civil injunction and damages (including the author's lost profits by reason of the infringement). Statutory damages for willful infringement may be as high as $50,000 even though the infringer makes no profit. While an exact reproduction obviously infringes the right, so does extensive paraphrasing.

It is also a federal crime willfully to infringe upon a copyright for profit (one year in jail, $10,000 fine or both).

WHAT ARE THE CHARACTERISTICS OF THE FEE SIMPLE ESTATE?

The *fee simple absolute estate* is the maximum or greatest interest that anyone can have in land or real property. Modernly, the fee simple absolute is a possessory estate that has the potential of lasting forever. The owner of the fee simple absolute has five distinct powers with respect to the land. The owner may: (1) use the land as he or she sees fit; (2) abuse or destroy the property; (3) exclusively possess the land; (4) take the fruits (e.g., crops, minerals) of the property; and (5) freely alienate (i.e., transfer) the land. The right to freely transfer property has always been considered a fundamental right of real property in the United States.

To say that the fee simple absolute estate has the potential of lasting forever means that the estate can be passed on indefinitely through generations of the owner's descendants or devisees. If the owner dies "intestate" (without a will) without having previously sold the real property, the state laws of intestacy will determine which relatives or heirs will receive the property (see Chapter 13). The heirs may be lineal heirs (direct up and down relatives, such as children, grandchildren, parents, and grandparents), or collateral heirs (indirect side-by-side relatives, such as brothers and sisters, uncles, aunts, cousins, etc.). A person who dies "testate" (with a will) can leave the property to his or her heirs or to any other designated person. It is only when a person dies without heirs and without a will specifying another person to take the property that the fee simple absolute will come to an end and "escheat" (i.e., pass) to the state. Theoretically, therefore, the fee simple absolute estate can last forever.

Restrictions on the Fee Simple Absolute Estate

However, even the owner of a fee simple absolute estate is substantially restricted in what he or she can do with the property by the following:

Eminent domain Eminent domain refers to the right of government to take private property for public use by means of a "condemnation" proceeding. The Fifth Amendment of the U.S. Constitution provides that property shall not be taken for public use without payment of just compensation to the property owner.

Police power "Police power" refers to government's inherent authority to do whatever is deemed necessary to protect public health, welfare, and morals. Under the police power, government acts to restrict fee simple landowners in the following ways:

Zoning The purpose of zoning laws is to promote wholesome housing. Landowners may thus be prohibited from constructing apartment houses or buildings for commercial or industrial use in areas of single-family housing. A second purpose of zoning laws is to promote commerce and industry. Within commercial districts, for example, there may be zoned areas for local grocery stores or convenience shopping only or areas for light industry versus heavy industry.

Violation of criminal statutes It is illegal to use property in a manner that violates criminal law (e.g., using the premises for gambling or prostitution or failing to observe statutes and ordinances dealing with noise control, litter, naturally growing things, stagnant water, etc.).

Environmental regulations and statutes Every landowner must observe the increasingly strict federal and state regulations and statutes prohibiting contamination of the environment with air and water pollution and uncontrolled solid waste disposal (see Chapter 12).

Discrimination laws A landowner may not use or transfer his or her property so as to discriminate on grounds of race, color, religion, national origin, etc.

Tax laws The power to tax real estate is deemed an inherent right of all state governments. If a real estate owner fails to pay his or her real property taxes, the owner's property may be sold and the taxes collected out of the proceeds.

Laws protecting owners of adjoining property A landowner may not use his or her real property so as to create a nuisance to adjoining landowners. It may be a nuisance, for example, to burn rubbish in the backyard, play loud music, or keep barking dogs on the property. If so, the nuisance may be enjoined (i.e., stopped) by court order, and the injured landowner may be awarded money damages.

Creditors' rights A person who fails to pay his or her lawful debts may be sued in court, and a judgment (court order requiring the debtor to pay) may be rendered against the debtor. If the debtor refuses to pay the judgment, his or her property, including any real property held in fee simple absolute, may generally be sold to satisfy the debt. (However, as you will see in Chapter 11 dealing with creditors and bankruptcy, all states exempt or exclude from seizure and sale a portion of the debtor's property, including his or her equity or interest up to a certain amount in a homestead or residence owned in fee simple absolute.)

WHAT IS A LIFE ESTATE?

A life estate is an estate limited in duration to the lifetime or combined lifetimes of one or more designated individuals. Generally, the measuring life is that of the grantee. For example, a conveyance "to John Little for life" gives John Little a freely transferable interest in the property for as long as he lives; upon his death, the land will revert to the grantor. The grantor who conveys a life estate retains a "reversion," i.e., a future interest that will become possessory only upon the death of the measuring life, in this case John Little. Because the grantor presently holds the future interest, he or she is free to dispose of it during life or at death by will or intestacy. Once the measuring life comes to an end and the future interest becomes possessory, the grantor (or his or her heir or transferee) will receive possession of the land in fee simple absolute.

Where the life estate is measured by the life of someone other than the grantee, the estate is called a life estate "pur autre vie" (a French phrase, meaning "for the life of another"). Say that a grantor conveys land "to John Little for the life of Shirley Short." By the terms of the conveyance, John Little receives a life estate "pur autre vie" (i.e., for the life of Shirley) that will terminate upon the death of Shirley Short, the measuring life. As long as Shirley lives, John Little is free to use the property or transfer the interest; and if John dies before Shirley, the interest will pass on to John's heirs by will or intestacy.

Life estates are very popular estates modernly; they are created not only by deed or other inter vivos transfer but also by will. One spouse, for example, may write a will leaving a surviving spouse a life estate in property, with a remainder interest (a presently owned future interest that will become possessory upon the death of the surviving spouse) in fee simple to the children.

Like a reversion, a remainder is a future interest that becomes possessory after the expiration or termination of a lesser estate created by the same conveyance. Unlike a reversion, a remainder does not revert to the grantor, but *remains away* from the grantor and passes to another party or parties as specified in the original land grant. For example, if a grantor conveys land "to John Little for life, and then to Shirley Short," John Little receives a life estate, Shirley Short receives a remainder in fee simply absolute that will become possessory upon John Little's death, and the grantor retains no reversion interest whatsoever.

Both reversions and remainders are called future interests; they are presently owned interests in property that will not become possessory until a future date or time. Because the reversion or remainder interest is presently owned, it may be presently sold or otherwise transferred. In short, the only thing "future" about a future interest is possession of the property. The salability of the reversion or remainder interest may depend to some extent on the age of the person holding the life estate, as a buyer might anticipate a shorter time to wait if that person is ninety as opposed to twenty.

WHAT IS CONCURRENT OWNERSHIP?

A person who owns a real or personal property right by himself or herself, without anyone else's sharing in the ownership, is said to own the property in *severalty*. Thus, the interests that you hold in personal property (whether the property is clothing, furniture, a book, a car, a patent right, or common stock) and those you hold in real property (whether the property is held in fee simple absolute or as a life estate, reversion, or remainder) are interests in severalty if you are the only person possessing such right or rights.

If you are not the only person possessing such rights but, instead, you share your ownership interest with one or more individuals, you do not own the property in severalty but, rather, concurrently (i.e., together) with those others. However, it is important to distinguish concurrent ownership from the situation in which one person owns one or more rights in property and another person owns entirely different rights in the same property (e.g., with regard to real property, the life tenant and the future interest holder). In this case, each party owns his or her rights in severalty, not concurrently. It is only when two or more people share ownership of the *same* right or rights in property that they are said to own the property concurrently. (We have already studied concurrent ownership by partners in a tenancy in partnership described in Chapter 6).

Concurrent ownership is often a practical alternative to ownership in severalty for the following reasons:

1. Concurrent ownership is a convenient way to invest with others or operate a business with others. For example, if you and perhaps ten of your friends form an investment club, pooling your resources to buy a diversified portfolio of stocks and bonds and an apartment house consisting of fifty units, how will each member of your club own the property purchased? Certainly, it is possible for each club member to obtain individual rights in the property (i.e., to own the rights in severalty), but this would make little sense. The better solution is for all members to own the investments you make together in a concurrent ownership form; each member with a one-eleventh interest in the entire properties.

2. Concurrent ownership enables spouses to share equally in the ownership of property acquired during marriage. In the typical marriage, both spouses work hard to acquire both real and personal property. Because both parties contribute substantially of their time and effort, it is only fair that the law provide a method of concurrent ownership between husband and wife enabling each spouse to own an undivided one-half interest in all the property acquired. Of course, if the spouses prefer, they can always divide the property equally and hold it in severalty.

In eight states (Arizona, California, Idaho, Louisiana, Nevada, New Mexico, Texas, and Washington) a form of concurrent ownership is recognized called "community property." In those states property that is acquired from the earnings of either spouse during a marriage will belong to both spouses equally in undivided one-half shares unless the spouses agree otherwise. In the rest of the United States, spouses will own their properties in severalty unless they elect to use some other form of concurrent ownership such as a joint tenancy with the right of survivorship or a tenancy in common.

3. Concurrent ownership may avoid the time and expense of probate. Some forms of concurrent ownership eliminate the need for probate of the concurrently held property upon the death of one of the co-owners.

Probate, as will be explained more fully in Chapter 13, is simply the legal process of transferring a decedent's property (all of his or her property held in severalty and some of his or her property held concurrently with others) to those people lawfully entitled to the property upon the decedent's death (i.e., those people named in the decedent's will or designated as the decedent's intestate heirs if the decedent leaves no will). Probate also serves to protect the interests of creditors of the deceased (nearly all decedents leave some bills, whether they are merely utility bills, doctor bills, or major debts evidenced by mortgages on real estate) and the interests of taxing authorities with respect to death, income, gift, and property taxes owing. In short, the probate process ensures that the right parties end up with the decedent's property. It is a desirable process that serves well to protect the decedent's interests and wishes with regard to the final disposition of his or her property.

To illustrate, imagine that your mother dies without a will, leaving you as her only surviving heir. Your mother's saving account in a local bank contains $50,000, and, as your mother's debts are paid in full, you are entitled to the full $50,000 free and clear of any creditor's claims. However, you cannot simply appear at the bank and demand your money—the bank has no means of determining whether you are the appropriate person to take it. It is up to the probate court to determine the legitimacy of your claim to your mother's properties (i.e., her estate) and ultimately to order distribution of the money to you.

In contrast to our orderly probate process, the author likes to recall a scene from the movie *Zorba the Greek* in which an old woman lay dying in a small village. The dying woman owned a substantial amount of property in the town, including a hotel with many furnishings. As the old woman approached death, the townspeople systematically removed each of her possessions until all she had left was the bed she lay dying on—even her clothes and other personal belongings had disappeared. Finally, several townspeople gathered around her bed waiting for her to die so as to be first in line for even the bed itself. That is one way of taking care of a decedent's property. Our system of probate is a much better way.

However, our probate system is also time consuming (in the usual case, eight to ten months) and expensive (usually 3 to 5 percent of the estate and sometimes more for administration costs, attorney's fees, appraiser's fees, etc.). For this reason, it is sometimes desirable to avoid probate, and one of the easiest ways to do so is to own property in certain forms of concurrent ownership. This is particularly true for husbands and wives who own their properties together.

HOW DO A TENANCY IN COMMON AND A JOINT TENANCY WITH THE RIGHT OF SURVIVORSHIP DIFFER?

A *tenancy in common* differs from ownership in severalty in one way—rather than one person's owning the interest, two or more people called tenants in common share undivided ownership of the property. Tenants in common need not own the same fractional share of the property (e.g., if A, B, C, and D own an apartment house or 100 shares of Standard Oil stock as tenants in common, A might own a one-half interest, B a one-third interest, and C and D one-sixth interests). Nor is it necessary that the tenants in common acquire their interests at the same time or from the same source. And tenants in common are free to transfer their interests at any time without regard to the other tenants' wishes.

As to inheritability, the interest of a tenant in common will pass to the tenant's lawfully designated beneficiaries or heirs upon the tenant's death just as if the property had been held in severalty. Thus, in the A, B, C, D example above, if A dies testate leaving her interest in the apartment house or in the stock to her daughter, Sally, Sally will become a tenant in common with B, C, and D, owning a one-half undivided interest in the property. As to distribution at death, an interest held in tenancy in common must be probated just like any interest held in severalty.

Modernly, any transfer of property to two or more persons is presumed to create a tenancy in common unless some other form of co-ownership is expressly indicated. There is also a presumption that the tenants take in equal shares unless there is evidence that the tenants were intended to share disproportionately.

In contrast to the tenancy in common, a *joint tenancy with the right of survivorship* requires that each "joint tenant" must acquire his or her interest at the same time; that each joint tenant's interest be created by the same instrument, that is, by the same deed of conveyance, contract of sale, or the like; that the interests must be identical in size and duration (all the parties must have either a life estate, an estate for years, or some other identical interest of the same duration). The *right of survivorship* is the single most important characteristic of the joint tenancy. This right means that upon the death of any joint tenant, the deceased tenant's interest passes, not to the tenant's lawfully designated beneficiaries or heirs (as in the case of the tenancy in common), but to the surviving joint tenants. In other words, if A, B, C, and D own an apartment house or a patent right as joint tenants with the right of survivorship and A dies, B, C, and D will automatically own A's interest. If B then dies, C and D will automatically own B's interest; and if C dies before D, D will automatically own all the property by himself in severalty. Where the right of survivorship exists, ownership of the property transfers automatically at the moment of death of the fellow cotenant. As a result, the need for probate is eliminated, and use of the joint tenancy with the right of survivorship is the easiest way to avoid probate.

Suppose that one joint tenant makes an inter vivos transfer of his or her interest to an outside party. The transferee, in this case, does not become a joint tenant with the right of survivorship but a tenant in common with the remaining joint tenants. This is because the transferee has received his or her interest at a different time and in a different transfer from the others who continue to be joint tenants as amongst themselves. Let's take an example. Assume that A, B, C, and D own a thirty-acre ranch as joint tenants with the right of survivorship. A transfers his interest to Sally who becomes a tenant in common with B, C, and D. B, C, and D, however, continue to own their interests as joint tenants with each other. If B and C die, D will own three-fourths of the property because of the survivorship characteristic; because there are no other surviving joint tenants, D will become a tenant in common with Sally who owns the other one-fourth undivided interest in the property. If D dies, her heirs will receive her three-fourths interest as tenants in common with Sally; if Sally dies, her heirs will receive her one-fourth interest as tenants in common with D or her heirs.

WHAT IS A DEED?

Whether real estate (land) is transferred by gift, sale, or exchange, a "deed" is used to effectuate the transfer. Students frequently make the mistake of thinking that deeds are contracts—they are not. A deed is simply an instrument required by law to evidence the transfer of real property by gift, contract, or sale or contract of exchange. It is a writing, signed by the grantor, whereby title (ownership) of real property is conveyed (i.e., transferred) from one person to another.

The requirements of a deed may be summarized as follows:

1. *In writing* The transfer of an interest in real property must be evidenced by a writing.
2. *Signed by the grantor* The written deed must be signed by the grantor—the party making the transfer.
3. *Description of the grantee* The grantee must be sufficiently described in the deed so that it may be ascertained with certainty who is to receive the land.
4. *Words of grant* The deed must contain words, called words of grant, indicating the grantor's intent to convey an interest in real property to the grantee. No special technical words are required—the word "grant" or the like will do. While many people use the somewhat technical "give, grant, bargain, and sell," this is not a requirement.
5. *Description of land conveyed* The test of whether the deed sufficiently describes the land to be transferred is whether the land may be located on the basis of the description with reasonable certainty. The description may be by "metes and bounds" (actual measurements and boundaries), by reference to government surveys, by recorded plats (maps or other representations of property subdivided into lots), by streets and numbers, by name of the property, by reference to adjacent property, or by any other nucleus of description.
6. *Acknowledgment* "Acknowledgment" refers to a formal declaration made by the grantor in front of a public officer, usually a notary public, that he or she has signed the deed and is transferring the property voluntarily.

Although very few states require acknowledgment, almost all states provide that an unacknowledged deed cannot be recorded. Thus, a purchaser who fails to obtain an acknowledged deed cannot record the deed and will not be protected against a subsequent purchaser of the same property who obtains and records an acknowledged deed (of course, in this case, the grantor will be in the wrong, and if the original purchaser can catch up with him or her, the purchaser will be able to recover money damages). While recording is not essential to making a deed valid as between the grantor and grantee, it does serve as "constructive notice" (i.e., inferred or implied notice) to the world at large that there is an outstanding interest in the land. The idea behind recording laws is that the ownership of real property should be determinable from the public record and that purchasers of land should be able to rely upon these records in entering into real estate transactions—they should not have to worry about secret, unrecorded deeds. Therefore, while a grantee who records will be protected against the claims of all subsequent transferees of the same property, a grantee who fails to record may lose his or her interest in the land to a subsequent "bona fide" purchaser. A "bona fide" purchaser is one who pays valuable consideration for the land (i.e., pays money or other value for the property) and who takes the land without notice, either actual or constructive, of the grantee's prior claim. Obviously, where the grantee records, there can be no bona fide purchasers, for the entire world is on constructive notice of the grantee's interest.

7. *Delivery* The grantor must deliver the deed to the grantee in order to complete the transfer of property. Without delivery the grantor retains title, and the grantee has no ownership interest in the land. Physical delivery of the deed coupled with the grantor's intent that the delivery be effective to transfer the real property is always sufficient. If the grantor retains physical possession of the deed, there arises a legal presumption against delivery that can only be rebutted by sufficient evidence to the contrary. Where the grantee is in physical possession of the deed, the presumption is in favor of delivery, and, to rebut the presumption, the grantor must introduce sufficient evidence of nondelivery. The fact that a deed has been recorded also raises a presumption of delivery, as does (at least in some states) the fact that the grantor has acknowledged the deed.

WHAT KINDS OF DEEDS ARE THERE?

Generally, there are four kinds of deeds used to convey interests in real property: quitclaim deeds; bargain and sale deeds; general warranty deeds; and special warranty deeds.

Quitclaim Deed

A quitclaim deed is an instrument purporting to convey only what interest, if any, the grantor has in a specified piece of real property. The deed does not purport to transfer the land itself, and the grantor who quitclaims property makes no promise, express or implied, that he or she has good title or ownership at all. The grantor is merely stating: "If I own any interest, and

I may, in fact, own no interest, I am transferring whatever I do own to you." Thus, upon execution of the quitclaim deed, whatever interest the grantor holds in the property will pass to the grantee; if the grantor holds no interest, nothing will be conveyed. In either event, the grantor has made no promise regarding the nature of his or her interest in the land and will not be responsible or liable if the grantee is later disappointed with the "transfer."

Usually a grantor who believes (but is not certain) that he or she holds an interest in real property that is likely to serve as a defect in title to the property will release his or her "rights" by executing a quitclaim deed.

Bargain and Sale Deeds

A bargain and sale deed is but one step above a quitclaim deed. While a grantor who executes a bargain and sale deed does purport to transfer land to the grantee (and not merely whatever interest, if any, he or she may own in the property), the grantor makes no promise, express or implied, that he or she has good title to the property, or any title at all. Because the grantee pays good value for the land without receiving any assurance (warranty) of title, the grantee is actually in no better position than the grantee of a quitclaim deed.

General Warranty Deed

A general warranty deed, on the other hand, not only purports to transfer the land itself—it also contains warranties (promises) that the grantor has good title to the property and that the grantor will protect the grantee from *any and all* claims that should arise from a defect in the grantor's ownership interest. With these warranties it is no wonder that investors in real property prefer a general warranty deed to quitclaim deeds and deeds of bargain and sale. The grantee who acquires ownership through a general warranty deed is assured of protection from the grantor in the event of future problems regarding title.

Special Warranty Deed

A special warranty deed normally contains the warranties found in the general warranty deed, with one major difference—the covenants found in the special warranty deed apply only to defects in title arising during the grantor's period of ownership of the land, not to defects that may have arisen prior to that time. In other words, the grantor promises only that he or she has not caused any defects in title—not, as in the case of the general warranty deed, that no one else has either. Thus, where title proves defective because of events occurring prior to the grantor's acquisition of title to the property, the grantor will not be liable to the grantee.

DOES A GRANTOR HAVE A DUTY TO CONVEY "MARKETABLE" TITLE?

A grantor who enters into a binding agreement to sell real property impliedly promises (covenants) that he or she will furnish the buyer with *marketable title* at the time of closing (i.e., at the time the buyer pays the purchase price and the seller delivers the deed to the buyer). Marketable title, often called *merchantable* title, means title reasonably free from doubt—title that a prudent buyer would accept. The idea behind marketable title is that a buyer should not be required to "purchase a lawsuit." Thus, an outstanding mortgage, lien (claim), or other defect in the property (including outstanding easements, profits, and covenants as will be defined later in the chapter) that is not listed in the contract of sale and is not accepted by the buyer will render the title unmarketable and will enable the buyer to refuse to go through with the purchase.

However, the buyer must insist upon and receive marketable title prior to paying for the land and accepting delivery of the deed, or he or she will be held to have waived the right. This is not to say that the buyer can call off the purchase agreement prior to the closing date because the seller does not have marketable title. There is always a possibility that the seller may obtain marketable title prior to that time, and the law will wait and see whether marketable title exists at the time of closing.

The contract of sale may specifically call for a "good record title." This means that the seller must provide marketable title based upon public land records. All states provide for public recordation of deeds and other documents affecting title to real property. The public records show the chain of ownership of the property and list any outstanding interests in the land.

Where "good record title" is demanded, title acquired by adverse possession will not be acceptable. Adverse possession (discussed in the next section) is a method of acquiring ownership of real property merely by possessing the property in a manner specified by statute for a designated period of time. Where "good record title" is not demanded, title acquired by adverse possession will qualify as marketable.

Before leaving the area of marketable title, it should be pointed out that the existence of an "encroachment" may also render title unmarketable. An encroachment, as it relates to marketable title, refers to the trespass on land of a physical structure or fixture. An encroachment may exist where: (1) a building or other fixture on the land sold intrudes in part on neighboring land; (2) a building or other fixture on the land sold intrudes upon an adjoining street or alley; or (3) a building or other fixture on adjoining land intrudes upon the land sold. In the case of (1) or (2), title will be unmarketable if the encroachment is likely to result in the institution of suit by either the neighboring landowner or the city for removal of the obstruction. Where the encroachment is very slight (e.g., where the landowner's garage extends one-half inch on to his or her neighbor's property), title will not be rendered unmarketable. It is the policy of the law to permit an obstruction to stand where the trespass is very slight, the cost of removal is great, and the benefit of removal to the landowner is negligible. In the case of (3), if the area of land occupied by the encroaching fixture is relatively insignificant, the title will most likely be held marketable, and the buyer will be allowed merely to deduct a portion of the purchase price to reflect the loss in land area.

Title insurance is insurance protection against loss arising from a defect in title or from lack of good title. Title insurance is generally available in one form or another throughout the United States. Basically, there are two types.

The Two Types of Title Insurance

Lawyer-title policies Here, the purchaser of property (or the seller on the purchaser's behalf where the contract of sale so provides) hires an attorney to conduct a title search and to furnish the purchaser with an opinion as to title as well as an abstract of title (an "abstract" is merely a summary of the record title, including all outstanding liens, mortgages, judgments, and similar claims). The abstract is turned over to a title insurance company which issues a policy on the basis of the abstract.

Title-plant policies Some title insurance companies issue policies on the basis of their own title search, rather than an attorney's abstract. Usually, the companies maintain duplicate land records in the plant's main office.

If the title insurance company is satisfied that good record title exists, the company will issue a policy insuring against loss that may arise from a defect in title. The company may specifically list in the policy any minor defects found on the record for which the company refuses to be liable. Unless the company takes exception to the existing defects of record, the company cannot escape liability for title defects which could have been discovered through the exercise of reasonable care. However, the company generally does not insure against the following:

1. unrecorded liens and easements;
2. rights of a person in possession on the basis of an unrecorded instrument;
3. rights that could be ascertained by inspection of the land, by proper survey, or by inquiry of a person in possession;
4. unrecorded mining claims and water rights;
5. violation of government zoning and use regulations; and
6. unpaid taxes or assessments.

In some cases, the title insurance company may be willing to sell such extended coverage for a substantial increase in premium.

In any event, the purchaser alone is insured against the covered defects, and the policy does not "run with the land" (i.e., the insurance protection is not transferred with a transfer of the property—any subsequent purchaser must buy his or her own title insurance).

Where a loss occurs and the title insurance company is liable, the insured landowner's recovery will be the actual market loss he or she suffers up to the maximum limits of the policy.

WHAT IS ADVERSE POSSESSION?

Adverse possession is a means of acquiring an ownership interest in real property merely by possessing the property in a manner prescribed by statute for a specified period of time. Thus, a person may acquire a life estate or a fee simple absolute interest in land belonging to another if he or she meets the following five conditions:

1. Actual possession;
2. Open and notorious possession;
3. Hostile intent;
4. Continuous possession throughout; and
5. Statutory time period.

Actual Possession

To begin with, the adverse possessor must actually occupy the property. This does not mean that he or she must in every case live on the property. What is required is that the adverse possessor exercise the kind of use and control over the land that would be expected of the true and lawful owner. Acts appropriate to the property, such as cultivating farmland and herding cattle on grazing land, are sufficient.

Open and Notorious Possession

Possession must be "open and notorious." This means that the possession must be so blantantly obvious that the rightful owner is put on notice that he or she had better take action to defend the property. This does not mean that the rightful owner must actually show up and discover the adverse possessor's presence on the land. All that is required is that the possession be so open and obvious that a reasonable inspection by the lawful owner would not fail to disclose its presence. Thus, a person who secretly cultivates land belonging to another or who stealthily lives on the property so as not to be discovered does not possess the land in the open and notorious manner required for adverse possession.

Hostile Intent

The possession also requires a "hostile" intent. Hostility, however, does not mean ill feeling—merely an intent to occupy and possess the land in disregard and denial of the true owner's ownership and title. Thus, a statement that "I know this land belongs to someone else, but I am claiming it as my own anyway" is sufficiently hostile. However, a statement that "I do not claim this land as my own even though I occupy it" lacks sufficient hostility.

Continuous Possession Throughout

The actual, open and notorious, hostile possession must continue for the entire statutory period. Continuous possession, however, does not mean constant possession. Again, what is required is the level of occupancy and use that could be expected of an average owner of the same or similar property. For example, a lakefront summer home that is snowed in during the winter may require occupancy and use only during the summertime.

However, where the adverse claimant at some point abandons the property, intending never to return, the adverse possession will come to an end. If the adverse possessor ever returns to the property, hoping to resume occupancy and use, he or she will have to start all over again for purposes of the statutory period.

Statutory Time Period

The adverse possession must continue for the period of time prescribed by statute—twenty years in most states, less in others (e.g., ten years in Oregon).

Once the statutory period of time has run, the original owner's title to the land is completely and automatically extinguished by operation of law, and new title or ownership rights are created in the adverse possessor. He or she owns good legal title, and the fact that his or her interest does not appear on record is of no consequence. Recording laws simply have no effect upon title acquired by adverse possession, and the adverse possessor is free, regardless of record title, to hold on to the property or to transfer it by deed, will, or intestacy. For example, suppose that Samantha Jones begins adversely possessing Seymour Langtry's forty-acre farm in 1950. In 1970, the statutory holding period is up, and Samantha acquires title to the property by adverse possession. In 1975, Seymour Langtry, whose name still appears on record as owner of the property, sells and deeds the forty-acre farm to Bill Smith who immediately records the deed. Who owns the land. Samantha Jones does—Bill Smith owns nothing. At the time Bill received the deed from Seymour, Seymour had nothing to convey; his interest in the farm was extinguished by operation of law in 1970. The fact that Seymour's name appeared as record title holder at the time of the transfer simply has no effect on Samantha's ownership rights. How could Bill Smith (or any other purchaser) have protected himself from this result? Prior to purchasing, he could have gone out to the property and inspected the land for the presence of adverse possessors.

Now let's change the facts a little. Suppose that Seymour Langtry owns, not a fee simple absolute, but a life estate interest in the farm, with the remainder interest in his son, Larry. Again, Samantha Jones begins adversely possessing the land in 1950. In 1970, Seymour's interest in the land is extinguished, and Samantha Jones automatically acquires ownership of Seymour's interest by adverse possession. If, in 1976, Seymour dies, does Samantha have a good defense to Larry Langtry's claims of fee simple ownership? No. By adversely possessing the land from 1950 to 1970, Samantha acquired title to a life estate pur autre vie (for the life of Seymour)—not to a fee simple absolute. This is because an adverse possessor acquires title only to whatever *present possessory interests* are owned by the lawful owner of the property at the time the adverse possession begins. Thus, to obtain title to the fee simple, Samantha must now adversely possess the land for another twenty years (during the period of Larry's fee simple ownership).

Finally, the statutory period for adverse possession does not run against government land. It is therefore impossible to acquire title by adverse possession to land belonging to the United States, the individual states, or any other political subdivision.

WHAT IS THE DIFFERENCE BETWEEN A LICENSE, EASEMENT, PROFIT, AND COVENANT?

License

A license is not an interest in land but is a mere privilege, personal to the licensee (the person possessing it), to go on to another's land for a specified purpose. It is oral or written permission to perform acts that would otherwise constitute a trespass.

A license is revocable at the will of the landowner; if the landowner decides to revoke, the license is instantly terminated. For example, a farmer who says to a hunter on Monday, "I give you permission to hunt pheasants on my land next week," can on Tuesday revoke the permission, and the hunter's license to hunt on the land will be automatically and instantly terminated. If the hunter persists in hunting, he or she will be liable for trespass.

Easement

An easement is a genuine, though nonpossessory interest in real property that may be owned in severalty or in a form of concurrent ownership. Like a license, an easement is a right to use another's land, but it is much more than a privilege and cannot be revoked by the landowner.

An easement may be classified in the same manner as a possessory estate—for years, for life, or in fee simple. Generally speaking, there are two kinds of easements: *easements appurtenant* and *easements in gross.* An easement appurtenant is one involving two adjoining parcels of land. One parcel, called the "dominant estate," is in some way benefited by the second parcel, or "servient estate." The servient estate is thus said to be burdened with the easement. For example, suppose that Seymour Langtry owns one acre of land in fee simple absolute. Seymour conveys one-half of the land in fee simple to Samantha Jones, and Seymour also conveys to Samantha an easement giving her the right to cross over Seymour's one-half to get to her property. Samantha's property, the dominant estate, is benefited by the easement of access across Seymour's land; Seymour's property, the servient estate, is burdened with the easement appurtenant. In the event that Samantha conveys her one-half interest or loses it by adverse possession, the easement appurtenant will be transferred along with the dominant estate.

An easement in gross, on the other hand, involves only one parcel of land belonging to someone other than the easement holder and benefiting the holder personally as opposed to benefiting a servient estate. Thus, an irrevocable right to hunt on another's property or to put up a billboard on the land constitutes an easement in gross (a revocable right to do these things would be merely a license). At common law, an easement in gross was considered personal to the grantee and could not be transferred either inter vivos or at death. Modernly, many states provide for the free transferability of commercial easements in gross, such as a commercial pipeline or utility line, but prohibit the transfer of noncommercial easements unless the deed of conveyance expressly states "to the grantee and his or her heirs or assigns." Still other states permit all easements in gross to be freely transferred whether they are commercial or noncommercial.

Other than implied or prescriptive easements, all easements must be created in writing (any attempt to create an easement orally will result in a mere license). Generally, a testator or grantor will directly grant an easement to a beneficiary or grantee in a will or deed of conveyance. In the absence of an express easement, an "implied" easement (also called an "easement by necessity") will arise where an easement is strictly necessary to the use or enjoyment of land conveyed or land retained by a grantor. Suppose that Seymour Langtry conveys the back one-half acre of his one-acre parcel to Samantha Jones. If the only way Samantha can reach her property from the public road or highway is by crossing the one-half acre retained by Seymour Langtry, the law will imply an easement by necessity permitting her to do so.

Easements may also be created by "prescription" (i.e., by adverse use). Acquiring such an easement is similar to acquiring title to a possessory estate in land by means of adverse possession. Like adverse possession, adverse use or prescription must be open and notorious, continuous and uninterrupted, and hostile as to the true owner. Again, this means that the adverse user must make no attempt to conceal his or her use of the land; that he or she must use the land continuously (although not necessarily constantly) for the entire statutory period; and that he or she must use the land in disregard and denial of the true owner's rights. Thus, if A walks over B's land whenever A happens to be going in that direction for a period of twenty years, A will acquire an easement by prescription. But if A has B's permission to cross over the property, A's use is not adverse to B's ownership rights (A has a license to use the land), and A cannot lay claim to a prescriptive easement.

Profit

A "profit" is very similar to an easement in that it is a genuine interest in real property as opposed to a mere license or privilege. It differs from an easement in that it gives, not an irrevocable right to *use* the land, but an irrevocable right *to take* something away from it, such as minerals, timber, water, oil, or the like. Of course, whenever a profit is granted, an implied easement is also created permitting the profit holder to go on to the property to accomplish the taking.

Covenant

A covenant is simply a promise to do something or not to do something. Covenants are frequently contained in deeds of conveyance as a means of restricting the grantee of property in his or her use of the land. For example, a grantee might promise "*not* to use the land for other than residential purposes," "*not* to build other than one-story structures on the land," "*to* maintain a fence," and "*to* rotate crops on the property." As such, the covenants are genuine nonpossessory interests in land. They belong to the grantor who has a legal right to enforce them.

Like express easements and profits, covenants must be created in writing in order to be valid. Generally, the writing is a deed which, as you will recall, is signed by the grantor and not by the grantee. However, the grantee is considered bound by any covenants contained in a deed by reason of accepting the deed. Any subsequent purchaser from the grantee is also bound by the covenants so long as the purchaser had either actual or constructive notice (from the recorded deed) of the covenants at the time of purchase. As a result, such covenants are said to "run with the land."

In conclusion, covenants designed to restrict the use of land on the basis of race, creed, color, or sex are in violation of federal and state discrimination laws and cannot be enforced in the courts.

WHAT DUTY DOES A LANDOWNER OWE A PERSON WHO COMES UPON HIS OR HER PROPERTY?

As a final restriction upon land ownership, the law imposes certain duties upon a landowner with regard to people who come upon his or her property. The duty is not the same in every case but varies with the class of individual who comes upon the land.

Trespassers

The landowner's duty to a trespasser is to warn the trespasser about hidden dangers on the property (e.g., a faulty stairwell) if and when the landowner discovers the trespasser's presence on the land. However, an exception arises in the case of trespassing children under what is called the "*attractive nuisance*" doctrine. If the landowner maintains a condition on his or her property that poses an unreasonable risk of harm to children and the owner can anticipate that children are likely to trespass on the land, then the owner will be liable if children do in fact trespass and suffer injury as a result of the condition. A good example of an attractive nuisance is a swimming pool that is inadequately fenced off. Generally, to recover under the attractive nuisance doctrine, a child must be of "tender years" (usually less than fourteen years of age).

Licensees

A licensee is a person who has a privilege to enter upon the landowner's property with the consent of the landowner but nothing more (e.g., members of the landowner's family, social guests who come to visit at the invitation of the landowner, door-to-door salesmen, etc.). The landowner's duty to a licensee is the same as his or her duty to a trespasser—that is, to warn the licensee of hidden dangers on the property once the landowner is aware of his or her presence on the land. Again, a higher duty may be imposed with respect to licensee children under the attractive nuisance doctrine.

Business Visitors, or Invitees

A business visitor or invitee is a person who comes upon the landowner's property upon the business of the landowner (e.g., a business customer, a restaurant patron, a TV repairer, etc.). The landowner owes a much higher duty to a business visitor than he or she owes to a trespasser or licensee. With regard to a business visitor, the landowner has a duty to make the premises safe—that is to say, to take reasonable precautions to protect the invitee from foreseeable dangers on the property.

MAY A PERSON USE FORCE TO DEFEND THREATS AGAINST HIS OR HER PROPERTY?

An individual is entitled to use reasonable force to protect his or her property. However, the law values human life (even that of a thief) more highly than it values property, and force likely to cause death or great bodily injury may never be used to protect property interests alone. Nor may such force be exerted indirectly in the form of spring guns or vicious watch dogs maintained on the premises to protect property. Of course, if more than property is threatened, i.e., if a person is himself or herself in great danger of physical harm, he or she may use reasonable force in self-defense. And while only the amount of force necessary to prevent the harm is privileged, if one is in danger of being killed he or she may kill in self-defense. However, force cannot be used once the danger has passed; revenge is not self-defense.

Cases

Did the "Fathers" own the coolers?

PREMONSTRATENSIAN FATHERS v. BADGER MUTUAL INSURANCE CO.

Supreme Court of Wisconsin, 1970.
46 Wis.2d 362, 175 N.W.2d 237.

This is an action to recover upon a fire insurance policy, the coverage clause of which provides:

> When the insurance under this policy covers a building, such insurance shall cover on the building, * * * all permament fixtures. * * *

The Premonstratensian Fathers, called Fathers, are the owners of a one-story building, insured by the property insurance policy in question, which is used as a supermarket. The building was originally constructed in 1958 by the Jacobs Realty Corporation. * * * Following the construction of the supermarket, the business has been continually run as a retail grocery business, offering a wide variety of canned goods, frozen goods, produce and meats.

* * * On March 7, 1960, Jacobs * * * deeded * * * the land and the improvements to the Fathers. On March 7, 1960, the Fathers leased the premises back

to the Jacobs Brothers Stores, Inc. for a term of twenty years. The lease further provided that the lessee was to provide fire insurance on the building and the fixtures in the name of the lessor. Following this lease, the premises were operated in exactly the same manner as it had been since the initial construction. The lessee then provided the insurance which is the subject of the instant lawsuit.

On June 1, 1964, the building and improvements were severely damaged by a major fire. Following the fire, the building was replaced with a new building, and the interior of the building is substantially the same as that prior to the fire and is still run as a supermarket. The defendant-insurers paid to the plaintiff the sum of $83,000 for the loss suffered to the building, but have refused to pay a claim in the amount of $23,551.02 for the destruction of five Hussman walk-in coolers which were situated in the building. The grounds upon which the insurers have refused to pay the claim of the Fathers, and upon which they relied in both the trial court and in this court are: (1) The coolers are not the property of the Fathers, and (2) even if the coolers are the property of the Fathers, they are not insured property. There is no issue as to the amount of the damages, or whether the policy was in full force and effect on the date of the fire. The trial court concluded that the coolers are insured property and granted judgment for the plaintiff.

The coolers which are the subject of this dispute are walk-in type coolers. There are five of these: two meat coolers, a deep-freeze, a produce cooler, and a dairy cooler. A further description of the coolers is set forth in the opinion.

Connor T. HANSEN, Justice

Although the insurers have divided their argument into two sections, the basis of the entire appeal is a consideration of the legal status of the coolers. If the coolers are determined to be common-law fixtures, and were such at the time of the construction of the building and the installation of the coolers, then they would have passed to the Fathers under the warranty deed of March 7, 1960, and they would be insured under the terms of the policy. The issue then is whether these coolers constitute fixtures.

The rule which has developed in Wisconsin as to what constitutes a fixture is not really a comprehensive definition, but rather a statement of the factors which are to be applied to the fact and circumstances of a particular case to determine whether or not the property in question does constitute a fixture:

> * * * Whether articles of personal property are fixtures, i.e., real estate, is determined in this state, if not generally, by the following rules or tests: (1) Actual physical annexation to the real estate; (2) application or adaptation to the use or purpose to which the realty is devoted; and (3) an intention on the part of the person making the annexation to make a permanent accession to the freehold.

It is the application of these tests to the facts of a particular case which will lead to a determination of whether or not an article, otherwise considered personal property, constitutes a common-law fixture, and hence takes on the nature of real property. * * *

Annexation

Annexation refers to:

> * * * the act of attaching or affixing personal property to real property and, as a general proposition, an object will not acquire the status of a fixture unless it is in some manner or means, albeit slight, attached or affixed, either actually or constructively, to the realty.

It has been held in Wisconsin that physical annexation, although a factor to be considered in the determination, is of relative unimportance:

> * * * it has often been said by this court that the matter of physical annexation of the article * * * is relatively unimportant. * * *

The trial court ably pointed out the physical facts which led to its conclusion that there is indeed annexation in this case. The more important of these are as follows: (1) The exterior walls of the cooler, in four instances, constituted the interior wall of another room. (2) In the two meat coolers, a meat hanging and tracking system was built into the coolers. These tracks were used to move large cuts of meats from the cooler area into the meat preparation areas, and were suspended from the steel girders of the building structure by means of large steel bolts. These bolts penetrated through the roof of the cooler supporting wooden beams, which, in turn, supported the tracking system. The tracking in the coolers was a part of a system of tracking throughout the rear portion of the supermarket. (3) The coolers were attached to hardwood plank which was, in turn, attached to the concrete floor of the supermarket. The attachment of the plank to the floor was accomplished through the use of a ramsetting gun. The planks were laid on the floor, and the bolts were driven through them into the concrete floor, where they then exploded, firmly fixing the coolers into place. * * *

These factors adequately support the conclusion that the coolers were indeed physically annexed to the premises. * * *

Adaptation

Adaptation refers to the relationship between the chattel and the use which is made of the realty to which the chattel is annexed. The use of the realty was that of a retail grocery, commonly known as a supermarket. This was the intent of the parties at the time of the construction of the building and the intent of the parties throughout the entire history of the business. The fact of operation has borne out this intent. In a business which carries fresh foods, frozen foods, produce, meats and butter, coolers used for storage and handling of these perishables are patently related to the use of the building. In fact, it would be hard to picture any equipment more closely related to the operation of a supermarket, where large quantities of perishables must, of necessity, be purchased for storage and processing.

* * *

Intent

This court has repeatedly held that intent is the primary determinant of whether a certain piece of property has become a fixture. The relevant intent is that of the party making the annexation. * * *

In its decision, the trial court found, as a reasonable and legitimate inference from all the facts and circumstances surrounding the placement of the coolers onto the realty, that there was an intention that the coolers became a permanent accession to the realty; that when Jacobs Realty Corporation conveyed the land together with all buildings and improvements thereon * * *, the intention still prevailed that the coolers were a permanent accession to the realty. * * *

* * * As this court has stated:

> * * * Although it is true that, in applying that doctrine, the question of whether such machines constitute fixtures is largely one of intent, that intent may be considered established conclusively by the fact that the machines in question were clearly adapted to, *and were in fact put by the owner of the realty and the machines to, the use to which he devoted the realty and the installed machines as an entirety.* * * * (Emphasis added.) * * *

Judgment affirmed.

"Operation Equality"—"all citizens have the same right to inherit, purchase, lease, sell, hold, and convey real and personal property."

BUSH v. KAIM

United States District Court, N.D.Ohio, E.D.1969.
297 F.Supp. 151.

LAMBROS, District Judge

This is a civil action arising under the Civil Rights Act of 1866, Title 42, U.S.C.A. § 1982. * * *

The plaintiffs, Reginald Bush, Jr., and Rita Mae Bush, are husband and wife; they are negroes; they have a four-month old daughter, Adrienne Bush.

Mr. Bush has recently been employed by the Mead-Johnson Laboratories as a medical sales representative. In connection with this employment, he was required to relocate in or near Cleveland, Ohio.

In order to secure suitable housing for himself and his family, he came to Cleveland on or about October 21, 1968. * * *

* * * In the Cleveland Plain Dealer edition of Saturday, November 9, 1968, Mr. Bush noticed the following advertisement: "Eastlake ranch, 2-bedrm, carpeted living rm, attached garage; spotless, $150. Reference 261–2820."

* * *

The defendants, Frank A. Kaim and Carolyn Kaim, are the owners of the property which was advertised as indicated above in the Cleveland Plain Dealer. This property is a single-family house located at 813 Stevens Blvd. in Eastlake, Ohio. This is the only rental property owned by these defendants. Mr. Kaim is a real estate agent and is experienced in the rental and sale of real property.

Mr. Bush called the number indicated in the advertisement at about 6:00 p.m. on the evening of Saturday, November 9th. He spoke with Carolyn Kaim. He asked to come out and view the property. Arrangements were made for him to come out that evening. Mrs. Kaim gave him directions to reach the property.

Bush arrived at about 8:30 that evening. Mr. Kaim met him at the door and showed him through the house. During the course of this tour and after they had been through a few rooms, Mr. Kaim told Bush that he had been showing the house to a number of other people and had received part of a rental deposit from a man to whom he had shown the house that day. Kaim also stated that he had not yet had time to tell his wife about this deposit, but that he was fairly certain the people who gave him the deposit would rent the house. Bush asked Kaim to call him the next day and let him know if the house had been taken. Although Mr. Kaim agreed to call the plaintiff, he never did so.

During the course of the meeeting between Kaim and Bush, Kaim asked Mr. Bush whom he worked for, and Bush told him. Mr. Kaim did not ask the size of Mr. Bush's family; he did not ask him his age; he did not ask for credit references; and he did not request Mr. Bush to fill out a rental application.

Mr. Bush became suspicious as a result of his meeting with Mr. Kaim. He called a Mrs. Talbot, who works for Operation Equality and told her what had occurred. He asked her to verify whether the house was in fact rented. She referred him to Mrs. Catherine Worley, a part-time employee of Operation Equality. Arrangements were made whereby Bush and Mrs. Worley would go out to the house on Monday to see if Bush could rent it. If they were unsuccessful, another Operation Equality volunteer would then appear at the house and attempt to rent it.

* * *

Mrs. Worley called Mrs. Joan M. Maguire, another Operation Equality volunteer. * * *

She had previously, in a phone conversation, instructed Mrs. Maguire to make an appointment to rent the house the following day. Mrs. Worley, Mrs. Maguire, and Mrs. Maguire's husband are white.

On Monday morning, Mrs. Worley called Mrs. Kaim sometime between 11:00 and 12:00 a.m. Mrs. Worley asked if the house was still available for rent. Mrs. Kaim said it was. She made an appointment to come out and view the house.

Mrs. Maguire also called up and asked if the house was for rent. The woman who answered the phone stated that it was. She then made an appointment to come out and view the house.

Mrs. Worley and Mr. Bush drove out to the house on Monday afternoon. They arrived at about 1:30. Mrs. Roland, who was at that time a tenant in the house, opened the door and allowed them to enter. Soon after, Mrs. Kaim arrived.

* * *

Mr. Bush introduced himself and Mrs. Worley. He stated that he had come to rent the house. * * *

* * * Mrs. Kaim declined to rent the property to Mr. Bush at that time. Mrs. Worley and Mr. Bush, unsuccessful in their attempt to rent the house, then left. They drove to the corner of the block, parked the car, and waited.

A few minutes later, Mrs. Maguire drove around the corner and proceeded to the Kaim house. She waved to Mrs. Worley and Mr. Bush as she drove by.

Mrs. Maguire was in the house for ten to fifteen minutes. Mrs. Kaim showed Mrs. Maguire around the house. * * *

* * *

Mrs. Maguire asked if the house had been rented, and Mrs. Kaim replied that it had not. Mrs. Kaim asked Mrs. Maguire if she wanted to rent the house. Mrs. Maguire said yes. Mrs. Maguire asked Mrs. Kaim if she would accept $50.00 as deposit, and Mrs. Kaim said yes. Mrs. Maguire gave Mrs. Kaim her personal check for $50.00 which Mrs. Kaim accepted.

* * *

The Court has studied the significant portions of the testimony of all the witnesses. The Court has concluded that the Kaims declined to rent to Mr. Bush solely for the reason that he was a negro and for no other reason. * * *

* * *

This action arises under the provisions of Title 42 U.S.C.A. § 1982, the so-called Civil Rights Act of 1866.

That Act provides:

> All citizens of the United States shall have the same right, in every State and Territory, as is enjoyed by white citizens thereof to inherit, purchase, lease, sell, hold, and convey real and personal property.

Plaintiffs allege that they have been denied the "same right" to lease property guaranteed them by Section 1982 solely on the basis of their race.

* * *

The landmark case interpreting Section 1982 is Jones v. Alfred H. Mayer Co., 392 U.S. 409, 88 S.Ct. 2186, 20 L.Ed.2d 1189 (1968). * * *

The precise issue before the Supreme Court in Jones v. Mayer was whether Section 1982 barred *all* racial discrimination, or merely discrimination which was the product of state action. The Court stated: "We hold that Section 1982 bars *all* racial discrimination, private as well as public, in the sale or rental of property, and that the statute, thus construed, is a valid exercise of the power of Congress to enforce the Thirteenth Amendment."

The issue of whether Section 1982 bars private discriminations in the sale or rental of houses can no longer be debated. This issue is conclusively settled by Jones v. Mayer.

* * *

The Court also set forth the standard to be utilized in determining whether an individual had been deprived of rights guaranteed him under Section 1982: "So long as a Negro citizen who wants to buy or rent a home can be turned away simply because he is not white, he cannot be said to enjoy 'the *same* right * * * as is enjoyed by white citizens * * * to * * * purchase [and] lease * * * real and personal property.' 42 U.S.C., § 1982." (Emphasis is Court's.) As the Court went on to state, Section 1982 "must encompass every racially motivated refusal to sell or rent." * * *

* * *

In sustaining his burden for proving that there has been a prohibited discrimination under the Act, the plaintiff must show each of the following elements: (1) that the owner (or responsible party) placed the property on the open market for sale or rental, (2) that the plaintiff was willing to rent or purchase the property on the terms specified by the owner, (3) the plaintiff communicated his willingness to the owner at a time when the property was available for sale or rent, (4) that the owner refused to rent or sell the property to the plaintiff on the terms which the owner indicated would otherwise be satisfactory, and (5) that there is no apparent reason for the refusal of the defendant to rent the property to the plaintiff other than the plaintiff's race.

The defendant may then come forward and rebut the evidence establishing any of these elements, or he may show that there were reasons other than the plaintiff's race underlying his refusal to rent to the plaintiff.

Section 1982 does not prohibit an owner from considering factors *other than* race in determining whether to sell or rent his property to a negro, or to any other person for that matter. An owner can refuse to rent or sell to anyone, negro, or white, for any reason he chooses so long as the motivating reason for this decision is not the individuals race or color."

The statute guarantees to negroes only the "same right" as is enjoyed by white citizens. It does not purport to grant to negroes rights which exceed those of white or other citizens. It provides merely that an owner may not refuse to rent to a negro solely on the basis of his race. Thus, an owner may refuse to rent to a negro for any reason he would refuse to rent to a white man. The statute merely prohibits him from refusing the negro solely because he is a negro.

* * * Such factors, which an owner might consider, include the credit standing of the applicant, his assets, his financial stability, his reputation in the community, his age, the size of his family, the ages of his children, his past experience as a lessee or tenant, the length of time he plans to occupy the premises, and whether he is or is not a transient.

* * *

* * * The Court may consider a number of things in determining whether the owner actually utilized relevant non-racial elements in deciding whether to rent to the plaintiff as opposed to another individual: (1) Did the owner request information relevant to these subjects from the plaintiff, (2) did the owner request such information from other applicants, (3) did he secure such information from other sources, (4) did he request this information from the plaintiff and/or from the other applicants during the period in which he was selecting a tenant, (5) did the owner make any attempt to follow up on this information or to check its accuracy, (6) did he perform this follow-up or checking process during the time in which he was deciding to whom to rent, (7) were there other applicants with better or more desirable ratings in these areas than the plaintiff.

The above are some of the elements which the Court may consider in determining whether the defendant's decision not to rent to the plaintiff was racially motivated or not. There may, of course, be other factors, and the above is not an exclusive list.

In the present case, certain differences other than race did exist between the Bushes and the Maguires. Nevertheless, although these differences did exist, the evidence establishes that the defendants did not consider them in refusing the plaintiffs. Rather, they based their decision not to rent to the plaintiffs solely upon considerations of race.

* * *

The Court seeks to restore to the plaintiffs that of which they have been deprived. The defendants held their property out for rental under certain terms and conditions. * * * The defendants, in refusing to rent to the plaintiffs, have deprived them of the right to enter into a lease for these premises under these terms and conditions. It was a rental of the property under these terms that the Kaims held forth to the white applicants; and it is a rental of the property under these terms that they have deprived the plaintiffs.

I

* * *

It is ordered that the defendants permit the plaintiffs to occupy the above-mentioned premises. * * *

While you are to be commended for your honesty, you do not get to keep the eight one-hundred dollar bills.

JACKSON v. STEINBERG

Supreme Court of Oregon, 1948.
186 Or. 129, 200 P.2d 376.

HAY, Justice

The plaintiff in this case in Mrs. Laura I. Jackson. The defendant is Karl Steinberg, who is engaged in the hotel business in Portland under the assumed business name of Arthur Hotel. Mrs. Jackson was employed by defendant as a chambermaid in his hotel.

The facts of the controversy are not disputed. Plaintiff entered defendant's employ on October 13, 1946. In describing her duties, she testified: "Well, where a guest checks out we are supposed to change the linen and dust and clean up the room, leave clean towels, and arrange the furniture like it should be, and take out anything that doesn't belong in there. Q. What do you do with that you take out? A. If it is of any value we take it to the desk clerk; if it isn't of any value we put in it the garbage." On December 30, 1946, while cleaning one of the guest rooms, she found eight one-hundred-dollar bills, United States currency, concealed under the paper lining of a dresser drawer. The bills were stacked neatly, and her attention was drawn to them only by reason of their bulk having made a slight bulge in the lining. She removed the bills and delivered them immediately to the manager of the hotel, in order that they might be restored to the true owner, if he could be found, and subject to her claims as finder. * * *

The hotel, during the period in question, was much patronized by seamen, some of who, after being paid off in the Port of Portland, brought considerable sums of money with them into the hotel, usually in bills of large denominations. Defendant made an unsuccessful effort to discover the owner of the bills, by communicating, or attempting to communicate, by mail, with each of the persons who had occupied this particular room from mid-October through December 31, 1946. Plaintiff then demanded of defendant that he return the money to her as finder, but he refused. She then, on July 10, 1947, filed this action in the district court for Multnomah County, to recover the sum of $800 of defendant as money had and received. * * *

Plaintiff had judgment in the District Court. * * * Defendant appeals from an adverse judgment.

Defendant's theory * * * is that the bills constitute mislaid property, presumed to have been left in the room by a former guest of the hotel, and that, as innkeeper, he is entitled to custody of the bills and bound to hold them as bailee for the true owner. Plaintiff, on the other hand, claims the right to the possession of the bills as treasure trove, as against all persons but the true owner.

Lost property is defined as that with the possession of which the owner has involuntarily parted, through neglect, carelessness, or inadvertence. It is property which the owner has unwittingly suffered to pass out of his possession, and of the whereabouts of which he has no knowledge.

Mislaid property is that which the owner has voluntarily and intentionally laid down in a place where he can again resort to it, and then has forgotten where he laid it.

Abandoned property is that of which the owner has relinquished all right, title, claim, and possession, with the intention of not reclaiming it or resuming its ownership, possession or enjoyment.

"Treasure trove consists essentially of articles of gold and silver, intentionally hidden for safety in the earth or in some secret place, the owner being unknown."

From the manner in which the bills in the instant case were carefully concealed beneath the paper lining of the drawer, it must be presumed that the concealment was effected intentionally and deliberately. The bills, therefore, cannot be regarded as abandoned property.

With regard to plaintiff's contention that the bills constituted treasure trove, it has been held that the law of treasure trove has been merged with that of lost goods generally, at least so far as respects the rights of the finder. * * *

The natural assumption is that the person who concealed the bills in the case at bar was a guest of the hotel. Their considerable value, and the manner of their concealment, indicate that the person who concealed them did so for purposes of security, and with the intention of reclaiming them. They were, therefore, to be classified not as lost but as misplaced or forgotten property, and the defendant, as occupier of the premises where they were found, had the right and duty to take them into his possession and to hold them as a gratuitous bailee for the true owner.

The decisive future of the present case is the fact that plaintiff was an employee or servant of the owner or occupant of the premises, and that, in discovering the bills and turning them over to her employer, she was simply performing the duties of her employment. She was allowed to enter the guest room solely in order to do her work as chambermaid, and she was expressly instructed to take to the desk clerk any mislaid or forgotten property which she might discover. It is true that, in the United States, the courts have tended to accede to the claims of servants to the custody of articles found by them during the course of their employment, where the articles are, in a legal sense, lost property. In Hamaker v. Blanchard, 90 Pa. 377, 35 Am.Rep. 664, a servant in a hotel found a roll of bank notes in the public parlor. It was held that, as the money was found on the floor of a room common to all classes of persons, there was no presumption that it was the property of a guest, and that, when the true owner was not found, the plaintiff was entitled to recover it from the innkeeper, to whom she had delivered it. In the case at bar, however, the bills were not lost property.

* * *

In finding for plaintiff herein, the circuit court judge held that his decision should be governed by Danielson v. Roberts, supra, 44 Or. 108, 74 P. 913, 65 L.R.A. 526, 102 Am.St. Rep. 627, and Roberson v. Ellis, 58 Or. 219, 114 P. 100, 102, 35 L.R.A.,N.S., 979. The present case may be distinguished from those cases, however. In the Danielson case, the plaintiffs were employed merely to clean out an old chicken house, in the process of which work they found buried treasure. In the Roberson case, the plaintiff was employed merely to remove from a warehouse certain goods and rubbish, and, while doing so, found some concealed gold coins. The finding of the treasure was, in neither case, within the scope of the employment of the finders. As stated in the Roberson case: "The handling of the property of other people, not connected with the defendant [the owner of the premises], was not in the line of the plaintiff's employment, and would neither impose responsibility nor confer privilege upon the defendant." In the present case, on the contrary, the search for mislaid or forgotten property was expressly within the scope of plaintiff's employment, and the delivery thereof to her employer was a part of her admitted duty.

* * *

Where money is found in an inn on the floor of a room common to the public, there being no circumstances pointing to its loss by a guest, the finder, even if an employee of the innkeeper, is entitled to hold the money as bailee for the true owner. It would seem that, as to articles voluntarily concealed by a guest, the very act of concealment would indicate that such articles have not been placed "in the protection of the house" and so, while the articles remain concealed, the innkeeper ordinarily would not have the responsibility of a bailee therefor. Upon their discovery by the innkeeper or his servant, however, the innkeeper's responsibility and duty as bailee for the owner becomes fixed.

In Flax v. Monticello Realty Co., 185 Va. 474, 39 S.E.2d 308, a hotel chambermaid found a diamond brooch, wrapped in tissue paper, concealed in a crevice in the margin of the mattress of a bed in one of the guest rooms. Thinking that the brooch belonged to the then occupant of the room, the maid placed it upon the bureau. There the guest found it, and laid claim to it as finder. He did, however, deposit it with the hotel manager in order that inquiry might be made to discover the owner. As the owner was not discovered, the guest demanded return of the brooch, and, on being refused, he brought an action in detinue against the hotel proprietor. Held, that an innkeeper is in direct and continued control of his guest rooms, which are to be considered as private rooms; that the brooch was unquestionably to be classified as mislaid and forgotten property; and that the innkeeper occupied the position of bailee for the true owner of the chattel.

The plaintiff in the present case is to be commended for her honesty and fair dealing throughout the transaction. Under our view of the law, however, we have no alternative other than to reverse the judgment of the lower court. It will be reversed accordingly.

*"Mickey Mouse, forever let us hold our banners high * * * M–I–C—K–E–Y—M–O–U–S–E."*

WALT DISNEY PRODUCTIONS v. MATURE PICTURES CORP.

United States District Court, S.D. New York, 1975.
389 F.Supp. 1397.

Kevin Thomas DUFFY, District Judge

This is an action for a preliminary injunction brought by the plaintiffs as owners of the copyright of Mickey Mouse March and seeking to prevent the use of that music by the defendants in a movie entitled "The Life and Times of the Happy Hooker" and/or "The Life and Times of Xaviera."

The "Mickey Mouse March" was an original song written by Jimmie Dodd and used generally in connection with the Mickey Mouse Club television series. Having at the request of the parties viewed major segments of the taped Mickey Mouse Club, it is clear that these programs were made for an audience comprised mainly of youngsters. The Mickey Mouse March apparently was the theme song for this television series.

In the movie produced and distributed by the defendants, there is a portion where three male actors sing some of the words of the Mickey Mouse March and for a period thereafter of approximately four to five minutes, the Mickey Mouse March is played as background music, while the female protagonist of the film appears to simultaneously gratify the sexual drive of the three other actors while the group of them is located on or near a billiards table. * * * Supposedly, according to the story line of the film, the three male actors were teenagers "whose father had arranged for her (the female protagonist) to be present as a birthday surprise to them." At the time the cast on the screen is quite bare except that the male actors are wearing "Mouseketeer" hats similar to those worn by the performers in the television productions of the "Mickey Mouse Club."

There can be no doubt that the music played as background in the defendants' film is the copyrighted "Mickey Mouse March." There is no doubt that the plaintiffs, as owners of the copyright, did not give defendants the right to use the song. There is no doubt that the defendants have used the copyrighted material for commercial gain.

The only real question presented is whether the use by defendants of the copyrighted material constitutes "fair use" as a parody.

Defendants claim the music is used to "highlight and emphasize the transition of such teenagers from childhood to manhood * * * in a highly comical setting," and as such is merely a "humorous take-off" on the music.

The exception of "fair use" as described in Rosemont Enterprises, Inc. v. Random

House, Inc., 366 F.2d 303, 307 (2d Cir. 1966) lies

> * * * in the constitutional purpose in granting copyright protection in the first instance, to wit, 'To promote the Progress of Science and the Useful Arts.' U.S.Const. art. 1, § 8. To serve that purpose, 'courts in passing upon particular claims of infringement must occasionally subordinate the copyright holder's interest in a maximum financial return to the greater public interest in the development of art, science and industry.' Whether the privilege may justifiably be applied to particular materials turns initially on the nature of the materials, e.g., whether their distribution would serve the public interest in the free dissemination of information and whether their preparation requires some use of prior materials dealing with the same subject matter.

Parody of a copyrighted article is one of the possible situations where the doctrine of fair use will come into play.

The permissible parody of the copyright article is not a complete copy of the original. It can only be permitted "[W]here the parodist does not appropriate a greater amount of the original work than is necessary to 're-call or conjure up' the object of his satire. * * *"

In the instant case, the use is far from the parody—there is a complete copy of the copyrighted material. The original song lasts for only two minutes, yet defendants used the work over and over again for substantially more time than is required to "conjure up the original." While defendants may have been seeking in their display of bestiality to parody life, they did not parody the Mickey Mouse March but sought only to improperly use the copyrighted material.

The defendants contend that no injunctive relief should be granted because there is no danger of irreparable damage being done through their use of the copyrighted material. In that contention they are totally wrong. Their use of the copyrighted material in the setting provided is such as to immediately compromise the work. Accordingly, a preliminary injunction will issue.

However, this Court recognizes that the issuance of this injunction could be used improperly to publicize either the "Mickey Mouse Club" or the "Life and Times of the Happy Hooker," and an order will enter providing that no such commercialization of this decision will be permitted under the penalty of contempt. Since the need for immediate relief is apparent, this Court will enter its own order simultaneously with the filing of this decision.

The last survivor gets all the money.

RUSHAK v. RUSHAK

Supreme Court, Appellate Division, Fourth Department, 1967.
28 A.D.2d 807, 281 N.Y.S.2d 940.

On January 14, 1952 Paraska Rushak opened the bank account which is the subject of the present litigation. Subsequently, in December 1959, she converted the account to a joint account, and a signature card was deposited with the bank bearing signatures of Paraska Rushak and her two sons, John and Stephen, stating that the account was jointly owned by the signatories, the survivor being entitled to the balance. The only deposits ever made in the account were made by Mrs. Rushak before the creation of the joint tenancy and the book was kept by her until her death on July 20, 1965. Five days later, on July 25, 1965, her son Stephen also died, leaving John as the surviving joint tenant. The appeal now before us is by John Rushak from a decree determining that the bank account belongs one-half to the estate of Stephen and one-half to John.

There can be no question * * * that in December 1959 Paraska Rushak created a joint tenancy with a right of ownership in the survivor. The fact that there were three, rather than the usual two, joint tenants does not change this result; nor is it affected by the death of one joint tenant. If, during the lifetime of the two surviving tenants, neither disposes of his joint interest, upon the death of the second joint owner the last survivor becomes the sole owner.

It is not important what the intention of either Stephen or John might have been after the death of Paraska as regards the ultimate disposition of the bank account, for they were not then creating a joint tenancy—or any interest—as between themselves. The joint tenancy with the right of survivorship had already been created in 1959 and that tenancy continued up to the death of Stephen, in the absence of any act by either of the brothers to terminate it. The joint ownership of personal property was analogous to a joint estate in lands and until terminated by act of the parties continued subject to the right of sole ownership in the survivor.

Decree unanimously reversed on the law and order granted decreeing that the joint bank account belongs to John Rushak. * * *

Upon learning of his terminal cancer he deeded the land to his "daddy," but was there a delivery of the deed?

HAGEN v. PALMER

Supreme Court of South Dakota, 1973.
87 S.D. 485, 210 N.W.2d 164.

DOYLE, Justice

This is an action to set aside a deed to a quarter section of land for lack of consideration and nondelivery of the deed with the proviso that the plaintiff pay to the defendant any sum due defendant on account of the purchase of said property, less the reasonable value of use of the land during the defendant's possession. The trial court entered judgment for the defendant and plaintiff appeals.

The plaintiff, Ethel C. Hagen, was formerly married to Paul Palmer, deceased, who was the son of Charles Palmer, the defendant in this action. They were married in 1951 and lived with the father until 1953 when they moved to a farming unit consisting of approximately 720 acres owned by the father. The land in dispute is contiguous to the unit owned by the father. On March 19, 1958, Paul Palmer purchased the land in question, one quarter section. He borrowed $600 from the bank and $5000 from his father in order to pay for the land. Paul and his wife Ethel resided on this unit, which included the part rented from the father and the quarter section purchased by Paul, until Paul Palmer died in July 1963. There was no formal lease or rent agreement between Charles Palmer and Paul Palmer. In November 1962, Paul Palmer learned that he had terminal cancer. On January 5, 1963, Paul Palmer and his wife Ethel Palmer executed a warranty deed conveying the quarter section of land in question to Charles Palmer. This warranty deed was drawn in an attorney's office, acknowledged by the attorney, mailed to the Register of Deeds of Hyde County where it was duly recorded and then returned to the attorney. The deed was subsequently mailed to the Paul Palmer residence and placed in their files. The defendant did not see the deed until it was shown to him at the trial. After the death of Paul Palmer, on July 29, 1963, his wife Ethel continued to live on the unit. However, the defendant, Charles Palmer, took possession of the parcel of land in question and leased it, collecting rent from 1964. He also paid the real estate taxes on the land from 1963 to date of trial. Ethel Palmer was the executrix of the estate of Paul Palmer, and the land in question was not included as part of the estate of Paul Palmer.

There are several propositions presented on appeal; however, the question of delivery of the deed is determinative of this lawsuit. The finding of fact and conclusion of law of the trial judge was that a preponderance of the evidence established that the deed executed by Paul and Ethel Palmer on January 5, 1963, was constructively delivered to the grantee, Charles Palmer. The trial court's finding, of course, will not be disturbed on appeal unless clearly erroneous.

The general rule concerning delivery is stated in Powell on Real Property, Vol. 6, ¶ 896, p. 249 at 252, as follows:

> The finding of delivery rests upon a judicial conclusion that the conduct of the grantor

> justifies a finding of his intent to treat the deed as an unrecallable instrument giving the grantee what the deed purports to convey him.

SDCL 43–4–9 states:

> Though a grant be not actually delivered into the possession of the grantee, it is yet to be deemed constructively delivered where the instrument is, by the agreement of the parties at the time of execution, understood to be delivered, and under such circumstances that the grantee is entitled to immediate delivery.

Whether there has been delivery is a question of intent to be found from all the facts surrounding the transaction. "The fact that a deed has been duly executed, acknowledged, and recorded is prima facie evidence of its delivery."

The evidence disclosed affirmative acts by the plaintiff from which the trial court could reasonably find an intent on her part and a knowledge of the intent of Paul Palmer to treat the deed as having been delivered to the grantee. Plaintiff was the executrix of the estate of Paul Palmer and his sole heir, and throughout the proceedings of said estate she made no claim that Paul Palmer had any interest in the land. The plaintiff, together with her husband, Oscar Hagen, leased and paid rent for this land in the year 1965. The defendant was permitted to take possession of the real estate, to lease it from 1964 and to retain all rental therefrom without any objection from the plaintiff. The defendant has also paid all real estate taxes on this property for the years 1963 to date of trial. There was testimony by the defendant that prior to Paul Palmer's death he had two conversations with his son regarding this parcel of land. The first conversation was in the fall of 1962 when Paul told his father, "'daddy, * * * I am going to give that quarter back to you. * * * I owe it to you.'" The second conversation occurred sometime between January 5, 1963 and July 1963, at which time Paul told his father that he had conveyed the property to him. Plaintiff, herself, testified that she knew that defendant was aware that Paul Palmer had put this parcel of land in the defendant's name and had informed him of this fact. There was testimony of a neighbor who stated that on January 5, 1963, the date of the deed, Paul Palmer had told him that he had transferred the parcel of land in question to his father because he owed money on it and felt he should turn it back to him.

The evidence disclosed that delivery and acceptance of the deed were accomplished by the parties. The plaintiff relies primarily on Cassidy v. Holland, 27 S.D. 287, 130 N.W. 771, in which this court held that:

> Where a deed is found in the possession of the grantor unexplained, the presumptions in relation to the delivery thereof are exactly opposite to those where the deed comes from the possession of the grantee.

In that case, however, the deed was not recorded and had never been out of the grantor's possession; consequently, the opinion does not apply to the facts in the present case.

* * *

In view of the trial court's express finding of constructive delivery of the deed, supported not only by the testimony of the defendant but by testimony of the plaintiff, and affirmative acts on the part of the plaintiff disclosing an intent that the deed had in fact been delivered, we conclude that judgment for the defendant be affirmed.

The defendants have established their "hostile, adverse claim of right to pasture and water livestock"—an easement by prescription.

SCHWENKER v. SAGERS

Supreme Court of Iowa, 1975.
230 N.W.2d 525.

HARRIS, Justice

This dispute concerns the extent of defendants' right to use a 30 foot wide strip of farmland. The trial court held defendants' rights were limited to ingress and egress to their adjoining land. The trial court issued a writ of injunction restraining defendants from, among other things, using the strip for keeping, feeding and watering livestock. We reverse and remand.

In 1943 defendants purchased a 50 acre tract in Jackson County, Iowa adjacent to land they already owned. To previous owners the 50 acre tract had been "landlocked"; that is, it did not abut a public roadway. Access to the 50 acre tract had been established over the 30 foot strip in question to an east-west public road to the south.

Plaintiff owned the tract from which the 30 foot strip was taken. The strip, which is also used for access purposes by persons other than the parties, amounts to a dirt farm lane. It is enclosed by fences with a gate at the point where it joins the public road. A short distance from the south boundary of defendants' 50 acre tract the strip is crossed by a stream. The stream does not otherwise touch defendants' property. Accordingly through long usage defendants and their predecessors in title utilized the strip for the purpose of watering livestock at the stream.

Although plaintiff disputes it, we believe defendants clearly established their claim they used the entire strip to water and pasture their livestock from the time they acquired the tract in 1943.

The actual use was a considerable enlargement of defendants' recorded rights to the strip, which they originally acquired by quit claim deed. Their immediate grantor acquired the strip by a deed which described an "easement to the use of the * * * [strip] as a roadway jointly with the grantor. * * *"

The right of plaintiff, defendants, and others to use the strip as a roadway is not disputed. At issue is defendants' expanded use of the strip for purpose of pasturing and watering livestock. Defendants claim their expanded right by way of prescription.

Until 1964 the question was not of great moment to the parties. In 1964 plaintiff acquired another tract to the north of defendants'. Use of the strip for ingress and egress had been reserved to the owner of that tract and was conveyed to plaintiff. Also in 1964 defendants rented their farm. Plaintiff claims the tenants keep more cattle than defendants did. It is apparent the trend to ever larger farm machinery has aggravated the problems incident to the shared use of the strip.

There are three generally recognized methods of creating an easement: (1) express written grant, (2) prescription and (3) implication. It is not controlling here that there was a more limited written grant as to the same strip in this case. The terms of the written grant are not denied by plaintiff. And defendants do not suggest that the written grant was sufficiently broad to authorize the use to which they were enjoined by the trial court. This is not a claim of easement by implication. Defendants' sole claim of easement in the strip for livestock use was by way of prescription.

"An easement by prescription is created 'by adverse possession, under claim of right or color of title, openly notoriously, continuously, and hostilely asserted against defendants for ten years or more.' [U]se of property does not establish adverse possession. One claiming an easement by prescription must prove by evidence, independent of his use, that an easement was claimed as a matter of right and that the title holder had express notice thereof."

An easement established for a limited use may be expanded by prescription.

Two principles are argued which should be laid aside, not as invalid, but because they are inapplicable. * * *

One principle limits the extent to which a shared easement may generally be used. It is a practical rule, necessary to accommodate the needs of others who share the easement, including the owner of the servient estate.

"The principles governing easement rights are simple and well established. [The easement holder] has the right to use the * * * strip in the manner and for the purposes it was intended to serve. He cannot use it in a way which imposes additional burdens on the owner of the land through which it runs. [The easement holder's] rights are not exclusive, and [servient owners] may use the easement strip for any purpose not inconsistent with [the] easement.

"Neither * * * may use the [strip] in violation of the rights of the other. * * *"

The foregoing principle might have aided plaintiff if the recorded easement had not been enlarged by prescription. It does not operate to reduce easement rights but only to define and regulate them. In short, the rule set out * * * could have been utilized to prevent defendants from acquiring expanded uses. But it is not appropriate to erase or erode rights to such uses after they have been established by prescription.

Another principle governs situations where the use is merely permissive at its inception. Where the use is undertaken by permission of the servient estate owner it is not adverse or under claim of right. Continued use does not, by mere lapse of time, become hostile or adverse. This principle does not prevent prescription from ever running in all cases where the original use was merely permissive. But it is necessary for the user to show the use has become adverse and ceased to be merely permissive. We have held one manner in which a permissive use becomes adverse is by transfer of the servient property.

The trial court noted the servient property in the instant case had been transferred to plaintiff within ten years prior to suit. On this basis it was held defendant had not shown adverse or hostile use for sufficient time to establish a prescriptive right. This was error. The fact less than ten years had run from transfer of the servient estate does not bar establishment of the prescriptive easement for two reasons. Neither the recorded easement nor the expanded easement were permissive in origin. In any event the expanded easement was clearly shown to be hostile and adverse to plaintiff's predecessors in title for a period far in excess of ten years.

IV. Enlargement by prescription of a limited easement is rare. We note and adopt the following:

"The comparatively few cases which a comprehensive search has revealed as involving the point clearly indicate that *where an easement is granted for use in a specified manner or for a specified purpose, an open and continuous use thereof, under a claim of right for the prescriptive period for purposes or in a manner beyond the scope of the grant, will create an easement of the larger scope by prescription,* although in the majority of such cases the enlarged easement was held in fact not to arise because of a lack of the elements necessary to create it." (Emphasis added.)

In the instant case defendants clearly establish their hostile, adverse claim of right to pasture and water livestock. The record shows defendants treated the strip as if they had bought it together with the 50 acre tract in 1943. There was a road gate at the end of the strip. The strip was thereby fenced together with a pasture on the 50 acre tract. Pasture and strip became one common ground where defendants thereafter regularly pastured and watered their cattle.

Defendants were able to show they had received, some 20 years prior to trial, a letter from Hillis Lee, a Maquoketa attorney. Mr. Lee then represented I. M. Bowley, a predecessor owner of the servient estate. Mr. Bowley threatened to put a gate across the strip so as to block access to the stream. At the time Mr. Bowley threatened to do so in order to impel defendants to participate in the upkeep of the north end of the strip. Defendants advised Mr. Lee they had a right to the use of the strip, specifically to the water, and refused to cooperate. The record shows that on the basis of their insistence Mr. Bowley's demands were dropped. They continued to use the strip during approximately 20 years that followed.

The trial court erred in ordering an injunction restraining defendants from using the strip for keeping, feeding and watering livestock.

Judgment of the trial court is reversed and the case is remanded for entry of a judgment in conformity herewith.

Spring guns and other man-killing devices are not justifiable against a petty thief.

KATKO v. BRINEY

Supreme Court of Iowa, 1971.
183 N.W.2d 657.

MOORE, Chief Justice

The primary issue presented here is whether an owner may protect personal property in an unoccupied boarded-up farm house against trespassers and thieves by a spring gun capable of inflicting death or serious injury.

We are not here concerned with a man's right to protect his home and members of his family. Defendants' home was several miles from the scene of the incident to which we refer infra.

Plaintiff's action is for damages resulting from serious injury caused by a shot from a 20-gauge spring shotgun set by defendants in a bedroom of an old farm house which had been uninhabited for several years. Plaintiff and his companion, Marvin McDonough, had broken and entered the house to find and steal old bottles and dated fruit jars which they considered antiques.

At defendants' request plaintiff's action was tried to a jury consisting of residents of the community where defendants' property was located. The jury returned a verdict for plaintiff and against defendants for $20,000 actual and $10,000 punitive damages.

* * *

Most of the facts are not disputed. In 1957 defendant Bertha L. Briney inherited her parents' farm land in Mahaska and Monroe Counties. Included was an 80-acre tract in southwest Mahaska County where her grandparents and parents had lived. No one occupied the house thereafter. Her husband, Edward, attempted to care for the land. He kept no farm machinery thereon. The outbuildings became dilapidated.

For about 10 years, 1957 to 1967, there occurred a series of trespassing and housebreaking events with loss of some household items, the breaking of windows and "messing up of the property in general." The latest occurred June 8, 1967, prior to the event on July 16, 1967 herein involved.

Defendants through the years boarded up the windows and doors in an attempt to stop the intrusions. They had posted "no trespass" signs on the land several years before 1967. The nearest one was 35 feet from the house. On June 11, 1967 defendants set "a shotgun trap" in the north bedroom. After Mr. Briney cleaned and oiled his 20-gauge shotgun, the power of which he was well aware, defendants took it to the old house where they secured it to an iron bed with the barrel pointed at the bedroom door. It was rigged with wire from the doorknob to the gun's trigger so it would fire when the door was opened. Briney first pointed the gun so an intruder would be hit in the stomach but at Mrs. Briney's suggestion it was lowered to hit the legs. He admitted he did so "because I was mad and tired of being tormented" but "he did not intend to injure anyone." * * *

Plaintiff lived with his wife and worked regularly as a gasoline station attendant in Eddyville, seven miles from the old house. He had observed it for several years while hunting in the area and considered it as being abandoned. He knew it had long been uninhabited. In 1967 the area around the house was covered with high weeds. Prior to July 16, 1967 plaintiff and McDonough had been to the premises and found several old bottles and fruit jars which they took and added to their collection of antiques. On the latter date about 9:30 p.m. they made a second trip to the Briney property. They entered the old house by removing a board from a porch window which was without glass. While McDonough was looking around the kitchen area plaintiff went to another part of the house. As he started to open the north bedroom door the shotgun went off striking him in the right leg above the ankle bone. Much of his leg, including part of the tibia, was blown away. Only by McDonough's assistance was plaintiff able to get out of the house and after crawling some distance was put in his vehicle and rushed to a doctor and then to a hospital. He remained in the hospital 40 days.

Plaintiff's doctor testified he seriously considered amputation but eventually the healing process was successful. Some weeks after his release from the hospital plaintiff returned to work on crutches. He was required to keep the injured leg in a cast for approximately a year and wear a special brace for another year. He continued to suffer pain during this period.

There was undenied medical testimony plaintiff had a permanent deformity, a loss of tissue, and a shortening of the leg.

* * *

Plaintiff testified he knew he had no right to break and enter the house with intent to steal bottles and fruit jars therefrom. He further testified he had entered a plea of guilty to larceny in the nighttime of property of less than $20 value from a private building. He stated he had been fined $50 and costs and paroled during good behavior from a 60-day jail sentence. Other than minor traffic charges this was plaintiff's first brush with the law. * * *

The main thrust of defendants' defense in the trial court and on this appeal is that "the law permits use of a spring gun in a dwelling or warehouse for the purpose of preventing the unlawful entry of a burglar or thief." * * *

In the statement of issues the trial court stated plaintiff and his companion committed a felony when they broke and entered defendants' house. * * * [T]he court referred to the early case history of the use of spring guns and stated under the law their use was prohibited except to prevent the commission of felonies of violence and where human life is in danger. * * *

* * * ["O]ne may use reasonable force in the protection of his property, but such right is subject to the qualification that one may not use such means of force as will take human life or inflict great bodily injury. Such is the rule even though the injured party is a trespasser and is in violation of the law himself."

* * * "An owner of premises is prohibited from willfully or intentionally injuring a trespasser by means of force that either takes life or inflicts great bodily injury; and therefore a person owning a premise is prohibited from setting out 'spring guns' and like dangerous devices which will likely take life or inflict great bodily injury, for the purpose of harming trespassers. The fact that the trespasser may be acting in violation of the law does not change the rule. The only time when such conduct of setting a 'spring gun' or a like dangerous device is justified would be when the trespasser was committing a felony of violence or a felony punishable by death, or where the trespasser was endangering human life by his act."

* * *

The overwhelming weight of authority, both textbook and case law, supports the trial court's statement of the applicable principles of law.

Prosser on Torts, Third Edition, pages 116–118, states:

> * * * the law has always placed a higher value upon human safety than upon mere rights in property, it is the accepted rule that there is no privilege to use any force calculated to cause death or serious bodily injury to repel the threat to land or chattels, unless there is also such a threat to the defendant's personal safety as to justify a self-defense. * * * spring guns and other man-killing devices are not justifiable against a mere trespasser, or even a petty thief. They are privileged only against those upon whom the landowner, if he were present in person would be free to inflict injury of the same kind.

* * *

In Volume 2, Harper and James, The Law of Torts, section 27.3, pages 1440, 1441, this is found: "The possessor of land may not arrange his premises intentionally so as to cause death or serious bodily harm to a trespasser. The possessor may of course take some steps to repel a trespass. If he is present he may use force to do so, but only that amount which is reasonably necessary to effect the repulse. Moreover if the trespass threatens harm to property only—even a theft of property—the possessor would not be privileged to use deadly force, he may not arrange his premises so that such force will be inflicted by mechanical means. If he does, he will be liable even to a thief who is injured by such device."

* * *

In Hooker v. Miller, 37 Iowa 613, we held defendant vineyard owner liable for damages resulting from a spring gun shot although plaintiff was a trespasser and there to steal grapes. At pages 614, 615, this statement is made: "This court has held that a mere trespass against property other than a dwelling is not a sufficient justification to authorize the use of a deadly weapon by the owner in its defense; and that if death results in such a case it will be murder, though the killing be actually necessary to prevent the trespass. The State v. Vance, 17 Iowa 138." At page 617 this court said: "[T]respassers and other inconsiderable violators of the law are not to be visited by barbarous punishments or prevented by inhuman inflictions of bodily injuries."

* * *

In addition to civil liability many jurisdictions hold a land owner criminally liable for serious injuries or homicide caused by spring guns or other set devices. See State v. Childers, 133 Ohio 508, 14 N.E.2d 767 (melon thief shot by spring gun); Pierce v. Commonwealth, 135 Va. 635, 115 S.E. 686 (policeman killed by spring gun when he opened unlocked front door of defendant's shoe repair shop); State v. Marfaudille, 48 Wash. 117, 92 P. 939 (murder conviction for death from spring gun set in a trunk); State v. Beckham, 306 Mo. 566, 267 S.W. 817 (boy killed by spring gun attached to window of defendant's chili stand); State v. Green, 118 S.C. 279, 110 S.E. 145, 19 A.L.R. 1431 (intruder shot by spring gun when he broke and entered vacant house. Manslaughter conviction of owner-affirmed); State v. Barr, 11 Wash. 481, 39 P. 1080 (murder conviction affirmed for death of an intruder into a boarded up cabin in which owner had set a spring gun).

* * *

The jury's findings of fact including a finding defendants acted with malice and with wanton and reckless disregard, as required for an allowance of punitive or exemplary damages, are supported by substantial evidence. * * *

* * *

Study and careful consideration of defendants' contentions on appeal reveal no reversible error.

Affirmed.

Review Questions

1. What are the requirements of a deed? What are the differences between the four basic types of deeds? What is the difference between marketable title and good record title? What are the two basic types of title insurance? What effect do recording laws have on adverse possession? What is required to achieve ownership by adverse possession? Explain your answers.

2. What is the difference between a personal and property right? Why is a leasehold not real property? Does a contract for the sale of minerals, crops, or timber constitute the sale of goods? What is the most important test in deciding whether something has become a fixture? Is this test ever disregarded? What other tests are used? Does it make any difference that the annexor is a tenant? Why might it be important that something is classified as real or personal property? Explain your answers.

3. In what five situations does a person acquire ownership of personal property by accession? What are the "loss of identity" and "relative value" rules? Does a willful wrongdoer ever get title by accession? When will a person acquire title by confusion? What are the requirements for an effective gift? How does the concept of gift causa mortis apply to property? How does a patent differ from a copyright? Explain your answers.

4. What is the difference between an easement, a license, and a lease? What factors do the courts look to in deciding whether a relationship is a lease or a license? Must a lease be in writing? An easement? What is the different between a tenancy for years and a tenancy from period to period? What laws protect against discrimination in renting real property? Who generally has the duty to repair leased premises? How does URLTA protect tenants? Explain your answers.

5. How does an easement appurtenant differ from an easement in gross? How does an easement in gross differ from a license? How are easements created? How does a profit differ from an easement? What does it mean when a covenant "runs with the land"? To what extent does a person have to worry about others getting hurt on his or her land? Can one use force to prevent people from stealing or trespassing on property? Explain your answers.

6. Is it possible to become the owner of a wild animal? Can someone who "finds" property become the owner of it? Does it make any difference whether it is classified as abandoned, lost, mislaid property, treasure trove, or property embedded in the soil? Does it make any difference that someone is an employee working on the premises where he or she "finds" the property or that the finder is a trespasser? Must a finder follow any statutory procedure? Is a finder entitled to compensation for finding? Explain your answers.

7. When will property escheat to the state? What are the characteristics of a fee simple absolute estate? Are there any restrictions on the ownership of such a fee? If one conveys away a life estate, what is retained? What is "future" about a future interest? Why might people own property concurrently? What is probate? What method of owning property concurrently will avoid probate? Explain your answers.

8. Define the following terms: attractive nuisance, covenant of quiet possession, constructive eviction, encroachment, gratuitous bailment, life estate pur autre vie, occupation, percentage lease, permissive waste, possession, remainder, surrender, tenancy in common, title, trademark, unlawful detainer proceeding.

Problems

1. Read and answer the following:

   a. Henry Dixon is the only passenger on a city bus. He finds an old black umbrella hooked over a seat (the owner intentionally left it there, no longer wanting the umbrella); a valuable ring lying on the floor; and a tote bag containing an expensive camera on the luggage rack above the seats. As between the bus company and Henry Dixon, who is entitled to the umbrella, the ring, and the tote bag? Explain.

   b. Henry works as a janitor at a local night club. While tidying up in the lounge, Henry finds a charm bracelet on the dance floor. As between the nightclub owner and Henry, who is entitled to the bracelet? Explain.

   c. After work, Henry goes to dinner at his friend Sheila's house. While playing horseshoes in Sheila's backyard, Henry discovers an empty wallet buried under the surface of the soil. As between Sheila and Henry, who is entitled to the wallet? Explain.

   d. On his way home, Henry trespasses over John Murphy's private property. Henry discovers a woman's handbag (containing no identification) under some bushes on the property. As between John and Henry, who is entitled to the handbag? Explain.

2. Patti Schroeder signs a written lease, agreeing to rent an apartment from "The Keyes Company" for a two-year period, the rent to be paid in monthly installments of $250. Patti is happy with the rented premises until one spring day when she forgets to close her glass sliding doors and an unexpected shower damages the apartment wall and floor. Patti insists that The Keys Company has a duty to keep the premises in repair, but the Company refuses to repair the water damage. A week later, and twelve months before the lease expires, Patti leaves the rented premises and moves in with her sister Cindy. Upon discovering that Patti has left, The Keys Company retakes possession of the apartment. In a back closet, the Company finds a color TV, some clothing, and other personal items forgotten by Patti; the Company sells the property and applies the proceeds towards Patti's unpaid rent. A few days later, and without informing Patti, the Company relets the premises for $200 a month. Twelve months later, the Company sues Patti for $750 (the $600 difference between the old rent and the new rent for the twelve-month period plus $150 for the water damage to the apartment). Patti seeks your advice.

   a. What type of tenancy did Patti enter into?

   b. As between The Keys Company and Patti, who is responsible for the water damage to the apartment? Explain.

   c. Did The Keys Company have a right to relet the premises when Patti moved in with her sister? Explain.

   d. Did the Company have a right to sell Patti's property? Explain.

   e. Is Patti responsible for the $600 rent deficit? Explain.

3. a. Jenny Walker works as a salesperson at "Price's Fabric Shop." One day when Mrs. Price is gone from the shop, Jenny steals eight yards of fine cream colored silk worth eighty dollars and sews it into a wedding dress worth $400. Jenny spends six weeks making the dress; she trims it in lace (of her own) and adds a new nylon zipper (also her own). When Mrs. Price discovers the theft, she sues to replevin the material in its "improved state." Decision? Would your answer differ if Jenny had "innocently" used Mrs. Price's material, believing it to be her own? Explain.

b. Tom Lovejoy fears that he is going to die when his doctor informs him that he must undergo coronary by-pass surgery. Before going into the hospital, Tom conveys his beach lot to his nephew, Frank Lovejoy; Tom delivers the deed to Frank. Tom also gives his watch and ring to his cousin, Karen Kramer. Tom undergoes surgery and recovers completely. He tells Frank that he wants his land back, but Frank refuses. He tells Karen that he wants his watch and ring back, and she refuses.

1. As between Tom and Frank, who is entitled to the beach lot? Explain.
2. As between Tom and Karen, who is entitled to the watch and the ring? Explain.
3. In the event that Karen has sold the watch and ring to a person who took the jewelry for value and in good faith, can Tom replevin the watch and ring? Explain.

c. Jay Gerber publishes and copyrights an English literature text entitled, *The World of Thomas Hardy.* The text is designed for college level courses, and Jay anticipates handsome royalties. Nellie Franklin, a literature professor at Digby State University, makes ten copies of the first chapter of the text and distributes them to her students for classroom use. The University Library makes a single copy of the entire text. When student interest in the text grows, the campus bookstore makes 200 copes of the entire text and puts them on sale. What are Jay Gerber's rights, if any, against Nellie Franklin, the University Library, and the campus bookstore? Explain.

4. Ted Spencer rents an apartment from The Keys Company on a monthly basis. The rent is $225 a month, and Ted is required to pay a one-time, refundable security deposit of $450. The apartment is inhabitable when Ted takes possession of the premises, but a few months later the heating system malfunctions, and the apartment is too cold for comfort. Ted complains to The Keyes Company, but the Company refuses to repair the heating. Ted reports the problem to the local housing authority (thinking that it may be a housing code violation), and he joins the neighborhood tenant's union to learn more about his rights as a tenant. Angry that Ted has contacted the housing authority and joined the tenant's union, The Keys Company gives Ted thirty days' notice of termination of the tenancy. When Ted pays no heed to the notice, the Company physically ousts him from the premises and locks him out. What is more, the Company refuses to refund Ted's security deposit. Assuming the Uniform Residential Landlord Tenant Act applies, answer the following:

a. What type of tenancy agreement did Ted enter into?
b. Did The Keys Company have a duty to repair the heating system? Explain. If your answer is yes, how could Ted have enforced this duty?
c. What legal rights, if any, does Ted have against the Company for the physical ouster, the lockout, and the refusal to refund the security deposit?
d. Assuming Ted would like to return to the apartment, does he have a legal right to repossession of the premises? Explain.

How would your answers to # 4 above differ if the URLTA were not in effect?

5. The Merchants and Mechanics County Bank expanded its services and facilities as a result of the economic growth of the community it serves. In this connection, it provided safe deposit facilities for the first time. A large vault was constructed as a part of the renovation and expansion of the bank building. Merchants purchased a bank vault door from Foolproof Vault Doors, Inc., for $65,000 and installed it at the vault entrance. The state in which Merchants was located had a real property tax but did not have a personal property tax. When the tax assessor appraised the bank building after completion of the renovation and expansion, he included the bank vault door as a part of the real property. Merchants has filed an objection claiming the vault door was initially personal property and remains so after installation in the bank.

There are no specific statutes or regulations determinative of the issue. Therefore, the question will be decided according to common law principles of property law.

Required: Answer the following, setting forth reasons for any conclusions stated.

a. What is the likely outcome as to the classification of the bank vault door?
b. The above situation involves a dispute between a tax authority and the owner of property. In what other circumstances might a dispute arise with respect to the classification of property as either real or personal property?

Source: CPA Exam, May 1979, #5.6.

6. Fosdick's land adjoins Tracy's land, and Tracy has been using a trail across Fosdick's land for a number of years. The trail is the shortest route to a roadway which leads into town. Tracy is asserting a right to continue to use the trail despite Fosdick's objections. In order to establish an easement by prescription, Tracy must show

a. Implied consent by Fosdick.
b. Use of the trail for the applicable statutory period.

c. His use of the trail with an intent to assert ownership to the underlying land.
d. Prompt recordation of the easement upon its coming into existence.

Source: CPA Exam, May 1983, #1(54).

7. Which of the following is true with respect to an easement created by an express grant?

a. The easement will be extinguished upon the death of the grantee.
b. The easement cannot be sold or transferred by the owner of the easement.
c. The easement gives the owner of the easement the right to the physical possession of the property subject to the easement.
d. The easement must be in writing to be valid.

Source: CPA Exam, May 1977, #3(36).

8. Wilmont owned a tract of waterfront property on Big Lake. During Wilmont's ownership of the land, several frame bungalows were placed on the land by tenants who rented the land from Wilmont. In addition to paying rent, the tenants paid for the maintenance and insurance of the bungalows, repaired, altered and sold them without permission or hindrance from Wilmont. The bungalows rested on surface cinderblock and were not bolted to the ground. The buildings could be removed without injury to either the buildings or the land. Wilmont sold the land to Marsh. The deed to Marsh recited that Wilmont sold the land, with buildings thereon, "subject to the rights of tenants, if any, . . ." When the tenants attempted to remove the bungalows, Marsh claimed ownership of them. In deciding who owns the bungalows, which of the following is *least* significant?

a. The leasehold agreement itself, to the extent it manifested the intent of the parties.
b. The mode and degree of annexation of the buildings to the land.
c. The degree to which removal would cause injury to the buildings or the land.
d. The fact that the deed included a general clause relating to the buildings.

Source: CPA Exam, May 1983, #1(53).

9. Smith purchased a tract of land. To protect himself, he ordered title insurance from Valor Title Insurance Company. The policy was the usual one issued by title companies. Accordingly

a. Valor will *not* be permitted to take exceptions to its coverage if it agreed to insure and prepared the title abstract.
b. The title policy is assignable in the event Smith subsequently sells the property.
c. The title policy provides protection against defects in record title only.
d. Valor will be liable for any title defect which arises, even though the defect could *not* have been discovered through the exercise of reasonable care.

Source: CPA Exam, May 1983, #1(55).

10. Purdy purchased real property from Hart and received a warranty deed with full covenants. Recordation of this deed is

a. Not necessary if the deed provides that recordation is *not* required.
b. Necessary to vest the purchaser's legal title to the property conveyed.
c. Required primarily for the purpose of providing the local taxing authorities with the information necessary to assess taxes.
d. Irrelevant if the subsequent party claiming superior title had actual notice of the unrecorded deed.

Source: CPA Exam, May 1983, #1(56).

The protection and enforcement of contracts through courts of civil law is the most crucial need of a peaceful society; without such protection, no civilization could be developed or maintained.

Ayn Rand
The Virtue of Selfishness

9

Contracts

WHAT ARE CONTRACTS AND HOW DO CONTRACTS RELATE TO PROPERTY?

A contract cannot be seen or touched or be otherwise perceived by the senses. It is a legal concept that exists only in the imagination. It is a thing conceived in the mind as creating legal rights and duties by reason of a bargain or promises between people. It is not a "writing." To be sure, many contracts are evidenced by a writing, but, even where the terms of the contract are written down, the writing itself is not the contract but merely proof of the contract which will always remain intangible.

Most contracts are, in fact, never written down. They are entirely products of the spoken word or of a wordless bargain or exchange. For example, if you purchase a magazine at the supermarket, you enter into a contract whether you orally state to the checker, "I'll take this magazine," or you simply place the magazine on the counter and the checker rings up the sale on the cash register. Similarly, if you place a quarter into a vending machine and receive a candy bar in return, you enter into a contract though nothing is said or put into writing. And the same is true if you place money into a parking meter to pay for an hour's parking (in this case, you enter into a contract with the city, you agreeing to pay a quarter in advance for the city's implied promise to rent you the space for an hour's time).

Whether a transaction is oral, wordless, or written, it constitutes a contract if it is recognized by law as creating legal rights and duties by reason of the bargain or promises (express or implied) of the agreeing parties.

Thus, "contracts" may be defined as legally recognized promises or bargains made by two or more persons including all rights and duties resulting from the promises or bargains.

Contracts often involve the transfer or sale of property or the performance of services in order to make a living and acquire property. Additionally, most contract rights are themselves property rights, as they may be freely transferred to others (such rights are correctly classified as *intangible* personal property rights) because they can be neither seen nor physically possessed. Yet, because they are transferable, they are property rights.

Contract rights are personal rights (rather than property rights) where they involve such close personal relationships or personal services that it would be unfair to permit their transfer. For example, you may have a binding contract to the personal services of a surgeon in taking out your appendix: neither you nor the surgeon can transfer that right to another. Or say that you have obtained approval for a loan based upon your good financial position and excellent credit rating—you obviously have no ability to transfer your right to the loan to another (his or her financial position and credit rating may be different).

The law requires four elements for a valid contract: (1) mutual assent, (2) consideration, (3) capacity, and (4) legality. Lacking any one of these four elements, the promises or bargains between parties will not create rights and duties and will not result in a valid contract.

WHY DO WE NEED THE CONTRACT CONCEPT?

People need commercial law so as to be able to plan and project, secure in the knowledge that their business dealings and agreements with others will be legally binding and enforceable. The basic tool or technique used by commercial or business law to accomplish this result is the contract. With the exception of illegal acts or promises, a person may use the contract device to commit to or have others commit to almost any present or future undertaking, including the sale of real or personal property, the performance of personal services, or the making of a loan. The law of contracts runs through every facet of modern society, reaching daily into all our lives. Our employment, our recreation, the properties we own, the creditors we owe—all are at some point subject to or governed by the law of contracts.

Through the concept of contracts, the law attempts to ensure that people will receive their reasonable expectations from the promises and bargains they enter into with others. The key word here is "reasonable." Where it is unreasonable to expect a party to carry out a promise exactly or to carry it out at all, the law will not require performance. For example, the law of contracts is unlikely to provide you with a legal remedy where your boyfriend or girlfriend fails to meet you for lunch "as promised," or where a friend who has "promised" to someday give you a valuable painting changes his or her mind. Most reasonable people in your position would not expect such promises to be legally binding or to result in legal remedies for "breach" of contract.

Contract law is complicated precisely because of the underlying notion of the law that not all promises should be legally binding. Obviously, it is very important for a person (particularly a business person) to know when the promises he or she makes or receives from others are binding and to what extent they are binding. As a result, many rules of contract law have been developed to determine when a person's promises or bargains will be binding and to what extent the machinery of the legal system will be available to assist the promisee in realizing his or her reasonable expectations if such promises or bargains are not carried out.

Of course, it is just as important to know when your promises or bargains will not be legally binding, and this is the starting point for a study of contracts—to know that promises and bargains will not be legally binding unless the four elements of mutual assent, consideration, capacity, and legality are present. In other words, you can promise a person anything, and the promise will mean nothing legally unless the four elements of a contract are present. While it may be bad manners to miss a luncheon date or a dance, it is not a breach of contract unless a contract was in fact formed (although it is unusual to form a contract regarding such subject matter, it is possible so long as all four elements of a valid contract are present).

So, start out with the basic realization that promises in and of themselves usually mean nothing legally unless they form a contract with the required mutual assent, consideration, capacity, and legality. The word "usually" is used because the law will sometimes recognize an exception to the general rule and hold a promise or bargain binding (at least in part) despite the fact that one or more of the four elements of a contract is lacking in order to achieve a fair and equitable result and meet a party's reasonable expectations.

WHAT ARE THE SOURCES OF CONTRACT LAW?

The basic law of contracts is common law (i.e., unwritten law resulting from court decisions). However, there are statutes in every state that affect contracts and control particular contract transactions. By far and away the most important legislation dealing with contracts is the Uniform Commercial Code which has been passed in full by forty-nine of the fifty states (and in part by Louisiana). The Code is divided into ten "Articles," each of which is divided into "Parts" and Sections. The "Articles" are entitled:

1. General Provisions;
2. Sales;
3. Commercial Paper;
4. Bank Deposits and Collections;
5. Letters of Credit;
6. Bulk Transfers;
7. Warehouse Receipts, Bills of Lading and Other Documents of Title;
8. Investment Securities;
9. Secured Transactions, Sales of Accounts, Contract Rights and Chattel Paper;
10. Effective Date and Repealer.

It should be noted that the Code applies to the sale of goods but does not apply to the sale of real property or to the use of real property as security (with the exception of fixtures). Nor does the Code apply to employment or other contracts involving services, to insurance contracts, suretyship transactions, or bankruptcy.

And even where the Code does apply, it may cover only part of the transaction—not all of its aspects. Common law and other statutory law may also come into play. The Code itself states at Section 1–103 that it is to be "supplemented" by the common law.

Thus, contract law is a blend of common law and statutory law. Though some of the specifics vary from state to state, the basic rules are largely the same.

WHAT IS MUTUAL ASSENT?

The first element necessary to formation of a contract is mutual assent. "Mutual assent" is synonymous with "agreement." What it requires is that each party manifest a willingness or agreement to be bound by his or her promise.

The law employs an objective test for determining the presence of mutual assent. Called the *objective theory of contracts,* the rule is that a contracting party may rely upon the apparent intentions of the other party without regard to the party's secret thoughts or subjective, but undisclosed, feelings or reservations. Thus, the test of mutual assent is what a reasonable person in the respective positions of each of the contracting parties would be led to believe by the words and conduct of the other party. So a person who subjectively intends not to enter into an agreement but who, by words or conduct, leads another reasonably to conclude that the requisite mutual assent is there, will be bound to the agreement despite his or her hidden intent to the contrary.

Now let's look at some examples. If, as a joke, Jeff Jackson offers to sell his $500 golf clubs to Jill Kelley for $25, and Jill, as a reasonable person, believes that the offer is genuine, mutual assent will be found despite Jeff's secret intention not to be bound by the agreement. However, if in light of all the circumstances, Jill should realize as a reasonable person that Jeff would not truly offer to sell the clubs for a mere fraction of their price, no mutual assent will be found, and Jeff will not be bound to follow through with the agreement. And of course, if Jill knows that Jeff's intent is to play a joke on her, mutual assent will not arise regardless of how reasonable it is to conclude from Jeff's words and conduct that he is serious about entering into an agreement.

The same rules apply to an expression of mutual assent made in anger or great excitement (e.g., a promise to pay $20,000 "to anyone who rescues my mother from the burning house"). For mutual assent to be found in such circumstances, it is necessary that the statement or expression create, in light of all the circumstances, an expectation of legally recognized rights in the mind of a reasonable person.

The objective theory of contracts also takes care of the social obligation situation. Suppose, for example, that Jeff Jackson promises Jill Kelley that he will have lunch with her on Tuesday or that he will take her to a dance at the college or country club. A reasonable person in Jill's position would realize that Jeff intends only a social obligation and not a binding legal promise with its attendant legal consequences for nonperformance. Understandably and logically, the law will not find the required mutual assent in such a situation.

HOW IS MUTUAL ASSENT USUALLY MANIFESTED?

Mutual assent is usually manifested by one party's making an offer and another party's making an acceptance of the offer.

An offer may be succinctly defined as a definite conditional undertaking. It is a *definite* proposal made by one party (the "offeror") to another party (the "offeree") indicating the offeror's present intent to enter into a contract (i.e., to *undertake* a legally recognized promise or obligation) *conditioned* upon the offeree's completion of the contract by acceptance.

It often happens that a party who desires to enter into a contract will not himself or herself make an offer, but will invite or request others to make offers that he or she can accept or disregard. This is particularly true of merchants (i.e., dealers in goods) who do not want to run the risk of making offers to sell a particular item to a large group of individuals or to the general public; if more than one of the offerees accepts, the offeror may face liability for breach of contract to all but the one offeree who receives the goods. Because such multiple liability is possible, it is very important for merchants to invite offers rather than to make offers to sell their goods.

Thus, it is that merchants or dealers in goods generally send out catalogs, price lists, or circular letters advertising their goods and prices but not offering to sell them. The advertisements are merely invitations to other merchants or members of the public to make an offer to buy the goods at the prices quoted. It is then up to the dealer to accept the offer or offers made; and, if the dealer does not have any goods in stock at the time the offer is made, he or she simply disregards the offer, and mutual assent does not arise.

This is not to say that merchants or dealers cannot make valid offers through their advertisements—merely that it is unusual for them to do so. To help protect merchants, there is a rebuttable presumption in the law that any advertisement placed in a newspaper, handbill, store window, catalog, price list, or circular letter is not an offer to sell but merely an invitation to another to make an offer to buy.

As a result, if you see an advertisement in your local newspaper that a local supermarket will be selling coffee, sugar, canned goods, and meats at specified prices on Saturday only, you are more than likely being invited, along with other potential customers, to come into the store on Saturday and make an offer to buy the advertised goods at the quoted prices. It is then up to the store to accept your offer at the check-out counter. In the unlikely event that the store has used language in the advertisement that clearly and unmistakably constitutes a definite conditional undertaking, the store has made an offer that you, as an offeree, have the power to accept.

HOW DEFINITE DOES A STATEMENT HAVE TO BE IN ORDER TO CONSTITUTE AN OFFER?

An offer does not have to contain every possible specific of an agreement in order to satisfy the requirement of definiteness. It need only be "reasonably" definite—that is, sufficiently definite that the court can determine the essential terms of the agreement as intended by the parties so as to meet the reasonable expectations of either party in damages. Suppose for example, that Bonita Businessperson and Thomas Artistic are graduating from college, Bonita with a degree in business administration and Thomas with a degree in art. Bonita plans to go into business for herself, while Thomas decides to paint still life for a living. If Bonita offers to pay Thomas a "fair share of the profits" from her business if Thomas will paint her a "masterpiece," the offer will fail for lack of definiteness. There is no way that a court can determine what a "fair share" of the profits from Bonita's new business might be, nor can the court pass judgment on what constitutes a "masterpiece" from Thomas.

It is generally agreed that the requirement of definiteness is satisfied if the court can determine four essential terms of the agreement: the parties to the contract, the subject matter of the contract, the time for performance by the parties, and the price, if any, involved in the transaction. It is not necessary that all four terms be spelled out expressly or exactly in the offer itself so long as the terms may be readily determined from the entire manifestations of the parties in both the offer and acceptance. In other words, the essential terms must be either expressly stated by the parties or unquestionably implied from their conduct. Suppose, for example, that a party telephones a plumber and requests him or her to come immediately and fix a pipe that has broken and flooded the caller's basement. Although nothing is said as to price, payment of a reasonable fee will be implied in fact from the caller's request for services. Because the price term is not mentioned at all, it is probable that the parties intended the term to be implied at the going rate of plumber's services.

UCC Provisions Regarding "Indefiniteness" in Contracts

It is important to realize that the Uniform Commercial Code has liberalized the requirement of definiteness insofar as contracts for the sale of goods are concerned. The specific Code provisions regarding "indefiniteness" in contracts for the sale of goods are summarized below.

Failure to state the price of goods Oftentimes, businesspeople leave the price term in a sales contract completely open or merely specify a procedure for determining price at some time in the future. And there may be good business reasons for doing so. The seller, on one hand, may believe that the market price is going to rise and so hope to sell at a higher price. The buyer, on the other hand, may believe that the market price is going to fall and so hope to conclude the purchase at a lower price (for a buyer purchasing inventory over a long period of time, the ability to buy at the lower price as the market price falls is crucial to remaining competitive with other dealers).

In recognition of the fact that "open price terms" are frequently necessary and desirable in business transactions, UCC Section 2–305, "Open Price Terms," provides as follows:

> (1) The parties if they so intend can conclude a contract for sale even though the price is not settled. In such a case the price is a reasonable price at the time for delivery if
>
> (a) nothing is said as to price; or
>
> (b) the price is left to be agreed by the parties and they fail to agree.
>
> * * *

Failure to specify place of delivery While most commercial sales (i.e., contracts entered into between businesspeople or merchants) expressly provide for the place and method of delivery of the goods, many private sales (i.e., contracts entered into between private persons) altogether omit any mention of delivery place. Where either a commercial or private sale of goods fails to specify the place of delivery, the transaction will not fail for lack of definiteness because of UCC Section 2–308 which provides:

> Unless otherwise agreed
>
> (a) the place for delivery of goods is the seller's place of business or if he has none, his residence. * * *

Failure to specify the time for shipment or delivery of the goods If the buyer and seller do not agree either expressly or impliedly on the time for delivery of the goods, UCC Section 2–309 provides that the time for delivery shall be a "reasonable" time. What is "reasonable" depends upon many factors including the nature of the goods (perishable or nonperishable), the nature of the market, the transportation conditions, the purpose for which the goods will be used, and the extent of the seller's knowledge of this purpose.

Failure to specify time of payment for the goods Where the time for payment is not specified by the parties, payment is due under UCC Section 2–310 at the time and place where the buyer receives the goods. The UCC provides for payment at the time of receipt of the goods in order to facilitate the buyer's right to inspect the goods prior to payment as provided for in Section 2–513. By deferring the buyer's duty to pay until the time and place of his or her receipt of the goods, the buyer can conveniently exercise his or her right of inspection just prior to payment.

Failure to state exactly the quantity of goods to be sold Often, a buyer of goods will contract for a seller's entire "output" or a seller will agree to supply a buyer with all his or her "requirements." Obviously, such contracts are inexact as to the quantity of goods to be sold, but they may be commercially desirable. A buyer, for example, may want to secure a source of supply that enables him or her easily to meet fluctuating market needs—

the convenience of dealing with only one seller is an added benefit. A seller, on the other hand, may find that the assurance of a market for his or her goods makes for better planning and scheduling of business operations and helps save storage and marketing costs, thus making for higher profits.

The UCC at Section 2–306 provides:

> (1) A term which measures the quantity by the output of the seller or the requirements of the buyer means such actual output or requirements as may occur in good faith, except that no quantity unreasonably disproportionate to any stated estimate or in the absence of a stated estimate to any normal or otherwise comparable prior output or requirements may be tendered or demanded.
>
> (2) A lawful agreement by either the seller or the buyer for exclusive dealing in the kind of goods concerned imposes unless otherwise agreed an obligation by the seller to use best efforts to supply the goods and by the buyer to use best efforts to promote their sale.

Under Subsection (1), a transaction for "output" or "requirements" is not too indefinite as it is held to mean the "actual good faith" output or requirements of the party.

Subsection (2) deals with "exclusive dealing" contracts wherein a buyer and seller agree that the buyer will have an exclusive right to sell the goods of the seller in a particular area or under a franchise. For example, Randall Retailer may be offered an exclusive right to sell in Walla Walla, Washington the products produced by the "Crispy Potato Chip and Dip" Company. At first glance, the offer appears too indefinite to create in Randall the right to complete an agreement upon acceptance. How much, for instance, is Randall supposed to sell under the terms of the offer? At what price? By imposing upon the seller an obligation to use his or her "best efforts" to supply the goods and upon the buyer an obligation to use his or her "best efforts" to sell the goods, Section 2–306 provides an objective standard by which these factors can be determined and saves the offer and subsequent acceptance from failure for lack of definiteness.

However, you will recall from Chapter 7 that "output," "requirements," and "exclusive dealing" contracts may result in unreasonable restraints of trade and such anticompetitive effect as to be violative of antitrust laws.

ARE THERE GUIDELINES FOR DETERMINING WHETHER PARTICULAR LANGUAGE CONSTITUTES AN OFFER?

While there is no one rule that tells us whether the particular words used by a person constitute an offer (indicating an intent to be bound), there are several "key" factors that may be helpful in making this determination.

Key Factors in Determining an Offer

To begin with, the primary test is this: Would a reasonable person in the position of the party hearing or reading the words believe that a contract would result upon his or her acceptance of the proposal? In answering this question, the courts look at four things.

The words used If the words of the proposal include "offer" or "promise," it is likely that an offer was intended. The words "I'm asking," or "first come, first served," or "I bid," are also suggestive of an offer. But the words, "Are you interested?," "Would you pay?," or "I'm thinking of selling" do not indicate an intent on the part of the speaker to become immediately bound.

How definite the words are The more definite the words and terms of the proposal, the more likely the proposal is an offer.

The circumstances in which the words are used Words spoken in a state of great excitement or fear rarely indicate true contractual intent even where words such as "offer" or "promise" are used. For example, a statement that "I promise to pay $50,000 to anyone who puts out the fire in my house" is probably not a valid offer. The same is true of a proposal obviously made in jest or in anger or as a political promise (e.g., "I promise to eliminate 10 percent of the bureaucrats in Washington, D.C., if you vote for me.").

The person to whom the proposal is made A statement made to a specific individual or to a small group of individuals is much more likely to constitute an offer than is a statement made to a large group of people or to the general public. This is not to say, however, that offers are never made to large groups or to the general public (an offer of reward, for example, is typically made to the public at large), but merely that they are more often made to small groups or a single individual.

MUST THE OFFEREE HAVE KNOWLEDGE OF THE OFFER TO ACCEPT IT?

The general rule is that an offeree must know of the existence of an offer before he or she can accept it. This means that the offer must be in some way communicated to the offeree either directly or indirectly (e.g., through a third party), or the offeree will not have the power to accept the offer.

For example, a person who performs an act called for in a public offer of reward generally cannot claim the reward unless he or she performed the act with knowledge of the offer. However, some courts hold that where the person learns of the reward after beginning performance, but before completing it, he or she may claim the reward by completing the called for act with the intention of accepting the offer. For example, suppose that Jeff Jackson finds a billfold and only later learns of a fifty dollar reward for "finding and returning" it. In a number of jurisdictions, Jeff will be permitted to collect the reward merely for returning the billfold to its true owner.

It is also held that identical cross-offers sent through the mail do not create mutual assent (offer and acceptance) because neither party has knowledge of the other's offer at the time of the mailing. Thus, where Jeff Jackson sends an offer by mail to Jill Kelley, offering to sell Jill his vacant lot on 4th Street for $6,000, and Jill, in ignorance of this offer, mails an offer to Jeff, offering to buy Jeff's vacant lot on 4th Street for $6,000, there is no mutual assent—no offer and acceptance—and there can be none until one of the parties accepts the other's offer.

However, insofar as the sale of goods is concerned, the rule on identical cross-offers is subject to UCC Section 2–204 which states that "an agreement sufficient to constitute a contract for sale may be found even though the moment of its making is undetermined." Thus, where parties act upon identical cross-offers for the sale of goods as though mutual assent is present and a valid contract exists, the courts will find a binding agreement on the basis of Section 2–204.

WHO MAY ACCEPT AN OFFER?

The offeror controls not only the terms of the offer but who can accept the offer. It is a rule of law that only the person or persons to whom the offer is made (i.e., the offeree or offerees) can accept, and this right to accept is nontransferable and nonassignable (a personal and not a property right).

Of course, an offer of reward is made to the general public and can be accepted by anyone who knows of the offer. However, once a party has accepted the offer by doing the requested act or acts, the offer cannot then be accepted by another.

The offeror will usually request acceptance in one of the following two ways:

1. *A promise for a promise—i.e., a "bilateral" contract.* Put simply, a *bilateral contract* is a promise for a promise: the offeror *promises* to do something or to refrain from doing something in exchange for the offeree's *return promise* to do something or not to do something. The offeree accepts the offer by making the requested promise, at which time mutual assent arises, and a contract comes into being creating present rights and duties even though both parties are to perform their promises at some time in the future. For example, suppose that Jeff Jackson makes the following offer to Jill Kelley: "I promise to transfer ownership of my Jack Palmer golf clubs together with my golf bag and cart to you on May 1 (three months from today's date) if you promise to mow my lawn once a week for the next three months." Jill responds: "I accept your offer and promise to mow your lawn once a week for the next three months." Here, Jeff's offer (his promise to transfer ownership) is conditioned upon Jill's return promise to mow Jeff's lawn. By making the requested promise, Jill has accepted the offer, and a bilateral contract comes into existence at the moment of acceptance even though both performances (the transfer of ownership and the mowing of the lawn) are to take place in the future.

An offeree thus accepts in a bilateral contract situation by making the requested promise.

2. *A promise for an act—i.e., a "unilateral" contract.* A *unilateral contract* is a promise for an act: here, the offeror promises to do something or not to do something in exchange for the offeree's performance of a requested act. The offeree accepts the offer by doing the requested act, at which time mutual assent arises, and a contract comes into being creating present rights and duties. Suppose, for example, that Jeff Jackson makes the following offer to

Jill Kelley: "I promise to transfer ownership of my Jack Palmer golf clubs together with my golf bag and cart to you on May 1 (three months from today's date) if you mow my lawn once a week for three months." Jeff's offer, in this case, is not conditioned upon Jill's return promise to mow Jeff's lawn but upon the actual act of mowing the lawn. Jill can accept the offer only by mowing the lawn for three months—not by promising to do so. Since no promise is demanded of Jill Kelley, she never becomes bound to perform. However, once Jill accepts the offer by performing the act, she becomes entitled to the promised performance of Jeff Jackson.

An offeree thus accepts in a unilateral contract situation by doing the requested act.

IS AN OFFER REVOCABLE?

It is often said that the offeror holds the power of life and death over an offer. What this means is that the offeror may generally revoke the offer at any time up until acceptance by the offeree by effectively communicating the revocation to the offeree.

An offer is revocable even where the offeror expressly promises not to revoke or expressly promises to hold the offer open for a definite time period. This is because promises in themselves are not binding: a binding promise requires all the elements necessary for a contract—mutual assent, consideration, legality, and capacity. An offer, by itself, does not even give rise to mutual assent. Thus, if Jeff Jackson offers to sell his golf clubs, bag, and cart to Jill Kelley for $500, Jeff can revoke the offer at any time prior to Jill's acceptance of the offer. Even if Jeff states, "I promise to sell you my golf clubs for $500, and I further promise that you can have ten days to think this over, during which time I will not revoke the offer," Jeff can still revoke the offer the following day. The offer in and of itself does not give rise to mutual assent, and, as you will learn in a later section of this chapter, there is also no consideration for Jeff's promise not to revoke.

Of course, Jeff and Jill can always enter into a *binding* agreement to keep the offer open for ten days. For example, suppose that Jeff states to Jill, "If you will pay me ten dollars I will promise not to sell my golf clubs to anyone else during the next ten-day period, during which time you may purchase the clubs for $500." If Jill accepts by paying Jeff the ten dollars, mutual assent arises. There is "consideration" or value given in the payment of the ten dollars, and, assuming all other elements of a contract are present, a binding agreement comes into being, and Jeff cannot revoke the offer to sell for the full ten-day period. During this ten-day period, Jill has an "option" to buy the clubs. And that is what a contract the subject matter of which is to keep an offer open is called—an *option contract.* An option contract is much more than a mere offer: it is a binding agreement, and it can be a very valuable asset. For example, the holder of an option to buy an acre of land for $50,000 anytime during the next six months may be able to sell the option for $60,000 in three months' time.

The Uniform Commercial Code, Section 2–205, "Firm Offers," creates an important exception to the general rule that an offer is revocable even though it contains an express promise that it will be kept open for a period of time.

> Section 2–205—An offer by a merchant to buy or sell goods in a signed writing which by its terms gives assurance that it will be held open is not revocable, for lack of consideration, during the time stated or if no time is stated for a reasonable time, but in no event may such period of irrevocability exceed three months.

Thus, a written offer to buy or sell goods made and signed by a merchant and containing an express promise that the offer will be kept open for a period of time is a "firm offer" and cannot be revoked by the merchant for the time stated or for three months, whichever is less, or, if no time is stated, for a "reasonable" time, again, not to exceed three months.

Apart from option contracts and firm offers, the general rule is that an offer is revocable at anytime up until the moment of acceptance. To be effective, the revocation must be communicated to the offeree prior to acceptance. Usually, the offeror directly notifies the offeree that the offer is being revoked. Any words or conduct by the offeror will serve to revoke the offer so long as a reasonable person in the position of the offeree would understand that the words or conduct constitute a revocation (this again, goes back to the objective theory of contracts). And sometimes the offeree on his or her own acquires reliable information that the offer has been revoked or that the offeror has entered into a completely inconsistent contract with another party. Such an indirect "communication" will also serve effectively to revoke the offer. Thus, Jeff Jackson's offer to sell his golf clubs to Jill Kelley is effectively revoked when Jill learns from Jeff's mother that Jeff has sold the clubs to Harvey Thompson.

In the case of a reward offer or other offer made to the general public through newspaper, television, or other advertising media, the law does not demand that revocation of the offer be effectively communicated to each of the potential offerees. Because such an offer is made to a number of persons whose specific identities are unknown to the offeror, it would be impossible for the offeror to determine just who had learned of the offer. To place upon him or her the burden of notifying all potential offerees would be unfair in the extreme. Thus, all that is required to revoke an offer made to the general public is publicity of revocation placed in the same advertising medium as the original offer and equal to the original offer in scope and style.

One final problem regarding revocation of offers revolves around revocation of an offer to enter into a unilateral contract (a promise for an act). The general rule that an offeror has the power of life and death over an offer up until the moment of acceptance by the offeree makes perfect sense insofar as a bilateral (a promise for a promise) contract is concerned. Acceptance in such situations (by the making of the requested promise) takes but a moment of the offeree's time. Nor is there a problem with regard to an offer to enter into a unilateral contract where the requested act can be performed summarily (for example, payment of fifty dollars in one lump sum). But where acceptance in the unilateral contract situation will take a period of time rather than a moment, it would not be fair to permit the offeror to revoke after the offeree has substantially begun to perform but before he or she has completed performance and accepted the offer. Accordingly, the courts hold that the offeror cannot revoke once the offeree has "substantially" (though not fully) performed, but must allow the offeree to complete the performance and so accept the offer.

Let's return to our previous example where Jeff Jackson promises to transfer ownership of his golf clubs to Jill Kelley if Jill mows Jeff's lawn once a week for the next three months. If Jill mows the lawn for four consecutive weeks, intending to accept the offer, Jeff cannot revoke even though Jill has yet to accept the offer by completing the requested act—Jeff must permit Jill to complete her performance since she has already substantially performed.

WHAT POSSIBLE RESPONSES ARE THERE TO AN OFFER?

Generally speaking, an offeree may respond to an offer in any one of the following six ways—by:

1. Rejection, which terminates the offer;
2. Acceptance, which results in mutual assent;
3. Something less than an acceptance, which has no legal effect;
4. A mere inquiry, which also has no legal effect;
5. Counteroffer, which, again, terminates the offer but is itself an offer which can be accepted by the original offeror; or
6. Something less than a common law acceptance or counteroffer which nevertheless constitutes a valid acceptance in some circumstances under the Uniform Commercial Code.

Rejection

A rejection is a definite statement by the offeree that he or she does not intend to accept the offer. A rejection serves to terminate the offeree's power of acceptance; it is effective only when it is communicated to the offeror.

Of course, where a merchant makes a firm offer as defined in UCC Section 2–205, the offeree's rejection of the offer will not terminate his or her power to accept; the firm offer must be kept open for the time stated, up to a maximum of three months.

Acceptance

To accept an offer is to respond in the manner requested by the offeror. An offeree accepts a bilateral contract by making the requested promise; he or she accepts a unilateral contract by performing the requested act. In either case, the result of a valid acceptance is the creation of mutual assent between offeror and offeree—the first element necessary for a contract.

Under the common law, an acceptance is not valid and effective unless it is unequivocal and unqualified. The acceptance must be exact, positive, and unconditional; a response that changes the terms of the offer in any respect is not an acceptance. (The only exception to this rule arises under Section 2–207 of the UCC as will be explained shortly.)

Something Less Than an Acceptance

Sometimes an offeree's response to an offer indicates an interest in the offer but is too equivocal or indefinite to qualify as an acceptance. In one case, for example, an offeree responded to an offer by sending a telegram to the offeror stating that the offer "constituted the low bid" and that the offeror "should come on the morning train." The court, in this case, rightfully concluded that the offeree's response was not an acceptance. Though the response indicated an interest in the offer, it simply said nothing more. So where Jeff Jackson offers to sell his Jack Palmer golf clubs together with his bag and cart for $500 to Jill Kelley, and Jill responds, "I am really interested and will work out the details with you in the next few days," there is a valid offer by Jeff but not acceptance by Jill. Jill's response contains no promise to buy the golf clubs at the stated price—her response is "something less than an acceptance" and has no legal effect whatsoever. Jill can still accept the offer so long as it remains open, and, of course, Jeff can freely revoke the offer at any time prior to her acceptance.

A Mere Inquiry

A mere inquiry is not an equivocal or indefinite expression of assent to an offer as is "something less than an acceptance"—rather, it is a question, suggestion, or request anticipating a change from the original terms of the offer. However, like "something less than an acceptance," a mere inquiry is not an acceptance and does not give rise to mutual assent; nor does it constitute a rejection of the offer so as to terminate the offeree's power to accept. A mere inquiry simply has no legal effect whatsoever. For example, an offeree often responds to an offer by inquiring whether or not the offeror will perform or sell on terms other than those contained in the offer. Responses such as, "Will you take less?", "Would you be able to deliver immediately rather than next week?", or "Would there be any change in price if I ordered a dozen instead of one?" are all mere inquiry responses. Because a mere inquiry has no legal effect, the offeree is still free after making such an inquiry to accept the original offer so long as he or she does so before the offeror revokes.

Counteroffer

If, in response to an offer, an offeree proposes his or her own definite, conditional undertaking containing terms different from or at variance with those of the original offer, the offeree has made a "counteroffer." The counteroffer serves to terminate the original offer and reverses the roles of the parties by creating in the original offeror the power to accept the counteroffer and so complete a binding agreement.

For example, if Jeff Jackson offers to sell his golf clubs to Jill Kelley for $500 and Jill responds, "I will give you $350 for the clubs," Jill has made a counteroffer (i.e., a definite conditional undertaking), and it is up to Jeff to decide whether or not to accept the offer. Jill's counteroffer has terminated Jeff's original offer, and Jill can no longer complete an agreement by agreeing to pay $500 for the clubs.

Something Less Than a Common Law Acceptance or Counteroffer under the UCC

The general rule that an acceptance must be unequivocal, unconditional, and exact or it will constitute something less than an acceptance or a counteroffer is qualified insofar as the sale of goods is concerned by UCC Section 2–207, "Additional Terms in Acceptance or Confirmation."

> Section 2–207 (1) A definite and seasonable expression of acceptance or a written confirmation which is sent within a reasonable time operates as an acceptance even though it states terms additional to or different from those offered or agreed upon, unless acceptance is expressly made conditional on assent to the additional or different terms.
>
> (2) The additional terms are to be construed as proposals for addition to the contract. Between merchants such terms become part of the contract unless: (a) the offer expressly limits acceptance to the terms of the offer; (b) they materially alter it; or (c) notification of objection to them has already been given or is given within a reasonable time after notice of them is received.

Section 2–207 of the Code was primarily enacted to put an end to the "battle of the forms" between merchant buyers and sellers. The "battle of the forms" refers to the confusion that resulted prior to the Code provision from each party's use of his or her own sales and purchase forms. For example, a buyer and seller will frequently engage in preliminary negotiation over the telephone. One party will then send a form prepared by his or her attorney to the other party and the other party will respond by returning his or her own form, carefully drafted to his or her own advantage. Generally, the forms will agree in some respects (e.g., as to price, quality, quantity, and delivery), but differ in others.

Following the common law rules expressed in the preceding pages, the forms taken together will produce something less than an offer and an acceptance—perhaps a counteroffer, something less than an acceptance, a mere inquiry, or a mish-mash of all of these. Generally, the parties will go ahead and perform the agreement, and so there will be no problem. But where the deal breaks down and the parties decide to stress the differences in their forms (each party looking for some means of release from his or her contractual obligations or some way of holding the other party to an agreement that he or she did not intend), the common law rules will be hard pressed for an answer.

To solve this problem with regard to the sale of goods, Section 2–207 of the Code provides that the offeree's injection of different terms will not necessarily constitute a rejection of the original offer nor a counteroffer that serves to terminate the original offer. Unless the original offer expressly limits acceptance to its terms, the additions to the offer will not prevent acceptance by the offeree but will be treated merely as proposals for addition to the contract. And where the transaction is between merchants, the new terms will automatically become part of the contract unless the new terms materially alter the contract or unless the offeror objects to the terms within a reasonable period of time.

For example, suppose that Millicent Manufacturer offers (on her form) "to sell 1,000 pairs of shoes at $10 per pair to be ready in 90 days," and Rudy

Retailer responds (on his form) by agreeing to buy on Millicent's terms but adds that the shoes "must be delivered to Martin's store and that a 2 percent discount is to be allowed if fully paid within 100 days." Millicent does not object to the new terms. Under the common law, Rudy's response does not give rise to mutual assent but is a counteroffer. However, under the UCC, mutual assent does arise, and the additional terms proposed by Rudy automatically become a part of the contract: both parties are merchants, the terms do not materially change Millicent's obligations, and Millicent does not appear to object.

If, in the example above, one or both of the parties are nonmerchants, the additional terms will not prevent acceptance by the offeree; however, the terms will be treated merely as proposals to the contract and will not become a part of the agreement unless the original offeror assents.

Remember, UCC Section 2–207 applies only to the sale of goods—the common law rules apply to all other transactions.

HOW ARE OFFERS TERMINATED APART FROM REVOCATION, REJECTION, OR COUNTEROFFER?

You will recall that, with the exception of firm offers and option contracts, an offeror may revoke an offer at any time by effectively communicating the revocation to the offeree. An offeree may also terminate an offer simply by communicating a rejection of the offer to the offeror or by responding with a counteroffer. Termination of an offer by revocation, rejection, or counteroffer is said to be termination by *act of the parties.*

Termination by Operation of Law

Termination of an offer may also occur *by operation of law* in the following situations.

Death or destruction of the subject matter An offer ceases to exist by operation of law if a person or thing essential to performance of the contemplated agreement either dies or is destroyed. So if Jeff Jackson offers to sell his Jack Palmer golf clubs for $500 to Jill Kelley and, before Jill can accept the golf clubs are destroyed in a fire at Jeff's home, the offer will automatically terminate, and Jill will no longer have any power to accept.

Death or insanity of the offeror or offeree An offer is personal to the offeror and offeree. It follows that if either party dies or becomes insane after the offer is made, but before acceptance, the offer will terminate by operation of law. Thus, if either Jeff Jackson or Jill Kelley dies or becomes insane after Jeff offers to sell his clubs, but before Jill accepts the offer, the offer will automatically terminate by operation of law.

Insanity occurring subsequent to the making of an offer must be distinguished from insanity existing at the time the offer is made. In the latter case, either the offeror or offeree will lack "capacity" to contract ("capacity" being the third element necessary for a contract), and a valid offer and acceptance cannot be made.

Death or insanity occurring subsequent to the making of an offer, but prior to acceptance, must also be distinguished from death or insanity occurring after the offer has been accepted. Assuming that all other elements necessary for a contract are present, the death or insanity will not affect the contract rights and obligations that have already come into being. They will be assets or liabilities of the decedent's or insane person's estate.

Supervening illegality of the proposed contract If the proposal contained in an offer becomes illegal after the offer is made, but prior to acceptance, the offer will terminate by operation of law. For example, where Jeff Jackson offers to sell his collection of handguns for $1,000 to Jill Kelley and, before Jill accepts, a law is passed making it illegal to sell handguns, Jeff's offer to Jill immediately terminates. It should be pointed out that where the law is passed only after Jill accepts Jeff's offer, the subsequent illegality will discharge performance of the parties' remaining contract obligations.

Lapse of time An offer terminates by operation of law upon the expiration of the time stated in the offer, and where no time is specified, at the end of a "reasonable" period of time. What is "reasonable" depends upon such factors as the nature of the subject matter involved, market fluctuations, and local usage and custom. Thus, if Jeff Jackson offers to sell his Jack Palmer golf clubs for $500, the offer will terminate by operation of law at the end of ten days, assuming that Jeff has not earlier revoked the offer. If Jeff fails to specify a time in the offer, the offer will terminate at the end of a reasonable time.

WHAT IS THE EFFECTIVE MOMENT OF ACCEPTANCE?

Most communications between an offeror and offeree are legally effective only when they are received by (i.e., communicated to) the recipient party. Thus, an offer is not effective until the offeree has actual knowledge of it, nor is a revocation effective to revoke an offer until the offeree knows of its existence. If the offeree makes a counteroffer, it, too, takes effect only upon its communication to the offeror; and if the offeree rejects the original offer, the rejection will serve to terminate the offer only when the offeror has actual knowledge of it.

The general principle that a communication between offeror and offeree must be received in order to be legally effective has but one exception—the so-called "deposited acceptance" rule. The rule states that, unless the offeror expressly provides to the contrary in his or her offer, the offeree's acceptance of the offer is effective when properly dispatched. Thus, unlike an offer, revocation, counteroffer, and rejection which are effective only when received, an acceptance is effective when sent. At the moment of proper dispatch, the acceptance gives rise to mutual assent between the offeror and offeree even though the offeror has no actual knowledge of the acceptance and will have none until it is received. The reasoning behind the rule is that when the mails or other means of communication are used, one of the parties—either the offeror or offeree—will have no knowledge of the effective time of acceptance. If the acceptance is effective when sent (as the deposited acceptance rule provides), the offeror will not know when mutual assent arises; if the acceptance is effective only when received, the offeree will not know when mutual assent occurs. As between the offeror and offeree, it is the offeror who invites acceptance, and so it is only fair that the offeror should bear the burden of "not knowing" unless he or she expressly provides to the contrary. Also, making acceptance effective at the time of dispatch closes the transaction more quickly and makes for prompt performance of the contract.

The deposited acceptance rule is limited in that the offeror may expressly provide in his or her offer that acceptance will be effective only when received.

And one important exception to the deposited acceptance rule arises where an offeree sends both an acceptance and a rejection to the offeror. If the offeree send the rejection first, the acceptance will be effective only when it is communicated to the offeror. Thus, if the rejection arrives first, the rejection will destroy the original offer, and the acceptance, once received, will operate only as a counteroffer. If, on the other hand, the acceptance arrives first, mutual assent will arise, and it will make no difference that the rejection is received a short time thereafter.

However, where the offeree sends the acceptance first and then the rejection, the acceptance will be effective upon dispatch, and the rejection will be of no effect unless it arrives before the acceptance and the offeree, relying upon it, changes his or her position (e.g., by selling the goods to someone else). The offeror, in the latter case, has no way of knowing that mutual assent has already occurred as a result of dispatch of the acceptance. The law will therefore protect the offeror and estop the offeree from asserting the existence of a contract.

WHAT ARE THE RULES OF MUTUAL ASSENT AS TO AUCTIONS?

The unique rules governing the creation of mutual assent at a public auction are summarized below:

1. The announcement or advertisement of the auction is not itself an offer. Rather it is an invitation to the public to come to the auction and make offers through the bidding process. Similarly, when the auctioneer puts the goods up for sale (often called putting the goods "on the block"), he or she is not making an offer to sell the goods but rather is inviting the public to make offers to purchase them.
2. A "bid" on the goods by a member of the public constitutes an offer.
3. The auctioneer makes an acceptance by dropping the hammer on a particular bid.
4. Unless the auction is explicitly advertised to be "without reserve," or unless the goods are explicitly put up for sale "without reserve," the auction is presumed to be "with reserve," meaning that the seller is free to reject any and all bids or withdraw the goods from sale at any time prior to acceptance by the auctioneer.
5. Because a seller who advertises that an auction is to be "without reserve" represents to the public that the goods will be sold to the highest bidder, the

seller is estopped from withdrawing the goods from sale once the bidding has begun. A bidder, on the other hand, makes no promise of any kind and is free to revoke his or her bid at any time up until the moment the hammer falls whether the auction is "with reserve" or "without reserve."
6. The seller may not personally bid on the goods unless he or she gives public notice of intent to do so prior to or at the time of the auction. This rule is designed to prevent the seller from fraudulently driving up the bid price by secretly bidding against "good faith" bidders. If the seller bids on the goods without giving notice, the sale is fraudulent, and the buyer may either disaffirm the sale or take the goods at the last good faith bid prior to acceptance by the auctioneer.

The above rules are provided under Section 2–328 of the Uniform Commercial Code which also provides that if a new bid is made just as the auctioneer is dropping the hammer on another bid, the auctioneer has the option of either closing the sale on the first bid or reopening the bidding. If the auctioneer chooses to reopen the bidding, the bid on which the hammer was falling will be discharged, although the bidder will be free to enter a new bid. The effect of this is to carve out an exception to the general rule that the dropping of the hammer constitutes an acceptance.

The UCC makes it clear that even though an auction "with reserve" is the usual and normal procedure, the point in time that determines whether an auction is "with" or "without reserve" is when the goods are "put up" for sale. To "put up" goods is to describe them to the people present at the auction and to open up bidding on the goods. Until the goods have been "put up" for sale, the goods may be withdrawn from the auction and never presented for sale regardless of whether the auction has been advertised as "with" or "without reserve." Of course, if the seller's "without reserve" advertisement constitutes a firm offer within the meaning of UCC 2–205 (firm offers were discussed in a prior section on revocation of offers), the seller will not be able to withdraw the goods during the time stated in the offer and, if no time is stated, for a reasonable time.

WHEN IS THERE NO MUTUAL ASSENT EVEN THOUGH THERE APPEARS TO BE A VALID OFFER AND ACCEPTANCE?

Mutual assent does not arise every time there looks to be a valid offer and acceptance. Sometimes there are other factors present that prevent the formation of mutual assent or agreement and warrant the conclusion that a contract was not intended. The following factors may prevent the creation of mutual assent even though there appears to be a valid offer and acceptance:

1. Mistake,
2. Undue influence;
3. Duress;
4. Fraud in the execution;
5. Fraud in the inducement; and
6. Other unconscionable act.

Mistake

A mistake is an erroneous belief relating to the facts as they exist at the time an agreement is made or entered into. The mistake must be as to *facts in existence,* or it will not prevent the creation of mutual assent. For example, a person who enters into a contract because of a mistaken prediction as to what will occur in the future makes no mistake as the term is used here. A great many agreements are made with full awareness of a future uncertainty, or with what might be called a "conscious ignorance" of the future. Though aware of the uncertainty, the parties estimate and weigh the possibilities and fix their values accordingly. If future events take an unexpected turn, the parties must still abide by their bargains.

However, if the parties were thinking of different things at the time of contracting, there is a latent (hidden) ambiguity, and there is no mutual assent and no contract. The most famous case involving a latent ambiguity is the old English case of Raffles v. Wichelhaus, 159 Eng.Rep. 375 (Exch. 1864), in which two parties to a sales contract agreed that a load of cotton should be delivered from Bombay on the ship "Peerless." As it turned out, each party was thinking of a different ship, there being two ships named "Peerless," each scheduled to arrive from Bombay at a different time. Since both parties in the "Peerless" case were thinking of different ships at the time of contracting, and since neither party was aware of the latent ambiguity or uncertainty, there was no mutual assent created despite the apparent offer and acceptance.

Latent ambiguity is thus an area of "mutual mistake"—that is, *both* parties to the contract must be mistaken. And they must be mistaken as to a *material* fact as opposed to a minor or collateral matter. Mutual assent will fail to arise only where the mutual mistake goes to the very heart or basis of the bargain.

Sometimes, a party will make an offer using words, symbols, or figures that are exact in meaning but that are based upon the offeror's mistaken belief as to existing facts. For example, an offeror might submit a bid on a construction job using figures that (unbeknownst to the offeror) are based upon mathematical errors or other erroneous computations.

Such a mistake is referred to in the law as a *unilateral mistake.* It is an error by the offeror in using clear unambiguous words that the offeror would not use if he or she had knowledge of the true facts. The offeror makes the unilateral mistake before he or she makes the offer: at the time of making the offer, the offeror is saying exactly what he or she intends to say and is conveying exactly the meaning that he or she intends to convey to the offeree. The offeror in the example above might intentionally submit a bid for $15,000, having incorrectly added up a column of figures to arrive at $15,000 rather than the correct total of $25,000. Certainly, the offeror has made a mistake, but it is a unilateral mistake the consequences of which may be entirely different from a mutual mistake.

When a unilateral mistake is made, there are two possible results:

1. If the offeree knows or has reason to know that the offeror has made a mistake, the result is the same as in the mutual mistake situation—that is,

there is no mutual assent and therefore no contract. It is often said that the offeree cannot "snap up the offer" knowing that it was made in mistake.
2. If the offeree neither knows nor has reason to know that a mistake has been made, mutual assent will arise based upon the terms proposed by the offeror. This result is in accord with the objective theory of contracts. A reasonable person in the position of an offeree who neither knows nor has reason to know that a unilateral mistake has been made would be led to conclude that the offer was made on the terms indicated. It follows that the unilateral mistake will not prevent a finding of mutual assent based upon those terms.

Suppose that an offeror uses an intermediary such as a telegraph company or interpreter to send his or her offer, and the intermediary makes a mistake in transmitting the offer to the offeree. Acceptance by the offeree will not give rise to mutual assent if the offeree knows or has reason to know that a mistake has been made. Again, the law will not permit the offeree to "snap up" an offer containing a palpable error.

But where the offeree is unaware of the error and has no reason to know of its existence, the majority rule is that there is mutual assent based upon the terms transmitted to the offeree. The reasoning behind the rule is that, since the offeror chose to use an intermediary, the offeror should bear the risk of any loss resulting from the intermediary's mistake.

Sometimes, an offeree who appears to assent to a written offer by signing it is really mistaken as to the contents of the offer because of a negligent failure to read the offer thoroughly before signing. The general rule is that the offeree is nevertheless legally bound to the terms *as they are written* unless the offeror knows or has reason to know of the offeree's mistake. This, again, is in accord with the objective theory of contracts: *by appearing to accept* the offer by signing the instrument (which may be a long and formal document), the offeree has led the offeror (along with any other reasonable person) to conclude either that the offeree is familiar with the terms of the offer and accepts them as is or that he or she is ignorant of the terms but accepts them anyway without knowing or caring what they are.

However, an offeree's mistake as to terms resulting from a failure to read the document before signing will not give rise to mutual assent or a valid contract where the effect of enforcing the agreement would be to work a tremendous hardship upon the party. This is particularly true in the case of a so-called *adhesion contract.* An adhesion contract is a "one-sided" contract in which the offeror and offeree occupy substantially unequal bargaining positions; the offeree, the party with inferior bargaining power, is forced to "adhere" to the terms dictated by the offeror in order to acquire some essential property or service.

Undue Influence

For undue influence to exist in a contract situation, one party must be under the domination of another, and the dominating party must use unfair persuasion to overcome the free will or judgment of the other party, causing the party to either make an offer or accept an offer.

For purposes of undue influence, one party is considered "dominated" by another where he or she is justified in assuming that the other will act only in his or her best interests. Thus, a relationship of trust or confidence between the parties, particularly a family or *fiduciary* relationship, will establish the necessary element of domination. Examples of such relationships include parent-child, attorney-client, trustee-beneficiary and doctor-patient. Of course, if it can be shown that one party is dominated by another even in the absence of a relationship of trust and confidence, that will be sufficient for purposes of undue influence.

Where undue influence is found to exist, the dominated party may avoid the contract. The contract is said to be voidable. A voidable contract generally has these three characteristics: (1) the contract is valid and remains so unless the power of avoidance is exercised; (2) a party having power to avoid the contract usually has the correlative power to ratify the contract (i.e., to agree with its terms and provisions); and (3) in the absence of specific words or actions indicating avoidance, the agreement may be held impliedly ratified.

Duress

Duress is any physical or mental coercion that deprives a person of his or her own free will and forces him or her to make an offer or accept an offer. Duress (mental or physical coercion or force) that reduces its victim to a mere mechanical instrument or automaton who is physically compelled to enter into an agreement against his or her will renders the transaction void (meaningless and of no legal effect). Here, the victim is not merely coerced but is physically forced to make an offer or accept an offer. Examples include a party who hypnotizes another and directs him or her to sign a contract that he or she does not intend to accept; a party who strong-arms a victim, taking his or her hand and physically forces him or her to sign; a party who furtively drugs or intoxicates another subsequently coaxing or persuading the victim to enter into an undesired agreement.

Where the victim of duress intentionally (as opposed to mechanically) enters into an agreement because of the threat or force employed, the agreement is merely voidable. Voidable duress requires three things:

- *An improper threat* Not all things are improper. For example, a threat to take a legitimate civil claim to court against another person is perfectly permissible.
- *A contract induced by the improper threat* The test is a subjective one: was the particular person who was subjected to the improper threat induced to enter into an agreement because of the threat?
- *No realistic alternative* Finally, a claim of voidable duress will be sustained only where the victim of the duress had no reasonable alternative (i.e., no "way out") but to submit to the coercion. For example, generally there is no voidable duress where a wrongdoer refuses to surrender another's personal property until the property owner agrees to pay the wrongdoer a specified sum of money (or enter into some other kind of agreement). There is no duress because the property owner whose goods have been wrongfully

withheld generally has a legal right (a realistic alternative) to go into court and demand their return. If the property owner elects to buy his or her way out of the situation rather than exercise his or her legal remedy, he or she cannot later sue for a "refund" on the basis of duress. Of course, there are situations where the property owner has no choice but to acquiesce to the wrongdoer's demands (e.g., where the property owner needs the goods immediately or the goods are perishable). In this case, the property owner's payment of money is made under duress, and the transaction is voidable.

Fraud in the Execution

Fraud in the execution (also called fraud in the factum) makes an agreement null and void—that is, of no legal effect whatsoever. Fraud in the execution occurs where a party who intends to enter into a transaction is fooled or tricked into entering into an entirely different transaction, or where a party who has no intention of entering into any agreement is fooled or tricked into signing an agreement. For example, suppose Percy Popstar is asked to sign an "autograph" on what turns out to be a carefully concealed legal document or check. The fraud in the execution (surreptitious substitution of the legal document or check) prevents the creation of mutual assent, and the transaction is utterly void and meaningless.

Fraud in the Inducement

In all cases, the victim of fraud in the execution has absolutely no intention of entering into the particular agreement that is fraudulently foisted upon him or her. The victim has no knowledge of the character or contents of the writing, and the entire transaction is void.

With regard to fraud in the inducement, on the other hand, the victim of the fraud intends to consent to the particular agreement, but only because a material fact has been misrepresented to him or her by the defrauding party. The agreement induced by the fraud is voidable, not void, and the defrauded party may go through with the agreement or avoid it at his or her option.

Fraud in the inducement such as will serve as a basis for avoiding an agreement requires four things:

1. A material misrepresentation;
2. Intent on the part of the party making the misrepresentation that the other party rely upon it;
3. Justifiable reliance by the other party (for example, it would not be justifiable to rely upon a statement one knows to be false); and
4. Inducement of the agreement by the misrepresentation (i.e., the misrepresentation must prompt the party to enter into the transaction).

Fraud in the inducement generally requires a false representation of a material fact as opposed to an *opinion*. A party may generally not rely upon another's statements as to value or quality—such statements are usually opinions only and not statements of fact. However, a party may be justified in relying upon a misrepresentation of opinion if the party has reason to believe that the opinion is made by one with expert knowledge (i.e., special skill or superior knowledge or judgment with respect to the subject matter). For example, it is reasonable to rely upon a jeweler's statement of opinion that a particular jewel is worth $5,000—the jeweler is a gems expert and possesses superior knowledge and judgment with respect to the nature and value of jewels.

Not only must the false representation be as to a fact, but the fact must be *material.* A fact is not material if it is of but peripheral importance to the agreement or if it makes little or no difference to anyone involved whether the fact is true or false.

Misrepresentations may result from concealment and nondisclosure. Concealment is an affirmative act intended to prevent another from learning a fact significant or relevant to a contemplated transaction, and it is equivalent to any affirmative misrepresentation made by written or spoken word. Examples of concealment include turning back the odometer (mileage meter) on an automobile, painting over defects so as to hide or cover them, and expunging (deleting) portions of relevant written records.

Ordinarily, neither party to a contemplated agreement is under any duty to disclose facts concerning the transaction, even where it is likely that one of the parties is unaware of one or more details. A party who is about to enter into an agreement is simply not expected to outline all the facts; thus, his or her failure to do so will not form the basis for fraud in the inducement.

However, in most states, a real property seller has a duty to disclose to a prospective purchaser any facts within his or her knowledge that are material to the sales transaction. A failure to disclose constitutes fraudulent misrepresentation. Thus, a purchaser may avoid his or her purchase of a home on the basis of fraud in the inducement if he or she discovers that the seller knowingly failed to disclose prior to the sale that the basement floods every winter, that the roof leaks when it rains, or that the building is infested with termites.

A person who is fraudulently induced to enter into a contract has a voidable agreement. Whenever an agreement is voidable (whether because of fraud in the inducement, duress, or undue influence), the wronged party has the option of rescinding the contract. To *rescind* is to restore the parties to the positions they were in prior to the agreement—to make it just as though no contract had ever been entered into. Rather than rescind the agreement and seek restitution, the defrauded party may affirm the agreement and request money damages. Rescission and affirmance are mutually exclusive alternative remedies: the injured party may do one or the other—he or she cannot do both.

To recover money damages, a party who elects to affirm a contract induced by fraud must bring a legal action in court for the tort involved. You will recall from Chapter 5 that a "tort" is any socially unreasonable conduct, and this certainly includes misrepresentation. Where the misrepresentation is intentionally made with knowledge of its falsity, either by written or spoken word or by active concealment of the truth, the tort involved is the tort of *deceit.* Where the misrepresentation is based on a careless failure to discover the falsity of the representation, the tort at issue is *negligence.* Generally speaking, only a party who is in the business of supplying information for the guidance of others (e.g., an accountant, stockbroker, lawyer, or the like) will be held responsible in money damages for his or her negligent misrepresentations.

Unconscionable Agreements

Even in the absence of mistake, undue influence, duress, or fraud, a transaction may be so unfair and "unconscionable" (inequitable) that the courts will refuse to find mutual assent and so refuse to enforce the agreement. Although it is impossible to state with precision when the doctrine of unconscionability will apply, pertinent case law in the area provides some guidelines:

1. Unconscionability is usually raised as a defense. Generally, the plaintiff asks the court to order the defendant to perform his or her part of the bargain or respond in money damages. The defendant, in turn, requests the court to rule that all or part of the contract is unconscionable and so relieve the defendant of his or her duty of performance.
2. Most unconscionable contracts involve poor and otherwise disadvantaged consumers (the courts have been particularly sympathetic to low income consumers). The courts generally refuse to apply the doctrine of unconscionability to contracts between merchants.
3. The agreement must be unconscionable at the time it is made. If it becomes unfair only at a later time because future events do not turn out as predicted by one of the parties, the agreement is not unconscionable as that term is used here and does not prevent the formation of mutual assent.
4. Many unconscionable contracts are adhesion contracts. You will recall that an adhesion contract is a contract in which the offeror and offeree occupy substantially unequal bargaining positions: the offeree, the party with inferior bargaining strength, is forced to "adhere" to the offeror's terms in order to acquire some essential commodity or service.
5. The fact that a party had little education and could not read the language of the contract is sometimes emphasized by the courts in finding unconscionability, as is the fact that the seller manufactured the contract forms using fine print.
6. Excessive price also suggests unconscionability, particularly where the markup is two or three times the cost of the product or where the product is sold at a price two or three times greater than the average retail price elsewhere.
7. Similarly, the fact that a consumer buyer is shown the written agreement form only after he or she has decided to buy is strong evidence of an adhesion contract.
8. Finally, provisions requiring a buyer to waive some of his or her legal remedies or his or her right to a jury trial in case of later controversy over the contract also indicate unconscionability.

WHY DOES THE LAW REQUIRE CONSIDERATION?

Consideration as an element required for a valid contract derives from the common law notion that not all promises should be legally enforceable. It is clearly undesirable legally to enforce all promises. Our courts are hardly likely to enforce (nor would we want them to enforce) a person's promise to stop smoking, to lose twenty pounds, to coach the junior high school girls' softball team, to bowl on the company team, to vote for a particular candidate, to work for another for free, or to sing in the church choir.

In fact, under our legal system, a promise that stands utterly alone is never legally enforceable. There must be something accompanying the promise that justifies enforcement. This "something" is called consideration and is based on a bargain theory requiring two things.

1. The consideration or "something" given for the promise must be bargained for between the parties—i.e., the consideration must be the motive for the promise, and the promise must be the motive for the consideration.
2. The consideration or "something" given for the promise must be legally sufficient. This is not to say that the consideration must be money or have economic value of any kind. Certainly, money or money's worth is frequently given in exchange for a promise and is legally sufficient consideration. However, just as often, the "something" given has no economic value but is still legally sufficient consideration: all that is needed is a commitment by the promisee to do something or refrain from doing something that he or she is not already obligated to do or to refrain from doing.

Thus, there is no consideration where either party promises to confer a gift upon the other; the motivation or bargain element is lacking. Also, it is often said that "past consideration is no consideration." What this means is that something done or given in the past cannot qualify as consideration for a present promise because the essential motivation or bargain element is lacking: the past act was obviously not performed in anticipation of and in return for the present promise and the present promise is obviously not given in anticipation of and in return for the past act.

Still, once the motivation is found, all that is necessary for legally sufficient consideration is the creation of some kind of obligation or responsibility on the part of the promisee in return for the promisor's promise. The result must be either a benefit to the promisor, a detriment to the promisee, or both. The fairness or adequacy of the consideration for the promise or the promise for the consideration is generally not relevant to the question of whether the consideration is legally sufficient. A mere promised change of positions by the parties will do so long as there results a benefit to the promisor or a detriment to the promisee.

Remember that a unilateral contract is a promise for an act. The promisee's acceptance is found in the doing of the act—and so is the consideration for the promise. A bilateral contract is a promise for a promise: one party promises to do something if another will make a requested return promise. The offeree accepts by making the return promise, and a bilateral contract springs into existence. The consideration for the contract is found in the promises made by the parties—each promise serves as consideration for the other.

Suppose that Lloyd Homeowner promises to pay Frank the Painter $1,000 if Frank will promise to paint Lloyd's house during the first week of July. Frank promises to do so, and a valid bilateral contract comes into being. Each promise serves as consideration for the other. Assume further that on July 1, Frank begins to paint Lloyd's house, but, that same afternoon, Frank informs Lloyd that he will not complete the job unless Lloyd promises to pay him $1,500 instead of the agreed upon $1,000. Lloyd agrees to pay the $1,500, whereupon Frank finishes painting the house. Lloyd, however, pays Frank only $1,000, stating that there was no consideration for the promise to pay an additional $500. Frank takes his claim for the additional money to court. Is Frank entitled to the additional $500? The answer is no. There is no benefit to Lloyd nor any detriment to Frank in his promise to paint the house for $1,500 since Frank is already legally bound to paint the house for $1,000. There is no consideration.

WHAT IS AN ILLUSORY PROMISE?

A promise is said to be illusory where the promisor, in actuality, promises nothing. In an illusory promise the promisor undertakes no obligation and sets no limit on his or her future course of conduct. Rather, the promisor leaves himself or herself an alternative (a way out) by which to escape any contract duty whatsoever. Thus, whenever a promise is phrased in the alternative, and the promisor has the right to choose a nondetrimental alternative (one that does not require him or her to change his or her position at all), the promise is illusory and will not serve as consideration for any other act or promise. For example, a person who says, "I promise to buy your car tomorrow unless I change my mind," has made an illusory promise because he or she can always choose the nondetrimental alternative (i.e., he or she can always change his or her mind).

Or suppose that Joe Fashion is in the business of manufacturing women's clothes, and Brenda Buyer is in the business of selling clothing at retail. Brenda promises to buy "whatever dresses I may wish to order" from Joe Fashion in return for Joe's promise "to sell Brenda up to 1,000 dresses during the next three months." Joe's promise is unenforceable because Brenda's promise is illusory. In other words, since Brenda's promise does not require her to do anything at all if she chooses not to, it will not serve as consideration (it does not benefit Joe and is not a detriment to Brenda) for Joe's promise to sell the dresses to Brenda. If Brenda tries to force Joe to sell by going to court, Joe will win in refusing to sell because the second element necessary for a contract is lacking, i.e., there is no consideration for his promise to sell.

Now suppose that Brenda Buyer promises to buy from Joe Fashion "all the dresses I will need" or "all that I will require." Brenda's promise, in this case, will serve as consideration for Joe Fashion's promise to sell. Brenda's promise is not illusory because she has definitely restricted her freedom of action: if she "needs" or "requires" any dresses, she must buy them from Joe Fashion or not buy them at all. While Brenda has the implied alternative of no longer operating her business, that, too, would be a legal detriment. Thus, the agreement between Brenda and Joe is an enforceable *requirements* contract, and Brenda can hold Joe Fashion to his promise to sell.

In a similar manner, a seller may promise to sell to a particular buyer his or her entire output from a plant or factory, using such words as "I promise to sell all that I produce." Again, the seller's promise in such an *output* contract is not illusory because the seller has set some limits to his or her future course of action: the seller can sell merchandise only to the particular buyer. Obviously, the seller may circumvent selling merchandise to the buyer by closing down his or her plant or factory, but this, too, would be a legal detriment to the seller.

Of course, there are good faith limits on the demands that can be made under either "requirements" or "output" contracts. The Uniform Commercial Code at Section 2–306 provides: "A term which measures the quantity by the output of the seller or the requirements of the buyer means such actual output or requirements as may occur in good faith, except that no quantity unreasonably disproportionate to any stated estimate or in the absence of a stated estimate to any normal or otherwise comparable prior output or requirements may be tendered or demanded.

In conclusion, a promise will escape being illusory only where the promisor sets some limits on his or her future course of action. If the promisor leaves himself or herself a nondetrimental alternative, the promise is illusory and will not serve as consideration for any other act or promise.

However, this is not to say that a promised performance can never be made subject to a condition. To be sure, many promised performances are made expressly dependent upon the prior happening of a condition. So long as the condition is not under the control of the promisor and there is a possibility of legal detriment or benefit, the promise is not illusory and will serve as consideration for another act or promise. For example, a promise that "I will buy your car tomorrow on the condition that I don't change my mind," is obviously illusory as the condition is totally under the promisor's control. But a promise that "I will buy your car but only if I am first able to sell my truck" is not illusory; the condition is not totally under the promisor's control, and a legal deteriment benefit may result.

Or say that Lola Executive learns that her employer, Countrywide Insurance Corporation, has tentatively decided to transfer her to another city within ninety days. Lola immediately enters into a contract with Martin Homebuyer. Lola promises to sell her house to Martin for $60,000 on the condition that Lola is transferred by her employer within the next ninety days; Martin promises to buy the house for the $60,000 price. As expected, Lola is transferred within ninety days, but Martin refuses to buy her house, stating that there was no consideration for his promise because "it was not certain that Lola would have to sell." Lola will be able to enforce Martin's promise because her promise to sell subject to the condition that she be transferred does serve as consideration for his promise to buy. The condition contained in Lola's promise is not under Lola's control, and Lola, the promisee of Martin's promise, suffers a legal detriment by reason of her promise.

Thus, a conditional promise is not illusory and will serve as consideration for another promise or act, so long as the promisor has no control over the happening of the condition and a legal detriment or benefit will result if the condition does occur (it is immaterial to the consideration issue that the condition later fails to occur, leaving both parties free of any obligation to perform).

Similarly, the fact that a promised performance is expressed in the alternative such as "I will either do this, or I will do something else" does not make the promise illusory, so long as all the alternatives involve a legal detriment to the promisor or a legal benefit to the promisee. Thus, Brenda Buyer's promise that she "will buy merchandise from Joe Fashion on or before a certain date or that she will notify Joe that she is not going to buy" is not illusory and will serve as consideration for Joe's promise to sell merchandise to Brenda. Here, Brenda has a choice of alternatives, but both are detrimental. Obviously, the giving of notice is not much of a detriment or burden, but the law does not require much of one. It requires only that the party making the promise set some limits to his or her future course of action—incur some obligation, however slight, that he or she did not previously have.

Related to this is the fact that UCC Section 1–203 stipulates that "every contract or duty within this Act imposes an obligation of good faith in its performance or enforcement." Thus, the giving of notice not to buy (i.e., to cancel or terminate the agreement) must be done in good faith and cannot be arbitrary or unreasonable. The common law imposes the same good faith duties in contracts that do not fall with the UCC, such as service contracts, contracts for the sale of land, and employment contracts.

Sometimes, though it appears that one party has promised nothing at all in return for another's promise, the party will still be held to have suffered a legal deteriment. Here the law *implies* a promise because the nature of the agreement indicates that a performance was intended. For example, in the case of *Wood v. Lucy, Lady Duff-Gordon*, 222 N.Y. 88, 118 N.E. 214 (1917), Lucy promised Wood an exclusive franchise or agency to market Lucy's products. Wood did not expressly promise anything in return, but he did have an organization suitable for the purpose of marketing the products. Lucy later refused to perform, claiming that there was no consideration for her promise to grant the exclusive franchise, whereupon Wood took the matter to court. The court ruled that Wood had impliedly promised to devote his organization to the marketing of Lucy's products; the implied promise was a legal detriment and, therefore, valid consideration.

The Uniform Commercial Code has specifically adopted this rule insofar as the sale of goods is concerned. Section 2–306(2) states: "A lawful agreement by either the seller or the buyer for exclusive dealing in the kind of goods concerned imposes unless otherwise agreed an obligation by the seller to use best efforts to supply the goods and by the buyer to use best efforts to promote their sale."

CAN DOING WHAT ONE ALREADY HAS AN OBLIGATION TO DO EVER SERVE AS CONSIDERATION FOR AN ACT OR PROMISE?

The general rule is that doing or promising to do what one already has a legal obligation or duty to do will never serve as consideration for another act or promise. Thus, we saw in our earlier example of Lloyd Homeowner and Frank the Painter that once Frank contracted to paint Lloyd's house for $1,000, he had a legal duty to do the job, and performance of that duty could not serve as consideration for Lloyd's promise to pay Frank $1,500 rather than $1,000 for the act of painting.

Similarly, a party who is already under a legal duty to perform the very act required in a unilateral contract situation suffers no legal detriment by performing his or her duty. For example, say that Cyrus Citizen offers a $5,000 reward for the apprehension of escaped criminal Frances Fugitive. Police officer Tim Daltry, who knows about the reward, catches Frances while on duty. Tim cannot collect the $5,000. While Tim has accepted the offer by doing the requested act, he was already under a duty to catch Frances, and there is no consideration for Cyrus's promise to pay the reward. Of course, if Officer Daltry apprehends Frances while outside the scope of his duties or after working hours, there would be a legal detriment to Daltry, a legal benefit to Cyrus, and consideration for Cyrus's promise to pay the reward.

Along the same line, suppose that a passenger aboard a large jumbo jet says to the airline pilot, "If you get us safely to Los Angeles, I will pay you $100." Again, the airline pilot is an employee of the airlines and is already under a legal duty to fly the jet safely to Los Angeles. In carrying out his or her duty, the pilot suffers no legal detriment, and the passenger receives no benefit since he or she is already entitled to the pilot's safe performance.

WILL A PROMISE NOT TO SUE ANOTHER SERVE AS SUFFICIENT CONSIDERATION FOR ANOTHER PROMISE OR ACT?

When two parties have a dispute, the law generally affords the injured party the legal remedy of taking the case to court—of bringing suit. A promise not to bring suit when there is a legitimate basis for doing so will serve as consideration for a return promise or act. The key word here is "legitimate." A promise to forego suit will constitute a legal detriment to the promisor only where the party honestly and reasonably believes in the case—i.e., where the party's claim has a reasonable possibility of success. Where the promisor simply has no basis for a legal claim, a promise to forego suit will not constitute a legal detriment, and the promise will not serve as consideration for any other promise or act.

By way of example, suppose that Nancy Prudence and Stanley Caution have a car accident at a busy intersection. Nancy believes that Stanley was negligent in driving too fast at the time of the collision. Stanley is not convinced that he was careless, but he promises to pay for all repairs to Nancy's car in return for Nancy's promise not to sue him for negligence. If Stanley later refuses to pay Nancy's repair bills, claiming that there was no consideration for his promise to pay them, Nancy will be able to enforce the promise in court. Nancy's promise not to sue constitutes a legal benefit to Stanley Caution. The only exception would be if Nancy had no legal basis whatsoever for bringing the lawsuit and knew she had none. In that case, Nancy would suffer no legal detriment in promising not to sue, nor would Stanley receive any legal benefit from such a promise.

WILL PART PAYMENT OF A DEBT SERVE AS CONSIDERATION FOR A PROMISE TO FORGET THE BALANCE OF THE DEBT?

Two important legal terms come into play when one party claims that another has promised to forget the balance of a debt in exchange for the first party's part payment of the debt. The terms are "liquidated debt" and "unliquidated debt." The term "liquidated" means to be ascertained, determined, fixed, settled, or agreed to. A debt is liquidated when it is certain what is due and how much is due. An unliquidated debt is one that is not ascertained in amount or remains unsettled. It is unliquidated if it is in dispute as to the proper amount.

The general rule is that part payment of a liquidated debt (a settled, undisputed debt) will not serve as consideration for a promise to forget the balance of the debt (i.e., a promise to discharge the whole debt) or for any other promise. The debtor who makes part payment suffers no legal detriment because he or she is already obligated to pay the full amount owing. And the creditor who receives part payment incurs no legal benefit because he or she is already entitled to receive payment in full.

By way of example, suppose that Linda Thompson goes to the J.C. Dollar Department Store and charges merchandise for $245. There is no dispute about the fairness or accuracy of the charges or the quality of the merchandise, and Linda admittedly owes J.C. Dollar the full $245. At the end of the month, when Linda's bill for the merchandise arrives, Linda makes out a check in the amount of $200 to the J.C. Dollar Department Store. On the back of the check, where the store must endorse (sign its name), Linda writes the following: "Endorsement of this check constitutes an acceptance of this check as full payment for all amounts owing and serves as consideration for a promise by the J.C. Dollar Department Store to forget the balance owing and accept $200 as full payment." Despite these words on the back of the check, the J.C. Dollar Department Store can endorse and cash the check and still proceed against Linda for the balance owing. There is simply no consideration for the store's "promise" to forget the balance.

Now suppose that, in addition to making part payment of the liquidated debt, Linda does something extra that she is not already legally obligated to do with the intent that the something serve as consideration for J.C. Dollar's promise to forget the balance of the debt. Here, Linda suffers a legal detriment, J.C. Dollar receives a legal benefit, and legal consideration for J.C. Dollar's promise exists. Obviously, the motivation or bargain element will not be present if the debtor adds something negligible and valueless (e.g., a debtor who says, "Here is part payment, and, oh, have a cigar on me.") The added "something" must be understood to constitute consideration for the creditor's promise to forget the balance of the debt owing. Additional facts that will serve as consideration include:

1. Part payment prior to maturity of the debt (i.e., part payment earlier than is called for by the terms of the credit agreement);
2. Part payment at a difference place than is called for under the terms of the agreement;
3. Part payment coupled with the giving of something else to the creditor, such as a book, painting, tool or other item;

4. Part payment in a medium other than money (e.g., by transferring to the creditor corporate stock worth two-thirds of the debt owing);
5. Part payment at the creditor's direction to a person other than the person listed in the credit agreement; and
6. Part payment by a person other than the debtor (this is a detriment to that person).

It should also be pointed out that one of the UCC exceptions to common law consideration (see subsequent section) may come into play in the area of part payment of a liquidated debt so as to make it impossible for the creditor to recover the balance of the debt. Section 1–107 of the Code provides that "any claim or right arising out of an alleged breach can be discharged in whole or in part by a written waiver or renunciation signed and delivered by the aggrieved party." Thus, insofar as liquidated debts arising out of the sale of goods are concerned, if the creditor signs and delivers to the debtor a written statement promising that he or she will forget the balance of the debt in exchange for part payment, the debtor will be completely discharged by part payment even though he or she unquestionably owes the full amount of the debt. While the UCC exception applies only to debts arising out of the sale of goods, statutes and common law in a few states have extended this same result to liquidated debts of all kinds.

In contrast to the rules regarding part payment of a *liquidated* debt, part payment of an *unliquidated* debt will always serve as consideration for the creditor's promise to forget the balance of the debt. An unliquidated debt is a debt disputed in good faith by the debtor. Because there is a bona fide dispute as to the amount owing, no duty to pay arises until the dispute is settled. It follows that whenever the debtor pays even a part of the disputed amount, the debtor suffers a legal detriment, the creditor receives a legal benefit, and there is consideration for the creditor's promise to forget the balance. Of course the dispute must be bona fide—a debtor cannot "convert" a liquidated debt into an unliquidated one by inventing a dispute. If the debtor does not truly disagree with the charges or find the merchandise or other subject matter of the contract faulty, the debt is not unliquidated.

For example, suppose that a party goes to a doctor, lawyer, CPA, plumber, or watch repairer but later refuses to pay the bill for the services because he or she feels that the charges are too high (they appear to exceed the usual and fair market value of such services). The debt is unliquidated. If the debtor makes part payment of the debt as settlement in full and the creditor accepts the payment, the debtor suffers a legal detriment, the creditor receives a legal benefit, and consideration exists for the creditor's promise to forget the balance of the debt. Of course, the creditor may refuse to accept part payment and go to court to obtain a judgment for the full amount of the debt. Any judgment the creditor obtains will be a liquidated debt, part payment of which will not serve as consideration for a promise by the creditor to forget the balance.

Or suppose that Linda Thompson purchases $245 worth of merchandise from the J.C. Dollar Department Store and later discovers that the merchandise is defective or not up to standard. Linda genuinely believes that the goods are not worth $245 and refuses to pay that amount. The debt is unliquidated, and any part payment accepted by J.C. Dollar as settlement in full will serve as valid consideration for the company's promise to forget the balance of the debt.

WHAT IS PROMISSORY ESTOPPEL?

Ninety-nine percent plus of all contracts involve the bargain theory of consideration. Generally, if bargain theory consideration is not present, there is no consideration and no contract. But occasionally, because of the circumstances surrounding a promise, the promisor will be "estopped" from claiming that there is no consideration. Generally speaking, there are four elements necessary for promissory estoppel:

1. The promisor must make a gratuitous promise (one lacking bargain theory consideration); the promise must be such that a reasonably prudent person in the promisor's position could *foresee* that the promise might induce reliance by the promisee (i.e., the reliance must be foreseeable);
2. The promisee must, in fact, rely upon the promise (i.e., take some action based on the promise), and the reliance must be reasonable under the circumstances;
3. The promisee must suffer a *substantial economic detriment* as a result of the reliance (notice that the detriment required is a large monetary loss); and
4. It must be necessary to enforce the promise to prevent injustice.

If A says to B, "I promise to give you $5,000 if you complete your college education" or "if you promise to complete your college education" there would be a valid contract supported by consideration in the bargain theory sense. B's completing his education or promising to do so would constitute legal detriment to B as the promisee of A's promise to pay. But where A states, "Well, I know you are going to college, and if you finish it up successfully, I am going to give you $5,000," A is asking nothing in return for his or her promise, and it is a gratuitous or gift promise only. Such a promise is generally not enforceable because there is no consideration in the bargain theory sense. But where B, in foreseeable reliance upon the gift promise, incurs substantial expenses, promissory estoppel will come into play, and A will be estopped from denying a lack of bargain theory consideration in any suit by B to enforce the promise. The promise is enforceable despite the lack of bargain theory consideration because the reliance was foreseeable, it was reasonable under the circumstances, it resulted in substantial economic loss, and it can be remedied only by enforcement of the promise.

WHAT IS THE MEANING OF QUASI CONTRACT?

A quasi contract is really no contract at all in the sense of mutual assent between the parties. Rather, it is an agreement implied in law to prevent unjust enrichment. The parties to a quasi contract reach no agreement and make no promises, but because one of the parties is substantially and unjustly benefited at the other's expense, the law imposes an obligation on the enriched party to restore the benefit. The typical example of a quasi contract arises where one party accidentally confers a benefit upon another who knowingly allows it to happen.

For example, suppose that Lloyd Homeowner contracts with Frank the Painter to have Frank paint his house while Lloyd is gone on vacation. Frank shows up to do the painting but mistakenly paints the house next door to Lloyd's, a house belonging to Sheila Letithappen. The fact that Sheila observes Frank in the process of painting her house but fails to voice any objection places the situation into one of quasi contract. To prevent unjust enrichment of Sheila, the law will imply a promise on her part to pay for the reasonable value of the benefits received—even though there is no mutual assent and no consideration in the bargain theory sense. Of course, if Sheila is also gone on vacation and does not know that Frank is painting her house, the benefit rendered to Sheila is purely accidental, and Frank the Painter can recover nothing at all.

Quasi contract may also arise where one party mistakenly pays money to another or erroneously delivers goods to another who knows or has reason to know that a mistake has been made. Of course, if what one receives is worthless or confers no benefit, there can be no recovery to the other in quasi contract, the recovery being based on "quantum meruit," meaning as much as is reasonably deserved even though there is no agreement.

WHEN WILL "PUBLIC POLICY" REQUIRE THE PERFORMANCE OF A PROMISE?

In a few situations, *public policy* considerations will require the enforcement of a promise despite the lack of bargain theory consideration, promissory estoppel, or quasi contract.

Debts Barred by the Statute of Limitations

Contract actions must usually be initiated within five years of the making of the contract, although the statute of limitations may be as short as three years in some states and as long as ten years in others. Whatever the time period involved, once the statute of limitations on a contract debt has run, the creditor is forever barred from bringing legal action to enforce the debt. Occasionally, however, a debtor will promise to pay the debt even though the statute of limitations has run. The courts, in this case, generally hold that a promise to pay a contract debt barred by the statute of limitations is enforceable without consideration.

Charitable Subscriptions

A charitable subscription is a promise to contribute or make a donation to a charity. Charities generally solicit subscriptions when undertaking special and costly projects (e.g., building a new church or charitable hospital). Most courts hold charitable subscriptions enforceable simply on the grounds of public policy. Such promises are binding despite the lack of bargain theory consideration, promissory estoppel, or quasi contract.

WHEN ARE PROMISES ENFORCEABLE UNDER THE UCC WITHOUT REGARD TO CONSIDERATION?

There are three main exceptions under the UCC where consideration is not required for enforceable promises.

Waiver or Renunciation of a Claim or Right after Breach of Contract

Section 1–107 of the UCC provides that "any claim or right arising out of an alleged breach can be discharged in whole or in part without consideration by a written waiver or renunciation signed and delivered by the aggrieved party." This means that a party who claims that another has breached (failed to perform) a commercial contract dealing with personal property may legally waive or discharge his or her rights against that party by signing and delivering a written promise to do so even though there is no consideration of any kind for the promise. Suppose that a buyer breaches a sales agreement by failing to make the agreed upon payments. If the seller promises in writing to settle for one-half of what is owing on the merchandise, the seller will be legally bound by the promise upon its delivery to the buyer even though there is no consideration for the promise.

Firm Offers

You will recall from our discussion of revocability of offers that UCC Section 2–205, "Firm Offers," provides as follows:

> An offer by a merchant to buy or sell goods in a signed writing which by its terms gives assurance that it will be held open is not revocable, for lack of consideration, during the time stated or if no time is stated for a reasonable time, but in no event may such period of irrevocability exceed three months.

Thus, a merchant's written and signed promise to hold an offer open is legally binding despite the absence of consideration. A written but unsigned or completely oral promise to keep an offer open, on the other hand, is not a firm offer and is not irrevocable unless common law consideration is present.

Modification, Rescission, and Waiver

Section 2–209 (1) of the UCC provides that "an agreement modifying a contract within this Article (sales) needs no consideration to be binding." This Code section is designed to facilitate needed modifications in sales contracts by eliminating the need for common consideration every time a change is made. The theory behind the Section is that the consideration given to support the original contract also serves to support the modified contract.

WHAT IS THE THIRD ELEMENT NECESSARY FOR A VALID CONTRACT?

The third element necessary for a valid contract is contractual capacity. Contractual capacity refers to the power that a person normally has to enter into a contract. Occasionally, however, a person is either totally or (as is more often the case) partially incapacitated (i.e., without the power to contract). For example, a person who is so infirm or disabled that he or she cannot understand the nature of an agreement is totally incapacitated, as is a mentally disturbed person whose affairs are handled by a court appointed guardian. Any "agreement" entered into by a totally incapacitated person is void (although quasi contract is sometimes utilized in such cases to prevent unjust enrichment).

The agreement of an infant, on the other hand, is not void but voidable. The infant is partially incapacitated. At common law, a legal infant was any person under the age of twenty-one years (the age of "majority" or adulthood). Modernly, many states have lowered the age of majority by statute, commonly terminating legal infancy at the age of eighteen (e.g., Kentucky and Oregon), nineteen (e.g., Alaska), or twenty (e.g., Hawaii).

The chief characteristic of legal infancy or minority is that a minor has no contractual capacity. In some states a minor who gets married acquires adult status and contractual capacity by virtue of the marriage. Generally, however, the fact that a minor is emancipated (i.e., on his or her own and outside of parental claim or control) does not confer contractual capacity or adulthood upon the minor, although a few states do provide a procedure whereby a child may be declared legally emancipated by a court and thereby receive contractual capacity.

A minor may either avoid or ratify his or her contracts. No particular language or conduct is required to disaffirm an agreement; the disaffirmance may be made at any time prior to ratification, even during the infancy of the minor—with one exception. Most courts hold that a minor cannot disaffirm his or her conveyance of real property until after the minor has reached the age of majority. The reason for the exception is that the transfer of the real property may be to the minor's benefit. Thus, the law seeks to protect the minor's interests by providing him or her with a longer period of time for determining whether to disaffirm or ratify.

Ratification is the opposite of avoidance and results in a legally binding contract. A minor cannot ratify an agreement until he or she has attained the age of majority; at that time, the minor may ratify by effectively surrendering his or her power of avoidance. This may be done by failing to disaffirm within a reasonable time after reaching adulthood, by expressly ratifying the contract, and by acting in a manner that amounts to ratification, such as by retaining or using and enjoying the property received under the contract.

A minor who disaffirms is legally obligated to return any property still in his or her possession that he or she received under the contract. If the minor no longer has the property or if it is impractical for the minor to return what he or she does have, the minor is not obligated to return the property or to compensate the other party to the contract in any way. The minor's obligation is thus one of *restoration in specie* (restoration of whatever actual property is left in whatever condition it is in).

Minors cannot disaffirm, in the case of a male minor, contracts to support illegitimate children, education loan contracts, life insurance contracts, certain banking transactions, and contracts for military enlistment. Also, a minor is liable in quasi contract for "necessaries" that he or she contracts for and receives. Generally, where the necessaries have yet to be furnished to the minor, he or she may still disaffirm the agreement and avoid paying for the items. This is because the nature of the minor's liability is quasi-contractual: because the minor has been unjustly enriched at another's expense, the law imposes an obligation on the minor to restore whatever benefits he or she has received; if the minor has received nothing, he or she has nothing to restore.

And because the remedy is in quasi contract, the minor is not liable for the contract price of the necessaries but only for the reasonable value of the items. Reasonable value refers to the average price in the community for such items—it does not refer to what a particular merchant or party is asking for the property. Thus, a party who furnishes necessaries to a minor may well lose a part of his or her profit.

What is a necessary depends upon the minor's particular circumstances in life. Generally, a minor will not be liable for a necessary unless it is a "necessary in fact," meaning that the item is essential to the minor's livelihood or well being and the minor's parent or guardian refuses to supply it. If the minor contracts for a "necessary" that his or her parent or guardian would have been willing to provide, the item is not "necessary in fact," and the minor may disaffirm the contract the same as any other.

In addition, the minor must personally contract for the necessaries in order to be held personally liable on the contract. Obviously, an emancipated minor will personally contract for more necessaries than will a minor who lives at home with his or her parents and a married minor will personally contract for even more. But whether the minor is emancipated or dependent, if a party furnishes necessaries to the minor on the basis of an agreement made with someone other than the minor, the minor is under no legal obligation to pay for the property.

Because each minor's necessaries differ, it is obviously impossible to list inclusively what is or is not a necessary. A few examples, however, might be helpful. Food, shelter, and clothing, for instance, are obviously necessaries; an automobile sometimes is but usually is not; medical services usually are; legal services incurred in defense of criminal or tort charges are certainly necessaries, but legal services incurred in defense of property rights may not be (with regard to property rights, it is generally held that a guardian must be appointed to protect these rights and to contract with an attorney where necessary). With regard to education, education through the secondary level is uniformly considered necessary; a trade school education is usually deemed necessary; but a college education is generally deemed not necessary.

DOES IT MAKE ANY DIFFERENCE THAT A MINOR COMMITS A TORT BY REASON OF HIS OR HER AGREEMENT?

While a minor is generally not obligated on his or her contracts (i.e., a minor may avoid his or her agreements), a minor is liable for his or her torts. Frequently, a minor who enters into a voidable contract commits a tort in the process.

First, a minor may, in breaching a voidable agreement, also commit a tort. For example, suppose that an adult takes his or her automobile to a minor who claims that he or she can service and repair the car. In the process of servicing and repairing the car, the minor negligently puts only part of the engine back together, carelessly forgetting to replace an essential part. The minor, in this case, has breached the contract; however, the minor has a legal right to disaffirm the contract and avoid liability for the breach. Yet the act of breaching the contract also constitutes the tort of negligence: the minor had a duty to repair the car properly, the minor breached the duty, and the minor's breach of duty resulted in damage to the other party's automobile. Can the minor be held liable for the tort even though he or she cannot be held liable on the contract? The answer is no. It is a rule of law that if the result of holding a minor liable for a tort is to achieve the same effect as enforcing the contract, the tort action will not be allowed. The tort in such a case is said to be "interwoven" with the contract and is simply not actionable. In the example, allowing the injured party to recover from the minor for his or her negligence would be tantamount to enforcing the contract. The tort is "interwoven" with the contract and is not actionable.

Second, a minor may misrepresent his or her age in order to persuade an adult to enter into an agreement (adults frequently refuse to contract with minors because of the right of minors to disaffirm). A minor who induces an adult to enter into a contract by lying about his or her age commits fraud in the inducement which constitutes the tort of deceit. While the minor's misrepresentation of age will not prevent the minor from disaffirming the contract, nearly all courts hold that the tort of deceit is not interwoven with the contract but is an independent, actionable tort. The reasoning here is that the tort occurred as an inducing factor prior to the making of the contract and that the payment of damages for deceit does not result in an indirect enforcement of the contract itself. So while the minor may disaffirm the contract, he or she will still be liable for tortious deceit.

WHAT IS THE FOURTH ELEMENT NECESSARY FOR A VALID CONTRACT?

Even where mutual assent, consideration, and contractual capacity are present, there may still be no contract because the subject matter of the agreement is illegal in light of statute or public policy. For example, suppose that Mary Embezzler enters into an agreement with Lee Hitman wherein Mary promises to pay Lee $10,000 in return for Lee's promise to kill Mary's partner, Walter. The first three elements necessary for a contract appear to be present in the example: there is a valid offer and acceptance (mutual assent); there is a change of position in the making of the promises (consideration); and both parties appear to be mentally competent and of majority age (capacity). However, if Lee carries out his promise and murders Walter, it would not only be ridiculous, but it would be terrible law to permit Lee to go to court to obtain enforcement of Mary's promise to pay him $10,000. Obviously, a fourth element—legality—must also be present if the agreement is to be a valid contract. In the example, there is a blatant absence of legality, and the agreement is invalid.

Agreements Which Are Illegal Bargains

Of course, there are far more subtle forms of illegality. The following agreements are typically held to be illegal bargains (it is improper to refer to an illegal agreement as an illegal contract; if the agreement is illegal, it is no contract at all).

Crimes Any agreement calling for the commission of a crime is obviously an illegal bargain. Thus, any agreement to commit murder, larceny, burglary, robbery, forgery, kidnapping, etc., is void.

Obstruction of justice Agreements to obstruct the administration of justice such as bribe giving or hindering prosecution are also illegal bargains.

Torts An agreement to commit a tort (any socially unreasonable conduct) is void as an illegal bargain.

Gambling In most states, most forms of gambling are illegal.

Bargains in restraint of trade Bargains in restraint of trade are illegal as follows:

Covenants not to compete Because public policy strongly favors having people work for a living, covenants not to compete are disfavored under the common law. Frequently, the seller of a business will agree not to compete with the buyer following the sale. Such a covenant not to compete is legal and enforceable only if it is reasonable as to *time* and *area* covered. In other words, the restraint upon the seller must not exceed the extent of the business goodwill purchased ("goodwill" being the favorable position that an established and well-conducted business organization holds with the public). If the restraint is to continue for an unduly long period of time or if it extends to territory in which the seller had no goodwill, the restraint will be unreasonable and to the extent that it is unreasonable, it will be unenforceable. By way of example, suppose that the owner of a small grocery store in a local community sells out to a large retail chain; the grocer agrees as part of the contract of sale to never again compete in the grocery business anywhere. The restraint is obviously unreasonable as to both time and area. What would be reasonable would be a promise not to compete in the local area for a period of five years and, to this extent, the restraint may be enforced.

Now suppose that a business with a great deal of domestic and international goodwill is sold; the buyer pays a large sum of money for the goodwill. A promise by the seller not to compete in a large area of the United States as well as in several foreign countries for a period of twenty-five years may well be reasonable under the circumstances.

Sometimes an employee will agree as part of an employment contract that, upon completion of the employment, he or she will not compete with his or her former employer either by going into business personally or by working for another. Generally speaking, such covenants not to compete are illegal. They will be enforced only where the former employee is using the employer's trade secrets or secret customer lists (learned during the employment) to compete with the employer. But even absent a covenant not to compete, an employee may not, after employment, disclose or make use of such employment secrets—the courts will always restrain an employee from doing so. Otherwise, however, the courts are reluctant to enjoin an employee from earning his or her customary livelihood. To obtain an injunction, the former employer must generally prove that he or she has suffered substantial economic harm because of the employee's activity in soliciting customers (or in otherwise depriving the employer of goodwill); the employer must also show that the employee has other means of supporting himself or herself and his or her family.

Agreements to monopolize As we have seen in Chapter 7, it is illegal under the law to monopolize or attempt to monopolize or to otherwise violate the Sherman Antitrust Act, the federal Clayton Act, and the federal Trade Commission Act.

WHAT IS THE EFFECT OF ILLEGALITY?

The effect of illegality may be summarized as follows: *First,* if an illegal agreement is severable into legal and illegal parts and the illegal part does not go to "the essence of the bargain," then the legal portion may be enforced, and the illegal part disregarded. The general rule is that an agreement is severable only if it is expressly or impliedly divisible into two or more parts. Each party's performance must be composed of installments and each installment of a party's performance must confer an advantage or benefit on the other party so as to induce performance of the next installment (i.e., each installment of a party's performance must serve as consideration for the next installment of the other party's performance).

A minority of courts hold that if a single (indivisible) promise is exchanged for one or more legal *and* one or more illegal considerations, the illegal considerations will be disregarded, and the promise will be enforced.

Second, where the agreement is not severable and the parties are equally culpable (i.e., both have knowledge of the illegality and have willingly participated in it), the parties are *in pari delicto* ("in equal fault") and neither will receive any help from the courts in enforcing the contract. Thus, neither party can legally require the other to perform. And it makes no difference that one party has performed, while the other has not: the performing party can neither rescind the agreement nor recover what he or she has given under quasi contract. The courts, in effect, leave the parties where they find them—in pari delicto—and neither party has any legal remedy whatsoever.

(However, under the doctrine of "locus penitentiae" some courts hold that if one of the parties repents and repudiates the illegal contract before any part of it is carried out, he or she will have a right to recover any value given under quasi contract.)

Third, if the parties are not equally culpable but one is innocent or relatively so, the innocent party may be able to recover in quasi contract for unjust enrichment. The proper word is "may" because the innocent party's recovery depends on whether the illegal agreement is *malum in se* (against good morals) or *malum prohibitum* (in violation of a statute or rule but not against good morals). A malum in se contract is void, and neither party, no matter how innocent, can obtain any help from the courts (it is just as if the parties are in pari delicto). Though the courts will not enforce a malum prohibitum contract, they will allow the innocent party to recover on the basis of quasi contract.

Fourth, sometimes, an agreement violates a statute that has been passed to protect a group of people. If one of the parties to the contract is a member of the protected group, that party will not be deemed in pari delicto. For example, say that a young child is employed in violation of child labor laws (laws outlawing oppressive child labor as defined in Chapter 7). The child employee can recover for the value of his or her work though the employment itself is illegal.

WHAT IS A CONDITION?

A *condition* is a fact or event, the happening or nonhappening of which creates or terminates a promisor's duty of performance under a contract. Because the promisor's duty is conditional, the promisor's failure to perform in light of a "failure of condition" (the nonoccurrence of a condition giving rise to a duty) is not a breach of contract. Thus, where a party's performance is subject to the prior happening of a condition, a failure of the condition lets the party "off the hook," and he or she does not have to perform. Nor is it a breach of contract for the promisor to terminate performance upon the occurrence of a condition cutting off his or her duty to perform.

Condition Precedent

A condition precedent is a condition that must occur before a party will have an absolute duty to perform under a contract. It is the happening of the condition that gives rise to the absolute duty; if the condition never occurs (i.e., if there is a failure of condition), the party is never obligated to perform. For example, suppose that Fred Farmer promises to buy a tractor for $20,000 from Dora Dealer, but only on the condition that Fred's wheat crop produces forty bushels to the acre and Fred is able to sell the crop for at least $50,000 by the first of December. Until and unless the condition occurs (i.e., until and unless Fred's wheat crop produces forty bushels to the acre, and Fred sells the crop for at least $50,000 prior to December 1), Fred has no legal obligation to buy the tractor. If the condition fails, Fred has no legal duty to perform.

Condition Subsequent

A condition subsequent is a condition the happening of which cuts off or extinguishes a previously held duty to perform or to continue performing. For example, suppose that Fred Farmer promises to plow Tom Neighbor's fields "as long as the weather holds, but if there is rain making the fields muddy, there is no further duty to plow." Because Fred is under a duty to plow until and unless the condition occurs (i.e., until and unless there is a break in the weather, and the fields become muddy), the condition is a condition subsequent: the happening of the condition will cut off or extinguish Fred's duty to perform.

WHAT IS THE STATUTE OF FRAUDS?

A valid contract may not be enforceable unless the party seeking to enforce the contract can produce a certain kind of written evidence. This is the subject matter of the Statute of Frauds. Every state has passed such a statute specifically providing that certain contracts are not enforceable in the absence of special written evidence.

Keys to the Statute of Frauds

There are four "keys" to understanding and properly applying the Statute of Frauds.

Limited applicability Understand that most oral contracts are enforceable. In most cases, the Statute of Frauds does not apply, and so long as there is mutual assent, consideration, capacity, and legality, the contract, though completely oral, is legally enforceable.

Effect Know that where the Statute of Frauds does apply, the contract is not void but merely unenforceable between the original parties to the contract. Even where the required written evidence is not available and the contract is not enforceable, the contract is still valid for all other purposes and as to all other people. Thus, a completely oral contract to sell an automobile for $600 (contracts for the sale of goods for $500 or more fall within the Statute) is effective to transfer ownership of the property, assuming neither party reneges on his or her promise. However, if one of the parties does renege and the other party takes him or her to court, the contract will be unenforceable because of the failure to comply with the Statute of Frauds. Of course, a person not a party to the contract cannot complain that the contract does not comply with the Statute: only one of the original parties to the agreement can set up the Statute as a defense to enforcement of the contract.

Six situations only Know that the Statute of Frauds applies in only six situations. The Statute requires special written evidence of the following: (a) promises to answer for the debt of another; (b) promises by a personal representative of a decedent's estate to answer for the decedent's debts out of the personal representative's own funds; (c) agreements made in consideration of marriage; (d) contracts for the sale of land; (e) contracts that cannot be performed within a year's time; and (f) sale of goods for $500 or more.

Written memo requirement Appreciate that the written evidence required by the Statute is but a memo, signed by the party being sued (the defendant), that embraces certain of the essential terms of the agreement. The contract need not be fully written; it is therefore misleading to say, as so many people do, that a contract that falls within the Statute of Frauds must be in writing. All that is required is a written and signed *memorandum* of the essential terms of the agreement. The memo must include: (1) the identity of the contracting parties; (2) a description of the subject matter of the contract; (3) the terms and conditions of the agreement; (4) a recital of the consideration (not a requirement in all states); and (5) the signature of the party to be charged (i.e., the defendant or party being sued). So long as the required information is present, the memo may consist of a letter, a telegram, a mere notation on a party's books of record. The memo may even be composed of several writings, so long as the writings refer to each other or to the same subject matter or are physically attached.

Two of the situations falling within the Statute of Frauds are promises to answer for the debt of another and promises by a personal representative of a decedent's estate to answer for the decedent's debts out of the personal representative's own funds. These are suretyship promises and require a written and signed memorandum in order to be enforceable. These are considered *collateral* promises as opposed to *primary* promises to answer for one's own debts. However, the "main purpose" or "leading object" rule states that where a promisor's main purpose or leading object in making a collateral promise is to secure an advantage for himself or herself or otherwise to benefit directly, the promise is not truly a promise to answer for the debt of another and so is enforceable without written evidence.

The agreements made in consideration of marriage that the Statute of Frauds apply to are antenuptial or prenuptial property settlement agreements (i.e., premarital promises to transfer money or property or anything else of value in exchange for marriage or a promise of marriage) and not mutual promises to marry which are valid contractual promises requiring no writing.

The Statute of Frauds provides that a contract that cannot be performed within a year's time must be supported by a written and signed memo if it is to be enforceable. This provision refers only to contracts that, by their very terms, cannot *possibly* be performed within one year from the making of the contract. The one-year period commences on the date the contract is entered into—not on the date the promised performance is to begin. And it is important to realize that the Statute of Frauds applies only to promises that cannot possibly be performed within a year's time. It makes no difference that performance of the contract is *likely* to continue for more than a year or that the contracting parties *envision* a lengthier period of performance. If there is any possibility that the contract may be fully performed within a year's time, the Statute of Frauds does not apply, and the contract is enforceable without any written evidence whatsoever. Thus, an oral promise "to buy your antique car as soon as I inherit my share of my uncle's estate" is an enforceable promise despite the lack of any written evidence. Though the promisor's uncle is likely to live for many years, it is possible that he will die within the year, and the promise could be fully performed within that time.

Also because the transfer of *any* interest in land falls within the Statute it is important to keep in mind the distinction between real and personal property and the many and varied interests in land that are possible including fee simples, life estates, future interests, easements, profits, etc.

A contract to sell real property or any interest in real property is unenforceable in the absence of a written memo signed by the party to be charged. A single exception to the rule arises where there has been a transfer of possession under an oral land sales contract. The transfer of possession of the land is considered sufficient part performance of the contract to remove it from the Statute of Frauds and to make the promise to transfer the land enforceable even in the absence of a written memo signed by the promisor. The idea is that the purchaser's taking of possession with the landowner's consent provides sufficient evidence of the existence of a contract so as to diminish the likelihood of fraud or perjury. A minority of courts require something more than the mere transfer of possession to remove the contract from the Statute's operation: in some jurisdictions, the purchaser must not only receive possession of the land but must erect permanent improvements on the property for which no adequate compensation in money damages is possible; in other jurisdictions, the purchaser must pay all or part of the purchase price in addition to receiving possession from the landowner.

While a sale of goods for $500 or more falls within the Statute of Frauds, the UCC at Section 2–201 requires less of a written memo to prove promises than is required for the other five subject matter areas covered by the Statute. In the sale of goods situation, the only essential memo term is *quantity,* and even it may be misstated (although recovery, in that case, will be limited to the misstated amount).

Also the Statute of Frauds may be satisfied in the sale of goods situation with other than a written memo (unlike the other five situations).

1. If the buyer *accepts and receives* all or part of the goods, the contract, though oral, is enforceable to the extent that the goods are accepted and received.
2. If the buyer makes *part payment* for the goods, the contract, though oral, is enforceable as to the goods paid for.
3. If the seller is required by the terms of the contract to manufacture *special goods* for the buyer (special goods are goods unsuitable for sale to others in the ordinary course of the seller's business), and the seller has made a substantial beginning in their manufacture or has contracted for their procurement, no writing is needed to support the promise to buy the goods.
4. If the contract is *between merchants* and one of the merchants within a reasonable time sends a written confirmation of the agreement to the other merchant, and that merchant fails to object in writing to the confirmation within ten days, the contract is enforceable against the merchant who receives the confirmation.

5. Finally, if the party to be charged admits in court or in the pleadings (complaint, answer, reply as described in Chapter 3) preliminary to court that a contract does, in fact, exist, the contract will be enforceable to the extent of the party's admission.

WHAT IS THE PAROL EVIDENCE RULE?

The parol evidence rule comes into play only where parties to a contract have reduced their agreement to a final and complete writing. For the rule to operate, the writing must be a fully written integrated agreement, the term "integrated" meaning that the parties intended the writing to be the final and complete expression of their contract.

Assuming that the parties sign such an agreement, the parol evidence rule states that the fully written integrated contract may not be changed, altered, varied, or modified by any oral or written evidence (apart from the writing) occurring prior to or at the time of the signing of the agreement. The reason for the rule is that parties who have reduced their agreement to a writing, intending it as the final expression of their contract, should be able to rely upon that expression without worry that one of the parties will later claim that something else was intended.

Keys to the Parol Evidence Rule

There are three "keys" to understanding the parol evidence rule.

Limited applicability The rule applies only to fully written integrated contracts. It does not apply to contracts that are partly oral and partly written. Nor does it apply to writings such as receipts or estimates or to oral contracts entered into independent of a fully written integrated contract. It is not unusual for parties to enter into more than one contract at the same time—one contract may be fully reduced to writing and a second may be oral and independent of the written contract. While the parol evidence rule operates to bar contradictory evidence about the written contract, it does not bar evidence about the independent oral agreement. For example, a party might agree to buy a movie theater from another, all the specifics of the agreement put into a fully written and integrated contract. At the same time, the party might orally agree to hire the former owner of the theater to work as a movie projectionist for a period of one year. The second contract is exactly that—a second and separate agreement having nothing to do with the first. Thus, while parol evidence of the first agreement is barred, parol evidence of the second is not.

Prior or simultaneous evidence The rule applies only to evidence occurring prior to or at the time of the signing of the fully written integrated contract. Evidence that occurs after the parties have signed the agreement is not barred (e.g., the parol evidence rule never operates to prevent the showing of a subsequent change or modification of the written contract).

Evidence that changes, alters, varies, or modifies The rule applies only to evidence that changes, alters, varies, or modifies the terms of the fully written integrated contract. Evidence that does not change or modify the terms is always admissible whether the evidence occurs prior to, simultaneously with, or subsequent to the signing of the written agreement. Evidence may always be offered, for example, to show the following:

- *That there is a condition precedent to the operation of the written contract.* Whether oral or written, the condition precedent does not alter or change the terms of the writing—it merely states that the written contract *as it is written* is not to operate until and unless a condition occurs.
- *That there was fraud, duress, mistake, undue influence, unconscionable act, forgery, incapacity, illegality, or failure of consideration (i.e., failure of a party to perform his or her obligations under the contract).* Proof of these things does not vary, alter, change, or modify the contract as it is written but simply provides a basis for relieving the other party of his or her obligation to perform under the contract.
- *That the written language of the contract is ambiguous and needs to be explained or interpreted.* To explain or interpret language is not to contradict, alter, change, or modify it.

WHAT OCCURS WHERE A CONTRACT IS VALID, ENFORCEABLE, AND CLEAR IN MEANING?

To this point, we have learned that a valid contract exists only where there is mutual assent, capacity, consideration, and legality; that there are sometimes conditions precedent or subsequent to obligations of performance under a contract; that some contracts require special written evidence to be enforceable; and that fully written integrated contracts cannot be changed by parol evidence. All of this brings us to the point of having a valid, enforceable contract, clear in meaning, and recognized as creating binding obligations of performance by the parties. What happens next?

Usually one of two things—either one or both parties are discharged of any further obligation of performance under the contract, or one of the parties breaches the agreement, thus incurring liability to the other party in money damages or other relief.

HOW IS A PARTY DISCHARGED FROM HIS OR HER CONTRACT OBLIGATIONS?

A party may be discharged from his or her contract obligations (i.e., freed of any further obligation to perform) in any of the following ways.

Voidable Contract

You already know that a contract may be voidable because of fraud, duress, undue influence, incapacity, or the like. When a contract is voidable, one of the parties has the option of affirming or rescinding the agreement. If the party elects to rescind or disaffirm, the party's obligations of performance under the contract are discharged.

Condition Subsequent

You know, too, that a condition subsequent is a condition the occurrence of which terminates a duty of performance under a contract. Upon occurrence of the condition, the party subject to the condition is discharged.

Complete Performance

Complete performance is the usual method of discharge of contract obligations. In most cases, the parties completely perform without controversy, and both parties are discharged through their performances.

Impossibility of Performance

A duty of performance will also be discharged if, after a contract is entered into, the promised performance becomes *objectively impossible* to perform. The impossibility must occur *after* the contract has been entered into; if it is objectively impossible to perform at the time the parties enter into the agreement, it is a matter of mutual mistake, and there is no mutual assent and no contract.

The impossibility must be *objective* as opposed to *subjective. Objective impossibility* refers to the inability of anyone to perform the particular promise made; *subjective impossibility* refers to the personal inability of the promisor to perform the promise, although another person would be able to perform. While objective impossibility serves to discharge the duty of performance under the contract, subjective impossibility has no effect, leaving the obligation to perform intact. Examples of objective impossibility include a performance that becomes illegal because of a subsequent change in the law; a promise that cannot be performed because of the destruction of the subject matter of the contract through no fault of the promisor (e.g., where Lloyd Homeowner's house burns down before Frank has a chance to paint it); and a promise that cannot be carried out because of the incapacitating illness or death of a person essential to the performance. In each of these cases, no one can carry out the promised performance—to do so is objectively impossible.

In contrast, suppose that Frank the Painter cannot afford to buy the paint to carry out his promise to paint Lloyd Homeowner's house. Frank's personal inability to perform is a subjective impossibility only (others can paint the house) and does not excuse or discharge his duty of performance under the contract.

Mutual Rescission

Where both parties have yet to perform under a contract, the parties may "agree" to forget the agreement. An agreement to forget an existing contract is termed a *mutual rescission.* The mutual rescission is itself a binding contract that serves to discharge all duty of performance under the agreement it rescinds or cancels: there is consideration for the mutual rescission in that each party gives up the promised performance of the other.

Modified or Substituted Contract

Just as parties may mutually rescind an agreement where both parties have yet to perform, the parties may also agree prior to performance to modify the original agreement or to substitute an entirely new contract in its place. So long as each party promises to do something or refrain from doing something that he or she was not previously bound to do or refrain from doing, there is consideration for the modified or substituted agreement.

Novation

Sometimes, a third party agrees to take the place of one of the original parties to a contract, and, with full consent of all old and new parties, the third party becomes bound on the agreement while the original party is fully discharged. The substituted contract that results in these circumstances is properly termed a *novation.* It is the agreement of all parties, both old and new, that is essential to a novation—all must agree that the new party is to substitute fully for the original party and that the original party is to be discharged fully from any further duty of performance under the old contract.

Release

A release is an agreement to give up or relinquish existing rights. Generally, one party to a contract may release another from his or her contractual obligations, thereby discharging the party from any further duty to perform. Such a release is really nothing more than a form of substituted contract. In most states, a release is effective only if it is in writing and supported by consideration. However, insofar as the sale of goods is concerned, you will recall that Section 1–107 of the Uniform Commercial Code provides that any claim arising out of an alleged breach of contract for the sale of personal property may be discharged without regard to consideration by a written release signed and delivered by the nonbreaching party.

Accord and Satisfaction

Like a release, an accord and satisfaction is merely another form of substituted contract. It is an agreement wherein a party with an existing duty of performance under a contract promises to do something other than perform the duty as a means of discharging the contract obligation. The promise or agreement to do something different is termed an *accord*; the carrying out of the accord results in a *satisfaction* that serves to discharge both the accord itself and the contract duty which is the subject of the accord. For example, returning to our contract between Frank the Painter and Lloyd Homeowner, suppose that Frank the Painter fully performs his part of the bargain by painting Lloyd's house. Instead of paying Frank the $1,000 as promised, Lloyd promises to give Frank his boat within the next thirty days' time if Frank will forego the $1,000 payment. Frank agrees, and an accord is entered into. The accord does not immediately operate to discharge Lloyd's duty to pay the $1,000; however, if the boat is delivered to Frank within the next thirty days, the delivery will operate as a satisfaction, discharging both the accord agreement and Lloyd's contract duty to pay $1,000.

Statute of Limitations

A party who fails to bring legal action for breach of contract within the time period fixed by the statute of limitations will be barred from recovering money damages or obtaining other relief. While the running of the statute of limitations does not discharge the contract duty owed, it does bar any possible remedy and so frequently has the same effect as a discharge. (But remember that a new promise to pay a debt barred by the statute of limitations is enforceable without consideration.)

WHAT IS THE EFFECT OF A BREACH OF CONTRACT?

Say that a party is under a contractual obligation to perform, and nothing has discharged the party from his or her duty of performance. A failure by the party to perform at the time and place called for in the agreement constitutes a breach of contract. Where the breach is *major*—often called a material breach—the nonbreaching party is discharged from any further duty of performance under the contract and may sue immediately for breach of the *entire* contract. Where the breach is *minor* (i.e., insignificant), the nonbreaching party is not excused from further performance under the contract; however, he or she may temporarily suspend performance until the minor breach is cured, in which case the party's duty of performance will be discharged. And where the breach is minor, the nonbreaching party may not sue for breach of the entire contract but may sue only for damages arising from the minor breach itself.

Sometimes, complete performance by a party is an implied condition precedent to the other party's duty to perform. Thus, where Frank the Painter promises to paint Lloyd Homeowner's house for $1,000, until and unless Frank paints the house, Lloyd is not obligated to pay any portion of the money. But suppose that Frank substantially performs (as by painting all of the house except for the window screens) and then is unable to finish painting through no fault of his own. Lloyd's duty to pay, in this case, is absolute, although Lloyd is entitled to set off a portion of the $1,000 as damages for the minor breach of contract (Frank's failure to complete the job). The doctrine of *substantial performance* applies only where the failure to complete a performance is innocent—it never applies to a willful failure to finish a job.

WHAT REMEDIES DOES THE NONBREACHING PARTY HAVE?

Generally speaking, there are three remedies available to the nonbreaching party.

Restitution

Earlier we have considered restitution as a remedy available upon rescission of a voidable contract and as a remedy utilized in the area of unjust enrichment. With regard to breach of contract, restitution refers to restoring the parties, insofar as is practicable, to the positions they were in prior to entering into the contract. To restore the *status quo ante* (the precontract state of affairs), the courts generally order the return of specific property to the nonbreaching party or award the nonbreaching party a sum of money measured by the value of the benefit received by the breaching party.

Specific Performance

Where money damages are not an adequate remedy, the courts may order specific performance of the contract. Specific performance is performance in the exact manner specified by the contract. Thus, a breaching party who is ordered specifically to perform must actually carry out his or her contractual promise. For example, a seller who breaches a land sale contract may be ordered specifically to perform by conveying the land to the purchaser. Specific performance is always available as a remedy for a seller's breach of a land sale agreement because land, by its very nature, is unique, and money damages are never adequate. Specific performance is not available, on the other hand, as a remedy for a purchaser's breach of a land sale agreement—the nonbreaching seller, in this case, may be adequately compensated with money damages. Nor is specific performance available where the nonperformed contract duty calls for a personal service. Forcing someone to work would violate the Thirteenth Amendment's prohibition of involuntary servitude.

Like land, unique chattels such as antiques, paintings, and the like may be the subject of specific enforcement. And so may common stock in a family or closed corporation (a corporation whose stock is not listed on a securities exchange and is not easily available). However, common stock in a publicly held corporation (a corporation trading on the public market) is not unique, and money damages are an adequate remedy.

Of course, if it is impossible for the breaching party to perform his or her contract duty, specific performance will not be ordered. The most obvious example is where a breaching party who has contracted to convey land to the nonbreaching party has since conveyed the land to a bona fide purchaser. The bona fide purchaser, not knowing of the previous contract, will be protected, and the nonbreaching party will be able to collect money damages only.

Damages

Usually, the nonbreaching party seeks, not restitution or specific performance, but compensatory money damages. The purpose behind compensatory money damages is to place the injured party (the nonbreaching party) in the position he or she would have been in had the contract been properly carried out. To the extent practicable, money damages compensate the injured party for his or her loss—they give the injured party the benefit of the bargain entered into.

Two important rules that come into play in determining the amount of money damages recoverable are the *rule of remoteness* and the rule requiring *mitigation of damages.*

An injured party's measure of recovery for breach of contract is limited by the rule of remoteness. The rule states that an injured party should be compensated only for losses that are reasonably foreseeable to the parties at the time they enter into the contract. The rule of remoteness was first announced in the English case of Hadley v. Baxendale, 156 Eng.Rep. 145 (1845). The plaintiffs in that case operated a flour mill in Gloucester, England. When a crank shaft broke in an engine furnishing power to the mill, the plaintiffs decided to send the shaft to a foundry in Greenwich so that a new shaft could be made using the broken one as a model. The plaintiffs contracted with the defendants to transport the broken shaft to Greenwich, but the defendants negligently delayed delivering the shaft for several days, with the result that the plaintiffs were forced to close down the mill for an extended period of time. The plaintiffs sued the defendants for their lost profits, but the court denied recovery, stating that the lost profits were too "remote" to be recoverable. The defendants could not reasonably foresee at the time of entering into the delivery contract that a delay in delivery would force closure of the mill. The court in *Hadley* concluded that *consequential* (remote or indirect) damages are recoverable only where both parties know of the special circumstances likely to result in the damages at the time of entering into the contract.

A related rule is that *speculative* (uncertain) damages are never recoverable for breach of contract (e.g., estimated lost profits where a breach of contract forces closure of a Broadway play). Nor are *punitive* (penalty) damages, and where the amount of loss is not reasonably certain of computation, any award of damages amounts to a penalty.

The nonbreaching party is legally obligated to make a reasonable effort to mitigate (i.e., reduce or lessen) the damages flowing from the breach of contract. If the party fails to do so, his or her recovery in money damages will be reduced by the amount of loss that could have been avoided. For example, where a buyer breaches a sales contract by refusing to accept the goods contracted for, the seller must make a reasonable effort to sell the goods elsewhere—he or she cannot simply sit back and allow the goods to spoil or deteriorate. And if the seller breaches the sales agreement by refusing to deliver the goods, the buyer must make a reasonable attempt to purchase substitute goods from another seller. Suppose that a seller is manufacturing goods for a buyer who repudiates the contract. The seller, in this case, must cease manufacturing if this is the best way to mitigate the damages; however, if more loss can be avoided by completing manufacture of the goods and selling to another buyer, the seller is legally obligated to finish the job and make reasonable efforts to sell elsewhere.

WHAT IS THE LAW REGARDING "ANTICIPATORY BREACH" OF A CONTRACT?

If either party to an *executory bilateral* contract announces in advance of his or her promised performance that he or she will not perform (i.e., repudiates the promised performance), the other party may treat the anticipatory repudiation as a present material breach of the contract and bring legal action immediately for breach of the *entire* agreement. The doctrine of anticipatory breach or repudiation is designed to prevent hardship to the party who is told in advance that a promised performance will not be forthcoming. Certainly, it would be extremely unfair to insist that the party wait until the time for performance, remaining all the while ready and able personally to perform, after the other party has stated that he or she will not carry out his or her part of the bargain. For example, suppose that Frank the Painter enters into a contract with Lloyd Homeowner on June 1 wherein Frank promises to paint Lloyd's house in the second week of August in return for Lloyd's promise to pay Frank $1,000. On June 15, Frank repudiates his promised performance stating, "I am not going to do the job in August." Obviously, it would make little sense to state that there is no breach of contract until August—it would not be fair to insist that Lloyd wait until that time, all the while remaining ready and able to pay Frank the $1,000 should he come through with his promised performance. What does make sense is to hold that Frank's anticipatory repudiation of his promise constitutes a present material breach of contract that discharges Lloyd from any further duty of performance under the contract and enables him to sue immediately for money damages. Thus, immediately upon Frank's repudiation, Lloyd may hire Tom Olson to paint the house, and if Tom charges Lloyd $1,500, Lloyd may sue Frank at once to recover the $500 in damages.

WHAT ARE THE RULES REGARDING "LIQUIDATED" DAMAGES?

Frequently, a contract will expressly stipulate that a specific amount of damages (i.e., a fixed or liquidated amount) must be paid in the event of a breach of contract. The enforceability of such a provision will depend upon whether it is a valid liquidated damages clause or an unenforceable penalty provision. If the provision represents a good faith effort by the contracting parties to determine in advance what the actual damages would be upon a breach of contract, the provision will be a valid and enforceable liquidated damages clause. Thus, if the amount agreed upon by the parties bears a reasonable relationship to the amount of probable loss as measured at the time of entering into the contract, the provision will be a valid and enforceable liquidated damages clause. And where the nature of the contract is such that it is difficult to determine in advance just what the actual damages are likely to be upon a breach of contract, any determination made by the parties will be upheld so long as it is made in good faith (e.g., it might be very difficult to determine probable damages resulting from a breach of a covenant not to compete for a ten-year period). Where a stipulated damages provision is held to be a valid liquidated damages clause, the nonbreaching party may generally recover the full stipulated amount without regard to what actual damages, if any, are suffered (a minority of courts hold that liquidated damages are not recoverable in the absence of actual damages).

Where a stipulated damages provision bears no reasonable relationship to the amount of probable loss as calculated at the time of entering into the contract, the provision is an unenforceable penalty provision. For example, suppose that Frank the Painter agrees to paint Lloyd Homeowner's house for $1,000. At the time of entering into the contract, both parties agree that if Frank does not complete the job within ten days, liquidated damages in the amount of $50 a day must be paid to Lloyd until the job is finished. The $50/day liquidated damages provision may well be reasonable in light of probable loss to Lloyd in the event that his house is not completely painted within ten days' time. But where the contract provides for liquidated damages of $500/day, it is difficult to discern any reasonable relationship to probable loss, and the provision appears to be an unenforceable penalty. Where a stipulated damages provision is held to be a penalty, the nonbreaching party is not entitled to recover the stipulated amount but must prove in court his or her actual damages.

Cases

*"High as a Georgia pine * * * mutual assent or just a bunch of two doggoned drunks bluffing to see who could talk the biggest and say the most"?*

LUCY v. ZEHMER

Supreme Court of Appeals of Virginia, 1954.
196 Va. 493, 84 S.E.2d 516.

BUCHANAN, Justice

This suit was instituted by W. O. Lucy and J. C. Lucy, complainants, against A. H. Zehmer and Ida S. Zehmer, his wife, defendants, to have specific performance of a contract by which it was alleged the Zehmers had sold to W. O. Lucy a tract of land owned by A. H. Zehmer in Dinwiddie county containing 471.6 acres, more or less, known as the Ferguson farm, for $50,000. * * *

The instrument sought to be enforced was written by A. H. Zehmer on December 20, 1952, in these words: "We hereby agree to sell to W. O. Lucy the Ferguson Farm complete for $50,000.00, title satisfactory to buyer," and signed by the defendants, A. H. Zehmer and Ida S. Zehmer.

The answer of A. H. Zehmer admitted that at the time mentioned W. O. Lucy offered him $50,000 cash for the farm, but that he, Zehmer, considered that the offer was made in jest; that so thinking, and both he and Lucy having had several drinks, he wrote out "the memorandum" quoted above and induced his wife to sign it; that he did not deliver the memorandum to Lucy, but that Lucy picked it up, read it, put it in his pocket, attempted to offer Zehmer $5 to bind the bargain, which Zehmer refused to accept, and realizing for the first time that Lucy was serious, Zehmer assured him that he had no intention of selling the farm and that the whole matter was a joke. Lucy left the premises insisting that he had purchased the farm.

[Judgment was for defendants]

* * *

W. O. Lucy, a lumberman and farmer, thus testified in substance: He had known Zehmer for fifteen or twenty years and had been familiar with the Ferguson farm for ten years. Seven or eight years ago he had offered Zehmer $20,000 for the farm which Zehmer had accepted, but the agreement was verbal and Zehmer backed out. On the night of December 20, 1952, around eight o'clock, he took an employee to McKenney, where Zehmer lived and operated a restaurant, filling station and motor court. While there he decided to see Zehmer and again try to buy the Ferguson farm. He entered the restaurant and talked to Mrs. Zehmer until Zehmer came in. He asked Zehmer if he had sold the Ferguson farm. Zehmer replied that he had not. Lucy said, "I bet you wouldn't take $50,000.00 for that place."

Zehmer replied, "Yes, I would too; you wouldn't give fifty." Lucy said he would and told Zehmer to write up an agreement to that effect. Zehmer took a restaurant check and wrote on the back of it, "I do hereby agree to sell to W. O. Lucy the Ferguson Farm for $50,000 complete." Lucy told him he had better change it to "We" because Mrs. Zehmer would have to sign it too. Zehmer then tore up what he had written, wrote the agreement quoted above and asked Mrs. Zehmer, who was at the other end of the counter ten or twelve feet away, to sign it. Mrs. Zehmer said she would for $50,000 and signed it. Zehmer brought it back and gave it to Lucy, who offered him $5 which Zehmer refused, saying, "You don't need to give me any money, you got the agreement there signed by both of us."

The discussion leading to the signing of the agreement, said Lucy, lasted thirty or forty minutes, during which Zehmer seemed to doubt that Lucy could raise $50,000. Lucy suggested the provision for having the title examined and Zehmer made the suggestion that he would sell it "complete, everything there," and stated that all he had on the farm was three heifers.

Lucy took a partly filled bottle of whiskey into the restaurant with him for the purpose of giving Zehmer a drink if he wanted it. Zehmer did, and he and Lucy had one or two drinks together. Lucy said that while he felt the drinks he took he was not intoxicated, and from the way Zehmer handled the transaction he did not think he was either.

December 20 was on Saturday. Next day Lucy telephoned to J. C. Lucy and arranged with the latter to take a half interest in the purchase and pay half of the consideration. On Monday he engaged an attorney to examine the title. The attorney reported favorably on December 31 and on January 2 Lucy wrote Zehmer stating that the title was satisfactory, that he was ready to pay the purchase price in cash and asking when Zehmer would be ready to close the deal. Zehmer replied by letter, mailed on January 13, asserting that he had never agreed or intended to sell.

Mr. and Mrs. Zehmer were called by the complainants as adverse witnesses. Zehmer testified in substance as follows:

He bought this farm more than ten years ago for $11,000. He had had twenty-five offers, more or less, to buy it, including several from Lucy, who had never offered any specific sum of money. He had given them all the same answer, that he was not interested in selling it. On this Saturday night before Christmas it looked like everybody and his brother came by there to have a drink. He took a good many drinks during the afternoon and had a pint of his own. When he entered the restaurant around eight-thirty Lucy was there and he could see that he was "pretty high." He said to Lucy, "Boy, you got some good liquor, drinking, ain't you?" Lucy then offered him a drink. "I was already high as a Georgia pine, and didn't have any more better sense than to pour another great big slug out and gulp it down, and he took one too."

After they had talked a while Lucy asked whether he still had the Ferguson farm. He replied that he had not sold it and Lucy said, "I bet you wouldn't take $50,000.00 for it." Zehmer asked him if he would give $50,000 and Lucy said yes. Zehmer replied, "You haven't got $50,000.00 in cash." Lucy said he did and Zehmer replied that he did not believe it. They argued "pro and con for a long time," mainly about "whether he had $50,000 in cash that he could put up right then and buy that farm."

Finally, said Zehmer, Lucy told him if he didn't believe he had $50,000, "you sign that piece of paper here and say you will take $50,000.00 for the farm." He, Zehmer, "just grabbed the back off of a guest check there" and wrote on the back of it. At that point in his testimony Zehmer asked to see what he had written to "see if I recognize my own handwriting." He examined the paper and exclaimed, "Great balls of fire, I got 'Firgerson' for Ferguson. I have got satisfactory spelled wrong. I don't recognize that writing if I would see it, wouldn't know it was mine."

After Zehmer had, as he described it, "scribbled this thing off," Lucy said, "Get your wife to sign it." Zehmer walked over to where she was and she at first refused to sign but did so after he told her that he "was just needling him [Lucy], and didn't mean a thing in the world, that I was not selling the farm." Zehmer then "took it back over there * * * and I was still looking at the dern thing. I had the drink right there by my hand, and I reached over to get a drink, and he said, 'Let me see it.' He reached and picked it up, and when I looked back again he had it in his pocket and he dropped a five dollar bill over there, and he said, 'Here is five dollars payment on it.' * * * I said, 'Hell no, that is beer and liquor talking. I am not going to sell you the farm. I have told you that too many times before.' "

Mrs. Zehmer testified that when Lucy came into the restaurant he looked as if he had had a drink. When Zehmer came in he took a drink out of a bottle that Lucy handed him. She went back to help the waitress who was getting things ready for next day. Lucy and Zehmer were talking but she did not pay too much attention to what they were saying. She heard Lucy ask Zehmer if he had sold the Ferguson farm, and Zehmer replied that he had not and did not want to sell it. Lucy said, "I bet you wouldn't take $50,000.00 cash for that farm," and Zehmer replied, "You haven't got $50,000 cash." Lucy said, "I can get it." Zehmer said he might form a company and get it, "but you haven't got $50,000.00 cash to pay me tonight." Lucy asked him if he would put it in writing that he would sell him this farm. Zehmer then wrote on the back of a pad, "I agree to sell the Ferguson Place to W. O. Lucy for $50,000.00 cash." Lucy said, "All right, get your wife to sign it." Zehmer came back to where she was standing and said, "You want to put your name to this?" She said, "No," but he said in an undertone, "It is nothing but a joke," and she signed it.

She said that only one paper was written and it said: "I hereby agree to sell," but the "I" had been changed to "We". However, she said she read what she signed and was then asked, "When you read 'We hereby agree to sell to W. O. Lucy,' what did you interpret that to mean, that particular phrase?" She said she thought that was a cash sale that night; but she also said that when she read that part about "title satisfactory to buyer" she understood that if the title was good Lucy would pay $50,000 but if the title was bad he would have a right to reject it, and that that was her understanding at the time she signed her name.

* * *

The defendants insist that the evidence was ample to support their contention that the writing sought to be enforced was prepared as a bluff or dare to force Lucy to admit that he did not have $50,000; that the whole matter was a joke; that the writing was not delivered to Lucy and no binding contract was ever made between the parties.

It is an unusual, if not bizarre, defense. When made to the writing admittedly prepared by one of the defendants and signed by both, clear evidence is required to sustain it.

In his testimony Zehmer claimed that he "was high as a Georgia pine," and that the transaction "was just a bunch of two doggoned drunks bluffing to see who could talk the biggest and say the most." That claim is inconsistent with his attempt to testify in great detail as to what was said and what was done. * * * The record is convincing that Zehmer was not intoxicated to the extent of being unable to comprehend the nature and consequences of the instrument he executed, and hence that instrument is not to be invalidated on that ground. It was in fact conceded by defendants' counsel in oral argument that under the evidence Zehmer was not too drunk to make a valid contract.

* * *

The appearance of the contract, the fact that it was under discussion for forty minutes or more before it was signed; Lucy's objection to the first draft because it was written in the singular, and he wanted Mrs. Zehmer to sign it also; the rewriting to meet that objection and the signing by Mrs. Zehmer; the discussion of what was to be included in the sale, the provision for the examination of the title, the completeness of the instrument that was executed, the taking possession of it by Lucy with no request or suggestion by either of the defendants that he give it back, are facts which furnish persuasive evidence that the execution of the contract was a serious business transaction rather than a casual, jesting matter as defendants now contend.

* * *

If it be assumed, contrary to what we think the evidence shows, that Zehmer was jesting about selling his farm to Lucy and that the transaction was intended by him to be a joke, nevertheless the evidence shows that Lucy did not so understand it but considered it to be a serious business transaction and the contract to be binding on the Zehmers as well as on himself. The very next day he arranged with his brother to put up half the money and take a half interest in the land. The day after that he employed an attorney to examine the title. The next night, Tuesday, he was back at Zehmer's place and there Zehmer told him for the first time, Lucy said, that he wasn't going to sell and he told Zehmer, "You know you sold that place fair and square." After receiving the report from his attorney that the title was good he wrote to Zehmer that he was ready to close the deal.

Not only did Lucy actually believe, but the evidence shows he was warranted in believing, that the contract represented a serious business transaction and a good faith sale and purchase of the farm.

In the field of contracts, as generally elsewhere, "We must look to the outward expression of a person as manifesting his intention rather than to his secret and unexpressed intention. 'The law imputes to a person an intention corresponding to the reasonable meaning of his words and acts.' "

At no time prior to the execution of the contract had Zehmer indicated to Lucy by word or act that he was not in earnest about selling the farm. They had argued about it and discussed its terms, as Zehmer admitted, for a long time. Lucy testified that if there was any jesting it was about paying $50,000 that night. The contract and the evidence show that he was not expected to pay the money that night. Zehmer said that after the writing was signed he laid it down on the counter in front of Lucy. Lucy said Zehmer handed it to him. In any event there had been what appeared to be a good faith offer and a good faith acceptance, followed by the execution and apparent delivery of a written contract. Both said that Lucy put the writing in his pocket and then offered Zehmer $5 to seal the bargain. Not until then, even under the defendants' evidence, was anything said or done to indicate that the matter was a joke. Both of the Zehmers testified that when Zehmer asked his wife to sign he whispered that it was a joke so Lucy wouldn't hear and that it was not intended that he should hear.

The mental assent of the parties is not requisite for the formation of a contract. If the words or other acts of one of the parties have but one reasonable meaning, his undisclosed intention is immaterial except when an unreasonable meaning which he attaches to his manifestations is known to the other party. Restatement of the Law of Contracts, Vol. I, § 71, p. 74.

> * * * The law, therefore, judges of an agreement between two persons exclusively from those expressions of their intentions which are communicated between them. * * *

An agreement or mutual assent is of course essential to a valid contract but the law imputes to a person an intention corresponding to the reasonable meaning of his words and acts. If his words and acts, judged by a reasonable standard, manifest an intention to agree, it is immaterial what may be the real but unexpressed state of his mind.

So a person cannot set up that he was merely jesting when his conduct and words would warrant a reasonable person in believing that he intended a real agreement.

Whether the writing signed by the defendants and now sought to be enforced by the complainants was the result of a serious offer by Lucy and a serious acceptance by the defendants, or was a serious offer by Lucy and an acceptance in secret jest by the defendants, in either event it constituted a binding contract of sale between the parties.

* * *

Reversed and remanded.

Should the existence of an agreement "depend upon the conflicting fine print of commercial forms which cross one another but never meet"? This was a "genuine battle of the forms."

GAYNOR–STAFFORD INDUSTRIES, INC. v. MAFCO TEXTURED FIBERS

Supreme Court, Appellate Division, First Department, 1976.
52 A.D.2d 481, 384 N.Y.S.2d 788.

BIRNS, Justice

Both parties to this appeal are merchants in the textile industry.

Beginning in April 1974 they entered into a series of contracts for the purchase by respondent from appellant of substantial quantities of textured polyester yarn. In each instance, respondent placed an oral order with appellant for the yarn. A written order acknowledgment from appellant of the oral order followed and thereafter respondent sent its own form of a written and signed purchase order to appellant. The yarn specified or described was subsequently delivered to respondent.

In October 1974 respondent asked for an extension of time to make payment, and then in November 1974 refused to pay for certain shipments which it asserted did not include "dyeable yarn."

On the face of appellant's order acknowledgments was a statement that "This acknowledges * * * receipt of your order," and the following language appeared:

> The acceptance of this order is conditional on the assent by the buyer to all of the conditions and terms on the reverse side hereof. Your assent will be assumed unless you notify us to the contrary immediately upon receipt of this acknowledgment or when you accept delivery, in whole or in part, of the goods described herein.

Respondent's written purchase orders stated at the bottom "Acknowledge promptly if you are unable to ship by date specified." Stamped on the face of each purchase order was the following:

> Unless confirmation is received from the seller, the option to retain or cancel this order remains with the buyer.

One purchase order (# 2706) sent by respondent, had a note on its face reading: "Confirmation of contract # 4375" which appears to indicate that respondent considered appellant's order acknowledgment # 4375 as "the contract" and its own purchase order merely as confirmation of that contract.

On the reverse side of each order acknowledgment was a provision (condition 14) that "all controversies arising out of or relating to this contract * * * shall be settled by arbitration * * * under the Rules of the General Arbitration Council of the Textile Industry. * * *"

Respondent contends, as it did below, that it was not aware of the arbitration clause nor bound by its inclusion on the reverse side of the order acknowledgment, and that the form used by appellant which included the arbitration clause should not be deemed superior to the form used by respondent which contained no arbitration clause.

Finally, it urges that the arbitration clause was a "material alteration" of the contract, thereby falling within the purview of Uniform Commercial Code section 2–207(2)(b).

Appellant asserts before us, as it did below, that the notation on the face of its order acknowledgments alerted or should have alerted respondent to the said arbitration clause and, moreover, that both appellant and respondent were engaged in textiles and respondent must have been aware arbitration was a trade practice in said business.

Because the sole issue before us is whether there was an agreement to arbitrate, the forms involved and the pertinent section of the Uniform Commercial Code must be examined and considered to determine the answer.

Section 2–207 of the Uniform Commercial Code provides:

> Additional Terms in Acceptance or Confirmation
>
> (1) A definite and seasonable expression of the acceptance or a written confirmation which is sent within a reasonable time operates as an acceptance even though it states terms additional to or different from those offered or agreed upon * * *.
>
> (2) The additional terms are to be construed as proposals for addition to the contract. Between merchants such terms become part of the contract unless:
>   (a) the offer expressly limits acceptance to the terms of the offer;
>   (b) they materially alter it; or
>   (c) notification of objection to them has already been given or is given within a reasonable time after notice of them is received.

* * *

Matter of Doughboy Ind. (Pantasote Co.), 17 A.D.2d 216, 233 N.Y.S.2d 488, cited by respondent [does not] justify respondent's position. Although that case was decided a short time before the Code became effective in September 1964, the court examined the official comments of the drafters of the Code under section 2–207 in reaching its decision. The parties in *Doughboy* were not in the textile business and had dealt with each other on only two occasions during a three-month period. There, the face of seller's form brought attention to the terms on the reverse side, which included an arbitration clause and recited that silence or failure to object to the terms would bind the buyer. The buyer remained silent. The buyer's form, however, stated "only signed consent will bind." The court below held that the arbitration clause was not binding in that it was a material alteration and, further, that the seller's arbitration clause and the provision in the buyer's form which stated that only signed consent would bind, were in conflict, thus initiating a genuine "battle of the forms." The court opined that the existence of an agreement to arbitrate should not depend upon the conflicting fine print of commercial forms which cross one another but never meet.

It is undisputed that the parties here were merchants who have had long experience in the textile industry and in fact had dealt with each other for seven months. Hence, Matter of Helen Whiting, Inc. (Trojan Textile Corp.), 307 N.Y. 360, 121 N.E.2d 367, although a pre-Code case, is helpful in disposing of the issue before us. The parties in *Whiting* were in the textile business. An arbitration clause appeared on the reverse side of the seller's form. The buyer claimed not to be bound thereby. The Court of Appeals observed: "From our own experience, we can almost take judicial notice that arbitration clauses are commonly used in the textile industry." Indeed, this Court has cited *Whiting* for the proposition that arbitration is common in the textile industry.

* * * Respondent's claim that the arbitration clause in appellant's form was a "material alteration" of the terms of the contract between the parties is negated by the rule in *Whiting*, supra, that arbitration is common in the textile industry. In these circumstances, the arbitration clause cannot be considered a "material alteration" (Uniform Commercial Code, § 2–207[2][b]) so as to be binding only where there is affirmative consent. Therefore, respondent's failure to notify appellant within a reasonable time af-

ter receipt of the order acknowledgments of its objection to the arbitration clause, gave said clause binding effect (Uniform Commercial Code, § 2–207[2][c]).

Accordingly, the judgment appealed from should be reversed * * * motion to compel arbitration should be granted.

"While she first exulted that she was entering the 'spring of her life,' she finally awakened to the fact that there was 'spring' neither in her life nor in her feet."

VOKES v. ARTHUR MURRAY, INC.

Court of Appeal of Florida, Second District, 1968.
212 So.2d 906.

PIERCE, Judge

This is an appeal by Audrey E. Vokes. * * *

Defendant Arthur Murray, Inc., a corporation, authorizes the operation throughout the nation of dancing schools under the name of "Arthur Murray School of Dancing" through local franchised operators, one of whom was defendant J. P. Davenport whose dancing establishment was in Clearwater.

Plaintiff Mrs. Audrey E. Vokes, a widow of 51 years and without family, had a yen to be "an accomplished dancer" with the hopes of finding "new interest in life." So, on February 10, 1961, a dubious fate, with the assist of a motivated acquaintance, procured her to attend a "dance party" at Davenport's "School of Dancing" where she whiled away the pleasant hours, sometimes in a private room, absorbing his accomplished sales technique, during which her grace and poise were elaborated upon and her rosy future as "an excellent dancer" was painted for her in vivid and glowing colors. As an incident to this interlude, he sold her eight ½-hour dance lessons to be utilized within one calendar month therefrom, for the sum of $14.50 cash in hand paid, obviously a baited "come-on."

Thus she embarked upon an almost endless pursuit of the terpsichorean art during which, over a period of less than sixteen months, she was sold fourteen "dance courses" totalling in the aggregate 2302 hours of dancing lessons for a total cash outlay of $31,090.45, all at Davenport's dance emporium. All of these fourteen courses were evidenced by execution of a written "Enrollment Agreement—Arthur Murray's School of Dancing" with the addendum in heavy black print, "No one will be informed that you are taking dancing lessons. Your relations with us are held in strict confidence," setting forth the number of "dancing lessons" and the "lessons in rhythm sessions" currently sold to her from time to time, and always of course accompanied by payment of cash of the realm.

These dance lesson contracts and the monetary consideration therefor of over $31,000 were procured from her by means and methods of Davenport and his associates which went beyond the unsavory, yet legally permissible, perimeter of "sales puffing" and intruded well into the forbidden area of * * * suggestion of falsehood, the suppression of truth, and the free exercise of rational judgment. * * * From the time of her first contact with the dancing school in February, 1961, she was influenced unwittingly by a constant and continuous barrage of flattery, false praise, excessive complements, and panegyric encomiums, to such extent that it would be not only inequitable, but unconscionable, for a Court exercising inherent chancery power to allow such contracts to stand.

She was incessantly subjected to overreaching blandishment and cajolery. She was assured she had "grace and poise"; that she was "rapidly improving and developing in her dancing skill"; that the additional lessons would "make her a beautiful dancer, capable of dancing with the most accomplished dancers", that she was "rapidly progressing in the development of her dancing skill and gracefulness," etc., etc. She was given "dance aptitude tests" for the ostensible purpose of "determining" the number of remaining hours instructions needed by her from time to time.

At one point she was sold 545 additional hours of dancing lessons to be entitled to award of the "Bronze Medal" signifying that she had reached "the Bronze Standard," a supposed designation of dance achievement by students of Arthur Murray, Inc.

Later she was sold an additional 926 hours in order to gain the "Silver Medal", indicating she had reached "the Silver Standard," at a cost of $12,501.35.

At one point, while she still had to her credit about 900 unused hours of instructions she was induced to purchase an additional 24 hours of lessons to participate in a trip to Miami at her own expense, where she would be "given the opportunity to dance with members of the Miami Studio."

* * *

At another point, while she still had over 1,000 unused hours of instruction she was induced to buy 151 additional hours at a cost of $2,049.00 to be eligible for a "Student Trip to Trinidad," at her own expense as she later learned.

Also, when she still had 1100 unused hours to her credit, she was prevailed upon to purchase an additional 347 hours at a cost of $4,235.74, to qualify her to receive a "Gold Medal" for achievement, indicating she had advanced to "the Gold Standard."

* * *

All the foregoing sales promotions, illustrative of the entire fourteen separate contracts, were procured by defendant Davenport and Arthur Murray, Inc., by false representations to her that she was improving in her dancing ability, that she had excellent potential, that she was responding to instructions in dancing grace, and that they were developing her into a beautiful dancer, whereas in truth and in fact she did not develop in her dancing ability, she had no "dance aptitude," and in fact had difficulty in "hearing the musical beat." The complaint alleged that such representations to her "were in fact false and known by the defendant to be false and contrary to the plaintiff's true ability, the truth of plaintiff's ability being fully known to the defendants, but withheld from the plaintiff for the sole and specific intent to deceive and defraud the plaintiff and to induce her in the purchasing of additional hours of dance lessons." It was averred that the lessons were sold to her "in total disregard to the true physical, rhythm, and mental ability of the plaintiff." In other words, while she first exulted that she was entering the "spring of her life," she finally was awakened to the fact there was "spring" neither in her life nor in her feet.

The complaint prayed that the Court decree the dance contracts to be null and void and to be cancelled, that an accounting be had, and judgment entered against the defendants "for that portion of the $31,090.45 not charged against specific hours of instruction given to the plaintiff." The Court held the complaint not to state a cause of action and dismissed it with prejudice. We disagree and reverse.

* * * Defendants contend that contracts can only be rescinded for fraud or misrepresentation when the alleged misrepresentation is as to a material fact, rather than an opinion, prediction or expectation, and that the statements and representations set forth at length in the complaint were in the category of "trade puffing," within its legal orbit.

It is true that "generally a misrepresentation, to be actionable, must be one of fact rather than of opinion." But this rule has significant qualifications, applicable here. * * *

> * * * A statement of a party having * * * superior knowledge may be regarded as a statement of fact although it would be considered as opinion if the parties were dealing on equal terms.

It could be reasonably supposed here that defendants had "superior knowledge" as to whether plaintiff had "dance potential" and as to whether she was noticeably improving in the art of terpsichore. And it would be a reasonable inference from the undenied averments of the complaint that the flowery eulogiums heaped upon her by defendants as a prelude to her contracting for 1944 additional hours of instruction in order to attain the rank of the Bronze Standard, thence to the bracket of the Silver Standard, thence to the class of the Gold Bar Standard, and finally to the crowning plateau of a Life Member of the Studio, proceeded as much or more from the urge to "ring the cash register" as from any honest or realistic appraisal of her dancing prowess or a factual representation of her progress.

* * *

Reversed.

"He promised his nephew that if he would refrain from drinking, using tobacco, swearing, and playing cards or billiards for money until he became 21 years of age, he would pay him the sum of $5,000."

HAMER v. SIDWAY

Court of Appeals of New York, Second Division, 1891.
124 N.Y. 538, 27 N.E. 256.

* * * The plaintiff presented a claim to the executor of William E. Story, Sr., for $5,000 and interest from the 6th day of February, 1875. * * * The claim being rejected by the executor, this action was brought. It appears that William E. Story, Sr., was the uncle of William E. Story, 2d; that at the celebration of the golden wedding of Samuel Story and wife, father and mother of William E. Story, Sr., on the 20th day of March 1869, in the presence of the family and invited guests, he promised his nephew that if he would refrain from drinking, using tobacco, swearing, and playing cards or billiards for money until he became 21 years of age, he would pay him the sum of $5,000. The nephew assented thereto, and fully performed the conditions inducing the promise. When the nephew arrived at the age of 21 years, and on the 31st day of January, 1875, he wrote to his uncle, informing him that he had performed his part of the agreement, and had thereby become entitled to the sum of $5,000. The uncle received the letter, and a few days later, and on the 6th day of February, he wrote and mailed to his nephew the following letter: "Buffalo, Feb. 6, 1875. W. E. Story, Jr.—Dear Nephew: Your letter of the 31st ult. came to hand all right, saying that you had lived up to the promise made to me several years ago. I have no doubt but you have, for which you shall have five thousand dollars, as I promised you. I had the money in the bank the day you was twenty-one years old that I intend for you, and you shall have the money certain. Now, Willie, I do not intend to interfere with this money in any way till I think you are capable of taking care of it, and the sooner that time comes the better it will please me. I would hate very much to have you start out in some adventure that you thought all right and lose this money in one year. The first five thousand dollars that I got together cost me a heap of hard work. You would hardly believe me when I tell you that to obtain this I shoved a jack-plane many a day, butchered three or four years, then came to this city, and, after three months' perseverance, I obtained a situation in a grocery store. I opened this store early, closed late, slept in the fourth story of the building in a room 30 by 40 feet, and not a human being in the building but myself. All this I done to live as cheap as I could to save something. I don't want you to take up with this kind of fare. I was here in the cholera season of '49 and '52, and the deaths averaged 80 to 125 daily, and plenty of small-pox. I wanted to go home, but Mr. Fisk, the gentleman I was working for, told me, if I left them, after it got healthy he probably would not want me. I stayed. All the money I have saved I know just how I got it. It did not come to me in any mysterious way, and the reason I speak of this is that money got in this way stops longer with a fellow that gets it with hard knocks than it does when he finds it. Willie, you are twenty-one, and you have many a thing to learn yet. This money you have earned much easier than I did, besides acquiring good habits at the same time, and you are quite welcome to the money. Hope you will make good use of it. I was ten long

years getting this together after I was your age. * * *" The uncle died on the 29th day of January, 1887, without having paid over to his nephew any portion of the said $5,000 and interest.

* * * The defendant contends that the contract was without consideration to support it, and therefore invalid. He asserts that the promisee, by refraining from the use of liquor and tobacco, was not harmed, but benefited; that that which he did was best for him to do, independently of his uncle's promise—and insists that it follows that, unless the promisor was benefited, the contract was without consideration. * * * The exchequer chamber in 1875 defined "consideration" as follows: "A valuable consideration, in the sense of the law, may consist either in some right, interest, profit, or benefit accruing to the one party, or some forbearance, detriment, loss or responsibility given, suffered, or undertaken by the other." Courts "will not ask whether the thing which forms the consideration does in fact benefit the promisee or a third party, or is of any substantial value to any one. It is enough that something is promised, done, forborne, or suffered by the party to whom the promise is made as consideration for the promise made to him." * * * Pollock in his work on Contracts, (page 166,) after citing the definition given by the exchequer chamber, already quoted, says: "The second branch of this judicial description is really the most important one. 'Consideration' means not so much that one party is profiting as that the other abandons some legal right in the present, or limits his legal freedom of action in the future, as an inducement for the promise of the first." Now, applying this rule to the facts before us, the promisee used tobacco, occasionally drank liquor, and he had a legal right to do so. That right he abandoned for a period of years upon the strength of the promise of the testator that for such forbearance he would give him $5,000. We need not speculate on the effort which may have been required to give up the use of those stimulants. It is sufficient that he restricted his lawful freedom of action within certain prescribed limits upon the faith of his uncle's agreement, and now, having fully performed the conditions imposed, it is of no moment whether such performance actually proved a benefit to the promisor, and the court will not inquire into it; but, were it a proper subject of inquiry, we see nothing in this record that would permit a determination that the uncle was not benefited in a legal sense. * * * In Talbott v. Stemmons, * * * the step-grandmother of the plaintiff made with him the following agreement: "I do promise and bind myself to give my grandson Albert R. Talbott $500 at my death if he will never take another chew of tobacco or smoke another cigar during my life, from this date up to my death. * * *" The [defendant] executor of Mrs. Stemmons [claimed] that the agreement was not based on a sufficient consideration. * * * In the opinion of the court it is said that "the right to use and enjoy the use of tobacco was a right that belonged to the plaintiff, and not forbidden by law. The abandonment of its use may have saved him money, or contributed to his health; nevertheless, the surrender of that right caused the promise, and, having the right to contract with reference to the subject-matter, the abandonment of the use was a sufficient consideration to uphold the promise." * * *

* * *

Was the college education a "necessary" for this minor?

JOHNSTONE v. JOHNSTONE

Appellate Court of Illinois, First District,
First Division, 1965.
64 Ill.App.2d 447, 212 N.E.2d 143.

BURMAN, Presiding Justice

This suit arises out of a claim filed by petitioner, Eloise Johnstone, against the minor's estate of her stepson, Robert B. Johnstone, Jr., for amounts expended by her and obligations incurred by her in financing his college education. She based her claim upon the contention that in modern society and under the circumstances of this case a college education falls within the legal definition of a "necessary"; and that since she furnished the only funds available for her stepson's college education he is liable to her under established principles of law. The court specifically found that petitioner's expenditures were not for "necessities," and dismissed her claim. Petitioner has appealed from this ruling.

Upon the minor's graduation from high school, he indicated his desire to continue his education at Dartmouth College in Hanover, New Hampshire. His father, Robert B. Johnstone, Sr., who was living at the time, approved of his son's plans, and in order to meet the costs of this education applied to the La Salle National Bank for a loan under the Bank's Assured College Education Plan. As an integral part of this plan, the Bank requires the Applicant Sponsor to purchase an insurance policy on his own life, naming the Bank as beneficiary. It appears from the record in this case that the poor health of the minor's father made him unable to qualify for such a policy, thereby preventing him from signing the loan as Applicant Sponsor. The application was signed by petitioner, the minor's stepmother, as Applicant Sponsor and the Minor's father signed as "Spouse of Applicant Sponsor."

Semi-annual payments of $750.00 by the Bank direct to Dartmouth College began in September of 1961, and continued through the sixth payment in December of 1963, at which time the minor's father died and payments by the Bank ceased. Prior to his death, Robert B. Johnstone, Sr., had made regular repayments to the Bank in the amount specified in the terms of the loan. At his death, the balance due the Bank was $2,101.50, for which the Bank has held petitioner responsible and which she has reduced by further payments. She seeks recovery from the minor's estate for this amount.

Two life insurance policies were left by the minor's decesed father. The first was a policy in the amount of $5,000, which named the petitioner as beneficiary. The other policy was in the amount of $10,000, and named petitioner and the minor as beneficiaries, each in the amount of $5,000. Petitioner seeks to recover against the minor's share of the proceeds of this policy. The record reveals that the father's estate is insolvent, and petitioner claims that all the monies she received from the policies will be used to pay claims against the estate.

It is well-established, as a general rule, that a minor or his estate may be liable for necessaries furnished him. As to the definition of a "necessary," our Supreme Court stated in McKanna v. Merry, 61 Ill. 177:

> There is no positive rule by means of which it may be determined what are, and what are not necessaries. Whether articles are of a class or kind for which infants are liable, or whether certain subjects of expenditure are necessaries, are to be judged of by the court. Whether they come within the particular class, and are suitable to the condition and estate of the infant, is to be determined by the jury as a matter of fact. * * * Blackstone defines necessaries to be 'necessary meat, drink, apparel, physic,' and says that an infant may bind himself to pay 'for his good teaching and instruction, whereby he may profit himself afterwards.' The articles furnished, or money advanced, must be actually necessary, in the particular case, for use, not mere ornament, for substantial good, not mere pleasure; and must belong to the class which the law generally pronounces necessary for infants.

In Crandall v. Coyne Electrical School, 256 Ill.App. 322, the court cited the McKanna case, and went on to say:

> It is recognized that a proper education is a necessary. But what is a proper education depends on circumstances. * * * A common school education is said to be a necessary in this country. (citing cases) In the latter case, it is said that circumstances, however, may exist where a more liberal edu-

> cation might properly be found a necessary as a matter of fact. (256 Ill.App. 322, at 324)

Thus, the trial judge in this case was charged with the responsibility of determining whether, on the basis of the evidence, a college education for this minor could be classified as a "necessary." But, as pointed out by Professor Williston, "What are necessaries is determined not simply by the nature of the thing, but by the need of that thing at that time by the infant in question." The evidence in this case showed the minor was at the top of his class in high school and that there was available to the minor a full tuition scholarship to the University of Chicago. The Court could have found from the evidence that the minor might have received from Dartmouth College either a scholarship or a loan on more favorable terms than the one received from La Salle National Bank. In light of these facts and the tests for "necessaries" set forth above, we cannot conclude that the Chancellor's findings were manifestly against the weight of the evidence, and therefore we cannot disturb his judgment.

Petitioner's claim is subject to a further objection. It has been the established rule in Illinois since Sinklear v. Emert, 18 Ill. 63, that a minor is liable for necessaries furnished him only if they are furnished on his credit, and not on the credit of another. Professor Williston states it thus:

> It is essential to recovery that necessaries shall have been furnished on the credit of the infant. If furnished on the credit of his parent or guardian, he is not liable. * * *

In this case, the record is clear that at the time the Johnstones entered into the loan agreement, the minor was not asked by either of them to repay the loan at any future time. Petitioner did not testify that she signed the note at the request of the minor, nor that she did so in reliance upon his credit. Indeed it appears that she obligated herself for the indebtedness at the request of her husband. The minor testified that while he knew a loan had been made he did not know, until after his father's death, that his stepmother was obligated on that loan. He further testified that his father told him that the loan was merely for the sake of convenience in view of the fact that his income fluctuated widely. Finally, the minor's father had paid regularly his tuition at a private high school, never indicating that the costs were beyond his ability to pay. In view of these facts, we conclude that petitioner has failed to prove that the funds for the minor's college education were furnished on his credit. For this reason, her appeal must fail, even assuming *arguendo* not only that the Dartmouth College education was a "necessary" in this case, but also assuming *arguendo* that petitioner is correct in her contention that a stepmother can recover for necessaries furnished despite the fact that a natural or adopting parent cannot.

Judgment affirmed.

Did plaintiff have a "legal" contract (entitling her to one-half of more than $1 million in earnings) when she gave up her singing career to become movie star Lee Marvin's "companion, homemaker, housekeeper, and cook"?

MARVIN v. MARVIN

Supreme Court of California, In Bank, 1976.
18 Cal.3d 660, 134 Cal.Rptr. 815, 557 P.2d 106.

TOBRINER, Justice

During the past 15 years, there has been a substantial increase in the number of couples living together without marrying. Such nonmarital relationships lead to legal controversy when one partner dies or the couple separates. Courts of Appeal, faced with the task of determining property rights in such cases, have arrived at conflicting positions: two cases held that the Family Law Act requires division of the property according to community property principles, and one decision has rejected that holding. We take this opportunity to resolve that controversy and to declare the principles which should govern distribution of property acquired in a nonmarital relationship.

We conclude: (1) The provisions of the Family Law Act do not govern the distribution of property acquired during a nonmarital relationship; such a relationship remains subject solely to judicial decision. (2) The courts should enforce express contracts between nonmarital partners except to the extent that the contract is explicitly founded on the consideration of meretricious sexual services. (3) In the absence of an express contract, the courts should inquire into the conduct of the parties to determine whether that conduct demonstrates an implied contract. * * *

In the instant case plaintiff and defendant lived together for seven years without marrying; all property acquired during this period was taken in defendant's name. When plaintiff sued to enforce a contract under which she was entitled to half the property and to support payments, the trial court granted judgment on the pleadings for defendant, thus leaving him with all property accumulated by the couple during their relationship. Since the trial court denied plaintiff a trial on the merits of her claim, its decision conflicts with the principles stated above, and must be reversed.

* * *

Plaintiff avers that in October of 1964 she and defendant "entered into an oral agreement" that while "the parties lived together they would combine their efforts and earnings and would share equally any and all property accumulated as a result of their efforts whether individual or combined." Furthermore, they agreed to "hold themselves out to the general public as husband and wife" and that "plaintiff would further render her services as a companion, homemaker, housekeeper and cook to * * * defendant."

Shortly thereafter plaintiff agreed to "give up her lucrative career as an entertainer [and] singer" in order to "devote her full time to defendant * * * as a companion, homemaker, housekeeper and cook"; in return defendant agreed to "provide for all of plaintiff's financial support and needs for the rest of her life."

Plaintiff alleges that she lived with defendant from October of 1964 through May of 1970 and fulfilled her obligations under the agreement. During this period the parties as a result of their efforts and earnings acquired in defendant's name substantial real and personal property, including motion picture rights worth over $1 million. In May of 1970, however, defendant compelled plaintiff to leave his household. He continued to support plaintiff until November of 1971, but thereafter refused to provide further support.

* * *

In Trutalli v. Meraviglia (1932) 215 Cal. 698, 12 P.2d 430 we established the principle that nonmarital partners may lawfully contract concerning the ownership of property acquired during the relationship. We reaffirmed this principle in Vallera v. Vallera (1943) 21 Cal.2d 681, 685, 134 P.2d 761, 763, stating that "If a man and woman [who are not married] live together as husband and wife under an agreement to pool their earnings and share equally in their joint accumulations, equity will protect the interests of each in such property."

* * *

Defendant first and principally relies on the contention that the alleged contract is so closely related to the supposed "immoral" character of the relationship between plaintiff and himself that the enforcement of the contract would violate public policy. He points to cases asserting that a contract between nonmarital partners is unenforceable if it is "involved in" an illicit relationship.

A review of the numerous California decisions concerning contracts between nonmarital partners, however, reveals that the courts have not employed such broad and uncertain standards to strike down contracts. The decisions instead disclose a narrower and more precise standard: a contract between nonmarital partners is unenforceable only *to the extent* that it *explicitly* rests upon the immoral and illicit consideration of meretricious sexual services.

* * *

Croslin v. Scott (1957) 154 Cal.App.2d 767, 316 P.2d 755 reiterates the rule established in *Trutalli.* * * * In *Croslin* the parties separated following a three-year nonmarital relationship. The woman then phoned the man, asked him to return to her, and suggested that he build them a house on a lot she owned. She agreed in return to place the property in joint ownership. The man built the house, and the parties lived there for several more years. When they separated, he sued to establish his interest in the property. Reversing a nonsuit, the Court of Appeal stated that "The mere fact that parties agree to live together in meretricious relationship does not necessarily make an agreement for disposition of property between them invalid. It is only when the property agreement is made in connection with the other agreement, or the illicit relationship is made a consideration of the property agreement, that the latter becomes illegal."

* * *

* * * In Hill v. Estate of Westbrook, supra, 95 Cal.App.2d 599, 213 P.2d 727, the woman promised to keep house for the man, to live with him as man and wife, and to bear his children; the man promised to provide for her in his will, but died without doing so. Reversing a judgment for the woman based on the reasonable value of her services, the Court of Appeal stated that "the action is predicated upon a claim which seeks, among other things, the reasonable value of living with decedent in meretricious relationship and bearing him two children. * * * The law does not award compensation for living with a man as a concubine and bearing him children. * * * As the judgment is, at least in part, for the value of the claimed services for which recovery cannot be had, it must be reversed." (95 Cal. App.2d at p. 603, 213 P.2d at p. 730.) Upon retrial, the trial court found that it could not sever the contract and place an independent value upon the legitimate services performed by claimant. We therefore affirmed a judgment for the estate. (Hill v. Estate of Westbrook (1952) 29 Cal.2d 458, 247 P.2d 19.)

In the only other cited decision refusing to enforce a contract, Updeck v. Samuel (1964) 123 Cal.App.2d 264, 266 P.2d 822, the contract "was based on the consideration that the parties live together as husband and wife." Viewing the contract as calling for adultery, the court held it illegal.

The decisions in the *Hill* and *Updeck* cases thus demonstrate that a contract between nonmarital partners, even if expressly made in contemplation of a common living arrangement, is invalid only if sexual acts form an inseparable part of the consideration for the agreement. In sum, a court will not enforce a contract for the pooling of property and earnings if it is explicitly and inseparably based upon services as a paramour. * * *

The principle that a contract between nonmarital partners will be enforced unless expressly and inseparably based upon an illicit consideration of sexual services not only represents the distillation of the decisional law, but also offers a far more precise and workable standard than that advocated by defendant. * * *

* * *

In summary, we base our opinion on the principle that adults who voluntarily live together and engage in sexual relations are nonetheless as competent as any other persons to contract respecting their earnings and property rights. Of course, they cannot lawfully contract to pay for the performance of sexual services, for such a contract is, in essence, an agreement for prostitution and unlawful for that reason. But they may agree to pool their earnings and to hold all property acquired during the relationship in accord with the law governing community property; conversely they may agree that each partner's earnings and the property acquired from those earnings remains the separate property of the earning partner. So long as the agreement does not rest upon illicit meretricious consideration, the parties may order their economic affairs as they choose, and no policy precludes the courts from enforcing such agreements.

In the present instance, plaintiff alleges that the parties agreed to pool their earnings, that they contracted to share equally in all property acquired, and that defendant agreed to support plaintiff. The terms of the contract as alleged do not rest upon any unlawful consideration. * * *

* * *

* * * As we have explained, the courts now hold that express agreements will be enforced unless they rest on an unlawful meretricious consideration. We add that in the absence of an express agreement, the courts may look to a variety of other remedies in order to protect the parties' lawful expectations.[24]

The courts may inquire into the conduct of the parties to determine whether that conduct demonstrates an implied contract or implied agreement. * * * [A] nonmarital partner may recover in quantum meruit for the reasonable value of household services rendered less the reasonable value of support received if he can show that he rendered services with the expectation of monetary reward.

* * *

The judgment is reversed. * * *

24. We do not seek to resurrect the doctrine of common law marriage, which was abolished in California by statute in 1895. Thus we do not hold that plaintiff and defendant were "married," * * * we hold only that she has the same rights to enforce contracts and to assert her equitable interest in property acquired through her effort as does any other unmarried person.

At 4:00 P.M. "workmen were all over the place, slapping on siding, laying the floors, bulldozing the yard, hooking up the utilities." Could the house have been "substantially completed" by 5:30 P.M.?

SURETY DEVELOPMENT CORP. v. GREVAS

Appellate Court of Illinois, Second District, First Division, 1963.
42 Ill.App.2d 268, 192 N.E.2d 145.

SMITH, Justice

When is a house a home? In our context a house is a home when it can be lived in. But when is that: When substantially completed or completely completed? We posit the question, because the answer is decisive.

Plaintiff sells prefabricated houses. Defendants selected one of their models, styled "Royal Countess, elevation 940." A contract was signed. The cost was $16,385.00; completion date September 27, 1961. Around 4:00 P.M. on that date defendants refused to accept the house asserting noncompletion. Plaintiff then sued for the balance due and defendants counter-claimed for their downpayment. Both alleged performance by them and non-performance by the other. The legal issue is therefore relatively simple: Who performed and who didn't. The facts are more elusive—plaintiff at times says one thing, defendants another. We narrate them briefly.

On the morning of the twenty-seventh, "Royal Countess, elevation 940" was far from being a house, let alone a home. Racing the clock, plaintiff initiated a crash program. When defendants arrived on the scene at 4:00, at plaintiff's behest for final inspection, the crash program was still crashing workmen were all over the place, slapping on siding, laying the floors, bulldozing the yard, hooking up the utilities, and so on. Defendants' tour was not a success, to put it mildly. Instead of a home, they found, to their dismay, a hive buzzing with activity. They did not tarry, in spite of the foreman's assurances that all would be right by 5:30. Nor did they come back. They should have. Believe it or not, the foreman was right. The job *was* substantially completed by 5:30, with only a service walk, some grading and blacktopping left undone.

The trial court found that the house had been substantially completed and concluded that there had been, therefore, substantial compliance with the contract and with this we agree. But because the house was not completely completed, it found that there had not been *complete* compliance. With this, too, we agree, but such finding is beside the point. Substantial—not complete—compliance in a construction contract is all that is required. By 5:30, there had been just that, in other words, substantial performance of the contract. Plaintiff's contretemps in having inspection set for 4:00 o'clock was hardly the way to make friends and influence people, but such happenstance is of no moment in determining whether or not there had been substantial compliance, unless such can be said to indicate bad faith. We do not think that it does. What it indicates is bad timing, not bad faith.

That substantial performance or compliance is the key needs no extensive citation. In Bloomington Hotel Company v. Garthwait, 227 Ill. 613, 81 N.E. 714, it was said:

> Literal compliance with the provisions of a contract is not essential to a recovery. It will be sufficient if there has been an honest and faithful performance of the contract in its material and substantial parts, and no willful departure from or omission of the essential points of the contract.

In 12 Ill.Law & Practice Contracts, § 402, p. 547, it is said:

> In building contracts a literal compliance with the provisions of the particular contract, and the plans, specifications and drawings, is not necessary to a recovery by the contractor. It is sufficient that there is a substantial performance in good faith or that there is an honest and faithful performance of the contract in its material and substantial parts, with no willful departure from, or omission of, the essential points of the contract.

No substantial sum was required to complete the items left undone. Nor were they of so essential a character that defendants could not have been ensconced in their new home that night if they had so desired. We have thus answered our question: A house is ready to be lived in, to become a home, when it has been substantially completed.

* * *

* * * [T]he court should have found for plaintiff and against defendants. * * * Accordingly, the judgment below is reversed and remanded with directions to enter judgment for plaintiff * * * and against defendants * * * and thereafter to determine plaintiff's damages.

Reversed and remanded with directions.

Review Questions

1. Is a contract a "writing"? Are most contracts evidenced by writings? In what six situations is written evidence important? What law requires this? Without such evidence are such agreements void? Exactly what written evidence is required? Is a sale of goods treated differently under this law than the other five situations? When can't a written agreement be changed by certain other evidence? What law so provides and what are its specifics?

What is the most important written law dealing with contracts? Does it apply to all contracts? Explain your answers.

2. Are minors' agreements void? Is there any special rule regarding a minor's real estate contract? Otherwise, is there a difference in timing for a minor's ratification versus his or her disaffirmance? What must a minor do upon disaffirming? Is a minor liable for anything ever? When is a covenant not to compete illegal? May an agreement be only partly illegal? What does it mean to be in pari delicto? Is an innocent party ever protected in an illegal agreement? Explain your answers.

3. Is a promise that stands alone usually enforceable? What is usually required under the bargain theory of consideration to make a promise binding? Why are output or requirements contracts not illusory? Will carrying out a pre-existing duty serve as consideration for a new promise? How about a promise not to sue? How about part payment of a pre-existing debt? How does promissory estoppel differ from the bargain theory of consideration? When does public policy require enforcement of promises? When does the UCC dispense with the bargain theory of consideration? Explain your answers.

4. Are contract rights personal or property rights? Why is the contract concept of law important to commercial activity? Are all promises binding? How does an offer differ from an invitation to make an offer? What four terms must generally be present to satisfy the requirement of definiteness in offers? How has the Uniform Commercial Code liberalized the requirements for definiteness in offers? Apart from definiteness, what other things are looked to by courts to decide if an offer is present? Do cross-offers result in mutual assent? In what two ways are offers usually accepted? Explain your answers.

5. How does duress differ from undue influence? How does mutual mistake differ from unilateral mistake? How does fraud in the inducement differ from fraud in the execution? When does the doctrine of unconscionability apply? Explain your answers.

6. What is the difference between a condition precedent and a condition subsequent? What is the usual method of discharging contract responsibility? What other ways discharge individuals from contract responsibility? What is the difference between objective and subjective impossibility? Will a minor breach of contract allow the other party to not perform at all? Does the term "status quo ante" apply to the remedy of specific performance? What is the purpose behind the contract remedy providing for compensatory damages? What rules come into play in a determination of compensatory damages? Is a person ever allowed to sue for breach of contract before the other person's performance is due? May the parties set potential damages by agreement at the time of entering into the contract? Explain your answers.

7. Are offers themselves ever binding? How are offers revoked? What are six ways that an offeree might respond to an offer, and what results from such responses? What does it mean that an offer terminates by operation of law? Are communications between the offeror and offeree effective when received or when sent? How does agreement result in an auction contract? Explain your answers.

8. Define the following terms: adhesion contract, auction without reserve, battle of the forms, consequential damages, contracts, deposited acceptance rule, firm offer, liquidated damages, necessary, novation, objective theory of contracts, obstruction of justice, quasi contract, restoration in specie, restitution, unilateral contract.

Problems

1. a. On February 1, Sharon Douglas offers to sell her stereo speakers to Gary Farrell for $450. What is the legal result of each of the following responses by Gary?

1. "I'm sure we can work something out over the next few days."
2. "I will give you $350."
3. "Would you accept payment in three monthly installments?"
4. On February 5, Gary writes Sharon, "I am not interested in your offer." On the morning of February 6, Gary changes his mind and telegrams Sharon, "I accept your offer." Sharon receives the letter at 2:00 P.M. on February 6. She receives the telegram at 3:00 P.M. on February 6.
5. On February 5, Gary sends a telegram to Sharon, stating: "I accept your offer." Before she receives the telegram, Sharon telephones Gary and states, "You can forget about the offer—I've decided not to sell my speakers after all."

b. Sam Ralston promises to pay Jerry Bailey $1,500 if Jerry builds Sam a drift boat for fishing on the Deschutes River. Jerry begins work on the boat, but after he is half finished, Sam calls and states, "I'm withdrawing my offer—you can forget about the boat." What kind of contract, if any, is at issue here? What are the rights and liabilities of the parties?

c. Read and answer the following:

1. Judy Banner promises to meet Cliff Winters for lunch at the "Byzantine Bistro." Judy does not show up as promised, and Cliff sues Judy for breach of contract. Result?
2. On May 1, Cliff Winters offers to sell his fine Arabian mare to Liz Gifford. Liz agrees to buy the mare and to take possession of the animal on June 5. The parties agree to decide upon price at a later time prior to delivery. Assuming the parties do not agree upon price prior to delivery, does the contract fail for lack of definiteness? Explain.
3. On May 1, Cliff Winters writes to his friend Sharon Douglas and offers to sell Sharon his used motorcycle for $300. On May 2, Cliff is fatally injured in an automobile accident. On May 3, Sharon posts a letter to Cliff, stating, "I accept your offer. Here is my

check for $300." What are Sharon's rights, if any, with regard to the used motorcycle? Explain. Would your answer differ if Sharon had posted her acceptance prior to Cliff's death in the automobile accident? Explain.

2. a. Ken Lovett offers to sell Peggy Rooney "forty acres of the best farmland in Westchester County." Believing that property taxes are going to be sharply reduced by the state legislature, Peggy accepts Ken's offer and purchases the land. When the state legislature fails to cut property taxes as expected, Peggy desires to get out of the contract. She also complains that the forty acres are not the best farmland in the county (they are not) and that the farmhouse roof leaks badly in several places (Ken had no knowledge of the leakage at the time he made the offer, but he did discover it just prior to sale). Can Peggy get out of the contract on the basis that the state legislature failed to reduce property taxes as expected? On the basis that the forty acres are not the best farmland in the county? On the basis that the farmhouse roof leaks? Explain fully.

b. Eddie Johnson is the last surviving son of elderly widower Victor Johnson. Eddie visits Victor often, and Victor looks to Eddie for advice and assistance in dealing with his considerable properties. After much coaxing, Eddie persuades Victor to sell him his foreign sportscar for $1,000; the car is worth $15,000. Producing a written document, Eddie tells Victor that he must sign over title to the car. Victor signs, not realizing that the writing is actually a deed of conveyance of his beachfront property to one Lucy Scruggs. Lucy, who believes that the sale is on the up-and-up, pays $60,000 for the land, giving it to Eddie as Victor's representative. Shortly thereafter Eddie drugs Victor, and taking his hand, signs his name on a deed conveying his valuable residence to Eddie. Discuss the validity of the sale of the sportscar to Eddie, the sale of the beachfront property to Lucy, and the conveyance of the residence to Eddie.

c. Barbara Biggs and Wendy Hiller, salespeople representing "Lifelong Pans, Inc.," knock on Gordon Snyder's door and persuade Gordon to let them in to demonstrate the superior quality of their product. Barbara and Wendy talk fast, and Gordon, who has had little formal education, doesn't understand all the sales terms they rush through. However, he is impressed with the sheen and durable appearance of the pans and agrees to purchase them despite his limited income. The women then produce a lengthy contract form, in very small print, for Gordon to sign; Gordon does not bother reading the form before signing. When Gordon later discovers that he has agreed to pay $600 for the pans (similar pans can be purchased locally for $150), he desires to get out of the contract. Counsel him.

d. John Hart owns two trucks—a red pickup worth $500 and a blue pickup worth $800. Discuss the legal effect of each of the following transactions:

1. John offers to sell his pickup to Rick Skinner for $500. Rick accepts John's offer. At the time of making the offer, John believes

he is selling the red pickup; at the time of accepting the offer, Rick believes he is buying the blue pickup.

2. John offers to sell his pickup to Rick for $500. Rick accepts John's offer, knowing that John intends to sell his red pickup. However, Rick later insists that it was the blue pickup he purchased.
3. John instructs the "Acme Telegram Service" to send the following message to Rick Skinner: "I offer to sell you my red pickup for $500." The Telegram Company makes an error in transmitting the message, and the offer reads: "I offer to sell you my blue pickup for $500." Rick does not know that John has two pickups. He accepts the offer.
4. Assume the same facts as in (3) above except that, this time, the Telegram Company sends the following erroneous transmission: "I offer to sell you my red pickup for $5.00." Again, Rick accepts the offer.

3. a. Sidney Streeter is doing well in his retail grocery business. He tells his favorite niece Sally Streeter that he is going to give her $10,000 at the end of the year so that she can start her own business. Over the course of the year, Sally rents an office building and purchases some office machinery and supplies on credit; she is counting on the $10,000 to pay off the debts (her own salary will not cover the purchases). However, Sidney dies before the end of the year, and his personal representative refuses to pay Sally the money. Is Sally entitled to the $10,000? Explain.

Suppose that Sidney had told Sally, "I promise to give you $10,000 at the end of the year if you attend business college this term." Assuming Sally attended business college, would she be entitled to the $10,000? Explain.

b. Does consideration (or an acceptable substitute for consideration) exist in the following situations? Explain your answers.

1. In return for Richard Klein's promise to pay her seventy-five dollars, Bonnie Miller promises "to shampoo Richard's carpets unless my rug shampooer breaks down."
2. The same as (1) above except that Bonnie promises "to shampoo Richard's carpets unless I decide I'm too busy."
3. Grateful that Keith Robel helped her fix a flat tire last week, Jody Welty telephones Keith and promises to pay him ten dollars when she receives her next paycheck.
4. Keith Robel owes a contract debt of $250 to Mike Mahoney. However, the statute of limitations has run on the contract, and Mike is barred from suing on the debt. Keith nevertheless pays Mike fifty dollars of the money and orally promises to pay the balance.
5. Phil Kennedy, who is in the painting business, paints Karen Spencer's fence by mistake, believing it to be that of her neighbor, Ruth Warrick. Karen is not at home at the time.
6. The same as (5) above except that Karen is at home; she sees Phil painting the fence but does not attempt to stop him.

c. Carol Thomas contracts to purchase a used television set from Todd Ritter for eighty-five dollars. By the terms of the contract, Carol must make payment thirty days after delivery of the set. After the set is delivered, Carol notifies Tom that she is short on cash and has only fifty dollars to pay him.

1. At Carol's insistence and in order to get at least a part of the money owing, Todd orally promises "to accept payment of fifty dollars thirty days after delivery of the set as settlement in full" of the debt. Carol pays Todd the fifty dollars, then Todd sues Carol for the thirty-five-dollar balance. Is there consideration for Todd's promise to accept the fifty dollars as payment in full? Explain, using a diagram to illustrate.
2. Todd promises "to accept payment of fifty dollars ten days after delivery of the set as settlement in full" of the debt, and Carol makes such payment. Is there consideration for Todd's promise to forget the balance of the debt? Explain, again using a diagram to illustrate.
3. Todd promises in writing "to accept payment of fifty dollars thirty days after delivery of the set as payment in full"; Todd signs the writing and delivers it to Carol, whereupon Carol pays Todd fifty dollars. Todd then sues Carol for the thirty-five-dollar balance. Result?

4. a. Seventeen-year-old Steve Cassidy has a used Chevy but also wants a motorcycle. He falsely tells Archie Palmer that he is eighteen (the age of majority in Steve's state) so that Archie will sell him a BMW motorcycle. A week later, Steve accidentally runs the cycle into a tree; he notifies Archie that he disaffirms the contract. Steve then contracts to paint Annie Hoffman's Volkswagen. Steve paints the car carelessly and ruins Annie's paint job. Steve notifies Annie that he disaffirms the contract. Steve then purchases some levis from "Farmer's Department Store" as well as an expensive watch and a solid gold medallion to wear around his neck. After a week, the jeans are dirty and Steve has lost the watch and medallion. Steve notifies Farmer's that he disaffirms the purchases. What are Steve's rights and duties vis-à-vis Archie, Annie, and Farmer's Department Store? Assume that Steve's parents contribute little to his support.

Finally, Steve contracts to sell his beach lot (a gift from his grandfather) to Muriel Morris. A month after Muriel takes possession of the land, Steve notifies her that he disaffirms the sale; Muriel ignores the notice. Three months later, Steve turns eighteen. On his nineteenth birthday, he again notifies Muriel that he disaffirms the sale. Who is entitled to the property? Explain.

b. Judge Tanner promises to dismiss Carl Cornwell's "Driving Under the Influence of Liquor" citation if Carl (who is a carpenter) will build her a solid oak desk. Carl builds the desk and delivers it to the judge's chambers. The judge accepts the desk, but then refuses to dismiss the citation. Can Carl legally compel dismissal of the citation? Assuming he cannot, can he obtain return of the desk? Explain your answers.

5. a. Fred Brown negotiates all summer with Nancy Lewis to buy a 40 percent interest in her hardware business. Several drafts of the agreement were written until both parties were satisfied, and both signed. A major problem in the negotiations was Nancy's worry that she and Fred might not get along and work well together. A year after the purchase Nancy decides she does not wish to continue in business with Fred and brings suit to rescind the agreement. She remembers discussions with Fred before the signing of the agreement in which Fred told her that he would let her return his money, and he would get out of the business if she ever didn't want to work with him. Fred says that there were discussions about this point but ultimately were resolved before their written agreement was signed. Will Nancy be able to make her point in court? What are the issues? Explain.

   b. Discuss the enforceability of each of the following contracts:
      1. John Dolan orally contracts to purchase a farm from Jean Farlow. John makes a downpayment on the purchase price and takes possession of the property.
      2. On October 1, 1984, Jan Maguire orally contracts to build Tom Tucker a house by October 1, 1987.
      3. David Olson owns 10 percent of the stock of "Olson Hardware, Inc." The corporation owes a past due debt of $5,000 to supplier Jo Ann Justice. David orally promises Jo Ann that he will pay the $5,000 debt and be responsible for future deliveries if Jo Ann will continue supplying the corporation.
      4. Edwin Hale orally contracts to purchase an $800 water heater from "Water Heaters Unlimited." Edwin makes a downpayment of $150.

6. Jake Blake contracts to reroof Harold Myer's house. What are Jake's and Harold's rights and duties in each of the following situations?

   a. After finishing 95 percent of the work, Jake gets bored and stops working. He demands payment for the work he has done.
   b. Jake finishes the work six days after the completion date called for in the contract. The contract provides that Jake must pay $1,000 per day for every day that he is late in finishing the work.
   c. Before the contract time for his performance arrives, Jake tells Harold, "I am not going to do the reroofing."
   d. The same as (c) above except that Jake later changes his mind and tells Harold, "I will do the reroofing after all."
   e. Jake breaches the contract by failing to reroof the house. Harold does not hire anyone else to do the work and rain leaks through the roof causing damage to Harold's upstairs bedrooms. Harold sues Jake for the damage.
   f. Harold promises to give Jake his used stationwagon if Jake will forego the promised $1,500 payment. Jake agrees, and Harold gives him the stationwagon upon completion of the reroofing.

g. By the terms of the contract, Jake is obligated "to reroof the house unless and until I am called back to work in Alaska." Shortly after Jake begins working, his union notifies him that he has been called back to work in Alaska.

7. a. Elrod is attempting to introduce oral evidence in court to explain or modify a written contract he made with Weaver. Weaver has pleaded the parol evidence rule. In which of the following circumstances will Elrod *not* be able to introduce the oral evidence?
1. The modification asserted was made several days after the written contract had been executed.
2. The contract indicates that it was intended as the "entire contract" between the parties, and the point is covered in detail.
3. There was a mutual mistake of fact by the parties regarding the subject matter of the contract.
4. The contract contains an obvious ambiguity on the point at issue.

b. Kent Construction Company contracted to construct four garages for Magnum, Inc., according to specifications provided by Magnum. Kent deliberately substituted 2 × 4s for the more expensive 2 × 6s called for in the contract in all places where the 2 × 4s would not be readily detected. Magnum's inspection revealed the variance, and Magnum is now withholding the final payment on the contract. The contract was for $100,000, and the final payment would be $25,000. Damages were estimated to be $15,000. In a lawsuit for the balance due, Kent will
1. Prevail on the contract, less damages of $15,000 because it has substantially performed.
2. Prevail because the damages in question were not substantial in relation to the contract amount.
3. Lose because the law unqualifiedly requires literal performance of such contracts.
4. Lose all rights under the contract because it has intentionally breached it.

c. Myers entered into a contract to purchase a valuable rare coin from Eisen. Myers tendered payment which was refused by Eisen. Upon Eisen's breach, Myers brought suit to obtain the coin. The court will grant Myers
1. Compensatory damages.
2. Specific performance.
3. Reformation.
4. Restitution.

Source: CPA Exam, May 1983, # 1(16), (19), (20).

8. a. In determining whether a bilateral contract has been created, the courts look primarily at
1. The fairness to the parties.
2. The objective intent of the parties.
3. The subjective intent of the parties.
4. The subjective intent of the offeror.

b. Dougal is seeking to avoid performing a promise to pay Clark $500. Dougal is relying upon lack of consideration on Clark's part sufficient to support his promise. Dougal will prevail if he can establish that
   1. The contract is executory.
   2. Clark's asserted consideration is worth only $100.
   3. Prior to Dougal's promise, Clark had already performed the requested act.
   4. Clark's only claim of consideration was the relinquishment of a legal right.

c. Justin made an offer to pay Benson $1,000 if Benson would perform a certain act. Acceptance of Justin's offer occurs when Benson
   1. Promises to complete the act.
   2. Prepares to perform the act.
   3. Promises to perform and begins preliminary performance.
   4. Completes the act.

Source: CPA Exam, May 1983, # 1(7), (8), (9).

9. a. The Statute of Frauds
   1. Codified common law rules of fraud.
   2. Requires that formal contracts be in writing and signed by the parties to the contract.
   3. Does *not* apply if the parties waive its application in the contract.
   4. Sometimes results in a contract being enforceable by only one party.

b. Certain oral contracts fall outside the Statute of Frauds. An example would be a contract between
   1. A creditor and a friend of the debtor, providing for the friend's guaranty of the debt in exchange for the creditor's binding extension of time for payment of the debt.
   2. A landlord and a tenant for the lease of land for ten years.
   3. A school board and a teacher entered into on January 1, for nine months of service to begin on Septembr 1.
   4. A retail seller of television sets and a buyer for the sale of a TV set for $399 C.O.D.

c. Silvers entered into a contract which contains a substantial arithmetical error. Silvers asserts mistake as a defense to his performance. Silvers will prevail
   1. Only if the mistake was a mutual mistake.
   2. Only if the error was *not* due to his negligence.
   3. If the error was unilateral and the other party knew of it.
   4. If the contract was written by the other party.

Source: CPA Exam, May 1983, # 1(12), (13), (14).

10. a. Luxor wrote Harmon offering to sell Harmon Luxor's real estate business for $200,000. Harmon sent a telegram accepting the offer at $190,000. Later, learning that several other parties were interested in purchasing the business, Harmon telephoned Luxor and made an unqualified acceptance on Luxor's terms. The telegram arrived an hour after the phone call. Under the circumstances
   1. Harmon's telegram effectively terminated the offer.

2. Harmon's oral acceptance is voidable because real estate is involved.
3. The offer was revoked as a result of Harmon's learning that others were interested in purchasing the business.
4. Harmon has made a valid contract at $200,000.

b. Fairbanks, an author, was approached by Nickle Corporation to ghostwrite the history of Nickle for $15,000. Larson, the president of Nickle, told Fairbanks the job was his if he would agree cleverly to defame its leading competitor, Mogul Corporation, using sly innuendo and clever distortion of the facts. Fairbanks wrote the history. It turned out that the Mogul passages were neither sly nor clever, and Mogul obtained a judgment against Nickle. Fairbanks is seeking to collect the final $5,000 installment on the contract. Nickle refuses to pay and seeks to recover the $10,000 it has already paid. In the event of a lawsuit
1. Fairbanks will recover $5,000.
2. The court will deny relief to either party.
3. Nickle will recover $10,000.
4. Fairbanks will recover in quantum meruit for the value of his services.

c. Glass Co. telephoned Hourly Company and ordered 2,000 watches at two dollars each. Glass agreed to pay 10 percent immediately and the balance within ten days after receipt of the entire shipment. Glass forwarded a check for $400, and Hourly shipped 1,000 watches the next day, intending to ship the balance by the end of the week. Glass decided that the contract was a bad bargain and repudiated it, asserting the Statute of Frauds. Hourly sued Glass. Which of the following will allow Hourly to enforce the contract in its entirety despite the Statute of Frauds?
1. Glass admitted in court that it made the contract in question.
2. Hourly shipped 1,000 watches.
3. Glass paid 10 percent down.
4. The contract is *not* within the requirements of the Statute.

Source: CPA Exam, May 1983, # 1(9), (10), (11).

10

Of the commercial law subject matters, perhaps most important to understand for the business person, from a risk perspective, are those dealing with insurance, negotiable paper, and agency.
John D. Watson

Insurance, Negotiable Instruments, and Agency

WHAT ARE THIRD PARTY BENEFICIARY CONTRACTS?

When you buy life insurance on your own life you enter into a third party beneficiary contract. It is but one example; very often people enter into contracts for the purpose of directly benefiting third persons who are not parties to the contracts. Such agreements are called *third party beneficiary contracts*, and the general rule is that a third party beneficiary may personally enforce the agreement even though he or she is not a party to it and has furnished no consideration for the promises made. This means that the third party beneficiary can sue in his or her own name to recover damages for breach of contract.

However, the third party beneficiary must be a *direct* beneficiary as opposed to an *incidental* one who benefits but remotely or indirectly from the contract and acquires no rights of enforcement whatsoever. For example, suppose that Mark Developer contracts with Barbara Builder to erect an expensive office building on Mark's property. The fact that Tom Neighbor's land will substantially increase in value by reason of performance of the contract makes Tom Neighbor an incidental beneficiary only. The increase in value is but a remote or indirect benefit of the construction contract, and if either Developer or Builder breaches the agreement, Tom Neighbor has no legal rights to complain.

There are two kinds of third party beneficiary contracts—*donee beneficiary* contracts and *creditor beneficiary* contracts. Where the promisee's primary purpose or intent in entering into the agreement is to confer a gift on the third party, the third party is a donee beneficiary, and the contract is a donee beneficiary contract. Where, on the other hand, the promisee's primary purpose or intent in entering into the agreement is to discharge an obligation owed to the third party, the third party is a creditor beneficiary, and the contract is a creditor beneficiary contract.

In a third party beneficiary contract, one party (the promisor) makes a promise to a second party (the promisee) for the benefit of a third party (the third party beneficiary). Once a donee or creditor beneficiary's rights vest under a contract (this occurs when the third party acquires knowledge of the contract made for him or her), the beneficiary can personally sue a defaulting promisor for money damages, specific performance, or other appropriate relief. Of course, the promisor may assert against the beneficiary any defense that he or she (the promisor) could assert against the promisee.

A donee beneficiary has no rights against the promisee if the promisor fails to perform as promised (it would not make sense to hold the promisee legally responsible because his or her attempted gift failed). A creditor beneficiary, on the other hand, can generally proceed against either the promisee on the original debt or the promisor on the third party beneficiary contract or against both parties (although the third party beneficiary can recover only once).

WHEN IS A LIFE INSURANCE CONTRACT A THIRD PARTY BENEFICIARY CONTRACT?

Life insurance policies are usually third party beneficiary contracts of the donee variety. Typically, the insured enters into a contract with the insurance company wherein the insured agrees to pay premiums to the company in exchange for the company's promise to pay money to a third party beneficiary upon the death of the insured. In all states, the donee beneficiary can bring legal action against the insurance company to enforce the policy, and any proceeds paid following the death of the insured belong to the beneficiary, not to the insured's estate.

While most life insurance policies are third party beneficiary contracts, this is not the case where a person, having an "insurable interest" in the life of another party, insures that person's life to protect his or her legally recognized interest.

WHAT IS THE NATURE OF INSURANCE?

Insurance is a contract but with a number of special rules peculiar to the law of insurance. For insurance, in its broadest sense, is an arrangement for transferring and distributing risk. "Risk" is the key to understanding insurance; it is the factor creating the need for insurance. A businesswoman, for example, may operate her business with a maximum of planning, care, and caution, yet be unable to prevent financial losses resulting from contingencies beyond her control. Similarly, a homeowner may construct his home with flame-retardant materials, eliminate all flammable wastes from his garage, instruct his children not to play with matches, yet still face fire and major destruction of his home from a defective light switch in the family room. Or a motorist may take a driver's education course, buckle up her seat belt at all times, drive carefully and cautiously, yet still be hit head on by a drunk driver. Or a hardworking executive may jog every day, watch his diet, have a yearly checkup, yet still drop dead from an unexpected heart attack. The risks of living go on and on.

The concept of insurance helps avert catastrophe by allowing a group of people to pool their risks and absorb individual losses on a group basis. Insurance is a contractual arrangement for transferring and distributing the risks of living. Usually, a company called an *insurer* contracts to pay for the loss of a person called an *insured* (or *beneficiary*) upon the happening of a specified, harmful contingency. Each insured pays *premiums* (specified monetary amounts) into a general fund; when any one insured experiences a loss, the fund covers the loss, and the individual is spared what might otherwise be an overwhelming financial setback. The insurer's promise to pay in the event of loss and the insured's promise to pay premiums and give proper notice of the loss are set forth in a written contract called a policy.

WHAT IS THE PRINCIPLE OF INDEMNITY?

Compensation for loss sustained without further benefit (i.e., nothing beyond the loss) is the principle of indemnity.

The reasoning behind the principle is that to permit an individual to realize gain from insurance proceeds would encourage two evils—gambling or wagering and destruction of insured lives and property. Public policy has long been opposed to gambling on the grounds that it induces idleness, vice, poverty, and crime. And intentional destruction of lives and property in order to collect insurance proceeds is certainly not in the public interest. By limiting recovery to actual loss only, the principle of indemnity eliminates the possibility of gain and successfully protects against gambling and destruction.

The principle of indemnity has given rise to two important legal doctrines: the insurable interest doctrine and the doctrine of subrogation.

Insurable Interest

It is a general rule of insurance law that the insured must have an *insurable interest* in the subject matter of the insurance contract. If he or she does not, the insured cannot enforce the insurance agreement.

Insurable interest in property A person possesses an insurable interest in property whenever damage or destruction of the property would result in measurable economic loss (in money value) to the person. The person's interest in the property can be less than total ownership. In fact it can be based on any one of the property interests described in Chapter 8, including real property fees, life estates, remainder interests, easements, profits, covenants, licenses, water rights, support rights, mineral rights, personal property chattels, or intangible personal property interests. The interest may be held in severalty or concurrently with others. Thus, all concurrent owners of property have insurable interests in the property whether the owners are partners holding partnership property or spouses holding community property or property held as joint tenants with the right of survivorship. A spouse also has an insurable interest in the property of the other spouse. And a stockholder of a corporation (see Chapter 6) has an insurable interest in the property owned by the corporation. Similarly, a lessee of real estate has an insurable interest in the rental property. And a security interest holder has an insurable interest in the property serving as collateral or security for a loan (see Chapter 12)—an unsecured creditor has no such interest. Also, and very importantly, a buyer of goods has an insurable interest in goods that have been "identified to the contract of sale" (i.e., selected or set aside by the seller—see Chapter 11). The buyer's insurable interest is part and parcel of the "special property" interest created in the buyer upon identification of the goods by the seller under UCC section 2–501. Even a person with a mere possessory interest in property has an insurable interest (e.g., a watch repairer has an insurable interest in any watch left in his or her possession for repair). And, finally, a building contractor has an insurable interest in any building under construction, as the contractor is legally liable to the owner for completion of the building.

The insurable interest in the property need exist only at the time the loss occurs and does not have to be present at the time the insurance contract was entered into.

Insurable interest in life Every person with lawful capacity has an insurable interest in his or her own life and may insure that life, naming anyone he or she chooses as beneficiary of the insurance policy. It is not necessary for the beneficiary to have an insurable interest in the insured's life since it is the insured who is taking out the policy.

For a person to obtain valid insurance, not on his or her own life, but on the life of another, the person taking out the policy must have an insurable interest in the life to be insured.

Generally, a person has an insurable interest in the life of his or her spouse and minor children; a minor has an insurable interest in the lives of his or her parents. Decisions go both ways on whether brothers and sisters have insurable interests in one another's lives. And courts frequently hold that adult children do not have insurable interests in the lives of their parents and vice versa. With regard to the debtor-creditor relationship, a creditor generally has an insurable interest in the debtor's life since death of the debtor may mean that the creditor will not be paid. However, if the amount of the insurance greatly exceeds the debt, the excess will be declared void for lack of an insurable interest. Because the death of a partner usually results in dissolution of the partnership firm (see Chapter 6), the partnership has an insurable interest in the lives of its partners. For the same reason, each partner has an insurable interest in the life of every other partner. And a business enterprise has an insurable interest in the life of "key" employees (employees crucial to the operation of the business). The interest is present because death of the employees could result in substantial financial loss to the business.

Unless it is clear that the insurer of another's life has an insurable interest in that life (i.e., will suffer a measurable economic loss by reason of the death), the courts will rule the insurance agreement void. The courts are particularly strict in the area of life insurance because the potential abuse of the insurance agreement is so great—wagering on human life and committing murder to collect the insurance proceeds.

Directly opposite to the insurable interest in property which must exist only at the time of loss, *the insurable interest in life must exist only at the time the policy is purchased.* The insurable interest need not be in existence at the time of the insured's death. For example, suppose that a wife purchases insurance on the life of her husband, naming herself as beneficiary. The fact that the wife later divorces her husband and has no insurable interest in his life at the time of his death does not render the insurance agreement void.

Subrogation

The second legal doctrine flowing from the principle of indemnity is the doctrine of subrogation. Like the insurable interest doctrine, the doctrine of subrogation is designed to prevent an insured from realizing a net gain from insurance proceeds (i.e., a benefit beyond compensation for loss sustained). The doctrine states, at least insofar as property insurance is concerned, that an insurance company that pays for an insured's loss is *subrogated* to the legal rights of the insured against the party who caused the loss. Thus, if an insured suffers a loss, he or she may look to his or her insurance company for payment. The insurance company, in turn, will receive whatever legal rights the insured may have (at least to the extent of the insurance coverage) to recover money damages in or out of court from the party who caused the loss. By transferring these rights to the insurance company, the doctrine of subrogation prevents the insured from recovering twice for the same loss (once from the insurance company and again from the party who caused the loss). The insured is thus denied a net gain from the loss, and the principle of indemnity is satisfied.

WHAT IS THE LAW REGARDING THE WRITING OF THE INSURANCE POLICY, ITS INTERPRETATION, AND EFFECT?

Most states, by statute, require insurance policies to be in writing; the statutes, to some extent, specify the required contents of the policies and even the size and style of type to be used in printing them. Minors generally cannot avoid contracts for life, disability, or health insurance. For purposes of mutual assent, it is the insured who makes the offer and the insurer who makes the acceptance.

Often, a substantial period of time elapses between a person's application for insurance and the insurance company's issuance of the policy. Obviously, if the insured has no insurance coverage during this time period, he or she may suffer a financially disastrous loss or undergo a change of circumstances that leaves him or her virtually uninsurable against future losses. For this reason, insurance agents frequently agree to provide temporary insurance coverage during the time interval between application for and issuance of the policy. Insofar as life insurance is concerned, an agent often uses a *conditional binding receipt* to make the insurance effective as of the date of application. A conditional binding receipt is a written memorandum of the essential terms of the life insurance contract. The memo provides that the insurance coverage is effective as of the date of application so long as certain conditions are met (usually, that the first premium is paid at that time and that the insured is insurable).

With regard to insurance other than life, applicant and agent frequently agree orally (often over the telephone) that the applicant will be insured temporarily during the period between application for and issuance of the policy. Such an agreement is called a *binder* and is usually followed by the agent's writing, signing, and sending to the insured a memorandum stating the essential terms of the policy. For example, it is not unusual for a new car purchaser to telephone an auto insurance agent from the car dealer's office and request comprehensive automobile insurance coverage. If the agent binds coverage over the phone, the purchaser will enjoy immediate protection and may drive home in his or her new car without undue worry or concern.

Like all other contracts, insurance contracts may be void or voidable on the basis of fraud, mistake, undue influence, unconscionability, etc. They may be subject to conditions precedent or subsequent, the occurrence or nonoccurrence of which will prevent the operation of the contract or discharge one or both parties from any further obligation of performance. The special terminology used in applying these general rules to insurance contracts is found primarily in the areas of *misrepresentation* and *warranty*.

Misrepresentation

If a prospective insured intentionally or innocently misrepresents a material fact that induces an insurer to enter into an insurance contract, the insurer has a right to rescind the agreement on the grounds of fraud (for intentional misrepresentation) or mistake (for innocent misrepresentation). For example, a prospective insured might misrepresent a material fact in answering questions on the insurance application form (such forms are often attached to the issued policy). The insurer, in this case, will have a right to rescind the contract upon discovering the misrepresentation. Rescission serves to place the parties in the positions they would have been in had there been no contract. Restitution is part and parcel of rescission, and the insurer must return all premiums paid by the insured in order to rescind (of course, the insurer is entitled to offset any expenses incurred by the company in processing and issuing the policy). And if the misrepresentation is intentional, the insurer may also bring suit against the insured for the tort of deceit.

Of course, to justify rescission, the misrepresentation must be as to a material fact (as opposed to an immaterial fact or an opinion). Whether or not a fact is material generally depends upon whether the insurer would have issued the policy had the truth been known.

Along the same line, an insurer may rescind an insurance agreement upon learning that the insured, in applying for the policy, intentionally failed to disclose a material fact unknown to the insurer that would have affected the insurer's willingness to accept the risk of loss. The insured's intentional failure to disclose a material fact is termed *concealment.*

Finally, insofar as life insurance is concerned, statutes generally require inclusion of what is called an *incontestable clause.* Typically, such a clause provides that after two years' time the insurer cannot contest or challenge the validity of the life insurance policy. Thus, after two years have elapsed, the issues of misrepresentation and concealment are generally meaningless. However, it should be pointed out that most life insurance policies expressly provide that where the insured misstates his or her age in applying for the policy, the amount payable upon the insured's death will be the amount of proceeds *the premiums paid would have purchased had the insured given his or her correct age.* Generally speaking, the courts will enforce such a provision though the policy contains an incontestable clause and more than two years have elapsed.

Warranty

A *warranty* is a representation made by either insurer or insured that is contained within the insurance policy itself. Generally, a warranty operates as a condition to create a duty of performance or discharge a duty of performance. For example, an automobile insurer may limit his or her liability for loss by means of the following language: "This policy applies only to accidents, occurrences, and loss during the policy period while the automobile is within the United States of America, its territories or possessions, or Canada, or is being transported between parts thereof." It is thus a condition precedent to recovery under the policy that the loss occur within the United States, its territories or possessions, or Canada, etc. (In face of such language, it is not surprising that most auto owners buy special insurance before venturing into Mexico.)

Similarly, a property insurer may limit his or her liability for loss by covering only the "contents" of a particular building or only the property situated at a particular location. Again, loss or damage to the particular described property is a condition precedent to recovery under the policy.

Warranties may generally be classified as either *affirmative warranties* or *promissory warranties.* An affirmative warranty is one stating a condition that must exist only at the time the contract is entered into. For example, the insured under a life insurance policy may be required to warrant as to his or her good health or lack of pre-existing disease or defect at the time of issuance of the policy. Good health is material to the risk insured against and is frequently a condition of life insurance coverage.

A promissory warranty, on the other hand, is one stating a condition that must be maintained throughout the period of the insurance policy. For example, the insured under a comprehensive property insurance policy may promise to take certain precautions against burglary or fire loss, such as hiring a nightwatchperson or installing and maintaining a sprinkler system. If the insured fails to keep his or her promise at any time throughout the period of the policy, the warranty is breached, and the condition subsequent operates to discharge the insurer from any further duty under the contract.

Interpretation of the Policy

Most people who purchase insurance have had little or no legal training. For this reason, the rules of interpretation provide that insurance policies are to be read and construed by the courts as they would be understood by the average person or businessperson—not by the person with legal training. Because the insurer writes the insurance contract, any ambiguities in the policy are interpreted against the insurer and in favor of the insured. This apparent "bias" of the courts in favor of the insured is not without good reason. Frequently, a person who wants insurance coverage (particularly life insurance) has little choice but to accept the policy as it is written. Confronted with an insurer whose attitude is "take it or leave it," the insured has next to no bargaining power. The contract, in this case, is one of adhesion, and the court may declare all or part of it unconscionable and unenforceable. For example, in the air travel insurance case of Lachs v. Fidelity & Casualty Co., 306 N.Y. 357, 118 N.E.2d 555 (1954), the court permitted recovery for a fatal crash occurring on a nonscheduled flight even though the vending machine and policy stated that recovery would be allowed only on scheduled flights. The provision limiting recovery was held unconscionable and unenforceable because it was couched in fine print in the policy and because the vending machine selling the insurance was placed near the airport counter where both scheduled and nonscheduled flights were processed.

WHAT ARE THE REQUIRED PROCEDURES IN THE EVENT OF INSURANCE LOSS?

All insurance policies contain provisions requiring the insured to give prompt notice of insurance-covered loss and to furnish proof of loss. Prompt notice is essential from the insurer's point of view because it affords the insurer reasonable opportunity to protect his or her rights as well as the interests of the insured (who may, on occasion, be held to liability beyond the limits of the policy). It is extremely important for the insured to comply fully and exactly with the notice and proof of loss terms. If the insured fails to comply and the failure prejudices the insurance company in determining the correct amount of the loss or in proceeding against the parties responsible for the loss, the insurance company may be excused from its duty of performance under the contract.

In addition to notice and proof of loss terms, liability insurance policies generally contain provisions requiring the insured to cooperate with and assist the insurer in investigating and defending insurance-covered tort claims against the insured. Generally, the insured must attend trials, assist in settlement efforts, help secure evidence, obtain attendance by witnesses, etc. The insured need not, however, cooperate at his or her own expense but may look to the insurer for the costs of cooperation and assistance. Again, any failure by the insured to comply fully and exactly with these terms may result in discharge of the insurer's duty of performance under the contract.

Liability insurance policies generally also contain provisions requiring the insurer to defend the insured against any insurance-covered claim brought against him or her. By this is meant that the insurer must defend the insured against any allegation that the insured has caused injury or damage to another as covered by the terms of the policy. Along this line, it is important to realize that the fact that a person has insurance or the amount of his or her insurance is neither relevant nor admissible in court in determining the existence and extent of liability. This rule of evidence is designed to prevent the jury from arbitrarily finding for the plaintiff because his or her insurance company can "easily" absorb the loss.

WHAT OTHER SPECIAL RULES ARE THERE REGARDING INSURANCE?

There are several special rules relating to insurance:

1. With regards to life insurance, as a practical matter the beneficiary of a life insurance policy should be a named individual rather than the estate of the insured. If the insured's estate is listed as the beneficiary, the insurance proceeds will be probated upon the death of the insured and will be reduced by any outstanding debts of the estate and charges of administration. On the other hand, if a named individual is listed as the beneficiary, the full insurance proceeds will by-pass probate and go directly to the beneficiary. To this end it is always a good idea for the insured to name both a primary and a contingent beneficiary to protect against the possibility of the primary beneficiary's predeceasing the insured.

2. Additionally, the general rule is that a beneficiary who kills the insured is not entitled to the insurance proceeds. Most courts award the proceeds as though the beneficiary predeceased the insured—thus, if there is a contingent beneficiary, he or she will be entitled to the money. A few courts hold that the proceeds belong to the estate of the murdered insured.

3. With regard to car insurance, some states issue drivers' licenses only upon proof of purchase of liability insurance. Other states have *financial responsibility laws* requiring drivers involved in accidents to furnish proof of their financial responsibility (usually by purchasing insurance or by posting a bond) as a condition to continued driving in the state. More and more states are moving toward requiring insurance for all drivers.

4. Another legal trend in the car insurance area is the adoption of *no-fault automobile insurance*. Under a no-fault plan, an insurance company pays, not for the loss of a third party bearing a lawful claim against the insured, but for the loss of its own policyholder without regard to fault of the parties. Because each party collects from his or her own insurance company, there is no need to waste time and money proving negligence in court. As a result, premiums are lower, and losses are handled more quickly. The first state to pass a no-fault plan was Massachusetts in 1970. Delaware followed in 1971 and since that time, approximately ten other states have adopted no-fault auto insurance. The no-fault plans generally provide coverage without regard to fault up to a certain monetary amount. If the damage suffered exceeds this amount, the injured party can still go to court and prove negligence or fault of the other party so as to collect the excess (liability insurance for such excess damage is also available).

5. With regard to fire insurance, generally, in order for a loss to be compensable, it must arise from an actual fire (not just heat but some flame or burning), and the fire must be *hostile* as opposed to *friendly.* A hostile fire is an accidental fire or an intentional one that has escaped, broken out, or become uncontrollable. A friendly fire is an intentional fire that remains under control. For example, if a person accidentally throws some valuable jewelry into a fireplace, the loss of the jewelry arises from a friendly fire and is not normally compensable. However, coverage for loss from a friendly fire may generally be obtained by payment of a higher premium.

6. As a part of fire insurance, many property owners purchase what is called a *homeowner's policy* which combines fire insurance with extended coverage, including coverage for theft loss, glass breakage, building collapse, accidental overflow of water or heating from plumbing or heating systems, and freezing perils. The homeowner's policy also includes liability insurance to protect the property owner against claims of bodily injury and property damage asserted by parties who come onto the insured's land.

7. Where a fire loss is found to be compensable, the insurer's liability is limited to the maximum amount stated in the policy or the total amount of damages sustained by the insured, whichever is less. Even if an insured has full coverage with two different insurers, the total amount of the loss is the maximum recoverable, and the insurers will share the loss.

8. Fire insurance coverage is based on the replacement value of the property, not on its original costs. Thus, a property owner must carefully determine how much insurance he or she needs to replace property or risk being underinsured. Premiums on fire insurance policies are generally paid annually to allow for inflation adjustment (so as to accurately reflect replacement costs). Frequently, fire insurance policies provide that the insurer may replace or restore the property to its former condition rather than pay the insured the cash value of the loss. The typical fire insurance policy on business property does not permit recovery for business interruption unless there is a special endorsement covering such loss.

9. In most states, an insurance company may include a *co-insurance clause* in a fire policy requiring the insured to maintain a certain amount of insurance on the property (usually a percentage of the property's value such as 80 percent). If the insured fails to insure his or her property for the required amount, the insurer will be liable only for its proportionate share of the amount of insurance required to be carried. With an 80 percent co-insurance clause, in the event that the insured fails to carry insurance amounting to 80 percent of the value of his or her property, and there is a fire, the insured must share the loss with the insurance company and can collect only that proportion of the loss which the amount of the insurance purchased bears to the amount of insurance called for under the co-insurance clause. For example, suppose that you own a business building with a fair market value of $150,000. Under the co-insurance clause, you are required to carry insurance covering 80 percent of this value—insurance of $120,000. If you do so, any fire loss you may suffer up to $120,000 will be fully paid for by the insurance company. But if you only insure your property for $105,000, and you thereafter suffer a fire loss of $80,000, you will be able to collect only $70,000 from the insurance company. You will have to absorb the remaining $10,000 loss yourself. The following formula applies:

$$\frac{\text{Amount of insurance carried}}{\text{Amount of insurance required}} \times \text{amount of loss} = \text{amount collectible from the insurance company}$$

Using the figures from our example: $\frac{\$105,000}{\$120,000} \times \$80,000 = \$70,000$

10. Finally, an insured who suffers a fire loss should do the following:

(a) The insured should immediately report the loss to the insurance company (sometimes the insurance adjuster will arrive before the fire department leaves);

(b) The insured should carefully safeguard his or her remaining property so that it is not stolen or vandalized;

(c) The insured should prepare an inventory of the damaged or destroyed property. This will be easy to do if the insured has on hand a prefire inventory of his or her property.

(d) Ultimately, the insured must submit a proof of loss form supported by the inventory (including pictures if possible) and other materials such as canceled checks showing all amounts paid for replacement items. The insurance policy usually provides for payment of the loss within sixty days of submission of the proof of loss. However, as a practical matter, the insurance company generally pays much faster than this. In most cases, an insurance adjuster is sent immediately to the location of the loss to help in determining the amount of loss and whether the company wants to rebuild or pay in cash. In the event the insured and insurer cannot agree on the loss, the policy may prescribe arbitration.

WHAT IS AN ASSIGNMENT OF CONTRACT RIGHTS?

Put simply, an assignment is a transfer of rights under an existing contract (e.g., Mary Smith enters into a contract with Richard Wiley, then transfers her rights under the contract to Sam Seymour). The party who transfers the rights (Mary Smith) is called the *assignor*, the party who receives the rights (Sam Seymour), the *assignee*. The general rule is that the assignee "stands in the shoes of the assignor" with respect to the transferred rights (i.e., the assignee is in the same position as the assignor and subject to the same defenses). Thus, if the other original party to the agreement (Richard Wiley) would have a defense to performance or a right to rescind the contract with the assignor, he or she will have the same right with regard to the assignee.

Later in this chapter we will contrast the position of an assignee who "stands in the shoes of the assignor" with that of a person who receives a *negotiable instrument* (e.g., a check, note, or draft) through a special form of transfer called a *negotiation*. Unlike the assignee, the party receiving the negotiable instrument *may* stand in a better position than his or her transferor (i.e., even if the nontransferring original party to the instrument has a defense to performance against the transferor, the defense may not be good against the transferee). The word "may" is emphasized because the transferee must qualify as a *holder in due course* in order to obtain rights superior to those of an assignee.

The vast majority of contract rights are freely transferable, and the law of assignments controls in most situations. It is only occasionally that the transferee of contract rights will receive rights superior to those of his or her transferor (namely, where the transferee is a holder in due course of a negotiable instrument).

The term "assignment" applies only to the transfer of rights under an existing contract. The transfer serves to extinguish the rights in the assignor and create the rights in the assignee: after the assignment, only the assignee may sue the nontransferring party to enforce the rights or to collect money damages for breach of contract.

The term "assignment" does not apply to and should not be used to describe an effort to transfer existing contract duties to another. Duties are not assigned—they are "delegated." To delegate a duty is to appoint another to perform the duty. Delegation does not extinguish the duties in the delegating party (the delegant); rather, the delegant remains liable for performance if the other party (the delegatee) fails to perform. Because there is no effective transfer of the duties, the term assignment does not apply.

Generally, any oral or written manifestation of intent by a party to *presently* transfer his or her rights under an existing contract to another person will constitute an assignment (the intent must be to transfer the interest now—not at some time in the future). No particular formality is required with limited exception. Most states have statutes requiring assignment of wages and assignment of interests in land to be in writing. Some states prohibit assignment of future wages; other states permit assignment of future wages but only upon the written consent of the employee's spouse or parent (if the employee is a minor) and only to the extent of necessaries furnished to the employee by the assignee.

An assignment need not be supported by consideration. Even a purely gratuitous assignment is valid, transferring to the assignee the rights of the assignor.

Situations Where Contract Rights Cannot Be Assigned

There are four situations where contract rights may not be assigned:

Where assignment would materially change the nontransferring party's duty A contract right to the personal services of another may not be assigned because it would not be fair to require the obligor (the nontransferring original party) to perform for someone other than the original party he or she contracted with. Also, the contract rights growing out of requirements and output contracts generally cannot be assigned. Obviously, the requirements or output of an assignee may vary greatly from those of an assignor. To permit assignment in such case would be to materially change the nontransferring party's duty under the contract.

Where assignment would materially change the nontransferring party's risk An assignment that materially changes the nontransferring party's risk under the contract is also invalid. For this reason, insurance policies are generally not assignable. And this makes good sense. Certainly, it would not be fair to allow an insured to transfer his or her right to life insurance coverage to another, thereby forcing the insurance company to insure a different person (who might have a heart condition or cancer). The same is true with regard to casualty, fire, auto insurance, etc. The assignee of such a policy might well present a more serious risk to the insurer.

This is not to say that the insured cannot transfer *ownership* of the life insurance policy to another. A policy holder will frequently transfer complete ownership of the policy to his or her beneficiary to prevent inclusion of the policy proceeds in his or her estate for purposes of death taxes. Death taxes are transfer taxes, and if the insured does not own his or her life insurance at death, there is nothing to transfer and nothing to tax. (Of course, if the insured irrevocably transfers his or her ownership of the policy with or without consideration, the insured can no longer change beneficiaries, borrow against the policy, surrender it for cash, or otherwise affect the policy without the assignee's consent.) There is no problem with assignment of ownership of the policy because such assignment does not vary the nontransferring party's risk. Assignment of the right to be insured, on the other hand, changes the risk substantially.

Nor is there any problem with assigning the right to collect the insurance proceeds in the event of loss. Payment to an assignee rather than to the insured or his or her named beneficiary does not constitute a material change of the insurer's obligations or risk.

Similar to insurance-covered risks where personal credit serves as a basis for the nontransferring party's promise, any substitution of debtors would vary the risk. Therefore, assignment is not allowed. For example, if a bank agrees to loan $10,000 to a prosperous businessman, the businessman cannot assign his right to the loan to someone who has a poor credit rating.

Where the assignment purports to transfer future rights in a nonexistent future contract Only present and future rights in *existing* contracts can be assigned. If a contract has yet to come into being, there is nothing to assign, and any purported assignment of future rights in the contract is invalid. For example, suppose that Harvey Weiss enters into a contract with an employment agency: Harvey assigns his first month's wages to the agency in return for assistance in finding a job. Since Harvey does not yet have a job, he has nothing to assign, and his purported transfer of future rights in a future contract of employment is invalid. However, if the agency finds Harvey a job, the court may order specific performance of the assignment to prevent unjust enrichment.

Where the contract expressly prohibits assignment Some contracts expressly provide that any attempted assignment will be void or will act as a condition subsequent to cut off the rights of the would-be assignor. Where this is so, any attempted transfer of rights will generally be ineffective.

In connection with landlord-tenant law (see Chapter 8), a tenant's interest in the leased premises is freely transferable in the absence of an agreement to the contrary. It is for this reason that many leases contain express prohibitions against assigning and/or subletting the leased premises. Subletting must be distinguished from assignment. A sublease is an agreement whereby the tenant-lessee sublets (transfers) all or part of the leased property at an agreed rental for a definite term but retains a reversionary interest in the property. In other words, the tenant-lessee does not transfer his or her entire interest in the real property to the sublessee. Rather the tenant transfers only a part of the property to the sublessee, or he or she transfers all of the property but for a period of time less than the period of the original lease. It is the tenant's retention of a reversionary interest that makes the transfer a sublease rather than an assignment. An *assignment* by a tenant-lessee is a transfer of his or her entire interest in the leased premises for the remainder of the lease period. In an assignment, the tenant retains no reversion in the leased premises.

With both a sublease and an assignment, the original tenant-lessee remains fully liable under the provisions of the original lease. However, with a sublease, the landlord must look to the original tenant for payment of the rent due under the lease—the subtenant pays the tenant not the landlord. With an assignment, on the other hand, the assignee becomes directly liable to the original landlord. It should be noted that a provision in a lease prohibiting assignment will not prohibit a sublease of the property, and vice versa. Because of this, many leases expressly prohibit both assignments and subleases of the property without the lessor's express written consent. And the fact that the lessor consents to one particular assignment or sublease does not constitute consent to subsequent assignments or subleases.

Just as there are contract rights that cannot be assigned, there are contract duties that cannot be delegated. The general rule is that delegation is not allowed where performance by the delegatee would vary materially from performance by the delegant. Thus, a party may not delegate a duty to perform personal services for another. As in the area of assignment, a performance by an artist, author, doctor, lawyer, teacher, accountant, etc., is simply too personal to be delegated. Of course, there are many duties that are not too personal to be transferred, such as a duty to pay money, to build or paint a building, to manufacture or transport goods. The test is whether performance by the original obligor is of the essence of the contract. If it is (e.g., where the original obligor has some special or unique talent), the nontransferring party has a substantial interest in having the original obligor perform personally, and delegation will not be allowed.

Remember, an assignee takes no new rights by virtue of an assignment. He or she merely "stands in the shoes" of the assignor—that is, in the same position as the assignor and subject to the same defenses as existed prior to the assignment.

WHAT ARE THE ASSIGNEE'S RIGHTS AGAINST THE ASSIGNOR IN THE EVENT OF NONPERFORMANCE BY THE NONTRANSFERRING PARTY?

In a purely gratuitous assignment, the assignee has no rights against the assignor in the event that the nontransferring obligor fails to perform or refuses to perform. However, where the assignment is for consideration (i.e., where it is contractual in nature), the assignee may have a cause of action against the assignor for breach of implied warranty. Even though the assignor does not expressly promise that the nontransferring party will perform, he or she is held by law to impliedly warrant (promise) the following:

1. That the assigned right actually exists and is subject to no limitations or defenses other than those stated or apparent at the time of the assignment;
2. That any document or paper shown to the assignee with regard to the assignment is genuine and what it purports to be; and
3. That the assignor has the right to assign and will do nothing in the future to defeat the assigned right (in other words, the assignor won't assign the same right to anyone else.

If the obligor's failure or refusal to perform can be traced to a breach of any of these implied warranties, the assignee may sue the assignor for money damages. Note that the assignor does not impliedly warrant that the obligor will, in fact, perform, or that he or she is solvent and capable of performing.

HOW DOES "ASSIGNMENT" AND "STANDING IN THE SHOES" OF THE ASSIGNOR DIFFER FROM "NEGOTIATION" AND HAVING THE RIGHTS OF A "HOLDER IN DUE COURSE"?

Earlier in this chapter we studied a special kind of contract—the insurance contract. We found that there are certain special rules that apply to insurance contracts, including rules on insurable interest, subrogation, concealment, and the like. We now take up another special form of contract—the *negotiable instrument.* The negotiable instrument is a contract designed to serve as a substitute for money and to help facilitate credit transactions. The basic kinds of negotiable instruments are *promissory notes, drafts* (or bills of exchange), and *checks* (a special type of draft that most of you are familiar with). Special rules apply to negotiable notes, drafts, and checks to enable them to flow freely through commerce without restriction. Obviously, if the ordinary rules of assignment were applied to such instruments, people would be unwilling to accept them in place of money or to extend credit on the basis of the instruments—the risk of a defense to payment would be too high, and the movement of the instruments through the channels of commerce would be too slow and cumbersome. The commercial importance of freely flowing negotiable instruments cannot be overemphasized. Checks, drafts, and notes serve as the basic means of payment in most commercial transactions; they facilitate the payment of bills and the movement of goods and services. For this reason, negotiable instruments are frequently referred to as *commercial paper.*

Consider the fact that commercial paper is to serve as a substitute for money. Now suppose that you purchase a television set from J. C. Dollar Department Store for $750 cash (you pay in seven $100 bills and one $50 bill). You take the TV home and find that it works on only half the channels. Obviously, J. C. Dollar has breached its part of the sales contract (buyers' remedies are discussed in Chapter 10), and your reasonable expectations have not been met. But should your remedy include the right to reacquire the exact same seven $100 bills and the exact same $50 bill? By now, the bills have probably been deposited in the bank and given back out to eight individuals. Certainly, it would be both ridiculous and impossible for J. C. Dollar to have to locate the exact same bills and return them to you. The bills have moved on into the channels of commerce, and that is the way negotiable instruments are designed to move. Of course, negotiable notes, drafts, and checks will never move quite as freely as currency itself, but they can be transferred far more easily than other kinds of contracts. Thus it is that if a negotiable instrument is transferred through a *negotiation* to one who qualifies as a *holder in due course*, the holder in due course will (with very limited exception) take the instrument free and clear of any defenses that the nontransferring party holds against the transferor. The instrument may thus continue to move through commerce free and clear of the defenses.

For the special rules of negotiability to come into play, the instrument involved must be a negotiable instrument. The Uniform Commercial Code, which very strictly controls negotiable instruments law, lists nine requirements of negotiability. Unless an instrument satisfies all nine requirements, the instrument is non-negotiable, and the law of assignments controls (in which case, a transferee of the instrument will always "stand in the shoes" of his or her transferor).

Even where the instrument is negotiable, the law of assignments will control unless the transferee of the instrument qualifies as a holder in due course. To be a holder in due course, one must first be a "holder." Section 1–201 of the Uniform Commercial Code defines "holder" as "a person who is in possession * * * of an instrument * * * drawn, issued or indorsed to him or to his order or to bearer or in blank." And the Uniform Commercial Code defines "holder in due course" at Section 3–302 as follows: "A holder in due course is a holder who takes the instrument (a) for value; and (b) in good faith; and (c) without notice that it is overdue or has been dishonored or of any defense against or claim to it on the part of any person."

Unlike an assignee, a holder in due course may have rights superior to those of his or her transferor. Section 3–305 of the Uniform Commercial Code states:

> To the extent that a holder is a holder in due course he takes the instrument free from
>
> (1) All claims to it on the part of any person; and
> (2) All defenses of any party to the instrument with whom the holder has not dealt except
>   (a) infancy, to the extent that it is a defense to a simple contract [incapacity of a minor as discussed in Chapter 8]; and
>   (b) such other incapacity, or duress, or illegality of the transaction as renders the obligation of the party a nullity [void transactions as discussed in Chapter 8]; and
>   (c) such misrepresentation as has induced the party to sign the instrument with neither knowledge nor reasonable opportunity to obtain knowledge of its character or its essential terms [fraud in the execution as discussed in Chapter 8]; and
>   (d) discharge in insolvency proceedings [see Chapter 11]; and

(e) any other discharge of which the holder has notice when he takes the instrument.

The defenses listed in subsection 2(a) through (e) are called *real defenses* and are the only defenses that may be asserted against a holder in due course. All other defenses are *personal defenses* which cannot be asserted. Of course, as between the original parties to the contract, it makes little difference whether a defense is real or personal—if the defense exists, it can be asserted. The distinction between real and personal defenses becomes important only when the negotiable instrument is transferred to a third party. If the transferee qualifies as a holder in due course, only real defenses can be asserted against him or her; if the transferee does not qualify as a holder in due course, any defense that is good against the transferor, whether real or personal, will be good against the transferee. Of course, if the transferor of the instrument is a holder in due course, the transferee will "stand in his or her shoes" and so acquire the rights of a holder in due course (this is known as the "shelter provision").

In summary, if you are trying to determine whether the special rules of negotiability apply, ask first—*is the instrument negotiable*? If the answer is no, the law of assignments controls, and you need go no further. If the answer is yes, ask a second question—*does the transferee of the instrument qualify as a holder in due course*? If the answer is yes, the rules of negotiability apply, and only real defenses will be good against the transferee. If the answer is no, the law of assignments controls, and any real or personal defenses good against the transferor will be good against the transferee. However, be sure to ask in this case—*does the transferee acquire the rights of a holder in due course under "shelter provision"*? If so, only real defenses will be good against the transferee; personal defenses will be cut off.

WHAT ARE THE TWO MAIN PURPOSES FOR COMMERCIAL PAPER?

As stated previously, negotiable instruments serve as substitutes for money in the world of commerce. Because of the special features of such instruments, people can accept them without fear that existing personal defenses will make it impossible to collect the instruments. Checks particularly are useful as monetary equivalents because they are payable on demand when presented to the bank where the drawer (the party who writes the check) keeps his or her account. Checks also permit the government to keep a much smaller supply of actual currency (money) in circulation. And using checks is safer and more convenient than using cash. People who write checks need not carry large amounts of money on their persons; and people are generally better off losing checks than they are losing cash (while lost money is nearly impossible to trace, a lost check, if unendorsed, usually cannot be converted into cash).

Negotiable instruments also serve a second purpose of helping to create credit (an important purpose in our society where most business is financed on credit). When one person pays another with a negotiable instrument that is payable at a fixed date in the future, the party who accepts the instrument is extending credit until the specified due date.

WHAT ARE THE NINE REQUIREMENTS OF NEGOTIABILITY?

Because negotiable instruments serve as substitutes for money and help facilitate credit transactions, the law requires that negotiability of an instrument be determinable merely by looking at the face of the instrument. Otherwise, people would not be willing to accept the instruments as money substitutes or as instruments creating credit—the risk of an existing defense to payment would be too great. Thus, the determination of negotiability is strictly a matter of form. If an instrument fully complies with the nine requirements of negotiability set out in Section 3–104 of the Uniform Commercial Code, the instrument is negotiable. If the instrument fails to satisfy any one of the nine requirements, the instrument is non-negotiable (in which case, the law of assignments controls). The nine requirements of negotiability are:

1. The instrument must be in writing;
2. The instrument must be signed;
3. The instrument must contain a promise to pay (if a note) or an order to pay (if a check or draft);
4. The promise or order must be unconditional;
5. The payment required must be of a sum certain;
6. The sum certain must be in money only;
7. The instrument must not contain any promise or order other than the promise to pay a sum certain in money;
8. The instrument must be payable on demand or at a definite time;
9. The instrument must be payable "to order" or "to bearer." (Often referred to as the "magic words" of negotiability, the words "to order" or "to bearer" appear on 99.9 percent of all negotiable instruments. However, the UCC at Section 3–310 says that "an instrument is payable to order when by its terms it is payable to the order or assigns of any person therein specified with reasonable certainty, or to him or his order, or when it is conspicuously designated on its face as 'exchange' or the like and names a payee." Occasionally, the word "assigns" or "exchange" is used and will satisfy this ninth requirement.)

WHAT IS A NEGOTIABLE PROMISSORY NOTE?

A negotiable promissory note is a written instrument in which one party (a *maker*) unconditionally promises to pay "to the order of" another party (a named *payee*) or to "bearer" (an unnamed *payee*) a sum certain in money upon demand or at a definite time in the future. The promissory note must be signed by the maker, and must contain no promise or order other than the promise to pay the specified sum.

As defined, a negotiable promissory note meets all nine requirements for negotiability. Where the note is made payable "to the order of" a named payee, the note is called *order paper*. The named payee must endorse the note (accomplished by signing on the back of the instrument) in order to negotiate it (i.e., transfer it so as to make the transferee a holder). Where the note is made payable to "bearer" (i.e., to any person who presents it for payment), the instrument is called *bearer paper*, and it may be freely negotiated without endorsement simply by delivery alone.

When are negotiable promissory notes used? Frequently, lenders of money require their borrowers to sign such notes; sometimes sellers of property accept negotiable promissory notes from purchasers who cannot afford immediately to pay the full cash price of the property. And in nearly all credit real estate transactions, the purchaser is required to sign both a negotiable promissory note and a mortgage. Let's consider an example. Suppose that Larry Taylor purchases a boat from George Johnson for $10,300. Larry pays $2,000 down and gives George a negotiable promissory note (payable at any time upon demand of the payee) for the balance. The instrument, a simple promissory note, is illustrated in figure 10–1.

Looking at the instrument, you can see that all nine requirements of negotiability are satisfied: the instrument is in writing; it is signed by the maker Larry Taylor; it contains an unconditional promise to pay a sum certain in money; it contains no other promise or order; and it is payable on demand to the order of a named payee, George Johnson (see figure 10–2).

Since the promissory note is order paper made payable to the order of George Johnson, the note can be negotiated only by (1) endorsement by George and (2) delivery to a third party (the endorsee). Without George's endorsement, a third party in possession of the instrument could not be a holder (and so obviously could not be a holder in due course), but could only be an assignee subject to any and all defenses that Larry might have against George (e.g., nondelivery of the boat).

FIGURE 10–1 A SIMPLE PROMISSORY NOTE

February 15, 1983

ON DEMAND the undersigned promises to pay to the order of

GEORGE JOHNSON

Eight thousand three hundred and no/100 -------DOLLARS

together with interest thereon from the date hereof until paid at

the rate of 9 percent per annum.

Lawrence Taylor

Lawrence Taylor

FIGURE 10–2 THE NINE REQUIREMENTS OF NEGOTIABILITY

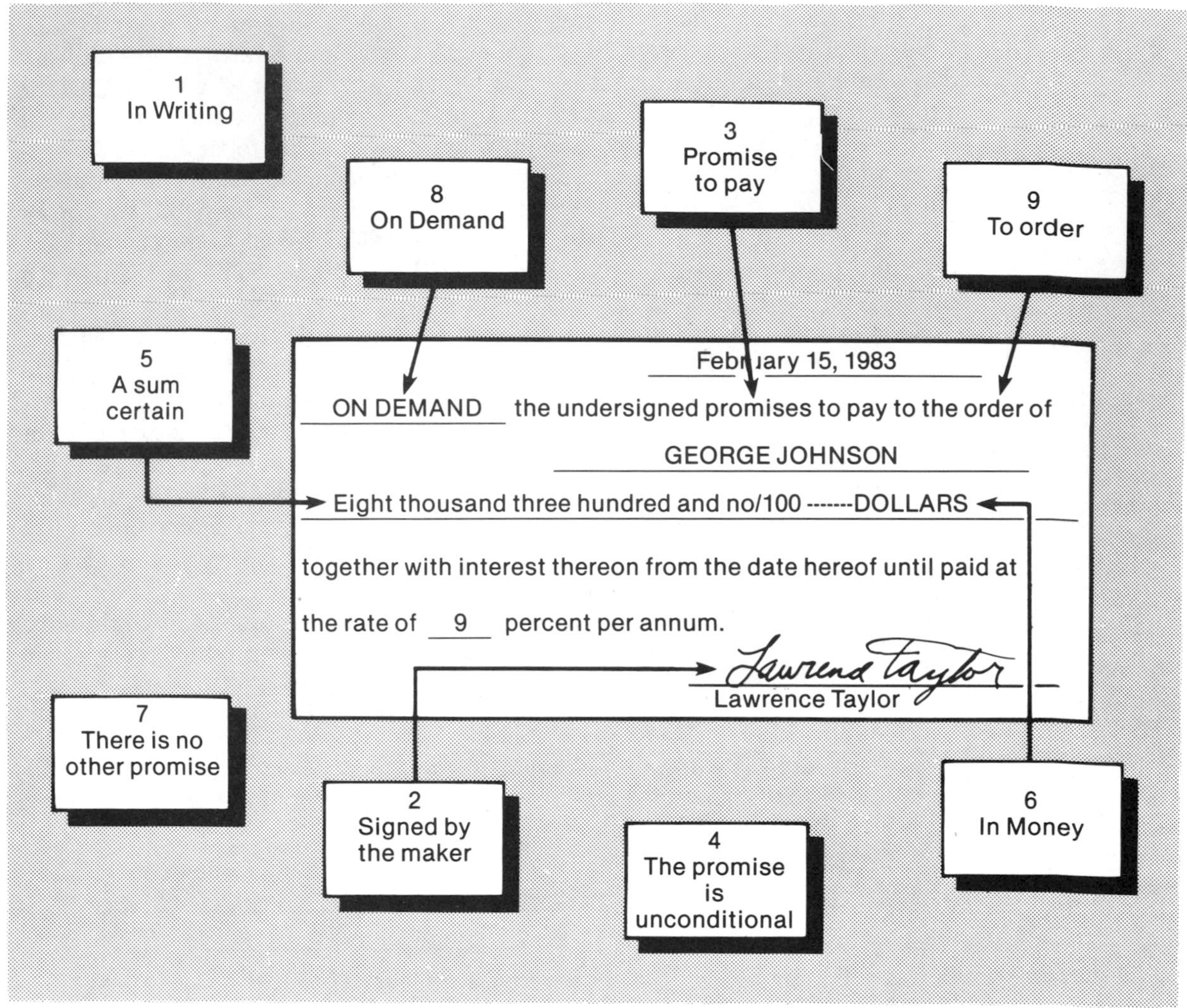

Now, let's vary the transaction so that Larry Taylor issues a promissory note payable, not on demand, but at a definite time in the future (this is more likely, in any case, since Larry does not appear to have present ability to pay the $8,300 balance). Let's also assume that Larry makes the note payable "to bearer" rather than to George Johnson. The instrument is illustrated in figure 10–3. Again, all nine requirements of negotiability are satisfied:

1. The instrument is in writing;
2. It is signed by the maker;
3. It contains a promise to pay;

FIGURE 10–3 A PROMISSORY NOTE PAYABLE TO BEARER

February 15, 1983

Ninety days after date, the undersigned promises to pay to

Bearer

Eight thousand three hundred and no/100 -------DOLLARS

Together with interest thereon from the date hereof until paid at

the rate of 9 percent per annum.

Lawrence Taylor

Lawrence Taylor

4. The promise is unconditional;
5. The promise is to pay a sum certain;
6. The sum certain is in money only;
7. The instrument contains no other promise or order;
8. It is payable at a definite time;
9. It contains "the magic words"—payable "to bearer."

WHAT IS A NEGOTIABLE DRAFT?

A *negotiable draft* is a written instrument in which one party (a drawer) unconditionally orders a second party (a drawee) to pay "to the order of" a named *payee* or "to bearer" a sum certain in money on demand or at a definite time in the future. The negotiable draft must be signed by the drawer, and must contain no promise or order other than the promise to pay. Thus, whereas a promissory note is a two-party (*maker* and *payee*) instrument involving a promise to pay, a draft is a three-party (*drawer, drawee,* and *payee*) instrument involving an order to pay. In every draft situation, there is one important underlying relationship:

> *The draft presupposes a debtor-creditor relationship between the drawee and the drawer.*

Obviously, a drawer cannot order a drawee to pay a sum certain in money unless the drawee is in some way indebted to the drawer. For example, most of you are familiar with one type of draft, the *check* (described in detail in a following section). The drawer of a check must deposit money in his or her checking account before writing the check ordering the drawee bank to pay "to order" or "to bearer." If the drawer fails to deposit money, the required debtor-creditor relationship does not exist (i.e., the bank is in no way indebted to the drawer), and the drawee bank is not obligated to pay upon the drawer's order. With regard to drafts other than checks, the drawee must either hold a similar account of funds belonging to the drawer, or he or she must owe the drawer money (e.g., the sale price in a purchase of goods from the drawer).

Drafts are generally classified as either time drafts or sight drafts. A *time draft* is a draft payable at a definite time in the future; a *sight draft* is a draft payable on demand (i.e., upon presentation to the drawee). Strictly speaking, a drawee incurs no liability for paying a draft until he or she has "accepted" the instrument. In the case of a time draft, the payee usually presents the draft to the drawee for acceptance well in advance of the instrument's due date. The drawee accepts the draft by writing his or her acceptance vertically across the face of the instrument. Having accepted the time draft, the *drawee-acceptor* returns the instrument to the payee who holds it until its due date (at which time the payee presents it again for payment).

Insofar as a sight draft is concerned, written acceptance is generally immaterial since the drawee accepts the draft on demand of the payee (i.e., upon the payee's presentation of the draft) simply by paying the instrument. An exception arises where the sight draft reads "payable thirty days after sight" or the like, in which case the payee must present the draft twice—once for acceptance and a second time, thirty days later, for payment.

As for the drawer's liability on the instrument, the drawer neither expressly promises nor expects to pay the sum certain to the payee—he or she merely orders the drawee to do so. However, if the drawee does not accept and pay the draft, the drawer will then generally become liable to pay the instrument.

Now let's return to our example. Suppose that Larry Taylor agrees to purchase George Johnson's boat for $10,300. Larry has only $2,000 to put down on the boat, but Mark Hopkins owes Larry $8,300 (due on March 15, 1983) for a parcel of real property Mark purchased from Larry. Larry puts $2,000 down on the boat and gives George the time draft illustrated in figure 10–4 for the balance.

As stated before, the drawee (Mark Hopkins) is not liable on the time draft until and unless he accepts the instrument. While it is true that the draft presupposes a debtor-creditor relationship between Mark Hopkins and Larry Taylor, Mark is not obligated to assume a new form of contract for paying off the previously existing debt (i.e., Larry cannot require Mark to pay other than in accord with the terms of the original debt agreement). Thus, Mark may refuse to accept the time draft, although he will still remain liable to Larry for the $8,300. However, it probably makes little difference to Mark whether he pays the $8,300 to Larry Taylor or George Johnson. He is therefore likely to accept the draft by writing the acceptance vertically across the face of the instrument as in figure 10–5.

FIGURE 10–4 A TIME DRAFT

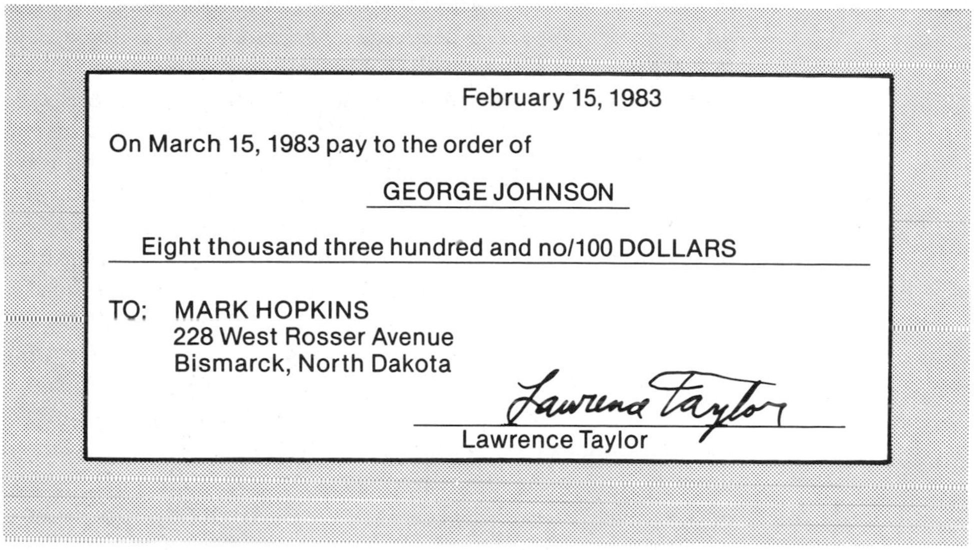

February 15, 1983

On March 15, 1983 pay to the order of

GEORGE JOHNSON

Eight thousand three hundred and no/100 DOLLARS

TO: MARK HOPKINS
228 West Rosser Avenue
Bismarck, North Dakota

Lawrence Taylor

Lawrence Taylor

FIGURE 10–5 ACCEPTANCE WRITTEN VERTICALLY ACROSS INSTRUMENT

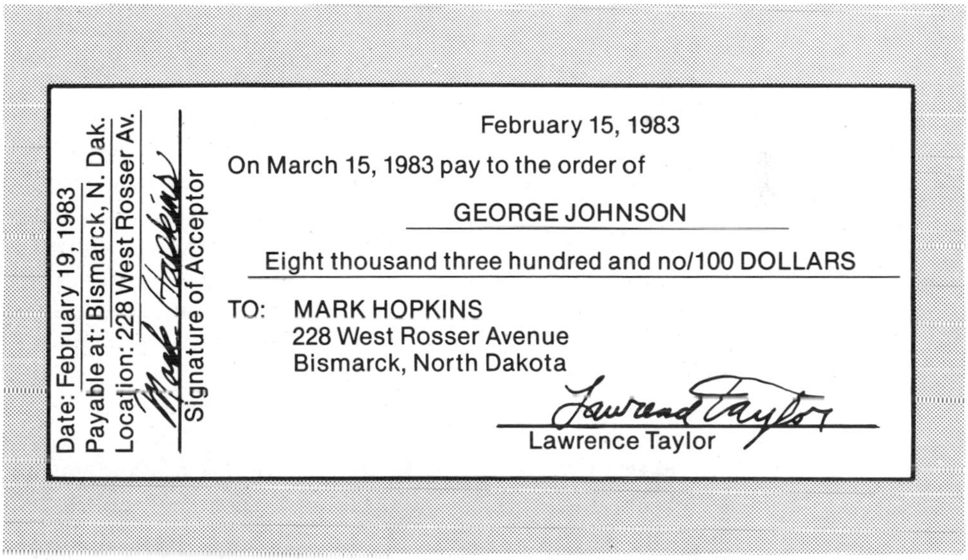

Date: February 19, 1983
Payable at: Bismarck, N. Dak.
Location: 228 West Rosser Av.
Mark Hopkins
Signature of Acceptor

February 15, 1983

On March 15, 1983 pay to the order of

GEORGE JOHNSON

Eight thousand three hundred and no/100 DOLLARS

TO: MARK HOPKINS
228 West Rosser Avenue
Bismarck, North Dakota

Lawrence Taylor

Lawrence Taylor

WHAT IS A TRADE ACCEPTANCE?

A *trade acceptance* is a special kind of draft used to finance the movement of goods in commerce. Whereas the drawer of a draft normally names some third party as a payee of the instrument, the drawer of a trade acceptance (usually a seller of merchandise) names himself or herself as payee. The seller draws the draft on a purchaser who cannot afford to pay the entire purchase price of goods immediately. By drawing the draft the seller facilitates the credit sale (i.e., the purchaser gets his or her goods) and produces a negotiable instrument that can be immediately discounted for cash to a bank or other financial institution (i.e., the seller gets his or her money—or, at least, most of it). Since both the drawer and drawee (once he or she has accepted) stand behind the trade acceptance, the draft is highly regarded by financial institutions, and it is relatively easy for the seller to obtain his or her money less the discount.

By way of example, assume that on February 15, 1983, Mary Manufacturer enters into a sales contract with Roger Retailer wherein Mary agrees to manufacture and deliver 2,000 men's shirts to Roger, and Roger agrees to pay Mary five dollars per shirt, or $10,000. The problem is that Roger is short on cash, while Mary needs immediate cash to meet her own obligations. To remedy the problem, Mary sells the goods to Roger, drawing a draft on him to pay the amount of the purchase price ($10,000) "to the order of Mary Manufacturer" on April 1, 1983. Mary presents the draft to Roger for written acceptance; she then endorses the instrument and discounts it at the bank (the bank deducts from the face value of the draft a charge for interest, risk, and handling). The result of the transaction is that Roger receives the goods he needs on credit, and Mary obtains immediate cash. The trade acceptance is illustrated in figure 10–6.

WHAT IS A CHECK?

A check is a draft drawn on a bank and payable on demand; it is not only the most common kind of draft, but it is the most widely used form of commercial paper. Each year, billions of checks are processed involving trillions (thousands of billions) of dollars. Generally, a drawer orders printed checks from the bank where he or she maintains an account. The drawer's name, address, and telephone number are printed on the face of the checks. The checks are numbered or left blank for the drawer to number, and there is a "memo" space for noting the particular reason for issuing the check (e.g., rent, groceries, electric bill, etc.). Also, the checks are specially marked with numbers representing the drawer's bank and indicating a combination by which the Magnetic Ink Character Recognition check collection system may pass the checks through a sorting computer so as to charge them to the proper account. The special numbers serve to facilitate the collection process and the movement of the checks through banking channels. Thus, Larry Taylor might simply write George Johnson a check for $10,300 to pay for the much sought-after boat. The check is illustrated in figure 10–7.

FIGURE 10–6 TRADE ACCEPTANCE

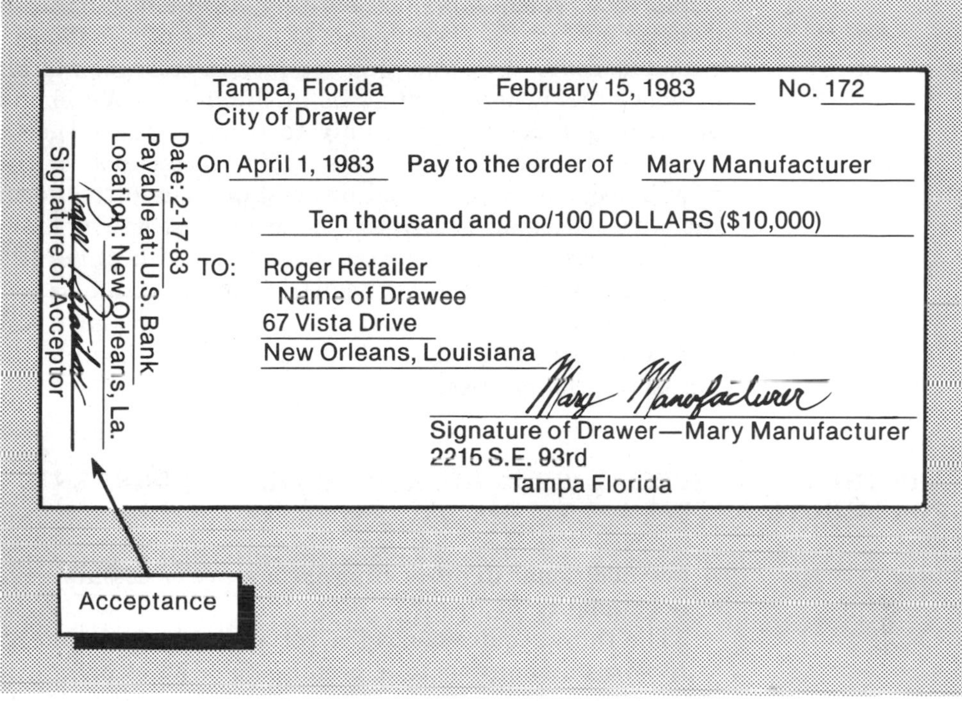

Tampa, Florida
City of Drawer

February 15, 1983

No. 172

On April 1, 1983 Pay to the order of Mary Manufacturer

Ten thousand and no/100 DOLLARS ($10,000)

TO: Roger Retailer
Name of Drawee
67 Vista Drive
New Orleans, Louisiana

Signature of Drawer—Mary Manufacturer
2215 S.E. 93rd
Tampa Florida

Date: 2-17-83
Payable at: U.S. Bank
Location: New Orleans, La.
Signature of Acceptor

FIGURE 10–7 A CHECK

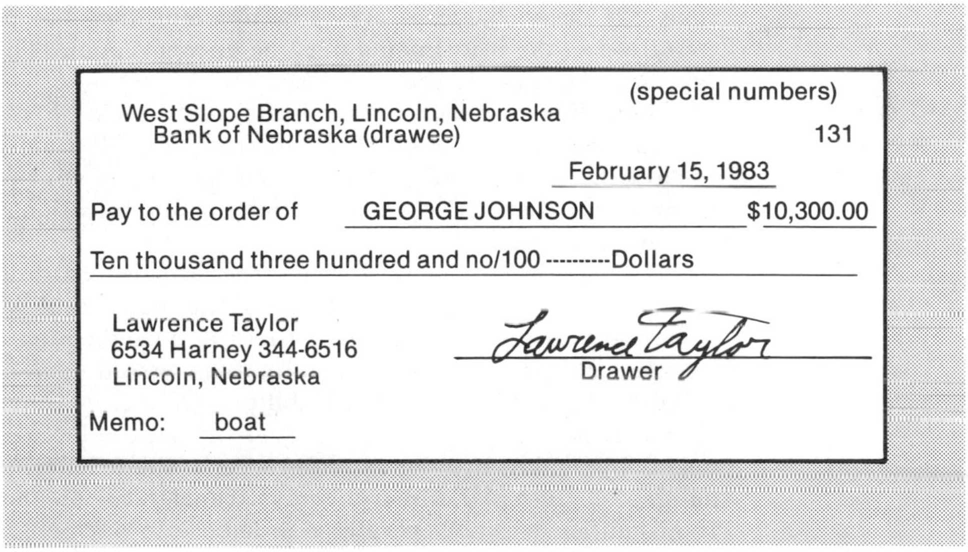

(special numbers)

West Slope Branch, Lincoln, Nebraska
Bank of Nebraska (drawee)

131

February 15, 1983

Pay to the order of GEORGE JOHNSON $10,300.00

Ten thousand three hundred and no/100 ----------Dollars

Lawrence Taylor
6534 Harney 344-6516
Lincoln, Nebraska

Drawer

Memo: boat

Negotiable notes, drafts, and checks serve as money substitutes and facilitate credit transactions. In Chapter 10, we will study about written instruments called *documents of title*, which may be either negotiable or non-negotiable, but which serve an entirely different purpose—they evidence the ownership of goods. Documents of title are of two types: *warehouse receipts*, which evidence the ownership of goods in storage, and *bills of lading*, which evidence the ownership of goods in shipment. Warehouse receipts and bills of lading are designed not only to transfer the ownership of goods but to represent the goods themselves. Thus, possession of the document of title may be equivalent to actual ownership; where the document is negotiable, the warehouseman or carrier (shipper) must deliver the goods to anyone in legal possession of the instrument. While negotiable documents of title serve an entirely different function from the commercial instruments (notes, drafts, checks) discussed in this chapter, they do have similar characteristics (e.g., they may be made out "to order" or "to bearer," they may cut off defenses of prior parties, etc.).

ARE THERE ANY SPECIAL RULES REGARDING THE REQUIREMENTS FOR NEGOTIABILITY?

A few additional items of information are necessary regarding the specifics of negotiability.

The third requirement of negotiability is that the instrument must contain words amounting to a promise (if a note) or an order (if a draft). A mere acknowledgment of a debt (e.g., "I.O.U. $10,000") does not constitute a promise to pay, nor does a mere "authorization" or "request" (e.g., "I request you to pay" or "I authorize you to pay") constitute an order to pay.

The fourth requirement of negotiability is that the promise or order to pay must be unconditional. As you will recall, negotiable instruments are designed to serve as substitutes for money and to facilitate credit transactions. If these objectives are to be accomplished, the promises and orders contained in the instruments must be unconditional. The instruments must represent obligations that are fixed and absolute—otherwise, people would not be willing to accept notes, drafts, and checks in place of money or to extend credit on the basis of the instruments. Put simply, people must be certain that there are no strings attached to payment of negotiable instruments—that there are no contingencies or qualifications that may somehow prevent payment.

The determination of whether the promise or order is unconditional must be made by looking at the face of the instrument without more. Thus, if on the face of the instrument there is no indication of any condition to payment, the fact that the original parties agreed upon a condition is immaterial to the instrument's negotiability. Of course, the condition will be effective as between the original parties (again, the fact that an instrument is negotiable makes little or no difference to the original parties and/or their assignees). But if the instrument is transferred to a holder in due course, the condition will not operate as a defense to payment. For example, suppose that Larry Taylor signs a negotiable promissory note, unconditional on its face, designating George Johnson as payee. As Larry signs the note, he says to George, "I will pay this money only if I am able to sell my apartment house in the next thirty days." If Larry fails to sell the apartment house within the designated time, the failure of condition will serve as a defense to payment against George or his assignee. However, it will not serve as a defense against a holder in due course of the instrument. Thus, if George or his assignee has transferred the instrument to a holder in due course, Larry will have to pay though the condition precedent has failed to occur. Of course, if the condition is stated on the face of the note, the note is non-negotiable, and a transferee of the instrument can have only the rights of an assignee (i.e., he or she will "stand in the shoes" of George Johnson).

Still, there are many items that can appear on the face of the instrument without rendering the instrument conditional. For example, a mere reference to the underlying transaction, document, or consideration upon which the instrument is based does not make the promise or order to pay conditional. Thus, a statement on the face of a promissory note that the note is executed "as per" or "in accordance with the written agreement made this date with the payee" does not impair negotiability. Nor is negotiability impaired where Larry Taylor states on the face of his promissory note that "this note is executed in consideration of the sale and delivery to me of George Johnson's boat." The Uniform Commercial Code states that conditions will not be implied or "read into" an instrument; thus, there is no implication that the consideration must be performed (i.e., that the boat must be sold and delivered) before Larry's duty to pay will arise. Again, as long as the note is in the hands of the original parties or their assignees, the defense of failure of consideration is a good one. But where the instrument has been transferred to a holder in due course, the maker (Larry Taylor) will have to pay despite the fact that there has been no sale and no delivery (of course, the maker in this case can bring suit against the payee [George Johnson] for breach of the underlying agreement).

Sometimes, however, a statement goes beyond a "mere reference" clearly and expressly to condition the promise or order on performance of the underlying transaction or consideration. Such a statement destroys negotiability. For example, a statement in a note that the instrument "*is subject to*" another document or "*is governed by*" another document or agreement is more than a mere reference—the statement clearly and expressly conditions the maker's promise to pay and, in doing so, renders the instrument non-negotiable.

A reference in an instrument to a particular fund from which payment is to be made does not condition the promise or order to pay unless it is stated that payment is to be made "*only*" from that fund (in which case, the promise or order is conditioned upon the existence of the particular fund, and the instrument is non-negotiable). Thus, the general rule is that a negotiable instrument must be based on the general credit of the obligor. However, there are two exceptions under the Uniform Commercial Code where an instrument may be negotiable even though it is limited to payment out of certain funds or assets. The first arises where an instrument issued by a governmental agency or unit is made payable only out of certain governmental funds or accounts. Such instruments are considered negotiable because the Uniform Commercial Code says they are. Secondly, an instrument issued by a partnership, unincorporated association, trust, or estate (see Chapter 12) is considered negotiable under the Code even though it is made payable solely out of the assets of the issuing party (unincorporated associations include fraternal groups, labor unions, nonprofit associations, credit unions, professional societies, and the like).

Finally, a promise or order is not made conditional by a recital that the instrument is part of a secured transaction. Thus, a statement that "this note is secured by a mortgage on the residence located at 3516 S.W. Lansing Street, Memphis, Tennessee" does not impair negotiability. The statement merely identifies the basic underlying transaction; it does not create any implied condition that the security given must be sufficient or the duty to pay will not arise.

The fifth requirement for negotiability is that the promise or order must be to pay a sum certain. Again, if commercial instruments are to accomplish the dual objectives of serving as money substitutes and facilitating credit transactions, the instruments must be payable on their face in a definite amount—that is, in a *sum certain.* Otherwise, people would be unable to determine the worth of the instruments; as a result, they would be unwilling to accept commercial paper in place of cash or to extend credit on the basis of the instruments.

However, this is not to say that the precise sum payable must always be stated with absolute certainty. It is enough if the party in possession of the instrument can determine the precise sum payable by looking at the face of the instrument and making whatever mathematical computations are necessary without going to any outside source. For example, a promissory note containing a promise to pay $10,000 on demand with interest at the rate of 10 percent satisfies the "sum certain" requirement. Though the amount of interest to be paid is unknown at the time the instrument is issued, it is a relatively simple matter for the party in possession of the note to compute the interest owing at the time he or she makes demand for payment. The same is true where an instrument provides for different rates of interest before and after a specified date, and where an instrument payable at a definite time provides for a fixed rate of discount if the instrument is paid prior to its due date and for a fixed rate of increase if the instrument is paid after its due date. In each case, the party in possession of the instrument can easily compute the sum certain owing at the time the payment is made.

The sixth requirement for negotiability is that the instrument must be payable in money. "Money" means a medium of exchange authorized or adopted by a *domestic or foreign government* as part of its *currency.* Thus, a promise to pay a sum certain in British sterling, French francs, Italian lira, Japanese yen, or any other recognized currency of a foreign government is a promise to pay in money. But a promise to pay "three ounces of gold" is not a promise to pay in money, and the instrument containing the promise is non-negotiable.

Even where the sum certain is stated in an officially sanctioned foreign currency, the instrument is deemed payable in an equivalent number of

American dollars unless the instrument *expressly requires* payment in the foreign currency.

The seventh requirement for negotiability is that the instrument must contain no promise or order other than the promise or order to pay a sum certain in money. An instrument is non-negotiable if it contains any promise or order in addition to the promise or order to pay a sum certain in money. Thus, a note in which the maker promises "to pay $5,000 *and* to paint the payee's house," is non-negotiable. So is a note in which the maker promises "to pay $5,000 *or* to paint the payee's house" (the fact that the promises are phrased in the alternative does not save the instrument's negotiability). The maker of a note must promise to pay money only; if, in addition to promising to pay money, he or she promises to render services, sell goods, give an option, or do anything else, the instrument, though a valid contract, is non-negotiable.

The eighth requirement is that the instrument must be payable on demand or at a definite time. If the time for payment of an instrument is otherwise definite, the fact that the instrument is subject to acceleration (i.e., subject to having payment fall due sooner) does not render the time indefinite. Such an instrument is actually more certain as to time of payment than is demand paper; unlike demand paper, there is a definite time beyond which payment of the instrument cannot run (i.e., the instrument is payable "on a certain date or sooner").

Thus, an instrument made payable on a specified date subject to acceleration at the option of one of the parties (either the maker, acceptor, or party in possession of the instrument) is payable at a definite time. This would include an instrument payable "on December 1, 1983 or sooner if the party in possession so chooses."

Similarly, an instrument made payable at a set time subject to acceleration automatically upon the happening of a specified event is also payable at a definite time. Frequently, for example, the full amount owing on an installment note will fall due automatically if any one installment of principal or interest is not paid on time.

Also an instrument made payable at a set date subject to extension at the option of the party in possession of the instrument is payable at a definite time. This is so even where no time limit is placed upon the extension. The reason is that the party in possession always has the right to waive the due date of the instrument regardless of whether he or she has an option to extend. To provide the party formally with such an option does not make the time for payment any more uncertain or affect negotiability in any way. However, the party in possession may never extend the time of payment over the objection of the maker or drawee.

Similarly, an option on the part of the maker or acceptor (as opposed to the party in possession) to extend payment for a further *definite period* of time does not make the time for payment uncertain or otherwise interfere with negotiability. So long as the extension is for a definite period, there is an ultimate date beyond which payment cannot run (the instrument is thus similar to an instrument payable at a definite time subject to acceleration). If the instrument grants the maker or acceptor an option to extend but fails to specify the length of extension, the time for payment is still certain as

Section 3–118(f) of the Uniform Commercial Code states: "Unless otherwise specified consent to extension authorizes a single extension for not longer than the original period." But where the instrument expressly provides that there is no limit on the time that the maker or acceptor may extend, the instrument is not payable on demand or at a definite time, and the instrument is non-negotiable (unlike the party in possession, the maker or acceptor has no right to "waive" the due date of the instrument.

Finally, the UCC at section 3–109(2) provides that "an instrument which by its terms is otherwise payable only upon an act or event uncertain as to time of occurrence is not payable at a definite time even though the act or event has occurred." Prior to passage of the Uniform Commercial Code, an instrument payable upon the happening of an event certain to occur, though uncertain as to time of occurrence, was considered payable at a definite time. For example, in pre-Code days, an instrument payable "when the first rain begins in the fall" or "when the first frost occurs" or "when the war ends" was payable at a definite time (all these events were certain to occur though uncertain as to time of occurrence). And it was common in pre-Code days for an individual to anticipate an inheritance by borrowing money and signing a negotiable note promising to repay the money six months after the death of a relative. Thus, a note payable "six months after the death of my grandfather, John" was payable at a definite time (and therefore negotiable) because the death of the maker's grandfather was certain to occur—the fact that the time of death was uncertain was immaterial as to negotiability.

However, under Subsection (2) of Section 3–109 of the Code, an instrument payable upon the happening of an event certain to occur, though uncertain as to time of occurrence, is not payable at a definite time and is not made so payable by the fact that the act or event has already occurred. Thus, a note payable "six months after the death of my grandfather, John" is uncertain as to time of payment and is non-negotiable. This is so even where the maker's grandfather is dead at the time the maker signs the note: negotiability must be determinable from the face of the instrument without more—it would not be fair to force a party to look outside the instrument to determine the time of payment.

Still, it is sometimes possible to accomplish the same result by making an instrument payable at a definite time subject to automatic acceleration upon the happening of a specified event. For example, a note might be made payable "ten years from today's date, or six months after the death of my grandfather, John if that event occurs before the expiration of the ten years." Here, there is an ultimate time certain ("ten years from today's date"), and the instrument looks like any other instrument payable at a definite time subject to automatic acceleration upon the happening of an event.

Finally, it should be added that an instrument payable upon the happening of an event *uncertain* to occur is not payable at a definite time and is therefore non-negotiable. Examples include instruments payable "when convenient" or "when I get married" or "when the corn crop is harvested" or "when my children graduate from college." As one of these events may never occur, there is no "time certain" for payment.

WHAT IS THE DIFFERENCE BETWEEN "ORDER" AND "BEARER" PAPER?

An instrument, whether a note, draft, or check, may be originally *issued* to a named party or to bearer. Section 3–102 of the Uniform Commercial Code defines "issuance" as the first delivery of an instrument to a holder. The instrument may then be *transferred* to other parties through what is termed a *negotiation.* Negotiation is accomplished in one of two ways depending on whether the instrument is bearer paper or order paper.

Bearer paper (commercial paper made payable "to bearer") is negotiated simply by delivery of the instrument. UCC Section 1–201 defines "delivery" as the voluntary transfer of possession of an instrument from one person to another. For example, suppose that Larry Taylor signs a negotiable promissory note for $10,300 to pay for the boat he is purchasing from George Johnson. Larry makes the instrument payable, not "to the order of George Johnson," but "to bearer." By issuing the note to George, the unnamed payee, Larry makes George a holder. George may now negotiate the note simply by delivering it to a third person. Thus, if George immediately discounts the note to Sally Streeter for $9,300, delivery of the note to Sally constitutes a negotiation, making Sally a holder of the instrument. (To "discount" an instrument is to sell it prior to its due date for an amount less than its face value.) If Sally, in turn, immediately discounts the note to Dick Drynan for $9,450, Sally's delivery of the note to Dick also constitutes a negotiation, and Dick becomes a holder of the note. In each case, delivery is all that is required to negotiate the bearer paper so as to make the transferee a holder.

It follows that even a thief or finder of bearer paper can negotiate the paper by delivering it to a third person who will become a holder of the instrument. (The thief or finder is also a holder, not on the basis of negotiation, but by reason of having taken possession of the bearer paper). Because bearer paper has much of the circulation potential and risk of money, it should be handled with the same care and caution.

Order paper (commercial paper made payable "to the order" of a named payee), on the other hand, can never be negotiated by a thief or finder; to negotiate such paper requires not only delivery of the instrument but also endorsement by the payee. The payee endorses the paper by signing his or her name on the back of the instrument. Returning to our example, suppose that Larry Taylor makes the $1,000 promissory note payable, not "to bearer," but "to the order of George Johnson." As before, George may immediately discount the note to Sally Streeter, but this time, in order to negotiate the instrument so as to make Sally a holder, George must both *endorse* the note and *deliver* the note to Sally. Delivery alone will not suffice. Of course, if Sally has given value for the instrument, she will have a specifically enforceable right to Larry's endorsement in the event that he delivers the instrument to her unendorsed.

Now whether an instrument is originally issued as order paper or bearer paper, it may be negotiated many many times before it is finally presented for payment. And a very interesting thing may occur as the instrument is transferred from party to party. Each time the paper is further negotiated, it may be changed from order paper to bearer paper, or vice versa, depending on the way the instrument is endorsed. For example, if a named payee endorses order paper *in blank* (i.e., signs only his or her name on the back of the instrument), the order paper is converted into bearer paper. Thus, before delivering the note to Sally Streeter, George Johnson might endorse the promissory note made payable to his order as in figure 10–8(a). The *blank endorsement* converts the order paper into bearer paper, and Sally Streeter may further negotiate the instrument by delivery alone.

The corollary is that a *special endorsement* (i.e., one directing the maker or drawee to pay a specific named individual) changes bearer paper into order paper. This is so whether the paper is originally issued "to bearer" or merely endorsed in blank. In our example, it is clear that Sally Streeter may further negotiate the promissory note to Dick Drynan by delivery alone. Suppose, however, that Sally decides to endorse the note. If she endorses in blank, the instrument will remain bearer paper; if she endorses specially, the instrument will change into order paper, and Dick may further negotiate the instrument only by both endorsing and delivering the note. Sally's special endorsement is illustrated in figure 10–8(b). You will note that a special endorsement need not contain the "magic words" of negotiability—"to order" or "to bearer." The "magic words" are required only on the face of the instrument; their use in endorsements is optional.

ARE THERE ANY SPECIAL RULES REGARDING THE REQUIREMENTS FOR BEING A HOLDER IN DUE COURSE?

Remember, a holder of a negotiable instrument is a holder in due course only when he or she takes the instrument: (1) for value, (2) in good faith, and (3) without notice that the instrument is overdue or subject to any claim or defense to payment.

FIGURE 10–8 (a) BLANK ENDORSEMENT AND (b) SPECIAL ENDORSEMENT

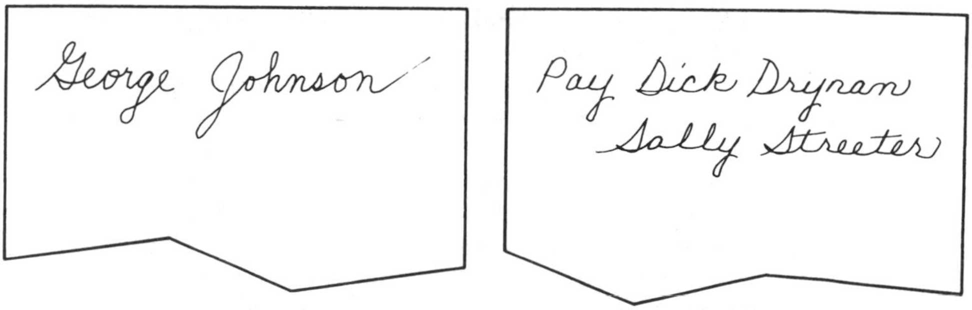

George Johnson

(a)

Pay Dick Drynan
Sally Streeter

(b)

Taking for Value

Value is a narrower concept than consideration required in a contract (see Chapter 8) in that it excludes an executory promise to perform in the future. Consideration sufficient to support a contract may be found simply in one's promise to do something that he or she is not already legally obligated to do. This will not, however, be sufficient to constitute value for being a holder in due course.

At the same time, value is a broader concept than consideration in that it will include the taking of an instrument as security for an existing debt. If a creditor takes an instrument merely as security for an existing debt (i.e., without extending the time for payment or incurring any other detriment in return for the instrument), consideration does not exist in the contract sense. Nevertheless, the Uniform Commercial Code provides that the creditor takes the instrument "for value." For example, suppose that Larry Taylor contracts to buy George Johnson's boat, Larry agreeing to pay $2,000 down and the balance of $8,300 in six months' time. When six months pass and payment is not made, George takes as security for the debt a promissory note from Larry payable in six months in the amount of $8,300. Under the Code, George has given value for the note.

Taking in Good Faith

Section 1–201(19) of the Uniform Commercial Code defines "good faith" as "honesty in fact in the conduct or transaction concerned." Thus the requirement that a holder take in good faith in order to qualify as a holder in due course means only that the holder must act honestly with regard to the transaction. The test of good faith is a subjective one—did the particular holder act in good faith in taking the instrument? If so, it will make no difference that a person of average shrewdness would have found the circumstances suspicious. And the fact that a holder learns of suspicious circumstances only after taking "honestly with regard to the transaction" does not destroy the good faith nature of the taking.

Taking without Notice

Though a holder acquires an instrument for value and in good faith, he or she will not be a holder in due course unless he or she also takes the instrument without notice that the instrument: (1) is overdue, (2) has been dishonored, or (3) is subject to any claim or defense.

A holder who knows or has reason to know any of the foregoing at the time of taking an instrument is denied holder in due course status because such knowledge puts the holder on alert that the instrument may not be enforceable—that, by taking the instrument, the holder may be getting involved in a lawsuit. Here, the test is an objective one: if, under the circumstances, the holder should realize that the instrument is overdue, has been dishonored, or is subject to a claim or defense, the holder takes "with knowledge" and does not qualify as a holder in due course. The fact that the holder does not have actual knowledge is immaterial.

A holder takes with knowledge that an instrument is *overdue* when the holder knows or has reason to know that any part of the principal amount has not been paid on time. Thus, if the instrument is payable at a definite time, the holder must acquire the instrument prior to midnight on the date set for payment. If the holder acquired the instrument later than this, he or she will have reason to know that the instrument is overdue. Where the instrument is payable in installments, the holder takes with knowledge that the instrument is overdue if he or she knows or has reason to know that the obligor has defaulted on any installment of principal (knowledge that the obligor has defaulted as to interest alone does not amount to taking with knowledge).

A holder takes an instrument with knowledge that it has been *dishonored* where the holder knows or has reason to know that demand for acceptance or payment of the instrument has been properly made upon the party expected to pay, and acceptance or payment has been refused. Usually, notation of the dishonor is made on the face of the instrument. For example, a dishonored check generally comes back stamped "insufficient funds" or "payment stopped" or "drawer has no account." Where a notation of dishonor appears on the instrument itself, the holder is put on notice of the dishonor and cannot qualify as a holder in due course. Where the dishonor does not appear on the face of the instrument, the holder may or may not qualify as a holder in due course depending on whether he or she has actual knowledge or reason to know of the dishonor.

Finally, a holder cannot qualify as a holder in due course where he or she knows or has reason to know at the time of taking the instrument that the instrument is *subject to a claim or defense* (e.g., a breach of contract between the original parties, a failure of consideration, mistake, fraud, duress, undue influence, unconscionable act, minority, illegality, or the like). However, it must be emphasized that a holder is under no duty to investigate whether a claim or defense to enforcement of an instrument exists. And the Uniform Commercial Code states that knowledge of certain facts without more does not constitute knowledge of a "claim" or "defense" within the meaning of the Code. For example, knowledge that the instrument was issued or negotiated in return for an executory promise does not impair the holder's status as a holder in due course. Obviously, where a promissory note states on its face that it "is given in return for the payee's promise to deliver his boat within sixty days," a holder cannot help but realize that the executory promise to deliver the boat *may* never be carried out—that there *may* be a failure of consideration. But unless the holder knows that a breach of contract or failure of consideration has *in fact* occurred, the holder takes without knowledge of a claim or defense and so may qualify as a holder in due course.

It should be pointed out that though a holder may not have notice of a claim or defense within the meaning of the Code, he or she may nonetheless know facts that make taking the instrument a bad faith transaction. For example, suppose that the holder knows that his or her transferor is in bad financial straits or has a bad business reputation or has been found guilty in the past of fraud or other criminal conduct. Knowledge of any or all of these things does not amount to notice of a claim or defense. However, it may show a lack of good faith on the part of the holder in taking the instrument (i.e., in light of the knowledge, the holder may have acted dishonestly). Where, under the circumstances, the holder must have known that there was something wrong but deliberately shut his or her eyes to avoid the truth, the result is commercial bad faith. Some courts reach the same result using what is called the *cumulation doctrine.* Under this doctrine, a sufficient accumulation of suspicious circumstances, though each circumstance is in and of itself inadequate to constitute notice, will support a conclusion that the holder had notice of a claim or defense and/or was acting in bad faith.

WHAT IS THE "SHELTER PROVISION"?

We stated previously that one who is not a holder in due course may still have the rights of a holder in due course by reason of taking the instrument from such a holder. This, of course, is in line with the law of assignments which provides that an assignee stands in the shoes of his or her assignor. The "shelter provision" (which is really simply an application of the law of assignments) states that where the assignor of a negotiable instrument is a holder in due course, the assignee of the instrument (and all subsequent transferees) will acquire the rights of such a holder. In other words, once a negotiable instrument is in the possession of a holder in due course, subsequent transferees need not worry about personally qualifying as such holders: the transferees will be effectively "sheltered" by the rights of the first holder in due course even though they take the instrument gratuitously (without giving value) and with notice of claims and defenses to enforcement. (It is sometimes helpful to think of the first HDC as holding a protective "umbrella" of rights over the heads of the subsequent transferees.)

Let's consider an example. Suppose that Larry Taylor negotiates a promissory note to Sally Streeter who qualifies as a holder in due course. Sally subsequently negotiates the note to Dick Drynan, who negotiates it to Buzz Cort, who negotiates it to Martha Hiatt, who negotiates it to Joe O'Reilly. Under the "shelter provision" it makes absolutely no difference whether Dick, Buzz, Martha, or Joe personally qualify as holders in due course. Each stands under Sally's protective "umbrella" and so has the rights of such a holder. (Again, the shelter provision is but an application of the law of assignments—each party in the example stands in the shoes of either a holder in due course or one with the rights of a holder in due course.)

The *single exception* to the shelter provision arises where a party attempts to improve his or her past or present position with respect to an instrument by taking the instrument from a holder in due course or from one with the rights of a holder in due course. Section 3–201 of the Code provides: "Transfer of an instrument vests in the transferee such rights as the transferor has therein, except that a transferee who has himself been a party to any fraud or illegality affecting the instrument or who as a prior holder had notice of a defense or claim against it cannot improve his position by taking from a later holder in due course."

Thus, a person who was party to a past fraud or illegality involving the instrument cannot better his or her position by standing under the protective umbrella held by the first holder in due course of the instrument. Nor can a prior holder with knowledge of a claim or defense better his or her position by standing under the HDC's umbrella of rights. For example, suppose that Larry Taylor fraudulently induces George Johnson to sign a promissory note, naming Larry as payee. Larry subsequently negotiates the note to Sally Streeter who qualifies as a holder in due course. Sally, in turn, transfers the note to Dick Drynan. At the time of the transfer, Dick knows about the fraud in the inducement; however, he had no part in the fraud, and thus he acquires the rights of a holder in due course under the shelter provision. Dick now transfers the note back to Larry Taylor, the original party to the fraud. Unlike Dick, Larry does not acquire the rights of a holder in due course. He falls within the exception to the shelter provision and will not be permitted to better his position by standing under Sally's protective umbrella. Had Dick previously received the note with knowledge of the fraud and later received it back from a holder in due course, he, too, would not have been able to improve his position.

WHAT ARE THE RULES ON "INCOMPLETE" OR "ALTERED" INSTRUMENTS?

On occasion, a maker or drawer will sign an instrument but leave portions of it blank. For example, the name of the payee may be left off the instrument, such as "pay to the order of ______"; the sum certain amount may be left blank; the instrument, though undated, may state that it is payable "90 days after date," etc. In each case, the instrument is incomplete and, therefore, non-negotiable.

To be complete, an instrument must sufficiently identify the parties to the contract and fully comply with the nine requirements of negotiability. If blanks are left in any material portion of the instrument, the instrument is incomplete and cannot be enforced until it is completed. Where the maker or drawer completes the instrument, the instrument will be enforced accordingly; where someone other than the maker or drawer fills in the blanks, the instrument will be enforced if it is completed in the manner intended by the maker or drawer. The legal presumption is that by signing the incomplete instrument, the maker or drawer has authorized another to fill in the gaps in the intended manner.

A holder who takes an incomplete instrument is held to take with knowledge of a possible claim or defense and so cannot qualify as a holder in due course. However, if the instrument is subsequently completed in the manner intended by the maker or drawer and presented to the primary party (maker or drawee-acceptor) for payment, the primary party cannot refuse to pay on the basis that the instrument, when issued, was incomplete. It is only where the instrument is completed in a manner not intended or authorized by the maker or drawer that the primary party will have a defense to payment good as against all but a holder in due course (e.g., where the sum certain blank is completed as $10,000 rather than the $1,000 intended by the maker or drawer).

Material Alteration

The holder of an instrument may find that the maker or acceptor (i.e., the primary party) refuses to pay on the grounds that the instrument has been altered. Alteration may take the form of an addition, change, or deletion of terms or, in the case of an incomplete instrument, an unauthorized completion. Section 3–407 of the Code defines "alteration" in this manner:

> Any alteration of an instrument is material which changes the contract of any party thereto in any respect, including any such change in (a) the number or relations of the parties; or (b) an incomplete instrument, by completing it otherwise than as authorized; or (c) the writing as signed, by adding to it or by removing any part of it.

Whether an alteration will serve as a defense to payment depends upon the nature of the alteration and the kind of holder trying to collect payment. The following rules prevail.

1. With regard to all holders other than holders in due course, a *fraudulent* and *material* alteration *made by a holder* of an instrument will discharge from liability any party whose contract is changed thereby. To result in discharge the alteration must be made by a holder or his or her confederate—"spoilation" (i.e., alteration by a meddling stranger) will not affect anyone's rights. Also, the alteration must be material; if the addition, change, deletion, or unauthorized completion in no way affects the contract of a previous signer, it is immaterial and will not result in discharge. And, notice that it is the previous signers who will be discharged; later parties are not discharged by alterations occurring prior to their involvement. If the alteration effects a change, however slight, in the contract of a previous party, the requirement of materiality is satisfied (e.g., adding one cent to the amount payable or advancing the due date of the instrument by one day). Finally, the alteration must be fraudulent. An addition, change, or deletion made with a benevolent motive as opposed to a fraudulent one (e.g., lowering an interest rate so as to confer a gift or benefit upon a party) will not serve to discharge anybody.

2. To say that an alteration that is immaterial, nonfraudulent, or made by one other than a holder will not discharge a party is not to say that the alteration will be given effect. The altered instrument will be enforced, but only according to its "original tenor" (i.e., according to the original terms of the instrument).

3. A subsequent holder in due course may in all cases enforce the altered instrument according to its original tenor—even where the alteration is fraudulent, material, and made by a holder. And where the maker or drawer has negligently and substantially contributed to the alteration, the holder in due course may enforce the instrument in its altered form (e.g., where the maker or drawer leaves numerous blanks in the instrument, making it easy for someone to change the figures).

4. Finally, where the alteration is an unauthorized completion of an incomplete instrument, a subsequent holder in due course may enforce the instrument either as intended or as completed. (Compare—as to all other fraudulent and material alterations made by a holder, a subsequent HDC can enforce the instrument only according to its original tenor with the exception of alterations substantially induced by the negligence of the maker or drawer.)

WHAT ARE THE PRESENTMENT WARRANTIES?

Generally the holder of the instrument presents it when due to the maker or drawee-acceptor who pays without question (the maker and drawee-acceptor are primary parties who have unconditionally contracted to pay the instrument).

However, sometimes the person primarily liable pays the wrong party or the wrong amount. Mistaken payment may generally be recovered back from any party who is not a holder in due course or who has not, in good faith, changed his or her position in reliance on the payment. However, under the so-called doctrine of finality, mistaken payment may not be recovered back from a holder in due course or a person who has, in good faith, changed his or her position in reliance on the payment unless the HDC or person has breached a warranty of presentment. Under the Uniform Commercial Code at Section 3–417, all persons obtaining payment and all prior transferors warrant that they have good title, which specifically means that there are no forged endorsements. So if there is a forged endorsement and payment has been made, payment may be recovered back from anyone including a holder in due course or a person changing position.

Additionally, all persons obtaining payment, *other than holders in due course,* warrant upon presentment that they have no knowledge that the maker's or drawer's signature has been forged or that the instrument has been materially altered.

So you must contrast the situation where a holder in due course is mistakenly paid after there has been a forged endorsement on the instrument, and the situation where the holder in due course is mistakenly paid after there has been a forged maker's or drawer's signature on the instrument. In the first situation, the party who has made the mistaken payment may recover the amount paid from the holder in due course. In the second situation, the party who has paid may not recover from the holder in due course and must look to the forger for repayment, assuming the forger may be found. The same result occurs regarding payment mistakenly made to a holder in due course on a material alteration.

WHAT ARE THE RULES REGARDING PERSONAL AND REAL DEFENSES?

Personal Defenses

The maker or acceptor of an instrument may refuse to pay on the basis of some personal defense. A personal defense is a defense that is good against all but a holder in due course; it is "personal" in the sense that it arises out of a breach of agreement between former parties to the instrument. The rule is that transfer of a negotiable instrument to a holder in due course "cuts off" personal defenses—anyone other than a holder in due course takes the instrument subject to the defenses. Personal defenses include:

Fraud in the inducement You will recall from Chapter 8 that fraud in the inducement refers to misrepresentation of a material fact. For example, suppose that George Johnson falsely represents to Larry Taylor that he paid $18,000 for his boat one year ago when, in fact, George paid only $10,000 for the boat. Relying on the misrepresentation, Larry purchases the boat, giving George a negotiable promissory note for $10,300. George's misrepresentation constitutes fraud in the inducement. If George or his assignee later tries to collect the note from Larry, Larry has a good defense to payment. However, the defense is personal, and if the note is subsequently transferred to a holder in due course, the holder in due course may enforce the note against Larry. And so may an assignee with the rights of a holder in due course under the shelter provision. Larry's only remedy, in this case, is to sue George for fraud—that is, if Larry can find George and George has enough money to make a suit worthwhile.

Failure of consideration Failure of consideration is also a personal defense. Say that Larry Taylor gives Geoerge Johnson a promissory note in payment for the boat, but George never delivers the boat to Larry. Here, there is a failure of consideration, and if George or his assignee tries to collect the note, Larry has a good defense to payment. But the personal defense will not be good as against a subsequent holder in due course of the instrument (or one with the rights of such a holder).

Nondelivery of the instrument Nondelivery of the instrument to the payee is also a personal defense good against all but a holder in due course. For example, suppose that Larry Taylor makes the promissory note out "to bearer," but the note is stolen before Larry can deliver it to George Johnson. Because the note is bearer paper, the thief can negotiate it by delivery alone; if he or she negotiates it to a holder in due course, the holder in due course will "cut off" the personal defense of nondelivery.

As will be explained later under the heading of "mixed defenses," there are several defenses that are sometimes personal and sometimes real (a "real" defense is a defense that is good even against a holder in due course) depending on the circumstances involved.

And it should be pointed out that several state legislatures have passed consumer protection statutes abolishing the "holder in due course doctrine" with regard to consumer goods financing. Too often in the past, an unscrupulous merchant would use fraudulent means to induce a buyer to purchase consumer goods, taking a negotiable instrument in return for the goods. The merchant would then sell the instrument to a holder in due course, and the buyer would have to pay despite the fraud in the inducement. The same thing resulted in cases of failure of consideration: the merchant who failed to perform would sell the buyer's negotiable instrument to a holder in due course, and the buyer would have to pay despite the fact that he or she received defective merchandise or no merchandise at all. Understandably, many state legislatures found this to be unacceptable. They enacted laws providing that, in the case of the sale of consumer goods, personal defenses such as fraud in the inducement and failure of consideration are not "cut off" by transfer of the instrument to a holder in due course.

Even in states without consumer statutes, the courts have held that if the holder of the instrument is *closely connected* to the seller of the consumer goods (e.g., where the holder is the finance company that finances all of the merchant's credit sales), the holder is charged with knowledge of the fraud or other defense and cannot qualify as a holder in due course. This is referred to as the "close connection" doctrine.

Real Defenses

Sometimes, the maker or acceptor of an instrument will refuse to pay on the basis of a real defense. Unlike a personal defense, a real defense is good against everyone, including a holder in due course (the defense goes to a defect so serious and so substantial that not even a holder in due course can cut it off). Real defenses include:

Fraud in the execution You will recall that fraud in the execution (also called fraud in the factum) usually involves the surreptitious substitution of one document for another. Thus, where the maker or drawer is tricked into signing an instrument without realizing that it is even a contract (e.g., signing an "autograph" that turns out to be a check), the maker or drawer will have a real defense to payment good against even a holder in due course.

Forgery Forgery (i.e., unauthorized signature) is also a real defense with one exception. Generally speaking, a forgery creates no legal obligation on the part of the party whose signature has been forged. That party—whether the maker, drawer, drawee, or endorser—will not have to pay even where the instrument has been transferred to a holder in due course. The exception arises where the party has negligently and substantially contributed to the forgery. Section 3–406 of the Code states that "any person who by his negligence substantially contributes to * * * the making of an unauthorized signature is precluded from asserting the * * * lack of authority against a holder in due course or against a drawee or other payor who pays the instrument in good faith and in accordance with the reasonable commercial standards of the drawee's or payor's business."

In contrast, forgery always creates obligation on the part of the wrongdoer who has forged the signature. Section 3–404 of the Code provides: "[Whereas] any unauthorized signature is wholly inoperative as that of the person whose name is signed unless he * * * is precluded from denying it * * * it operates as the signature of the unauthorized signer in favor of any person who in good faith pays the instrument or takes it for value." Thus, as to the parties who in good faith pay the instrument or take it for value, the forger is fully liable on the instrument in the capacity in which he or she signed (e.g., if he or she forged the maker's signature, he or she will be primarily liable; if he or she forged an endorsement, he or she will be liable as an endorser). Of course, the forger's liability will be of little practical value if the forger cannot be found or if he or she has insufficient funds to pay the instrument.

Infancy Infancy, too, is a real defense good as against even a holder in due course. You will recall from Chapter 8 that a minor's contracts are generally voidable. To the same extent that a minor may rescind his or her agreements, he or she may rescind negotiable instruments arising out of the agreements. For example, if, under local law, a minor has the right to rescind a contract for purchase of a stereo, he or she also has the right to refuse to pay a negotiable note signed to pay for the stereo. This is so even where the note has been transferred to a holder in due course. And where local law provides that a minor is liable for the fair value of necessaries, the minor cannot refuse to honor a note signed to pay for the necessaries. Infancy or minority is thus a defense to payment of an instrument only where it would justify the minor in rescinding the underlying transaction.

Mixed Defenses

As stated previously, some defenses are sometimes personal and sometimes real depending on the circumstances involved. They are called *mixed defenses* and include duress, incapacity (other than infancy), illegality, and discharge of contract duties. As you will recall from Chapter 8, the first three of these defenses will make a contract either void or voidable. If the duress, incapacity (other than infancy), or illegality is such as to make the contract void, the defense is a real defense good as against even a holder in due course. If the defense merely makes the contract voidable, the defense is personal and is cut off by a holder in due course.

Discharge of an instrument is frequently encountered as a defense. One type of discharge—discharge in bankruptcy—is a real defense and is good against everyone, including a holder in due course. (You will learn in Chapter 11 that most of a bankrupt individual's debts are discharged in a bankruptcy proceeding, including debts represented by negotiable instruments.)

Discharge by payment of the negotiable instrument is a personal defense *unless* the payment is noted on the instrument (or unless the party who pays takes up the instrument and destroys it, in which case the problem of subsequent transfer is altogether eliminated). Of course, where the payment or other discharge of parties is apparent on the instrument itself, any holder who takes the instrument takes "with notice" of the discharge and so cannot qualify as a holder in due course with respect to the discharged party or parties.

WHAT ARE THE RESPONSIBILITIES OF ENDORSERS?

Secondary liability usually goes to any *endorser* of a negotiable instrument. By endorsing (signing) the instrument, the endorser assumes contractual liability thereon. This is so even where the endorsement is not required to negotiate the instrument (e.g., where the party chooses to endorse bearer paper in blank or specially).

With secondary liability the endorser is saying: "I will pay but only if the primary party does not pay." The endorser's contract is to pay according to the tenor of the instrument *at the time of the endorsement.* Thus, if the instrument is altered prior to the endorsement, the endorser must pay according to the altered terms. If the instrument is altered after the endorsement, the endorser is not liable, and, in fact, may be discharged if the alteration changes the terms of his or her contract. The endorser's contract runs not only to the immediate endorsee (the party to whom he or she endorses the paper) but also to any subsequent holder who takes the instrument (and who may have to pay upon the instrument's dishonor).

However, there are three conditions precedent to the endorser's liability:

1. The holder of the instrument must present it to the primary party for acceptance or payment *within a reasonable time* after the endorsement;
2. The primary party must dishonor the instrument; and
3. The holder must protest (a "protest" is a formal notice of dishonor required *only* when dealing with *drafts* [and including checks] drawn or payable in a *foreign country*—it is frequently referred to as a "notice of dishonor with trimmings" because it is a formal certificate of notice usually notarized by a notary public or made under the hand and seal of a United States consul or vice consul) or notify the endorser of the dishonor *within a reasonable time* after the dishonor.

Section 3–414 of the Uniform Commercial Code defines the contract of an endorser as follows:

> (1) Unless the indorsement otherwise specifies (as by such words as "without recourse") every indorser engages that upon dishonor and any necessary notice of dishonor and protest he will pay the instrument according to its tenor at the time of the indorsement to the holder or to any subsequent indorser who takes it up, even though the indorser who takes it up was not obligated to do so.
> (2) Unless they otherwise agree indorsers are liable to one another in the order in which they indorse, which is presumed to be the order in which their signatures appear on the instrument.

A holder's failure to present an instrument *within a reasonable time* after its endorsement or to notify the endorser of the instrument's dishonor *within a reasonable time* after dishonor will serve to completely discharge the endorser. A "reasonable time" is measured from the time each endorser signs the instrument. A presentment for payment may be prompt enough to bind the last endorser but too slow to bind a prior endorser who is discharged as a result.

Quite often, there are several endorsements on an instrument. Since, upon dishonor and notice the holder may proceed against any one of the endorsers without proceeding against the others, it becomes important to know whether an endorser who is required to pay has any rights against the other endorsers. The rule is that the endorsers are liable to each other in the order in which their signatures appear on the instrument; each endorser may hold his or her prior endorser, back to the first endorser (barring untimely presentment or notice by the holder which has discharged some or all of the endorsers). Thus, in most cases, the first endorser is ultimately required to pay the instrument, although he or she, in turn, may collect from the drawer (on a draft) if the drawer is financially solvent and has no defense to payment good as against the endorser.

A drawer of a draft is also secondarily liable with similar conditions precedent to liability. Thus, if a drawee dishonors a draft and the three conditions precedent are met, the drawer must pay the draft upon its dishonor by the drawee.

Time of presentment is governed by Section 3–503 of the Code. With regard to the liability of a drawer, a check is presented within a "reasonable time" if presented within thirty days after date of issue of the check. With regard to the liability of an endorser, a "reasonable time" for presentment is "within 7 days" of the endorsement. If the liability of secondary parties is not to be impaired, notice of dishonor of an instrument must be given by a bank by midnight of the next banking day following dishonor and by any other person by midnight of the third business day following dishonor.

WHAT IS A QUALIFIED ENDORSEMENT?

An endorser may avoid secondary liability by endorsing without recourse. Such an endorsement is called a *qualified endorsement* because the endorser who signs "without recourse" disclaims liability on the endorsement contract. The endorser, in effect, states, "I do not agree to pay the instrument upon dishonor by the primary party even if timely presentment is made and notice of dishonor given." Words other than "without recourse" may be used to accomplish a qualified endorsement if the words clearly indicate an intent to disclaim the endorsement contract. However, an endorser seldom uses other words because if there is any question as to the endorser's intent, the words will be considered a regular and not a qualified endorsement. The only safe way to make a qualified endorsement is to endorse "without recourse."

A drawer may also avoid secondary liability by drawing "without recourse."

In direct contrast to a qualified endorsement is an endorsement with words of guaranty added. Here, the endorser does more than engage to pay the instrument upon its dishonor (assuming all conditions precedent have been met)—he or she guarantees payment. The practical effect of the guaranty depends on the words used by the endorser. If the endorser adds words like "payment guaranteed" to his or her endorsement, the endorser's liability is like that of a co-maker: the endorser promises that if the instrument is not paid when due, he or she will immediately pay it without any conditions precedent. Unlike the usual unqualified endorser, this endorser has no right to insist upon presentment to the maker or drawee or notice of dishonor.

An endorser who adds words like "collection guaranteed," on the other hand, merely guarantees the solvency of the principal obligor. Like the endorser who guarantees *payment,* this endorser waives the conditions precedent of presentment and notice of dishonor. However, the endorser creates several new conditions to liability. The endorser, in effect, states, "I will pay the instrument if it is not paid when due *provided that* (1) the holder reduces his or her claim against the maker or acceptor to judgment, and the judgment is returned unsatisfied; or (2) the maker or acceptor has become insolvent; or (3) it is otherwise apparent that it is useless to proceed against the maker or acceptor."

WHAT ARE THE TRANSFER WARRANTIES?

It is possible to have a situation where the primary party and all secondary parties (endorsers) are financially unable to pay, have a good defense to payment, or are discharged from liability or where the endorsers have endorsed without recourse so as to avoid secondary liability. Can the holder collect payment from anyone in this situation? On what basis?

The holder may be able to collect payment from a party on the basis of breach of *implied warranty of transfer.* Apart from an original party (i.e., a maker, drawer, or drawee), any party who transfers an instrument for value, whether through an assignment or a negotiation, is held to make certain implied warranties. If the party endorses the instrument prior to transfer, the warranties run to all subsequent good faith holders of the instrument. If the party does not endorse prior to transfer (e.g., where the party transfers bearer paper by delivery alone), the warranties run only to the party's immediate transferee. The idea is that a negotiable instrument is "property," and a purchaser of "property" is entitled to certain basic protections (i.e., the purchaser should have legal recourse in the event the property turns out to be something other than what it appears to be).

Warranty liability exists independently of secondary liability (irrespective of endorsement). A party who endorses an instrument prior to transferring it may be liable both on his or her endorsement (assuming he or she is financially solvent and has no defense to payment) and on the basis of breach of implied warranty. However, as to the party's warranty liability, there are no conditions precedent of presentment, dishonor, protest, or notice of dishonor; the party is liable immediately upon breach of any one of the five warranties set forth in Section 3–417 of the Uniform Commercial Code.

Warranty of Title

By transferring an instrument, a party impliedly warrants that he or she has good title (or is authorized to obtain payment or acceptance on behalf of one who has good title) and that the transfer is otherwise rightful. The warranty of title is designed to protect the transferee who ultimately discovers that his or her transferor did not own the instrument. This may occur, for example, where an instrument is stolen and transferred with or without a forged endorsement. In the case of order paper, suppose that Larry Taylor makes out a negotiable promissory note payable "to the order of George Johnson." After Larry delivers the note to George, Charlie Sneakthief steals the instrument, forges George's blank endorsement, and sells the note to Sally Streeter. Sally, in turn, transfers the "bearer paper" by delivery alone to Mark Hopkins who takes the note for value and in good faith. Mark presents the note to Larry Taylor for payment; however, Larry has been informed of the theft by George Johnson and refuses to pay. Larry's personal defense of nondelivery is good against Mark who does not qualify as a holder in due course (endorsement by George is required to negotiate the note so as to make someone a holder and, therefore, a holder in due course). Looking to secondary parties, can Mark collect from anyone on the basis of endorsement? You know that he cannot collect from George Johnson (forgery is a real defense), and he cannot collect from Sally Streeter who did not endorse. While he could collect from Charlie Sneakthief who is liable in the capacity in which he signed, Charlie has left town and has little or no money to boot. However, Mark can hold Sally Streeter liable for breach of implied warranty of title; by transferring the note without an endorsement, Sally impliedly warranted good title to Mark, her immediate transferee. Of course, Charlie Sneakthief is also liable for breach of implied warranty of title both as to Sally (his immediate transferee) and as to Mark (Charlie's forged endorsement is effective to make the warranty run to subsequent good faith holders). But again, Charlie has left town, so the remedies are of little value. Thus, it is Sally Streeter who must bear the loss here, and that is only fair since it was Sally who first dealt with forger Charlie Sneakthief.

Would the result differ if the instrument involved were bearer paper? Yes—only Charlie Sneakthief would be liable for breach of implied warranty of title and only as to his immediate transferee. Remember, a holder in due course who receives bearer paper from a thief obtains good title and can pass good title to another. Thus, Sally Streeter has good title at the time of her transfer to Mark Hopkins and so has not breached the warranty of title.

Warranty That All Signatures Are Genuine or Authorized

One who transfers an instrument for value also warrants that all signatures on the instrument are genuine or authorized. Where it is the signature of a payee or endorsee that is forged, the transferor breaches both the warranty of title and the warranty of genuine signatures (e.g., Sally Streeter breaches both warranties when she sells the note containing George Johnson's forged endorsement to Mark Hopkins).

Warranty against Material Alteration

A party who purchases a negotiable instrument assumes that he or she will be able to enforce the instrument according to its tenor at the time of the purchase. Yet, if the instrument has been materially altered, the liability of previous signers may be limited to the tenor of the instrument at the time of their signature, or their liability may be altogether discharged. To protect the transferee in this situation, the Uniform Commercial Code provides that a party who transfers an instrument for value warrants that the instrument has not been materially altered. Thus, even if the transferor has a good defense to secondary liability, he or she may still be liable on the basis of warranty.

Warranty against Defenses

This is the only transfer warranty that differs in the case of a qualified endorsement. Any transferor for value other than a qualified endorser (i.e., one who endorses "without recourse") warrants absolutely that no defenses of any party are good against him or her. A qualified endorser warrants merely that *he or she has no actual knowledge of any defense good as against him or her.* To protect the transferee, qualified endorsers are sometimes asked to make express warranties against defenses.

Warranty against Knowledge of Insolvency Proceedings

Finally, a transferor for value warrants that he or she has no knowledge of any insolvency proceeding (e.g., bankruptcy) instituted with respect to the maker or acceptor (or drawer of an unaccepted instrument). This warranty goes no further than what it says. The transferor does not warrant that the maker, acceptor, or drawer is a good credit risk or that he or she is in good shape financially—the transferor merely states, "I have no knowledge of any formal insolvency proceeding instituted with respect to the party."

Thus, you have the basic procedure for collecting the sum certain on a negotiable instrument. Start by going against the primary party, and if he or she pays the instrument, that is the end of it. If the primary party is financially unable to pay or sets up a good defense to payment (remember, a holder in due course cuts off personal defenses), proceed against any secondarily liable parties. Of course, the secondary parties may also be financially unable to pay or may have good defenses to payment or may have avoided secondary liability by endorsing or drawing without recourse. In this case, look to see whether any transferor for value of the instrument is liable on the basis of breach of warranty (whether title, signatures, alterations, defenses, or insolvency). If the transferor for value has endorsed the instrument, the warranties will run to all subsequent good faith holders of the instrument; if the transferor has not endorsed, the warranties will run only to his or her immediate transferee.

WHAT IS AN ACCOMMODATION PARTY?

Usually, a party who signs a negotiable instrument does so because of personal involvement in the underlying transaction (e.g., the party is buying or selling something). An *accommodation* party, on the other hand, signs only to support some other party to the instrument. For example, a merchant may extend credit to a party who is a bad credit risk only if the party produces an accommodation party with good credit to sign with him or her—usually, as an endorser (secondary party) or co-maker (primary party). The accommodation party is liable in whatever capacity he or she signs. And it makes no difference whether the accommodation party signs before or after the instrument is transferred or whether all the parties are aware that an accommodation was intended.

Generally speaking, lack of consideration is no defense to the accommodation party's liability. The Uniform Commercial Code provides that consideration need not move to the accommodation party to make him or her bound on the instrument (usually, consideration moves to the accommodated party, i.e., the party who needs the support). This is so even where the accommodation party signs the instrument *after* it has been taken by the creditor in payment for the goods or services; so long as the creditor took the instrument for value before it was due, the accommodation party will become bound despite the lack of new or additional consideration.

Finally, the accommodation party is always a *surety* (see Chapter 11). Thus, he or she is not liable to the accommodated party, and, if he or she is required to pay the instrument, he or she will have a right to reimbursement from the accommodated party.

WHAT IS A RESTRICTIVE ENDORSEMENT?

To this point, we have dealt with three kinds of endorsements—***blank***, *special*, and *qualified*, (versus unqualified) endorsements. You will recall that a blank endorsement (the endorser's signature alone) converts order paper into bearer paper, and a special endorsement (endorsement to a named payee) converts bearer paper into order paper. A qualified endorsement (one "without recourse") eliminates the endorser's secondary liability and somewhat limits his or her warranty liability. Now we move to yet another kind of endorsement—a *restrictive* (versus nonrestrictive) endorsement. Section 3–205 of the UCC defines "restrictive endorsement" as follows:

> An indorsement is restrictive which either (a) is conditional; or (b) purports to prohibit further transfer of the instrument; or (c) includes the words "for collection," "for deposit," "pay any bank," or like terms signifying a purpose of deposit or collection; or (d) otherwise states that it is for the benefit or use of the indorser or of another person.
>
> No restrictive indorsement prevents further transfer or negotiation of the instrument.
>
> * * * [A]ny transferee under an indorsement which is conditional or includes the words "for collection," "for deposit," "pay any bank," or like terms * * * must pay or apply any value given by him for or on the security of the instrument consistently with the indorsement and to the extent that he does so he becomes a holder for value. In addition such transferee is a holder in due course if he otherwise complies with the requirements * * * on what constitutes a holder in due course.

WHAT IS THE BASIS OF THE LEGAL RELATIONSHIP BETWEEN A BANK AND ITS CUSTOMERS?

A party who opens a checking account with a bank enters into a contract with the bank wherein it is agreed that the bank will provide collection and payment services for the party in return for a service charge and use of the depositor's money. The contractual relationship is one of debtor-creditor: the bank becomes a debtor of the depositor by virtue of receiving the deposited funds; the depositor becomes a creditor of the bank by reason of depositing the funds. Both bank and depositor benefit substantially from the relationship. The bank charges for its services and acquires the use of the depositor's money. The depositor receives the benefit of the two most important bank functions—collection and payment. The bank's duty is to collect checks presented by the depositor for deposit and to pay from the depositor's account only according to the order of the depositor.

Again, the bank's contractual duty is to pay *only* according to the customer's order. Obviously, materially altered items or items containing forgeries are not *according to the customer's order* and are not "properly payable" (an exception, to be explained shortly, arises where the drawer has negligently and substantially contributed to the forgery or alteration). Thus, if a drawee bank makes final payment of a materially altered check (say, one on which the sum certain has been raised from $100 to $1,000), the bank cannot charge the altered amount to the drawer's account; the bank can charge against the account only to the extent of the check's original tenor ($100). Nor can the drawee bank charge a paid check bearing a forged endorsement, with two exceptions. The exceptions are known as the fictitious payee and imposter problems.

Fictitious Payees

As an exception to the general rule, the payor bank may charge against the drawer's account an instrument bearing a forged endorsement of a *fictitious payee.* The fictitious payee situation arises where a trusted employee of the drawer secures the drawer's signature on a check made out to the order of a nonexistent or actual person not intended by the employee to have any interest in the check proceeds. For example, the employee may be in charge of making up the monthly payroll. He or she simply adds to the payroll the name of a fictitious payee who is really not an employee at all. The drawer, who signs perhaps 100 to 200 employee paychecks a month, signs the check made payable to the fictitious payee without even realizing it. The "trusted" employee then forges the fictitious payee's endorsement, and the bank pays the check. Section 3–405 of the Uniform Commercial Code provides that the bank may charge the check against the employer-drawer's account. The theory is that the employer-drawer should bear the loss resulting from his or her employment of a person who cheats and pads the payroll. The employer-drawer's only recourse is against the employee who cheated him or her.

Imposters

Similarly, it is the drawer who must bear the loss where he or she is fooled into issuing a check to an imposter who pretends to be the named or intended payee. If the imposter forges the payee's endorsement and cashes the check, the check will be chargeable against the drawer's account.

Apart from the fictitious payee and imposter exceptions, a forged or altered instrument may be charged to a drawer's account only where the drawer has negligently and substantially contributed to the forgery or alteration. Thus, if a drawer negligently leaves large gaps in a check with the result that the instrument is easily altered, the altered check will be chargeable against the drawer's account. However, the negligence must substantially contribute to the alteration. If the payee chemically erases all the writing and writes an entirely new check, the drawer's negligence in leaving gaps is immaterial, and the drawer is not liable on the instrument as altered. Other examples of negligence include failing to look after a signature stamp or other automatic signature device with the result that someone uses the device to "manufacture" checks and carelessly mailing a check to someone other than the payee but with the same name as the payee who endorses the check and cashes it.

Also banks furnish checking account customers with periodic statements of account transactions at which time canceled checks are also returned. Section 4–406 of the Code imposes certain duties upon bank customers upon their receipt of the bank statements and canceled checks. The Section is designed to protect banks against losses that could be avoided by prompt customer inspection for forgeries and alterations. The customer-drawer must do two things:

1. He or she must promptly examine the statement and canceled checks; and
2. He or she must promptly notify the bank of any apparent forgery or alteration.

If the customer-drawer fails to exercise the required care, the forged or altered instrument may be charged to his or her account. And so may any other item subsequently forged or altered by the same wrongdoer and paid by the bank within fourteen days of the customer's receipt of the bank statement. These rules are only fair, as the customer's failure to act promptly deprives the bank of reasonable opportunity to catch the wrongdoer and to be on the alert for additional forgeries or alterations by the same party.

However, Section 4–406(1)–(2) is qualified in that the bank cannot hold the customer liable for negligence where the bank itself has failed to exercise ordinary care in paying the check. Section 4–406(3) states that "the preclusion under subsection (2) does not apply if the customer establishes lack of ordinary care on the part of the bank paying the item."

And, finally, Section 4–406(4) provides: "Without regard to care or lack of care of either the customer or the bank a customer who does not within one year from the time the statement and items are made available to the customer discover and report his unauthorized signature or any alteration on the face or back of the item or does not within 3 years from that time discover and report any unauthorized indorsement is precluded from asserting against the bank such unauthorized signature or indorsement or such alteration." In other words, even where the customer is entirely blameless and the bank completely negligent, the customer must assert an unauthorized drawer's signature or alteration within one year of receipt of the statement containing the forgery or alteration or forever lose his or her right to do so. With regard to forged endorsement, the customer-drawer has up to three years to assert the defense. The time limit is shorter in the first instance because the drawer has little excuse for not realizing that his or her own signature has been forged or his or her own instrument altered. It is more reasonable that the drawer should be unaware of a forged endorsement.

CAN A CUSTOMER–DRAWER "STOP PAYMENT" OF A CHECK?

Occasionally, a bank customer writes a check, then discovers that he or she has been defrauded by the payee or that the check has been lost or stolen. The customer, in this case, will want to order the bank to "stop payment" of the check. The customer-drawer (or his or her personal representative in the case of a deceased customer-drawer) is the only person who can order payment stopped. The payee cannot do so. The customer-drawer must give the order at such time as to afford the bank reasonable opportunity (usually, two hours at maximum) to act before "final payment" of the item is made. Note that under Section 4–403 of the UCC, an oral stop payment order is binding for only fourteen days. Usually, the customer-drawer will call the bank and give the stop payment order orally: there is a need for haste so as to prevent the check from being cashed. But unless the customer-drawer follows up with a written stop payment order, the order will cease to be binding after fourteen days. A written order, on the other hand, is binding for six months and may be renewed for additional periods of time.

Of course, stopping payment of an item affects only the relationship between the drawer and the bank (it keeps the bank from charging the check against the drawer's account). It does not affect the underlying transaction which gave rise to the check. Thus, if the payee is entitled to payment because of underlying contract or other rights, the payee can successfully sue upon dishonor of the instrument and hold the drawer for the amount owing. And if the check is dishonored while in the hands of a holder in due course, the drawer will have to pay the HDC unless the drawer has a real as opposed to a personal defense to payment.

It must be emphasized that a bank is obligated to follow a timely given stop payment order. If it disregards the order and pays the check, the bank will be liable to the customer-drawer for any loss he or she suffers as a result. The bank, in turn, will be subrogated to the customer-drawer's rights against the payee or other party.

The bank itself will never become liable to the payee by reason of following the stop payment order. If there is a dispute regarding the underlying transaction, it must be settled between the customer and the payee without involvement by the bank.

WHAT IS THE DIFFERENCE BETWEEN A CERTIFIED CHECK AND A CASHIER'S CHECK?

After writing a check but before issuing it, the drawer may have his or her bank *certify* the instrument. Similarly, the payee or subsequent holder of a check may present the instrument to the drawee bank, not for payment but for *certification*. Certification is the drawee bank's signed engagement to honor the check when it is presented for payment; certification constitutes formal acceptance by the bank, making the bank primarily liable on the instrument (ordinarily, checks are not accepted but are paid on demand as are other demand drafts). At the very moment of certification, the bank charges the amount of the check against the drawer's account. The result—the bank has its money, and the holder of the check is secure in the knowledge that the bank's assets stand behind the instrument.

Thus, it is often prudent to require payment by certified check, and, in fact, many contracts do require payment by either certified check or *cashier's check.* A cashier's check is a check issued by the bank itself; unlike a certified check, it is not drawn on a customer's account. Anyone can go into a bank and purchase a cashier's check—the cost is the amount of money for which the check is to be drawn plus an amount charged by the bank for the service of providing the check.

Agency

WHAT IS AN AGENT?

An *agent* is a person who is authorized to make contracts on behalf of another called a *principal.* A properly authorized agent enters into contracts on behalf of the principal, and the principal is bound just as though he or she had made the contracts personally.

Ordinarily, anything a person can do legally himself or herself, he or she can also do through an agent (however, the subject of the agency must not be illegal or contrary to public policy). In the business world, the concept of agency is essential; rather than enter into each and every contract personally, a businessperson can authorize others to contract for him or her. Imagine the difficulties, for example, if the owner of a large department store or supermarket had to wait personally on each and every customer. The business would have little chance to survive, much less expand. Under the concept of agency, the store owner can authorize salesclerks to sell goods to customers (on the owner's behalf) and can authorize a general business manager to purchase inventory from wholesalers (again on the owner's behalf). With agency, it makes no difference what kind of contract is involved—it can be a sale of goods, a purchase of land, an agreement to perform services, etc.

With regard to negotiable instruments, Section 3–403 of the UCC provides that an agent may sign for the maker or drawer. However, Section 3–403 must be read in conjunction with Section 3–401 which states that "no person is liable on an instrument unless his signature appears thereon." Thus, if an agent signs his or her own name on a negotiable instrument without naming the principal (the maker or drawer the agent represents), the principal will not be liable on the instrument.

If the agent signs only the principal's name on the negotiable instrument, the principal alone is bound. If the agent signs only his or her own name without more, the agent alone is liable, and parol evidence is not admissible to identify the principal. Of course, if the agent is ultimately required to pay the instrument, he or she can sue the principal for reimbursement (including reasonable expenses).

In all other cases where the agent signs his or her own name on the negotiable instrument, the agent will be personally liable unless he or she both (1) identifies the principal on the instrument, and (2) indicates on the instrument that he or she is signing in a representative capacity. If the agent does both things, the principal again is solely liable. For example, suppose that Larry Taylor authorizes Sally Streeter to purchase George Johnson's boat for $10,300. Larry instructs Sally to put $2,000 down on the boat and sign a promissory note for the balance. If Sally signs the note—"Sally Streeter, agent for Larry Taylor"—only Larry Taylor will be bound on the instrument. If Sally signs—"Sally Streeter, Agent"—Sally will be personally liable on the instrument. However, because Sally has indicated the fact of agency without naming the principal, the instrument contains a patent ambiguity, and parol evidence is admissible to identify the principal in suits between the original parties (and/or their assignees). Once the principal is identified, he or she alone will be liable on the instrument to the original payee or his or her assignee. But if the party suing on the instrument is not an assignee, but a holder in due course, parol evidence is not admissible, and the holder in due course can collect on the instrument from the agent. The HDC cannot collect from the principal as his or ner name does not appear on the instrument as required by Section 3–401(1) of the UCC. Thus, if after selling the boat to Sally Streeter, George Johnson discounts the promissory note (signed by "Sally Streeter, Agent") to a holder in due course, the HDC will be able to collect on the note from Sally. Sally will not be allowed to introduce oral or written evidence showing that Larry Taylor is her principal and the holder in due course will not be able to proceed against Larry on the instrument. (If the HDC can't collect from Sally it may be possible to proceed as an assignee against Larry on the basis that George Johnson has assigned his rights in the underlying transaction regarding the boat.)

The use of an agent always involves risks for the principal. So long as an agent acts within the scope of his or her authority, the principal will be "stuck" (i.e., bound) by the agent's contracts even if the principal does not like the contracts. The "key" to understanding the concept of agency is one word—*authority.* An agent exists only because of the *authority* given to him or her by the principal. As used in the law of agency, the term authority has a very special meaning.

WHAT IS MEANT BY THE TERM "AUTHORITY"?

For an agent to bind a principal in contract, the agent must have the "authority" to do so. While authority is often created by contract, a contract is not required to establish an agency relationship. Authority rests, not on contract, but on the *consent* of the principal. It is *consent* that is the basis of authority. Say you tell your fifteen-year-old daughter that she can use your credit card to do some shopping at the local department store. Your daughter clearly has no contract right to use the card; neither of you intend to create a contract, and there is no mutual assent, consideration, or capacity (your daughter being only fifteen). Yet your daughter has your *consent* to use your card, and, as your agent, she can bind you to pay for her charges. The same would be true if you told her to fill up your car with gas and charge it to your account at the local service station. Again, there would be no "breach of contract" if your daughter did not purchase the gas; at the same time, she has your *consent* (i.e., your authority) to purchase it and, as your agent, can bind you to pay for it.

And it makes no difference that your daughter is a minor or otherwise lacks capacity to contract. Contractual capacity on the part of the agent is not required—the agent binds the principal in contract, not himself or herself. The general rule is that anyone can be an agent who is capable of performing the functions involved. (Thus it is that many sixteen and seventeen-year-olds work in gas stations selling gas, and in fast food restaurants selling hamburgers.) Of course, an agent cannot be so bereft of mind that he or she cannot perform the work of the agency.

As for the principal's capacity, anyone can be a principal who is not fully and completely incapacitated. Where the principal is partially incapacitated, his or her agent's contracts will be void or voidable according to the ordinary rules of contract law. For example, if a minor contracts through an agent, he or she can disaffirm the contracts just as he or she had made them personally (see Chapter 8).

Real Authority and Apparent Authority

The two general classifications of authority are *real authority* and *apparent authority.* So long as the agent had either kind of authority for entering into the contract, the principal will be "stuck"—period. Real authority and apparent authority may be defined as follows:

Real authority Real authority is authority manifested by the principal to the agent either expressly or by implication. Two kinds of real authority are express and incidental. A principal confers express authority upon an agent when he or she explicitly authorizes the agent, either orally or in writing, to contract on his or her behalf. However, it is not necessary for a principal to spell out every detail of an agent's authority. By virtue of giving an agent express authority to contract, a principal also consents to any authority that is normally incidental to carrying out the contracting. Real authority may also be implied by the conduct of the principal.

Apparent authority Though a person has no real authority (express, incidental, or implied) to act as another's agent, he or she may nevertheless have apparent authority to do so. Apparent authority is authority that results from an appearance of authority *created by the principal;* it is authority that is normal to the appearance created.

Apparent authority is based on the objective theory of contracts as explained in Chapter 8; the secret or hidden intentions of a party (here, the principal) will not control over what is objectively manifested to others (here, the third parties who deal with the agent). Regardless of a principal's private intentions, if he or she creates in a party an appearance of authority, the principal will be bound by the acts of the party that are normal to that appearance. The test of apparent authority is thus twofold:

- First, what appearance did the principal create?
- Second, was the agent's effort to bind the principal normal to that appearance?

It should be emphasized that the appearance of authority *must be created by the principal*—either giving the agent some secretly limited express authority or by intentionally or negligently placing the unauthorized person in an apparent position of authority. It follows that a person who fraudulently "manufactures" evidence to prove that he or she represents another has no authority (either real or apparent) and no ability to bind the principal in contract. It would not make sense to hold otherwise: the purported principal (who may not even know the purported agent) has neither authorized the party to act nor in any way contributed to creating the appearance of authority. A third party who deals with such an "agent" will have no legal recourse against the "principal" (it is a risk we all face—the risk of being fooled by others).

One problem in the area of apparent authority is that it is frequently difficult to determine just what is "normal" to a particular appearance or occupation. Where the matter is disputed in court, expert witnesses in similar positions of authority may be called to testify. The courts have established what authority is "normal to the appearance" of the following occupations and professions:

A business manager A business manager has authority to do what is normally done in similar businesses in carrying out the day-to-day business operation. This includes authority to buy and sell (e.g., inventory), to purchase equipment and supplies for normal business operations, to employ counsel, and to hire and fire daily employees. It does not include authority to mortgage business property, to make any negotiable paper on behalf of the company (e.g., to borrow money from a bank), or to expand or terminate the business or alter it any way.

A real estate dealer or broker A prospective buyer or seller of land usually employs a real estate dealer or broker to find a willing seller or buyer for the property. Generally speaking, a real estate dealer or broker is not an agent at all but is an independent contractor who is paid a commission for doing a job. It follows that the dealer or broker has no apparent authority to bind his or her employer in any way; he or she cannot bind the employer to a contract of sale or purchase, nor can he or she accept payment of all or part of the purchase price of the property on behalf of the employer. The dealer's or broker's only job is to find a willing buyer or seller—period. Upon successful completion of the job, he or she is entitled to his or her commission regardless of whether a contract of sale or purchase is ultimately concluded.

A loan agent With one exception, an agent who is authorized to negotiate a loan of money to a third party has no apparent authority to collect repayment of either the loan principal or interest (even if the agent has real authority to collect interest, he or she has no apparent authority to collect principal). The exception arises where the agent retains possession of the promissory note evidencing the loan. The debtor, here, is protected in making repayment to the agent. Authority (real or apparent) to accept repayment means authority to accept money only—not goods, land, checks, promissory notes, etc. Of course, an agent may always have real authority to accept other than money; an agent who is authorized to accept a check in repayment has no apparent authority to endorse the check and present it for payment.

A traveling salesperson of goods A salesperson who travels from "door to door" in an effort to sell his or her company's products normally does not carry the goods with him or her but simply takes orders for the goods. The goods themselves are delivered later, independent of the salesperson's selling activity. A traveling salesperson who carries no goods has no apparent authority to accept the purchase price of the goods. Say that a saleswoman visits your home and takes your order for a twelve-piece cutlery set. The saleswoman has no apparent authority to receive the purchase price. If you pay her and she absconds with the money, you will have to pay a second time to the principal. (The fact that the saleswoman had samples with her is immaterial—a traveling salesperson has no apparent authority to sell a principal's samples).

On the other hand, a traveling salesperson who carries goods (not just samples) with him or her and delivers them over to the buyer at the time of purchase has apparent authority to accept the purchase price. Paying the salesperson, in this case, is the same as paying the principal. If the salesperson absconds with the money, it is the principal who will suffer the loss. (Even here, however, the salesperson does not have apparent authority to accept payment for goods sold previously to the buyer on a credit basis—again, the buyer must make credit payments directly to the principal's bookkeeping department.)

Of course, it should be realized that a principal is always free to give an agent *more* authority than what is normal to the appearance of a particular occupation or profession. What a principal cannot do without running the risk of being held liable on the basis of apparent authority is to give the agent *less* authority than what is normal. A principal who gives less authority should make it very clear to third parties that the agent's authority has been restricted.

Marriage in and of itself does not establish any agency relationship. However, the long-term conduct of the spouses in mixing incomes and accounts and in paying each other's bills often results in one or both parties having real authority to contract for the other. In other words, a large amount of authority is usually created in a marriage after a time. A husband and wife may have joint bank accounts, joint charge accounts, jointly owned property, and so forth. The wife may charge her husband's account for luxury items as well as for household supplies, and the husband may pay the bills over a long period of time. If the wife is the income producer, she may pay her husband's bills over a long period of time. Through such conduct, real authority (for the most part implied) will result, and one or both parties will be an agent of the other.

WHAT IS THE DIFFERENCE BETWEEN A GENERAL AND A SPECIAL AGENT?

It is sometimes useful to classify an agent as either a *general agent* or a *special agent.* A general agent is one who is authorized to contract regarding more than a single transaction and/or for a continuing period of time. A special agent is one who is authorized to conduct but a single transaction not involving any continuity of service. For example, if you authorize an agent to sell your car, the party is a special agent—the sale is one transaction involving only a short period of service. On the other hand, if you employ an agent to manage your business, the party is a general agent: he or she will represent you in many transactions over a considerable period of time.

A general agent has much more by way of implied, incidental, and apparent authority than does a special agent. And, as will be explained later in the chapter, there are special requirements for terminating a general agent's (as opposed to a special agent's) authority.

WHAT ARE THE DUTIES OF AN AGENT TO A PRINCIPAL?

An agent is a *fiduciary* of his or her principal—i.e., an agent is in a position of trust and confidence with the principal. As a fiduciary, an agent owes a high duty of care and responsibility to the principal. The agent's fiduciary duties include the following.

The Agent's Fiduciary Duties

The duty of loyalty An agent has a duty to act with complete and utmost loyalty and fidelity regarding his or her responsibilities to the principal. The law very strictly enforces this duty; it will not allow the agent to have any conflict of interest with the principal. Thus, an agent may not represent one whose interests conflict with those of the principal (e.g., a party looking to contract with the principal). The law has long recognized that "no man can serve two masters." An agent cannot properly (and loyally) represent the interests of his or her principal if, at the same time and with regard to the same transaction, the agent is trying to represent another's interests. An exception is made where both principals, being fully informed of the agent's dual representation, consent that he or she act for both of them.

The duty of loyalty also prohibits an agent from secretly acting for himself or herself in the transaction (called "self-dealing"). For example, an agent who is authorized to sell a car for his or her principal cannot sell the car to himself or herself; an agent authorized to buy a car cannot buy from himself or herself. Again, an exception is made where the principal is fully informed and consents to the transaction.

It is also "self-dealing" for an agent to use information acquired during the course of the agency to make a profit for himself or herself at the principal's expense—the agent may not compete with his or her principal.

Anytime an agent breaches the duty of loyalty by self-dealing, the principal has a right to avoid the transaction even though he or she has not been injured. Say that a principal employs an agent to sell her car for $5,000; the agent buys the car at the stated price for himself. Upon discovering that the agent is the buyer, the principal may avoid the contract of sale or let it stand at her option. The fact that the principal received $5,000 for the car—all that she asked for—is immaterial.

An agent who breaches his or her duty of loyalty also forfeits any fee, commission, or other compensation provided for by the terms of the agency.

The duty to obey the principal's instructions An agent also has a fiduciary duty to comply exactly with any instructions given by the principal; the agent will be liable to the principal for any loss resulting from a failure to follow instructions.

The duty to account An agent has a duty to account carefully (and timely) for any money, property, or profits in his or her possession belonging to the principal. To say that the accounting must be "timely" means that the agent must notify the principal of actual receipts and expenditures within a reasonable time after they occur. Formal books of account are not required as long as the agent can produce vouchers or other evidence showing the receipts and expenditures.

The agent also has a duty not to mix any of his or her own money or property with that of the principal. If the agent does commingle funds or property and the principal suffers a loss, the agent will be liable. And, of course, if the property is so intermixed that the separate monies or properties cannot be identified and separated, the agent will lose the whole of the property to the principal under the law of "confusion" (see Chapter 8 on "confusion").

Sometimes, a sales agent is a factor, i.e., a commercial agent employed by a principal to sell merchandise. The principal consigns the goods to the factor for sale; the factor is a bailee of the property (see Chapter 10). The factor is paid on a commission basis for any goods that are sold (the commission is called a "factorage"). Sometimes when selling consigned goods on credit, the factor, for an additional commission, will guarantee the solvency of the purchaser and his or her performance under the contract. The factor, in this case, is called a *del credere agent.* A *del credere agent* is liable to his or her principal only in cases where the purchaser defaults.

IS THE PRINCIPAL EVER LIABLE FOR TORTS COMMITTED BY HIS OR HER AGENT?

The general rule is that a principal is not liable for torts committed by his or her agent. However, there is one major exception. If an agent who is authorized to make true representations about the subject matter of the agency (in most cases, such authority is implied or apparent) makes a fraudulent misrepresentation, the principal will be liable for the tort of deceit. It is just as though the principal personally made the misrepresentation. (In other words, so long as an agent is authorized to make true representations, the principal is bound by the agent's unauthorized misrepresentations—though the principal had no knowledge of the fraud and certainly would not have approved of it!) The injured third party may avoid the contract because of the misrepresentation or hold the principal liable in damages.

IS AN AGENT OBLIGATED TO INFORM THIRD PARTIES THAT HE OR SHE REPRESENTS A PRINCIPAL?

In our discussions to this point, we have assumed a *disclosed agency* situation—i.e., the third party who deals with the agent has knowledge of the *existence* and of the *identity* of the principal. Where the agency is disclosed, the principal alone is liable on the contract; the agent can neither sue nor be sued on the agreement (unless the contract specifically provides to the contrary, as where the agent guarantees performance by the principal).

Sometimes, however, the third party has no knowledge of the existence of the agency (and ergo no knowledge of the principal's identity). The third party truly believes that the agent represents only himself or herself. In this situation, the agency is said to be *undisclosed.*

An undisclosed agency is perfectly legal and proper (assuming the subject matter of the agency is legal and not contrary to public policy). The law has long recognized that a party may have sound business reasons for dealing "behind the scenes" as an undisclosed principal. For example, say that a successful real estate developer wants to buy all the land in a particular downtown block; ultimately, the developer wants to construct a twenty-story office building upon the property. The land is currently rundown with old buildings, and its market value is quite low. By using an undisclosed agent, the developer will be able to purchase the land at its current market value. In contrast, if the agency is disclosed and the landowners learn that a successful developer wants to buy the property, the land values may soar, and the development may not occur.

The examples go on and on. A businessperson in a small town might want to expand his or her commercial interests or holdings without drawing attention to the fact. A public figure (e.g., a television personality) might want to invest in a business or property development without public knowledge of the investment. In each case, an undisclosed agency will make the transaction possible (and there is nothing "deceitful" or "evil" about it!).

Thus, the general rule is that an undisclosed agent has no duty to inform the third party about the agency. Once the undisclosed principal comes forward, the principal's rights under the contract are the same as those of a disclosed principal. In other words, the principal may sue in his or her own name and right, and the third party is obligated to treat him or her as the other contracting party in all respects. And this is not unfair to the third party. In most cases, it makes no difference that there is an undisclosed principal involved. If a third party contracts to sell a house or car to an agent representing an undisclosed principal, the third party loses nothing by accepting the purchase price from the undisclosed principal and transferring title to him or her (rather than to the agent). Thus, the general rule is that it is no defense to performance that the third party had no knowledge of the agency and would not have dealt with the undisclosed principal had he or she had knowledge. There are only two exceptions to this rule:

1. *Where the contract is personal in nature.* An undisclosed principal has no right or ability to enforce a contract that is personal in nature. For example, a contract may call for personal services. Say that undisclosed agent Wayne Newton contracts to perform musically for a third party. Undisclosed principal Dolly Parton cannot later demand to perform on the basis that she is the real party to the contract.

Or a contract may be based on personal credit. Say that a third party bank agrees to loan $50,000 to undisclosed agent Molly Millionaire. Undisclosed principal Bill Bankrupt has no right to demand a personal loan of $50,000 from the banker.

In each case, the third party, if he or she chooses, may enforce the contract against the agent.

2. *Where the undisclosed agent falsely asserts that he or she does not represent an undisclosed principal.* Any false assertion by the agent that the real principal has no interest in the transaction will serve as the basis for fraud in the inducement. Thus, if the third party asks the undisclosed agent whether he or she represents a principal and the agent says "no," the agent's misrepresentation will constitute fraud, permitting the third party to rescind the contract. (Of course, to constitute fraud, the misrepresentation must be material; if the third party really does not care whether an agency relationship exists, the misrepresentation is immaterial and nonfraudulent.)

In some cases, it is so apparent that the third party would not deal with a particular undisclosed principal that the agent has an affirmative duty to disclose the existence of the agency (even though not asked). The agent's failure to make disclosure constitutes fraud, against justifying rescission of the contract.

As to who is liable on the contract in the undisclosed agency situation, both the principal *and* the agent are liable. It follows that, in the event of breach of contract the third party may sue either the principal (once disclosed) *or* the agent *or* both. However, in most states, a judgment against one of the parties precludes a judgment against the other (i.e., the third party may complete the court process against only one of the parties). A few states provide that if a judgment against one is uncollectible (for example, because of the party's insolvency), the third party may obtain a judgment against the other.

In nearly all states, if the third party obtains a judgment against the agent *before* learning of the principal's existence, the judgment against the agent will not bar a second judgment against the principal. After the agency is disclosed, the third party may sue the principal and obtain a judgment against him or her as well. However, the third party may collect only one of the judgments: collection of one bars collection of the other. (Of course, the party who ultimately pays may be able to obtain reimbursement from the other depending on the circumstances of the case and the underlying agency contract, if any.)

Where the third party elects to sue the undisclosed principal, the principal may assert in defense any and all defenses that would be available to the agent, including fraud, duress, failure of consideration, objective impossibility, etc.

Additionally, remember, if there is a negotiable instrument involved (note, draft, or check) the undisclosed principal may assert as a defense to payment that his or her name does not appear on the instrument. Of course, if the third party is forced to collect payment from the agent, the agent may, in turn, seek reimbursement from the principal based, not on the negotiable instrument (the principal's name does not appear on the instrument), but on the underlying agreement between the parties.

One final defense available to the undisclosed principal is that, prior to the third party's knowledge of the principal's existence, the principal completely settled his or her accounts with the agent in reasonable reliance upon the third party's conduct. By way of example, suppose that Ray Chamberlain hires Tom Parker to go out and buy him a new delivery truck. Ray tells Tom not to disclose that he is acting for Ray because Ray believes that Tom will get a better deal if the seller does not know Ray is really the buyer. Tom goes out and talks to several dealers and finally enters into an agreement to purchase a truck for $12,500. Though payment is to be made in thirty days, the dealer mistakenly gives Tom a receipt showing that the truck has been paid for in full; the dealer delivers the truck to Tom. Tom, in turn, delivers the truck along with the receipt to Ray Chamberlain who pays Tom not only his commission for making the purchase but also the $12,500 it appears Tom has paid the dealer. Tom subsequently disappears with the money; the dealer learns of Ray's identity as the principal and brings an action against him for the purchase price. Ray has a good defense to payment in that he settled his accounts with Tom in reasonable reliance upon the dealer's conduct in providing Tom with a receipt marked "paid in full." The dealer's only remedy is to locate Tom and bring legal action against him.

DOES AN AGENT MAKE ANY WARRANTIES TO THIRD PARTIES?

One who purports to be an agent impliedly warrants to third parties that he or she has authority to represent the principal with regard to the particular transaction. If the agent's authority does not extend to the transaction or if he or she has no authority at all, the agent breaches the *implied warranty of authority* and is liable to the third party in damages.

An agent (real or purported) does not impliedly warrant, however, that the principal is honest or solvent or that he or she (the principal) will perform the contract. Nor does the agent impliedly warrant that the principal has full capacity (an exception arises where the agent knows for a fact that the principal is incapacitated and that the third party is ignorant of the fact). However, the agent does impliedly warrant that the principal is alive (not dead) and has, at least, partial capacity.

The third party's measure of damages for breach of warranty is the amount of money it will take to place the party in the position he or she would have been in had there been no breach. Thus, an agent who breaches the implied warranty of authority may escape paying damages because the purported principal is insolvent and incapable of performing; even if the "agent" had authority, the third party would be in no better position—remember, the agent does not warrant the principal's solvency.

WHAT IS RATIFICATION?

Sometimes, an agent exceeds his or her authority and attempts to bind a principal to a contract that is clearly unauthorized. Less often, a person who is not an agent at all purports to bind a "principal" to a contract. Though in each case the "agent" clearly has no authority to bind the "principal," the principal may still be bound on the basis of *ratification.* Ratification means acceptance, express or implied, of the contract. It comes into play *only where no authority of any kind—real or apparent—can be found with regard to the particular transaction* (where there is authority, the principal is bound because of the authority, and it is incorrect to talk of ratification).

Ratification is an "all or nothing" proposition. A purported principal is not free to ratify portions of a contract and reject the rest. He or she must accept the entire contract or none of it. If the purported principal ratifies, he or she becomes bound on the contract and acquires full rights to enforce the agreement against the third party. The effect of ratification is to treat the transaction as though the agent had authority from the outset (the purported agent is thus off the hook insofar as the implied warranty of authority is concerned).

Ratification is possible, however, only where the purported agent was, in fact, attempting to contract on the purported principal's behalf. If the agent was actually trying to contract on his or her own behalf, the principal cannot ratify (remember, offers are not assignable—one person may not accept another's offer by purporting to be a "principal"). For the same reason, an undisclosed principal can never ratify a contract. The law says it is simply going too far to state, first, that an undisclosed agency relationship exists; second, that the agent had no authority to bind the undisclosed principal with regard to the particular transactions; and, third, and on top of it all, that the undisclosed principal has ratified the unauthorized contract.

How a Contract is Ratified

Generally speaking, ratification occurs in one of two ways.

The principal wants to ratify the contract and does so either expressly or by implication The purported principal may like the terms of the unauthorized contract and want to ratify it. Upon learning of the contract, the purported principal is in the position of an offeree with the third party as an offeror. Like any other offeree, the purported principal has a reasonable time to either accept or reject the offer; however, up until the moment of acceptance, the third party may revoke the offer.

The principal does not want to ratify the contract but has done something resulting in ratification It happens far more often that the purported principal wants to escape liability on the contract but is estopped (prevented) from denying the agent's authority. Typically, this occurs where the principal has accepted some benefit from the contract without immediately informing the third party of the purported agent's lack of authority. Thus, where the purported principal accepts delivery of the subject matter of the contract and retains and uses it for a period of time, the principal will be held to have ratified the contract by his or her conduct.

An example is found in Wilkins v. Waldo Lumber Co., 130 Me. 5, 153 A. 191 (1931). In that case, a party purporting to be an agent for a lumber company (but clearly lacking any real or apparent authority from the company) entered into a contract to buy standing timber from a third party. On learning of the contract, the lumber company not only contracted to sell part of the timber to another party, but actually milled some of the timber into lumber and delivered it to the party. The lumber company then tried to get out of the original contract on the grounds that the purported agent had no authority to contract on the company's behalf. Understandably, the court held that the lumber company had, by its conduct, ratified the contract and was bound by its terms. However, it must be remembered that there can be no ratification unless the purported principal has full knowledge of all facts relevant to the contract.

HOW IS THE AGENCY RELATIONSHIP TERMINATED?

The agency relationship, which is created through the consent of the principal, may be terminated in one of two ways (1) by operation of law; or (2) by act of the parties.

Termination by Operation of Law

The principal-agent relationship automatically and instantly ends by operation of law when any of the following occurs:

The death of the principal or agent The agent's authority automatically terminates by operation of law upon the principal's death; the deceased principal's personal representative is responsible for carrying on the principal's business affairs after death. The agent's authority also ends instantly on the agent's death; it does not pass to the agent's heirs or personal representative.

The insanity of the principal or agent The agency relationship also terminates instantly by operation of law at any time either party—principal or agent—is formally adjudged insane by a court of law. If the principal becomes insane but has not been declared so by a court, the principal's contracts (including those entered into by the agent) are voidable, the principal lacking capacity to contract. And remember, the agent does not warrant the principal's capacity. The agent is liable for failing to inform the third party of the principal's incapacity only where the agent knows for a fact that the principal is incapacitated and that the third party has no knowledge of the incapacity.

While the agent himself or herself need not have capacity to contract in order to contract on behalf of the principal, the agent cannot be so bereft of mind as to be incompetent to do the act required of the agency. Where the agent becomes so bereft of mind, the agency terminates by operation of law.

Bankruptcy of the principal or agent Similarly, the agency terminates automatically and instantly at any time bankruptcy proceedings begin for either principal or agent. With the commencement of such proceedings, the bankrupt's assets are turned over to the trustee in bankruptcy who is authorized to look after the bankrupt's affairs (see Chapter 11 on bankruptcy).

War between the countries of the principal and agent In nearly all cases where the principal and agent are residents or nationals of different countries, the outbreak of war between the two countries makes it impossible or illegal for the agency relationship to continue; the agency terminates by operation of law.

Destruction of the subject matter of the agency If the agency pertains to specific property and the property is lost or destroyed, the agency terminates as a matter of necessity.

Termination by Act of the Parties

The parties may themselves terminate the agency relationship as follows:

The original agreement may provide for a fixed term of agency or for termination upon the happening of a certain event The parties being free to contract, they may provide in their original agreement (assuming they have one) that the agency relationship will terminate in one year, in eighteen months, at the end of the "fishing season," etc.

Accomplishment of the object of the agency Where the agent is authorized to do a particular thing—e.g., to sell a car—the agency will end when the task is accomplished.

Mutual assent of both parties The parties may at any time mutually agree to end the relationship.

Renunciation by the agent The agent may terminate the agency relationship at any time by giving oral or written notice of termination to the principal. Of course, if the agency is contractual in nature, the agent's renunciation may constitute a breach of contract, allowing the principal to bring an action for damages against the agent.

Revocation of authority by the principal Conversely, the principal may at any time revoke the agent's authority. Again, if the agency is contractual, the revocation may constitute a breach of contract, allowing the agent to sue the principal for money damages.

WHEN IS NOTICE TO THIRD PARTIES REQUIRED TO TERMINATE AN AGENT'S APPARENT AUTHORITY?

When a *disclosed, general* agency is terminated *by act of the parties,* the general agent continues to have apparent authority to bind the principal in contract unless and until notice of termination is given to third parties. Remember, a general agent is one who is authorized to contract for a principal with regard to more than a single transaction and/or for a continuing period of time; a special agent is one authorized to conduct but a single transaction not involving any continuity of service.

Notice is required in the case of a general agent (and not a special agent) because a general agent is likely to establish a pattern or course of dealing with third parties. Absent notice that the principal has fired the agent or that the agent has quit the agency, etc., the third parties have no reason to suspect that the agent's authority has been terminated. Thus, the law operates to protect the third parties at the expense of the principal who fails to give notice.

The required notice consists of the following:

1. Individual notice to each of the agent's steady customers; and
2. Public notice of termination of the agency (typically, the notice is placed in a local newspaper, but any reasonable method of giving public notice will do).

Additionally, the principal must make a reasonable effort to recover from the agent any company stationery, forms, business cards, etc., that would indicate a continuing authority on the part of the agent to contract in the principal's behalf (a failure to recover such items may give rise to apparent authority in the agent).

IS THE AGENT'S AUTHORITY EVER IRREVOCABLE?

One type of agency authority cannot be revoked—"an agency power coupled with an interest" (sometimes called "an agency coupled with security"). Here the agency power is given to the agent to enable him or her to protect an interest that is separate from the subject of the agency. Typically, the interest stems from some prior relationship or dealings between the principal and agent. For example, the agent may have advanced or loaned money to the principal some months prior to the agency—the agent's "interest," here, is repayment of the money. Or the agent may have performed work for the principal at a prior date—the agent's "interest" being compensation for the work performed. The principal gives the agent an unrelated agency power (e.g., authority to sell the principal's house or car) so that the agent can protect his or her interest (i.e., collect payment of the monies owing). Because the agency is coupled with an interest, the principal cannot revoke it, and it will not terminate even upon the death, insanity, or bankruptcy of the principal or agent.

A good example of an agency coupled with an interest is found in Chrysler Corp. v. Blozic, 267 Mich. 479, 255 N.W. 399 (1934). There, a hospitalized and dying principal had only life insurance proceeds with which to pay his hospital bill. Before he died, the principal authorized the hospital to collect the insurance money and apply it to his bill. Of course, in the ordinary agency situation, the agency would terminate by operation of law upon the principal's death. Here, however, the agency was coupled with an interest (the hospital's right to payment of the bill) and was not revoked by the death of the principal. The hospital needed the agency power to secure payment of the bill.

An agency coupled with an interest must be distinguished from the situation where an agent is to be paid a commission for doing the work of the agency. Obviously, the agent has an "interest" in receiving his or her commission. But it is not an interest separate from the subject of the agency, and the agency is not one coupled with an interest (i.e., the agency is not irrevocable).

Cases

An aunt murders her two-and-one-half-year-old niece after insuring her life. Insurable interest?

LIBERTY NATIONAL LIFE INSURANCE CO. v. WELDON

Supreme Court of Alabama, 1957.
267 Ala. 171, 100 So.2d 696.

LAWSON, Justice

This is a suit by Gaston Weldon, who sues as the father of Shirley Dianne Weldon, deceased, his minor daughter, under § 119, Title 7, Code 1940, the so-called homicide statute, against Liberty National Life Insurance Company, a corporation; National Life & Accident Insurance Company, a corporation; and Southern Life & Health Insurance Company, a corporation.

We will sometimes hereafter refer to Gaston Weldon as the plaintiff, to his deceased child as Shirley, and to the defendant insurance companies as Liberty National, National Life and Southern Life.

Shirley died on May 1, 1952, when she was approximately two and one-half years of age. Prior to her death each of the defendant insurance companies had issued a policy wherein Shirley's life was insured. The policy of Liberty National in the amount of $500 was issued on December 1, 1951. National Life's policy in the amount of $1,000 was issued on or about April 23, 1952. The policy of Southern Life in the amount of $5,000 was issued in the latter part of March, 1952. Each of those policies was issued on an application of Mrs. Earle Dennison, who was an aunt-in-law of Shirley, that is, she was the widow of a brother of Shirley's mother. Each of the policies provided that the death benefits be paid to Mrs. Dennison. * * *

The theory on which plaintiff seeks to recover damages from the defendants is that Mrs. Dennison had no insurable interest in Shirley's life and that the defendants knew or should have known that fact; and, that by reason of the wrongful and negligent issuance of the "illegal" policies of insurance Mrs. Dennison murdered Shirley with the hope of collecting the insurance proceeds.

The case was submitted to the jury on plaintiff's amended complaint which consisted of six counts, in each of which damages were claimed in the amount of $100,000. * * * Counts 3 to 6 inclusive are grounded on negligent acts on the part of the defendants, with Counts 3 and 6 alleging that the acts of the defendants placed the insured child in a zone of danger, with unreasonable risk of harm to her and that the defendants in issuing the alleged illegal contracts of insurance knew, or by the exercise of reasonable diligence should have known, that the beneficiary, Mrs. Dennison, had no insurable interest in the life of the insured. * * * Each of the counts contains an averment to the effect that the wrongful or negligent acts of the defendant insurance companies concurred or united in proximately contributing to or causing the death of plaintiff's minor child.

* * * There were verdict and judgment for the plaintiff in the amount of $75,000. The motions for new trial filed by each of the defendant insurance companies having been overruled, each of them has appealed to this court.

* * *

Assignment of Error No. 8 of each appellant challenges the action of the trial court in overruling their motions for change of venue. In support of those motions, wherein they averred in effect that they could not get a fair and impartial trial in Elmore County, the defendants relied in the main on a newspaper story concerning this suit which appeared in the October 22, 1953, issue of the Wetumpka *Herald,* a newspaper widely circulated in Elmore County. The newspaper story pointed out the theory on which the plaintiff sought to recover damages from the defendants, the amount of damages claimed, the ruling of the trial court on the demurrers, the date the case was set for trial, and the fact that it involved questions of considerable interest to the legal profession and to the insurance business. The story also called attention to the fact, already known by most people in Alabama, that Mrs. Dennison had been electrocuted for the murder of Shirley and that she was the first white woman to be electrocuted for crime in Alabama. The newspaper account was concluded with these words in parentheses: "Not the $64,000 question but the $100,000 question."

* * * Newspaper publicity does not necessarily constitute grounds for a change of venue. Littlefield v. State, supra. We see nothing in the newspaper account which would justify us in holding that the trial court abused its discretion in denying the motions for change of venue. Nor could we put the trial court in error on the mere statement of counsel for the defendants below that the defendants could not get a fair trial in Elmore County because the people of that county were aroused over the fact that Mrs. Dennison had murdered Shirley.

* * *

The evidence in this case shows beyond peradventure that Shirley was murdered by Mrs. Dennison. We will briefly summarize the facts which tend to support that statement. In the early afternoon of May 1, 1952, Mrs. Dennison drove to plaintiff's home, in rural Elmore County, where she found the plaintiff, his wife and their two children, Orville and Shirley. Shortly after Mrs. Dennison's arrival the plaintiff and his son left the home to attend to some duties around the farm. At the time of their return home Mrs. Dennison was engaged in serving some soft drinks which she had purchased at a nearby store. Mrs. Dennison divided an orange drink between Orville and Shirley. Shirley's drink was poured into a little cup that Mrs. Dennison provided. Shortly after she consumed her drink Shirley became very nauseated. After the nausea subsided Mrs. Dennison left the room but returned in a short time shaking a partially filled bottle of Coca-Cola, from which she gave Shirley a drink. Shirley again became violently nauseated and that condition continued until she became almost unconscious. At the mother's insistence Shirley was taken to Wetumpka in search of a doctor. She was admitted to a hospital in Wetumpka shortly after her arrival there. She died within a comparatively short time after she was admitted to the hospital.

Dr. Rehling, the Director of the Department of Toxicology of this state, testified that an autopsy which he performed revealed arsenic in fatal quantities in Shirley's body and expressed the opinion that the child died as the result of arsenic taken through her mouth. He testified that he found traces of arsenic on articles of clothing worn by Shirley and by Mrs. Dennison at the time the drinks were served and he further testified that he found traces of arsenic in the cup from which Shirley drank. The appellants do not contend here that the evidence was not altogether ample to support a jury finding that Mrs. Dennison murdered the little girl.

The evidence is also clear to the effect that Mrs. Dennison murdered the child in order to collect insurance benefits payable to her upon the child's death. We will not undertake to set out all of the evidence which tends to support that statement, for the defendants do not contend that such was not the case. We simply call attention to one incident which we think clearly shows why Mrs. Dennison poisoned the child. Mrs. Dennison was a nurse in the hospital to which Shirley was admitted and she was directed by the doctor in charge of Shirley to administer aid to the patient. By late afternoon when it was apparent that Shirley was dying, Mrs. Dennison left the hospital and drove approximately twelve miles to the home of an insurance agent to pay the premium on the Liberty National policy which was about to lapse.

So it is clear that the harm which came to plaintiff's little girl was not caused by the direct act of any of the defendants, but by the intervening act of Mrs. Dennison, who has paid with her life for her horrible crime.

But as before indicated, the plaintiff says, in effect, that such harm would not have come to his little girl if the defendants had not wrongfully or negligently issued to Mrs. Dennison the alleged illegal policies covering Shirley's life.

The plaintiff has proceeded against these defendants on the theory that Mrs. Dennison did not have an insurable interest in the life of Shirley and hence the policies involved were illegal and void as against public policy; that the defendants were negligent in the issuance of the policies in that they knew there was no such interest or failed to exercise reasonable diligence to ascertain that fact before issuing the policies, although there was a duty upon them to do so; and that the failure to perform that duty was in fact the proximate cause of the child's death.

The evidence was sufficient to show a lack of insurable interest. * * * [A]n in-law relationship in and of itself does not sustain an insurable interest.

Most certainly the evidence in this case does not show as a matter of law that Mrs. Dennison had an insurable interest in Shirley because she had a reasonable expectation of possible profit or advantage to her from the continued life of Shirley. Helmetag's Adm'r v. Miller, 76 Ala. 183; Commonwealth Life Ins. Co. v. George, supra. Mrs. Dennison did not provide a home for Shirley. They lived in different towns several miles apart. Shirley lived in the home of her parents with her brother and sister and received her entire support from her parents. * * *

From the evidence presented the jury was well justified in finding that none of the defendants before issuing the policies of insurance made reasonable effort to ascertain whether Mrs. Dennison did in fact have an insurable interest in Shirley's life.

* * *

The conclusions which we have reached above, namely, that the evidence was sufficient to show that Shirley was murdered and the policies were void because of lack of insurable interest and were, in effect, negligently issued do not, of course, determine the liability of the defendants. For all negligence is not actionable. To be actionable it must be the breach of a duty which the defendant owed the plaintiff as an individual or one of a class and the plaintiff must not only show causal connection between the negligent breach of the duty but that such negligence was the proximate cause of the injury.

* * *

The position of the defendants seems to be that if murder results the insurance companies are, of course, sorry that the insured met with such a fate, but they have no liability if there is no insurable interest although they can treat such policies as completely void. If an early death from natural causes makes the policy unprofitable, the defendants can and do refuse to pay the beneficiary for the reason that such policies are void. In other words, the defendants seem to be of the opinion that the insurable interest rule is to protect insurance companies. We do not agree. The rule is designed to protect human life. Policies in violation of the insurable interest rule are not dangerous because they are illegal; they are illegal because they are dangerous.

As we have shown, it has long been recognized by this court and practically all courts in this country that an insured is placed in a position of extreme danger where a policy of insurance is issued on his life in favor of a beneficiary who has no insurable interest. There is no legal justification for the creation of such a risk to an insured and there is no social gain in the writing of a void policy of insurance. Where this court has found that such policies are unreasonably dangerous to the insured because of the risk of murder and for this reason has declared such policies void, it would be an anomaly to hold that insurance companies have no duty to use reasonable care not to create a situation which may prove to be a stimulus for murder.

* * *

* * * [T]he wrongful or negligent acts of the three insurance companies concurred or united in proximately contributing to or causing the death of plaintiff's minor child. * * *

* * *

Section 119, Title 7, Code 1940, the statute under which this action was brought, provides that for the wrongful death of a minor child the persons there entitled to sue, if entitled to a verdict, "shall recover such damages as the jury may assess." The damages are entirely punitive, imposed for the preservation of human life. As the wording of the statute indicates, the amount of damages rests largely in the discretion of the jury. However, this discretion is not an unbridled or arbitrary one, but "a legal, sound and honest discretion." In arriving at the amount of damages which should be assessed, the jury should give due regard to the enormity or not of the wrong and to the necessity of preventing similar wrongs. The punishment by way of damages is intended not alone to punish the wrongdoer, but as a deterrent to others similarly minded.

The verdict rendered in this case is large, perhaps the largest to come before this court in a case brought under the so-called homicide statute, §§ 119 and 123, Title 7, Code 1940. But the trial court refused to disturb the amount of the verdict and we have held that when such is the case we will not order a reduction unless the verdict is so excessive as to indicate passion, prejudice, corruption or mistake. We are unwilling to say that the amount of damages awarded by way of punishment of these three appellants for wrongfully and negligently issuing illegal policies of insurance, the issuance of which the evidence clearly shows led to the murder of plaintiff's young daughter, is so excessive as to indicate passion, prejudice, corruption or mistake, and as we have heretofore shown, the jury in fixing the amount of the verdict was charged with the duty of giving consideration to the necessity of preventing the same wrongs by others similarly minded.

* * *

Affirmed.

The instrument is not negotiable, so the law of assignment applies.

HAGGARD v. MUTUAL OIL & REFINING CO.

Court of Appeals of Kentucky, 1924.
204 Ky. 209, 263 S.W. 745.

CLARKE, J.

The single question presented by this appeal is whether or not the following check is a negotiable instrument:

$2,500.00. Winchester, Ky., July 10, 1920.

The Winchester Bank, of Winchester, Ky.: Pay to Arco Refinery Construction Company twenty-five hundred and no/100 dollars, for a/c constructing refinery, switch, and loading racks, Win.Ky.

Mutual Oil & Refining Co.,
By C.L. Bell, Pres.

Subdivision 4 of section 3720b, which is the Negotiable Instruments Act (Acts 1913, p. 213), § 1, provides that:

> An instrument to be negotiable must conform to the following requirements: * * * (4) Must be payable to the order of a specified person or to bearer.

Since, as the check itself shows, and as is admittedly true, the maker, in issuing the check, drew a line through the printed words "or bearer," we need only to examine it to ascertain whether or not it was "payable to the order of a specified person," for unless so, it lacked one of the essentials prescribed for negotiability.

Section 8 of the act (section 3720b8 of the Statutes) defines when an instrument is payable to order as follows:

> The instrument is payable to order where it is drawn payable to the order of a specified person or to him or his order.

It will be noticed that the above check is not payable to the order of the payee, nor to the payee or its order, but is payable simply to the payee. It therefore seems to us too clear for dispute that this check is not payable to order, and is therefore, as the lower court held, not negotiable.

In other words, we think it is clear that subsection 8 means, as it says, that the instrument must be payable either (1) to the order of the payee, or (2) to the payee or order. * * *

* * *

Counsel for appellant concede that this section has been construed by this court and others in the above cases to require the use of the words "order or bearer" or other words of similar legal import in order to make a note or other bill negotiable, but they insist that there is such a material difference between a note and a check as that these cases are not applicable to one in which, as here, the bill is a check.

But in this they are clearly mistaken. Section 185 of the act (Ky.St. § 3720b185) expressly declares that a check is a bill of exchange payable on demand, and that, except as otherwise therein provided, the provisions of the act applicable to a bill of exchange payable on demand shall apply to a check, and, as it is not otherwise therein provided, it is clear that sections 1 and 8 of the act apply to a check as well as to any other bill of exchange, and to be negotiable it also must employ some such words as "order" or "bearer" indicating negotiability.

It results, therefore, that a check, just as any other bill of exchange that is made payable simply to the payee and not to his order or to bearer, is not negotiable, and that appellant, to whom this check was assigned by the payee, took same subject to all defenses which were available between the original parties.

[Defendant's defense of lack] of consideration [is a good defense against the original assignor and the assignee.]

The "holder in due course" has "super plaintiff" status.

ILLINOIS VALLEY ACCEPTANCE CORP. v. WOODARD

Court of Appeals of Indiana, First District, 1973.
159 Ind.App. 50, 304 N.E.2d 859.

ROBERTSON, Presiding Judge

The plaintiff-appellant (Acceptance) is appealing the denial of its attempt to collect upon a trade acceptance made by the defendant-appellee (Woodard). The primal issue raised concerns Acceptance's status as a holder in due course of a negotiable instrument.

Woodard was a part time salesman for Moody Manufacturing Company (Moody), a manufacturer of grain bins and grain handling equipment. In May of 1966, Moody, as "borrower," had entered into a Finance Agreement with Acceptance listed as "the lender." This agreement made provision, among other things, for Moody to sell acceptable accounts to Acceptance for face value with 15% being reserved for deductions, expenses, accumulated interest, etc. On the 24th of December, 1968, Woodard signed, as acceptor, the trade acceptance which is the subject of this litigation. Moody was the drawer and payee. At that time it was in blank with the face value subsequently being filled in for the face amount of $8,815.62. In the four or five years prior to 1968, Woodard had signed several trade acceptances in blank for Moody for the purposes of covering the purchase of materials which he sold. The face amount was ultimately to be filled in when it was determined how much he had ordered. The December, 1968, trade acceptance was endorsed by Moody's secretary and given to Acceptance several days after Woodard had signed it. Between February and April, 1970, and several months past the due date, Moody went bankrupt. When Acceptance presented the instrument for payment it was refused by Woodard. Additionally, Woodard never received the materials presented by the trade acceptance, nor was he aware it had been negotiated by Moody to Acceptance.

Acceptance filed its complaint for collection of the trade acceptance against Woodard. * * * Woodard * * * raised the defenses of fraud and want of consideration. Acceptance filed a response alleging itself to be a holder in due course, which would defeat Woodard's professed defenses. Acceptance then filed a motion for summary judgment with an affidavit made by the vice-president of Acceptance in support thereof. The pertinent parts of the affidavit read:

> 4. That since May 17, 1966, Illinois Valley Acceptance Corp. would periodically purchase from Moody Manufacturing Company trade acceptances, promissory notes or other negotiable instruments.
>
> 5. That on or about December 26, 1968, Illinois Valley Acceptance Corp., for the cash consideration of Seven Thousand Four Hundred Ninety-Three Dollars and Twenty-Eight Cents ($7,493.28), purchased from Moody Manufacturing Company a certain trade acceptance shown as 'No. Inv. # 302', dated December 24, 1968, due November 30, 1969 and accepted on December 24, 1968 by ROBERT WOODARD, the same being payable at PEOPLES STATE BANK, Fairbanks, Indiana. * * *
>
> * * *
>
> 7. That on December 26, 1968, Affiant knew of no reason or fact which would indicate to him that the trade acceptance attached to the Complaint in this cause was anything other than a valid and enforceable trade acceptance, issued by Moody Manufacturing Company, and accepted by ROBERT WOODARD in the ordinary course and scope of their respective businesses, and that same was a valid, legitimate and enforceable negotiable instrument.

The affidavit concluded with statements to the effect that the trade acceptance had been refused and that Acceptance was the lawful owner and holder of the trade acceptance.

Woodard filed no response. The trial court overruled the motion for summary judgment and some time thereafter proceeded to trial with subsequent judgment against Acceptance. Acceptance's overruled motion to correct errors raises two issues; whether the trial court erred in overruling its motion for summary judgment, and whether the judgment is contrary to the evidence and the law. As previously indicated, the answer to both is tied to Acceptance's classification as a holder in due course of the questioned trade acceptance.

* * *

This case is to be decided under the provisions of the Uniform Commercial Code. * * * Acceptance's acknowledged status as a holder was not sufficient for it to recover because Woodard raised the defenses of fraud and failure of consideration, each a valid defense. These defenses, however, may have been cut off if Acceptance was a holder in due course. The holder in due course takes the instrument "free from all defenses of any party to the instrument with whom the holder has not dealt," subject to several exceptions. To avail itself of this "super-plaintiff" status, Acceptance had the burden of establishing by a preponderance of the evidence that it was "in all respects a holder in due course." "In all respects" means that Acceptance had to establish the existence of each of the elements set forth in IC 1971, 26–1–3–302, Ind.Ann.Stat. § 19–3–302. It provides:

> (1) A holder in due course is a holder who takes the instrument
>
> (a) for value; and
>
> (b) in good faith; and
>
> (c) without notice that it is overdue or has been dishonored or of any defense against or claim to it on the part of any person.

The evidence, when examined with the foregoing requisites in mind, establishes Acceptance as a holder in due course. Briefly summarized that evidence shows the trade acceptance being endorsed over to Acceptance by Moody. Moody in turn received a draft for 85% of the face value of the trade acceptance. There was nothing irregular with the appearance of the trade acceptance and the transaction was similar to other prior transactions between the parties. At that time Acceptance had no knowledge that the trade acceptance had been signed in blank and that the goods had not been delivered.

A portion of Woodard's arguments appears to be directed to the questions of good faith and notice. Both are statutorily defined:

> (19) 'Good faith' means honesty in fact in the conduct or transaction concerned.

Notice, insofar as applicable, is defined as:

> (1) The purchaser has notice of a claim or defense if
>
> (a) the instrument is so incomplete, bears such visible evidence of forgery or alteration, or is otherwise so irregular as to call into question its validity, terms or ownership or to create an ambiguity as to the party to pay; or
>
> (b) the purchaser has notice that the obligation of any party is voidable in whole or in part, or that all parties have been discharged.

The gist of Woodard's cross examination of Acceptance's vice-president was directed to when Acceptance became aware of Moody's bankruptcy and to the Finance Agreement between Moody and Acceptance. We believe that the bankruptcy has no relevancy because of its nonexistence at the time the trade acceptance was endorsed over to Acceptance. The Finance Agreement, introduced into evidence by Woodard, may have been an attempt to establish something akin to the doctrine of close connectedness, characterized by Woodard as the lack of an arms-length transaction, for the purpose of showing that Acceptance was so closely related to Moody commercially that it knew, or should have known, either Moody was in poor financial shape or that it had not delivered the goods represented by the trade acceptance. Acceptance's summary judgment affidavit as well as the testimony given at the trial belies such a relationship.

Woodard further argues that there was no value given for the trade acceptance and that the Finance Agreement between Moody and Acceptance was merely a borrowing agreement. The evidence shows that Acceptance paid Moody 85% of the face value of trade acceptance and held the remainder in reserve. There can be little question that the value concept was satisfied. * * *

Woodard also argues that Acceptance failed to show the instrument was negotiated because the evidence is in conflict as to whether there was delivery of the instrument. Delivery is an element required by IC 1971, 26–1–3–202, Ind.Ann.Stat. § 19–3–202, and is defined as a voluntary transfer of possession. We fail to find any conflicting evidence on delivery of the trade acceptance from Moody to Acceptance.

Woodard's affirmative defense of want of consideration is not available against a holder in due course.

Turning next to the question of fraud § 19–3–305(2)(c) allows a defense against a holder in due course based upon "such misrepresentation as has induced the party to sign the instrument with neither knowledge nor reasonable opportunity to obtain knowledge of its character or its essential terms." The comments subsequent to this statute state that fraud in the essence or fraud in the factum is a valid defense against a holder in due course with the theory being that the "signature is ineffective because he did not intend to sign such an instrument at all." Woodard's past conduct in signing blank trade acceptances for Moody negates a defense based on the foregoing. Woodard testified he was familiar with the forms and knew they constituted a promise to pay.

In determining whether a verdict is contrary to the law the proper rule is:

> * * * only where the evidence is without conflict and can lead to but one conclusion, and the trial court has reached an opposite conclusion, that the decision of the trial court will be set aside on the ground that it is contrary to law.

It is our conclusion that the evidence conclusively demonstrated Acceptance to be a holder in due course. We, accordingly, reverse and remand for judgment to be entered for the plaintiff-appellant Illinois Valley Acceptance Corp., and against the defendant-appellee Robert Woodard.

Reversed and remanded.

A "without recourse" endorsement does not eliminate all obligations.

HARTFORD LIFE INSURANCE CO. v. TITLE GUARANTEE CO.

United States Court of Appeals, District of Columbia Circuit, 1975.
520 F.2d 1170.

WEIGEL, District Judge

This case turns upon facts which are somewhat complicated and include prior litigation before this Court. In In re Parkwood, Inc., 149 U.S.App.D.C. 67, 461 F.2d 158 (1971), we invalidated a loan entered into in violation of the District of Columbia Loan Shark Law, D.C.Code § 26–601 et seq. The effect of the decision was to render uncollectable the unpaid balance of approximately $79,000.00. * * *

In October, 1960, Walker & Dunlop, a real estate broker and mortgage banker, loaned $100,000 to Suburban Motors, Inc. The loan, evidenced by a promissory note, was to bear interest at an annual rate of 6½% and was secured by a deed of trust on real property owned by Suburban. * * * In January, 1961, pursuant to an understanding reached before the loan was made, Walker & Dunlop transferred the note and deed of trust to Hartford, endorsing the note "without recourse."

In March, 1962, Suburban sold the property, subject to the deed of trust, to Adams Properties, Inc., a subsidiary of Parkwood, Inc. In July, 1966, these companies filed petitions for reorganization under the Bankruptcy Act. Later that year, Hartford filed a proof of claim as a secured creditor of Adams for the balance due on the note—some $79,000.00.

In May 1968, the Trustee appointed for Adams objected to the claim on the ground that the loan had been made in violation of the Loan Shark Act, Section 601. That statute makes it unlawful to charge yearly interest on a secured loan at a higher rate than 6% unless a license has been procured to charge the higher rate. [I]n In re Parkwood, supra, this Court found * * * that the loan was subject to the Act, and that the loan and accompanying deed of trust were void. Hartford's proof of claim was disallowed.

Hartford instituted this action in December, 1972. In its amended complaint, Hartford seeks to recover its loss from Walker & Dunlop on * * * breach of warranty. * * *

The District Court held that the causes of action against Walker & Dunlop * * * were barred * * * by the "without recourse" endorsement on the note which

Walker & Dunlop had transferred to Hartford. * * *

* * *

The District Court * * * erred in ruling that Hartford's claims against Walker & Dunlop were barred by the "without recourse" endorsement on the note transferred by Walker & Dunlop to Hartford.

The legal effect of a "without recourse" endorsement is defined by the Uniform Commercial Code. D.C.Code § 28:3–417(3), (2)(d). Thus, whether or not this endorsement bars Hartford's claims against Walker & Dunlop must be determined with reference to the principles of commercial law established therein.

A "without recourse" endorsement is a qualified endorsement; it does not eliminate all obligations owed by the transferor of an instrument to his transferee. By endorsing the note "without recourse", Walker & Dunlop still warranted to Hartford that it had no knowledge of any fact which would establish the existence of a good defense against the note. Walker & Dunlop breached this warranty. At all times it was fully aware of the facts relevant to our later determination that the note was unenforceable because of the illegality of the underlying loan. * * *

* * *

* * * [W]e hereby reverse the order granting * * * judgment in favor of Walker & Dunlop. * * *

A dishonest employee forged endorsements of fictitious payees.

MAY DEPARTMENT STORES CO. v. PITTSBURGH NATIONAL BANK

United States Court of Appeals,
Third Circuit, 1967.
374 F.2d 109.

Before HASTIE, GANEY and SEITZ, Circuit Judges

Opinion of the Court

This is an appeal from summary judgment entered for the defendant after these facts were established without contradiction. An employee of the plaintiff, May Department Stores Co., fraudulently caused the plaintiff to draw its checks payable to fictitious suppliers. The wrongdoing employee then forged the endorsements of the fictitious payees, cashed the checks at the defendant bank and converted the proceeds. The bank charged the sums thus paid against the plaintiff's account.

The plaintiff then sued the bank for illegally charging its account with amounts paid on forged endorsements. On the record before it, and in the absence of any allegation or showing of countervailing circumstances by the plaintiff, the district court properly concluded that the bank was protected by the following provision of the Uniform Commercial Code as in force in Pennsylvania.

> (1) An indorsement by any person in the name of a named payee is effective if
>
> * * *
>
> (c) an agent or employee of the drawer has supplied him with the name of the payee intending the latter to have no such interest. 12A P.S. § 3–405(1)(c).

The judgment will be affirmed.

Appellant's wife had neither express nor implied authority to draw on her husband's trading account.

TAYLOR v. MERRILL LYNCH, PIERCE, FENNER & SMITH, INC.

Court of Appeals of District of Columbia,
1968.
245 A.2d 426.

MYERS, Associate Judge

Appellee is a securities dealer with whom appellant kept a trading account, in his name only. Appellant's estranged wife, residing in the state of Washington, who was not authorized to draw on the account, wrote to appellee saying that an emergency had arisen and asked to withdraw $1,000.00. At that time the account contained a balance of $1,072.14. Appellee drew a check for $1,000.00, payable to appellant, mailed it to his wife at her residence, and debited appellant's account. Apparently the wife signed appellant's name as endorser and cashed the check. Upon learning of the withdrawal, appellant filed suit alleging that appellee owed him $1,072.14. Appellee answered and admitted owing $72.14, but argued that it had paid $1,000.00. From a trial finding in appellee's favor, the present appeal is taken. The only question before us is whether, as a matter of law, the established facts make out the affirmative defense of payment.

Generally, payment of a debt so as to extinguish it may be made only to the creditor or to someone to whom the creditor directs payment to be made. One making payment to an agent has the burden of showing that the latter had express or apparent authority to receive such payment on behalf of a creditor. * * *

In the instant case, it is not contended that appellant's wife had either express or implied authority to draw on her husband's trading account. The only question is whether making the check payable to appellant under the present circumstances constituted payment to him. We hold that it did not.

Appellee drew the check on the instructions of a person who had no authority to give that instruction. In addition, appellee mailed the check to appellant's wife at an address different from the address at which it had been corresponding with appellant. Furthermore, appellee did not inform appellant of its action, and it was not until appellant received a periodic statement that he was apprised of the withdrawal. Under the circumstances, we are of the opinion that appellee's actions do not amount to payment, despite its issuance of the check payable to appellant.

Reversed with directions to enter judgment for appellant in the amount of $1,072.14.

If there was no authority, was there ratification?

STUDLEY, INC. v. GULF OIL CORP.

United States District Court, S.D. New York, 1968.
282 F.Supp. 748.

Opinion

POLLACK, District Judge

Gulf Oil Corp. leased space in the Sperry Rand Building in New York City for a ten year period with renewal options. It was represented in the negotiations for the lease by the brokerage firm of Cushman & Wakefield to where the landlord has paid brokerage commissions.

The plaintiff in this case, a real estate brokerage firm, asserted that it was improperly deprived of a brokerage commission on the lease by the misconduct of Gulf Oil Corp. and brought suit against Gulf Oil Corp. for damages.

This case was submitted to a jury together with special questions and it rendered a verdict in favor of the plaintiff for $25,000. The defendant, Gulf Oil Corp. has moved to set the damage verdict aside. * * *

* * *

The plaintiff's * * *

* * * claim—for breach of contract—was that the defendant employed the plaintiff as its real estate agent to locate office space for it in New York City with the understanding that, if the plaintiff procured an acceptable lease for it, "defendant would enter into a lease * * * and * * * plaintiff would be the broker in the transaction", and thereby become eligible for payment of a commission by the owner of the property or the landlord.

The plaintiff alleged that the contract with it was made by one Burkhiser, the director of defendant's department of General Services stationed in Pittsburgh, Pennsylvania.

The plaintiff further contended that if Burkhiser was not authorized either actually or apparently to commit the defendant to the alleged agreement made on its behalf, the defendant had ratified the agreement by accepting the services of the plaintiff with full knowledge of the alleged agreement.

The plaintiff contended that the defendant breached the agreement by failing to act in good faith and by failing to designate the plaintiff as broker upon entering into a lease with the landlord, Rock-Uris and by failing to advise Rock-Uris of the plaintiff's role in the transaction resulting in a lease of space in the Sperry Rand Building. The plaintiff claimed that it would have received a commission from Rock-Uris, but for Gulf's breach and sought as damages the amount of the compensation it would have earned.

* * *

With respect to the * * * claim the case was submitted to the jury on the following special questions:

> 1. "Did Gulf authorize Burkhiser to enter into an agreement with Studley binding it to represent to Rock-Uris that Studley was responsible for the lease to Gulf in the Sperry Rand Building?"
>
> The jury's answer to this first question was "No."
>
> 2. *"Did Gulf ratify with knowledge thereof any arrangements made by Burkhiser with Studley pertaining to the lease to Gulf in the Sperry Rand Building?"*
>
> 3. "Did Gulf breach any agreement with Studley made with Gulf's authority or ratified by it with knowledge thereof?"
>
> The jury answered each of the second and third questions "Yes."
>
> 6. "To what award, if any, is plaintiff entitled from Gulf?"
>
> The jury's answer to the sixth question was "$25,000."

The defendant contends that there is no evidence whatsoever in the record of a ratification of the unauthorized arrangement made by Burkhiser.

* * *

Consideration of the question raised is aided by a brief review of the facts including the scope and nature of the services rendered by Studley.

In September, 1962 Gulf Oil Corp. was seeking office space in New York City. In response to a request by Burkhiser, Studley furnished Burkhiser with a list of buildings in the Rockefeller Center area in which there was space for rent; the list gave the rentals being requested. The data identified buildings that were completed or in the process of construction and nearing completion. One of the buildings included in Studley's list was the Sperry Rand Building at 1290 Avenue of the Americas, which was nearing completion.

The data supplied by Studley was essentially the information circulated publicly by renting agents of the buildings involved. None of the data involved any special or confidential information; it was all of the type which building owners and their renting agents circulate generally to lists of brokers and to business organizations generally or to those known to be interested in leasing commercial space. In addition to furnishing such a list Studley walked with Burkhiser to inspect the Pan American Building at 200 Park Avenue which was then completed and walked to the site of the Sperry Rand Building which was still in process of construction. There also were telephone calls between Studley and Burkhiser which kept the contact alive during the ensuing weeks.

Unknown to Burkhiser, a senior officer of the defendant stationed in its New York Office, one Cadman, had independently been negotiating for space through another broker, Cushman & Wakefield. The existing lease which the defendant had on space in Canada House was about to terminate; either it had to be renewed by October 31, 1962 or other space procured. Cushman & Wakefield were the renting agents for Canada House and were also the renting agents for the Sperry Rand Building. Although the emphasis was on attempting to work out a renewal of the space arrangement at Canada House, according to defendant, Cushman & Wakefield had, prior to Burkhiser's contacts with Studley, already called to the attention of Mr. Cadman the Sperry Rand Building and the possibilities of acquiring space therein for the defendant.

The defendant's determination to move its quarters crystallized at a meeting of Gulf Oil executives in Florida during the week of October 22, 1962. Shortly before that date or during that week Mr. Cadman notified Cushman & Wakefield that it desired to proceed actively with the consideration of space in the Sperry Rand Building.

* * *

Thereafter, on Octobert 30, 1962, a meeting was called in Mr. Cadman's office in New York attended by a representative of Cushman & Wakefield and by the technical staff of the defendant whose function it was to plan the specifications and layout and furnishing of space rented by the defendant. Included in the latter group was Burkhiser, who as the director of General Services Administration, was concerned with such problems.

It was at this meeting of October 30, 1962 that Burkhiser made the first disclosure to Cadman of his arrangements with Studley which the jury has stamped as forming an unauthorized contract. * * *

Mr. Cadman then told Burkhiser that he agreed to go along with Cushman & Wakefield because he believed that Gulf was exposed first by Cushman & Wakefield to the Sperry Rand Building.

* * *

No act or statement of the defendant or any authorized person on its behalf thereafter gives any indication that the defendant adopted or made use of any of the services rendered by Studley or recognized or intended to recognize or adopt the unauthorized arrangements as obligations of the defendant. Due to the generality of the services it cannot be said realistically that Gulf *thereafter* utilized Studley's services or reports, or derived benefits therefrom.

In the ensuing weeks, Studley did not attempt to or speak with any authorized officer of Gulf and Gulf gave no indication to Studley of any intention or willingness to adopt its services or any obligation for its services or any obligation to request the landlord to consider or recognize Studley as the representative of Gulf in the matter of the lease of space in the Sperry Rand Building.

The plaintiff has failed to point to any evidence of ratification on which to impose an obligation on Gulf herein. * * *

* * *

> Ratification is a form of subsequent authorization and is based upon the principle of approval with knowledge of the facts to be ratified. If a principal with such knowledge that there is an agreement outstanding and with knowledge of what that agreement is then accepts the benefits of an agent's action, the principal is responsible for agreement of the agent whether originally authorized or not. * * *
>
> * * * ratification is the affirmance by a principal of a prior act or commitment which does not bind him but which was done or professedly done on his account, and the ratification occurs when the principal learns of the commitment and then affirmatively elects to adopt it as if originally authorized by him.

* * *

Thus, ratification exists upon the concurrence of three elements: (1) acceptance by the principal of the benefits of the agent's act, (2) with full knowledge of the facts, and (3) circumstances or an affirmative election indicating an intention to adopt the unauthorized arrangement.

The knowledge required of the principal must be full and complete. If the principal's knowledge of the facts is partial or imperfect he will not be held to have ratified the unauthorized act, and the proof of adequate knowledge should be reasonably clear and certain.

The affirmative election to adopt must be evidenced by either express or implied intention to adopt.

> A ratification of the unauthorized act of an agent or of a stranger who claims to act as such, if it exists, must be found in the intention of the principal, either express or implied. If that intention cannot be shown, no ratification can be held to have been established. * * * Where one who has assumed to act as an agent for another has no authority to do so, but is a mere volunteer, a failure to disavow his acts will not amount to a ratification, unless under such circumstances as indicate an intention to do so.

* * *

The earliest occasion which presents any possibility of knowledge of the contract on the part of Gulf was the October 30 meeting between Cadman * * * and Burkhiser. * * * There was no evidence that Cadman either acknowledged Burkhiser's authority or adopted the alleged contract with Studley for Gulf. Indeed, it would be unreasonable for the triers of fact to find and conclude that Cadman at one and the same time intended to ratify the alleged contract for Gulf and yet sought to have the commission paid to another broker. * * *

The evidence adequately supports the jury's finding on the first special question, that Burkhiser's arrangement with Studley lacked authority. However, there is no support for the finding of a ratification.

There is only one reasonable conclusion with respect to the question of ratification, which conclusion is reached without weighing the credibility of the evidence. There is a total absence of evidence on which to find ratification expressly or by implication, or of an intent to ratify, or of an election to adopt the unauthorized arrangement, or of a ratification by estoppel.

Plaintiff, having failed to establish the alleged contract, is not entitled to the award of damages.

The jury's findings of a ratification and a breach of a ratified but unauthorized contract and its damage verdict in plaintiff's favor are set aside. * * *

So ordered.

The company clothed Mrs. Chaffee with the attributes of agency enabling her to sell without arousing the defendant's suspicions.

CALIFORNIA LIFE INSURANCE CO. v. MULTNOMAH COUNTY SCHOOL DISTRICT

40, Civil No. 63–130, Memorandum Opinion, Oct. 27, 1964.

SOLOMON, Judge

Plaintiff, the California Life Insurance Company, issues policies that insure schools and school districts against loss or damage resulting from injury to students and faculty while engaged in various school activities. The company sells its insurance through general agents, one of whom was National Scholastic Underwriters, Inc. (National). This controversy concerns the sale of insurance to the defendant, Multnomah County School District (School District), by an employee of National, Sara Ann Chaffee, a duly authorized representative of the Company and licensed to sell insurance by the State of Oregon. Mrs. Chaffee issued a policy to the School District for the 1962–63 school year containing altered endorsements to which the Company contends it never consented. The Company brings this action to have the altered endorsements declared void.

Mrs. Chaffee, as an agent for the company, wrote a policy for the School District for the 1962–1963 year which contained substantially the same coverage as the 1961–62 policy, which she had also written. The Company claims that it notified Mrs. Chaffee that she could not write any policies for the 1962–1963 period, but the School District was not notified of that fact, and she was permitted to retain supplies containing policy forms and endorsements. The School District purchased its insurance from Mrs. Chaffee, unaware of her lack of authority.

Where the authority of an insurance agent is terminated, it is the duty of the insurance company to notify those who are dealing with this person of such termination. If the insureds continued to deal with such person as an agent, not knowing of the termination, the company will be bound by his acts. * * *

Here the company terminated Mrs. Chaffee's authority to write policies some six months prior to her having written the 1962–1963 policy. Defendant was not notified of the termination and was unaware of it. In addition, the Company, by permitting Mrs. Chaffee to retain all the supplies, clothed her with the attributes of agency and enabled her to sell these policies without arousing the defendant's suspicions. * * *

Judgment is for the defendant.

Review Questions

1. How do negotiable instruments facilitate the flow of commerce? What exactly does it mean that the determination of negotiability is strictly a matter of form? How does a note differ from a draft? A check? Is an IOU negotiable? Is there a difference between saying a note or draft is executed "according to" another contract versus saying it is "subject to" another contract? May a party promise to pay money and do something else and still create a negotiable instrument? If an instrument provides that the time for payment may be extended, will it be non-negotiable? What if it is payable only upon an event uncertain as to time of occurrence? Explain your answers.

2. What legal rights result to an incidental beneficiary of a contract? What is the difference between a donee and an incidental beneficiary? Is life insurance always a third party beneficiary contract? What legal doctrines result from the principle of indemnity? Do incontestable clauses apply to all kinds of policies? How does an affirmative warranty differ from a promissory warranty? What rules apply to the interpretation of insurance policies? What must an insured do if he or she has any kind of loss? What if it is a loss from a fire? Explain your answers.

3. In what two situations is the defense that an agency was undisclosed a good defense for a third party? What is the most important warranty made by one purporting to be an agent? What measure of damages is used for breach of this implied warranty? When does ratification come into play? What is the result of ratification? What must a principal do to end an agency? When will agency end automatically? Is it ever irrevocable? Explain your answers.

4. Are most contract rights assignable? What about contract duties? Regarding a lease what is the difference between assignment and sublease? How does the law of assignments sometimes give an assignee the rights of a holder in due course even though the assignee is not himself or herself a holder in due course? What difference does it make? Explain your answers.

5. What is meant by "negotiation"? Can a thief negotiate? Will "order" paper always remain "order" paper? How about "bearer" paper? What does it mean to take for value, in good faith, and without notice? Are there "exceptions" within the operation of the shelter provision? Are any defenses good against a holder in due course? Does "alteration" include "unauthorized completion" ? Do alterations always result in complete discharge of prior parties? If a party makes payment on any instrument to one not entitled to payment, will the party who paid be able to recover the money back? Explain your answers.

6. How must an agent sign a negotiable instrument to prevent personal liability? What is the basis of authority? As to ultimate result for the principal, does it make any difference whether the agent has real or apparent authority? What is the twofold test of apparent authority? Is a real estate broker usually an agent? To what extent is an agent also a fiduciary? How is the tort of deceit different from other torts committed by an agent? Explain your answers.

7. What is secondary liability? How does it result? What are the conditions precedent? How may secondary liability be avoided? Exactly what liability does a person incur by transferring a negotiable instrument? Does it make any difference that the instrument is bearer paper, order paper, or qualifiedly endorsed? When can a bank pay a check on a forged endorsement and properly charge the drawer's account? Does a bank customer have any responsibility regarding his or her bank statement? How does a "stop payment" order affect the underlying transaction that gave rise to the check? Explain your answers.

8. Define the following terms: accommodation party, agency coupled with an interest, assignee, blank endorsement, certified check, close connection doctrine, co-insurance clause, conditional binding receipt, del credere agent, doctrine of finality, friendly fire, general agent, mixed defenses, principle of indemnity, protest, restrictive endorsement, special agent, special endorsement, shelter provision, trade acceptance.

Problems

1. Although Art Carswell has no interest in the property, he purchases fire insurance on his sister Marsha's residence. Six months later, Art buys the house from Marsha. One day, while burning trash in the fireplace, Art accidently throws his wristwatch into the fire, damaging it beyond repair. A week later, Art intentionally sets fire to the downstairs portion of the house so that he can have it rebuilt (and redecorated) at the insurance company's expense. The following week, Art builds a fire in the upstairs fireplace; the fire goes out of control, escapes from the fireplace, and seriously damages the living and dining rooms. The insurance company refuses to reimburse Art for any of these losses. The company states that Art had no insurable interest at the time of purchasing the insurance, and that even if he had had such an interest, none of these particular losses would be compensable. Discuss the validity of the insurance company's arguments. Is Art entitled to coverage? Explain.

2. a.

> As per our agreement of March 1st, I promise to pay to Ray and Susan Martin, or their assigns
>
> Four thousand and no/100 DOLLARS ($4,000.00)
>
> with interest at the current rate OR deliver them a 1984 Chevrolet Monza, payment or delivery to be made on December 15, 1984, except that I reserve the right to extend the date of payment or delivery.
>
> *Cathy Carpenter*
>
> Cathy Carpenter, Agent
> for Carter's Autos, Inc.

Is this instrument negotiable or non-negotiable? Discuss in detail, with specific reference to each of the requirements of negotiability. Who is liable as a maker of the instrument? Explain.

b. Dennis Barker breaks into Frank McClanahan's office and steals the following negotiable instruments: a check made payable by Frank "to the order of Frances Sweeney" in the amount of $500; a promissory note made payable by Frank "to bearer" in the amount of $1,000; and a check made payable by Mike Murphy "to the order of Frank McClanahan" in the amount of $750 (Frank has signed only his name on the back of the instrument). Dennis sells all three instruments to Betty Benson for $1,750. Betty has no idea that the instruments are stolen. She accepts delivery of the instruments, not realizing that Dennis has forged Frances Sweeney's endorsement on the check made payable to Frances's order. Was Dennis Barker a "holder" of the instruments? Is Betty Benson a "holder" of the instruments? Can Betty collect payment of the instruments despite the fact that they were stolen from Frank McClanahan? Explain your answers fully.

c. Suppose that Betty gives the $1,000 promissory note made payable to bearer to her nephew, Harley Benson. Unlike his aunt, Harley knows that the note was stolen; however, he did not participate in the theft. Harley sells the instrument for $650 to Jack Southwell who did participate in the theft with Dennis Barker. Could Harley have enforced the instrument despite the fact that it was stolen? Can Jack Southwell enforce the instrument? Explain in detail.

3. Nancy Bagley draws a negotiable draft on Margie Davis payable "to the order of Jonathan Beal" in the amount of $300. Jonathan skillfully changes the "3" into an "8" so that the draft appears to be payable in the amount of $800. The following transactions occur:

1. Jonathan endorses the draft in blank without recourse and delivers it to Lorna Roberts in satisfaction of an $800 debt he owes Lorna.
2. Lorna, who is unaware of the alteration, gives the draft to her niece, Myrna, who needs the money for college.
3. Myrna presents the draft to Margie for payment; Margie pays Myrna the $800, and Myrna uses the money to pay her college tuition.

(1) Johnathan Beal
Without Recourse

(2) (no endorsement)

(3) (no endorsement)

Margie thereafter discovers that the draft has been altered. What are Margie's rights, if any, against Myrna Roberts, Lorna Roberts, and Jonathan Beal? Explain fully.

Suppose that Margie is insolvent and cannot pay when Myrna presents the draft to her for payment. What are Myrna's rights, if any, against Nancy Bagley? Would your answer differ if Nancy had negligently and substantially contributed to the alteration (e.g., by writing the monetary amount in pencil so that it could be easily changed)? Would it differ if Margie had gone insolvent during an unreasonable delay by Myrna in presenting the draft for payment? Explain your answers.

Assuming that Nancy Bagley is also insolvent or has a good defense to payment, what are Myrna's rights, if any, against Lorna Roberts and Jonathan Beal? Explain fully.

Is Myrna required to proceed against Nancy before proceeding against Lorna and Jonathan? Explain.

4. a.

ON APRIL 15th, 1984, I promise to pay to the order of DOUGLAS CRENSHAW

One thousand one hundred fifty DOLLARS ($1,150.00)

Julie Bradley
Julie Bradley

1. Doug endorses in blank and delivers the note to Mary O'Connall for $850.
2. Mary specially endorses to Ron Weiss and delivers the note to Ron in payment for a used car.
3. Ron endorses in blank and gives the note to his son, Howard.
4. Howard specially endorses to Jean Peacock and delivers the note to her in exchange for $950.

(1) Doug Crenshaw
(2) Pay Ron Weiss
Mary O'Connall
(3) Ron Weiss
(4) Pay Jean Peacock
Howard Weiss

Who is primarily liable on this instrument? Explain. Who is secondarily liable? Explain. Who is liable on the basis of warranty? Explain.

b. Suppose that Charlie receives his bank statement containing the canceled check bearing his forged drawer's signature, but does not examine the statement until six weeks have passed. At that time, he informs the bank that his signature has been forged and that the check should not be charged to his account. Charlie then learns that a second check also forged by Mike Pratt was charged to his account six days after he received the bank statement containing the first forged instrument. Can First State Bank charge the first forged check to Charlie's account? Can it charge the second forged check to his account? Explain.

5. Sullivan Products hires Molly Taylor to act as its traveling salesperson in the small and sparsely populated Harrow County. Molly travels from "door to door" taking orders for goods; she carries only samples with her (the company sends the goods later by company truck). Without informing Sullivan Products, Molly also agrees to sell goods in Harrow County for Wyler Products; Wyler's goods directly compete with those of the Sullivan Company. One day, while traveling through Harrow County, Molly persuades Nancy Homer to purchase a Sullivan food processor. To obtain the order, Molly falsely tells Nancy that the processor is manufactured by Hytone, Inc. (a highly respected producer of good quality products) and simply sold under the Sullivan label. The processor is actually manufactured by the Sullivan Company. The same day, Molly sells an electric meat slicer to Harvey Mix who knows that the product is manufactured by Sullivan Products. Molly accepts Harvey's $150 check as payment for the meat slicer. Molly cashes the check and pockets the proceeds. She then delegates her sales duties for the Sullivan Company to Harry Owen and skips town.

a. Was Molly within her rights in agreeing to represent Wyler Products? Explain.

b. Who, if anyone, can Nancy hold liable for Molly's false assertion about the food processor? Explain.

c. Sullivan Products delivers a meat slicer to Harvey Mix and demands payment of $150. In a suit by the Company against Harvey to recover payment, who will prevail? Explain.

d. Did Molly have authority to delegate her sales duties to Harry Owen? Explain.

6. a. Nancy is asserting rights as a third party donee beneficiary on a contract made by Johnson and Harding. In order to prevail, Nancy must prove that
   1. The contract specifically named her as the beneficiary.
   2. She gave consideration for the donative promise.
   3. She is related by blood or marriage to the promisee.
   4. The terms of the contract and surrounding circumstances manifest a clear intent to benefit her.

b. The assignment of a contract right
   1. Will *not* be enforceable if it materially varies the obligor's promise.
   2. Is invalid unless supported by consideration.
   3. Gives the assignee better rights against the obligor than the assignor had.
   4. Does not create any rights in the assignee against the assignor until notice is given to the obligor.

Source: CPA Exam, May 1983, # 1(17)(18).

7. a. The insurable interest in property
   1. Can be waived by consent of the parties.
   2. Is subject to the incontestability clause.
   3. Must be present at the time the loss occurs.
   4. Is only available to owners, occupiers, or users of the property.

b. The underlying rationale which justifies the use of the co-insurance clause in fire insurance is
   1. It provides an insurable interest in the insured if this is *not* already present.
   2. To require certain minimum coverage in order to obtain full recovery on losses.
   3. It prevents arson by the owner.
   4. It makes the insured more careful in preventing fires since the insured is partially at risk in the event of loss.

Source: CPA Exam, May 1983, # 1(36)(37).

c. Hazard & Company was the owner of a building valued at $100,000. Since Hazard did not believe that a fire would result in a total loss, it procured two standard fire insurance policies on the property. One was for $24,000 with the Asbestos Fire Insurance Company and the other was for $16,000 with the Safety Fire Insurance Company. Both policies contained standard pro rata and 80 percent co-insurance clauses. Six months later, at which time the building was still valued at $100,000, a fire occurred which resulted in a loss of $40,000. What is the total amount Hazard can recover on both policies and the respective amount to be paid by Asbestos?
   1. $0 and $0.
   2. $20,000 and $10,000.
   3. $20,000 and $12,000.
   4. $40,000 and $20,000.

Source: CPA Exam, May 1980, # 1(48).

8. a.

> September 2, 1984
>
> I, Henry Hardy, do hereby acknowledge my debt to Walker Corporation arising out of my purchase of soybeans and promise to pay to Walker or to its order, SIX HUNDRED DOLLARS, thirty days after presentment of this instrument to me at my principal place of business.
>
> *Henry Hardy*
>
> Henry Hardy
>
> Re: $600.00—Soybean purchase

The above instrument is

1. Non-negotiable.
2. A negotiable promissory note.
3. A trade acceptance.
4. A negotiable bill of lading.

b.

> No. 003
>
> November 1, 1984 62-105/251
>
> Pay to the order of Alex & Co. $1,000.00
>
> One Thousand and 00/100 Dollars
>
> Ten days after presentment
>
> Security Trust Company
> Austin, Texas
>
> Memo: For purchases of securities
>
> *Herbert Stein*
>
> Herbert Stein

The above instrument is

1. Non-negotiable.
2. A draft.
3. A trade acceptance.
4. A check.

c.

October 5, 1984

To: Henry Futterman Suppliers
281 Cascade Boulevard
Spokane, Washington 99208

$950.00

Pay to the order of Alex & Co. Nine hundred fifty and 00/100 dollars one month after acceptance.

Alex & Co.

By *Charles Alex*

Managing Partner

Alex & Co.
264 Liberty Avenue
Philadelphia, Pa. 19117

Accepted by: *Laura Futterman*
Treasurer
Henry Futterman Suppliers

Date: October 15, 1982

The above instrument is

1. Non-negotiable since the payee is also the drawer.
2. A time promissory note.
3. A trade acceptance which imposes primary liability upon Henry Futterman Suppliers after acceptance.
4. A negotiable investment security under the Uniform Commercial Code.

Source: CPA Exam, November 1982, # 1(35), (36), (37).

9. a. Dunhill fraudulently obtained a negotiable promissory note from Beeler by misrepresentation of a material fact. Dunhill subsequently negotiated the note to Gordon, a holder in due course. Pine, a business associate of Dunhill, was aware of the fraud perpetrated by Dunhill. Pine purchased the note for value from Gordon. Upon presentment, Beeler has defaulted on the note.

Required: Answer the following, setting forth reasons for any conclusions stated.

1. What are the rights of Pine against Beeler?
2. What are the rights of Pine against Dunhill?

Source: CPA Exam, May 1983, # 5(a).

b. The following three endorsements appear on the back of a negotiable promissory note made payable to Harold Dawson. The note is in the possession of Maxim Company.

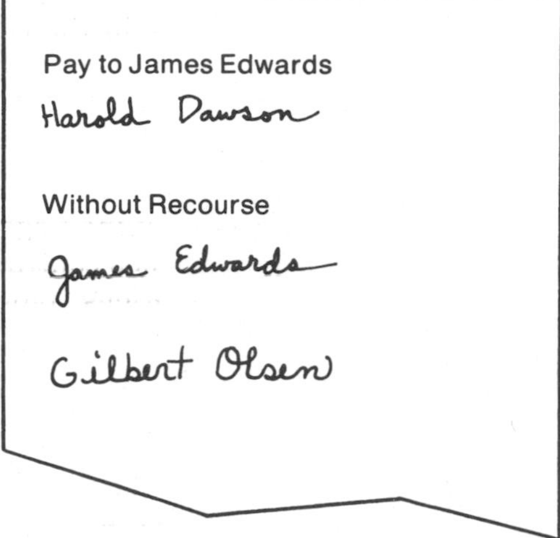

The instrument has been dishonored after due presentment by Maxim. Proper notice of dishonor has been given to all parties. Which of the following is correct?

1. James Edwards' signature on the instrument was *not* necessary.
2. James Edwards has effectively negated all warranty liability to any subsequent party except Gilbert Olsen.
3. James Edwards has neither contractual nor warranty liability as a result of his endorsing without recourse.
4. Gilbert Olsen's signature was *not* necessary effectively to negotiate the instrument to Maxim.

Source: CPA Exam, November 1982, # 1(42).

c. Dodger fraudulently induced Tell to issue a check to his order for $900 in payment for some nearly worthless securities. Dodger took the check and artfully raised the amount from $900 to $1,900. He promptly negotiated the check to Bay who took in good faith and for value. Tell, upon learning of the fraud, issued a stop order to its bank. Which of the following is correct?

1. Dodger has a real defense which will prevent any of the parties from collecting anything.
2. The stop order was ineffective against Bay since it was issued after the negotiation to Bay.
3. Bay as a holder in due course will prevail against Tell but only to the extent of $900.
4. Had there been no raising of the amount by Dodger, the bank would be obligated to pay Bay despite the stop order.

Source: CPA Exam, November 1982, #1 (43).

10. a. Wallace, an agent for Lux, made a contract with Doolittle which exceeded Wallace's authority. If Lux wishes to hold Doolittle to the contract, Lux must prove that
1. Lux ratified the contract before withdrawal from the contract by Doolittle.
2. Wallace was acting in the capacity of an agent for an undisclosed principal.
3. Wallace believed he was acting within the scope of his authority.
4. Wallace was Lux's general agent even though Wallace exceeded his authority.

b. Terrence has been Pauline's agent in the liquor business for ten years and has made numerous contracts on Pauline's behalf. Under which of the following situations could Terrence continue to have power to bind Pauline?
1. The passage of a federal constitutional amendment making the sale or purchase of alcoholic beverages illegal.
2. The death of Pauline without Terrence's knowledge.
3. The bankruptcy of Pauline with Terrence's knowledge.
4. The firing of Terrence by Pauline.

Source: CPA Exam, May 1983, # 1(1)(2).

c. Mathews is an agent for Sears with the express authority to solicit orders from customers in a geographic area assigned by Sears. Mathews has no authority to grant discounts or to collect payments on orders obtained. When Mathews secured an order from Davidson, he agreed to a price of $1,000 less a 10 percent discount if Davidson makes immediate payment. Davidson had previously done business with Sears through Mathews but this was the first time that a discount-payment offer had been made. Davidson gave Mathews a check for $900 and thereafter Mathews turned in both the check and the order to Sears. The order clearly indicated that a 10 percent discount had been given by Mathews. Sears shipped the order and cashed the check. Later Sears attempted to collect $100 as the balance owed on the order from Davidson. Which of the following is correct?
1. Sears can collect the $100 from Davidson because Mathews contracted outside the scope of his express or implied authority.
2. Sears can *not* collect the $100 from Davidson because Mathews as an agent with express authority to solicit orders had implied authority to give discounts and collect.
3. Sears can *not* collect the $100 from Davidson as Sears has ratified the discount granted and payment made to Mathews.
4. Sears can *not* collect the $100 from Davidson because, although Mathews had *no* express or implied authority to grant a discount and collect, Mathews had apparent authority to do so.

Source: CPA Exam, May 1982, # 1(7).

d. Davidson is the agent of Myers, a fuel dealer. Myers is an undisclosed principal. Davidson contracts with Wallop to purchase 30,000 tons of coal at twenty dollars per ton. Which of the following is correct?

1. If Davidson acts outside the scope of his authority in entering into this contract, Myers can *not* ratify the contract.
2. Wallop is bound to this contract only if Davidson acts within the scope of his authority.
3. If Davidson acts within the scope of his authority, Wallop can *not* hold Davidson personally liable on the contract.
4. Should Davidson refuse to accept delivery of the coal, Wallop will become an agent of Myers by substitution.

Source: CPA Exam, November 1982, # 1(7).

11

The last twenty years have seen the teaching of marketing, as well as marketing strategy itself, greatly affected by new consumer protection laws and UCC rules on sales, documents of title, and letters of credit.

D. James Manning
Professor of International Marketing

Bailments, Sales, and Consumer Protection

WHAT IS A BAILMENT?

A *bailment* may be defined as *the rightful possession of another's personal property*. The owner of the property is called the *bailor*, the party in possession is the *bailee*. There are four "keys" to understanding bailments.

1. Realize that only personal property can be bailed. It is not possible to create a bailment with real property. Only books, clothes, cars, stock certificates, promissory notes, money, and other personal property can be bailed.
2. Appreciate that the bailee's possession must be "rightful" (a party in wrongful possession of stolen property is not a bailee).
3. Understand that legal possession demands two things: actual physical control over the property plus intent to assume or exercise control. The intent to possess (i.e., to assume custody and control over the property) is essential to a bailment. A person who exercises physical control over personal property without intending to possess it has mere "custody" and not "possession." And custody is not sufficient to create a bailment. For example, suppose that Susie Customer is shopping at Super Value Department Store. If Susie picks up a silk scarf to examine it, Susie has custody only; she lacks the intent to assume control that is necessary for a bailment. Similarly, if John Clerk of the Super Value Store carries items of merchandise from place to place in the store as part of his job, he has custody only (though John has physical possession, like Susie he lacks the intent to control required for a bailment). Now suppose that Susie decides to try on a new coat in the store. John helps Susie remove her coat, and he places it on a counter from which it disappears. Here, the Super Value Store through its employee John Clerk

has manifested an intent to exercise control over the coat, and a bailment exists. If, on the other hand, Susie takes off her own coat and lays it on the counter with the result that the coat disappears, there is no physical possession by the store, no intent, and no bailment. The same is true where Susie personally hangs her coat on a hook in a restaurant—the restaurant is not a bailee of the coat. However, if Susie forgets her coat at the restaurant and the restaurant owner or his or her employee puts the coat away for Susie, a bailment comes into being. And, of course, if the restaurant provides a hat and coat checkroom staffed by an employee of the restaurant, the restaurant manifests the required intent to assume control and is a bailee of any checked item, including Susie's coat. Now suppose that on her way home Susie sees a billfold lying in the street. Again, if Susie merely picks up the billfold, examines it, and throws it back down in the street, Susie has custody only, and a bailment relationship does not come into being. But if, after examining the billfold, Susie takes it home with her, Susie holds the property as a finder and bailee for the true owner (see Chapter 8 regarding "finders").

4. Finally, recognize that the possession must be of a chattel belonging to someone else. The bailee must realize that he or she has possession of another person's personal property or a bailment relationship will not exist.

You can see from the finder example that a contract is not required for a bailment although, as a practical matter, contracts often give rise to bailment relationships. For example, if Susie Customer rents a car from Skimpy Budget Car Rental or takes her watch in for repairs or her clothes into the laundry, there is in each case a contract creating a bailment. The bailments arising from express and implied contracts may be distinguished from bailments which are *gratuitous* (not supported by consideration). Gratuitous bailments may be *voluntary* (the bailor intentionally delivers personal property to the bailee); *involuntary* (the bailor unintentionally turns over possession of the property as where Susie forgets her coat in the restaurant and the restaurant owner—the involuntary bailee—takes possession of it); or *constructive* (the bailor loses the property and the finder—the constructive bailee—takes possession of it).

WHAT ARE A BAILEE'S DUTIES?

A bailee has three basic duties with regard to the bailed personal property.

To Use the Chattel According to the Contract

First, the bailee has a duty to use the chattel only in accord with the bailment contract, and, if there is no contract, only in a manner that is fair and reasonable under the circumstances. In other words, the bailee must use the chattel for proper bailment purposes only. If the bailee uses the property for an improper purpose (i.e., uses it in any manner inconsistent with and in defiance of the bailor's ownership rights), the bailee will be liable to the bailor for misuse of the chattel (and for any damage or destruction resulting from the misuse) and breach of the bailment relationship. For example, suppose that Bill Bradley bails a television set to Randy Johnson for storage only. If Randy willfully destroys the set or uses it for his own purposes (as opposed to storing it), Randy will be liable in damages for misuse of the goods and breach of the bailment relationship.

To Exercise Care over the Chattel

Second, the bailee has a duty to exercise care over the bailed chattel. Apart from liability for misuse the bailee is not liable for damage or destruction of the chattel in the absence of negligence (as you will recall, negligence demands four things—a duty, a breach of duty, a causal connection between the breach and the damage, and actual damage measurable in dollar terms). So long as the bailee uses the chattel for a proper purpose and exercises care over the chattel, the risk of damage or destruction is entirely on the bailor. However if the bailee is negligent (i.e., violates his or her duty of care) and the chattel is damaged or destroyed as a result of the negligence, the bailee will again be liable to the bailor. For example, suppose that Susie Customer uses a rented car for normal driving purposes only. If the car is struck by lightning or is stolen without any fault on Susie's part, Susie will not be liable for damage; the risk of loss is entirely on the bailor. But if Susie drives the car while intoxicated and, as a result, runs it into a telephone pole, Susie will be liable; Susie's negligence has shifted the risk of damage or destruction back to the bailee.

The bailee's duty is to exercise the degree of care that a reasonable person under the same or similar circumstances would exercise. The circumstances include the nature of the bailed chattel, its apparent value, its proper uses, the location of the bailment, etc. To help in determining whether a bailee has exercised reasonable care, some courts have classified bailments into three categories, each requiring a different degree of care and imposing liability for a variant degree of negligence. The three traditional classifications are as follows:

A bailment for the mutual benefit of both the bailor and the bailee Where both parties benefit from the bailment relationship, the bailment is referred to as a mutual benefit bailment (also called a "bailment for hire" or a "commercial bailment"). For example, where Susie Customer rents a car from Skimpy Budget Car Rental, Susie (the bailee) benefits by reason of having a car to drive, and Skimpy Budget Car Rental (the bailor) benefits by virtue of receiving the rental payment. The bailment is properly termed a mutual benefit bailment.

The bailee in a mutual benefit bailment is required to exercise *ordinary care* and is liable for *ordinary negligence.* Courts frequently define "ordinary care" as "what a reasonable person would do in caring for his or her own goods of a similar kind under similar circumstances"; "ordinary negligence" is a failure to exercise ordinary care. Thus, if Susie Customer parks the rented car in front of her house instead of in her garage and a hit-and-run driver damages the vehicle, Susie is not liable to the bailor. Susie has exercised ordinary care (a reasonable person would park his or her own car on the street); therefore, her actions do not amount to ordinary negligence. On the other hand, if Susie leaves the keys to the rented car in the ignition with the result that the car is stolen, Susie is liable to the bailor. Susie has failed to exercise ordinary care (a reasonable person would not leave ignition keys in his or her car) and is liable for ordinary negligence.

What constitutes ordinary care necessarily varies with the circumstances of the particular bailment (e.g., a bailee is obviously expected to use more care for a chattel of great value than for a relatively inexpensive chattel).

A bailment for the sole benefit of the bailee Here the bailee alone benefits from the bailment relationship (typically, the mere loan of a chattel to the bailee). The bailee is required to exercise *extraordinary* or *great care* (as opposed to ordinary care) and is liable for *slight negligence* (as opposed to ordinary negligence). But not even a borrower-bailee is an insurer of the bailed goods. Some negligence, however slight, must be shown if the bailee is to be held liable. For example, suppose that Susie Customer borrows a friend's car and leaves it parked in the street instead of parking it in her garage. If the car is damaged by a hit-and-run driver, Susie may well be liable for failure to use extraordinary care. At most, Susie has been slightly negligent in leaving the car parked in the street; however, slight negligence is all that is necessary for liability where the bailment is for the sole benefit of the bailee. Still, Susie is not an insurer of the car. If she locks the car in her garage and the garage is struck by lightning, destroying the vehicle, Susie will not be liable because she has not been negligent.

A bailment for the sole benefit of the bailor This kind of bailment is frequently referred to as a "gratuitous bailment" since only the bailor benefits—the bailee holds the property gratuitously (i.e., without receiving anything in return). For example, a finder of lost property is a gratuitous bailee who holds the property for the sole benefit of the true owner. Similarly, where Susie Customer gratuitously stores Bill Bradley's car in her garage while Bill is vacationing in Europe, Susie holds the car solely for the benefit of Bill Bradley. The general rule is that a gratuitous bailee who cares for another's goods or chattels without receiving payment or other benefit in return must exercise only *slight care* (as opposed to ordinary or great care) and is liable only for *gross negligence* (as opposed to slight or ordinary negligence). Courts have met with considerable difficulty in trying to define the term "gross negligence." One court defined it in this way:

> Gross negligence is substantially and appreciably higher in magnitude than ordinary negligence. It is materially more want of care than constitutes simple inadvertence. It is an act or omission respecting legal duty of an aggravated character as distinguished from a mere failure to exercise ordinary care. It is very great negligence, or the absence of slight diligence, or the want of even scant care. It amounts to indifference to present legal duty and to utter forgetfulness of legal obligations so far as other persons may be affected. It is a heedless and palpable violation of legal duty respecting the rights of others. Altman v. Aronson, 231 Mass. 588, 121 N.E. 505 (1919).

But such definitions are not very helpful when dealing with actual fact situations. For example, we concluded that Susie Customer's conduct in leaving the keys to the rented car in the ignition (with the result that the car was stolen) amounts to ordinary negligence. But does Susie's conduct constitute gross negligence? You can appreciate the problem. Because of it, modern authorities have tended to stop analyzing bailments—particularly mutual benefit bailments and bailments for the sole benefit of the bailor—in terms of degrees of care and negligence. Instead the courts now state that negligence in such cases is nothing more than a failure to bestow the care which the property in its situation demands; the omission of the reasonable care required is the negligence which creates the liability; and whether this existed is a question of fact for the jury to determine. Thus, under the modern approach, the fact that a bailee receives no payment or other benefit for taking care of the bailed property is but one of the many circumstances to be considered in determining how much care is required of the bailee and whether he or she has been negligent in causing injury or loss to the chattel.

Sometimes the parties to a bailment desire to vary the duty of "reasonable care under the circumstances" imposed by law upon the bailee. The parties, by contract, may generally impose a lesser or greater duty of care. For example, a bailee will frequently insert a contract provision limiting his or her liability to a fixed amount in the event of damage or loss or the bailee will insert a provision exempting himself or herself from liability. The limitation or exemption may apply to all kinds of loss or damage, or it may be limited to a few specific kinds such as loss or damage resulting from "leakage, freezing, or flooding" (e.g., where the parties anticipate that "leaking, freezing, or flooding" is likely to occur despite any reasonable precautions taken). Most courts uphold such provisions so long as they are clearly called to the bailor's attention or are placed so that a reasonable person in the position of the bailor would notice them. Thus, a large sign stating "not responsible for theft or damage to articles checked" is effective to disclaim liability for negligence when placed at the entrance to a restaurant had and coat checkroom. However, the same statement in small print on the back of a standard claim check is not effective to disclaim liability for negligence unless it is clearly called to the customer's attention.

Of course, a bailee can never limit his or her liability for willful or intentional injury to the bailed chattel. Nor can the bailee exempt himself or herself from such liability. Any provision purporting to do so is contrary to public policy and, thus, unenforceable. Along the same line, many courts prohibit a bailee from limiting or exempting his or her liability for gross negligence. And some courts prohibit any and all limitation or exemption of liability as being contrary to public policy.

Finally, the parties to a bailment may choose to increase the bailee's responsibility by contract. For example, a bailee might agree, in return for consideration, to assume absolute responsibility for goods—to become, in effect, an insurer of the property. The "insurer" bailee has a duty to return the goods in an undamaged condition under all circumstances; he or she is liable for any loss or damage no matter what the cause. Contract provisions imposing a greater duty of care upon the bailee are generally upheld unless they are unconscionable as defined in Chapter 8.

In any event, a bailee may purchase liability insurance to protect against liability for loss or damage of the bailed goods. The bailee in every case has an insurable interest in the bailed property; however, he or she is under no obligation to the bailor to insure the goods.

To Redeliver the Chattel to the Bailor

Third, the bailee has a duty to redeliver the chattel to the bailor (or his or her appointee). The bailee's duty is absolute. No reasonable care standard is applied; if the bailee improperly delivers the chattel to one other than the bailor (or his or her appointee), the bailee will be liable regardless of how much care he or she has exercised.

However, the bailee will not be liable if, knowing that a third person claims ownership of the chattel, the bailee delivers the chattel into the "custody of the law" (i.e., takes the chattel to court for a determination of who is entitled to the property). The bailee will, in fact, be liable to the third person if the bailee redelivers the chattel to the bailor and it later turns out that the third person and not the bailor owns the item.

The bailee's duty is to redeliver the *identical* goods bailed to him or her. The single exception is where the goods are "fungible" goods as defined in Chapter 8. You will remember that each fungible unit is the equivalent of any other like unit. Frequently, when a bailor deposits fungible goods with a bailee, the bailee places the goods in common mass of like fungibles. The bailee agrees to redeliver not the identical goods deposited but merely an equal amount of like goods taken from the common mass. The bailor-depositors of the goods making up the common mass own the property as tenants in common (see Chapter 8 on "tenants in common.") Any individual depositor may have an option to sell his or her deposit and receive back cash rather than the deposited fungibles; such an option does not impair the bailment relationship.

HOW DOES THE BAILOR PROVE THAT THE BAILEE WAS NEGLIGENT?

You know that if bailed goods are lost, damaged, or destroyed while in the possession of the bailee, the bailor can recover from the bailee only if the bailee has been negligent. Yet, in many situations, it is difficult, if not impossible, for the bailor to prove any lack of care on the bailee's part (where the bailee fails to return the bailed chattel or returns it in a damaged condition, how is the bailor to know, much less prove, what happened to the property?). If required to prove negligence, the bailor would seldom recover.

For this reason, the law does not require the bailor to prove that the bailee was negligent. It requires only that the bailor establish the existence of the bailment (possession in the bailee) along with the bailee's failure to return the goods on demand or his or her return of the property in a damaged state. This is called making out a *prima facie* case against the bailee. The effect of making out a prima facie case is to establish a rebuttable presumption that the bailee was negligent and that his or her negligence caused the loss or damage. If the bailee fails to rebut the presumption (i.e., fails to prove that he or she was not negligent), judgment will be entered on behalf of the bailor.

For example, suppose that Susie Customer leaves a car rented from Skimpy Budget Car Rental in her garage while she goes on vacation. While Susie is away, a fire breaks out in the garage, and the car is destroyed. Though there is no evidence as to how the fire started or whether Susie was to blame, Skimpy Budget Car Rental can make out a prima facie case against Susie by proving that the car was rented and not returned. Since Susie cannot disprove negligence, she will lose the case. On the other hand, if Susie can prove that the fire was caused by lightning striking the garage, Susie will rebut the presumption of negligence and win the case.

WHAT IS THE BAILMENT CONTAINER RULE?

When the bailed chattel is a closed container or other item containing property not visible to the bailee, the bailee is responsible for the chattel's contents only where he or she knows or should know as a reasonable person (e.g., because of the nature of the container) that the contents are present. For example, suppose that you park your car with a bailee and the car is stolen or damaged as a result of the bailee's negligence. Obviously, the bailee will be liable for the loss of the car. But will he or she be liable for the loss of property contained in the trunk of the car? As to ordinary automobile accessories such as a jack and a spare tire, the answer is yes, because the bailee should reasonably expect such items to be present in the trunk. But the bailee will not be responsible for the loss of golf clubs contained in the trunk unless you informed him or her of their presence and he or she took possession of the car anyway.

WHAT ARE THE BAILMENT RESPONSIBILITIES OF A COMMON CARRIER OF GOODS?

A person who is in the business of transporting goods for others (whether by truck, plane, ship, etc.) is called a *carrier*. If a carrier holds himself or herself out to transport goods for any and all members of the public, he or she is a *common carrier*: a common carrier is one engaged in transporting goods for the general public without discrimination and for compensation. If a carrier does not hold himself or herself out to transport goods for the general public but merely agrees to carry goods for a limited number of customers under contract, the carrier is a *private contract carrier*.

Both common carriers and private contract carriers are bailees (both are in possession of another's personal property during the carriage); however, their responsibilities are very different. A private contract carrier is in the position of a mutual benefit bailee and is responsible for loss or damage only if he or she fails to exercise reasonable care under the circumstances. A common carrier, on the other hand, is strictly liable for the goods once they have been delivered to the carrier and have been accepted by him or her for immediate transportation.

Exceptions to the Common Carrier's Strict Liability

There are five exceptions to the common carrier's strict liability.

Act of God This is any sudden, violent, natural phenomenon that damages or destroys the goods in the custody of the carrier. The force must be natural, extraordinary, and unforeseeable, (e.g., a fire caused by lightning). A force of human origin is not an act of God (e.g., a fire resulting from arson). If the carrier knows of the natural force's approach, the carrier has a duty to exercise reasonable care to protect the shipper's goods. And if the carrier in any way contributes to the loss caused by the act of God (whether a flood, tornado, earthquake, etc.), the carrier will be liable for the full value of the loss or destruction.

Act of a public enemy If a public enemy (i.e., a military force of a hostile nation) causes loss or damage to goods in possession of a common carrier, the carrier will not be liable in the absence of negligence. "Public enemy" does not encompass common criminals; an ordinary highjacker of a carrier truck, cargo plane, or vessel is not a public enemy nor is a rioting mob. However, "public enemy" does include a hijacker or pirate involved in an international conspiracy against a recognized governmental power.

Act of a public authority Similarly, a carrier is not strictly liable for loss or damage caused by an act of a state, federal, or local government agency. For example, a public health agency might halt the carrier to inspect the goods; the delay might result in loss or damage for the shipper. Or a county sheriff might seize the goods to satisfy a judgment obtained by a creditor of the shipper. In any case, the carrier has a duty to notify the shipper of any potentially injurious action by the state so that the shipper can take steps to protect his or her interest.

The inherent nature of the goods The carrier also escapes strict liability where the loss or damage stems from the inherent nature of the bailed goods. Fruits and vegetables, for example, may spoil or deteriorate while being transported without any fault on the part of the carrier—the carrier is not liable for this natural, normal spoilage. Nor is a carrier of live animals responsible if the animals die of fright or refuse to eat and starve to death because they are highly strung and nervous creatures.

Of course, if the carrier in any way contributes to the loss or destruction, the carrier will be liable on the basis of negligence. For example, if the carrier can tell by seeing the goods that they will spoil during the carriage, the carrier is under a duty to refuse to transport the property. If the carrier accepts the goods and they spoil en route, the carrier will be liable. Similarly, the carrier of live animals will be liable if he or she fails to provide the animals with proper food and water and proper shelter from the elements. All perishables must be properly carried to prevent deterioration.

To protect themselves, most common carriers provide special refrigerated and heated cars which are available to shippers at a higher rate. A shipper who fails to take advantage of the special cars but ships his or her goods in ordinary cars so as to pay the lower charge cannot later recover from the carrier on the basis that special cars should have been provided.

The fault of the shipper-bailor Finally, if the shipper himself or herself causes the loss, the carrier will not be liable. The most common example is where a shipper defectively packages goods, and the goods spoil or deteriorate as a result. Of course, if the defect in packaging is apparent, the carrier is under a duty to refuse to transport the goods; if the carrier accepts the goods and the goods spoil or deteriorate as a result of the packaging, the carrier will be liable.

A second example is where a shipper gives faulty directions to a carrier. Unless the carrier knows or should know that the directions are incorrect, the carrier will not be liable for any delay or damage that results.

Because common carriers deal with the public, they are closely regulated by government agencies. The federal Interstate Commerce Commission (ICC) regulates common carriers engaged in interstate transportation (see Chapter 5); state and local agencies regulate intrastate carriers. Under the law, a shipper is entitled to demand that a common carrier accept and carry his or her goods at a reasonable rate (subject to regulation and approval by the regulatory agencies) and subject to the insurer's liability. A common carrier must accept and carry goods without discrimination. However, a carrier is not bound to accept and carry:

1. Goods beyond the capacity of the carrier;
2. Goods of a kind which the carrier does not normally carry and has no facilities to carry;
3. Goods injurious to person or property;
4. Goods that have been defectively packed or loaded; or
5. High risk goods requiring unusual care in transport.

Also, the common carrier may limit his or her strict liability by contract with the shipper. While the carrier may not enter into a valid agreement to absolve himself or herself of negligence, the carrier may lawfully contract to exempt himself or herself from liability for accidental loss or certain specific hazards (e.g., employee strikes, fires resulting from causes other than an act of God or carrier negligence).

The common carrier may also contract to limit his or her liability to a certain fixed amount or percentage of the value of the goods. Notice that, in each case, the word "contract" has been used: a carrier's limited liability agreement with a shipper is enforceable only if the carrier gives consideration for the agreement in the form of a reduced rate for the shipment with limited liability. In other words, the agreement will be upheld only if the carrier offers the shipper a choice between limited and unlimited liability and gives the shipper a decrease in rate for the former. A carrier who offers only one rate of coverage cannot escape strict liability. Along this line, the Interstate Commerce Act and many state statutes require or authorize carriers to file *tariffs* (books or tables of rates and limitations) with the appropriate federal (the ICC) and state regulatory agencies. Air carriers file tariffs with the Civil Aeronautics Board (CAB). A shipper is held to be on notice of any rate or limitation contained in a published tariff filed by a carrier and approved by the appropriate federal or state agency.

Sometimes, a common carrier takes freight for shipment, then ships the goods over more than one line or through connecting carriers. The law provides that the original ("originating") carrier may not limit his or her strict liability for losses occurring on the other lines or carriers. By accepting the freight for shipment, the originating carrier assumes responsibility for its entire transport. The liability of a connecting carrier, on the other hand, is limited to the period of the carrier's possession of the goods (of course, if the originating carrier is held liable for a connecting carrier's portion of the transport, the originating carrier may be able to recover from the connecting carrier).

Finally, the common carrier is under an absolute duty to deliver the goods to the right person (remember, a bailee's third duty is to redeliver the bailed goods only to the bailor or his or her appointee). If the carrier delivers the goods to the wrong person, the carrier will be liable for any loss or damage that results.

A common carrier of passengers is required to exercise the highest degree of care, skill, and diligence in providing for their safety. It follows from this extremely high duty of care that the carrier is liable for the slightest negligence resulting in loss or damage to a passenger. For example, if the owner-operator of a passenger bus fails to provide safe areas for boarding and alighting from the vehicle and a passenger is injured while getting on or off the bus, the carrier will be liable.

WHAT ARE THE BAILMENT RESPONSIBILITIES OF A WAREHOUSEPERSON?

A *warehouseperson* is a person who is in the business of storing the goods of others for compensation. A public warehouseperson holds himself or herself out generally to serve the public without discrimination. Because of their public calling, warehousepersons are subject to special statutory regulation as to rates, storage facilities, and proper safety precautions.

Unlike a common carrier, a warehouseperson is not strictly liable for the goods in his or her possession. Rather, the warehouseperson is deemed to be an ordinary mutual benefit bailee and must exercise only ordinary care and is liable for ordinary negligence. Like a common carrier, a warehouseperson may limit his or her liability to a specified maximum. To do so, the warehouseperson must offer the customer a choice between full liability for the storage at one rate and limited liability at a lower rate. The warehouseperson must state the limitation for each item or each unit of weight (e.g., "our maximum liability for this fur coat will be $500" or "our maximum liability for each bushel of corn will be $50") rather than use a blanket limitation such as "our maximum liability will be $1,500."

It should be pointed out that a common carrier of goods may have only a warehouseperson's liability at certain times. You will recall that the carrier's strict liability arises when goods have been *delivered* to the carrier and *accepted* by the carrier for *immediate transportation*. If the goods are delivered to the carrier but are not yet ready for immediate carriage because something remains to be done by the shipper (e.g., the shipper must deliver more goods or give further instructions, etc.), the carrier will be liable only as a warehouseperson until the goods are ready for shipment.

It should also be mentioned that a common carrier's strict liability may terminate at a point in time prior to the actual receipt of the goods by the party (called the "consignee") to whom they are shipped. Where an express company or other common carrier delivers the goods to the consignee's residence or place of business, the carrier's strict liability continues until the moment of delivery. But where a carrier completes transporting the goods, then puts the goods in storage for the consignee, the carrier's liability again becomes that of a warehouseperson. For example, a railroad company generally transports goods to the point of destination, then deposits the goods in the station or warehouse for delivery to the consignee. Once the consignee is notified that the goods are ready for delivery and has reasonable time to react to the notification, the carrier's liability changes from that of strict insurer to mutual benefit bailee.

WHAT ARE DOCUMENTS OF TITLE AND WHEN ARE THEY NEGOTIABLE?

Without warehousepersons and common carriers there could be little business or commerce. Each year, literally billions of dollars worth of goods have to be stored and/or transported. On the one hand, there are goods that must be aged or cured in storage; many crops must be stored after harvest to await delivery to the consumer; goods pledged as loan collateral must be stored until the loans are repaid. On the other hand, raw materials must be sent to both foreign and domestic processing and manufacturing plants, and manufactured goods must be shipped to retailers both at home and abroad.

The warehousing and transporting of goods is essential to the working of our national economy. While these functions are largely governed by the law of bailments, the economy's need for a free flow of goods demands the ability to pass ownership (title) of the goods even while they are in the possession of the warehouseperson or common carrier. This is where the special written contracts of the warehouseperson and common carrier come into play. Called "warehouse receipts" when issued by a warehouseperson and "bills of lading" when issued by a common carrier, these written contracts are properly designated *documents of title.* When issued in negotiable form, the documents of title can be used to transfer ownership of the goods though the goods remain in the possession of the warehouseperson or carrier bailee. Negotiable documents of title have similar characteristics to the negotiable notes, drafts, and checks discussed in Chapter 10. Just as a negotiable note, draft, or check may be transferred to a *holder in due course* who acquires superior rights in the instrument, a negotiable document of title may be transferred to a *bona fide purchaser* who acquires superior rights both in the document itself and in the goods covered by the document. The bona fide purchaser (bfp) succeeds to ownership without having to worry about the claims of prior parties.

And both negotiable and non-negotiable documents of title can be pledged as security or collateral for a loan though the goods remain in the warehouseperson's or carrier's possession.

A warehouseperson who stores goods for a price issues a "warehouse receipt" to the owner-bailor of the property. The receipt is first of all a written contract between the parties wherein the bailor promises to pay the storage charge, and the bailee acknowledges receipt of the goods and promises properly to care for the goods and deliver them according to the bailor's direction. The warehouse receipt is second of all a "document of title" which may be used to transfer ownership of the goods though the goods never leave the bailee's warehouse.

A common carrier also issues a written contract called a "bill of lading" to the bailor-shipper of goods. A bill issued by an originating carrier and specifying one or more connecting carriers is called a *through bill of lading.* Like the warehouse receipt, the bill of lading evidences the contract between the parties; the bill is an order for delivery of the goods in which the shipper promises to pay the carriage charge, and the carrier promises properly to care for the goods and transport and deliver them as provided by the shipper. The bill of lading also serves as a receipt for the goods to be transported; the bill describes the condition, quantity, and weight of the goods and names the party to whom they are to be delivered (the consignee). Finally, the bill of lading is a document of title which may be used to transfer ownership of the goods even while the goods are in transit (i.e., while they are being transported by the carrier).

The Difference Between a Negotiable and Non-negotiable Document of Title

A negotiable document of title represents legal ownership of the goods covered by the document—the owner of a negotiable warehouse receipt or negotiable bill of lading is entitled to the goods. When is a warehouse receipt or bill of lading negotiable? You will recall from Chapter 10 that notes, drafts, and checks must satisfy nine requirements if they are to be negotiable instruments that serve as money substitutes. A "money instrument" must be in writing; it must contain an unconditional promise or order to pay a sum certain in money on demand or at a definite time; it must be signed by the maker or drawer; and it must be made payable to "order" or to "bearer."

Like "money instruments," negotiable documents of title ("goods instruments") must contain the magic words to "order" or to "bearer." However, unlike money instruments, goods instruments need satisfy no other requirements in order to be negotiable. If a warehouse receipt or bill of lading makes the goods deliverable to "bearer" or to the "order" of a named person, the document of title is negotiable. If the warehouse receipt or bill of lading does not contain the magic words, the document is non-negotiable. It is as simple as that.

Negotiable documents of title are negotiated in much the same manner as negotiable notes, drafts, and checks. "Order" documents of title are negotiated by endorsement and delivery; "bearer" documents are negotiated by delivery alone. As with money instruments, a blank endorsement (signature alone) of an "order" document converts it to bearer paper. A special endorsement (endorsement to a specified person) of a "bearer" document converts it to order paper. Other kinds of endorsements (e.g., conditional and qualified) do not apply to documents of title.

The result of duly negotiating a negotiable document of title is to transfer the right to delivery of the goods covered by the document and, along with this right, ownership of the goods themselves. Like negotiation of a money instrument to a HDC, due negotiation of a negotiable document of title may create rights in the purchaser of the document superior to those of his or her transferor.

A purchaser who takes a goods instrument through a negotiation in good faith, without notice, for value, and in the regular course of business or financing and not in settlement or payment of a money obligation is referred to as a bona fide purchaser. With limited exception, a bona fide purchaser acquires ownership (title) both of the document of title and of the goods covered by the document. The bfp's ownership (title) is good as against the whole world. This is so notwithstanding that the transferor had no right to negotiate the document to the bona fide purchaser (e.g., where the transferor had rightful possession of the document but no authority to negotiate it, or where the transferor obtained the document by defrauding the true owner). Like the holder in due course who acquires superior rights in a money instrument, the bona fide purchaser of the document may acquire rights superior to those of his or her transferor—the bfp's rights are good even against the true owner.

As far as the requirements of a bfp are concerned, you already know how documents of title are negotiated. And you are familiar with the requirements of taking in good faith, without notice, and for value—these are the same requirements for a holder in due course of a money instrument. However, the last requirement of a bona fide purchaser of a document of title—*taking in the regular course of business or financing and not in settlement or payment of a money obligation*—is new and requires some explanation. To begin with, the law regarding bona fide purchasers is designed to facilitate the speedy flow of goods in commerce. A bfp who acquires superior rights in bailed goods can further negotiate the document of title covering the goods, and the transferee will succeed to ownership free of the claims of prior parties. Because the objective of the law is to protect only commercial transactions, the law requires that the bfp take the document in the regular course of business or financing and not in settlement or payment of a money obligation. In other words, the bfp must acquire the document in a usual and ordinary commercial transaction, the purpose of which is to move the goods in commerce. A transfer out of the regular course of business (including a transfer of a document merely to pay off or settle a money debt) is not a transfer that will make a person a bona fide purchaser.

With limited exception, a bona fide purchaser who takes a negotiable document of title through a negotiation cuts off claims of prior parties both as to the document of title and as to the goods covered by the document. For example, a bona fide purchaser of a bearer document of title acquires complete ownership rights to the document and to the goods covered by the document even though the true owner has already sold the document or the goods to another. The same is true where the true owner is deprived of the bearer document through misrepresentation, fraud, accident, mistake, duress, loss, or conversion; if a bona fide purchaser takes the document through a negotiation (delivery alone) the bfp acquires title good as against the whole world, including the true owner or his or her transferor.

Of course, if the document is order paper, a thief or finder cannot negotiate it (endorsement as well as delivery is required), and any subsequent purchaser or transferee cannot qualify as a bona fide purchaser. The fact that the thief or finder has forged the required signature does not improve the transferee's position: the transferee is an assignee who "stands in the shoes" of his or her transferor. The transferee's only remedy, for what it is worth, is against the forger.

Suppose that a thief steals goods (as opposed to stealing a bearer document of title) and takes the goods to a warehouseperson or common carrier who issues a negotiable warehouse receipt or bill of lading. The law provides that the thief cannot divest the true owner of title to the goods by now negotiating the "goods instrument" to a bona fide purchaser. This is like a "real defense" good as against a holder in due course: though a purchaser qualifies as a bfp (i.e., takes the negotiable document of title through a negotiation, in good faith, without notice, for value, and in the regular course of business), he or she does not acquire paramount title in the property.

Another "real defense" arises where fungible goods covered by a negotiable warehouse receipt are sold and delivered by a warehouseperson (who is also in the business of buying and selling such fungibles) to a buyer in the ordinary course of business. Though the warehouse receipt has been duly negotiated to a bfp, the bfp will not prevail against the buyer in the ordinary course of business. Of course, the warehouseperson who wrongfully sells the fungibles will be liable to the bailor or his or her transferee (bfp or otherwise) who holds the warehouse receipt. Generally, the problem is compounded by the fact that the warehouseperson had the fungibles stored in a common mass of like fungibles belonging to other bailors. Ordinarily, warehoused goods under a particular warehouse receipt must be kept separate to permit easy identification and delivery, but fungibles may be commingled. Assuming the warehouseperson-bailee who wrongfully sells the bailed fungibles has insufficient fungibles remaining in the common mass to cover every bailor's interest, the bailors (or their transferees) are entitled to their proportionate share of the common mass as tenants in common.

But apart from the "stolen goods" and "sale of fungibles" exceptions, the bona fide purchaser of a document of title acquires paramount title to the document and to the goods covered by the document. The bona fide purchaser's title is good as against the whole world, including the true owner.

In contrast, the purchaser of a non-negotiable warehouse receipt or bill of lading receives only the rights of his or her transferor (the purchaser is an assignee "standing in the shoes" of his or her transferor). For example, suppose that Jake Howard fraudulently induces Mary Smith to part with goods, then warehouses the goods so as to create a non-negotiable warehouse receipt. Jake subsequently sells the receipt to Jean Kent, whereupon Mary finds and claims her goods. As between Jean and Mary, Mary prevails; her defense of fraud is good not only against Jake but also against his assignee, Jean, and Mary is entitled to the return of her property. (Of course, if Jake had obtained a negotiable warehouse receipt and duly negotiated it to Jean—a bfp—Jean, and not Mary, would prevail.

WHAT IS A PLEDGE?

A "pledge" is a special kind of bailment. A pledge is the placement of personal property in the possession of another as security or collateral for some act by the bailor. Usually, the act secured is the repayment of a loan; the bailee makes the loan because the bailor deposits personal property with the bailee as collateral; the pledged property secures repayment of the money. The bailee-pledgee of the personal property must exercise the ordinary care of a mutual benefit bailee. He or she has the right to exclusive possession of the property during the term of the pledge and can use the property in any manner contemplated by the pledge agreement (any substantial misuse will constitute a conversion of the property). Once the pledgor has performed the required act (e.g., has repaid the loan), the pledge automatically terminates, and the pledgor is entitled to the return of his or her property. In the event that the pledgor fails to perform as promised (e.g., fails to repay the loan), the pledgee has the right to sell the pledged personal property and collect the money owning.

In the usual bailment pledge, there is actual delivery of possession of the personal property. But where the goods are represented by a document of title, delivery of the document is sufficient.

And sometimes the owner of goods wants to use the goods as security for a loan, but it is not feasible to transfer the goods to a warehouse. You will understand the problem if you imagine thousands of logs piled in the forest, or vast quantities of raw materials sitting in a manufacturing yard, or a large inventory of automobiles held by a dealer for sale to retailers. Obviously, it would be very difficult to pledge the goods if they first had to be placed in a warehouse. Most lenders do not have warehouse facilities available, yet they are willing to lend on such goods if their security interest in the goods can be protected. The solution is a procedure known as *field warehousing*. Rather than move the goods to a warehouse, the "warehouse" is set up in the "field" (i.e., where the goods are located). Generally, part of the owner's plant or yard is blocked off and put under the control of the warehouseperson; sometimes, only a fence is placed around the goods. What is essential is that the warehouseperson have control over the property so that the lender can be assured that his or her security interest is protected. Once control is established, the warehouseperson can issue a warehouse receipt; the receipt can be pledged as security for the loan, and the owner of the goods can receive the needed cash from the lending institution.

Usually, where the warehouseperson does not have the goods in his or her warehouse but controls them only in the field, he or she will issue a non-negotiable warehouse receipt. It is not desirable to issue a negotiable receipt because the debtor-owner-bailor will frequently need to have part of the warehoused goods released to him or her so as to be able to continue business operations—for example, the logs will have to be milled, the raw materials manufactured, the automobiles sold. With a negotiable receipt, the warehouseperson has a duty to collect the receipt at the time of delivery of the goods; in the case of partial delivery, the warehouseperson must conspicuously note the extent of delivery on the face of the receipt (this protects the parties from subsequent transfer of a collected document to a bfp). Thus, the warehouseperson cannot rightfully deliver part of the goods to the owner-bailor without asking the pledgee physically to hand over the document of title and risk losing his or her security. With a non-negotiable receipt, the lender can retain possession of the document and simply authorize the warehouseperson to release goods in the desired quantity. Also, with a non-negotiable receipt, additional inventory can be added to the field warehoused goods as it is purchased or as it arrives for use in the business.

Bills of lading are also pledged as security for cash loans. Sellers of goods frequently enter into transactions where the buyer is to pay cash for goods only upon their arrival at the buyer's place of business. The goods may not arrive for many days or even weeks—yet, the seller needs the cash immediately for business or other reasons. The seller can obtain the money (less a discount) at the time of shipment by pledging the bill of lading covering the goods with a lender. The procedure is as follows. The seller directs the carrier to issue a negotiable bill of lading to the "order" of the seller covering the goods to be transported to the buyer. The seller also draws a draft on the buyer for the amount of the purchase price. The seller then specially endorses both the negotiable bill of lading and the draft to the "order" of the lender. The lender, in turn, pays the seller an amount of money equal to the purchase price of the goods minus a discount reflecting the lender's profit. The lender then forwards the draft and the bill of lading to his or her representative in the area where the buyer is located. After the goods arrive in the area, the lender's representative presents the draft and the bill of lading and collects the purchase price.

So you see, documents of title are used not only to transfer ownership of goods, but also to finance business and business transactions.

WHAT ARE DOCUMENT OF TITLE DELIVERY REQUIREMENTS?

A warehouseperson or carrier is absolutely liable for misdelivery of goods (i.e., if a warehouseperson or carrier delivers goods to the wrong person, the warehouseperson or carrier will be liable without regard to negligence). If the bill of lading is non-negotiable (i.e., if it is not made deliverable to "bearer" or to the "order" of a named person), it is termed a *straight bill of lading*. A straight bill of lading specifies a consignee to whom the goods are to be delivered—the carrier is contractually obligated to deliver the goods to that person only.

Unlike a bona fide purchaser of a negotiable bill of lading, a party in possession of a straight bill has no paramount claim to title of the document. If the carrier delivers the goods to a person in possession of the bill other than the named consignee, the carrier will be liable for conversion of the bailed property. And it is not necessary for the named consignee to present or surrender the straight bill of lading in order to pick up the goods. The consignee has a right to receive the goods, and the carrier has an obligation to deliver them without surrender of the document.

With a negotiable bill of lading, the rules are entirely different. Here the carrier undertakes to deliver the goods, not to a named consignee, but to anyone who qualifies as a holder of the document. Again, the carrier is protected only if he or she complies with the terms of the bill; in the case of a "bearer" bill, the carrier must deliver the goods to any person in possession of the document; where the document is an "order" bill, the carrier must deliver the goods to any person in possession of the bill properly endorsed. And where the bill of lading is negotiable, the carrier is also obligated to take up and cancel the bill upon delivery of the goods.

WHAT IS THE DIFFERENCE BETWEEN A BAILMENT AND A SALE?

As you know, a *bailment* is the rightful possession of another's personal property. A bailment is a transfer of possession only—not a transfer of ownership; when the bailment comes to an end, the bailee must return the identical property bailed to the bailor. A sale, on the other hand, is the transfer of ownership of goods from a seller to a buyer for a consideration known as a price. A sale can be effected (i.e., ownership or title can be transferred) with or without a transfer of possession.

So, in a bailment, possession—not ownership—is transferred; in a sale, ownership is transferred, sometimes with and sometimes without a transfer of possession.

WHAT IS THE EFFECT OF "IDENTIFICATION" OF THE GOODS TO THE CONTRACT OF SALE?

A sale is a contract by which the ownership of goods is transferred from a seller to a buyer. Obviously, if a sale is to occur, the specific goods to be sold must at some point be identified. The process of selecting or setting aside the specific goods is referred to as "identification" of the goods to the contract. Identification requires two things: first, the goods must be in existence; and second, the specific chattel or chattels to be transferred from the seller to the buyer must be singled out. Other than this, no specific procedure is required—it is sufficient that the specific goods be in some way earmarked for the buyer.

Occasionally, goods are identified at the time the contract is entered into. Here, both buyer and seller have in mind certain specific goods that are to be sold, and the buyer bargains for the specific goods. More often, however, identification takes place after the contract is entered into. At the time of the sale, the seller merely agrees to furnish a specified number of items from his or her general inventory; the seller segregates the specific items to be sold at a later point in time. For example, suppose that Susan Seller agrees to sell fifty TV sets from her general stock of 1,000 such sets to Barry Buyer. At the time of entering into the contract, Susan makes no effort to single out or set aside the specific sets to be sold to Barry; thus, identification does not occur at this point. It occurs later when Susan segregates the fifty sets to be delivered to Barry. Of course, if at the time of contracting Susan gives Barry a list of fifty serial numbers identifying the specific sets that he will receive, identification takes place at that time.

Identification of the goods to the contract has important legal consequences for the buyer. Section 2–501 of the Uniform Commercial Code provides that the buyer acquires a "special property and insurable interest" in the goods at the time they are identified. The buyer's "special property" consists of three rights: the right to inspect the identified goods, the right to replevin the goods under some circumstances, and the right to recover damages from any third party who converts the goods or otherwise interferes with the property. These rights of the buyer do not exist absent identification.

As for the buyer's insurable interest in the goods, you will recall that a person must have an insurable interest in property in order to purchase insurance on the property (see Chapter 10). The Uniform Commercial Code creates an insurable interest in the buyer upon identification of the goods on the rationale that as soon as the buyer knows or can determine which specific goods he or she will receive, the buyer can enter into other contracts regarding the goods requiring insurance protection. For example, Barry Buyer may contract to provide the fifty identified TV sets for a new motel operation.

It should be realized that the buyer's "special property and insurable interest" are far less than the complete ownership of the goods that the buyer will acquire upon completion of the sale: the "special property and insurable interest" exist independently of ownership (title) which is almost certain to remain in the seller (along with the risk of loss for damage or destruction of the goods) for a period of time after identification. The seller owner retains his or her own insurable interest in the property until such time as ownership passes to the buyer. And if the seller retains a "security interest" in the goods (see Chapter 12), his or her insurable interest will continue until the goods are paid for.

AS BETWEEN THE BUYER AND THE SELLER, WHO MUST BEAR THE LOSS IF THE GOODS ARE LOST, DAMAGED, OR DESTROYED?

Obviously, goods start out at the risk of the seller. A seller may have a whole warehouse full of inventory that he or she intends to sell. If the warehouse burns to the ground, destroying the goods, the seller will have to absorb the loss and look to insurance coverage for reimbursement. Potential but as yet unknown buyers would not share in the loss.

At some point, however, a buyer enters into the picture. And, at some point, the risk of loss may pass from the seller to the buyer. If the goods to be sold under the contract are lost, damaged, or destroyed while the risk is in the seller, the seller must bear the loss; but if the risk has passed to the buyer, the buyer must bear the loss. As to when the risk of loss passes, the Uniform Commercial Code provides that title is not determinative; the fact that ownership of the goods has not yet passed to the buyer does not mean that risk of loss has not yet passed, and vice versa. Rather, the Uniform Commercial Code deals with risk of loss from an event or situation standpoint. One of the parties—either buyer or seller—may be at fault in causing the loss. Or, as is more often the case, neither party may be at fault—as where the loss or damage results from an act of God (e.g., a flood, earthquake, tornado, or the like), an unavoidable accident (e.g. a fire that starts without negligence of any kind), or a negligent or wrongful act of a third party (e.g., a delay in shipment by a common carrier). The seller may have fulfilled all of his or her duties with regard to shipment of the goods, or he or she may have duties remaining. And either party, buyer or seller, may have breached the contract of sale, etc. Three situations may arise.

Fault of One of the Parties

The goods may be lost, damaged, or destroyed through fault of one of the parties. Where either the buyer or the seller is "at fault" in causing the loss or damage, the party at fault bears the risk of loss and is liable to the other party for any loss that he or she suffers. "Fault" includes negligent as well as willful wrong.

Before the Risk of Loss Passes

More often, the goods are lost, damaged, or destroyed through no fault of the parties. If the loss or damage occurs before the risk of loss has passed from the seller to the buyer, the seller will be liable to the buyer unless his or her inability to perform (i.e., to deliver the goods in the condition promised) constitutes an "objective impossibility" or is "commercially impracticable" (see Chapter 9). In almost all cases where the goods are lost, damaged, or destroyed prior to identification (as where the seller's entire inventory is destroyed by fire) or after identification, where identification takes place after the contract is entered into (the usual situation), it is only subjectively impossible for the seller to perform (the goods could be obtained from other sources).

Occasionally, however, the goods are identified to the contract at the time the contract is entered into. Here, as you will recall, both buyer and seller have certain specific goods in mind as the subject matter of the sale at the time the contract is entered into. The buyer bargains for the specific goods, and, if the goods are lost, damaged, or destroyed, it will be objectively impossible for the seller to perform (no one could deliver the specific goods bargained for). The contract will thus be avoided, and the seller will be excused from performance (however, both buyer and seller may be protected by insurance as both have insurable interests in the property, the buyer by virtue of his or her "special property and insurable interest," the seller by virtue of his or her ownership).

Where goods *identified when the contract is entered into are not totally, but only partially lost or destroyed* (again without fault of the parties and before the risk of loss has passed to the buyer), the buyer has the right to demand inspection of the goods and at his or her option either avoid the contract or accept the goods in their damaged state with due allowance from the contract price for the damage or deterioration (UCC 2–613).

After the Risk of Loss Passes

Even though neither party is at fault, once the risk of loss has passed from the seller to the buyer, it becomes the buyer's problem if the goods are lost, damaged, or destroyed; the buyer will have to pay the seller the full contract price for the goods even though they arrive in a damaged or deteriorated condition or don't arrive at all. Of course, the buyer, in turn, may be able to recover from a third party (e.g., a common carrier) who is strictly liable or at fault in causing the loss.

WHEN DOES THE RISK OF LOSS PASS FROM SELLER TO BUYER?

As to *when* the risk of loss passes from the seller to the buyer, the Uniform Commercial Code very specifically controls according to the following situations or events.

No Common Carrier or Other Bailee

In most sales contracts, there is no common carrier or other bailee involved, and the parties make no agreement as to risk of loss. The seller simply delivers the goods to the buyer. For example, if you purchase a pair of shoes from a department store, the store employee will hand you the shoes, and you will take them home with you. If you purchase a refrigerator-freezer from the store, the store will deliver the appliance to you in a company truck (as opposed to a common carrier). If you buy a used set of dishes at a neighborhood garage sale, the seller will relinquish possession of the dishes, and you will take possession.

At some point in time, the risk of loss for damage or destruction of the shoes, the refrigerator-freezer, or the dishes passes to you, the buyer. If the seller is a *merchant*, the risk of loss passes to you upon *receipt* of the goods, "receipt" meaning physical possession. If the seller is a *nonmerchant*, the risk of loss passes to you upon *tender of delivery* of the goods without regard to your actual receipt of the goods ("tender" is simply a conditional offer to perform—a statement that "I am ready to perform if you are"). Thus, if the nonmerchant-seller tenders delivery of the goods (says "here they are, take them), and you, the buyer, refuse to accept delivery, the risk of loss will nevertheless pass to you at the moment of tender.

Returning to our examples, suppose that you accidentally leave your new shoes on a counter in the same department store while making another purchase. If the shoes are stolen from the counter, you must bear the loss. The risk of loss passed to you at the time you received actual possession of the shoes from the department store merchant-seller.

Now suppose that the department store delivery truck arrives at your home and the driver of the truck tenders delivery of the refrigerator-freezer. You refuse delivery. The truck leaves to return to the store but is in an accident on the way back, and the refrigerator-freezer is badly damaged. Here, the department store merchant-seller must bear the loss—you, the buyer, have not *received* the goods, and receipt is necessary for the risk of loss to pass to you from the merchant-seller. (Of course, the merchant-seller is likely to sue you for breach of contract if you have no valid reason for refusing delivery.)

On the other hand, suppose that the nonmerchant neighborhood seller brings the used dishes to your home in his or her stationwagon and there "tenders delivery" to you. Again, you refuse delivery, the seller is in an accident on the way home, and the dishes are destroyed. Here, you must bear the loss. The seller being a nonmerchant, the risk of loss passed to you upon tender of delivery without regard to your actual receipt of the goods.

Shipment by Common Carrier

Most *business* contracts for the sale of goods call for the goods to be shipped to the buyer by common carrier. Here, the risk of loss passes to the buyer at one of two times depending on whether the contract is a "shipment" contract or a "destination" contract. In a *shipment contract,* the seller is required to deliver the goods merely to a carrier at the place of shipment rather than to a particular destination. The risk of loss passes to the buyer when the goods are "duly delivered" to the carrier. If the seller "duly delivers" the goods to the carrier, (i.e., delivers them to the carrier in the condition contracted for and makes proper arrangements for their carriage), the goods will be "conforming" (i.e., in accord with the terms of the contract). The goods being conforming, the buyer will have no right to reject them even if they arrive in a spoiled or damaged condition. The risk of loss has passed to the buyer (upon due delivery of the goods to the carrier), and the buyer will have to pay the full contract price for the goods and seek recovery from the carrier or other third party.

Of course, if the goods are not in the condition contracted for when delivered to the carrier (e.g., if they are already spoiled or damaged), the goods are *nonconforming* (i.e., not in accord with the terms of the contract), and there is no due delivery. The risk of loss remains in the seller, and the buyer has the right to reject the goods upon their arrival in the spoiled or damaged state. (UCC Section 2–504).

In a *destination contract*, on the other hand, the seller must deliver the goods to a particular destination: the risk of loss does not pass to the buyer until the goods are there *duly tendered* to the buyer. Remember, a tender is a conditional offer. Under UCC Section 2–503, tender of delivery demands that the seller, at a reasonable hour, put and hold conforming goods (i.e., goods in accord with the terms of the contract) at the buyer's disposal and provide the buyer with such notice and documents as are reasonably necessary to enable the buyer to take possession of the goods. Upon due tender, the risk of loss passes to the buyer—this is so whether or not the buyer takes actual delivery of the goods (as where the buyer is unwilling to accept delivery).

Sale contracts calling for shipment to the buyer by common carrier are presumed to be shipment and not destination contracts unless the contract expressly provides to the contrary. The fact that a seller is required to pay freight to the point of destination does not in and of itself make a contract a destination contract, nor does the fact that goods are to be delivered "C.O.D." (meaning "collect on delivery," with the buyer required to pay for the goods and their transportation before delivery will be made).

However, the use of other commercial shipment terms such as "F.O.B.," "F.A.S.," or "C.I.F." may be controlling as to whether a particular contract is a shipment or destination contract. Remember always that in a shipment contract the risk of loss passes to the buyer upon due delivery of the goods to the carrier; in a destination contract, the risk of loss passes to the buyer upon due tender of delivery at the specified destination point.

F.O.B. The term "F.O.B.," standing for "free on board," is used as a delivery term rather than a price term. When the contract calls for the seller to ship the goods "F.O.B. place of shipment," the agreement is a shipment contract, and the seller is required only to bear the risk and expense of putting the goods into the possession of the carrier; the seller is not obligated to bear the expense of loading. As in other shipment contracts, the risk of loss passes to the buyer once the goods are duly delivered to the carrier. So if the contract is "F.O.B. the seller's place of business" or "F.O.B. the seller's factory" or "F.O.B. Chicago" (where Chicago is the point of shipment), the contract is a shipment contract, and the risk of loss passes to the buyer upon due delivery of the goods to the carrier.

In contrast, if the language used is "F.O.B. place of destination" (e.g., "F.O.B. buyer's place of business"), the contract is a destination contract, and the risk of loss does not pass to the buyer until the seller makes proper tender of delivery at the destination point.

F.A.S. The letters "F.A.S." mean "free alongside" and are generally used in maritime shipping contracts (i.e., in contracts calling for the goods to be shipped over the water on oceangoing or other vessels). A seller who agrees to ship "F.A.S." must deliver the goods free of expense to the buyer alongside (on the dock next to) the vessel on which they are to be loaded (the buyer bears the expense of loading); the seller must there tender a receipt for the goods in exchange for which the carrier is under a duty to issue a bill of lading. The risk of loss passes to the buyer when the goods are duly delivered alongside the vessel. (UCC Section 2–319).

C.I.F. and C. & F. "C.I.F." and "C. & F." contracts are also maritime shipment contracts. The letters "C.I.F." stand for "cost, insurance, and freight," the letters "C. & F." for "cost and freight." Under a "C.I.F." contract, the buyer promises to pay a price for the goods that includes not only the cost of the goods but also all freight charges to the named destination, as well as all insurance costs in providing for safe delivery of the shipment. The seller, in turn, must at his or her own expense and risk put the goods into the possession of the carrier at the port of shipment; obtain negotiable bills of lading to cover their transportation to the named destination; have the goods loaded; pay the costs of loading; obtain a receipt from the carrier showing that the freight has been paid or provided for; obtain an appropriate certificate of insurance on behalf of and for the benefit of the buyer; prepare an invoice and other necessary documents and forward and tender the documents, properly endorsed, to the buyer. The risk of loss passes to the buyer upon due delivery of the goods to the carrier.

Under a "C. & F." contract the buyer promises to pay a price including the cost of the goods and all freight charges to the named destination—the price does not include the cost of insurance. With the exception of duties relating to insurance, the seller has the same duties under a C. & F. contract that he or she has under a C.I.F. contract. Again the risk of loss passes to the buyer upon due delivery of the goods to the carrier.

With regard to both C.I.F. and C. & F. contracts, when all proper documents including the negotiable bill or bills of lading have been tendered to the buyer, the buyer is obligated to pay the full purchase price of the goods though the goods themselves have not arrived. In fact, a tender of the actual goods without a tender of the document would not constitute full performance by the seller, and the buyer would not be obligated to accept or pay for the goods. (This is true in any case where documents are needed to take possession of the goods, whether the contract is F.A.S., F.O.B. vessel, etc.)

Ex-ship Finally, an "ex-ship" contract is a destination contract. A seller who agrees to deliver goods "ex-ship" agrees to bear full risk and expense until the goods leave the ship's tackle (i.e., until they are unloaded). The risk of loss passes to the buyer when the goods are unloaded. As always, the seller must furnish the buyer any documents that are required to enable the buyer to take possession of the goods (UCC Section 2–322).

Delivery of Goods Without Being Moved

Sometimes, the goods are in the possession of a bailee and are to be "delivered" into the buyer's ownership without being moved (i.e., after the sale is complete, the goods will still be in the bailee's possession but will be owned by the buyer rather than by the seller). Section 2–509 of the UCC provides that the risk of loss passes to the buyer in this situation, upon the buyer's receipt of any document of title covering the goods (usually, the goods are in the hands of a professional warehouseperson and are covered by a warehouse receipt), or, if there is no document, upon the bailee's acknowledgment of the buyer's right to possession of the goods.

An exception arises where the seller himself or herself is the bailee. It is generally held that if the seller retains possession of the goods after the sale, the risk of loss will pass according to the "usual" rule discussed in (1) above (i.e., upon delivery in the case of a merchant-seller or upon tender of delivery in the case of a nonmerchant seller).

Agreement as to Risk of Loss

The rules discussed above in numbers (1), (2), and (3) may be altered by agreement of the parties as to risk of loss. The buyer and seller are left free to readjust their rights and risks in any manner agreeable to them (UCC Section 2–509(4)).

Sale on Approval or Sale or Return

Goods may be transferred in a "sale on approval" or a "sale or return." In a "sale on approval," goods are delivered to a buyer for a stated period of time or, if no time is stated, for a reasonable time, during which the buyer may use the goods for the purpose of determining whether or not to purchase them. Ownership and risk of loss remain in the seller until the buyer accepts the goods. Generally, the buyer accepts by notifying the seller that he or she "approves" the sale. And the buyer will be deemed to accept if he or she fails to return the goods to the seller within a reasonable time (or to notify the seller of their return) or if he or she exercises dominion over the goods inconsistent with the purpose of determining approval (e.g., selling the goods to another). Upon acceptance, title and risk of loss pass to the buyer, and the buyer becomes liable for the purchase price of the goods.

In a "sale or return," on the other hand, goods are delivered to the buyer who has an option to return them to the seller. Here, ownership and risk of loss pass to the buyer according to rules (1) through (4) above. However, in a sale or return, the buyer can revest ownership and risk of loss in the seller by returning the goods. The return is at the buyer's risk and expense.

Sometimes it is difficult to determine whether a particular contract is a sale on approval or a sale or return. To aid in such situations, Section 2–326 of the UCC provides that if the goods are delivered primarily for the buyer's use, the transaction is a sale on approval, but if the goods are delivered primarily for resale by the buyer, the transaction is a sale or return. For example, in a "sale on consignment," a seller transfers goods to a buyer for purposes of resale; the seller purports to retain ownership of the goods, and any goods that go unsold must be returned to the seller. Under Section 2–326, a sale on consignment is a sale or return (the goods are delivered primarily for resale by the buyer) and ownership and risk of loss pass to the buyer accordingly. (A sale on consignment is considered a sale or return primarily to protect creditors of the buyer who have no way of knowing that the goods "belong" to another.)

Breach of Contract of Sale

There are three situations where the risk of loss rules discussed in (1) through (5) above do not apply because one of the parties—either buyer or seller—has breached the contract of sale.

The first situation arises where the seller breaches the contract by sending *nonconforming* goods, and the buyer rejects the goods. UCC Section 2–601 states in part that "if the goods or the tender of delivery fail in any respect to *conform* to the contract, the buyer may (a) reject the whole; or (b) accept the whole; or (c) accept any commercial unit or units and reject the rest." As for the risk of loss, UCC Section 2–510(1) states that "where a tender or delivery of goods so fails to conform to the contract as to give a right of rejection the risk of their loss remains on the seller until cure or acceptance." Thus, where goods are nonconforming, the risk of loss remains on the seller until he or she "cures" the nonconformity by sending conforming goods (the buyer, in this case, may set off a reasonable amount from the purchase price or may pay the full purchase price and sue the seller for breach of contract of sale).

The second situation occurs where the seller breaches the contract by sending nonconforming goods, and the buyer accepts the goods before discovering the nonconformity. If the nonconformity is "substantial" (i.e., if it substantially impairs the value of the goods to the buyer), the buyer may upon discovering it revoke his or her acceptance under UCC Section 2–608 and treat the risk of loss as being in the seller to the extent that the buyer does not have insurance covering the loss. For example, suppose that auto manufacturer Paula Pontiac agrees to sell ten cars to auto retailer Junior Samples. The cars arrive in apparently good order, and Junior accepts the cars. However, as it turns out, each car has 100 minor defects that "substantially" impair the value of the cars to Junior. Upon discovering the defects, Junior can revoke his acceptance. It follows that if the cars are destroyed in Junior's parking lot by an unexpected flood, Junior can treat the risk of loss as being in Paula Pontiac to the extent that Junior has no insurance coverage for the loss.

However, it should be realized that the buyer must notify the seller of his or her intention to revoke within a reasonable time after discovering the nonconformity. If the buyer unreasonably delays in notifying the seller and continues to use the goods, the buyer will lose the right to revoke.

The third and final situation arises where the buyer *wrongfully* repudiates or otherwise breaches the contract of sale after the goods have been identified to the contract but before the risk of loss has passed to the buyer. To the extent that the seller is uninsured for loss or damage to the property, the seller may treat the risk of loss as being in the buyer for a "commercially reasonable time" after the repudiation or other breach. Assume, for example, that Paula Pontiac has the ten cars ready for shipment to Junior Samples. The day prior to shipment, Junior wrongfully repudiates the contract by informing Paula that he will not accept or pay for the cars. That night the cars are destroyed in Paula's parking lot by an unexpected flood. Though the risk of loss has not yet passed to Junior Samples (the cars have not been delivered to the carrier), Paula can treat the risk of loss as being in Junior to the extent that Paula's insurance does not cover the loss.

Now suppose that the cars are destroyed by flood, not on the night of Junior's wrongful repudiation but six months later. Six months is not a "commercially reasonable time" as prescribed by Section 2–510(3), and Junior will not be liable for any part of the loss.

DOES THE BUYER HAVE A RIGHT TO INSPECT THE GOODS PRIOR TO ACCEPTANCE OR PAYMENT?

In almost all cases, the buyer has a right to inspect the goods prior to accepting or paying for them—the seller has no basis for objection if the buyer refuses to accept or pay until inspection is made. The UCC at Section 2–513 provides that the buyer may inspect the goods at any reasonable time and place and in any reasonable manner, either before or after delivery. However, if the buyer fails to inspect within a reasonable time after receipt of the goods, the buyer will lose the right to inspect. Sometimes, it is impossible to tell from a mere visual inspection (by simply looking at the goods) whether the goods are conforming or nonconforming. The buyer, in this case, also has a right to test a reasonable amount of the goods in any manner reasonable under the circumstances. The expenses of inspection must be borne by the buyer; however, he or she can recover the expenses from the seller if the goods do not conform and the buyer rejects them.

On occasion, the buyer is obligated under the terms of the contract to pay for the goods upon receipt of the shipping documents (as opposed to receipt of the goods themselves). This is referred to as "paying against documents of title"—usually bills of lading. The buyer, in this situation, generally has no right to demand inspection of the goods prior to making payment; this makes sense, as the shipping documents commonly arrive and are tendered to the buyer while the goods are still in transit. However, if the goods by the terms of the contract are to be "available for inspection" at the time the payment falls due, the buyer will have a right to inspect before making payment.

Similarly, in a "C.O.D." contract (meaning "collect on delivery"), the buyer has no right of inspection prior to payment unless the agreement expressly provides for such a right.

Nor does a buyer who is obligated to pay "against documents" or "C.O.D." have any right to possession of the goods prior to making payment in full. However, payment under these circumstances does not constitute acceptance of the goods, and if the goods turn out to be nonconforming, the buyer may still reject them and recover from the seller any payment made along with damages incurred.

WHAT ARE THE BUYER'S REMEDIES IF THE SELLER SENDS NONCONFORMING GOODS?

The Buyer's Right to Reject the Goods

If the goods or the tender of delivery fail *in any respect to conform* to the contract, the buyer may reject the whole or accept any commercial unit and reject the rest. Thus, if the goods sent by the seller are not in accordance with the terms of or obligations under the contract, the buyer may reject the goods—that is, refuse to keep them. The buyer must notify the seller of his or her decision to reject within a reasonable time after delivery or tender of the goods. And the notification must be specific; the buyer must disclose the nature of the defect if it is curable or he or she will be barred from asserting the defect as a reason for rejecting the goods.

The buyer who rejects all the goods tendered or delivered because all or part of the goods are nonconforming in effect cancels (i.e., puts an end to) the contract of sale. This is a significant remedy in that the buyer is freed from all obligation under the contract and may recover from the seller any part of the purchase price paid along with any damages incurred by reason of the nonconforming delivery. The buyer who accepts part of the goods and rejects the rest "cancels" only a portion of the contract; the buyer may "set off" (i.e., deduct) from the purchase price owing on the accepted goods any damages incurred by reason of the nonconformity.

The buyer who rejects goods may have certain duties with regard to the goods. If, prior to rejection, the buyer has taken physical possession of the goods, the buyer must exercise reasonable care over the property for a time sufficient for the seller to remove the goods. If the buyer is a merchant and the seller has no business representative or place of business at the place of rejection, the buyer must follow the seller's reasonable instructions with regard to the goods and, in the absence of such instructions, must sell the goods for the seller's account if they are perishable or threaten to decline in value speedily. Of course, the buyer may deduct from the sales proceeds or otherwise collect from the seller his or her expenses in caring for and selling the goods. (Section 2–603 of the UCC).

The parties, by agreement, may limit the UCC remedies of either buyer or seller or may provide for an "exclusive" remedy for either party. In the event that such an "exclusive" or "limited" remedy fails of its essential purpose, the Code remedies may be utilized.

The buyer's right to reject is also subject to the seller's *right to "cure"* (i.e., remedy) the nonconformity. So long as the contract time for performance has not yet expired, the seller who makes an improper tender or delivery has a right to cure the nonconformity by delivering conforming goods. And even where the contract time for performance has expired, the seller will have a reasonable time to effectuate cure if the seller had "reasonable grounds to believe" that the goods would be acceptable.

Obviously, to effectuate cure the seller must know of the nonconformity; it is for this reason that UCC Section 2–602 requires the buyer seasonably to notify the seller of his or her intention to reject the goods, and UCC Section 2–605 requires the buyer to specifically list the defects prompting the rejection. Upon cure by the seller, the buyer loses his or her right of rejection.

Following Acceptance, the Buyer's Right to Revoke Acceptance

Sometimes, the buyer accepts the goods and only afterwards discovers that they are nonconforming. Usually, where nonconforming goods are accepted, the acceptance occurs by virtue of the buyer's failing to make an effective rejection. Remember, the buyer must under the UCC, reject the goods within a reasonable time after their delivery and must give timely notice of the rejection to the seller. A failure effectively to reject results in acceptance.

Under certain circumstances a buyer who accepts goods, then subsequently discovers the goods to be nonconforming, may revoke his or her acceptance. However, revocation of acceptance is not as easily accomplished as rejection of the goods in the first instance. Whereas a buyer may reject goods that are nonconforming *in any respect*, the buyer may revoke acceptance of goods only if the goods are *substantially nonconforming*. In other words, to justify revocation, the nonconformity must substantially impair the value of the goods to the buyer. Where this is the case, the buyer may revoke his or her acceptance as to all the goods or any commercial unit of the goods, whereupon the buyer will be in the same position as though he or she had rejected the goods from the outset. Thus, the buyer who revokes his or her acceptance as to all the goods, in effect, cancels the sale and is freed from all obligation under the contract; the buyer may recover from the seller any damages sufferd by reason of the nonconforming delivery. The buyer who revokes his or her acceptance as to part of the goods cancels only that portion of the contract and must pay for the goods accepted; however, the buyer may "set off" from the purchase price owing any damages incurred because of the nonconformity.

Like the buyer's right of rejection, the buyer's right of revocation of acceptance is subject to the seller's right to "cure" the defect. Since the buyer who revokes is in the same position as if he or she had rejected the goods, it follows that the seller has a right to "cure" under UCC Section 2–508. If the contract time for performance by the seller has not yet expired, the seller has an absolute right to "cure"; if the contract time for performance has expired, the seller has a right to cure only if he or she had "reasonable grounds to believe" at the time of performing that the goods would be acceptable to the buyer.

Finally, if the buyer who revokes has "physical possession" of the goods at the time of revocation of acceptance, the buyer will have the same duties with regard to the goods as if he or she had rejected them.

The Buyer's Right of Resale to Recover Prepayments

Following rejection or revocation of acceptance of all or part of the contract of sale, the buyer has a right to recover any prepayments made on the purchase price. Where the buyer cancels but a portion of the sale, the buyer may generally "recover" the prepayments simply by "setting off" the prepaid amounts from the monies still owing under the contract. Sometimes, however, this is insufficient to reimburse the buyer, and where the buyer has prepaid all of the purchase price or has canceled the entire contract, the remedy of "set off" has no application.

Short of going to court, how is the buyer in this situation to recover his or her prepayments? In demanding repayment, the buyer has one very important "bargaining tool"—he or she has physical possession of the nonconforming goods. Under UCC Sections 2–711(3) and 2–706(6) a buyer who has prepaid all or part of the purchase price may offer to restore the nonconforming shipment to the seller in return for repayment of the monies paid; if the seller refuses, the buyer may sell the goods to recover his or her prepayments. The buyer must remit to the seller any resale proceeds in excess of the buyer's prepayments and costs in selling the goods.

The Buyer's Right to "Cover" or Sue for Damages

Following rejection or revocation of acceptance, the buyer has a right to "cover" or sue for money damages for nondelivery. A buyer who rightfully rejects nonconforming goods or justifiably revokes acceptance of the goods has a right to effect "cover" under Section 2–712 of the Uniform Commercial Code. To effect *"cover"* means to go out into the market and purchase substitute goods. So long as the buyer acts reasonably and in good faith, the buyer may recover from the seller any excess of the cover price over the contract price (along with any incidental or consequential damages, less expenses saved by reason of buying in another market).

Both merchant and nonmerchant buyers have a right to effect "cover" following rightful rejection of goods or justifiable revocation of acceptance. Of course, there can be a problem if the buyer, following rejection or revocation of acceptance, notifies the seller and immediatley effects cover, only then to receive notice from the seller that the seller intends to cure the defect under UCC Section 2–508. It would appear that the buyer must be careful not to cover until he or she is certain that the seller cannot cure the nonconformity under Section 2–508.

As an alternative to cover, a buyer who has rightfully rejected goods or justifiably revoked acceptance of them has a right under UCC Section 2–713 to sue for money damages for nondelivery. The buyer's measure of damages for nondelivery is the difference between the market price at the time when the buyer learned of the breach and the contract price (together with any incidental or consequential damages less expenses saved in consequence of the seller's breach). The market price is determined as of the *place* of arrival where the goods are rejected after arrival or acceptance of them is revoked.

Frequently, the buyer's measure of damages for nondelivery will be the same as his or her measure of damages following cover. However, this is not always so; market price for purposes of nondelivery is determined as of the time the buyer learns of the breach, for purposes of cover, at the time of cover. Obviously, the market price may differ at these two times, particularly where the buyer waits several days or even weeks after learning of the breach to effect cover (remember, though the buyer must cover within a reasonable time, he or she is free to shop around for a good bargain).

In any case, whether the buyer covers and sues for damages or sues for money damages for nondelivery, the buyer is entitled as part of his or her measure of damages to any incidental or consequential damages incurred (less expenses saved because of the seller's breach). The test for recovery of consequential (remote or indirect) damages is whether the loss was reasonably foreseeable by the seller at the time of contracting. However, there is no requirement that the loss be actually foreseen by the seller. In the case of Lewis v. Mobil Oil Corp., 438 F.2d 500, 510 (8th Cir.1971), the court stated with regard to the buyer's lost profits:

> Where a seller provides goods to a manufacturing enterprise with knowledge that they are to be used in the manufacturing process, it is reasonable to assume that he should know the defective goods will cause a disruption of production, and loss of profits is a natural consequence of such disruption. Hence, loss of profits should be recoverable under these circumstances.

In addition to lost profits, consequential damages might include such items as legal expenses, repair expenses, amounts paid to third parties as a result of the seller's breach, etc.

The rule that any reasonably foreseeable loss is recoverable is subject to one qualification: consequential damages will not be allowed where the buyer could have prevented the loss by cover or other action. For example, lost profits will not be allowed as consequential damages where the buyer could have avoided the loss by effecting cover (i.e., by purchasing substitute goods on the open market). This qualification stems from the rule of mitigation of damages which requires the aggrieved party in a breach of contract situation to do whatever is reasonable to "mitigate" the damages.

The Buyer's Right to Damages for Breach of Warranty

Following acceptance of the goods, the buyer has a right to damages for breach of express or implied warranty. In nearly all sales, the seller makes express and/or implied "warranties" to the buyer. As you will recall from

Chapters 8 (dealing with "warranty" deeds for the transfer of land) and 9 ("warranties" in connection with insurance policies), a "warranty" is simply a promise that a proposition of fact is true. With regard to sales of goods, the seller warrants (promises) as true certain facts about the character, quality, or title of the goods. Frequently, the seller's warranties are express—i.e., stated either orally or in writing. For example, the seller or his or her saleperson may make oral warranties to the buyer or place the warranties right in the contract of sale. And all of you are familiar with the "warranty" cards that accompany the purchase of small appliances, sporting equipment, and other items. The cards contain the seller's express warranties as to the goods; generally, the buyer is asked to fill out the cards and return them either to the seller or manufacturer.

No special words or intent are required to create an express warranty. Thus, the statement that an item is an "air conditioner" will operate as an express warranty though the words "warrant" or "promise" are not used.

However, to constitute an express warranty, the statement must be one of fact and not merely a statement of "opinion" or "puffing" of wares. As you will recall from Chapter 8, it is sometimes difficult to distinguish between statements of fact and puffing. A statement that "this car is the best on the market" is obviously "puffing" and not an express warranty, while a statement that "this car is mechanically perfect" may well be a statement of fact constituting an express warranty.

Express warranties may arise from the seller's use of samples or models. Also, the timing of the affirmation of fact (the express warranty) is immaterial so long as the language, the sample, or the model is fairly to be regarded as "part of the basis of the bargain."

In addition to express warranties, the seller may make certain *implied warranties* regarding quality of the goods or implied warranties against infringement of patents or trademarks. An implied warranty is one that arises by operation of law without regard to any express affirmation of fact made by the seller; whether or not the seller makes any express warranties, he or she is held to imply certain promises simply by virtue of making the sale. Thus, a seller who sends nonconforming goods may breach an express warranty, an implied warranty, or both. A breach of either kind of warranty will provide the buyer with a complete remedy for the nonconforming delivery.

Two implied warranties—the *implied warranty of merchantability* and the *implied warranty against infringement*—apply only to merchants. Insofar as these warranties are concerned, a "merchant" is "a person who deals in goods of the kind" involved in the transaction (UCC Section 2–314—Official Comment). Thus, a plumber, electrician, or carpenter who installs parts as part of his or her services makes no implied warranties about those parts. And statutes in more than half the states provide that blood donors make no implied warranties about the quality or "merchantability" of their blood. Only those who are actually in the business of selling "goods of that kind"—department stores, grocery stores, hardware stores, etc.—qualify as "merchants" for purpose of making the implied warranties. Of course, merchants dealing with each other in supplying inventory are making the implied warranties.

Goods to be merchantable must be at least such as:

1. Pass without objection in the trade under the contract description;
2. In the case of fungible goods are of fair average quality within the description;
3. *Are fit for the ordinary purposes for which such goods are used;*
4. Run within the variations permitted by the agreement of even kind, quality, and quantity within each unit and among all units involved;
5. Are adequately contained, packaged, and labeled as the agreement may require; and
6. Conform to the promises or affirmations of fact made on the container or label if any.

Thus, the delivery by Hood River Apple Company of 800 crates of Grade C apples constitutes a breach of the implied warranty of merchantability when Grade A apples had been ordered. The Grade C apples obviously cannot "pass without objection in the trade under the contract description" and are not "fit for the ordinary purposes" of Grade A apples.

It should be realized that the implied warranty of merchantability applies to the sale of used goods as well as new goods. The Official Comment to Section 2–314 of the Uniform Commercial Code states: "A contract for the sale of secondhand goods, however, involves only such obligation as is appropriate to such goods for that is their contract description." In other words, the older and more used the goods are, the less of a warranty there will be. In the case of Overland Bond and Investment Corp. v. Howard, 9 Ill.App.3d 348, 292 N.E.2d 168 (1972), the plaintiff purchased a used 1965 automobile in June of 1970. The day after the plaintiff purchased the car, the transmission fell out of the automobile and had to be repaired. A week later, the brakes went out. Upon suit by the buyer, the court held that the defendant seller had breached the implied warranty of merchantability: the used car could not "pass without objection in the used car trade" and was not "fit for the ordinary purposes" for which used cars are utilized. The car was, therefore, unmerchantable and the merchant-seller liable.

The second implied warranty applying only to merchants—the implied warranty against patent or trademark infringement—is found at Section 2–312 of the Code:

> Unless otherwise agreed a seller who is a merchant regularly dealing in goods of the kind warrants that the goods shall be delivered free of the rightful claim of any third person by way of infringement or the like but a buyer who furnishes specifications to the seller must hold the seller harmless against any such claim which arises out of compliance with the specifications.

The implied warranty against patent or trademark infringement is unique in that, where the buyer furnishes the plans or specifications for the goods to be assembled, prepared, or manufactured, the warranty is imposed on the buyer rather than on the seller. The buyer, in such case, is held impliedly to warrant that the manufacture or assembly of the items will not infringe on another's patent or trademark rights.

A third implied warranty—*the implied warranty of fitness for a particular purpose*—applies to both merchant and nonmerchant sellers. Uniform

Commercial Code Section 2–315 provides: "Where the seller at the time of contracting has reason to know any particular purpose for which the goods are required and that the buyer is relying on the seller's skill or judgment to select or furnish suitable goods, there is an implied warranty that the goods shall be fit for such purpose." Thus, there are three conditions required for the warranty to arise: (1) the seller must know or have reason to know of the buyer's *particular* purpose; (2) the seller must know or have reason to know that the buyer is relying on the seller's skill or judgment to select suitable or proper goods; and (3) the buyer must, in fact, rely upon the seller's skill and judgment in selecting the goods.

The implied warranty of merchantability assures the buyer of goods "fit for the *ordinary* purpose for which such goods are used"; the implied warranty of fitness for a particular purpose assures the buyer of goods fit for a *"particular"* or *"special"* purpose. Again, the former warranty applies only to merchant sellers while the latter applies to all sellers, merchants and nonmerchants alike.

In the event that the seller breaches an express or implied warranty by sending nonconforming goods, the buyer upon *acceptance* of the goods may bring legal action against the seller to recover money damages. As far as the buyer's measure of damages is concerned, it makes no difference whether one warranty is breached or five are breached, or whether the warranties are express or implied—the buyer's measure of damages is the same in any case. All that is required is that the buyer notify the seller within a "reasonable time" that there may be a breach of warranty. What is a "reasonable time" varies depending on the circumstances. In the case of a merchant-buyer, commercial standards are controlling; in the case of a consumer-buyer, less stringent standards are applied with the result that the consumer-buyer has a longer period of time for giving notice.

Under Section 2–714(2), the buyer's measure of damages for breach of warranty is the difference between the "value of the goods accepted and the value they would have had as warranted." And where the buyer in the breach of warranty situation still owes the seller any or all of the purchase price of the accepted goods, the buyer may "set off" (i.e., deduct) from the amount owing any damages incurred by reason of the breach of warranty. As explained previously, the "set off" remedy is not confined to any particular situation but applies any time a buyer owing money under a contract of sale suffers damages by reason of the seller's breach of contract.

Finally, Section 2–714(3) of the Code provides that the buyer's measure of damages for breach of warranty includes any incidental or consequential damages, and Section 2–715(2)(b) states that consequential damages may be recovered for "injury to person or property proximately resulting from any breach of warranty." Thus, whereas consequential damages are generally recoverable only where they are reasonably foreseeable by the seller at the time of contracting, there is no foreseeability requirement insofar as Section 2–715(2)(b) is concerned. Thus, if the buyer accepts nonconforming goods and is subsequently injured as a result of the defective condition of the property, the buyer will be able to recover from the seller under Section 2–715(2)(b) though the injury was not foreseeable at the time of contracting.

One special problem for the buyer in the warranty area is *"disclaimer"* of warranty liability by the seller. First of all, if the goods contain patent (i.e., obvious) defects and the buyer inspects the goods prior to sale, the buyer waives the implied warranties with respect to the patent defects. The same is true where the buyer refuses to inspect the goods following a demand by the seller that he or she do so: by making the demand, the seller puts the buyer on notice that there may be patent defects; by not inspecting, the buyer assumes the risk of the defects.

Second, if the parties by their course of performance or previous dealings have excluded or modified the implied warranties, or if the warranties are excluded or modified by custom or usage within the particular trade, the implied warranties will be excluded or modified accordingly.

Third, and closely related to the second, the seller may effectively disclaim the implied warranties by using "catchall" terms such as "*as is*" or "*as they stand,*" "*with all faults,*" etc.

Fourth, *apart from using "catchall" language,* the seller may specifically disclaim the implied warranties of merchantability and fitness for a particular purpose as follows:

Disclaimer of the implied warranty of merchantability The implied warranty of merchantability may be disclaimed by the seller either orally or in writing. Whether oral or written, the disclaimer *must specifically mention the word "merchantability"*; if in writing, the disclaimer must be conspicuous.

These two requirements are very strictly enforced by the courts. If the word "merchantability" is not found in the disclaimer, the disclaimer will be ineffective to exclude the implied warranty. Thus, a statement that "any claim for defects is waived unless made within ten days" does not serve to disclaim or limit the implied warranty of merchantability because the word "merchantability" is nowhere found in the disclaimer.

Similarly, though a written disclaimer specifically mentions the word "merchantability," the disclaimer is ineffective to exclude or limit the implied warranty unless it is conspicuous. The Code, at Section 1–201(10) defines conspicuous as "a term or clause * * * so written that a reasonable person against whom it is to operate ought to have noticed it. * * * Language in the body of a form is 'conspicuous' if it is in larger or other contrasting type or color."

Disclaimer of the implied warranty of fitness for a particular purpose Unlike the implied warranty of merchantability which may be disclaimed either orally or in writing, the implied warranty of fitness for a particular purpose may be disclaimed *only in writing,* and the disclaimer must be conspicuous. Unlike the word "merchantability," the word "fitness" need not appear in the disclaimer. A conspicuous written statement that "there are no warranties which extend beyond the description on the face hereof" is sufficient to disclaim the implied warranty of fitness for a particular purpose even though it would be insufficient to disclaim merchantability.

Remember, the implied warranty of fitness is made by both merchant and nonmerchant sellers; the disclaimer requirements apply equally to both.

Remember, too, that a disclaimer of the implied warranty will be stricken by the courts if it is found to be unconscionable.

Fifth, the implied warranty against patent or trademark infringement may be disclaimed only by specific wording or by circumstances giving the buyer reason to know that such infringement may exist. Thus, while "catchall" language such as "with all faults" or "as is" will be effective to disclaim the implied warranties of merchantability and fitness for a particular purpose, it will not be effective to disclaim the implied warranty against patent or trademark infringement absent knowledge of possible infringement on the part of the buyer.

WHAT ARE THE BUYER'S RIGHTS IF THE SELLER BECOMES INSOLVENT AND IS UNABLE TO PERFORM?

The Uniform Commercial Code defines "insolvency" at Section 1–201(23) as follows: "A person is 'insolvent' who either has ceased to pay his debts in the ordinary course of business or cannot pay his debts as they become due or is insolvent within the meaning of the federal bankruptcy law." A person is "insolvent" within the meaning of the federal Bankruptcy Act if his or her liabilities exceed his or her assets (see Chapter 12).

Where the seller becomes insolvent and is unable to deliver the goods to the buyer, the buyer will have a right under certain circumstances to "capture" the goods (i.e., demand and obtain them from the seller). There are three specific requirements for the right of capture to exist: (1) the goods must be *identified* to the contract of sale; (2) the buyer must have *prepaid* all or part of the purchase price of the goods (where the buyer has prepaid only part of the price, he or she must tender to the seller the balance owing and keep the tender open); (3) the seller must have become insolvent within ten days after receiving the first installment on the purchase price.

The right of capture allows the buyer to demand and obtain the goods without going to court. However, the right does not carry with it a right to use force or self-help in claiming the property. If the seller refuses to recognize the buyer's right and deliver over the property, the buyer must go to court and replevin the goods.

Of course, where the seller is unable to deliver goods because of insolvency, the buyer will have other possible remedies in addition to capture or replevin—most notably, the right to effect cover or sue for money damages for nondelivery. However, these other remedies are generally of little value to the buyer since they involve seeking money damages; where the seller is insolvent, money damages are unlikely to be forthcoming. And in a bankruptcy proceeding the buyer is unlikely to get all of his or her prepayments back. Thus, being able to get the goods themselves is the best remedy.

CAN THE BUYER EVER GET SPECIFIC PERFORMANCE FROM THE SELLER?

Occasionally, the buyer cannot cover because adequate substitute goods are not available on the open market. In this unusual situation, the goods are deemed "unique," and the buyer may sue for specific performance—that is, for replevin of the specific goods.

HOW DOES THE UCC TREAT ANTICIPATORY BREACH?

Insofar as the sale of goods is concerned, the UCC extends the doctrine of anticipatory breach or repudiation (see Chapter 8) to include any contract of sale in which there remains some duty of performance owing by at least one of the parties. Section 2–610 states:

> When either party repudiates the contract with respect to a performance not yet due the loss of which will substantially impair the value of the contract to the other, the aggrieved party may:
>
> (a) for a commercially reasonable time await performance by the repudiating party; or
>
> (b) resort to any remedy for breach * * * even though he has notified the repudiating party that he would await the latter's performance and has urged retraction; and
>
> (c) in either case suspend his own performance.

Many times, however, it is not clear whether the particular words or acts of a party constitute a repudiation of the sales contract. An oral or written communication from the party may be ambiguous as to the party's intent or ability to perform. Or the party may appear to be insolvent and incapable of performing. If the other party, believing there has been a repudiation of the contract, suspends his or her own performance (or indicates an intent to do so), that party, if mistaken, will himself or herself be liable for breach of contract or anticipatory repudiation. To prevent this from happening, the UCC provides a method for determining whether a repudiation has, in fact, occurred. Under Section 2–609, if one party has a reasonable basis for feeling insecure about the other's performance, he or she may demand *adequate assurance* of due performance. If the other party fails to provide such assurance within a reasonable time not exceeding thirty days, that party will be deemed to have repudiated the contract.

While the aggrieved party has a right to resort immediately to any remedy for breach in the case of repudiation by the other, he or she is not required to do so. So long as the party takes no action, the other is free to retract (i.e., withdraw) his or her repudiation under UCC Section 2–611 and reinstate his or her rights under the contract. In other words, an anticipatory repudiation is revocable unless and until the aggrieved party has (1) canceled the contract; (2) changed his or her position materially in response to the repudiation; or (3) indicated in some other way that he or she has accepted the repudiation as final.

WHAT ARE THE RIGHTS OF THE SELLER IF THE BUYER BREACHES THE SALES CONTRACT?

If the buyer fails to make a payment due on or before delivery or repudiates the contract in advance of delivery, the seller may withhold delivery of the goods. To withhold delivery in no way affects any other remedies available to the seller. And if the seller who has contracted to sell goods on credit to a buyer discovers prior to delivery that the buyer is insolvent, the seller may demand payment in cash for the goods and withhold delivery until cash payment is made. If the seller has already delivered part of the goods at the time of learning of the buyer's insolvency, he or she may demand payment in cash for all the goods (both those delivered and those to be delivered) and withhold further delivery until such payment is made.

Sometimes, the seller does not discover that the buyer is insolvent until after he or she has delivered the goods on credit to the buyer. Obviously, the remedy of withholding delivery is not available to the seller in this case. But if the buyer was insolvent at the time of receipt of the goods, the seller may *reclaim* (the seller's right of reclamation) the property as provided by Section 2–702 of the Uniform Commercial Code. To reclaim the goods, the seller must demand their return within ten days after the buyer receives them. The ten-day limitation does not apply where the buyer misrepresented his or her solvency in writing to the seller within three months prior to delivery. Just as an aggrieved buyer may not use force or self-help to *capture* goods, an aggrieved seller may not use force or self-help to *reclaim* goods. If the buyer refuses to honor the seller's right of reclamation, the seller must go to court to replevin the goods. Successful reclamation (whether the goods are given up voluntarily by the buyer or obtained through replevin) excludes all other remedies with respect to the property, although the seller is still entitled to incidental damages. UCC Section 2–710 states: "Incidental damages to an aggrieved seller include any commercially reasonable charges, expenses or commission incurred in * * * connection with return * * * of the goods." The transfer of the goods to a bona fide purchaser for value (i.e., one who buys the goods for value without notice of the seller's rights) cuts off the seller's rights of reclamation: the bfp prevails over the seller as to possession of the goods, and the seller must resort to some other remedy.

If the seller learns of the buyer's insolvency after delivering the goods to a carrier for shipment, the seller may "stop" the goods while they are in transit and retake possession of them. The seller may thereafter withhold delivery of the goods pending cash payment and, if such payment is not forthcoming, may resort to any other available remedy. Referred to as the right of *stoppage in transit*, this seller's remedy is provided by Section 2–705 of the UCC (which also extends the right to situations where the goods are in the possession of a bailee other than a carrier—e.g., a warehouseperson).

The seller may exercise his or her right of stoppage in transit by notifying the carrier or other bailee to stop delivery. The notice must be such as to give the carrier or other bailee sufficient time to locate the goods and prevent their delivery. Upon receiving a timely "stop" notice, the carrier must hold and deliver the goods according to the seller's direction. If the goods are covered by a negotiable document of title, the carrier is not obligated to obey the "stop" order until the seller surrenders the document. However, it should be pointed out that if the buyer sells the goods while they are in transit to a bona fide purchaser, the bfp will cut off the seller's right of stoppage in transit. The same is true where the buyer obtains a negotiable document of title covering the goods and negotiates it to a bona fide purchaser. This is so whether the document is negotiated to the bfp before or after the seller has notified the carrier to stop delivery (UCC Section 7–502(2)).

The buyer's creditors, however, do not qualify as bona fide purchasers for purposes of cutting off the seller's right of stoppage in transit.

Probably the easiest thing for the seller to do when the buyer wrongfully refuses to accept the goods, fails to make a payment due on or before delivery of the goods, or repudiates the contract in advance of the time for performance is simply to resell the goods to another party. The seller's right of resale arises where the buyer wrongfully refuses to accept the goods, fails to make a payment due on or before delivery, or repudiates the contract in advance. So long as the seller resells the goods "in good faith" and in a "commercially reasonable manner" (UCC Section 2–706), the seller may recover from the buyer the difference between the resale price and the contract price together with any allowable incidental or consequential damages, less expenses saved by reason of the buyer's breach. In the event the resale price is greater than the contract price, the seller may keep the excess proceeds, having no obligation to account to the buyer for profits made on the resale. If, at the time of the breach, the goods have not yet been identified to the contract, the seller may identify the goods and then resell them.

Sometimes, however, the seller is unable to resell the goods or prefers not to resell them. As an alternative to resale, the seller may bring legal action for *money damages for nonacceptance or repudiation* (this remedy is the seller's counterpart to the buyer's right to sue for money damages for nondelivery under UCC Section 2–713).

Where the seller is in the process of manufacturing the goods at the time the buyer breaches the contract (by failing to make an advance payment or repudiating the contract), the seller may do one of two things. First, he or she may cease manufacturing and identify the goods though they are still incomplete; it must be clear that the goods were intended for the particular contract with the buyer. The seller may then sell the identified goods for their scrap or salvage value. Or, second, the seller may complete the manufacturing process if such is commercially reasonable and then identify the goods for resale. The seller may recover from the buyer the difference between the resale price and the contract price.

In just three situations the seller may recover the full purchase price that the buyer was obligated to pay under the contract:

1. Where the buyer has, in fact, accepted the goods;
2. Where the goods are lost or damaged *after* the risk of loss has passed to the buyer; or
3. Where, following the buyer's breach, the seller is unable to resell the identified goods through reasonable efforts.

MAY THE BUYER AND SELLER AGREE TO REMEDIES AND/OR DAMAGES NOT PROVIDED BY THE UCC?

The parties, by agreement, may provide for remedies in addition to or in place of those provided by the UCC. The parties may designate such remedies as "exclusive" remedies for either the buyer or seller. The parties may also limit or alter the measure of damages recoverable to return of the goods and repayment of the price or to repair and replacement of nonconforming goods or parts. However, at least minimum adequate remedies must be available. Any clauses purporting to modify or limit the remedial provisions of the Code in an unconscionable manner are not enforceable. And, where an apparently fair and reasonable clause, because of circumstances, fails in its purpose or operates to deprive either party of the substantial value of the bargain, it must give way to the general remedy provisions of the Code.

Along the same line, Section 2–718 of the Code permits the parties to set *liquidated damages.* You will recall the discussion of liquidated damages from Chapter 8. Where a liquidated damages provision bears no reasonable relationship to the amount of probable loss as calculated at the time of entering into the contract, the provision is not a valid liquidated damages clause but is an unenforceable penalty provision.

Even in the absence of a liquidated damages provision, if the seller justifiably withholds delivery of the goods because of a breach by the buyer, the seller may retain any deposit made on the purchase price up to 20 percent of the price, or $500, whichever is less (UCC Section 2–718).

WHAT HAPPENS WHEN A PERSON PURPORTS TO SELL GOODS THAT HE OR SHE DOES NOT OWN?

The question of when ownership (title) passes from a seller to a buyer is not very important under the Uniform Commercial Code. Risk of loss problems and buyer's and seller's remedies for breach of contract all are specifically controlled by the Uniform Commercial Code without regard to who has title to the goods or when or whether title passes from the seller to the buyer.

Yet at some point in the sales transaction (assuming there is no problem or dispute) the seller has complete title (ownership) to the goods and, through the sale, transfers this title (ownership) to the buyer. UCC Section 2–401 provides the rules for passing of title, stating that once the goods are identified, title passes from the seller to the buyer at whatever time the parties intend that title should pass. If the parties have not explicitly agreed as to the time of passage of title, the Code provides that title passes when the seller has completed whatever performance is required of him or her with respect to physical delivery of the goods. Thus, in a "shipment" contract, title passes to the buyer upon shipment; in a "destination" contract, title passes upon proper tender of the goods at destination. If delivery is to be made without moving the goods and the seller is to deliver a document of title, title passes at the time and place of delivery of the document; if the goods are already identified at the time of contracting and no document of title is involved, title passes at the time of contracting. Of course, if a negotiable document of title is involved, title to the goods will pass whenever the document of title is negotiated to a bona fide purchaser.

Title, however, cannot pass until the goods are in existence. So if future goods are specified—for example, an agreement to sell "all the apples produced by Hood River Apple Company over the next three years"—title to the goods cannot pass until the goods are grown regardless of any contrary expression of intent by the buyer and seller.

Although title is generally not a consideration in most sales disputes, it becomes a crucial factor when someone purports to sell goods he or she does not own. There are always three parties involved: (1) the *purported seller* who does not have title to the goods; (2) the *buyer* who believes he or she is acquiring title from the seller; and (3) the *true owner* of the property who does have title. The various rights, duties, and liabilities of the parties will depend on the circumstances. Sometimes, the "buyer" will prevail against the true owner even though the seller had no title to transfer; other times, the true owner will prevail. In any event, one of the parties—either buyer or true owner—will have a cause of action against the purported seller, the true owner on the basis of conversion of the property, the buyer on the basis of breach of warranty of title.

Four situations must be considered.

The Seller Is a Thief, Finder, or Nonmerchant Bailee

Sometimes, the purported seller is a thief, finder, or nonmerchant bailee of the goods, and the goods are not covered by a negotiable document of title. Regardless of his or her good faith, a person who purchases goods (not covered by a negotiable document of title) from a thief, finder, or nonmerchant bailee of the goods, acquires *no rights of title whatsoever.* The thief, finder, or nonmerchant bailee (e.g., one who borrowed the goods) simply has no ability to transfer any rights in the property. It follows that the true owner may replevin the goods from the buyer or even sue the buyer for conversion of the goods.

A person who buys goods from a thief, finder, or nonmerchant bailee "intends" to exercise control over the property inconsistent with the true owner's rights; thus, the party is liable for conversion (see Chapter 4). Rather than replevin the goods, the true owner may "force" their sale to the buyer, requiring him or her to pay the fair market value of the property. It is no defense to payment that the buyer has already paid once—to the purported seller. Where the true owner cannot find the buyer, he or she may, of course, sue the purported seller for conversion.

Assuming the true owner recovers from the buyer—either by way of a conversion action or a suit to replevin the goods—the buyer may, in turn, recover from the purported seller on the basis of breach of warranty of title. Section 2–312 of the UCC provides that a seller impliedly warrants that he or she conveys good title and that his or her transfer is rightful. Like other warranties, the implied warranty of title may be specifically excluded or disclaimed by the seller.

The Goods Are Wrongfully Sold by a Merchant

Occasionally, goods are entrusted to a merchant who regularly deals in goods of that kind, and the merchant, in the regular course of his or her business, wrongfully sells the goods to a good faith purchaser for value ("bona fide purchaser"). Section 2–403(2) of the UCC, called the *entruster rule*, provides that if the goods are "entrusted" to a merchant who deals in goods of that kind, the merchant automatically acquires the power to transfer all the rights of the entruster of the goods to a buyer in the ordinary course of business.

Generally speaking to "entrust" is to acquiesce in any retention of possession of the goods by the merchant. For example, if you leave your watch at a jeweler's place of business for repair (i.e., you entrust it to the jeweler for repair) and the jeweler sells the watch to a customer in the regular course of business, the buyer will acquire title (ownership) to the watch.

Note well that the entruster rule provides that the merchant has the power to transfer all the rights *of the entruster*. Thus, if the entruster is not the owner of the goods but is only a bailee (not authorized by the owner to entrust the goods), a finder, or a thief, the merchant can transfer only the rights of the bailee, finder, or thief—the bfp in this case will not obtain full ownership (title). It is only where the true owner entrusts the goods (or authorizes another to entrust them) that the merchant will acquire power to transfer complete ownership (title).

Also, the entruster rule applies only to a merchant who deals regularly in goods of the kind entrusted to him or her. And it applies only if the entrusted goods are sold by the merchant "in the ordinary course of business"—not in some unusual situation or isolated transaction.

Where the entruster rule operates to transfer title, the true owner may neither replevin the goods from the buyer nor bring an action for conversion against him or her. However, the true owner may certainly bring an action for conversion against the merchant who sold the entrusted goods.

A Nonowner Negotiates a Negotiable Document of Title

A finder, thief, or other nonowner may negotiate a regularly issued negotiable document of title covering goods (i.e., a negotiable bill of lading or warehouse receipt) to a bona fide purchaser for value. As you will recall, where a regularly issued negotiable document of title covering goods—either a negotiable bill of lading or a negotiable warehouse receipt—is negotiated to a bona fide purchaser for value, the bfp obtains title to the document (and to the goods covered by the document) good as against the whole world including the true owner.

Of course, for a thief, finder, or other nonowner to be able to negotiate a document of title, the document must be in "bearer" form. As you will recall, a document is in bearer form if it is issued as bearer paper and contains no special endorsement or if it is issued as order paper but is endorsed in blank.

Of course, the negotiable document of title must be *regularly issued*. If the document is a forgery or if the document was issued to a thief who shipped or warehoused stolen goods so as to create the document (here, the thief steals *goods* as opposed to a regularly issued negotiable document of title), no rights can be created in the goods by transfer of the document. A person who buys such an instrument receives no interest (no title) in the goods, and his or her only recourse is against the person who sold him or her the document.

Finally, where the document of title is nonnegotiable, transfer the document (a mere receipt for the goods) has no effect on ownership of the property.

The Seller is a Person with Voidable Title

A person with voidable title to goods may sell them to a bona fide purchaser for value. A person is said to have *voidable* title where he or she acquires goods in such a way that the transferor has power to rescind the transaction and reacquire ownership. Thus, a person has voidable title where he or she obtains ownership of goods through fraud, trick, imposture, or use of bad checks. The defrauded party in each case has a right to avoid the sale because of the deception. However, if the party with voidable title sells the goods to a bona fide purchaser for value before the defrauded party avoids, the bfp will prevail. UCC Section 2–403 provides that sale to a bfp transfers complete and valid title to the purchaser though the seller had voidable title at the time of sale.

By way of example, say that Floyd Fraud visits Sea Scape Art Gallery and buys a painting for $1,000, paying with a worthless check. Floyd immediately turns around and sells the painting for $800 to Roberta Collector, who takes the painting without knowledge of the bad check. Under UCC Section 2–403, Roberta receives full title to the painting even though Floyd Fraud had only voidable title. The same would be true had Floyd acquired ownership in any of the following ways:

1. Floyd impersonated another so as to induce Sea Scape Gallery to part with the painting; fooled by Floyd's impostering, Sea Scape transferred the painting to Floyd.
2. Sea Scape specified that the sale was to be "strictly cash," then took a check from Floyd in payment; the check was later dishonored.
3. Floyd otherwise fraudulently induced Sea Scape Gallery to part with the painting; Floyd's conduct was larcenous under the criminal law.

Remember, a "bona fide purchaser" is a person who purchases goods for value, in good faith, and without notice of any defect in the seller's title or of any adverse claim to the goods. To give "value" means to provide any consideration sufficient to support a simple contract (see Chapter 9 for a definition of bargain theory consideration). Whether a person takes "in good faith" (i.e., without notice of any claim or defect) is to be determined subjectively. Thus, the fact that a reasonable person would have discovered a particular claim or defect is immaterial if the buyer did not discover it. At the same time, if the claim or defect is so patent (i.e., obvious) that the buyer could not have missed it, the buyer will be held to have taken "with knowledge" though he or she claims otherwise.

WHAT ARE LETTERS OF CREDIT?

We conclude our study of "sales" with a description of *letters of credit.* A letter of credit is a special device used often in sales transactions both as a method of payment and as a means of financing the sale. Letters of credit originated in international trade to reduce the sales risks of both the buyer and seller of goods. Today, such letters are widely used internationally, and they are used increasingly in domestic trade (frequently, in transactions not even involving the sale of goods, such as the construction of apartment houses or manufacturing plants).

For example, suppose that Rita Retailer is a new, but so far successful new car dealer in Denver, Colorado. George Nikota is a Japanese businessman who has been manufacturing "Nikota" brand cars for only a few months; the "Nikota," which sells for $7,000 in Japan, will sell for $8,500 in the American market. Rita Retailer believes (backed by some good marketing statistics) that she can easily sell 500 "Nikota" cars in the Denver market during the upcoming year. Rita writes to George, offering to buy 500 of the automobiles on credit, but George rejects the offer, feeling that Rita has insufficient business experience to warrant such a credit sale. Rita looks for a new solution. She does not want to pay for the cars in advance (even assuming she could afford to do so) because she wants assurance they will arrive in the Denver market in early July—crucial if the "Nikotas" are to be put on the market before the new car releases of the American manufacturers in early fall. Rita thus proposes to pay cash for the cars when they arrive in Denver and ownership is transferred to her.

To reduce the risks for both George and Rita, a "letter of credit term" is added to the contract of sale requiring Rita to obtain a letter of credit from a bank or other reputable financial institution (the "letter" to be used along with a negotiable bill of lading and a sight draft). Generally speaking, a buyer called the "bank customer" applies for the letter of credit from a bank (the "issuer"), paying whatever deposit and/or service charge is required. The bank issues the letter in favor of the seller (the "beneficiary" designated by the buyer). In the letter, the bank agrees to pay a draft drawn by the beneficiary upon the customer (or the issuer bank) when the beneficiary presents the draft to the bank and shows compliance with any and all conditions stated in the letter of credit. "Conditions" of the letter might include that the beneficiary present certain documents to the bank—usually a bill of lading describing the goods as they are described in the letter of credit, a certificate of insurance covering the goods, and a certificate of inspection (issued by a disinterested inspection agency) certifying that the goods have arrived, have been inspected, and are without defect.

A letter of credit is not a "negotiable instrument"; the letter is conditioned by nature, and the beneficiary must comply with the conditions before her or she has a right to payment.

An irrevocable letter of credit is independent of the underlying contract between the buyer and the seller. So long as all conditions of the letter are satisfied, the issuer must pay the draft regardless of what happens between the customer and beneficiary as regards the contract of sale. For example, suppose that the only condition of a letter of credit is that the beneficiary present along with the draft a bill of lading properly describing the goods—a certificate of inspection is not required. If the beneficiary duly presents the draft and bill of lading (i.e., meets the condition of the letter), the issuer will be obligated to pay the draft though the buyer complains that the goods are nonconforming.

On the other hand, though the letter is irrevocable, if the beneficiary fails to fully and exactly comply with the conditions of the letter, the issuer is obligated *not* to pay the draft and will be liable to the customer if it does so (e.g., the issuer will be liable for paying the draft where the goods described in the bill of lading are not the same as those described in the letter of credit).

Let's return to our example. George Nikota is worried that he may not be paid when the cars arrive in Denver; Rita Retailer is concerned that the cars may arrive nonconforming. By adding a letter of credit to the transaction, both parties may reduce their risks. Suppose that George insists as part of the contract of sale that Rita obtain an irrevocable letter of credit from a reputable bank naming George as beneficiary. Rita applies for the letter, depositing all or part of the cash price of $3,500,000 with the bank and paying a small service charge. (The bank may allow Rita to pay a substantial part of the amount with interest at a later time allowing Rita to first sell all or part of the cars.) The bank issues the letter in favor of George. The conditions of the letter are that George (or his representative) present the draft along with a bill of lading properly describing the goods, a certificate or policy of insurance covering the goods, and a certificate of inspection certifying that the goods have arrived, have been inspected, and are without defect (this, of course, is to protect Rita). Because the letter is irrevocable, the bank must pay the draft so long as George complies with all the requirements of the letter. George thus has his $3,500,000; Rita has her 500 cars in good condition.

The result of using the letter of credit was to reduce the sales risks of both seller and buyer; the seller was assured of payment so long as he complied with the conditions of the letter; the buyer was assured of conforming goods by demanding a certificate of inspection.

Of course, as stated previously, letters of credit may contain any kind of condition and may be used for purposes other than sales. A letter of credit, for example, might be used in connection with the building of an apartment house. Say the beneficiary of the letter is building the apartment house for the bank customer. The condition of the letter is that the beneficiary present construction certificates showing that certain progress has been made toward completion of the complex. Perhaps the foundation must be completed before the first draft is honored; then the framing must be finished; then the roofing; etc.

Consumer Protection

WHAT IS THE CONSUMER MOVEMENT?

SALEM PIANO FIRM NAMED IN $2 MILLION FEDERAL SUIT [1]

A civil complaint was filed Tuesday in U.S. District Court in Portland seeking penalties of up to $2 million against a Salem-based piano and organ retailer for alleged false advertising and violations of the Truth in Lending Act.

The suit, which charges 347 violations, was initiated by U.S. Atty. Sidney Lezak. Defendants are Tallman Piano Store, Inc., and Piano Organ Acceptance Corp., both Oregon corporations; and Tallman's Pianos-Organs, Inc., a Washington corporation doing business in Burien.

1. Reprinted with permission of *The Oregonian.*

> Also named as a defendant is Richard L. Taw, described as an officer, director and shareholder of the corporations and as the person who controls their practices.
>
> The alleged violations, the complaint charges, have taken place since Jan. 6, 1973, the effective date of a Federal Trade Commission cease and desist order issued to prohibit the firms from violating provisions of the FTC.
>
> Among the alleged violations in the government's suit are charges that the firms advertised used pianos and organs and implied they were new; advertised that merchandise was guaranteed, but gave no pertinent details of the guarantees; misrepresented savings available to purchasers; and failed to disclose full and accurate details on price, interest and payments in making credit sales.
>
> The complaint asks the court to impose a civil penalty on each of the alleged 347 violations, and to permanently enjoin the defendants from future violations of the FTC order and the Truth in Lending Act.

Consumerism is defined as the organized effort to seek redress, restitution, and remedy for dissatisfaction related to the acquisition of goods or services. Society has rejected the once pre-eminent doctrine of *caveat emptor* which states "let the buyer beware" and puts him on his own in the marketplace. In place of the doctrine has emerged a consumer bill of rights. In his first consumer message to Congress in 1962, President John F. Kennedy enunciated the four basic consumer rights, including: 1. *The Right to Safety*—to be protected against the marketing of goods that are hazardous to health or life; 2. *The Right to be Informed*—to be given sufficient facts to make an informed choice and to be protected against fraudulent, deceitful, or grossly misleading information, advertising, and labeling practices; 3. *The Right to Choose*—to be provided access, wherever possible, to a variety of good quality products and services at fair, competitive prices; and 4. *The Right to be Heard*—to be assured that consumer interests will receive full and sympathetic consideration in the formulation of government policy and fair, speedy treatment in its administrative tribunals. Congress committed itself to this bill of rights in a legislative program that defines and protects the rights of consumers.

The term "consumer movement" refers to a kaleidoscopic collection of formal and informal associations of varying strength, duration, and purpose. The movement was initially concerned with the consumer's physical safety and needs, but with increased leisure time, rising incomes, higher educational levels, and general affluence, the consumer is actually demanding better products than those presently available—regardless of the economic and technical ability of firms to provide them. The mounting political support for the forces of consumerism and the popular success of the consumer "crusade" have increased the movement's effectiveness and reinforced its importance.

The consumer movement is primarily concerned with legal power. The consumer needs laws to enforce standards of safety and reliability; he or she needs laws that compel the sellers of goods or services accurately to disclose the nature and quality of their products; and he or she needs appropriate and timely enforcement of these laws. Other major retailing functions that have attracted consumer interest include sanitation, consumer information, price, credit, and, more recently, repair and warranty service. This chapter deals with consumer rights—the right to be heard, the right to safety, and the right to be informed. The final right—the right to choose—is primarily safeguarded by strict adherence to a system of free and private enterprise, which topic was taken up in Chapter 7 dealing with antitrust and labor law.

WHAT IS THE RIGHT TO BE HEARD?

The consumerist wants his or her position heard and acted upon. To get results, the consumer must pressure the corporation by means more sophisticated than the simple purchase or nonpurchase of an item. In asserting its views, the consumer movement has become intimately bound up with the government agencies established to protect its interests; as a result, it directs a large proportion of its activities toward influencing government action. Large, private foundations have also furnished support. The Carnegie Foundation, for example, helps finance Ralph Nader's Center for the Study of Responsive Law; the Ford Foundation acts as sponsor for the Center for Law and Social Policy; Airtime, an organization dedicated to getting truthful information on the air, is being initially funded by members of the Rockefeller family; and the Stein Family Fund provides assistance for the Project on Corporate Responsibility.

Consumerists have used the following tactics to effect their right to be heard.

Exposé

The consumerist first employed the exposé (a means of revealing "inside information" through the press). A 1965 exposé published by Ralph Nader, entitled *Unsafe At Any Speed,* revealed the faults of the auto industry. Nader reported:

> For over half a century, the automobile has brought death, injury, and the most inestimable sorrow and deprivation to millions of people. With Medea-like intensity, this mass trauma began rising sharply four years ago reflecting new and unexpected ravages by the motor vehicle. A 1959 Department of Commerce report projected that 51,000 persons would be killed by automobiles in 1975. That figure will probably be reached in 1965, a decade ahead of schedule.
>
> Highway accidents were estimated to have cost this country in 1964, 8.3 billion dollars in property damage, medical expenses, lost wages, and insurance overhead expenses. Add an equivalent sum to compromise roughly the indirect costs and the total amounts to over two per cent of the gross national product. But these are not the kind of costs which fall on the builders of motor vehicles (excepting a few successful law suits for negligent construction of the vehicle) and thus do not pinch the proper foot. Instead, the costs fall to users of vehicles, who are in no position to dictate safe automobile designs.[2]

---

2. From *Unsafe At Any Speed* by Ralph Nader. Copyright © 1965 by Ralph Nader.

Nader, however, did not stop at writing the exposé; he also encouraged members of Congress who supported his findings to work towards administrative change and new legislation. His specific action proposals resulted in the National Traffic and Motor Vehicles Act of 1966.

The Lawsuit

The lawsuit is traditionally viewed as the final or last step to be taken when parties cannot settle out of court. The consumerist rejects this viewpoint. He or she asks, instead, how the legal process can be used to further the consumer movement. And the consumerist answers the question in this way: first, it can publicize the consumer controversies. A few years ago, for example, John F. Banzhaf III, professor of law at George Washington University, filed a complaint with the Federal Communications Commission maintaining that if WCBS—New York carried cigarette ads, it also had to carry antismoking messages under the fairness doctrine. CBS argued that the doctrine did not apply and that while they were under no obligation to carry the ads, they did cover the antismoking point of view in their news broadcasts and other programming. The FCC ruled against CBS, and the Court of Appeals sustained its ruling. As a result, some $200 million worth of antismoking advertising went on the air. While the complaint focused on but one station, the decision provided a clear legal precedent, and every station across the country had to comply with its requirements. Congress, influenced as well, passed legislation completely prohibiting cigarette ads on TV.

The damage suit is also used to make companies compensate consumers who are injured while using their products. And it may become an increasingly popular way to call a corporation to account for its misdeeds. Thirty years ago, product liability cases were only infrequently before the courts. But by 1963, the number had grown to 50,000 suits annually, and by 1972, the figure had climbed well over 500,000. The annual cost of product-related injuries presently exceeds some $5.5 billion. And this rapid increase in the number of suits has been accompanied by a parallel increase in settlement costs. A product liability suit involving death or severe injury may result in a verdict of half a million dollars or more. In fact, U.S. manufacturers lose more than $250 million each year in the form of damage awards, fines, and product recalls. Nearly half of all the businesses that file for bankruptcy give product-liability related problems as a prime factor in their failure.

Lobbying

Lobbying is an attempt to influence government policies. But the consumerist does more than bring pressure upon government legislators: he or she also attempts to influence the manner in which government conducts its own business (e.g., its hiring and purchasing policies). Certainly, government must change before it can demand the same of private groups. Its efforts to clean its own house first in the areas of civil rights and equal employment practices are a good example of its willingness to do so. But when necessary, actions have been taken to "embarrass" agencies into a quality oriented, environmentally sound buying policy. The government, for example, was heavily "encouraged" to use recycled paper.

Boycott

While the consumerist has been somewhat successful in inspiring boycotts of harmful products, his or her efforts to discourage the purchase of a good quality item in protest of unrelated but disfavored company policies have generally failed. The California grape boycott in which consumers did stop purchasing grapes because of the grape growers' policy toward farm workers is a notable exception. Boycotts are often initiated by an effective exposé that convinces the consumer that a particular product works against his or her own self-interest.

Advertising

Advertising is a consumer tactic borrowed from industry itself. Two of its forms are worth noting: first is public interest advertising such as the Cancer Society series; the other is competitive advertising by a producer of similar goods that stresses the unsafe or ineffective condition of a competitor's product. Consumerists believe that this is a valid basis for competition and that industry has too long ignored such issues in its advertising.

WHAT IS THE RIGHT TO SAFETY?

The right to safety is the right to be protected against the marketing of goods that are hazardous to health or life. Each year, greater numbers of consumers spend their rising incomes on manufactured products. And as the risk of harm through the purchase and use of a defective product grows, so, too, does the right to safety increase in importance. The mounting number of consumer deaths and injuries has aroused the federal government's concern. According to the National Commission of Product Safety, 20 million Americans are injured annually, 30,000 are killed, and 110,000 are permanently disabled in their own homes as a result of incidents connected with consumer products.

The federal legislation with greatest impact on protecting the consumer's right to safety is the Consumer Product Safety Act of 1972. This Act created a five-member Consumer Product Safety Commission (CPSC) (see Chapter 5).

The Consumer Product Safety Act prohibits the manfuacture, sale, distribution, or import of any consumer product that does not conform to product safety standards or that has been banned as a hazardous product. The manufacturer is required to accompany his or her product with a certificate that states the applicable standard and that assures the consumer of the product's conformance to that standard.

Product Liability

On February 6, 1978, a superior court jury in Santa Ana, California ordered the Ford Motor Company to pay damages of $127,800,000 to a teenager who suffered severe burns over 95 percent of his body when the gasoline tank of a

1972 Ford Pinto exploded (the young man was required to undergo some fifty-two operations). The jury determined that the young man's extensive injuries were caused by a defective product (the Pinto) manufactured by the Ford Motor Company. The evidence at the trial (which lasted seven months) showed that the Pinto was hit in the rear by another vehicle moving at only about thirty-five miles per hour. Because of faulty welding the gas tank of the car was punctured on impact, with the result that ignited gasoline leaked into the passenger compartment. The compartment was entirely engulfed by flames, and the plaintiff was severely burned. The evidence also showed that the Ford Motor Company had prior knowledge of the defect: before putting the particular Pinto model on the market, the company had conducted crash tests on the car, and the car had failed the tests. In August of 1977, consumer advocate Ralph Nader charged that Ford had allowed the sale of the Pintos in a defective condition. The attorney for the injured plaintiff was quoted after the jury verdict as saying:

> We were charging that Ford Motor Co. had consciously, knowing that those tests had failed, put out that model to save 10 bucks a car at the risks of hundreds of more injuries like the plaintiffs. * * * This is probably the loudest noise that the jury has made in any civil suit in American jurisprudence.

A person injured by a defective product may sue for money damages on any one of three theories of liability:

1. Negligence,
2. Breach of warranty, or
3. Strict liability in tort.

Negligence The plaintiff must establish four elements to prove negligence.

1. The plaintiff must show that the defendant had a duty to act according to a certain standard of conduct.
2. Once duty is established, the plaintiff must prove that the defendant breached the duty—that he or she failed to conform to the required standard of conduct.
3. The plaintiff must also prove that the defendant's breach of duty caused the injury. The defendant's conduct causes the injury only where it is a material element or substantial factor in bringing the injury about.
4. Finally, the plaintiff must prove that he or she suffered actual loss or damage.

While it is still the law that a manufacturer is under a duty to make his or her products carefully and a person injured by reason of a defective product may bring an action based on negligence, this remedy is frequently unsatisfactory because it is often difficult or impossible for the injured party to prove the four elements of negligence. The manufacturer alone may know what was done in making the product, or the product itself may be so deteriorated (following the accident) that it is impossible to tell whether it was defectively made. For this reason, the courts have looked increasingly to two additional theories of liability—a contract theory based on warranty and a second tort theory based, not on negligence, but on strict liability.

Warranty Earlier in the chapter, we dealt with warranties only as they related to a buyer's remedies when the seller sends him or her nonconforming goods. A seller's breach of warranty may also result in personal injury or property damage to the buyer and/or third parties. Thus, breach of warranty is a second basis for holding a manufacturer (or retailer) liable for damages resulting from defective products.

While, at first glance, damages for breach of warranty would appear to encompass any personal injury or property damage caused by a defective product, this is not always the case. Like the tort of negligence, a contract action for breach of warranty is often an unsatisfactory remedy—the defendant manufacturer or seller may have any one of the following three defenses to such an action:

1. Failure to give proper notice to the defendant;
2. Lack of privity of contract; or
3. Disclaimer of warranty.

Although a consumer injured by a defective product has a substantial "reasonable time" for giving notice to the seller (this makes sense as the consumer may be in the hospital for many weeks or even months following the injury), if a reasonable time passes without notice being given, the injured consumer may not proceed on the basis of breach of warranty but must look to another remedy for relief.

Breach of warranty is a contract theory of liability. Whereas a tort action for negligence requires no underlying agreement between the parties (a tort simply being any kind of socially unreasonable conduct), a breach of warranty action, being based on contract, demands an underlying agreement. Thus, the general rule is that in order to sue for breach of warranty (i.e., for breach of contract), the plaintiff must have entered into a contract of sale with the party to be sued. Parties who have contracted with each other are said to be in "privity" of contract; parties who have not contracted with each other lack "privity" of contract. And lack of privity of contract is a defense to a breach of warranty action. For example, the neighbor child injured by the defective lawn mower may not sue the manufacturer or retailer of the mower on the basis of breach of warranty—the child lacks privity of contract with both parties. The same is true of a pedestrian who is injured by a defective automobile. The injured party, in each case, lacks privity of contract with the manufacturer or retailer of the product.

In many states the UCC (Section 2–318) eliminates the privity requirements for members of the buyer's family or household or guests in the buyer's home, if it is reasonable to expect that they will use, consume, or be affected by the particular product.

Finally, a party who suffers personal injury and/or property damage because of a defective product may be unable to recover for breach of warranty because the seller has effectively disclaimed warranty responsibility. The Code does not prevent the seller from completely disclaiming warranty liability so long as the buyer is fully aware of the disclaimer. Assuming the disclaimer is held valid, the injured party (whether it is the buyer himself or herself or a third party) will be unable to recover for breach of warranty. However, a manufacturer or retailer who warrants a consumer product to a consumer by means of a written warranty cannot disclaim any implied warranty covering the product by reason of the Magnuson-Moss Act discussed in a later section of this chapter.

Strict liability in tort Because negligence and breach of warranty are often unavailable or unsatisfactory remedies for a person injured by a defective product, the law has developed still a third basis for recovery—strict liability in tort. The landmark case recognizing strict liability in tort for the sale of a dangerously defective product is Greenman v. Yuba Power Products, Inc., 59 Cal.2d 57, 27 Cal.Rptr. 697, 377 P.2d 897 (1963). In that case, the plaintiff's wife purchased a combination power tool from the defendant retailer and gave it to her husband. The plaintiff was using the tool as a lathe for turning a large piece of wood (to be made into a chalice) when, suddenly, a chunk of the wood flew out of the machine and struck the plaintiff in the head causing serious injury. In sustaining damages of $65,000 against the manufacturer, the appellate court stated:

> * * * [T]o impose strict liability on the manufacturer under the circumstances of this case, it was not necessary for the plaintiff to establish * * * warranty. * * * A manufacturer is strictly liable in tort when an article he places on the market, knowing that it is to be used without inspection for defects, proves to have a defect that causes injury to a human being.

Thus, a manufacturer who places a defective product on the market is strictly liable for any damage the product causes. The same is true of any other seller of the product so long as the seller is *in the business of selling such goods* (e.g., a retailer). In order to recover, the injured plaintiff need prove only the following: (1) that the defendant seller sold the product in a defective condition making the product unreasonably dangerous to the user or consumer or his or her property; (2) that the defective product reached the user or consumer without substantial change in its condition; and (3) that the plaintiff suffered personal injury or property damage as a result of the defect.

Obviously, not all products that are dangerous to use are "defective." A knife, though perfectly constructed, might easily cut a finger; a hammer might smash a thumb. Roller skates, though sturdy, might increase one's risk of falling (of course, if the skates fall apart on first use, they are probably defective, in which case the seller will be liable for any injury that results).

While the early strict liability decisions limited recovery to loss for personal injury, the modern rule is that strict liability encompasses both personal and property loss (including damage to the defective product itself). Thus, if a defective furnace explodes, injuring the neighbors and burning up their property, all the personal injury and property damage will be part of the manufacturer's strict liability.

The early strict liability cases also limited recovery to "users" and "consumers" of the defective product—bystanders injured by the product were not protected. Again, the majority of jurisdictions now extend protection even to bystanders, stating that industry is responsible for all foreseeable harm caused by its defective products. For example, in Piercefield v. Remington Arms Co., 375 Mich. 85, 133 N.W.2d 129 (1965), a bystander was injured when a defective shotgun discharged. The decision was in favor of the bystander. Similarly, in Sills v. Massey-Ferguson, Inc., 296 F.Supp. 776 (N.D.Ind.1969), a bystander was awarded damages after being hit by an object thrown some 150 feet by a defective lawn mower manufactured by the defendant.

By way of defense, the seller may show that his or her product was not used in the normal way: the seller will not be liable if the product was put to some abnormal or unforeseeable use. Thus, an automobile driver who is recklessly speeding when a defective tire blows out on his car cannot recover for his personal injuries on the basis of strict liability. However, it is no defense to a seller's liability that a long period of time elapsed before the defect in the product came to light—it frequently takes a long time for a defect to result in injury, particularly where the defect is in the design of the product. At the same time, a number of states have passed statutes of limitation that require such actions to be brought within a certain time after purchase of the product (e.g., Oregon—within two years of the injury or eight years of purchase of the product whichever comes first). And a consumer is held by law to know that certain products have a normal life expectancy and will ultimately wear out (e.g., a consumer is expected to realize that automobile tires will wear out and become dangerous if they are not replaced after a reasonable time).

Nor may a manufacturer of a completed product escape liability by tracing the defect to a component part supplied by another party (although the manufacturer would certainly be able to recover from the supplier for providing him or her with the defective product). The manufacturer is liable for the defect regardless of its source. It follows that the manufacturer remains strictly liable though he or she delegates the final steps of the manufacturing process to a retailer and the defect is traced to the retailer's part in the process (here, of course, the manufacturer will be able to recover from the retailer).

Finally, it should be pointed out that a retailer, too, is strictly liable for any defective product he or she sells though the retailer has nothing to do with the manufacturing process. If the injured party chooses to sue the retailer, the retailer may generally recover from the manufacturer. The reasoning here is that the cost of protection for the consumer can be adjusted by contract between the manufacturer and retailer in the course of their continuing business relationship.

WHAT IS THE RIGHT TO BE INFORMED?

The right to be informed is the right to be given sufficient facts to make an informed choice—to be protected against fraudulent, deceitful, or grossly misleading information, advertising, labeling, or other practices.

Truth in Lending

The Consumer Credit Protection Act of 1968 ("Truth in Lending") has had great impact on the consumer's right to be informed. The Act includes credit disclosure regulations that require lenders to spell out their finance charges; it prohibits extortionate credit transactions; and it places certain limitations on the garnishment of wages.

The purpose of truth in lending is to inform borrowers and customers of the cost of credit so they can compare these costs with those of other credit sources. The law fixes no maximum or minimum credit charge. But it does require disclosure of credit terms—the finance charge and the annual percentage rate are the two most important disclosures required. These terms tell a customer at a glance how much he or she is paying for his credit and what its relative cost is in percentage terms. The law applies to any individual or organization that extends or arranges credit for which a finance charge is or may be payable or which is repayable in more than four installments. This includes banks, savings and loan associations, department stores, credit card issuers, credit unions, automobile dealers, consumer finance companies, residential mortgage brokers, hospitals, and craftsmen (e.g., plumbers and electricians), as well as doctors, dentists and other professional people.

Most credit cards and revolving charge accounts in retail stores are based on open end credit in which finance charges are made on unpaid monthly balances. The new account customer must receive these specific items in writing: 1. the conditions under which a finance charge may be imposed, and the period of time in which payment can be made before a finance charge will be incurred; 2. the method used to determine the balance on which the finance charge is made; 3. how the finance charge is calculated; 4. the periodic rates used, and the range of balances to which each applies; 5. the conditions under which additional charges may be made and how they are calculated; 6. descriptions of any lien that may be acquired on a customer's property; and 7. the minimum payment that must be made on each billing.

The customer must receive the following information on his or her monthly statement:

1. The unpaid balance at the start of the billing period;
2. The amount and date of each credit extension and identification of each item purchased;
3. Customer payments and other credits (including returns, rebates and adjustments);
4. The finance charge shown in dollars and cents;
5. The rates used to calculate the finance charge plus the range of balances to which they apply;
6. The annual percentage rate;
7. The unpaid balance on which the finance charge was calculated; and
8. The closing date of the billing cycle and the unpaid balance at that time.

Credit other than "open end" includes both loans and sales credit. These are cases where the total amount of credit, the number of payments, and the due dates are agreed upon by the creditor and the customer for a specified period of time. This is the method typically used in buying or financing the purchase of "big ticket" items (e.g., a finance company loan to buy an automobile, a credit extension from a store to buy a washing machine, television set, or other major appliance—or even a single payment loan). The customer must be furnished the following information in writing: (1) the total dollar amount of the finance charge (except in the case of a credit transaction to finance purchase of a dwelling); (2) the date on which the finance charge begins to apply, if this differs from the date of transaction; (3) the annual percentage rate; (4) the number, amounts, and due dates of payments; (5) the total payments (except in the case of first mortgages on dwelling purchases); (6) the amount charged for any default or delinquency or the method used to calculate that amount; (7) a description of any security held; (8) a description of any penalty charge for prepayment of principal; and (9) how the unearned part of the finance charge is calculated in case of prepayment. Charges deducted from any rebate or refund must also be stated.

The customer who obtains a loan must also be given an itemized account of the credit extension, including all charges that are part of the credit extension but not a part of the finance charge. The customer must be informed of any prepaid finance charges or required deposit balances.

In the case of a credit sale, the following additional information must be provided: 1. the cash price; 2. the down payment (including trade in); 3. the difference between the two; 4. an itemization of all other charges included in the amount financed but not part of the finance charge; 5. the unpaid balance; 6. the amounts deducted as prepaid finance charges or required deposit balances; 7. the amount financed; and 8. the total cash price, finance and all other charges (this does not apply to sale of a building).

A person who fails to make the disclosures required under this law may be sued by the customer for twice the amount of the finance charge—for a minimum of $100 up to a maximum of $1,000—plus court costs and attorneys' fees. A criminal conviction for willful or knowing noncompliance may result in a fine up to $5,000, imprisonment for one year, or both.

Real estate credit in any amount is covered under truth in lending when it is extended to an individual for other than business purposes (with the exception of agriculture). Two special provisions apply:

1. The total amount of the finance charge on a credit sale or first mortgage loan to finance the purchase of the customer's dwelling need not be shown.
2. In many instances, a customer may cancel a credit arrangement within three business days *if his or her residence is used as collateral* for credit. This provision applies to residences only and the creditor must notify the customer of his or her right to cancel. The customer cancels the transaction: (1) by signing and dating the notice received from the creditor (as required by law), and either mailing it to the creditor at the address shown on the notice or delivering it to him or her personally or by messenger; or (2) by sending a telegram to the creditor at the address shown on the notice (a brief description of the transaction to be canceled should be included); or (3) by writing down a brief description of the transaction to be canceled and either mailing it to the creditor at the address shown on the notice or delivering it to him or her personally or by messenger. *A telephone call placed to the creditor will not cancel the transaction. Written notice of cancellation is required. And a first mortgage to finance purchase of a residence carries no right to cancel at all.* A first mortgage for any other purpose, and even a second mortgage on the same residence, may be canceled, however.

Because these special rules apply when a residence is used as collateral, a craftsman who charges "finance charges" should wait three days before starting work unless there is an emergency. A customer may waive the right to cancel if credit is needed to meet a bona fide, personal, financial emergency and if failure to start repairs would endanger the customer or his or her family or property.

Truth in lending also affects advertising that aids or promotes the extension of consumer credit regardless of who the advertiser may be. An association which advertises that its members extend consumer credit, for example, is subject to the provisions of this law. All types of advertising are included—television, radio, newspapers, magazines, leaflets, flyers, catalogs, public address announcements, direct mail literature, window displays, and billboards. An advertisement may state that the down payment, installment plan, or amount of credit can be arranged only if this is the advertiser's usual business practice. And specific credit terms may be included only if all other terms are clearly and visibly stated.

The federal credit card law is an amendment to the Truth in Lending Act. It limits the cardholder's liability to fifty dollars on lost or stolen credit cards even where the consumer does not promptly notify the card's issuer of its loss or unauthorized use. Liability ends in all cases upon notification of loss to the issuer. Federal law also provides that unordered merchandise received in the mail may be kept and used or disposed of with no legal obligation to the sender. The law does not prohibit the solicitation of donations for address labels or decorative stamps sent through the mail by charitable organizations nor does it prohibit the mailing of free samples, provided they are conspicuously labeled as such.

THE MAGNUSON–MOSS WARRANTY FEDERAL TRADE COMMISSION IMPROVEMENT ACT OF 1975

In 1975, to provide increased protection for consumers, Congress passed the Magnuson-Moss Act. Section 2302(a) of the Act provides:

> In order to improve the adequacy of information available to consumers, prevent deception, and improve competition in the marketing of consumer products any warrantor warranting a consumer product to a consumer by means of a written warranty shall, to the extent required by rules of the Federal Trade Commission fully and conspicuously disclose in simple and readily understood language the terms and conditions of such warranty.

Under the Act, the term "consumer product" means any tangible personal property which is purchased primarily for personal, family, or household purposes. The term "consumer" means a buyer (other than for purposes of resale) of a consumer product and any subsequent transferee of the product during the duration of any written or implied warranty covering the product. Section 2301(6) defines "written warranty" as follows:

> (A) Any written affirmation of fact or written promise made in connection with the sale of a consumer product by a supplier [manufacturer or retailer] to a

buyer which relates to the nature of the material and workmanship and affirms or promises that such material is defect free or will meet a specified level of performance over a specified period of time, or

(B) Any undertaking in writing in connection with the sale by a supplier of a consumer product to refund, repair, replace, or take other remedial action with respect to such product in the event that such product fails to meet the specifications set forth in the undertaking which written affirmation, promise, or undertaking becomes part of the basis of the bargain between a supplier and a buyer for purposes other than resale of the product.

Empowered by Section 2302, the Federal Trade Commission has set down certain minimum disclosure requirements with regard to written warranties of consumer products. FTC Regulation 16 CFR 701.3 states:

(a) Any warrantor warranting to a consumer by means of a written warranty a consumer product costing the consumer more than $15.00 shall clearly and conspicuously disclose in a single document in simple and readily understood language, the following items of information:

(1) The identity of the party or parties to whom the written warranty is extended, if the enforceability of the written warranty is limited to the original consumer or is otherwise limited to persons other than every consumer owner during the term of the warranty;

(2) A clear description and identification of products, or parts, or characteristics, or components or properties covered by and where necessary for clarification, excluded from the warranty;

(3) A statement of what the warrantor will do in the event of a defect, malfunction or failure to conform with the written warranty, including the items or services the warrantor will pay for or provide, and, where necessary for clarification, those which the warrantor will not pay for or provide;

(4) The point in time or event in which the warranty term commences, if different from the purchase date, and the time or other measurement of warranty duration;

(5) A step-by-step explanation of the procedure which the consumer should follow in order to obtain performance of any warranty obligation;

(6) Information respecting the availability of any informal dispute settlement mechanism elected by the warrantor [a "mechanism" being any informal, independent, dispute settlement procedure incorporated into the terms of a written warranty];

(7) Any limitation on the duration of implied warranties, disclosed on the face of the warranty * * * accompanied by the following statement:

"Some states do not allow limitations on how long an implied warranty lasts, so the above limitation may not apply to you.";

(8) Any exclusions of or limitations on relief such as incidental or consequential damages, accompanied by the following statement:

"Some states do not allow the exclusion of or limitation of incidental or consequential damages, so the above limitation or exclusion may not apply to you.";

(9) A statement in the following language:

"This warranty gives you specific legal rights, and you may also have other rights which vary from state to state."

The FTC has no power under the Magnuson-Moss Act to require sellers to warrant their products or to prescribe the duration of written warranties. However, if a seller does not give a written warranty, the warranty must contain all the information in (1) through (9) above, and the seller must make the warranty information available to the buyer prior to sale.

Section 2303 of the Magnuson-Moss Act further requires the warrantor of consumer goods costing the consumer more than ten dollars clearly and conspicuously to designate any written warranty covering the goods as either a "full (statement of duration, e.g., one-year) warranty" or a "limited warranty." To be labeled a "full warranty," a written warranty must meet the following minimum federal standards:

1. The warrantor must agree to remedy the consumer product (repair or replace it or, if this is not possible, refund the consumer's money) within a reasonable time and without charge in the case of defect, malfunction, or other breach of the written warranty;
2. The warrantor may not limit the duration of any implied warranty covering the product;
3. The warrantor may not exclude or limit consequential damages for breach of any written or implied warranty unless the exclusion or limitation conspicuously appears on the face of the warranty;
4. If the product still contains a defect or malfunction after a reasonable number of attempts by the warrantor to remedy the defects, the warrantor must allow the customer to elect a refund or replacement of the article without charge.

A warrantor who gives a "full" written warranty may not impose upon the consumer any condition precedent to repair, replacement, or refund other than notification of the breach of warranty (e.g., the warrantor may not require as a condition precedent return of a "warranty registration card"). A warrantor who labels a written warranty as a "full warranty" will be bound by the minimum federal standards.

No warrantor of a consumer product may condition his or her written or implied warranty of the product on the consumer's use (in conjunction with the product) of an article or service identified by brand, trade, or corporate name unless that article or service is provided free of charge to the consumer.

As to disclaimer or modification of implied warranties, Section 2308 of the Magnuson-Moss Act states:

> (a) No supplier may disclaim or modify (except as provided in subsection (b) of this section) any implied warranty to a consumer with respect to such consumer product if (1) such supplier makes a written warranty with respect to such consumer product, or (2) at the time of sale, or within 90 days thereafter, such supplier enters into a service contract with the consumer which applies to such consumer product. [A "service contract" is a contract in writing to perform over a fixed period of time or for a specified duration service relating to the maintenance or repair, or both of a consumer product.]
>
> (b) For purposes of this [law] * * * implied warranties may be limited in duration to the duration of a written warranty of reasonable duration,

> if such limitation is conscionable and is set forth in clear and unmistakable language and prominently displayed on the face of the warranty [but remember, a warrantor who gives a "full warranty" may not limit the duration of implied warranties].
>
> (c) A disclaimer, modification, or limitation made in violation of this section shall be ineffective for purposes of this * * * and state law.

Thus, if a manufacturer or retailer gives a written warranty (as defined by the Magnuson-Moss Act) covering consumer goods, the manufacturer or retailer cannot exclude any implied warranty covering the goods. However, if the written warranty is a "limited" one, the manufacturer or retailer can limit the duration of the implied warranty.

Finally, the Magnuson-Moss Act authorizes the FTC to investigate and enjoin violations of the Act (including deceptive warranty advertising). And the Act provides a civil action remedy for any consumer who is injured by a warrantor's failure to comply with the Magnuson-Moss Act or with any written or implied warranty thereunder. The consumer may sue in state court (and in certain cases in federal court) and recover damages as well as the costs and expenses of the action.

Cases

The automobile was stolen from a self-service parking lot.

WALL v. AIRPORT PARKING CO. OF CHICAGO

Supreme Court of Illinois, 1969.
41 Ill.2d 506, 244 N.E.2d 190.

HOUSE, Justice

Defendant, Airport Parking Company of Chicago, operator of a self-parking lot at O'Hare Airport as lessee of the city of Chicago, appealed to the Appellate Court, First District, from a judgment against it in favor of the insurer of an automobile stolen from the lot. The Appellate Court reversed, and we granted leave to appeal.

The cause was submitted on an agreed statement of facts. The lot is wholly enclosed, well lighted, paved and marked into parking spaces. Motorists enter through automatic gates and there receive a ticket bearing the date and time of arrival. They park in any available parking space, lock their automobiles, and retain the keys. When ready to depart they walk into the lot, pick up their vehicle and leave via an exit where the ticket is handed to an attendant to compute and collect the parking charges.

This is a case of first impression in this court although there is a great variety of holdings in the area of the liability of operators of parking-lot facilities, mostly by courts of intermediate jurisdiction. From this welter of decisions there emerge two principal classes of relationship between the automobile owner and the lot operator. One is that of the leasing of a parking space with no bailment being created. The other is a delivery of the vehicle into the possession and control of the lot operator thereby creating a bailment.

Typical of the first class of cases is where the owner parks his own car either at a place designated by an attendant or chosen by himself, retains the keys, and does not actually deliver the car to the lot operator. In the second class of cases, a bailment is usually created where the keys are left in the parked vehicle (at the request of the parking-lot attendant to permit moving it for the entrance or exit of other vehicles on the lot) and where tickets are issued identifying the car for redelivery. In final analysis, however, parking-lot cases do not readily lend themselves to precise categorization of whether the motorist is leasing space on the one hand, or whether delivery of the vehicle onto a parking lot creates a *prima facie* bailment. As was said by the Court of Appeals of New York in Osborn v. Cline, 263 N.Y. 434, 189 N.E. 483, 484: "Whether a person simply hires a place to put his car or whether he has turned its possession over to the care and custody of another depends on the place, the conditions and the nature of the transaction." In a case very similar to this, except that parking was in an enclosed parking garage and valuables in the car rather than the car itself were stolen, the Pennsylvania Supreme Court said: "Since here plaintiffs reserved possession of the car at all times by retaining the keys thereto, defendant acquired no dominion over the vehicle nor any right to control removal of it; hence there was no bailment." Taylor v. Philadelphia Parking Authority, 398 Pa. 9, 156 A.2d 525, 527.

In recent years a new type of self-service vehicular parking lot has developed, particularly at the larger airports of this country. The one here involved is typical. A motorist gains admission to the lot through one or more automatic entrance gates, which open when he takes a machine dispensed ticket from an automatic dispenser. The ticket is stamped with the day and hour of arrival, but it does not identify any particular automobile or owner. No attendant is present nor is the motorist directed where to park, except that he is expected to park within the lines marking individual parking spaces. The motorist retains the keys. There is nothing to prevent him from moving the car from place to place within the confines of the lot as often as he chooses. He may not have (and probably has not) seen an attendant until he re-enters his car and proceeds to an exit where an attendant computes and collects the charges for the period of time the vehicle has been on the lot. This checking-out process is his only necessary contact with the lot operator or attendants.

In order to establish a bailor-bailee relationship there must be either an express agreement (there is none here) or an agreement by implication, which may be gathered from the circumstances surrounding the transaction, such as the benefits to be received by the parties, their intentions, the kind of property involved, and the opportunities of each to exercise control over the property. There must not only be a delivery of possession, but there must also be an acceptance, either actual or constructive, before there can be a bailment. Applying these criteria to the facts here we find that the self-parking-lot operator primarily offers spaces for parking with a minimum amount of labor, which presumably is reflected in the fees charged for use of the facilities. There undoubtedly is more protection to the users of the facilities than is afforded by street parking in that the parking lot is fenced, well lighted, attended around the clock by one to five attendants, and is patrolled by the Chicago police squad cars from time to time. But space rather than security is the primary purpose of a self-service parking lot. The motorist is, of course, benefited by having parking space reasonably close to the airport.

By its very nature a self-service parking lot must be open at all times to the public and the operator has no control over who uses the lot. True, temporary possession in the sense that the motorist leaves a vehicle on the lot may be said to have been given up, but actual control is retained by the act of locking the vehicle and taking the keys, thereby preventing its movement. There is no acceptance of the vehicle by the lot owner. Plaintiff asserts that National Safe Deposit Co. v. Stead, 250 Ill. 584, 95 N.E. 973, is analogous. There, the safe deposit company held itself out as safeguarding valuables, and security was that which was being bought by the public. Valuables were stored in vaults and entry was through iron gates manned by armed guards. It was inherent in the nature of the service offered that the primary objective was to safeguard customers. That case is not persuasive.

We are of the opinion that use of self-service parking lots, such as the one here involved, does not create a bailor-bailee relationship and the lot operator is not subject to the liability imposed by the rules relating to bailments.

* * *

Judgment affirmed.

Hurricane Betsey and the slash pine seed.

WEST BROTHERS, INC. v. RESOURCE MANAGEMENT SERVICE, INC.

Supreme Court of Alabama, 1968.
283 Ala. 78, 214 So.2d 431.

MERRILL, Justice

* * *

This appeal is from a judgment in the amount of $1,105.35 in favor of appellee, hereinafter designated the shipper, against appellant, hereinafter designated the carrier. * * *

* * *

The action is for recovery of damages for the alleged late delivery by the carrier of a shipment of slash pine seed tendered to it at Birmingham for transportation to New Orleans for connection with a steamship for further movement to Buenos Aires, Argentina. The shipment was received by the carrier on the morning of September 10, 1965, for delivery in New Orleans on September 13 to meet a sailing date of September 14. However, the shipment was lost and was not found until September 23.

Hurricane Betsey struck New Orleans just before midnight on September 9, and the carrier's yard was flooded. The shipment actually arrived in New Orleans on September 15. The steamship's sailing was delayed and postponed until September 21. On September 16, around 7:00 o'clock P.M., the shipper was notified by its freight forwarder that the shipment had not arrived, and at approximately the same time the carrier advised the shipper by telephone that it had no record of the shipment. The next day, September 17, the carrier again advised the shipper that it had no record of the shipment and could not locate the seed. September 18, according to the carrier's evidence, was the last date that the seed comprising the shipment could have any market value or viability, because it would lose its germinative capacity when removed from refrigeration for over a week at the then prevailing temperatures. On September 20, the shipper removed a new shipment of seed from cold storage in Birmingham and delivered the seed to New Orleans in a pickup truck. On September 21, the ship, with the seed on board, sailed for Argentina. On September 23, the shipper was again advised by the carrier that it had no record of the shipment and that the shipper should file a claim. Later that same day, the shipper was advised by the carrier that the seed had been located in Hattiesburg, Mississippi, at carrier's home office.

The shipper's evidence shows (1) that it delivered the seed to the carrier, (2) that at the time of such delivery the seed was in good condition, and (3) that at the time the seed was made available either for delivery to the consignee under the bill of lading or return to the shipper, the seed was worthless.

The carrier argues that its evidence shows that it is excused from liability because (1) the admitted delay in forwarding the shipment was caused by an act of God, (2) the damage to the seed resulted from an inherent defect in the seed, and (3) the shipper failed to prove its damages.

A carrier's liability for damage to goods shipped in interstate commerce is governed by the Carmack Amendment to the Interstate Commerce Act, 49 U.S.C.A. § 20(11). And this amendment pre-empts the field and supercedes all state common law rights arising from a breach of a bill of lading contract for the interstate carriage of goods. * * *

In Missouri Pacific Railroad Co. v. Elmore & Stahl, 377 U.S. 134, it is said:

> * * * The Carmack Amendment of 1906, § 20(11) of the Interstate Commerce Act, makes carriers liable 'for the full actual loss, damage, or injury * * * caused by' them to property they transport, and declares unlawful and void any contract, regulation, tariff, or other attempted means of limiting this liability. It is settled that this statute has two undisputed effects crucial to the issue in this case: First, the statute codifies the common-law rule that a carrier, though not an absolute insurer, is liable for damage to goods transported by it unless it can show that the damage was caused by '(a) the act of God; (b) the public enemy; (c) the act of the shipper himself; (d) public authority; (e) or the inherent vice or nature of the goods.' Second, the statute declares unlawful and void any 'rule, regulation, or other limitation of any character whatsoever' purporting to limit this liability. Accordingly, under federal law, in an action to recover from a carrier for damage to a shipment, the shipper establishes his prima facie case when he shows delivery in good condition, arrival in damaged condition, and the amount of damages. Thereupon, the burden of proof is upon the carrier to show both that it was free from negligence and that the damage to the cargo was due to one of the expected causes relieving the carrier of liability.

* * *

Under the facts already stated, the shipper made out a prima facie case and the burden of proof passed to the carrier to show that it was free from negligence and that the damage was due to one of the excepted causes.

We think the mere fact that the carrier, after unquestionably receiving the shipment of two drums of pine seed, could neither find it, or a bill of lading or any record of the shipment for some thirteen days, when the carrier had been notified that the seed was due to be loaded on a steamship sailing from New Orleans on the fourth day from the time the shipment was received by the carrier, makes out a case of negligence on the part of the carrier.

In support of its contention that the delay was caused by an act of God, the carrier adduced evidence that after the first and second impact of hurricane Betsey just before midnight on September 9, the wind died down, but the water began to rise in carrier's terminal yard in New Orleans and rose nearly five feet. The office, sleeping quarters and pickup and delivery equipment were flooded; there was no mobile power, power and telephone lines were down and there was no way to notify the home office at Hattiesburg of the difficulty.

L.D. Nation, the then manager of carrier's New Orleans terminal, and other employees were stranded at the terminal until the next afternoon (Friday, September 10) when they were evacuated by boat. The home office at Hattiesburg was notified around 7:00 P.M. on Friday. The shipment of seed was finally located and sent to Hattiesburg.

An act of God is not a complete, blanket defense in a carrier liability case. By its very definition an act of God implies an entire exclusion of all human agency from causing the loss or damage. And an act of God absolves a carrier from liability only if there is no contributing human negligence. [T]he Supreme Court of Washington said:

> * * * The carrier's contributing, concurring, subsequent or superseding neglect is sufficient to make it liable notwithstanding proof of a latent defect, act of God or one of the other limited number of excepted causes which may relieve a carrier of liability to an owner.
>
> The general rule is summarized at 13 C.J.S. Carriers § 80, p. 159:
>
> [I]t is very generally declared that, if the negligence of the carrier concurs with the excepted cause in producing a loss or injury, the carrier is not exempted from liabiity by showing that the immediate cause was the

> act of God, or some other excepted cause. As otherwise expressed, the carrier is responsible where the loss is caused by an act of God or other excepted cause, if the carrier's negligence mingles with it as an active and cooperative cause.

Since the carrier was not free from negligence in the instant case in losing the shipment, it cannot avoid liability on the defense that the delay was caused by an act of God.

The same reason applies to the defense that the seed, if damaged at all, were damaged as a proximate result of their inherent nature.

The carrier argues that the shipper failed to prove any recoverable damages. It argues that the shipper could not recover the invoice price of the seed because it did not lose its sale.

> The general common law rule of damages in cases of unreasonable delay and damage to goods in shipment is the difference in the market value of the goods at the date and in the condition they were contracted to arrive at their destination and the date on and the condition in which they actually arrived.

* * *

Here, the testimony was that the seed was worthless when found by the carrier and under the Carmack Amendment, the carrier was liable for the "full actual loss, damage or injury to such property caused by it."

The trial court did not err in admitting the invoice showing the price of the seed to be $985.60 or in fixing the shipper's damage to the seed at that amount.

The carrier also argues that the trial court erred in awarding special or consequential damages in the amount of $119.75, the actual expenses incurred by the shipper in transporting the second shipment of seed from Birmingham to the boat at New Orleans in the pickup truck.

The general rule is that a carrier is not chargeable with or liable for special damages resulting from delay in transportation or delivery of goods entrusted to it for shipment, unless notice of the special circumstances rendering prompt delivery and transportation essential is given at or before the time of making the contract of shipment.

The undisputed testimony of shipper's agent, Harry E. Murphy, as to notice to the carrier of special circumstances was:

> Q When you undertook to make arrangements for transportation of this seed with West Brothers Company, what did you do?
>
> A Well, I came down on a Friday morning to deliver the seed and specifically went to the offices and told them I had their seed to be shipped to New Orleans, needed to be there on the 14th, and in view of the reported hurricane that occurred in New Orleans, could they handle it, and they said, yes. We underlined the bill to be sure that it got there on the 14th.
>
> * * *
>
> Q All right. Let's go back to the time that you delivered this seed to West on the 10th. Did you have any discussion with any of the representatives there at the West terminal with reference to the perishable nature of this freight?
>
> A Yes. I did.
>
> Q Would you recount what you can recall at that discussion?
>
> A Well, I told them that the seed was of a perishable type, a perishable nature, and that at any extended period it would lose its viability and 'Could you assure that you could get it down there by the 14th?' That would be a safe period of time. They said, yes. And then the emphasis was, I keep recalling, 'We'll make sure. Don't worry about it' or something to that effect. Well, 'We'll scratch it underneath this bill of lading that you gave me to emphasize,' and then that's the reason we went out to the dock for the man to particularly be acquainted with the fact to be sure it was going to get there on the 14th."

Also, the carrier's freight bill on the seed shipment shows the following notation: "SHIP SAILS TUESDAY MORNING SEPT 14TH" and under that notation the word "RUSH" appears nine times.

We think this is clearly an occasion for the assessment of the special damages in the sum of $119.75.

Affirmed.

The "special property" interest.

DRAPER v. MINNEAPOLIS-MOLINE, INC.

Appellate Court of Illinois, Third District, 1968.
100 Ill.App.2d 324, 241 N.E.2d 342.

CULBERTSON, Justice

This appeal presents questions concerning the Uniform Commercial Code, * * * and stems from a judgment entered in favor of the plaintiff, Robert Draper, against the defendant, Minneapolis-Moline, Inc. * * *

On December 30, 1966, plaintiff entered into a written contract with Larry Meiners, a farm equipment dealer who handled defendant's products, for the purchase of a new Minneapolis-Moline tractor and a new six bottom plow for use on plaintiff's farm. By the terms of the contract various extras, including a cab and radio, were to be installed on the tractor by the dealer; plaintiff was to trade in an old tractor and an old plow; and delivery was to be "by" April 1, 1967. The net purchase price of $5,300.00 was to be paid on delivery. Subsequently, on a date not entirely clear from the record, the old and the new plows were exchanged but nothing was paid on the contract.

At the time the contract was entered into, the dealer did not have the required tractor in stock, but received one from defendant on or about January 26, 1967. This machine was delivered under * * * agreement * * * which gave Meiners the right to sell the tractor at retail in the ordinary course of business, and provided that * * * the machine could be repossessed if the dealer defaulted in the terms for payment.

Shortly after the dealer received the machine, plaintiff came to the store and was shown the tractor and was told that it was his. At the trial plaintiff recalled that the last three digits of the serial number on the tractor shown to him were "804," and this coincided with the number shown on the purchase agreement between the dealer and defendant. The dealer had not as yet received the cab called for by the contract and this appears to have delayed delivery of the tractor to the plaintiff. On one occasion, apparently in February, 1967, the dealer offered to let plaintiff take the tractor without the cab but plaintiff refused the offer.

During the last week of February, 1967, the completion of a routine audit disclosed the dealer to be greatly in arrears for substantial sums of money owed to defendant. When it became apparent that he was not financially able to correct or alleviate the situation, defendant repossessed all of its products on the store premises for which it had not been paid, including the tractor plaintiff had been told would be delivered to him under his contract. At the time plaintiff had neither turned in his old tractor nor had he paid anything to the dealer. Plaintiff then negotiated directly with defendant to complete the deal, but the negotiations fell through because defendant, as a manufacturer, was in no position to accept a trade-in or to provide and install the contract extras. It is undisputed that plaintiff thereafter did his spring plowing with his old tractor, and that he incurred expenses of $396.70 he would not have had if the new tractor had been available to him. This action against defendant for damages soon followed.

The authority for plaintiff's action is found in Section 2–722 of Article 2 of the Uniform Commercial Code which, in substance, gives to one having a special property interest in goods a right of action against a third party who "so deals with goods which have been identified to a contract for sale as to cause actionable injury to a party to that contract." The quoted language, we believe, intends that a third party would be liable for conversion, physical damage to the goods, or interference with the rights of a buyer in the goods. Section 2–103(1)(a) of Article 2 states that in such Article: " 'Buyer' means a person who buys *or contracts to buy goods,*" and it is thereafter provided in Section 2–501(1) in pertinent part:

> The buyer obtains a special property and an insurable interest in goods by identification of existing goods as goods to which the contract refers *even though the goods so identified are non-conforming* and he has an option to return or reject them. Such identification can be made at any time and in any manner explicitly agreed to by the parties. In the absence of explicit agreement identification occurs
>
> (b) if the contract is for the sale of future goods * * * when goods are shipped, marked or otherwise designated by the seller as goods to which the contract refers.

While defendant makes a mild argument that the tractor did not conform to the contract because the extras had not been installed when it was pointed out by the dealer, we think it manifest from the evidence that there was a complete and sufficient identification of the tractor to the contract within the purview of Section 2–501(1). It is apparent, too, that defendant's conduct made it impossible for the dealer to deliver the tractor to plaintiff, and that defendant so dealt with the goods as to interfere with plaintiff's special property interest.

* * *

* * * [J]udgment * * * affirmed * * * for the plaintiff in the amount of $396.70.

The Revel Craft Playmate Yacht was destroyed by fire.

HAYWARD v. POSTMA

Court of Appeals of Michigan, Div. 3, 1971.
31 Mich.App. 720, 188 N.W.2d 31.

V.J. BRENNAN, Judge

From a judgment in favor of the plaintiff buyer in an action to determine risk of loss under a sales contract, defendant appeals.

On February 7, 1967, the plaintiff agreed to purchase a 30-foot Revel Craft Playmate Yacht for $10,000. The total purchase price included a number of options which the dealer was to install after he received the boat from the manufacturer. The parties agreed that defendant would deliver the boat to a slip on Lake Macatawa in or about April, 1967.

On March 1, 1967, shortly after the boat arrived at the dealer's showroom, plaintiff executed a security agreement in favor of the defendant seller along with a promissory note in the amount of $13,095.60. The note was subsequently assigned to Michigan National Bank. Clauses 7 and 8 of the security agreement provided:

> (7) Buyer will at all times keep the Goods in first class order and repair, excepting any loss, damage or destruction which is fully covered by proceeds of insurance;
>
> (8) Buyer will at all times keep the Goods fully insured against loss, damage, theft and other risks, in such amounts and companies and under such policies * * * satisfactory to the secured party, which policies shall specifically provide that loss thereunder shall be payable to the secured party as its interest may appear. * * *

In April of 1967, prior to delivery of the boat, a fire on defendant's premises destroyed part of his inventory of boats including the Revel Craft Playmate. Neither party had obtained insurance although both the seller and the buyer had an insurable interest in the boat. Plaintiff requested the defendant to pay off the promissory note or reimburse him for payments made, and when he refused, the plaintiff started suit in Kent county circuit court. The lower court held that the seller bore the risk of loss and entered judgment for plaintiff.

There is little dispute as to the facts of this case; the entire controversy centers around a single provision of the Uniform Commercial Code. Under the Code, risk of loss is no longer determined by which party has title to the goods at the time of the loss. It is determined, instead, by rules in the Code covering specific fact situations independent of title. The question of risk of loss in the absence of breach of the sale contract is covered in § 2509 which provides in subsection (3):

> * * * risk of loss passes to the buyer on his receipt of the goods if the seller is a merchant; otherwise the risk passes to the buyer on tender of delivery.

But for the next subsection of the Code, the solution to this case would be clear, since it is undisputed that the seller was a merchant and that the buyer had not received the goods.

The Code further provides at § 2509(4) that:

> The provisions of this section are subject to contrary agreement of the parties and to the provisions of this article on sale on approval (section 2327) and on effect of breach on risk of loss (section 2510).

It is the seller's claim that clause 8, supra, in the security agreement declaring that the buyer must "at all times keep the Goods fully insured" is equivalent to a contrary agreement of the parties. We do not agree.

The general approach of Article 2 of the code is that freedom of contract prevails; the greater part of it is concerned with detailing what happens where the contract is silent on a particular point. Such is the purpose of § 2509(3). This provision was meant to cover the common situation where parties have not agreed on who shall bear the risk of loss. In deciding that the seller should bear the risk of loss while the goods are still in his hands, the drafters give the following explanation in Code Comment # 3:

> The underlying theory of this rule is that a merchant who is to make physical delivery at his own place continues meanwhile to control the goods and can be expected to insure his interest in them. The buyer, on the other hand, has no control of the goods and it is *extremely unlikely* that he will carry insurance on goods not yet in his possession. (Emphasis supplied.)

The code drafters correctly observe that it would be highly unusual for the average consumer to carry insurance on an item of personal property weeks or even months before it is delivered to him. The question in our case, then, is whether boilerplate language in a security agreement to the effect that the buyer agrees to keep the goods insured at all times is sufficient to apprise the buyer that he bears the risk of loss on goods he has contracted for, but has not yet received. We think not.

On the contrary, we feel that a contract which shifts the risk of loss to the buyer before he receives the goods is so unusual that a seller who wants to achieve this result must make his intent very clear to the buyer. Fine print in a security agreement concerning insurance does not achieve this result. Clause 8 is entirely vague when it states that insurance is to be carried "at all times." Common experience would dictate that the words "at all times" mean "at all times after one gets possession." This interpretation of the clause is borne out if we consider the language immediately preceding it:

> (7) Buyer will at all times keep the Goods in first class order and repair, excepting any loss, damage or destruction which is fully covered by proceeds of insurance.

Clause 7, including its mention of insurance which is later expanded upon in clause 8, apparently assumes that the buyer (debtor) is in possession of the collateral. One cannot keep in repair what he does not have. Finally, risk of loss is nowhere mentioned in clause 8, and under the circumstances it cannot readily be inferred. We, therefore, hold that the parties to this contract had not agreed that the buyer would bear the risk of loss prior to his receipt of the goods and that the seller bears the loss under § 2509(3).

* * *

We do not mean to say that parties may not validly agree on who bears the risk of loss; rather, we hold that if they intend to shift that burden to the buyer before his receipt of the goods, they must do so in clear and unequivocal language.

For the foregoing reasons, the judgment of the lower court is affirmed.

Affirmed.

The Old Colony truck driver refused to deliver the merchandise inside the door of defendant's store.

NINTH STREET EAST, LIMITED v. HARRISON

Connecticut Circuit Court, First Circuit, 1968.
5 Conn.Cir. 597, 259 A.2d 772.

Norton M. LEVINE, J.

This is an action to recover the purchase price of merchandise sold to defendant by plaintiff. Plaintiff is a manufacturer of men's clothing, with a principal place of business in Los Angeles, California. Defendant is the owner and operator of a men's clothing store, located in Westport, Connecticut, known as "The Rage."

Pursuant to orders received by plaintiff in Los Angeles on November 28, 1966, defendant ordered a variety of clothing items from plaintiff. On November 30, 1966, plaintiff delivered the merchandise in Los Angeles to a common carrier known as Denver-Chicago Trucking Company, Inc., hereinafter called Denver, and received a bill of lading from the trucker. Simultaneously, plaintiff mailed defendant four invoices, all dated November 30, 1966, covering the clothing, in the total sum of $2216. All the invoices bore the notations that the shipment was made "F.O.B. Los Angeles" and "Via Denver-Chicago." Further, all four invoices contained the printed phrase, "Goods Shipped at Purchaser's Risk." Denver's bill of lading disclosed that the shipment was made "collect," to wit, that defendant was obligated to pay the freight charges from Los Angeles to Westport. Denver subsequently transferred the shipment to a connecting carrier known as Old Colony Transportation Company, of South Dartmouth, Massachusetts, hereinafter called Old Colony, for ultimate delivery at defendant's store in Westport. The delivery was attempted by Old Colony at defendant's store on or about December 12, 1966. A woman in charge of the store, identified as defendant's wife, requested the Old Colony truck driver to deliver the merchandise inside the door of defendant's store. The truck driver refused to do so. The dispute not having been resolved, Old Colony retained possession of the eight cartons comprising the shipment, and the truck thereupon departed from the store premises.

Defendant sent a letter, dated December 12, 1966, and received by plaintiff in Los Angeles on December 20, 1966, reporting the refusal of the truck driver to make the delivery inside defendant's store. This was the first notice to plaintiff of the nondelivery. The letter alleged that defendant needed the merchandise immediately for the holidays but that defendant nevertheless insisted that the merchandise must be delivered inside his store, as a condition of his acceptance. Plaintiff tried to reach defendant by phone, but without success. Similarly, its numerous attempts to locate the shipment were fruitless. Plaintiff filed a claim against Denver for the lost merchandise, but up to the date of trial had not been reimbursed, in whole or in part, by the carrier. Defendant never recovered possession of the merchandise at any time following the original refusal.

The sole special defense pleaded was, "The Plaintiff refused to deliver the merchandise into the Defendant's place of business." Therefore defendant claimed that he is not liable for the subsequent loss or disappearance of the shipment, or the purchase price thereof, and that the risk of loss remained with plaintiff.

The basic problem is to determine the terms and conditions of the agreement of the parties as to transportation, and the risks and hazards incident thereto. The court finds that the parties had originally agreed that the merchandise would be shipped by common carrier F.O.B. Los Angeles, as the place of shipment, and that the defendant would pay the freight charges between the two points. The notations on the invoices, and the bill of lading, previously described, make this clear. The use of the phrase "F.O.B.," meaning free on board, made this portion of the agreement not only a price term covering defendant's obligation to pay freight charges between Los Angeles and Westport but also a controlling factor as to risk of loss of the merchandise upon delivery to Denver and subsequently to Old Colony as the carriers. * * * [A]n F.O.B. term must be read to indicate the point at which delivery is to be made unless there is specific agreement otherwise and therefore it will normally determine risk of loss."

* * *

The arrangements as to shipment were at the option of plaintiff as the seller. § 2–311(2). Plaintiff duly placed the goods in possession of a carrier, to wit, Denver, and made a reasonable contract for their transportation, having in mind the nature of the merchandise and the remaining circumstances. Notice of the shipment, including the F.O.B. provisions, was properly given to defendant, as required by law, pursuant to the four invoices. Uniform Commercial Code § 2–504, comment 5.

The law erects a presumption in favor of construing the agreement as a "shipment" contract, as opposed to a "destination" contract. § 2–503; Uniform Commercial Code § 2–503, comment 5. Under the presumption of a "shipment" contract, plaintiff's liability for loss or damage terminated upon delivery to the carrier at the F.O.B. point to wit, Los Angeles. The court finds that no persuasive evidence was offered to overcome the force of the statutory presumption in the instant case. Thus, as § 2–509(1) indicates, "[w]here the contract requires or authorizes the seller to ship the goods by carrier (a) if it does not require him to deliver them at a particular destination, the risk of loss passes to the buyer when the goods are duly delivered to the carrier." Accordingly, at the F.O.B. point, when the risk of loss shifted, Denver and Old Colony, as carriers, became the agents or bailees of defendant. The risk of subsequent loss or delay rested on defendant, and not plaintiff. A disagreement arose between defendant's wife and the truck driver, resulting in nondelivery of the merchandise, retention thereof by the carrier, and, finally, disappearance of the shipment. The ensuing dispute was fundamentally a matter for resolution between defendant and the carriers, as his agents. Nothing in the outcome of that dispute could defeat or impair plaintiff's recovery against defendant.

Defendant has urged that, since plaintiff pressed a damage claim against the carrier, this constitutes an assertion of an ownership interest by plaintiff, and responsibility for loss thereof, inconsistent with plaintiff's present claim against defendant. The court does not agree. Even though the risk of loss, subsequent to delivery to the carrier, had passed to defendant, plaintiff nevertheless had the privilege of pressing the damage claim against the trucker. Any recovery on the claim would, however, be held by plaintiff, subject to its own interest, as a fiduciary for defendant. § 2–722(b). In this connection, the evidence demonstrated that plaintiff first made an effort to secure defendant's cooperation in asserting the damage claim but was unsuccessful.

* * *

In view of defendant's wrongful rejection, following the shifting of the risk of loss to him, he is liable to plaintiff for the entire purchase price of the merchandise. Thus, § 2–709 provides in part: "(1) When the buyer fails to pay the price as it becomes due the seller may recover . . . the price (a) * * * of conforming goods lost or damaged within a commercially reasonable time after risk of their loss has passed to the buyer." * * *

The issues are found for plaintiff. Judgment may therefore enter for plaintiff to recover of defendant the sum of $2216, plus taxable costs.

A thirty-eight foot pleasure boat—the RIVER QUEEN.

GALLAGHER v. UNENROLLED MOTOR VESSEL RIVER QUEEN

United States Court of Appeals,
Fifth Circuit, 1973.
475 F.2d 117.

Before COLEMAN, MORGAN and RONEY, Circuit Judges.

Plaintiffs sued to recover possession of their 38-foot pleasure motor boat, RIVER QUEEN, which one defendant, a marina operator, had sold to the other defendants. Judgment was entered for plaintiff against the purchasers on the finding that the marina operator had no right to sell the plaintiff's vessel, and against the marina operator in favor of the purchasers who had paid for the boat which they could not keep.

The purchasers appeal on the ground that they acquired all rights to RIVER QUEEN under Section 2.403(b) of the Uniform Commercial Code which provides:

> (b) Any entrusting of possession of goods to a merchant who deals in goods of that kind gives him power to transfer all rights of the entruster to a buyer in ordinary course of business.

We find no error in the District Court's conclusion that

> * * * Plaintiffs did not entrust the vessel RIVER QUEEN to Defendant Smith as a merchant within the meaning of Section 2.403 of the Uniform Commercial Code. Plaintiffs rented a stall at Defendant Smith's marina to keep this vessel. This defendant operated several businesses at this one location. His business of renting stalls for vessels was separate and apart from his business as a boat repair. [By inference, the court concluded that the renting of stalls was also separate and apart from his business as a boat merchant.] The River Queen was kept at this marina pursuant to a verbal rental contract.

* * *

Affirmed.

Percy Grubb's loan.

GRUBB v. OLIVER ENTERPRISES, INC.

United States District Court, N.D. Georgia,
Atlanta Division, 1972.
358 F.Supp. 970.

MOYE, District Judge

On December 17, 1970, Percy Grubb borrowed $55.94 from the Dollar Loan Company. The disclosed annual percentage rate of interest on the loan was 65.46 percent. Although Grubb was obligated to repay Dollar Loan $55.94, he received cash in hand of only $17.27. Dollar Loan Company kept the balance in order to apply $22.73 to a prior unpaid loan, collect statutorily authorized interest charges of $5.59, and pay Grubb's premiums of $10.07 on a credit accident and health insurance plan. Evidently this loan was insufficient to satisfy Grubb's long range financial needs because on April 14, 1971, Grubb returned to Dollar Loan and negotiated another small loan for $55.94 out of which he received cash in hand of $35.27 after similar deductions were made by the Dollar Loan Company.

* * * The question before the Court is whether Dollar Loan Company violated the Truth in Lending Act by using the words "loan fee" on its disclosure statements instead of the words "prepaid finance charge" as required by Regulation Z. * * *

The Georgia Industrial Loan Act authorizes Dollar Loan Company to charge two types of interest. First, Dollar Loan can charge eight percent (8%) interest per year on the face amount of the note. Second, and in addition to the first type of interest, Dollar Loan is authorized to charge a "fee" for making the loan: eight percent (8%) of the first $600 and four percent (4%) of the excess. This fee is collected at the time the loan is made and is not refunded to the borrower except insofar as it is required to be applied to any new loan which the borrower may negotiate with that lender within 15 days after prepaying the old loan (all of which must be within a six-month or two-year period, as applicable). In the instant case, Dollar Loan charged Percy Grubb interest of $1.11 and a "loan fee" of $4.48 on a note in the amount of $55.94. Percy Grubb contends that the $4.48 "loan fee" should have been referred to on Dollar Loan's disclosure statement as a "prepaid finance charge" in order to comply with the requirements of the Truth in Lending Act and Regulation Z. Dollar Loan contends that the $4.48 "loan fee" is not a prepaid finance charge and is properly disclosed by the term "loan fee."

The Truth in Lending Act and the regulations prescribed thereunder were designed to require creditors to make certain uniform disclosures in consumer credit transactions in order to "assure a meaningful disclosure of credit terms so that the consumer will be able to compare more readily the various credit terms available to him and avoid the uninformed use of credit." Percy Grubb's loan is covered by Regulation Z, * * * which specifies the disclosures creditors must make and uniform terminology they must use when extending loans and other nonsale credit. * * *

* * *

* * * Regulation Z state[s], in essence, that a finance charge which is paid separately to the creditor or withheld by the creditor from the proceeds of the credit extended, must be disclosed using the words "prepaid finance charge." The "fee" for making a loan which is authorized by the Georgia Industrial Loan Act is a finance charge which is paid separately to the creditor or withheld by the creditor from the proceeds of the credit extended and therefore must be labeled and disclosed as a "prepaid finance charge." * * * To rule otherwise would frustrate the purposes of the Act and allow creditors to use varying terminology which would confuse the average person who attempts to compare his credit alternatives.

Moving to the issue of damages, the Court awards plaintiff $200 pursuant to Section 1640 of the Act which provides that the civil liability for violating the Act shall be "twice the amount of the finance charge" with a minimum award of $100 and a maximum award of $1,000. Since Dollar Loan violated the Act in connection with two loans, Mr. Grubb is entitled to the $100 minimum award for each loan which amounts to a total award of $200.

* * * After due consideration of the evidence and argument presented by counsel for both parties, the Court awards the plaintiff's attorney $1,750 in attorney's fees for which the defendant is hereby liable.

* * *

Review Questions

1. Does a bailment always involve a contract? Does it ever involve real property? What uses may a bailee make of the bailed property? How much care must a bailee take of the bailed property? To what extent may the legal duties of care be varied by contract? Is there any exception to the duty of the bailee to redeliver the identical chattels to the bailor? How does a bailor make out a prima facie case against the bailee, and what is its effect? Is a bailee responsible for the contents of a bailed item? Explain your answers.

2. What are the four basic consumer rights? What tactics are used by consumerists? What are the three legal theories used to establish product liability? What are the problems for a plaintiff in using these different theories? What is the purpose of "truth in lending"? What are the two most important disclosures under this law? Are there special requirements for real estate credit? Does "truth in lending" affect advertising relating to consumer credit? Are there any special requirements for written warranties under the Magnuson-Moss Act? Are there rules relating to warranty disclaimer under the Magnuson-Moss Act? Explain your answers.

3. Is a common carrier always strictly liable for goods bailed to the carrier? Are there any goods a common carrier is not bound to carry? May a carrier's strict liability be limited by contract? Is a warehouseperson strictly liable for the goods stored? Does a common carrier ever have a warehouseperson's liability? What are the two basic documents of title? When is such a document negotiable? What one additional requirement is necessary for a bona fide purchaser of a document of title versus a holder in due course of a money instrument? In what two situations does a bona fide purchaser of a document of title not acquire title to the goods covered by the contract? In what position is a purchaser of a non-negotiable document of title? How are documents of title used as security? Are there different delivery requirements depending on the type of document of title involved? Explain your answers.

4. What two things are required for "identification" of goods to a contract of sale? What is the result of such identification? What happens if the goods are destroyed after a sales contract is entered into but before the risk of loss has transferred to the buyer? At what point in time does the UCC say the risk of loss passes to the buyer under a sale of goods? Is a buyer allowed to inspect the goods before paying for them? Explain your answers.

5. What rules apply if either a buyer or a seller repudiates a future promised performance? How can either party be certain there has been a repudiation? When may a seller withhold delivery? When may a seller reclaim goods or get them back while they are still being transported to a buyer? Does it make any difference that the buyer has already sold them? How does the seller's right to resell the goods differ from his or her right to bring an action for money damages because the buyer would not accept them? What if the seller is still in the process of manufacture? Is the seller ever able to recover the full purchase price? May the buyer and seller forecast damages or set special remedies? Is the seller entitled to retain any prepayments after justifiably withholding delivery? Explain your answers.

6. When is title a consideration in sales disputes? How do letters of credit work? Explain your answers.

7. How does a buyer's right to reject goods differ from his or her right to revoke after acceptance? What seller's right is the buyer's right to reject or revoke after acceptance subject to? When does a buyer "set off" or "resell"? When can the buyer purchase substitute goods? Does the buyer have an alternative? Will the measure of damages be the same? Is there still a third alternative a buyer may use, and is the measure of damages still different? What implied warranties apply to merchants only? How about nonmerchants? How may implied warranties be disclaimed? Does insolvency in a seller ever give the buyer additional rights? When can the buyer get specific performance? Explain your answers.

8. Define the following terms: anticipatory breach, bailment, capture, commercial bailment, common carrier, consumerism, consumer product, cover, cure, destination contract, entruster rule, field warehousing, full warranty, implied warranty of merchantability, sale on approval, sale or return, shipment contract, stoppage in transit, straight bill of lading, tariff.

Problems

1. a. Blackburn Trucking Company accepts a truckload of mandarin oranges for delivery to Little Rock. Explain whether the Company is liable for loss or damage to the oranges in each of the following situations:

1. An escaped convict hijacks the truck and runs it off the road with the result that the oranges are badly squashed and damaged.
2. The oranges are overripe when they're delivered to the carrier, and they spoil en route. (In your answer, assume first that the Trucking Company knew that the oranges were overripe when it accepted them for shipment, and second that it did not know.)
3. Lightning strikes the truck which bursts into flame, destroying all of the oranges.
4. Joe Gibbs, the driver for Blackburn Trucking, is drunk and carelessly runs the truck into a ditch. While Joe is waiting for help, a tornado strikes, destroying the truck and what's left of the oranges.
5. A state health inspector delays shipment and half the oranges spoil before they arrive in Little Rock.

b. Edie Evans delivers three carloads of onions to Great Lincoln Railroad for shipment to Newberg. The Railroad issues Edie a negotiable bill of lading covering the onions. Edie endorses the bill in blank and forwards it to John Johanson who has purchased the onions. When the onions arrive in Newberg, John presents the bill of lading to the Railroad, and the Railroad delivers the onions to John. However, the Railroad neither takes up the bill of lading nor marks it "delivered in full," and John subsequently sells the bill to Paula Kern, a produce wholesaler who is unaware that delivery has been made under the bill. In a suit by Paula against Great Lincoln Railroad, who will prevail? Explain. Would your answer differ if the bill were non-negotiable? Explain.

c. Kevin McBride stores thirty portable TV sets with Farrell Storage, Inc. Farrell issues Kevin a negotiable warehouse receipt covering the sets made deliverable to Kevin's order. James Denny breaks into Kevin's office and steals the receipt, forges Kevin's blank endorsement, and presents the receipt to Farrell Storage which delivers the sets to Denny. In a suit by Kevin against Farrell Storage, who will prevail? Explain. Would your answer differ if the warehouse receipt were originally made deliverable "to bearer"? Explain.

Now suppose that James Denny steals thirty portable TV sets from Kevin McBride and warehouses them so as to obtain a negotiable warehouse receipt. Denny later delivers the receipt to the warehouseman and recollects the sets. What rights, if any, does Kevin McBride have against the warehouseman? Explain fully. Assuming Denny does not recollect the sets but, instead, transfers the warehouse receipt to Ann Pringle who pays value for the receipt and takes without knowledge of the theft, what are Ann's rights, if any, to the TV sets? Explain fully.

2. a. Debra Warren contracts in writing to purchase two prize-winning, registered Hereford bulls from Hank Turner, a Texas rancher. By the terms of the contract, Hank must ship the bulls "F.O.B. Pendleton, Oregon" where Debra owns a cattle ranch. Hank ships the two registered bulls via West Central Railroad; he procures a negotiable bill of lading covering the animals from the Railroad and forwards it to Debra in Oregon. While the West Central train carrying the bulls is passing through Utah, an unexpected flash flood causes the train to derail, and one of the bulls is killed (the other escapes injury).

1. As between Debra and Hank, who bears the risk of loss regarding the bulls during the shipment to Oregon? Explain.
2. Following the derailment, what are Debra's rights, if any, against Hank Turner? Explain fully.
3. How would your answers to (1) and (2) differ if the contract had called for shipment "F.O.B. Dallas, Texas"?

b. Jack Buell, a radio dealer in Miami, Florida telephones radio manufacturer Ron Fletcher in Detroit, Michigan on June 1 and orders 500 Z-Mac radios at a cost of $10,000, the radios to be shipped to Jack in September "F.O.B. Central Atlantic Railroad, Detroit, Michigan." On June 5, Ron sends the following note to Jack:

Dear Jack:

This is to confirm that per our agreement of June 1, I will ship 500 radios to you in September via the Central Atlantic Railroad, the total contract price for the radios to be $10,000.

Yours truly,

Ron Fletcher

Jack does not respond to the note. In September, Ron delivers the 500 Z-Mac radios to the carrier and obtains a negotiable bill of lading from the Railroad which he forwards to Jack in Miami. The carrier, however, is negligent in loading the radios, and more than half of them arrive in Miami in a damaged condition.

1. As between Jack and Ron, who bears the risk of loss regarding the radios during shipment to Miami? Explain. Would your answer differ if Ron had shipped 500 T-Mac radios instead of the Z-Mac models ordered by Jack? Explain.

2. Suppose that Jack orders the radios because he needs them for the Christmas trade and cannot obtain them elsewhere. The contract calls for Ron to deliver the radios "F.O.B. Miami, Florida." What action can Jack take even before the radios leave Detroit to protect himself from the possibility of loss or destruction of the radios during shipment?

c. As between the buyer and the seller, who must bear the loss in each of the following situations:
   1. Peggy Newman contracts to purchase a baby grand piano from Overmyer's Music Shop. The store's delivery truck arrives at Peggy's home on Saturday, and employees of the store attempt to deliver the piano. Though the piano is conforming in all respects, Peggy refuses delivery. The delivery truck is involved in an accident on its way back to the store, and the piano is destroyed.
   2. David Bushey contracts to purchase Alan Jensen's old snow skis. As per the terms of the contract, Alan brings the skis over to David's house and attempts to deliver them. However, David is not home at the time so Alan takes the skis back home with him. That night a fire breaks out in Alan's garage, and the skis, which are stored there, are totally destroyed.
   3. Retailer Marian McKinney contracts to purchase 150 occasional chairs from Comfort Furniture, Inc., the chairs to be shipped to Marian "F.A.S. The Voyager." Comfort Furniture delivers the chairs alongside "The Voyager," and the crew of the ship begins to load the goods. The crew is careless in loading, and some of the chairs are damaged.
   4. Again, Marian McKinney contracts to purchase 150 occasional chairs from Comfort Furniture. This time, however, the chairs are in the possession of Waterman Storage Company, and Comfort Furniture merely delivers to Marian a negotiable warehouse receipt covering the chairs. After Marian receives the receipt but before she notifies the Storage Company of her right to the chairs, the chairs are destroyed in a warehouse explosion.

3. a. Sporting goods retailer Amy Burrows contracts to purchase 150 fishing rods for $2,500 from Wiseman Fish-Outfitters, Inc. What are Amy's legal rights and remedies in each of the following situations?
   1. By the terms of the contract, Amy must pay the $2,500 in two equal installments of $1,250—the first installment due prior to delivery of the fishing rods, the second due at the time of delivery. Five days after Amy pays the first installment, Wiseman Fish-Outfitters, Inc. goes insolvent and although the Company has already set aside the 150 rods to be sent to Amy, it does not deliver the rods.
   2. Wiseman, Inc. ships 100 fishing rods to Amy (instead of the 150 called for in the contract). Amy has prepaid $500 on the purchase price.
   3. Wiseman, Inc. ships 150 fishing rods to Amy, but the rods are poorly constructed and not at all like the samples that Wiseman showed to Amy before she entered into the contract.

4. Three months before delivery is due under the contract, Amy hears rumors that Wiseman, Inc. is insolvent. The rumors come from a reliable source, and Amy fears that the fishing rods may not be delivered.

b. Dale Fitzsimmons contracts to purchase a truckload of Idaho potatoes from Sara McCracken for $1,200. What are Sara's legal rights and remedies in each of the following situations?

1. The contract calls for Sara to sell the potatoes to Dale on credit. Before delivering the potatoes to the carrier for shipment, Sara learns that Dale is insolvent.
2. The same as in (#1) except that Sara has already delivered the potatoes to the carrier when she learns of Dale's insolvency; the carrier is en route to Dale's place of business.
3. Sara delivers a truckload of conforming Idaho potatoes to Dale; Dale refuses to accept the potatoes.
4. Sara sells the potatoes to Dale on credit. Five days after she delivers the goods, Sara discovers that Dale was insolvent at the time of receiving the potatoes and cannot pay for them. This surprises Sara as Dale assured her in writing prior to delivery that he was financially solvent.
5. The same as in (#4) except that Dale has already resold the potatoes to Joseph Roberts who paid $1,500 for them and took them without knowledge of Dale's financial problems.
6. By the terms of the contract, Dale is obligated to pay $500 of the purchase price in advance of delivery of the potatoes. Dale fails to make the $500 payment when due. Sara, at this time, has not yet set aside the specific potatoes to be sent to Dale.
7. Thirty days before Sara is to ship the potatoes, Dale notifies her that he no longer wants the potatoes and will not accept them if they are delivered.

4. a. Sharon Steinberg makes the following purchases at "Costless" Variety Store: a five-speed "Eatwell" brand electric mixer, a "Foreversharp" brand chef's knife, and a spray bottle of "Cleanwell" brand glass and window cleaner. Sharon's daughter, Shelley, is using the mixer to beat up a chocolate cake mix when one of the beaters flies out of the mixer and strikes Shelley in the eye, injuring her. The cake mix splatters on Shelley's new dress, ruining it. The same day, Sharon cuts her hand on the blade of the chef's knife while removing it from the package. And Sharon's husband, Bob, mistakes the glass and window cleaner for hairspray and sprays it on his hair with the result that a goodly portion of his hair falls out.

1. What are Shelley's rights, if any, against "Eatwell," Inc., the manufacturer of the mixer? Against "Costless" Variety Store? Discuss all possible bases of liability. Would your answer differ if Shelley waited until six months after her injury to bring the matter to the attention of Eatwell and Costless? Explain. Would your answer differ if the package containing the mixer stated in bold print: "All warranties, whether express or implied, are disclaimed." Explain.

2. What are Sharon's rights, if any, against "Foreversharp," the manufacturer of the chef's knife? Against "Costless" Variety Store?
3. What are Bob's rights, if any, against "Cleanwell," the manufacturer of the glass and window cleaner? Against "Costless" Variety Store?

b. Professional thief Ben Boggs breaks into the home of wealthy widow Gertrude Lents and steals Gertrude's fine diamond brooch. Ben sells the Brooch to Judith Corbin (who is unaware that the brooch is stolen) for $1,500. Boggs then purchases a used car from Fred Fisher for $750; Boggs pays by check, and Fred accepts the check though the sale was to be "strictly cash." Ultimately, the check is dishonored and returned to Fred, but, by that time, Boggs has resold the car to Eunice Byers who paid $700 cash for the car. Eunice took without knowledge of the prior transaction or the bad check.
   1. Upon discovering that her brooch has been sold to Judith Corbin, what are Gertrude's rights, if any, against Judith? Assuming that Judith must return the brooch to Gertrude, what are Judith's rights, if any, against Ben Boggs? Explain fully.
   2. What are Fred Fisher's rights, if any, against Eunice Byers? Assuming that Eunice must return the car to Fred, What are Eunice's rights, if any, against Ben Boggs? Explain fully.

c. Julie Benson borrows an expensive camera from Paul Cotton to take with her on vacation. While photographing some bears in Yellowstone Park, Julie accidentally drops the camera, and the lens is broken. Julie decides to repair the camera before returning it to Paul. She takes it to Tyler's Camera Shop and leaves it there for repair along with her own less expensive camera which is also broken. Ted Tyler, the shop proprietor, repairs the cameras and then sells them to Glenn Davies, a customer who sees the cameras on the shelf and thinks they are part of Ted's inventory. When Paul and Julie learn of the sale, they are incensed. What are their rights, if any, against Glen Davies? Against Ted Tyler? Discuss fully. What are Glen Davies's rights, if any, against Ted Tyler? Discuss fully.

d. Andrew Cross, a San Francisco clothing retailer, contracts in writing to purchase 10,000 ladies' tops at a total contract price of $30,000 from Mike Korasu, a Hong Kong-based clothing manufacturer. The contract contains a letter of credit term requiring Andrew to obtain an irrevocable letter of credit from First State Bank in San Francisco, naming Mike as beneficiary. Andrew applies for the letter, depositing $17,000 as security for repayment. The bank issues the letter in favor of Mike. The conditions of the letter are that Mike (or his representative) present to the bank a draft drawn on Andrew Cross for $30,000 along with a negotiable bill of lading properly describing the goods. Mike's San Francisco representative presents the draft and bill of lading to the issuer bank. Although the bill of lading describes only "6,000 ladies' tops," the bank nonetheless honors the $30,000 draft. What are Andrew's rights, if any, against First State Bank? What are First State Bank's rights, if any, against Mike Korasu?

e. Assume that Mike Korasu's representative presents the draft and bill of lading properly describing the "10,000 ladies' tops." Does Andrew have any right to "stop payment" of the draft in the event that the tops arrive nonconforming? Explain. What contract provision could Andrew have insisted upon to prevent such a problem?

5. a. Much to her dismay Cheryl Babcock discovered that the finance charge on her $3,000 household loan had been inaccurately disclosed on the written statement of credit terms. When Cheryl complained to the loan company about this "gross misrepresentation," she was met with vague indifference. What is Cheryl's legal remedy?

b. On April 1, Roscoe Woolley took out a second mortgage on his residence in order to clear up "once and for all" his mounting pile of personal debts. When Roscoe's wife, Louise, convinced her husband that such a drastic measure was uncalled for, Roscoe agreed to cancel the mortgage (he was notified by the mortgagor that he had three business days in which to do so). On the morning of April 3, Roscoe called his "creditor's" office and left a message with the secretary that he wished to cancel the transaction. Is Roscoe free of the mortgage? Explain.

6. *Part a.* Sure Rain Apparel, Inc., manufactures expensive, exclusive rain apparel. One model is very popular and sold widely throughout the United States. About six months after their initial sale to distributors, Sure started receiving complaints that there was a noticeable fading of the color of the material. Many of the distributors seek to return the goods, recover damages, or both. Sure denies liability on the following bases: (1) there was an "Act of God," (2) there was no breach of warranty since the fading was to be expected in any event, and (3) any and all warranty protection was disclaimed unless expressly stated in the contract.

The contract contained the following provisions relating to warranty protection:

First: The manufacturer warrants that the material used to make the raincoats is 100% Egyptian long fiber cotton.

Second: The manufacturer guarantees the waterproofing of the raincoat for one year if the directions as to dry cleaning are followed.

Third: There are no other express warranties granted by the seller, except those indicated above. This writing is intended as a complete statement and integration of all express warranty protection.

Fourth: The manufacturer does not purport to give any implied warranty of merchantability in connection with this sale. The express warranties above enumerated are granted in lieu thereof.

Fifth: There are no warranties which extend beyond the description above.

The fourth and fifth provisions were conspicuous and initialed by the buyers.

Several buyers have commenced legal actions against Sure based upon implied warranties and express oral warranties made prior to the execution of the contract.

Required: Answer the following, setting forth reasons for any conclusions stated.

1. Is Sure liable for breach of warranty?

Part b. Nielson Wholesalers, Inc., ordered 1,000 scissors at $2.50 a pair from Wilmot, Inc., on February 1, 1982. Delivery was to be made not later than March 10. Wilmot accepted the order in writing on February 4. The terms were 2/10, net/30, F.O.B. seller's loading platform in Baltimore. Due to unexpected additional orders and a miscalculation of the backlog of orders, Wilmot subsequently determined that it could not perform by March 10. On February 15, Wilmot notified Nielson that it would not be able to perform, and canceled the contract. Wilmot pleaded a reasonable mistake and impossibility of performance as its justification for canceling. At the time the notice of cancellation was received, identical scissors were available from other manufacturers at $2.70. Nielson chose not to purchase the 1,000 scissors elsewhere but instead notified Wilmot that it rejected the purported cancellation and would await delivery as agreed. Wilmot did not deliver on March 10, by which time the price of the scissors had risen to $3.00 a pair. Nielson is seeking to recover damages from Wilmot for breach of contract.

Required: Answer the following, setting forth reasons for any conclusions stated:

1. Will Nielson prevail and, if so, how much will it recover?
2. Would Nielson be entitled to specific performance under the circumstances?
3. Assuming that Wilmot discovers that Nielson was insolvent, will this excuse performance?

Source: CPA Exam, November 1982, # 5(a), (b).

7. On February 1, 1983, Nugent Manufacturing, Inc. contracted with Costello Wholesalers to supply Costello with 1,000 integrated circuits. Delivery was called for on May 1, 1983. On March 15, 1983, Nugent notified Costello that it would not perform and that Costello should look elsewhere. Nugent had received a larger and more lucrative contract on February 27, 1983, and its capacity was such that it could not fulfill both orders. The facts

a. Are *not* sufficient clearly to establish an anticipatory repudiation.
b. Will prevent Nugent from retracting its repudiation of the Costello contract.
c. Will permit Costello to sue immediately after March 15, 1983, even though the performance called for under the contract was not until May 1, 1983.
d. Will permit Costello to sue only after May 1, 1983, the latest performance date.

Source: CPA Exam, May 1983, # 1(42).

8. The Uniform Commercial Code deals differently with negotiable documents of title than with commercial paper. Which of the following will prevent a due negotiation of a negotiable document of title?

a. The transfer by delivery alone of a title document which has been endorsed in blank.

b. The receipt of the instrument in payment of an antecedent money obligation.
c. The taking of a bearer document of title from one who lacks title thereto.
d. The fact that the document of title is more than one month old.

Source: CPA Exam, May 1983, # 1(43).

9. a. A claim has been made by Donnegal to certain goods in your client's possession. Donnegal will be entitled to the goods if it can be shown that Variance, the party from whom your client purchased the goods, obtained them by

1. Deceiving Donnegal as to his identity at the time of the purchase.
2. Giving Donnegal his check which was later dishonored.
3. Obtaining the goods from Donnegal by fraud, punishable as larceny under criminal law.
4. Purchasing goods which had been previously stolen from Donnegal.

Source: CPA Exam, May 1982, # 1(47).

b. Webster purchased a drill press for $475 from Martinson Hardware, Inc. The press has proved to be defective, and Webster wishes to rescind the purchase based upon a breach of implied warranty. Which of the following will preclude Webster's recovery from Martinson?

1. The press sold to Webster was a demonstration model and sold at a substantial discount; hence, Webster received no implied warranties.
2. Webster examined the press carefully, but as regards the defects, they were hidden defects which a reasonable examination would *not* have revealed.
3. Martinson informed Webster that they were closing out the model at a loss due to certain deficiencies and that it was sold "with all faults."
4. The fact that it was the negligence of the manufacturer which caused the trouble and that the defect could *not* have been discovered by Martinson without actually taking the press apart.

Source: CPA Exam, November 1982, # 1(47).

10. a. Falcon, by telegram to Southern Wool, Inc., ordered thirty bolts of cloth, first quality, 60% wool and 40% dacron. The shipping terms were F.O.B. Falcon's factory in Norwalk, Connecticut. Southern accepted the order and packed the bolts of cloth for shipment. In the process it discovered that one-half of the bolts packed had been commingled with cloth which was 50% wool and 50% dacron. Since Southern did not have any additional 60% wool cloth, it decided to send the shipment to Falcon as an accommodation. The goods were shipped, and later the same day Southern wired Falcon its apology informing Falcon of the facts and indicating that the fifteen bolts of 50% wool would be priced at $15 a bolt less. The carrier delivering the goods was hijacked on the way to Norwalk. Under the circumstances, who bears the risk of loss?

1. Southern, since they shipped goods which failed to conform to the contract.

2. Falcon, since the shipping terms were F.O.B. Falcon's place of business.
3. Southern, because the order was *not* a signed writing.
4. Falcon, since Falcon has title to the goods.

Source: CPA Exam, November 1982, # 1(48).

b. Sanders Hardware Company received an order for $900 of assorted hardware from Richards & Company. The shipping terms were F.O.B. Lester Freight Line, seller's place of business, 2/10, net/30. Sanders packed and crated the hardware for shipment, and it was loaded upon Lester's truck. While the goods were in transit to Richards, Sanders learned that Richards was insolvent in the equity sense (unable to pay its debts in the ordinary course of business). Sanders promptly wired Lester's office in Denver, Colorado, and instructed them to stop shipment of the goods to Richards and to store them until further instructions. Lester complied with these instructions. Regarding the rights, duties, and liabilities of the parties, which of the following is correct?
   1. Sanders's stoppage in transit was improper if Richards's assets exceeded its liabilities.
   2. Richards is entitled to the hardware if it pays cash.
   3. Once Sanders correctly learned of Richards's insolvency, it had no further duty or obligation to Richards.
   4. The fact that Richards became insolvent in no way affects the rights, duties, and obligations of the parties.

Source: CPA Exam, November 1982, # 1(50).

Neither a borrower, nor a lender be;
For loan oft loses both itself and friend,
And borrowing dulls the edge of husbandry.
Shakespeare,
Hamlet, Act I, Scene 3

12

Bankruptcy, Secured Creditors, and Accountants' Responsibilities

Bankruptcy

WHAT IS THE NATURE OF BANKRUPTCY?

Despite these words of the immortal Shakespeare, people have been borrowing and lending for thousands of years. Even the earliest civilizations recognized the legal relationship of debtor and creditor. Recognition, however, did not mean leniency for the debtor who would not or could not pay his or her debts. Up until the last few hundred years the law dealt harshly with the delinquent debtor. For example, the early Roman Law (as founded on the Twelve Tables about 450 B.C.) provided that a creditor who was unable to collect on his or her claim from a debtor could cut up the debtor's body and divide the pieces—or better yet, leave the debtor alive and sell him or her into slavery. Even after the law prohibited dismemberment for failure to pay debts, it still allowed the debtor to pledge his or her person, spouse, or children as security for debts, and if payment was not made as promised, the pledged persons were turned over to the creditor to work in bondage. This practice went on for hundreds of years.

Under the English common law system that we have inherited, it was never possible for a debtor to pledge his or her person or family as security for debts. But under the Statute of Merchants (1285), a debtor who did not pay his or her debts could be immediately imprisoned, and it was not necessary for the creditor to look first to the debtor's property for payment. It was not until the eighteenth century that the practice of jailing debtors and holding them "hostage" until their debts were paid was finally abolished.

The debtor's position further improved in 1705 when the first bankruptcy laws came into existence. These laws gave the honest debtor an opportunity to secure a discharge of his or her debts and to retain a portion of his or her estate exempt from the claims of creditors.

Modern bankruptcy law, which we will study in this chapter, accomplishes the same results. It permits a debtor who is "snowed under" by his or her debts to go through bankruptcy and start over unencumbered by past financial obligations. Bankruptcy, however, does not wipe the slate clean of all debts. Though most debts are discharged (i.e., eliminated) in bankruptcy, the bankrupt remains liable for any unpaid alimony and child support; for taxes that fall due within three years preceding the bankruptcy; for liabilities arising out of obtaining money or property by false pretenses or from securing a loan or credit on the basis of a materially fraudulent statement of financial condition; for debts resulting from the bankrupt's willful or malicious injuries to the person or property of another; and for educational loans due within five years preceding the bankruptcy.

And the debtor who goes bankrupt must give up most of his or her property. Any property he or she owns under a secured transaction or installment sale backed by a lien on the goods (subjects covered in detail in the following sections) may be repossessed by the specific creditor involved (e.g., the mortgagor of the bankrupt's home may foreclose on the house). Assets not subject to a lien are turned over to the court and sold, and the proceeds are used to pay off the bankrupt's debts. Still, the debtor is not stripped totally naked; some of his or her property is exempt from sale for his or her debts. For example, the bankrupt can generally keep his or her home if it is not worth too much, some household furnishings and personal clothing, and some tools and other property used in a trade or profession. But most of the bankrupt's debts and most of his or her property are gone. What is more, having been given a new start in life, the debtor cannot repeat the bankruptcy process for a period of six years following discharge.

Each year over 200,000 hard-pressed individuals and companies in the United States go into court and declare themselves bankrupt.

Of course, not everyone who is having financial difficulties wants or needs to have his or her debts completely discharged (i.e., go through straight bankruptcy). An individual who has a few good assets and can work to pay off his or her debts should do so in order to retain a portion of his or her property and because the bankruptcy court cannot discharge a bankrupt's debts again for six years (if more serious financial problems arise during the six year period, the bankrupt will not be able to escape his or her creditors).

WHAT KINDS OF CREDITORS ARE THERE?

Creditors fall into three basic categories: general, governmental, and lien creditors. All three kinds of creditors share in common a desire to be paid as soon as possible, but each, under the law, is provided with different rights and remedies.

A *government creditor* is any government entity to which a debt is owed, whether the debt arises out of a contract with the government or is based on a tax owing. A government creditor can be either a lien creditor or a general creditor depending on whether or not the government has a lien against the debtor's property. A lien is simply a charge on the debtor's property that secures the lien creditor's claim. The lien gives the creditor the right to have his or her claim satisfied from the specific property which is subject to the lien before the property can be used to satisfy the claims of general creditors (creditors having no lien or security on the debtor's assets). However, a creditor is a lien creditor only to the extent of the value of his or her lien on specific property. If the value of the property subject to the lien is insufficient to satisfy the creditor's claim, the creditor will become a general creditor as to the balance owing.

HOW DO LIENS ARISE?

Liens are created in several different ways, the first of which is by agreement. Frequently, for example, liens are created between parties to a sales contract for the purchase of goods. Here, a party may want to purchase goods but does not have the cash price or sufficient credit standing to buy the goods on open credit. So instead, the party makes a down payment on the purchase price and promises to pay the balance to the seller in installments over a specified period of time. The seller during this time may retain a lien or security interest in the goods, and the buyer enjoys possession and use of the goods while he or she pays off the credit balance. As will be seen later in this chapter, *one way* the creditor can protect his or her security interest (which lasts until the full balance is paid) is by filing a "financing statement" (usually in the Secretary of State's Office, although the place of filing varies from state to state). The financing statement generally includes the names and addresses of the parties to the agreement, a description of the collateral (the property to which the lien attaches), and the signatures of the parties. By filing this statement, the secured creditor puts the world on notice that the described collateral, though it is in the debtor's possession, is subject to the creditor's lien. However, the financing statement must be filed before the debtor is petitioned in bankruptcy. A filing made after that time is invalid, and the creditor who makes the filing remains a general, unsecured creditor.

The *security interest* as described above is the lien created by agreement when personal property is used as collateral. When the secured property is real estate (land and buildings), the lien created by the agreement is called a *mortgage*.

Liens are created not only by agreement but by judicial process as well. These so called "judicial liens" result from a creditor's efforts to collect his or her debt. As you will see in the following sections, many of these efforts involve activity prior to obtaining a courtroom judgment. Prejudgment efforts resulting in liens include "attachment" and "garnishment." And if the creditor obtains a judgment against the debtor, the judgment, too, will create a lien. Suppose the debtor fails to pay the judgment, and the creditor must resort to postjudgment procedure such as "execution." Again, a lien may result. Where any of these—prejudgment, judgment, and postjudgment efforts—result in liens, the liens are called judicial liens.

Finally, liens may be created by statute. The most common statutory liens include: (1) the employee's lien on the employer's personalty to secure payment of back wages; (2) the materialman's and mechanic's liens on land and improvements on land to secure the compensation of those who contributed labor or materials to improving the land; and (3) tax liens on the property of people who have not paid their lawful taxes.

Any lienholder, whether he or she holds a consensual lien (security interest or mortgage), a judicial lien (because of the creditor's efforts to collect the debt), or a statutory lien (an employee's lien, mechanic's lien, or tax lien), stands in a much better position regarding the debtor's assets than does a general creditor, at least to the extent that the lien holder's security covers his or her claim.

WHAT IS THE FAIR DEBT COLLECTION PRACTICES ACT?

Congress passed the Fair Debt Collection Practices Act in 1978. The Act prohibits collection agencies from engaging in many unscrupulous practices that previously plagued debtors. Some of the prohibited practices include:

1. Harassing or abusive telephone calls to the debtor, particularly at his or her place of employment;
2. Falsely implying that the debtor's wages are about to be seized;
3. Falsely implying that the collector is a lawyer;
4. Making unauthorized calls to the debtor's employer, neighbors, and friends.

On its face the Act applies only to collection agencies (companies in the business of collecting creditor's claims)—not to creditors or collection lawyers. However, Congress has declared that the practices are contrary to the public interest, and that is all that is required to establish that each abusive and unfair debt collection practice (whether by a collection agency, a creditor, or a collection lawyer) comes within the meaning of Section 5(a) of the Federal Trade Commission Act. The Act authorizes the FTC to investigate unfair and deceptive practices that are found to be against the public interest and to outlaw and punish the commission of such practices. Any debtor who feels that he or she has been unfairly or abusively treated by his or her creditors should contact the Federal Trade Commission in Washington, D.C., or the nearest FTC regional office.

WHAT ARE THE PREJUDGMENT REMEDIES?

There are three prejudgment remedies that a creditor can sometimes pursue before his or her claim is reduced to judgment. These are attachment, garnishment, and prejudgment receivership. Each is a procedure that enables the creditor to preserve property belonging to the debtor until the creditor can prove the validity of his or her claim. The idea here is to prevent the debtor from disposing of his or her property or from concealing or destroying it so it cannot be used to pay off the debt. The creditor may have a legitimate claim that he or she can reduce to judgment by bringing an action against the debtor in a court of law. And the debtor may have sufficient property with which to satisfy the claim once the judgment is granted by the court. What the creditor worries about is what the debtor might do with the property during the time the court is considering the case and before the judgment is rendered against the debtor. Suppose the debtor disposes of the property, conceals it, or destroys it. Prejudgment remedies are designed to prevent this from happening.

These remedies are available only upon the commencement of the case against the debtor (filing the complaint—see Chapter 3).

Attachment

A writ of attachment seizes the debtor's property so as to secure the creditor's claim in case judgment is later rendered in the creditor's favor. Attachments are strictly controlled by statute in all our states. They are generally granted only if (1) the plaintiff is unable to obtain personal service on the defendant (Chapter 2) because the defendant is out of the state hiding or is a nonresident; or (2) where there are special or extraordinary circumstances indicating that the defendant is about to dispose of or secret his or her property to defraud creditors. Where either situation is present, the plaintiff-creditor can get the clerk of the court in which the action is being processed to issue a writ of attachment by filing a bond and an affidavit stating that the statutory grounds for attachment exist. The order of attachment is then directed to the sheriff of the county in which the defendant's property is located. The order instructs the sheriff to satisfy the plaintiff's claim once the judgment has been granted by the court.

The act of the sheriff in taking the property into custody is called a *levy*. Where real property is involved, the sheriff is generally required to post notice of the attachment on the property and to leave a copy of the attachment order with the person in possession of the land. With personal property that can be physically possessed, the sheriff takes the property into actual custody.

A levy on property creates a lien on the property. But although the lien dates from the time of the levy, it becomes effective only if the attaching creditor in fact secures a judgment against the debtor. Once a judgment is granted, the lien gives the attaching creditor a secured creditor's position as to that specific property and thus a preferred position as against other competing creditors who are unsecured.

The debtor can obtain a termination of the attachment by posting a bond called a "discharging" bond in which the debtor promises to pay the claim if judgment is entered against him or her; the issuer of the bond promises to pay if the debtor does not.

The creditor, however, must exercise care in using attachment as a prejudgment remedy. If the debtor can prove that the plaintiff-creditor maliciously obtained the order of attachment without probable cause for believing that the statutory grounds existed, the debtor can sue the creditor for the tort of malicious and wrongful attachment.

Prejudgment Garnishment

An order of attachment directs the sheriff to seize the defendant's property. In a prejudgment garnishment, the order is directed at a third party, called the garnishee, who either owes the debtor money or other property or who is in possession of property belonging to the debtor. The garnishment informs the garnishee that the plaintiff-creditor has a right to satisfy a claim out of what the garnishee holds for the debtor or owes to him or her. The order directs the garnishee to hold the property or to refuse to pay the principal debtor until the creditor's case has been decided and the resulting judgment in favor of the creditor (if, in fact, it is in his or her favor) has been satisfied by the principal debtor.

Most often, the garnishment order is directed to the debtor's employer or to the bank at which the debtor has a savings or checking account. Like an attachment, the garnishment generally creates a lien when the creditor obtains a judgment against the debtor. And once again, tort actions may lie for improper garnishment.

Prejudgment Receivership

A receivership is generally created to preserve or manage property removed from the possession of a debtor. Thus, in an attachment, the sheriff seizes the debtor's property in order to make it available to satisfy the creditor's claim if and when the creditor obtains a judgment. In a prejudgment garnishment a third party holding property belonging to the debtor is ordered to keep the property for use in satisfying the creditor's claim, again, if and when the creditor obtains a judgment. In the case of an order appointing a receiver and creating a receivership, a third party is given possession of the debtor's property along with authority to preserve and manage it. The receiver may be authorized, for example, to continue the operation of a business, to collect rents, or even to sell the property.

A receivership differs from an attachment and garnishment in that the creditor does not obtain a lien on the property subject to the receivership.

ARE THERE ANY LIMITATIONS ON THE USE OF ATTACHMENT, GARNISHMENT, AND PREJUDGMENT RECEIVERSHIP?

The U.S. Supreme Court has ruled that the use of prejudgment remedies must conform to the requirements of "due process" of law. This means that before the debtor's property can become subject to attachment, garnishment, or receivership, the debtor must be notified of the claim against him or her and must be given an opportunity to be heard on the matter. The notice and hearing requirement is designed to establish the validity of the creditor's claim before the debtor can be deprived of his or her property in any manner.

Exceptions

But there are exceptions. The U.S. Supreme Court has stated that notice and hearing may be constitutionally dispensed with in "extraordinary situations" demanding special protection for state or creditor interests. Thus, a government agency may seize property in order to protect the public welfare—and it may do so without notice and hearing. So, too, may property be attached or garnished or become subject to prejudgment receivership where such action is necessary to obtain jurisdiction over a nonresident who cannot be reached by the usual service of summons. Finally, if it can be shown that there is immediate danger that a debtor will destroy or conceal disputed goods, the prejudgment remedies may be resorted to without preliminary notice or hearing.

The use of garnishment is additionally limited by the federal Consumer Credit Protection Act ("Truth in Lending Act") passed in 1968 and containing a section on garnishment. The Act exempts a certain amount of an individual's disposable earnings for any work week from being subject to garnishment. The exemption is the greater of:

1. 75 percent of the individual's disposable earnings for that week; or
2. Thirty times the federal minimum hourly wage prescribed under the Wage and Hour Act at the time such earnings are payable (the minimum wage was $3.35 an hour in 1984).

The Act also prohibits an employer from discharging an employee because his or her earnings have been garnished for a single indebtedness. And it provides that where state law is more restrictive than the federal law, the provisions of the state law will govern.

HOW DOES THE CREDITOR OBTAIN A JUDGMENT?

If the debtor fails to pay despite pressures from the creditor (and despite the use of any prejudgment remedies available), the creditor will have to seek a courtroom judgment against the debtor (Chapter 3). However, upon serving the debtor with a copy of the summons and complaint, the creditor would probably prefer that the debtor fail to respond at all. For if the debtor fails to respond, a default judgment will be entered against him or her. A default judgment provides a fast and relatively inexpensive remedy for the creditor, and such judgments are fairly common. Many debtors do in fact fail to respond after service of process upon them, and many judgments are entered by default against debtors.

A valid judgment creates a lien on the debtor's *real property* (only in the three southern states of Alabama, Georgia, and Mississippi is a judgment lien good against both the real and personal property of the debtor). The judgment lien gives the creditor a position of priority as to the specific real property to which the lien attaches over other creditors whose claims arise after the judgment.

Once a creditor obtains a valid judgment, he or she can actually collect the money through either "execution" or "after-judgment garnishment."

Execution

A writ of execution is issued upon a judgment creditor's request by the clerk of the court in which the judgment was granted. The granting of the writ requires no hearing; it is a completely ministerial act, and the court clerk exercises no discretion in granting the writ. Based on the writ of execution, the sheriff levies on the property described and, after appraisal and notice of sale, sells the property at public auction. In most states the writ of execution extends to both the real and personal property of the debtor, and it applies for a period of from sixty to ninety days, during which time the property must be sold. After the expenses of the sale are subtracted from the sales proceeds, the judgment creditor is paid, assuming there are no lien creditors who take priority over him or her with respect to the specific property sold (if there are such creditors, they will be paid first). Any excess that remains goes to the judgment debtor.

After-Judgment Garnishment

An execution results in sale of the debtor's property. But sometimes the debtor has no property to sell. Where this is the case, the creditor will still be able to collect the judgment if he or she can pinpoint property, funds, or earnings belonging to the debtor in the hands of some third party. Once the judgment creditor locates the property, he or she can obtain a writ of garnishment from the court by filing an affidavit declaring that he or she has a judgment unpaid by the judgment debtor and that the garnishee holds some of the debtor's property or earnings. The writ of garnishment is then served on the garnishee who must answer within a certain time and set out what property or earnings of the debtor he or she holds. If the garnishee fails to answer the writ of garnishment, the court will either enter a judgment against the garnishee for the amount alleged to be in his or her possession, or it will compel the garnishee to answer by use of contempt proceedings. If the garnishee answers and denies that he or she has such property or earnings, the issue as to whether the garnishee does or does not will be tried in court like any other case. If the garnishee admits to possession, the court will issue a judgment against the garnishee for the property or earnings, and the property will be ordered turned over to the court for sale to satisfy the claim of the judgment creditor. But remember, the Consumer Credit Protection Act (Truth in Lending) exempts a minimum of 75 percent of the debtor's weekly earnings from garnishment. And it prohibits an employer from discharging an employee because of garnishment of earnings for a single debt.

DO OTHER LAWS EXEMPT PART OF THE DEBTOR'S PROPERTY FROM BEING SUBJECT TO HIS OR HER DEBTS?

We have seen that part of a debtor's wages are exempt from garnishment under the Consumer Credit Protection Act. Exemptions, however, do not stop there. Statutes in all states exempt certain other properties of the debtor from being subject to sale for his or her debts. The purpose of such laws is to prevent the debtor and his or her family from becoming public charges.

To begin with, all states exempt certain personal property from the claims of creditors (in some cases, the property is exempt up to a certain value only). An exemption is generally created for life insurance, as well, and for wages up to a certain amount (the amount can be greater than the federal law requires, but it cannot be less).

A typical state statute might provide for the following exemptions:

1. For a head of a family or a person sixty-five years of age or older, equity (ownership interest) in a home of up to $20,000. For any other person, equity up to $10,000. Or, in the alternative, equity up to $5,000 in a house trailer in which the debtor or his or her family lives. (The exemption covering the family home is called the "homestead" exemption. In most states, the debtor can claim this exemption only if he or she has a family, uses the property as a residence, and possesses an ownership interest in the home. However, if there is a mortgage on the property, the mortgage is not affected by the exemption statute, and the financial institution financing the purchase of the home can foreclose on the property and sell it notwithstanding that the home falls within the "homestead" exemption as to other creditors.)
2. All household furnishings, appliances, and personal wearing apparel are exempt if they are reasonably necessary to and personally used by the debtor or his or her family (including a piano, radio, TV set, shotgun, rifle, and enough provisions and fuel to cover the debtor's needs for up to three months' time).
3. Equity up to $300 in an automobile so long as the vehicle is not worth more than $1,000.
4. Savings of up to $1,000 in a financial institution (savings account).
5. Life insurance that can be purchased with premiums of up to $500 a year.
6. Up to $2,500 of actual cash value, over and above all liens and other creditors' interests, of tools and any other property used by a debtor in his or her trade, business, or profession (including, for example, a boat, truck, or car that the debtor uses for business purposes).

A debtor who wants to take advantage of these exemptions when a writ of execution has been issued to sell his or her property must claim the exemption within a certain period of time after the levy.

Also, the exemptions do not apply equally to all creditors. A federal tax lien is good as against all property owned by the deficient taxpayer. And if a debtor puts up exempt property as collateral for a loan, the debtor is generally deemed to have waived his or her right of exemption with respect to that loan.

In addition to the state exemptions described above, social security and veterans benefits are exempt under federal statute.

CAN A DEBTOR DEFEAT CREDITORS' RIGHTS BY CONVEYING PROPERTY AWAY TO FRIENDS OR RELATIVES?

The answer is no. The law has long stated (since the Statute of 13 Elizabeth enacted in 1570) that a debtor is not free to conceal or transfer his or her property so as to prevent creditors from satisfying their legal claims. Such a transfer is a *fraudulent conveyance*—that is, a conveyance intended to delay, hinder, or defraud creditors. A fraudulent conveyance is void and of no effect against the persons hindered, delayed, or defrauded. Fraudulent conveyances include not only selling the property to others but also giving it away at a creditor's expense. A debtor must be just before he or she is generous. The leading case involving fraudulent conveyances dates back to 1601 in England and is known as *Twyne's* case. The court in this case considered a debtor's efforts to transfer his property in order to defraud a creditor. The court found six specific "signs and marks" of fraud, which have become known in modern law as "badges of fraud." The following six circumstances, the court stated, indicated the debtor's intent to defraud:

1. The conveyance was general (the debtor did not even except such items as wearing apparel and other necessities thus arousing a suspicion that no real intention to transfer property was present);
2. The debtor remained in possession of the property after the transfer and continued to deal with the property as his own (if a real transfer was intended, the debtor would not have kept possession);
3. The conveyance was made while a creditor's action was pending against the debtor (a transfer made after litigation has begun or immediately prior to anticipated litigation is also highly suspicious);
4. The transaction was secret;
5. The transferee took only a legal interest in the property and held the property for the equitable benefit of the transferor, in effect creating a trust (see Chapter 12) for the debtor (the passage of bare legal title hinders and delays the judgment creditor by depriving him or her of legal remedies while, at the same time, allowing the debtor to keep the complete beneficial interest);
6. The deed itself contained statements that it was made honestly and truly and that it was bona fide (such unusual recitals are suspicious).

Today, all jurisdictions recognize these "badges of fraud" in determining whether a particular conveyance has been made to defeat creditors. Courts also carefully scrutinize intrafamily transfers, voluntary transfers, transfers without consideration, and transfers made immediately prior to the start of litigation against the debtor. If a fraudulent conveyance has been made, the defrauded creditor can either bring a legal action to set the conveyance aside, or he or she can completely ignore the transfer and levy on and sell the property despite the conveyance. Generally, where the creditor has a lien on the property, he or she can also recover damages in tort against anyone who hinders him or her in the execution of the lien.

APART FROM BANKRUPTCY, WHAT LEGAL ALTERNATIVES ARE AVAILABLE TO DEBTORS?

State law provides the debtor with a number of alternatives to bankruptcy, including assignments for the benefit of creditors, a composition for the benefit of creditors, and, in some states, a state wage earner receivership.

Assignments for the Benefit of Creditors

A debtor may voluntarily assign (transfer) all his or her assets (with the exclusion of exempt property) to another party who is given the job of liquidating the assets and distributing the proceeds to the creditors. Any surplus remaining in the hands of the assignee (the party to whom the property is transferred) after the creditors are paid goes back to the debtor.

Of course, it is possible that the creditors may not wish to have the debts and assets administered through a general assignment. If this is so, the creditors can force the debtor into bankruptcy (involuntary bankruptcy is discussed in a following section). If the creditors force the debtor into bankruptcy after the assignment has been made, the assignee is required to turn over the debtor's estate to the bankruptcy receiver or trustee. Since assignment is informal, it may be less expensive and less time consuming than formal bankruptcy proceedings. And because assignment is flexible, it may result in higher sales proceeds (sufficient to pay off the creditors in full and still leave the debtor with some excess). But while bankruptcy costs more and results in less, it does result in a discharge of the debtor's debts which an assignment for the benefit of creditors does not do. Thus, in the assignment situation, if the creditors are not paid in full out of the sales proceeds of the transferred assets, the debtor remains liable for the deficiencies. This inability to obtain a discharge is the biggest disadvantage of making a general assignment. It is for this reason that assignments for the benefit of creditors are seldom used.

Composition of Creditors

A composition of creditors is simply a contract between the debtor and his or her creditors and between and among the creditors themselves that each creditor will accept a lesser sum immediately in full payment of the total amount owing. Thus, unlike an assignment for the benefit of creditors, a composition of creditors effects a discharge of the debtor from the remaining debts he or she owes to creditors who agree to the plan. The discharge occurs at the time the debtor pays the creditors in accord with the plan. And as a composition is not statutory in nature, there is nothing to prevent a debtor whose debts have been discharged by composition from later going through bankruptcy (a debtor whose debts have been discharged in bankruptcy, on the other hand, cannot go through bankruptcy again for another six years).

Extension

An extension is much like a composition in that it, too, is based on an agreement or contract between or among the debtor and his or her creditors. It is unlike a composition in that the debtor pays his or her creditors not in part but in full. An extension simply gives the debtor more time—that is, it results in payment in full but over a period of time extended beyond the original due date. Sometimes the debtor bargains for a combination composition and extension contract with his or her creditors which permits the debtor to pay less in full satisfaction of the debts over an extended period of time. This is not a true composition contract because the creditors are not immediately paid, nor is it a true extension since it does not result in full payment to creditors.

State Wage–Earner Receivership

Statutes in a few states provide for a voluntary state wage earner receivership. In Ohio, for example, the court will appoint someone, upon the debtor's request, to act as a receiver in collecting all nonexempt wages of the debtor and distributing them pro rata among the debtor's creditors until all debts are paid in full. During the time the wage earner receivership is in effect, all repossessions and wage garnishments against the debtor are prohibited (as will be seen in a following section, a similar type of federal receivership may be available under Chapter 13 of the federal Bankruptcy Act).

WHAT IS BANKRUPTCY?

Bankruptcy law may be divided into two main areas. The first is the so-called "straight bankruptcy" which, as described earlier, is designed to liquidate the debtor's property, pay off his or her creditors, and discharge the debtor from any remaining debts. Straight bankruptcy can be either "voluntary" or "involuntary." The Bankruptcy Act deals with straight bankruptcy in Chapters 3, 5, and 7.

The second main area of bankruptcy law is "debtor rehabilitation." Debtor rehabilitation does not work to liquidate the debtor's property and discharge the debtor's debts. Rather, it serves to reorganize his or her holdings and instruct his or her creditors to look to the debtor's future earnings for payment. The Bankruptcy Act deals with debtor reorganization and rehabilitation in Chapters 11 and 13.

WHAT IS STRAIGHT BANKRUPTCY?

Straight bankruptcy does two things:

1. It liquidates the debtor's nonexempt property. To accomplish this, the bankruptcy court usually appoints a "trustee" whose job is to collect the bankrupt's property, sell it, and distribute the proceeds among the bankrupt's creditors. Where the debtor has very little property or the situation is otherwise uncomplicated, a trustee may not be needed and will not be appointed.
2. It discharges the bankrupt from any remaining debts, including "contingent" debts, that are not specifically excluded from discharge by the Bankruptcy Act.

Section 101(4) of the Bankruptcy Act says that a claim "means (A) the right to payment, whether or not such right is reduced to judgment, liquidated, unliquidated, fixed, contingent, matured, unmatured, disputed, undisputed, legal, equitable, secured, or unsecured."

Nearly all straight bankruptcies are voluntarily initiated by the debtor. Involuntary bankruptcies initiated by the debtor's creditors are unusual by comparison. The debtor begins a voluntary straight bankruptcy by filing a petition with the federal district court in the area where the debtor's domicile, residence, or principal place of business has existed for the longest period of time during the preceding 180 days. The debtor's solvency is immaterial, as is the amount of his or her liabilities, so long as the debtor has debts. The debtor must include in the petition a list of all his or her creditors so that they may be sent a notice of the first creditors' meeting.

Once the debtor has filed the petition, he or she is automatically declared a bankrupt (called an "order for relief"), and the first creditors' meeting is called.

Where the straight bankruptcy is involuntary, the debtor can be declared a bankrupt and the first creditors' meeting can be called only if the following conditions are met:

1. The bankruptcy petition must be filed by the proper number of creditors holding certain minimum claims that are not contingent as to liability. If the debtor has twelve or more creditors, at least three of them must join in filing the petition; if the debtor has less then twelve creditors, a single creditor may legally file. In determining whether the debtor has twelve or more creditors, several kinds of creditors are not counted, including the debtor's own employees or relatives; fully secured creditors; officers, directors, or stockholders of the debtor; and any creditor who has received a lien, transfer, or preference that can be avoided under the law. The creditors who file (whether three or more or a single creditor) must hold claims that are not contingent as to liability and that amount to at least $5,000 beyond the value of any property securing such claims.

2. Also, the debtor must be properly served with the petition. If the debtor is properly served but does not respond to the petition, he or she may be declared a bankrupt by default. If the debtor responds and controverts the petition, he or she may be declared a bankrupt in a judicial trial only if it is shown that (1) the debtor is generally not paying his or her debts as they fall due, or (2) a custodian took possession of the debtor's property within 120 days of the filing of the petition under a general assignment for the benefit of creditors, a receivership, or the like. If the debtor successfully controverts the creditors' petition (by showing that he or she is generally paying his or her debts as they fall due and that his or her property has not been taken over by or transferred to any custodian as described above), then the debtor may have judgment against the creditors who filed the petition for costs, attorneys' fees, and other damages including punitive damages if the creditors filed in bad faith.

HOW DOES STRAIGHT BANKRUPTCY PROCEED ONCE THE DEBTOR HAS BEEN ADJUDGED A BANKRUPT?

Once the debtor has been adjudged a bankrupt, the straight bankruptcy procedure is the same whether the debtor originally filed for bankruptcy voluntarily or was forced into bankruptcy upon the petition of his or her creditors. The debtor's creditors file their claims, and the claims are either allowed or disallowed. Claims for unmatured interest are not allowed, and claims for rent on leases of real estate will be allowed only for one year's rent beyond what was owing at the time of the filing of the petition (e.g., if the debtor had a lease to pay rent on a building for four more years at the time of the filing, the lessor's claim would only be allowed for unpaid rent due under the lease at the time of the filing plus one year's rent). The same is true for long-term employment contracts.

Once the creditor's claims have been determined, the first creditors' meeting is scheduled; all creditors are notified as to when the meeting will take place. At the first meeting, the creditors question the bankrupt regarding the location and value of his or her assets. The creditors hope to discover, through their questions, whether the debtor has made any fraudulent conveyances or preferential transfers (discussed hereafter). In addition to questioning the debtor, the creditors also elect a trustee to act as their representative. Creditors holding at least 20 percent of the total claims must vote in the election, and the trustee must receive a majority of the votes. If no one person receives a majority, the court will appoint a trustee. The trustee's job, in any case, is to collect the bankrupt's assets. After conducting whatever investigation is necessary to uncover the assets, the trustee is empowered to avoid, in court, any transfers that prove to be fraudulent or preferential.

The trustee may set aside a transfer made or obligation incurred by the debtor within one year of the filing of the bankruptcy petition if the debtor made the transfer or incurred the obligation with actual intent to defraud or if the debtor received less than reasonably equivalent consideration for the transfer or obligation and was insolvent at the time (or became insolvent as the result of the transfer or obligation).

The trustee may also set aside any *preferential transfer* made by the debtor. A preferential transfer is a transfer of the bankrupt's nonexempt property for the benefit of a creditor on account of an antecedent (previous) debt. The transfer is preferential only if the debtor was insolvent at the time he or she made the transfer. Section 101(26) of the Bankruptcy Act defines "insolvent" as a "financial condition such that the sum of [one's] debts is greater than all of [one's] property, at a fair valuation, exclusive of (i) property transferred, concealed, or removed with intent to hinder, delay, or defraud [one's] creditors; and (ii) property that may be exempted from property of the estate." To be preferential the transfer must also operate to permit the transferee creditor to obtain a greater percentage of his or her claim than some other creditor in the same class. Since, by definition, a "preference" requires a transfer on account of an antecedent debt, the creation of a new debt through execution of a mortgage or by buying more goods on account would not be a preference. Nor would a gift transfer constitute a preference since a gift would not involve a creditor (however, a gift might well constitute a fraudulent conveyance). Also, to be preferential the transfer must generally be made within ninety days before the bankruptcy filing but may go up to one year prior to filing if an insider (e.g., relative, partner, officer or director of a bankrupt corporation) is involved.

With regard to a transfer made on or within ninety days before the date of filing of the bankruptcy petition, the transferee need not know or have reason to believe that the debtor is insolvent at the time of the transfer.

With regard to a transfer made to an insider between ninety days and one year before the date of filing, the insider must have reasonable cause to believe that the debtor is insolvent at the time of the transfer or the transfer will not be preferential.

It is the duty of the trustee in bankruptcy to sell the property of the bankrupt's estate so as to be able to distribute the money to the bankrupt's creditors. After all the bankrupt's nonexempt property is liquidated, the bankrupt's estate is formally closed. The trustee makes a final report which, when approved by the court, permits cash disbursement of the sales proceeds to the creditors. Any remaining debts of the bankrupt are discharged, with the exception of those specifically excluded by the Bankruptcy Act.

IS ANY OF THE BANKRUPT'S PROPERTY EXEMPT FROM THE BANKRUPTCY SALE?

It was pointed out earlier in the chapter that all states exempt certain property from the claims of creditors. These exemptions apply to bankruptcy proceedings as well. Thus, all or part of the bankrupt's equity in his or her home, auto, household furnishings, savings, life insurance, tools, etc., are exempt from the bankruptcy sale even where the bankrupt's other assets are nowhere near sufficient to cover the bankrupt's debts. Also, the Bankruptcy Act specifically provides that, unless a state prohibits their use, the debtor may choose as an alternative to the exemptions provided by his or her own state law certain exemptions provided by the federal bankruptcy law. Because the federal exemptions are generally more liberal than the individual state exemptions, most of the states have prohibited the use of the federal exemptions. Thus, in most jurisdictions only the state exemptions may be used.

In any event, the exempt properties are not subject to sale for the debtor's debts with two exceptions: all the debtor's property—even exempt property—can be reached to satisfy tax debts and support obligations (alimony and child support).

WHAT IS A "DISCHARGE" IN BANKRUPTCY?

One of the main purposes of the Bankruptcy Act is to discharge debtors from their remaining debts so that the debtor can start over fresh in life. To "discharge" a debt is completely to eliminate it. This means that once a bankrupt's debts are discharged in bankruptcy, he or she has no further obligation with respect to payment. Debts listed by the debtor may be discharged even though the creditor files no proof of claim. Still, not all debts are dischargeable in bankruptcy, and sometimes an objection to discharge may be raised with the result that there is no discharge at all.

The Bankruptcy Act spells out several grounds for denying a debtor a discharge in bankruptcy. Section 727(c) of the Act states that either the trustee or a creditor may object to discharge on any of the following grounds:

1. The debtor's effort to conceal or destroy property within one year before the filing of the petition or after the petition is filed;

2. The debtor's effort to destroy or falsify financial records or his or her failure to keep or preserve such records or information;
3. The debtor's fraudulent act in making false oaths, false claims, attempting to obtain money or property by false pretenses, or in withholding information relating to his or her property or financial affairs;
4. The debtor's failure to explain satisfactorily any loss or deficiency of assets to meet his or her liabilities;
5. The debtor's refusal to obey an order of the court requiring him or her to answer questions material to the bankruptcy proceeding. Of course, the bankrupt has a constitutional, Fifth Amendment right to refuse to answer where the answer might tend to incriminate him or her. But if the court grants the debtor immunity so that there can be no incrimination, his or her continued failure to answer will serve as grounds for denial of discharge.
6. The debtor's previous discharge in bankruptcy within the last six years (measured from filing date to filing date).

If the bankruptcy court finds that any one of the six grounds listed above exists, the court will deny the debtor a discharge, and the debtor will leave the bankruptcy proceeding still owing the same debts that he or she owed prior to the proceeding (of course, the debts will be less in amount since the creditors will have received a distribution from sale of the debtor's nonexempt property).

As stated previously, not all debts are dischargeable in bankruptcy. Section 523 of the Bankruptcy Act specifically excepts nine types of debts from discharge, and any creditor who can show that his or her claim falls within one of these nine categories can collect any unpaid portion of the claim from the debtor personally. The nine statutory exceptions include:

1. Back taxes the debtor-bankrupt owes (unless the taxes became due and owing more than three years before the bankruptcy) or taxes for which no tax returns were filed.
2. Debts that arise from obtaining money by false pretenses or false representation (including "innocent" misrepresentation) and debts that result from obtaining credit on the basis of materially false financial statements.
3. Debts that are not properly scheduled, unless the creditor has notice of the bankruptcy proceeding before the time to file claims has expired. This means that if the bankrupt fails to schedule all of his or her creditors and gives an incomplete list of creditors to the bankruptcy court, the debts owing to the unscheduled creditors will not be discharged unless the creditors have other actual notice of the proceeding.
4. Debts resulting from the bankrupt's misconduct as a public or corporate officer or as a result of breach of fiduciary duty. This would include, for example, debts arising from fraud, embezzlement, or larceny.
5. Unpaid support obligations such as alimony, maintenance, or child support.
6. Claims resulting from the debtor-bankrupt's willful and malicious injury of another.
7. Fines or other penalties owed to the government and not classified as taxes.

8. Educational loans due within the last five years unless this would result in undue hardship to the debtor or his or her dependents.
9. Debts that could have been listed in a previous bankruptcy proceeding of the debtor or for which discharge was waived in a previous bankruptcy proceeding.

Section 524 of the Bankruptcy Act entitled "Effect of Discharge" states clearly that discharged debts are no longer collectible and also makes it clear that promises made by a debtor after discharge to pay discharged debts are not enforceable. The debtor may enter into an agreement *prior to discharge* to pay such debts, but even then he or she may rescind the agreement for a period of thirty days. Also, before entering into the agreement, a hearing must be held in which the court explains that the debtor need not promise to repay the debt. And if the debt is a "consumer debt," the court must approve the agreement as not involving undue hardship for the debtor and as being in the debtor's best interests. Section 101(7) defines a "consumer debt" as a "debt incurred by an individual primarily for a personal, family, or household purpose."

Once a discharge has been granted, there are only three grounds for its revocation. A creditor, trustee, or other interested party can obtain a revocation of discharge if he or she can prove that the discharge was obtained through fraud; or that the bankrupt fraudulently failed to tell the trustee that he or she had other properties; or that the bankrupt failed to answer material questions during the bankruptcy proceedings or within one year after discharge. Generally, the court has power to revoke a discharge upon proof of any one of these three grounds for a period of one year following entry of discharge.

IN WHAT ORDER ARE CREDITORS PAID?

The bankrupt's creditors are paid after the trustee has reduced all the bankrupt's nonexempt property into cash. The secured creditors always have the first right to payment, at least insofar as the security covers their claims. To the extent that a secured creditor's security does not cover his or her claim, the secured creditor becomes a general creditor. When there is more than one secured creditor as to the same specific property (i.e., more than one creditor has a lien against the same property), state law governs the order of payment. Generally, the "first in time, first in right" rule controls as to liens on the same property (later sections of this chapter deal with the "secured creditor" in detail). And, again, when the proceeds from the particular property run out, the lien (secured) creditor becomes a general creditor for the balance.

In the case of a federal tax lien which attaches to all the debtor's property, Section 6323(a) of the federal Internal Revenue Code recognizes and protects "purchasers, holders of security interests, mechanics lienors, and judgment lien creditors" whose secured interests arose before notice of the tax lien was filed. In other words, specific liens on particular parts of the property, which liens arose prior to perfection of the tax lien (by proper filing), will take priority over the tax lien as to the particular property involved.

So you see that lien creditors are also general creditors to the extent that their liens do not cover their claims. And government, for example, is a general creditor for any unpaid taxes that remain unassessed at the time the bankruptcy procedure begins. This is so because a tax lien is conditioned on three things: first, assessment by the government of the taxes owing; second, demand upon the taxpayer for payment of the taxes; and third, a failure by the taxpayer to pay. The tax lien itself dates from the time the assessment is made. But suppose that a taxpayer inaccurately reports his or her income and understates his or her taxes by a considerable amount. Months or even years may go by before an audit of the taxpayer's return uncovers the deficiency. Even after the taxpayer has been notified by the government that he or she owes more taxes, another ninety days must pass before the tax deficiency can be legally assessed. By this time the taxpayer may have gone into bankruptcy. The government, in this case, will not have a lien (as no assessment has been made) but will have only the rights of a general creditor as to the taxes owing. Even so, the government will be in a better position than some general creditors because the federal Bankruptcy Act categorizes general creditors' claims according to priority. Once the secured creditors have been paid, what cash is left will go to the general creditors, but in the following order:

1. *First priority*—administrative expenses of handling the bankruptcy. Included are filing fees, costs and expenses incurred in the trustee's administration of the bankruptcy, and any money spent to recover property rightfully belonging to the bankrupt's estate. But remember, even these expenses will not be paid until the claims of all lien creditors have been fully satisfied. However, to the extent that a secured creditor was benefited by an administrative expenditure (e.g., where the trustee incurred an expense to preserve secured property), the trustee may recover the expense from the secured creditor.
2. *Second priority*—in an involuntary bankruptcy proceeding only, debts incurred in the ordinary course of the debtor's business or financial affairs after filing of the bankruptcy but before the appointment of the trustee.
3. *Third priority*—certain wage claims arising within ninety days preceding the filing of the bankruptcy petition or the termination of the debtor's business, whichever occurs first. Wages are covered only to the extent of $2,000 per any one claimant. Wages of all types of employees (including management) are covered. Also "wages" include claims for vacations, severance, and sick pay as well as the usual wages, salaries, or commissions.
4. *Fourth priority*—unsecured claims for contributions to employee benefit plans up to $2,000 for each employee but less any amount paid such employee for wages under the third priority.
5. *Fifth priority*—unsecured claims up to a maximum of $900 arising from deposits of money made by people with the debtor in order to purchase or rent property or to purchase services for personal, family, or household use which property or services were not delivered or provided.

6. *Sixth priority*—taxes legally due and owing within three years of the bankruptcy to the United States or to any state or other political subdivision. These are taxes for which the government has no lien or secured status.

Only after these six priority claims have been fully covered do the rest of the general creditors share in the balance of the proceeds.

WHAT IS THE DIFFERENCE BETWEEN STRAIGHT BANKRUPTCY AND DEBTOR RELIEF UNDER DEBTOR REHABILITATION PROVISIONS?

In addition to straight bankruptcy, the Bankruptcy Act offers the debtor alternative methods by which he or she may work to pay off his or her debts without losing all of his or her property. The methods are similar to the composition, extension, and wage earner receivership agreements found in most states. As you will recall, a composition is a contract between the debtor and his or her creditors and among the creditors themselves by which the creditors agree to accept a lesser sum immediately in full payment of the amount owing. An extension is an agreement between and among the debtor and his or her creditors whereby the debtor agrees to pay his or her debts in full but over an extended period of time.

Chapters 11 and 13 of the Bankruptcy Act deal with "debtor rehabilitation." Chapter 11, entitled "Reorganization," allows a debtor to set up a payment plan involving such devices as composition, extension, and receivership; Chapter 11 is available to debtor individuals, corporations, and partnerships alike. Chapter 13, entitled "Adjustment of Debts of an Individual with Regular Income," provides relief for individual debtors who desire to effect a composition or extension out of future earnings or wages. A debtor may use either Chapter 11 or 13 even after straight bankruptcy proceedings have begun if deemed appropriate by the court (the straight bankruptcy is simply "converted" into a Chapter 11 or 13 case).

HOW DOES A CHAPTER 11 REORGANIZATION WORK?

A Chapter 11 "reorganization" permits a debtor to work out a court supervised plan with his or her creditors usually in the nature of a composition (reduction in debt), an extension (more time to pay off the debt), or a receivership (involving the continuing management of the debtor's business or property). Chapter 11 is purely voluntary on the part of the debtor and can be utilized by an individual, a partnership, or a corporation. The debtor elects to go under Chapter 11 by filing a petition in the U.S. District Court where the debtor would file for straight bankruptcy. Frequently, the court permits the debtor to continue operating his or her own business during the time the Chapter 11 reorganization is in effect.

The debtor must then within 120 days file a plan stating the terms of the proposed reorganization. The debtor may propose almost anything, including changes or modifications in the rights of the creditors (both secured and unsecured)—even their division into different classes (e.g., creditors with claims of less than $1,000 or creditors with wage claims, rent claims, or the like). The debtor will generally state how he or she plans to make a living or carry on his or her business and what payment schedule he or she intends to follow during the period of extension. A debtor corporation may provide, as part of the plan, for the issuance of new securities or for the amendment of the corporate charter.

The debtor's creditors may either accept or reject the plan. Section 1126 of the Act provides that a class of creditors accepts the plan where there is majority creditor approval in number and two-thirds in amount of claims. Thus, if there are fifty creditors in a particular class, at least twenty-six must approve. And if the aggregate amount of claims within the class is $30,000, the approval must come from creditors holding claims of at least $20,000.

If a class of creditors is not "impaired," then no acceptance of the plan by this class is required. A class of claims is impaired under a plan unless the plan leaves unaltered the legal, equitable, and contractual rights to which such claim or interest entitles the holder of such claim or interest.

Section 1125 of the Act provides that the creditors must be sent copies or summaries of the plan prior to their voting on it.

Under Chapter 11, a trustee need not be appointed. The Act provides that a trustee will be appointed under the Chapter only for cause such as fraud, incompetence, or (if a company) gross mismanagement or if the court otherwise decides that it is in the best interests of the creditors or shareholders (in the case of a corporate debtor). Where a trustee is not appointed, the debtor continues to possess his or her assets and continues to operate any business involved in the reorganization. However, at any time after commencement of the case, the court may, upon petition of any interested party, appoint an "examiner" with similar powers to the trustee if the court determines this to be in the best interest of the creditors or if the debtor's unsecured debts exceed $5 million.

Whether or not a trustee is appointed, the law does require the appointment of at least one creditors' committee made up of unsecured creditors (including those holding the seven largest claims of the type represented by the committee). The committee's job is to work with the trustee or debtor in possession in carrying out the reorganization plan.

The bankruptcy court "confirms" the debtor's plan only if it is satisfied that the proposal is in the best interests of the creditors; that the debtor will faithfully carry out the plan; that the plan provides for payment to creditors in the order of priority as described earlier in the chapter; and that the creditors have either accepted the plan or, if they have not accepted, will receive or retain as much as they would have received or retained under a straight bankruptcy proceeding.

Even after a plan has been confirmed by the court, the case may be converted to straight bankruptcy if the plan proves to be unworkable.

The effect of confirmation, apart from exceptions provided in the plan itself, is to discharge the debtor in the same manner as does a straight bankruptcy proceeding.

WHAT IS CHAPTER 13 OF THE BANKRUPTCY ACT?

Chapter 13 of the Bankruptcy Act provides debtor rehabilitation for an "individual with regular income." Section 101(24) defines an "individual with regular income" as an individual "whose income is sufficiently stable and regular to enable such individual to make payments under a plan under Chapter 13." An individual debtor elects to go under Chapter 13 by filing (with the U.S. district court) a "plan" providing for the use of all or part of the debtor's future earnings for payment of his or her debts. Generally, the proposed payment period may not exceed three years. Under Chapter 13, the court appoints a trustee to administer the plan. The plan must recognize and provide for payment in full of all priority claims. Other debts may be classified in the same manner as under Chapter 11.

The rights of both secured and unsecured creditors can be modified with the single exception of a secured interest in the debtor's residence.

After notice to the creditors, a confirmation hearing must be held, and any creditor or party in interest may object to confirmation. However, creditor approval is not required—it is up to the court to decide whether or not to confirm the plan.

Generally, the plan will ask for a combination composition and extension, affording the debtor a longer time to pay a lesser amount of his or her debts. However, the amount of cash or property to be distributed to unsecured creditors under the plan must not be less than the amount the creditors would receive under a straight bankruptcy proceeding. Each secured creditor must either accept the plan, or the plan must allow the creditor to retain his or her lien and ultimately receive the secured amount, or the plan must provide for the creditor to receive the actual property securing the claim.

Once the debtor has made all payments called for under the plan, the court will order a discharge of his or her remaining debts (with the exception of those that are not dischargeable). If the debtor fails to make all the required payments, discharge will be denied unless (1) the debtor is blameless, and (2) the creditors are in as good a position as they would have been under a straight bankruptcy proceeding.

In many cases a Chapter 13 "plan" is preferable to straight bankruptcy. While straight bankruptcy results in discharge of the bankrupt's debts, the bankrupt will usually lose all of his or her property. In a Chapter 13 proceeding, on the other hand, the debtor receives a discharge but is usually able to retain at least a portion of his or her assets.

ARE THERE ANY OTHER ASPECTS TO THE BANKRUPTCY ACT?

The Bankruptcy Act accomplishes two other important things:

First, Section 104 of the Act provides that the dollar amounts stated in the Act will be adjusted periodically to reflect changes in the value of the dollar. The Section states:

> The judicial Conference of the United States shall transmit to the Congress and to the President before May 1, 1985, and before May 1 of every sixth year after

May 1, 1985, a recommendation for the uniform percentage adjustment of each dollar amount in this title.

Second, the Act provides for the creation of "Bankruptcy Courts" as special courts to handle bankruptcy matters. The Act states that a Bankruptcy Court shall be created in every judicial district where there is located a federal district court (district courts are located in every state and in the District of Columbia). The Bankruptcy Courts come into existence on April 1, 1984 with bankruptcy judges appointed by the president of the United States, subject to Senate confirmation, and serving for terms of fourteen years.

Finally, Section 1930 of the Bankruptcy Act prescribes filing fees in the amount of sixty dollars for a case under Chapter 7 (straight bankruptcy) or Chapter 13 (adjustment of debts of an individual with regular income) and $200 for a reorganization case under Chapter 11 (unless the case involves a railroad in which event the fee is $500).

Security Devices to Protect Creditors

HOW EASY IS IT TO BORROW MONEY OR BUY ON CREDIT?

He who goes a borrowing, goes a sorrowing.

Benjamin Franklin
Poor Richard's Almanac

In 1941, consumer credit in the United States totaled $9 billion (i.e., the entire consumer population owed a total of $9 billion on homes, cars, and loans). Today, the consumer credit figure is well over $500 billion and going up. Credit is easy to obtain in our society because merchants know that charge account customers and customers who buy on time under installment contracts tend to return to the same stores where they have existing accounts and can get possession of what they want now and pay later. Perhaps 80 percent of all goods sold by furniture stores, appliance stores, and jewelry stores are financed with consumer credit. About 60 percent of all clothing sales and from 60 to 70 percent of all department store sales are also credit financed. Approximately three-fourths of all cars purchased in the United States are purchased under some credit arrangement. And nearly all people who buy homes make a down payment of from 5 to 25 percent of the purchase price and owe the balance; they pay off their "mortgage" on the property in equal monthly installments over a period of twenty-five to thirty years.

People know that buying on time costs more because of interest and other finance charges. A person who takes out a $40,000 mortgage to finance a home will end up paying more than $100,000 for the home over a thirty-year period. So why do people borrow? Quite simply, they want to have the use of homes, cars, refrigerators, clothes and other property NOW—the "now use" of these items is considered to be worth the extra costs of borrowing.

And for the most part, credit works well and materially adds to the enjoyment of life. Benjamin Franklin's quote from *Poor Richard's Almanac* is not necessarily valid anymore. More than 50 percent of the nation's families are in debt but are not "sorrowing" because of it. Rather, borrowing enables them to enjoy homes, cars, TV sets, and college educations for their children. This is not to say that people never get into financial difficulty because of too much borrowing. As you know many people do overextend themselves financially and end up having to go through bankruptcy. Still, this is the exception rather than the rule—most people borrow, repay, borrow again, and enjoy life all the more because of it.

But not only consumers borrow money. Businesses, too, often need to borrow cash in order to expand or diversify, or they need to purchase inventory on credit simply to stay in business. Thus, a business that has many credit customer accounts may itself have many creditors. Business financing is a natural, ongoing part of business involving many millions of dollars of debtor-creditor transactions daily.

Despite the fact that credit is needed and that it increases sales, there would be no credit if creditors could find no protection in the law for their interests. Understandably, creditors would be unwilling to loan money to finance the purchase of "big ticket" items (expensive items such as refrigerators, TV sets, automobiles, homes, entire inventories and other large items posing a considerable risk of loss) if they had no *legal* assurance of repayment. Knowing this, the law provides creditors with legal procedures and devices to protect them from losing the values they have extended. Earlier we considered several creditor procedures that protect creditors, whether secured or unsecured, including attachments, garnishments, judgments, assignments for the benefit of creditors, and so on. Now we will look closely at a number of legal devices that enable creditors to feel more "secure" about their lending. The most important of such methods or devices include allowing a creditor to reach specific property owned by the debtor before any other creditor can reach it; those permitting a creditor to collect the debt from a third party if the primary debtor refuses to pay or cannot pay; and those protecting the creditors of a business in the event that the entire business or a major part of it is sold to another party.

WHAT TRANSACTIONS ARE COVERED BY ARTICLE 9 OF THE UCC?

Article 9 of the UCC covers all transactions involving the creation of a security interest in personal property. The Article applies regardless of the form of the transaction and irrespective of the terms the debtor and creditor use to describe it. Section 9–102 allows (and governs) the creation of security interests in *any personal property*. Personal property includes, first of all, "goods," which encompass not only chattels but also growing crops, standing timber to be cut and removed, and the unborn young of animals. "Goods" include "consumer goods," "farm products," and "inventory."

Under Section 9–102, a security interest can also be created in *fixtures.* As you will recall from Chapter 8, a "fixture" is an article that started out as personal property but was connected to real property in such a manner or with such intent that it became a part of the real property—a real property "fixture." Section 9–313 of the UCC provides that a person who holds a security interest in goods that later become fixtures may be protected even after the goods have become real property. The same Section states that no security interest can be created in ordinary building materials that are incorporated into an improvement on land (i.e., made an integral and inseparable part of the improvement, as to put bricks into a wall).

Article 9 of the UCC applies not only to the use of goods as collateral but also to other kinds of personal property, including "documents, instruments, general intangibles, chattel paper or accounts." Thus, a security interest can be created in "documents," meaning documents of title such as bills of lading and warehouse receipts (as studied in Chapter 10).

A security interest can also be created in "instruments," meaning negotiable promissory notes and drafts (see Chapter 9) and security certificates representing investments in stocks, bonds, and other securities (see Chapter 6). For example, a shareholder will often put up his or her common stock as collateral when taking out a bank loan.

"General intangibles" such as goodwill, trademarks, copyrights, patents, or even blueprints or literary rights can also serve as collateral for the creation of a security interest.

So can "chattel paper." "Chattel paper" is any writing that sets forth the terms of a security agreement and contains the debtor's promise to pay the secured party. The most common source of chattel paper is a purchase money security interest in personal property. Section 9–107 of the Code defines a "purchase money security interest" as follows:

> A security interest is a "purchase money security interest" to the extent that it is (a) taken or retained by the seller of the collateral to secure all or part of its price; or (b) taken by a person who by making advances or incurring an obligation gives value to enable the debtor to acquire rights in or the use of collateral if such value is in fact so used.

Subsection (a) describes the typical "conditional sale" in which a purchaser buys goods on credit and signs a statement in which he or she promises to pay the purchase price (usually in installments) and agrees to give the seller a security interest in the goods until they are paid for. The statement the buyer signs is "chattel paper." Frequently, the secured party seller uses the chattel paper as collateral in order to obtain a loan or buy on credit. The chattel paper, in this case, not only embodies the original security interest in the goods (i.e., the security interest that resulted when the goods were sold on credit to the buyer whose promise to repay is contained in the paper), but it also serves as collateral in the second financing transaction between the holder of the chattel paper and the buyer of the paper.

With regard to the use of "accounts" as collateral, most businesses sell on credit to customers without using any security device. A business simply bills its customers periodically for the amounts owing on their accounts (e.g., most people have one or more charge accounts and a number of utility company accounts for electric, water, gas, and telephone service). The UCC defines an "account" at Section 9–106 as "any right to payment for goods sold or leased or for services rendered which is not evidenced by an instrument or chattel paper, whether or not it has been earned by performance." Sometimes a business uses its "accounts receivable" (i.e., the amounts owing to the business from its customers) as collateral for taking out a loan or buying on credit. The secured party lender, in this case, will have priority as to the accounts only if he or she complies with all Article 9 requirements for protecting the interest.

It should be pointed out that both accounts and chattel paper may also be sold outright (as opposed to being used as collateral for obtaining a loan or buying on credit). Accounts and chattel paper are usually sold at a discount in the same way negotiable instruments that are not yet due are sold. Where the sale is made in order to finance the seller's ongoing business operations (e.g., to purchase inventory), the sale is treated as a secured transaction under UCC Section 9–102(1)(b). In other words, the buyer's interest in the accounts and chattel paper is considered to be a security interest only, and the buyer must comply with all Article 9 requirements in order to have priority over other creditors of the seller who claim ownership of or a security interest in the accounts or chattel paper.

Sometimes what appears to be a personal property lease agreement (i.e., rental of personal property for a term) is really an Article 9 security transaction. Leases are often structured so that the lessee is entitled to purchase the "leased" goods at the end of the term. If the "purchase price" to be paid is nominal (so little as to be negligible in relation to the value of the property), the substance of the transaction is a sale and not a lease. In other words, the so-called lessor sells the property to the so-called lessee but calls the transaction a lease so as to protect himself or herself until full payment is made (by retaining title the so-called lessor prevents other creditors of the lessee from reaching the leased property).

Under Article 9, such a lease arrangement is a security agreement, and the so-called lessor will take priority over other creditors of the "lessee" only if he or she complies with the requirements of Article 9. The same result follows where the so-called lessee has an option to renew at the end of the lease term for a nominal rental. By way of example, suppose that Bill Businessperson "leases" a new Chevrolet from Linda Lease-A-Car Company. The monthly rental is set at $150, and Bill is given an option to purchase the car for $150 at the end of the four-year term (or an option to renew the lease for another four years by making one additional rental payment of $150). Here, the substance of the "rental" transaction looks to be a sale (the purchase or renewal price is nominal), and the lease is a security agreement. Linda must thus comply with requirements of Article 9 if she is to take priority over other creditors of Bill Businessperson with regard to the leased auto (e.g., upon default in "rental" by an insolvent Bill Businessperson).

In conclusion, Article 9 covers any security transaction involving the use of any kind of personal property as collateral. The Article does not apply to the use of real property as collateral (this is the subject of "mortgages" as discussed later in this chapter).

Secured Transactions in Personal Property

The Code uses the following terminology to describe secured transactions in personal property:

Security interest The Code defines "security interest" as every interest "in personal property or fixtures which secures payment or performance of an obligation." UCC 1–201(37). Pledges, chattel mortgages, conditional sales—all are included within the definition and will create superior rights in the secured party if the rules of Article 9 are complied with.

Security agreement The "security agreement" is the agreement which creates the security interest. The security agreement is required in every case no matter what the form of transaction (pledge, chattel mortgage, conditional sale, etc.). It is usually in writing but may be oral if the secured party has possession of the collateral as in a pledge (the specifics of the security agreement are considered in the following section).

Secured party The "secured party" is the lender, seller, purchaser, or other person in whose favor the security interest is created; he or she possesses the security interest in the collateral according to the terms of the security agreement.

Debtor The "debtor" is the party who must pay or otherwise perform the obligation embodied in the security agreement.

Financing statement Sometimes, but not always, the secured party must file a document called a financing statement describing the collateral in order to maintain a position of priority over other creditors of the debtor. The financing statement should not be confused with the security agreement. The financing statement is much less detailed, it is not required in every case (the security agreement is), and it does not create the security interest but merely gives public notice of the interest when filed in the proper local or statewide office.

No matter what terminology the parties themselves use to describe their personal property security transaction, the provisions of Article 9 are controlling.

WHAT IS MEANT BY THE STATEMENT THAT AN ARTICLE 9 SECURITY INTEREST "ATTACHES" TO THE COLLATERAL?

Under the UCC, "attachment" of a security interest is synonymous with *creation* of the interest. Unless and until a security interest attaches, the interest simply does not exist. Attachment (creation) of a security interest requires three things: (1) the debtor and the secured party must enter into a security agreement (sometimes oral, but usually in writing); (2) the secured party must give value for the security interest; and (3) the debtor must have rights in the collateral.

A Security Agreement

In all cases the debtor and the secured party must enter into a security agreement. Where the collateral is in the secured party's *possession,* the security agreement *does not have to be in writing*—a completely oral agreement will suffice. This is the typical pledge transaction where the debtor transfers possession of the collateral to the secured party. For example, someone who pawns his or her guitar for $100 is likely to receive only a pawn ticket and not a written security agreement. Still, the pawn shop will have a security interest in the guitar by virtue of having possession of it and by reason of having entered into an oral security agreement.

But sometimes it is impractical or undesirable for the secured party to have possession of the collateral. Where, pursuant to agreement, the collateral is not in the secured party's possession, the security interest will attach only if the parties have a written security agreement that describes the collateral and is signed by the debtor (under UCC Section 1–201(39), "signed" includes any symbol executed or adopted by a party with present intention to authenticate a writing). The requirement of a writing in the absence of possession by the secured party is like the Statute of Frauds requirement (see Chapter 8) with regard to certain contracts: a contract that falls within the Statute is enforceable only if it is supported by a written memo signed by the party to be charged. Thus, where the secured party does not have possession of the collateral, the security interest is enforceable only if it is evidenced by a written security agreement signed by the debtor. It is not necessary for the secured party to sign, although as a practical matter most secured parties do.

The written security agreement must contain a reasonably definite description of the collateral, UCC Section 9–110 stating that "any description of personal property * * * is sufficient whether or not it is specific if it reasonably identifies what is described." For example, in one case a written security agreement that described the collateral in general terms as "the contents" of the debtor's luncheonette and all "property used in" operation of the luncheonette was held sufficiently definite to cover a cash register used in operation of the business. National Cash Register Co. v. Firestone and Co., Inc., 346 Mass. 255, 191 N.E.2d 471 (1963).

Where the security interest covers crops or timber, the written security agreement must also include a description of the land involved. Again, a detailed legal description is not required so long as the security agreement reasonably identifies the land. A description by street number or location is usually sufficient.

It is not necessary for the written agreement expressly to mention "proceeds." It is presumed that the parties intend the security interest to extend to any proceeds (cash or other property) that result when the specific collateral is sold or exchanged.

Two provisions—an "after-acquired property" clause and a "future advance" clause—are often used in written security agreements to facilitate the financing of inventory and accounts receivable. The first allows the security interest to extend to the debtor's after-acquired property; the second permits the interest to cover additional loans to be made in the future by the secured party.

After-acquired property and future advance clauses work together with the provisions of Section 9–205 of the UCC to enable the debtor whose inventory is subject to a security interest to transfer and dispose of individual items of the inventory while acquiring other inventory with which to replace it. The security interest, in this case, is on the whole of the inventory (whatever items the inventory consists of at any particular time); periodically, the secured creditor loans additional money on the inventory. The arrangement is called a *floating lien*: the lien is said to "float" over the collateral, attaching to each item of inventory as it comes into the debtor's possession and ending when the item is sold (or if the item is an account, when the account is collected). Thus, in a "floating lien," there is a constant turnover of collateral, with the security interest resting on a shifting stock of goods or accounts. The secured party makes present and future advances to the debtor with the advances secured by both present and after-acquired inventory and/or accounts.

The Secured Party Must Give Value

A "person gives value for rights if he acquires them (a) in return for a binding commitment to extend credit or for the extension of immediately available credit whether or not drawn upon and whether or not a chargeback is provided for in the event of difficulties in collection; or (b) as security for or in total or partial satisfaction of a pre-existing claim; or (c) by accepting delivery pursuant to a pre-existing contract for purchase; or (d) generally, in return for any consideration sufficient to support a simple contract." UCC Section 1–201(44).

As you can see, the term "value" has a much broader meaning with regard to the creation of a security interest than it has with regard to the consideration required for a valid contract. However, under Section 1–201(44)(b), "a person gives 'value' for rights if he or she acquires them as security for a pre-existing claim." Thus, a person who takes a security interest for an antecedent debt (i.e., past consideration furnished by the secured party) gives "value" within the meaning of the Section. For example, say that Bill Businessperson purchases a car from Cora Cardealer on an open credit with no agreement regarding any security. One month later, Bill is unable to pay for the car, and he enters into a security agreement with Cora, giving Cora a security interest in the car. Though Cora extended the credit a month ago, she is considered to give "value" now for purposes of creating the security interest, and the interest attaches to the automobile. (Cora, of course, is not promising to do anything new or different, and there is no consideration in the contract sense.)

The Debtor Must Have Rights in the Collateral

To say that the debtor must have rights in the collateral is not to say that he or she must own the property (i.e., have legal title to it). It is true that in most cases the debtor owns the property that he or she puts up as collateral and has rights in the property on the basis of title. But title is not required. The debtor may have far less than complete ownership of the property and still have "rights" in the collateral for purposes of creating a security interest. For example, a person who contracts to buy goods acquires a "special property" interest in the goods at the time they are identified to the contract of sale (see Chapter 11). This "special property" is not complete ownership, but it will serve as "rights in the collateral" for purposes of creating a security interest in the goods.

Having considered each of the three requirements for attachment in detail, let's look now at an example. Say that Bill Businessperson enters into a written agreement with Lisa Lender wherein Lisa agrees to loan Bill $25,000 on July 1, the loan to be secured by Bill's factory equipment (which Bill owns and is using in the business); at the same time, Lisa agrees to loan Bill another $15,000 on his inventory together with an automobile Bill plans to buy in the next few weeks. On July 1, Lisa loans Bill $25,000; on August 15, she loans Bill another $15,000; and, on September 1, Bill purchases the car. Lisa has a security interest in the factory equipment, in the inventory, and in the car—however, each interest attached (i.e., came into existence) at a different time. Lisa's security interest in the equipment attached on July 1 because all three requirements for attachment were met on that date: the parties had a written security agreement; Lisa gave value in the amount of $25,000; and Bill had rights in his factory equipment. Lisa's security interest in the inventory attached on August 15: though the security agreement was entered into on July 1, Lisa did not give value (loan the $15,000) until August 15. And, finally, Lisa's security interest in the car attached on September 1: though the security agreement was reached on July 1, and though Lisa gave value on August 15, the debtor Bill did not have rights in the collateral (the car) until September 1

WHAT IS MEANT BY THE STATEMENT THAT AN ARTICLE 9 SECURITY INTEREST IS "PERFECTED"?

A creditor who extends credit in relation to personal property looking to obtain a security interest in the property will end up in one of three positions.

1. The security interest may not attach (because one or more of the three requirements for attachment have not been met), in which case the creditor will receive no security interest. The creditor will be in the same position as any other unsecured creditor. If the debtor does not pay, the creditor may sue the debtor to obtain a money judgment. However, if the debtor is unable to pay the judgment, the creditor's only right will be to share in the debtor's nonexempt assets with other general, unsecured creditors of the debtor.

2. The security interest may attach, but it may not be perfected. Here, the creditor will be secured and have something more than an unsecured creditor—but not much more. A secured creditor with an unperfected security interest will have rights to proceed against the specific collateral if the debtor does not pay (i.e., if the debtor defaults). However, the creditor will enjoy little protection as against other unperfected security interest holders if his or her interest attached first, his or her claim will generally be subordinate to that of perfected security interest holders and bona fide purchasers for value (i.e., purchasers who take the collateral for value without knowledge of the security interest).

3. The security interest may attach and it may be perfected, in which case the creditor will be in the best position possible with respect to the collateral. The holder of a security interest who does whatever is necessary to "perfect" the interest maximizes his or her rights against third party claimants to the same collateral. In most cases the holder of a perfected security interest will have priority over the claims of subsequent lien creditors of the debtor or a creditor's representative such as a receiver, trustee in bankruptcy, or assignee for the benefit of creditors. The secured party will also prevail over holders of unperfected security interests perfected at a later date and time. In many cases the holder of a perfected security interest will even prevail over a bona fide purchaser of the collateral.

Sometimes, however, not even perfection will serve to protect the creditor. Section 9–307(1) of the UCC provides that a person who buys goods in the ordinary course of business from a seller who deals in goods of that kind will take the goods free of any existing security interest (perfected or unperfected) even where the buyer knows of the interest at the time of the purchase. To come under the Section, the sale must be in the regular course of the seller's business, and the buyer must give value for the goods (and, here, value does not include total or partial satisfaction of a pre-existing debt or claim). Usually, the buyer is purchasing some product or item from the dealer's inventory. Thus, a person who buys a typewriter from a dealer in the ordinary course of business will take the typewriter free of any existing security interest in the typewriter, whether perfected or unperfected.

As to how a security interest is perfected, the UCC provides for three methods of perfection: (1) taking possession of the collateral; (2) filing a "financing statement" giving public notice of the security interest with the appropriate state or local agency; and, in some cases, (3) by simple attachment of the security interest.

Taking Possession of the Collateral

In the typical pledge situation, the secured party's *possession* of the collateral without more serves to perfect the security interest. You will recall that a pledge is a bailment or delivery of personal property by way of security for a debt or other promised performance. Not only goods may be pledged, but also money, documents of title (e.g., warehouse receipts and bills of lading), negotiable instruments (e.g., promissory notes and drafts and investment securities), and chattel paper (when transferred to third parties to secure a second credit transaction).

Remember that the secured party's possession of the collateral (pursuant to agreement with the debtor) eliminates the need for a *written* security agreement—the secured party's possession of the collateral also serves to perfect the security interest (i.e., maximize the secured party's rights with respect to collateral). *Everything that can be done to secure a creditor is thus achieved by possession alone.* This is a very important fact to remember.

A security interest is perfected by possession from the moment possession is taken; it remains perfected only as long as the possession continues.

Of course, the secured party, as a bailee, must use reasonable care in storing and preserving the collateral. He or she may charge the debtor for any reasonable expenses incurred in caring for the property, including insurance costs (the collateral secures payment of these expenses as well as payment of the original debt).

Security interests in money or negotiable instruments (including negotiable money instruments and negotiable investment securities) can only be perfected by taking possession of the collateral. On the other hand, some intangible items such as accounts receivable cannot be pledged because they are not represented by any tangible document or instrument. Perfection as to such collateral is by filing only.

Quite often, when inventory is used as collateral, possession (and hence perfection) is accomplished by the use of "field warehousing" as discussed in Chapter 11. The secured party in the "floating lien" situation takes over part of the debtor's facilities and controls what is sold from the inventory and what is added to it.

Filing a Financing Statement

It is frequently impractical for the secured party to take possession of the collateral. The secured party, in this case, can perfect his or her security interest by filing a *financing statement.* A financing statement is a document designed to put the debtor's creditors "on notice" that a security agreement is in effect as to certain of the debtor's property.

The statement briefly notes the secured party's interest in the property and describes in general terms the type of collateral included under the security agreement. The secured party files the financing statement in the local or statewide government office as prescribed by the UCC. While the secured party may use the written security agreement as the financing statement, most secured parties prefer not to. The security agreement is generally much more detailed than the financing statement (which gives little specific information about the underlying transaction), and most parties prefer not to have the "detail" of their transaction on file publicly.

Under Section 9–403(2) of the Code, a properly filed financing statement is effective for a period of five years from the date of filing. Unless a new financing statement or a *continuation statement* is filed before the expiration of the five-year period, the security interest will become unperfected. Where this occurs, all third parties having liens against the collateral will gain priority over the interest. In most cases the secured party elects to file a continuation statement because, unlike the original financing statement, it does not have to be signed by the debtor (only the secured party must sign it). The continuation statement must identify the original financing statement by file number. The statement adds another five-year period of perfection to the security interest; succeeding continuation statements may be filed to add additional five-year periods.

Before moving on to perfection by attachment alone, it should be pointed out that Section 9–302(3) of the UCC expressly exempts from Article 9 *filing* requirements security interests in property subject to a state certificate of title law. In many states automobiles, boats, motor homes, and the like are subject to laws requiring that a security interest in the property be noted on a certificate of title covering the property (or be otherwise filed centrally under the statute). Compliance with the certificate of title law is the exclusive method of perfection in this case, and filing in the normal way under the UCC is ineffective.

Perfection by Attachment of the Security Interest

In a few situations there is yet a third method of perfection, and that is by mere attachment (creation) of the interest. In other words, mere attachment of the security interest will serve to perfect the interest. The most important such transaction is the purchase money security interest in consumer goods. You will recall that in a purchase money security interest the secured party advances money or credit to the debtor to enable him or her to purchase the collateral. Where the transaction involves the purchase of consumer goods (i.e., goods used or bought primarily for personal, family, or household purposes), it is not necessary for the secured party to file a financing statement to perfect his or her security interest. The security interest is perfected automatically upon its attachment to the collateral. UCC Section 9–302(1)(d).

This is not to say that a written security agreement is not required—a written agreement is always required unless the secured party has possession of the collateral. And, of course, in the purchase money security interest situation, the very purpose of the transaction is to give the debtor possession of the consumer goods. By way of example, suppose that Harvey Consumer buys a TV set on credit so that his family can watch television. Harvey agrees to pay off the purchase price in installments; he signs a written security agreement giving the seller a security interest in the set until the purchase price is paid. The creditor-seller has a perfected security interest in the TV set upon attachment. Because the interest is a purchase money security interest in consumer goods, no filing is required.

The general rule is that a secured party with a perfected interest has priority over all subsequent claimants to the same collateral. However, where perfection occurs by attachment alone in the case of consumer goods, there is one "subsequent" claimant against whom the secured party will not be protected. And that is a buyer who subsequently purchases the goods from any seller without knowledge of the security interest and for his or her own personal, family, or household use. A subsequent consumer buyer who purchases the goods without knowledge of the security interest will take them free of the interest unless the secured party has also perfected by filing a financing statement.

For example, suppose that Harvey Consumer sells the TV set to his neighbor Sheila, who plans to use the set for family viewing purposes. Sheila has no knowledge of the creditor-seller's purchase money security interest in the set (perfected by attachment only) and takes the set free of the interest. However, if the creditor-seller had filed a financing statement covering the set (and not relied on attachment alone for perfection), Sheila's interest in the set would be subject to the creditor-seller's interest.

This should be contrasted with the situation where a buyer purchases goods in the ordinary course of business from a dealer in goods of that kind. As stated previously, the buyer takes the goods free of any existing security interest (perfected or unperfected) in them even where the buyer has knowledge of the interest at the time of the purchase. Filing, in this case, won't protect the secured creditor.

WHAT ARE THE PRIORITIES OF ARTICLE 9 SECURED CREDITORS?

Sometimes more than one person claims a security interest in the same collateral. As to who has priority with respect to the collateral, the general rule is that the first secured party to "file or perfect" has priority.

Thus, the first party to file or perfect his or her security interest will have priority. As you know, a secured party may file a financing statement before his or her security interest attaches (remember, attachment requires three things: a security agreement, the giving of value by the secured party, and the debtor's acquiring rights in the collateral). So long as the security interest ultimately comes into being, the early "filing" date will govern priorities under the "first to file or perfect" rule. For example, suppose that on July 1, Debra Debtor arranges to borrow $20,000 from Frank Financer, the loan to be made on August 1 and to be secured by Debra's collection of valuable paintings; Debra is to retain possession of the paintings. Frank files a financing statement on July 1 describing the paintings as collateral. On July 10, Debra transfers possession of the paintings to Artis Artcollector as security for a $20,000 loan made by Artis to Debra on that day. On August 1, Frank Financer loans Debra $20,000. Nine months later, Debra is insolvent and cannot repay either loan. As between Frank and Artis, who has priority with regard to the paintings? You know that Artis took possession of the paintings on July 10, the day she loaned the $20,000 to Debra; thus, her security interest in the collateral both attached and was perfected on that day. Frank, on the other hand, filed a financing statement on July 1, but did not loan the $20,000 (i.e., give value) until August 1; thus, his security interest in the collateral did not attach until August 1 (and therefore could not be perfected until that time). However, Section 9–212 of the UCC states that the "first to file *or* perfect" takes priority, and Frank, though his security interest attached and was perfected after Artis's, was first to file or perfect. He therefore takes priority as to the collateral. Assuming the paintings bring $18,000 when sold, Frank will receive all of the money and Artis none of it. (And it makes no difference whether Frank knew of Artis's interest at the time he advanced the $20,000 to Debra.)

On the other hand, if Artis had taken possession of the paintings (i.e., perfected her interest) before Frank filed, then Artis would have priority as to the collateral because she was first to *perfect* or file.

ARE THERE ANY SPECIAL PROBLEMS FOR THE ARTICLE 9 SECURED CREDITOR IF HIS OR HER DEBTOR GOES BANKRUPT?

Bankruptcy procedure is designed to distribute all of a bankrupt's nonexempt assets to his or her creditors and to discharge the bankrupt's remaining debts. A trustee in bankruptcy is elected to represent the creditors; the trustee is responsible for collecting and liquidating the bankrupt's assets and for distributing the cash to the bankrupt's unsecured creditors. Because of this, the interests of the trustee may often be adverse to that of a party claiming a security interest in a particular asset owned by the bankrupt. Obviously, if the asset is used first to pay off the secured party's interest, there will be less money available for distribution to the unsecured creditors.

When the interests of the trustee and a secured party conflict, the trustee may attempt to set aside the secured party's lien on the debtor's property. Section 9–301 of the Code states: "* * * [A]n unperfected security interest is subordinate to the rights of (b) A person who becomes a lien creditor before the security interest is perfected, * * *" And Section 544 of the federal Bankruptcy Act states in part: "(a) The trustee shall have, as of the commencement of the case * * * the rights and powers of * * * (1) a creditor that extends credit to the debtor at the time of the commencement of the case, and that obtains, at such time, and with respect to such credit, a judicial lien on all property on which a creditor on a simple contract could have obtained a judicial lien, whether or not such a creditor exists. * * *"

Section 544 is known as the "strong-arm" clause because it places the trustee in bankruptcy in the position of a lien creditor even though the creditors the trustee represents are general unsecured creditors (i.e., creditors without liens). Putting Section 9–301(b) of the UCC together with the "strong-arm" clause of the federal Bankruptcy Act (Section 544), you can see that the trustee in bankruptcy takes priority over a secured creditor with an *unperfected* interest.

For example, suppose that Martha Supplier sells machinery on credit to Bill Businessperson for use in his business. Martha takes a purchase money security interest in the machinery pursuant to agreement on January 15, the date of the sale. However, Martha neglects to file a financing statement (and filing is the only way this interest can be perfected since Martha does not have possession and the collateral is other than consumer goods). On March 15, an insolvent Bill Businessperson files a petition in bankruptcy. On April 1, Martha files a financing statement covering the purchase money security agreement. Under the "strong-arm" clause, the trustee in bankruptcy is in the position of a lien creditor as of March 15—the date the petition in bankruptcy was filed. Since Martha Supplier did not perfect by filing until April 1, the trustee in bankruptcy will take the machinery under the "strong-arm" clause, and Martha will be relegated to the status of an unsecured creditor (i.e., she will be entitled to share ratably with other unsecured creditors in Bill Businessperson's nonexempt assets). If, on the other hand, Martha had perfected the security interest prior to March 15, she would prevail over the trustee.

While the trustee in bankruptcy cannot attack a perfected security interest under the "strong-arm" clause, he or she can attack a perfected interest on the grounds that it is a "preferential transfer" under Section 547 of the Bankruptcy Act. The trustee in bankruptcy may avoid (set aside) any preferential transfer made by the bankrupt within ninety days of the bankruptcy filing (and up to one year if the transferee is an "insider" who had reasonable cause to believe that the debtor was insolvent at the time of the transfer). Thus, an insolvent debtor who gives a security interest in collateral to an unsecured creditor on account of an antecedent debt within ninety days of bankruptcy makes a preferential transfer which may be set aside by the trustee in bankruptcy. By way of example, suppose that Martha Supplier sells $5,000 worth of goods on open account to Bill Businessperson (Martha is thus a general unsecured creditor). The sale takes place on December 20. By February 1, Bill has become insolvent and cannot pay any of the $5,000 owing on the account. Martha agrees to take a security interest in goods belonging to Bill valued at $5,000 on account of the antecedent debt (remember, an antecedent debt constitutes "value" for purposes of attachment of a security interest). Martha files a financing statement covering the security interest the same day. On April 15, Bill Businessperson files a petition in bankruptcy. The trustee in bankruptcy may set aside Martha Supplier's security interest on the grounds that it is a preferential transfer. The result is that Martha will be back in the position of a general unsecured creditor.

Finally, the trustee in bankruptcy may try to proceed under Section 548 of the Bankruptcy Act which allows the trustee to set aside any fraudulent transfer made by the bankrupt within one year of the filing of the bankruptcy petition. However, to prevail, the trustee must show that the security interest was given fraudulently (i.e., without fair consideration or with the intent to hinder, delay, or defraud creditors).

WHAT CAN THE ARTICLE 9 SECURED CREDITOR DO BY WAY OF ENFORCEMENT IF THE DEBTOR "DEFAULTS"?

Apart from priority or bankruptcy problems, what are the secured party's rights when the debtor fails to make payment when due or otherwise breaches the terms of the security agreement (as by making an unauthorized sale of the collateral)? Many times, the security agreement expressly provides that if the debtor misses an installment payment, the secured party has a right to *accelerate* payment (i.e., require immediate payment of the entire balance owing). Or the secured party may simply treat the debtor as being in default.

Where a default occurs, the secured party obviously has all the rights of any general unsecured creditor. Thus, the secured party can go to court and reduce his or her claim against the debtor to judgment. The secured party may then execute the judgment on all the debtor's nonexempt assets, including the specific collateral securing the debt. If the debtor is solvent, proceeding against him or her as an unsecured creditor will result in full payment, and it will make little difference that the creditor is secured.

However, over and above the rights of an unsecured creditor, the secured party has certain special rights against the collateral itself under Article 9 of the Uniform Commercial Code. Sections 9–501 through 9–507 provide that, upon default, the secured creditor may take what is called "default action" against the specific collateral. And in the great majority of cases the secured party will want to proceed against the specific collateral rather than obtain a general judgment against all the debtor's nonexempt property. If the secured creditor places himself or herself in the position of an unsecured creditor and it turns out that the debtor is insolvent, the creditor will end up sharing the debtor's nonexempt assets with all the debtor's other general creditors. The secured creditor may end up receiving only a small part of the amount owing. Proceeding against the collateral itself, on the other hand, will generally result in full (or at least substantial) payment for the creditor. And many times it can be accomplished without going to court.

Upon default by the debtor, Section 9–503 allows the secured party personally to take possession of the collateral without going to court if this can be done without a breach of the peace. For example, where the security interest is in the debtor's automobile, the secured party may, on default by the debtor, remove the automobile from its street or parking lot location without notifying the debtor or obtaining his or her permission. However, the secured party may not remove the collateral over the debtor's express objection even though physical violence is not required to effect removal. Nor may the secured party enter the debtor's place of business or his or her home or garage without the debtor's consent in order to remove the collateral. Any breaking and entering is improper, as are threats and active deception (e.g., posing as a law enforcement officer in order to remove the collateral).

Where repossession is not physically possible (e.g., where the collateral is very heavy equipment), the Code authorizes the secured party to render the equipment inoperative on the debtor's premises and/or dispose of it there without a breach of the peace. If a breach of peace is inevitable, the secured party must resort to the courts.

If the collateral is a fixture and the secured party has priority over all competing claims to the real property, the secured party may, on default, remove the fixture from the realty. However, the secured party must reimburse any owner or mortgage holder (other than the debtor) for physical damage caused the real property by reason of the removal. An owner or mortgage holder who would be entitled to reimbursement in the event of damage may refuse the secured party permission to remove the fixture until he or she has given adequate security for payment of the repairs (as by posting a "repair" bond). For example, suppose that Martha Supplier sells twenty-five "built-in" style ranges on credit to Arnie Apartment Owner, Martha retaining a security interest in the ranges and making a "fixture filing" covering the interest before the ranges are installed in Arnie's apartment house. Clark Mortgagee holds a mortgage on the apartment house, but Martha's security interest as to the ranges takes priority over the mortgage. Upon default by Arnie in paying for the ranges, Martha may remove the ranges from the apartment house subject only to a duty to reimburse Clark Mortgagee for any physical damage to the real property caused by the removal. However, Clark has a right to insist, prior to removal of the ranges, that Martha give adequate security for payment of repairs.

Once the collateral has been rightfully repossessed, the secured party generally has two alternatives.

Retain the Collateral

In most cases, the secured party may simply retain the collateral in satisfaction of the debt—this is called *strict foreclosure.* The secured party must notify the debtor in writing of his or her intent to foreclose, and where the collateral is other than consumer goods, the secured party must also send written notice to any other secured creditor who has notified the secured party in writing of a claim to the collateral. If, after sending notice, the secured party does not receive a written objection to his or her retention of the collateral within twenty-one days from any of the parties who have been notified, the secured party may retain the collateral in satisfaction of the debt. Where the secured party retains the collateral, the obligation is completely discharged, and the secured party abandons any claim to a deficiency. If, on the other hand, the secured party receives a written objection within the twenty-one day period, he or she must proceed to the second alternative and sell the collateral in satisfaction of the debt.

Also, the secured party cannot retain the collateral but must sell it if the collateral is consumer goods and the debtor has paid 60 percent of the cash price (in the case of a purchase money security interest) or 60 percent of the loan (in the case of a security interest other than a purchase money security interest). The reasoning is that, if the debtor has paid more than 60 percent of the cash price or loan, he or she can probably have the collateral sold for more than what is owing (the 40 percent) and receive the surplus. If the secured party fails to sell the collateral within ninety days of the repossession, the debtor may bring a tort action for conversion (see Chapter 4) against the secured party.

Sell the Collateral

As an alternative to retaining the collateral, the secured party may always choose to sell the collateral and apply the sales proceeds to the unpaid debt. And in some cases the secured party must do this, as where written objection is made to his or her retention of the collateral or the debtor has paid 60 percent of the purchase price.

Where the secured party chooses to sell the collateral, every aspect of the sale "including the method, manner, time, place and terms must be commercially reasonable." The secured party must give notice of the sale to the debtor and to any other secured party who has given notice to the secured party of having a claim to the collateral (except in the case of consumer goods where notice need be given only to the debtor). The sale of the collateral to a purchaser for value transfers all of the debtor's rights in the collateral to the purchaser and discharges the security interest (along with any junior security interest in the collateral).

As to the sales proceeds, they must be applied in the following order:

1. To pay the secured party's reasonable expenses (including attorneys' fees) in repossessing and disposing of the collateral;
2. To pay the debt owed to the security party;
3. To pay the debt owed to any junior security interest holder (i.e., a person with a security interest that is subordinate to the secured party's) who has made a written demand and furnished reasonable proof of the security interest; and
4. Finally, any remaining surplus must be turned over to the debtor.

In many states if the sale does not result in sufficient proceeds to cover the secured party's reasonable expenses along with the amount of the debt owing, the debtor will be liable to the secured party for the deficiency. However, statutes in a number of states (including California, Illinois, and Washington) provide that a creditor who repossesses and sells consumer goods may not collect any deficiency in proceeds from the debtor. The secured party, in these states, must elect between obtaining a judgment against the debtor and attempting to collect the full debt or repossessing and reselling the collateral with the risk of a deficiency in proceeds.

A secured party who fails to comply with the default provisions of Article 9 (as by using force to repossess the collateral, failing to give proper notice of sale to the debtor, selling the collateral in some "commercially unreasonable" way, etc.) is liable to the debtor for any losses that he or she suffers. UCC 9–507(1). If the collateral is consumer goods, UCC Section 9–506(1) allows the debtor to recover a minimum of the credit service charge plus 10 percent of the principal amount of the debt or the time price differential plus 10 percent of the cash price. For example, suppose that a debtor borrows $5,000 to buy a camper-truck for use on a cross-country vacation; the creditor takes a purchase money security interest in the camper. The debtor, who is to pay $9.00 per $100 over a period of three years, defaults in payment. The secured party repossesses the camper, using physical force to do so. Under UCC Section 9–507(1), the debtor may sue the secured party for a minimum of $500 (10 percent of the $5,000 principal) plus $1,380 (the $9.00 credit charge × 50 hundreds × 3 years) for a total of $1,850. And if the debtor has suffered actual loss greater than this, he or she may recover the full amount of the loss.

A debtor whose property has been repossessed has a "right of redemption" under Section 9–506 of the Uniform Commercial Code. The right of redemption is the right to free the collateral from any lien or encumbrance and gain absolute ownership by payment of the amount due. The debtor exercises the right by tendering an amount sufficient to cover the debt as well as any expenses incurred by the secured party in repossessing the collateral (e.g., attorneys' fees or other legal expenses). However, the right must be exercised before the secured party has sold the collateral or entered into a contract to do so. And it must be exercised before the secured party has taken steps to retain the collateral in satisfaction of the debt (as by giving the required notice to the debtor and other claimants to the property).

WHAT IS THE LAW OF MORTGAGES?

The Uniform Commercial Code does not govern mortgages (i.e., the use of real property as security). Rather, state common law and statutory law (other than the UCC) controls. Generally speaking, real property secures much larger debts than personal property, and the debts are usually paid off over a longer period of time (twenty to thirty years as opposed to the comparatively shorter time periods involved when personal property serves as collateral).

In broad terms, a *mortgage* is a conveyance of land given as security for payment of a debt. The debtor (the "mortgagor") borrows money from the creditor (the "mortgagee") and conveys his or her real property to the mortgagees as security for the loan. Right at the outset, it is important to understand that the "conveyance" aspect of the transaction must be minimized.

For all intents and purposes, the debtor (mortgagor) retains complete ownership of the land—he or she retains possession and use of the land though having created a lien or encumbrance on the property. This lien or security aspect is the dominant feature of a mortgage. When the mortgage debt is repaid, the mortgagee's interest in the land immediately and automatically terminates, and the mortgagor once again holds the property free of the lien. The immediate and automatic extinguishment of the mortgagee's security interest upon payment of the debt is called the *condition of defeasance* and is a part of every mortgage.

No prescribed words are necessary to create a mortgage. However, in most cases the basic structure of the mortgage is very similar to that of a deed (see Chapter 8). The mortgage must be evidenced by a writing sufficient to satisfy the Statute of Frauds. The writing must reasonably identify the mortgagee and describe the debt and land involved. The writing need not contain all the specifics of the agreement: usually, the parties do not want all the details put into the writing because the writing is generally recorded in the public records. For example, the exact amount of the debt need not be stated so long as the debt is described with sufficient particularity so that it is identifiable.

The lack of detail in the writing is unimportant because most mortgages are also represented by a negotiable promissory note. In other words, there is usually (but not always) both a mortgage and a note, and the note specifies the "sum certain" and the interest rate (see Chapter 9).

Because an unacknowledged mortgage cannot be recorded, a mortgagee should always insist that the mortgagor acknowledge the mortgage. Also like a deed, a mortgage must be delivered. An effective delivery is made when the mortgagor surrenders the mortgage in complete form to the mortgagee with the intention that it operate as a security interest in the real property.

A mortgagor frequently executes a mortgage on land contemporaneously with acquiring ownership of the property in order to secure the purchase price. This is the typical home purchase transaction. A mortgage that is executed to secure the purchase price of land is referred to as a *purchase money mortgage.* A special rule applies to such mortgages. The general rule is that a purchase money mortgage takes priority over all prior claims existing against the mortgagor at the time of the purchase. By way of example, suppose that Barbara Borrower buys land, putting $8,000 down and mortgaging the purchased land for $20,000 to provide the balance of the purchase price. The mortgage Barbara gives the mortgagee will take preference over any existing judgments, liens, or other debts outstanding against Barbara at the time of the purchase. However, the special priority of the purchase money mortgage is subject to the recording acts: if, after taking the mortgage, the mortgagee fails to record it, the mortgagee's interest will be subordinate to *subsequent,* recorded interests.

Mortgages, like deeds, should always be recorded. While recording is not essential to making a deed or other instrument valid as between the grantor and grantee, it does serve as "constructive notice" (i.e., inferred or implied notice) to the world at large that there is an outstanding interest in the land. Like a grantee who records, a mortgagee who records is protected against the claims of all subsequent mortgagees and other security interest holders. A mortgagee who fails to record may be in a position subordinate to later mortgagees.

A *deed of trust* is a security device that is commonly used (particularly in nine states) instead of a regular mortgage. Instead of giving a mortgage to a creditor the borrower deeds the land to a third party (the trustee) who holds title to the land solely for the purpose of returning it to the borrower once the loan is paid off. If the borrower fails to repay the loan, the trustee is empowered to sell the property at a public auction without going through the courts and apply the proceeds of the sale to the debt. Generally, the mortgagee notifies the trustee of any default by the mortgagor, whereupon the trustee is required to publish notice of the sale for the benefit of the debtor and prospective purchasers.

In many ways using a trust deed makes it easier for the mortgagee (the creditor) to collect his or her money upon default by the debtor. With a regular mortgage, as you will learn shortly, a judicial proceeding is often required to effect a sale of the property upon default.

Also a trust deed provides special protections for both mortgagor and mortgagee. Whereas a regular mortgage involves two parties, a trust deed is a three-party transaction: mortgagor, mortgagee, and trustee. The trustee is very similar to an escrow agent in that he or she is an independent party who will act only upon objective proof of default. If there are surplus proceeds resulting from sale of the property, the trustee will turn them over to the mortgagor.

A trust deed is also advantageous in that it facilitates the borrowing of large sums of money. For example, a corporation might borrow money from several individuals through the use of bonds secured by real estate owned by the corporation. While it would be impractical to give each shareholder a separate mortgage, it is a simple matter to deed the land to a trustee with a deed of trust securing the bonds purchased by the investors.

Whether a mortgage is cast in regular form or as a deed of trust, it is regarded as a mere lien upon the property—that is to say, a mere security interest in the land, with the mortgagee having no right to possession of the property. This right of possession remains in the mortgagor unless and until there has been a rightful foreclosure and sale of the property. Of course, the parties may always agree as part of the mortgage contract that the mortgagee is to have possession of the land, but this seldom occurs.

Generally, under the terms of the mortgage agreement, the mortgagor has a duty to pay the taxes that come due upon the real property, to keep the property in repair, and to keep it properly insured (it is well settled in the law that both the mortgagor and mortgagee have insurable interests in the mortgaged land—see Chapter 9. If the mortgagor fails to pay the taxes, make repairs, or provide adequate insurance, the mortgagee may generally accelerate payment and declare the entire debt due. This permits the mortgagee to foreclose and have the property sold to satisfy the mortgage debt. Or, rather than accelerate, the mortgagee may simply pay such expenses and add them to the amount of the debt secured by the mortgage.

Sometimes a real property owner places more than one mortgage on the same property. Under the recording acts, a person who takes a mortgage for value without knowledge of a prior, unrecorded mortgage *and* records his or her mortgage will have priority over the prior interest. In other words, if the debtor-mortgagor cannot pay either debt, the holder of the subsequent, recorded mortgage will take priority over the prior, unrecorded mortgage. But remember, to be protected under the recording acts, a person must take *for value* and *without notice* and must subsequently *record* his or her interest. Many times, these requirements are not met, and the prior mortgage will take priority even though it is unrecorded (the general rule being, without regard to the recording acts, that the first mortgage takes priority over subsequent mortgages, liens, or encumbrances).

The typical mortgage provides a definite time when the debt must be paid. The mortgage is said to reach "maturity" at that time. Very often when the mortgage debt is a large one, the mortgage agreement calls for payment in installments (with each installment being part interest and part principal). A mortgage payable in installments generally contains an *acceleration* clause stating that, upon failure of the mortgagor to pay any installment when due, the entire debt shall become due and payable immediately.

Many times, the mortgagor has an option to pay off the debt at its maturity date or to prepay it at an earlier time. However, in the absence of a specific provision allowing prepayment, the mortgagor has no right to insist that the mortgagee accept payment prior to the maturity date. Many mortgages allow prepayment subject to the condition that the mortgagor pay a penalty upon prepayment. Such prepayment penalties are generally upheld on the basis that the mortgagee entered into the mortgage contract expecting to receive interest over a number of years, and where prepayment is made, the mortgagee loses this interest.

At some point in time the mortgage debt will mature, and the mortgagor will either pay the debt or be in default. If the mortgagor pays the debt, the mortgagee's security interest in the real estate will automatically terminate (remember, the mortgagee's interest is subject from the outset to termination by payment of the debt). No conveyance by the mortgagee is required to perfect the mortgagor's estate: the mortgagee's interest in the land immediately reverts to the mortgagor by operation of law.

Nevertheless, statutes in many states require a mortgagee who has received payment to file a "satisfaction" of the mortgage (i.e., a statement that the mortgage has been paid) in the public mortgage records. If the mortgagee fails to file a satisfaction within a specified period of time following a request by the mortgagor that he or she do so, the mortgagee will be liable in damages to the mortgagor (for a definite sum set by statute and for any additional damages the mortgagor sustains by reason of the failure to file).

In most cases the mortgage is paid, a "satisfaction" is entered, and the transaction is complete. Sometimes, however, the mortgagor fails to make payment when the obligation matures and is considered to be in default.

Upon default by the mortgagor, the mortgagee does not automatically acquire ownership of the land. However, this was not always the case. In England, in the fourteenth century and for a couple hundred years thereafter, if a mortgage debt was not paid when due, the default served to extinguish the mortgagor's interest in the land, and the mortgagee automatically succeeded to ownership of the property by operation of law. After a time the law recognized that this was too harsh a result and permitted the mortgagor who had defaulted to reacquire ownership of the land by paying the debt in full (along with interest). This was called the mortgagor's *equity of redemption* and was a right that could be sold by the mortgagor or even passed on to his or her heirs at death.

Of course, the result of the mortgagor's equity of redemption was to place the mortgagee in a position of uncertainty: the mortgagor or his or her heir could come in and repurchase the property at any time. To remedy this situation, the law developed a new practice called a "foreclosure suit" which allowed the mortgagee to go to court to obtain a judge's order stating that the mortgagor's equity of redemption would be cut off if it was not exercised within a specified period of time (typically, six months to one year). If the mortgagor failed to redeem the property within this time, the equity of redemption was forever barred, and the mortgagee became the owner absolute of the real property. Today, this method of foreclosure is known as *strict foreclosure.*

Most courts disfavor the strict foreclosure remedy because of the harsh result of turning the land over to the mortgagee even though it may be worth considerably more than the debt owing, with the result that the mortgagor loses his or her surplus equity. The preferred remedy is foreclosure by judicial sale of the property with any surplus proceeds (proceeds over and above the amount of the debt) turned over to the mortgagor. Thus, the most common way for the mortgagee to obtain his or her money upon default by the mortgagor is through sale of the property. The specifics of the statutes regulating "judicial sale" vary from state to state but generally call for public sale of the property after compliance with certain notice requirements as to time, place, manner, and terms of the sale. The sale itself is usually done at the direction of the county sheriff in the county where the land is located. Generally, the court must confirm the sale and will not do so if it determines that the price received for the property was so low as to be unconscionable. However, the court will not refuse to confirm simply because a depression exists or because a higher price might be received at a later time—it will refuse to confirm only where the price is so low as to raise a presumption of unfairness or a lack of protection for the mortgagor.

If the sales proceeds are not sufficient to cover the mortgage debt (and related costs and interest), the mortgagee may in some states obtain a judgment against the mortgagor for the deficiency. However, most states have either abolished or sharply restricted deficiency judgments. Too often, the mortgaged property does not bring its true value at a forced sale. And sometimes the mortgagee himself or herself is the purchaser. To allow a mortgagee to buy the property at less than its actual value and then to obtain a deficiency judgment is to allow a recovery beyond the amount of the mortgage debt. The states are particularly strict in prohibiting deficiency judgments in the case of purchase money mortgages. In a purchase money mortgage, the seller-mortgagor sells the land on credit to the purchaser, taking a mortgage in the land as security for the purchase price. If a foreclosure ultimately results and there is a deficiency, it can be inferred that the seller-mortgagee originally sold the land at a price beyond its true value and thus overreached (i.e., took advantage of) the buyer-mortgagor.

Occasionally, the sale of the land will result in surplus proceeds beyond the mortgage debt and related costs and interests. Such surplus belongs to the mortgagor.

A foreclosure sale cuts off the mortgagor's equitable right of redemption. However, in twenty-six states the mortgagor has a statutory right of redemption following a foreclosure sale enabling him or her to redeem the property (by paying the sales price plus reasonable costs and expenses) for a certain period of time (usually one year). Statutory redemption nullifies the foreclosure sale and restores title of the land to the mortgagor. The mortgagor's *statutory right of redemption* should not be confused with his or her equitable right of redemption prior to the foreclosure sale. Statutes recognizing the statutory right of redemption include: Alabama, Arizona, Arkansas, California, Colorado, Idaho, Illinois, Indiana, Iowa, Kansas, Kentucky, Maine, Michigan, Minnesota, Missouri, Montana, Nevada, New Mexico, North Dakota, Oregon, South Dakota, Tennessee, Utah, Vermont, Washington, and Wyoming. In all other states, the foreclosure sale is final and cannot be set aside.

WHO IS RESPONSIBLE FOR PAYING THE MORTGAGE DEBT WHEN THE MORTGAGOR SELLS THE MORTGAGED PROPERTY?

That is, what is the difference between selling land "subject to the mortgage" and selling it with the mortgage "assumed"?

Since the mortgagor owns the mortgaged property subject only to a security interest in the mortgagee, the mortgagor may freely sell or otherwise transfer the property. However, the mortgagor can never delegate his or her duty of performance under the mortgage. Thus, the mortgagor will always be liable on the mortgage even if he or she sells the property.

Whether or not the purchaser of the property will also be liable on the mortgage will depend on whether the purchaser took the land "subject to the mortgage" or took it with an "assumption" of the mortgage.

A purchaser takes the land "subject to the mortgage" when he or she pays the mortgagor the value of the property less the amount of the mortgage debt owing but does not assume any personal liability for the mortgage debt. The purchaser, in this case, is not bound on the mortgage either to the mortgagor or mortgagee. Of course, the land still serves as security for the mortgage debt. But if there is a deficiency following a foreclosure sale, the mortgagee cannot look to the purchaser for the deficiency but can go only against the mortgagor.

In contrast, a purchaser takes the land and "assumes" the mortgage when he or she pays the mortgagor the value of the land less the amount of the mortgage debt owing and also promises the mortgagor that he or she will pay the mortgage debt. The purchaser's promise is said to be an "assumption" of the mortgage debt. Of course, the mortgagor is not relieved of his or her own duty to pay the debt, but where the purchaser "assumes" the mortgage, the mortgagor does have a right to insist that the purchaser make payment. The mortgagee can look to either party for payment—the mortgagor on the basis of the original mortgage agreement, and the purchaser on the basis of being a third party beneficiary of the assumption agreement (see Chapter 9) or by reason of suretyship (see next section). If the mortgagee collects from the mortgagor, the mortgagor has a right to reimbursement from the purchaser.

It is apparent that the purchaser of mortgaged real property is in a better position (i.e., a less risky one) if he or she takes the land "subject to the mortgage" rather than with an "assumption" of the mortgage.

WHAT IS SURETYSHIP?

There is yet a third way for a creditor to provide security for a debt or other promised performance—a method not involving the use of personal or real property as security. Rather, a third person, called a *surety,* agrees to repay the debt (or perform the promise) owed to the creditor assuming the debtor (the *principal*) does not. This security device is known as the suretyship contract and it always involves three parties: the debtor-principal, the creditor, and the surety.

By way of example, suppose that Sylvia Student wants to borrow $3,000 from a bank to help her with her college expenses. Sylvia applies for a loan but finds that she does not have sufficient credit standing to obtain an unsecured loan or adequate real or personal property to use as collateral in obtaining a loan. Sylvia goes to her employer, Bill Businessperson, who agrees to "back" the loan with his own personal credit; this time not only Sylvia promises to repay the loan to the bank, but Bill also promises to repay the loan. And this time the bank, knowing of Bill's sound financial position, agrees to make the loan.

Thus, in the suretyship relationship, the surety becomes legally bound to the creditor on the principal's debt, with the result that both parties are liable. The creditor is entitled to payment from the principal or the surety; however, the ultimate burden of the debt remains on the principal who must reimburse the surety if the surety is required to pay it. In our example, Sylvia is the principal and thus has the ultimate duty to pay the loan to the creditor bank. However, the bank may also look to the surety, Bill, for payment.

The surety's obligation to the creditor may be absolute and unconditional so that the creditor has an option to go against either the surety or the principal in the first instance. Or the surety's promise may be conditioned upon the creditor's first trying to collect from the principal. Suretyship may also be tied into the use of property as security as where a third person provides collateral to secure the debt of another.

Thus, in the broad sense, the term "suretyship" includes any relationship wherein one person agrees to answer for the debt of another—for example, assuming a mortgage, endorsing a check, or signing a note as an accommodation maker.

Though suretyship is a contract, it is to some extent unique as a legal concept—it has been a part of law even to the time of the Bible. Originally, a surety was used personally as a human hostage to secure payment of a debt; if the debt was not paid, the surety would be imprisoned, tortured, or even put to death. After a time the person of the surety ceased to be used as the security, and, instead, the surety's promise became the security. Still, it was not considered particularly intelligent to become a surety and promise to pay for another's debt. The Bible, Proverbs 11:15 states: "He that is surety for a stranger shall smart for it; and he that hateth suretyship is sure." The fact is, sureties were often inexperienced and did the foolish thing and ended up having to pay for their friend's debts. It is partly for this reason that there are special protections in the law for the surety.

WHAT ARE THE SPECIAL RULES OF SURETYSHIP?

The following special rules and principles apply to the suretyship contract.

Statute of Frauds

You will recall from Chapter 9 that certain promises are enforceable under the Statute of Frauds only if they are supported by a written memo signed by the party to be charged. The suretyship obligation is one such promise and must be evidenced by a written memo signed by the surety in order to be enforceable.

Creditor's Collection Procedure

The general rule is that the creditor does not have to proceed first against the principal upon default but may proceed directly and immediately against the surety to collect the debt. In other words, the surety cannot force the creditor to try to collect first from the principal. States following the general rule include Connecticut, Delaware, Louisiana, Maine, Massachusetts, Michigan, Minnesota, New Hampshire, New Jersey, New Mexico, Oregon, Rhode Island, South Carolina, Vermont, Wisconsin, and others.

In about half the states the general rule has been changed by judicial decision or statute. In the following states, if the surety notifies the creditor to proceed first against the principal, and the creditor does not do so but attempts to collect instead from the surety, the surety will be discharged: Alabama, Arizona, Arkansas, California, Colorado, Georgia, Illinois, Indiana, Iowa, Kentucky, Mississippi, Missouri, Montana, New York, North Carolina, North Dakota, Ohio, Oklahoma, Pennsylvania, South Dakota, Tennessee, Texas, Virginia, Washington, West Virginia, and Wyoming.

Exoneration

To exonerate means to free from responsibility. The principal owes a duty to the surety to perform as soon as performance is due so that the surety will be exonerated and will not be sued by the creditor. Thus, it is a principle of surety law that a surety may compel his or her principal to perform the obligation when it is due. If the principal fails to perform, the surety may bring a suit against the principal and obtain a decree from the court requiring the principal to pay the creditor. This is so even though the principal has a duty to indemnify (reimburse) the surety if the surety is required to pay the debt. Reimbursement is not an adequate remedy because the surety may suffer considerable loss by reason of having to raise the money to pay the debt.

Reimbursement

A surety who pays the principal's debt has a right of reimbursement from the principal. And the right is not conditioned upon the surety's being forced to pay the debt. The surety may voluntarily make payment, then go to court to seek reimbursement from the principal.

However, a surety is not allowed to make a profit at the principal's expense. If the surety discharges the debt by giving the creditor his or her personal promissory note, the majority rule is that the surety may sue the principal for the face value of the note even though the surety has not yet paid the note.

Subrogation

Subrogation is the substitution of one person in the legal position of another with respect to a lawful claim, demand, or right. Subrogation was discussed in Chapter 10 (dealing with insurance) as follows: "[A]n insurance company that pays for an insured's loss is subrogated to the legal rights of the insured against the party who caused the loss." Upon paying the principal's debt, the surety has a right to be subrogated to the creditor's lawful claims against the principal. Subrogation entitles the surety to use any legal remedy against the principal that the creditor could have used and to enjoy any benefit or advantage that the creditor would have had in proceeding against the principal. Thus, if the creditor was holding the debtor-principal's collateral as security, the surety will have the creditor's right to proceed against the collateral by reason of the subrogation. The surety will succeed to any position of priority that the creditor has against the debtor. If the suretyship relates to a mortgage and the surety pays the mortgage debt, the surety has all the rights of the mortgagee. (It should be noted that a creditor need not proceed against the collateral first before looking to the surety for payment.)

Contribution

Where there are co-sureties and one surety pays the principal's entire debt or more than his or her share of the debt, that surety is entitled to contribution from his or her co-sureties to the extent of their ratable shares. Co-sureties are liable jointly and severally and may be sued by the creditor as a group or individually.

The right of contribution exists between all who are liable as sureties as to the *same obligation* of a principal; it does not exist where the sureties are liable on *different obligations* of a principal.

WHAT IS THE PURPOSE OF THE BULK SALES LAW?

As we have seen, creditors may protect themselves by using property as security or by having a third party serve as surety for a debtor. Still, many creditors sell on open account without using any security device. This is particularly true of suppliers who provide inventory merchandise. Most inventory suppliers sell to merchants on credit, expecting to be paid in the ordinary course of business as the inventory is sold to customers. As long as the merchant-debtor's business operates smoothly and the merchant pays the supplier as the inventory is sold, the supplier has nothing to worry about. However, if the merchant decides to sell his or her business or a "major part" of his or her materials, supplies, merchandise, or other inventory, the supplier may justifiably worry about whether or not he or she will be repaid. As long as the inventory is present, the supplier, upon default by the buyer, can use all of the creditor remedies to collect his or her debt from the merchant. As you will recall, these include the prejudgment remedies of attachment, garnishment, and prejudgment receivership—remedies designed "to prevent the debtor from disposing of his or her property, or from concealing or destroying it, so it cannot be used to pay his or her debt."

The difficulty arises where the merchant, without warning, sells the entire business (or a major part of it) and there is no longer any inventory to attach or place in receivership. What is more, the merchant-debtor may have squandered the proceeds resulting from sale of the business and/or left the state. In the ordinary case, the merchant's creditors cannot reach the transferred assets in the buyer's hands unless the creditors can show that the transfer was a fraudulent conveyance or preferential transfer. A good faith purchaser of the assets would take them free of the creditors' claims.

Yet, if the creditors have adequate warning of a planned bulk sale, they can take action prior to the sale to protect their interests. The purpose of bulk sales law under Article 6 of the UCC is to provide such notice. Bulk sales law does not prescribe specific remedies for creditors; rather, it is designed to give notice to suppliers and other creditors of a going business that the business or a major part of it is going to be sold. Once notified, the creditors can take whatever action they deem necessary (if any) to protect their interests. Of course, in many cases the creditors will take no special action because they know that the seller is solvent and responsible and will pay them anyway. But if the creditors fear that they will not be paid, they may pressure the seller and buyer to pay them off as part of the bulk sale transaction, or they may resort to any other available legal remedies (including the prejudgment remedies).

The law applies only to businesses whose principal business is the sale of merchandise from stock, including businesses that manufacture what they sell. And the law applies to the transfer of a *major part* of a business's materials, supplies, merchandise, or other inventory. The Code nowhere defines "major part"—rather, the courts must, in each case, look at the impact the transfer will have on creditors. Some courts apply an arbitrary rule, stating that anything over 50 percent of a business's materials, supplies, merchandise, or other inventory is a "major part" of the business (meaning over 50 percent of the value of the materials, supplies, merchandise, etc.). However, it would appear that less than this could also be a major part; thus, a seller of a business would be well advised to follow the bulk sales requirements whenever he or she is transferring a substantial bulk of materials, supplies, merchandise, or other inventory.

Equipment is included under the bulk sales rules only if it is transferred in connection with a bulk transfer of inventory.

WHAT MUST BE DONE TO COMPLY WITH ARTICLE 6 WHEN A "BULK SALE" IS MADE?

The "bulk sales" requirements of Article 6 come into play when a person whose principal business is selling merchandise from stock decides to sell his or her business (or transfer a major part of his or her materials, supplies, merchandise, or other inventory). Article 6 sets forth the following four requirements, imposing duties on both the seller and buyer in the bulk sales situation:

1. The buyer-transferee of the business must require the seller-transferor to furnish him or her with a list of the existing creditors of the business. The list must include all creditors, whether trade creditors (those who furnish inventory on credit); creditors who claim on the basis of other contracts, torts, or tax claims; even creditors who claim amounts that are disputed by the seller. Each creditor's name and business address must be listed together with the amount of his or her claim. And the list must be signed and sworn to by the seller.
2. The buyer and seller must together prepare a schedule of the property to be transferred.
3. The buyer must preserve the creditors' list and property schedule for six months following the transfer. During this time, the buyer must either permit creditors to inspect and copy from the list and schedule at all reasonable hours or the creditor must file the list and schedule in a public office (such as the county clerk's office) in the area where the business is located.
4. The buyer must give notice of the sale to the listed creditors and any other parties known to have claims against the business. The notice must either be delivered personally or "sent" by registered or certified mail at least ten days before the buyer takes possession of the property transferred in bulk.

In addition to the above four requirements, some eighteen states have passed as part of Article 6 optional Section 6–106 requiring that part of the bulk sales proceeds be distributed to the transferor's creditors. States having passed this Section include Alaska, Florida, Idaho, Kansas, Kentucky, Maryland, Mississippi, Montana, New Jersey, North Dakota, Oklahoma, Pennsylvania, South Dakota, Tennessee, Texas, Utah, Washington, and West Virginia.

WHAT IS THE RESULT OF FAILURE TO COMPLY WITH THE BULK SALES RULES?

Assuming the buyer and seller fully comply with the bulk sales rules of Article 6, the creditors of the business, having been notified of the bulk sale, can do whatever they deem necessary (if anything) to protect their interests. It may be that the seller-transferor is solvent and responsible and that the creditors will be paid off completely with no difficulty. The creditors, in this case, are likely to do nothing.

However, if it appears that the inventory is being sold for far less than it is actually worth or that the seller is going to flee the state with all the proceeds of the sale, the creditors will want to act immediately to protect themselves. If the creditors do nothing and the bulk sale is made in full conformity with Article 6, the creditors will have no claim to the goods transferred in bulk to the transferee buyer.

A creditor who is worried about an impending bulk sale may try to get the parties to agree to pay him or her off as part of the bulk sale transaction. If this does not work, the creditor may threaten legal action. However, unless there has been a breach of contract, the creditor will have no basis for going to court to obtain a judgment (in other words, the debt must be overdue or the creditor will have no cause to complain). And to use a prejudgment remedy (e.g., attachment), the creditor must show that he or she is in imminent danger of losing his or her claim by reason of the transferor's hiding the proceeds, spending them, or leaving the state. Of course, the creditor may threaten to force the transferor into bankruptcy, but to do this, the creditor must show that the transferor has debts of at least $5,000 and that he or she is not paying his or her debts as they fall due or has had his or her property taken over by a legal custodian. If the creditor cannot show this, he or she can do nothing more to fight the bulk sale (the creditor, in this case, probably has little to worry about anyway by reason of the sale).

But suppose that the parties (buyer and seller) fail to comply fully with the requirements of Article 6. The UCC states that noncomplying transfers are ineffective. The result is that the seller's creditors can still reach the inventory or other goods transferred just as if they never left the seller's hands. Thus, though the goods are in the possession of the buyer-transferee, the creditors can levy upon the goods and have them sold to satisfy judgments against the seller-transferor. The creditors can also obtain an injunction against the transferee to prevent him or her from reselling the goods or, if the goods have already been resold, to prevent the transferee from disposing of the proceeds.

Of course, a bona fide purchaser of the goods (i.e., one who takes the goods for value without knowledge of the failure to comply with the bulk sales rules) will acquire ownership (title) of the property free of the creditors' claims. Any other person taking the property will be an assignee only in the same position as the transferee.

Any action or levy by a creditor under the bulk sales law must be brought or maintained within six months after the date on which the transferee takes possession of the goods unless the transfer has been concealed.

In the latter case, creditors' actions or levies may be maintained up to six months after discovery of the bulk transfer.

In conclusion, remember that the bulk sales rules are designed to give the creditors of a business prior notice that a bulk sale is going to occur so that the creditors can take whatever action they deem necessary to protect their interests. It is important to remember that the bulk sales rules do not affect any remedies a creditor might have as a secured creditor (under Article 9 of the UCC or as a mortgage holder) or any remedies a creditor might have by reason of the federal Bankruptcy Act or state creditor remedy law.

Accountants' Professional Responsibilities

WHAT IS THE BASIC RESPONSIBILITY OF A PUBLIC ACCOUNTANT?

Accountants are very often involved with transactions involving their clients and the clients' creditors. The key word in describing the role of a public accountant is the word "independent." The work of the public accountant in *independently* examining, verifying, and certifying business accounts and financial data and statements makes it possible for the private enterprise system to function. The private enterprise system is based on the continuing confidence of investors and creditors in the reliability of such statements.

A public accountant is responsible not only to the client who pays his or her fee but also to investors, creditors, and other members of the public who rely on his or her reports. The federal securities laws (see Chapter 6) impose both civil and criminal liability on auditors for certain failures of responsibility. To help guide accountants, the American Institute of Certified Public Accountants (AICPA) promulgates "generally accepted accounting principles" (GAAP) and "generally accepted auditing standards" (GAAS). However, the Securities and Exchange Commission (SEC), which administers the securities laws, takes the position that the auditor's obligation goes beyond the GAAP and GAAS. The SEC states that it is the auditor's duty to (1) detect any gross overstatement of assets and profits, and (2) to communicate the results of his or her audit so that even lay investors (people without accounting training) can make meaningful investment decisions.

The courts agree with the SEC stating that the test is not simply whether GAAP and GAAS have been followed but whether the financial statements, data, and disclosures tell the investor what he or she needs to know in order to make a meaningful decision regarding whether or not to invest. If they do not, the accountant may be liable despite the fact that he or she has complied with GAAP and GAAS. Judge MacMahon stated it this way in the case of Hertzfeld v. Laventhol, Krekstein, Horwath & Horwath, CCH Fed.Sec.L.Rep. # 94,574 (S.D.N.Y.1974):

> Much has been said by the parties about generally accepted accounting principles and the proper way for an accountant to report real estate transactions. We

> think this misses the point. Our inquiry is properly focused not on whether Laventhol's report satisfies esoteric accounting norms, comprehensible only to the initiate, but whether the report fairly presents the true financial position of Firestone, as of November 30, 1969, to the untutored eye of an ordinary investor.

It may be concluded that the courts will not hesitate to require a higher standard than GAAP or GAAS, particularly where the investing public is reading and relying on the accountant's financial data and reports.

Three types of improper accounting that can result in both civil and criminal liability are "artful accounting," "creative accounting," and "salami accounting." "Artful accounting" refers to the incomplete disclosure of information or the hiding of information so that an investor or creditor looking at the financial report is not likely to see it. An important disclosure may be buried in a footnote, or it may be phrased in such sophisticated financial terminology that a lay person (one not educated in accounting) cannot understand it. For example, saying that certain customers' accounts are "subject to realization" may be an artful way of saying that they are uncollectible.

"Creative accounting" means structuring transactions so as to create a false picture of financial health (e.g., creating "paper profits" through transactions with your own subsidiaries).

Finally, "salami accounting" is taking up a past accounting error gradually over future periods so as to prevent immediate, full disclosure of the error (the error is said to be "sliced very thin" and taken up gradually into the financial picture so as not to distort "the mainfare").

Because public accounting is important to the economic system and affects the public welfare, it is regulated by statute in all states. For example, all states regulate the use of the title "certified public accountant" (CPA). To become a CPA an accountant must pass a twenty-four-hour exam prepared and graded by the American Institute of Certified Public Accountants. The exam contains two parts on accounting practice, and one part each on accounting theory, auditing, and business law. Many states additionally require an accountant to have from one to six years of accounting experience and/or a college degree in specified courses to become a CPA. And an increasing number of states require continuing education as a condition to continued licensing of CPAs.

The American Institute of Certified Public Accountants regulates its membership with the Code of Professional Ethics. The courts look upon these rules as minimum standards required of all public accountants. Because they are minimum standards, the courts and the Securities and Exchange Commission are free to impose additional standards with regard to financial data and statements submited in connection with the federal securities laws.

Whether civil or criminal liability is at issue, the courts are involved in regulating the accounting profession. In determining an accountant's liability, it is necessary to look at: (1) the CPA's responsibility to his or her client; and (2) the CPA's responsibility to third parties.

WHAT IS THE CPA's RESPONSIBILITY TO HIS OR HER CLIENT?

The CPA's responsibility to his or her client is based on the *contract* between the parties. The CPA is an independent contractor (see Chapter 7) who promises to perform certain services for a fee. The CPA's duty under the contract is to perform the services properly and with due care. For example, a contract to perform an audit implies duties to verify the cash, confirm accounts receivable, check the physical inventories, and follow generally accepted accounting principles (GAAP) and auditing standards (GAAS). If the CPA fails to carry out these duties properly and with due care, the CPA not only breaches the contract but also commits the tort of negligence (malpractice).

And it may make a difference whether a client brings an action based on contract versus tort. For example, contract damages are designed to put the parties in the positions they would have been in had the contract been carried out (subject to the rule of remoteness). Tort damages for negligence, on the other hand, include any damages proximately caused by the breach of duty and, if gross negligence is involved, may even include punitive damages. Also, the statute of limitations time period for bringing suit generally differs for contract and tort actions. It should be pointed out that the problem has been obviated under modern pleading statutes which allow a plaintiff to sue for both breach of contract and the tort of negligence in one legal action.

An accountant's responsibility to his or her client may be summarized as follows:

1. The standard of care required of an accountant is that of an average accountant performing his or her work with reasonable care. An accountant is not an insurer or guarantor and is not liable for an honest error in judgment, assuming reasonable care has been exercised. However, reasonable care means more than simply verifying the arithmetical accuracy of a client's financial data and statements. The accountant must inquire into the *substantial accuracy* of the data, using reasonable care and skill in making inquiries and investigations. Also, the accountant's own accounting procedures and mathematical computations must be *substantially accurate;* if they are not, this shows a lack of due care. In addition, the accountant must not certify material that he or she knows to be inaccurate. And the accountant must use reasonable care and skill in forming his or her opinion about the material's accuracy. This is not to say that an auditor must approach his or her work with suspicion—an auditor is a "watchdog," not a "bloodhound"—but merely that he or she must use more care if his or her suspicions are aroused.

Along the same line, an accountant is not strictly liable for discovering fraud, but a negligent failure to uncover fraud will result in liability (e.g., where the fraud is undetected because of the failure to follow GAAP or GAAS).

2. An auditor has a duty to *communicate* the information obtained from his or her audit to the client (and to any third parties the auditor knows will rely on the information). While a CPA is an independent contractor, he or she has contract duties of loyalty and honesty to the client. Thus, if the

CPA discovers that fraud exists, he or she has a duty to disclose this fact to the client.

3. An accountant who is being sued by a client for negligence may assert the client's contributory negligence as a defense to liability (e.g., a client who fails to follow his or her accountant's advice or refuses to allow the accountant to perform necessary procedures may be guilty of contributory negligence).

4. An accountant who materially breaches a contract with a client is not entitled to any fee and may be sued by the client for breach of contract and/or the tort of negligence. If the breach is willful or grossly negligent, the client may recover punitive damages in the tort action (such damages are not recoverable in a breach of contract action).

If the breach is minor (e.g., a minor error or inaccuracy in the report), the accountant will still be entitled to a fee, but the client may "set off" reasonable damages from the amount owing.

5. Apart from negligence, an accountant will be liable for the intentional tort of deceit if he or she actively deceives the client or shows a reckless disregard for the truth (i.e., gross negligence bordering on intentional deceit). An example of "reckless disregard" would be failing to carry out a vital procedure such as bank reconciliation. The accountant, in this case, may be sued not only for actual damages but also for punitive damages.

6. Where the accountant dies or becomes disabled and is unable to perform the contract, the contract obligations of both parties are discharged. The contract calls for services of a personal nature, and it would be objectively impossible for anyone else to perform.

7. To avoid liability to third parties when doing "unaudited" financial statements or mere "write-up" work (bookkeeping functions or creating basic financial records), an accountant must make it clear: (1) that the work is not based on an audit; (2) that it is for the internal use of the client only; and (3) that the accountant expresses no opinion about the substantial accuracy of the work. Under AICPA standards, an accountant is associated with any unaudited financial statements or write-up work he or she prepares whether the work is on plain paper or letterhead. To disclaim liability to third parties, the accountant must mark each page of the work "unaudited" and must make a disclaimer of opinion either on the work itself or on a separate sheet. Where a financial statement is prepared on an accountant's letterhead without any qualifications, anyone using the material can assume it is the result of an audit and impose liability on this basis.

Even with unaudited financial statements or write-up work, the accountant is still under a duty of loyalty and honesty to the client and must disclose any information (e.g., evidence of fraud) resulting from the work.

8. With regard to tax work, a CPA must sign any tax return that he or she prepares whether or not he or she receives a fee for the work. However, the CPA must not sign until he or she is completely satisfied that all relevant information has been provided and all relevant questions have been answered. In signing a tax return, a CPA need not provide a disclaimer of opinion for unaudited data or the like; a tax return is not a financial statement, and the preparer's signature does not constitute an opinion as to the taxpayer's financial condition or the accuracy of his or her financial statements. However, if the CPA is negligent in preparing the return or fails to file it on time, he or she will be liable for malpractice and will have to pay any penalties and interest assessed by the government.

Incorrect tax advice will also result in liability for negligence. For example, in the case of Rassieur v. Charles, 354 Mo. 117, 188 S.W.2d 817, (1945), an accountant incorrectly advised his client that she had realized a taxable profit on the sale of certain securities and should sell certain other securities so as to create a tax loss before the end of the year. The client had, in fact, incurred a tax loss on the sale of the securities and suffered increased loss as a result of selling the additional securities. The court ruled that the accountant was liable for the difference in the sales price of the stock and its repurchase price when the correct facts came to light.

An accountant who discovers that he or she has given incorrect tax advice has a duty to advise the client of the error immediately. An accountant who is performing continuous services for a client also has a duty to inform the client of any changes in the law affecting previous tax advice (an accountant who is not performing continuous services is not expected to follow up with changes in the law when the contract relationship with the client no longer exists).

9. At common law there exists no accountant-client privilege (like that of a doctor-patient, attorney-client, priest-penitent, etc.—see Chapter 3) that may be invoked by a client to prevent disclosure of his or her communications to the accountant. Thus, if an accountant is subpoenaed to testify in state or federal court about a client's communications, the accountant may not refuse to testify the way that a doctor, lawyer, or priest may refuse with regard to the communications of a patient, client, or penitent. The reasoning here is that it is not in the public interest to impede the courts in the administration of justice by preventing them from calling accountants as witnesses.

However, fifteen states and Puerto Rico have passed statutes creating a limited accountant-client privilege, including Arizona, Colorado, Florida, Georgia, Illinois, Iowa, Kentucky, Louisiana, Maryland, Michigan, Missouri, Nevada, New Mexico, Pennsylvania, and Tennessee. There is no accountant-client privilege in any federal court other than in Puerto Rico. The statutes vary in many respects. Some cover all public accountants, while others cover only CPAs; some apply to all accounting sources, while others are restricted in coverage. Some do not apply to criminal cases or bankruptcy proceedings. All are alike in that they protect only communications that are *intended* to be confidential.

The Rules of Ethics of the American Institute of CPAs prohibits the disclosure of confidential client data unless (1) the client consents; (2) the disclosure is necessary to avoid violation of generally accepted accounting principles (GAAP) or auditing standards (GAAS); (3) the disclosure is in response to an enforceable subpoena from a state or federal court (and there is no statute creating an accountant-client privilege); or (4) the disclosure is in response to an inquiry by the Ethics Division or Trial Board of the AICPA or any state CPA or other regulatory agency.

It is interesting to note that a taxpayer may refuse to surrender his or her tax records and documents to a court of law or other investigatory authority on the basis of the Fifth and Fourteenth Amendments' privilege against self-incrimination. However, the privilege does not apply if the taxpayer entrusts the records or documents to a third party such as an accountant, and the third party may not withhold possession on the basis of the taxpayer's privilege.

Finally, it should be pointed out that an accountant *may not* retain client records in order to enforce payment of a fee.

10. An accountant's "working papers" belong to the accountant and not to the client. The American Institute of Certified Public Accountants defines "working papers" in the following language:

> Working papers are the records kept by the independent auditor of the procedures he followed, the tests he performed, the information he obtained, and the conclusions he reached pertinent to his examination. Working papers, accordingly, may include work programs, analyses, memoranda, letters of confirmation and representation, abstracts of company documents, and schedules of commentaries prepared or obtained by the auditor [from Statement of Auditing Standards No. 1, p. 68, AICPA guidelines].

However, an accountant's ownership of "working papers" is basically custodial, and the accountant may not transfer the papers to a third party without the client's consent. Nor may the accountant turn over the papers to a government agency (e.g., the Internal Revenue Service) without the client's consent unless in response to an enforceable subpoena. The accountant has a duty to keep the information contained in the papers confidential. Thus, before selling his or her accounting practice, an accountant must obtain his or her clients' permission to transfer their working papers.

Where a partner in an accounting firm dies, the working papers of the firm belong to the surviving partners (see Chapter 6 for ownership of partnership properties). The working papers of a deceased sole proprietor accountant, on the other hand, must be destroyed once the deceased's estate has no further use for them.

11. Internal accounting and auditing manuals described by an accounting firm are considered "trade secrets" under the law, and a court will require their production only upon a showing by the plaintiff of some actual need or necessity for the manuals in the case before the court. In the case of Rosen v. Dick, CCH Fed.L.Rep. # 94,989 (1975) the court held that the plaintiff had made such a showing, saying:

> The internal accounting and auditing manuals of Andersen are properly termed "trade secrets." Clearly, they are carefully protected internally and are the product of much effort on the part of Andersen. However, in this case, I think a showing of necessity had been made. In order to show fraud, or negligence, even measured against generally accepted accounting practices, plaintiff must establish by a preponderance of the evidence that Andersen's actions did not meet that standard. It will be necessary for plaintiff to be aware of these procedures to conduct a meaningful deposition of the accountants who worked on the audits in question. Evidence that is acquired from those depositions will have a direct bearing on the outcome of the case. I find sufficient need, therefore, to overcome the trade secret barrier, protected, of course, by the proper restrictive order.

12. An accountant who performs auditing services is generally covered by a fidelity bond purchased through a surety company. Usually, an accountant also carries malpractice insurance to cover losses resulting from negligence (e.g., losses resulting from the auditor's negligent failure to discover fraud). In many cases, if the surety company has to pay on the fidelity bond, it will be entitled to reimbursement from the accountant's malpractice insurance. Typically, the surety company has a right to reimbursement for loss resulting from the accountant's dishonest, criminal, or grossly negligent acts but not for loss resulting from his or her ordinary negligence.

Frequently, a client carries insurance against embezzlement within his or her company. If the insurer has to pay for a loss, the insurer will be subrogated to the rights of the insured against the embezzler and any other party who contributed to the loss. Thus, if the insured's accountant negligently failed to discover the embezzlement, the insurer will have a right (the insured's right) to sue the accountant and recover for the negligence.

WHAT IS THE CPA's RESPONSIBILITY TO THIRD PARTIES?

In addition to an accountant's client, many third parties also rely on the accountant's reports, including creditors, suppliers, investors, and regulatory agencies. The accountant's liability to such third parties for negligence or fraud in preparing reports is summarized below.

Negligence

Whether a third party can hold an accountant liable for ordinary negligence depends on the relationship existing between the accountant and the third party. The early rule was that a third party could recover from an accountant for ordinary negligence only if the third party was identified as the primary beneficiary of the audit contract. In other words, the accountant had to know prior to submitting the work that it was being done primarily for the benefit of a particular identified third party.

The modern rule, stated in the case of Ryan v. Kanne, 170 N.W.2d 395 (Iowa 1969), is that a third party can recover from an accountant for ordinary negligence, whether or not the third party was identified as the primary beneficiary of the contract, so long as the accountant knew that the reports were intended for the use or guidance of a third party and the third party was identified before the accountant submitted the reports. In the *Ryan* case, the CPAs had orally guaranteed the accuracy of "accounts payable" within $5,000; the accounts were off by more than $20,000. Though no third party had been identified as the primary beneficiary of the contract, the accountants knew that particular third parties would be using and relying on the report in deciding whether or not to invest in the client's business. Judgment was awarded against the accountants for some $30,000 despite their contention that the third parties were not parties to the contract. The court said:

> When the accountant is aware that the balance sheet to be prepared is to be used by a certain party or parties who will rely thereon in extending credit or in as-

> suming liability for obligations of the party audited, the lack of privity should be no valid defense to claim for damages due to the accountant's negligence. We know of no good reason why accountants should not accept the legal responsibility to known third parties who reasonably rely upon financial statements prepared and submitted by them.

The trend in the law is to carry the accountant's potential liability for ordinary negligence still further and hold him or her responsible even to unidentified third parties so long as: (1) the accountant knew the reports would be used by third parties; (2) the accountant had knowledge of the *class* of users (e.g., banks) and the *type of transaction* (e.g., loans) contemplated; and (3) the third party who suffers the loss is a member of the class and he or she *relied* on the reports in entering into the contemplated transaction.

Fraud

The general rule stated in the case of Ultramares Corp. v. Touche, 255 N.Y. 170, 174 N.E. 441 (1931), is that an accountant is liable for fraudulent or deceitful reports to any and all third parties who rely upon the reports to their loss. The third parties do not have to be intended users, and they do not have to be identified (compare this with the accountant's liability to third parties for ordinary negligence).

As used here, fraud encompasses not only intentional deceit but also reckless misstatement or omission of facts (gross negligence). Fraud based on gross negligence is referred to as "constructive fraud." An example would be certifying financial statements without any basis for a belief in their accuracy. In State Street Trust Co. v. Ernst, 278 N.Y. 104, 15 N.E.2d 416 (1938), the court stated:

> Accountants, however, may be liable to third parties, even where there is lacking deliberate or active fraud. A representation certified as true to the knowledge of the accountants when knowledge there is none, a reckless misstatement, or an opinion based on grounds so flimsy as to lead to the conclusion that there was no genuine belief in its truth, are all sufficient upon which to base liability. A refusal to see the obvious, a failure to investigate the doubtful, if sufficiently gross, may furnish evidence leading to an inference of fraud so as to impose liability for losses suffered by those who rely on the balance sheet. In other words, heedlessness and reckless disregard of consequence may take the place of deliberate intention.
>
> In Ultramares * * * we said with no uncertainty that negligence, if gross, or blindness, even though not equivalent to fraud, was sufficient to sustain an inference of fraud. Our exact words were: "In this connection we are to bear in mind the principle already stated in the course of this opinion that negligence or blindness, even where not equivalent to fraud, is none the less evidence to sustain an inference of fraud. At least this is so if the negligence is gross."

Remember that when fraud or constructive fraud is proved, the accountant is liable to anyone who suffered loss as a result of the fraud.

Right of Contribution

In most states, an accountant who incurs liability to third parties has a right of contribution against any parties who wrongfully helped cause the loss (e.g., the client or other party).

Indication of Responsibility

Where two or more accountants audit portions of the same report, the report must clearly indicate who bears responsibility for which part of the work. And an accountant may not rely on the unaudited data of another accountant where the data could materially affect his or her opinion as to the total financial statement or report. If the accountant does rely on the data, he or she must *disclaim* an opinion or face liability to third parties for making statements without knowledge or in reckless disregard of the truth.

Notification of Inaccuracy

The trend in the law is to hold an accountant responsible for notifying parties known to be relying on his or her completed reports of any information that subsequently comes to light, making the reports inaccurate or misleading.

The Securities Act of 1933

As you know from Chapter 6, the Securities Act of 1933 (the "truth in securities" law) regulates sales of securities to the public in interstate commerce. The primary purpose of the Act is to protect the investing public. Unless an exemption can be found, the Act requires registration of sales of securities with the Securities and Exchange Commission and demands the filing of a registration statement, including a prospectus, containing financial statements certified by an independent public accountant.

Under Section 11 of the Act, an accountant who misrepresents or omits a material fact in a registration statement or prospectus filed under the Act is civilly liable to third parties who purchase the covered securities. The purchaser need not prove fraud, negligence, or reliance in order to recover (except that the purchaser must prove reliance where he or she bought the securities after the issuance of an earnings statement covering a period of at least twelve months following the effective date of the registration statement). However, an accountant can avoid liability under Section 11 by showing "due diligence"—i.e., by showing that, after reasonable investigation, the accountant had reason to believe that the statements contained in the statement were true and complete at the time the registration statement became effective. Note that the accuracy of the statement is measured as of the statement's effective date. This puts a duty of due diligence on the accountant up to the time the registration statement becomes effective. In other words, the accountant has a continuing duty to investigate under the effective date of the registration statement. And if the accountant discovers or learns of new information which materially affects the accuracy of the financial statements filed with the SEC, he or she must file amended statements with the SEC.

A purchaser must bring a civil action under Section 11 within one year after discovering the misrepresentation or omission (or within one year after it should have been discovered), but in no event more than three years after the security was offered to the public. The purchaser's measure of damages (and the accountant's liability) is the difference between the amount paid for the security and its market value at the time of suit. If the purchaser has resold the security, his or her measure of damages will be the difference between the amount paid and the resale price. However, in no case can the measure of damages exceed the price at which the security was offered to the public.

Section 11 does not apply to periodic reports filed with the SEC or annual reports distributed to shareholders.

The Securities Exchange Act of 1934

Under the Securities Exchange Act of 1934, any company having at least 500 shareholders and total assets of $3 million must register its securities with the SEC and furnish the Commission with an annual report, including financial statements certified by an independent public accountant. Several thousand companies provide continuous disclosure under the Act regarding their investment securities.

An accountant may incur liability under Section 18 of the Act which provides civil liability for making any false or misleading statement in any document required to be *filed* under the Act. Liability extends to any person who *relies* on the false statement in purchasing or selling a covered security.

Liability under Section 10(b) and Rule 10b–5 of the Act is much broader. Section 10(b) and Rule 10b–5 provide civil liability for making any false statement or using any other deceptive device in connection with the purchase or sale of any security. These rules apply to all securities, whether listed on a national exchange or traded over-the-counter and regardless of whether they are subject to the filing requirements of the securities laws. However, an accountant is liable under the rules only upon a showing of *willful* or *intentional* conduct designed to deceive or defraud investors (i.e., the accountant must have knowledge of the fraud, which in some cases may include a situation where the accountant acted in reckless disregard of the truth—constructive fraud).

Criminal Liability

A class action is the favored remedy where several third parties are injured by an accountant's fraud, negligence, or securities law violation and there is a common question of law or fact (see Chapter 2).

Accountants have potential criminal liability under both state and federal statutes. Many states have statutes providing criminal penalties for willfully falsifying reports or making false statements in a prospectus. Penalties may include fines up to $10,000 and/or imprisonment of up to five years under the Securities Act of 1933, the Securities Exchange Act of 1934, the Federal False Statements Statute, and the Federal Mail Fraud Statute.

A CPA who aids or assists others in violating the federal laws may be subject to criminal liability for conspiracy to commit an offense against the United States. And an accountant who willfully prepares false tax returns or assists others in evading their taxes is subject to fine and imprisonment under the federal tax laws.

The courts will "infer" that an accountant has acted "willfully" where his or her actions show a reckless disregard for the truth. And compliance with generally accepted accounting principles (GAAP) is not a defense to a criminal charge where the auditor had knowledge of but failed to disclose improper activities of the client that would affect the audited financial statements. An auditor who makes an honest mistake is under a duty to disclose the error when he or she discovers it; failure to disclose may result in both civil and criminal liability (as failure to disclose evidences an intent to mislead).

Cases

Notice and opportunity to be heard must be given before garnishment.

SNIADACH v. FAMILY FINANCE CORP. OF BAY VIEW

Supreme Court of the United States, 1969.
395 U.S. 337, 89 S.Ct. 1820, 23 L.Ed.2d 349.

Mr. Justice DOUGLAS delivered the opinion of the Court.

Respondents instituted a garnishment action against petitioner as defendant and Miller Harris Instrument Co., her employer, as garnishee. The complaint alleged a claim of $420 on a promissory note. The garnishee filed its answer stating it had wages of $63.18 under its control earned by petitioner and unpaid, and that it would pay one-half to petitioner as a subsistence allowance [1] and hold the other half subject to the order of the court.

Petitioner moved that the garnishment proceedings be dismissed for failure to satisfy the due process requirements of the Fourteenth Amendment. The Wisconsin Supreme Court sustained the lower state court in approving the procedure. The case is here on a petition for a writ of certiorari.

The Wisconsin statute gives a plaintiff 10 days in which to serve the summons and complaint on the defendant after service on the garnishee. In this case petitioner was served the same day as the garnishee. She nonetheless claims that the Wisconsin garnishment procedure violates that due process required by the Fourteenth Amendment, in that notice and an opportunity to be heard are not given before * * * seizure of the wages. What happens in Wis-

1. Wis.Stat. § 267.18(2)(a) provides:

When wages or salary are the subject of garnishment action, the garnishee shall pay over to the principal defendant on the date when such wages or salary would normally be payable a subsistence allowance, out of the wages or salary then owing in the sum of $25 in the case of an individual without dependents or $40 in the case of an individual with dependents; but in no event in excess of 50 per cent of the wages or salary owing. Said subsistence allowance shall be applied to the first wages or salary earned in the period subject to said garnishment action.

consin is that the clerk of the court issues the summons at the request of the creditor's lawyer; and it is the latter who by serving the garnishee sets in motion the machinery whereby the wages are frozen. They may, it is true, be unfrozen if the trial of the main suit is ever had and the wage earner wins on the merits. But in the interim the wage earner is deprived of his enjoyment of earned wages without any opportunity to be heard and to tender any defense he may have, whether it be fraud or otherwise.

Such summary procedure may well meet the requirements of due process in extraordinary situations. But in the present case no situation requiring special protection to a state or creditor interest is presented by the facts; nor is the Wisconsin statute narrowly drawn to meet any such unusual condition. * * *

The question is not whether the Wisconsin law is a wise law or unwise law. Our concern is not what philosophy Wisconsin should or should not embrace. We do not sit as a super-legislative body. In this case the sole question is whether there has been a taking of property without that procedural due process that is required by the Fourteenth Amendment. We have dealt over and over again with the question of what constitutes "the right to be heard" within the meaning of procedural due process. * * * [W]e said that the right to be heard "has little reality or worth unless one is informed that the matter is pending and can choose for himself whether to appear or default, acquiesce or contest." In the context of this case the question is whether the interim freezing of the wages without a chance to be heard violates procedural due process.

A procedural rule that may satisfy due process for attachments in general does not necessarily satisfy procedural due process in every case. The fact that a procedure would pass muster under a feudal regime does not mean it gives necessary protection to all property in its modern forms. We deal here with wages—a specialized type of property presenting distinct problems in our economic system. We turn then to the nature of that property and problems of procedural due process.

A prejudgment garnishment of the Wiconsin type is a taking which may impose tremendous hardship on wage earners with families to support. Until a recent Act of Congress [Truth in Lending Law], § 304 of which forbids discharge of employees on the ground that their wages have been garnished, garnishment often meant the loss of a job. Over and beyond that was the great drain on family income. As stated by Congressman Reuss:

> The idea of wage garnishment in advance of judgment, of trustee process, of wage attachment, or whatever it is called is a most inhuman doctrine. It compels the wage earner, trying to keep his family together, to be driven below the poverty level.

Recent investigations of the problem have disclosed the grave injustices made possible by prejudgment garnishment whereby the sole opportunity to be heard comes after the taking. Congressman Sullivan, Chairman of the House Subcommittee on Consumer Affairs who held extensive hearings on this and related problems stated:

> What we know from our study of this problem is that in a vast number of cases the debt is a fraudulent one, saddled on a poor ignorant person who is trapped in an easy credit nightmare, in which he is charged double for something he could not pay for even if the proper price was called for, and then hounded into giving up his pound of flesh, and being fired besides.

The leverage of the creditor on the wage earner is enormous. The creditor tenders not only the original debt but the "collection fees" incurred by his attorneys in the garnishment proceedings:

> The debtor whose wages are tied up by a writ of garnishment, and who is usually in need of money, is in no position to resist demands for collection fees. If the debt is small, the debtor will be under considerable pressure to pay the debt and collection charges in order to

> get his wages back. If the debt is large, he will often sign a new contract of 'payment schedule' which incorporates these additional charges.

Apart from those collateral consequences, it appears that in Wisconsin the statutory exemption granted the wage earner is "generally insufficient to support the debtor for any one week."

The result is that a prejudgment garnishment of the Wisconsin type may as a practical matter drive a wage-earning family to the wall. Where the taking of one's property is so obvious, it needs no extended argument to conclude that absent notice and a prior hearing this prejudgment garnishment procedure violates the fundamental principles of due process.

Reversed.

Does Arizona's Motor Vehicle Act conflict with the federal bankruptcy law?

PEREZ v. CAMPBELL

Supreme Court of the United States, 1971.
402 U.S. 637, 91 S.Ct. 1704, 29 L.Ed.2d 233.

Mr. Justice WHITE delivered the opinion of the Court.

This case raises an important issue concerning the construction of the Supremacy Clause of the Constitution—whether Ariz. Rev.Stat.Ann. § 28–1163(B) (1956), which is part of Arizona's Motor Vehicle Safety Responsibility Act, is invalid under that clause as being in conflict with the mandate of * * * the Bankruptcy Act, providing that receipt of a discharge in bankruptcy fully discharges all but certain specified judgments. * * *

On July 8, 1965, petitioner Adolfo Perez, driving a car registered in his name, was involved in an automobile accident in Tucson, Arizona. The Perez automobile was not covered by liability insurance at the time of the collision. The driver of the second car was the minor daughter of Leonard Pinkerton, and in September 1966 the Pinkertons sued Mr. and Mrs. Perez in state court for personal injuries and property damage sustained in the accident. On October 31, 1967, the petitioners confessed judgment in this suit, and a judgment order was entered against them on November 8, 1967, for $2,425.98 plus court costs.

Mr. and Mrs. Perez each filed a voluntary petition in bankruptcy in Federal District Court on November 6, 1967. Each of them duly scheduled the judgment debt to the Pinkertons. The District Court entered orders on July 8, 1968, discharging both Mr. and Mrs. Perez from all debts and claims provable against their estates, including the Pinkerton judgment.

During the pendency of the bankruptcy proceedings, the provisions of the Arizona Motor Vehicle Safety Responsibility Act came into play. * * * § 28–1142 provides that within 60 days of the receipt of an accident report the Superintendent of the Motor Vehicle Division of the Highway Department shall suspend the driver's license of the operator and the registration of the owner of a car involved in an accident "unless such operator or owner or both shall deposit security in a sum which is sufficient in the judgment of the superintendent to satisfy any judgment or judgments for damages resulting from the accident as may be recovered against the operator or owner." * * *

Article 4 of the Arizona Act, which includes the only provision at issue here, deals with suspension of licenses and registrations for nonpayment of judgments. Interestingly, it is only when the judgment debtor in an automobile accident lawsuit—usually an owner-operator like Mr. Perez—fails to respond to a judgment entered against him that he must overcome two hurdles in order to regain his driving privileges. Section 28–1161, the first section of Art. 4, requires the state court clerk or judge, when a judgment has remained unsatisfied for 60 days after entry, to forward a certified copy of the judgment to the superintendent. This was done in the present case, and on March 13,

1968, Mr. and Mrs. Perez were served with notice that their drivers' licenses and registration were suspended pursuant to § 28–1162(A). Under other provisions of Art. 4, such suspension is to continue until the judgment is paid, and § 28–1163(B) specifically provides that "[a] discharge in bankruptcy following the rendering of any such judgment shall not relieve the judgment debtor from any of the requirements of this article." In addition to requiring satisfaction of the judgment debt, § 28–1163(A) provides that the license and registration "shall remain suspended and shall not be renewed, nor shall any license or registration be thereafter issued in the name of the person * * * until the person gives proof of financial responsibility" for a future period. Again, the validity of this limited requirement that some drivers post evidence of financial responsibility for the future in order to regain driving privileges is not questioned here. Nor is the broader issue of whether a State may require proof of financial responsibility as a precondition for granting driving privileges to anyone before us for decision. What is at issue here is the power of a State to include as part of this comprehensive enactment designed to secure compensation for automobile accident victims a section providing that a discharge in bankruptcy of the automobile accident tort judgment shall have no effect on the judgment debtor's obligation to repay the judgment creditor, at least insofar as such repayment may be enforced by the withholding of driving privileges by the State. It was that question, among others, which petitioners raised after suspension of their licenses and registration by filing a complaint in Federal District Court seeking declaratory and injunctive relief and requesting a three-judge court. They asserted several constitutional violations, and also alleged that § 28–1163(B) was in direct conflict with the Bankruptcy Act and was thus violative of the Supremacy Clause of the Constitution. In support of their complaint, Mr. and Mrs. Perez filed affidavits stating that the suspension of their licenses and registration worked both physical and financial hardship upon them and their children. * * *

* * * [T]he construction of the Bankruptcy Act is * * * clear. This Court on numerous occasions has stated that "[o]ne of the primary purposes of the bankruptcy act" is to give debtors "a new opportunity in life and a clear field for future effort, unhampered by the pressure and discouragement of preëxisting debt." There can be no doubt that Congress intended this "new opportunity" to include freedom from most kinds of preexisting tort judgments.

* * * [W]e proceed immediately to the constitutional question whether a state statute that protects judgment creditors from "financially irresponsible persons" is in conflict with a federal statute that gives discharged debtors a new start "unhampered by the pressure and discouragement of preëxisting debt." As early as Gibbons v. Ogden, 9 Wheat. 1 (1824), Chief Justice Marshall stated the governing principle—that "acts of the State Legislatures * * * [which] *interfere with,* or are contrary to the laws of Congress, made in pursuance of the constitution," are invalid under the Supremacy Clause. * * *

From the foregoing, we think it clear that § 28–1163(B) of the Arizona Safety Responsibility Act is constitutionally invalid. The judgment of the Court of Appeals is reversed and the case is remanded for further proceedings consistent with this opinion.

It is so ordered.

Was the debt fraudulent or dischargeable?

IN RE COKKINIAS

United States Bankruptcy Court,
D. Massachusetts, 1983.
28 B.R. 304.

GLENNON, Bankruptcy Judge

Before me is a complaint to determine the dischargeability of a debt filed by Daniel Barch. This action arises from a loan transaction entered into in July of 1981. * * *

I find the facts to be as follows. The debtor, John P. Cokkinias ("Cokkinias") and the plaintiff, Daniel J. Barch ("Barch") met sometime in the middle of 1980. They had no business dealings with each other. They were purely casual friends, i.e., they socialized at the Y.M.C.A., played golf together, etc. Both men were knowledgeable businessmen; Cokkinias had been in the real estate business for forty years while Barch was the owner of Compudata, a data processing service.

On the evening of July 8, 1981, Cokkinias telephoned Barch, at home, and stated he had a serious problem he had to discuss with Barch. Barch replied he would be in his office shortly and Cokkinias should telephone him there. Soon thereafter, Cokkinias called Barch and stated he was in immediate need of money which, if loaned, could not be repaid for approximately six months. Without asking the reason for the demand, and without asking for any security in return, Barch replied that he would leave a $5,000 check with one of his employees which Cokkinias could pick up that same evening. Cokkinias picked up the check and cashed it the next day. The check was drawn on the account of Compudata, the company owned by Barch.

About two weeks later, Barch called Cokkinias and stated that upon the advice of his accountant, Cokkinias would need to sign some type of papers in recognition of the loan. Barch's accountant was afraid that absent such papers, the Internal Revenue Service might deem the transaction a dividend with adverse tax consequences to Compudata. Cokkinias agreed to later meet Barch at the offices of Leonard Michelman ("Michelman"), Barch's attorney. Cokkinias arrived at Michelman's office before Barch. Michelman showed Cokkinias a document labelled "NOTE". The word "MORTGAGE" preceeding "NOTE" was crossed out. Where the type of security pledged was to be typed in, the word "NONE" appeared. According to the terms of the "NOTE," $5,000 was payable on demand and due September 1, 1981, with interest at the rate of 15 percent per annum. At the bottom of the note, below the signature lines, the names John P. Cokkinias and Mary Gail B. Cokkinias (the debtor's wife) were typed in. The note was dated July 21, 1981. Neither the debtor, nor his wife, signed this document.

* * *

In September 1981, Cokkinias met Barch and stated he would sign an agreement to pay $200 per month until the balance (including interest) was paid. He had yet to make any payments in satisfaction of the loan. A document captioned "Sales Agreement", dated September 1, 1981, was signed by both parties. Under the terms of this agreement, Cokkinias was to begin making payments of $200 on October 1, 1981. Thereafter, $200 was due on the first of every month until the principal amount of $5,000, plus 15 percent annual interest were paid down. Cokkinias made only one payment. On October 5, 1981, Cokkinias filed his Chapter 7 petition.

* * *

11 U.S.C. § 523(a) provides:

> A discharge under section 727, 1141 or 1328(b) of this title does not discharge an individual debtor from any debt—* * *
>
> (2) for obtaining money, property, services, or an extension, renewal, or refinance of credit, by—
>
> (A) false pretenses, a false representation or actual fraud, other than a statement respecting the debtor's or an insider's financial condition; or (B) use of a statement in writing—
>
> (i) that is materially false;
>
> (ii) respecting the debtor's or an insider's financial condition;
>
> (iii) on which the creditor to whom the debtor is liable for obtaining such money, property, services, credit reasonably relied; and
>
> (iv) that the debtor caused to be made or published with intent to deceive. * * *

This court has recently concluded that the requirements which must be met in order for a debt to be declared nondischargeable pursuant to § 523(a)(2)(A) are:

> (1) a false representation by the debtor;
> (2) known to be false at the time it was made;
> (3) made with the intention and purpose of deceiving the creditor;
> (4) which was reasonably relied upon by the creditor;
> (5) which resulted in loss or damage to the creditor as a result of the false representation. * * *

For a debt to be declared nondischargeable under this subsection, *each* of the five elements set forth above must be proven. For, it is well settled that the exceptions to discharge are to be strictly construed in favor of the debtor so as to afford the honest debtor the fresh start protection promised by the Bankruptcy Code. * * *

In the instant action, the five requirements have not been satisfied. At the time of the loan transaction, the debtor did not knowingly make a false statement to Barch and therefore, there could be no statement upon which Barch relied. I recognize that even a misrepresentation of an intent to pay in the future may be sufficient grounds to satisfy, in part, § 523(a)(2)(A). However, it appears that on the evening of the loan transaction, Cokkinias did not misrepresent his intention to pay. Nor did he misrepresent his intention to provide security to Barch for the loan. That evening is the critical point in time at which the representation referred to in § 523(a)(2)(A) is to be examined. By his own admission, Barch testified the reasons he requested the debtor to sign a document evidencing the loan was to satisfy his accountant, and possibly the Internal Revenue Service. The fact that the debtor "said something about equity agreement, or something", (Hearing Transcript January 4, 1982 at 18) at the time the loan transaction was made, is insufficient in terms of satisfying § 523(a)(2)(A). The elements which must be shown to have existed, as set forth above, are not met without a showing of specific facts.

The Court is not now passing on whether *subsequent* to the loan transaction the debtor may have made a false statement which caused § 523(a)(2)(A) to be operable. Such a determination is irrelevant. The law is clear on this point. "[I]f the property was obtained prior to the making of any false representation, subsequent misrepresentation will have no effect upon the discharge of the debt . . . The plaintiff must prove that the claimed fraud existed at the *inception* of the debt and that [he] relied upon it." * * *

The creditor, as an experienced businessman, was not without the knowledge or ability to secure protection for himself at the time the loan was made. Admittedly, it is not often that a businessman would lend $5,000 to a casual friend without receiving any type of security in return for the loan. However, it is not for the Court to intervene on behalf of Barch and now offer him an escape from his own mistake. "[A p]laintiff cannot conduct business without due care and then maintain that as a result of deception it extended credit." * * * The discharge provided by 11 U.S.C. § 727 is to be granted to an honest debtor filing for protection under Chapter 7 unless the debtor is guilty of the conduct set forth in the § 523 exceptions.

* * *

Therefore, in accordance with the above:

Judgment shall enter in favor of the debtor; the loan of July 8, 1981 is dischargeable;

* * *

So Ordered.

An alleged concealment of assets.

IN RE MARTIN

United States Court of Appeals,
Seventh Circuit, 1983.
698 F.2d 883.

CUDAHY, Circuit Judge

This appeal arises from bankruptcy proceedings initiated in 1980 by appellee Martin seeking relief as a voluntary debtor under Title 11 of the United States Code. Appellants First Federated Life Insurance Co. and Dennis E. Quaid, the largest creditor and the trustee of the estate, respectively, filed complaints in the bankruptcy proceedings seeking a denial of discharge because of an alleged concealment of assets. Trustee Quaid also sought to have the disputed assets conveyed to Quaid, as trustee. The bankruptcy acourt * * * entered judgment for the appellees. The bankruptcy court subsequently granted appellee Ronald Martin a discharge in bankruptcy and this appeal followed. We reverse and remand the judgment below.

The resolution of this case essentially rests on whether or not the appellee Ronald Martin had an interest in a condominium, occupied by Ronald Martin, but asserted to be the property of his father, Alex Martin.[2]

At trial, the facts were developed as follows: Ronald Martin testified that, in the aftermath of a divorce in 1975, he sought to locate a place to live which would be a good investment for either him or his father. In early 1976, the property in question, a condominium located in Lincolnwood, Illinois, was purchased for $67,500 of which $15,000 was a cash down payment and the balance the proceeds of a mortgage loan. The note for the mortgage loan was signed by the debtor's parents, Alex and Josephine Martin. * * * The bankruptcy court found that Ronald Martin lived in the condominium, paid all mortgage, maintenance, and insurance charges, voted as a condominium owner, and deducted the interest payments on his own federal income tax returns.

The ultimate source of the $15,000 used to make the down payment on the condominium has been a matter of some dispute. The bankruptcy court found that the down payment was made in three installments from Alex Martin's checking account. The source of the funds in the checking account was, in turn, documented to be a money market fund account owned by Ronald Martin. At this point, the further source of the funds becomes more confusing. The debtor asserts that the funds in the money market fund account were given to him by his father, Alex Martin. Alex Martin claimed that he had given the $15,000 in cash to his son for the purpose of purchasing the condominium. This transfer took place approximately three months prior to the actual purchase of the condominium. No explanation was given as to why Alex transferred the money in cash so long before the purchase. The appellants assert that the funds used to buy the condominium were, in fact, Ronald's, that the story concerning the $15,000 cash transfer was not credible, and that there was, therefore, a secret agreement between the debtor and his father for the father to hold the property in his own name and that of his wife as nominees for Ronald.

The bankruptcy court found that there was no credible proof that the $15,000 which was used to make the down payment was not entirely Ronald's. The court further noted that (referring to the debtor and his father): "Seldom has this Court observed witnesses whose credibility was lower. It was not so much that they appeared to be lying as it was that they seemed to be indifferent to the truth."

There is no suggestion that Ronald Martin was insolvent at the time of these transactions. The bankruptcy court also found that Ronald Martin had an income at that time of over $100,000 a year; his father's income, on the other hand, was found to be only approximately $6,000 a year.

It is well settled that findings of fact made in a bankruptcy proceeding will not be set aside by a reviewing court unless "clearly erroneous." * * * This is a well-established rule of law rooted on the reasonable thesis that a trial judge is best able to appre-

2. It has apparently been generally assumed by the parties that the property in question has a value substantially in excess of the outstanding mortgage debt upon it, and that if the trustee can establish ownership of it he will be able to generate substantial funds for the benefit of creditors.

ciate the nuances of demeanor and evidentiary content that go into determinations of the credibility of witnesses. The facts of this case illustrate the merit of this rule. Due to a lack of documentary evidence, the events and transactions involved here had to be reconstructed largely from oral evidence. The bankruptcy judge, in the course of testimony by the debtor, his father, and other witnesses, was in a unique position to form judgments about what actually may, or may not, have happened. The bankruptcy judge's assessments of credibility, which are critical to the outcome of the case, are based upon personal observation and evaluation of the witnesses which are impossible for us to replicate on appeal. Thus, in a case such as this, we are extremely reluctant to disturb the findings of fact of the bankruptcy judge and would do so only if we thought them clearly erroneous. Therefore, we must conclude that the source of the funds used to buy the condominium was indeed Ronald Martin.

We think, however, that the legal principles applied to the facts as found were incorrect, and that this must change the result. There are at least two independent grounds upon which a discharge must be denied to this debtor. First, Section 727a(5) of the Bankruptcy Code provides that the court should grant the debtor a discharge, unless "the debtor has failed to explain satisfactorily . . . any loss of assets or deficiency of assets to meet the debtor's liabilities." * * * Section 727a(5) is broadly drawn and clearly gives a court broad power to decline to grant a discharge in bankruptcy where the debtor does not adequately explain a shortgage, loss, or disappearance of assets.

* * *

In *Baum*, a case involving a bankrupt real estate broker and contractor, the court upheld the bankruptcy referee's denial of a discharge on the basis that the debtor had failed to adequately explain the shrinkage in his assets in the 21-month period prior to filing for bankrupcty. This court stated that * * * the bankrupt's explanation "must consist of more than . . . [a] vague, indefinite, and uncorroborated hodgepodge of financial transactions." 359 F.2d at 814. This principle seems to us to be directly applicable to the case at hand.

* * *

Accepting as we do the bankruptcy court's finding that the money used to buy the condominium was Ronald Martin's, there has been a "loss or deficiency" of substantial assets unaccompanied by any explanation from the debtor why such an unusual transaction occurred. In fact, the debtor's explanation, such as it is, seems to dig him deeper into a hole. Martin has persisted in maintaining that he received $15,000 cash from his father. This persistent effort at explanation makes it all the more difficult to accept the bankruptcy court's speculation that the condominium could have been intended as a gift from Ronald to his father. In any event, the creditors satisfied their burden of proof under section 727a(5), and we hold that the bankruptcy court should not have granted a discharge given the debtor's failure to satisfy his obligation under that section.

In addition, even if this were not a case within the ambit of section 727a(5), it would be controlled by 11 U.S.C. § 727a(3), under which a continuing concealment of assets is grounds for the denial of a discharge. In fact, the claim most strongly pressed by the appellants has been that the purchase, and subsequent ownership status, of the condominium constituted such a continuing concealment of the debtor's assets. Thus, even if we did not find section 727a(5) controlling, section 727a(3) would dictate a remand to the bankruptcy court.

* * *

The creditors here have proved a transfer of funds by the debtor, with a continuous subsequent use by the debtor of the property acquired with these funds. In *In re Kauffman*, 675 F.2d 127 (7th Cir. 1981), this court found a very similar set of circumstances sufficient to constitute proof of a continuing concealment and denied the debtor in that case a discharge. 675 F.2d at 128. The court stated: "The transfer of title with attendant circumstances indicating that the bankrupt continues to use the property is sufficient to constitute a concealment." * * * The creditor's proof as to the debtor's actions, while perhaps insufficient to satisfy the ultimate burden of persuasion in the fact of a credible explanation by the debtor, is sufficient in this case to shift to the debtor an obligation to come forward with such an explanation of his actions. Unless and until the debtor could provide such a credible explanation, a discharge should have been denied under the continuing concealment provisions of section 727a(3).

* * *

It is clearly unsatisfactory to grant the debtor a discharge in a case such as this, where the debtor "stonewalls" the creditor and refuses to credibly explain to the court his puzzling or suspect transactions. The speculation of the bankruptcy judge or the creditors as to what may actually have been occurring is not an adequate substitute for a believable explanation by the debtor. The evidence in this case which could satisfactorily explain the events in question is far more likely to lie in the hands of a debtor than of the creditor. The debtor presumably knows why what is usually a simple matter (either the purchase of a condominium or an intrafamily gift) has taken on such a byzantine character. To the extent that the debtor can explain these events he has an obligation to come forward and do so—he cannot abuse the bankruptcy process by obfuscating the true nature of his affairs and then refusing to provide a credible explanation.

* * *

We therefore reverse the order of September 21, 1981, granting the debtor a discharge. We *Remand* the case for further proceedings not inconsistent with this opinion, including, in the discretion of the bankruptcy court, the reopening of the matter for receipt of additional evidence.

Chapter 11 reorganization.

IN RE CONCRETE PIPE MACHINERY CO.

United States Bankruptcy Court,
D. Iowa, 1983.
28 B.R. 537.

THINNES, Bankruptcy Judge

Concrete Pipe Machinery Company is currently a Debtor in Possession in a Chapter 11 Bankruptcy proceeding filed with this Court on July 12, 1982, and is seeking Court approval to reject the collective bargaining agreement it has with the General Drivers, Warehousemen and Helpers Union Local #383 of Sioux City, Iowa. Concrete Pipe contends that rehabilitation would be severely hampered or perhaps impossible if it must continue to abide by the terms of the collective bargaining agreement. Additionally, Concrete Pipe is investigating the possibilities of selling the company. None of the potential buyers, however, are willing to bid on the company with the collective bargaining agreement in place.

During its period of greatest activity, Concrete Pipe employed well over 100 persons. Now the average is approximately two per week with a maximum of six. If there is any hope to restore some of the lost jobs, the collective bargaining agreement must be rejected by Concrete Pipe to insure a chance for rehabilitation, or to facilitate a sale of the company to a financially sound purchaser. For this reason alone, the balance of equities favors rejection of the collective bargaining agreement. * * * Additionally, the Court notes that Congress has made a policy decision not to insulate collective bargaining agreements from the general provisions of Bankruptcy Code § 365. * * * Therefore, collective bargaining agreements should receive no more protection than other executory contracts which may be rejected or assumed. * * * Finally, the record indicates that there is a compelling need to reject this contract, with little or no concomitant adverse effect to the employees. * * *

By rejecting the collective bargaining agreement, the Debtor would have, at the very least, a greatly improved chance of reorganization. Conversely, the debtor will almost surely be forced to liquidate if not allowed to reject the agreement. The employees covered by the collective bargaining agreement stand to lose very little. Over 95 percent have already lost their jobs, and the few remaining workers may not be employed for very long. There is also a potential benefit for the employees in that a rehabilitated debtor could provide jobs for many of those laid off. Under any of the tests discussed above, the Debtor should be allowed to reject the collective bargaining agreement and increase its potential for reorganization.

* * *

[So ordered.]

Lease or sale?

IN RE TULSA PORT WAREHOUSE CO., INC.

United States Court of Appeals,
Tenth Circuit, 1982.
690 F.2d 809.

SEYMOUR, Circuit Judge

We are once again called upon to consider a question proven to be a prime source of litigation in the field of commercial law: when is a purported lease in fact a security agreement subject to the requirements of Article 9 of the Uniform Commercial Code (UCC)?

In this case, Tulsa Port Warehouse Company (bankrupt or lessee) entered into four automobile "Non-Maintenance Lease Agreements" with defendant Chuck Naiman Buick Company (lessor), which were subsequently assigned to defendant General Motors Acceptance Corporation (GMAC). Following the bankruptcty of the lessee, the trustee in bankruptcy and GMAC engaged in the classic battle to determine the priority of their interests in the vehicles. It is undisputed that GMAC did not comply with the requirements of Article 9 relating to the perfection of a security interest. If the leases are in fact security agreements, GMAC's interest in the automobiles is subordinate to that of the trustee. * * * The bankruptcy court resolved the issue in favor of the trustee, and the district court affirmed that decision.

Under the open-end leases [1] at issue, which are identical in all pertinent respects, the bankrupt leased the automobiles for commercial or business use for either a twenty-four or thirty-six month period. The monthly charge was determined as follows: first, the agreed depreciated value of the vehicle at the end of the lease term was deducted from the original value; second, to this remainder, designated "total amount of fixed monthly rentals for the lease term to be credited against original value," was added the item "total amount of fixed monthly rentals *not* to be credited against original value."

* * *

The lease agreements did not further identify this latter amount or indicate how it was calculated.[2] Finally, the sum of these two items was divided by the number of

1. The lessor uses closed-end and open-end leases. Under the closed end leases, the lessee returns the vehicle to the lessor at the end of the lease term and the obligations of both come to an end. Under the open-end lease, however, the relationship between the lessor and lessee does not end. Rather, it involves the sale of the vehicle and an adjustment between the lessor and lessee based on the sales price, as more fully described hereinafter.

2. The bankruptcy court that this item "euphemistically describes ordinary interest without disclosure as to its rate." The district court also found the amount to constitute interest.

months in the lease term to produce the amount due monthly.[3]

The open-end leases contain no option to purchase. Each lease includes termination and default provisions under which the lessee is obligated at termination to return the vehicle to the lessor. At that time, the lessor is required to dispose of the vehicle at wholesale in a commercially reasonable manner. If the amount realized at this sale exceeds the agreed depreciated value, the lessee receives the surplus. If the sale amount is less than the agreed depreciated value, the lessee is liable to the lessor for the deficit.

In Oklahoma, "[w]hether a lease is intended as security is to be determined by the facts of each case." This court has recently set out the analytical framework for determining whether an agreement is a true lease or a secured transaction. * * * We pointed out that when a lease does not contain a purchase option, the lease "will still be deemed one intended as security if the facts otherwise expose economic realities tending to confirm that a secured transfer of ownership is afoot."

In considering the persistent lease versus secured transfer question, the courts have identified a number of significant factors tending to suggest that a sale has occurred: (1) whether the lease creates an equity in the lessee, * * * (2) whether the lessee is obligated to provide comprehensive insurance in favor of the lessor, * * * (3) whether the lessee pays sales tax, * * * (4) whether the lessee pays all taxes, maintenance, and repairs; * * * and (5) whether the lessee holds the lessor harmless, * * * or assumes the risk of loss. * * *

With respect to the creation of an equity interest in the lessee in this case, the bankruptcy court and the district judge approved the discussion in Bill Swad Leasing Co. v. Stikes (In re Tillery), 571 F.2d 1361 (5th Cir. 1978). In Tillery, the court considered an open-end lease agreement substantially similar to the ones before us and concluded that "[t]he termination formula recognizes the equity of the 'Lessee,' in the vehicle because he is required to bear the loss or receive the gain from its wholesale disposition." Although defendants argue vigorously on appeal that Tillery was wrongly decided, we agree with its analysis on this issue.

Moreover, many of the other factors tending to indicate that a lease is in reality a secured transaction are present in this case. The lessee is required to obtain comprehensive insurance in favor of the lessor; pay sales tax and all other licenses, registration, and title fees; pay for all maintenance and repairs; and indemnify the lessor against all loss. As a practicial matter, the lessee holds all the incidents of ownership except bare legal title.

Defendants conceded at oral argument that there is no economic difference to the lessor between the lease arrangement here and a secured transfer of property. Under the lease, the lessor is assured of receiving the entire original value of the vehicle plus an amount that realistically must be viewed as interest. The fact that a portion of the original value may be paid by a third party wholesale purchaser after termination of the lease is of no economic significance to the lessor, particularly when the surplus or deficit from this sale is borne by the lessee. We agree with the trial judge's conclusion that "[t]he practical effect of this arrangement is

3. For example, under one of the 36 month leases for a Buick Regal, the monthly rental was computed as follows:

1.	Original value of vehicle	$7,798.00
2.	Agreed depreciated value at end of least term	3,450.00
3.	Total amount of fixed monthly rentals for the full base term to be credited against original value	4,348.00
4.	Total amount of fixed monthly rentals *not* to be credited against original value	1,730.96
5.	Fixed monthly rental charges	6,087.96
6.	Sales or use tax	243.00
7.	Total monthly rental charge	$6,321.96
8.	Monthly rental payments	$ 175.61

the same as if lessee purchased the car, then sold it two or three years later and used the proceeds to pay off the note."

In sum, we conclude that the agreements were transfers of property subject to a security interest. One purpose of Article 9 of the UCC is to provide notice of such prior interests to third parties dealing with personal property. To promote that end, buyer and seller should be prevented "from masquerading their secured installment sale as a 'lease,' thereby placing it beyond the reach of UCC provisions governing secured transactions."

Judgment affirmed.

The purchaser at the "bulk sale" received an affidavit of "no creditors."

ADRIAN TABIN CORP. v. CLIMAX BOUTIQUE, INC.

Supreme Court, Appellate Division, Second Department, 1972.
40 A.D.2d 146, 338 N.Y.S.2d 59.

SHAPIRO, Justice

The novel issue posed by this appeal is whether a purchaser at a bulk sale, who receives an affidavit of "no creditors" is nevertheless under a duty to make careful inquiry as to the possible existence of creditors, of whom he has no actual knowledge. The plaintiff, a creditor of the seller, was not notified of the sale and hence seeks an adjudication that, as to it, the sale is void.

Defendant L.D.J. Dresses, Inc. (hereinafter referred to as "the seller") operated a dress shop in Jamaica, Queens. The seller was indebted to the plaintiff, a garment supplier, at the time it sold its business in bulk to defendant Paul Warman, who in turn sold the business to defendant Climax Boutique, Inc., in which he was a principal. (Warman and Climax will hereafter be referred to as "the purchasers".)

Prior to the consummation of the bulk sale the purchasers received an affidavit from Joseph Marino, the president of the seller, which stated that the seller was not indebted to anyone and had no creditors. The purchasers caused a lien search to be conducted and determined that there were no outstanding liens.

At the trial, the purchasers' attorney testified as follows:

> I knew * * * the attorney for the seller for at least fifteen years, knew him well, had seen him in court maybe once a month for fifteen years so knew his voice well. In fact I had matters with him too from the past. At the closing * * * [the seller's attorney] and I spoke on the telephone and I said, "What about the general creditors? you have told me already there are none but I think I should have some necessary affidavit to cover." Then he said, "Well, to begin with," he said, "I am going to give you a bill of sale sworn to by the seller and notarized by me as an attorney that there are absolutely no creditors. He has shown me checks that he had sent to all his creditors because I checked it with him in order to close out the business for the end of the year and I am satisfied that there are none and as an attorney I would never let my client sign such a affidavit if I thought there were, and there are no creditors."

The parties stipulated that the purchasers had no knowledge of the plaintiff prior to the sale.

In setting aside the sale the Special Term noted that the purchasers had not requested an examination of the seller's books and had not questioned the source of the garments involved in the sale. It held that the purchasers had not made careful inquiry of the seller as to existing creditors and that, failing such careful inquiry, the purchasers had acted at their peril. The appeal is from the ensuing judgment. * * *

A bulk sale is ineffective against creditors of the seller unless the purchaser requires the seller to furnish a list (signed and sworn to or affirmed) of his existing creditors (Uniform Commercial Code, § 6–104) and notifies such creditors of the impending sale (Uniform Commercial Code, §§ 6–105, 6–107). * * *

* * * Subdivision (3) of section 6–104 of the Uniform Commercial Code provides that "responsibility for the completeness and

accuracy of the list of creditors rests on the transferor, and the transfer is not rendered ineffective by errors or omissions therein *unless the transferee is shown to have had knowledge*" (emphasis supplied). Section 1–201 of the Uniform Commercial Code, the general definitions section of that code, provides, in subdivision (25), that "a person 'knows' or has 'knowledge' of a fact when he has actual knowledge of it." It is therefore apparent that a bulk sale may not be set aside as to creditors not listed by the seller in the affidavit requested by the purchaser, of whom the purchaser had no actual knowledge. As the purchasers concededly had no actual knowledge of the plaintiff, the possibility of whose existence as a creditor was denied by the seller in an affidavit (the purchasers having no reason to disbelieve the truthfulness of the affidavit), the bulk sale may not be set aside as to the plaintiff.

We note, in passing, that even were the purchasers under a duty to make careful inquiry, they complied with that responsibility in this case by making a lien search and by making inquiry of the seller's attorney, who represented that all creditors had been paid and that he had seen the checks sent out to them in payment of the seller's obligations.

The judgment should be reversed.

* * *

Nay committed suicide and left a note describing the accounts as "spurious."

ERNST & ERNST v. HOCHFELDER

Supreme Court of the United States, 1976.
425 U.S. 185, 96 S.Ct. 1375, 47 L.Ed.2d 668.

Mr. Justice POWELL delivered the opinion of the Court.

The issue in this case is whether an action for civil damages may lie under § 10(b) of the Securities Exchange Act of 1934 and Securities and Exchange Commission Rule 10b–5, 17 CFR § 240.10b–5, in the absence of an allegation of intent to deceive, manipulate, or defraud on the part of the defendant.

Petitioner, Ernst & Ernst, is an accounting firm. From 1946 through 1967 it was retained by First Securities Company of Chicago (First Securities), a small brokerage firm and member of the Midwest Stock Exchange and of the National Association of Securities Dealers, to perform periodic audits of the firm's books and records. In connection with these audits Ernst & Ernst prepared for filing with the Securities and Exchange Commission (the Commission) the annual reports required of First Securities under § 17(a) of the 1934 Act, 15 U.S.C. § 78q(a).[1] It also prepared for First Securities responses to the financial questionnaires of the Midwest Stock Exchange (the Exchange).

Respondents were customers of First Securities who invested in a fraudulent securities scheme perpetrated by Leston B. Nay, president of the firm and owner of 92% of its stock. Nay induced the respondents to invest funds in "escrow" accounts that he represented would yield a high rate of return. Respondents did so from 1942 through 1966, with the majority of the transactions occurring in the 1950's. In fact, there were no escrow accounts as Nay converted respondents' funds to his own use immediately upon receipt. These transactions were not in the customary form of dealings between First Securities and its customers. The respondents drew their personal checks payable to Nay or a designated bank for his account. No such escrow accounts were reflected on the books and records of First Securities, and none was shown on its periodic accounting to respondents in connection with their other investments. Nor were they included in First Securities' filings with the Commission or the Exchange.

This fraud came to light in 1968 when Nay committed suicide, leaving a note that described First Securities as bankrupt and

1. * * * During the period relevant here, Commission Rule 17a–5, 17 CFR § 240.17a–5, required that First Securities file an annual report of its financial condition that included a certificate stating "clearly the opinion of the accountant with respect to the financial statement covered by the certificate and the accounting principles and practices reflected therein."

the escrow accounts as "spurious." Respondents subsequently filed this action for damages against Ernst & Ernst in the United States District Court for the Northern District of Illinois under § 10(b) of the 1934 Act. The complaint charged that Nay's escrow scheme violated § 10(b) and Commission Rule 10b–5, and that Ernst & Ernst had "aided and abetted" Nay's violations by its "failure" to conduct proper audits of First Securities. As revealed through discovery, respondents' cause of action rested on a theory of negligent nonfeasance. The premise was that Ernst & Ernst had failed to utilize "appropriate auditing procedures" in its audits of First Securities, thereby failing to discover internal practices of the firm said to prevent an effective audit. The practice principally relied on was Nay's rule that only he could open mail addressed to him at First Securities or addressed to First Securities to his attention, even if it arrived in his absence. Respondents contended that if Ernst & Ernst had conducted a proper audit, it would have discovered this "mail rule." The existence of the rule then would have been disclosed in reports to the Exchange and to the Commission by Ernst & Ernst as an irregular procedure that prevented an effective audit. This would have led to an investigation of Nay that would have revealed the fraudulent scheme. Respondents specifically disclaimed the existence of fraud or intentional misconduct on the part of Ernst & Ernst.[5]

After extensive discovery the District Court granted Ernst & Ernst's motion for summary judgment and dismissed the action. The court rejected Ernst & Ernst's contention that a cause of action for aiding and abetting a securities fraud could not be maintained under § 10(b) and Rule 10b–5 merely on allegations of negligence. It concluded, however, that there was no genuine issue of material fact with respect to whether Ernst & Ernst had conducted its audits in accordance with generally accepted auditing standards.

The Court of Appeals for the Seventh Circuit reversed and remanded, holding that one who breaches a duty of inquiry and disclosure owed another is liable in damages for aiding and abetting a third party's violation of Rule 10b–5 if the fraud would have been discovered or prevented but for the breach. 503 F.2d 1100 (1974). The court reasoned that Ernst & Ernst had a common-law and statutory duty of inquiry into the adequacy of First Securities' internal control system because it had contracted to audit First Securities and to prepare for filing with the Commission the annual report of its financial condition required under § 17 of the 1934 Act and Rule 17a–5, 17 CFR § 240.17a–5. The Court further reasoned that respondents were beneficiaries of the statutory duty to inquire and the related duty to disclose any material irregularities that were discovered. * * *

We granted certiorari to resolve the question whether a private cause of action for damages will lie under § 10(b) and Rule 10b–5 in the absence of any allegation of "scienter"—intent to deceive, manipulate, or defraud.[12] We conclude that it will not and therefore we reverse.

5. In their response to interrogatories in the District Court respondents conceded that they did "not accuse Ernst & Ernst of deliberate, intentional fraud," merely with "inexcusable negligence." App. 81.

12. Although the verbal formulations of the standard to be applied have varied, several courts of appeals have held in substance that negligence alone is sufficient for civil liability under § 10(b) and Rule 10b–5. See, e.g., White v. Abrams, 495 F.2d 724, 730 (CA9 1974) ("flexible duty" standard); Myzel v. Fields, 386 F.2d 718, 735 (CA8 1967), cert. denied, 390 U.S. 951, 88 S.Ct. 1043, 19 L.Ed.2d 1143 (1968) (negligence sufficient); Kohler v. Kohler Co., 319 F.2d 634 (CA7 1963) (knowledge not required). Other courts of appeals have held that some type of scienter—i.e., intent to defraud, reckless disregard for the truth, or knowing use of some practice to defraud—is necessary in such an action. See, e.g., Clegg v. Conk, 507 F.2d 1351, 1361–1362 (CA10 1974), cert. denied, 422 U.S. 1007, 95 S.Ct. 2628, 45 L.Ed.2d 669 (1975) (an element of "scienter or conscious fault"); Lanza v. Drexel & Co., 479 F.2d 1277, 1306 (CA2 1973) ("willful or reckless disregard" of the truth). But few of the decisions announcing that some form of negligence suffices for civil liability under § 10(b) and Rule 10b–5 actually have involved only negligent conduct.

In this opinion the term "scienter" refers to a mental state embracing intent to deceive, manipulate, or defraud. In certain areas of the law recklessness is considered to be a form of intentional conduct for pur-

Federal regulation of transactions in securities emerged as part of the aftermath of the market crash in 1929. The Securities Act of 1933 was designed to provide investors with full disclosure of material information concerning public offerings of securities in commerce, to protect investors against fraud and, through the imposition of specified civil liabilities, to promote ethical standards of honesty and fair dealing. The 1934 Act was intended principally to protect investors against manipulation of stock prices through regulation of transactions upon securities exchanges and in over-the-counter markets, and to impose regular reporting requirements on companies whose stock is listed on national securities exchanges. Although the Acts contain numerous carefully drawn express civil remedies and criminal penalties, Congress recognized that efficient regulation of securities trading could not be accomplished under a rigid statutory program. As part of the 1934 Act Congress created the Commission, which is provided with an arsenal of flexible enforcement powers.

Section 10 of the 1934 Act makes it "unlawful for any person * * * (b) [t]o use or employ, in connection with the purchase or sale of any security * * * any manipulative or deceptive device or contrivance in contravention of such rules and regulations as the Commission may prescribe as necessary or appropriate in the public interest or for the protection of investors." 15 U.S.C.A. § 78j. In 1942, acting pursuant to the power conferred by § 10(b), the Commission promulgated Rule 10b–5, which now provides:

> Employment of manipulative and deceptive devices.
>
> It shall be unlawful for any person, directly or indirectly, by the use of any means or instrumentality of interstate commerce, or of the mails, or of any facility of any national securities exchange,
>
> (1) To employ any device, scheme, or artifice to defraud,
>
> (2) To make any untrue statement of a material fact or to omit to state a material fact necessary in order to make the statements made, in the light of the circumstances under which they were made, not misleading, or
>
> (3) To engage in any act, practice, or course of business which operates or would operate as a fraud or deceit upon any person, in connection with the purchase or sale of any security."

Although § 10(b) does not by its terms create an express civil remedy for its violation, and there is no indication that Congress, or the Commission when adopting Rule 10b–5, contemplated such a remedy, the existence of a private cause of action for violations of the statute and the rule is now well established. During the 30-year period since a private cause of action was first implied under § 10(b) and Rule 10b–5, a substantial body of case law and commentary has developed as to its elements. Courts and commentators long have differed with regard to whether scienter is a necessary element of such a cause of action, or whether negligent conduct alone is sufficient. In addressing this question, we turn first to the language of § 10(b), for "[t]he starting point in every case involving construction of a statute is the language itself."

Section 10(b) makes unlawful the use or employment of "any manipulative or deceptive device or contrivance" in contravention of Commission rules. The words "manipulative or deceptive" used in conjunction with "device or contrivance" strongly suggest that § 10(b) was intended to proscribe knowing or intentional misconduct.

In its *amicus curiae* brief, however, the Commission contends that nothing in the

poses of imposing liability for some act. We need not address here the question whether, in some circumstances, reckless behavior is sufficient for civil liability under § 10(b) and Rule 10b–5.

Since this case concerns an action for damages we also need not consider the question whether scienter is a necessary element in an action for injunctive relief under § 10(b) and Rule 10b–5. Cf. SEC v. Capital Gains Research Bureau, Inc., 375 U.S. 180, 84 S.Ct. 275, 11 L.Ed.2d 237 (1963).

language "manipulative or deceptive device or contrivance" limits its operation to knowing or intentional practices. In support of its view, the Commission cites the overall congressional purpose in the 1933 and 1934 Acts to protect investors against false and deceptive practices that might injure them. The Commission then reasons that since the "effect" upon investors of given conduct is the same regardless of whether the conduct is negligent or intentional, Congress must have intended to bar all such practices and not just those done knowingly or intentionally. The logic of this effect-oriented approach would impose liability for wholly faultless conduct where such conduct results in harm to investors, a result the Commission would be unlikely to support. But apart from where its logic might lead, the Commission would add a gloss to the operative language of the statute quite different from its commonly accepted meaning. The argument simply ignores the use of the words "manipulative," "device," and "contrivance," terms that make unmistakable a congressional intent to proscribe a type of conduct quite different from negligence. Use of the word "manipulative" is especially significant. It is and was virtually a term of art when used in connection with securities markets. It connotes intentional or willful conduct designed to deceive or defraud investors by controlling or artificially affecting the price of securities.

* * *

The 1933 and 1934 Acts constitute interrelated components of the federal regulatory scheme governing transactions in securities. * * * "[T]he interdependence of the various sections of the securities laws is certainly a relevant factor in any interpretation of the language Congress has chosen * * *." Recognizing this, respondents and the Commission contrast § 10(b) to other sections of the Acts to support their contention that civil liability may be imposed upon proof of negligent conduct. We think they misconceive the significance of the other provisions of the Acts.

* * *

The structure of the Acts does not support the Commission's argument. In each instance that Congress created express civil liability in favor of purchasers or sellers of securities it clearly specified whether recovery was to be premised on knowing or intentional conduct, negligence, or entirely innocent mistake. For example, § 11 of the 1933 Act unambiguously creates a private action for damages when a registration statement includes untrue statements of material facts or fails to state material facts necessary to make the statements therein not misleading. Within the limits specified by § 11(e), the issuer of the securities is held absolutely liable for any damages resulting from such misstatement or omission. But experts such as accountants who have prepared portions of the registration statement are accorded a "due diligence" defense. In effect, this is a negligence standard. An expert may avoid civil liability with respect to the portions of the registration statement for which he was responsible by showing that "after reasonable investigation" he had "reasonable ground[s] to believe" that the statements for which he was responsible were true and there was no omission of a material fact.[26] § 11(b)(3)(B)(i). See, e.g., Escott v. BarChris Const. Corp., 283 F.Supp. 643, 697–703 (S.D. N.Y.1968). The express recognition of a cause of action premised on negligent behavior in § 11 stands in sharp contrast to the language of § 10(b), and significantly undercuts the Commission's argument.

We also consider it significant that each of the express civil remedies in the 1933 Act allowing recovery for negligent conduct is subject to significant procedural restrictions not applicable under § 10(b). Section 11(e) of the 1933 Act, for example, authorizes the court to require a plaintiff bringing a suit

26. Other individuals who sign the registration statement, directors of the issuer, and the underwriter of the securities similarly are accorded a complete defense against civil liability based on the exercise of reasonable investigation and a reasonable belief that the registration statement was not misleading.

under § 11, § 12(2), or § 15 thereof to post a bond for costs, including attorneys' fees and in specified circumstances to assess costs at the conclusion of the litigation. Section 13 specifies a statute of limitations of one year from the time the violation was or should have been discovered, in no event to exceed three years from the time of offer or sale, applicable to actions brought under § 11, § 12(2), or § 15. * * * We think these procedural limitations indicate that the judicially created private damage remedy under § 10(b)—which has no comparable restrictions [29]—cannot be extended, consistently with the intent of Congress, to actions premised on negligent wrongdoing. Such extension would allow causes of action covered by § 11, § 12(2), and § 15 to be brought instead under § 10(b) and thereby nullify the effectiveness of the carefully drawn procedural restrictions on these express actions. We would be unwilling to bring about this result absent substantial support in the legislative history, and there is none.[30]

We have addressed, to this point, primarily the language and history of § 10(b). The Commission contends, however, that subsections (2) and (3) of Rule 10b–5 are cast in language which—if standing alone—could encompass both intentional and negligent behavior. These subsections respectively provide that it is unlawful "[t]o make any untrue statement of a material fact or to omit to state a material fact necessary in order to make the statements made, in light of the circumstances under which they were made, not misleading * * *" and "to engage in any act, practice, or course of business which operates or would operate as a fraud or deceit upon any person. * * *" Viewed in isolation the language of subsection (2), and arguably that of subsection (3), could be read as proscribing, respectively, any type of material misstatement or omission, and any course of conduct, that has the effect of defrauding investors, whether the wrongdoing was intentional or not.

We note first that such a reading cannot be harmonized with the administrative history of the rule, a history making clear that when the Commission adopted the rule it was intended to apply only to activities that involved scienter. More importantly, Rule 10b–5 was adopted pursuant to authority granted the Commission under § 10(b). The rulemaking power granted to an administrative agency charged with the administration of a federal statute is not the power to make law. Rather, it is " 'the power to adopt regulations to carry into effect the will of Congress as expressed by the statute.' " Thus, despite the broad view of the Rule advanced by the Commission in this case, its scope cannot exceed the power granted the Commission by Congress under § 10(b). When a statute speaks so specifically in terms of manipulation and deception, and of implementing devices and contrivances—the commonly understood terminology of intentional wrongdoing—and when its history reflects no more expansive intent, we are quite unwilling to extend the scope of the statute to negligent conduct.

* * *

The judgment of the Court of Appeals is

Reversed.

29. Since no statute of limitations is provided for civil actions under § 10(b), the law of limitations of the forum state is followed as in other cases of judicially implied remedies. See Holmberg v. Armbrecht, 327 U.S. 392, 395, 66 S.Ct. 582, 584, 90 L.Ed. 743, 746 (1946), and cases cited therein. Although it is not always certain, which state statute of limitations should be followed, such statutes of limitations usually are longer than the period provided under § 13.

30. Section 18 of the 1934 Act creates a private cause of action against persons, such as accountants, who "make or cause to be made" materially misleading statements in reports or other documents filed with the Commission. 15 U.S.C.A. § 78r. We need not consider the question whether a cause of action may be maintained under § 10(b) on the basis of actions that would constitute a violation of § 18. Under § 18 liability extends to persons who, in reliance on such statements, purchased or sold a security whose price was affected by the statements. Liability is limited, however, in the important respect that the defendant is accorded the defense that he acted in "good faith and had no knowledge that such statement was false or misleading."

Review Questions

1. Does Article 9 of the UCC cover the use of any kind of property for security purposes? Are sales or lease arrangements ever considered Article 9 security transactions? What are the requirements for attachment of a security interest under Article 9? When does a security agreement have to be in writing? What two provisions are often used in written security agreements to facilitate the financing of inventory and accounts receivable? Does taking a security interest for an antecedent debt constitute giving value under Article 9? To have "rights in the collateral" is it necessary to have title? Explain your answers.

2. What is the dominant feature of a mortgage? Must a mortgage be in writing? Does the mortgagee have right to possession? May the mortgagee's debt be paid off early? What is the preferred remedy of foreclosure of a mortgage? What is the statutory right of redemption? What is the position of a purchaser of mortgaged land as far as the mortgage debt? Does suretyship usually involve the use of property as security? Is an oral suretyship promise enforceable? Must the creditor try to collect from the principal debtor before going against the surety? How does subrogation apply to suretyship? If a surety pays, does he or she have a right to collect back from the principal debtor? What specific remedies are provided to creditors under the Bulk Sales law? When does this law apply? What are the four requirements? If they are not met, what may existing creditors do? Within what period of time? Explain your answers.

3. In bankruptcy does a debtor lose all of his or her property? Are all of his or her debts discharged? Will a debtor ever be denied a discharge in bankruptcy? Will a discharge ever be revoked? Do tax liens have priority over other liens? Are all general creditors treated the same or are some paid before others? How does Chapter 11 differ from Chapter 13 of the Bankruptcy Act? Explain your answers.

4. What is the difference between general, governmental, and lien creditors? What are the three ways in which a lien may be created? May a creditor ever affect a debtor's property prior to obtaining a judgment against the debtor? When does a levy become an effective lien? How can a debtor terminate an attachment? What is the difference between prejudment garnishment and prejudgment receivership? Do prejudgment remedies violate due process of law requirements? Are all of a person's earnings subject to garnishment? Does a judgment create a lien on the debtor's property? Why do states exempt certain properties of a debtor from a sale to satisfy debts? Do the exemptions apply to all creditors? Explain your answers.

5. What is the key word in describing the role of the accountant? How does the SEC define an auditor's duty? What is meant by artful, creative, and salami accounting? Upon what two legal theories might a client sue his or her accountant? What is the accountant's standard of care? Is an accountant strictly liable for not discovering fraud? When might an accountant be liable for punitive damages? How does an accountant avoid liability for "unaudited" financial statements? What is an accountant's responsibility regarding tax work? Does an accountant have a privilege like a lawyer? When may an accountant disclose confidential data? Who owns working papers used by an accountant? What is the difference in liability of an accountant to third parties based on negligence versus fraud? What special liabilities might result to accountants because of the securities laws? Explain your answers.

6. What is the effect of a fraudulent conveyance? What circumstances indicate there has been a fraudulent conveyance? What is the disadvantage of an assignment for the benefit of creditors? Does this same disadvantage apply to a composition of creditors? How does an extension differ from a composition? What two things does straight bankruptcy accomplish? What conditions must be met for an involuntary bankruptcy? Are there any restrictions on the allowance of creditors' claims? Does the trustee in bankruptcy have any power to avoid previous transfers of assets made by a bankrupt? Explain your answers.

7. What three positions may a creditor end up in when attempting to obtain a security interest under Article 9? Which is best? How is it achieved? What is the basic rule regarding priorities of Article 9 secured creditors? When does the trustee in bankruptcy take priority over a secured creditor under Article 9? Has the trustee any other basis for attacking Article 9 creditors? May an Article 9 creditor ever repossess the collateral? What alternatives are available to such a creditor? If force is used by the Article 9 creditor, does the debtor have any remedy? Is there an Article 9 right of redemption? Explain your answers.

8. Define the following terms: after-judgment garnishment, chattel paper, condition of defeasance, constructive fraud, continuation statement, deed of trust, execution, exoneration, Fair Debt Collection Practices Act, floating lien, GAAP, GAAS, homestead exemption, individual with regular income, malicious and wrongful attachment, perfected security interest, preferential transfer, purchase money mortgage, state wage earner receivership, strong-arm clause.

Problems

1. a. Carl Henry is driving along Wiltshire Road in his sportscar when Jenny Metcalfe negligently collides with his car; Jenny is driving an old pickup truck at the time. Carl suffers minor injuries in the accident, and the damage to his car is estimated at $1,195. Carl consults a lawyer and decides to sue Jenny for $3,500. However, before bringing suit, Carl learns that Jenny is planning to leave town to escape paying him: her plans include picking up her two-week paycheck in the amount of $280 from Connor Medical Supply; withdrawing her $2,000 in savings from First State Bank; loading up her pickup with her few personal belongings and leaving the state. What action, if any, can Carl take immediately to protect his interests?

Assume that Jenny has no plans to leave town. Carl sues her for negligence and obtains a judgment in the amount of $3,500. When Jenny refuses to pay the judgment, Carl seeks your advice. How can Carl enforce the judgment?

b. Harvey Fine has been forced into straight bankruptcy by his creditors. The court appoints Mona Carswell to serve as trustee.

1. Can Mona set aside any of the following prebankruptcy transfers made by Harvey? Explain fully.
   a. Eight months before the involuntary bankruptcy petition was filed, Harvey repaid a $20,000 personal loan to his brother, Morton. The loan, which was unsecured, was originally made to enable Harvey to go into business on his own. At the time of repayment, Morton knew that Harvey's liabilities exceeded his assets; it was for this reason that Morton insisted upon repayment in full.
   b. Two months before the involuntary petition was filed, Harvey paid off $3,000 owing on open account to Francine McCrea, a business supplier and personal friend of Harvey's. At the time of repayment, Harvey's liabilities exceeded his assets, but Francine did not know this.
   c. Seven months prior to filing of the petition, Harvey gave his mountain cabin to his daughter, Sheila. The deed stated that the transfer was "bona fide and honestly and truly made." After the transfer, Harvey continued to use the cabin on weekends. At the time of the transfer to Sheila, Harvey's liabilities exceeded his assets, but Sheila did not know this.
2. In the bankruptcy proceeding, several of Harvey's creditors object to two claims which have been filed with the court. Will the following claims be allowed? Explain fully.
   a. Nancy Green claims $13,000 in rent owing under a lease of property (office space) to Harvey: $1,000 is for past due rent at the time of filing of the petition, and $12,000 represents the $500/month rent due for the two years remaining on the lease.
   b. Mitch Conaway claims $15,000 for personal injuries suffered in an automobile accident caused by Harvey's negligence. The claim has never been reduced to judgment.
3. Which of the following of Harvey's debts will be discharged in bankruptcy? Explain.
   a. Back taxes owing for the five-year period prior to filing of the petition.
   b. $6,000 in unpaid alimony and child support.
   c. $2,500 that Harvey embezzled three years ago when he worked as treasurer of Sebert Corporation.
   d. A $3,000 judgment against Harvey for negligent driving.
   e. A $5,000 unsecured contract debt for the purchase of office machinery.
   f. A $1,500 claim for damages resulting from Harvey's intentional assault and battery upon the claimant.
4. Suppose that six months after Harvey's discharge in bankruptcy, Mona discovers that Harvey failed to disclose the existence and

whereabouts of certain substantial properties belonging to him. What is Mona likely to do?

5. Suppose that during the straight bankruptcy proceeding, it becomes clear that Harvey's sole proprietorship operation could be successful if provided with sound management and supervision and that Harvey could pay off his debts with future earnings from the operation. Discuss any viable alternative Harvey has under federal bankruptcy law to going through with the straight bankruptcy.

2. a. On March 1, Marla Mitchell obtains a $10,000 civil judgment (arising out of a negligence action) against Sid Smith. On April 1, Ben Barker loans Sid $55,000 to enable him to purchase a two-bedroom rental property. Sid executes a mortgage on the property in favor of Ben, with the mortgage evidenced by a negotiable installment note. Ben does not record the mortgage. Sid subsequently executes a second mortgage against the property in favor of Jim Zell in return for a $10,000 loan. Jim, who has no knowledge of the first mortgage, immediately records his mortgage. As between Marla and Ben, who has priority with respect to the property in the event that Sid fails to pay them? As between Ben and Jim? As between Marla and Jim? Explain your answers fully. Assuming Sid defaults on the mortgage agreements, what foreclosure remedies are available to Ben and Jim? What rights, if any, does Sid have following foreclosure?

b. By the terms of its security agreement with Fisher Furniture Company, First State Bank has a security interest in "all inventory now or hereafter acquired by Fisher Furniture Company." The security agreement further states that "the security interest herein created shall also secure all other indebtedness, obligations, and liabilities of Fisher Furniture to First State Bank, now existing and hereafter arising, including future advances." On August 5, First State Bank files a financing statement covering the interest. The statement purports to cover Fisher's "inventory": it makes no mention of "inventory hereafter acquired," nor does it refer to "future advances," On August 20, Pete Seely purchases a five-piece set of livingroom furniture from the Fisher Company for $2,500. What type of security interest does First State Bank have in Fisher's inventory? Explain fully. Does the fact that the financing statement makes no mention of "inventory hereafter acquired" or "future advances" impair the Bank's security agreement in any way? Explain. Does Pete Seely take the furniture subject to the Bank's security interest? Explain.

c. Dana Smith purchases a refrigerator-freezer on credit from Apple Appliance, Inc. The Apple Company takes a security interest in the refrigerator-freezer but does not file any financing statement regarding the interest. Dana uses the appliance for a few weeks in her home and then sells it to her neighbor Fred Stoner for $450 cash. Fred, who plans to use the appliance in his own home, is unaware of Apple's security interest. Does Fred take the set subject to Apple's security interest? Explain.

d. On September 10, Jane Dolan agrees to loan David Jackson $5,000 on September 20, the loan to be secured by David's collection of valuable coins; by the terms of the written security agreement, David is to keep possession of the coins. Jane files a financing statement covering the security interest on September 11. On September 15, David borrows $6,000 from Bill Bosley; the same day, David tranfers possession of the coins to Bill as security for the loan. On September 20 Jane loans David $5,000. As between Jane and Bill, who has priority with respect to the coins? Explain fully.

3. The MIB Corporation has been petitioned into bankruptcy. The petition was filed February 1, 1977. Among its creditors are the following:

a. *Viscount Machine, Inc.*
Viscount put an $8,600 deposit down on certain heavy machinery to be purchased from MIB. MIB was petitioned into bankruptcy, and the machinery (which was never identified to the contract) was not delivered.

b. *Second National County Bank*
Second National holds a first mortgage on the real estate where MIB has its principal plant, office, and warehouse. The mortgage is for $280,750 representing the unpaid balance due on the original $350,000 mortgage. The property was sold for $290,000, its fair market value as established by bids received by the trustee. The mortgage was taken out two years ago and duly filed and recorded at that time.

c. *Marvel Supply Company*
Marvel, a major supplier of parts, delivered $10,000 worth of parts to MIB on January 17, 1977. Upon delivery Marvel received 50 percent cash and insisted on the balance by the end of the month. When the balance was not paid, Marvel obtained from MIB a duly executed financing statement which Marvel filed on February 2, 1977.

d. *Sixty-one wage earners*
Sixty machine operators employed in MIB's plant and warehouse were not paid for the final month. Each has a claim for $400 which equals $24,000 in total. Also, the Executive Assistant to the president of the Corporation was not paid for the final month and has a claim for $2,400 against MIB.

e. *Federal, state, and local taxing authorities*
MIB owes $6,800 in back taxes.

f. *Administration costs*
These total $12,000.

g. *Various general creditors*
Excluding items A through F above, general creditors have allowable claims of $1,614,900. The bankrupt's total estate consists of $850,000 of assets in addition to the real estate described in B.

Required: Answer the following, setting forth reasons for any conclusions stated.

1. Discuss the legal implications and the resulting rights of each of the persons or entities described above in A through G as a result of the facts given and the application of bankruptcy law to them.

2. What is the bankruptcy dividend (percentage on the dollar) that each general creditor will receive? Show calculations in good form.

Source: Modified from CPA Exam, May 1977, #7(a) to reflect 1979 Bankruptcy Act.

4. a. A voluntary bankruptcy proceeding is available to
   1. All debtors provided they are insolvent.
   2. Debtors only if the overwhelming preponderance of creditors have not petitioned for and obtained a receivership pursuant to state law.
   3. Corporations only if a reorganization has been attempted and failed.
   4. Most debtors even if they are not insolvent.

b. An involuntary petition in bankruptcy
   1. Will be denied if a majority of creditors in amount and in number have agreed to a common law composition agreement.
   2. Can be filed by creditors only once in a seven-year period.
   3. May be successfully opposed by the debtor by proof that the debtor is solvent in the bankruptcy sense.
   4. If not contested will result in the entry of an order for relief by the bankruptcy judge.

Source: CPA Exam, May 1983, #1(21), (22).

c. The Bankruptcy Reform Act of 1978 provides that certain allowed expenses and claims are entitled to a priority. Which of the following is *not* entitled to such a priority?
   1. Claims of governmental units for taxes.
   2. Wage claims, but to a limited extent.
   3. Rents payable within the four months preceding bankruptcy, but to a limited extent.
   4. Unsecured claims for contributions to employee benefit plans, but to a limited extent.

Source: CPA Exam, May 1982, #1(20).

5. a. An otherwise valid petition for involuntary bankruptcy has been filed against Mohawk Corporation. This will be sufficient to obtain an order for relief against Mohawk provided
   1. Mohawk is generally not paying debts as they become due.
   2. A custodian has been appointed to take charge of substantially all of Mohawk's debts within four months of filing.
   3. The creditor or creditors can establish that Mohawk is bankrupt in the bankruptcy sense.
   4. The majority of creditors join in the filing if there are more than two creditors involved.

Source: CPA Exam, November 1982, #1(16).

b. If a secured party's claim exceeds the value of the collateral of a bankrupt, he will be paid the total amount realized from the sale of the security and will
   1. Not have any claim for the balance.
   2. Become a general creditor for the balance.
   3. Retain a secured creditor status for the balance.

4. Be paid the balance only after all general creditors are paid.

Source: CPA Exam, May 1981, #1(43).

c. On January 10, 1978, Edwards gave Cantrell a mortgage on his office building to secure a past due $40,000 obligation which he owed Cantrell. Cantrell promptly recorded the mortgage. On March 15, 1978, a petition in bankruptcy was filed against Edwards. Simpson, the trustee in bankruptcy, desires to prevent Cantrell from qualifying as a secured creditor. In seeking to set aside the mortgage, which of the following statements is correct?
   1. The mortgage cannot be set aside since it is a real property mortgage and recorded.
   2. Even if the mortgage is set aside, Cantrell has a priority in respect to the office building.
   3. The mortgage can only be set aside if the mortgage conveyance was fraudulent.
   4. The mortgage can be set aside if it was taken with knowledge of the fact that Edwards was insolvent in the bankruptcy sense.

Source: CPA Exam, May 1978, #1(25).

6. a. Attachment and perfection will occur simultaneously when
   1. The security agreement so provides.
   2. There is a purchase money security interest taken in inventory.
   3. Attachment is by possession.
   4. The goods are sold on consignment.

b. Perfection of a security interest by a creditor provides added protection against other parties in the event the debtor does not pay his debts. Which of the following is not affected by perfection of a security interest?
   1. A buyer in the ordinary course of business.
   2. A subsequent personal injury judgment creditor.
   3. The trustee in a bankruptcy proceeding.
   4. Other prospective creditors of the debtor.

c. On November 10, 1982, Cutter, a dealer, purchased 100 lawnmowers. This comprised Cutter's entire inventory and was financed under an agreement with Town Bank which gave the bank a security interest in all lawnmowers on the premises, all future acquired lawnmowers, and the proceeds of sales. On November 15, 1982, Town Bank filed a financing statement that adequately identified the collateral. On December 20, 1982, Cutter sold one lawnmower to Wills for family use and five lawnmowers to Black for its gardening business. Which of the following is correct?
   1. The security interest may not cover after-acquired property even if the parties so agree.
   2. The lawnmower sold to Wills would not ordinarily continue to be subject to the security interest.
   3. The lawnmowers sold to Black would ordinarily continue to be subject to the security interest.
   4. The security interest does not include the proceeds from the sale of the lawnmowers to Black.

d. Fogel purchased a TV set for $900 from Hamilton Appliance Store. Hamilton took a promissory note signed by Fogel and a security interest for the $800 balance due on the set. It was Hamilton's policy not to file a financing statement until the purchaser defaulted. Fogel obtained a loan of $500 from Reliable Finance which took and recorded a security interest in the set. A month later, Fogel defaulted on several loans outstanding, and one of his creditors, Harp, obtained a judgment against Fogel which was properly recorded. After making several payments, Fogel defaulted on a payment due to Hamilton, who then recorded a financing statement subsequent to Reliable's filing and the entry of the Harp judgment. Subsequently, at a garage sale, Fogel sold the set for $300 to Mobray. Which of the parties has the priority claim to the set?
   1. Reliable.
   2. Hamilton.
   3. Harp.
   4. Mobray.

Source: CPA Exam, May 1983, #1(47), (48), (49), (51).

e. Norwood Furniture, Inc., found that its credit rating was such that it was unable to obtain a line of unsecured credit. National Bank indicated that it would be willing to supply funds based upon a "pledge" of Norwood's furniture inventory which was located in two warehouses. The bank would receive notes and bearer negotiable warehouse receipts covering the merchandise securing the loans. An independent warehouseman was to have complete control over the areas in the warehouse set aside as field warehousing facilities. The Hastings Field Warehousing Corporation was selected to serve as the independent warehouseman. It was to retain keys to the posted area in which the inventory was contained. Negotiable bearer warehouse receipts were issued to Norwood when it delivered the merchandise to Hastings. The receipts were then delivered by Norwood to National to secure the loans which were made at 80 percent of the market value of the furniture indicated on the receipts. Upon occasion, Norwood would take temporary possession of the furniture for the purpose of packaging it, surrendering the warehouse receipt for this limited purpose. As orders were filled out of the field warehouse inventory, the requisite receipt would be relinquished by National, the merchandise obtained by Norwood, and other items substituted with a new receipt issued.

   Required: Answer the following, setting forth reasons for any conclusions stated.

   1. Based upon the facts given, is the field warehousing arrangement valid?
   2. When does a security interest in the negotiable warehouse receipts attach?
   3. What, if anything, is necessary to perfect a security interest in goods covered by negotiable warehouse receipts?
   4. What are the dangers, if any, that National faces by relinquishing the warehouse receipts to Norwood?

7. a. Prior to a bulk transfer, the creditors of the transferor are entitled to
1. Examine the books and records of the transferee in order to determine creditworthiness.
2. Require that the transferee post an adequate surety bond guaranteeing proper performance.
3. Prevent the proposed bulk transfer from taking place if the creditors will meet the terms offered by the transferee in the transfer agreement.
4. Notice at least ten days before the transferee takes possession of the goods or pays for them, whichever occurs first.

b. Johnstone purchased all the inventory, machinery, and fixtures of Lomax. Johnstone failed to comply with the requirements of the Bulk Transfers Article of the Uniform Commercial Code. Dark subsequently purchased some of the used machinery from Johnstone. Dark
1. Must give notice to Lomax's creditors who sold the machinery to Lomax.
2. Will take free of the claims of Lomax's creditors irrespective of Dark's good faith or notice since the creditors must seek recourse from Johnstone exclusively.
3. Will have a voidable title even if he took in good faith and without notice.
4. Takes subject to any title defect if he had notice of Johnstone's failure to comply.

c. Which of the following transfers by a transferor is subject to the Bulk Transfers Article of the Uniform Commercial Code?
1. The transfer of property to creditors to provide security for performance of an obligation.
2. The transfer to a buyer of some equipment used in the business along with the major part of the inventories, materials, and supplies.
3. A transfer made to a vendor in settlement of a security interest.
4. A transfer made to a creditor pursuant to settlement of a judicial lien.

Source: CPA Exam, May 1983, #1(28), (29), (30).

8. a. Recordation of a real property mortgage
1. Is required to validate the rights of the parties to the mortgage.
2. Will not be effective if improperly filed even if the party claiming superior title had actual notice of its existence.
3. Perfects the interest of the mortgagee against subsequent bona fide purchasers for value.
4. Must be filed in the recordation office where the mortgagee's principal place of business is located.

b. Moch sold her farm to Watkins and took back a purchase money mortgage on the farm. Moch failed to record the mortgage. Moch's mortgage will be valid against all of the following parties **except**
1. The heirs or estate of Watkins.
2. A subsequent mortgagee who took a second mortgage since he had heard there was a prior mortgage.

3. A subsequent bona fide purchaser from Watkins.
4. A friend of Watkins to whom the farm was given as a gift and who took without knowledge of the mortgage.

c. Peters defaulted on a purchase money mortgage held by Fairmont Realty. Fairmont's attempts to obtain payment have been futile, and the mortgage payments are several months in arrears. Consequently, Fairmont decided to resort to its rights against the property. Fairmont foreclosed on the mortgage. Peters has all of the following rights *except*
   1. To remain in possession as long as his equity in the property exceeds the amount of debt.
   2. An equity of redemption.
   3. To refinance the mortgage with another lender and repay the original mortgage.
   4. A statutory right of redemption.

Source: CPA Exam, May 1983, #1(58), (59), (60).

d. Golden sold his moving and warehouse business, including all the personal and real property used therein, to Clark Van Lines, Inc. The real property was encumbered by a duly recorded $300,000 first mortgage upon which Golden was personally liable. Clark acquired the property subject to the mortgage but did not assume the mortgage. Two years later, when the outstanding mortgage was $260,000, Clark decided to abandon the business location because it had become unprofitable and the value of the real property was less than the outstanding mortgage. Clark moved to another location and refused to pay the installments due on the mortgage. What is the legal status of the parties in regard to the mortgage?
   1. Clark took the real property free of the mortgage.
   2. Clark breached its contract with Golden when it abandoned the location and defaulted on the mortgage.
   3. Golden must satisfy the mortgage debt in the event that foreclosure yields an amount less than the unpaid balance.
   4. If Golden pays off the mortgage, he will be able to successfully sue Clark because Golden is subrogated to the mortgagee's rights against Clark.

Source: CPA Exam, May 1981, #1(53).

e. Newfeld purchased a parcel of land in New City from Stoneham Realty. His plan was to construct a professional building and parking lot on the property. In order to do this, Newfeld needed financing and approached the New City National Bank for a first mortgage loan. The proposal looked good to New City National, and they loaned Newfeld $200,000 to help finance the venture. Newfeld engaged builders who accomplished the construction of the building and the parking lot. After two years of ownership and operation of the building and lot, Newfeld decided to sell. Robbins agreed to purchase Newfeld's interest but indicated she was not willing to assume the existing mortgage. It was finally agreed that the entire property would be transferred to Robbins subject to the New City National's first mortgage. Robbins subsequently defaulted.

Required: Answer the following, setting forth reasons for any conclusions stated.

1. Who is expected to make the payments during the remaining life of the mortgage?
2. What rights does New City Bank have against Robbins and Newfeld upon default?
3. Assume that the bank has to resort to foreclosure and that after the debt, interest, and all expenses have been paid, there is $2,000 remaining. Who is entitled to this amount?

Source: CPA Exam, May 1980, #4(c).

9. a. A distinction between a surety and a co-surety is that only one is entitled to
   1. Compensation.
   2. Subrogation.
   3. Contribution.
   4. Notice upon default.

b. A release of a co-surety by the creditor
   1. Will have *no* effect on the obligation of the other co-surety.
   2. Will release the other co-surety entirely.
   3. Will release the other co-surety to the extent that his right to contribution has been adversely affected.
   4. Need *not* be a binding release in order to affect the rights of the parties.

c. The right of subrogation
   1. May permit the surety to assert rights he otherwise could *not* assert.
   2. Is denied in bankruptcy.
   3. Arises only to the extent that it is provided in the surety agreement.
   4. Can *not* be asserted by a co-surety unless he includes all other co-sureties.

Source: CPA Exam, May 1983, #1(25), (26), (27).

d. Hardaway Lending, Inc., had a four-year $800,000 callable loan to Superior Metals, Inc., outstanding. The loan was callable at the end of each year upon Hardaway's giving sixty days written notice. Two-and-one-half years remained of the four years. Hardaway reviewed the loan and decided that Superior Metals was no longer a prime lending risk, and it therefore decided to call the loan. The required written notice was sent to and received by Superior sixty days prior to the expiration of the second year. Merriweather, Superior's chief executive officer and principal shareholder, requested Hardaway to continue the loan at least for another year. Hardaway agreed, provided that an acceptable commercial surety would guarantee $400,000 of the loan and Merriweather would personally guarantee repayment in full. These conditions were satisfied, and the loan was permitted to continue.

The following year the loan was called, and Superior defaulted. Hardaway released the commercial surety but retained its rights against Merriweather and demanded that Merriweather pay the full amount of the loan. Merriweather refused, asserting the following:

- There was no consideration for his promise. The loan was already outstanding, and he personally received nothing.
- Hardaway must first proceed against Superior before it can collect from Merriweather.
- Hardaway had released the commercial surety, thereby releasing Merriweather.

Required: Answer the following, setting forth reasons for any conclusions stated.

Discuss the validity of each of Merriweather's assertions.

Source: CPA Exam, November 1980, #3(a).

10. a. Whitlow & Company is a brokerage firm registered under the Securities Exchange Act of 1934. The Act requires such a brokerge firm to file audited financial statements with the SEC annually. Mitchell & Moss, Whitlow's CPAs, performed the annual audit for the year ended December 31, 1979, and rendered an unqualified opinion which was filed with the SEC along with Whitlow's financial statements. During 1979 Charles, the president of Whitlow & Company, engaged in a huge embezzlement scheme that eventually bankrupted the firm. As a result substantial losses were suffered by customers and shareholders of Whitlow & Company, including Thaxton who had recently purchased several shares of stock of Whitlow & Company after reviewing the company's 1979 audit report. Mitchell & Moss's audit was deficient; if they had complied with generally accepted auditing standards, the embezzlement would have been discovered. However, Mitchell & Moss had no knowledge of the embezzlement nor could their conduct be categorized as reckless.

Required: Answer the following, setting forth reasons for any conclusions stated.

What liability to Thaxton, if any, does Mitchell & Moss have under the Securities Exchange Act of 1934?

b. Jackson is a sophisticated investor. As such, she was initially a member of a small group who was going to participate in a private placement of $1 million of common stock of Clarion Corporation. Numerous meetings were held among management and the investor group. Detailed financial and other information was supplied to the participants. Upon the eve of completion of the placement it was aborted when one major investor withdrew. Clarion then decided to offer $2.5 million of Clarion common stock to the public pursuant to the registration requirements of the Securities Act of 1933. Jackson subscribed to $300,000 of the Clarion public stock offering. Nine months later, Clarion's earnings dropped significantly and as a result the stock dropped 20 percent beneath the offering price. In addition, the Dow Jones Industrial Average was down 10 percent from the time of the offering.

Jackson has sold her shares at a loss of $60,000 and seeks to hold all parties liable who participated in the public offering including Allen, Dunn, and Rose, Clarion's CPA firm. Although the audit was performed in conformity with generally accepted auditing standards, there were some relatively minor irregularities. The financial statements of Clarion Corporation, which were part of the registration statement, contained minor misleading facts. It is believed by Clarion and Allen, Dunn, and Rose that Jackson's asserted claim is without merit.

Required: Answer the following, setting forth reasons for any conclusions stated.

1. Assuming Jackson sues under the Securities Act of 1933, what will be the basis of her claim?
2. What are the probable defenses which might be asserted by Allen, Dunn, and Rose in light of these facts?

Source: CPA Exam, November 1980, #4(a)(1), (b)(1)(2).

c. Pelham & James, CPAs, were retained by Tom Stone, sole proprietor of Stone Housebuilders, to compile Stone's financial statements. Stone advised Pelham & James that the financial statements would be used in connection with a possible incorporation of the business and sale of stock to friends. Prior to undertaking the engagement, Pelham & James were also advised to pay particular attention to the trade accounts payable. They agreed to use every reasonable means to determine the correct amount.

At the time Pelham & James were engaged, the books and records were in total disarray. Pelham & James proceeded with the engagement applying all applicable procedures for compiling financial statements. They failed, however, to detect and disclose in the financial statements Stone's liability for certain unpaid bills. Documentation concerning those bills was available for Pelham & James's inspection had they looked. This omission led to a material understatement ($60,000) of the trade accounts payable.

Pelham & James delivered the compiled financial statements to Tom Stone with their compilation report which indicated that they did not express an opinion or any other assurance regarding the financial statements. Tom Stone met with two prospective investors, Dickerson and Nichols. At the meeting, Pelham & James stated that they were confident that the trade accounts payable balance was accurate to within $8,000.

Stone Housebuilders was incorporated. Dickerson and Nichols, relying on the financial statements, became stockholders along with Tom Stone. Shortly thereafter, the understatement of trade accounts payable was detected. As a result, Dickerson and Nichols discovered that they had paid substantially more for the stock than it was worth at the time of purchase.

Required: Answer the following, setting forth reasons for any conclusions stated.

Will Pelham & James be found liable to Dickerson and Nichols in a common law action for their damages?

Source: CPA Exam, May 1982, #3(b).

13

In this world nothing is certain
but death and taxes.
Benjamin Franklin

Trusts, Estates, Taxes, and Environmental Law

WHAT IS A TRUST?

In a trust, one person holds property for the benefit of another. A trust arrangement is often desirable for a spouse or child who is incapable of managing property or who is simply unwilling to assume such responsibility. With the property placed in trust, the trustee (the person who holds the property) is solely responsible for managing and caring for the property, while the spouse or child (the "beneficiary" of the trust) is entitled to all the benefits and income derived from the property. And trust provisions can be very flexible to suit the needs of the particular situation. The trustee, for example, may be given broad discretion to make investments or very little discretion. The beneficiaries may have a right to all the income or only a portion and they may or may not have a right to reach the trust property itself. Thus it is that a person who leaves a will frequently writes a trust into the will for the benefit of his or her surviving spouse or minor children. The testator (person leaving the will) may prefer that a trustee manage the property for the benefit of his or her lawfully designated beneficiaries rather than have responsibility for management directly on the beneficiaries. In the case of minor children, it is not unusual for the testator to provide that the trust continue until the children reach the age of twenty-one, twenty-five, or thirty.

Black's Law Dictionary defines "trust" as follows.

> A right of property, real or personal, held by one party for the benefit of another. * * * Any arrangement whereby property is transferred with intention that it be administered by trustee for another's benefit.[1]

1. Henry Campbell Black, *Black's Law Dictionary*, rev. 4th ed. (West Publishing Co., 1968), p. 1680.

There are five elements necessary to create an express trust, including: (1) intent to create a trust; (2) a valid trust purpose; (3) designation of a trust property (called the trust "res" or "corpus"); (4) designation of a trustee (a person who holds a trust res for the benefit of another called a "beneficiary"); and (5) determination of one or more trust beneficiaries.

The trustor's intent must be *presently* to create a trust, or a trust will not arise. This means that the trustor must intend that the trust take effect immediately rather than at some future date. Additionally, the trustor must intend to create a legal obligation in the trustee to hold the property for the benefit of another. The trustor's "hope," "wish," "request," or "suggestion" that the transferee hold for the benefit of another is generally insufficient. Such language is termed "precatory" language (words "requesting" or "suggesting" rather than clearly and positively commanding) and will not give rise to an express trust. Thus, where Ed Brown transfers his ranch to "my wife, Leona, with the hope that she will use the ranch to care for our children," there is no express trust created, and Leona is free to disregard Ed's wishes.

However, there are exceptions where even precatory language will result in creation of an express trust. Where the result of ruling out a trust is to place complete ownership and beneficial use of the property in a stranger as opposed to a spouse or child, a trust is likely to be upheld even where the language is merely "wishful" or "hopeful." This is particularly so where the precatory instructions are given to a personal representative (an executor or administrator of a decedent's estate) who is not also a natural beneficiary of the transferor.

Generally speaking, a trust may be created for any lawful purpose. Most often the purpose is to provide for the welfare of some private individual, such as the trustor's spouse or child. Where a transferor of property attempts to create a trust for what the law determines to be an improper purpose, the trust will be held invalid because it is contrary to public policy. Thus, trusts designed to induce criminal or tortious acts, or to encourage immorality or divorce are invalid. Similarly, trusts created for the purpose of hindering or defrauding creditors are impermissible and invalid. As you know, creditors have a right to set aside any such transfer as a fraudulent conveyance.

The property placed into trust is called trust *res* or *corpus*. Generally, any transferable property may form a part of the trust res or corpus whether the property is real or personal, tangible or intangible, presently possessory or a future interest.

To become a trustee, a person must have capacity not only to take ownership of the property but to manage it properly as well. While the trustor may specifically name or designate a trustee, the trust will not fail for lack of definiteness if the trustor should fail to do so. The court, under such circumstances, will simply appoint an appropriate trustee. And the court will appoint a new trustee any time the death or resignation of a trustee gives rise to a vacancy of the trusteeship during the active period of the trust.

As to the trustee's ownership interest in the trust res, it is "bare legal title" only. Bare legal title permits the trustee to manage and use the property to the extent necessary to carry out the trust purpose. Generally, the trust instrument will spell out in detail the trustee's powers with regard to the property (e.g., the instrument may provide that the trustee has the power of sale). Because the trustee's interest is one of bare legal title, with all beneficial ownership belonging to the beneficiaries of the trust, creditors of the trustee cannot reach the trust res or corpus in any way.

A private express trust will fail in the absence of a named or identifiable beneficiary, called a *cestui qui trust*, who is capable of enforcing the trust terms. Again, the beneficiary need not be specifically named or even be in existence at the time the trust is created so long as enough information is given so that the beneficiary may be identified either now or later with reasonable certainty. Thus, a transfer of property by Ed Brown to "the First National Bank of New York in trust for the benefit of my son, Tom Brown, for his life, and remainder in trust to Tom's children" is valid even though Tom Brown has no children at the time of creation of the trust—it will be easy enough to identify the children at a later date. If children are never born to Tom Brown, the trust res or corpus will simply go back to Ed Brown or his heirs by means of a resulting trust (to be explained later in this chapter).

Where one or more persons are designated beneficiaries by means of reference to a "class" of persons, the class must be sufficiently described that the court can determine who is entitled to enforce the trust. The terms "children," "brothers and sisters," and "family" (i.e., a spouse and children) are sufficiently definite. "Relatives" may be too indefinite. "Friends" is unquestionably vague, and the trust will fail for lack of definiteness.

Any person, including a minor and an incompetent, may be a beneficiary. In addition to having enforcement rights against the trustee, a beneficiary has an actual property interest (the beneficial use of the property) in the trust res or corpus. The interest may be for years, for life, or forever. It may be contingent, vested, or subject to a condition. Where there is more than one beneficiary, the co-beneficiaries are presumed to hold their interests as tenants in common unless the trustor has expressly indicated that they are to hold in another form of concurrent ownership.

In the absence of a provision to the contrary, a beneficiary is free to transfer his or her interest in the trust to another. The beneficiary may borrow money on the interest or even transfer the interest in trust for the benefit of some other person. Where the beneficiary has more than a life estate interest, the beneficiary may transfer the interest at death by will or intestacy. And creditors of the beneficiary can reach the interest to satisfy their lawful claims (an exception arises under a "spendthrift" trust as will be explained in a later section).

HOW ARE TRUSTS CREATED?

A property owner may create a trust simply by declaring that he or she holds property for the benefit of another, in which case the trustor is also the trustee. Where the trustee is someone other than the trustor, delivery of the trust res to the trustee is required. A trust is not a contract, and no consideration between or among the parties is required. A trust may be credited orally or in writing. The only difficulty with an oral trust is in the area of real property. While the oral trust is valid, it will be unenforceable under the Statute of Frauds in the event that the trustee does not voluntarily comply with the trustor's orders. But as long as the trustee is willing to perform the trust, no one can object that the trust is oral—not the trustor, not the beneficiaries, nor any other party whether related or unrelated to the transaction.

WHAT ARE SOME PARTICULAR TYPES OF TRUSTS?

Spendthrift Trusts

A beneficiary's ownership interest in the trust res is generally transferable and can usually be "reached" by the beneficiary's creditors. However, the trustor may use what is termed a "spendthrift" trust to limit the beneficiary's interest, making it nontransferable and not subject to the claims of creditors. A "spendthrift" trust may be defined as a trust that prohibits the beneficiary from voluntarily or involuntarily transferring his or her interest in the trust res. Thus, the beneficiary of such a trust may not sell or give away his or her right to trust income or principal, nor can the beneficiary's creditors reach the trust in any way.

As a practical matter, spendthrift trusts are used to protect financially incompetent beneficiaries from their own financial mismanagement. Such trusts are recognized in almost all states. However, a few states, such as California, permit creditors of the spendthrift to reach at least a part of the trust income, although not any of the trust res or corpus. Of course, once trust income or principal is paid to a spendthrift beneficiary, it becomes an asset just like any other and may be transferred or reached by creditors.

On the grounds of public policy some courts permit certain creditors of the beneficiary to reach the trust even where there is a valid spendthrift provision. For example, the wife or child of a "husband/father beneficiary" may reach the trust income or principal insofar as is necessary for their support. Additionally, anyone who furnishes "necessaries" for the beneficiary may reach the trust. And tax claims of state and federal governments are routinely permitted against the trust income and principal.

In conclusion, it should be pointed out that a trustor cannot create a spendthrift trust for himself or herself. It would be contrary to public policy to permit a person by means of a trust device to place his or her property beyond the reach of creditors.

Discretionary Trusts

A "discretionary" trust is one in which the trustee has absolute discretion to either pay or refuse to pay trust income or principal (i.e., trust res or corpus) to a beneficiary. Generally, where the trustee decides not to pay, he or she is bound by the terms of the trust to distribute to another beneficiary instead. A discretionary trust does not prohibit a beneficiary from transferring his or her interest, nor does it make it impossible for creditors of the beneficiary to reach the beneficiary's interest. What it does do is render such actions meaningless unless and until the trustee decides to exercise discretion in favor of the beneficiary.

The discretionary trust is used often in states that do not recognize spendthrift trusts. To accomplish a result similar to the spendthrift provision, the trustor will name an alternative beneficiary who can be counted on to come to the spendthrift beneficiary's assistance should the latter get into financial trouble (in which case distribution to the spendthrift would be of benefit only to his or her creditors). For example, Ed Brown might transfer property in trust to Linda Thompson who is given discretion to pay trust income and portions of the principal to either Ed's son, Tom Brown, or Ed's friend and Tom's godfather, Jim Johnson. If Tom Brown gets into financial difficulties and his creditors attach his interest in that trust, Linda Thompson can exercise discretion in favor of Jim Johnson. Jim, who is Tom's godfather and has Tom's interests at heart, can be counted on by Ed to take care of Tom through a sense of moral obligation.

Protective Trusts

A "protective" trust is an ordinary trust that automatically becomes discretionary (giving the trustee discretion to distribute the trust income to any or all of a group of beneficiaries, including the original beneficiary) at such time as the original beneficiary becomes insolvent or attempts to transfer his or her interest in the trust or a creditor of the beneficiary attempts to reach the trust interest. A good example of a protective trust is found in the following transfer by Ed Brown:

> To the United States National Bank in trust for my son Tom Brown, but if Tom ever cannot pay his debts as they fall due, or if Tom's creditors ever try to reach his interest in this trust, or if Tom ever tries voluntarily to transfer his interest in this trust to another, then in trust for Tom Brown, his wife Mary, or Tom's older sister Suzie, or his younger sister Betty, as the trustee believes best under the circumstances.

As in all protective trusts, the only way that Tom, the original beneficiary, can be certain of receiving benefits is by remaining solvent and making no effort to transfer his trust interest.

Support Trusts

A "support trust" is one in which the trustee has the power to pay the beneficiary only so much of the trust income as is necessary for the beneficiary's support, education, and maintenance. The trust income may be spent for these purposes and no others. Like the spendthrift beneficiary, the support beneficiary cannot transfer his or her interest in the trust, nor may creditors of the beneficiary reach the interest. Payment by the trustee to the beneficiary's transferee or creditor would not accomplish the support of the beneficiary, and, under the terms of the support trust, every payment must do this and only this.

Blended Trusts

A "blended" trust is a trust designed by its terms to benefit a group of people rather than individual beneficiaries (e.g., "in trust for the Jones family"). The trust is nonseparable or "blended," meaning that no one member of the group has an individual interest distinct and separable from the interest of the group. Accordingly, no one member can transfer an interest in the property, and no creditor of an individual member may reach the trust income or corpus.

Charitable Trusts

Unlike the private express trust, a charitable trust will not fail for lack of a definite, designated beneficiary. All that is required is that the trust be created for the benefit of some group (which may be indefinite in number) large enough to produce a public benefit. The fact that a single individual or a small group is the direct recipient of the trust fund monies will not be fatal to the charitable trust so long as the recipient is selected from a group "substantial" enough in size to produce the required public benefit. For example, a charitable trust will be upheld in a transfer of funds in trust to the Milton Meyer School of Business for the establishment of an annual scholarship program for well-qualified business students who show an interest in the insurance profession. The fact that one or two students will be singled out each year as scholarship recipients does not destroy the charitable nature of the trust.

As to the requirement of a charitable purpose, it is generally agreed that a valid charitable trust may be created for any of the following purposes: (1) relief of poverty; (2) advancement of education; (3) advancement of religion; (4) promotion of health; (5) government or municipal purposes; and (6) purposes resulting in benefit to the community (e.g., animal care, maintenance of public cemetaries or fountains). Whatever the charitable purpose it must be clearly expressed in the trust instrument; a trust created simply "for charity," "for benevolent purposes," or "for the benefit of all mankind" will fail for indefiniteness.

The trustee of a charitable trust need not be a charitable organization—in most cases the trustee is a financial institution or other financial expert. In any case the trustee must be empowered to use the trust funds only for the charitable, nonprofit-making purpose.

In some states a trustor may be prohibited by statute from creating charitable trusts by will. Such statutes, called "Mortmain" or "fear of hell" statutes, are designed to protect a decedent's close relatives (e.g., a spouse and children) from the decedent's "eve of death" decision to leave his or her property to charity in an effort to increase his or her chances for "eternal salvation." The statutes vary from state to state; some prohibit the decedent trustor from leaving more than one-third to one-half of his or her estate to charity, while others prohibit any charitable gifts in a will executed by the decedent within a short period of time (typically thirty days) before death. In all states such statutes do not apply unless the decedent is survived by close relatives who would otherwise stand to inherit the property. And many states have altogether eliminated Mortmain statutes, thus abolishing any statutory restriction on testamentary gifts to charities.

Because a charitable trust may last forever, it sometimes happens that a charitable trust "outlives" its charitable purpose (for example, where a trust is established to found and maintain a "girls' " school, and the girls' school is ultimately made coeducational). Where this occurs, the courts may turn to the special charitable trust doctrine of *cy pres* which enables the courts to apply the charitable trust funds to another, similar charitable purpose in the event the original trust purpose cannot be carried out. *Cy pres* applies only to charitable trusts, and it will not be invoked where the trustor clearly intended strictly to limit use of the trust funds to the original charitable purpose. Where the doctrine is found to apply, the courts will make every effort to locate a charitable purpose as close to the trustor's original purpose and intent as possible. In the example above, the courts might well find that the trustor's intent would be to continue to benefit the school even though it had become coeducational.

Finally, a charitable trust containing a provision discriminating on the basis of race or sex will fail for violating the U.S. Constitution.

Resulting Trusts

A "resulting" trust is a trust that arises by operation of law when a person transfers property, intending that someone other than the transferee should have the beneficial interest but failing clearly to express such intent. Basically, there are three situations where a resulting trust will arise:

Failure of an express trust Where a trustor intends to create an express trust but the trust for some reason fails (e.g., because it fails to designate a beneficiary or because land is involved and there is no evidentiary writing), the court will imply a resulting trust in favor of the trustor on the basis that the trustor intended either to create a valid express trust or to keep the property for himself or herself. The transferee of the property, in such case, will hold the property in a resulting trust for the transferor ("trustor") or his or her estate.

Fulfillment of the trust purpose Similarly, where a trustor transfers more property in trust than is needed to accomplish the trust purpose, any excess trust res will be held in a resulting trust for the trustor or his or her estate. Again, the theory is that the trustor intends any surplus to revert to his or her own use, rather than to the benefit of the trustee. For example, suppose that Ed Brown transfers property to Jim Johnson in trust for Ed's son, Tom Brown, for life. If, at Tom's death, there is property remaining in the trust, a resulting trust will be declared in favor of Ed Brown or his successors in interest. Jim Johnson will have no claim to the property.

Another example arises where there are charitable trust funds remaining after the specific charitable purpose of the trust has been carried out. Assuming that the doctrine of cy pres cannot be applied to extend the trust, the trustee will hold the leftover property in a resulting trust for the benefit of the original trustor or his or her estate.

Purchase money resulting trust A resulting trust will so be declared in favor of a person who pays all or a substantial part of the purchase price for property while another person succeeds to legal ownership and title of the property (e.g., where Ed Brown hands Jim Johnson $25,000 and tells him to pay the money to Bill Girod who will then transfer ownership of his three-bedroom home to Jim, or where Ed simply pays $25,000 with instructions that he should transfer title to the property to Jim Johnson). Where this occurs, the person acquiring legal title to the property will hold the property in trust for the benefit of the person who supplied the purchase price.

Purchase money resulting trusts are not favored by the courts, and where possible, the courts will find that the purchaser did not intend such a trust to arise. Thus, a purchase money resulting trust will generally be ruled out where there is a close family relationship between the person who furnishes the purchase price and the person who acquires legal title. The person acquiring title, in this case, is said to be a natural object of the purchaser's bounty (particularly so in the case of a spouse or child), and it is natural to assume that a gift of the property was intended and not a trust relationship. This strong presumption in favor of gifts, coupled with the fact that many "purchasers" intend merely to loan money rather than obtain the benefit of the property, serves to defeat the purchase money resulting trust in a good majority of cases.

Along the same line, where the effect of finding a resulting trust in favor of the purchaser would be to help the purchaser accomplish an unlawful purpose, such as defrauding creditors or evading taxes, a purchase money resulting trust will not be declared. For example, suppose that Ed Brown purchases a 100-acre farm and directs that the property be legally transferred to Ed's friend, Jim Johnson, because Ed is in trouble with his creditors and wants to prevent them from "reaching" the farm property. Ed cannot later ask the court to declare a purchase money resulting trust in his favor. Rather, the entire conveyance will be set aside as a fraudulent conveyance.

Suppose that Ed Brown pays $75,000 and Jim Johnson pays $25,000 towards the purchase price of a 150-acre ranch which is transferred over into the legal ownership of Johnson. In the event a purchase money resulting trust is declared, Jim Johnson will hold a three-fourth's undivided interest in the property in trust for Ed Brown. Remember, the "purchaser" does not have to pay the entire price—only a substantial part.

Constructive Trusts

A "constructive" trust, like a resulting trust, is one that arises by operation of law. However, a constructive trust is imposed by the courts not to comply with the trustor's probable intent (as is a resulting trust), but to prevent a wrong or remedy an injustice that our legal system will not tolerate. Thus, where a murderer inherits property from his or her victim's estate, the courts will impose a constructive trust in favor of those next entitled to the property, with the murderer in the position of the trustee. A constructive trust will also be declared where a person uses improper methods such as fraud, force, or trickery to acquire another's property: the transferee will hold the property in constructive trust for the person who was fooled, tricked, or otherwise improperly influenced into parting with his or her property.

Similarly, a constructive trust will be imposed where a *fiduciary*, a person who stands in a position of responsibility, trust, and confidence with another, takes advantage of his or her "special situation" to gain or acquire control of property that rightfully belongs to the other party. Thus, if an agent who is employed to purchase property for a principal takes title to the property in his or her own name, the courts will impose a constructive trust on the property in favor of the principal. The agent has breached his or her fiduciary relationship and should not be permitted to benefit from the wrongdoing. Similarly, a corporate officer who uses his or her special position to acquire property that the corporation has expressed an interest in will be required to hold the property in a constructive trust for the corporate shareholders. And an employee who acquires title to property on the basis of confidential information disclosed to him or her during the course of employment will be required to hold the property in a constructive trust for the employer.

HOW LONG DOES A RESULTING TRUST OR CONSTRUCTIVE TRUST LAST?

Generally, where a resulting or constructive trust has been declared, the courts will order the "trustee" to transfer the "trust res" to the "beneficiary" as soon as practicable. Once the transfer is accomplished, the trust will terminate by operation of law as one and the same person will hold both bare legal title and beneficial use (with such a merger of the legal and beneficial interests, there is no need for the trust to continue).

WHAT ARE THE POWERS OF A TRUSTEE?

A trustee has whatever powers are specifically spelled out in the trust instrument (if any), as well as whatever powers are "necessary or appropriate" to accomplishing the purpose of the trust. Thus, even in an oral trust or in a written trust containing no specific powers, the trustee will be deemed to have the following implied powers unless they are expressly withheld at the time of the creation of the trust.

The Implied Powers of a Trustee

Power of sale The trustee has an implied power to sell both the real and personal property making up part of the trust res.

Power to lease The trustee also has an implied power to lease trust property for reasonable periods of time under reasonable lease provisions. Where the trust is to terminate at a specific future date, it is not reasonable to lease the property for a period that will extend beyond the duration of the trust. Where the trust has no fixed term, the trustee is still under a duty of care to see that the property is not leased for a period that will extend beyond the "probable" period of the trust.

Power to pay expenses The trustee has an implied power to incur and pay for the reasonable expenses of managing the trust corpus. Under this power the trustee may take whatever action is necessary to utilize and preserve the trust property, including making improvements to the property.

The power to borrow against the trust res, on the other hand, is never implied and must be expressly conferred at the time of creation of the trust. Also, the power to accumulate income is not an implied power, and in the absence of express power to accumulate, the trustee must at reasonable intervals pay all of the net income from the trust to the income beneficiary pursuant to the terms of the trust.

Is the trustee required to exercise the trust powers? Occasionally, a trust will include what are called "imperative" powers that the trustee must exercise. For example, the trustee may be directed to purchase the beneficiary a new automobile every three years. The trustee has no choice in the matter and must either exercise the power (i.e., make the purchases) or the court will order him or her to do so. More typically, however, the powers granted to the trustee are "discretionary," and the trustee is free to either exercise a particular power or ignore it completely. The court, in this case, may require the trustee to make a decision (exercise discretion) as to whether or not to exercise the power, but the court will never interfere with the decision the trustee makes.

WHAT ARE THE DUTIES OF THE TRUSTEE?

A trustee stands in a fiduciary relationship to the cestui que trust (i.e., the trust beneficiary). The trustee's fiduciary duties with regard to management of the trust include the following.

The Trustee's Fiduciary Duties

Duty of loyalty The duty of loyalty refers to the trustee's duty to manage the trust solely in the interest of the beneficiary. The duty is one of absolute loyalty, and the trustee must scrupulously avoid obtaining any personal advantage because of his or her position as trustee. Thus, the trustee may not use or deal with the trust property for his or her own profit or for any other purpose unconnected with the trust.

Duty properly to manage the trust The trustee is generally required to exercise that degree of care and skill in managing the trust that a reasonably prudent businessperson would exercise in dealing with his or her own property. Of course, where the trustee represents that he or she has greater skill than a man or woman of ordinary prudence, the trustee will be held to the higher standard of care (for example, a higher standard of care may be required of a lawyer or investment broker). And where the trustee is a corporate trustee (e.g., a bank with a trust department), some courts demand a higher degree of care and skill on the theory that corporate trustees hold themselves out as being specially qualified to manage trust funds.

Duty to safeguard the trust res The trustee is also obligated properly to secure and safeguard the trust res. Again, the standard of care required is that of a reasonably prudent person in caring for his or her own property and safeguarding it from loss or deterioration. Thus, the trustee is required to pay all bills and property taxes on time and to provide for needed repairs. And if claims are made against the trust assets, jeopardizing the trust corpus, the trustee must hasten to the defense of the trust property.

Duty to earmark The trustee must take special care to keep the trust assets separate from his or her individual assets and the assets of any other trust that he or she is managing. This is called the trustee's "duty to earmark," and the trustee will be liable for any losses that result from a failure to earmark trust funds or assets. However, most states do allow corporate trustees to place property from several trusts in a single common fund to allow for greater flexibility in purchasing common investments.

Duty to invest A trustee is generally obliged to manage the trust and invest the trust properties so as to produce income from the assets of the trust res. The trustee must use reasonable care and skill in making the investments; he or she will be liable for any losses sustained because of a failure to exercise reasonable care. If the trustee simply fails to invest, he or she will be liable for the amount of income that would have been produced had suitable investments been made. Typically, real property must be rented or farmed, and where the property cannot be made productive, it must be sold (of course, the trustor is always free to provide in the trust instrument that the land is to be held on to whether or not it is productive). Unproductive chattels must also be sold, and money must be invested. In making investments, the trustee may be guided by one of the following three standards:

Express direction The trust instrument may specifically authorize the trustee to make investments of a particular nature, or it may limit the trustee to a particular class or type of investment.

Statutory or legal list In some states there are statutory lists, or "legal lists" as they are sometimes called, that specify the kinds of investments that a trustee can make (the lists are usually confined to the more conservative investments such as government bonds or guaranteed savings). Some of the statutes take a "mandatory" approach and require the trustee to invest only in the areas prescribed. Other statutes are "permissive" and allow the trustee to invest in areas not on the list so long as the investment is proper and prudent for the particular trust purpose. In "straying" from the "permissive" list, the trustee must still use the statute as his or her guide and must exercise great care in choosing an alternative investment.

Prudent investor rule A majority of states restrict trustee investment, not by statutory list but by the prudent investor rule. Under the prudent investor rule, a trustee is required to use good faith and sound discretion in making investments—he or she must generally do what a prudent businessperson would do in making a permanent disposition of his or her own funds considering both the probable income from and the probable safety of the investment. Thus, in making investments, the "prudent" trustee must consider a variety of factors, including liquidation of the investment (i.e., reduction to cash), diversification, security, and taxation. The trustee must also continuously review whatever investments are made to ensure that they do not become unproductive.

It should be pointed out that government bonds are safe investments whether a statutory list or prudent investor rule is followed. The same is true with respect to a well-secured first mortgage on land, although a second mortgage on real property would not necessarily be acceptable. Unsecured loans are generally improper under either rule, and so is investment in real property except where the land is necessary to some other trust purpose such as running a particular business. As to corporate common stocks, they are generally excluded from statutory investment lists, but are permissible investments under the prudent investor rule.

Duty properly to account The trustee has a duty to keep accurate accounts and to present accurate accountings to the beneficiary. Suppose that A delivers property to B to be held in trust for the life of C, all income from the trust res to be distributed quarterly to C and, upon C's death, the trust res or "principal" to be distributed to remainderman D. Here, the trust instrument provides that one beneficiary, C, is to receive only income from the trust res, while another beneficiary, D, is to receive "principal." If the trust instrument also specifies that it is up to the trustee to determine what is "income" and what is "principal" and what expenses are to be charged to "income" and what expenses to "principal" for purposes of accounting, the trustee's determinations will be deemed conclusive so long as the trustee makes the decisions in good faith.

However, where the trust instrument does not provide that the trustee is to make these determinations on his or her own, the trustee is governed by the following rules which are designed to protect the interests of both life beneficiary and remainderman:

1. The life beneficiary is entitled to all trust "income," and the remainderman is entitled to all trust "capital" or "principal."
2. All "ordinary" receipts such as rent, interest, and cash dividends are trust income.
3. All "extraordinary" receipts such as monies resulting from the sale of trust assets are trust capital or principal.
4. In a testamentary trust that takes effect upon the trustor's death, all trust earnings resulting from the moment of death are payable as income to the life beneficiary even though the trustee may not receive the trust res until several months after the trustor's death because of the time involved in probate. Thus, trust earnings during the period of probate will not increase the size of the trust res but will be distributed as income to the life beneficiary.

5. A variety of rules have been applied in the situation where a life beneficiary dies, and, at the moment of his or her death, there exists earned (i.e., accrued) income on the trust property that has not yet been received by the trustee. The common law rule was that unless the trustee had actually received the income at the time of the life beneficiary's death, the income would become a part of the trust res for the benefit of the remainderman, and the life beneficiary's estate would not be entitled to any of it. The only exception to this rule was for interest deemed earned on a day-to-day basis—whoever was entitled to the interest each day would receive it. Thus, interest that had accrued on a $10,000 savings account for three months prior to the life beneficiary's death would belong to the life beneficiary's estate whether or not the trustee had received the interest at the time of the beneficiary's death.

In contrast to the common law rule, the Revised Uniform Principal and Income Act, a statute in effect in many states today, provides that all income is apportionable except dividends. This means that the life beneficiary's estate is entitled to all income accrued up to the moment of death regardless of receipt by the trustee.

As for dividends all "ordinary" cash dividends are treated as income and not as principal. "Extraordinary" dividends, on the other hand, may be either income or principal (at least to a certain extent) depending upon the rule that is followed in the particular jurisdiction. The majority "Massachusetts Rule" states that all cash dividends, whether ordinary or extraordinary, are income belonging to the life beneficiary, while all stock dividends, which are always extraordinary, are a part of trust capital or principal. A stock dividend, which is always extraordinary, refers to the payment of a dividend in stock rather than in money.

The "Pennsylvania Rule" (a minority view) is that extraordinary dividends, stock or cash, are "principal" payments to the extent that they reduce the book value of the shares from what it was when the stock was acquired by the trust. The minority differs considerably from the majority: to the extent that an extraordinary cash dividend reduces the acquisition date book value of the shares of stock held in trust, the dividend forms a part of the trust capital or principal and will ultimately be distributed to the trust remainderman. Any balance remaining will be currently distributed as income to the life beneficiary. Acquisition date book value is found by totaling the assets of the dividend distributing corporation as of the date the trust acquired stock in the corporation, deducting all corporate liabilities as of the same date, and dividing the difference by the number of shares of stock outstanding at the time.

Because of the many difficulties inherent in determining whether a particular cash dividend has been paid out of corporate earnings or profits so as not to reduce the acquisition date book value of trust held shares, most states follow the Massachusetts Rule and hold that such dividends are, in their entirety, trust income fully payable to the life beneficiary regardless of reduction in book value.

6. Proceeds from the sale of trust assets generally become a part of trust capital or principal. The only time any portion of the proceeds will be allocable to trust income is where the trustee unreasonably delays in selling unproductive trust property. The trustee has a duty to sell unproductive property so as to convert that part of the trust corpus to productive use. Under the Revised Uniform Principal and Income Act, "unproductive" property is defined as property producing an annual income of less than 1 percent of its original appraised value or market cost. If the trustee delays in selling such property, he or she must apportion the proceeds of the sale between trust income and principal so as to reflect the income that would have resulted had the trustee sold the property immediately and properly invested the proceeds.

7. The general rule is that current expenses are chargeable against trust income while extraordinary expenses (expenses that benefit only the remainderman) are chargeable against trust principal. Thus, extraordinary expenses incurred at the time of creation of a trust in putting the trust property into an income-producing condition are chargeable to the trust capital account. Thereafter, current repairs, maintenance expense, and current insurance premiums are chargeable to trust income. As for taxes, ordinary taxes are payable out of trust income, while assessments for permanent improvements that will last until the trust remainderman comes into possession are payable out of principal. Mortgage interest, another current expense, is chargeable to income, while payment against the mortgage debt is chargeable to principal. Costs incurred in selling trust assets and in defending title to such assets is also chargeable to the principal account (this being "for the benefit" of the capital account).

Administration expenses of the trust, including compensation for the trustee's services, are generally apportioned between income and principal accounts. Some statutes provide that the administration expenses should be evenly divided between the two accounts, while other statutes maintain that the costs should be split on the basis of the services rendered and the respective benefits received by the life beneficiary and trust remainderman. Allocation of expenses under the latter statutes is thus left to the discretion of the trustee and the courts.

As a means of keeping the corpus intact for the remainderman, most courts also require the trustee to deduct from the income account for depreciation of the trust assets and to add the amount deducted to the principal account. Depreciation, of course, refers to the decline in value of an asset as the result of normal wear and tear or the like. By deducting depreciation loss from the income account and adding back into the principal reserve, the trust remainderman will ultimately receive a well-preserved res rather than a trust corpus depleted in value by the mere passage of time.

WHAT IS A WILL?

A will as defined by *Black's Law Dictionary*, is:

> The legal expression or declaration of a person's mind or wishes as to the disposition of his property, to be performed or take effect after his death. * * * [It is] a revocable instrument by which a person makes disposition of his property to take effect after his death. * * * [It is] a written instrument executed with the formalities of law, whereby a person makes a disposition of his property to

> take effect after his death. * * * [T]he form of an instrument is of little consequence in determining whether it is a will, but if it is executed with formalities required by statute, and if it is to operate only after death of maker, it is a "will." [2]

A will, therefore, may be defined as a written instrument executed in accordance with the formalities prescribed by state statute whereby a property owner (called a "testator") directs the disposition of his or her real and personal property to take effect upon death. Because a will does not effectively transfer property until the testator's death, the testator is free to revoke or modify the will at any time during life. As a result of this right to revoke, the beneficiaries named in the will have no interest in the property until the testator dies and, until that time, are said to have but a "mere expectancy."

Although wills are revocable and legally ineffective until death, the law provides that the meaning of words and phrases used in a will are to be construed or interpreted according to the language usage and law in effect at the time of execution of the will rather than at the time of the testator's death. However, the law to be applied is generally the law in effect at the time of the testator's death.

Generally, there are four requirements for a valid will: (1) testamentary intent; (2) testamentary capacity at the time of execution of the will; (3) execution without fraud, duress, undue influence, or mistake; (4) execution in full compliance with the statutory formalities. If any one of these four requirements is lacking, the decedent's property will pass as if there is no will.

Testamentary Intent

The testator must intend that the instrument presently operate as his or her last will and testament. This means that the testator must specifically intend (a) to provide for the disposition of his or her property, (b) to take effect only upon death, (c) according to the terms of the written "will." Testamentary intent is a subjective test, and if it can be shown that a particular decedent did not have the required intent presently to create a will, the will will fail despite the fact that, on its face, the instrument appears proper in every respect.

Where a will is executed in full compliance with statutory formalities, a presumption arises that the instrument was also executed with the required testamentary intent. In most states, the presumption is rebuttable, and evidence tending to show lack of intent is always admissible.

Testamentary intent is lacking where the words used in the writing indicate an intent to execute a will at some time in the future rather than presently to provide for the disposition of property at death. For example, suppose that Sidney Smith signs and witnesses a document that states, "It is my intention to make a will, leaving all my property to my friend, Mary Lewis."

---

2. Henry Campbell Black, *Black's Law Dictionary*, rev. 4th ed. (West Publishing Co., 1968), p. 1772.

The document is not a valid will because Sidney Smith indicates no intent that the signed and witnessed writing serve as his last will and testament—Sidney's expressed intention is to execute a will in the future.

However, the requirement of a *present* intent does not prohibit a testator from including will provisions that are conditioned upon the happening of some specified event or contingency. For example, one spouse will often provide by will that the other spouse is to receive real and personal properties only if he or she survives the testator-spouse. Similarly, it is perfectly proper for Sidney Smith to execute a will containing a provision that his properties are to be transferred to Mary Lewis only if Mary marries him. If the condition occurs (i.e., if Mary marries Sidney), Mary will be entitled to Sidney's property upon his death; if the condition does not occur, the will provision will be inoperative, and Mary will receive nothing.

The only time a condition will not be acceptable in a will is where the condition is contrary to public policy. Thus, a provision in a will providing for a transfer of property to Mary Lewis "only if Mary divorces her husband, Lance," is contrary to public policy and will be legally disregarded. In most jurisdictions the named beneficiary (in this case Mary) will still be entitled to the property after deletion of the condition so long as all four requirements for a valid will are otherwise present.

Testamentary Capacity

To make a valid will, a person must be of sound mind. "Sound mind" does not demand a superior intelligence or even an average mentality. All that is required is that the testator have, if not actual knowledge, at least the capacity generally to understand and remember: (a) the nature and extent of his or her property; (b) the people who are the natural objects of his or her bounty or generosity (e.g., relatives and close friends); and (c) the disposition that he or she is making of the property. It is essential that the testator have the capacity to understand and interrelate these factors so as to come up with an orderly plan for the disposition of his or her property.

Because of the requirement of testamentary capacity, many wills begin with a statement by the testator that he or she is of "sound mind." Such language suggests that the testator has the required testamentary capacity to make a will, but evidence tending to show the contrary is always admissible. In some states a showing of capacity must be made before a will will be admitted to probate. In most states, however, there is a rebuttable presumption of competency that effectively forces those who would contest capacity to disprove its existence.

While a person may lack capacity to make a will for many reasons, the most common reasons are lack of legal age, presence of mental deficiency, and presence of mental derangement or delusion.

Underage All states provide by statute that a person under a certain age (usually eighteen or twenty-one) cannot make a valid will.

Mental deficiency As previously stated, the test of mental competency is whether a person has the mental capacity to understand and interrelate the nature and extent of his or her property, the natural objects of his or her bounty, and the disposition of property that he or she is making. It takes no great mental giant to satisfy this test, and a person possessing but minor mental deficiencies will not be prevented from making a will on the grounds of testamentary incapacity. Thus, a person who is incompetent to manage a business or even his or her own affairs is not necessarily incompetent to make a valid will.

Mental derangement or delusion A delusion or irrational belief held by a testator will invalidate only that portion of the will affected. However, a belief is irrational only where it is so contrary to reason and good sense that it indicates mental derangement. Thus, if the testator had any rational basis, however tenuous, for the belief, it will not be considered irrational. If the testator had any facts to reason from (incorrect though the reasoning might be), the belief will not be considered a mental delusion. But a testator who disinherits his only daughter because he concluded without benefit of any facts that his wife of thirty-five years was once unfaithful and gave birth to the girl as a result, is probably suffering from an insane delusion regarding the child, and the disinheritance provision will likely be disregarded.

Absence of Fraud, Duress, Undue Influence, and Mistake

A person who believes that a testator executed a will as a result of fraud, duress, undue influence, or mistake may petition the probate court upon the testator's death to disregard the will in whole or in part. If the person who alleges the existence of one of these four factors proves facts sufficient to substantiate the charge, the probate court will set aside the affected portions of the will, which may very well be the will in its entirety.

Fraud Fraud, as it relates to the execution of a will, refers to an intentional misrepresentation of a material fact made with intention that a testator rely upon the misrepresentation in executing a will and, in fact, resulting in the testator's execution of a will in justifiable reliance thereon. Again, there are two kinds of fraud: fraud in the execution and fraud in the inducement.

Fraud in the execution, also called "fraud in the factum," usually involves the surreptitious substitution of one document for another. For example, a testator may be tricked into signing a document without realizing that the instrument is a will. Or the testator may be fooled into signing one will, believing it to be another. In both cases the testator is deceived as to the nature of the instrument or its contents and has no testamentary intent as that term is defined in law.

A testator who intentionally and knowingly signs and executes a will in justifiable reliance upon another's fraudulent misrepresentation is a victim of fraud in the inducement. For example, suppose that Sidney Smith's son, Robert, is killed in an automobile accident while touring Europe. If one Gina Smith suddenly shows up and persuades Sidney to execute a will in her favor by falsely representing that she is Robert's widow, Sidney's will will be a product of fraud in the inducement. In this case the testator has not been deceived as to the nature of the instrument, nor does he lack the required testamentary intent. Rather, his testamentary intent and execution have been fraudulently induced, and the resulting will or affected portions are invalid.

Upon a showing of fraud in the execution or fraud in the inducement, the probate court will set aside the will in whole or in part. The court may also use the remedy of constructive trust to carry out the testator's probable intent. Thus, where the testator has been fraudulently persuaded to change beneficiaries, the court may impose a constructive trust for the benefit of the party who would have received the property but for the fraud. For example, where Sidney Smith is persuaded to execute a will in favor of his niece, Freda, rather than his son, Robert, on the basis of Freda's fraudulent assertion that Robert has been killed in Europe, the court may impose a constructive trust in favor of Robert. A constructive trust may be imposed whether the fraud affects the entire will or merely a portion of the will.

Duress Duress is physical or mental coercion that deprives a testator of his or her own free will and forces the testator to execute a will or portions of a will that he or she would not otherwise execute. The key word here is "coerce." Where duress or coercion can be established, the will or its affected portions will be declared invalid by the court.

Undue influence Like duress, undue influence demands an over-powering of the testator's own free will. However, it does not require the element of coercion or actual force that is needed for a showing of duress. Undue influence may be defined as persuasion, pressure, or influence, short of actual force but stronger than mere advice, that so overpowers the testator's own free will that he or she cannot act intelligently, understandingly, and voluntarily but acts, instead, subject to the will or purposes of another in executing a will. Generally, the courts require a combination of the following four factors as proof of undue influence: (1) the testator was in a weakened physical or mental state and thus susceptible to the undue persuasion of others; (2) the person accused of exercising undue influence was in a position to benefit or gain personally from its exercise; (3) the person had an opportunity to exercise the undue influence; and (4) the will, as written, provided for an unnatural disposition of the testator's property, rather than a disposition to the natural objects of the testator's bounty, such as a spouse and children.

Undue influence does not require the existence of a confidential or fiduciary relationship (e.g., attorney and client or trustee and beneficiary) between testator and influencer, but the presence of such a relationship certainly makes undue influence easier to establish. This is because a person who stands in a relationship of trust and confidence with the testator is likely to have more opportunity unduly to influence the provisions of the testator's will than is a complete stranger or casual friend. Thus, where a person in a confidential or fiduciary's relationship benefits from provisions in a testator's will at the expense of the objects of the testator's natural bounty, the court is likely to declare the provisions invalid as a result of undue influence. The courts will impose a constructive trust for the benefit of the testator's close friends or relatives.

Mistake A testator who mistakenly signs an instrument not realizing that it is a will has no testamentary intent, and the will is void. However, the will of a testator who merely makes a mistake as to who his or her living relatives are or what their health and financial status might be will not be invalid in whole or in part unless the mistake appears on the face of the will. For example, if, upon hearing that his cousin, Ruth, has died in Europe, Sidney Smith provides by will, "I leave all my property to the American Red Cross," the will will not be set aside if it later turns out that Ruth is alive and well. However, if Sidney provides, "I leave all my property to the American Red Cross because my cousin, Ruth, has died in Europe," and Ruth later turns up alive, the will will be declared invalid and a constructive trust imposed for her benefit.

Proper Statutory Formalities

The statutory formalities for execution of a will are essentially the same from state to state. Typically, there are four: (1) signature of testator; (2) publication by the testator; (3) competent witnesses; and (4) signature of witnesses.

Signature The testator may sign the will in any manner so long as he or she intends what is written to serve as his or her complete signature. A full name, a nickname, or initials may be used; even a mark or rubber stamp will be sufficient if the testator intends it to serve as his or her signature. If the testator is too ill to sign the will or is illiterate and cannot sign, he or she can direct another person to sign for him or her; so long as the other person signs in the presence of and at the direction of the testator, the signature will be valid. Again, a full name, a nickname, initials, a rubber stamp, or mark will be acceptable.

Some states do not require the testator to sign at the end of the will (a signature at the end of an instrument is called a "subscription"). Thus, a full name, a nickname or a rubber stamp anywhere on the instrument will serve as a valid signature so long as that is the testator's clear intent. Other states do require a subscription and hold that if anything appears after the testator's signature other than an attestation clause (a statement by the witnesses affirming the testator's signature), the entire will is void (a minority of these states hold that only the provisions appearing after the signature are void). Of course, even where subscription is not required, the testator cannot simply add on to the will or make changes in the will after the will has been executed. Change or modification must be accomplished by a valid *codicil* (i.e., a properly executed amendment as will be explained in a later section).

Finally, the testator must either sign in the presence of the required witnesses or acknowledge (i.e., declare as genuine) in their presence a signature previously placed on the instrument by himself or herself or by another at his or her direction.

Publication Required in but a minority of states, "publication" refers to a declaration by the testator to the assembled witnesses that the instrument is the testator's will. The publication may be by words or conduct so long as the nature of the instrument is communicated to the witnesses. Usually, the attestation clause will acknowledge that the testator has declared the writing to be his or her last will and testament. In no case is it necessary for the witnesses to be familiar with the contents of the will.

Witnesses A will must generally be witnessed by two (in a few states, three) competent witnesses. The testator must sign or acknowledge the will and publish the will, where necessary, in their assembled presence. A "competent" witness is a witness old enough and of sufficient mental capacity to understand the nature of what he or she is witnessing. No minimum age is required.

So long as a person is mature enough to understand the proceedings so as to be able to testify in court regarding them should the need ever arise, the person's youth will be no bar to competency. Also, the fact that a witness who was competent at the time of execution of the will later becomes incompetent will not affect the validity of the will.

A witness must have no beneficial interest in the will—that is, he or she must receive no direct interest by the terms of the instrument. However, the effect of an "interested" party's witnessing the will is not to invalidate the entire will but only the gift to that particular witness. Thus, a person who by the terms of the will is to receive $5,000 in cash cannot witness the will, or he or she will forfeit the interest. However, a person who stands but indirectly to benefit from the will (e.g., a spouse or creditor of a beneficiary) is not an "interested" party and may freely serve as a witness. Similarly, an attorney who prepares a will is not considered an interested party merely because he or she will ultimately receive a probate fee from the testator's estate. Nor is an intestate heir (one who would receive property if the testator had no will) an interested party unless, of course, he or she is also named as a beneficiary under the will.

The only time a gift to an interested witness will be upheld is where more than the required number of witnesses attest to the will, and the interested witness can be legally disregarded. A disregarded witness is called a "supernumerary" witness (i.e., an extra witness over and above the statutory requirement). Where more than one witness is interested, all must be supernumerary or none will be: unless there are sufficient witnesses apart from the interested parties to satisfy the statutory requirement, all gifts to the interested witnesses will be voided.

Signature of witnesses The witnesses must also sign the will, attesting to the testator's signature and to the publication, where required. Where publication is called for, the witnesses must attest to (affirm) their knowledge of the nature of the instrument. Where it is not required, the witnesses need only attest to the testator's execution of a document—not to their knowledge of the kind of document.

Most states require the witnesses to sign the will in the presence of the testator, although not necessarily within each other's presence. As to what constitutes "presence," the courts use two tests: the "scope of vision" test and the "conscious presence" test. A witness is present for purposes of the "scope of vision" test only if he or she signs the will in the testator's physical presence and within the scope of his or her vision. Whether or not the testator *actually* sees, he or she must be *able* to see the will, the witnesses, and the signing.

The "conscious presence" test, on the other hand, is satisfied where the testator can either see or hear what is being done, the testator is conscious of what is occurring, and the signing is a continuous transaction that takes but a brief moment of time.

It generally makes no difference whether the witnesses sign before or after the testator signs or whether their signatures appear on the will before or after his or her signature appears (although their signatures almost always appear after). Although it is usually not required by statute, most wills contain a formal "attestation clause" immediately after the testator's signature and immediately preceding the signatures of the attesting witnesses. The attestation clause expressly affirms the testator's signature or acknowledgment in the presence of the witnesses, as well as his or her publication of the document (where required) as his or her last will and testament. A typical attestation clause might read as follows:

> The foregoing instrument, consisting of three pages, was on the date above mentioned, signed, published and declared by the said Sidney Aaron Smith as and for his Last Will and Testament, in the presence of us, who at his request, and in his presence, and in the presence of each other, do hereunto subscribe our names as witnesses thereto.

In most jurisdictions the use of an attestation clause serves to raise a rebuttable presumption of proper execution of a will; a person who would contest the will for lack of proper execution must show facts to rebut the presumption and substantiate the charge.

The four requirements of a valid will—testator's signature, publication, competent witnesses, and attestation—are designed to accomplish several things. First, they are designed to prevent fraud and forgery in the execution of a will and to provide the best evidence possible for establishing testamentary intent. Second, they are ritualistically fashioned to impress upon the testator the importance of his or her act in providing for an orderly, death-time disposition of property. And, finally, they are structured to reduce the likelihood of undue influence or duress being exercised upon the testator (particularly the requirement of competent witnesses who are disinterested in the testamentary plan).

Where a testator makes reference in a will to another document such as a deed, a letter, or a prior invalid will, the document will become part of the will though it is not executed with the testamentary formalities so long as the document was in existence at the time of execution of the will, the will specifically describes the document so that it may be readily identified, and the testator expresses an intent in the will that the document become part of it. Where these conditions are met, the document is said to be *incorporated by reference* into the will. For example, where Sidney Smith's will provides, "To my son, Robert, I leave the personal property described in a letter to Robert, dated March 3, 1978, the letter to be found in my safety deposit box," the letter referred to in the will is incorporated by reference and becomes a part of the will. However, where Sidney's will provides, "I want my son, Robert, to have some specific items of personal property that I will list in a letter sometime within the next year, said letter to be placed into my safety deposit box," the letter will not be incorporated by reference because it was not in existence at the time the will was executed.

The "extrinsic facts" doctrine provides that a testator may determine beneficiaries or their interests by reference in a will to extrinsic acts or events so long as the acts or events have an "independent legal significance" apart from the will itself. An act or event has independent legal significance where it is fundamentally nontestamentary in nature. For example, Sidney Smith may provide by will, "I leave $1,000 to each employee working on my ranch at the time of my death." Determination of beneficiaries by reference to employment at a particular time is perfectly proper because employees are ordinarily selected because of their business skills—not because they are desired as beneficiaries. The act of employment thus has an independent significance apart from its impact on Sidney's testamentary disposition. The same is true where Sidney's will provides, "I leave all my property to whichever of my children I am living with at the time of my death." Again, it is unlikely that Sidney will live with a particular child merely to designate him or her as a beneficiary.

However, where Sidney provides by will, "I am going to write a letter sometime in the future and designate which of my children are to receive my property," the determination of beneficiaries by letter has no independent legal significance apart from furthering Sidney's testamentary scheme, and the determination cannot be upheld on the basis of the "extrinsic facts" doctrine. Nor can the provision be upheld as a valid incorporation by reference; the letter was not in existence at the time the will was written.

Trusts are frequently written into wills as a means of providing property management for beneficiaries such as a spouse or children who are either too young or incompetent to manage their own property or simply unwilling to do so. A trust created by will is called a *testamentary trust* and takes effect only upon the testator's death. A testamentary trust must satisfy the requirements of a valid trust as well as the requirements of a valid will.

A provision in a will providing that all or a portion of the testator's property should be added to the trust res or corpus of a trust established during the lifetime of the decedent is called a "pour-over" trust provision. For example, Sidney Smith might provide by will that $50,000 and 750 shares of General Motors stock should be added to the trust res of an inter vivos trust Sidney created ten years ago for the benefit of his invalid younger sister, Angela. Upon Sidney's death, the "pour-over" trust provision would operate to transfer the designated property into the trust res or corpus to be administered and distributed as part of the inter vivos trust.

Pour-over trust provisions may be upheld on the basis of incorporation by reference (i.e., the inter vivos trust is made a part of the will by the testator's express reference to it), or as an act of independent significance under the "extrinsic facts" doctrine (i.e., the inter vivos trust is fundamentally nontestamentary in nature and has independent significance apart from the testator's dispository scheme).

WHAT IS A POWER OF APPOINTMENT?

An owner of property may give another person the power to designate who should own the property. Such a power is called a power of appointment. A power of appointment may be created by deed or by will. The property owner who creates the power of appointment is called the donor of the power; the person to whom the power is given is the donee. The power of appointment may give the donee the power to exercise the appointment in favor of the donee himself or herself or in favor of the donee's estate. Such a power is called a *general power.* A general power is very close to ownership itself since the donee may appoint the property to himself or herself during life or control its disposition upon death. Because of this, a general power is said to be "tantamount to ownership," and the value of the property is included in the donee's estate for purposes of death taxes.

A general power of appointment is most frequently created by will. This is particularly true of a donor-testator who wants to leave the income from property to one person for life and also to give that person the power to reach the principal of the property when he or she dies. Typically, this is what one spouse might do for a surviving spouse in his or her last will and testament. For example, Mary Wife's Last Will and Testament might read as in figure 13–1.

Note that in Article IV(2), Mary has created a general power of appointment in her husband Stanley, the donee of the power. Mary also adds the following provision to enable Stanley to have complete power to reach the trust principal during his lifetime:

> During the lifetime of my said husband, he shall have the absolute power to withdraw all of the principal of the trust estate or portions thereof from time to time. Such withdrawals shall be made by an instrument in writing, signed by my husband and filed with the trustee. Any principal so withdrawn shall be distributed to my said husband free of the trust herein provided.

Clearly, a general power of appointment gives the donee what is "tantamount to ownership" of the property. Still, use of the trust and the power of appointment allows for management by other than the trust beneficiary.

In contrast to a general power of appointment (which may be exercised in favor of the donee or his or her estate) is a *special power of appointment.* A special power is one that cannot be exercised in favor of the donee or his or her estate but may be exercised only in favor of identifiable person(s) other than the donee. For example, suppose that Mary Wife used this language in Article VI(2):

> (2) Upon the death of my husband all the assets of the trust fund then remaining shall be distributed as my said husband shall appoint by his Last Will and Testament, which power he may only exercise in favor of our children Tom, Dick, Harry, Mary, and Anne.

Here, Mary has created a special power of appointment. The husband, as donee of the power, may exercise it only in favor of the named children. A special power is *exclusive* if the donee is authorized to exclude one or more of

FIGURE 13–1 LAST WILL AND TESTAMENT

LAST WILL AND TESTAMENT
OF
MARY WIFE

I, MARY WIFE, do hereby make, publish, and declare this to be my Last Will and Testament, and do revoke all wills and codicils heretofore made by me.

I.

I nominate and appoint my husband, STANLEY HUSBAND, as executor of my estate.

II.

I direct my Executor to pay from my estate all inheritance, estate, transfer, and succession taxes which become payable by reason of my death and authorize him to contest or compromise any claims for such taxes.

. . .

IV.

I give, devise, and bequeath all of my property, both real and personal to the trustee hereinafter named, in trust on the terms and conditions and for the uses and purposes following:
. . . The trust fund shall be held by my trustee on the following terms:

(1) The net income shall be paid to or applied for the benefit of my husband in quarterly or more frequent installments during his lifetime. In addition, my trustee shall have the authority, in his discretion, to pay to or apply on behalf of my husband such principal sums as he may determine to be necessary and proper for his maintenance and welfare in order that he may maintain the standard of living to which he was accustomed at the time of my death.

(2) Upon the death of my husband all the assets of the trust fund then remaining shall be distributed as my said husband shall appoint by his Last Will and Testament, which power he may exercise in favor of his estate or of any other person or persons. In default of such appointment, or subject to any partial appointment by my husband, the trust fund remaining shall be distributed outright in equal shares to my children then living at my husband's death.

the designated appointees from receiving any of the property. If some benefit must be conferred upon all of the appointees, then the power is *nonexclusive.* Most courts hold that, unless the creating instrument expressly provides that the donee must include all appointees, the special power is exclusive, and the donee may completely exclude one or more of the appointees or give the property entirely to one appointee. (A minority of courts hold that a power is presumed to be nonexclusive.) Thus, in the example above, most courts would hold this to be an exclusive power, and Stanley could exercise the power in his will so as to exclude one or more of the children.

Whether the special power is exclusive or nonexclusive, if the donee fails to exercise the power, the designated appointees will take equally.

WHAT IS A CODICIL?

A "codicil" is a legally effective amendment to a will. Whether a codicil is a separate instrument (the usual case) or simply an addition to the original will itself, the codicil must be executed with full testamentary formalities—that is, signature of the testator, publication where required, and attestation by two or three competent witnesses.

Generally, a valid codicil has the effect of republishing or re-executing the original will. This means that the will, as amended by the codicil, will be interpreted as of the date of the codicil rather than as of the date of execution of the will. This change in effective date of interpretation may have a substantial impact on specific provisions of the will. For example, suppose that Sidney Smith provides by will that Sandy Granstrom is to receive $1,000 in cash from his estate. Unfortunately, Sandy witnesses the will, and because she cannot qualify as a supernumerary, she stands to forfeit her $1,000 interest. However, if Sidney later executes a codicil to the will that Sandy does not witness, the gift to Sandy will be valid because the effect of the codicil is to republish the will as of the later date; the courts will look only to the attesting witnesses of the codicil, and the prior attestation will be disregarded.

Or suppose that Sidney Smith provides by will, "I am going to write a letter sometime in the future and designate which of my children is to receive my property." You will recall that the letter, once written, cannot be incorporated by reference into the will because the letter was not in existence at the time of execution of the will. However, if, after the letter is written, Sidney executes a codicil to the will, the letter will be incorporated by reference because the effect of the codicil is to republish the will as of the codicil's effective date, and the letter is in existence at the time.

The only time republication will not apply is where its application is clearly contrary to the testator's expressed intent.

HOW ARE TESTAMENTARY GIFTS LEGALLY DESIGNATED?

A gift of personal property under a will is called a "bequest" or "legacy"; a gift of real property is called a "devise." Bequests and devises may be classified as follows.

Bequests and Devises

Specific bequest or devise A specific bequest or devise under a will is a gift of identifiable property. For example, a gift of "my 12-gauge Browning over and under shotgun" or "my apartment house located at 12th and Market in Mandan, North Dakota" is, in the first instance, a specific bequest of the shotgun and, in the second, a specific devise of the land.

Unless a will provides otherwise, the beneficiary of a specific bequest or devise is entitled to the specified gift free and clear of the testator's debts (the testator's debts will be satisfied out of the general assets of the estate). This is called the beneficiary's "right to exoneration." An exception to the right arises where the specified property is subject to a security interest in another party, in which case the beneficiary takes the property subject to the interest. Thus, if in the example above the apartment house is mortgaged, the beneficiary will take the real property subject to the mortgage.

General bequest or devise A general bequest or devise is not a gift of specific, identifiable property but a gift of fixed or calculable value that may be satisfied out of any of the general assets of a decedent's estate (e.g., a bequest of $2,500 or of "all the personal property I own at the time of my death" or a devise of "all of my land").

Demonstrative bequest A demonstrative bequest is both specific and general. It is a gift of personal property, usually money, that is to be paid first out of a particular fund and, second, out of the general assets of the estate to the extent that the particular fund is insufficient. An example of a demonstrative bequest is "a gift of $2,500 to my son, John, from my savings account at the First National Bank but, if that fund is insufficient, out of my other properties."

Residuary bequest and devise A residuary bequest and devise is a gift of whatever personal and real property is left after all specific, general, or demonstrative gifts have been satisfied. The residuary gift must be worded so as to pass all the testator's remaining property (however, it is possible for a testator to satisfy this requirement by bequeathing all his or her remaining personal property to one person and all his or her remaining real property to another). While no special words or language are required to create a residuary gift, the words "the rest, residue, and remainder of my property" are usually employed.

WHAT IS ADEMPTION BY EXTINCTION?

To "adeem" is to destroy. Ademption by extinction is the destruction of a specific bequest or devise that occurs when the specified personal property or realty is not to be found in the testator's estate upon his or her death. The gift in this case fails completely, and the beneficiary who was to receive the property receives nothing. Where only a portion of the property is missing, the gift is adeemed *pro tanto* (to the extent of that portion), and the beneficiary is entitled to whatever portion remains.

Ademption by extinction applies only to specific bequests and devises. A minority of courts make its operation dependent upon the intent of the testator: unless it can be shown that the testator transferred or otherwise disposed of the property with the intent that the specific bequest or devise be destroyed, ademption by extinction will not operate to deprive the beneficiary of his or her interest. For example, if a testator *in a minority jurisdiction* makes a specific bequest of an automobile, then sells the car for $5,000 and places the proceeds into a savings account, the beneficiary of the specific bequest will probably receive the $5,000.

Wherever possible, the courts will classify gifts as general bequests and devises rather than specific gifts of property in order to avoid the hardship of ademption by extinction.

WHAT IS ADEMPTION BY SATISFACTION?

General and demonstrative bequests are considered "adeemed by satisfaction" where the testator, subsequent to execution of the will, makes an inter vivos gift to the designated beneficiary, intending the gift to satisfy in whole or in part the testamentary bequest. Ademption by satisfaction does not apply to specific bequests because an inter vivos transfer of the property to the beneficiary would remove the property from the estate and result in ademption by extinction. (Although the doctrine of ademption by satisfaction would appear logically to apply to general devises of real property, the courts have so far chosen not to apply it in this area.)

Unlike ademption by extinction, which in a majority of jurisdictions takes place regardless of the testator's intent, ademption by satisfaction will occur only where the testator intends the inter vivos gift to reduce or take the place of the testamentary bequest. If the testator does not intend this result, the general or demonstrative bequest will still be valid.

Where ademption by satisfaction is found to apply, the value of the inter vivos gift will be deducted from the bequest, and the beneficiary will receive whatever balance, if any, remains. Some special rules apply where a class gift is involved. For example, suppose that Robert Smith provides by will, "I leave $50,000 to my children." After Robert executes the will, two of his children get into financial difficulty and persuade Robert to give them some of the money before he dies. Prior to death, Robert transfers a total of $5,000 to his son, James, and $8,000 to his daughter, Carla, intending that the transfers be deducted from the testamentary bequest. Robert transfers nothing to his other two children, Mark and Karen. Upon Robert's death the doctrine of ademption by satisfaction applies because Robert intended the inter vivos transfers to reduce the testamentary bequests to his son and daughter. Because a class gift is involved, the court will throw everything into *hotchpot*. This means that the court will add together the total value of the inter vivos gifts ($13,000) and the original amount of the testamentary bequest ($50,000). The court will then divide the total by the number of people in the class ($63,000 divided by 4) to come up with the amount of money or property ($15,750) that each member of the class should receive. Class members who have received a portion of their share inter vivos (James and Carla) will have that amount ($5,000 and $8,000 respectively) subtracted from their share of the hotchpot. Thus, upon Robert's death, James will receive a total of $10,750; Carla will receive $7,750; and Mark and Karen will each receive $15,750. As you can see, the result of applying ademption by satisfaction is to treat all members of the class equally, taking into account that some of the members received a portion of their interest inter vivos.

IN WHAT ORDER ARE TESTAMENTARY GIFTS DISTRIBUTED?

Testamentary gifts are distributed in the following order: first, specific bequests and devises (a demonstrative gift is specific to the extent of the specified fund); second, general bequests or devises (including a demonstrative gift in excess of the specified fund); and, third, and last, residuary gifts.

WHAT HAPPENS WHEN THERE ARE INSUFFICIENT ASSETS?

Where there are insufficient assets fully to satisfy all gifts, the courts generally resort to *abatement* (i.e., proportionate reduction) of gifts within a particular class. The order of abatement is normally just the reverse of the order of distribution—that is, residuary gifts are first reduced, then general gifts, then, finally, specific bequests and devises. In some states, all personal property gifts are abated before real property gifts; in other states, specific and general gifts are abated ratably rather than general gifts first.

Where abatement of a class gift is required, each class member generally loses a proportionate share of the property. Suppose that Robert Smith provides by will that his children are to receive $50,000 upon his death, but Robert dies leaving only $40,000 available for distribution to his two sons and two daughters. Assuming no inter vivos gifts have been made, each child's $12,500 share will be ratably reduced by $2,500 for a total of $10,000 for each child.

In some states where the class consists only partially of blood relatives of the testator, the shares of the blood relatives will be paid in full and the shares of the other class members will be abated. Thus, if in our example above, two of the class members are Robert's children and two are friends of the family, Robert's children will each receive a full $12,500 while Robert's friends will receive but $7,500 each ($12,500–$5,000).

WHAT IS A LAPSED GIFT?

A lapsed gift is a gift that fails because the named beneficiary is either unwilling to accept the gift or unable to take the property because he or she is dead at the time the will takes effect. If the will does not specify an alternative beneficiary, a lapsed gift, specific, general, or demonstrative gift will become a part of the residuary; a lapsed residuary gift will be treated as intestate property and will pass according to the state intestacy laws (intestacy is discussed in a later section).

A class gift will not lapse so long as any members of the class are alive and willing to take the property. Thus, if Robert Smith leaves "$50,000 to my children," the gift will be valid even if three of Robert's four children die before Robert dies so long as the fourth and last child is willing to accept the $50,000 at the time of Robert's death. However, where Robert leaves "$50,000 to my children James, Carla, Mark, and Karen," the court may construe the gift, not as a class gift, but as a specific bequest of $12,500 to each child; the gift of any child who dies before Robert dies will thus lapse in the absence of an alternative beneficiary.

Most states have now passed "antilapse" statutes which generally provide that a testamentary gift to a blood relative of the testator will not lapse in the event that the relative predeceases the testator. Rather, the gift will pass to the deceased beneficiary's heirs or beneficiaries.

ARE THERE ANY RESTRICTIONS ON A TESTATOR'S DISPOSITION OF HIS OR HER PROPERTY?

With the following limited exceptions, a testator is free to dispose of his or her property in any manner he or she chooses so long as the proper will formalities are observed.

Spouses

In most states a surviving spouse has a statutory right to claim a designated portion or share (usually one-fourth or one-half) of a deceased spouse's property regardless of the provisions of the decedent's will. Thus, if the surviving spouse receives nothing by the terms of the will, he or she can make an "election" against the will and receive from one-fourth to one-half of the estate. The same is true where the surviving spouse receives some property by the terms of the will but less than his or her statutory share; he or she can elect against the will, renouncing all the testamentary gifts provided, and receive, again, from one-fourth to one-half of the decedent spouse's estate. A surviving spouse who makes a "renunciation" of the gifts provided by will may lose the specific bequests and devises made in his or her favor, but the spouse will gain an increased overall share of the estate property.

Where a surviving spouse chooses to elect against the will, the probate court must generally abate the testamentary gifts made to others (residuary gifts first, then general gifts, then specific gifts) in order to provide the spouse with his or her proper statutory share.

It might also be pointed out that election against the will and renunciation are usually not provided for by statute in community property states: as each spouse already has an undivided ownership interest in all property, other than separate property, acquired during the marriage, a statutory forced share is not considered necessary.

Children

"Pretermitted heir" statutes in nearly all states provide that where the testator's child is not mentioned in a will, the will will be disregarded to the extent that the child will be permitted to receive his or her intestate share of the decedent's property (i.e., that share he or she would be entitled to receive had the testator left no will). For example, suppose that Robert Smith executes a will leaving property to his sons, James and Mark, and his daughter Carla. Robert leaves nothing to his daughter Karen—in fact, he fails to mention her anywhere in the will. Upon Robert's death, the probate court will declare Karen to be a "pretermitted" (i.e., omitted) heir and permit her to take her intestate share of Robert's property. If necessary, the gifts to

James, Mark, and Carla will be abated to provide Karen with her lawful share.

The "pretermitted heir" statute applies whether the pretermitted child was born before or after execution of the will. The theory behind the statute is that the testator has merely forgotten to provide for the child and that, in disregarding the child's omission from the will, the law is simply carrying out the testator's intent.

It follows that the pretermitted heir statute does not apply where it is apparent from the will that the testator clearly intended to disinherit the child. For example, a specific statement in a will that "I hereby disinherit my son, Robert," is sufficient to accomplish the task—the "pretermitted heir" statute will not be used to defeat the testator's expressed intent.

Debtors

The "doctrine of retainer" is the rule of law that a monetary bequest to a debtor of the testator (and thus a debtor of the testator's estate) should be reduced by the amount of the debt outstanding. For example, suppose that Sidney Smith loans $5,000 to his friend, Peter Carson; Peter still owes Sidney the money at the time of Sidney's death. If Sidney's will provides that Peter is to receive $10,000 from Sidney's estate, the doctrine of retainer will operate to reduce the $10,000 bequest by the $5,000 debt outstanding for a total bequest to Peter of $5,000.

Creditors

A testamentary bequest to a creditor of the testator in an amount equal to or greater than the debt owing is rebuttably presumed to be in satisfaction of the debt. Unless the creditor can show that the testator intended the bequest to be separate from and in addition to satisfaction of the debt, the creditor cannot collect twice from the testator's estate.

Charities

Finally, as pointed out earlier, Mortmain Statutes in some states restrict or prohibit a testator's testamentary gifts to charity. You will recall that some of the statutes provide that a testator may give no more than one-third or one-half of his or her estate to charity. Other statutes declare that any testamentary gift made within a short period of time before the testator's death (such as thirty days) is invalid. Of course, many states have modernly repealed such laws and permit the free and unrestricted testamentary transfer of property to charity so long as the proper will formalities, including testamentary intent and capacity, are present.

WHAT IS A HOLOGRAPHIC WILL?

A *holographic* will is a written will that lacks the statutory requirements for formal execution. Holographic wills are recognized as valid in a *minority* of states so long as the following three requirements are met in addition to testamentary intent:

1. The will must be written entirely in the testator's own handwriting;
2. The will must be dated in the handwriting of the testator;
3. Finally, the will must be signed in the testator's own handwriting.

WHAT IS A "TOTTEN" TRUST?

In Chapter 8 we discussed the joint tenancy with the right of survivorship and learned that property held with the survivorship characteristic passes, not to the deceased cotenant's heirs or beneficiaries, but to the surviving cotenant or cotenants automatically by operation of law. Because the interest passes automatically at the moment of death, the deceased joint tenant has nothing left to transfer by will or intestacy, and a will provision purporting to transfer property held concurrently with the right of survivorship is void and of no effect. One elderly woman, for example, hired an attorney to draft her a will leaving her $80,000 cash estate to her nine grandchildren. At the same time, however, and without realizing the legal effect of her actions, the woman placed the $80,000 into a savings account which she held jointly with her son and daughter, all with the right of survivorship. When the woman died a few months later, the $80,000 automatically passed to her son and daughter, the surviving joint tenants—despite the terms of the will, the woman's grandchildren received nothing. As you can see, a person who owns all his or her property concurrently with the right of survivorship has no need for a will. Such ownership is a very effective will substitute and a popular one as well.

Also a property owner who places all his or her property into an inter vivos trust may effectively avoid the need for a will. For example, it is not unusual for a trustor to transfer property in trust for the lifetime benefit of himself or herself and, upon his or her death, for the benefit of a surviving spouse or children. Such a trust is an effective will substitute. And frequently, an insured will transfer ownership of a life insurance policy to a trustee for the benefit of another. Upon the death of the insured, the life insurance proceeds become a part of the trust res (the proceeds are payable directly to the trust, the named beneficiary of the insurance policy) and will be managed by the trustee according to the conditions and purposes stated in the trust. Life insurance trusts are not considered testamentary even though there is an absence of any significant trust res prior to the trustor-insured's death. They are nontestamentary and valid will substitutes even where the insured retains the power to revoke or modify the trust or to change its beneficiaries.

The so-called "Totten" trust, also called the "savings bank deposit trust" or "tentative trust," may also be an effective will substitute. Suppose, for a moment, that Sidney Smith deposits $10,000 in an account at the First National Bank for "Sidney Smith in trust for my son, Robert." Has Sidney created a valid trust in favor of Robert with himself appointed as trustee? If so, does Robert have an immediate right to the money or any portion of it, or do Robert's rights arise only when Sidney dies? If Robert's rights do not arise until Sidney's death and if Sidney has unlimited power over the $10,000 until that time, the transfer would appear testamentary in nature and, in the absence of the proper will formalities, would be invalid.

Nevertheless, a majority of states follow the "tentative trust doctrine" established in the New York case of Matter of Totten, 179 N.Y. 112, 71 N.E. 748 (1904) (the case from which the term "Totten" trust derives). The tentative trust doctrine provides that a deposit of funds by a person in his or her own name as trustee for another creates a revocable inter vivos trust. The depositor can revoke the trust in whole or in part at any time simply by making withdrawals from the account. And so long as the depositor is alive, his or her creditors can reach the deposit even though the depositor is technically deemed a trustee for another. Whatever is left in the account (if anything) at the time of the depositor's death will go to the named beneficiary if he or she is still alive.

Because the deposit is held to create a valid, though revocable inter vivos trust and because the balance of the account will pass to the named beneficiary rather than remain in the decedent-depositor's estate, the Totten trust is an effective will substitute and one readily available to property owners of even the most limited means.

It should be pointed out that if the named beneficiary of the trust predeceases the depositor, the trust will terminate, and the beneficiary's heirs or beneficiaries will have no rights to the account balance upon the depositor-trustor's death.

Also, if the depositor-trustor specifically provides by will that the account balance is to go to someone other than the trust beneficiary, the will will control, and the trust beneficiary will receive nothing. However, a statement that "all my property" is to go to some other named individual is not sufficiently specific to affect the rights of the Totten trust beneficiary—the statement must specifically refer to the Totten trust account. Finally, the revocable Totten trust will become irrevocable if the depositor-trustor turns control of the account over to the beneficiary by giving the beneficiary the savings account passbook.

Why is a transfer of property that appears so testamentary in character given the legal status of a valid, revocable inter vivos trust and will substitute in a majority of jurisdictions? Despite the fact that the depositor retains almost unlimited control over the deposited funds and despite the fact that the beneficiary has no interest, if any, until the depositor-trustor dies, the Totten trust is a socially desirable device that enables people of limited means to obtain the advantages of a will without the expense and delay of a testamentary disposition of property.

In the minority of jurisdictions where Totten trusts are not recognized because of their testamentary nature, the account balance is deemed an asset of the decedent-depositor's estate, and the account beneficiary has no rights to the property.

Will substitutes, including Totten trusts, are used to avoid probate. Probate, as explained in Chapter 3, is simply the process of legally transferring a deceased person's property to the deceased's lawfully designated heirs or beneficiaries. The probate process ensures that the right people end up with the property, and it serves to protect creditors of the deceased, including governmental taxing authorities.

However, probate is a time-consuming process (usually eight to ten months), and it is also expensive (perhaps 3 to 5 percent of the value of the estate). Because of this, many people use will substitutes to avoid probate. Property that is given away during life is not in the decedent's estate at death and so is not subject to probate. Nor is property that is placed in trust or held jointly with the right of survivorship probated as part of the decedent's estate. But absent an effective will substitute, a decedent's property is probated whether he or she dies with or without a will (intestate). Dying intestate, the property will go to surviving heirs according to state statute (see figure 3–6 in Chapter 3), the deceased's property going first to children, then to grandchildren, then to great-grandchildren. It is only when there are none of these that the property will go to brothers and sisters, etc. Only when there are no living relatives does the property escheat to the state. And while a wife or husband is not an "heir" because not a blood relative, a wife or husband does receive all or part of the decedent's property; generally all of it if there are no children, and half of it if there are children and the decedent dies intestate.

By way of example, suppose that Robert Smith dies intestate (i.e., without a will), leaving a surviving wife, Peg, an unmarried daughter, Karen, and two grandchildren, Peter and Brian, the children of Robert's son, Mark, who predeceased Robert (see figure 13–2). Because Robert has no will, state statute determines who gets the property. While state intestacy laws differ from state to state, a typical statute might provide for the following distribution of property.

Note that the grandchildren Peter and Brian take the share of their deceased father Mark. They are said to take their father's share "per stirpes" which means by right of representation.

In most states if the heirs are all in the same class (i.e., all children or all grandchildren, etc.), they do not take "per stirpes," but rather "per capita"

FIGURE 13–2 PER STIRPES

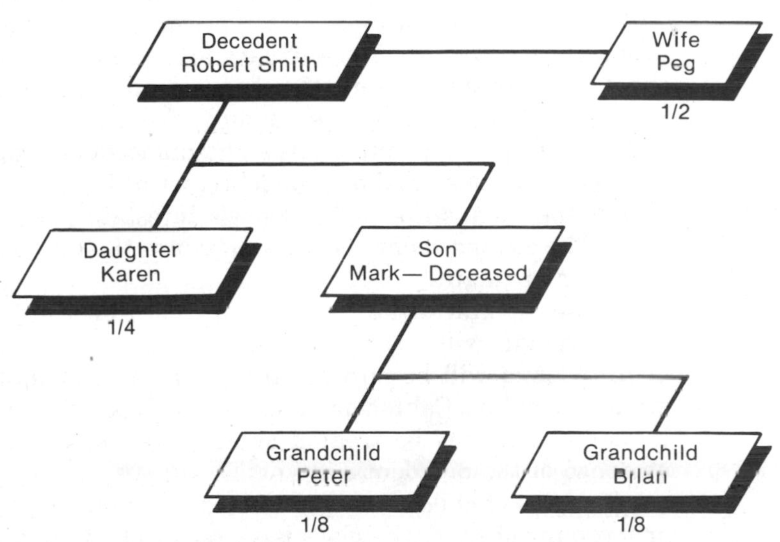

FIGURE 13–3 PER CAPITA

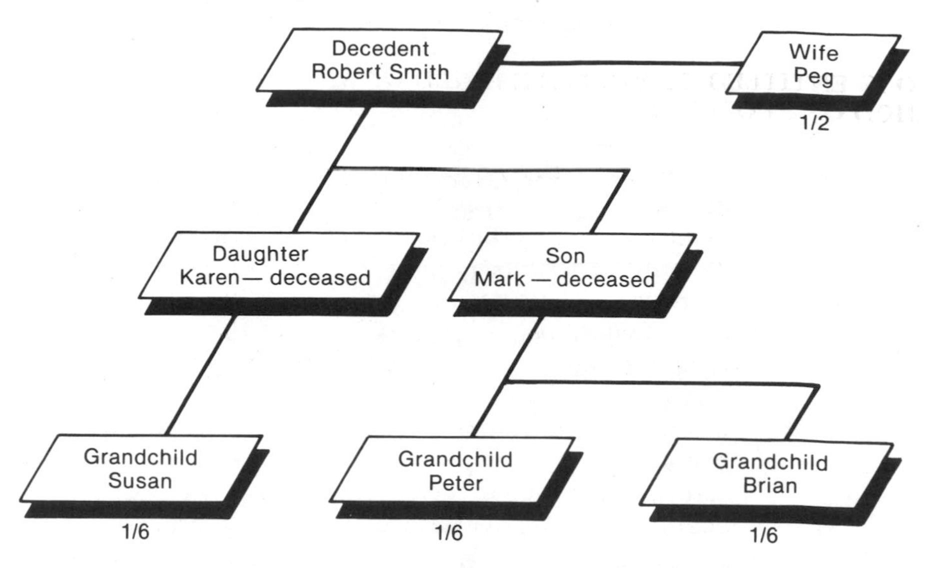

which means in their own right in equal shares. Thus, in our example, if daughter Karen was also deceased leaving a surviving child Susan, the three grandchildren, being in the same class, would take "per capita" and each receive one-sixth of the estate as in figure 13–3.

WHAT IS AN "ADVANCEMENT?"

An advancement is very much like an ademption by satisfaction. As you will recall, ademption by satisfaction comes into play when a testator gives property inter vivos to a beneficiary named in his or her will, intending that the gift satisfy the testamentary bequest in whole or in part (the testamentary bequest is reduced by the amount of the inter vivos gift). Similarly, an "advancement" is an inter vivos gift made by a property owner (who later dies intestate) to a child or grandchild with the intention that the gift constitute prepayment toward the donee's intestate portion of the decedent's estate. The advancement operates to reduce the intestate share of the value of the inter vivos gift.

However, unless the decedent *intends* that the gift reduce the intestate share, the gift will not qualify as an advancement, and the decedent's child or grandchild will be entitled to his or her full intestate share. In a few states, including California, a gift to any person who would qualify as an intestate heir may be treated as an advancement only if there is written evidence of the decedent's intent.

If a class of children or grandchildren qualifies as intestate heirs and one or more members of the class have received an advancement, the respective shares of the individual members will be calculated by the "hotchpot" method as described in the section on ademption by satisfaction.

WHO IS ENTITLED TO INCOME EARNED BY AN ESTATE DURING THE PERIOD OF PROBATE?

Obviously, a decedent's property will continue to produce income during the period of administration or probate of the estate, which may take many months or even years. Such income is taxable to the estate which is a taxable entity that must report its income and pay income taxes like any other taxpayer. The estate reports its income on what is called a "fiduciary income tax return." (Inter vivos and testamentary trusts must also report their income on a "fiduciary income tax return" and pay income taxes just like any other taxable entity. A trust which by its terms must distribute income to beneficiaries receives a deduction for the income distributed to the beneficiaries who must report the income they receive on their own personal returns.) Of course, income earned and taxed to the estate will not be taxed again when it is distributed to the beneficiaries of the estate at the end of the probate period.

As to who is entitled to the earnings and profits of the estate during this period, it is necessary to return to our previous classification of testamentary gifts.

Specific Gifts

Specific gifts, such as bank accounts, stocks, bonds, real estate, etc., carry with them the right to all earnings and profits produced by the specific property *after* the death of the testator (any accrued but unpaid *interest* on the property at the time of the testator's death also goes to the specific beneficiary). For example, rent due and owing prior to the testator's death is not payable to the specific devisee of the rental property, but rent falling due after the testator's death is. Similarly, dividends declared on stock prior to the testator's death do not belong to the stock beneficiary, but dividends declared after the testator's death do. Suppose that there is a split of stock resulting in an increased number of shares—does the stock beneficiary have a right to the added shares? The beneficiary will have a right to the shares whether the stock split is declared before or after the testator's death so long as the gift of stock is truly a *specific* bequest of particular shares rather than a *general* bequest that may be satisfied out of any number of shares. For example, if Sidney Smith bequeaths "my 100 shares of General Motors stock to my son, Robert," and, prior to Sidney's death, the stock splits two for one, Robert will be entitled to the full 200 shares upon Sidney's death because the specific 100 shares Sidney intended Robert to receive are now represented by 200 shares. However, a bequest of "100 shares of General Motors stock to my son, Robert" is probably a general gift of stock that may be satisfied out of any General Motors stock in Sidney's estate, and Robert would not be entitled to any additional stock resulting from a stock split prior to Sidney's death. The courts, in any case, will try to give effect to the testator's probable intent. And a gift of stock in a closely held or family corporation will more than likely be held a specific rather than a general bequest.

General Gifts

In most states, general bequests begin to bear interest at the legal rate in favor of the general gift beneficiary starting one year after the testator's death.

Residuary Gifts

Residuary gifts do not bear interest. However, all earnings and profits that do not belong to the specific gift beneficiaries and that are not payable as interest to the general gift beneficiaries belong to the residuary beneficiary.

IN WHAT ORDER ARE CLAIMS AGAINST AND INTERESTS IN THE DECEDENT'S ESTATE SATISFIED?

While probate statutes vary somewhat from state to state, the following order of payment is typical:

1. Expenses of administration, including court costs (probate fees), attorneys' fees, and personal representative fees;
2. The decedent's funeral expenses;
3. Medical bills and other expenses of the decedent's last illness;
4. Family support allowances provided during the administration of the estate for the support of the decedent's surviving spouse and children;
5. Taxes owing to the government;
6. Any wages owing to employees of the decedent for work during the three months immediately preceding their employer's death;
7. All mortgages or secured liens or claims against the estate in the order of their priority;
8. All inter vivos judgments against the decedent in the order of their priority (first in time, first in priority);
9. All other valid claims against the estate;
10. And finally, the beneficiaries or heirs are paid.

With regard to payment of beneficiaries or heirs, if the decedent died testate, the specific gifts are distributed first, then the general, and, finally, the residuary. If the decedent died intestate, the intestate heirs are paid their respective shares or portions of the estates.

In most states, taxes must be equitably apportioned against the shares of all beneficiaries of the estate unless the decedent's will provides otherwise. As a result, it is very common to find a provision in a will that all taxes are to be paid out of the residuary portion of the estate so as not to affect the specific, demonstrative, and general bequests and devises.

WHAT HAPPENS IF A DECEDENT AND HIS OR HER BENEFICIARIES ARE KILLED IN A SIMULTANEOUS DEATH?

For a person to receive property under a will or by virtue of the laws of intestacy, it is necessary for the person to survive the decedent, if only for a moment of time. Sometimes, however, where a common disaster occurs, it is difficult to determine who died first. Thus, the Uniform Simultaneous Death Act, the law in effect in a great many states, provides that where it is impossible to determine who died first in a common accident, the property of *each* decedent will be distributed as if he or she had survived. The effect of the Act is to prevent a double probate. For example, suppose that Sidney Smith executes a will leaving one-half of his property to his wife, Mary, and one-half to his son, Robert. Sidney's wife, Mary executes a will leaving one-half of her estate to Sidney and one-half to Robert. Subsequently, Sidney, Mary, and Robert all die in an automobile accident with no evidence of who died first. Under the USDA, Sidney will be deemed to have survived both his wife and his son insofar as his estate is concerned, and Mary will be deemed to have survived both her husband and son with regard to her property. As a result, all gifts under both wills will lapse, and both Sidney and Mary will be deemed to have died intestate.

Life and accidental insurance are handled the same way: where both insured and beneficiary die in the same accident, it is presumed that the beneficiary died first so as to permit distribution of the insurance proceeds to the alternate beneficiary.

CAN A DECEDENT'S MURDERER INHERIT FROM THE DECEASED?

No. Just as a joint tenant who murders his or her cotenant will not be permitted to acquire ownership of the cotenant's property by the right of survivorship, a person who murders another cannot share in his or her victim's estate either as a beneficiary under the decedent's will or as the decedent's lawful intestate heir. The murderer will not be permitted to profit from his or her wrongful act. Generally, he or she will be treated as though he or she predeceased the decedent, in which case the murderer's gifts under the will will lapse, and his or her intestate gifts will be distributed to the victim's other intestate heirs.

CAN PROPERTY BE PLACED IN TRUST SO AS TO MAKE THE INCOME TAXABLE TO SOMEONE OTHER THAN THE GRANTOR?

Yes, if certain conditions are met. A taxpayer in a high tax bracket may want to reduce his or her income tax liability by placing income-producing property into what is termed a "grantor trust" for the benefit of a family member (or perhaps a close friend) who is in a much lower tax bracket. A taxpayer can effectively "split his or her income" in this manner only if he or she places the property into trust for a minimum of ten years; so long as the grantor-trustor has no reversionary interest in the trust during this period of time, all income from the trust will be taxed to the trust beneficiary—not to the trustor.

Of course, the grantor-trustor may provide for a reversionary interest in himself or herself after the ten-year period, and a provision in the trust that the property will revert to the grantor prior to this time if the income beneficiary dies within the ten-year period is also permissible. However, other than this, the grantor must have no power to direct the beneficial enjoyment of the trust income during the ten-year period, either to himself or herself or to others.

In conclusion, use of a "grantor trust" is particularly desirable for individuals in high income tax brackets with minor children in low income tax brackets (although the grantor will be taxed on any portion of the trust income that is used for the support or maintenance of the children as the grantor is already legally obligated to provide for their support).

WHAT ARE TAXES?

The Congress shall have power: To lay and collect taxes, duties, imports, and excises to pay the debts and provide for the common defense and general welfare of the United States.

> *Taxes are what we pay for civilized society. I like to pay taxes. With them I buy civilization.*
>
> Oliver Wendell Holmes

Taxation is a very complicated legal concept. Its source is found in the constitutional provision set out above giving Congress the power to require payment of taxes. State constitutions have similar provisions providing for state and local taxation. Both federal and state legislative bodies have enacted taxing statutes so that governments can operate. Originally, the tax system was used merely to pay for the ordinary and regular expenses of government, but the rise of a modern and complex society has wrought a great increase in the number, extent, and intensity of public functions by all units of government—local, state, and national. For better or worse, government has taken on increasing responsibility for the protection and welfare of the people—chief responsibility for carrying out the four legitimate functions of the law. But along with responsibility has come the need for a much heavier tax burden. More and more revenue is needed to pay for the programs of government. This revenue must come from taxes.

A tax may be defined as a compulsory contribution levied by the state upon persons, property, income, and privileges for the purpose of defraying the expenses of government. Only an authorized legislative body may levy a tax, and it must do so according to established legal principles. But these rules and principles only begin with the tax statutes themselves. Administrative agencies created by the statutes, such as the Internal Revenue Service and state tax commissions, make thousands of rules each year regarding the tax law. Equitable concepts, national policy objectives, special interest group pressure (e.g., oil industry, farmers, charitable organizations, and legal administrators themselves), along with the hundreds of thousands of administrative and judicial decisions have all shaped tax law into the highly complex labyrinth of rules, exceptions to the rules, and exceptions to the exceptions that we have today. Obviously, it's impossible to deal completely with the concept of tax law in part of a single chapter. But we can present the various bases for taxation that exist in the country today, as well as the government programs that form an important part of our legal environment. We will mention a few common tax problems that affect all of us, businessman and homemaker alike, and suggest ways to handle them. We will also present a summary of inheritance, estate, and gift taxes (taxes on the transfer of property at death and on its transfer by gift). Certainly, a basic understanding of taxation and public regulation is essential to successful living in our society.

For a tax to be valid, it must be levied not only by a duly constituted "public authority" but for the public good—or, as frequently stated by the courts, for a "public purpose" (i.e., it may not be levied to run a private business in our free enterprise system). But courts have upheld the use of public funds for private business in times of emergency. Municipal funds, for example, were used to operate a fuel yard during a particularly severe winter and to keep a North Dakota state bank open in a serious postwar depression. Federal "public purpose" expenditures include subsidies to private agriculture and credit to private individuals for business and home building.

WHAT ARE TAX RATE STRUCTURES?

There are a variety of tax bases. A tax base is an object upon which a tax is levied and to which a tax rate is applied. The tax base in the income tax is "net income." After determining your "net income," you apply the tax rate—the percentage of the tax base that must be paid by the taxpayer to the government. The amount of tax is determined simply by multiplying the base by the tax rate. The property tax base is the assessed value of the property: after the county assessor determines that value, the tax rate is applied to determine your property tax. The sales tax base is the value of the goods purchased.

Taxation involves three basic rate structures. A tax rate structure is a pattern that shows how a rate behaves as the tax base increases or decreases. Thus as the value of property goes up, the tax rate can either go up or down. Or as a person's income increases, the tax rate can also increase.

Progressive Rate Structure

In a progressive rate structure, the rate increases as the base increases. Progressive tax rates are found in income, estate, and inheritance taxes in the United States. Thus, as your income goes up, so too does your tax rate increase until you reach the point where 50 to 60 percent of every dollar you make is paid to the government in taxes. The same is true for very large estates. If you die, leaving to your survivors an estate worth $100,000 or less, you may have little or no death tax to pay. But if you leave an estate of

$10 million, the government may tax a portion of it at 50 percent and collect several millions of dollars in taxes.

Proportional Rate Structure

In a proportional rate structure, the rate remains constant whether the base is large or small and regardless of whether it increases or decreases. This structure is generally applied to property and sales taxes. So a general property tax on your home is at the same rate no matter what the value of your home is. You may pay 2 percent a year on a house worth $20,000 (tax of $400), or 2 percent of a $50,000 home, with a resulting tax of $1,000.

Regressive Rate Structure

In a regressive rate structure, the rate decreases as the base increases. Actually, there are no regressive rate structures used in this country (sales and property taxes are applied using a proportional rate). But people frequently use the term regressive to describe sales and property taxes because this kind of tax takes a larger proportion of the small or middle income producer's money than it does of the individual with a very high income. For example, someone who makes only $4,000 to $5,000 a year probably spends much of his income on items subject to a sales tax, while the person making $40,000 to $50,000 is less likely to spend the same proportion of his income on similar items. The tax, therefore, is said to be regressive. But, remember, the person who makes only $4,000 or $5,000 a year pays little or no income tax, while the person making $40,000 to $50,000 pays a substantial portion of his income to the government.

Tax rate structures have always been a subject of controversy. Some people claim that the sales tax is too hard on the "little guy"; others support it because it makes everyone pay something for the government services he receives. Defenders of the progressive tax rate believe that every person should contribute to the government according to his ability to do so. Its critics find that it stifles initiative and penalizes thrift and industry. But one wise man who remains anonymous perhaps said it best: "Taxes," he said, "are a changing product of earnest efforts to have others pay them." What it boils down to is that nobody really likes to pay taxes, but nearly everyone wants more and better services from the government. But government needs more revenue if programs are to be initiated and paid for. For better or for worse, our system is basically one of progressive taxation. It is "for better" because taxpayers in the middle and upper income tax brackets help the government provide services and benefits for low income producers and achieve national goals of growth and development. It is "for worse" because progressive taxes dangerously diminish desire to work and incentive to invest—essential elements of a free enterprise system. If the progressive tax system goes too far, and takes too much, private initiative may be destroyed.

As Benjamin Franklin said, "In this world nothing is certain but death and taxes." Our tax system and its results in terms of government programs and services are very much a part of our legal environment. With

FIGURE 13–4 TAX RATE STRUCTURES

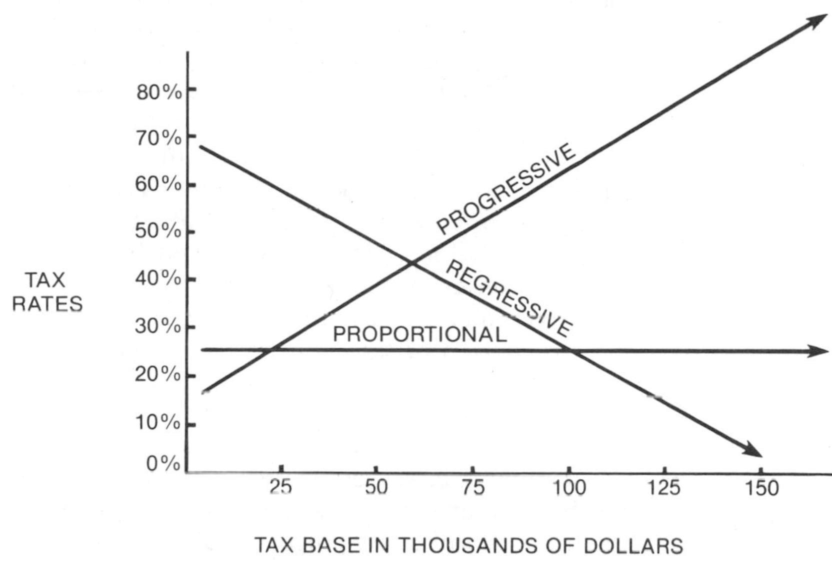

this in mind, let's take a brief look at the kinds of taxation that exist in this country today.

WHAT ARE THE MAIN WAYS TO TAX?

Property Taxes

The Constitution states at Article 1, § 9, Cl. 5 that direct taxes must be apportioned according to population. This means that the state with the largest population must pay the most tax, and the state with the lowest must pay the least. Tax on real estate has always been recognized as a "direct tax," but it is very difficult to levy property tax according to population. As a result, there is no federal property tax. And property tax is seldom levied on a statewide basis; most states rely on income and/or sales tax revenue. But property tax is the very substance of local tax structure. School districts rely heavily upon them—particularly real estate taxes on homes (school districts in many states also receive substantial aid from state revenues—income or sales taxes).

While property tax is generally levied on real property (land, buildings, and other improvements on land), some personal property is also included within the tax (e.g., business inventories). The property tax base is the "value" of the property on assessment day. Legislatures in the various states use such terms as "fair market value" or "actual cash value" in determining the value of particular pieces of property. Frequently, if value is at issue (and a taxpayer can always challenge the assessed value in court), the court will use this test of "fair market value"—what a willing buyer would pay a willing seller when neither is under any compulsion to buy or sell.

There are perhaps 150,000 to 200,000 local units in the United States that are involved with the administration, collection, and use of property tax. Cities, towns, counties, school districts, water districts, drainage irrigation districts, flood control districts, park districts, sewage disposal districts—all receive property tax revenues.

The "primary assessment" district (usually the county) is the governmental unit that carries out the original assessment activity for all other governmental units within a fixed area. The primary assessment district determines the value of the property and levies and collects the tax. The smaller governmental units, including the school district, park district, or sewage district share in the revenue collected. General administrative procedure in execution of the property tax is as follows:

Original assessment Generally, the assessor is required by statute to value all property within a district on a particular day (April 1 and May 1 are common dates in several states). The actual assessment work, however, is done throughout the year as the assessor locates the property and values it. The assessor gives the property its final value on assessment day. Any property acquired after that date is not taxed until the next assessment date—and then, only if the assessor adds the property to his records. Assessment is a continuous job of keeping district valuations up to date.

Review of assessment Generally, district boards of review have power to alter the assessment on grounds of unjust valuation, but it is up to the property owner himself to prove that his property has been assessed at a higher value than the general level of community assessments. This right to contest the assessor's valuation is guaranteed to the property owner by due process of law.

Actual assessment organization varies greatly throughout the country. In small areas the entire organization may consist of one elected official (usually called the assessor) and two or three helpers. In larger areas, a complicated organizational structure employing a great number of people may exist. Employees may be divided into groups that deal strictly with certain types of property (e.g., business or residential). Or the assessor's office may further divide into geographical areas. In any case his or her office is always equipped with district maps that show the size and location of lots within the area and each area's key land values as well. Many offices maintain files that list the history of each piece of property located within the district, including its change of owners, sale prices, and improvements.

Statutes usually require the holders of personal property that is used for business or for the production of income (e.g., apartment house owners) to file an annual statement showing what property is in their possession on assessment day. This frequently applies to farmers, who must file an inventory listing the machinery and livestock they own and use for farming along with its present value. The age, type, location, and income-producing capability of the property are all relevant in assessing its value.

The assessor's valuation of the property is the base upon which the tax rate is applied to determine property tax. But coming up with that value is by far the most difficult problem in property taxation. Land values are usually determined with reference to recent sale of the land or similar land. And a parcel of land that produces substantial income is valued much higher than barren land that produces nothing. With buildings, replacement cost is taken into account. And where inventories are concerned, the assessor frequently refers to the value shown for the inventory in the balance sheet of the business or in other business records. Most businesses keep fairly accurate records of inventory value as a matter of sound business practice. For a manufacturing company, the value of labor and material that has gone into an uncompleted item is used to determine its value.

General levy The authority to tax property must first come from a legislative body with constitutional power to create the tax. This authority to tax is called the "general levy." It states that a tax may be levied against property, and it sets either a definite amount for collection or a definite rate of taxation to be applied against the property tax base.

Determination of rate for each unit Once the general levy has passed, the specific tax rate to be applied against property within the district must be determined. This may be complicated if there is a general levy for a statewide tax, plus local levies for a particular school district and/or additional levies for a drainage or fire district. If the state rate is .3 percent, the county 2.2 percent, the city 1.5 percent, and the school district 2.9 percent, there is a total combined rate of 6.9 percent. This total rate is then applied to the assessed value of property within the district. Of course, these rates are based on what is authorized in the levy for each district; they are originally determined by looking at the projected need—what will it take to operate the school or to provide fire protection? Many states require district voter approval of operating budgets and levies before the rate may be applied and the tax collected.

Collection of the property taxes Property taxes are usually collected at the local level. The funds are then distributed to the particular governmental units. Payment of the tax may be on a quarterly or other installment plan basis, and often a discount is provided if the entire tax is paid in one lump sum by a certain date. Where the tax is not paid on time, a delinquent penalty (e.g., 6 percent of the tax) may be imposed. And where the tax is not paid at all, the state may sell the property to the highest bidder (over a certain minimum price) and thus collect the taxes, interest, and penalties.

Judicial review Of course, taxpayers who feel they have been unjustly treated may always seek judicial review of assessment and other taxing authority procedures.

On many occasions, certain property is exempted altogether from application of the tax. Society is best served, for example, by exempting charities from property tax; they provide services and benefits that the government itself would otherwise be responsible for. Some industries also escape property taxation (to influence their location), as do some individuals such as veterans, who are thus rewarded for the services they rendered to their country.

And in almost every case, a tax sale resulting from nonpayment of delinquent tax is not a final and irrevocable loss of the property. The tax statute provides a means known as "redemption" by which the taxpayer may defeat the tax sale and get his property back. He does this by repaying the purchase price of the property at the tax sale along with interests and costs in a period of time that runs from several months to a year or more.

Income Taxes

The Sixteenth Amendment to the Constitution, ratified in 1913, states that "Congress shall have power to lay and collect taxes on incomes from whatever source derived, without apportionment among the several states; and without regard to any census or enumeration." What this means is that the federal government need not apportion income tax according to population. The amendment, however, fails to state what "income" is. The Internal Revenue Code (federal taxing statutes) defines income in but a general way; the Internal Revenue Service (a federal agency) has specifically defined it in regulations that interpret and effect the statutes.

The first step in arriving at taxable income (the tax base) is to determine gross income. Certain receipts are legally excluded from income, including gift receipts. To constitute income, some consideration (whether past, present, or future) must move from the recipient to the other person. That is, the taxpayer must work, give up something, or do something for what he or she receives, or the receipt is a gift, not income. Of course, even a gift, if large enough, is subject to gift tax laws. And prizes and awards are generally considered income because the recipient must do something, however small, to become eligible to win them. Inheritances are not income, but, again, they are subject to estate or death tax if sufficiently large. Even receipts obtained illegitimately are income as long as the taxpayer does something to earn them. This includes dishonest, fraudulent, and criminal income. Al Capone, for example, was sent to jail for failure to pay his taxes; he was accused but never convicted of other crime. Receipts from illegal gambling, bootlegging, racketeering, prostitution, and extortion must all be reported as part of gross income.

Frequently, what is received is a return of investment. This "return of capital" is not income. So if you buy a vacant lot for $5,000 and sell it two years later for $8,000, you are taxed only on $3,000; $5,000 is a return of capital. The Internal Revenue Code generally provides that the amount of gain from the sale or other disposition of an asset is the difference between the sale price and the cost.

Receipts in kind, though not monetary in form, are also income. Thus if you are paid for your work with either goods or services, you must list the "fair market value" of the goods or services as part of your gross income.

Many rules specifically deal with what receipts are income or to what extent they are. Of course, many items are obviously income—wages, salaries, fees, commissions, partnership income, business income, interest, rents, royalties, dividends, and so forth. As a taxpayer, you must subject every form of receipt to the same question: "Does this receipt constitute an item of income?" If the item is an unusual one, you may have to look to the appropriate statute or regulation or consult with a tax advisor to find out.

Whether you make out your own return or seek assistance from someone else, you are responsible for calculating the amount of your income tax liability each taxpaying period. You must report your true net income and maintain sufficient records to insure the accuracy of your return. The basic mechanics of tax reporting involve four steps: (1) determining gross income; (2) deducting from gross income all allowable deductions and exemptions to arrive at net or taxable income; (3) applying the tax rate to this taxable income (the tax base) to determine tax liability; and (4) applying the credits allowed, including taxes already paid, to determine the specific amount you owe the government or the amount the government must refund you because of overpayment.

Determining gross income The following items are commonly excluded from gross income (in addition to the receipts we have already mentioned).

Interest on government bonds It is a long-established constitutional principle that the federal government may not tax the interest on state and municipal bonds. On the other hand, states cannot tax the interest on federal bonds either. A bond is a written or printed instrument that evidences a debt owed by a government (also used in business by corporations). The government issues the bond in order to borrow money. In this way, cities, counties, and other local, state, and federal governments can raise revenue in addition to tax monies to pay for the expenses and projects of government. The bond states that the issuer (the government) will pay the principal (the sum borrowed) back when the bond matures at some future date (usually some years into the future). A fixed amount of interest is also paid at regular intervals until the principal is returned. A person in a high income tax bracket under the progressive income tax system (where he pays tax on income at a rate to as high as 50 percent federal) may choose to invest in government bonds. While the interest rate is rather low, the interest itself is not taxable. All of this, however, is subject to provisions in the tax law that require payment of some minimum tax. These provisions are designed to prevent any person from having an all tax-exempt income.

Life insurance proceeds Life insurance proceeds received on the death of an insured decedent are not taxable income. But the proceeds are taxed as part of the decedent's estate for death or estate tax purposes (considered later in this chapter) if the insured owns the policy at the time of his death.

Gifts, bequests, and inheritances These are also subject only to gift or death taxes—they are not taxed as income.

Compensatory damages Compensatory damages recovered in a tort action are not taxable income. They are awarded simply to put the plaintiff back in the position he was in prior to the injury. And this is true even where the action is settled out of court (e.g., money paid out by an insurance company in settlement of injury is not taxed as income). But punitive damages, awarded for malicious or outrageous conduct, are taxable.

Payments from certain government programs Such payments, which include veterans benefits based on disability, welfare payments, and social security benefits, are generally not taxable.

Child support payments Child support payments received by a divorced spouse are not taxable income, but alimony payments are.

Other There are other special exclusions in the tax law, including all return of capital. And, of course, the exclusions change from time to time and differ from state to state where income tax is used as a means of raising revenue.

Deductions and exemptions Income tax law is designed to tax net income only. Unjust criticism is often leveled against the individual who pays little tax with comments like the following: "He had a hundred thousand dollars of income and paid no tax." Having a gross income of a hundred thousand dollars or even of a million dollars is of little significance if your expenses and other deductions total or exceed that same amount. Production of income may be costly; all reasonable and necessary costs are generally deductible from gross income. Business deductions typically include expenses for supplies, management, labor, rentals, travel, advertising, insurance, property taxes, depreciation, and depletion. Depreciation is the estimated yearly decrease in value from normal wear and tear of an asset used in business or for the production of income. It may be computed by any one of several methods. Thus a business truck purchased for $8,000 may wear out completely in four years' time. The expense is legitimate and may be deducted yearly for four years in equal parts of $2,000. If the truck has a lifespan of eight years, then only $1,000 may be properly deducted each year, and if the truck will not wear out completely, then adjustment must be made for its salvage value. Depletion is a deduction allowed for assets like oil, gas, minerals, or timber that are used up or wasted in removal from their natural state. The basic deposit is reduced each year, and at the end of the extraction period, it's fully removed. As long as the depletion allowance is based on the cost of the natural resource, it's quite similar to depreciation and is merely a recovery of the original investment—or a return of capital. But when it is based on a fixed percentage of annual gross extractions, it results in great profit to owners of the natural resource without regard to the amount of original investment. Thus for many years federal law permitted the oil industry to deduct 27½ percent of their gross oil extractions each year so long as anything was extracted. Obviously, that law was designed to do more than return the cost of investment. It encouraged high risk oil exploration by allowing a considerable portion of oil industry receipts to go untaxed. But as profits increased, Congress acted to bring the depletion allowance down. Whether this will result in substantially lessened oil exploration remains to be seen. What is apparent is that tax laws frequently have other purposes in addition to raising revenue. They are sometimes designed to encourage certain activities or to discourage them (e.g., witness the deterrent effect of a very high tax on gambling activity). And as previously noted, charitable exemptions encourage these organizations to provide services the government itself would otherwise be responsible for.

Nearly all taxpayers take the following deductions whether they are engaged in business or not: (1) charitable contributions; (2) interest paid (so a person who owns his own home may deduct the interest paid on his mortgage); (3) certain taxes (all property taxes are deductible); (4) medical expenses; (5) casualty losses (although a minimum amount for both medical and casualty losses may not be deductible, and there is often a maximum deduction for both charitable contributions and medical expenses); and (6) certain miscellaneous deductions such as employee expenses (e.g., union dues, special work clothing, and travel expenses other than commuting to and from work), childcare expenses, and expenses incurred in preparation of tax returns or other tax service. All of these items are deducted to arrive at net taxable income.

But suppose you have none of these deductions or that your total deductions amount to less than a certain minimum figure known as the "standard deduction." When this occurs, you may take the standard deduction instead—i.e., you may subtract a certain percentage of your income up to a specified maximum in lieu of itemizing your personal deductions. The standard deduction figure changes from time to time to keep apace with growing inflation.

There are several personal exemptions additionally provided for by statute. As a taxpayer, you can deduct a certain figure for yourself, your spouse (if a joint return is filed), for each dependent, and again for yourself or your spouse if one or both of you is over sixty-five or blind. This figure also changes to reflect the increased cost of living. Recently, it has been $1,000 per exemption. So if you are thirty-five years old with a spouse and five children, you receive seven such exemptions, but if you are thirty-five and single, you get only one.

Applying the proper rate Applying the rate against the base is largely mechanical, but you must be careful to use the schedule that applies to you and that will produce the least amount of tax. Of course, this depends on whether you are a married person filing a joint return (i.e., filing together as husband and wife), a single person, or an unmarried head of a household with a dependent living with you. And if your income increases suddenly and very substantially over a previous year, you may want to file a return based on averaging your income over the previous five years. You are legally permitted to treat the increase as though you earned it not in one year, but in several.

Taking applicable credits Finally, credits for taxes paid or for special credits specified in the tax law must be taken against the tax owed. By the time you file your return, you have probably already paid substantial taxes on your income either because your employer withheld taxes from your wages or because you made quarterly payments to the government based on estimated income for a current year (taxpayers who receive income other than wages are frequently required by law to make such quarterly payments). These amounts are deducted to determine the net tax payable or the net refund due from the government. Employers also withhold social security taxes (see Chapter 7 for a discussion of social security).

How to Avoid Difficulty in Income Tax Reporting

There are certain rules you should follow in reporting your income tax if you wish to avoid difficulties with the Internal Revenue Service and state tax departments. Not only will the government be less likely to challenge you, but if it does call you in, you will be able to sustain the items on your return.

1. Fill in all the necessary schedules, supplementary forms, and explanations with reasonable detail;
2. Wherever an unusual item is likely to raise a question, attach a supplementary explanation;
3. Preserve all records, receipts, letters, canceled checks, and other documents or items that are relevant to proving your position;
4. Retain a copy of the return for your own future reference;
5. Be consistent each year and from year to year on any continuous item such as depreciation or depletion;
6. If you want to save money, be honest and fair in taking deductions and in reporting your income. Failure to report an item may result in assessment of interest and other penalties. And intentional evasion of taxes is a criminal offense punishable by federal imprisonment. Remember that most tax administrators are fair and reasonable so long as you try to be honest and accurate in your reporting.

The income tax has other applications as well. Corporations pay substantial amounts of income taxes on their net incomes. In fact, their income is subject to a "double" taxation: dividends paid out to shareholders are taxed again on the shareholder's individual return. The estate of a decedent also pays income tax. When a person dies, his assets continue to earn income. While the estate is being probated and until the estate is closed, it is a taxable entity and must file what is called a fiduciary income tax return.

The income tax is the backbone of the United States tax system. It is the most rational and scientific of all tax instruments, and it raises the bulk of government revenue. It is unique in that almost all Americans voluntarily comply with its requirements—and in a generally efficient and honest way. Although it is progressive, it is reasonably fair and equitable; those individuals with the most incentive and personal industry are properly rewarded for their efforts. And finally, it is a flexible tax. It may be adjusted to raise more revenue and to achieve constructive social and economic objectives as well.

Miscellaneous Other Taxes

Estate and gift taxes Estate and gift taxes tax the transfer of property from one generation to another. Our legal system recognizes private ownership of property; each of us owns some property, and we have a right to pass it along to others as we please. We can give it away by inter vivos gift (i.e., a gift of property from one living person to another), or we can pass it on at our death by will or by operation of the laws of intestacy. In each case the transfer of property is legally taxable. Either the gift tax or death tax will apply. The death tax taxes either the transfer of property (called an estate tax) or it taxes the receipt of property (called an inheritance or succession tax). The difference between the two is easily understood when you compare them to the pitching and catching of a baseball—the estate tax is on the pitcher who pitches the ball, and the inheritance tax is on the catcher who catches it. Death and gift tax revenue is small in comparison to the income tax. But for the individual who accumulates substantial wealth, it may be very significant. The tax on an estate worth several million dollars, for example, can be as high as a 50 to 60 percent (federal and state) progressive rate. As a result, the wealth passed down to the next generation may be substantially diminished with the goverment taking a considerable share of the estate.

The federal death tax is an estate tax. That is, it taxes the transfer of the estate assets to the persons named in the will or to those who receive under the laws of intestacy. State death taxes are either estate or inheritance taxes, or they are a combination of the two. Some states, for example, require payment of an estate tax for the transfer of any estate. But if someone not immediately related to the deceased receives the property, he must pay an additional inheritance tax. So if the decedent's spouse, children, or parents take the property, then the state death tax alone applies; while if someone else takes it, an additional inheritance tax payment is imposed.

The Economic Recovery Act of 1981 changed the estate and gift tax law substantially. The law decreased the tax rates and provided a new unlimited marital deduction for decedents dying after 12/31/81. Still, the mechanics of the estate tax are similar to those of the income tax. The gross value of the estate must first be established. This includes all the decedent's assets (e.g., real property, stocks and bonds, personal assets, life insurance, business interests, general powers of appointment, etc.). The assets must be listed and valued as of the date of death (federal law presently allows use of an alternate valuation date six months later in case the estate assets suddenly go down in value).

Once the total value of the estate is determined, certain deductions are allowed. The federal law permits deduction of all expenses, indebtedness, and taxes owing at the date of death. It would be manifestly unjust to tax the gross assets without such an allowance, since the decedent may owe more than he or she owns. The allowance includes any attorney's fees, transfer expenses, and appraiser's fees incurred during the course of probate. Any theft or casualty losses are also deductible if they occur during the administration of the estate. And transfers to charity are fully deductible. Thus if a decedent leaves his or her entire estate to a charity—a school, hospital, or religious organization—there will be no death tax. Finally, there is a marital deduction under federal law.

The 1981 Economic Recovery Act removed all limits on the marital deduction for estate (and gift) taxes. As long as the property passes to the decedent's (or donor's) current spouse, its value is 100 percent deductible. Thus, if a spouse leaves all of his or her property to a surviving spouse, there is no taxable estate.

There is a unified rate schedule for estate and gift taxes, meaning that the same rate of tax is applied whether property is given away during life or at death. The tax rate on taxable estates starts at 18 percent for the first $10,000 and progresses at 2 to 4 percent increments to 65 percent for estates over $5 million. However, the 1981 Act reduces the maximum tax rate on estates and gifts to 50 percent over a four-year period. Thus, for gifts made and decedents dying in 1982, the maximum rate was 65 percent; for 1983, it is 60 percent; for 1984, it is 55 percent; and for 1985 and later, it is 50 percent. The Act also provides that no federal gift tax or death tax is payable unless lifetime taxable gifts or death-time taxable estate exceeds $225,000 in 1982; $275,000 in 1983; $325,000 in 1984; $400,000 in 1985; $500,000 in 1986; and $600,000 in 1987 or later. In addition, regarding taxable gifts, the law provides that taxable gifts do not include the first $10,000 a year given to any one donee. This is called the gift tax annual exclusion allowing donors unlimited gifts up to $10,000 a year to any number of individual donees with no gift tax liability.

Consumption taxes Consumption taxes fall upon the consumer who uses goods or services. The taxes are levied against expenditures for consumption in four general areas: (1) customs, (2) excise, (3) sales, and (4) use. While consumption taxes have a proportional rate structure (i.e., a uniform rate for all), it is frequently argued that they are regressive in effect—that they hit lower income groups the hardest and take away a larger percentage of their income in comparison with the middle and upper income groups. Others favor these taxes because they increase consumer awareness of the costs of government and force everyone to pay something for the services he receives.

Customs Customs or tariffs are levied on goods that cross national boundaries. They are of two types: (1) specific duties, and (2) ad valorem duties. Specific duties are those levied on certain goods, such as ten cents on a package of cigars or two dollars on a gallon of Scotch whiskey. Ad valorem duties are those levied on the value of goods imported—such as 25 percent on the value of imported TV sets or automobiles. Customs may be designed to raise revenue without discouraging imports, or they may be set high to protect domestic manufacturers from an influx of low-priced foreign goods.

Excise taxes These are taxes on the making or selling of goods. Unlike the sales tax, this tax is paid directly by the producer or distributor of the goods—not by the buyer. But the ultimate incidence of the tax is on the consumer, since the tax is reflected indirectly in the purchase price of the goods. Excise taxes are frequently levied on items like alcoholic beverages and tobacco. The tax serves not only to raise revenue but to discourage use of the product as well. Many urge that all "harmful" goods should properly bear excise tax. Marijuana, for example, might best be controlled if sold by the government with a very high excise tax to eliminate illegal traffic in the drug and to raise revenue for the control of so-called "hard drugs." Excise taxes are also found on luxury and semiluxury items like leather goods, entertainment, jewelry, and transportation (railroad and airline tickets).

Great care must be exercised in use of the excise tax so that particular industries are not injured.

Sales tax The sales tax is a more general tax levied on all goods or on all goods with some minor exceptions such as food. While the retail sales tax is extensively used by some state governments, other states have refused to adopt it. This is because the sales tax administration depends largely on the seller-retailer who must collect the tax, keep good records, file accurate reports, and send in the sales tax money to the state on a regular basis. If this is not easily accomplished, the state will find administration of the tax very expensive, as it will have to establish a large and effective investigation and auditing division to get the job done. Generally exempted from the sales tax are goods already under excise taxes such as gasoline, liquor, and tobacco. Some states exempt sales to charitable and religious institutions; others exempt food. But none seems to exempt clothing, although it, too, appears to be a necessary item. The consumer pays the sales tax directly when he makes his purchase.

Use Many states that don't have a sales tax border states that do. A buyer in the sales tax state could avoid paying the tax altogether by purchasing goods in the bordering state. To prevent this, use taxes are imposed on the use, storage, or consumption of all goods that would be subject to the sales tax if bought within the state.

Motor vehicle and highway taxes (the gas tax) Much of the United States highway system has been constructed and maintained from the taxation of motorists. Two state taxes generally apply—the license tax for the vehicles themselves, and the gasoline tax. Motor vehicle license tax bases vary greatly from state to state for passenger cars, trucks, buses, and other vehicles. Sometimes the base is the weight of the vehicle, its horsepower, its cost, or it may simply be a flat rate. In most states, weight is the predominant factor. State agencies are generally responsible for making rules and administering the motor vehicle license law.

The gasoline tax also varies from two cents a gallon on up. And the federal government adds on a federal gasoline tax. Of course, both the vehicle license tax and the gas tax are consumption or excise taxes. We treat them separately here because the funds are generally used only for the highway system. The gas tax reaches the tourist who uses the highways to come through the state. It is a convenient tax to pay, and it makes the people who use the road pay for it.

SHOULD YOU ARGUE WITH THE GOVERNMENT OVER YOUR TAXES?

Arthur Godfrey once said the following: "I'm proud to pay taxes in the United States. Only thing is—I would be just as proud for half the money."

As a taxpayer, you have a legal duty to pay your taxes in full—but not a penny more. If the government makes a mistake in computing your taxes, you have not only a right but a duty to protest. This willingness to protest unwarranted assessments enables the tax system to work properly and to reach its intended result: payment of a fair share but no more.

The best way to win a tax case, however, is to avoid the dispute altogether. The courtroom should be the last resort. If you make clear explanations on your returns, avoid careless mistakes in computation, and follow the advice of competent tax counsel, you can eliminate most problems in advance and avoid the "dreaded" audit.

But if you are called in for an audit (i.e., if you are told to appear before a tax investigating agency of the government), it's wise to remember that the examiner is a human being too. You'll have a much easier time if you try to cooperate in resolving the dispute. It's also important to close the controversy as soon as possible. Not only is it easier to do so at an earlier stage, but it is much less expensive as the government is usually willing to compromise at this level to save the time and expense of a courtroom battle. Once a taxpayer decides to go to court, the government seldom gives in on any point.

Occasionally, it's impossible to reach a settlement with the administrative agency. In this case, if your position is sound and there is a good deal of money involved, you should take your case to court. State tax matters are adjudicated in the court of general jurisdiction or in the state tax court if there is one. If the controversy is with the federal government, you have three courts to choose from. You may refuse to pay the additional tax and ask the federal Tax Court to redetermine the deficiency. Or you may pay the tax and immediately sue for refund in either the federal district court (federal question) or the U.S. Claims Court (claims against the United States). And it often pays to go to court. The taxpayer's record discloses a total or partial victory in about 50 percent of the cases. Besides, any expenses incurred in the determination, collection, or refund of any tax are legally deductible. So if you choose to fight out your controversy, you may deduct your expenses.

FIGURE 13–5 THE BUDGET DOLLAR

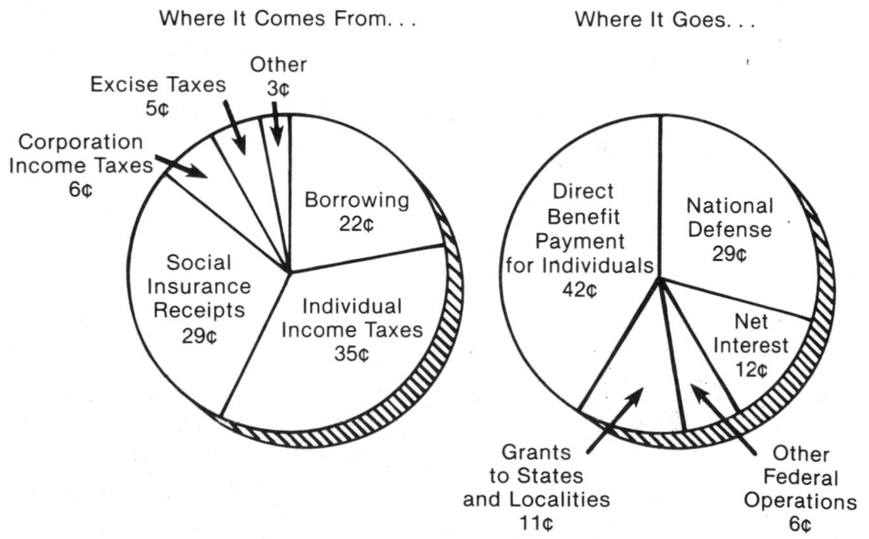

Environmental Protection

WHAT ARE THE SOURCES OF ENVIRONMENTAL LAW?

> A statement of environmental policy is more than a statement of what we believe as a people and as a nation. It establishes priorities and gives expression to our national goals and aspirations. It provides a statutory foundation to which administrators may refer to for guidance in making decisions which find environmental values in conflict with other values.
>
> What is involved is a congressional declaration that we do not intend, as a government or as a people, to initiate actions which endanger the continued existence or the health of mankind. That we will not intentionally initiate actions which will do irreparable damage to the air, land, and water which support life on earth.
>
> Senator Henry Jackson
> Washington

Environmental protection was traditionally the job of state and local governments as it was considered a proper exercise of their "police" power. In the early days of public awareness of the problem, state and local laws prevailed, and it was generally agreed that pollution control should be handled at the lowest possible level of government. Federal involvement with the environment has been gradual (with the exception of radiation pollution which has been viewed as a national concern from the very beginning of nuclear energy development). But in recent years, the federal government has taken on increasing responsibility for pollution control and enforcement. Federal pollution control began, not with an assertion of federal regulatory power, but through sponsorship of grant-in-aid programs. Under these programs, states that agree to follow federal standards receive federal funds for use in protecting the environment.

Federal authority to impose environmental regulations and controls stems from three constitutional powers: the power to tax and spend, the commerce power, and the treaty power. Initially, the federal government used the power to tax and spend in an effort to regulate pollution indirectly. While the spending power may be used only for the "general welfare," the environment is actually the epitome of what is "general." The power to tax is equally broad, and an "effluent charge" (i.e., a pollution tax measured by the cost of cleaning up the quantity and type of effluent the polluter emits with the proceeds used for required treatment operations) would undoubtedly be upheld.

Under the commerce power, Congress can regulate virtually every activity that tends to contaminate the environment. Air or water pollution (even of intrastate, non-navigable streams) that injures crops, farm animals, or fish, impedes aerial or possibly even surface transportation, or discourages employment or recreation travel is damaging to interstate commerce, and Congress can act to control it.

Finally, the treaty power may be exercised where other grants of power are insufficient. The president, for example, can agree with another nation to refrain from certain conduct harmful to the environment. Congress can then implement the treaty through legislation that, previously, it had no power to enact.

The key federal agency dealing with the environment is the Environmental Protection Agency (EPA), established December 2, 1970 (see Chapter 5). It brought together for the first time in a single agency the major environmental problems of air and water pollution, solid wastes management, pesticides, radiation, and noise.

WHAT IS THE NATIONAL ENVIRONMENTAL POLICY ACT?

The passage of the National Environmental Policy Act of 1969 (NEPA) requires all federal agencies to prepare an "environmental impact" statement if any of their proposed activities might significantly affect the environment. Senator Henry Jackson of Washington introduced the original 1969 version of the bill—Senate Bill 1075. Its purpose was threefold: 1) to establish a national environmental policy; 2) to authorize research concerning natural resources; and 3) to establish a council of environmental advisors.

Section 101(b) of NEPA provides that:

> (b) In order to carry out the policy set forth in this Act, it is the continuing responsibility of the Federal Government to use all practicable means, consistent with other essential considerations of national policy, to improve and coordinate Federal plans, functions, programs, and resources to the end that the Nation may—
>
> (1) fulfill the responsibilities of each generation as trustee of the environment for succeeding generations;
>
> (2) assure for all Americans safe, healthful, productive and esthetically and culturally pleasing surroundings;
>
> (3) attain the widest range of beneficial uses of the environment without degradation, risk to health or safety, or other undesirable and unintended consequences;
>
> (4) preserve important historic, cultural, and natural aspects of our national heritage, and maintain, wherever possible, an environment which supports diversity, and a variety of individual choice;
>
> (5) achieve a balance between population and resource use which will permit high standards of living and a wide sharing of life's amenities; and
>
> (6) enhance the quality of renewable resources and approach the maximum attainable recycling of depletable resources.

Section 102 requires federal agencies to discuss their action proposals with federal and state agencies well versed in environmental matters and to prepare an environmental impact statement on the conclusions they arrive at. Agencies are thus forced to internalize consideration of the environmental repercussions of their activities. Exceptions are made only for agencies that deal with security and military institutions, as courts have traditionally been reluctant to interfere with decisions of the Executive on matters of national security. Yet the courts had no difficulty in applying NEPA to security sensitive, underground nuclear testing in Committee for Nuclear Responsibility v. Schlesinger, 404 U.S. 917, 92 S.Ct. 242, 30 L.Ed.2d 191, 1 E.L.R. 20534 (1972). At issue was Project Cannikin which involved the testing of a five megaton nuclear warhead by detonating it deep beneath Amchitka, an island in the Aleutian chain off Alaska. The Atomic Energy Commission assumed that NEPA applied and prepared both a draft and a final environmental impact statement. Plaintiffs contested the adequacy of the Commission's final statement, relying primarily upon a series of secret government studies not included in the NEPA review process. The studies, some of which were ordered public late in the litigation, allegedly cast greater doubt on the safety and environmental soundness of the test than did the Commission's "official" environmental impact statement. The Court made clear in the Cannikin case that any agency attempts to bypass NEPA will be closely policed and that exceptions to its provisions will be made only under the most compelling circumstances.

Problems may also develop where temporary or emergency actions are involved. There is no time for NEPA review or for preparation of an environmental impact statement, for example, when wage and price controls are needed immediately. In Cohen v. Price Commission, 337 F.Supp. 1236, 2 E.L.R. 20178 (S.D.N.Y.1972), Judge Weinfeld ruled that the "long range" aims of NEPA and its "prolonged decision-making process" were incompatible with the nature of the Price Commission (which was to exist only until March 1973) and its need to "act upon matters within its authority with dispatch." So, where the New York Transit Authority's grave financial condition necessitated a speedy decision on the legality of a fare increase, the court found that there was "substantial doubt" that Congress intended the Commission to operate in accordance with the Act and denied plaintiff's plea for a preliminary injunction.

Title II of the Act establishes the Council on Environmental Quality in the Executive Office of the president. The Council is designed to provide the president with objective advice and to supervise closely federal activities affecting the environment. Its long-range activities include establishing a system for monitoring environmental indicators and maintaining environmental records to insure complete availability of data for anticipated problems and trends.

Section 201 of NEPA requires the president to submit an annual Environmental Quality report to Congress.

WHAT ARE THE SPECIFIC PROBLEM AREAS FOR ENVIRONMENTAL LAW?

Water Quality

Water pollution is a serious threat to life, health, and the nation's productivity. Oceans, rivers, streams, lakes, estuaries, underground aquifers, and wetlands are essential, in one way or another, to all forms of life and play a central role in much of our economic activity and recreation. The Clean Water Act of 1972 is the basic authority for water pollution control programs. The goal of the Act is to make national waters fishable and swimmable, and the major provisions require:

1. Municipal pollution control through a program of federal grants for construction or modification of sewage treatment plants. The federal government funds 75 percent of a project's cost.

2. Regional planning to choose the best waste treatment methods for a particular area and to estimate the effects of future growth on waste treatment facilities. All major metropolitan areas must establish planning agencies, and each state is required to prepare a water quality management plan.
3. Effluent limitations defining the amount and kinds of material that can be discharged into the nation's waters. The limitations apply to both municipal and industrial sources of water pollution.
4. Water quality standards established by EPA and applicable to all surface waters. Standards are set according to the use of the water—agricultural, industrial, recreational, or drinking—and include maximum levels for temperature, oxygen supply, microbiological content, toxic pollutants, etc.
5. Dredge and fill permits to regulate dredging, filling of wetlands, or dumping of dredged material affecting navigable waters of the United States. Permits are granted by the Army Corps of Engineers, subject to EPA approval. The Marine Protection, Research, and Sanctuaries Act of 1972 authorizes EPA to regulate ocean dumping of wastes by designating areas where dumping is permitted, issuing permits for dumping, and assessing penalties for unauthorized dumping.

Drinking Water

EPA conducts a special program to protect the safety of drinking water. Water-borne disease still occurs, and chemicals and pesticides sometimes find their way into drinking water. To deal with these problems, Congress passed the Safe Drinking Water Act of 1974. Major provisions require:

1. Drinking water regulations established by EPA to protect public health and welfare.
2. State enforcement of drinking water standards established by EPA. EPA can assume that responsibility if a state fails to enforce the standards.
3. Protection of underground water supplies against contamination by underground injection of wastes and other materials.

Waste

Industrial, commercial, and residential sources generate tremendous quantities of waste. In one year, solid wastes from residential and commercial sources are estimated at 130 million metric tons (1 metric ton = 2,200 pounds), enough to fill the New Orleans Superdome from floor to ceiling twice a day, weekdays and holidays included. Additionally, some 350 million metric tons of industrial wastes are generated. Disposing of these wastes is costly and poses major environmental risks.

A particularly serious problem is proper disposal of hazardous wastes, such as toxic chemicals, caustics, pesticides, and other flammable, corrosive, or explosive materials. Hazardous wastes are generated in the United States at a rate of approximately 57 million metric tons a year. The dangers such wastes can create have been illustrated by the tragedy at Love Canal at Niagara Falls, New York. Hundreds of residents were forced to abandon homes built over or near an abandoned chemical dump site. Some of the chemicals identified at Love Canal are known to cause cancer, birth defects, and other serious health problems. There are thousands of improper disposal sites—both active and abandoned—scattered throughout the United States.

In 1976 Congress passed the Resource Conservation and Recovery Act (RCRA). This was major new legislation to deal with both municipal and hazardous waste problems and to encourage resource recovery and recycling. The statute requires states to develop and implement waste disposal plans. To set the stage for establishment of environmentally sound disposal practices, states are to inventory all existing waste disposal sites and determine whether the sites are in sound condition. Federal financial and technical assistance is provided to the states through EPA for these planning and implementation efforts.

To carry out RCRA's provisions for dealing with hazardous wastes, EPA has developed a national hazardous waste management system to monitor the movement of significant quantities of hazardous wastes from cradle to grave. Under the system, hazardous waste generating facilities must identify the wastes they create and report the means of disposal. Transport of wastes will be regulated and tracked. Treatment and disposal sites must have permits to operate, and their design must be adequate to prevent the waste from moving through the soil and reaching water sources. Active sites will be monitored constantly. Closed sites are to be capped, but monitoring must continue as well. The owner will be required to assume limited financial responsibility for damage during active operations and to set aside funds for monitoring after the site is closed.

Congress also has enacted legislation to deal with the nation's legacy of hazardous waste dump sites abandoned in past years. The federal government and industry will join in establishing a "superfund" to pay for the cleanup of sites that become public health threats.

Pesticides

Pesticides are chemical substances used to control unwanted funguses, weeds, bacteria, insects, rodents, and other pests. Over a billion pounds of pesticides, employing more than 1,400 chemical compounds are used annually in the United States. While use of pesticides has been an important part of modern farming methods and public health vector control, some pesticides have the potential to cause severe health problems and environmental damage. Acute poisoning, cancer, sterility, and other toxic effects have been traced to pesticide use. Farmworkers, pesticide applicators, pesticide production employees, home users, and residents of communities near sprayed areas can be exposed to pesticides and suffer adverse effects from improper handling and application. Pesticides have also done serious damage to the natural environment.

Congress passed the original Federal Insecticide, Fungicide, and Rodenticide Act in 1947. This bill was subsequently strengthened and amended in 1972, 1975, and 1978. Regulation of pesticides under this Act is handled by EPA's Office of Pesticides and Toxic Substances.

The pesticide control program has three major components—registration of pesticides, training of pesticide applicators, and monitoring and research.

All pesticides must be registered with EPA before being marketed. Based on available scientific data concerning their safety and effectiveness, the Agency reviews and approves labeling, stating directions for use, precautions, and warnings. EPA also sets maximum safe levels for pesticide residues in human and animal food. Some pesticides have been discovered to be so toxic that their use must be banned altogether. Others may be restricted to use on a limited number of crops or at certain times in the growing season or only by certified applicators.

To make certain that pesticides are properly used, the Act requires EPA to develop an applicator training program, leading to the certification of persons permitted to apply restricted-use pesticides. Of the nearly two million persons certified under this program, most are individual farmers. In general, applicator training and certification are conducted as EPA-approved state programs.

The agency sponsors extensive research on pesticides and monitors pesticide levels in the environment. Researchers consider both acute and long-term effects in their epidemiological studies of pesticide effects. In addition, EPA, the National Science Foundation, and the Department of Agriculture are sponsoring research into environmentally safe, integrated pest management techniques that minimize the use of chemical pesticides.

Toxic Substances

Toxic substances can cause death, disease, birth defects, and miscarriages in human beings, and create severe problems in the natural environment even in extremely small quantities. Levels of some substances measured in parts per *billion* can make water unfit for drinking. Other substances are so toxic that the environment may not be able to absorb even such small quantities without serious damage. Toxic substances include a number of manufactured chemicals, as well as naturally occurring heavy metals, such as mercury, cadmium, and lead, which are mined and released into the environment.

The damage done to human beings and their environment through uncontrolled releases of toxic substances has already been vast. Major bodies of water, such as the Great Lakes, the Hudson River in New York, and the Housatonic River in Massachusetts and Connecticut, have been severely damaged and perhaps permanently lost as commercial fisheries as a result of pollution from polychlorinated biphenyls (PCBs). Hundreds of thousands of people are expected to die of lung diseases from inhaling asbestos.

In light of the serious problems caused by toxic substances in the environment, Congress passed the Toxic Substances Control Act in 1976. This bill was meant to supplement and reinforce the authorities EPA already had in its air, water, pesticides, and waste disposal laws for dealing with toxic substances. The Toxic Substances Control Act deals with two major kinds of problems. First, newly created chemicals or chemicals entering into commerce for the first time may do serious damage to human beings and their environment before their possible dangers are even known. EPA estimates that several hundred new chemicals or chemical compounds are introduced into commerce each year. Second, many chemicals and substances already in commerce may require more stringent control. EPA estimates that 70,000 chemicals and substances are now in commercial use.

To deal with the problem of new, potentially toxic substances, the Act imposes a system of premarket notification to EPA if a company wishes to market a new chemical, or significantly expand existing uses of a chemical already on the market. EPA may then require testing of the chemical for toxic effects and may ban production unless the manufacturer shows that the chemical does not present "an unreasonable risk of injury to health or the environment." EPA also requires testing of chemicals already in commerce. The results may lead to restrictions on use or even to an outright ban on the manufacture of chemicals found to be extremely dangerous. The Act essentially bans all further manufacture of PCBs and places restrictions on disposal of equipment containing that unusually toxic substance.

Air Quality

Air pollution is a serious threat to human health, affecting millions of Americans, particularly in urban areas. In some parts of the country, children must be warned during pollution alerts not to play outdoors, as the air is unfit for breathing during strenuous exercise. Property is also affected by air pollution. Paint and building stone are corroded by air pollutants and vegetation is stunted.

The increased burning of fossil fuels for energy—producing massive amounts of sulfur oxides and nitric oxides—has increased the acidity of rain, killing fish in remote lakes, dissolving the limestone and marble of buildings, and threatening forests and crops. Acid rain often falls hundreds of miles from pollution sources and across international boundaries.

Direct sources of air pollution divide into two categories: stationary sources, such as factories, power plants, and smelters; and mobile sources, such as automobiles, buses, trucks, locomotives, and airplanes. Some facilities, such as major highways and shopping centers, are called indirect sources because traffic concentrates at those places and increases local pollution levels.

The Clean Air Act, as amended in 1970 and 1977, provides the basic legal authority for the nation's air pollution control programs. Major provisions require:

1. National ambient air quality standards for specific air pollutants to protect public health and welfare. Standards have been set for sulfur dioxide, particulates, oxides of nitrogen, carbon monoxide, hydrocarbons, ozone, and lead.
2. State clean air plans stipulating steps that will be taken to achieve satisfactory air quality. EPA must review the plans and, if necessary, require revisions or substitute its own plan.
3. New source performance standards for new or modified stationary sources of air pollution. Emission limitations are established for specific types of sources such as power plants and cement plants.
4. Hazardous air pollutants national standards limiting emissions of such substances as asbestos, beryllium, mercury, vinyl chloride, and benzene from both new and old stationary sources.

5. Prevention of significant deterioration of air quality in areas which have pristine or good to moderate air quality. Subject to EPA approval, states identify areas of good, moderate, and poor air quality (Class I, Class II, and Class III). Class I, which includes all national parks and wilderness areas, permits no additional air pollution. The Class II designation allows additional pollution up to prescribed limits, and Class III areas must conform to general national standards.
6. Automobile emission controls to achieve a 90 percent reduction in carbon monoxide and hydrocarbon emissions (based on 1970 emission levels). Nitrogen oxide emissions are to be reduced by 75 percent by 1985.

Noise

Noise is a serious environmental problem in many urban areas where it degrades the quality of life and can seriously threaten health and well-being. It can permanently impair hearing and cause a number of other physical and psychological problems. It is estimated that nearly 15 million workers are exposed to an eight-hour average sound level of greater than seventy-five decibels, a level at which there is risk of hearing damage. Millions of other Americans are exposed to levels above seventy-five decibels as operators of passengers of transportation or recreation vehicles. In surveys conducted by the Department of Housing and Urban Development, noise is mentioned three times as frequently as crime by residents listing undesirable conditions of neighborhoods. EPA has identified fifty-five decibels as the day-night average sound level which should not be exceeded in order to protect the general population against activity interference. More than 100 million Americans live in areas where the decibel level exceeds this amount.

The EPA Noise Abatement and Control Program is administered under the Noise Control Act of 1972, as amended by the Quiet Communities Act of 1978.

The primary functions of EPA under the legislation are (1) establishment of standards and promulgation of regulations concerning major sources of noise (this includes noise emission standards for products identified by EPA as major sources of noise, e.g., lawnmowers, air drills, garbage trucks, motorcycles, etc., and labeling regulations for consumer products which produce noise capable of affecting the public health and welfare, and for products sold on the basis of their effectiveness in reducing noise); (2) research into the causes, effects, and control of noise; and (3) state and local assistance programs designed to help states and localities deal with their own noise problems. EPA submits regulatory proposals to the Federal Aviation Administration on the problem of aviation noise and provides technical assistance to airports and other entities with regard to airport noise abatement and control.

Radiation

Ionizing radiation can be a serious environmental contaminant. High levels of exposure cause acute radiation poisoning and death. Lower levels of exposure may lead to cancer and genetic problems years later. Ionizing radiation comes from such sources as uranium mining and milling, nuclear power wastes, and radioactive materials used in medicine. The health effects of non-ionizing radiation, such as microwaves and radiation from high voltage power lines, are not as well understood, but it also may be hazardous.

In general, EPA is responsible for setting standards to protect the general environment from radiation, including that released from nuclear power plants and from the processing of uranium and phosphate. Occupational guides apply to the interior of nuclear power plants and other nuclear facilities. EPA, in cooperation with the Food and Drug Administration, provides guidance to other federal agencies on the use of x-rays in medicine. The Agency is developing standards for disposal of high-level nuclear wastes, for the control of hazards at active and inactive uranium mill tailing sites, nuclear accident protective action guidelines, clean-up guidelines for areas contaminated by plutonium, and guidance for occupational exposure to radiation. It is evaluating the need to set standards for non-ionizing radiation sources.

EPA assesses radiation technologies developed by federal agencies. Of particular concern are the various proposals for handling radioactive waste. EPA is responsible for reviewing environmental impact statements required by the National Environmental Policy Act and determining whether proposed technologies are environmentally acceptable. These reviews include major facilities licensed by the Nuclear Regulatory Commission.

Finally, EPA monitors radiation in the environment, such as that resulting from above-ground nuclear weapons tests. An air monitoring network of twenty-two continuously operating samplers measures ambient radioactivity. EPA also monitors drinking water supplies and computes radiation exposure to the public from both ionizing and non-ionizing radiation.

WHAT REMEDIES MAY BE USED IN CONTROLLING THE ENVIRONMENT?

The recent awakening of our nation's environmental conscience has been truly dramatic. Yet despite the intensive activity at all levels of government, environmentalists remain dissatisfied, especially with the performance of federal administrative agencies where, as in any large organization, fundamental change is sometimes slow and frustrating. A number of articulate environmental spokespersons have asserted that a different approach is required—that the most expeditious and effective method of protecting the environment would be to allow individual citizens or public interest groups to bring lawsuits directly against alleged polluters, and to empower the courts to re-examine fully on the merits all administrative decisions affecting the environment.

Class Actions

Rule 23 of the Federal Rules of Civil Procedure provides that a class action can be brought where a wrong has been committed against a group of persons so numerous that it is impracticable to bring all the parties before the court (see Chapter 3).

The class action is a potentially useful tool in the fight for a decent environment. It is especially effective against the polluter who has heretofore found it to his or her economic benefit to continue environmentally destructive practices and let the general public suffer. The polluter's thinking goes something like this: while it would cost a great deal of money to control or abate the pollution, letting it continue harms each member of the public "just a little." And since no one member is injured sufficiently to make the expense of litigation worthwhile, the polluter profits from his or her socially reprehensible conduct. Use of the class action, however, restores balance within our legal system by allowing the adversary system to work. Thus the polluter who saves a million dollars in abatement costs by inflicting a few dollars' damage on each of a million citizens may still be brought to court, and profitably so, in a class action suit.

Nuisance

A nuisance may be either public or private. A private nuisance, as you will recall from Chapter 8, is a civil wrong based on an interference with someone's property right. A public nuisance is a catchall criminal offense involving interference with the rights of the community at large, though a public nuisance may also give rise to a tort action maintained by a private individual.

In the case of a private nuisance, only the person whose property rights have been invaded can bring the action—and the invasion of rights must be substantial. Each property owner, however, has a right to use his or her property in any manner the owner chooses so long as the use does not interfere with the similar rights of other owners. So, in determining whether one owner has substantially interfered with the rights of another, the courts must balance the interests of both owners involved. This is often referred to as a "balancing of the equities." For example, in Madison v. Ducktown Sulphur, Copper & Iron Co., 113 Tenn. 331, 83 S.W. 658 (1904) (a private nuisance action brought by farmers for property damage resulting from operation of a mining processing enterprise), the court recognized that it would have to shut down the plant completely in order to prevent further harm to the farms of little value. Not only would this make the manufacturing property nearly worthless, but it would destroy nearly half of the county's property tax base and create massive unemployment. After "balancing" these "equities," the court refused to issue an injunction but sought instead to rectify the wrong by allowing the defendant to pay money damages to the plaintiffs for his unabatable nuisance. The weakness of the balancing doctrine for use in protecting the environment is apparent: the powerful polluter will never be stopped unless he or she injures an equally large economic interest.

Public nuisance developed historically as an omnibus criminal offense that allowed the government to prevent interference with the rights of the community. The term "public nuisance" has been used to embrace a wide variety of so-called improper activities, including interference with the public morals (e.g., houses of prostitution, illegal gambling houses, or illegal bars), the creation of odors, air pollution, noise, parking problems, or danger to the public safety.

The law has long recognized the right of a private citizen to bring a tort action for a public nuisance. In order to do so, however, the private party must establish three elements. First, he or she must show that the nuisance is "public," i.e., that it affects the interest of the general public as opposed to that of only a few individuals. Second, the party must show that he or she has suffered special damages over and above the ordinary damage caused to the public at large. And third, he or she must show injury different in kind, rather than in degree, from that of the general public. Of course, it is easy to show particular injury when you have suffered physical injury because of the nuisance, but there are several other grounds as well (e.g., where the plaintiff suffered a pecuniary loss not inflicted upon the community). Public nuisance actions will also lie for interference with the use of land.

The individual confronted with a nuisance—either public or private—has three possible remedies. He or she can seek money damages or equitable relief by injunction or can abate the nuisance by self-help. Where the nuisance is temporary, the plaintiff's measure of damages is the value of the use of the property (or its loss of rental) for the period of time that the nuisance is in existence; if the nuisance is permanent, the plaintiff may recover for the permanent loss in value of the property. But an award of money damages is not a very satisfactory remedy for environmental torts. Wherever possible, the equity court should exercise its power to enjoin the nuisance. And the more unreasonable the defendant's conduct under the circumstances of the case, the more likely the court is to do so. The plaintiff who carefully demonstrates for the court just what abatement steps could be effectively taken in his or her situation increases the chances of obtaining an equitable remedy. An added advantage of the equity power is that it can be used to prevent a threatened harm that has not yet materialized.

Finally, the right to abate the nuisance by self-help exists for only a short period of time after knowledge of the nuisance is acquired. The doctrine is further limited in that only the minimum abatement necessary to protect the individual from special damage is allowed. What is reasonable necessarily depends upon all the circumstances. But caution—abatement through self-help is an emergency measure and should be used only where any delay in abatement would create a danger of serious harm.

New Remedies

One of the new remedies in environmental litigation is the so-called "inverse condemnation." Where the government acts to damage seriously or diminish materially the value of property, the owner of the property may sue the government defendant for its full value, even where there has been no physical occupancy or formal taking through the power of eminent domain. "Inverse condemnation" cases generally arise where highway construction has severely restricted the plaintiff's use of his or her property or where damage from low-flying aircraft has materially diminished its value.

Another new environmental remedy is based on the public trust doctrine. This doctrine states that the government has a duty as a trustee of the people to protect our nation's natural resources. If the government breaches its trust, court action may be instituted. One of the most famous cases to invoke this doctrine was Illinois v. Illinois Central Railroad, 146 U.S. 387, 13 S.Ct. 110, 36 L.Ed. 1018 (1892), in which the state of Illinois, suing to prevent the city of Chicago from giving away most of its harbor to the Illinois Railroad, prevented the transfer as a breach of the public trust. The public trust doctrine has been applied not only to public lands and waters but to cases involving wildlife protection and public roads. Whether this doctrine will be further extended to protect public rights to pure air and water and to an undefiled environment remains to be seen.

Cases

After Alice gave the ring back, Angelo claimed a "resulting trust."

PRASSA v. CORCORAN

Supreme Court of Illinois, 1962.
24 Ill.2d 288, 181 N.E.2d 138.

DAILY, Justice

The plaintiff, Angelo Prassa, instituted this action in the superior court of Cook County against his ex-fiancee, Alice Patricia Corcoran, and her father, H. James Corcoran, seeking to impress a trust on an improved parcel of real estate, title to which is jointly in plaintiff and Alice, for an accounting, and for a decree compelling conveyance of the property to him. Alice Corcoran appeals from a decree finding that a resulting trust arose in favor of the plaintiff and directing that she execute a deed in favor of the plaintiff. * * *

The uncontroverted evidence indicates plaintiff and defendant became engaged to be married in July, 1959. As a token of the engagement plaintiff gave her a ring. In contemplation of the marriage it was decided that a two-flat building in which they could live after marriage be purchased. It was at the suggestion of defendant's father that plaintiff decided to purchase the apartment building in which Alice resided with her parents. It was planned that after the marriage plaintiff and Alice would live in the second floor apartment and her parents would continue to live downstairs. Negotiations were handled by defendant's father and the sellers, but it was contemplated by the parties that plaintiff alone would pay the consideration for the building. Having reached an agreement on the price, a contract was prepared by the attorney for the sellers. On September 1, 1959, plaintiff and his fiancee signed the contract and plaintiff paid the sellers' attorney $2,000 as earnest money. The balance of $18,750 was to be paid by plaintiff on the passing of the deed. Defendant signed the contract "Alice Patricia Prassa" even though at the time she was a single woman. Pursuant to the contract, the sellers, on October 1, delivered a warranty deed conveying the property in question to "Angelo Prassa and Alice Patricia Prassa, his wife, not in tenancy in common but in joint tenancy." The plaintiff then paid to the sellers the balance of the purchase price in cash. Plaintiff testified he told the sellers or their representatives how he wanted the contract and deed to be made out, the manner chosen being due to the fact that "we were going to get married the following month and we figured why go through all the expense of having it changed after we were married." Plaintiff had no conversation with the defendant as to how she was to be designated in the documents, but had only discussed it with her father and the lawyer. Defendant testified she signed the documents in the manner directed by the plaintiff. She had never signed her name that way before and was not aware of any legal rights possessed by her under the contract until the present litigation ensued.

On November 4 plaintiff and his fiancee, in the course of decorating and furnishing the apartment which they were going to occupy, had a dispute. She gave the engagement ring back to the plaintiff. Plaintiff that same evening attempted to return the ring to defendant, but she refused it. Defendant's parents were informed of the occurrence that evening. The following day plaintiff sent flowers to Alice and visited her that evening for the purpose of attempting a reconciliation. Plaintiff told her if she wouldn't take the ring he wouldn't come back. She again refused to accept the ring. Three days later Alice called plaintiff telling him that she would now accept the ring. At this time plaintiff agreed to drive her to work and discuss the matter. Thereafter unavailing discussions between themselves and with a clergyman were held concerning possible reconciliation. They were fruitless and upon defendant's refusal to convey to plaintiff her interest in the building, plaintiff instituted this suit.

The character of the trust relied upon by plaintiff is that of a resulting trust created by operation of law. The applicable rules of law have been frequently stated. A resulting trust arises by operation of law where one person pays or furnishes the consideration for a deed conveying real estate to another. Whether or not such a trust arises depends in every case upon the intention, at the time of the conveyance, of the person who furnishes the purchase price. Such a trust arises, if it arises at all, the instant the legal title is taken, and is founded upon the natural equity that he who pays for the property should enjoy it, unless he intended by the vesting of title to confer a beneficial interest upon the grantee. The payment of the consideration raises a *prima facie* presumption in favor of a resulting trust. This presumption, however, may be rebutted by parol proof of an intention on the part of the payor that the grantee shall take the beneficial interest and not merely the legal title. No general rule can be stated that will determine when a conveyance made to one other than the person furnishing the consideration will carry with it a beneficial interest and when it will be construed to create a trust, but the intention must be gathered from the facts and circumstances as shown by the record in each case. Where a deed absolute in terms and without condition or reservation conveys real estate to two persons as joint tenants, the language of the deed is sufficient to show an express intent to convey both the legal title and the beneficial interests to the two grantees as joint tenants, but if the purchase price was paid by only one of such grantees, this indicates an intention that that grantee is the only one beneficially interested in the property, and under such facts, the expressed intent as shown by the deed must give way to the rule of equity which protects the party paying the purchase price by raising a resulting trust in his favor.

* * *

Where * * * the uncontroverted evidence is that the plaintiff paid the original payment and sole consideration for the property, and that title to the property in question was conveyed to the plaintiff and defendant, as joint tenants, such facts bring this case within the resulting trust doctrine. * * *

Upon the foregoing facts and considerations the law raises a *prima facie* presumption in favor of a resulting trust, and imposes upon the grantee the burden of going forward with the evidence and showing an intention on the part of the grantor that she was to have some beneficial interest in the property.

* * * [T]here is clear proof in support that plaintiff did not intend to vest in defendant a beneficial interest in the property at the time of the conveyance.

The contract and deed indicate that the intended interest of the defendant in the property was to be as plaintiff's wife and not as Alice Patricia Corcoran. Such conclusion is also evident from Alice's concern over whether she should sign the contract in that manner and then doing so pursuant to plaintiff's verbal request. Defendant herself testified that plaintiff had told her prior to the conveyance that he "had saved money for a home when he was to marry"; moreover, the property was to serve as a home for plaintiff and defendant as well as her parents. Plaintiff's testimony that he chose the particular form of the contract for convenience is additional corroboration of a nondonative intention at the time of the conveyance.

Although a resulting trust cannot be predicated upon a condition subsequent to the conveyance, subsequent conduct and attitude toward the act in question and the property acquired may be used to shed light upon the true intention of the plaintiff. Defendant's father, who was integrally involved in the negotiations and consummation of the purchase transaction, testified that after the marriage appeared definitely off he stated that he wished to buy the property from plaintiff "for what he (plaintiff) paid for it." Alice testified that pursuant to her father's offer she made efforts to secure funds with which to purchase the building. From such evidence the only reasonable inference to be drawn is in support of an intention held by plaintiff not to make a gift prior to consummation of marriage. This certainly is not to suggest that a gift cannot be given by one engaged individual to the other in contemplation of marriage. Rather, under the circumstances here presented, the chancellor was warranted in finding that plaintiff did not intend a gift. In determining that no gift was contemplated and therefore not consummated during the period of engagement, it is immaterial which of the parties was responsible for the breaking of the engagement.

* * *

Decree affirmed.

Were the "Happy Birthday" checks from dad properly charged to the trust?

JIMENEZ v. LEE

Supreme Court of Oregon, In Banc, 1976.
274 Or. 457, 547 P.2d 126.

O'CONNELL, Chief Justice

This is a suit brought by plaintiff against her father to compel him to account for assets which she alleges were held by defendant as trustee for her. Plaintiff appeals from a decree dismissing her complaint.

Plaintiff's claim against her father is based upon the theory that a trust arose in her favor when two separate gifts were made for her benefit. The first of these gifts was made in 1945, shortly after plaintiff's birth, when her paternal grandmother purchased a $1,000 face value U.S. Savings Bond which was registered in the names of defendant "and/or" plaintiff "and/or" Dorothy Lee, plaintiff's mother. It is uncontradicted that the bond was purchased to provide funds to be used for plaintiff's educational needs. A second gift in the amount of $500 was made in 1956 by Mrs. Adolph Diercks, one of defendant's clients. At the same time Mrs. Diercks made identical gifts for the benefit of defendant's two other children. The $1,500 was deposited by the donor in a savings account in the names of defendant and his three children.

In 1960 defendant cashed the savings bond and invested the proceeds in common stock of the Commercial Bank of Salem, Oregon. Ownership of the shares was registered as "Jason Lee, Custodian under the Laws of Oregon for Betsy Lee [plaintiff]." At the same time, the joint savings account containing the client's gifts to defendant's children was closed and $1,000 of the proceeds invested in Commercial Bank stock.[1] Defendant also took title to this stock as "custodian" for his children.

1. The specific disposition of the balance of this account is not revealed in the record. Defendant testified that the portion of the gift not invested in the stock "was used for other unusual needs of the children." Defendant could not recall exactly how the money was used but thought some of it was spent for family vacations to Victoria, British Columbia and to satisfy his children's expensive taste in clothing.

The trial court found that defendant did not hold either the savings bond or the savings account in trust for the benefit of plaintiff and that defendant held the shares of the Commercial Bank stock as custodian for plaintiff under the Uniform Gift to Minors Act (ORS 126.805–126.880). Plaintiff contends that the gifts for her educational needs created trusts in each instance and that the trusts survived defendant's investment of the trust assets in the Commercial Bank stock.

It is undisputed that the gifts were made for the educational needs of plaintiff. The respective donors did not expressly direct defendant to hold the subject matter of the gift "in trust" but this is not essential to create a trust relationship. It is enough if the transfer of the property is made with the intent to vest the beneficial ownership in a third person. That was clearly shown in the present case. Even defendant's own testimony establishes such intent. When he was asked whether there was a stated purpose for the gift, he replied:

> * * * Mother said that she felt that the children should all be treated equally and that she was going to supply a bond to help with Elizabeth's educational needs and that she was naming me and Dorothy, the ex-wife and mother of Elizabeth, to use the funds as may be most conducive to the educational needs of Elizabeth.

Defendant also admitted that the gift from Mrs. Diercks was "for the educational needs of the children." There was nothing about either of the gifts which would suggest that the beneficial ownership of the subject matter of the gift was to vest in defendant to use as he pleased with an obligation only to pay out of his own funds a similar amount for plaintiff's educational needs.

Defendant himself demonstrated that he knew that the savings bond was held by him in trust. In a letter to his mother, the donor, he wrote: "Dave and Bitsie [plaintiff] & Dorothy are aware of the fact that I hold $1,000 each for Dave & Bitsie in trust for them on account of your E-Bond gifts." It is fair to indulge in the presumption that defendant, as a lawyer, used the word "trust" in the ordinary legal sense of that term.

Defendant further contends that even if the respective donors intended to create trusts, the doctrine of merger defeated that intent because plaintiff acquired both legal and equitable title when the savings bond was registered in her name along with her parents names and when Mrs. Diercks' gift was deposited in the savings account in the name of plaintiff and her father, brother and sister. The answer to this contention is found in II Scott on Trusts § 99.4, p. 811 (3d ed. 1967):

> A trust may be created in which the trustees are A and B and the sole beneficiary is A. In such a case it might be argued that there is automatically a partial extinguishment of the trust, and that A holds an undivided half interest as joint tenant free of trust, although B holds a similar interest in trust for A. The better view is, however, that there is no such partial merger, and that A and B will hold the property as joint tenants in trust for A. * * *

Having decided that a trust was created for the benefit of plaintiff, it follows that defendant's purchase of the Commercial Bank stock as "custodian" for plaintiff under the Uniform Gift to Minors Act was ineffectual to expand defendant's powers over the trust property from that of trustee to that of custodian.[4]

4. If defendant were "custodian" of the gifts, he would have the power under the Uniform Gift to Minors Act (ORS 126.820) to use the property "as he may deem advisable for the support, maintenance, education and general use and benefit of the minor, in such manner, at such time or times, and to such extent as the custodian in his absolute discretion may deem advisable and proper, without court order or without regard to the duty of any person to support the minor, and without regard to any other funds which may be applicable or available for the purpose." As custodian defendant would not be required to account for his stewardship of the funds unless a petition for accounting were filed in circuit court no later than two years after the end of plaintiff's minority. ORS 126.875. As the trustee of an educational trust, however, defendant has the power to use the trust funds for educational purposes only and has the duty to render clear and accurate accounts

Defendant's attempt to broaden his powers over the trust estate by investing the trust funds as custodian violated his duty to the beneficiary "to administer the trust solely in the interest of the beneficiary."

The money from the savings bond and savings account are clearly traceable into the bank stock. Therefore, plaintiff was entitled to impose a constructive trust or an equitable lien upon the stock so acquired. Plaintiff is also entitled to be credited for any dividends or increment in the value of that part of the stock representing plaintiff's proportional interest. Whether or not the assets of plaintiff's trust are traceable into a product, defendant is personally liable for that amount which would have accrued to plaintiff had there been no breach of trust. Defendant is, of course, entitled to deduct the amount which he expended out of the trust estate for plaintiff's educational needs. However, before he is entitled to be credited for such expenditures, he has the duty as trustee to identify them specifically and prove that they were made for trust purposes. A trustee's duty to maintain and render accurate accounts is a strict one. This strict standard is described in Bogert on Trusts and Trustees § 962, pp. 10–13 (2d ed. 1962):

> It is the duty of the trustees to keep full, accurate and orderly records of the status of the trust administration and of all acts thereunder. * * * 'The general rule of law applicable to a trustee burdens him with the duty of showing that the account which he renders and the expenditures which he claims to have been made were correct, just and necessary. * * * He is bound to keep clear and accurate accounts, and if he does not the presumptions are all against him, obscurities and doubts being resolved adversely to him.' He has the burden of showing on the accounting how much principal and income he has received and from whom, how much disbursed and to whom, and what is on hand at the time.

Defendant did not keep separate records of trust income and trust expenditures. He introduced into evidence a summary of various expenditures which he claimed were made for the benefit of plaintiff. It appears that the summary was prepared for the most part from cancelled checks gathered together for the purpose of defending the present suit. This obviously did not meet the requirement that a trustee "maintain records of his transactions so complete and accurate that he can show by them his faithfulness to his trust."

In an even more general way defendant purported to account for the trust assets in a letter dated February 9, 1966, written to plaintiff shortly after her 21st birthday when she was in Europe where she had been receiving instruction and training in ballet. In that letter defendant revealed to plaintiff, apparently for the first time, that her grandmother had made a gift to her of a savings bond and that the proceeds of the bond had been invested in stock. Without revealing the name of the stock, defendant represented that it had doubled in value of the bond from $750 to $1,500. The letter went on to suggest that plaintiff allocate $1,000 to defray the cost of additional ballet classes and that the remaining $500 be held in reserve to defray expenses in returning to the United States and in getting settled in a college or in a ballet company.

Defendant's letter was in no sense a trust accounting. In the first place, it was incomplete; it made no mention of Mrs. Diercks' gift. Moreover, it was inaccurate since it failed to reveal the true value attributable to the Commercial Bank stock. There was evidence which would put the value of plaintiff's interest in the stock at considerably more than $1,500.[9]

showing the funds have been used for trust purposes. See ORS 128.010: Restatement (Second) of Trusts § 172 (1959).

9. It appears that with the accumulation of cash and stock dividends the total value of plaintiff's interest at the time she received defendant's letter would amount to as much as $2,135. This figure is an approximation derived from the incomplete stock price information before us. It is important only to demonstrate that defendant did not render an adequate accounting. Our calculation does not include the value of plaintiff's interest in stock purchased with the proceeds of Mrs. Diercks' gift.

Defendant contends that even if a trust is found to exist and that the value of the trust assets is the amount claimed by plaintiff there is sufficient evidence to prove that the trust estate was exhausted by expenditures for legitimate trust purposes. Considering the character of the evidence presented by defendant, it is difficult to understand how such a result could be reached. As we noted above, the trust was for the educational needs of plaintiff. Some of the expenditures made by defendant would seem to fall clearly within the purposes of the trust. These would include the cost of ballet lessons, the cost of subscribing to a ballet magazine, and other items of expenditure related to plaintiff's education. But many of the items defendant lists as trust expenditures are either questionable or clearly outside the purpose of an educational trust. For instance, defendant seeks credit against the trust for tickets to ballet performances on three different occasions while plaintiff was in high school. The cost of plaintiff's ticket to a ballet performance might be regarded as a part of plaintiff's educational program in learning the art of ballet, but defendant claims credit for expenditures made to purchase ballet tickets for himself and other members of the family, disbursements clearly beyond the purposes of the trust.

Other expenditures claimed by defendant in his "accounting" are clearly not in furtherance of the purposes of the trust. Included in the cancelled checks introduced into evidence in support of defendant's claimed offset against the trust assets were: (1) checks made by defendant in payment of numerous medical bills dating from the time plaintiff was 15 years old (these were obligations which a parent owes to his minor children); (2) checks containing the notation "Happy Birthday" which plaintiff received from her parents on her 17th, 18th and 22nd birthdays; (3) a 1963 check with a notation "Honor Roll, Congratulations, Mom and Dad"; (4) defendant's check to a clothier which contains the notation "Betsy's Slacks and Sweater, Pat's Sweater, Dot's Sweater", (defendant attempted to charge the entire amount against the trust); (5) defendant's check to a Canadian Rotary Club for a meeting attended when he joined plaintiff in Banff after a summer ballet program; (6) $60 sent to plaintiff to enable her to travel from France, where she was studying ballet, to Austria to help care for her sister's newborn babies. There were also other items improperly claimed as expenditures for plaintiff's educational benefit, either because the purpose of the outlay could not be identified or because defendant claimed a double credit.[11]

It is apparent from the foregoing description of defendant's evidence that the trial court erred in finding that "Plaintiff in these proceedings has received the accounting which she sought and * * * is entitled to no further accounting." The trial court also erred in finding that "Defendant did not hold in trust for the benefit of Plaintiff" the product traceable to the two gifts.

The case must, therefore, be remanded for an accounting to be predicated upon a trustee's duty to account, and the trustee's burden to prove that the expenditures were made for trust purposes. There is a moral obligation and in proper cases a legal obligation for a parent to furnish his child with higher education. Where a parent is a trustee of an educational trust, as in the present case, and he makes expenditures out of his own funds, his intent on one hand may be to discharge his moral or legal obligation to educate his child or on the other hand to follow the directions of the trust. It is a question of fact in each case as to which of these two purposes the parent-trustee had in mind at the time of making the expenditures. In determining whether defendant has met this strict burden of proof, the trial court must adhere to the rule that all doubts are resolved against a trustee who maintains an inadequate accounting system.

11. The double counting occurs where defendant claims credit for cashier's checks sent to plaintiff while she was staying in Europe and at the same time also claims credit for his personal checks used to purchase the cashier's checks.

The decree of the trial court is reversed and the cause is remanded for further proceedings consistent with this opinion.

She feared that if we went to the attorney who prepared her former will, her daughter would find out about it and "raise Hell."

IN RE ESTATE OF WEIR

Court of Appeals of Oregon, 1975.
21 Or.App. 476, 535 P.2d 119.

TONGUE, Judge Pro Tem

This is a proceeding to contest the will of Sophia Weir, a resident of Coos County. The mental capacity of the Testator is conceded, but it is contended that the will was the result of the undue influence of the sole beneficiary, Wayne Clawson, alias Bill Wolf. As in most will contest cases, the facts are of extreme importance.

The Facts

A previous will was executed by Mrs. Weir on December 28, 1971, naming one of her two daughters, Louise Carlton, as her sole beneficiary. At that time Mrs. Weir and a hired man lived on her farm. In May 1972, Wayne Clawson became manager of the farm. He had come to Oregon from California where he had a criminal record of several convictions, with the result that he had assumed the name of Bill Wolf. From June 1972, until her death on November 23, 1973, Mrs. Weir and Wolf occupied the old two-story house on the farm.

Mrs. Weir was then 77 years of age and in poor health suffering from diabetes, high blood pressure, chronic urinary infection, diarrhea and progressive cataracts; but she was mentally "sharp" and strong willed, according to the testimony. Shortly after Wolf came to the farm Mrs. Weir fell and broke her hip. She was a heavy woman and thus had to be helped. As a result of these disabilities, Mr. Wolf helped her take her baths and helped her to bed, among other things. He took good care of her, according to the testimony.

Shortly after he became manager of the farm Mr. Wolf had an attorney prepare a "management agreement," which he took to the farm, where it was signed by him and Mrs. Weir. By the terms of that agreement Mr. Wolf was to be the manager of the farm for five years, with "full authority" to manage it "within [his] sole discretion." The agreement also provided that as compensation he was to be furnished living quarters, rent free, for the five-year period, as well as title to all timber on the premises, to be removed within five years. There was no testimony as to the amount or value of that timber.

Mrs. Carlton, Mrs. Weir's daughter, became concerned about developing problems between herself and Mr. Wolf when she visited her mother on the farm. Although there is no evidence that she knew of the management agreement, she took her mother to the office of the attorney who had prepared her previous will. That attorney testified that he talked to Mrs. Weir alone and that she told him that she wanted to stay on the ranch and have Mr. Wolf take care of her, but that she did not want him to be in a "position to lay claim to the ranch as a result of services provided for her." She said nothing, however, about the written management agreement.

He then wrote a letter to Mr. Wolf as attorney for Mrs. Weir stating his understanding that "in return for taking care of Mrs. Weir and her ranch operation," Mr. Wolf was to receive "full tenancy at the premises," subject to termination at any time, and stating that if this was not a correct statement of the agreement between him and Mrs. Weir, to "contact me at your early convenience to discuss what you feel to be the true and correct nature of the agreement." Mr. Wolf did not respond to that letter because, as he testified, he thought it "not important enough."

Considerable testimony was offered from several witnesses to the effect that as of that time Mrs. Weir did not want to sell the farm, which had been "in the family" for over 100 years, but wanted to keep it in "the family" for "the kids," in accordance with the provisions of her previous will leaving it to her daughter and that she made such statements as late as within three months prior to her death. Mr. Wolf, however, testified that she never told him that she wanted to keep the farm in the family, but said that "they would never take care of it," but would sell it and were "just waiting for her to die."

There was testimony that in "conversations" with Mrs. Weir, Mr. Wolf was critical of Mrs. Carlton for failing to devote sufficient attention to her mother; that this was the subject of "frequent conversations," and that Mrs. Weir was also critical of her daughter. Mrs. Carlton apparently visited her mother once each week "for the eggs" and also drove her to see the doctor. There were also difficulties between Mr. Wolf and one of Mrs. Carlton's sons, who was accused by Wolf of stealing from Mrs. Weir.

It also appears that a friend of Mr. Wolf, a Mr. Ogden, also originally from California, where he had once been convicted of a crime, was a frequent visitor at the farm. He stayed there on his days off from work "almost every week," and played cribbage and pinochle with Mrs. Weir. Another frequent visitor to the farm was Eldred Clawson, father of Mr. Wolf, who was retired and "came up" from California to visit his son. He also had a criminal record in California. According to Mr. Ogden, he, Mr. Wolf and Wolf's father, Mr. Clawson, were all "living" at the farm in November 1973 when the contested will was executed and when Mrs. Weir died.

Except for the testimony of one other witness, the only evidence of any statements by Mrs. Weir prior to the preparation and execution of the contested will indicating a change of her previous desire to leave the farm "in the family" was the testimony of Mr. Wolf himself. He testified that over a period of "a couple of months" he and Mrs. Weir "talked over the possibility of [his] becoming the owner of the place" and that she "asked me if I would keep the place going if I owned it and I told her I would try my very best." Mr. Wolf also told his friend, Mr. Ogden, that he would "like to own something like this" and also told his father that Mrs. Weir said that there was a possibility that she would "will the place to him." He denied, however, that he had any conversations with her about preparing a will to accomplish that purpose.

There was also testimony that on occasion Mr. Wolf would give Mrs. Weir an affectionate pat or hug and refer to her as "Mom." He also testified that Mrs. Weir trusted him, had "much confidence" in him, and that she confided most of her problems to him.

Just when and under what circumstances she finally decided to change her previous will is not entirely clear, even under the testimony of the proponents of the contested will. Mr. Ogden testified that he typed the will on a typewriter that he had taken to the farm and that he got the information for the will from Mrs. Weir, who said she was "very unhappy" with her daughter; that this was the reason for changing her will, and that she definitely wanted to make a new will and leave it to Mr. Wolf." He testified that he suggested that she go to a lawyer but that she asked him to "do it." He also said that he typed two or three drafts of the one-page will and that Mrs. Weir finally said that "it would do all right." Ogden also said that he got the description of the farm for the purposes of the will from tax statements that were "on the table" and that he did not know if they were provided by Mr. Wolf.

Mr. Wolf's father, Mr. Clawson, who also had lived at the farm for some time before the contested will was executed, said that he heard no discussions between Mrs. Weir, Ogden and Wolf about the will and knew nothing about it other than that Ogden typed it "upstairs" and then brought it down to show her to read and make any necessary changes.

Mr. Wolf testified that he gave the tax statement to Ogden for the purposes of using in the will its description of the farm, but that he did so at the request of Mrs. Weir, and that he did not tell Ogden what to "say" in the will, but that Mrs. Weir did. He also testified that about one month before he had tried, "at her request," to get the attorney who prepared his management contract to come to the farm and prepare a will, but that the attorney refused to do so and suggested that Mrs. Weir come to his office. Wolf said that he also previously talked to another attorney, who declined to prepare the will and suggested that he go to another attorney. Mr. Wolf testified that Mrs. Weir did not want anyone to know about the new will and feared that if she went to the attorney who prepared her former will her daughter would find out about it and would "raise Hell." These were the reasons, according to Mr. Wolf, that she asked Ogden to "do it."

Apparently the will was typed by Ogden on Sunday, November 18, 1973. On the following day Mr. Wolf requested a notary public whom he had previously known to come to the farm to notarize the will. Upon arrival of the notary, and in the presence of Mr. Ogden and Mr. Clawson, Wolf's father, the will was signed by Mrs. Weir and was witnessed by them. According to the testimony, Mr. Wolf, the sole beneficiary of the will, was "in and out" of the room both when the will was prepared and when it was signed and witnessed. According to the notary, Wolf spoke to Mrs. Weir at that time as "Mom" and asked if he could get her another cup of coffee.

The notary and the other witnesses, Ogden and Clawson, identified their signatures and that of Mrs. Weir, but were not asked the usual questions whether she appeared to have the necessary testamentary capacity and whether she appeared to be acting of her own free will. They testified, however, that the notary read the will to Mrs. Weir before she signed it. There was other testimony that because of cataracts she had considerable difficulty in reading.

On November 23, 1973, four days after the execution of the will on November 19, Mrs. Weir died in the farmhouse of an apparent heart attack. Mr. Wolf was alone with her at that time. At that time the natural heirs of Mrs. Weir, in addition to the daughter who had been named as the sole beneficiary in her previous will, included another daughter and several grandchildren.

In its decree denying the "petition to revoke probate" of the will of November 19, 1973, and in admitting that will to probate "in solemn form" the trial court made no findings of fact other than general findings that Mrs. Weir was competent and that "said will was not the result of undue influence."

It was established by the evidence that the will was the product of undue influence.

The Supreme Court of Oregon held in In re Reddaway's Estate, that:

> Definitions of undue influence couched in terms of the testator's freedom of will are subject to criticism in that they invite us to think in terms of coercion and duress, when the emphasis should be on the unfairness of the advantage which is reaped as the result of wrongful conduct. "Undue influence does not negative consent by the donor. Equity acts because there is want of conscience on the part of the donee, not want of consent on the part of the donor." Said in another way, undue influence has a closer kinship to fraud than to duress. It has been characterized as "a species of fraud."
>
> * * * This court has held that where a confidential relation exists between a testator and the beneficiary, slight evidence is sufficient to establish undue influence. The rule is more specifically stated in In re Southman's Estate, as follows:
>
>> The existence of a confidential relationship * * * when taken in connection with other suspicious circumstances may justify a suspicion of undue influence so

> as to require the beneficiary to go forward with the proof and present evidence sufficient to overcome the adverse inference. * * *

It will be noted that the burden does not exist unless there are circumstances in addition to the confidential relation. * * *

As in *Reddaway,* we find that there was a confidential relationship between Mrs. Weir and Mr. Wolf and that the "relationship [was] such as to indicate a position of dominance by the one in whom confidence [was] reposed over the other." As in *Reddaway,* we also find that in this case "suspicious circumstances are abundant."

In *Reddaway* the Oregon Supreme Court listed and discussed the various "factors of importance" to be considered in determining whether undue influence was exercised. Upon considering those various factors we find that enough of them were sufficiently established so as to require the conclusion that the will of Sophia Weir was the product of undue influence by Bill Wolf, for reasons which we shall next discuss.

(1) *Procurement, i.e., "participation [by] the beneficiary in the preparation of the will."* Wolf provided for Ogden the description of the farm for the purposes of the will, despite his contention that he did so at the request of Mrs. Weir. Aside from the fact that Wolf's friend Ogden typed the will and Wolf's own father and his friend Ogden witnessed the will, he also procured a notary public to witness the will and was "in and out" of the room during its execution, at which time he called Mrs. Weir "Mom" and offered to get her a cup of coffee.

(2) *Independent advice.* No independent advice was provided to Mrs. Weir relative to the preparation of the will.

(3) *Secrecy and haste.* One reason that no lawyer was engaged to prepare the will was the desire to keep it a secret. The circumstances are such as also to indicate considerable haste in its preparation. The only reason for waiting until the next day for the execution of the will was the mistaken belief of Wolf that it had to be witnessed by a notary public.

(4) *Change in decedent's attitude toward others.* As in *Reddaway,* there was a change in the attitude of the testator toward her own child. Although Wolf testified that the reason for the change was her displeasure with her daughter, it is "just as probable" in this case that Wolf "played a part in effecting this change in attitude," as it was that similar conduct played a similar part in *Reddaway.*

(5) *Change in the testator's plan of disposing of her property.* As in *Reddaway,* there was such a change in the plan of the testator and there was evidence of a previously "settled intent in the disposition of [her] estate" and of a "variance" between the testator's previous will and the will in question.

(6) *Unnatural or unjust gift.* Although, as recognized in *Reddaway,* one may make a legal disposition of his estate which reasonable men would regard as "unfair," it is a "circumstance" to be weighed in determining whether undue influence existed. This is not a case in which the beneficiary who cared for an ill and aged testator was rewarded by the will for faithful service and would otherwise have received little or no compensation. Wolf already had procured a five year "management agreement," including title to all timber on the property.

(7) *Susceptibility to influence.* Finally, as in *Reddaway,* this testator, although a person of "strong will," was physically sick and infirm and was susceptible to influence by reason of her dependence upon Wolf as the result of her physical infirmities.

As in *Reddaway,* there was also other evidence in the record which was relevant to the issue of undue influence, including other "suspicious circumstances," but the combination of the foregoing circumstances is sufficient, in our judgment, to require that this court sustain the contention of the contestants that undue influence was exercised upon this testator.

* * * [T]he will of Sophia Weir was the product of undue influence by Bill Wolf.

Accordingly, the decree of the trial court is reversed and this case is remanded for further proceedings not inconsistent with this opinion.

A "Totten" trust.

IN RE PETRALIA'S ESTATE

Supreme Court of Illinois, 1965.
32 Ill.2d 134, 204 N.E.2d 1.

HERSHEY, Justice

In 1948 Antonio Petralia opened a savings account in the First National Bank of Chicago, naming himself as "trustee" for the benefit of his daughter, Dominica Di Maggio, to whom the balance in the account at his death was to be paid. After Petralia's death, Dominica Di Maggio, plaintiff herein, instituted a citation proceeding against the defendant administrator of the estate of Antonio Petralia in the probate court of Cook County in which she claimed title to the account. The probate court held that a valid trust had been created and that under the terms thereof the plaintiff was entitled to the balance of $17,189.15 in the account. The Appellate Court affirmed, and we granted leave to appeal.

This is the first occasion on which we have been called upon to consider the validity of savings bank or "Totten" trusts. The defendant urges the court to reverse the judgments below on two grounds: (1) that the execution of the signature card was insufficient to establish an intent on the part of Antonio Petralia to create a trust; and (2) "that the form of trust attempted to be executed by the savings accounts trusts is an attempt at a testamentary disposition and not operative, due to the failure to conform with the Statute of wills."

The record indicates that for a number of years prior to 1948 Antonio Petralia was the sole owner of a regular savings account which he had opened in his name at the First National Bank of Chicago. On November 8, 1948, he closed the account and transferred all the funds therein to the savings account trust which is the subject of this litigation. The new account was entitled "Tony Petralia, Trustee," and on the first side of the signature card appeared the signature "Tony Petralia" with the word "trustee" written beneath. On the reverse side of the card was the following language:

> All deposits in this account are made for the benefit of Domenica Di Maggio to whom or to whose legal representative said deposits or any part thereof, together with the interest thereon, may be paid in the event of the death of the undersigned Trustee.

The signature "Tony Petralia" again appeared below the language on a line designated "trustee". Beneath the signature was written "Mrs. Domenica Di Maggio", "July 29, 1909" and "Daughter."

Introduced in evidence were facsimile ledger sheets of the First National Bank which showed that from the date the account was opened to the date of his death, Antonio Petralia alone made numerous deposits to and infrequent withdrawals from the account. The balance in the account steadily increased.

In support of his contention that the execution of the signature card was insufficient to show an intent to create a trust, the administrator emphasizes the fact that the printed agreement on the card provided that the bank "may", rather than "shall", pay the balance to the plaintiff at his death. The use of the word "may" is said to show a lack of intent that the plaintiff was definitely to receive the benefit of the account.

The reason for the inclusion of the word "may" in the agreement is not clear. * * * Whatever the reason for the use of the word "may", however, we think that the general tenor of the agreement indicates an intent to create a trust and that the settlor intended that the funds be paid to his daughter at his death. This conclusion is confirmed by the fact that the settlor changed his regular savings account to a savings account in trust form, an act which would have been unnecessary if he intended to maintain the account solely for his own benefit. We think it significant also that Antonio Petralia did not in fact withdraw the funds in the account and use them for his own benefit during his lifetime but instead followed a regular pattern of making deposits, thereby steadily increasing the size of the account, apparently for the benefit of his daughter. Although there was testimony by Antonio Petralia's nephew that Petralia had told him the account was opened so that his daughter could make deposits for him, the fact that Petralia alone made all deposits greatly discredits the persuasiveness of such evidence. We think there was ample evidence to support the trial court's finding that Antonio Petralia intended to create a trust.

This brings us to a consideration of the defendant's contention that the trust was invalid as an attempted testamentary disposition without compliance with the Statute of Wills. Since the trust agreement was not executed in accordance with the formalities required by the Statute of Wills, the determinative issue becomes whether a valid *inter vivos* trust was created. One of the requirements for the establishment of a valid *inter vivos* trust is that the beneficiary acquire a present interest during the lifetime of the settlor. The defendant argues that since the settlor alone retained the power to withdraw interest and principal from the account during his lifetime, the trust was illusory and testamentary in that the beneficiary never obtained any present interest during the settlor's lifetime.

It is true that Antonio Petralia, as settlor and trustee, retained extensive control over the savings account trust which he established. However, in this respect it is not significantly different in substance from other revocable *inter vivos* trusts which have been held valid in this and other jurisdictions. The nature of the beneficiary's present interest under such trusts is well stated in 1 Scott, The Law of Trusts, 353–354: "The declaration of trust immediately creates an equitable interest in the beneficiaries although the enjoyment of the interest is postponed until the death of the settlor, and although the interest may be divested by the exercise of the power of revocation." The fact that the beneficiary's actual enjoyment of the trust is contingent on Antonio Petralia's death without first having revoked the trust by withdrawing the balance in the account does not negate the existence of a present interest in the plaintiff during her father's lifetime, even though that interest may have been highly destructible.

We conclude that the instrument executed by Antonio Petralia on November 8, 1948, was sufficient to create a valid and enforceable *inter vivos* savings account trust. In so holding we accept the position adopted by the American Law Institute in § 58 of the Restatement (Second) of Trusts: "Where a person makes a deposit in a savings account in a bank or other savings organization in his own name as trustee for another person intending to reserve a power to withdraw the whole or any part of the deposit at any time during his lifetime and to use as his own whatever he may withdraw, or otherwise to revoke the trust, the intended trust is enforceable by the beneficiary upon the death of the depositor as to any part remaining on deposit on his death if he has not revoked the trust."

The judgment of the Appellate Court affirming the order of the probate court of Cook County is affirmed.

Judgment affirmed.

Does a husband who murders his wife have a right to share in her estate when she dies intestate?

ESTATE OF KALFUS v. KALFUS

Superior Court of New Jersey,
Chancery Division, 1963.
81 N.J.Super. 435, 195 A.2d 903.

PASHMAN, J.S.C.

This is a summary proceeding to determine the * * * the rights of defendant Richard H. Kalfus under the New Jersey statute of descent and distribution. A brief factual résumé is necessary to an understanding of the present controversy.

On November 20, 1962 Domenica Kalfus was murdered by her defendant husband. Domenica died intestate. Following a plea defendant was sentenced to the New Jersey State Prison, where he is presently confined, for a term of 15 to 20 years.

Domenica died seized of an estate comprising personal property and the equity in the family home in Cliffside Park which she owned in fee simple. The equity in the house was approximately $25,500 and the personal estate about $6,800. She was survived by her husband and two infant children, Michele, age seven, and Jane, age three. Bernard Natalino, a brother of the deceased intestate, was appointed guardian of the infants and administrator of the estate. This court ordered the real property sold as being in the best interests of the infants, and the proceeds of the sale were deposited into court pending a determination of the following * * * question. * * *

Does a husband who murders his wife have a right to share in her personal estate where the wife dies intestate?

* * *

Under our statute of descent and distribution, an intestate's husband is entitled to one-third of the intestate's personal property if a child or children also survive the deceased parent.

* * *

In the insurance cases the courts have impressed a constructive trust on the proceeds of the policy by invoking the age-old maxim of the common law that "no man can profit by his own wrongdoing."

* * *

[T]heory allows the legal title to pass but equity treats the wrongdoer as a constructive trustee because of his unconscionable conduct, and will compel the wrongdoer to convey the property to the heirs or next of kin of the deceased.

This * * * view was adopted in Sherman v. Weber, where the nature of the property was a tenancy by the entirety, and in Whitney v. Lott, a situation involving a devise from deceased wife, to husband-murderer. More recently the doctrine of constructive trust was used in Neiman v. Hurff, where a husband murdered his wife. The husband and wife held real property as tenants by the entirety and shares of stock as joint tenants.

In the Whitney case the effect of the statute of wills was circumvented by the use of the constructive trust whereby title would pass, subject however to the imposition of the trust *ex maleficio.*

* * * Even in the absence of a specific statute, it has been held that a murderer cannot inherit from his victim under the statute of descent and distribution.

* * *

Based upon the reasoning of our courts in analogous situations and upon the cases in those jurisdictions which deny recovery to a murderer who takes the life of a spouse or the person from whom he or she is to inherit under the statutes of descent and distribution, this court holds that * * * defendant is a constructive trustee of the aforementioned property because of his unconscionable method of acquiring the property. He is therefore ordered to transfer and convey the legal title to the property to the minor plaintiffs.

* * *

Counsel may submit a judgment in accordance with this opinion.

The Establishment Clause does not extend to this type of tax deduction.

MUELLER v. ALLEN

Supreme Court of the United States, 1983.
— U.S. —, 103 S.Ct. 3062, 77 L.Ed.2d 721.

JUSTICE REHNQUIST delivered the opinion of the Court.

Minnesota allows taxpayers, in computing their state income tax, to deduct certain expenses incurred in providing for the education of their children. * * * The United States Court of Appeals for the Eighth Circuit held that the Establishment Clause of the First and Fourteenth Amendments was not offended by this arrangement. * * * We now affirm.

Minnesota, like every other state, provides its citizens with free elementary and secondary schooling. * * * It seems to be agreed that about 820,000 students attended this school system in the most recent school year. During the same year, approximately 91,000 elementary and secondary students attended some 500 privately supported schools located in Minnesota, and about 95% of these students attended schools considering themselves to be sectarian.

Minnesota, by a law originally enacted in 1955 and revised in 1976 and again in 1978, permits state taxpayers to claim a deduction from gross income for certain expenses incurred in educating their children. The deduction is limited to actual expenses incurred for the "tuition, textbooks and transportation" of dependents attending elementary or secondary schools. A deduction may not exceed $500 per dependent in grades K through six and $700 per dependent in grades seven through twelve. * * *

Petitioners—certain Minnesota taxpayers—sued in the United States District Court for the District of Minnesota claiming that [Minnesota law] violated the Establishment Clause by providing financial assistance to sectarian institutions. They named as respondents the Commissioner of the Department of Revenue of Minnesota and several parents who took advantage of the tax deduction for expenses incurred in sending their children to parochial schools. The District Court granted respondent's motion for summary judgment, holding that the statute was "neutral on its face and in its application and does not have a primary effect of either advancing or inhibiting religion." * * * On appeal, the Court of Appeals affirmed, concluding that the Minnesota statute substantially benefited a "broad class of Minnesota citizens."

Today's case is no exception to our oft-repeated statement that the Establishment Clause presents especially difficult questions of interpretation and application. It is easy enough to quote the few words comprising that clause—"Congress shall make no law respecting an establishment of religion." It is not at all easy, however, [to] apply this Court's various decisions construing the Clause to governmental programs of financial assistance to sectarian schools and the parents of children attending those schools. Indeed, in many of these decisions "we have expressly or implicitly acknowledged that 'we can only dimly perceive the lines of demarcation in this extraordinarily sensitive area of constitutional law.' " * * *

One fixed principle in this field is our consistent rejection of the argument that "any program which in some manner aids an institution with a religious affiliation" violates the Establishment Clause. * * * For example, it is now well-established that a state may reimburse parents for expenses incurred in transporting their children to school, *Everson* v. *Board of Education,* 330 U.S. 1, 67 S.Ct. 504, 91 L.Ed. 711 (1947), and that it may loan secular textbooks to all schoolchildren within the state, *Board of Education* v. *Allen,* 392 U.S. 236, 88 S.Ct. 1923, 20 L.Ed.2d 1060 (1968).

Notwithstanding the repeated approval given programs such as those in *Allen* and *Everson,* our decisions also have struck down arrangements resembling, in many respects, these forms of assistance. See, *e.g., Lemon* v. *Kurtzman, Levitt* v. *Committee for Public Education, Meek* v. *Pittenger, Wolman* v. *Walter.*[3] In this case we are asked to decide whether Minnesota's tax deduction bears

3. In *Lemon* v. *Kurtzman, supra,* the Court concluded that the state's reimbursement of nonpublic schools for the cost of teacher's salaries, textbooks, and instructional materials, and its payment of a salary supplement to teachers in nonpublic schools, resulted in excessive entanglement of church and state. In *Levitt* v. *Committee for Public Education, supra,* we struck down on Establishment Clause grounds a state program reimbursing

greater resemblance to those types of assistance to parochial schools we have approved, or to those we have struck down. Petitioners place particular reliance on our decision in *Committee for Public Education* v. *Nyquist,* where we held invalid a New York statute providing public funds for the maintenance and repair of the physical facilities of private schools and granting thinly disguised "tax benefits," actually amounting to tuition grants, to the parents of children attending private schools. As explained below, we conclude that [the Minnesota law] bears less resemblance to the arrangement struck down in *Nyquist* than it does to assistance programs upheld in our prior decisions and those discussed with approval in *Nyquist.*

The general nature of our inquiry in this area has been guided, since the decision in *Lemon* v. *Kurtzman,* 403 U.S. 602, 91 S.Ct. 2105, 29 L.Ed.2d 745 (1971), by the "three-part" test laid down in that case:

> First, the statute must have a secular legislative purpose; second, its principle or primary effect must be one that neither advances nor inhibits religion . . . ; finally, the statute must not foster "an excessive government entanglement with religion."

While this principle is well settled, our cases have also emphasized that it provides "no more than [a] helpful signpost" in dealing with Establishment Clause challenges. * * *

Little time need be spent on the question of whether the Minnesota tax deduction has a secular purpose. Under our prior decisions, governmental assistance programs have consistently survived this inquiry even when they have run afoul of other aspects of the *Lemon* framework. * * * This reflects, at least in part, our reluctance to attribute unconstitutional motives to the states, particularly when a plausible secular purpose for the state's program may be discerned from the face of the statute.

A state's decision to defray the cost of educational expenses incurred by parents—regardless of the type of schools their children attend—evidences a purpose that is both secular and understandable. An educated populace is essential to the political and economic health of any community, and a state's efforts to assist parents in meeting the rising cost of educational expenses plainly serves this secular purpose of ensuring that the state's citizenry is well-educated. Similarly, Minnesota, like other states, could conclude that there is a strong public interest in assuring the continued financial health of private schools, both sectarian and non-sectarian. By educating a substantial number of students such schools relieve public schools of a correspondingly great burden—to the benefit of all taxpayers. In addition, private schools may serve as a benchmark for public schools, in a manner analogous to the "TVA yardstick" for private power companies. As Justice Powell has remarked:

> Parochial schools, quite apart from their sectarian purpose, have provided an educational alternative for millions of young Americans; they often afford wholesome competition with our public schools; and in some States they relieve substantially the tax burden incident to the operation of public schools. The State has, moreover, a legitimate interest in facilitating education of the highest quality for all children within its boundaries, whatever school their parents have chosen for them. *Wolman* v. *Walter,* 433 U.S. 229, 262, 97 S.Ct. 2593, 2613, 53 L.Ed.2d 714 (POWELL, J., concurring in part, concurring in judgment in part, and dissenting in part).

All these justifications are readily available to support § 290.09(22), and each is sufficient to satisfy the secular purpose inquiry of *Lemon.*

nonpublic schools for the cost of teacher-prepared examinations. Finally, in *Meek* v. *Pittenger, supra,* and *Wolman* v. *Walter, supra,* we held unconstitutional a direct loan of instructional materials to nonpublic schools, while upholding the loan of textbooks to individual students.

We turn therefore to the more difficult but related question whether the Minnesota statute has "the primary effect of advancing the sectarian aims of the nonpublic schools." * * * In concluding that it does not, we find several features of the Minnesota tax deduction particularly significant. First, an essential feature of Minnesota's arrangement is the fact that § 290.09(22) is only one among many deductions—such as those for medical expenses, Minn.Stat. § 290.09(10) and charitable contributions, Minn.Stat. § 290.21—available under the Minnesota tax laws. Our decisions consistently have recognized that traditionally "[l]egislatures have especially broad latitude in creating classifications and distinctions in tax statutes," *Regan* v. *Taxation with Representation,* — U.S. —, 103 S.Ct. 1997, 76 L.Ed.2d 129 (1983), in part because the "familiarity with local conditions" enjoyed by legislators especially enables them to "achieve an equitable distribution of the tax burden." * * * Under our prior decisions, the Minnesota legislature's judgment that a deduction for educational expenses fairly equalizes the tax burden of its citizens and encourages desirable expenditures for educational purposes is entitled to substantial deference.

Other characteristics of § 290.09(22) argue equally strongly for the provision's constitutionality. Most importantly, the deduction is available for educational expenses incurred by *all* parents, including those whose children attend public schools and those whose children attend non-sectarian private schools or sectarian private schools. * * *

In this respect, as well as others, this case is vitally different from the scheme struck down in *Nyquist.* There, public assistance amounting to tuition grants, was provided only to parents of children in *nonpublic* schools. This fact had considerable bearing on our decision striking down the New York statute at issue; we explicitly distinguished both *Allen* and *Everson* on the grounds that "In both cases the class of beneficiaries included *all* schoolchildren, those in public as well as those in private schools." * * * Moreover, we intimated that "public assistance (*e.g.,* scholarships) made available generally without regard to the sectarian-nonsectarian or public-nonpublic nature of the institution benefited," might not offend the Establishment Clause. We think the tax deduction adopted by Minnesota is more similar to this latter type of program than it is to the arrangement struck down in *Nyquist.* Unlike the assistance at issue in *Nyquist,* § 290.09(22) permits *all* parents—whether their children attend public school or private—to deduct their childrens' educational expenses. * * * [A] program, like § 290.09(22), that neutrally provides state assistance to a broad spectrum of citizens is not readily subject to challenge under the Establishment Clause.

We also agree with the Court of Appeals that, by channeling whatever assistance it may provide to parochial schools through individual parents, Minnesota has reduced the Establishment Clause objections to which its action is subject. It is true, of course, that financial assistance provided to parents ultimately has an economic effect comparable to that of aid given directly to the schools attended by their children. It is also true, however, that under Minnesota's arrangement public funds become available only as a result of numerous, private choices of individual parents of school-age children. For these reasons, we recognized in *Nyquist* that the means by which state assistance flows to private schools is of some importance: we said that "the fact that aid is disbursed to parents rather than to . . . schools" is a material consideration in Establishment Clause analysis, albeit "only one among many to be considered." It is noteworthy that all but one of our recent cases invalidating state aid to parochial schools have involved the direct transmission of assistance from the state to the schools themselves. * * * Where, as here, aid to parochial schools is available only as a result of decisions of individual parents no "imprimatur of State approval," can be deemed to have been conferred on any particular religion, or on religion generally.

We find it useful, in the light of the foregoing characteristics of § 290.09(22), to compare the attenuated financial benefits flowing to parochial schools from the section to the evils against which the Establishment Clause was designed to protect. These dangers are well-described by our statement that "what is at stake as a matter of policy [in Establishment Clause cases] is preventing that kind and degree of government involvement in religious life that, as history teaches us, is apt to lead to strife and frequently strain a political system to the breaking point." * * * It is important, however, to "keep these issues in perspective":

> At this point in the 20th century we are quite far removed from the dangers that prompted the Framers to include the Establishment Clause in the Bill of Rights. * * * The risk of significant religious or denominational control over our democratic processes—or even of deep political division along religious lines—is remote, and when viewed against the positive contributions of sectarian schools, and such risk seems entirely tolerable in light of the continuing oversight of this Court. * * *

The Establishment Clause of course extends beyond prohibition of a state church or payment of state funds to one or more churches. We do not think, however, that its prohibition extends to the type of tax deduction established by Minnesota. The historic purposes of the clause simply do not encompass the sort of attenuated financial benefit, ultimately controlled by the private choices of individual parents, that eventually flows to parochial schools from the neutrally available tax benefit at issue in this case.

Petitioners argue that, notwithstanding the facial neutrality of § 290.09(22), in application the statute primarily benefits religious institutions. Petitioners rely, as they did below, on a statistical analysis of the type of persons claiming the tax deduction. They contend that most parents of public school children incur no tuition expenses, see Minn.Stat. § 120.06, and that other expenses deductible under § 290.09(22) are negligible in value; moreover, they claim that 96% of the children in private schools in 1978–1979 attended religiously-affiliated institutions. Because of all this, they reason, the bulk of deductions taken under § 290.09(22) will be claimed by parents of children in sectarian schools. Respondents reply that petitioners have failed to consider the impact of deductions for items such as transportation, summer school tuition, tuition paid by parents whose children attended schools outside the school districts in which they resided, rental or purchase costs for a variety of equipment, and tuition for certain types of instruction not ordinarily provided in public schools.

We need not consider these contentions in detail. We would be loath to adopt a rule grounding the constitutionality of a facially neutral law on annual reports reciting the extent to which various classes of private citizens claimed benefits under the law. Such an approach would scarcely provide the certainty that this field stands in need of, nor can we perceive principled standards by which such statistical evidence might be evaluated. Moreover, the fact that private persons fail in a particular year to claim the tax relief to which they are entitled—under a facially neutral statute—should be of little importance in determining the constitutionality of the statute permitting such relief.

Finally, private educational institutions, and parents paying for their children to attend these schools, make special contributions to the areas in which they operate. "Parochial schools, quite apart from their sectarian purpose, have provided an educational alternative for millions of young Americans; they often afford wholesome competition with our public schools; and in some States they relieve substantially the tax burden incident to the operation of public schools." * * * If parents of children in private schools choose to take especial advantage of the relief provided by

§ 290.09(22), it is no doubt due to the fact that they bear a particularly great financial burden in educating their children. More fundamentally, whatever unequal effect may be attributed to the statutory classification can fairly be regarded as a rough return for the benefits, discussed above, provided to the state and all taxpayers by parents sending their children to parochial schools. In the light of all this, we believe it wiser to decline to engage in the type of empirical inquiry into those persons benefited by state law which petitioners urge.

Thus, we hold that the Minnesota tax deduction for educational expenses satisfies the primary effect inquiry of our Establishment Clause cases.

Turning to the third part of the *Lemon* inquiry, we have no difficulty in concluding that the Minnesota statute does not "excessively entangle" the state in religion. The only plausible source of the "comprehensive, discriminating, and continuing state surveillance," necessary to run afoul of this standard would lie in the fact that state officials must determine whether particular textbooks qualify for a deduction. In making this decision, state officials must disallow deductions taken from "instructional books and materials used in the teaching of religious tenets, doctrines or worship, the purpose of which is to inculcate such tenets, doctrines or worship." Making decisions such as this does not differ substantially from making the types of decisions approved in earlier opinions of this Court. In *Board of Education* v. *Allen,* 392 U.S. 236, 88 S.Ct. 1923, 20 L.Ed.2d 1060 (1968), for example, the Court upheld the loan of secular textbooks to parents or children attending nonpublic schools; though state officials were required to determine whether particular books were or were not secular, the system was held not to violate the Establishment Clause. * * * The same result follows in this case.

For the foregoing reasons, the judgment of the Court of Appeals is

Affirmed.

The windfall profit tax does not violate the Uniformity Clause.

UNITED STATES v. PTASYNSKI

Supreme Court of the United States, 1983.
— U.S. —, 103 S.Ct. 2239, 76 L.Ed.2d 427.

JUSTICE POWELL delivered the opinion of the Court.

The issue is whether excluding a geographically defined class of oil from the coverage of the Crude Oil Windfall Profit Tax Act violates the Uniformity Clause.

During the 1970s the Executive Branch regulated the price of domestic crude oil. * * * Depending on its vintage and type, oil was divided into differing classes or tiers and assigned a corresponding ceiling price. Initially, there were only two tiers, a lower tier for "old oil" and an upper tier for new production. As the regulatory framework developed, new classes of oil were recognized.[1]

In 1979, President Carter announced a program to remove price controls from domestic oil by September 30, 1981. By eliminating price controls, the President sought to encourage exploration for new oil and to increase production of old oil from marginally economic operations. * * * He recognized, however, that deregulating oil prices would produce substantial gains (referred to as "windfalls") for some producers. The price of oil on the world market had risen markedly, and it was anticipated that de-

1. In addition to lower- and upper-tier oil, the Federal Energy Administration recognized essentially four other classes of crude oil: stripper oil, Alaska North Slope oil, oil produced on the Naval Petroleum Reserve, and incremental tertiary oil. See H.R.Rep. No. 96–304, p. 12 (1979). Alaska North Slope oil was considered a separate class of oil because its disproportionately high transportation costs forced producers to keep the wellhead price well below the ceiling price. See 42 Fed.Reg. 41566–41568 (1977).

regulating the price of oil already in production would allow domestic producers to receive prices far in excess of their initial estimates. Accordingly, the President proposed that Congress place an excise tax on the additional revenue resulting from decontrol.

Congress responded by enacting the Crude Oil Windfall Profit Tax Act of 1980. * * * The Act divides domestic crude oil into three tiers and establishes an adjusted base price and a tax rate for each tier. * * * The base prices generally reflect the selling price of particular categories of oil under price controls, and the tax rates vary according to the vintages and types of oil included within each tier. * * * The House Report explained that the Act is "designed to impose relatively high tax rates where production cannot be expected to respond very much to further increases in price and relatively low tax rates on oil whose production is likely to be responsive to price." * * *

The Act exempts certain classes of oil from the tax, one of which is "exempt Alaskan oil." It is defined as:

> any crude oil (other than Sadlerochit oil) which is produced—
>
> (1) from a reservoir from which oil has been produced in commercial quantities through a well located north of the Arctic Circle, or
>
> (2) from a well located on the northerly side of the divide of the Alaska-Aleutian Range and at least 75 miles from the nearest point on the Trans-Alaska Pipeline System.

Although the Act refers to this class of oil as "exempt Alaskan oil," the reference is not entirely accurate. The Act exempts only certain oil produced in Alaska from the windfall profit tax. Indeed, less than 20% of current Alaskan production is exempt. Nor is the exemption limited to the State of Alaska. Oil produced in certain offshore territorial waters—beyond the limits of any State—is included within the exemption.

The exemption thus is not drawn on state political lines. Rather it reflects Congress' considered judgment that unique climatic and geographic conditions require that oil produced from this exempt area be treated as a separate class of oil. * * * As Senator Gravel explained, the development and production of oil in arctic and subarctic regions is hampered by "severe weather conditions, remoteness, sensitive environmental and geological characteristics, and a lack of normal social and industrial infrastructure." * * * These factors combine to make the average cost of drilling a well in Alaska as much as 15 times greater than that of drilling a well elsewhere in the United States. * * * Accordingly, Congress chose to exempt oil produced in the defined region from the windfall profit tax. It determined that imposing such a tax "would discourage exploration and development of reservoirs in areas of extreme climatic conditions." * * *

Six months after the Act was passed, independent oil producers and royalty owners filed suit in the District Court for the District of Wyoming, seeking a refund for taxes paid under the Act. On motion for summary judgment, the District Court held that the Act violated the Uniformity Clause, Art. I, § 8, cl. 1. * * * It recognized that Congress' power to tax is virtually without limitation, but noted that the Clause in question places one specific limit on Congress' power to impose indirect taxes. Such taxes must be uniform throughout the United States, and uniformity is achieved only when the tax " 'operates with the same force and effect in every place where the subject of it is found.' " * * *

Because the Act exempts oil from certain areas within one State, the court found that the Act does not apply uniformly throughout the United States. It recognized that Congress could have "a rational justification for the exemption," but concluded that "[d]istinctions based on geography are simply not allowed." The court then found that the unconstitutional provision exempting Alaskan oil could not be severed from the remainder of the Act. It therefore held the entire windfall profit tax invalid.

We * * * now reverse.

Appellees advance two arguments in support of the District Court's judgment. First, they contend that the constitutional requirement that taxes be "uniform throughout the United States" prohibits Congress from exempting a specific geographic region from taxation. They concede that Congress may take geographic considerations into account in deciding what oil to tax. * * * But they argue that the Uniformity Clause prevents Congress from framing, as it did here, the resulting tax in terms of geographic boundaries. Second, they argue that the Alaskan oil exemption was an integral part of a compromise struck by Congress. Thus, it would be inappropriate to invalidate the exemption but leave the remainder of the tax in effect. Because we find the Alaskan exemption constitutional, we do not consider whether it is severable.

The Uniformity Clause conditions Congress' power to impose indirect taxes. It provides that "all Duties, Imposts and Excises shall be uniform throughout the United States." Art. I, § 8, cl. 1. The debates in the Constitutional Convention provide little evidence of the Framers' intent, but the concerns giving rise to the Clause identify its purpose more clearly. The Committee of Detail proposed as a remedy for interstate trade barriers that the power to regulate commerce among the States be vested in the national government, and the Convention agreed. * * * Some States, however, remained apprehensive that the regionalism that had marked the Confederation would persist. There was concern that the national government would use its power over commerce to the disadvantage of particular States. The Uniformity Clause was proposed as one of several measures designed to limit the exercise of that power. * * * As Justice Story explained:

> [The purpose of the Clause] was to cut off all undue preferences of one State over another in the regulation of subjects affecting their common interests. Unless duties, imposts, and excises were uniform, the grossest and most oppressive inequalities, vitally affecting the pursuits and employments of the people of different States, might exist. The agriculture, commerce, or manufactures of one State might be built up on the ruins of those of another; and a combination of a few States in Congress might secure a monopoly of certain branches of trade and business to themselves, to the injury, if not to the destruction, of their less favored neighbors. * * *

* * *

This general purpose, however, does not define the precise scope of the Clause. The one issue that has been raised repeatedly is whether the requirement of uniformity encompasses some notion of equality. It was settled fairly early that the Clause does not require Congress to devise a tax that falls equally or proportionately on each State. Rather, * * *, a "tax is uniform when it operates with the same force and effect in every place where the subject of it is found."

* * *

[T]he Uniformity Clause requires that an excise tax apply, at the same rate, in all portions of the United States where the subject of the tax is found. Where Congress defines the subject of a tax in nongeographic terms, the Uniformity Clause is satisfied. * * * We cannot say that when Congress uses geographic terms to identify the same subject, the classification is invalidated. The Uniformity Clause gives Congress wide latitude in deciding what to tax and does not prohibit it from considering geographically isolated problems. * * * But where Congress does choose to frame a tax in geographic terms, we will examine the classification closely to see if there is actual geographic discrimination.

In this case, we hold that the classification is constitutional. As discussed above, Congress considered the windfall profit tax a necessary component of its program to encourage the exploration and production of oil. It perceived that the decontrol legislation would result—in certain circumstances—in profits essentially unrelated to the objective of the program, and concluded that these profits should be taxed. Accordingly, Congress divided oil into various classes and gave more favorable treatment to those classes that would be responsive to increased prices.

Congress clearly viewed "exempt Alaskan oil" as a unique class of oil that, consistent with the scheme of the Act, merited favorable treatment. It had before it ample evidence of the disproportionate costs and difficulties—the fragile ecology, the harsh environment, and the remote location—associated with extracting oil from this region. We cannot fault its determination, based on neutral factors, that this oil required separate treatment. Nor is there any indication that Congress sought to benefit Alaska for reasons that would offend the purpose of the Clause. Nothing in the Act's legislative history suggests that Congress intended to grant Alaska an undue preference at the expense of other oil-producing States. This is especially clear because the windfall profit tax itself falls heavily on the State of Alaska.

Had Congress described this class of oil in nongeographic terms, there would be no question as to the Act's constitutionality. We cannot say that identifying the class in terms of its geographic boundaries renders the exemption invalid. Where, as here, Congress has exercised its considered judgment with respect to an enormously complex problem, we are reluctant to disturb its determination. Accordingly, the judgment of the District Court is

Reversed.

The psychological aftermath of the Three Mile Island accident falls outside the scope of the National Environmental Policy Act.

METROPOLITAN EDISON CO. v. PEOPLE AGAINST NUCLEAR ENERGY

Supreme Court of the United States, 1983.
— U.S. —, 103 S.Ct. 1556, 75 L.Ed.2d 534.

JUSTICE REHNQUIST delivered the opinion of the Court.

The issue in these cases is whether petitioner Nuclear Regulatory Commission (NRC) complied with the National Environmental Policy Act, (NEPA), when it decided to permit petitioner Metropolitan Edison Co. to resume operation of the Three Mile Island Unit 1 nuclear power plant (TMI–1). The Court of Appeals for the District of Columbia Circuit held that the NRC improperly failed to consider whether the risk of an accident at TMI–1 might cause harm to the psychological health and community well-being of residents of the surrounding area. We reverse.

Metropolitan owns two nuclear power plants at Three Mile Island near Harrisburg, Pennsylvania. Both of these plants were licensed by the NRC after extensive proceedings, which included preparation of Environmental Impact Statements (EIS). On March 28, 1979, TMI–1 was not operating; it had been shut down for refueling. TMI–2 was operating, and it suffered a serious accident that damaged the reactor. Although, as it turned out, no dangerous radiation was released, the accident caused widespread concern. The Governor of Pennsylvania recommended an evacuation of all pregnant women and small children, and many area residents did leave their homes for several days.

After the accident, the NRC ordered Metropolitan to keep TMI–1 shut down until it had an opportunity to determine whether the plant could be operated safely. The NRC then published a notice of hearing specifying several safety related issues for consideration. The notice stated that the Commission had not determined whether to consider psychological harm or other indirect effects of the accident or of renewed operation of TMI–1. It invited interested parties to submit briefs on this issue.

Petitioner People Against Nuclear Energy (PANE), intervened and responded to this invitation. PANE is an association of residents of the Harrisburg area who are opposed to further operation of either TMI reactor. PANE contended that restarting TMI–1 would cause both severe psychological health damage to persons living in the vicinity, and serious damage to the stability, cohesiveness, and well being of the neighboring communities.[2]

The NRC decided not to take evidence concerning PANE's contentions. * * * PANE filed a petition for review in the Court of Appeals, contending that both NEPA and the Atomic Energy Act, require the NRC to address its contentions. Metropolitan intervened on the side of the NRC.

The Court of Appeals concluded that the Atomic Energy Act does not require the NRC to address PANE's contentions. It did find, however, that NEPA requires the NRC to evaluate "the potential psychological health effects of operating" TMI-1 which have arisen since the original EIS was prepared. It also held that, if the NRC finds that significant new circumstances or information exist on this subject, it shall prepare a "supplemental [EIS] which considers not only the effects on psychological health but also effects on the well being of the communities surrounding Three Mile Island." * * *

All the parties agree that effects on human health can be cognizable under NEPA, and that human health may include psychological health. The Court of Appeals thought these propositions were enough to complete a syllogism that disposes of the case: NEPA requires agencies to consider effects on health. An effect on psychological health is an effect on health. Therefore, NEPA requires agencies to consider the effects on psychological health asserted by PANE. PANE, using similar reasoning, contends that because the psychological health damage to its members would be caused by a change in the environment (renewed operation of TMI-1), NEPA requires the NRC to consider that damage. Although these arguments are appealing at first glance, we believe they skip over an essential step in the analysis. They do not consider the closeness of the relationship between the change in the environment and the "effect" at issue.

Section 102(C) of NEPA, directs all federal agencies to

> include in every recommendation or report on proposals for legislation and other major Federal actions significantly affecting the quality of the human environment, a detailed statement by the responsible official on—
>
> (i) the environmental impact of the proposed action, [and]
>
> (ii) any adverse environmental effects which cannot be avoided should the proposal be implemented . . . .

To paraphrase the statutory language in light of the facts of this case, where an agency action significantly affects the quality of the human environment, the agency must evaluate the "environmental impact" and any unavoidable adverse environmental effects of its proposal. The theme of § 102 is sounded by the adjective "environmental": NEPA does not require the agency to assess *every* impact or effect of its proposed action, but only the impact or effect on the environment. If we were to seize the word "environmental" out of its context and give it the broadest possible definition, the words "adverse environmental effects" might embrace virtually any consequence of a governmental action that some one thought "adverse." But we think the context of the statute shows that Congress was talking about the

2. Specifically, PANE contended, Pet.App.115-116:

> 1.) Renewed operation of . . . TMI-1 would cause severe psychological distress to PANE's members and other persons living in the vicinity of the reactor. The accident at [TMI-2] has already impaired the health and sense of well being of these individuals, as evidenced by their feelings of increased anxiety, tension and fear, a sense of helplessness and such physical disorders as skin rashes, aggravated ulcers, and skeletal and muscular problems. Such manifestations of psychological distress have been seen in the aftermath of other disasters. The possibility that [TMI-1] will reopen severly aggravates these problems. As long as this possibility exists, PANE's members and other persons living in the communities around the plant will be unable to resolve and recover from the trauma which they have suffered. Operation of [TMI-1] would be a constant reminder of the terror which they felt during the accident, and of the possibility that it will happen again. The distress caused by this ever present spectre of disaster makes it impossible . . . to operate TMI-1 without endangering the public health and safety.

physical environment—the world around us, so to speak. NEPA was designed to promote human welfare by alerting governmental actors to the effect of their proposed actions on the physical environment.

The statements of two principal sponsors of NEPA, explaining to their colleagues the Conference Report that was ultimately enacted, illustrate this point:

> What is involved [in NEPA] is a declaration that we do not intend as a government or as a people to initiate actions which endanger the continued existence or the health of mankind: That *we will not intentionally initiate actions which do irreparable damage to the air, land and water* which support life on earth.
>
> [W]e can now move forward *to preserve and enhance our air, aquatic, and terrestrial environments* . . . to carry out the policies and goals set forth in the bill to provide each citizen of this great country a healthful environment. * * *

Thus, although NEPA states its goals in sweeping terms of human health and welfare, these goals are *ends* that Congress has chosen to pursue by *means* of protecting the physical environment.

To determine whether § 102 requires consideration of a particular effect, we must look at the relationship between that effect and the change in the physical environment caused by the major federal action at issue. For example, if the Department of Health and Human Services were to implement extremely stringent requirements for hospitals and nursing homes receiving federal funds, many perfectly adequate hospitals and homes might be forced out of existence. The remaining facilities might be so limited or so expensive that many ill people would be unable to afford medical care and would suffer severe health damage. Nonetheless, NEPA would not require the Department to prepare an EIS evaluating that health damage because it would not be proximately related to a change in the physical environment.

Some effects that are "caused by" a change in the physical environment in the sense of "but for" causation, will nonetheless not fall within § 102 because the causal chain is too attenuated. For example, residents of the Harrisburg area have relatives in other parts of the country. Renewed operation of TMI–1 may well cause psychological health problems for these people. They may suffer "anxiety, tension and fear, a sense of helplessness," and accompanying physical disorders, because of the risk that their relatives may be harmed in a nuclear accident. However, this harm is simply too remote from the physical environment to justify requiring the NRC to evaluate the psychological health damage to these people that may be caused by renewed operation of TMI–1.

Our understanding of the congressional concerns that led to the enactment of NEPA suggests that the terms "environmental effect" and "environmental impact" in § 102 be read to include a requirement of a reasonably close causal relationship between a change in the physical environment and the effect at issue. This requirement is like the familiar doctrine of proximate cause from tort law. * * * The issue before us, then, is how to give content to this requirement. This is a question of first impression in this Court.

The federal action that affects the environment in this case is permitting renewed operation of TMI–1. The direct effects on the environment of this action include release of low-level radiation, increased fog in the Harrisburg area (caused by operation of the plant's cooling towers), and the release of warm water into the Susquehanna River. The NRC has considered each of these effects in its EIS, and again in the EIA. Another effect of renewed operation is a risk of a nuclear accident. The NRC has also considered this effect.

PANE argues that the psychological health damage it alleges "will flow directly from the risk of [a nuclear] accident." But a *risk* of an accident is not an effect on the physical environment. A risk is, by definition, unrealized in the physical world. In a causal chain from renewed operation of TMI–1 to psychological health damage, the element of risk and its perception by PANE's members are necessary middle links. We believe that the element of risk lengthens the causal chain beyond the reach of NEPA.

Risk is a pervasive element of modern life; to say more would belabor the obvious. Many of the risks we face are generated by modern technology, which brings both the possibility of major accidents and opportunities for tremendous achievements. Medical experts apparently agree that risk can generate stress in human beings, which in turn may rise to the level of serious health damage. For this reason among many others, the question whether the gains from any technological advance are worth its attendant risks may be an important public policy issue. Nonetheless, it is quite different from the question whether the same gains are worth a given level of alteration of our physical environment or depletion of our natural resources. The latter question rather than the former is the central concern of NEPA.

Time and resources are simply too limited for us to believe that Congress intended to extend NEPA as far as the Court of Appeals has taken it. * * * The scope of the agency's inquiries must remain manageable if NEPA's goal of "ensur[ing] a fully informed and well considered decision," is to be accomplished.

If contentions of psychological health damage caused by risk were cognizable under NEPA, agencies would, at the very least, be obliged to expend considerable resources developing psychiatric expertise that is not otherwise relevant to their congressionally assigned functions. The available resources may be spread so thin that agencies are unable adequately to pursue protection of the physical environment and natural resources. As we said in another context, * * * "[w]e cannot attribute to Congress the intention to . . . open the door to such obvious incongruities and undesirable possibilities."

This case bears strong resemblance to other cases in which plaintiffs have sought to require agencies to evaluate the risk of crime from the operation of a jail or other public facility in their neighborhood. * * * The plaintiffs in these cases could have alleged that the risk of crime (or their dislike of the occupants of the facility) would cause severe psychological health damage. The operation of the facility is an event in the physical environment, but the psychological health damage to neighboring residents resulting from unrealized risks of crime is too far removed from that event to be covered by NEPA. The psychological health damage alleged by PANE is no closer to an event in the environment or to environmental concerns.

The Court of Appeals thought that PANE's contentions are qualitatively different from the harm at issue in the cases just described. It thought PANE raised an issue of health damage, while those cases presented questions of fear or policy disagreement. We do not believe this line is so easily drawn. Anyone who fears or dislikes a project may find himself suffering from "anxiety, tension, fear, [and] a sense of helplessness." Neither the language nor the history of NEPA suggest that it was intended to give citizens a general opportunity to air their policy objections to proposed federal actions. The political process, and not NEPA, provides the appropriate forum in which to air policy disagreements.

We do not mean to denigrate the fears of PANE's members, or to suggest that the psychological health damage they fear could not, in fact, occur. Nonetheless, it is difficult for us to see the differences between someone who dislikes a government decision so much that he suffers anxiety and stress, someone who fears the effects of that decision so much that he suffers similar anxiety and stress, and someone who suffers anxiety and stress that "flow directly," * * * from the risks associated with the same decision. It would be extraordinarily difficult for agencies to differentiate between "genuine" claims of psychological health damage and claims that are grounded solely in disagreement with a democratically adopted policy. Until Congress provides a more explicit statutory instruction than NEPA now contains, we do not think agencies are obliged to undertake the inquiry. * * *

The Court of Appeals' opinion seems at one point to acknowledge the force of these arguments, but seeks to distinguish the situation suggested by the related cases. First, the Court of Appeals thought the harm alleged by PANE is far more severe than the harm alleged in other cases. It thought the severity of the harm is relevant to whether NEPA requires consideration of an effect. This cannot be the case. NEPA addresses environmental effects of federal actions. The gravity of harm does not change its character. If a harm does not have a sufficiently close connection to the physical environment, NEPA does not apply.

Second, the Court of Appeals noted that PANE's claim was made "in the wake of a unique and traumatic nuclear accident." We do not understand how the accident at TMI–2 transforms PANE's contentions into "environmental effects." The Court of Appeals "cannot believe that the psychological aftermath of the March 1979 accident falls outside" NEPA. On the contrary, NEPA is not directed at the effects of past accidents and does not create a remedial scheme for past federal actions. It was enacted to require agencies to assess the future effects of future actions. There is nothing in the language or the history of NEPA to suggest that its scope should be expanded "in the wake of" any kind of accident.

For these reasons, we hold that the NRC need not consider PANE's contentions. NEPA does not require agencies to evaluate the effects of risk, *qua* risk. The judgment of the Court of Appeals is reversed, and the case is remanded with instructions to dismiss the petition for review.

It is so ordered.

Review Questions

1. How does a charitable trust differ from a private express trust? For what purposes may a charitable trust be created? What happens if the purpose of a charitable trust has come to an end? In what three situations will a resulting trust arise? In what situation will a resulting trust not arise even though a person pays for property for which legal title is held by someone else? How does a constructive trust differ from a resulting trust? When do constructive trusts arise? What happens to the trust res of a constructive or resulting trust? Does a trustee have any implied powers apart from those specifically spelled out in the trust? What are the fiduciary responsibilities of a trustee? In making investments, what three standards might guide a trustee? Where there are life and remainderman beneficiaries, what rules determine what is income or principal? In this regard, are there special problems when a life beneficiary dies? Explain your answers.

2. What is the purpose of will substitutes? How may concurrent ownership be used as an effective will substitute? An inter vivos trust? Life insurance trust? "Totten" trust? Is a decedent's property probated if he or she dies without a will? What is the difference between "per stirpes" and "per capita"? What is the difference between an advancement and an ademption by satisfaction? Is an estate a taxable entity? Will income earned by an estate be taxed to the beneficiaries of the estate? Who gets the income earned by an estate? In this regard, how are stock splits treated? Is there any priority in the payment of claims against a decedent's estate? How about the beneficiaries? Who pays the taxes? What is the result if a beneficiary murders the testator? Explain your answers.

3. What five elements are necessary to create a trust? Will the use of precatory language ever result in the creation of a trust? Is trust property limited to real estate? If the trustee dies, must the trust end? Is it possible for creditors of the trustee to reach the trust res? Is it possible for beneficiaries of a trust to not yet be in existence when the trust is created? How definite must the description of beneficiaries be? Do they have property interests? Transferable interests? Is a trust a contract? Do trusts have to be in writing? For whom and for what purpose may spendthrift trusts be created? How does a discretionary trust differ from a spendthrift trust? Is it possible to pay trust income only for a beneficiary's support, maintenance, and education? Explain your answers.

4. What are the requirements for a valid will? What are they designed to accomplish? What presumption arises if a will is properly executed? May a testator include will provisions that are conditioned upon the happening of an event? What are the most common reasons why a person may lack capacity to make a will? What is the difference between mental deficiency and mental derangement? Between fraud in the execution and fraud in the inducement? What is required to show undue influence? When will mistake invalidate a will? What are the usual formalities for execution of a will? What happens if a witness to a will is also a beneficiary of the will? What does it mean to be in the "presence" of the testator? What generally results from the use of an attestation clause? On what basis may pour-over trust provisions be upheld? What is the difference between a general and a special power of appointment? What is the effect of a valid codicil? Explain your answers.

5. What is required for a tax to be valid? What is a tax base? How do the three basic tax rate structures differ? Why is there no federal real estate tax? What is the general administrative procedure in execution of property taxes? How are real estate values determined by taxing authorities? Is property ever exempted from the property tax? Why is the income tax not a direct tax? Are any receipts excluded from the meaning of income? Are receipts from illegal income taxable? What are the four basic steps in income tax reporting? Are any damages recovered in a tort action taxable? Do tax laws ever have purposes other than the raising of revenue? What deductions are usually taken in lieu of the standard deduction? What steps should a taxpayer take to avoid difficulties in tax reporting? What is the difference between an estate tax and an inheritance tax? What are the mechanics of the estate tax? How much may be deducted of what is given or left to a spouse? How do gift and estate tax rates differ? How much may be given away before a gift tax applies? What are the four general areas of consumption taxes? What is the difference between an excise tax and a sales tax? Does a sales tax generally provide for any exemptions? Where does the federal budget dollar come from and how is it used? Explain your answers.

6. How did federal pollution control begin? What constitutional powers are the basis of federal environmental law? What is the key federal agency dealing with the environment? What is the purpose of NEPA? Are there any exceptions to NEPA requirements regarding "impact" statements? What are the major legal protections for the environment relating to water quality? Drinking water? Waste? Pesticides? Toxic substances? Air quality? Noise? Radiation? Why is the class action useful as an environmental law remedy? When may a private party bring a tort action for public nuisance? What remedies might result? What new remedies have been used in environmental litigation? Explain your answers.

7. What is the difference between a bequest and a legacy and how may they be classified? When does ademption apply to bequests or devises? Are there special problems in ademption of class gifts? Is the order of abatement the same as the order of distribution? What generally happens to property comprising a lapsed gift? Do statutes ever change this result? May a spouse disinherit the other spouse by will? Might this result in an application of abatement principles? May a testator disinherit a child by will? What is the doctrine of retainer? Are there special rules regarding creditors of a testator? Explain your answers.

8. Define the following terms: ademption pro tanto, ad valorem duty, bare legal title, blended trust, cestui que trust, demonstrative bequest, duty to earmark, environmental impact statement, exclusive special power of appointment, extrinsic facts doctrine, fiduciary income tax return, hotchpot, grantor trust, imperative powers, inverse condemnation, mere expectancy, Mortmain statutes, progressive rate structure, protective trust, pretermitted heir, public trust doctrine, republication, sound mind, supernumerary witness, tax, trust, Uniform Simultaneous Death Act, use tax, will.

Problems

1. What trusts, if any, arise in the following situations? Explain.

a. Minnie Waverly hands her adult son, Robert, a check for $5,000 and orally tells him, "Here, Robert, I hope you will use this to help put Cindy (Robert's daughter) through college."

b. Lori Saunders dies leaving a will which provides for the transfer of $50,000 in real and personal property "to First State Bank for the care and benefit of the Hank Simmons family."

c. Marsha Hunter conveys a parcel of real property to Mike Lolly. Marsha orally tells Mike, "You are to hold this land in trust for Grace Goodfellow."

d. Nick Jones dies leaving a will which provides for the transfer of $100,000 "to First State Bank for the care and benefit of my friends."

2. Discuss the legal implications of each of the following:

a. Pat Cross provides by will, "I leave all my property to my sister, Jean, because my daughter, Kathy, was killed in a climbing accident." Kathy, in fact, survived the accident and appears on the scene to contest the will.

b. Pat Cross provides by will, "I leave all my property to my daughter, Kathy." When Pat is informed that Kathy was killed in a climbing accident, he tears up the will. Pat dies, and it is discovered that Kathy is still alive.

c. Pat Cross dies without a will and without any surviving heirs.

d. Pat Cross provides by will, "I leave $5,000 to each of my children who are living in the City of Missoula at the time of my death."

e. In his will, Pat Cross directs that $55,000 be added to an inter vivos trust established by Pat five years ago for the benefit of his grandson, Richard.

f. Pat Cross provides by will, "I leave $75,000 to my children." After Pat executes the will, his daughter Kate gets into financial trouble and asks Pat for $8,000. Pat gives her the money. Pat then dies, leaving four children—Kathy, Kate, Jon, and Sandy.

3. It's that time of year again as John Vanderbeek sits down to figure out his federal income taxes. A brief survey of the year's financial records reveals the following:

a. John's wages as a junior executive in one of the city's finest banks totaled $12,500.

b. John embezzled funds from the bank in the sum of $3,000.

c. John's father, Cyril, died and left him $25,000.

d. John won first prize of $1,000 in a company golfing tournament.

e. John recovered compensatory damages in the amount of $1,700 in a tort action for negligence.

f. John's great aunt, Zelda, gave him a birthday gift of $200.

Which of the above receipts must be included within John's "gross income" for purposes of the federal income tax? Suppose that after pondering the problem, John is unable to come up with an answer. What should he do?

4. a. Cybill Burden is angry. Without notice, the county assessor has just upped the assessed value of her home $25,000 simply because her husband, Fred, built on those two much-needed extra bedrooms. Cybill wants to complain, but does she have a right to challenge the assessor's decision? And if she takes her complaint to court, how will the value of her home be determined?

b. Bud Knowles has adamantly refused to pay his property tax in protest of rising costs and increased government spending at federal, state, and local levels of government. When threats of delinquent penalties fail to move the renitent taxpayer, taxing officials decide to sell Knowles's property and take their share from the proceeds. But are they legally justified in doing so? And, if so, is Knowles's loss a final and irrevocable one?

c. The president's tax advisors have suggested a federal property tax as a good way of raising that "extra" revenue. Comment on their proposal. How about a progressive income tax with exceedingly steep rates?

d. Loretta Stenzel is called in for an audit when unusual business expenses and changed methods of depreciation appear on her federal income tax return without explanation and sharply reduce her income tax liability. Incensed, Loretta prepares herself for confrontation with the IRS. Counsel her on the best way to settle this dispute.

If settlement is impossible, would you advise Loretta to go to court? What procedural alternatives are available to her if she decides to "fight it out"?

5. a. A majority of the residents in a small midwestern state desire to discourage the heavy consumption of carbonated soft drinks in hopes of reducing premature dental decay. Suggest a tax plan that will serve this purpose well. Why have similar plans been criticized as "regressive"?

b. A heavy sales tax has just been imposed in Wade Hammond's home state. Loathe to pay those extra few pennies, Hammond plans to cross state lines and purchase his goods in a nearby non-sales tax state. Can the sales tax state protect its interests in face of this reluctant taxpayer? Explain.

c. Hugh Wiggins's will divided Hugh's sizable estate equally between his son, Hugh, Jr., and his long-time friend (but no relation), Jay Hunnicutt. Upon the senior Wiggins's death, the state taxed the decedent's estate on both transfers of property, and it additionally taxed Hunnicutt on the share he received. Name and explain the kind of tax involved here. How could Hugh, Sr. have avoided paying a portion of this tax?

d. Plagued with serious financial difficulties in the operation of his used car dealership, Romney Marshall convinces his brother, Dellbert, the local tax assessor and tax administrator, to levy a "special" property tax just to help Romney out. Dellbert agrees to the plan but fails to obtain either legislative or voter approval. A valid tax? Explain.

6. a. The Solar Power Commission has prepared an environmental impact statement concerning the construction of a solar power plant in the southwestern United States. What items must this statement include to conform to the requirements of NEPA?

b. Suppose a severe energy shortage has made immediate construction of the power plant crucial to the country's continued existence. What effect, if any, does this have upon the NEPA requirements?

c. State officials are angered when the City of Hearndon decides to sell historic Lansdowne Park to a commercial condominium development corporation. But do they have any legal right to interfere? Explain.

7. a. The last will and testament of Jean Bond left various specific property and sums of money to relatives and friends. She left the residue of her estate equally to her favorite niece and nephew. Which of the various properties described below will become a part of Bond's estate and be distributed in accordance with her last will and testament?

1. A joint savings account which listed her sister, who is still living, as the joint tenant.
2. The entire family homestead which she had owned in joint tenancy with her older brother who predeceased her and which was still recorded as jointly owned.
3. Several substantial gifts that she made in contemplation of death to various charities.
4. A life insurance policy which designated a former partner as the beneficiary.

Source: CPA Exam, May 1981, #1(50).

b. The intestate succession distribution rules

1. Do not apply to property held in joint tenancy.
2. Do not apply to real property.
3. Effectively prevent a decedent from totally disinheriting his wife and children.
4. Apply to situations where the decedent failed to name an executor.

Source: CPA Exam, November 1978, #1(34).

8. a. Martins created an irrevocable fifteen-year trust for the benefit of his minor children. At the end of the fifteen years, the principal reverts to Martins. Martins named the Bloom Trust Company as trustee and provided that Bloom would serve without the necessity of posting a bond. In understanding the trust and rules applicable to it, which of the following is correct?

1. If Martins dies ten years after creation of the trust, it is automatically revoked and the property is distributed to the beneficiaries of his trust upon their attaining age twenty-one.
2. Martins may revoke the trust after eleven years, since he created it, and the principal reverts to him at the expiration of the fifteen years.
3. The facts indicate that the trust is a separate legal entity for both tax and nontax purposes.
4. The trust is *not* a separate legal entity for federal tax purposes.

Source: CPA Exam, May 1982, #1(57).

b. James Gordon decided to create an inter vivos trust for the benefit of his grandchildren. He wished to bypass his own children and to provide an independent income for his grandchildren. He did not, however, wish to completely part with the assets he would transfer to the trust. Therefore, he transferred the assets to the York Trust Company, in trust for the benefit of his grandchildren irrevocably for a period of twelve years. Which of the following is correct regarding the trust?

1. The trust will fail for want of a proper purpose.
2. The trust income will not be taxable to Gordon during its existence.

3. Gordon retains beneficial title to the property transferred to the trust.
4. If Gordon demands the return of the trust assets prior to the twelve years, York must return them to him since he created the trust and the assets will eventually be his again.

Source: CPA Exam, November 1979, #1(44).

9. a. The Martin Trust consisted primarily of various income-producing real estate properties. During the year, the trustee incurred various charges. Among the charges were the following: depreciation, principal payments on various mortgages, and a street assessment. Which of the following would be a proper allocation of these items?

1. All to income, except the street assessment.
2. All are to be allocated equally between principal and income.
3. All to principal.
4. All to principal, except depreciation.

Source: CPA Exam, November 1981, #1(51).

b. Madison died fifteen years after executing a valid will. In it she named her daughter, Janet, as the executrix of the will and bequeathed two-thirds of her estate to her husband after all taxes, expenses, and fees were paid, and the balance equally to her children. The approximate size of Madison's estate is $1 million. Which of the following is correct?

1. Immediately upon Madison's death, Janet has the legal right to act for and on behalf of the estate even though the will has not been admitted to probate and she has not yet been appointed as executrix.
2. All the property bequeathed to Madison's husband will be excluded from her estate for federal estate tax purposes.
3. Upon execution of her will, Madison's beneficiaries had a vested interest in her property.
4. Had Madison died without making a will, her husband would have received everything.

Source: CPA Exam, November 1981, #1(53).

10. You have been assigned by a CPA firm to work with the trustees of a large trust in the preparation of the first annual accounting to the court. The income beneficiaries and the remaindermen are in dispute as to the proper allocation of the following items on which the trust indenture is silent:

1. Costs incurred in expanding the garage facilities of an apartment house owned by the trust and held for rental income.
2. Real estate taxes on the apartment house.
3. Cost of casualty insurance premiums on the apartment house.
4. A two-for-one stock split of common stock held by the trust for investment.
5. Insurance proceeds received as the result of a partial destruction of an office building which the trust owned and held for rental income.

6. Costs incurred by the trust in the sale of a tract of land.
7. Costs incurred to defend title to real property held by the trust.

Required:

a. Explain briefly the nature of a trust, the underlying concepts in the allocation between principal and income, and the importance of such allocations.
b. Indicate the allocations between principal and income to be made for each of the above items.

Source: CPA Exam, May 1976, #7(b).

APPENDIX A

Glossary

A

abandoned property Property intentionally and permanently given up by its owner.

abatement Proportionate reduction of testamentary gifts within a particular class.

abstract of title A summary of the record title of real property, including all outstanding liens, mortgages, judgments, and similar claims.

acceptance Response to an offer in the manner requested by the offeror; valid and effective only if it is unequivocal and unqualified.

accession A means of acquiring ownership or title to personal property that is "added to" property already in existence.

accommodation party An additional party who endorses an instrument thereby becoming secondarily liable for repayment if the maker fails to pay.

acknowledgment A formal declaration made by the grantor in front of a public officer that he or she has signed a deed and is transferring the property voluntarily.

ACTION The principal federal agency responsible for administering volunteer programs; oversees Foster Grandparents Program, Retired Senior Volunteer Program, Urban Crime Prevention Program, and Peace Corps.

actus reus The criminal act required for commission of a crime.

ademption by extinction The destruction of a specific bequest or devise that occurs when the specified personal property or realty is not to be found in the testator's estate upon his or her death.

ademption by satisfaction Where the testator, subsequent to execution of the will, makes an inter vivos gift to the designated beneficiary of a general or demonstrative bequest, intending the gift to satisfy in whole or in part the testamentary bequest.

ademption pro tanto The partial destruction of a specific bequest or devise that occurs when a portion of the specified personal property or realty is missing, resulting in the beneficiary's being entitled to whatever portion is left.

adhesion contract A one-sided contract in which the offeror and offeree occupy substantially unequal bargaining positions. The offeree is forced to adhere to the terms dictated by the offeror in order to acquire some essential property or service.

adjective law Procedural law by which rights and duties may be enforced.

adjudication The act of settling disputes and controversies; one of the four distinct categories of activity involved in lawmaking.

administrative agency Any government authority that is not a court or legislature but that acts like one by making rules or deciding cases.

administrative law Law resulting from the work of an administrative agency.

administrative law judge A federal administrative agency hearing examiner.

advancement An inter vivos gift made by a property owner who subsequently dies intestate to a child or grandchild with the intention that the gift constitute prepayment toward the donee's intestate portion of the decedent's estate.

adversary system Refers to the adversarial nature of legal procedure in the United States wherein the parties, as opponents or adversaries, are responsible for presenting their own sides of the case, the judge acts as referee, and the jury is factfinder.

adverse possession A method of acquiring ownership of real property by merely possessing the property in a manner prescribed by statute for a specific period of time.

affectation doctrine Doctrine providing that Congress has the power, under the commerce clause, to regulate any activity which has any appreciable effect upon interstate commerce.

Affirmative Action A program initiated by the federal government to eliminate discrimination in employment against women and minorities. By threatening to terminate supply and research contracts, the federal government has pressured employers to take specific steps to hire and promote minorities and women in percentages roughly equal to their representation in the local community.

affirmative warranty Warranty stating a condition that need exist only at the time the contract is entered into.

after-acquired property clause A clause in a security agreement allowing the security interest to extend to the debtor's after-acquired property.

Age Discrimination in Employment Act Federal act that protects workers aged forty to seventy from arbitrary age discrimination in hiring, discharge, pay, promotions, fringe benefits, and other aspects of employment.

agent A person who is authorized to make contracts on behalf of another called a principal.

aggravated assault The crime of causing serious bodily injury to another or causing such injury purposely, knowingly, or recklessly under circumstances manifesting extreme indifference to the value of human life.

anarchism The belief that there should be no government.

answer The defendant's written response to the plaintiff's complaint in the pleading stage of litigation that either admits or denies the specific facts alleged in the plaintiff's complaint.

apparent authority Authority that results from an appearance of authority created by the principal.

appellant The legal name given to the party who appeals a trial court decision not in his or her favor.

appellate court A court whose function is to review trial court decisions for error.

appellate stage of litigation Reviews trial court proceedings for error.

appellee The legal name given to the winning party in the trial court during appeal of the decision by the appellant; also referred to as the respondent.

arbitration As an alternative to court, use of a neutral third party (arbitrator) to resolve a dispute by issuing a binding decision as to law and fact.

aristocracy A power structure or form of government wherein control is lodged in the hands of a few wealthy individuals of supposedly superior intelligence, ability, and character.

arraignment A criminal hearing wherein the accused is informed in public of the charges against him or her and given an opportunity to plead to the charges.

arrest Taking a person into custody to answer for the commission of a crime; the starting point for criminal procedure.

arson, the crime of Starting a fire or causing an explosion with the purpose of destroying or damaging any property.

artful accounting The incomplete disclosure of information or the hiding of information so that an investor or creditor looking at the financial report is not likely to see it.

articles of incorporation A formal written statement of corporate purpose, powers, and ownership rights that must be filed with the state preliminary to issuance of a corporate charter.

articles of partnership A formal written partnership agreement.

assault, the tort of Any act that places a person in actual apprehension or fear of an imminent battery.

assignee Party who receives the rights of an existing contract that is transferred.

assignment A transfer of rights under an existing contract from one of the original parties to a third party.

assignment for the benefit of creditors A debtor's voluntary transfer of all of his or her assets (with the exclusion of exempt property) to another party who is given the job of liquidating the assets and distributing the proceeds to the creditors.

assignor The party who transfers the rights of an existing contract.

assumption of a mortgage A purchaser takes land and assumes the mortgage when he or she pays the mortgagor the value of the land less the amount of the mortgage debt owing and also promises the mortgagor that he or she will pay the mortgage debt.

assumption of risk Voluntarily incurring a known or obvious risk; often asserted as a defense to tort liability.

attempt In criminal law, a substantial step that goes beyond mere preparation taken in a course of conduct planned to culminate in the commission of a crime.

autocracy A power structure or form of government wherein one person, called a dictator, takes complete power and control without the consent of the people subject to that control.

B

bailee The party in possession of bailed goods.

bailment The rightful possession of another's personal property.

bailment container rule The rule that where a bailed chattel is a closed container or other item containing property not visible to the bailee, the bailee is responsible for the chattel's contents only where he or she should know as a reasonable person that the contents are present.

bailment for the sole benefit of the bailee A bailment that benefits only the bailee. The bailee is required to exercise extraordinary care and is liable for slight negligence.

bailment for the sole benefit of the bailor A bailment that benefits only the bailor. The bailee must exercise slight care and is liable for gross negligence.

bailor The owner of bailed property.

bargain and sale deed A deed purporting to convey the grantor's interest in land but making no promise that he or she has good title to the property.

battery, the tort of An unpermitted, offensive, or unprivileged touching of another's person.

bearer paper An instrument that is made payable "to bearer" and can be freely negotiated without endorsement.

bed-bug letter A written notice from the SEC that a securities registration statement is not acceptable.

bequest A gift of personal property under a will.

best evidence rule Requires an attorney who refers to a written document, contract, or other writing to produce that writing as a courtroom exhibit because the writing itself is the best evidence of its contents.

bilateral contract A promise for a promise. The offeror promises to do something in exchange for the offeree's return promise to do something or not to do something.

bill A formal writing containing an idea for a law to be submitted to a legislature.

bill of attainder A law inflicting punishment on a person or group without judicial trial.

bill of lading A document evidencing the receipt of goods for shipment issued by a person engaged in the business of transporting or forwarding goods.

Bill of Rights The first ten amendments to the U.S. Constitution.

binder An oral agreement between applicant and issuer, with regard to insurance other than life, that the applicant will be insured temporarily during the period between application for and issuance of the policy.

blank endorsement An endorsement by a named payee wherein the named payee signs his or her name on the back of the instrument, converting it from order to bearer paper.

blended trust A trust designed by its terms to benefit a group of people rather than individual beneficiaries.

blue sky laws State securities laws designed to protect people from promoters of worthless securities and from deceit and fraud in securities transactions.

bona fide purchaser One who takes property for value and in good faith without knowledge or notice that there is anything wrong with the title or that there are any defenses to its validity.

bond A borrower's written promise given in return for money to pay a fixed sum of money at a specified future time with stated interest payable at fixed intervals.

book value of stock The value of corporate assets less liabilities divided by the number of shares of stock issued by the corporation.

breach of contract A failure by a party under contractual obligation to perform at the time and place called for in the agreement.

briefs Written arguments prepared by the attorneys for both sides in the appellate stage of litigation containing the parties' arguments and authorities (citations of supporting cases and statutes) as to why the case should be reversed or affirmed.

broker A person engaged in the business of effecting transactions in securities for the account of others.

bulk transfer Any transfer in bulk and not in the ordinary course of the transferor's business of a major part of the materials, supplies, merchandise, or other inventory.

business judgment rule Rule stating that a director is personally liable for an erroneous business judgment that results in loss to a corporation only if the director acted fraudulently or in bad faith.

burglary, the crime of Entering a building or occupied structure with purpose to commit a crime therein, unless the premises are at the time open to the public or the actor is privileged to enter.

C

capital surplus Any amount paid for par value stock over and above its par value.

capture Obtaining the identified goods from the seller without going to court.

case or controversy requirement Requirement that a real case or controversy (i.e., an honest and actual antagonistic fight for one's rights between adverse parties) must exist before a court will exercise judicial review or otherwise render an opinion.

C. & F. A maritime shipment contract where the buyer promises to pay a price for the goods that includes their cost and freight charges.

C.I.F. A maritime shipment contract where the buyer promises to pay a price for the goods that includes their cost, the freight charges, and insurance for the goods until they are delivered.

C.O.D. Means collect on delivery with the buyer being required to pay for the goods and their transportation before delivery is made.

cashier's check A check issued by the bank itself.

certified check A check that is formally accepted by the bank, which makes the bank primarily liable on the instrument.

challenge for cause The excuse or dismissal of a prospective juror for any reason that would likely make the juror unable to reach an impartial decision.

charitable trust A trust created for a charitable purpose; the trustor must intend to transfer a trust res to a trustee to be held for the benefit of another.

chattel An article of personal property.

chattel mortgage A security interest in the debtor's personal property that does not require a transfer of possession of the property to the creditor.

chattel paper Any writing that sets forth the terms of a security agreement and contains the debtor's promise to pay the secured party.

check A draft drawn on a bank and payable on demand.

checks and balances system The legal system designed to diffuse control and responsibility among the several branches of government in the United States by providing both formal and informal checks on the exercise of power.

choice of law rules See conflict of law rules.

chose in action An intangible personal property right (i.e., one without material substance).

chose in possession A tangible personal property right (i.e., one with material substance).

circumstantial context Referring to a statute, all the relevant factors and conditions that were in existence at the time the statute was passed, including social, political, economic, and technological circumstances.

class action An action brought by or against one or more members of a class or group of people sharing a common interest.

Clayton Act Federal act passed in 1914 prohibiting certain practices if they might substantially lessen competition, including price discrimination, mergers and consolidations, tie-in sales, and exclusive dealing arrangements.

closed shop Union membership is a condition of employment with membership required before hiring.

closely held corporation A corporation whose shares have not been offered or sold to the public but are held by a relatively small group of private shareholders.

codicil A properly executed and legally effective amendment to a will.

co-insurance clause A clause in a fire insurance policy requiring the insured to maintain a certain amount of insurance on the property.

collateral note A note secured by a pledge of personal property.

collateral promise A promise to discharge or answer for the debt of another.

"collection guaranteed" Words that an endorser may add to his or her endorsement promising that if the instrument is not paid when due, he or she will pay the instrument provided that the holder reduces his or her claim against the maker or acceptor to judgment and the judgment is returned unsatisfied, or the maker or acceptor has become insolvent, or it is otherwise apparent that it is useless to proceed against the maker or acceptor.

collective bargaining The settlement of industrial disputes through peaceful negotiations between employers and employee representatives.

commercial bribery Bribing an employee to influence conduct relating to his or her employer's business.

commercial paper Checks, drafts, and notes (negotiable instruments) serving as basic means of payment in most commercial transactions.

commercial tort Socially unreasonable conduct that adversely affects a consumer, competitor, or other party. Examples include infringing on another's trademark or trade name, imitating product design or packaging, misappropriating another's trade secret, false advertising and misrepresentation, product defamation, producer defamation, invasion of privacy, and "prima facie" tort.

common carrier One engaged in transporting goods for the general public without discrimination and for compensation.

common law Unwritten, judge-made law that comes into play when a judge has no written law to guide him or her in making a decision or settling a dispute and so must look to precedents (judge-made decisions from the past) to serve as a guide or rule.

common stock The ordinary stock of a corporation.

community property In community property states, all property, other than separate property, acquired by the spouses during the existence of the community (i.e., the marriage) belongs to both spouses equally in undivided one-half shares.

comparative negligence statutes Statutes in effect in over half the states that reject the rule of contributory negligence as a complete bar to recovery and, instead, apportion damage according to fault (the plaintiff's damages are reduced in proportion to his or her own negligence).

compensatory damages Damages designed to compensate or recompense an injured party for his or her loss.

complaint A pleading that initiates a civil action by complaining about a defendant's actions and setting forth reasons why the defendant should be compelled to respond to the plaintiff.

complaint, criminal A sworn written statement by a police officer, based on the officer's observations and evidence, charging that there is probable cause to believe that a person has committed a criminal offense; the complaint is filed before a judge and a warrant for arrest issued.

composition of creditors A contract between the debtor and his or her creditors and between the creditors themselves that each creditor will accept a lesser sum immediately in full payment of the total amount owing.

compulsory subjects of collective bargaining Areas where bargaining is required by statute; includes wages, hours, and other terms and conditions of employment.

concealment An active effort to hide facts; an affirmative act intended to prevent another from learning a fact significant or relevant to a contemplated transaction. With regard to insurance, an insured's intentional failure to disclose a material fact.

concept From the Latin "conceptus" or "thing conceived," a general thought or idea; a mental formulation on a broad scale and in some detail.

concurrent ownership Owning real or personal property with one or more other individuals.

condition A fact or event the happening or nonhappening of which creates or terminates a promisor's duty of performance under a contract.

condition concurrent Conditions, either express or implied by law, that must be performed at the same time.

condition of defeasance The immediate and automatic extinguishment of the mortgagee's security interest upon payment of the mortgage debt.

condition precedent A condition that must occur before a party will have an absolute duty to perform under a contract.

condition subsequent An event the happening of which terminates any further duty of performance under a contract.

conditional binding receipt A written memorandum of the essential terms of the life insurance contract that provides that the insurance coverage is effective as of the date of application so long as certain conditions are met.

conflict of law rules Rules that guide judges in determining which state's law to apply in disputes where parties are from different states or where one or more events relating to the case occurred outside the state where the case is brought; also called "choice of law" rules.

conforming goods Goods in accord with the terms of the contract.

confusion Title to personal property may be acquired by confusion when goods owned by different parties are intermingled so that the property of each is no longer distinguishable.

conservator A special guardian appointed by petition of the ward when the ward feels unable for whatever reason to care properly for his or her own business or property.

consideration The requirement that a party either do something that he or she was not already bound to do, or that the party promise to do something or not do something that he or she was not already bound to do or to refrain from doing. The second element required for a valid contract.

consignee The person to whom goods are shipped by a common carrier.

consignment A bailment arrangement in which the owner of goods delivers them to a bailee with authority to sell the goods on behalf of the owner.

consolidation Occurs when a new corporation is formed from one or more existing corporations; the new or consolidated corporation absorbs the existing corporations which cease to exist as separate entities.

conspiracy, the crime of An unlawful combination or agreement between or among two or more people to commit a crime.

constitution A formal written document embodying the supreme law of an area governed; sets out in formal, written terms the fundamental system of power (the rules and principles) for that area.

constructive bailment A bailment where the bailor loses the property and the finder takes possession of it.

constructive eviction When a landlord so seriously interferes with the tenant's use and enjoyment of the land that the tenant is forced to leave the property.

constructive notice Inferred or implied notice.

constructive trust A trust that is neither express nor implied but is created by law to prevent a wrong or remedy an injustice.

Consumer Product Safety Commission An independent federal regulatory agency responsible for implementing the Consumer Product Safety Act, the Federal Hazardous Substance Act, the Poison Prevention Packaging Act, the Flammable Fabrics Act, and the Refrigerator Safety Act.

consumption tax A tax on the use of goods or services; includes customs, excise, sales, and use taxes.

contract Legally recognized promises or bargains made by two or more persons and including all rights and duties resulting from the promises or bargains.

contractual capacity The power that a person has to enter into a contract.

contributory negligence Relating to a plaintiff's negligence action against a defendant, negligent conduct by the plaintiff that contributes to the harm he or she suffers; acts as a complete bar to recovery in some states.

conversion, the tort of Intentional interference with another's personal property serious enough to justify a forced sale of the property to the wrongdoer.

conversion rights Rights of preferred stockholders to convert their stock to common stock at certain times or under certain circumstances.

corporate charter A written instrument in certificate form creating a corporation and permitting it to operate.

corporate opportunity doctrine Doctrine stating that a director or officer cannot take personal advantage of a business opportunity that would be advantageous to the corporation without first offering the corporation a right of first refusal.

corporate promoter A person who participates in forming a corporation, selling its stock, and organizing its initial business activities.

corporate veil The corporate entity in that it acts like a "veil" to shield the shareholders from corporate debts and other obligations, affording them limited liability.

corporation An artificial being created for the carrying on of business; invisible, intangible, and existing only in contemplation of law. Being the mere creation of law, it possesses only those properties which its charter confers upon it.

corrupt system Any power structure or form of government wherein the people in authority benefit by reason of having the power at the expense of the people subject to that authority.

counteroffer Response to an offer in which the offeree proposes his or her own definite conditional undertaking containing terms different from or at variance with those of the original offer.

covenant An absolute and unconditional promise to perform; a promise to do something or not to do something.

cover The purchase of substitute goods in the event the seller breaches the sales contract.

"covered" corporation A corporation subject to registration and continuing disclosure with the SEC under the Securities Exchange Act of 1934 (any corporation whose securities are listed on a national securities exchange and any corporation with at least 500 shareholders of equity securities and total assets of at least $3 million).

creative accounting To structure transactions so as to create a false picture of financial health.

creditor beneficiary contract Contract in which the promisee's primary intent in entering into the agreement is to discharge an obligation owed or believed to be owed to the third party.

crime Any act or omission prohibited by public law in order to protect the public.

criminal homicide Under the Model Penal Code, purposely, knowingly, or negligently causing the death of another human being; includes murder, manslaughter, and negligent homicide.

criminal mischief Purposely or recklessly tampering with tangible property of another so as to endanger person or property.

criminal solicitation Intentionally enticing, advising, inciting, ordering, or otherwise encouraging another person to commit a crime.

criminal trespass Knowingly entering or remaining in any place for which notice against trespass is given.

cross-examination After the direct examination of a witness, the follow-up questioning of that witness by the other side; often called the "truthfinder."

cumulative preferred stock Stock in which the shareholder's right to the stated dividend will carry over to the next year (and subsequent years) until it is paid.

cumulative voting Under cumulative voting, each share of common stock has as many votes as there are directors to be elected, and a shareholder can distribute his or her votes among the candidates in any way he or she chooses.

custody Actual physical control of property but no intent to control.

customs tax A tax or tariff levied on goods that cross national boundaries.

cy pres doctrine A special charitable trust rule which states that the courts may apply the charitable trust funds to another similar charitable purpose in the event the original trust purpose cannot be carried out.

D

dealer of securities Any person who is engaged in the business of offering, selling, dealing, or otherwise trading in securities issued by another.

debenture A bond that is not secured by specific assets.

debtor The party who must pay or otherwise perform the obligation embodied in the security agreement.

decree A court order issued by a judge in an equity suit calling for something other than the payment of money.

deed An instrument required by law to evidence the transfer of real property by gift, contract of sale, or contract of exchange.

deed of trust A security device in which the borrower deeds the land to a third party (the trustee) who holds title to the land solely for the purpose of returning it to the borrower once the mortgage is paid off.

deep pocket doctrine Doctrine stating that public policy is furthered if an injured person is presented with the most effective relief available. As a justification for the rule of respondeat superior, the deep pocket doctrine states that since the employee's financial resources are extremely limited in comparison with those of the employer, the injured party should be able to proceed against the employer who, in terms of finances, has the "deeper pocket."

defamation, the tort of Publication to a third party of any communication that holds another up to public hatred, contempt, or ridicule or that causes others to shun or avoid him or her; includes libel and slander.

defendant The legal name given to the party being sued in a lawsuit.

delegation doctrine The delegation or transfer of powers to an administrative agency is constitutional so long as adequate standards are provided within the enabling statute that narrow and confine the agency's power so that the courts can determine generally what the agency is to accomplish and so long as procedural due process is guaranteed.

democracy A system of government wherein the supreme power is in the hands of the people.

demonstrative bequest A gift under a will of personal property, usually money, that is to be paid first out of a particular fund and, second, out of the general assets of the estate to the extent that the particular fund is insufficient.

demurrer A motion to dismiss a case on the basis that even if the facts stated in the plaintiff's complaint are true, no rule of law allows for recovery; says "so what" to the plaintiff's complaint.

deposited acceptance rule Rule stating that unless the offeree expressly provides to the contrary in his or her offer, the offeree's acceptance of the offer is effective when properly dispatched.

deposition Testimony of a party or witness taken under oath but out of court as a part of discovery procedure prior to trial.

derivative suit An action brought by one or more shareholders on behalf of a corporation to recover damages for the corporation.

destination contract The seller must deliver the goods to a particular destination, and he or she bears the risk and expense until such delivery.

devise A gift of real property under a will.

dictator A ruler with unlimited power.

direct beneficiary One who benefits directly from the contract and who acquires rights of enforcement as well.

direct examination The initial questioning of a witness by the party or attorney who called the witness to the stand.

discharged Freed of any further obligation to perform his or her contract obligations.

discharging bond Bond used to terminate an attachment in which the debtor promises to pay the claim if judgment is entered against him or her (the issuer of the bond promises to pay if the debtor does not).

disclaimer of warranty When the seller absolves or tries to absolve him or herself from liability on the basis of warranty.

discovery stage of litigation Follows the pleading stage of litigation; investigates the facts, prepares evidence, and attempts to settle the controversy before trial.

discretionary trust A trust in which the trustee has absolute discretion either to pay or refuse to pay trust income or principal to a beneficiary.

discount note Note where the maker promises to pay the lender in installments a lump sum representing both loan principal and interest; the maker receives a cash amount less than the face value of the note because the interest to be paid is deducted from the face value and only the balance remaining is given to the maker.

disparagement, the tort of False assertions about another's product made with intent to injure the other's business.

dissolution of a partnership The change in the relation of the partners caused by any partner's ceasing to be associated in the carrying on as distinguished from the winding up of the business.

distraint A landlord's right to lock a tenant out of the rented real property.

distress A landlord's right to seize his or her tenant's personal property.

diversity of citizenship One of two areas of subject matter jurisdiction in the federal district courts providing for jurisdiction in disputes between citizens of different states where the amount in controversy equals or exceeds $10,000.

dividend A distribution of cash or other property made by a corporation to its shareholders; the means by which shareholders participate in corporate earnings.

division of markets Any agreement among businesses performing similar services or dealing in similar products to divide up and share the available market.

doctrine of finality Payment or acceptance of any instrument is final in favor of a holder in due course or a person who has in good faith changed his or her position in reliance on the payment (except for liability for breach of warranty on presentment).

document of title Includes bill of lading, dock warrant, dock receipt, warehouse receipt or order for the delivery of goods, and also any other document which in the regular course of business is treated as adequately evidencing that the person in possession of it is entitled to receive, hold, and dispose of the document and the goods it covers.

donee beneficiary contract Contract in which the promisee's primary intent in entering into the agreement is to confer a gift on the third party.

double jeopardy Under the Fifth and Fourteenth Amendments of the U.S. Constitution, no person can be placed in double jeopardy (i.e., tried twice for the same criminal offense).

draft A writing that is a negotiable order to pay.

due diligence The standard of reasonableness required of a prudent person in the management of his or her own property.

due process Guaranteed by the Fourteenth Amendment of the U.S. Constitution before life, liberty, or property may be taken away, due process requires: (1) power limited or based on one of the three sources of law; (2) reasonable notice and hearing; (3) courts available to resolve disputes; (4) proper jurisdiction of courts; (5) use of proper rules of evidence and procedure in court; and (6) safeguarding of constitutional rights.

duress Any physical or mental coercion that deprives a person of his or her own free will and forces the person to act contrary to his or her free will.

duty A legal obligation to act or to refrain from acting.

E

easement A genuine, though nonpossessory, interest in real property. It is a right to use another's land that cannot be revoked by the landowner.

easement appurtenant An easement involving two adjoining parcels of land in which the dominant estate is in some way benefited by the servient estate.

easement by necessity An easement arising when an easement is strictly necessary to the use or enjoyment of land.

easement by prescription An easement acquired by adverse use of the property.

easement in gross An easement involving one parcel of land belonging to someone other than the easement holder which benefits the holder personally.

ejusdem generis A rule of construction providing that where a general word in a statute follows particular and specific words of the same nature as itself, the general word takes its meaning from them and is presumed to be restricted to the same genus as those words.

eminent domain The right of the government to take private property for public use by means of a condemnation proceeding.

enabling statute A statute creating an administrative agency and authorizing it to operate within standards that satisfy the delegation doctrine.

encroachment The trespass on land of a physical structure or fixture.

endorse To sign one's signature on an instrument thereby assuming contractual liability.

entrapment by police officers Causing someone to commit a crime by implanting the criminal idea in his or her mind.

entrepreneur theory Theory that since the employer has created the risk of harm by hiring the employee, the employer should assume full financial responsibility if the employee's tortious, scope of employment conduct causes injury to a third party.

entrust To acquiesce in any retention of possession of the goods by the merchant.

entruster rule Any entrusting of possession of goods to a merchant who deals in goods of that kind gives the merchant power to transfer all rights of the entruster to a buyer in the ordinary course of business.

Equal Employment Opportunity Commission Created by Title VII of the federal Civil Rights Act of 1964, this commission is responsible for the enforcement of Title VII which prohibits employment discrimination on the basis of race, color, religion, sex, or national origin. The EEOC also administers the Age Discrimination in Employment Act and the Equal Pay Act.

Equal Pay Act The federal act prohibiting sex discrimination in the payment of wages to women and men performing substantially equal work in the same establishment.

equity Refers to court-ordered relief other than money damages in cases where money is an inadequate remedy; giving justice and doing right.

equity of redemption The right of a mortgagor who has defaulted to reacquire ownership of the land subject to the mortgage by paying the debt in full.

escheat The passage or transfer of a deceased person's property to the state when he or she dies without a will and without heirs to inherit the property.

estate tax A death tax on the transfer of property at death.

estop To deny someone the ability to assert a particular fact or defense.

excise tax A tax on the making or selling of goods paid by the producer or distributor of the goods.

exclusionary rule Evidence obtained during an unlawful search cannot be used in criminal prosecution (i.e., it is "excluded" from the courtroom).

exclusive dealing contract Contract wherein a buyer and seller agree to sell the goods of the seller in a particular area or under franchise.

execution of the law The act of carrying the law into effect and enforcing the general rules; one of the four distinct categories of activity involved in lawmaking.

executory contract A contract wherein there remains some duty of performance owing by at least one of the parties.

expert witness The only kind of witness who may give his or her opinion in court, an expert is a person who possesses substantial knowledge about a particular field or endeavor.

Export-Import Bank Known as Eximbank, the federal agency that facilitates and aids in financing exports of United States goods and services.

ex post facto law A law making criminal an act that was innocent when done or inflicting a greater punishment than the law annexed to the crime at the time of its commission.

express contract An oral or written contract.

express trust A trust that comes into existence when a party externally manifests an intent to create a trust.

ex-ship A destination contract where the risk of loss passes to the buyer when the goods are unloaded at the specified location.

extension An extension allows the debtor to pay his or her creditors in full but over a period of time extended beyond the original due date.

extradite Bringing a criminal suspect who has crossed state lines back to the state where the crime took place; involves the governor of one state making formal demand upon the governor of the other state for the suspect's return.

F

F.A.S. Means free alongside and a seller who agrees to ship F.A.S. must deliver the goods free of expense to the buyer alongside the vessel on which they are to be loaded.

F.O.B. Free on board.

factor A consignee in the business of selling goods on consignment (also called a commission merchant).

Fair Labor Standards Act The federal act guaranteeing workers certain minimum employment standards, including a minimum wage and maximum length work week; the law also outlaws oppressive child labor.

false imprisonment, the tort of Confining another within a certain area and refusing to let him or her leave.

family law Law dealing with marriage, children, and divorce.

Federal Communications Commission Commission created to regulate interstate and foreign communications by wire and radio, including radio and television broadcasting; telephones, telegraph, and cable television operations; two-way radio and radio operators; and satellite communications.

Federal Emergency Management Agency Provides a wide range of emergency management activities in both peace and war. Coordinates civil emergency preparedness for nuclear attack, monitors nuclear power plant accidents and nuclear security emergencies, and operates the federal aid programs for presidentially declared disasters and emergencies.

Federal Food, Drug, and Cosmetic Act Prohibits misbranded and adulterated food and drugs from being sold or transported in interstate commerce.

Federal Maritime Commission An independent regulatory agency responsible for U.S. domestic offshore and foreign waterborne commerce.

Federal Mediation and Conciliation Service An independent agency that provides mediation assistance in preventing and settling collective bargaining controversies.

federal question A question concerning the federal Constitution, a federal treaty, or a federal statute.

Federal Reserve System The central bank of the United States, administers and establishes monetary and credit policy.

Federal Trade Commission An independent federal law enforcement agency charged by Congress with protecting consumers and business persons against anticompetitive behavior and unfair and deceptive business practices.

fee simple absolute A possessory estate that has the potential of lasting forever; the maximum interest one can have in land (the whole bundle of sticks).

felony Any crime punishable by death, by term of imprisonment exceeding one year, or by imprisonment in a state prison facility as opposed to a county or city jail.

fiduciary A person who has a legal duty to act primarily for the benefit of another with whom he or she stands in a position of responsibility, trust, and confidence.

financial responsibility laws State laws requiring drivers involved in accidents to furnish proof of their financial responsibility (usually by purchasing insurance or by posting a bond) as a condition to continued driving in the state.

financing statement A brief statement describing the collateral subject to a security agreement. It is designed to put the debtor's creditors on notice that a security interest is in effect as to certain of the debtor's property.

firm offer Written offer to buy or sell goods made and signed by a merchant and containing an express promise that the offer will be kept open for a period of time.

fixture An article, once personal property, that has become so closely connected to real property that it becomes a part of the land.

floating lien A security agreement in which there is a constant turnover of collateral, with the security interest resting on a shifting stock of goods or accounts.

foreclosure suit A court action brought by the mortgagee to obtain a judge's order stating that the mortgagor's equity of redemption will be cut off if it is not exercised within a specified period of time.

Foreign Corrupt Practices Act Federal act requiring "covered" corporations to develop and maintain an adequate system of internal accounting controls and making it unlawful for all American business firms to make use of the mails or any other means of interstate commerce in furtherance of any corrupt payment to a foreign official or politician to use his or her power or influence to assist such American firms in obtaining or retaining business for themselves or any other person.

forgery Unauthorized signature.

forum non conveniens Means that the place selected for trial is not convenient and is a grounds for change of venue.

fraudulent conveyance A conveyance that is intended to delay, hinder, or defraud creditors; it is void and of no effect against the persons defrauded, hindered, or delayed.

Freedom of Information Act Federal act providing that "any person" has the right to see and copy government records.

Full Faith and Credit Clause Article IV, Section 1 of the U.S. Constitution providing that "full faith and credit shall be given in each state to the public acts, records, and judicial proceedings of every other state."

fungible goods Goods of the same quality and value, any one unit of which is the same as any other unit, which are customarily sold by weight and measure.

future-advances clause A clause in a security agreement allowing the security interest to cover additional loans to be made in the future by the secured party.

G

general agent An agent authorized to contract for more than a single transaction and/or for a continuing period of time.

General Accounting Office Assists Congress by reviewing the operations of essentially all government agencies. Audits and evaluates programs, activities, and financial operations of federal departments and agencies and their contractors and grantees.

general bequest A gift of personal property of a fixed or calculable value that may be satisfied out of the general assets of a decedent's estate.

general denial An answer stating that every single allegation in the complaint is false; generally improper since there is usually something in the complaint that is true.

general devise A gift of real property of a fixed or calculable value that may be satisfied out of the general assets of a decedent's estate.

general lien A lien that secures payment of any and all debts owed by the debtor to the secured party creditor.

general power of appointment A power of appointment wherein the donee is given power to exercise the appointment in favor of himself or herself or his or her estate; said to be "tantamount to ownership."

General Services Administration Created by Congress in 1949 to handle the government's internal business affairs. Scope includes acting as government's builder and landlord, wholesaler and retailer, transportation expediter, communications and data-processing expert, property and utilities manager, and historian and record keeper.

general warranty deed A deed transferring the land to a grantee and warranting that the grantor has good title to the property.

gift A voluntary transfer of ownership of property without consideration.

gift causa mortis A conditional gift of personal property made by a person anticipating imminent death.

good faith Honesty in fact in the conduct or transaction concerned.

good record title Marketable title based on public land records.

goods All things which are movable at the time of identification to the contract of sale, including animals, their unborn young, growing crops, timber, and other things to be severed from land or realty.

government creditor Any government entity to which a debt is owed, whether the debt arises out of a contract with the government or is based on a tax owing.

grand jury A "board of inquiry" composed of citizens that investigates or listens to evidence presented by a prosecutor to determine if sufficient evidence exists to indict someone for commission of a crime.

grantor trust Trust created when a taxpayer in a high tax bracket reduces his or her income tax liability by placing income-producing property into trust for at least ten years for the benefit of a family member or close friend who is in a much lower tax bracket.

gratuitous bailment A bailment not supported by consideration.

group boycott An agreement among a group of competitors not to deal with a person or firm outside the group.

guardian In a guardianship, the party appointed to look out for the ward's interests.

guardian ad litem A guardian appointed to represent a ward in a single legal proceeding.

guardianship A legal relationship created by the courts to protect and manage the person and/or property of a living person who is too young, too old, too ill, or too incompetent to handle his or her affairs.

H

hearing examiner Conducts administrative agency hearings in a manner similar to a judge and prepares an initial decision both as to law and fact which may be appealed to the agency head; also called an administrative law judge.

heir A blood relative entitled to inherit from a deceased's estate.

holder A person who is in possession of an instrument drawn, issued, or endorsed to him or her or to his or her order or to bearer or in blank.

holder in due course A holder who takes a negotiable instrument for value, in good faith, and without notice that it is overdue or has been dishonored or that there is any defense against or claim to it on the part of any person.

holographic will A will written entirely in the testator's own handwriting.

homeowner's policy Combines fire insurance with extended coverage including coverage for loss from theft, glass breakage, collapse of building, accidental overflow of water or heating from plumbing or heating systems, and freezing perils. This also provides property owners with liability insurance for protection against claims of bodily injury and property damage asserted by parties coming onto the land.

honorary trust A trust created for a noncharitable purpose with no specific designated beneficiary capable of compelling enforcement of the trust.

horizontal restraint of trade An agreement between or among competitors on the same level of industry to eliminate or lessen the competition between or among themselves.

I

identification of goods Selection of the specific goods to be sold under a contract of sale.

illegal per se Referring to antitrust violations, means illegal on its face and not requiring any case-by-case inquiry into the reasonableness of the restraint.

illegal subjects of collective bargaining Areas forbidden to the employer and union who cannot bargain here because it would be illegal to do so.

illusory promise A "promise" where, in actuality, the promisor promises nothing, undertaking no obligation and setting no limit on his or her future course of conduct.

implied in fact contract A contract in which the mutual asset is manifested by conduct alone.

implied warranty against patent or trademark infringement A seller who is a merchant regularly dealing in goods of the kind warrants that the goods shall be free of the rightful claim of any third person by way of infringement or the like, but a buyer who furnishes specifications to the seller must hold the seller harmless against any such claim which arises out of compliance with the specifications.

implied warranty of fitness for a particular purpose If the seller at the time of contracting has reason to know any particular purpose for which the goods are required and that the buyer is relying on the seller's skill or judgment to select or furnish suitable goods, there is an implied warranty that the goods shall be fit for such purpose.

implied warranty of merchantability A seller of goods who deals in goods of that kind warrants the goods to be fit for the general purpose they are to be used for.

incidental beneficiary One who benefits only indirectly from the contract and who acquires no rights of enforcement whatsoever.

incontestable clause Clause providing that after two years' time, the insurer cannot contest or challenge the validity of the life insurance policy.

indemnity insurance A collateral contract assurance by which one person engages to secure another against an anticipated loss or to prevent him or her from being damnified by the legal consequences of an act; also compensation for a loss already sustained.

independent contractor One who works physically for the employer but is under no control of the employer other than as to the results to be accomplished.

indictment A formal written accusation by a grand jury that a person has committed a crime; also called a "true bill."

inflation A time of generally rising prices for goods and costs of production.

infliction of mental or emotional distress, the tort of Outrageous acts that induce feelings of grief, anxiety, or shame even when unaccompanied by physical injury.

information, criminal A prosecutor's formal written accusation of a crime that reasonably apprises the accused of the charges so that he or she has an opportunity to prepare and present a defense; an alternative to grand jury indictment following an arrest made pursuant to a criminal complaint.

information return A tax return filed by a partnership, specifying how much income the partnership had for the year and what each partner's share of the income was.

inheritance tax A death tax paid by the recipient of property on the death of another; also called a succession tax.

initiative A method allowing voters some direct control over lawmaking in the sense of a pure democracy; provides that anyone may write a proposed law, and if he or she gets the required number of signatures supporting it in a petition, the proposal must be brought either before the legislature or before the people for a vote.

injunction A court order embodied in an equitable decree to do something or to refrain from doing something.

insider profits See short swing profits.

insolvent A person is insolvent when he or she cannot pay his or her debts as they fall due, or has ceased to pay his or her debts in the ordinary course of business, of it the person comes within the meaning of insolvency in the federal Bankruptcy Act (liabilities exceed assets).

insurable interest in life A person has an insurable interest in his or her own life and also in the life of another to the extent that death of that other will result in measurable economic loss to the person.

insurable interest in property Whenever damage or destruction of property will result in measurable economic loss to a person, the person has an insurable interest in the property.

insurance An arrangement for transferring and distributing risk.

insurance agent A person authorized by an insurance company to negotiate and enter into insurance contracts on behalf of the company.

insurance broker An independent contractor whose business it is to determine what insurance needs are present, then place those insurance needs with the appropriate companies.

insurance policy A written contract of the insurer's promise to pay in the event of loss and the insured's promise to pay premiums and give proper notice of the loss.

insurer A company that contracts to pay for a person's loss.

interest in the partnership A partner's interest in partnership profits and surplus as of any given date; always personal property.

interlocking directorate The situation in which a director serves on the boards of two corporations that deal with each other.

interlocutory injunction A temporary injunction granted before a hearing on the merits of the case to provide immediate relief pending the case's outcome.

International Communication Agency Federal agency created to facilitate an understanding of a nation's policies and intentions through an exchange of information, people, and ideas.

interpretation of the law The act of determining the meaning of written and common law rules and pinpointing where they should be applied; one of the four distinct categories of activity involved in lawmaking.

interrogatories Written questions that must be answered under oath by a party to a legal action as part of the discovery procedure prior to trial.

Interstate Commerce Commission An independent federal agency responsible for regulating interstate surface transportation to assure that the American public has adequate and efficient transportation systems.

inter vivos gift A gift made when the donor is alive.

interwoven tort When the result of holding a minor liable for a tort is to achieve the same effect as enforcing the contract, the tort action is not allowed. The tort is said to be "interwoven" with the contract.

intestate Dying without a will.

invasion of the right to privacy, the tort of Use of a person's name, portrait, or picture without his or her consent for purposes of trade or advertising; intruding on another's solitude or seclusion; publicly disclosing private facts about a person; or placing a person in a false light in the public eye.

issuer of securities Any person who issues or proposes to issue a security.

J

joint liability Liability together as a group; all parties must be named in any court action to enforce the obligation.

judgment A court order issued by a judge in a civil action for money damages.

judicial review Defined in the case of *Marbury v. Madison*, the power of the judicial branch of government to determine that legislative or executive acts are unconstitutional and therefore illegal; often called the power to make law by striking down other law.

jurisdiction A court's very power, right, or authority to interpret and apply the law and settle a dispute; a court must have both subject matter jurisdiction and jurisdiction over the person of the defendant.

jurisdiction over the person of the defendant Authority of a court to issue a judgment or decree binding on the defendant; obtained by proper service of process.

justifiable reliance A party who relies upon another's misrepresentation must have reasonable basis for doing so or fraud in the inducement will not be found.

K

kidnapping, the crime of Unlawfully removing another from his or her place of residence or business or unlawfully confining another for a substantial period in a place of isolation for ransom, or as a shield or hostage, or to facilitate commission of any felony or flight thereafter.

L

laissez-faire Social theory, prevalent in the United States in the 1800s, that people are best served by letting them go about their business with as little government interference as possible.

Landrum-Griffin Act Federal act passed in 1959 to protect the rights and interests of individual workers as well as the public from infringement by powerful union leaders; outlaws corrupt union practices.

lapsed gift A gift under a will that fails because the named beneficiary is either unwilling to accept the gift or is unable to take the property because he or she is dead at the time the will takes effect.

law A system of control over the conduct of people.

law merchant Another term for mercantile law.

leading question A question that contains the answer in the question, suggests the answer the attorney wants to hear, or is a question that can be answered yes or no; generally not allowed in direct examination.

lease A binding agreement by a landlord to rent real property to a tenant coupled with a conveyance to the tenant of the right to exclusive possession of the property.

legacy A gift of personal property under a will.

legal concept A specific category or division of law that has been authoritatively defined by the legislative, executive, or judicial branches of government.

legislation General rules of conduct consciously, formally, and solemnly written by an authorized branch of government; may be made on the national level by Congress, on the state level by a state legislature, or on a local level by a county commission or city council.

legitimate system of government A system wherein the people have freely consented to the power structure within the system.

lessee One who leases property from another.

lessor One who leases property to another.

letter of credit A special device used often in sales transactions both as a method of payment and as a means of financing the sale. It is an engagement by a bank or other person made at the request of a customer that the issuer/bank will honor drafts or other demands for payment upon compliance with the conditions specified in the credit.

levy The act of the sheriff in taking the judgment debtor's property into his or her custody.

libel Written defamation.

license A privilege of one person, called a licensee, to go onto another's land for a specific purpose.

lien A claim or charge against real or personal property that secures payment of a debt or performance of some other act.

lien creditor A creditor holding a lien against the debtor's property. A lien creditor has the right to have his or her claim satisfied from the specific property against which he or she holds the lien before the property can be used to satisfy the claims of general creditors.

life estate A possessory estate that is limited in duration to the lifetime or combined lifetimes of one or more designated individuals.

life estate pur autre vie A life estate measured by the life of someone other than the grantee.

limited liability Refers to the limited nature of a shareholder's liability; it is limited to his or her investment in the corporation, and the shareholder's personal assets are not at stake.

limited partnership A partnership consisting of one or more general partners and one or more limited partners. The limited partner is liable only to the extent of his or her investment in the partnership.

liquidated damages Where a contract includes a provision stipulating a specific amount of damages.

liquidated debt A debt where it is certain what is due and how much is due.

litigation The carrying on of a lawsuit.

lobbying An attempt to influence government policies.

locus in quo Place in which a chattel is found.

long arm statute A state statute allowing service of process outside the state under certain circumstances and requiring the defendant who is served to return and defend the action or lose by default.

lost property Property unintentionally or accidentally lost or left behind by its owner.

M

maker The party issuing a promissory note.

malum in se Against good morals.

malum prohibitum In violation of a statute or rule but not against good morals.

manslaughter Under the Model Penal Code, criminal homicide which would otherwise be murder is manslaughter when committed under the influence of extreme mental or emotional disturbance for which there is a reasonable explanation or excuse.

marketable title Title reasonably free from doubt; title that a prudent buyer would accept.

market value of stock The price that a willing buyer would pay a willing seller for the stock with neither party under any compulsion to buy or sell.

marshaling of assets The arrangement or ranking of assets in a certain order toward payment of debts.

master-servant The relationship of employer to employee.

maxims Equitable rules of fairness (often called "rules of conscience") applied by judges in equity suits. An example is "equity aids the vigilant."

mediation Use of a person skilled in settling disputes to help in resolving a problem by offering an unbiased and nonbinding viewpoint.

mens rea The criminal intent required for commission of a crime.

mercantile law Also called the "law merchant," mercantile law refers to the business law rules, customs, and usages generally accepted by European merchants and traders and ultimately taken into the English common law system in the eighteenth century.

merchant A person who deals in goods of the kind or otherwise by his or her occupation holds himself or herself out as having knowledge or skill peculiar to the practices or goods involved in the transaction or to whom such knowledge or skill may be attributed by his or her employment of an agent or broker or other intermediary who by his or her occupation holds himself or herself out as having such knowledge or skill. UCC 2–104.

mere inquiry A question, suggestion, or request anticipating a change from the original terms of the offer.

merger A merger takes place when an existing corporation absorbs one or more existing corporations; the absorbing corporation survives the merger; the absorbed corporations cease to exist.

Miranda Rights The following warnings which must be given prior to custodial interrogation: You have a right to remain silent. Anything you say can be used against you in a court of law. You have a right to an attorney prior to questioning, and if you can't afford one, one will be appointed for you.

misdemeanor Any crime other than a felony punishable by term of imprisonment not exceeding one year generally to be served in a county or city jail.

mislaid property Property that the owner has intentionally put down in a particular location only to forget subsequently where he or she has placed the property.

mistake An erroneous belief relating to the facts as they exist at the time that an agreement is made or entered into.

mitigation of damages rule The injured party is legally obligated to make a reasonable effort to minimize the damages flowing from the breach of contract.

mixed defense A defense that is sometimes personal and sometimes real depending on the circumstances involved.

mobocracy The overthrow of government resulting in unreasoning mobs of people exercising power and control at the expense of freedom.

Model Penal Code The comprehensive criminal code passed in all or in part by more than thirty of the states.

monarchy A dictatorship wherein the dictator, called a monarch, occupies an inherited throne.

money A medium of exchange authorized or adopted by a domestic or foreign government as part of its currency.

monopoly power The power to control prices or exclude competitors in a particular market; illegal only if exercised deliberately or purposefully.

mortgage A conveyance of land given as security for the payment of a debt. The debtor borrows money from the creditor and conveys his or her real property to the creditor as security for the loan.

mortgagee The creditor in a mortgage agreement.

mortgagor The debtor in a mortgage agreement.

most significant relationship rule The modern conflict of law rule that calls for the judge to look to the contacts and interests of each state involved and apply the law of the state having the most significant relationship with the parties and issues and whose interests would be most furthered by the application of its law.

motion for directed verdict A request made by the defendant in a civil action immediately after the plaintiff has rested his or her case asking the judge to direct that a verdict be entered in favor of the defendant because the plaintiff has not proved sufficient facts to win.

murder Under the Model Penal Code, criminal homicide committed purposely or knowingly or recklessly under circumstances manifesting extreme indifference to the value of human life.

mutual assent The agreement of the parties, usually manifested by an offer and an acceptance.

mutual benefit bailment A bailment in which both parties benefit from the bailment relationship. The bailee is required to exercise ordinary care and is liable for ordinary negligence.

mutual mistake When both parties involved in a contract agreement are mistaken as to a material fact; the mistake prevents formation of mutual assent.

mutual rescission An agreement to forget an existing contract.

N

National Labor Relations Act Federal act passed in 1935 that guarantees employees the right (1) to form, join, or assist labor organizations, (2) to bargain collectively with the employer, and (3) to engage in concerted activity for the purpose of collective bargaining or mutual aid and protection.

National Mediation Board An independent agency created to handle all labor management collective bargaining problems in the railroads and airlines.

negligence, the tort of Unintentional conduct that falls below the standard established by law for the protection of others against unreasonably great risk of harm to either person or property.

negligent homicide Criminal homicide involving very reckless or culpably negligent conduct.

negotiable draft A written instrument in which one party (drawer) unconditionally orders a second party (drawee) to pay "to the order of" a named payee or "to bearer" a sum certain in money on demand or at a definite time in the future.

negotiable instrument A contract designed to serve as a substitute for money and to help facilitate credit transactions.

negotiable promissory note A written instrument in which one party unconditionally promises to pay "to the order of" another party or "to bearer" a sum certain in money upon demand or at a definite time in the future.

negotiation The subsequent transfer of a negotiable instrument to a third party so as to make the party a holder; order paper is negotiated by endorsement and delivery, bearer paper by delivery alone.

no arrival, no sale contract The seller must ship the goods, but if they do not arrive, the seller will not be liable; the seller makes no promise that the goods will arrive.

no fault divorce laws Laws eliminating the traditional grounds for divorce and making fault irrelevant to the divorce proceeding; a party need allege only that "irreconcilable differences have caused the irremediable breakdown of the marriage."

no-par value stock Stock that is issued without any stated value on the certificate.

Norris-LaGuardia Act The federal act passed in 1932 providing that the worker "though he should be free to decline to associate with his fellows must have full freedom of association, self-organization, and designation of representatives of his own choosing, to negotiate the terms and conditions of his employment, and must be free from the interference, restraint, or coercion of employers of labor in these activities."

notice-and-comment rule making Informal rule making by an administrative agency requiring: (1) the agency must give prior notice, usually in the *Federal Register*, with a description of the subjects and issues involved; (2) the agency must provide interested persons an opportunity to participate by submitting written comments; and (3) the final rules issued by the agency must be accompanied by a concise general statement of its reasons for the rules.

novation Where, with the agreement of all parties, a new party fully substitutes for one of the original parties to a contract, and the original party is fully discharged from any further duty of performance under the old contract.

Nuclear Regulatory Commission Federal independent regulatory agency responsible for reactors using nuclear materials. Purpose is to assure that reactors are properly and safely designed, constructed, and operated to guarantee against hazards to the public from leakage or accident.

nuisance, the tort of Use of property in a manner that unreasonably interferes with another's use and enjoyment of his or her land.

nuncupative will An oral will.

O

objective impossibility Impossibility of anyone to perform the particular promise made.

occupation Acquiring title to personal property by taking possession of either wild things or abandoned property.

offer A definite conditional undertaking, i.e., a *definite* proposal made by one party (the offeror) to another party (the offeree) indicating the offering party's present intent to enter into a contract, conditioned upon the offeree's completion of the contract by acceptance, his or her power to accept being created by the offer itself.

oligarchy A corrupt aristocracy.

oppressive child labor A condition of employment under which any employee under the age of sixteen years is employed by an employer other than a parent in any occupation, or any employee between the ages of sixteen and eighteen is employed by any employer in any occupation which the Secretary of Labor shall find and by order declare to be particularly hazardous for the employment of children between such ages or detrimental to their health or well-being.

option contract A contract in which the subject matter is to keep an offer open.

order to pay A direction to pay which must be more than an authorization or request. It must identify the person to pay with reasonable certainty.

order paper A note made payable "to the order of" a named payee; the payee must endorse it in order to negotiate it.

original tenor Original terms of the instrument.

ownership Generally referred to as title which confers upon the owner the exclusive right to use, possess, and dispose of the property owned.

P

"palming off" goods Falsely representing that goods are originals rather than copies in a manner likely to confuse or deceive the public.

pari delicto Equal fault; parties to an illegal bargain are generally said to be in "pari delicto."

pari materia A rule of construction providing that statutes which are consistent with one another and which relate to the same subject matter (i.e., are in pari materia) should be construed together and effect be given to them all, although they may contain no reference to one another and were passed at different times.

parol evidence Oral testimony; however in parol evidence rule, it encompasses both oral and written evidence contradictory to the fully and finally written contract.

parol evidence rule States that a fully written, integrated contract may not be changed, altered, varied, or modified by any oral or written evidence (apart from the writing) occurring prior to or at the time of the signing of the agreement.

participating preferred stock Preferred stock in which the shareholder is entitled to participate in any dividends paid to the common stockholders beyond the preferred shareholder's own annual rate.

parties to the crime Rule of criminal law stating that if several persons combine or conspire to commit a crime, or if they command or counsel a crime or aid and abet in any attempt to commit a crime, each is responsible for all acts committed by all parties in execution of the common purpose so long as the acts are a natural or probable consequence of the unlawful combination or undertaking.

partnership An association of two or more persons to carry on as co-owners a business for profit.

partnership at will A partnership with no fixed term of duration.

partnership for term A partnership with a fixed term of duration.

partnership property All property originally brought into the partnership stock or subsequently acquired by purchase or otherwise on account of the partnership.

par value stock Stock that is assigned a specific value which is stated on the certificate.

payee A named party to whom a negotiable instrument is made payable.

"payment guaranteed" Words that an endorser may add to his or her endorsement, promising that if the instrument is not paid when due, he or she will immediately pay it without any conditions precedent.

peremptory challenge The excuse or dismissal of a prospective juror without stating any reason; generally each side has a fixed number of such challenges.

permissive subjects of collective bargaining Subjects that fall within the discretion of the employer and the union who may choose whether or not to bargain about them.

personal defense A defense good as against all holders but a holder in due course; "personal" in the sense that it arises out of a breach of agreement between former parties to the instrument.

personal property Tangibles (choses in possession) and intangibles (choses in action).

personal right A nontransferable right that can be exercised only by the person possessing it.

plaintiff The legal name given to the party who initiates a lawsuit.

pleading stage of litigation Notifies the parties and the court in writing of the nature of the case before them; defines the controversy between the parties and narrows and formulates the issues in dispute.

pledge The placement of personal property in the possession of another as security for some act by the bailor.

pocket veto The automatic veto of a bill that occurs when a bill is submitted to the president for signature less than ten days before Congress adjourns and the president fails to sign it within the period remaining.

police power The inherent authority of the government to do whatever is deemed necessary to protect public health, welfare, and morals.

possession To possess personal property legally, a person must intend to exercise control over the chattel and he or she must physically control the chattel to an appreciable extent.

power of appointment A power to designate who should own property; may be created by deed or will.

precedent A past judicial decision that serves as a guide for subsequent or future decisions.

pre-emptive right The right of a shareholder to purchase a percentage of any new issue of stock equal to his or her present holdings.

preferential transfer A transfer of the bankrupt's nonexempt property for the benefit of a creditor on account of a previous or antecedent debt.

preferred stock Stock with a preference as to earnings and/or net assets.

prejudgment remedy A procedure that enables the creditor to preserve the property belonging to the debtor until the creditor can prove the validity of his or her claim.

price fixing An agreement between or among competitors to raise, depress, fix, peg, or stabilize the price of a commodity.

prima facie A fact presumed to be true unless disproved by some evidence to the contrary.

primary promise A promise to answer for one's own debt.

principle of indemnity Compensation for loss sustained without further benefit.

Privacy Act Federal act allowing individuals to inspect any files that administrative agencies have on them.

private contract carrier One who carries goods for a limited number of customers under contract but does not hold himself or herself out to transport goods for the general public.

private law Law dealing with the legal relationships existing between individuals (e.g., tort and contract law).

privileged communications Confidential communications (made between persons in certain relationships) that do not have to be disclosed in court (e.g., doctor and patient, clergy and penitent, attorney and client).

probate The legal process of transferring a decedent's property to those persons lawfully entitled to the property upon the decedent's death.

product liability The area of law dealing with the special strict liability of the seller of any product in a defective condition unreasonably dangerous to the user or consumer or to his or her property.

profit An irrevocable right to take something away from the land, such as minerals, trees, etc.

progressive tax rate A tax rate that increases as the tax base increases.

promissory estoppel Where the bargain theory of consideration does not apply, the promisor will still be held to his or her promise if the promisee has substantially changed his or her position in reliance upon the promise.

promissory warranty Warranty stating a condition that must be maintained throughout the period of the insurance policy.

property right A transferable right that can be disposed of by gift, sale, or assignment.

proportional tax rate A tax rate that remains constant whether the base is large or small and regardless of whether it increases or decreases.

protective trust An ordinary trust that automatically becomes discretionary (giving the trustee discretion to distribute the trust income to any or all of a group of beneficiaries, including the original beneficiary) at such time as the original beneficiary becomes insolvent or attempts to transfer his or her interest in the trust, or a creditor of the beneficiary attempts to reach the trust interest.

proxy A power of attorney given by a shareholder to another party authorizing the party to exercise the voting rights of the shares.

public law Law involving the rights of society as a whole and encompassing the legal concepts of criminal, administrative, and constitutional law; legal representation is by government agency.

publicly held corporation A corporation whose shares have been offered and sold to the public.

punitive damages Penalty damages designed to punish the wrongdoer and deter others from acting in a similar manner; they vary in amount according to the outrageousness of the wrongdoer's conduct.

Q

qualified endorsement An endorsement "without recourse" which eliminates all secondary liability for that particular endorser.

quasi contract An agreement implied in law to prevent unjust enrichment.

quitclaim deed A deed purporting to convey only what interest, if any, the grantor has in a specified piece of real property.

quo warranto action An action by the state forcing a corporation into involuntary dissolution and requiring forfeiture of the corporate charter.

R

Racketeer Influenced and Corrupt Organizations Act Part of the Organized Crime and Control Act, RICO makes it a crime to invest funds acquired through a pattern of racketeering in an enterprise engaged in interstate commerce.

real authority Authority manifested by the principal to the agent either expressly or by implication.

real defense A defense good against even a holder in due course.

real property Land and things permanently attached to land such as buildings and their fixtures.

reasonable doubt Relating to the burden of proof in a criminal action, the lack of an abiding conviction, to a moral certainty, of the truth of the charge.

reasoning by example The special kind of reasoning involved in the making of common law, requiring three steps: (1) a past case (precedent) is recognized as being similar to the current case; (2) the rule of the precedent case is stated; and (3) the rule of the precedent case is applied to the current case.

recession A downward trend in the cycle of business characterized by a decline in production and employment, which in turn causes a decline in household income and spending.

reclamation The seller's right to reclaim goods given to the buyer upon discovery of the buyer's insolvency.

recognizance, release on one's own Release without monetary bail in cases where the judge believes there is no danger of the accused's not appearing for arraignment.

redemption of shares Occurs when a corporation purchases shares of its stock from shareholders and cancels the shares.

referendum A method allowing voters some direct control over lawmaking in the sense of a pure democracy; requires or permits a law proposed by the legislative branch of government to be submitted to the people for approval.

regressive tax rate A tax rate that decreases as the tax base increases.

rejection A definite statement by the offeree that he or she does not intend to accept the offer.

release An agreement to give up or relinquish existing rights.

remedy at law Money damages.

remittitur A reduction in the amount of monetary damages awarded in a civil action.

removal The defendant's right to transfer a case from a state trial court of general jurisdiction to a federal district court where the request is made prior to the start of the trial and where the case could have been brought originally in the federal district court.

renunciation The holder of an instrument may discharge any party by renouncing his or her rights by a writing signed and delivered or by surrender of the instrument to the party to be discharged.

republic A democracy wherein the people exert their power indirectly through elected representatives.

repurchase of shares A corporation repurchases shares when it buys shares of its stock from shareholders but does not cancel the shares. The stock is held by the corporation itself and is known as treasury stock.

resale price maintenance A seller's setting by contract the price at which the buyer can resell his or her product; illegal per se.

rescission The avoidance or annulment of a contract.

residuary bequest A gift of whatever personal property is left after all specific, general, and demonstrative gifts have been satisfied.

residuary devise A gift of whatever real property is left after all specific, general, and demonstrative gifts have been satisfied.

res judicata The principal of law that a final decision in a civil action is conclusive and that further suits involving the same question of law between the same parties may not take place.

respondeat superior doctrine The rule of law that a master or employer must respond in damages for all torts committed by his or her employees while acting within the scope of employment; justified by the "deep pocket" doctrine and the "entrepreneur" theory.

respondent Another name for the appellee.

restitution The restoration of anything to its rightful owner. With regard to breach of contract, the restoration of the parties, insofar as is practicable, to the positions they were in prior to entering into the contract.

restoration in specie Restoration of whatever actual property is left in whatever condition it is in.

restrictive endorsement An endorsement is restrictive which either is conditional or purports to prohibit further transfer of the instrument or includes the words "for collection," "for deposit," "pay any bank," or like terms signifying a purpose of deposit or collection or otherwise states that it is for the benefit or use of the endorser or of another person.

resulting trust A trust that arises by operation of law where a person transfers property, intending that someone other than the transferee should have the beneficial interest, but failing clearly to express such intent.

retainer doctrine The rule of law that a monetary bequest to a debtor of the testator should be reduced by the amount of the debt outstanding.

reverse unilateral contract An act for a promise: the offeror offers to perform an act in return for a requested promise from the offeree to do something or not to do something.

reversion A future interest retained by a grantor who conveys away less than he or she owns.

right A legal capacity to act or to demand action or forbearance on the part of another.

right of redemption The right of the debtor to free the collateral from any lien or encumbrance and regain absolute ownership by payment of the amount due.

right of survivorship Upon the death of any joint tenant, the deceased tenant's interest passes, not to the tenant's lawfully designated beneficiaries or heirs, but to the surviving joint tenants.

robbery, the crime of In the course of committing theft, inflicting serious bodily injury upon another or threatening another with or purposely putting him or her in fear of such injury or committing or threatening to commit immediately any first- or second-degree felony.

rule making The creation of principles or rules governing conduct; one of the four distinct categories of activity involved in lawmaking.

rule of reason Relating to antitrust violations, means that an alleged violation is illegal only if it unreasonably restrains trade and requires a case-by-case examination into the reasonableness of the restraint.

rule of remoteness An injured party should be compensated only for losses that are reasonably foreseeable to the parties at the time they enter into the contract.

rule making on a record Formal rule making by an administrative agency requiring a trial type hearing with testimony and cross-examination.

rule of avoidable consequences A person injured by another's negligence must do whatever he or she can to avoid furthering the damage after the initial injury.

rules of construction Common law rules that aid judges in interpreting the meaning of statutes.

S

salami accounting Taking up a past accounting error gradually over future periods so as to prevent immediate full disclosure of the error.

sale A contract by which the ownership of goods is transferred from a seller to a buyer.

sale on approval The goods are delivered to a buyer for a stated period of time during which the buyer may use the goods for the purpose of determining whether or not to purchase them.

sale or return Goods are delivered to a buyer with an option to return them to the seller. The goods must be delivered primarily for resale.

sales tax A general tax levied on all goods at the time of sale or on all goods with some minor exceptions such as food.

satisfaction of a mortgage A statement that the mortgage has been paid.

scope of employment An employee is within the scope of employment when intending to serve the employer and doing the work in the usual and normal way.

secured party The lender, seller, purchaser, or other person in whose favor the security interest is created.

Securities and Exchange Commission A commission created by the Securities Exchange Act of 1934 to enforce and administer all federal securities laws.

security Any note, stock, treasury stock, bond, debenture, evidence of indebtedness, certificate of interest, or participation in any profit-sharing agreement, collateral-trust certificate, preorganization certificate or subscription, transferable share, investment contract, voting-trust certificate, certificate of deposit for a security, fractional undivided interest in oil, gas, or other mineral rights, or in general, any interest or instrument commonly known as a "security," or any certificate of interest or participation in temporary or interim certificate for, receipt for, guarantee of, or warrant or right to subscribe to or purchase any of the foregoing.

security interest Every interest in personal property or fixtures which secures payment or performance of an obligation.

self-dealing An agent self-deals when he or she acts for himself or herself in a transaction.

self-defense A person's privilege to use whatever force is reasonably necessary to prevent harmful contact or confinement.

seller's right to cure The seller can cure (i.e., remedy the nonconformity) if the contract time for performance has not yet expired or if the contract has expired but the seller had reasonable grounds to believe that the goods would be acceptable.

separate property In a community property state, property belonging entirely to one spouse who is free to sell the property or otherwise use or dispose of it without regard to the wishes of the other spouse.

separation of powers To prevent abuse of power, the division of government into three equal branches—executive, legislative, judicial—with separate spheres of power such that no branch may invade the power sphere of another; aided by the checks and balances system.

servant Person employed to render services of any type to a master (employer) subject to the master's right of control.

service of process Delivery of a summons and a copy of the complaint to the defendant in a civil action.

severalty Owning real or personal property without anyone else's sharing in the ownership.

several liability Where each of the parties specifically promises to be individually bound, using language such as "each of us makes this promise severally, not jointly."

shelter provision Provides that where the assignor of a negotiable instrument is a holder in due course, the assignee will acquire the right of such a holder as will subsequent transferees of the instrument.

Sherman Act Federal act passed in 1890 which makes unlawful every contract, combination, or conspiracy in restraint of trade in interstate or foreign commerce; also prohibits monopolizing and attempts to monopolize.

shipment contract The seller is required to deliver the goods merely to a carrier at the place of shipment rather than to a particular destination.

short swing profits Under Section 16 of the Securities Exchange Act of 1934, any profits made by an insider as the result of the purchase or sale of a covered corporation's stock within six months of each other.

sight draft A draft payable on demand (upon presentation to the drawee).

slander Oral defamation.

Small Business Administration Federal agency which provides a wide range of services to small businesses including loans, help in obtaining and fulfilling government contracts, and management courses.

small claims court A court where small monetary claims (typically $700 to $1,000) may be brought by a plaintiff and defendant who represent themselves before a judge with a minimum of formality and expense; there are no attorneys or jury, and the judge's decision is usually a final one.

sole proprietorship A business that is owned and operated by one person.

special agent An agent authorized to conduct but a single transaction not involving any continuity of service.

special endorsement An endorsement directing the maker or drawee to pay a specific named individual.

special power of appointment A power of appointment that cannot be exercised in favor of the donee or his or her estate but may be exercised only in favor of identifiable person(s) other than the donee.

special property right The right acquired by the buyer upon identification of the goods to the contract of sale. Includes three rights as set out in the UCC: (1) the right to inspect the goods; (2) the right to replevin the goods; and (3) the right to recover damages from any third party who converts the goods or otherwise interferes with the property.

specific bequest A gift of identifiable personal property under a will.

specific devise A gift of identifiable real property under a will.

specific performance Performance in the exact manner specified by the contract.

spendthrift A person whose excessive drinking, idleness, gambling, or debauchery spends, wastes, or so lessens his or her estate that the person or his or her family is exposed to want or suffering.

spendthrift trust A trust that prohibits the beneficiary from voluntarily transferring his or her interest in the trust.

standing, doctrine of A person who brings a case to court asserting a violation of a constitutional or statutory right must have standing (i.e., must show a direct and immediate personal injury to himself or herself as a result of the challenged action, meaning a "personal stake" in the outcome as opposed to a societal problem).

"stand in the shoes" of the assignor The assignee of contract rights stands in the same position as the assignor and stands subject to the same defenses as existed prior to the assignment.

stare decisis, doctrine of Doctrine referring not only to the use of precedents but to the principle itself that precedents should be followed in subsequent cases involving the same legal question.

statute A formal written enactment of a legislative body, whether federal, state, city, or county.

statute of frauds A statute specifically providing that certain contracts are not enforceable in the absence of special written evidence.

statute of limitations A statute specifying a time period in which legal action on a particular claim must be initiated.

statutory right of redemption The right of a mortgagor following a foreclosure sale to redeem the property by paying the sales price plus reasonable costs and expenses for a certain period of time (usually one year).

stock subscription An agreement by a party called a subscriber to purchase a certain amount of capital stock of a corporation.

stoppage in transit The seller's right to stop the goods while they are in transit and retake possession of them.

straight bankruptcy A proceeding designed to liquidate the debtor's property, pay off his or her creditors, and discharge the debtor from his or her debts. It can be either voluntary (started by the debtor) or involuntary (started by the debtor's creditors).

straight bill of lading A non-negotiable bill of lading that specifies a consignee to whom the goods are to be delivered—the carrier is contractually obligated to deliver the goods to that person only.

strict foreclosure The situation in which a debtor defaults and the secured party simply retains the collateral in satisfaction of the debt.

strict liability Liability for conduct that is unintentional and without fault.

strong-arm clause Gives the trustee in bankruptcy the position of a lien creditor even where the creditors the trustee represents are general unsecured creditors.

Subchapter S Internal Revenue Code provision allowing certain "small business corporations" to elect to be taxed as a partnership.

subjective impossibility Personal inability of the promisor to perform the promise made.

subject matter jurisdiction Authority of a court to hear a particular *kind* of case.

subrogation The substitution of one person in the place of another with reference to a lawful claim, demand, or right so that the substituted party succeeds to the rights of the other in relation to the debt or claim and its rights, remedies, or securities.

substantive law Law defining rights and duties.

summons A written notice to a defendant that he or she is being sued so that the defendant can appear and defend against the action.

support trust A trust in which the trustee has the power to pay the beneficiary only so much of the trust income as is necessary for the beneficiary's support, education, and maintenance.

surety A third person who agrees to repay the debt owed to the creditor, assuming the debtor does not.

suretyship A contract wherein a third person agrees to repay the debt owed to the creditor, assuming the debtor does not.

suretyship promise A promise to answer for the debt of another; legally enforceable only if the promise is supported by a written memo signed by the promisor.

T

Taft-Hartley Act Federal act passed in 1947 that enables government to combat union "unfair labor practices" and to intervene in strikes that threaten the national welfare.

tax A compulsory contribution levied by the state upon persons, property, income, and privileges for the purpose of defraying the expenses of the government.

tax base An object upon which a tax is levied and to which a tax rate is applied.

tax rate The percentage of the tax base that must be paid to the government by the taxpayer.

tenancy at sufferance The "estate" that results when a tenant in lawful possession of property under one of the other three leasehold estates remains in possession of the leased property after expiration of the term of the lease.

tenancy at will An estate that is terminable at the will of either landlord or tenant.

tenancy for years A tenancy that has a fixed or definite beginning and end at the time of its creation.

tenancy from period to period An estate that continues from year to year or successive fractions of a year until terminated by proper notice from either party.

tenant A renter of land, buildings, or apartments.

tender A conditional offer to perform.

testamentary capacity Requirement for a valid will that a person be of sound mind; he or she must be able to understand generally and remember the nature and extent of his or her property, the people who are natural objects (relatives and friends) of his or her bounty or generosity, and the disposition that he or she is making of the property.

testamentary intent Requirement for a valid will that the testator must intend that the instrument presently operate as his or her last will and testament.

testamentary transfer Transfer of a person's property at the time of his or her death.

testate Dying with a will.

textual context Relating to statutory interpretation, refers to looking not only at the sentence in which a word appears but also at the larger units into which the statute is further divided including the paragraph, the section, the chapter, and the entire statute.

The Government in the Sunshine Act Federal act requiring most meetings of government agencies to be open to the public.

third party beneficiary contract Contract entered into for the purpose of directly benefiting a third person who is not a party to the contract.

time draft A draft payable at a definite time in the future.

title Ownership of real or personal property.

title insurance Insurance protection against loss arising from a defect in title or from a lack of good title.

tort Any socially unreasonable conduct for which a court of law will grant money damages or other relief.

tort of deceit Tort where a misrepresentation is intentionally made with knowledge of its falsity either by written or spoken word or by active concealment of the truth.

totalitarianism A system of government wherein the power structure controls every aspect of the lives of the people subject to it.

totten trust A revocable inter vivos trust created when a person deposits funds in his or her own name as trustee for another; also called a "savings bank deposit trust" or "tentative trust."

trade acceptance A special kind of draft used to finance the movement of goods in commerce; the drawer of this type of draft names himself or herself as payee.

Travel Act Federal act making it a crime to travel in interstate or foreign commerce or use any facility in interstate or foreign mail to carry on unlawful activity involving gambling, liquor, narcotics, prostitution, extortion, bribery, or arson.

treasure trove Coin, bullion, or paper money that is found buried in the ground.

treasury stock Stock held by a corporation following corporate repurchase of shares.

treaty A formal written agreement between the United States and one or more foreign nations or sovereigns.

trespass to chattels, the tort of Intentional interference with another's personal property not serious enough to justify a forced sale of the property.

trespass to land, the tort of Any physical entry upon the surface of another's land.

trial court The court wherein a matter in dispute is first considered and resolved using witnesses, exhibits, and other evidence and with procedure based on the adversary system.

trial stage of litigation In-court resolution of a civil action using the adversary system.

trust A right of property, real or personal, held by one party for the benefit of another.

trust beneficiary The person entitled to all the benefits and income derived from trust property.

trustee The person who holds the trust property and is solely responsible for managing and caring for the property.

trustor The party creating a trust.

trust "res" or "corpus" The property placed into trust.

"truth-in-lending" Federal act requiring all lenders to spell out their finance charges—to inform borrowers and customers of the cost of credit.

tying agreement The agreement that results when a seller refuses to sell one product (the tying product) to a customer unless the customer agrees to buy a second product (the tied product) as well.

tyranny A corrupt autocracy or monarchy.

U

UCC Uniform Commercial Code.

ultra vires act An act by a corporation that goes beyond the powers of the corporation.

unconscionable contract A contract containing provisions extremely unfair to one party to the contract who had little bargaining power in entering into the agreement.

underwriter A financing specialist who is paid to offer advice regarding the need for public financing, the best types of securities to offer, the best time to offer them, and the best offering price.

undue influence Persuasion, pressure, or influence short of actual force but stronger than mere advice that so overpowers the dominated person's free will or judgment that he or she cannot act intelligently and voluntarily but acts, instead, subject to the will or purposes of the dominating party.

unemployment compensation State and federal law designed to provide income to qualifying individuals who are out of work and for whom suitable replacement work is not available.

unfair competition The use of economic advantage to destroy the livelihood of another.

Uniform Commercial Code Detailed business law code (set of statutes) adopted in all or in part by all the states (with some variation so that "uniform" is really a misnomer) covering many areas of commercial law with greatest emphasis on the law of sales and the use of checks and promissory notes.

Uniform Simultaneous Death Act Provides that where it is impossible to determine who died first in a common accident, the property of each decedent will be distributed as if he or she had survived.

unilateral contract A promise for an act; the offeror promises to do something or not to do something in exchange for the offeree's performance of a requested act.

union shop Union membership is compulsory but only after employment.

United States Commission on Civil Rights An independent, bipartisan, fact-finding agency established under the Civil Rights Act of 1957 to investigate sworn allegations of certain citizens being deprived of the right to vote by reason of color, race, religion, sex, age, handicap, or national origin or by reason of fraud.

United States Environmental Protection Agency Formed in 1970 to consolidate in one agency much of the federal authority and expertise in controlling pollution and dealing with other threats to life and the environment. Scope includes areas of air, water, solid waste, noise, radiation, and toxic substances.

United States Office of Personnel Management Central personnel agency of the federal government charged with recruiting, training, job classification, employee productivity, and pay and benefit administration.

unlawful detainer proceeding A statutory procedure by which a landlord can legally evict a tenant in default on his or her rent.

unliquidated debt A debt not ascertained in amount; not determined; remaining unsettled.

use tax A tax on the use, storage, or consumption of all goods that would be subject to a sales tax if bought within the state.

V

venue Refers to the proper or best place for trial when more than one court has jurisdiction.

vertical restraint of trade An agreement between or among competitors on different levels of industry to eliminate or lessen competition.

veto The power of the president to disapprove (i.e., veto) a bill passed by Congress; Congress may override a veto by a two-thirds vote.

voidable contract A contract which may be either ratified or rescinded.

voidable transaction A transaction that one of the parties may avoid or ratify at his or her option.

void transaction One that has absolutely no force and effect and is incapable of legal enforcement.

voir dire examination Qualifying examination of prospective jurors designed to discover possible prejudice and otherwise weed out undesirable juror candidates.

W

ward The party in a guardianship who has the incapacity.

warehouseman A person in the business of storing the goods of others for compensation.

warehouse receipt A receipt for goods issued by a person engaged in the business of storing goods for hire.

warrant for arrest A court order authorizing a law officer to take a person into custody to answer for the commission of a crime; may be obtained by grand jury indictment or by the filing of a criminal complaint showing probable cause for arrest.

warranty A promise that a proposition of fact is true.

warranty of title A seller of goods impliedly warrants that he or she has good title to the goods and that the transfer is rightful.

watered stock Stock issued by a corporation for less than full and adequate consideration.

will A written instrument executed in accordance with the formalities prescribed by state statute whereby a property owner (testator) directs the disposition of his or her real and personal property to take effect upon death.

without recourse Words that may be used by a drawer in signing a draft or check so as to completely eliminate the drawer's secondary liability.

workers' compensation statutes Laws that provide for the injured worker to receive an amount of money (worked out in advance by a state agency) to use for medical expense and support after each and every accident that arises out of and in the course of employment.

working papers The records kept by an independent auditor of the procedures followed, tests performed, information obtained, and conclusions reached pertinent to his or her examination.

writ of attachment An order to seize a debtor's property in order to secure the claim of a creditor.

writ of certiorari A petition asking the U.S. Supreme Court to hear a case on appeal because there is a federal question involved; the writ is discretionary with the Court.

writ of execution A routine court order directing the appropriate officer (usually the sheriff) to take and sell as much of the defendant's property as is necessary to pay a judgment.

writ of habeas corpus A court order requiring the police to produce an arrested person in court and show cause for holding him or her or let the person go.

written law Law found in one of three formal documents—a constitution, a treaty, or a statute.

APPENDIX B

The Constitution of the United States

Preamble

We the People of the United States, in Order to form a more perfect Union, establish Justice, insure domestic Tranquility, provide for the common defence, promote the general Welfare, and secure the Blessings of Liberty to ourselves and our Posterity, do ordain and establish this Constitution for the United States of America.

Article I

Section 1. All legislative Powers herein granted shall be vested in a Congress of the United States, which shall consist of a Senate and House of Representatives.

Section 2. [1] The House of Representatives shall be composed of Members chosen every second Year by the People of the several States, and the Electors in each State shall have the Qualifications requisite for Electors of the most numerous Branch of the State Legislature.

[2] No Person shall be a Representative who shall not have attained to the Age of twenty five Years, and been seven Years a Citizen of the United States, and who shall not, when elected, be an Inhabitant of that State in which he shall be chosen.

[3] Representatives and direct Taxes shall be apportioned among the several States which may be included within this Union, according to their respective Numbers, which shall be determined by adding to the whole Number of free Persons, including those bound to Service for a Term of Years, and excluding Indians not taxed, three fifths of all other Persons. The actual Enumeration shall be made within three Years after the first Meeting of the Congress of the United States, and within every subsequent Term of ten Years, in such Manner as they shall by Law direct. The Number of Representatives shall not exceed one for every thirty Thousand, but each State shall have at Least one Representative; and until such enumeration shall be made, the State of New Hampshire shall be entitled to chuse three, Massachusetts eight, Rhode Island and Providence Plantations one, Connecticut five, New York six, New Jersey four, Pennsylvania eight, Delaware one, Maryland six, Virginia ten, North Carolina five, South Carolina five, and Georgia three.

[4] When vacancies happen in the Representation from any State, the Executive Authority thereof shall issue Writs of Election to fill such Vacancies.

[5] The House of Representatives shall chuse their Speaker and other Officers; and shall have the sole Power of Impeachment.

Section 3. [1] The Senate of the United States shall be composed of two Senators from each State, chosen by the Legislature thereof, for six Years; and each Senator shall have one Vote.

[2] Immediately after they shall be assembled in Consequence of the first Election, they shall be divided as equally as may be into three Classes. The Seats of the Senators of the first Class shall be vacated at the Expiration of the Second Year, of the second Class at the Expiration of the fourth Year, and of the third Class at the Expiration of the sixth Year, so that one third may be chosen every second Year; and if Vacancies happen by Resignation, or otherwise, during the Recess of the Legislature of any State, the Executive thereof may make temporary Appointments until the next Meeting of the Legislature, which shall then fill such Vacancies.

[3] No Person shall be a Senator who shall not have attained to the Age of thirty Years, and been nine Years a Citizen of the United States, and who shall not, when elected, be an Inhabitant of that State for which he shall be chosen.

[4] The Vice President of the United States shall be President of the Senate, but shall have no Vote, unless they be equally divided.

[5] The Senate shall chuse their other Officers, and also a President pro tempore, in the Absence of the Vice President, or when he shall exercise the Office of President of the United States.

[6] The Senate shall have the sole Power to try all Impeachments. When sitting for that Purpose, they shall be on Oath or Affirmation. When the President of the United States is tried, the Chief Justice shall preside: And no Person shall be convicted without the Concurrence of two thirds of the Members present.

[7] Judgment in Cases of Impeachment shall not extend further than to removal from Office, and disqualification to hold and enjoy any Office of honor, Trust, or Profit under the United States: but the Party convicted shall nevertheless be liable and subject to Indictment, Trial, Judgment, and Punishment, according to Law.

Section 4. [1] The Times, Places and Manner of holding Elections for Senators and Representatives, shall be prescribed in each State by the Legislature thereof; but the Congress may at any time by Law make or alter such Regulations, except as to the Places of chusing Senators.

[2] The Congress shall assemble at least once in every Year, and such Meeting shall be on the first Monday in December, unless they shall by Law appoint a different Day.

Section 5. [1] Each House shall be the Judge of the Elections, Returns, and Qualifications of its own Members, and a Majority of each shall constitute a Quorum to do Business; but a smaller Number may adjourn from day to day, and may be authorized to compel the Attendance of absent Members, in such Manner, and under such Penalties as each House may provide.

[2] Each House may determine the Rules of its Proceedings, punish its Members for disorderly Behavior, and, with the Concurrence of two thirds, expel a Member.

[3] Each House shall keep a Journal of its Proceedings, and from time to time publish the same, excepting such Parts as may in their Judgment require Secrecy; and the Yeas and Nays of the Members of either House on any question shall, at the Desire of one fifth of those Present, be entered on the Journal.

[4] Neither House, during the Session of Congress, shall, without the Consent of the other, adjourn for more than three days, nor to any other Place than that in which the two Houses shall be sitting.

Section 6. [1] The Senators and Representatives shall receive a Compensation for their Services, to be ascertained by Law, and paid out of the Treasury of the United States. They shall in all Cases, except Treason, Felony and Breach of the Peace, be privileged from Arrest during their Attendance at the Session of their respective Houses, and in going to and returning from the same; and for any Speech or Debate in either House, they shall not be questioned in any other Place.

[2] No Senator or Representative shall, during the Time for which he was elected, be appointed to any civil Office under the Authority of the United States, which shall have been created, or the Emoluments whereof shall have been increased during such time; and no Person holding any Office under the United States, shall be a Member of either House during his Continuance in Office.

Section 7. [1] All Bills for raising Revenue shall originate in the House of Representatives;

but the Senate may propose or concur with Amendments as on other Bills.

[2] Every Bill which shall have passed the House of Representatives and the Senate, shall, before it becomes a Law, be presented to the President of the United States; If he approve he shall sign it, but if not he shall return it, with his Objections to the House in which it shall have originated, who shall enter the Objections at large on their Journal, and proceed to reconsider it. If after such Reconsideration two thirds of that House shall agree to pass the Bill, it shall be sent together with the Objections, to the other House, by which it shall likewise be reconsidered, and if approved by two thirds of that House, it shall become a Law. But in all such Cases the Votes of both Houses shall be determined by yeas and Nays, and the Names of the Persons voting for and against the Bill shall be entered on the Journal of each House respectively. If any Bill shall not be returned by the President within ten Days (Sundays excepted) after it shall have been presented to him, the Same shall be a Law, in like Manner as if he had signed it, unless the Congress by their Adjournment prevent its Return in which Case it shall not be a Law.

[3] Every Order, Resolution, or Vote, to Which the Concurrence of the Senate and House of Representatives may be necessary (except on a question of Adjournment) shall be presented to the President of the United States; and before the Same shall take Effect, shall be approved by him, or being disapproved by him, shall be repassed by two thirds of the Senate and House of Representatives, according to the Rules and Limitations prescribed in the Case of a Bill.

Section 8. [1] The Congress shall have Power To lay and collect Taxes, Duties, Imposts and Excises, to pay the Debts and provide for the common Defence and general Welfare of the United States; but all Duties, Imposts and Excises shall be uniform throughout the United States;

[2] To borrow money on the credit of the United States;

[3] To regulate Commerce with foreign Nations, and among the several States, and with the Indian Tribes;

[4] To establish an uniform Rule of Naturalization, and uniform Laws on the subject of Bankruptcies throughout the United States;

[5] To coin Money, regulate the Value thereof, and of foreign Coin, and fix the Standard of Weights and Measures;

[6] To provide for the Punishment of counterfeiting the Securities and current Coin of the United States;

[7] To Establish Post Offices and Post Roads;

[8] To promote the Progress of Science and useful Arts, by securing for limited Times to Authors and Inventors the exclusive Right to their respective Writings and Discoveries;

[9] To constitute Tribunals inferior to the supreme Court;

[10] To define and punish Piracies and Felonies committed on the high Seas, and Offenses against the Law of Nations;

[11] To declare War, grant Letters of Marque and Reprisal, and make Rules concerning Captures on Land and Water;

[12] To raise and support Armies, but no Appropriation of Money to that Use shall be for a longer Term than two Years;

[13] To provide and maintain a Navy;

[14] To make Rules for the Government and Regulation of the land and naval Forces;

[15] To provide for calling forth the Militia to execute the Laws of the Union, suppress Insurrections and repel Invasions;

[16] To provide for organizing, arming, and disciplining, the Militia, and for governing such Part of them as may be employed in the Service of the United States, reserving to the States respectively, the Appointment of the Officers, and the Authority of training the Militia according to the discipline prescribed by Congress;

[17] To exercise exclusive Legislation in all Cases whatsoever, over such District (not exceeding ten Miles square) as may, by Cession of particular States, and the Acceptance of Congress, become the Seat of the Government of the United States, and to exercise like Authority over all Places purchased by the Consent of the Legislature of the State in which the Same shall be, for the Erection of Forts, Magazines, Arsenals, dock-Yards, and other needful Buildings;—And

[18] To make all Laws which shall be necessary and proper for carrying into Execution the foregoing Powers, and all other Powers vested by this Constitution in the Government of the United States, or in any Department or Officer thereof.

Section 9. [1] The Migration or Importation of Such Persons as any of the States now existing shall think proper to admit, shall not be prohibited by the Congress prior to the Year one thousand eight hundred and eight, but a Tax or duty may be imposed on such Importation, not exceeding ten dollars for each Person.

[2] The privilege of the Writ of Habeas Corpus shall not be suspended, unless when in Cases of Rebellion or Invasion the public Safety may require it.

[3] No Bill of Attainder or ex post facto Law shall be passed.

[4] No Capitation, or other direct, Tax shall be laid, unless in Proportion to the Census or Enumeration herein before directed to be taken.

[5] No Tax or Duty shall be laid on Articles exported from any State.

[6] No Preference shall be given by any Regulation of Commerce or Revenue to the Ports of one State over those of another: nor shall Vessels bound to, or from, one State be obliged to enter, clear, or pay Duties in another.

[7] No money shall be drawn from the Treasury, but in Consequence of Appropriations made by Law; and a regular Statement and Account of the Receipts and Expenditures of all public Money shall be published from time to time.

[8] No Title of Nobility shall be granted by the United States: And no Person holding any Office of Profit or Trust under them, shall, without the Consent of the Congress, accept of any present, Emolument, Office, or Title, of any kind whatever, from any King, Prince, or foreign State.

Section 10. [1] No State shall enter into any Treaty, Alliance, or Confederation; grant Letters of Marque and Reprisal; coin Money; emit Bills of Credit; make any Thing but gold and silver Coin a Tender in Payment of Debts; pass any Bill of Attainder, ex post facto Law, or Law impairing the Obligation of Contracts, or grant any Title of Nobility.

[2] No State shall, without the Consent of the Congress, lay any Imposts or Duties on Imports or Exports, except what may be absolutely necessary for executing it's inspection Laws: and the net Produce of all Duties and Imposts, laid by any State on Imports or Exports, shall be for the Use of the Treasury of the United States; and all such Laws shall be subject to the Revision and Controul of the Congress.

[3] No State shall, without the Consent of Congress, lay any Duty of Tonnage, keep Troops, or Ships of War in time of Peace, enter into any Agreement or Compact with another State, or with a foreign Power, or engage in War, unless actually invaded, or in such imminent Danger as will not admit of delay.

Article II

Section 1. [1] The executive Power shall be vested in a President of the United States of America. He shall hold his Office during the Term of four Years, and, together with the Vice President, chosen for the same Term, be elected, as follows:

[2] Each State shall appoint, in such Manner as the Legislature thereof may direct, a Number of Electors, equal to the whole Number of Senators and Representatives to which the State may be entitled in the Congress; but no Senator or Representative, or Person holding an Office of Trust or Profit under the United States, shall be appointed an Elector.

[3] The Electors shall meet in their respective States, and vote by Ballot for two Persons, of whom one at least shall not be an Inhabitant of the same State with themselves. And they shall make a List of all the Persons voted for, and of the Number of Votes for each; which List they shall sign and certify, and transmit sealed to the Seat of the Government of the United States, directed to the President of the Senate. The President of the Senate shall, in the Presence of the Senate and House of Representatives, open all the Certificates, and the Votes shall then be counted. The Person having the greatest Number of Votes shall be the President, if such Number be a Majority of the whole Number of Electors appointed; and if there be more than one who have such Majority, and have an equal Number of Votes, then the House of Representatives shall immediately chuse by Ballot one of them for President; and if no Person have a Majority, then from the five highest on the List the said House shall in like Manner chuse the President. But in chusing the President, the Votes shall be taken by States the Representation from each State having one Vote; A quorum for this Purpose shall consist of a Member or Members from two thirds of the States, and a Majority of all the States shall be necessary to a Choice. In every Case, after the Choice of the President, the Person having the greater Number of Votes of the Electors shall be the Vice President. But if there should remain two or more who have equal

Votes, the Senate shall chuse from them by Ballot the Vice President.

[4] The Congress may determine the Time of chusing the Electors, and the Day on which they shall give their Votes; which Day shall be the same throughout the United States.

[5] No person except a natural born Citizen, or a Citizen of the United States, at the time of the Adoption of this Constitution, shall be eligible to the Office of President; neither shall any Person be eligible to that Office who shall not have attained to the Age of thirty-five Years, and been fourteen Years a Resident within the United States.

[6] In case of the removal of the President from Office, or of his Death, Resignation or Inability to discharge the Powers and Duties of the said Office, the Same shall devolve on the Vice President, and the Congress may by Law provide for the Case of Removal, Death, Resignation or Inability, both of the President and Vice President, declaring what Officer shall then act as President, and such Officer shall act accordingly, until the Disability be removed, or a President shall be elected.

[7] The President shall, at stated Times, receive for his Services, a Compensation, which shall neither be increased nor diminished during the Period for which he shall have been elected, and he shall not receive within that Period any other Emolument from the United States, or any of them.

[8] Before he enter on the Execution of his Office, he shall take the following Oath or Affirmation: "I do solemnly swear (or affirm) that I will faithfully execute the Office of President of the United States, and will to the best of my Ability, preserve, protect and defend the Constitution of the United States."

Section 2. [1] The President shall be Commander in Chief of the Army and Navy of the United States, and of the militia of the several States, when called into the actual Service of the United States; he may require the Opinion, in writing, of the principal Officer in each of the Executive Departments, upon any Subject relating to the Duties of their respective Offices, and he shall have Power to grant Reprieves and Pardons for Offenses against the United States, except in Cases of Impeachment.

[2] He shall have Power, by and with the Advice and Consent of the Senate to make Treaties, provided two thirds of the Senators present concur; and he shall nominate, and by and with the Advice and Consent of the Senate, shall appoint Ambassadors, other public Ministers and Consuls, Judges of the supreme Court, and all other Officers of the United States, whose Appointments are not herein otherwise provided for, and which shall be established by Law; but the Congress may by Law vest the Appointment of such inferior Officers, as they think proper, in the President alone, in the Courts of Law, or in the Heads of Departments.

[3] The President shall have Power to fill up all Vacancies that may happen during the Recess of the Senate, by granting Commissions which shall expire at the End of their next Session.

Section 3. He shall from time to time give to the Congress Information of the State of the Union, and recommend to their Consideration such Measures as he shall judge necessary and expedient; he may, on extraordinary Occasions, convene both Houses, or either of them, and in Case of Disagreement between them, with Respect to the Time of Adjournment, he may adjourn them to such Time as he shall think proper; he shall receive Ambassadors and other public Ministers; he shall take Care that the Laws be faithfully executed, and shall Commission all the Officers of the United States.

Section 4. The President, Vice President and all civil Officers of the United States, shall be removed from Office on Impeachment for, and Conviction of, Treason, Bribery, or other high Crimes and Misdemeanors.

Article III

Section 1. The judicial Power of the United States, shall be vested in one supreme Court, and in such inferior Courts as the Congress may from time to time ordain and establish. The Judges, both of the supreme and inferior Courts, shall hold their Offices during good Behaviour, and shall, at stated Times, receive for their Services a Compensation, which shall not be diminished during their Continuance in Office.

Section 2. [1] The judicial Power shall extend to all Cases, in Law and Equity, arising under this Constitution, the Laws of the United States, and Treaties made, or which shall be made, under their Authority;—to all Cases affecting Ambassadors, other public Ministers and Consuls;—to all Cases of admiralty and maritime Jurisdiction;—to Controversies to which the United States shall be a Party;—to Controversies between two or more States;—between a State and Citizens of another State;—between Citizens of different States;—between Citizens of the same State claiming Lands under the Grants of different States, and between a State, or the Citizens thereof, and foreign States, Citizens or Subjects.

[2] In all Cases affecting Ambassadors, other public Ministers and Consuls, and those in which a State shall be a Party, the supreme Court shall have original Jurisdiction. In all the other Cases before mentioned, the supreme Court shall have appellate Jurisdiction, both as to Law and Fact, with such Exceptions, and under such Regulations as the Congress shall make.

[3] The trial of all Crimes, except in Cases of Impeachment, shall be by Jury; and such Trial shall be held in the State where the said Crimes shall have been committed; but when not committed within any State, the Trial shall be at such Place or Places as the Congress may by Law have directed.

Section 3. [1] Treason against the United States, shall consist only in levying War against them, or, in adhering to their Enemies, giving them Aid and Comfort. No Person shall be convicted of Treason unless on the Testimony of two Witnesses to the same overt Act, or on Confession in open Court.

[2] The Congress shall have Power to declare the Punishment of Treason, but no Attainder of Treason shall work Corruption of Blood, or Forfeiture except during the Life of the Person attainted.

Article IV

Section 1. Full Faith and Credit shall be given in each State to the public Acts, Records, and judicial Proceedings of every other State. And the Congress may by general Laws prescribe the Manner in which such Acts, Records and Proceedings shall be proved, and the Effect thereof.

Section 2. [1] The Citizens of each State shall be entitled to all Privileges and Immunities of Citizens in the several States.

[2] A Person charged in any State with Treason, Felony, or other Crime, who shall flee from Justice, and be found in another State, shall on demand of the executive Authority of the State from which he fled, be delivered up, to be removed to the State having Jurisdiction of the Crime.

[3] No Person held to Service or Labour in one State, under the Laws thereof, escaping into another, shall, in Consequence of any Law or Regulation therein, be discharged from such Service or Labour, but shall be delivered up on Claim of the Party to whom such Service or Labour may be due.

Section 3. [1] New States may be admitted by the Congress into this Union; but no new State shall be formed or erected within the Jurisdiction of any other State; nor any State be formed by the Junction of two or more States, or Parts of States, without the Consent of the Legislatures of the States concerned as well as of the Congress.

[2] The Congress shall have Power to dispose of and make all needful Rules and Regulations respecting the Territory or other Property belonging to the United States; and nothing in this Constitution shall be so construed as to Prejudice any Claims of the United States, or of any particular State.

Section 4. The United States shall guarantee to every State in this Union a Republican Form of Government, and shall protect each of them against Invasion; and on Application of the Legislature, or of the Executive (when the Legislature cannot be convened) against domestic Violence.

Article V

The Congress, whenever two thirds of both Houses shall deem it necessary, shall propose Amendments to this Constitution, or, on the Application of the Legislatures of two thirds of the several States, shall call a Convention for proposing Amendments, which, in either Case, shall be valid to all Intents and Purposes, as part of this Constitution, when ratified by the Legislatures of three fourths of the several States, or by Conventions in three fourths thereof, as the one or the other Mode of Ratification may be proposed by the Congress; Provided that no Amendment which may be made prior to the Year One thousand eight hundred and eight shall in any Manner affect the first and fourth Clauses in the Ninth Section of the first Article; and that no State, without its Consent, shall be deprived of its equal Suffrage in the Senate.

Article VI

[1] All Debts contracted and Engagements entered into, before the Adoption of this Constitution shall be as valid against the United States under this Constitution, as under the Confederation.

[2] This Constitution, and the Laws of the United States which shall be made in Pursuance thereof; and all Treaties made, or which shall be made, under the Authority of the United States, shall be the supreme Law of the Land; and the Judges in every State shall be bound thereby, any Thing in the Constitution or Laws of any State to the Contrary notwithstanding.

[3] The Senators and Representatives before mentioned, and the Members of the several State Legislatures, and all executive and judicial Officers, both of the United States and of the several States, shall be bound by Oath or Affirmation, to support this Constitution; but no religious Test shall ever be required as a Qualification to any Office or public Trust under the United States.

Article VII

The Ratification of the Conventions of nine States shall be sufficient for the Establishment of this Constitution between the States so ratifying the Same.

ARTICLES IN ADDITION TO, AND AMENDMENT OF, THE CONSTITUTION OF THE UNITED STATES OF AMERICA, PROPOSED BY CONGRESS, AND RATIFIED BY THE LEGISLATURES OF THE SEVERAL STATES PURSUANT TO THE FIFTH ARTICLE OF THE ORIGINAL CONSTITUTION.

Amendment I [1791]

Congress shall make no law respecting an establishment of religion, or prohibiting the free exercise thereof; or abridging the freedom of speech, or of the press; or the right of the people peaceably to assemble, and to petition the Government for a redress of grievances.

Amendment II [1791]

A well regulated Militia, being necessary to the security of a free State, the right of the people to keep and bear Arms, shall not be infringed.

Amendment III [1791]

No Soldier shall, in time of peace be quartered in any house, without the consent of the Owner, nor in time of war, but in a manner to be prescribed by law.

Amendment IV [1791]

The right of the people to be secure in their persons, houses, papers, and effects, against unreasonable searches and seizures, shall not be violated, and no Warrants shall issue, but upon probable cause, supported by Oath or affirmation, and particularly describing the place to be searched, and the persons or things to be seized.

Amendment V [1791]

No person shall be held to answer for a capital, or otherwise infamous crime, unless on a presentment or indictment of a Grand Jury, except in cases arising in the land or naval forces, or in the Militia, when in actual service in time of War or public danger; nor shall any person be subject for the same offence to be twice put in jeopardy of life or limb; nor shall be compelled in any criminal case to be a witness against himself, nor be deprived of life, liberty, or property, without due process of law; nor shall private property be taken for public use, without just compensation.

Amendment VI [1791]

In all criminal prosecutions, the accused shall enjoy the right to a speedy and public trial, by an impartial jury of the State and district wherein the crime shall have been committed, which district shall have been previously ascertained by law, and to be informed of the nature and cause of the accusation; to be confronted with the witnesses against him; to have compulsory process for obtaining witnesses in his favor, and to have the Assistance of Counsel for his defence.

Amendment VII [1791]

In Suits at common law, where the value in controversy shall exceed twenty dollars, the right of trial by jury shall be preserved, and no fact tried by jury, shall be otherwise re-examined in any Court of the United States, than according to the rules of the common law.

Amendment VIII [1791]

Excessive bail shall not be required, nor excessive fines imposed, nor cruel and unusual punishments inflicted.

Amendment IX [1791]

The enumeration in the Constitution, of certain rights, shall not be construed to deny or disparage others retained by the people.

Amendment X [1791]

The powers not delegated to the United States by the Constitution, nor prohibited by it to the States, are reserved to the States respectively, or to the people.

Amendment XI [1798]

The Judicial power of the United States shall not be construed to extend to any suit in law or equity, commenced or prosecuted against one of the United States by Citizens of another State, or by Citizens or Subjects of any Foreign State.

Amendment XII [1804]

The Electors shall meet in their respective states and vote by ballot for President and Vice-President, one of whom, at least, shall not be an inhabitant of the same state with themselves; they shall name in their ballots the person voted for as President, and in distinct ballots the person voted for as Vice-President, and they shall make distinct lists of all persons voted for as President, and of all persons voted for as Vice-President, and of the number of votes for each, which lists they shall sign and certify, and transmit sealed to the seat of the government of the United States, directed to the President of the Senate;—The President of the Senate shall, in the presence of the Senate and House of Representatives, open all the certificates and the votes shall then be counted;—The person having the greatest number of votes for President, shall be the President, if such number be a majority of the whole number of Electors appointed; and if no person have such majority, then from the persons having the highest numbers not exceeding three on the list of those voted for as President, the House of Representatives shall choose immediately, by ballot, the President. But in choosing the President, the votes shall be taken by states, the representation from each state having one vote; a quorum for this purpose shall consist of a member or members from two-thirds of the states, and a majority of all states shall be necessary to a choice. And if the House of Representatives shall not choose a President whenever the right of choice shall devolve upon them before the fourth day of March next following, then the Vice-President shall act as President, as in the case of the death or other constitutional disability of the President.—The person having the greatest number of votes as Vice-President, shall be the Vice-President, if such number be a majority of the whole number of Electors appointed, and if no person have a majority, then from the two highest numbers on the list, the Senate shall choose the Vice-President; a quorum for the purpose shall consist of two-thirds of the whole number of Senators, and a majority of the whole number shall be necessary to a choice. But no person constitutionally ineligible to the office of President shall be eligible to that of Vice-President of the United States.

Amendment XIII [1865]

Section 1. Neither slavery nor involuntary servitude, except as a punishment for crime whereof the party shall have been duly convicted, shall exist within the United States, or any place subject to their jurisdiction.

Section 2. Congress shall have power to enforce this article by appropriate legislation.

Amendment XIV [1868]

Section 1. All persons born or naturalized in the United States, and subject to the jurisdiction thereof, are citizens of the United States and of the State wherein they reside. No State shall make or enforce any law which shall abridge the privileges or immunities of citizens of the United States; nor shall any State deprive any person of life, liberty, or property, without due process of law; nor deny to any person within its jurisdiction the equal protection of the laws.

Section 2. Representatives shall be apportioned among the several States according to their respective numbers, counting the whole number of persons in each State, excluding Indians not taxed. But when the right to vote at any election for the choice of electors for President and Vice President of the United States, Representatives in Congress, the Executive and Judicial officers of a State, or the members of the Legislature thereof, is denied to any of the male inhabitants of such State, being twenty-one years of age, and citizens of the United States, or in any way abridged, except for participation in rebellion, or other crime, the basis of representation therein shall be reduced in the proportion which the number of such male citizens shall bear to the whole number of male citizens twenty-one years of age in such State.

Section 3. No person shall be a Senator or Representative in Congress, or elector of President and Vice President, or hold any office, civil or military, under the United States, or under any State, who having previously taken an oath, as a member of Congress, or as an officer of the United States, or as a member of any State legislature, or as an executive or judicial officer of any State, to support the Constitution of the United States, shall have engaged in insurrection or rebellion against the same, or given aid or comfort to the enemies thereof. But Congress may by a vote of two-thirds of each House, remove such disability.

Section 4. The validity of the public debt of the United States, authorized by law, including debts incurred for payment of pensions and bounties for services in suppressing insurrection or rebellion, shall not be questioned. But neither the United States nor any State shall assume or pay any debt or obligation incurred in aid of insurrection or rebellion against the United States, or any claim for the loss or emancipation of any slave; but all such debts, obligations and claims shall be held illegal and void.

Section 5. The Congress shall have power to enforce, by appropriate legislation, the provisions of this article.

Amendment XV [1870]

Section 1. The right of citizens of the United States to vote shall not be denied or abridged by the United States or by any State on account of race, color, or previous condition of servitude.

Section 2. The Congress shall have power to enforce this article by appropriate legislation.

Amendment XVI [1913]

The Congress shall have power to lay and collect taxes on incomes, from whatever source derived, without apportionment among the several States, and without regard to any census or enumeration.

Amendment XVII [1913]

[1] The Senate of the United States shall be composed of two Senators from each State, elected by the people thereof, for six years; and each Senator shall have one vote. The electors in each State shall have the qualifications requisite for electors of the most numerous branch of the State legislatures.

[2] When vacancies happen in the representation of any State in the Senate, the executive authority of such State shall issue writs of election to fill such vacancies: *Provided*, That the legislature of any State may empower the executive thereof to make temporary appointments until the people fill the vacancies by election as the legislature may direct.

[3] This amendment shall not be so construed as to affect the election or term of any Senator chosen before it becomes valid as part of the Constitution.

Amendment XVIII [1919]

Section 1. After one year from the ratification of this article the manufacture, sale, or transportation of intoxicating liquors within, the importation thereof into, or the exportation thereof from the United States and all territory subject to the jurisdiction thereof for beverage purposes is hereby prohibited.

Section 2. The Congress and the several States shall have concurrent power to enforce this article by appropriate legislation.

Section 3. This article shall be inoperative unless it shall have been ratified as an amendment to the Constitution by the legislatures of the several States, as provided in the Constitution, within seven years from the date of the submission hereof to the States by the Congress.

Amendment XIX [1920]

[1] The right of citizens of the United States to vote shall not be denied or abridged by the United States or by any State on account of sex.

[2] Congress shall have power to enforce this article by appropriate legislation.

Amendment XX [1933]

Section 1. The terms of the President and Vice President shall end at noon on the 20th day of January, and the terms of Senators and Representatives at noon on the 3d day of January, of the years in which such terms would have ended if this article had not been ratified; and the terms of their successors shall then begin.

Section 2. The Congress shall assemble at least once in every year, and such meeting shall begin at noon on the 3d day of January, unless they shall by law appoint a different day.

Section 3. If, at the time fixed for the beginning of the term of the President, the President elect shall have died, the Vice President elect shall become President. If the President shall not have been chosen before the time fixed for the beginning of his term, or if the President elect shall have failed to qualify, then the Vice President elect shall act as President until a President shall have qualified; and the Congress may by law provide for the case wherein neither a President elect nor a Vice President elect shall have qualified, declaring who shall then act as President, or the manner in which one who is to act shall be selected, and such person shall act accordingly until a President or Vice President shall have qualified.

Section 4. The Congress may by law provide for the case of the death of any of the persons from whom the House of Representatives may choose a President whenever the right of choice shall have devolved upon them, and for the case of the death of any of the persons from whom the Senate may choose a Vice President whenever the right of choice shall have devolved upon them.

Section 5. Sections 1 and 2 shall take effect on the 15th day of October following the ratification of this article.

Section 6. This article shall be inoperative unless it shall have been ratified as an amendment to the Constitution by the legislatures of three-fourths of the several States within seven years from the date of its submission.

Amendment XXI [1933]

Section 1. The eighteenth article of amendment to the Constitution of the United States is hereby repealed.

Section 2. The transportation or importation into any State, Territory, or possession of the United States for delivery or use therein of intoxicating liquors, in violation of the laws thereof, is hereby prohibited.

Section 3. This article shall be inoperative unless it shall have been ratified as an amendment to the Constitution by conventions in the several States, as provided in the Constitution, within seven years from the date of the submission hereof to the States by the Congress.

Amendment XXII [1951]

Section 1. No person shall be elected to the office of the President more than twice, and no person who has held the office of President, or acted as President, for more than two years of a term to which some other person was elected President shall be elected to the office of President more than once. But this Article shall not apply to any person holding the office of President when this Article was proposed by the Congress, and shall not prevent any person who may be holding the office of President, or acting as President, during the term within which this Article becomes operative from holding the office of President or acting as President during the remainder of such term.

Section 2. This article shall be inoperative unless it shall have been ratified as an amendment to the Constitution by the legislatures of three-fourths of the several States within seven years from the date of its submission to the States by the Congress.

Amendment XXIII [1961]

Section 1. The District constituting the seat of Government of the United States shall appoint in such manner as the Congress may direct:

A number of electors of President and Vice President equal to the whole number of Senators and Representatives in Congress to which the District would be entitled if it were a State, but in no event more than the least populous state; they shall be in addition to those appointed by the states, but they shall be considered, for the purposes of the election of President and Vice President, to be electors appointed by a state; and they shall meet in the District and perform such duties as provided by the twelfth article of amendment.

Section 2. The Congress shall have power to enforce this article by appropriate legislation.

Amendment XXIV [1964]

Section 1. The right of citizens of the United States to vote in any primary or other election for President or Vice President, for electors for President or Vice President, or for Senator or Representative in Congress, shall not be denied or abridged by the United States, or any State by reason of failure to pay any poll tax or other tax.

Section 2. The Congress shall have power to enforce this article by appropriate legislation.

Amendment XXV [1967]

Section 1. In case of the removal of the President from office or of his death or resignation, the Vice President shall become President.

Section 2. Whenever there is a vacancy in the office of the Vice President, the President shall nominate a Vice President who shall take office upon confirmation by a majority vote of both Houses of Congress.

Section 3. Whenever the President transmits to the President pro tempore of the Senate and the Speaker of the House of Representatives his written declaration that he is unable to discharge the powers and duties of his office, and until he transmits to them a written declaration to the contrary, such powers and duties shall be discharged by the Vice President as Acting President.

Section 4. Whenever the Vice President and a majority of either the principal officers of the executive departments or of such other body as Congress may by law provide, transmit to the President pro tempore of the Senate and the Speaker of the House of Representatives their written declaration that the President is unable to discharge the powers and duties of his office, the Vice President shall immediately assume the powers and duties of the office as Acting President.

Thereafter, when the President transmits to the President pro tempore of the Senate and the Speaker of the House of Representatives his written declaration that no inability exists, he shall resume the powers and duties of his office unless the Vice President and a majority of either the principal officers of the executive department or of such other body as Congress may by law provide, transmit within four days to the President pro tempore of the Senate and the Speaker of the House of Representatives their written declaration and the President is unable to discharge the powers and duties of his office. Thereupon Congress shall decide the issue, assembling within forty-eight hours for that purpose if not in session. If the Congress, within twenty-one days after receipt of the latter written declaration, or, if Congress is not in session, within twenty-one days after Congress is required to assemble, determines by two-thirds vote of both Houses that the President is unable to discharge the powers and duties of his office, the Vice President shall continue to discharge the same as Acting President; otherwise, the President shall resume the powers and duties of his office.

Amendment XXVI [1971]

Section 1. The right of citizens of the United States, who are eighteen years of age or older, to vote shall not be denied or abridged by the United States or by any State on account of age.

Section 2. The Congress shall have power to enforce this article by appropriate legislation.

Proposed Constitutional Amendment *

Section 1. For purposes of representation in Congress, election of the President and Vice President, and Article V of this Constitution, the District constituting the seat of government of the United States shall be treated as though it were a State.

Section 2. The exercise of the rights and powers conferred under this article shall be by the people of the District constituting the seat of government and shall be as provided by Congress.

Section 3. The twenty-third Amendment to the Constitution is hereby repealed.

Section 4. This article shall be inoperative, unless it shall have been ratified as an amendment to the Constitution by the legislatures of three-fourths of the several States within seven years from the date of its submission.

* Congress submitted this proposed amendment to the states for ratification in August 1978.

Index

A

B

C

D

E

F

G

H

I

J

L

Q

R

V

W

Z

†